GMAT® Prep Plus 2019

KAPLAN

PUBLISHING

New York

© 2018 by Kaplan, Inc.

Published by Kaplan Publishing, a division of Kaplan, Inc.
750 Third Avenue
New York, NY 10017

ISBN: 978-1-5062-3489-2

10 9 8 7 6 5 4 3 2 1

Additional resources available at www.kaptest.com/gmatbookresources

PART THREE: VERBAL SECTION AND STRATEGIES

PART FOUR: QUANTITATIVE SECTION AND STRATEGIES

PART SIX: TEST DAY AND BUSINESS SCHOOL

PART SEVEN: APPENDICES

How to Use This Book

WELCOME TO KAPLAN'S GMAT PREP PLUS 2019

Congratulations on your decision to pursue an MBA or other graduate management degree and thank you for choosing Kaplan for your GMAT preparation.

You've made the right choice in acquiring this book—you're now armed with a comprehensive GMAT program that is the result of decades of researching the GMAT and teaching many thousands of students the skills they need to succeed. You have what you need to score higher; the next step is to make the commitment to your study plan, which, according to the GMAT test maker, averages about 100 hours of preparation for 600+ and 700+ scorers.

Let's start by walking you through everything you need to know to take advantage of this book and your online resources.

YOUR BOOK

There are two main components to your *GMAT Prep Plus* study package: your book and your online resources. This book contains:

- Detailed instruction covering the essential verbal, math, and writing concepts
- Time-tested and effective Kaplan Methods and strategies for every question type
- A pretest (Chapter 3) featuring full-length Quantitative and Verbal sections, designed to help you diagnose your strengths and weaknesses
- Over 350 practice questions, followed by detailed answer explanations

YOUR ONLINE RESOURCES

Your Kaplan online resources give you access to additional instruction and practice materials to reinforce key concepts and sharpen your GMAT skills. The following list summarizes the resources available to you:

- Five full-length computer-adaptive practice tests (CATs)

- Analysis of your performance on each practice test, including detailed answer explanations

- Practice sets for the Verbal, Quantitative, Analytical Writing, and Integrated Reasoning sections of the GMAT

- A 200-question Qbank for additional targeted practice

- Video workshops featuring veteran GMAT instructors

- The GMAT Strategy Sheet

GETTING STARTED

Studying for the GMAT can be daunting, and with so many resources available to you, it may not be clear where to begin. Don't worry; we'll break it down one step at a time, just as we'll do with the GMAT questions that you will soon be on your way to mastering.

GETTING STARTED

1. Register your online resources.
2. Sign up for a free Live Online event.
3. Take a GMAT practice test to identify your strengths and weaknesses.
4. Create a study plan.
5. Learn and practice using this book and your online resources.
6. Work through the five computer-adaptive practice tests to gauge your progress.

STEP 1: REGISTER YOUR ONLINE RESOURCES

Register your online resources using these simple steps:

1. Go to **kaptest.com/booksonline**.

2. Follow the on-screen instructions. Please have a copy of your book available.

Access to the online resources is limited to the original owner of this book and is nontransferable. Kaplan is not responsible for providing access to the online resources to customers who purchase or borrow used copies of this book. Access to the online resources expires one year after you register.

STEP 2: SIGN UP FOR A FREE LIVE ONLINE EVENT

Kaplan's GMAT Live Online events are interactive, instructor-led GMAT training sessions that you can join from anywhere you can access the Internet.

Live Online events are held in a state-of-the-art virtual classroom in real time, just like a physical classroom experience. You'll interact with your teacher and other classmates using audio, instant chat, whiteboard, polling, and screen sharing. And just like in-person courses, a GMAT Live Online event is led by an experienced Kaplan instructor.

To register for a free GMAT Live Online event, go to **KaplanGMAT.com** and search for a free event. Look for events such as GMAT Bootcamps and GMAT Lessons. (The free GMAT practice tests draw from the same question pool as the tests in your online resources, so you should use the online tests that come with this book.) Live Online events are available for all locations.

STEP 3: TAKE A GMAT PRACTICE TEST

It's essential to take a practice test early on. Doing so will give you the initial feedback and diagnostic information that you will need to achieve your maximum score. Taking a full-length test right at the start can be intimidating, but remember: your practice test scores don't count. During your first practice test—and all of your practice tests—turn off your cell phone, give the test your full attention, and learn from your performance.

Your diagnostic test is Practice Test 1, which is found in your online resources. Practice Test 1, like all of Kaplan's online full-length tests, is a computer-adaptive test (CAT), which is the same format as the actual GMAT. The computer-adaptive format feels and scores differently than a paper test, so the more you practice with CATs, the better off you'll be. However, for your convenience, we've also included a pretest in Chapter 3 of this book. The pretest includes full-length Quantitative and Verbal sections and will give you a chance to familiarize yourself with the various question types. It will also allow you to gauge the content you know and identify areas for practice and review.

Review the detailed answer explanations to better understand your performance. Our explanations label each question according to its question type and topic; these labels align with the material covered throughout this book. Look for patterns in the questions you answered correctly and incorrectly. Were you stronger in some areas than others? This analysis will help you target your practice time to specific concepts.

STEP 4: CREATE A STUDY PLAN

Use what you've learned from your initial practice test to identify areas for closer study and practice. Take time to familiarize yourself with the key components of your book and online resources. Think about how many hours you can consistently devote to GMAT study. We have found that most students have success with about three months of committed preparation before Test Day.

Consider the following statistic as you build your study plan: according to the GMAT test makers, the average 600+ or 700+ scorer prepares for the GMAT for about 100 hours. We recommend you add 20 percent to this figure and plan to put in 120 total hours of practice before Test Day. Roughly estimated, if you spend an average of 2 hours per chapter in this book, that gets you to 40 hours. The five computer-adaptive practice tests are each about 3.0 hours, if you do the writing section and Integrated Reasoning, followed by about 1.5 hours of review. All told, that gets you to about 60 hours of preparation. That 60 hours may be enough for some test takers, and it will be more than enough to give you an indication of where you stand relative to your GMAT goals. The most convenient way to bulk up your study plan is to enroll in Kaplan's GMAT Self-Paced course, which includes approximately 160 hours of preparation. For more information on GMAT Self-Paced and the other preparation options (including instructor-led courses) available from Kaplan, visit **KaplanGMAT.com**.

Schedule time for study, practice, and review. One of the most frequent mistakes is to take practice tests and not review them thoroughly—review time is your best chance to gain points. Many people find it works best to block out short, frequent periods of study time throughout the week. Check in with yourself often to make sure you're not falling behind your plan or forgetting about any of your resources.

STEP 5: LEARN AND PRACTICE

Your book and online resources come with many opportunities to develop and practice the skills you'll need on Test Day. Read each chapter of this book and complete the practice questions. Depending on how much time you have to study, you can do this work methodically, covering every chapter, or you can focus your study on those question types and content areas that are most challenging for you. You will inevitably need more work in some areas than in others, but know that the more thoroughly you prepare, the better your score will be.

Remember also to take and review the practice sets in your online resources. These additional test-like questions allow you to put into practice the skills you are learning. As always, review the explanations closely.

Initially, your practice should focus on mastering the needed skills and not on timing. Add timing to your practice as you improve fundamental proficiency.

STEP 6: WORK THROUGH THE FIVE COMPUTER-ADAPTIVE PRACTICE TESTS

As you move through your GMAT studies, take advantage of the five full-length practice tests available in your online resources. You will learn more about CATs in Chapters 1 and 2 of this book. The Kaplan CATs are realistic practice tests, and taking full-length tests is the best way to prepare fully for what you will face on the real GMAT. Take your first computer-adaptive test relatively early in your prep and continue taking practice tests at regular intervals until your Test Day.

Always review your practice test results thoroughly to make sure you are addressing the areas that are most important to your score. Allot time to review the detailed explanations so that you can learn from your mistakes before taking your next practice test.

If you find that you would like access to more of Kaplan's CATs and quizzes, as well as in-depth instruction on the question types and strategies, look into the variety of practice resources and course options available at **KaplanGMAT.com**.

Thanks for choosing Kaplan. We wish you the best of luck on your journey to business school.

KaplanGMAT.com

The material in this book is accurate and up-to-date at the time of printing. However, the Graduate Management Admission Council may have instituted changes in the tests or test registration process after this book was published. Be sure to read carefully the materials you receive when you register for the test.

If there are any important late-breaking developments, we will post that information online at **KaplanGMAT.com**.

kaptest.com/publishing

If there are changes or corrections to the materials in this book, these can be found at **kaptest.com/publishing**.

PART ONE

The GMAT

CHAPTER 1

Introduction to the GMAT

- **GMAT Format**
- **GMAT Scoring**
- **GMAT Attitude**
- **GMAT Checklist**

Let's start with the basics. The GMAT is, among other things, an endurance test. It is a computerized test consisting of 127 minutes of multiple-choice math and verbal questions, a 30-minute reasoning section, and a 30-minute analytical essay. Add in the administrative details, plus two 8-minute breaks, and you can count on being in the testing center for about 3.5 hours.

It's a grueling experience, to say the least. And if you don't approach it with confidence and rigor, you'll quickly lose your composure. That's why it's so important that you take control of the test, just as you take control of the rest of your business school application process.

Here are the basics.

GMAT FORMAT

The GMAT consists of four sections, and you can choose your section order on Test Day. Before you begin your test, you'll be presented with three orders and asked to select one:

- Analytical Writing Assessment (AWA), Integrated Reasoning (IR), Quantitative, Verbal
- Verbal, Quantitative, Integrated Reasoning, Analytical Writing Assessment
- Quantitative, Verbal, Integrated Reasoning, Analytical Writing Assessment

If you do not choose an order, then after 1 minute, the first order—beginning with Analytical Writing—will be chosen for you.

The order you take the sections in will not appear on your score report, and the test maker's research has not shown section order gives one test taker a statistical advantage over another. If you are especially concerned about a particular section and want to take it when you are mentally freshest, then choose the order that puts that section first. If you want to build confidence by completing other sections first, then choose an order that puts that section later. And if you don't care what order you take the sections in, that's perfectly okay—just choose whichever order you have practiced most.

The Analytical Writing Assessment (AWA) requires you to complete an essay, typing it into the computer using a simple word processing program. You are given 30 minutes for this essay, during which you have to analyze the flawed reasoning behind a given argument and recommend how to improve the argument.

The Integrated Reasoning section is 30 minutes long. This section has 12 questions, each of which may require more than one response. The questions in this section ask you to draw conclusions based on information in tables, interpret graphs, understand information presented across different layouts, and find two answers that lead to a single solution.

The Quantitative section contains 31 questions in two formats, Problem Solving and Data Sufficiency, which are mixed together throughout the section. The Verbal section contains 36 questions in three formats, Reading Comprehension, Sentence Correction, and Critical Reasoning, which are also mixed throughout the section.

GMAT Exam Section	Questions	Time
Analytical Writing Assessment	1	30 min
Integrated Reasoning	12	30 min
Quantitative	31	62 min
Verbal	36	65 min
Total Testing Time		**3 hours, 7 minutes**

Length of Sections on the GMAT

You will also get two optional 8-minute breaks between sections. Also, note that a few "experimental" questions will be scattered throughout; they look just like the other questions but won't contribute to your score.

Order A	Order B	Order C
Analytical Writing Assessment	Verbal	Quantitative
Integrated Reasoning		
8-minute break (optional)		
Quantitative	Quantitative	Verbal
8-minute break (optional)		
Verbal	Integrated Reasoning	Integrated Reasoning
	Analytical Writing Assessment	Analytical Writing Assessment

Breaks on the GMAT by Section Order

We'll talk more about each of the question types in later chapters. For now, note the following: you'll be answering 79 multiple-choice questions in about 2.5 hours. Clearly, you'll have to move fast. But you can't let yourself get careless. Taking control of the GMAT means increasing the speed of your work without sacrificing accuracy.

GMAT SCORING

The most important score on the GMAT is the total score, which ranges from 200 to 800. This score is the GMAT result that schools look at primarily. More than half of all GMAT test takers score within 100 points of 556, the approximate mean. Pulling yourself out of that cluster is an important part of distinguishing your application.

Percentile	Score
99%	760–800
94%	720
88%	700
75%	650
64%	620
51%	580

Some GMAT Percentiles vs. Total Scores

The total score is calculated from "scaled scores" from the Quantitative section and Verbal section. These scores are meant to provide a timeless, absolute measure of skill. For example, a Quant score of 40 in 2008 represents the same level of ability as does a Quant score of 40 in 2018.

While the scaled scores haven't changed over time, the population of test takers has. Quant performance has gone up, and Verbal performance has gone down. While Verbal section scores still follow a fairly even distribution, Quantitative scaled scores now skew high. Thus, percentiles have shifted.

Schools view your percentile performance (which is the same thing as a "percent ranking") overall and on each section of the GMAT. The relationship between the section percentiles and the overall percentile is not simple. We're frequently asked, "One of my scaled scores is 83rd percentile and the other is 84th percentile. How can my overall score be 87th percentile?" An example shows how this works. Imagine that of 100 students taking the test, 50 people got a 51 Quant and an 11 Verbal, while the other 50 people got an 11 Quant and a 51 Verbal. You take the same test and get 40 Quant and 40 Verbal. You'd be 50th percentile on each section, because 50 percent of test takers in this sample group scored worse than you. However, your total score would put you higher than anyone else on the test—99th percentile.

Quantitative		Verbal	
Percentile	**Score**	**Percentile**	**Score**
96%	51–60	99%	45–51
86%	50	98%	44
75%	49	96%	42
69%	48	94%	41
63%	47	91%	40
60%	46	89%	39
57%	45	85%	38
52%	44	83%	37
50%	43	81%	36

Some Percentiles vs. Scaled Scores
for the Quantitative and Verbal Sections

Let's note two key takeaways about percentiles. The first is that your overall score is about balanced performance on the two sections. Generally, you will not win on the GMAT by nailing one section and hoping your performance will overcome a deficit on the other. The second key point is that admissions officers often look at Quant and Verbal percentiles separately and may reject a candidate who does not meet a certain threshold for either subscore. This is especially true for Quantitative percentiles, particularly at programs with a strong analytical focus.

The Analytical Writing Assessment (AWA) is scored separately from the rest of the GMAT. Unlike the total and scaled scores, AWA scores aren't available on Test Day. When you do get your score, it will take the form of a number from 1 to 6 in increments of 0.5 (you get a zero if you write off topic or in a foreign language). The magic number here is 4. Although you should strive for the best score possible, an essay graded 4 is considered "satisfactory" according to the grading rubric, and an essay graded 3 is not.

AWA	
Percentile	**Score**
89%	6
80%	5.5
54%	5
42%	4.5
18%	4
12%	3.5
5%	3
4%	2.5
3%	1.5–2
2%	0.5–1

Percentiles vs. Scaled Scores for the AWA

Percentiles give a slightly different perspective on the AWA. An AWA score of 4 ranks at a shockingly low 18th percentile. To break the median, you have to score a 5 or higher. The good news is that few programs, in our experience, use the AWA score to differentiate candidates' competitiveness. It's more of a reality check against the writing skills that you demonstrate in your application essays. Here's a little-noticed fact: business schools receive the actual text of your AWA essay in the official score report.

Finally, you'll receive a score for the Integrated Reasoning section. As with the Quant and Verbal sections, Integrated Reasoning scores are available on Test Day. Like the AWA, the Integrated Reasoning section has its own scoring scale, independent from the 200 to 800 scale. You'll receive a score from 1 to 8, in whole-point increments. The magic number this time is 5, as this is the score at which you beat the median.

You will definitely want to show schools that you're in the better half of the Integrated Reasoning field, but at the same time, an exceptional 200–800 score will do more for your application than will an exceptional Integrated Reasoning score, and you should prioritize your study time accordingly.

The 1–8 score is derived from just 12 questions, nearly all of which have multiple parts, and there is no partial credit. Integrated Reasoning questions come in four types, described in more detail in the Integrated Reasoning chapter of this book: Graphics Interpretation, Multi-Source Reasoning, Table Analysis, and Two-Part Analysis.

Integrated Reasoning	
Percentile	**Score**
93%	8
82%	7
70%	6
55%	5
40%	4
26%	3
12%	2
0%	1

*Percentiles vs. Scaled Scores for the Integrated
Reasoning Section*

Unlike the Quantitative and Verbal sections of the GMAT, the Integrated Reasoning section isn't adaptive: you'll see a predetermined sequence of 12 questions no matter how many you get right and wrong as you go along. However, despite not being adaptive, the Integrated Reasoning section does not let test takers skip questions or return to previously answered questions. As a result, it's often advantageous to guess and abandon a hard question early in the section to ensure that no easy questions are left unanswered at the end of the section.

SCORE REPORTS

Within 20 days after your test date, your official score report will be available online. You'll receive an email when yours is ready. Reports will only be mailed to candidates who request that service. The official score report includes your scores for the Analytical Writing Assessment, Integrated Reasoning, Verbal, and Quantitative sections, as well as your total score and percentile ranking.

Your report also includes the results of all the GMAT exams you've taken in the previous five years, not including cancellations. Any additional reports are US$35 each. All score report requests are final and cannot be canceled.

GMAT ATTITUDE

In the chapters that follow, we'll cover techniques for answering the GMAT questions. But you'll also need to go into the test with a certain attitude and approach. Here are some strategies.

USE THE NOTEBOARDS

Test takers are given noteboards, which are spiral-bound booklets of laminated paper, and a black wet-erase pen. Here are the specs so you know what to expect on Test Day.

Noteboard

- 5 sheets, 10 numbered pages
- Spiral-bound at top
- Legal-sized (8.5″ × 14″) in United States, Canada, and Mexico; A4 elsewhere
- First page has test instructions and is not suitable for scratchwork
- Pages 2–10 consist of a gridded work surface
- Pale yellow in United States, Canada, and Mexico; may be a different color elsewhere

Pen

- Black fine-print Staedtler wet-erase pen

You will not be given an eraser, and you are not allowed to reuse the noteboard. Each time you fill up your noteboard during the test, the administrator will replace your used noteboard with a clean one. You can also request a new pen, if necessary. The noteboard cannot be removed from the test room during or after the exam, and you must return it to the administrator when your exam is complete.

We know how important it is for test takers to be as prepared as possible for the actual testing experience. That's why we have always recommended that students use separate scratch material with our GMAT preparation program, including with the practice questions and tests in this book. We suggest that you use an eraser board (or anything with a similar surface) and a nonpermanent marker while doing the practice tests. Even if you practice with the noteboard and marker until you are comfortable, there are still some snags you may encounter on Test Day. Here are some tips on how to handle them:

1. **Erasable ink you're not supposed to erase:** Say you make a mistake during a calculation or you smudge your work with your hand. The noteboard's surface won't lend itself to quick-and-easy erasing. You can't write on top of the smudge or error because you'll just be left with a blob of ink that you can't read. So what should you do? Just start over. Seriously. Think of it this way—you won't waste precious time in a futile attempt to save a sinking ship. Left-handed test takers (and some right-handed ones, too) might find that their writing styles make them particularly susceptible to smudging. If this sounds like you, practicing with the eraser board will help you work out any such problems before Test Day.

2. **A problematic pen:** Difficulties with pens are not common. Keep in mind that you should recap your pen when you are not using it so that it doesn't dry out. However, you could get a pen that's simply dry from the get-go or dries out quickly no matter how careful you are. Don't sweat it. The best thing to do is just to get a new pen. Should you be saddled with a pen that leaves wayward blobs of ink, don't waste time with this either. Ask the administrator for a new pen as soon as it starts to act up.

More Noteboard Strategies

Using one booklet for an entire section and requesting a replacement during breaks is the most efficient method for using the noteboards. Since you are given nine pages to write on, this technique can be used without difficulty, especially with planning and practice. However, should you need a new noteboard (or pen) during a section, hold the used one in the air to clarify immediately the nature of the request (rather than just raising your hand).

Be Systematic

Use your noteboard to organize your thinking. If you eliminate choices, draw an answer choice grid, cross off choices as you rule them out, and guess intelligently. Make sure to leave enough time to answer every question in the section. You'll be penalized for questions you don't get to.

Pace Yourself

Of course, the last thing you want to happen is to run out of time before you've done all the questions. Pace yourself so that this doesn't happen. We're not saying you have to spend exactly 120 seconds, for instance, on every Critical Reasoning question. But you should have a sense of how much time to spend on each question. (We'll talk about general timing guidelines later.)

TURN OFF THE CLOCK

The timer in the corner of the GMAT screen can work to your advantage, but if you find yourself looking at it so often that it becomes a distraction, turn it off for 10 or 15 minutes and try to refocus. Even if you lose track a bit without the clock, there is no replacement for focus and accuracy. Some people work best with the clock off from the beginning. If that's you, be sure to check in with the clock every five questions. You don't want to fall too far behind. No matter what your preference is for the clock, when there are 5 minutes left, the clock turns on permanently, counts down the seconds, turns red, and flashes.

DON'T WASTE TIME ON QUESTIONS YOU CAN'T DO

Skipping a tough question is easier said than done. It's natural to want to plow through a test and answer every question as it appears. But that doesn't pay off here. We'll discuss in Chapter 2 why it's sometimes best to move on and avoid running out of time on a section. A strategic guess may be necessary to get a top score on the GMAT.

REMAIN CALM

It's imperative that you remain calm and composed during the test. You can't let yourself get rattled by one hard question to the degree that it throws off your performance on the rest of the section.

When you face a tough question, remember that you're surely not the only one finding it difficult. The test is designed to challenge everyone who takes it. Having trouble with a difficult question isn't going to ruin your score, but getting upset and letting it throw you off track will. When you understand that part of the test maker's goal is to reward those who keep their composure, you'll recognize the importance of keeping your cool when you run into challenging material.

GMAT CHECKLIST

The GMAT is offered by appointment, at your convenience, almost every day of the year. You will be required to register online before making an appointment.

CHOOSE A TESTING CENTER

Before you register, find a testing center that's convenient for you and determine whether that site has available seats. Each testing center operates on its own schedule and can accommodate varying numbers of test takers. To locate a testing center near you, go to **mba.com**.

REGISTER AND SCHEDULE YOUR APPOINTMENT

Available time slots change continuously as people register for the test. You will find out what times are available at your chosen testing center when you register. You may be able to schedule an appointment within a few days of your desired test date, but popular dates (especially weekends) fill up quickly.

Admissions deadlines for business schools vary. Check with the schools and make your test appointment early enough to allow your scores to be reported before the schools' application deadlines.

You may register and schedule your appointment online, by phone, by mail, or by fax:

- Online: Go to **mba.com** and create an account.
- Phone (you may be charged a US$10 fee):

- The Americas: Call toll-free (within the United States and Canada only) 800-717-GMAT (4628), Monday to Friday, 7:00 a.m. to 7:00 p.m. Central Standard Time.
  - Asia Pacific: +852-3077-4926, 9:00 a.m. to 6:00 p.m. AEST
  - China: 86-10-82345675, Monday to Friday, 8:30 a.m. to 5:00 p.m. China Standard Time
  - India: +91 120 439 7830, 9:00 a.m. to 6:00 p.m. Indian Standard Time
  - Europe/Middle East/Africa: +44 (0) 161 855 7219, 9:00 a.m. to 5:00 p.m. GMT
- Fax or postal mail (slowest options):
  - Look up your desired test center(s) in the Test Center List and download the GMAT Appointment Scheduling form, available at **mba.com**.
  - Fill out the GMAT Appointment Scheduling form.
  - If you wish to fax your form, use the appropriate fax number:
    - The Americas: (952) 681-3680 or (952) 681-3681
    - Asia Pacific and India: +91-120-4001660
    - China: 86-10-61957800
    - Europe/Middle East/Africa: +44 (0) 161 855 7301
  - If you wish to mail your form, send your completed form to the following address. Keep in mind that mail from some countries can take as long as eight weeks to arrive in the United States:

    Pearson VUE—GMAT Program
    PO Box 581907
    Minneapolis, MN 55458-1907
    USA

The fee to take the GMAT is US$250 worldwide (at the time of printing). It is payable by credit card online or by mailing in a check. If you have questions about GMAT registration, visit **mba.com** or call 800-717-GMAT (4628).

Identify Yourself Correctly

When scheduling your test appointment, be sure that the spelling of your name and your stated date of birth match the ID you will present at the testing center. If those do not match, you will not be permitted to take the test, and your test fee will be forfeited.

RESCHEDULING OR CANCELING AN APPOINTMENT

If you need to reschedule the date, time, or location of your appointment, there is a US$60 fee (as this book goes to press) as long as you reschedule at least seven days before your original appointment. If you need to reschedule fewer than seven days before your original date, you have to pay the full registration amount again. Rescheduling can be done online at **mba.com** or by calling one of the numbers listed previously. If you reschedule over the phone, you may be subject to an additional fee. You cannot reschedule an appointment by mail or fax.

If you need to cancel your appointment, you will receive a US$80 refund (as this book goes to press) as long as you cancel at least seven days before your original appointment. If you cancel fewer than seven days before your original date, you forfeit the entire registration fee. For registration fees paid by credit card, the refund amount will be credited to the card. If the fee was paid by check or money order, you will receive a check in the mail. Cancellations can be made online at **mba.com** or by calling one of numbers listed previously, based on your location. If you cancel over the phone, you may be subject to an additional fee. You cannot cancel an appointment by mail or fax.

THE DAY OF THE TEST

You should arrive at your testing center 30 minutes before the time of your scheduled appointment. You must complete a number of security measures before you will be allowed to take the exam. A late arrival (15 minutes or more) may result in your being turned away from the testing center and forfeiting your test fee.

Presentation of Proper Identification

You will be asked to present ID—no exceptions. The following are the only acceptable forms:

- Passport
- Government-issued driver's license or (US only) laminated learner's permit
- Government-issued national/state/province identity card (including European ID card)
- Military ID card
- Permanent resident/green card (US only)

If you aren't a citizen of the country in which you take your test, you'll probably need your passport. In some countries, a passport will always be required. Visit **mba.com** for the current requirements.

The ID must be current (not expired) and legible, and it should contain all four of the elements listed below. If you do not have one ID with all four of these elements, you will need to bring a second ID (also from the list above) that shows the missing elements.

1. Your name in the Roman alphabet. It must be exactly the same as what you provided when you made your appointment, including the order and placement of the names.
2. Your date of birth. The date of birth must also exactly match the date provided when you made your appointment.
3. A recent, recognizable photograph
4. Your signature

If these elements do not match what the test administrator has on file for you, you will not be allowed to take the GMAT, and your test fee will be forfeited.

Before you schedule your test appointment, make sure you understand all the requirements that are particular to your situation and have acquired or renewed the ID you will use. Also, note that if your ID is found to be fraudulent or invalid after you take the exam, your scores will be canceled and your test fee forfeited.

Palm Scan, Signature, and Photograph

Once your government-issued ID is approved, the administrator will take your palm scan, signature, and photograph using digital equipment. The testing rooms are also equipped with audio and video recorders, which are active during the exam. If you do not complete the entire check-in process or refuse to be recorded, you will not be allowed to take the GMAT, and your test fee will be forfeited.

Agreements

When you arrive at the center, you will be asked to agree to the GMAT Test Taker Rules & Agreement. Once you are seated at a workstation, you will electronically confirm that you agree to the GMAT Non-Disclosure Agreement and General Terms of Use statement. If you do not agree, you will not be allowed to take the GMAT, and your test fee will be forfeited. If you are caught violating the agreement, the business schools that you're applying to will be informed of this fact.

Prohibited Items

The following items cannot be brought into the testing room:

- Electronics such as cell phones, media players, personal data assistants (PDAs), cameras, radios, and photographic devices
- Any timepieces, including wristwatches, stopwatches, and watch alarms
- Notes, scratch paper, books, pamphlets, dictionaries, translators, and thesauruses
- Pens and pencils
- Measuring tools such as rulers
- Calculators and watch calculators

Essentially, you can't bring anything that may cause distractions, provide aid during testing, or be used to remove exam content from the testing room. (Note that you are not permitted to use a calculator for the Quantitative section, though there is an onscreen calculator available for the Integrated Reasoning section.) It is possible that your testing center has storage space available, such as lockers, where you can leave possessions that are prohibited from the testing room. However, this may not be the case at all centers. Call your testing center to inquire about storage and plan accordingly.

Disruptive Behavior

You will not be allowed to smoke, eat, drink, or use a cell phone in the testing room. In fact, you won't be allowed to use a phone or send a text message at all once the test has begun, even during breaks.

You also cannot leave the testing room without the administrator's permission. Some testing centers provide earplugs to keep noise to a minimum; if this interests you, call your testing center for details. Should you have any questions or problems during the exam, raise your hand and wait for the administrator to approach you.

Breaks

The length of your appointment is approximately 4 hours. Two breaks are scheduled into the exam. Each time you leave and return to the testing room, your palm will be scanned. If you exceed the allotted break time, the excess time will be deducted from the next section of your exam. For more information on administrative regulations and testing procedures, visit **mba.com**.

Know the Names of Up to Five Business Schools You Wish to Receive Your Scores

You may select up to five schools to receive your scores before you take the test. Your registration fee will cover that cost. Before Test Day, decide which schools you want to get your GMAT scores and bring that list with you. You will not be able to change the list once you have made your selection.

CHAPTER 2

Understanding the CAT

- The CAT Explained
- Are the First Questions More Important?
- The Importance of Pacing
- Other CAT Strategies

The GMAT is a computer-adaptive test, or CAT. The test is called "adaptive" because, in the course of a section, the test notices whether you answered the previous question correctly or incorrectly and "adapts" in its selection of the next question.

A few basic rules make the adaptive format possible:

- You're presented with one question at a time, and you must answer it to move on to the next question.
- You can't return to previously answered questions within a section.
- You can't skip questions—or rather, the only questions that can be skipped or omitted are any questions at the end of a section that you leave unanswered.
- Within a section (Quantitative or Verbal), the questions are not grouped by topic or type. You don't, for example, finish Reading Comprehension and then move on to Sentence Correction and then to Critical Reasoning; those three question types are interspersed with one another throughout the section.

THE CAT EXPLAINED

Here's how the adapting works. You start the section (Quantitative or Verbal) with questions of about medium difficulty; about half of test takers get them right, and half get them wrong. Those who answer correctly begin to get harder questions, and those who answer incorrectly get easier items. This pattern continues: Throughout the section, if you got the previous question right, generally you'll get a harder question next. Conversely, if you got the previous question wrong, generally you'll get an easier one next. In this way, you'll follow a generally upward, downward, or flat trajectory through the questions. The test homes in on the difficulty level that is best matched to your performance; at that difficulty level, generally, you'll be getting about half the questions correct and half incorrect. How high on the difficulty scale you end up is one of the criteria that determine your score, along with how many questions you answer and other factors.

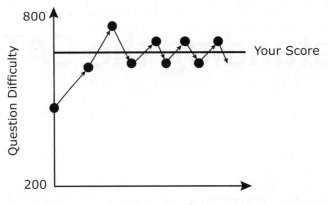

A Rough Schematic of How Adaptive Scoring Works on a CAT

The adaptive design of the test has two purposes:

1. **Accuracy:** A CAT is allegedly more accurate than a "linear" (i.e., nonadaptive) test because it zeros in on a test taker's ability level. Lucky guesses cause the GMAT to give lucky testers harder questions that they cannot answer correctly, thus eliminating any gains resulting from chance. Conversely, unlucky arithmetic errors on tough problems give unlucky testers easier problems, and these unlucky testers should be able to get the easier questions right, thus correcting the nonrepresentative drop in score.

2. **Time:** CATs can be made shorter than comparable linear tests, and the shorter duration is a benefit both to you and the test maker. The reason for this efficiency is that a CAT does not waste questions. If you get most of the questions right, you pretty much never see an easy one, and if you get most of the questions wrong, you pretty much never see a hard one. On a linear test such as the SAT, on the other hand, everyone gets the same mix of easy and hard questions. On such a test, students struggling on the easy questions will do little better than chance on the challenging problems, while high-scoring students will get close to 100 percent of the easy questions correct. Thus, giving low-scoring questions to high-scoring students (and vice versa) doesn't actually provide much useful statistical data. In this respect, many questions are "wasted," whereas the CAT can afford to be a much shorter test at equal accuracy.

Those points define the basic pattern of the CAT, but there are additional bells and whistles in the algorithm. One of the most important details to be aware of is that the test does not always adjust difficulty level question by question. Therefore, avoid the temptation to assess the difficulty level of a question you're on or to infer whether you got the previous question correct. Even if you could precisely assess a question's difficulty level (and you can't, in practice, for reasons we discuss partly later), you wouldn't be able to draw any conclusions, since the test doesn't always adapt immediately.

The experimental questions are another refinement to the CAT formula. Some of the questions in each section do not count toward your score. The test maker must try future questions out on people who do not know that they are experimental in order to determine the validity and difficulty of the questions. We'll talk more about this topic later, but we'll give away one headline early: do not try to guess which questions are experimental.

ARE THE FIRST QUESTIONS MORE IMPORTANT?

One of the most frequently asked questions about GMAT scoring is "Are the first 10 or so questions more important than the rest?"

As we've discussed, the GMAT adaptive algorithm starts with medium-difficulty questions. If you get questions right, your next questions are harder, and if you get questions wrong, your next questions are easier. The swings are relatively large at first but then become smaller as the test zeros in on an estimate of your performance. For that reason, you may find it tempting to spend lots of extra time at the beginning of the test.

The short word on that idea: don't.

The test maker concedes that the computer-adaptive testing algorithm uses the first 10 questions to obtain an initial estimate of your ability. The key word, though, is *initial*. As you continue to answer questions, the algorithm self-corrects by computing an updated estimate on the basis of how many questions you have answered, and then it administers items that are closely matched to this new estimate of your ability. Your final score is based on your responses, the difficulty of all the questions you answered, and the number of questions left unanswered. Taking additional time on the first 10 questions will not "game the system" and can hurt your ability to finish the test.

The test maker insists that, despite persistent rumors to the contrary, you can't outsmart the GMAT by spending extra time at the beginning. The reason for this is timing: if you answer more questions correctly than you should in more time than you should, then you will face much harder questions, under more time pressure, in the remaining three quarters of the section. Your short-term gains will be erased.

However, you still want to adjust your test-prep strategy to account for those early swings. Specifically, remember that even when your test-taking skills have become so strong that most of your test will be made up of challenging, high-reward problems, you'll still have to go through some simpler problems to get there—don't rush or become overconfident just because those first few questions are easier.

A good comparison is to a sporting event. Are the first innings or is the first quarter of a game more important than the following ones? Perhaps, since the early part of the game sets the tone for the game and gives the leading team options. But doing well during the first part of a game does not guarantee a win; you need to start strong *and* finish strong.

The cost of not finishing strong on the GMAT is substantial. If you don't answer all the questions, a penalty is assessed that will precipitously lower your score. In fact, this effect is more exaggerated in the case of high scorers. As an example, provided by GMAC, if you are at the 91st percentile but then fail to answer five questions, your score could drop to the 77th percentile. A score difference of that magnitude is substantial.

THE IMPORTANCE OF PACING

The GMAT is a test of both accuracy and speed. There is a substantial penalty for not finishing a section, as we've seen. But there is no need to think of the GMAT as a race. In fact, according to the test maker, the GMAT is created to be optimally timed so that most test takers finish the first time they sit for the test. Those who don't finish the GMAT the first time often retake the test, and almost all finish the second time.

You want to be in the group that finishes the test on the first try. Also, while you don't want to rush or make sloppy guesses, you do need to finish the test on time in order to maximize your score.

The graph below is an illustration of the penalty incurred by test takers who leave a string of unanswered questions at the end of a CAT section. Even if you had previously been performing well on questions at a high level of difficulty, running out of time will lead to a severe drop in your score. Fortunately, pacing can be improved through practicing some key principles of time management.

Spending Extra Time at the Beginning of a Section Can Lead to Failure at the End of the Section

You can pace yourself on both the Quantitative and Verbal sections, broadly speaking, by dividing each section into three parts:

- The first 10 questions
- The last 10 questions
- Everything in between

Each part has its own strategy.

- **The first 10 questions:** Given what we've covered above, you now have an idea of how to pace yourself on the first 10 questions. To recap: the first questions are likely to produce some large swings in your score, but you may see larger swings later on, and it's important to finish just as strong as you start. The theme of these 10 questions: proceed diligently, keep an eye out for pitfalls, and avoid preventable errors.

- **The middle segment:** Regardless of how the first 10 questions go, you're almost certain to find some challenges in this segment. Most test takers will "top out." Topping out means that you will be unable to solve any more difficult problems and you will begin to hover around your skill level, getting about half of the questions right and half of them wrong. The great danger at this point in the test is that you will feel you ought to be able to "get" every problem and you will spend too much time on some of them. Since time spent here takes away from the time you have for the later questions in the section, you may need to guess on a few questions to stay on pace. Fortunately, if you've budgeted your minutes well, you will have some time to give your guesses a little thought. The theme of the middle segment: stay on pace, keep your morale high, and make strategic guesses where necessary.

- **The final 10 questions** are the home stretch. You're trying to finish before the bell rings. Here you must pick your battles. Make an effort not to guess on more than one or two questions in a row. As the end draws nigh, alternate any guesses that you need to make, rather than saving them for a series at the end. Doing so will increase your options to solve without guessing, decrease the odds of accidentally running out of time, and most likely reduce the score drop from questions answered incorrectly. The theme of this segment: choose your questions and finish on time.

Now you're done. You've maximized your payoff. It can be exciting to set a pace and stick to it, and guessing on the trickiest questions can reduce your anxiety and frustration.

OTHER CAT STRATEGIES

In addition to the strategies mentioned earlier about pacing, keep in mind other CAT-specific strategies that will have a direct, positive impact on your score:

- Because the level of difficulty of questions on the CAT is not predictable, always be on the lookout for answer-choice traps.

- Because each right or wrong answer affects the next question you get, the CAT does not allow you to return to questions you've already answered. In other words, you cannot go back to double-check your work. So be as sure as you can be about your answer before moving on.

- If you're given a question you cannot answer, you'll have to guess. Guess intelligently and strategically by eliminating any answer choices that you know are wrong and guessing among those remaining. The faster you can determine that you can't answer a question, the more time you'll save by guessing; that's more time to spend on other questions that you *can* get right.

- Don't get rattled if you keep seeing really tough questions. It can mean you're doing very well. Keep it up—you're on your way to a great GMAT score!

Practice these strategies every time you take a CAT in your online resources, and you'll have the right mindset for success on Test Day.

 GO ONLINE

kaptest.com/login

PART TWO

Pretest

CHAPTER 3

GMAT Pretest

HOW TO TAKE THIS TEST

Before taking this pretest, find a quiet place where you can work without interruptions for a little over 2.5 hours. Make sure you have a comfortable desk, scratch paper, and something to write with. Be prepared to time yourself. You may take an 8-minute break between the sections.

This is not a full-length practice GMAT. Rather, this pretest comprises the two multiple-choice sections on the GMAT: the Quantitative and Verbal sections. These are the two sections that determine your 200–800 score, which is the most important score for business school admissions. (We have not included the Analytical Writing or Integrated Reasoning sections on this pretest, as we believe it is a better use of your time to first learn about and practice these question types in the relevant chapters of this book. You will have the opportunity to practice the Analytical Writing and Integrated Reasoning sections as part of full-length practice tests in your online resources.)

This pretest is designed to accurately reflect the question types and content of the GMAT Quantitative and Verbal sections. The most important benefits you'll get from taking this test are familiarity with the test content and the ability to assess your strengths and areas of opportunity. As you review this test, take note of the question types and topics that gave you the most trouble so that you can prioritize your studies in those areas for the maximum score improvement.

Since this pretest is not adaptive, it cannot be used to estimate your ability level. To get an estimate of your current score, as well as to experience the online test interface, take the Diagnostic Test in your online resources at **kaptest.com/login**. (If you have not yet registered your book, go to **kaptest.com/booksonline** to do so.) As you learn the Kaplan Methods and strategies taught in this book, take more full-length computer-adaptive tests in your online resources to gauge your progress.

GO ONLINE

kaptest.com/login

To make it easier to check your answers, use the answer sheet that follows to record your responses to the questions. You'll find the answer key and explanations in the chapter following the test. As is the case throughout this book, answer choices are referred to as **(A)**, **(B)**, **(C)**, **(D)**, and **(E)**, even though the test questions are formatted as you'll see them on Test Day: preceded by ovals, not letters.

Since the computer-adaptive GMAT does not allow test takers to skip questions or answer questions out of order, you can emulate that experience on this paper pretest by answering each question in order, guessing where necessary, and not going back to check your work on previous questions.

Good luck!

GMAT PRETEST ANSWER SHEET

Remove (or photocopy) this answer sheet and record your answers on it to make them easier to check against the answer key once you've finished the test.

Quantitative

1. _____   20. _____
2. _____   21. _____
3. _____   22. _____
4. _____   23. _____
5. _____   24. _____
6. _____   25. _____
7. _____   26. _____
8. _____   27. _____
9. _____   28. _____
10. _____   29. _____
11. _____   30. _____
12. _____   31. _____
13. _____
14. _____
15. _____
16. _____
17. _____
18. _____
19. _____

Verbal

1. _____   22. _____
2. _____   23. _____
3. _____   24. _____
4. _____   25. _____
5. _____   26. _____
6. _____   27. _____
7. _____   28. _____
8. _____   29. _____
9. _____   30. _____
10. _____   31. _____
11. _____   32. _____
12. _____   33. _____
13. _____   34. _____
14. _____   35. _____
15. _____   36. _____
16. _____
17. _____
18. _____
19. _____
20. _____
21. _____

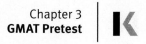
Quantitative Section

31 Questions

Time—62 minutes

In the Quantitative section, there are two types of questions: Problem Solving and Data Sufficiency.

Directions: For each **Problem Solving** question, solve the problem and select the best of the answer choices given.

Each **Data Sufficiency** problem consists of a question and two statements, labeled (1) and (2), which contain certain data. Using these data and your knowledge of mathematics and everyday facts (such as the number of days in July or the meaning of the word *counterclockwise*), decide whether the data given are sufficient for answering the question and then select one of the following answering choices:

O   Statement (1) ALONE is sufficient, but statement (2) alone is not sufficient to answer the question asked.

O   Statement (2) ALONE is sufficient, but statement (1) alone is not sufficient to answer the question asked.

O   BOTH statements (1) and (2) TOGETHER are sufficient to answer the question asked, but NEITHER statement ALONE is sufficient to answer the question asked.

O   EACH statement ALONE is sufficient to answer the question asked.

O   Statements (1) and (2) TOGETHER are NOT sufficient to answer the question asked, and additional data specific to the problem are needed.

<u>Note</u>: In Data Sufficiency problems that ask for the value of a quantity, the data given in the statements are sufficient only when it is possible to determine exactly one numerical value for the quantity.

Example:

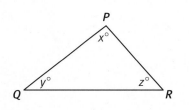

In ΔPQR, what is the value of x?

(1) $PQ = PR$

(2) $y = 40$

Explanation: According to Statement (1), $PQ = PR$; therefore, $\triangle PQR$ is isosceles and $y = z$. Since $x + y + z = 180$, it follows that $x + 2y = 180$. Since Statement (1) does not give a value for y, you cannot answer the question using Statement (1) alone. According to Statement (2), $y = 40$; therefore, $x + z = 140$. Since Statement (2) does not give a value for z, you cannot answer the question using Statement (2) alone. Using both statements together, since $x + 2y = 180$ and the value of y is given, you can find the value of x. Therefore, BOTH Statements (1) and (2) TOGETHER are sufficient to answer the question, but NEITHER statement ALONE is sufficient.

For **all** questions in the Quantitative section you may assume the following:

Numbers: All numbers used are real numbers.

Figures:

- For Problem Solving questions, figures are drawn as accurately as possible. Exceptions will be clearly noted.

- For Data Sufficiency questions, figures conform to the information given in the question, but will not necessarily conform to the additional information given in Statements (1) and (2).

- Lines shown as straight are straight, and lines that may appear jagged are also straight.

- The positions of points, angles, regions, etc. exist in the order shown, and angle measures are greater than zero.

- All figures lie in a plane unless otherwise indicated.

You may review these directions at any time during the Quantitative section.

1. Two different prime numbers between 10 and 30 are multiplied together, and the product is squared. What is the least possible result?

   ○ 20,449
   ○ 27,225
   ○ 32,402
   ○ 38,025
   ○ 53,361

2. If $b \neq 0$ and $-1 < \dfrac{a}{b} < 1$, which of the following CANNOT be true?

   ○ $a + b < 0$
   ○ $(a + b)(a - b) > 0$
   ○ $a - b > 0$
   ○ $(a + b)(a - b) < 0$
   ○ $a + b > 0$

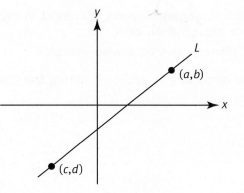

3. What is the difference between the y-intercept and the x-intercept of line L in the figure above?

   (1) The equation of line L is $2x - 3y = 6$.
   (2) $\dfrac{d - b}{c - a} = \dfrac{2}{3}$

   ○ Statement (1) ALONE is sufficient, but statement (2) is not sufficient.
   ○ Statement (2) ALONE is sufficient, but statement (1) is not sufficient.
   ○ BOTH statements TOGETHER are sufficient, but NEITHER statement ALONE is sufficient.
   ○ EACH statement ALONE is sufficient.
   ○ Statements (1) and (2) TOGETHER are NOT sufficient.

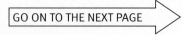

GO ON TO THE NEXT PAGE

4. A class studying genetics is growing pea plants that have either purple or white flowers and either tall or short stems. The laboratory contains 800 plants with purple flowers and 350 plants with white flowers. Of the plants with purple flowers, 70 percent have tall stems. If 480 plants have short stems, then how many plants in the laboratory are tall with white flowers?

    ○ 110
    ○ 190
    ○ 240
    ○ 350
    ○ 670

5. If j and k are both integers, and $j + k = 9n$, is n an integer?

    (1) $j + k$ is a multiple of 9.
    (2) $9n - j$ is an integer.

    ○ Statement (1) ALONE is sufficient, but statement (2) is not sufficient.
    ○ Statement (2) ALONE is sufficient, but statement (1) is not sufficient.
    ○ BOTH statements TOGETHER are sufficient, but NEITHER statement ALONE is sufficient.
    ○ EACH statement ALONE is sufficient.
    ○ Statements (1) and (2) TOGETHER are NOT sufficient.

6. Which of the following could equal zero for some value of x?

    I. $3x^2 - 12$
    II. $x^2 + x^4 + 1$
    III. $x^2 + 7x + 6$

    ○ I only
    ○ III only
    ○ I and II only
    ○ I and III only
    ○ I, II, and III

GO ON TO THE NEXT PAGE

7. If p is a negative number greater than -2, what is the value of p?

   (1) $|p^2 - 5| = 4$

   (2) $\dfrac{\left(p + \frac{1}{2}\right)(p + 1)}{p + 0.5} = 0$

   ○   Statement (1) ALONE is sufficient, but statement (2) is not sufficient.

   ○   Statement (2) ALONE is sufficient, but statement (1) is not sufficient.

   ○   BOTH statements TOGETHER are sufficient, but NEITHER statement ALONE is sufficient.

   ○   EACH statement ALONE is sufficient.

   ○   Statements (1) and (2) TOGETHER are NOT sufficient.

8. At a certain university, the football team receives 4 times more funding than does the basketball team. Together, the football and basketball teams receive 3 times as much funding as do all other sports programs combined. What is the ratio of funding for the basketball team to funding for all other sports programs, not including the football team?

   ○   1:5

   ○   1:4

   ○   3:5

   ○   3:4

   ○   5:3

GO ON TO THE NEXT PAGE

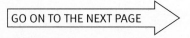

9. If $\dfrac{3a - 2ce}{3} = \dfrac{4b - 2de}{2}$, then $\dfrac{e}{3} =$

    ○ $\dfrac{9a - 8b}{6c - 4d}$

    ○ $\dfrac{6a - 3b}{2c - 3d}$

    ○ $\dfrac{3a - 6b}{2c - 3d}$

    ○ $\dfrac{a - 2b}{6c - 9d}$

    ○ $\dfrac{a - 2b}{2c - 3d}$

10. In a certain garden, x percent of f flowers are annuals, y percent of those a annuals are begonias, and z percent of those b begonias are infected with a fungus. How many begonias in the garden are infected?

    (1) $x = 50$, $y = 20$, and $z = 70$.

    (2) $a:b = 5:1$, $a:f = 1:2$, $100:(100 - z) = 10:3$, and $f = 100$.

    ○ Statement (1) ALONE is sufficient, but statement (2) is not sufficient.
    ○ Statement (2) ALONE is sufficient, but statement (1) is not sufficient.
    ○ BOTH statements TOGETHER are sufficient, but NEITHER statement ALONE is sufficient.
    ○ EACH statement ALONE is sufficient.
    ○ Statements (1) and (2) TOGETHER are NOT sufficient.

GO ON TO THE NEXT PAGE ⇒

11. In 15 minutes, Joanna can read p pages of her economics book. How many minutes will it take her to read r pages of her marketing book, if she reads both books at the same rate?

    ○ $\dfrac{r}{15p}$

    ○ $\dfrac{15r}{p}$

    ○ $\dfrac{15}{rp}$

    ○ $\dfrac{15p}{r}$

    ○ $\dfrac{p}{15r}$

12. A farmer who grows only two crops, corn and soybeans, has the same combined target output every year. This year, corn makes up 40 percent of the crop and weighs 24 tons. Next year, however, the farmer wants corn to be only 15 percent of the total tonnage. How many more tons of soybeans must the farmer grow next year to maintain the same target output?

    ○ 9
    ○ 15
    ○ 25
    ○ 36
    ○ 51

GO ON TO THE NEXT PAGE

13. If m^3 and t^3 are negative, does $p = 0$?

  (1) $p^2 - \left(\dfrac{t}{m}\right)^2 = 0$

  (2) $|t| = m^{\frac{1}{3}} \left(\sqrt[3]{p}\right)^3$

  ○ Statement (1) ALONE is sufficient, but statement (2) is not sufficient.
  ○ Statement (2) ALONE is sufficient, but statement (1) is not sufficient.
  ○ BOTH statements TOGETHER are sufficient, but NEITHER statement ALONE is sufficient.
  ○ EACH statement ALONE is sufficient.
  ○ Statements (1) and (2) TOGETHER are NOT sufficient.

14. A photographer has visited exactly 42 countries, all of which have been in Africa, Europe, or Asia. If the photographer has been to 6 more countries in Europe than in Asia, and twice as many in Africa as in Europe, how many countries in Asia has the photographer visited?

  ○ 4
  ○ 6
  ○ 12
  ○ 18
  ○ 24

15. Next year, Company S plans to make a new product, which it will sell for $50 per unit. The fixed cost of production is estimated to be $8,400, and the variable cost will be 30 percent of the per-unit selling price. What is the smallest number of units that Company S needs to sell for its total revenue to exceed its total cost?

  ○ 168
  ○ 169
  ○ 239
  ○ 240
  ○ 241

GO ON TO THE NEXT PAGE

16. If x and y are integers and $z = |x - 2| - |y + 2|$, does $z = 0$?

    (1) $\dfrac{9}{5} < x < \dfrac{7}{2}$ and $-3 \leq y < -\dfrac{21}{11}$

    (2) $2 \leq x < \dfrac{7}{3}$ and $-\dfrac{22}{7} < y < -\dfrac{13}{7}$

    ○ Statement (1) ALONE is sufficient, but statement (2) is not sufficient.
    ○ Statement (2) ALONE is sufficient, but statement (1) is not sufficient.
    ○ BOTH statements TOGETHER are sufficient, but NEITHER statement ALONE is sufficient.
    ○ EACH statement ALONE is sufficient.
    ○ Statements (1) and (2) TOGETHER are NOT sufficient.

17. How many organizational structures can be formed that consist of Division A; at least one of Divisions B and C; at least two of Divisions D, E, and F; and at least two of Divisions G, H, J, and K?

    ○ 60
    ○ 90
    ○ 99
    ○ 120
    ○ 132

18. If a and b are integers, and $ab = 210$, then what is the value of a?

    (1) $13 < a < 16$
    (2) $\dfrac{a}{15}$ is an integer, and $\dfrac{b}{14}$ is an integer.

    ○ Statement (1) ALONE is sufficient, but statement (2) is not sufficient.
    ○ Statement (2) ALONE is sufficient, but statement (1) is not sufficient.
    ○ Statements (1) and (2) TOGETHER are NOT sufficient.
    ○ BOTH statements TOGETHER are sufficient, but NEITHER statement ALONE is sufficient.
    ○ EACH statement ALONE is sufficient.

GO ON TO THE NEXT PAGE

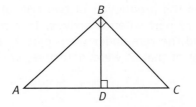

19. In the figure above, if ∠*ABC* is a right angle and *BD* bisects *AC*, then what is the ratio of *BC* to *AC*?

    ○ $\dfrac{\sqrt{2}}{4}$

    ○ $\dfrac{\sqrt{2}}{3}$

    ○ $\dfrac{1}{2}$

    ○ $\dfrac{\sqrt{2}}{2}$

    ○ $\dfrac{2\sqrt{3}}{3}$

20. Paula has a collection of used books worth $104. How many are histories?

    (1) Paula has only mysteries and histories; each mystery is worth $1, and each history is worth $25.

    (2) Paula has exactly 4 mysteries in her collection that together cost a total of $4.

    ○ Statement (1) ALONE is sufficient, but statement (2) is not sufficient.
    ○ Statement (2) ALONE is sufficient, but statement (1) is not sufficient.
    ○ BOTH statements TOGETHER are sufficient, but NEITHER statement ALONE is sufficient.
    ○ EACH statement ALONE is sufficient.
    ○ Statements (1) and (2) TOGETHER are NOT sufficient.

GO ON TO THE NEXT PAGE

21. A manufacturer outsources the production of two critical parts, part W and part Z. The manufacturer inspects every part when it arrives. In a recent shipment, 60 percent of the parts were part W, and the remainder were part Z. If 0.1 percent of part W were defective and 0.05 percent of part Z were defective, what percentage of the total shipment was defective?

    ○ 0.0075%
    ○ 0.06%
    ○ 0.075%
    ○ 0.08%
    ○ 0.8%

22. The average weight of 10 bags of apples is 2.50 kg per bag. Of the 10 bags, 4 weigh 2.65 kg, 3 weigh 2.40 kg, and 1 weighs 2.20 kg. If the difference between the weights of the 2 remaining bags is 0.40 kg, what is the weight of the lightest bag of the 10?

    ○ 2.10 kg
    ○ 2.20 kg
    ○ 2.25 kg
    ○ 2.30 kg
    ○ 2.40 kg

23. How many employees of Company R are surveyors?

    (1) Exactly $\frac{5}{8}$ of the employees of Company R are not surveyors.
    (2) The 18 architects in Company R constitute 25 percent of the company's total employees.

    ○ Statement (1) ALONE is sufficient, but statement (2) is not sufficient.
    ○ Statement (2) ALONE is sufficient, but statement (1) is not sufficient.
    ○ BOTH statements TOGETHER are sufficient, but NEITHER statement ALONE is sufficient.
    ○ EACH statement ALONE is sufficient.
    ○ Statements (1) and (2) TOGETHER are NOT sufficient.

GO ON TO THE NEXT PAGE

24. If $2(s - r) = -2\left(\dfrac{r^2 - s^2}{s^2 - r^2}\right)$ and $s^2 - r^2 \neq 0$, then $s - r =$

   ○ -2
   ○ -1
   ○ 0
   ○ 1
   ○ 2

25. A ferry crosses a lake and then returns to its starting point by the same route. The first time it crosses the lake, the ferry travels at 15 kilometers per hour. The ferry's return trip takes 3 hours. How many hours does the ferry take for the first leg of the trip?

   (1)   The ferry's average speed for the entire round trip is 12 kilometers per hour.
   (2)   The distance the ferry covers to cross the lake once is 30 kilometers.

   ○   Statement (1) ALONE is sufficient, but statement (2) is not sufficient.
   ○   Statement (2) ALONE is sufficient, but statement (1) is not sufficient.
   ○   BOTH statements TOGETHER are sufficient, but NEITHER statement ALONE is sufficient.
   ○   EACH statement ALONE is sufficient.
   ○   Statements (1) and (2) TOGETHER are NOT sufficient.

26. If $a^5 \geq -32$ and a is an integer, what is the value of a?

   (1) $6a + 18 \leq 12$
   (2) $a^2 > 2$

   ○   Statement (1) ALONE is sufficient, but statement (2) is not sufficient.
   ○   Statement (2) ALONE is sufficient, but statement (1) is not sufficient.
   ○   BOTH statements TOGETHER are sufficient, but NEITHER statement ALONE is sufficient.
   ○   EACH statement ALONE is sufficient.
   ○   Statements (1) and (2) TOGETHER are NOT sufficient.

GO ON TO THE NEXT PAGE

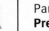
27. A rectangular wooden block with dimensions of 10 inches wide by 10 inches long by 20 inches high is painted blue on all surfaces. The block is placed upright (resting on a square base) and cut in half from top to bottom parallel to two sides of the block. What fraction of the surface area of each resulting half is <u>not</u> painted blue?

   ○ $\frac{1}{8}$

   ○ $\frac{2}{9}$

   ○ $\frac{1}{4}$

   ○ $\frac{2}{7}$

   ○ $\frac{1}{2}$

28. How many multiples of 7 are there among the integers 100 through 1,000 inclusive?

   ○ 127
   ○ 128
   ○ 132
   ○ 142
   ○ 143

29. In the equation $d = kc - 3$, k is a constant. If possible solutions to the equation are in the form (c,d), then is $(1,-2)$ a solution?

   (1) $k^2 = 1$
   (2) $(0,-3)$ is a solution.

   ○ Statement (1) ALONE is sufficient, but statement (2) is not sufficient.
   ○ Statement (2) ALONE is sufficient, but statement (1) is not sufficient.
   ○ BOTH statements TOGETHER are sufficient, but NEITHER statement ALONE is sufficient.
   ○ EACH statement ALONE is sufficient.
   ○ Statements (1) and (2) TOGETHER are NOT sufficient.

GO ON TO THE NEXT PAGE ⟹

30. Flo and Ethan commute separately to the same office. Flo's commute is four-fifths the distance of Ethan's, and Ethan's commute takes two-thirds more time than does Flo's. If it takes Flo 0.4 hours to travel to work, by what percentage is Ethan's average speed lower than Flo's?

    ○ $12\frac{1}{2}\%$

    ○ 25%

    ○ $33\frac{1}{3}\%$

    ○ $37\frac{1}{2}\%$

    ○ 50%

31. If $0 < x < 1$, which of the following has the greatest value?

    ○ $(x^2 - 1)^{-1}$

    ○ $x^{-\frac{1}{2}}$

    ○ $(x + 1)^{-2}$

    ○ x^{-2}

    ○ $(x^2 + 1)^{-1}$

YOU MAY NOW TAKE AN 8-MINUTE BREAK.

STOP

Verbal Section

36 Questions

Time—65 minutes

There are three types of questions in the Verbal section: Critical Reasoning, Reading Comprehension, and Sentence Correction.

Directions: For each question, select the best answer of the choices given.

Each of the **Critical Reasoning** questions is based on a short argument, a set of statements, or a plan of action.

Each of the **Reading Comprehension** questions is based on the content of a passage. After reading the passage, answer all questions pertaining to it on the basis of what is **stated** or **implied** in the passage.

Each of the **Sentence Correction** questions presents a sentence, part or all of which is underlined. Beneath the sentence you will find five ways of phrasing the underlined part. The first of these repeats the original; the other four are different. Follow the requirements of standard written English to choose your answer, paying attention to grammar, word choice, and sentence construction. Select the answer that produces the most effective sentence; your answer should make the sentence clear, exact, and free of grammatical error. It should also minimize awkwardness, ambiguity, and redundancy.

You may review these directions at any time during the Verbal section.

1. The *lira da braccio*, an ancestor of the modern-day violin that has a sound post that helps generate the distinctively <u>expressively tonality that is a characteristic of the violin family of instruments, are</u> seen in Renaissance artwork in which it is often played by prominent characters of Greek myth.

   ○ expressively tonality that is a characteristic of the violin family of instruments, are
   ○ expressively tonality that is a characteristic of the violin family of instruments, is
   ○ expressive tonality that is a characteristic of the violin family of instruments, are
   ○ expressive tonality that is a characteristic of the violin family of instruments, is
   ○ expressive tonality that is a characteristic of the violin family of instruments, was

2. Last month, a group of salespeople from Excello attended a seminar on persuasive speaking. In the weeks following the seminar, the salespeople who attended the seminar have made more sales, on average, than those who did not attend the seminar. To increase sales, the sales manager plans to send the remaining salespeople to the same seminar next month.

   Which of the following, if true, would most support the prediction that the sales manager's plan will achieve its goal?

   ○ Last month's seminar focused solely on tactics relevant to the work at Excello.
   ○ Total sales at Excello last month were higher than sales from the month prior to the seminar.
   ○ To prepare for the seminar, the attending salespeople read a book on improving communication skills.
   ○ Over the last month, Excello's sales were greater than the sales of its largest competitor.
   ○ Invitations to last month's seminar were not accepted solely by salespeople with above-average sales.

3. Brand management in the personal care industry, <u>like any industry, is the art of defining consumer perceptions of the utility and value promised by the product line</u> and the personality projected by the company.

   ○ like any industry, is the art of defining consumer perceptions of the utility and value promised by the product line
   ○ similar to how any industry does it, is the art of defining consumer perceptions of the utility and value promised by the product line
   ○ like brand management in any industry, is the artistic defining of consumer perceptions of the product line's promises of utility and value
   ○ as in any industry, is artfully defining consumer perceptions of the utility and value promised by the product line
   ○ as in any industry, is the art of defining consumer perceptions of the utility and value promised by the product line

GO ON TO THE NEXT PAGE

4. During the latter stages of the insurrection, the revolution's leaders resorted to ever more violent means, including public execution of members of the upper class, <u>to establish their authority, and they suppressed</u> dissent ruthlessly.

   ○ to establish their authority, and they suppressed
   ○ that established their authority, and it suppressed
   ○ of establishing their authority and to suppress
   ○ to establish their authority, and they were suppressing
   ○ so that their authority was established, and it suppressed

5. The city of Northtown collects an average of $2.2 million in business taxes per year. Neighboring Southtown collects an average of $1.8 million in business taxes per year. Both cities assess business taxes on net profits. In an attempt to attract new businesses to Southtown, the spokesperson for the chamber of commerce of that city uses these statistics to claim that Southtown's lower business tax rate offers a more favorable environment for business than can be found in Northtown.

   Which of the following, if true, would most seriously undermine the spokesperson's argument?

   ○ Most tax revenue collected in Northtown comes from business taxes.
   ○ Most tax revenue collected in Southtown comes from business taxes.
   ○ The net profits generated by Northtown businesses are currently twice those of Southtown businesses.
   ○ Northtown has twice the population of Southtown.
   ○ Southtown businesses generate twice as much sales revenue as do Northtown businesses.

6. Establishing goals for a nonprofit organization is often different <u>than setting</u> goals for a profit-making enterprise because the stakeholders of the former may be more varied.

   ○ than setting
   ○ than the setting of
   ○ from
   ○ from setting
   ○ from the setting of

GO ON TO THE NEXT PAGE ⟹

7. A grain-processing company has started experimenting with catfish farming in an attempt to reduce waste by using the by-products of its grain processing as fish food. Catfish whose diet includes grain by-products have been found to reach marketable size in five months, and restaurants have expressed interest in having a reliable source for catfish.

   The answer to which of the following questions is LEAST directly relevant to the grain-processing company's consideration of whether fish farming is a preferable alternative to discarding grain by-products?

   ○ How does the cost of discarding grain by-products compare to the operating costs of a fish farm?

   ○ How many pounds of catfish are served by restaurants locally and nationally each year?

   ○ Are there government regulations that apply to the production and transportation of fish?

   ○ Do catfish require nutrients not supplied by grain by-products?

   ○ In how many months do wild catfish reach marketable size?

8. Although her X-ray photographs <u>had laid the foundation for describing the structure of DNA, Rosalind Franklin, an accomplished chemist, did not receive the Nobel prize when it was awarded for this achievement</u> in 1962.

   ○ had laid the foundation for describing the structure of DNA, Rosalind Franklin, an accomplished chemist, did not receive the Nobel prize when it was awarded for this achievement

   ○ had laid the foundation for its description, the structure of DNA did not result in accomplished chemist Rosalind Franklin receiving the Nobel prize awarded for it

   ○ of the structure of DNA had laid the foundation for their description, the accomplished chemist Rosalind Franklin was not awarded the Nobel prize for this achievement

   ○ were the foundation for describing the structure of DNA, the Nobel prize was not awarded to accomplished chemist Rosalind Franklin for it

   ○ were an achievement by Rosalind Franklin, an accomplished chemist, it did not receive the Nobel prize for laying the foundation for describing the structure of DNA

GO ON TO THE NEXT PAGE

Questions 9–12 refer to the passage.

Women around the world graduate from college at higher rates than men. However, women's participation in the workforce, especially in the ranks of senior management, continues to lag far behind that of men. Research indicates that, as women marry and start families, their earnings and opportunities for promotion decrease. While the difficulties that

5   women encounter as they attempt to balance work and family life are frequently discussed, and are beginning to be addressed by employers, it is interesting to note that the difficulties faced by working married men are seldom raised.

Scott Coltrane, a researcher at the University of Oregon, has found that, while the earnings of women tend to go down with each additional child, the earnings of married men

10   not only exceed those of both unmarried men and divorced men but also tend to go up with each additional child. One reason for this disparity may be that, as the size of the family grows, men rely on women to manage most of the responsibilities of housekeeping and child raising. While within the past few decades men have assumed a greater share of household responsibilities, in the United States, women still spend nearly twice as much

15   time as men do in caring for children and the home. The time diaries of highly educated dual-income U.S. couples show that men enjoy three and a half times the leisure time as their female partners do.

If married men earn higher salaries and have more leisure time than their female counterparts do, what difficulties do these working men face? Research indicates three

20   possible problems. First, the perceived responsibility of providing for a family drives men to work more hours and strive for promotion. Many men report feeling dissatisfied because the level of performance that is required to earn promotions and higher salaries prevents them from spending time with their families. Second, these demands on men also contribute to higher levels of marital discord. In a 2008 survey, 60 percent of U.S. fathers

25   reported work-family conflicts, compared to 47 percent of mothers.

The pressure to be perceived as a good provider contributes to the third reason that married men may struggle. While women's decisions to use family leave benefits, move to part-time employment, or leave the workforce to care for children are seen as valuable contributions to family life and, by extension, society, men's decisions to do the same are frequently viewed

30   by their employers as signs of weakness. Studies suggest that men who take advantage of paternity leave policies are viewed as weak or inadequate by both women and men. Research conducted in Australia found that men's requests to work flexibly were denied at twice the rate of those of women.

GO ON TO THE NEXT PAGE ⟹

9. The author of the passage is primarily concerned with

    O   advocating changes in employers' practices regarding female employees with children

    O   examining some of the reasons that married men may experience problems related to their employment

    O   describing the psychological consequences for men of earning high salaries

    O   taking issue with those who believe that women should not earn more than men

    O   analyzing the indirect effects of discrimination against women on married men

10. The passage provides information in support of which of the following assertions about married men who work?

    O   The ability to provide for their families is the most important aspect of employment for married men.

    O   Married men in high-status positions are easily able to integrate their careers and family lives.

    O   Married men who achieve greater earnings while having a larger family are more satisfied on average than their wives.

    O   The perceived demands on men to earn enough income to support a family may have harmful effects on family life.

    O   As married men achieve higher earnings, they are able to take more time off from work to spend with their families.

11. The author of the passage discusses Coltrane's research primarily in order to

    O   illustrate the benefits that employers extend to their married male employees

    O   identify a benefit of work that married men experience that is accompanied by some potential costs

    O   defend the family leave policies and flexible work schedules that some employers offer

    O   modify the prevailing view that women experience disadvantages in the workplace after marrying and having children

    O   point out several ways in which women experience discrimination in the workplace

GO ON TO THE NEXT PAGE

12. According to the passage, married men generally receive higher salaries and have a better chance of being promoted than do single men because

    O   employers consider married men to be more diligent and responsible than single men

    O   married men have usually accrued more experience than have single men

    O   married men may be able to rely on their spouses to address child care and household responsibilities

    O   higher pay typically corresponds with greater job security and enhanced benefits

    O   employers recognize the difficulties of providing for a larger number of children and seek to ease this burden

13. Science fiction has been described as the genre that by addressing the future, <u>that it concerns ideas of large scope rather than the ephemeral thoughts</u> and emotions of individuals.

    O   that it concerns ideas of large scope rather than the ephemeral thoughts

    O   that concerns ideas of large scope instead of the ephemeral thoughts

    O   concerns ideas of large scope rather than the ephemeral thoughts

    O   so concerns ideas of large scope instead of the ephemeral thinking

    O   it concerns ideas of large scope but not the ephemeral thoughts

14. Nina Simone, <u>whose distinctive technique is credited as to her early classical training, is known to be famous for</u> her renditions of blues, jazz, and folk compositions as well as for her impassioned civil rights activism.

    O   whose distinctive technique is credited as to her early classical training, is known to be famous for

    O   whose distinctive technique is credited to her early classical training, is known for

    O   who had a distinctive technique that is credited with her early classical training, is known for

    O   credited with a distinctive technique due to her early classical training, is known for

    O   who is credited to her early classical training on account of her technique, is known as

GO ON TO THE NEXT PAGE ⟹

15. Earlier this year, our city's three main reservoirs had unusually low water levels. As a result, city officials initiated a program that encouraged residents to reduce their water usage by 20 percent. Since the program was announced, the water level at all three reservoirs has returned to normal. Our city officials should be applauded for their role in preventing a crisis.

    Which of the following, if true, casts the most doubt on the efficacy of the officials' program?

    O   The current water level in the reservoirs is lower than it was at the same time last year.

    O   Other nearby reservoirs recovered from lower water levels this year, even though those reservoirs provide water to cities that did not enact water restriction policies.

    O   Residents reduced their water usage for lawn maintenance significantly more than they did for washing clothes.

    O   Imposing stiff penalties on residents who did not conserve water would have resulted in even higher water levels in the reservoirs.

    O   Water usage in the city dropped steadily during the first two weeks of the program before leveling off.

16. To attract new visitors, the local zoo is planning to offer new experiences. One proposal involves allowing visitors to assist in feeding the big cats, such as the lions and the tigers. However, unlike the zookeepers, visitors do not spend time interacting with the cats and becoming familiar to them. Enacting this plan would be like inviting people to enter the home of a well-armed stranger without knocking.

    Which of the following statements, if true, would most strengthen the argument?

    O   Visitors have not spent as much time studying the behavior of big cats as the zookeepers have.

    O   Those who would be most interested in opportunities to assist in feeding big cats are already regular visitors and would not bring along new visitors.

    O   Burglars who are attacked by an occupant during a home invasion usually incur serious injuries requiring emergency treatment.

    O   People who visit zoos have less experience interacting with wild animals than do people who do not visit zoos.

    O   Feeding big cats requires entering their habitat, which can only be done safely after previous interaction with the animals.

GO ON TO THE NEXT PAGE

17. <u>As one step in their plan to engender greater goodwill in the community, the town council organized a series of public meetings when residents could air grievances about the opacity of decision making, a tendency to award contracts to cronies, and their failure to follow through on promised reforms.</u>

    ○ As one step in their plan to engender greater goodwill in the community, the town council organized a series of public meetings when residents could air grievances about the opacity of decision making, a tendency to award contracts to cronies, and their failure to follow through on promised reforms.

    ○ As one step in its plan to engender greater goodwill in the community, the town council organized a series of public meetings at which residents could air grievances about the opacity of decision making, a tendency to award contracts to cronies, and a failure to follow through on promised reforms.

    ○ As one step in its plan to engender greater goodwill in the community, the town council organized a series of public meetings at which residents could air grievances about the opacity of decision making, tendency to award contracts to cronies, and failing to follow through on promised reforms.

    ○ As one step in its plan to engender greater goodwill in the community, a series of public meetings was organized by the town council so that residents could air grievances about the opacity of decision making, a tendency to award contracts to cronies, and a failure to follow through on promised reforms.

    ○ The town council, as one step in their plan to engender greater goodwill in the community, organized a series of public meetings for residents at which they could air grievances about their opacity of decision making, tendency to award contracts to cronies, and failure to follow through on promised reforms.

GO ON TO THE NEXT PAGE

18. Reducing the population of Japanese beetles is done <u>most easily by applying pesticides to turf-dwelling young larva in late summer than applications</u> to mature larva in spring or adult beetles at any time of year.

- O   most easily by applying pesticides to turf-dwelling young larva in late summer than applications
- O   most easily by the application of pesticides to turf-dwelling young larva in late summer than that
- O   more easily by applying pesticides to turf-dwelling young larva in late summer than
- O   easier through the application of pesticides to turf-dwelling young larva in late summer than
- O   more easily by applying pesticides to turf-dwelling young larva in late summer rather than applying

GO ON TO THE NEXT PAGE

Questions 19–21 are based on the following passage.

It is believed that half or more of the languages spoken on Earth will be extinct within a century. UNESCO, which monitors endangered languages, says that "with each vanishing language, an irreplaceable element of human thought in its multiform variations is lost forever." As the world becomes more interconnected, many languages, as well as the
5   culture captured within them, may be lost.

There is a strong link between language and cultural identity. In nineteenth-century Japan, attempts to assimilate the Ainu people into Japanese culture included banning their language; some indigenous languages in both North American and Australia suffered the same fate. Many of those languages are lost or dying. With loss of language comes
10   loss of links to the past and feelings of belonging to a community, which research has linked to mental health. One study of Aboriginal communities found that youth suicide rates dropped to almost zero when the residents had conversational knowledge of native languages.

One problem endangered languages face is lack of official recognition. Residents of a
15   country are expected to know its official language or languages, but many countries do little to recognize minority regional languages. Take Basque, a language spoken in both Spain and France. In France, only French is recognized as an official language. In Spain, the constitution allows for regional recognition of official languages besides Spanish, so in Basque-speaking parts of the country, both Spanish and Basque are official languages.
20   It is not surprising, therefore, that UNESCO cites Basque as "vulnerable" in Spain but "critically endangered" in France.

Consider, in contrast, the case of Finnish. This tongue is not endangered, even though Finland was ruled from the Middle Ages until 1917 by first Sweden and then Russia and, during this period, Swedish was used as the language of administration and
25   government. In 1919, a newly independent Finland constitutionally adopted both Finnish and Swedish as official languages, legally recognizing its native language as important to its burgeoning national identity. As of 2013, Finnish was spoken by 89 percent of the population of Finland.

In order to preserve languages that will otherwise be lost, linguists have proposed
30   creating a database of endangered languages. But how would an academic repository serve the often marginalized groups that speak such languages? While directed toward a noble goal, this project would fail to address the issue of language's critical role in preserving a sense of cultural identity.

GO ON TO THE NEXT PAGE ⟹

19. According to the passage, Basque is more endangered in France than in Spain because

    ○ France has suppressed Basque in order to maintain a French cultural identity
    ○ there are more Basque speakers in Spain than in France
    ○ Basque has no governmental recognition as an official language in France
    ○ multiple languages are recognized as official throughout Spain
    ○ Basque-speaking regions in Spain have developed a separate cultural identity

20. Which of the following statements, if true, would support the assertion that Finnish was "important to [Finland's] burgeoning national identity" (lines 26–27)?

    ○ Speaking Finnish after 1919 became a point of pride for those in Finland, whereas it previously had often been a source of shame.
    ○ Both Swedish and Finnish were taught in Finnish schools after 1919, just as they had been before the new constitution was adopted.
    ○ Finland adopted a new flag and national anthem after the new constitution was approved in 1919.
    ○ Some people in Finland continued to use Swedish as their preferred language even after Finnish was adopted as an official language.
    ○ Those who worked to modernize Finnish in the late nineteenth century so it would achieve broader acceptance favored the western dialect over the eastern.

21. Which of the following statements most clearly exemplifies the aspect of language extinction that UNESCO considers problematic?

    ○ As one of the world's oldest languages, Basque is worth preserving as a living historical artifact as well as a modern spoken language.
    ○ Because scholars have been unable to translate the Linear A script, the intellectual capital of the culture that produced it remains inaccessible.
    ○ Because Socrates did not leave behind any written works, his ideas have been preserved only through secondhand sources.
    ○ Most linguists term Korean a "language isolate" because it is not known to be related to any other languages.
    ○ Because it has no equivalent word in many languages, "serendipity" is a particularly difficult term to translate.

GO ON TO THE NEXT PAGE ⇒

22. The recently discovered planet Kepler-90i was found via machine learning, a form of artificial intelligence <u>in which the identification of planets learned by computers is done from data by finding in the Kepler telescope instances of recorded signals from planets beyond our solar system,</u> known as exoplanets.

    ○ in which the identification of planets learned by computers is done from data by finding in the Kepler telescope instances of recorded signals from planets beyond our solar system

    ○ in which computers learn to identify planets by finding in the Kepler telescope instances of recorded signals from planets beyond our solar system

    ○ in which computers learn to identify planets by finding in data from the Kepler telescope instances of the planet's recorded signals from beyond our solar system

    ○ in which computers learn to identify planets by finding in data from the Kepler telescope instances of recorded signals from planets beyond our solar system

    ○ in which the identification of planets is learned by computers by finding in data from the Kepler telescope instances of recorded signals from planets beyond our solar system

23. A business owner noticed that many of her employees exhibited signs of fatigue throughout the workday. To combat this, the business owner has partnered with a local gym to offer employees a discounted rate on annual memberships. The business owner is confident this program will help, as studies have shown that people who exercise regularly have higher energy levels than people who do not.

    Which of the following, if true, would most seriously call into question the claim that the business owner's plan will reduce fatigue?

    ○ Making minor changes to one's diet can boost energy as effectively as can regular exercise.

    ○ The discount offered is so small that most employees will not be encouraged to purchase an annual membership.

    ○ Employees with higher energy levels are not necessarily more productive at work.

    ○ The local gym would have to offer more classes to accommodate the increase in membership.

    ○ There is no way to eliminate fatigue altogether.

GO ON TO THE NEXT PAGE

24. Since 2007, the Department of Defense has maintained a program designed to investigate unidentified flying objects, <u>despite the views of many scientists who considered</u> that these phenomena will be found to have natural explanations.

    ○ despite the views of many scientists who considered
    ○ despite the views of many scientists who consider
    ○ despite the views of many scientists believe
    ○ despite the views of many scientists who believe
    ○ although scientists believed

25. Although carotene and xanthophyll pigments are present in leaves throughout the year, these pigments are not usually visible until <u>the days shorten, temperature drops, and the breaking down of the chlorophyll in the leaves reveals</u> the yellow and orange colors.

    ○ the days shorten, temperature drops, and the breaking down of the chlorophyll in the leaves reveals
    ○ the days shorten, the temperature drops, and the chlorophyll breakdown in the leaves is to reveal
    ○ the days shorten, the temperature drops, and the chlorophyll in the leaves breaks down, revealing
    ○ the days are shorter, the temperature is lower, and less chlorophyll in the leaves due to breakdown reveals
    ○ the days shorten, the temperature drops, and chlorophyll breaks down revealing in the leaves

26. To protect the environment, paper towels in public restrooms should be banned and replaced with hot-air dryers. The use of such dryers would reduce the need to cut down trees to turn into paper towels; furthermore, since fewer paper towels would be needed, the environmental impact of the emissions from the paper-manufacturing process would be lessened.

    Which of the following is an assumption upon which the above proposal depends?

    ○ The operating expenses related to hot-air dryers are no higher than those related to paper towels.
    ○ The manufacture and operation of hot-air dryers use fewer natural resources than do the manufacture and use of paper towels.
    ○ Hot-air dryers are the only viable alternative to paper towels in public restrooms.
    ○ Hot-air dryers are at least as effective as paper towels.
    ○ The operators of public restrooms are willing to replace paper towels with hot-air dryers.

GO ON TO THE NEXT PAGE

27. Coffee beans that are imported into the United States from Zantria regularly outsell those imported from Kuanta. Coffee plants in Zantria are grown in the mountains, while plants in Kuanta are grown in the lowlands. To improve sales, farmers in Kuanta should start growing plants in that country's mountains, which have a nearly identical climate to that of Zantria.

Which of the following, if true, casts the most doubt on the conclusion of the argument?

○ In a blind taste test, coffee experts rated coffee made from Kuanta's beans as more flavorful than that made from Zantria's beans.

○ The coffee plants in Zantria are of the species *C. arabica*, while those in Kuanta are *C. canephora*.

○ Coffee plants in the lowlands of Kuanta are threatened by a fungal infection, which could reduce the supply of beans.

○ At retail outlets in the United States, the average price of Kuanta's coffee beans is lower than the average price of Zantria's beans.

○ The coffee beans imported from Zantria are available in a full range of light, medium, and dark roasts.

GO ON TO THE NEXT PAGE ⟹

28. In 2017, completing the journey in six less days than was previously done, the record for sailing around the world alone was broken by French sailor François Gabart.

   O   In 2017, completing the journey in six less days than was previously done, the record for sailing around the world alone was broken by French sailor François Gabart.

   O   Completing the journey in six fewer days than was previously done, the record for sailing around the world alone in 2017 was broken by French sailor François Gabart.

   O   Completing the journey in six fewer days than the previous record, the record for sailing around the world alone was broken by French sailor François Gabart in 2017.

   O   In 2017, completing the journey in six fewer days than the previous record holder, French sailor François Gabart broke the record for sailing around the world alone.

   O   In 2017, completing the journey in six less days than the previous record, French sailor François Gabart broke the record for sailing around the world alone.

GO ON TO THE NEXT PAGE

Questions 29–32 are based on the following passage.

Bog bodies, most of them dating from between 500 BCE and 100 CE, have been found across northwestern Europe. They are remarkably well preserved in many cases, sometimes down to wrinkles and scars on their leathery, reddish-brown skin. They have not been kept intact in the same way as Egyptian mummies, deliberately embalmed
5 through painstaking human technique, but have likely been perpetuated by an accident that archaeologists who study the Iron Age might call a happy one.

The wetlands in which the bodies are found are exclusively sphagnum moss bogs. These exist in temperate climes where the winter and early spring weather is cold, leaving the water in the bogs below 40° F during those months, and the bogs are all near sources of
10 salt water. Together these elements create the perfect environment for the preservation of skin and internal organs.

The biochemistry of preservation in bogs has several components. Both the cold temperatures and dense peat from the moss, which constitutes a mostly anaerobic environment, prevent significant bacterial growth in the water. As layers of moss die and
15 deteriorate in the water, they create humic acid, also known as "bog acid"; the acidic environment further inhibits bacteria.

Interestingly, this acid often erodes the bones of bog bodies, leaving only the skin and organs, in a process quite the opposite of that which acts upon bodies outside of bogs. The dead layers of moss also release sphagnan, a carbohydrate that attaches itself to the
20 skin of the bodies, preventing rot and water damage.

Besides bodies, bogs have also preserved books, boats, and even bread and "bog butter"—waxy dairy- or meat-based substances sometimes found stored in barrels in the bogs, which likely served as the equivalent of Iron Age refrigerators, preserving food just as they preserve human skin. Much can be learned about our ancestors from the Iron
25 Age and even earlier due to the unique ability of sphagnum moss bogs to preserve so thoroughly that which has fallen into them: scholars have studied such diverse featues of early human life as medical conditions like arthritis and parasitic infection, diet, and how far from home people traveled. The bogs offer a fascinating window into the past.

GO ON TO THE NEXT PAGE

29. According to the passage, all of the following conditions are conducive to the preservation of bog bodies EXCEPT

  ○ long winters

  ○ low air temperatures

  ○ proximity to salt water

  ○ cool water

  ○ sphagnum moss

30. The primary purpose of the passage is to

  ○ explain the ways in which bog bodies are different from other preserved bodies, such as mummies

  ○ challenge the position that the preservation of bodies in bogs is probably the result of intentional effort

  ○ discuss the characteristics of sphagnum moss bogs that allow bodies to be found in a condition that permits unique study

  ○ argue that scholars would not understand significant aspects of human life during the Iron Age had bog bodies not been discovered

  ○ analyze the differences between sphagnum moss bogs and the types of environments in which bodies decay

31. In the context of the passage as a whole, the third paragraph serves primarily to

  ○ evaluate the relative importance of the elements discussed in the second paragraph

  ○ provide support for an argument presented in the fourth paragraph about the significance of the subject of the passage

  ○ outline the creation of the environment that produces the effect that is the topic of the passage

  ○ elaborate on the mechanisms underlying an effect achieved by elements introduced in the second paragraph

  ○ explain the prominence of a particular academic discipline in the study of the topic of the passage

GO ON TO THE NEXT PAGE ⇒

32. According to the passage, bacterial growth is inhibited by all of the following EXCEPT

   O   an anaerobic environment
   O   the presence of sphagnum moss
   O   breakdown of layers of dead moss
   O   cold water temperature
   O   release of sphagnan from dead moss

33. In recent years, the use of herbarus, a natural remedy that is recommended by practitioners of alternative medicine, has become more popular for the treatment of anxiety, and there has been a corresponding decrease in the incidence of anxiety in countries where the sale of herbarus is legal. Studies have shown that people who take herbarus for anxiety under the supervision of an alternative health care practitioner are less likely to have difficulty performing important life activities than are people who choose to take a pharmaceutical prescribed by a physician, but people who take herbarus are, on the recommendation of their health care provider, more likely to use multiple treatment modalities in combination.

   If the statements above are all true, they most strongly support which of the following conclusions?

   O   People who choose to take herbarus to treat anxiety report higher overall satisfaction with their quality of life than do people who take a medication prescribed by a physician.
   O   Since the popularity of using herbarus to treat anxiety has increased, there has been a decline in the number of people who take physician-prescribed pharmaceuticals.
   O   Most people believe that herbs and other natural remedies, including herbarus, are better for the treatment of anxiety than are physician-prescribed medications.
   O   If the popularity of using herbarus to treat anxiety were not growing, the number of people with symptoms of anxiety would be increasing.
   O   A practitioner of alternative medicine is likely to use different protocols in treating an individual who reports feeling anxious than would a physician seeing the same patient.

GO ON TO THE NEXT PAGE

34. The self-portraits of Frida Kahlo can be considered both introspective explorations of a psyche that ranged free, unbounded by historical notions of cultural identity and <u>feminine, as well as subverting</u> traditional European portraiture.

- ○ feminine, as well as subverting
- ○ being feminine, and subverted
- ○ that was feminine, and subversions of
- ○ the femininity, as well as subverted
- ○ femininity, and subversions of

35. Sales of yoga mats from Daniel's yoga studio this year were double those of the prior year. However, average enrollment per class at Daniel's studio decreased from the prior year, despite Daniel's studio being the only yoga studio in town.

Which of the following, if true, most helps to explain the discrepancy in sales?

- ○ Daniel offered a greater variety of yoga mats for sale than he had offered the previous year.
- ○ The prices of yoga mats in Daniel's studio increased from the previous year.
- ○ Daniel began to teach additional styles of yoga this year, increasing the number of classes offered and attracting new students.
- ○ Daniel increased the cost of each of his yoga classes from the previous year.
- ○ Daniel's studio requires that an individual bring his or her own yoga mat to each of the classes.

GO ON TO THE NEXT PAGE

36. The rise of alternative funding opportunities, such as microloans, crowdfunding, and peer-to-peer networks, <u>have enabled many small entrepreneurs to rapidly grow successful companies specializing in products that are of interest only to niche markets</u>.

    ○ have enabled many small entrepreneurs to rapidly grow successful companies specializing in products that are of interest only to niche markets

    ○ have enabled many small entrepreneurs to rapidly grow successful companies only specializing in products that are of interest to niche markets

    ○ has enabled many small entrepreneurs to rapidly grow successful companies specializing in products that are of interest only to niche markets

    ○ has enabled many small entrepreneurs to rapidly grow only successful companies specializing in products that are of interest to niche markets

    ○ has enabled many small entrepreneurs to grow successful companies specializing rapidly in products that are of interest only to niche markets

CONGRATULATIONS! THIS CONCLUDES YOUR GMAT PRETEST.

STOP

CHAPTER 4

Pretest Answers and Explanations

HOW TO REVIEW THIS TEST

The primary purpose of this pretest is to allow you to evaluate your strengths and weaknesses—or, as we call them, your areas of opportunity. If you have ample time before Test Day, you will benefit from working through each chapter in this book thoroughly, taking full advantage of the strategic explanations, and using your online resources at **kaptest.com/login** for further practice. If, however, you have more limited time to prepare, you may need to prioritize your studies to make sure you address the areas in which you are struggling the most—thereby making the most of your opportunities for score improvement.

In either case, understanding your strengths and weaknesses is an essential starting point for your GMAT prep. Each explanation is preceded by one label for the question type (e.g., Data Sufficiency, Sentence Correction) and, often, one or more labels for the question topic (e.g., Arithmetic: Exponents, Verbs). These labels correspond to question types or content areas covered in this book. As you review the explanations, note what question types and topics you found most challenging. Fill in the tables in the next section to help identify these areas. Then as you work through this book and your online resources, place particular focus on these questions and concepts.

The explanations themselves are valuable learning tools. Review the questions you answered incorrectly *and* those you got right. Rework the questions you got wrong so you can be sure to know exactly what to do when you see a similar one in the future. For the questions you got correct, did you answer correctly for the right reasons, or did you follow a lucky hunch? Does the explanation offer an alternative, more efficient path to the right answer that you can add to your arsenal? Or maybe you aced the problem and should take note of your process so that you can repeat it on similar problems!

As you review these explanations, you may not initially understand everything that they describe. Don't worry about this at first—the GMAT tests many different concepts, and you haven't yet begun to learn all the valuable Kaplan Methods and strategies contained in this book. You may find it useful to return to these explanations later in your studies, once you've read and practiced with this book and your online resources. It's likely that by that point, things that were once confusing to you will have become much clearer. It will also be a great confidence boost to see how far you've come in your mastery of the GMAT.

And finally, don't concern yourself with how many questions you got right or missed on this test. You've still got a lot to learn about the GMAT, but you have the best tools to help you on your journey—and taking and reviewing this pretest is a great first step. Just remember to be patient with yourself as you make mistakes. Everyone does; it's normal. But consider this: every wrong answer you choose, *and then learn from*, reduces the chance that you'll get a similar question wrong on the one and only day when wrong answers matter. So make mistakes willingly and even happily now, while they don't count. Just resolve to learn from every one of them.

Happy studying!

ANSWER KEY

	Quantitative				Verbal		
1.	A	20.	C	1.	D	22.	D
2.	B	21.	D	2.	E	23.	B
3.	A	22.	B	3.	E	24.	D
4.	A	23.	C	4.	A	25.	C
5.	A	24.	D	5.	C	26.	B
6.	D	25.	D	6.	D	27.	B
7.	D	26.	C	7.	E	28.	D
8.	C	27.	D	8.	A	29.	A
9.	E	28.	B	9.	B	30.	C
10.	B	29.	E	10.	D	31.	D
11.	B	30.	B	11.	B	32.	E
12.	B	31.	D	12.	C	33.	E
13.	D			13.	C	34.	E
14.	B			14.	B	35.	C
15.	E			15.	B	36.	C
16.	E			16.	E		
17.	E			17.	B		
18.	B			18.	C		
19.	D			19.	C		
				20.	A		
				21.	B		

PRETEST SELF-ASSESSMENT TOOL

After using the answer key to check your answers, circle the questions you got correct in the tables below and fill in the blanks in the last column. These tables will give you an estimate of your relative strengths and weaknesses so you can target your study effectively.

Since a paper-based test cannot adapt to your performance the way the computer-adaptive GMAT does, it is not possible to generate a reliable score estimate from your pretest. Indeed, since the actual test will give progressively less difficult questions to a low-scoring student until that student begins to get questions right and progressively more difficult questions to a high-scoring student until that student begins to miss questions, it's not unusual for students with very different scores to end up getting about the same percentage of questions right. The difference in score is due to the difficulty of the questions answered correctly. However, the test makers can write a fairly easy or a very challenging question testing virtually any skill, so if you missed a high percentage of, for example, algebra questions or Sentence Correction questions on this pretest, it's a good bet that investing more time in studying algebra or Sentence Correction will pay off.

To take a full-length, computer-adaptive diagnostic test that estimates your current score, visit your online resources.

GO ONLINE

kaptest.com/login

QUANTITATIVE REASONING

Question Type	Pretest Question Numbers	# Correct
Problem Solving (Chapter 10)	1, 2, 4, 6, 8, 9, 11, 12, 14, 15, 17, 19, 21, 22, 24, 27, 28, 30, 31	_____ out of 19
Data Sufficiency (Chapter 11)	3, 5, 7, 10, 13, 16, 18, 20, 23, 25, 26, 29	_____ out of 12
Content Area	**Pretest Question Numbers**	**# Correct**
Algebra (Chapter 12)	6, 7, 9, 11, 14, 15, 20, 24, 29	_____ out of 9
Arithmetic (Chapter 13)	13, 16, 26, 31	_____ out of 4
Number Properties (Chapter 14)	1, 2, 5, 18	_____ out of 4
Proportions (Chapter 15)	8, 10, 12, 21, 23	_____ out of 5
Statistics (Chapter 16)	17, 28	_____ out of 2
Math Formulas (Chapter 17)	4, 22, 25, 30	_____ out of 4
Geometry (Chapter 18)	3, 19, 27	_____ out of 3

VERBAL REASONING

Question Type	Pretest Question Numbers	# Correct
Critical Reasoning (Chapter 6)	2, 5, 7, 15, 16, 23, 26, 27, 33, 35	_____ out of 10
Reading Comprehension (Chapter 7)	9, 10, 11, 12, 19, 20, 21, 29, 30, 31, 32	_____ out of 11
Sentence Correction (Chapter 8)	1, 3, 4, 6, 8, 13, 14, 17, 18, 22, 24, 25, 28, 34, 36	_____ out of 15

EXPLANATIONS

QUANTITATIVE SECTION EXPLANATIONS

1. A

Question Type: Problem Solving
Question Topic: Number Properties ▶ Factors and Primes

You'll want to start with the lowest possible product of two prime numbers between 10 and 30. Thus, you want the lowest prime numbers between 10 and 30, which are 11 and 13. Mathematically, the next step would be to multiply these and square the product. If you suspect that would involve far too much calculation, that's a great GMAT instinct—look for a pattern that will help you get to the solution more efficiently. Since you have $11 \times 13 \times 11 \times 13$, you might notice that the last digit of each number will multiply together to yield $1 \times 1 \times 3 \times 3 = 9$, which eliminates all but **(A)** 20,449. If you didn't notice this, you might have used the fact that since a prime number, by definition, has no factors other than 1 and itself, 11×13 cannot have any other prime factors. Therefore, you can eliminate any answer that's a multiple of a smaller prime. **(B)** and **(D)** are multiples of 5, and **(C)** is a multiple of 2. In multiples of 3, the digits sum to a multiple of 3; **(E)** has digits that sum to 18, so it's a multiple of 3 and can be eliminated. Since **(A)** is the only answer choice you haven't eliminated, 20,449 must be correct.

2. B

Question Type: Problem Solving
Question Topic: Number Properties ▶ Positives and Negatives

The answer choices compare various expressions to 0, so consider positive and negative number properties as you seek the choice that must be false. The inequality in the question stem means that the absolute value of a is less than the absolute value of b (a is closer to 0); the two values may have the same or different signs.

(A) and **(E)** are very similar and relatively easy to evaluate. Since both a and b could be negative, their sum could be less than 0; since they could be positive, their sum could be greater than 0. Eliminate both of these choices.

(C) is a good one to tackle next. This statement is true if $a > b$. The inequality in the question stem allows for a to be positive while b is negative (e.g., $a = 1$ and $b = -2$), so this choice could be true—eliminate it.

(B) and **(D)** contain the same quadratic expression: $(a + b)(a - b)$. Restate this as $a^2 - b^2$. Any non-zero value raised to an even exponent is positive, so the fact that a and/or b could be negative can be ignored. The absolute value of b is greater than that of a, so $b^2 > a^2$. Thus, $a^2 - b^2$ must be negative and cannot be positive. The statement $(a + b)(a - b) > 0$ cannot be true, so **(B)** is correct.

3. A

Question Type: Data Sufficiency
Question Topic: Geometry ▶ Coordinate Geometry

Statement (1) provides the equation of line L. Since the x-intercept is where the line crosses the x-axis, $y = 0$ there. Similarly, since the y-intercept is where the line crosses the y-axis, $x = 0$ there. Thus, you could determine each intercept by substituting 0 for the other in the line's equation. You would then subtract the x-intercept from the y-intercept to get a single value to answer the question. Eliminate **(B)**, **(C)**, and **(E)**.

Statement (2) provides the ratio between the difference in the y values to the difference in the x values of the two points shown. This is line L's slope. Knowing a line's slope does not tell you where that line crosses the x-axis or the y-axis, so this statement is insufficient. **(A)** is the correct answer.

4. A

Question Type: Problem Solving
Question Topic: Math Formulas ▶ Overlapping Sets

These overlapping set problems are often best solved by organizing the data into a chart:

	Tall stems	Short stems	Total
Purple flowers	$0.7(800) = 560$		800
White flowers	?		350
Total		480	

In any column or row that contains two values, you can add or subtract to find the amount in the missing cell, working your way toward the cell with your answer. There are multiple paths to the answer.

	Tall stems	Short stems	Total
Purple flowers	560	$800 - 560 = 240$	800
White flowers	$670 - 560 = \mathbf{110}$ *or* $350 - 240 = \mathbf{110}$	$480 - 240 = 240$	350
Total	$1{,}150 - 480 = 670$	480	$800 + 350 = 1{,}150$

Thus, there are 110 tall pea plants with white flowers.

5. A

Question Type: Data Sufficiency
Question Topic: Number Properties ▸ Multiples

The question stem says that j and k are both integers and provides a relationship among n, j, and k. If n were an integer, then $9n$ would be an integer multiple of 9, and the sum of j and k would be a multiple of 9. Thus, the stem is really asking, "Is the sum of j and k a multiple of 9?"

Statement (1) tells you that the sum of j and k is a multiple of 9, which answers the question with a yes. Eliminate **(B)**, **(C)**, and **(E)**.

Statement (2) states that the difference between $9n$ and j is an integer. Since the question asks about n, rearrange the equation in (2) to see whether n must be an integer, remembering from the question stem that j is an integer:

$$9n - j = \text{integer} \rightarrow n = \frac{\text{integer} + j}{9}$$

$$= \frac{\text{integer} + (\text{another integer})}{9}$$

$$= \frac{\text{a new integer}}{9}$$

Since determining whether n is an integer hinges on whether "a new integer" is a multiple of 9, and since that unknown integer might or might not be such a multiple, it is unclear from Statement (2) whether n is necessarily an integer. The correct choice is **(A)**.

6. D

Question Type: Problem Solving
Question Topic: Algebra ▸ Quadratic Equations

No statement is markedly easier to work with than the others, and Statement I shows up the most, so start there. Factor the expression into $3(x^2 - 4) = 3(x + 2)(x - 2)$. If x is 2 or −2, the expression is 0. Statement I must be part of the correct answer, so eliminate **(B)**.

Evaluate II next. Notice that both variable terms, x^2 and x^4, will never be negative, since a base raised to an even exponent is never negative. Therefore, the expression cannot be less than 1. Eliminate **(C)** and **(E)**.

Evaluate III by factoring $x^2 + 7x + 6$ into $(x + 6)(x + 1)$. The expression will be 0 if $x = -6$ or $x = -1$. **(D)** is correct.

7. D

Question Type: Data Sufficiency
Question Topic: Algebra ▸ Isolating a Variable, Quadratic Equations

The question stem tells you that p is a negative number that is greater than -2, so $-2 < p < 0$.

Solve the equation in Statement (1) for p. Recall that absolute value is always positive, so the expression inside the absolute value bars may be positive or negative. If $p^2 - 5 = 4$, then $p^2 = 9$, making p equal to ± 3. Alternatively, if $p^2 - 5 = -4$, then $p^2 = 1$, making p equal to ± 1. Since the question stem specifies that $-2 < p < 0$, the only permissible value for Statement (1) is -1. This statement is sufficient. Eliminate **(B)**, **(C)**, and **(E)**.

Since the fraction in Statement (2) equals 0, the numerator $\left(p + \frac{1}{2}\right)(p + 1) = 0$, so $p = -\frac{1}{2}$ or -1. Note that a value of $-\frac{1}{2}$ would make the denominator 0, so the only value of p that works for Statement (2) is -1. Since each statement is sufficient on its own, **(D)** is correct.

8. C

Question Type: Problem Solving
Question Topic: Proportions ▸ Ratios

Picking values is a great strategy to answer ratio questions when no actual values are given. Numbers need not be realistic; pick easy-to-use values. Let the funding for the basketball team be \$3. Since the football team receives 4 times as much, its funding is \$12. Together, these two teams have \$15 in funding, which is 3 times as much as that of all of the other sports combined. Therefore, the other programs receive \$5. Finally, the ratio of funding for the basketball team to that for all other sports is 3:5.

Alternatively, select variables to represent the funding unknowns (such as f for football, b for basketball, and p for other sports programs). Then, $f = 4b$, since football gets 4 times more than basketball. Together, these two teams' funding is $f + b$, and, substituting $4b$ for f, the total amount is $4b + b = 5b$. That's 3 times the amount given to the other programs, p, so $5b = 3p$. Rewriting the equation to solve for $b{:}p$, you obtain the ratio 3:5.

9. E

Question Type: Problem Solving
Question Topic: Algebra ▸ Isolating a Variable

To isolate the variable e, cross multiply: $2(3a - 2ce) = 3(4b - 2de)$. Distributing 2 on the left side of the equation and 3 on the right side gives $6a - 4ce = 12b - 6de$.

Collect all terms that contain e on one side of the equation: $-4ce + 6de = 12b - 6a$.

Factoring out e yields $e(-4c + 6d) = 12b - 6a$.

Dividing both sides by $(-4c + 6d)$ results in $e = \frac{-6a + 12b}{-4c + 6d}$. Divide each term on the right by 2: $e = \frac{-3a + 6b}{-2c + 3d}$.

Thus, $\frac{e}{3} = \frac{1}{3}e = \left(\frac{1}{3}\right)\left(\frac{-3a + 6b}{-2c + 3d}\right) = \frac{-a + 2b}{-2c + 3d}$. None of the choices match, but **(E)** is close. Multiplying this expression by $\frac{-1}{-1}$ does not change its value but does change the sign of each term, resulting in $\frac{a - 2b}{2c - 3d}$.

10. B

Question Type: Data Sufficiency
Question Topic: Proportions ▸ Percents

To translate the question stem into algebra, recall that "of" means multiply. Translate piece by piece:

- There are f flowers.
- $x\% \times f$ are annuals (a).
- $y\% \times x\% \times f$ are begonias (b).
- $z\% \times y\% \times x\% \times f$ are infected begonias.

Call the number of infected begonias B. So $B = z\% \times y\% \times x\% \times f$. Also $a = x\% \times f$ and $b = y\% \times x\% \times f$. That's seven variables and three equations. There are four more variables than equations, so to solve, you'll need four more distinct equations.

Statement (1) provides three equations, namely the values of the three percents. However, it doesn't provide the total f flowers. Therefore, you couldn't calculate the number of infected begonias. Eliminate **(A)** and **(D)**.

Statement (2) provides four distinct equations; three are proportions and one gives the value of f. This is sufficient, and the answer is **(B)**. To see why, you can think through the solution: From the ratio of f to a, you could determine the value of a. Then from the ratio of a to b, you could determine the value of b, which is $y\% \times x\% \times f$. From the proportion containing z, you could determine the value of z. Finally, from the values of b and z, you could determine B.

11. B

Question Type: Problem Solving
Question Topic: Algebra ▶ Translating Words into Expressions and Equations

First, find the rate at which Joanna is reading. Reading p pages in 15 minutes gives a rate of $\frac{p}{15}$ pages per minute. Then, to get the time for her to read r pages at the same rate, use the formula Work = Rate × Time, where r is the work and $\frac{p}{15}$ is the rate:

$$r = \frac{p}{15} \times \text{time}$$

$$\frac{15}{p} \times r = \text{time}$$

$$\frac{15r}{p} = \text{time}$$

So the answer is **(B)**. You could also pick numbers. Say she reads $p = 5$ pages of her economics book in 15 minutes. Then she reads $r = 10$ pages of her marketing book in twice as much time, 30 minutes. When you plug in 5 for p and 10 for r in the choices, only **(B)** equals 30.

12. B

Question Type: Problem Solving
Question Topic: Proportions ▶ Mixtures

First, use the fact that 24 tons of corn makes up 40% of the target output to find the target output amount t:

$$0.40t = 24$$

$$\frac{4}{10}t = 24$$

$$4t = 240$$

$$t = 60$$

The total output is 60 tons. Next year, corn will only be 15% of the total output, so that will be 15% × 60 = 9 tons, which is 15 fewer tons than for the current year. Therefore, to maintain the target output, the farmer will need to grow 15 more tons of soybeans.

13. D

Question Type: Data Sufficiency
Question Topic: Arithmetic ▸ Exponents

The question stem states that the cube of m and the cube of t are both negative. Since a positive base raised to an odd exponent would be positive and a base of zero would be zero, m and t must be negative. Information that allows you to answer the question about p with a definite yes or a definite no will be sufficient.

Rewrite Statement (1) as $p^2 = \left(\frac{t}{m}\right)^2$. If $p = 0$, then $p^2 = 0$, and $\left(\frac{t}{m}\right)^2$ would also have to equal 0. However, since t is negative, it does not equal 0, and thus $\left(\frac{t}{m}\right)^2$ cannot equal 0. Since p cannot equal 0, this statement answers the question with a no. Eliminate **(B)**, **(C)**, and **(E)**.

In Statement (2), the expression on the right simplifies to mp. The absolute value of t on the left cannot be 0 (since $t \neq 0$). Therefore, neither of the factors m and p can be 0. Statement (2) also answers the question with a no. **(D)** is correct.

14. B

Question Type: Problem Solving
Question Topic: Algebra ▸ Systems of Linear Equations

Let S represent the number of countries in Asia, F the number in Africa, and E the number in Europe. Since there are 42 countries total, $F + E + S = 42$. Also, since the photographer has been to 6 more countries in Europe than in Asia, $E = S + 6$. Twice as many in Africa as in Europe gives $F = 2E$.

It follows that, since $E = S + 6$, $F = 2E = 2(S + 6)$. So, by substitution,

$$F + E + S = 42$$
$$2(S + 6) + (S + 6) + S = 42$$
$$2S + 12 + S + 6 + S = 42$$
$$4S + 18 = 42$$
$$4S = 24$$
$$S = 6$$

Therefore, the photographer has been to 6 countries in Asia.

15. E

Question Type: Problem Solving
Question Topic: Algebra ▸ Translating Words into Expressions and Equations

Translate this word problem into algebra. The variable cost is 30% of the selling price of $50, or $0.30 \times \$50 = \$15$. If you let n represent the number of units sold, the total cost is $\$15n + \$8,400$, and the total revenue is $\$50n$. Find the breakeven point by setting the total cost equal to the total revenue:

$$50n = 8,400 + 15n$$
$$35n = 8,400$$
$$n = 240$$

At 240 units, the total revenue equals the total cost. So, revenue will exceed cost if 1 more unit, or 241 total units, is sold.

16. E

Question Type: Data Sufficiency
Question Topic: Arithmetic ▸ Absolute Value, Inequalities

Given the equation $z = |x - 2| - |y + 2|$, if $z = 0$, then $|y + 2| = |x - 2|$. This is the case when x and y have the same magnitude but different signs. For example, if $x = -2$, y must equal 2 so that $|2 + 2| = |-2 - 2| = 4$. The question stem says that x and y are integers, so while the statements have inequalities involving scary fractions, you'll only need to consider integer values in those ranges. Pay careful attention to whether the inequality is "less than" or "less than or equal to."

In Statement (1), the only integers in the range for x are 2 and 3, and the only integers in the range for y are -3 and -2. Thus, the values of x and y could, but do not necessarily have to be, opposites of each other. Eliminate **(A)** and **(D)**.

From Statement (2), you can conclude that x must equal 2 and that y must equal -3 or -2. Thus, y's value could be but does not necessarily have to be the opposite value of x. Eliminate **(B)**.

Combining Statements (1) and (2), you know that x must equal 2 because that is the only value for x that works for both statements. However, y could equal -3 or -2. Since y's value could be -2 and be the opposite of x, but y could also be -3, the correct answer is **(E)**.

17. E

Question Type: Problem Solving
Question Topic: Statistics ▸ Combinations and Permutations

Since Division A must be part of the organization, there is only 1 way to choose that unit.

If at least one of B and C must be in the organization, B, C, or both could be in it, making for 3 possible ways to choose from these divisions.

At least two of D, E, and F must be part of the organization. If two join, there are 3 possible outcomes: D and E, D and F, or E and F. Or all three could be included, which is 1 more outcome. So, there are 4 possible ways to choose this group of units.

Finally, at least two of G, H, J, and K must be included. If two are included, $_4C_2 = \frac{4!}{(2!)(4-2)!} = \frac{4 \times 3 \times \cancel{(2!)}}{2 \times 1 \times \cancel{(2!)}} = 6$ possible outcomes. If three of these divisions are used, there are four ways to leave one division out, so that's 4 possible outcomes. If all four are included, that's 1 more outcome. Thus, there are 11 possible ways to choose divisions from this group.

To find the number of organizational structures that can be formed from these various groups, multiply the numbers of ways of selecting each group: $1 \times 3 \times 4 \times 11 = 132$.

18. B

Question Type: Data Sufficiency
Question Topic: Number Properties ▸ Factors and Multiples

The question stem says that both a and b are integers and that their product is 210. Thus, a and b are factors of 210.

Statement (1) states that a is between but does not include 13 and 16; thus, a could equal 14 or 15. Since b must remain an integer when multiplied by a, divide 210 by 14 and 15 to see whether an integer b results: $\frac{210}{14} = 15$, so $\frac{210}{15}$ must equal 14. Since a could equal 14 or 15, as either value results in b being an integer, eliminate **(A)** and **(D)**.

Statement (2) says that both $\frac{a}{15}$ and $\frac{b}{14}$ are integers; in other words, 15 is a factor of a, and 14 is a factor of b. Thus, ab, or 210, has a factor of 14 and a factor of 15. Since $210 = (15)(14)$, if a is a multiple of 15, it must be 15. You can conclude from Statement (2) that a has only one value: 15. Thus, the correct answer is **(B)**.

19. D

Question Type: Problem Solving
Question Topic: Geometry ▸ Triangles

Line segment AD divides right triangle ABC into two right triangles. Since AD bisects AC, it also bisects the angle opposite that side, so it splits right angle ABC into two 45° angles. Each of the two smaller triangles then consists of a 90° angle at vertex D, a 45° angle at vertex B, and a $180° - (90° + 45°) = 45°$ angle at the third vertex. Thus, vertices A and C are 45°, and the large triangle is a 45-45-90 triangle. This means that the corresponding side ratios are $x : x : x\sqrt{2}$. Leg BC is represented in this ratio by x and hypotenuse AC by $x\sqrt{2}$, making the ratio of BC to AC $\frac{x}{x\sqrt{2}}$. Cancel the x terms and rationalize the denominator:

$$\frac{\cancel{x}\left(\sqrt{2}\right)}{\cancel{x}\sqrt{2}\left(\sqrt{2}\right)} = \frac{\sqrt{2}}{2}$$

20. C

Question Type: Data Sufficiency
Question Topic: Algebra ▶ Systems of Linear Equations

The question stem says that Paula's used book collection is worth \$104 and indicates that some are histories: $C_H N_H + C_O N_O = 104$, where C is the average cost per book, N is the number of books, H is "histories," and O is "other books." You need to be able to solve for N_H.

Statement (1) tells you that Paula has only mysteries at \$1 apiece and histories at \$25 apiece. Now $(25)(N_H) + (1)(N_M) = 104$, where M is "mysteries." However, with two variables and one equation, there is not enough information to solve for N_H. If Paula has, say, 4 mysteries, then she has 4 histories; if she has 29 mysteries, then she has 3 histories, and so on. Eliminate **(A)** and **(D)**.

Statement (2) states that there are exactly 4 mysteries worth \$4. However, the remaining \$100 could be made up of any number of combinations of non-mystery books. Eliminate **(B)**. Since neither statement is sufficient alone, try combining the statements.

Combining Statements (1) and (2), you know that Paula has only mystery and history books. The mysteries cost a total of \$4, and the histories cost \$25 each. So $(25)(N_H) + (1)(4) = 104$, which could be solved for the number of histories. **(C)** is correct.

21. D

Question Type: Problem Solving
Question Topic: Proportions ▶ Percents

Since the question involves percentages of an unknown number of parts, pick a number for the total number of parts; 100 is a good choice, since percents are the amount per 100. Thus, 60 were part W and 40 were part Z. The number of defective Ws was $60 \times 0.001 = 0.06$, and the number of defective Zs was $40 \times 0.0005 = 0.02$. (Do not worry that it looks like somehow there can be less than a whole defective part. You don't have to use "realistic" numbers; 100 was chosen to simplify the calculations.) So, out of 100, there were a total of $0.06 + 0.02 = 0.08$ defective parts. Since "out of 100" is the same as percent, 0.08% is correct.

22. B

Question Type: Problem Solving
Question Topic: Math Formulas ▶ Averages

The formula for calculating an average is $\text{Average} = \frac{\text{Sum of values}}{\text{Number of values}}$. Rearrange this to Sum of values = Average × Number of values. Since the average weight of the bags is 2.50 kg, the total weight is $10 \times 2.50 = 25.00$. The total weight of the 8 bags for which the weights are known is $(4 \times 2.65) + (3 \times 2.40) + (1 \times 2.20) = 10.60 + 7.20 + 2.20 = 20.00$. The weight of the 2 remaining bags is $25.00 - 20.00 = 5.00$. One of these weighs 0.40 kg more than the other. If the weight of the lighter bag is L, then $L + (L + 0.40) = 5.00$; $2L = 4.60$; $L = 2.30$. This is more than the weight of the 2.20 kg bag, so the 2.20 kg bag is the lightest.

23. C

Question Type: Data Sufficiency
Question Topic: Proportions ▸ Ratios, Percents

The question stem gives no numerical information, so look at the statements.

Statement (1) says that $\frac{5}{8}$ of the employees are not surveyors, which means the remaining $\frac{3}{8}$ of the employees are surveyors. However, there is no way to calculate an actual number of surveyors. Eliminate **(A)** and **(D)**.

Statement (2) is enough to find the total number of employees ($18 = 0.25R$, so $R = 72$), but not how many of the employees are surveyors. Statement (2) by itself is insufficient, so eliminate **(B)**. Since neither statement worked by itself, try combining them.

Combining Statements (1) and (2), you know the total number of employees (72) from Statement (2), and you know what fraction of those employees are surveyors $\left(\frac{3}{8}\right)$ from Statement (1). You could thus calculate the total number of employees who are surveyors (the calculation is $\frac{3}{8} \times 72 = 27$). **(C)** is correct.

24. D

Question Type: Problem Solving
Question Topic: Algebra ▸ Isolating a Variable, Quadratic Equations

The fact that $x - y = -(y - x)$ is an important idea for the GMAT. For example, you may use this property to reexpress algebraic expressions to match the given answer choices. Here, a variation can be used to simplify the equation in the question stem, $2(s-r) = -2\left(\frac{r^2 - s^2}{s^2 - r^2}\right)$, to solve for $s - r$. Begin by dividing both sides by 2:

$$s - r = -1\left(\frac{r^2 - s^2}{s^2 - r^2}\right)$$

To multiply -1 by the numerator, simply reverse the terms:

$$s - r = \frac{s^2 - r^2}{s^2 - r^2}$$

Cancel common factors:

$$s - r = 1$$

25. D

Question Type: Data Sufficiency
Question Topic: Math Formulas ▶ Rates and Speed

This question asks for a value: how long is the first leg of the trip? This question involves one of the common math formulas you should memorize for Test Day: Distance = Rate × Time.

Make a table to organize the information you know from the question stem:

	Distance	Rate	Time
First leg	d	15 kph	t
Second leg	d	r	3 hours

The question asks for the time (t) of the first leg of the trip, and you have one equation involving t: $d = 15t$. Information that provides a value for d or that provides a second equation with d and t will be sufficient to solve.

Statement (1) gives the average speed for the entire trip, allowing you to write a second equation involving d and t. Although you wouldn't do the math on Test Day, here's how it works. Since Total distance = Average speed × Total time, $2d = 12 \times (t + 3) = 12t + 36$. From the first leg of the trip, you know that $d = 15t$, so substitute $15t$ for d to find that $2(15t) = 12t + 36$, $30t = 12t + 36$, $18t = 36$, and $t = 2$. Thus, with two variables and two equations, you could solve for each of the variables. Eliminate **(B)**, **(C)**, and **(E)**.

Statement (2) gives a value for d, which is exactly what you need to solve directly for t. Since both statements are sufficient individually, **(D)** is correct.

26. C

Question Type: Data Sufficiency
Question Topic: Arithmetic ▶ Exponents, Inequalities

From the question stem, you know that a must be an integer greater than or equal to $\sqrt[5]{-32}$, or $a \geq -2$. To have sufficiency, you need information that will allow you to narrow this range down to one possible value for a.

Statement (1) gives an inequality that you could solve for a, resulting in the inequality $a \leq -1$. Since a is an integer, it could be either -1 or -2. That's two values, so eliminate **(A)** and **(D)**.

Statement (2), $a^2 > 2$, means that $a > 1$ or that $a < -1$. The information in the question stem, $a^5 \geq -32$, tells you that $a \geq -2$. So a could either be any integer greater than 1, or it could be -2. Eliminate **(B)**. Since neither statement alone was sufficient, try combining the statements.

Combining Statements (1) and (2), you know from Statement (1) that $a \leq -1$ and from Statement (2) that either $a = -2$ or $a > 1$. The only integer value that works in both statements is -2, so this must be the value of a. **(C)** is correct.

27. D

Question Type: Problem Solving
Question Topic: Geometry ▸ Solids

Draw a sketch to help visualize the scenario. In the figure above, which shows the rectangular block after it has been cut into halves, the shaded parts represent the painted surfaces; the three unseen sides of the labeled half (the back, bottom, and right side) are also shaded. Only the left side of the labeled piece—the surface that used to be inside the block—is unpainted wood. Each half is itself a rectangular solid with dimensions of 5 inches × 10 inches × 20 inches. The surface area formula for a rectangular solid is $2(l \times w) + 2(l \times h) + 2(w \times h)$. For each half-block, that's $2(10 \times 5) + 2(10 \times 20) + 2(5 \times 20) = 700$ square inches. The surface area that's not painted blue is the area exposed by the cut (the unshaded area), which is $10 \times 20 = 200$ square inches. Thus, the fraction of the surface area of each piece that's not painted blue is $\frac{200}{700} = \frac{2}{7}$.

28. B

Question Type: Problem Solving
Question Topic: Statistics ▸ Sequences of Integers

First, find the smallest multiple of 7 in the given range. Since $100 \div 7 = 14$ with a remainder of 2, $7 \times 15 = 105$ is that value. Next, determine the greatest multiple of 7 that is less than or equal to 1,000. Since $1,000 \div 7 = 142$ with a remainder of 6, then $7 \times 142 = 994$ is the greatest number in the sequence. Thus, the question can be thought of as, "How many numbers are in the sequence of consecutive integers between 15 and 142 inclusive?" The rule for determining the number of consecutive integers in a sequence is Greatest − Least + 1. For this question, that is $142 - 15 + 1 = 128$.

29. E

Question Type: Data Sufficiency
Question Topic: Algebra ▸ Isolating a Variable

To determine whether any particular ordered pair (c,d) is a solution to the equation $d = kc - 3$, you need to find the value of k. Specifically, to find out whether $(1,-2)$ is a solution, you need to know whether $-2 = 1k - 3$. That's the same as asking whether $k = 1$.

Statement (1) indicates that $k^2 = 1$. Solving for k yields $k = \pm 1$. Since k could be 1 but it could also be −1, eliminate **(A)** and **(D)**.

Statement (2) states that $(0, -3)$ is a solution to the equation in the stem. Thus, $-3 = k \times 0 - 3 = -3$. Since k could take on any value in this situation, eliminate **(B)**.

Combining Statements (1) and (2), you know from (2) that k could equal any value, and (1) only restricts its value to ± 1. Since you still cannot determine exactly one value for k, the answer is **(E)**.

30. B

Question Type: Problem Solving
Question Topic: Math Formulas ▸ Rates and Speed

The question stem provides information about two peoples' commutes. By briefly sketching a chart on your noteboard, you can organize and simplify this information. Since Ethan travels $\frac{2}{3}$ more time than Flo, convert Flo's time of 0.4 to $\frac{2}{5}$ to facilitate the calculation. Call the distance of Ethan's commute d.

	Distance (miles)	Rate (mph)	Time (hrs)
Ethan	d		$\frac{2}{5} + \left(\frac{2}{3}\right)\left(\frac{2}{5}\right) = \left(\frac{6}{15}\right) + \left(\frac{4}{15}\right) = \left(\frac{10}{15}\right) = \frac{2}{3}$
Flo	$\frac{4}{5}d$		$\frac{2}{5}$

Use the formula Distance = Rate × Time to determine the two rates. The calculations may be easier if you pick a number for d—say d is 10. Divide the two commuters' distances by their respective times:

Ethan's rate is $10 \div \frac{2}{3} = 10 \times \frac{3}{2} = 15$.

Flo's rate is $\left(\frac{4}{5}\right)(10) \div \frac{2}{5} = \left(\frac{4}{5}\right)(10) \times \frac{5}{2} = 20$.

Your chart now looks like this:

	Distance (miles)	Rate (mph)	Time (hrs)
Ethan	10	15	$\frac{2}{3}$
Flo	8	20	$\frac{2}{5}$

Finally, use the percent difference formula, Percent difference $= \frac{\text{Amount of difference}}{\text{Base amount}}(100\%)$, to determine the percent difference between Ethan's and Flo's average speeds. You are comparing Ethan's rate to Flo's, so Flo's rate is the base:

$$\frac{15 - 20}{20}(100\%) = -\frac{5}{20}(100\%) = -25\%$$

Ethan's speed is 25% less than Flo's speed.

31. D

Question Type: Problem Solving
Question Topic: Arithmetic ▸ Exponents and Radicals

The question stem says that x is a positive fraction less than 1. The answer choices involve negative exponents. Recall that raising a base to a negative exponent is equivalent to taking the reciprocal of the base raised to a positive exponent. If you rewrite the choices with positive exponents, it will be easier to compare them:

(A) $\dfrac{1}{x^2 - 1}$

(B) $\dfrac{1}{x^{\frac{1}{2}}}$

(C) $\dfrac{1}{(x+1)^2}$

(D) $\dfrac{1}{x^2}$

(E) $\dfrac{1}{x^2 + 1}$

First, because $x < 1$, the denominator $x^2 - 1$ in **(A)** must be negative, making this fraction negative; all the other choices must be positive, so eliminate **(A)**. Now look for the fraction that involves dividing 1 by the smallest positive value, keeping in mind that x decreases in value when raised to larger, not smaller, exponents. **(B)** stands out as raising x to the smallest exponent, so eliminate this choice.

Compare the remaining choices pairwise. Squaring $(x + 1)$ results in a larger denominator than squaring x, so **(C)** has a larger denominator than **(D)**; eliminate **(C)**. Then $x^2 + 1$ is greater than x^2, so the denominator in **(E)** is greater than in **(D)**. **(D)** $\frac{1}{x^2}$ has the smallest denominator and thus has the largest value.

VERBAL SECTION EXPLANATIONS

1. D

Question Type: Sentence Correction
Question Topic: Verbs; Modification

The underlined portion of the sentence begins with the adverb "expressively," which is incorrectly modifying the noun "tonality." Nouns must be modified by adjectives. Moreover, the underlined portion ends with a plural verb, "are," but the subject of the verb, "[t]he *lira da braccio*," is singular. Eliminate **(A)**. Also eliminate **(B)** for beginning with "expressively" and **(C)** for using the plural "are." **(E)** uses the singular past tense "was." This choice might be tempting because the sentence refers to the Renaissance, but the following clause speaks of the instrument in the artwork in the present tense ("it is often played"). The instrument is still seen in the art today, so "is" in **(D)** is correct.

2. E

Question Type: Critical Reasoning ▶ Strengthen

The sales manager's goal is to increase sales by having the salespeople who didn't attend the seminar on persuasive speaking attend the next seminar. The implied opinion is that the seminar will make employees better salespeople; in other words, it will cause sales to increase. The evidence provided for this argument is that the salespeople who did attend the seminar had better sales than did nonattendees. However, this is only a correlation. There could be some other reason for the good performance (e.g., other seminars, better leads, luck). It's also possible the author's logic is backward: perhaps the attendees were already above average. Maybe that's why they were chosen to attend the seminar in the first place, or perhaps more highly motivated people both choose to attend seminars and get more sales. The sales manager assumes these factors did not play an important role in the increased sales and that the seminar was responsible. The correct answer will eliminate one or more of these alternative causes from consideration.

(E) is correct as it eliminates one alternative reason that attendees had better sales, strengthening the conclusion that the seminar helps sales. **(A)** doesn't establish that these tactics actually helped sales—perhaps the salespeople already knew these tactics. Moreover, this choice describes the last seminar, but the argument is about the benefits of attending the next seminar. **(B)** does not help make the case for attending the seminar. The author's argument rests on the assumption that those who attended the seminar improved while those who didn't attend did not improve. **(B)** does not address the comparison. Indeed, if overall sales were up, then it's possible everyone did better and not just people who attended the seminar. **(C)** weakens the argument by bringing up a potential alternative explanation. Maybe the book was responsible and not the seminar itself. **(D)** is an irrelevant comparison. How Excello compares to other companies has nothing to do with whether the seminar was effective.

EXPLANATIONS

3. E

Question Type: Sentence Correction
Question Topic: Comparison; Parallelism

The word "like" that begins the underlined portion of the sentence indicates that the sentence is comparing two things. Comparisons must be logical and parallel. Here, "[b]rand management" should logically be compared to some kind of management, but instead it is compared to "any industry." Eliminate **(A)**. **(B)** substitutes "similar to" for "like" but still doesn't compare "management" to management. **(C)** solves the comparison problem by inserting the term "brand management" into the second part of the comparison. However, when one thing "is" another, the two things must be expressed in parallel form, and "[b]rand management...is the artistic defining" is not parallel. Eliminate **(C)**. **(D)** and **(E)** solve the comparison problem by using "as" to compare how brand management is in one industry to how brand management is in any industry. However, **(D)** breaks parallelism after the comma with "[b]rand management...is artfully defining," since "brand management" is a regular noun while "defining" is an *-ing* verb form acting as a noun. **(E)** uses the same noun form in both parts of the structure—"brand management...is the art"—so it is correct.

4. A

Question Type: Sentence Correction
Question Topic: Pronouns; Verbs

The revolution's leaders committed violent acts for the purpose of establishing their authority—"to establish their authority"—and they also suppressed dissent. The infinitive form "to establish" is idiomatically correct, the plural pronouns "their" and "they" correctly refer to "leaders," and "suppressed" is in the correct past tense. **(A)** is correct. By replacing "to" with "that," **(B)** subtly changes the meaning of the sentence, and the singular pronoun "it" is incorrect. By dropping the pronoun altogether, **(C)** forms a compound predicate, which would have to be parallel, but "establishing" and "to suppress" do not have the same form. **(D)** uses the past progressive "were suppressing," which would only be correct to describe an action that was ongoing when another action happened; the leaders "resorted" to violence and "suppressed" dissent in the same time frame, and both take the simple past tense. **(E)** uses a wordier construction and commits a pronoun error with "it."

5. C

Question Type: Critical Reasoning ▸ Weaken

The question stem asks you to identify the fact that will most undermine, or weaken, the spokesperson's argument. Begin by identifying the conclusion and supporting evidence. The spokesperson claims that Southtown's lower business tax rate creates a better business environment. The evidence is the lower amount of business taxes collected in Southtown. Thus, the spokesperson is equating lower total business tax receipts with a lesser impact on an individual business that might start up in Southtown. However, while the amount of taxes collected is lower, that doesn't mean that Southtown has the lower tax rate. Perhaps Southtown has fewer businesses and collected the smaller amount by taking a larger percentage of taxes from those businesses. A good prediction would be "anything that says Southtown may have a smaller amount of business profits to tax or a higher rate of taxation."

(C) matches the prediction and is correct. if Northtown has twice the business profits and doesn't collect twice the tax revenue of Southtown, then Northtown has the lower tax rate. Thus, a business that started in Northtown would pay less taxes. The argument is only about the impact of business taxes, so whether a smaller or larger proportion of all taxes are business taxes has nothing to do with tax rates and is irrelevant to the conclusion; eliminate **(A)** and **(B)**. **(D)** is irrelevant because the size of the population does not necessarily correspond to the amount of business profits or business taxes collected. **(E)** is irrelevant because business taxes are not assessed on sales but on profits, and if they were assessed on sales, this choice would strengthen, not weaken, the argument.

6. D

Question Type: Sentence Correction
Question Topic: Comparison

The fact that the word "than" is underlined is a clue that there may be a comparison problem here. When one thing (a noun) is said to differ from another, the correct phrase is *different from*, not *different than*. In this sentence, the *–ing* words "[e]stablishing" and "setting" are verb forms that function as nouns, so the sentence should read, "Establishing goals…is often different from setting goals …" That's **(D)**. The word "than" in **(A)** and **(B)** would be properly used to introduce a new clause and would have to be followed by both a noun and a verb. **(C)** compares "[e]stablishing" to "goals," which would not be parallel. By introducing "the" and "of," **(E)** violates parallelism and is unnecessarily wordy.

7.   E

Question Type: Critical Reasoning ▸ Evaluation

You need to find the one question whose answer would *not* help you decide whether the grain-processing company should discard its grain by-products or recycle those products to produce catfish. One piece of evidence for success of the plan is that fish with grain by-products in their diets reach marketable size; this establishes that catfish eat the by-products and grow large enough to be sold. Another piece of evidence is that restaurants want a steady supply of catfish. These facts are both promising, but do they make operating a fish farm a better choice than just throwing away the by-products? As with any question that asks you to evaluate a plan, consider other factors that might influence whether the plan is the better choice or feasible at all.

(E) is the correct answer because the time it takes for catfish to mature in the wild is irrelevant to whether the company should farm them. Even if catfish mature much more quickly in the wild, they may be difficult to harvest, expensive to transport, or not found in sufficient numbers. Even if they mature much more slowly, they may be less prone to disease and thus be a more reliable supply, or they may taste better. An answer to this question about wild catfish does not help evaluate the plan concerning farmed catfish. With **(A)**, if the costs of operating the fish farm were less than the costs of discarding the by-products, the plan would be more attractive. **(B)** is an important question that speaks to how much fish the company could sell to earn revenue and offset the costs of running the farm. An answer to **(C)** would provide information about regulations that could increase the costs and reduce the feasibility of fish farming. Although the author says that some fish fed with grain by-products grow up, it doesn't say their entire diet is grain by-products. Thus, an answer to **(D)** would provide information about whether the grain company would need to buy other foods or supplements, making the project more expensive.

8.   A

Question Type: Sentence Correction
Question Topic: Pronouns

The underlined portion begins with the past perfect verb "had laid," so first check whether this verb tense is correct. In fact it is, because the photographs "laid the foundation" before another action in the past, the awarding of the Nobel prize. That more recent past action is correctly stated with the simple past tense, "did not receive...it was awarded." The pronoun "it" appears, so make sure the pronoun unambiguously refers to a singular, nonhuman antecedent. "It" refers clearly to "the Nobel prize," so no problem there. Finally, the overall structure of the sentence is logical: her photographs laid a foundation for a scientific discovery, but Franklin did not win a prize for the discovery. There is no error, and **(A)** is correct.

The other choices have various errors, but you can efficiently eliminate them by focusing on the use of pronouns. In **(B)**, the final "it" seems to refer to "the structure of DNA," but describing the DNA earned the prize, not the structure itself. In **(C)**, the plural pronoun "their" could only refer to the plural noun "photographs," but the photographs were not being described. It's hard to know what the "it" at the end of **(D)** might refer to. And the "it" in **(E)** would refer to the "photographs," but "it" is singular and "photographs" is plural; moreover, Franklin (not her photographs) would have been awarded the Nobel.

On the left, we've shown how keywords help to identify the major elements of the passage and its structure and what you could skim over. On the right, we've shown what you might be thinking as you read the passage strategically.

Passage for Questions 9–12

PASSAGE	ANALYSIS
Women around the world... **While** the difficulties that women encounter... are frequently discussed... **it is interesting to note** that the difficulties faced by working married men are seldom raised.	Introduces difficulties faced by working women. Topic of this passage is the difficulties faced by working married men.
Scott Coltrane... has found that, **while** the earnings of women tend to go down... the earnings of married men **not only** exceed those of both unmarried men and divorced men **but also** tend to go up with each additional child. **One reason**...	Married men earn more with additional children. One reason is provided. The rest of the paragraph expands on that reason.
If married men... difficulties? Research indicates **three possible problems. First,** the perceived responsibility of providing for a family drives men to work more hours and strive for promotion... **Second**... higher levels of marital discord...	Opening question signals a return to the topic introduced in the first paragraph. Three reasons married men are struggling will be discussed. First reason: married men work harder and longer to provide for their families, so they lose family time. Second reason: more marital problems.
[T]he **third reason... While** women's decisions... valuable contributions, men's decisions... signs of weakness.	Third reason: men's decisions to limit work are not valued like those of women.

EXPLANATIONS

Passage Map

Here is an example of the notes that you might have made as you read:

¶1: Married men (MM) face difficulties in the workplace

¶2: MM earn more, have more leisure

¶3: MM work harder and longer to support families, experience more marital discord

¶4: MM don't get same flexibility in workplace

Topic: *Working married men*

Scope: *Difficulties faced by* ___↑

Purpose: *Explain the reasons behind* ___↑

9. B

Question Type: Reading Comprehension ▶ Global

The correct answer to a question about the primary concern of the passage must reflect the passage as a whole. Your prediction for the answer would be something like "Explain the difficulties that are faced by working married men."

(B) matches the prediction and is correct. **(A)** incorrectly addresses the difficulties that women face. While these issues are mentioned in the passage, the author discusses them to contrast women's issues with those of married men. In addition, the author's tone is neutral; the author doesn't advocate anything. **(C)** misstates the main idea of the passage. The focus of the text is on the issues that are faced by working married men, some of whom happen to earn high salaries. **(D)** is not discussed in the passage. In addition, the author doesn't take issue with others' views. **(E)** is also not discussed in the passage, which does not attribute the difficulties of married men to discrimination against women.

10. D

Question Type: Reading Comprehension ▶ Inference

The passage discusses married men who work in the second, third, and fourth paragraphs, providing most details in the last two paragraphs. As you evaluate the choices, strictly compare each to the passage, keeping the author's overall purpose in writing in mind.

Lines 9–11 and 20–21 suggest that married men earn more to provide for their families. Lines 21–25 describe two negative effects on the families of married men—the men don't have enough time to spend with their families, and those men have higher levels of marital discord. Taken together, these parts of the passage support **(D)**.

(A) goes beyond what is stated in the passage and is incorrect. The passage suggests that married men work more hours and earn more money to support their families as their families grow, but the passage never indicates that this is the *most* important aspect of employment for married men.

(B) is the opposite of what the passage states and is incorrect. The third and fourth paragraphs discuss the difficulties faced by working married men.

EXPLANATIONS

Since the second paragraph outlines some of the advantages that married men have over their female counterparts, you may suspect that the author would agree with **(C)**, but no support for this comparison of their satisfaction levels is actually given in the passage.

(E) contradicts the passage and is thus incorrect. One of the complaints of married men, mentioned in lines 21–23, is that their job responsibilities prevent them from spending time with their families.

11. B

Question Type: Reading Comprehension ▶ Logic

The words "in order to" indicate this question is asking *how* or *why* the author used a feature of the passage, not about the content of the feature itself. Refer to your notes on the second paragraph and consider how the author used Coltrane's research to achieve the purpose of the passage. A good prediction of the correct answer would be "to explain that earning more money may not be enough for married men to be satisfied with their jobs."

(B) matches the prediction and is correct.

(A) describes the content of Coltrane's research, but the primary purpose of the paragraph is not to highlight the advantages enjoyed by working married men but rather to set the stage for a discussion of the reasons married men may be dissatisfied in their jobs.

The second paragraph does not address family leave policies and flexible work schedules **(C)**; these are discussed in the fourth paragraph.

The author mentions some disadvantages that women face after marrying and having children **(D)**, such as lower pay with each child. The author does not argue against the idea that women experience disadvantages.

While Coltrane's research could be construed as support for the idea that discrimination against women exists in the workplace **(E)**, the author neither attributes the problems women face to discrimination in the workplace nor describes Coltrane's research as indicative of discrimination. Also, again, the purpose of discussing this research is to describe men's experiences, not women's.

12. C

Question Type: Reading Comprehension ▶ Detail

The comparison of the salaries of married men to those of single men is found in lines 9–11, and a proposed explanation is found in lines 11–13: "One reason...may be that, as the size of the family grows, men rely on women to manage most of the responsibilities of housekeeping and child raising." **(C)** is a paraphrase of that sentence and is thus correct.

The remaining choices may be plausible in everyday life, but none of them are mentioned in the passage, so they are all incorrect.

13. C

Question Type: Sentence Correction
Question Topic: Other (Clauses and Connectors)

The clause starting "that it concerns ideas" and going all the way to the end of the sentence describes the genre of science fiction. Since the sentence before the comma already has a "that," which stands for the word right before it, "genre," there is no need for another "that" after the comma or for the pronoun "it." Eliminate **(A)**. To see clearly what sort of connector is needed, try reading the sentence without the unessential prepositional phrase "by addressing the future." In fact, no connector words are needed after the comma: "Science fiction has been described as the genre that … concerns ideas …" **(C)** is correct. Like the original sentence, **(B)** repeats "that," and **(E)** loses the "that" but retains the "it." **(D)** uses "so" improperly and changes "thoughts" to "thinking," which is not parallel with its partner "emotions."

14. B

Question Type: Sentence Correction
Question Topic: Idioms and Usage

The underlined portion of the sentence includes an unidiomatic phrase, "credited as to," and the redundant "known to be famous for." Eliminate **(A)**. The first part of **(C)** is wordier than the original, and "credited with" gives credit for her classical training to her technique, when the relationship is the other way around. **(D)** rearranges the words to say that Simone is given credit for a distinctive technique because she received classical training; this distorts the original's meaning. **(E)** says Simone herself is a result of her classical training, but it is her technique that was the result of her training. **(B)** uses the correct "credited to" and the succinct "known for," and this choice is correct.

15. B

Question Type: Critical Reasoning ▶ Weaken

The question stem asks for something that reduces the likelihood that the officials' program was effective. The program called for reduced water usage, and the water levels did return to normal. However, this a classic example of an unsupported cause-and-effect argument. The author assumes that the program caused the levels to return to normal and that nothing else was responsible. Your prediction should be along the lines of "something other than the program led to the increased water level."

(B) does this. It doesn't outright state what the other factor was. However, if other reservoirs in the area recovered without a water usage program in place, then some other factor was likely involved. **(A)** makes an irrelevant comparison between this year and last year. Even if last year's levels were higher, it's still possible that the program helped the reservoirs return to normal this year. **(C)** is another irrelevant comparison: as long as people reduced water usage overall, the program still could have worked. **(D)** suggests that there could have been a more effective plan, but that doesn't mean that the city officials' plan was ineffective. And the timing of the drop in water usage, in **(E)**, does not affect the argument that the plan caused the reduction and that this reduction caused reservoir levels to rise.

16. E

Question Type: Critical Reasoning ▶ Strengthen

The author uses an analogy to argue that allowing visitors to help feed the big cats would be dangerous. The reason is that the cats don't get to know the visitors as they do the zookeepers. But what if people could help feed the cats without actually interacting with the animals? That would take away the danger, making the author's argument fall apart. So, to strengthen the argument, show that feeding the cats involves a risk of physical contact.

(E) does exactly that, making it correct. **(A)** states that visitors are not as knowledgeable as the zookeepers. However, the argument hinges on how well the cats know the people feeding them, not the other way around. Moreover, this statement does not provide a link between interaction and safety while feeding the animals, so it adds no value to the argument. **(B)** addresses the wrong idea. The zoo may be looking to attract new visitors, but the author is only concerned about safety, not whether the zoo is successful in increasing attendance. **(C)** confirms the potential danger of entering a stranger's home unannounced. However, the author brings up this situation as an analogy, and knowing more about the danger of committing a home invasion does not confirm that feeding big cats is equivalently dangerous. **(D)** mentions people's experience interacting with wild animals in general, while the argument is about whether the big cats in this zoo will have had prior exposure to the visitors. More importantly, this comparison of visitors to non-visitors is irrelevant as it still does not make a connection between greater interaction and safety.

17. B

Question Type: Sentence Correction
Question Topic: Pronouns; Parallelism; Modification

When faced with choices that are this long, it is often easier to focus on one element of the sentence at a time. The opening phrase says something is happening as "one step in their plan." Whose plan? The town council's—but a council is singular and must be represented by the singular pronoun "its." Eliminate **(A)** and **(E)**, as both include "their plan." Scan the remaining choices in parallel until you see a difference. **(D)** has "a series of public meetings" after the comma, indicating that the series of meetings sought to engender greater goodwill. This isn't logical, so eliminate this choice. The difference between **(B)** and **(C)** comes in the list at the end. Examine the list for parallel structure and notice the lack of parallel structure in **(C)** with "the opacity...tendency...and failing." The list in **(B)** has parallel structure, and this choice is correct.

18. C

Question Type: Sentence Correction
Question Topic: Comparison

The words at the beginning of the underlined portion, "most easily," indicate that a comparison is being made. Specifically, the comparison is about how reducing a population of insects is easier if done by attacking young larva instead of by attacking older larva or adults. This is a two-part comparison between *one way* and *other ways*, so the correct word is "more," not "most." Eliminate **(A)**, and eliminate **(B)** for the same reason. **(D)** begins with the adjective "easier," which does not correctly modify the verb "done." One thing is done *more easily than* another, so the second part of the construction must use "than." **(E)** uses "than applying" at the end, which does not integrate correctly with the non-underlined text that follows. That leaves **(C)**, which begins with "more easily" and ends with "than," correctly forming the comparison.

On the left, we've shown how keywords help to identify the major elements of the passage and its structure and what you could skim over. On the right, we've shown what you might be thinking as you read the passage strategically.

Passage for Questions 19–21

PASSAGE	ANALYSIS
As the world becomes more interconnected...languages, as well as the culture...may be lost.	Many languages/cultures = in danger of extinction.
[S]trong link between **language** and **cultural identity...With** loss of language comes loss of links to the past and feelings of belonging to a community.	Language and identity are linked. Examples given.
One problem...is lack of official recognition. Residents...expected to know...official language or languages, **but** many countries do little to recognize minority...languages...**It is not surprising, therefore**...	Official vs regional languages—Basque as example
Consider, **in contrast**...Finnish...not endangered **even though** Finland was ruled...by first Sweden and then Russia...Finland...constitutionally adopted...Finnish...**important** to its burgeoning national identity.	Identity and language—Finnish as example
[L]inguists have proposed creating a database of endangered languages... **While** directed toward a noble goal, this project would **fail** to address the issue of language's **critical** role in preserving a sense of cultural identity.	Saving endangered languages in a database wouldn't help those who will lose their native tongue/cultural identity.

Passage Map

Here is an example of the notes that you might have made as you read:

¶1: Languages/culture endangered

¶2: Language = cultural identity

¶3: Official/not official; ex: Basque in Fr & Sp

¶4: Finnish; made official

¶5: Database won't preserve cultural identity

Topic: Language and cultural identity

Scope: Preservation of ___↑

Purpose: Explain importance and problems & argue against one solution ___↑

19. C

Question Type: Reading Comprehension ▶ Detail

Basque is mentioned in the third paragraph, so research the answer there. This paragraph is about the importance of official recognition to the survival of a language. It is officially recognized in Spain but not in France, and the author links this difference to Basque's status as "vulnerable" in Spain but "critically endangered" in France.

(C) states the reason for Basque's more precarious situation in France and is correct. While France does not recognize Basque as an official language, nothing in the passage suggests Basque has been actively suppressed there, eliminating **(A)**. Nothing is said of how many speakers there are in each country, so **(B)** can be eliminated. **(D)** and **(E)** may or may not be true, but neither is a reason why, according to the passage, Basque is more endangered in France than in Spain.

20. A

Question Type: Reading Comprehension ▶ Strengthen

Research the line reference, reading the entire sentence for context. The author states that the acknowledgment of Finnish as key to national identity took place in 1919, when the new constitution was adopted. Look for a piece of evidence that associates the use of the Finnish language with a revitalization of national pride.

(A) describes a key change in feelings about Finnish, from negative to positive, in 1919 and supports the assertion; this is correct. **(B)** and **(D)** are examples of the status quo continuing after Finnish was adopted, so neither adds support to the assertion that the language was important to developing nationalism. **(C)** notes national symbols that may have expressed or promoted nationhood, but this choice does not support the idea that the Finnish language was important. If anything, **(E)** would be a weakener as it implies cultural divisions within Finland instead of national unity.

21. B

Question Type: Reading Comprehension ▶ Application

This question asks you to evaluate a statement that is not in the passage in terms of how well it reflects an idea that is in the passage. First, research the first paragraph where UNESCO's assertion appears. This can be paraphrased as, *When a language is lost, ideas are also lost.* The correct answer will reflect this idea.

In **(B)**, the inability to translate a script has resulted in the loss of the ideas of the people who wrote it. This matches the prediction and is correct. **(A)** speaks only about the value of the language itself, not about the value of the ideas it communicates. **(C)** is a counterexample to UNESCO's concern; though there is no way to read the thoughts of Socrates in his own words, his ideas are preserved in the writings of others, diminishing the importance of whether his original language has survived. **(D)** and **(E)** are not related to losing language or the ideas that it carries. Ideas expressed in Korean are accessible to those who learn that language, and the concept expressed by "serendipity" is accessible to those who understand the word; both Korean and the English word "serendipity" are alive and well.

22. D

Question Type: Sentence Correction
Question Topic: Modification

In the original sentence, the placement of the modifying phrase "learned by computers" makes it unclear whether the "identification" or the "planets" are learned by the computers. Furthermore, the construction "the identification of planets learned by computers is done" is passive and awkward. Since the computers identify planets, ideally "computers" will precede "identify" in the sentence. Moreover, the sentence states that computers found instances of recorded signals *"in* the telescope," which is illogical. A telescope is used to make observations, and in these data the computer could find signals from planets. Eliminate **(A)**. There is a long string of prepositional phrases in this sentence, so look for the choice that puts each phrase next to the thing it modifies. **(E)** begins in nearly the same passive, confusing manner as **(A)**, so eliminate this choice. Eliminate **(B)**, which also has the computer finding recorded signals in the telescope. Eliminate **(C)** because the non-underlined phrase "known as exoplanets" must modify the noun closest to it, but the "signals from beyond our solar system" are not "known as exoplanets." **(D)** is correct.

23. B

Question Type: Critical Reasoning ▸ Weaken

There are a few good ways to approach this question. As with all Weaken questions, begin by understanding the argument. The business owner argues that partnering with a local gym to offer employees a discounted membership will help reduce fatigue. As evidence, the owner cites a correlation between exercise and high energy levels. The owner assumes that exercise is what causes these people to have high energy levels. To weaken such an assumption, it could be shown that the high energy levels were caused by something else (e.g., caffeine, protein diets, medication). It could also be shown that the author has misunderstood the direction of causality: perhaps people exercise because they already have more energy, not the other way around. Or perhaps increased exercise and increased energy are both just effects of another variable (e.g., motivation).

Besides an assumption about causality, there is another assumption. The owner makes a plan based on a prediction, which means the author assumes there are no factors that would affect the predicted outcome of the plan. To weaken this assumption, you could find a problem with the plan—something that shows it might not help reduce fatigue. Maybe employees will get the gym membership but not exercise more (how many people join a gym but don't actually go?), or maybe the membership will be unappealing even with the discount. And that's what **(B)** does. It shows how the discount will not encourage people to go to the gym, making it less likely they will feel more energetic.

(A) suggests there are other ways to achieve the same results, but that doesn't mean the owner's plan won't work. **(C)** is irrelevant. Higher productivity might be a nice side effect, but it's not the owner's stated goal. She is discounting gym memberships to reduce fatigue. **(D)** is irrelevant. Any extra burden on the gym has no effect on whether the plan will work. If anything, this supports the owner's thinking by implying that people will exercise more. **(E)** uses extreme language. The issue is whether fatigue can be reduced, not whether it can be eradicated completely.

24. D

Question Type: Sentence Correction
Question Topic: Verbs; Idioms and Usage

The phrase "[s]ince 2007" is a clue that verb tenses are being tested. "Since 2007" and "has maintained" indicate the program began in the past and is still continuing, so eliminate **(A)** and **(E)** because these choices use the past tense verbs "considered" and "believed," respectively. Another issue in the original sentence is the idiomatic usage of "consider." On the GMAT, "consider" is used without a following connecting word or phrase. A correct use of "consider" in this sentence would be *many scientists who consider these phenomena to have natural explanations*. Since "that" is not underlined and so can't be changed, eliminate **(B)**. **(C)** incorrectly states "the views...believe ..." The *views* don't believe, the *scientists* believe. **(D)** is correct.

25. C

Question Type: Sentence Correction
Question Topic: Parallelism

Items in a list must be in identical grammatical format, and the original sentence has two noun-verb pairings—"days shorten" and "temperature drops"—followed by an *–ing* construction. Also, the first item is preceded by "the," the second item lacks a "the," and then "the" reappears in front of the third item. Eliminate **(A)**. In **(B)**, "is to reveal" is not parallel with "shorten" and "drops." Eliminate **(D)** since in the first two list items, this choice uses more words to say the same thing, and the phrasing of the last item makes it unclear what is breaking down to reduce the amount of chlorophyll in the leaves. **(E)** uses "the" before the first two items but drops it in the third item; also, moving "in the leaves" further from "chlorophyll" makes it less clear where the chlorophyll is. **(C)** has all items in identical form—"shorten...drops...breaks down"—and is correct.

26. B

Question Type: Critical Reasoning ▸ Assumption

The question stem, in addition to asking for an assumption, indicates that a proposal has been made. To recommend the proposal, the author must assume that its benefits outweigh any disadvantages. The proposal is a ban on paper towels, which would be replaced by hot-air dryers; the purpose of this ban is to reduce environmental impact, since this plan would use fewer resources and reduce emissions. A good prediction would be that there's nothing about hot-air dryers that would make them worse for the environment than paper towels.

(B) matches this prediction and is thus correct; since one of the stated goals of the plan is to protect the environment and this will be achieved, in part, by cutting down fewer trees, the author must be assuming that hot-air dryers use fewer natural resources than do paper towels. If increased use of hot-air dryers would cause, for example, the mining of metals for their manufacture or of coal or uranium to produce electricity, then their environmental impact might not be less than that of paper towels, and the argument falls apart. **(A)** is irrelevant; the fact that costs won't increase might be an additional benefit of the proposal, but since the argument is strictly about environmental impact, the author isn't assuming anything about the cost of the change. **(C)** is incorrect because it's not

EXPLANATIONS

necessary for dryers to be the only alternative to towels for them to be the better alternative. **(D)** is wrong because effectiveness is irrelevant to an argument that is based on environmental concerns. **(E)** may be tempting because it might seem that the proposal won't be effective if people aren't willing to implement it; however, the proposal is to ban paper towels, so whether or not people are willing to replace them is irrelevant.

27. B

Question Type: Critical Reasoning ▶ Weaken

To weaken the argument, you need to find the choice that contradicts an assumption of the argument. The conclusion is that moving coffee plant production in Kuanta from the lowlands will increase sales. The evidence is that Zantria coffee, which has higher sales, is grown in the mountains. The assumption is that Zantria coffee is more popular because it's grown in the mountains, so moving production to the mountains would have the same effect on Kuanta coffee; in other words, there's nothing else that could be causing the sales gap. To weaken a cause-and-effect assumption, look for an answer that suggests another cause. In this case, then, the prediction would be "another difference between the two types of coffee that could explain the difference in sales."

That's why **(B)** is correct. If the coffee plants in the two countries are of a different species, then that difference might explain their relative popularity; perhaps they taste different, or maybe one type is more trendy right now. At any rate, this presents an alternative explanation. There's no way to know whether the opinion of experts, in **(A)**, correlates with the opinion of coffee consumers in general. Even if it did, this would actually strengthen the argument by eliminating one alternative reason for Zantria coffee's better sales; if Zantria coffee doesn't sell better because it tastes better, then maybe it is the coffee farms' location that makes the difference. **(C)**, if anything, would strengthen the argument; if the coffee plants in the lowlands are threatened, then moving them to another location may be a good idea. Even so, however, the possible destruction of beans by the fungus in the future does not speak to why Kuanta coffee isn't selling as well now. **(D)** would strengthen the argument; one reason Kuanta coffee might sell less well than Zantria coffee would be if Kuanta coffee were more expensive. If this explanation is eliminated, then it's more likely that the coffee farms' location is the culprit. **(E)** may be tempting; it seems to provide a reason other than where the beans were grown that could explain the gap in sales. There's no way to know, however, whether Kuanta's beans are also available in different roast levels or even whether this is something that consumers appreciate.

28. D

Question Type: Sentence Correction
Question Topic: Idioms and Usage; Modification

The original sentence contains several errors. An efficient approach when a large amount of text is underlined is to focus on one error, evaluate the choices, and then proceed to the next error. First, because days are countable, the journey was completed in six *fewer* days. Eliminate **(A)** and **(E)**. Next, the modifying phrase between commas, "completing the journey...done," must refer to the first noun that follows the phrase, but "the record" did not complete the journey. Eliminate **(B)** and **(C)** for committing this error. **(D)** is correct.

EXPLANATIONS

On the left, we've shown how keywords help to identify the major elements of the passage and its structure and what you could skim over. On the right, we've shown what you might be thinking as you read the passage strategically.

Passage for Questions 29–32

PASSAGE	ANALYSIS
Bog bodies...**remarkably** well preserved...**not**...like Egyptian mummies, deliberately embalmed...**but** likely perpetuated by an accident...	Bog bodies are preserved, probably accidentally.
The wetlands...are **exclusively** sphagnum moss bogs...weather is cold...saltwater...**Together** these elements create the **perfect environment** for the preservation...	Makeup of the bogs where bodies are found promotes preservation.
The biochemistry of preservation...has **several components**... cold temperatures and dense peat...acidic environment **further** inhibits bacteria...**also** release sphagnan...preventing rot and water damage...	Bog environment interacts with bodies in several ways that keep them preserved.
Besides bodies, bogs have also preserved...**Much can be learned** about our ancestors...of medical conditions...of diet, of how far from home people traveled...	The scholarly value of bog bodies

Passage Map

Here is an example of the notes that you might have made as you read:

¶1: *Bog bodies = accidentally preserved?*

¶2: *Conditions of bogs*

¶3: *Biochemistry that allows preservation*

¶4: *Other things preserved; value for learning*

Topic: *Bog bodies*

Scope: *How sphagnum moss bogs preserve* ⤴

Purpose: *Describe and explain* ⤴

E X P L A N A T I O N S

29. A

Question Type: Reading Comprehension ▸ Detail

The necessary conditions for preserving bodies are discussed in the second paragraph: sphagnum moss, cold temperatures that lead to cool water, and nearby salt water "[t]ogether…create the perfect environment."

While a cold winter and early spring are important for preservation, the passage does not say the length of this season is a factor, so **(A)** is correct. The other choices are all mentioned in this paragraph as promoting the preservation of bodies.

30. C

Question Type: Reading Comprehension ▸ Global

Use the author's purpose in the passage map, rather than reviewing the passage itself, to predict the correct answer.

(C) is a neat summation of the purpose and is correct. While the author mentions at the beginning of the passage a presumed difference between bog bodies and mummies, contrasting bog bodies with other remains isn't the purpose of the passage, eliminating **(A)**. Similarly, while the author mentions that bog bodies were probably preserved by accident, the author never implies that anyone thinks any differently, let alone mounts an argument for the idea; **(B)** can be eliminated. **(D)** reflects only a few details from the last paragraph of the passage and not the passage as a whole. Moreover, while the passage says that bog bodies have helped scholars understand the lives of Iron Age humans, it does not go so far as to claim that this information would be unknown if not for the bog bodies. The passage explains what is distinct about sphagnum moss bogs but never discusses other environments, so analyzing differences between them, as in **(E)**, cannot be the primary purpose.

31. D

Question Type: Reading Comprehension ▸ Logic

According to the passage map, the third paragraph discusses the biochemistry of the bogs that are involved in preservation. Research of the paragraph itself shows that it describes the ways in which the moss and cold water, first mentioned in the preceding paragraph, produce the relatively inert environment of the bog.

(D), though phrased in more abstract language, matches this prediction and is correct. The author doesn't indicate that some factors are more important than others, so **(A)** is out. The author does say in the last paragraph that bog bodies are important, but the third paragraph does not provide support for this assertion; eliminate **(B)**. In **(C)**, "the environment…that produces the effect that is the topic" is the bog, but this paragraph describes how the bog works on bodies, not how the bog is formed. **(E)** distorts the author's use of "biochemistry"; while a grasp of biochemistry is undoubtedly helpful to understand how sphagnum moss bogs preserve bodies, the role of this paragraph is not to explain the importance of biochemistry but to explain how certain bogs preserve bodies.

32. E

Question Type: Reading Comprehension ▸ Detail

"[B]acterial growth" is mentioned in the third paragraph, so research this part of the text. Cold temperatures, the creation by the dense sphagnum moss of "a mostly anaerobic environment," and the release of humic or "bog" acid by the deterioration of dead layers of moss all inhibit bacterial growth.

(E) is mentioned in the passage. However, sphagnan prevents "rot and water damage" by binding to the skin. The text does not say it acts against bacteria. This is the correct answer. **(A)**, **(B)**, **(C)**, and **(D)** all match relevant details in the passage and can be eliminated.

33. E

Question Type: Critical Reasoning ▸ Inference

The correct answer will be fully supported by the text, so as you read, mentally catalog the facts presented, as these can support inferences. The first sentence describes two trends: an increase in the use of herbarus to treat anxiety and a decrease in the incidence of anxiety where herbarus is legal. The second sentence reports on studies that compare outcomes of people who take herbarus under the care of an alternative practitioner and of people who take a drug prescribed by a doctor. Identify the choice that aligns with one or more of these facts.

According to the studies cited in the passage, people who take herbarus under the care of an alternative practitioner are likelier to use more than one type of treatment than are people who see a physician for their anxiety. It follows then that alternative healers treat people with anxiety differently than do physicians. This makes **(E)**, which says that a practitioner of alternative medicine is likely to use different protocols, the correct answer. **(A)** discusses people's satisfaction with their lives, which the passage does not mention; the passage only talks about medical outcomes such as less anxiety in the population and less difficulty performing life activities for individuals. For **(B)**, the author provides no data about the number of physician-prescribed drugs; even though the author states that the popularity of herbarus has increased, the number of prescriptions for conventional medications could also have increased or remained the same. **(C)** is a comparison not supported by the passage. The passage doesn't say why people are increasingly opting to use herbarus; perhaps it's less expensive than other drugs or there is some other reason people prefer it. **(D)** might seem tempting, but it is not necessarily true that the incidence of anxiety would increase if not as many people opted for herbarus. The number might stay the same, or perhaps the association between herbarus and mental health actually operates in reverse, with people who have less severe anxiety that is more likely to resolve without medical treatment opting to use natural remedies.

34. E

Question Type: Sentence Correction
Question Topic: Parallelism

The construction "*both* introspective explorations …" needs to be completed by *and* to be idiomatically correct, and the *and* must be followed by a noun that is parallel with "explorations." Thus, "as well as" is incorrect, and so is "subverting." Moreover, the two halves of the phrase "of cultural identity and feminine" should be in parallel form, but since "identity" is a noun and "feminine" is an adjective, this phrase is incorrect as written. Eliminate **(A)**. With "being feminine," "that was feminine," and "the femininity," **(B)**, **(C)**, and **(D)**, respectively, violate the parallelism of the "of cultural identity and …" phrase. **(B)** and **(D)** also use "subverted," which is not parallel with "explorations," and **(D)** uses the unidiomatic "as well as." **(E)** completes both parallel constructions correctly.

35. C

Question Type: Critical Reasoning ▸ Explain

Despite a decline in enrollments in each yoga class at the studio, sales of yoga mats increased. Consider possible explanations: it might be that more people are taking up yoga outside a studio or at a studio outside of town, people are using yoga mats for non-yoga-related activities, more classes are being offered such that per-class enrollment is down but overall enrollment is up, or people now want a different mat for each day of the week—or perhaps there are other explanations. There's no way to know exactly what will show up in the correct answer, so predict "anything that would increase demand for yoga mats."

An increase in the number of classes as well as the addition of new students, **(C)**, explains the discrepancy. Even if per-class enrollment is down, more classes means overall enrollment could be up, and new students probably don't already have mats and need to buy them. **(A)** only explains the increase in sales if you further assume that people like to buy different types of mats when they are available, and there is no evidence for this. **(B)** deepens the mystery; if the price of mats has gone down, then all else being equal, you'd expect sales to go up. **(D)** may explain the decrease in yoga class enrollment, but it does not address the increase in yoga mat sales. **(E)** would only work if this requirement were new this year; however, the stimulus does not say this is the case.

36. C

Question Type: Sentence Correction
Question Topic: Verbs; Modification

The original sentence contains an error in subject-verb agreement. The subject "rise" requires the singular verb "has enabled." Eliminate **(A)** and **(B)**. Read the remaining three choices in parallel. The first difference is in the position of "rapidly." **(E)** moves "rapidly" to describe the rate of specialization instead of the rate of growth, changing the meaning of the sentence. Continue reading **(C)** and **(D)**. By placing "only" before "successful companies," **(D)** says that entrepreneurs have started nothing but successful companies, but the intention of the original sentence is that these companies are successful even though their products have limited markets. **(C)** is correct.

PART THREE

Verbal Section and Strategies

CHAPTER 5

Verbal Section Overview

- Composition of the Verbal Section
- Pacing on the Verbal Section
- How the Verbal Section Is Scored
- Core Competencies on the Verbal Section
- Introduction to Strategic Reading

COMPOSITION OF THE VERBAL SECTION

A little more than half of the multiple-choice questions that count toward your overall score appear in the Verbal section. You have 65 minutes to answer 36 Verbal questions in three formats: Reading Comprehension, Sentence Correction, and Critical Reasoning. These three types of questions are mingled throughout the Verbal section, so you never know what's coming next. Here's what you can expect to see:

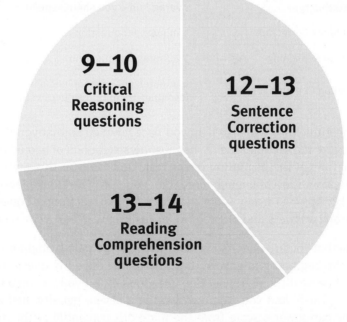

9–10
Critical Reasoning questions

12–13
Sentence Correction questions

13–14
Reading Comprehension questions

The Approximate Mix of Questions on the GMAT Verbal Section

You may see more of one question type and fewer of another. Don't worry: the GMAT is a standardized test, so the number of each kind of question won't vary too far from what you expect and have studied for.

In the next three chapters, you'll learn strategies for each of these question types. But first, let's look at some techniques for managing the Verbal section as a whole.

PACING ON THE VERBAL SECTION

The GMAT will give you about four Reading Comprehension passages. With less than 2 minutes per question on the Verbal section, where will you find the time to read those passages?

Part of the answer is that the Reading Comprehension chapter of this book will give you great tips about how to read the passages efficiently. Another big part, though, is how you will handle Sentence Correction. Follow the Kaplan Method for Sentence Correction, which you will see in the chapter devoted to that question type, and through practice you will bring your average time down to 60 seconds per Sentence Correction question. Moving through Sentence Correction questions efficiently will allow you the time you'll need to read long Reading Comprehension passages and take apart complex arguments in Critical Reasoning.

Here are Kaplan's timing recommendations for the Verbal section of the GMAT. While it's far more important at first that you practice to build mastery of the strategies, it's also a good idea to keep these timing recommendations in mind. Then, by incorporating more timed practice as you progress in your GMAT prep, you will grow comfortable reading and answering questions at the suggested pace, setting yourself up for success on Test Day.

Verbal Section Timing	
Question type	**Average time you should spend**
Sentence Correction	1 minute per question
Critical Reasoning	2 minutes per question
Reading Comprehension	4 minutes per passage and a little less than 1.5 minutes per question

Following these timing guidelines will also help you pace yourself so that you have time to work on the questions at the end of the section. One of the most persistent bits of bad advice out there is that you should take more time at the beginning of the test. Don't fall for this myth! Running short of time at the end of the test will cost you much more than you may gain from a few extra right answers up front. The test maker imposes heavy score penalties for not reaching all questions in a section, and long strings of wrong answers due to guessing or rushing will hurt your score as well.

What this all means is that you are under some conflicting pressures. It might seem like a good idea to take extra time at the beginning to ensure that you get all the early questions right, since then the test would give you those difficult, high-value questions. But if you use up a lot of time early on, you won't have time to finish, and your score will suffer a severe penalty. Just a handful of unanswered final questions can lower a score from the mid-90th percentile to the mid-70th percentile. Plus, if you spend all that time early on, you won't have time to solve the hard questions you may receive as a result of your careful work, so you won't be able to take advantage of their extra value.

So if taking more time at the beginning isn't a good idea, does that mean you should rush through the beginning? This is also not the case. Rushing almost guarantees that you will miss some crucial aspect of a question. If you get a lot of midlevel questions wrong, the test will never give you those difficult, high-value questions that you want to reach.

If you are stuck on a question, make a guess. Even the best test takers occasionally guess, and it's still possible to achieve an elite score if you are strategic about when and how you guess. If you start to fall behind pace, look for good guessing questions. That way, you'll reach the end of the section and have the time to earn the points for all the questions that you are capable of answering correctly and efficiently. What kinds of questions are good candidates for guessing? Ones that you know play to your weaknesses, ones that require lots of reading, or ones that look like they will involve separate evaluation of each answer choice.

STRATEGIC GUESSING

Whether because you're running short of time or you've encountered a question that totally flummoxes you, you will have to guess occasionally. But don't simply guess at random. First, try to narrow down the answer choices. This will greatly improve your chances of guessing the right answer. When you guess, you should follow this plan:

1. **Eliminate answer choices you know are wrong.** Even if you don't know the right answer, you can often tell that some of the choices are wrong. For instance, on Sentence Correction questions, you can eliminate **(A)** as soon as you find an error in the original sentence, thus reducing the number of choices to consider.

2. **Avoid answer choices that make you suspicious.** These are the choices that just "look wrong" or conform to a common wrong-answer type. For example, if an answer choice in a Reading Comprehension question mentions a concept you don't remember from the passage, chances are it is wrong. (The next three chapters contain more information about common wrong-answer types on the Verbal section.)

3. **Choose one of the remaining answer choices.** The fewer options you have to choose from, the higher your chances of selecting the right answer.

EXPERIMENTAL QUESTIONS

Some questions on the GMAT are experimental. These questions are not factored into your score. They are questions that the test maker is evaluating for possible use on future tests. To get good data, the test maker has to test each question against the whole range of test takers—that is, high and low scorers. Therefore, you could be on your way to an 800 and suddenly come across an easy question, leading you to question how you think you are doing.

Don't panic; just do your best on the question in front of you and keep going. The difficulty level of the experimental questions you see has little to do with how you're currently scoring. Remember, there is no way for you to know whether a question is experimental or not, so approach every question as if it were scored.

Furthermore, keep in mind that it's hard to judge the difficulty level of a question. A question that seems easy to you may simply be playing to your personal strengths and be very difficult for other test takers. So don't waste time speculating about the difficulty of the questions you're seeing and what that implies about your performance. Rather, focus your energy on answering the question on the screen as efficiently as possible.

HOW THE VERBAL SECTION IS SCORED

The Verbal section of the GMAT is quite different from the Verbal sections of paper-and-pencil tests you may have taken. The major difference between the test formats is that the GMAT computer-adaptive test (CAT) adapts to your performance. Each test taker is given a different mix of questions, depending on how well he or she is doing on the test. In other words, the questions get harder or easier depending on whether you answer them correctly or incorrectly. Your GMAT score is not determined by the number of questions you get right but rather by the difficulty level of the questions you get right.

When you begin a section, the computer

- assumes you have an average score (about 550), and
- gives you a medium-difficulty question. About half the people who take the test will get this question right, and half will get it wrong. What happens next depends on whether you answer the question correctly.

If you answer the question correctly,

- your score goes up, and
- you are given a slightly harder question.

If you answer the question incorrectly,

- your score goes down, and
- you are given a slightly easier question.

This pattern continues for the rest of the section. As you get questions right, the computer raises your score and gives you harder questions. As you get questions wrong, the computer lowers your score and gives you easier questions. In this way, the computer homes in on your score.

If you feel like you're struggling at the end of the section, don't worry! Because the CAT adapts to find the outer edge of your abilities, the test will feel hard; it's designed to be difficult for everyone, even the highest scorers.

CORE COMPETENCIES ON THE VERBAL SECTION

Unlike most subject-specific tests you have taken throughout your academic career, the scope of knowledge that the GMAT requires of you is fairly limited. In fact, you don't need any background knowledge or expertise beyond fundamental math and verbal skills. While mastering those fundamentals is essential to your success on the GMAT—and this book is concerned in part with helping you develop or refresh those skills—the GMAT does *not* primarily seek to reward test takers for content-specific knowledge. Rather, the GMAT is a test of high-level thinking and reasoning abilities; it uses math and verbal subject matter as a platform to build questions that test your critical-thinking and problem-solving capabilities. As you prepare for the GMAT, you will notice that similar analytical skills come into play across the various question types and sections of the test.

Kaplan has adopted the term "Core Competencies" to refer to the four bedrock thinking skills rewarded by the GMAT: Critical Thinking, Pattern Recognition, Paraphrasing, and Attention to the Right Detail. The Kaplan Methods and strategies presented throughout this book will help you demonstrate these all-important skills. Let's dig into each of the Core Competencies in turn and discuss how each applies to the Verbal section.

CRITICAL THINKING

Most potential MBA students are adept at creative problem solving, and the GMAT offers many opportunities to demonstrate this skill. You probably already have experience assessing situations to see when data are inadequate; synthesizing information into valid deductions; finding creative solutions to complex problems; and avoiding unnecessary, redundant labor.

In GMAT terms, a critical thinker is a creative problem solver who engages in critical inquiry. One of the hallmarks of successful test takers is their skill at asking the right questions. GMAT critical thinkers first consider what they're being asked to do, then study the given information and ask the right questions, especially, "How can I get the answer in the most direct way?" and "How can I use the question format to my advantage?"

For instance, as you examine a Reading Comprehension passage, you'll interrogate the author: "Why are you writing about Walt Whitman?" or "Why have you included this detail in paragraph 2?" For Sentence Correction questions, you'll ask: "Why do three of the five answer choices share the same grammatical construction?" or "Is there a better way to express the idea?" For Critical Reasoning, you'll ask the author of the argument: "What's your main point?" or "What evidence have you presented to convince me to agree with you?"

Those test takers who learn to ask the right questions become creative problem solvers—and GMAT champs. Let's see how to apply the GMAT Core Competency of Critical Thinking to a sample Critical Reasoning question:

1. One problem with labor unions today is that their top staffs consist of college-trained lawyers, economists, and labor relations experts who cannot understand the concerns of real workers. One goal of union reform movements should be to build staffs out of workers who have come up from the ranks of the industry involved.

    The argument above depends primarily upon which one of the following assumptions?

    ○ Higher education lessens people's identification with their class background.

    ○ Union staffs should include more people with firsthand industrial supervisory experience.

    ○ Some people who have worked in a given industry can understand the concerns of workers in that industry.

    ○ Most labor unions today do not fairly represent workers' interests.

    ○ A goal of union reform movements should be to make unions more democratic.

This question asks you to identify what the author is assuming. You'll learn more about assumptions in the Critical Reasoning chapter of this book, but for now, know that an "assumption" is something the author *must* believe but doesn't state directly. A skilled critical thinker will approach this task by asking questions to uncover the author's unstated assumption.

First of all, what does the author want to see happen? The author argues that unions should get more "workers who have come up through the ranks" into leadership. What's her reason for this claim? She asserts that the lawyers and experts don't understand what real workers worry about.

So if her solution is to get more rank-and-file workers into top union staffs, then what must she think these rank-and-file are capable of? The author is assuming that, unlike the college-trained experts, "workers who have come up through the ranks" can understand the concerns of the "real workers" whom the unions are supposed to represent. Scanning the answer choices, the one that matches this prediction is choice **(C)**.

Notice how efficiently you can move through a question like this one when you engage in critical inquiry—no rereading, no falling for answer choice traps, no time wasted. As you move through this book, you'll learn how to identify the most helpful questions to ask depending on how the test question is constructed.

PATTERN RECOGNITION

Most people fail to appreciate the level of constraint standardization places on test makers. Because the test makers must give reliable, valid, and comparable scores to many thousands of students each year, they're forced to reward the same skills on every test. They do so by repeating the same kinds of questions with the same traps and pitfalls, which are susceptible to the same strategic solutions.

Inexperienced test takers treat every problem as if it were a brand-new task, whereas the GMAT rewards those who spot the patterns and use them to their advantage. Of course, Pattern Recognition is a key business skill in its own right: executives who recognize familiar situations and apply proven solutions to them will outperform those who reinvent the wheel every time.

Even the smartest test taker will struggle if he approaches each GMAT question as a novel exercise. But the GMAT features nothing novel—just repeated patterns. Kaplan knows this test inside and out, and we'll show you which patterns you will encounter on Test Day. You will know the test better than your competition does. Let's see how to apply the GMAT Core Competency of Pattern Recognition to a sample Sentence Correction question:

2. A major pharmaceutical company, in cooperation with an international public health organization and the medical research departments of two large universities, is expected to announce tomorrow that it will transfer the rights to manufacture a number of tuberculosis drugs to several smaller companies.

- ○ is expected to announce tomorrow that it will transfer the
- ○ are expected to announce tomorrow that they will transfer their
- ○ are expected to announce tomorrow that they will transfer the
- ○ is expected to announce tomorrow that they will transfer the
- ○ is expected to announce tomorrow that there would be a transfer of the

Many people will look at this problem and start thinking about grammar classes they haven't had for years. Then they'll plug every answer choice back into the sentence to see which one works best. Did you find yourself doing that during your diagnostic test?

There are two important patterns at work in this question that you should recognize from now on. First, choice **(A)** on Sentence Correction questions will always repeat the underlined portion of the original sentence. You should only ever choose **(A)** if there's no error in the original sentence. If you've already read the original sentence, there's never any reason to spend time reading through choice **(A)**.

Second, notice the pronoun *it* in the underlined portion. Pronouns are one of seven grammar and usage topics that together make up 93 percent of the Sentence Correction issues on the GMAT.

Whenever a pronoun appears in the underlined portion of the sentence, you should check whether it's correct. Here, ask yourself what *it* refers to. In this case, *it* is the pharmaceutical company. Notice in scanning the answer choices that they, too, fall into patterns: some use *it*, and others use *they*. Recognizing this pattern lets you know what question to ask next: "To refer to a company, is the correct pronoun *it* or *they*?" For a singular noun, the correct pronoun is *it*. Eliminate **(B)**, **(C)**, and **(D)**, which all use *they*.

Having narrowed down the choices to just two, **(A)** and **(E)**, you can eliminate **(E)** because it uses an awkward, lengthy phrase that makes it less clear *who* will "transfer the rights." The answer is **(A)**; the sentence is correct as written.

Notice how efficiently you can find the correct answer when you recognize the patterns. Meanwhile, your competition, not recognizing how the GMAT works, would waste time floundering through each answer choice in turn.

PARAPHRASING

Yet another Core Competency is Paraphrasing: the GMAT rewards those who can reduce difficult, abstract, or polysyllabic prose to simple terms. Paraphrasing is, of course, an essential business skill: executives must be able to define clear tasks based on complicated requirements and accurately summarize mountains of detail.

The test isn't going to make it easy for you to understand questions and passages. But you won't be overwhelmed by the complicated prose of Critical Reasoning or Reading Comprehension questions if you endeavor to make your own straightforward mental translations. Habitually putting complex ideas and convoluted wording into your own simple, accurate terms will ensure that you "get it"— that you understand the information well enough to drive to the correct answer.

Let's see how to apply the GMAT Core Competency of Paraphrasing to the first paragraph of a sample Reading Comprehension passage. You will return to this passage in full in the Reading Comprehension chapter of this book. For now, use the first paragraph to see how Paraphrasing helps you synthesize ideas by putting them in your own words:

> The informal sector of the economy involves activities that, in both developed and underdeveloped countries, are outside the arena of the normal, regulated economy and thus escape official record keeping. These activities, which include such practices as off-the-books hiring and cash payments, occur mainly in service industries such as construction, hotels, and restaurants. Many economists think that the informal sector is an insignificant supplement to the larger formal economy. They base this belief on three assumptions that have been derived from theories of industrial development. But empirical evidence suggests that these assumptions are not valid.

One of the most crucial ways to paraphrase on the GMAT is to summarize the main idea of a paragraph. When you learn about passage mapping in the Reading Comprehension chapter of this book, you will see how helpful it is to write a short summary of each paragraph. Clearly, however, you do not want to waste time copying down whole sentences or phrases from the passage verbatim. Paraphrasing helps you simultaneously identify quick, short ways to record main ideas and reinforce your understanding of those ideas.

You don't need to be an expert on economic policy to identify the main ideas in this paragraph and put them into your own words. The paragraph defines the informal sector, gives examples, then sets the stage for a debate between "many economists" and the author over how big or important the informal sector is.

On Test Day, you might write the following shorthand notes in your passage map for this paragraph:

¶1: Informal sector jobs; examps; econs think minor (based on 3 assumps); author disagrees

As you work through the Verbal chapters of this book, you will learn more about Paraphrasing for Reading Comprehension passages. You will also develop techniques for Paraphrasing the content of Critical Reasoning questions and interpreting the gist of what a Sentence Correction sentence is trying to say so that you can choose the answer choice that most accurately and concisely expresses that meaning.

ATTENTION TO THE RIGHT DETAIL

Details present a dilemma: missing them can cost you points. But if you try to absorb every fact in a Reading Comprehension passage or Critical Reasoning stimulus, you may find yourself swamped, delayed, and still unready for the questions that follow, because the relevant and irrelevant details are all mixed together in your mind. Throughout this book, you will learn how to discern the essential details from those that can slow you down or confuse you. The GMAT test maker rewards examinees for paying attention to "the right details"—the ones that make the difference between right and wrong answers.

Attention to the Right Detail distinguishes great administrators from poor ones in the business world as well. Just ask anyone who's had a boss who had the wrong priorities or who was so bogged down in minutiae that the department stopped functioning.

Not all details are created equal, and there are mountains of them on the test. Learn to target only what will turn into correct answers. Let's see how to apply the GMAT Core Competency of Attention to the Right Detail to a sample Critical Reasoning question:

3. Police officers in Smith County who receive Special Weapons and Tactics (SWAT) training spend considerable time in weapons instruction and practice. This time spent developing expertise in the use of guns affects the instincts of Smith County officers, making them too reliant on firearms. In the past year in Smith County, in 12 of the 14 cases in which police officers shot a suspect while attempting to make an arrest, the officer involved had received SWAT training, although only 5 percent of the police force as a whole in the county had received such training.

    Which of the following, if true, most strengthens the argument above?

    O   In an adjacent county, all of the cases in which police shot suspects involved officers with SWAT training.

    O   SWAT training stresses the need for surprise, speed, and aggression when approaching suspects.

    O   Only 15 percent of Smith County's SWAT training course is devoted to firearms lessons.

    O   Among officers involved in the arrest of suspects in Smith County in the past year, the proportion who had received SWAT training was similar to the proportion who had received SWAT training in the police force as a whole.

    O   Some Smith County officers without SWAT training have not been on a firing range in years.

You will learn more about strengthening arguments in the Critical Reasoning chapter of this book; for now, focus on finding the detail that makes a difference.

SWAT training, the author concludes in the second sentence, is making Smith County officers too reliant on firearms. The evidence in the third sentence presents you with many different numbers and figures. However, the important thing to note here is the shift in scope between the conclusion, which is about Smith County police officers in general, and the evidence, which is about the 14 cases that involved shootings during an arrest.

That "scope shift" signals that you've found the right detail to focus on. If the author is using data from arrests to make a point about the effects of SWAT training on the police force as a whole, it will make a difference if, for example, a disproportionate number of officers involved in making arrests have received SWAT training. Since you're looking for the answer choice that strengthens the argument, you need one that equates officers making arrests to officers at large.

Choice **(D)** is the correct answer. If **(D)** is true, then the officers in the 14 cases are representative of officers as a whole, and the argument is strengthened.

Notice that paying Attention to the Right Detail—the one that the question hinges upon—enables you to form a prediction of what the correct answer will contain. Selecting an answer then becomes a straightforward matter of finding the choice that matches your prediction, rather than a time-consuming process of debating the pros and cons of each answer choice in turn. Throughout this book, you will learn to distinguish the important from the inconsequential on the GMAT.

INTRODUCTION TO STRATEGIC READING

Since you're reading this book and aspire to go to business school, it goes without saying that you can read. What needs saying is that the way of reading for which you've been rewarded throughout your academic and professional careers is likely not the best way to read on Test Day.

Normally, when you read for school, pleasure, or even work, the main things you try to get from the text are the facts—the story, who did what, what's true or false. That way of reading may have served you well throughout your life, but on the GMAT you must read strategically.

Because Kaplan knows the test so well, we've identified the key structures that will get you points on the test. More importantly, we've identified the keywords that signal those structures and tell you what to do with them. Strategic Reading means using structural keywords to zero in on what the test will ask you about. Usually, it's great to read in order to broaden your horizons. On Test Day, you haven't got time for anything that doesn't pay off in right answers.

KEYWORDS

- Keywords determine the structure of a passage.
- Keywords highlight lines in the text that are crucial to the author's message.

As you see from the bullet points, keywords help you see the structure of the passage. That, in turn, tells you what part of the text is crucial to the author's point of view, which is what the test consistently rewards you for noticing.

On the GMAT, questions could give the same facts, but the correct answers could vary depending on the author's point of view. To see how this works, take a look at the following two facts about Bob:

Bob got a great GMAT score.

He is going to East Main State Business School.

The meaning depends on the keyword that links these facts. Fill in the supported inference for each case:

Bob got a great GMAT score. Therefore, he is going to East Main State Business School.

    Supported inference about East Main State: _____

Bob got a great GMAT score. Nevertheless, he is going to East Main State Business School.

    Supported inference about East Main State: _____

For the first example, you can infer that East Main State must be a good school, or at least Bob must think it is; because he got a good score, that's where he's going. Based on the second example, however, you can infer that East Main State must not be the kind of school where people with good scores usually go; it must not be very competitive to get in there. Notice that the facts didn't change. The keywords "therefore" and "nevertheless" made all the difference to the correct GMAT inference.

This distinction is important because almost all GMAT questions hinge on keywords. Because it cannot reward test takers for outside knowledge, the GMAT cannot ask what you already know about East Main State—but it *will* ask questions to assess how well you understand what the author says about East Main State.

In Reading Comprehension and Critical Reasoning, keywords highlight the author's opinion and logic, and they may indicate contrast, illustration, continuation, and sequence. As you continue your GMAT prep, pay close attention to keywords you encounter and what they tell you about the relationship between the information that comes before and after the keywords. Here are the most important categories of keywords and some examples of words that fall into each category.

KEYWORD CATEGORIES

Contrast: Nevertheless, despite, although, but, yet, on the other hand

Continuation: Furthermore, moreover, additionally, also, and

Logic: Therefore, thus, consequently, it follows that, because, since

Illustration: For example, we can see this by, this shows, to illustrate

Sequence/Timing: First, second, finally, in the 1920s, several steps, later

Emphasis/Opinion: Unfortunately, happily, crucial, very important, a near disaster, unsuccessful, she even _____

To see how keywords separate the useful from the useless on the GMAT, take a look at the following Critical Reasoning question—without the answer choices for the moment. You will learn more about analyzing arguments in the Critical Reasoning chapter of this book, but for now, the following questions will guide you through the process of breaking down an argument using keywords:

What does this word tell us about the relationship between "artistic quality" and "marketing tool"? _____

What does this word tell us about the purpose of this sentence? _____

4. In recent years, many advertisements have won awards for their artistic quality. But since advertising must serve as a marketing tool, advertising executives must exercise their craft with an eye to the effectiveness of their advertisement. For this reason, advertising is not art.

What reason is this phrase referring to?

_____

_____

Paraphrase this argument: _____

_____

_____

_____

The argument above depends on which of the following assumptions?

What is the author assuming? _____

_____

Let's walk through the above questions in boxes, starting with the question that refers to the word "but." You may have noted that "but" is a contrast keyword. This tells you that the author believes the terms "artistic quality" and "marketing tool" to be opposed or incompatible.

The next question refers to the word "since," which falls under the logic category of keywords. Like the word "because," "since" signals a reason; in terms of an argument, "since" introduces the author's evidence.

The phrase "for this reason" refers to the evidence that came immediately beforehand—that ad executives must be concerned with effectiveness. "For this reason" also signals that the final sentence contains the argument's conclusion.

The next box asks you to paraphrase the argument. This means that you should put the evidence and conclusion into your own succinct words: *ads aren't art [conclusion], because they must take effectiveness into account [evidence].*

Before looking at the answer choices, you need to predict exactly what you're looking for: "What is the author assuming?" Look for the gap in your paraphrase above. The author must believe that something judged on its effectiveness cannot be art.

Now take a look at the answer choices and identify which one matches your prediction.

4. In recent years, many advertisements have won awards for their artistic quality. But since advertising must serve as a marketing tool, advertising executives must exercise their craft with an eye to the effectiveness of their advertisement. For this reason, advertising is not art.

    The argument above depends on which of the following assumptions?

    O   Some advertisements are made to be displayed solely as art.

    O   Some advertising executives are more concerned than others with the effectiveness of their product.

    O   Advertising executives ought to be more concerned than they currently are with the artistic dimension of advertising.

    O   Something is not "art" if its creator must be concerned with its practical effect.

    O   Artists are not concerned with the monetary value of their work.

Choice **(D)** matches the prediction and is the correct answer.

By attending to the keywords, you zeroed in on just what's important to the test maker—with no wasted effort or rereading. Strategic Reading embodies all four GMAT Core Competencies: Critical Thinking, Pattern Recognition, Paraphrasing, and Attention to the Right Detail.

CHAPTER 6

Critical Reasoning

A study of 20 overweight men revealed that each man experienced significant weight loss after adding SlimDown, an artificial food supplement, to his daily diet. For three months, each man consumed one SlimDown portion every morning after exercising and then followed his normal diet for the rest of the day. Clearly, anyone who consumes one portion of SlimDown every day for at least three months will lose weight and will look and feel his best.

Which one of the following is an assumption on which the argument depends?

○ The men in the study will gain back the weight if they discontinue the SlimDown program.

○ No other dietary supplement will have the same effect on overweight men.

○ The daily exercise regimen was not responsible for the effects noted in the study.

○ Women won't experience similar weight reductions if they adhere to the SlimDown program for three months.

○ Overweight men will achieve only partial weight loss if they don't remain on the SlimDown program for a full three months.

Above is a typical Critical Reasoning question. In this chapter, we'll look at how to apply the Kaplan Method to this question, discuss the logical structures being tested, and go over the basic principles and strategies that you want to keep in mind on every Critical Reasoning question. But before you move on, take a minute to think about what you see in this question and answer some questions about how you think it works:

- The question refers to the paragraph as an "argument." What does this term mean?

- What does it mean for an argument to depend on an assumption?

- Notice that the question comes after the argument. Is it a better idea to read the argument or the question first?

- What GMAT Core Competencies are most essential to success on this question?

PREVIEWING CRITICAL REASONING

THE QUESTION REFERS TO THE PARAGRAPH AS AN "ARGUMENT." WHAT DOES THIS TERM MEAN?

Over 70 percent of Critical Reasoning questions are based on arguments, so understanding what they are and how they work will be of great help on Test Day.

When the GMAT refers to an *argument*, it doesn't mean a conversation in which two people shout at each other. An argument in Critical Reasoning means any piece of text in which an author puts forth a set of ideas or a point of view and attempts to support it. A statement such as "Small dogs make better pets than large dogs" is not an argument—it's just an opinion. An argument must make some attempt to persuade. For instance, if this opinion statement included a reason or two to support its point of view, then it would become a simple argument: "Small dogs make better pets than large dogs, because small dogs are easier to clean up after and generally have longer life spans than large dogs." Later in this chapter, you will learn to refer to these main parts of the argument as the *conclusion* (the author's main point) and the *evidence* (the support for that point).

WHAT DOES IT MEAN FOR AN ARGUMENT TO DEPEND ON AN ASSUMPTION?

In everyday life, the verb *to assume* is used to mean "to take for granted" or "to presume" that something is the case. Likewise, *to depend on* something is to "need" or "rely on" that thing. Fortunately, the meaning of the word *assumption* in the context of a GMAT argument is much the same. Critical Reasoning questions that ask for an argument's assumption could be paraphrased as follows: "What important fact does the author of the argument take for granted but not directly state?" or "What else would need to be true in order for this argument to hold?" Throughout this chapter, you will see how identifying the central assumption is key to answering Critical Reasoning questions that involve arguments.

NOTICE THAT THE QUESTION COMES AFTER THE ARGUMENT. IS IT A BETTER IDEA TO READ THE ARGUMENT OR THE QUESTION FIRST?

It might be your natural instinct to start reading from the beginning of the paragraph, but the most efficient approach is to read the question (which we call the *question stem*) before the paragraph that precedes it (which we call the *stimulus*). By starting with the question stem and identifying the task it poses, you will be able to read the stimulus strategically—targeting the information you need to answer the question without wasting time rereading.

WHAT GMAT CORE COMPETENCIES ARE MOST ESSENTIAL TO SUCCESS ON THIS QUESTION?

As you may have surmised from the previous paragraphs, Critical Reasoning questions are full of rewards for test takers with a firm handle on all four Core Competencies—the bedrock analytical skills that the GMAT measures. Critical Thinking will enable you to analyze the structure of arguments, such as the one at the beginning of this chapter, and identify any gaps or errors in the author's logic. Your Pattern Recognition skills will help you take advantage of patterns of argumentation that come up again and again, as well as enable you to spot common wrong answer types quickly. Paraphrasing is essential to untangling tough text, such as the description of study results in this stimulus, by putting it in your own words. Finally, Attention to the Right Detail will let you zero in on the most important parts of Critical Reasoning stimuli, often signaled by keywords, and determine which facts are crucial to the correct answer. In this chapter, you will learn how to apply these skills to every type of Critical Reasoning question you may see on Test Day.

Here are the main topics we'll cover in this chapter:

- Question Format and Structure
- The Basic Principles of Critical Reasoning
- The Kaplan Method for Critical Reasoning
- Critical Reasoning Question Types
- Advanced Strategies: Three Special Cases

QUESTION FORMAT AND STRUCTURE

About 10 Critical Reasoning questions appear on the Verbal section of the GMAT. Critical Reasoning (CR) tests reasoning skills involved in making arguments, evaluating arguments, and formulating or evaluating a plan of action. These questions are based on materials from a variety of sources, though you will not need to be familiar with any subject matter beforehand.

Specifically, you are measured on your ability to reason in the following areas:

- **Understanding the argument's construction:** Recognizing the basic structure of an argument, properly drawn conclusions, underlying assumptions, explanatory hypotheses, or parallels between structurally similar arguments
- **Evaluating the argument:** Analyzing an argument, recognizing elements that would strengthen or weaken it, identifying reasoning errors or aspects of the argument's development
- **Formulating and evaluating a plan of action:** Recognizing the relative appropriateness, effectiveness, and efficiency of different plans of action, as well as factors that would strengthen or weaken a proposed plan of action

The directions for Critical Reasoning questions are short and to the point. They look like this:

Directions: Select the best of the answer choices given.

On the GMAT, in business school, and in your career, you'll need the ability to recognize and understand complex reasoning. It's not enough to sense whether an argument is strong or weak; you'll need to analyze precisely why it is so. This presumes a fundamental skill that's called on by nearly every Critical Reasoning question—the ability to isolate and identify the various components of any given argument. And that brings us to the basic principles of Critical Reasoning.

THE BASIC PRINCIPLES OF CRITICAL REASONING

Here are the basic skills that you need to succeed on CR questions.

UNDERSTAND THE STRUCTURE OF AN ARGUMENT

As you learned earlier in this chapter, an argument is an author's attempt to convince you of a point. You must know how arguments are structured so that you can break them down into their core components. Every GMAT argument is made up of two basic parts:

1. The conclusion (the point that the author is trying to make)
2. The evidence (the support that the author offers for the conclusion)

Success on these questions hinges on your ability to identify the parts of the argument. There is no general rule about where the conclusion and evidence appear in the argument—the conclusion could be first, followed by the evidence, or it could be the other way around. Consider the following CR stimulus:

> The Brookdale Public Library will require extensive physical rehabilitation to meet the new building codes passed by the town council. For one thing, the electrical system is inadequate, causing the lights to flicker sporadically. Furthermore, there are too few emergency exits, and those few that exist are poorly marked and sometimes locked.

Suppose that the author of this argument was allowed only one sentence to convey her meaning. Do you think she would waste her time with the following statement? Would she walk away satisfied that her main point was communicated?

> The electrical system [at the Brookdale Public Library] is inadequate, causing the lights to flicker sporadically.

No. Given a single opportunity, she would have to state the first sentence to convey her real purpose:

> The Brookdale Public Library will require extensive physical rehabilitation...

That is the conclusion. If you pressed the author to state her reasons for making that statement, she would then cite the electrical and structural problems with the building. That is the evidence for her conclusion.

But does that mean that an evidence statement like "The electrical system is inadequate" can't be a conclusion? Not necessarily—it's just not the conclusion for this particular argument. Every idea, every new statement, must be evaluated in the context of the stimulus in which it appears.

For the statement above to serve as the conclusion, the stimulus could be the following:

> The electrical wiring at the Brookdale Public Library was installed more than 40 years ago and appears to be corroded in some places [evidence]. An electrician, upon inspection of the system, found a few frayed wires as well as some blown fuses [evidence]. Clearly, the electrical system at the Brookdale Public Library is inadequate [conclusion].

To succeed in Critical Reasoning, you'll have to be able to determine the precise function of every sentence in the stimulus. The easiest way to do this is to use structural signals, or "keywords" as we call them at Kaplan, to identify conclusion and evidence. You read about keywords in the Verbal Section Overview chapter of this book. Keywords such as *because, for, since, as a result of,* and *due* to are clear indications of evidence; keywords such as *therefore, hence, thus, so, clearly,* and *consequently* usually signal the conclusion. Notice how the word *clearly* in the argument above provides a strong signal that the last sentence is the conclusion.

Not every Critical Reasoning stimulus will have these keywords, but most do; look for them every time, because using them to identify the conclusion and evidence will greatly increase not only your ability to get the right answer but also your ability to do so quickly.

STUDY THE QUESTION FIRST

As you learned earlier in this chapter, you should always look over the question stem before you read the stimulus. Doing so will give you some idea of what you need to look for as you read. Suppose the question with the first library argument above asked:

> The author supports her point about the need for rehabilitation at the Brookdale Library by citing which of the following?

If you had read the question before the stimulus, you'd know what to look for in advance—only the evidence, the "support," provided. You wouldn't have to pay much attention to the conclusion at all! But suppose the question were this:

> The author's main point is best expressed by which of the following?

In this case, you'd do the opposite—you'd focus only on the conclusion and wouldn't care much about the evidence.

Reading the question first allows you to save valuable time because you will know how to attack the stimulus. As you'll soon see, this technique will be especially handy when you have a great working knowledge of the strategies for the different types of Critical Reasoning questions.

READ STRATEGICALLY

As you learned in the Verbal Section Overview chapter of this book, Strategic Reading means reading for structure and for the author's point of view, since these are the things the GMAT most rewards test takers for noticing. On Critical Reasoning questions in particular, this means using keywords to identify the most important parts of the stimulus (often an argument) and paraphrasing the main ideas. Let's examine how to read strategically on Critical Reasoning questions.

Paraphrase the Argument

In Critical Reasoning, you should paraphrase the author's main argument to yourself after reading the stimulus. As discussed in the Verbal Section Overview chapter, the Core Competency of Paraphrasing is a valuable tool. If you can't accurately paraphrase the stimulus, you probably don't understand it yet. Frequently, the authors in Critical Reasoning say pretty simple things in complex ways. So if you mentally translate the verbiage into a simpler form, the whole thing will become more manageable.

In the first library argument, for instance, there's no advantage to grappling with the full complexity of the author's stated conclusion:

> The Brookdale Public Library will require extensive physical rehabilitation to meet the new building codes passed by the town council.

Instead, you want to paraphrase a much simpler point: *the library will need fixing up to meet new codes*.

Similarly, the evidence is pretty bulky:

> For one thing, the electrical system is inadequate, causing the lights to flicker sporadically. Furthermore, there are too few emergency exits, and those few that exist are poorly marked and sometimes locked.

You could paraphrase it like this: *the library's electrical system is bad, and the emergency exits are too few, hard to find, and locked*.

So the whole argument might be said simply as follows: the library's electrical system is bad, and the emergency exits are too few, hard to find, and locked. Therefore, the library will need fixing up to meet new codes.

Often, by the time you begin reading through the answer choices, you run the risk of losing sight of the gist of the stimulus. So restating the argument in your own words will not only help you get the author's point in the first place but also help you hold on to it until you've found the correct answer. Keep in mind that it's the *meaning* of the answer choices that matters. Since Critical Reasoning questions hinge on logic, you will be better able to choose the correct answer if you have paraphrased the ideas in the stimulus; doing so will keep you from becoming derailed if the correct choice doesn't use the exact wording you might expect.

Hunt for Potential Problems with the Argument

You must read actively, not passively, on the GMAT. Active readers are always attacking the passage, analyzing the text and forming reactions as they go along. Instead of accepting an argument at face value, they look for potential problems. Active reading pays huge dividends on most Critical Reasoning questions.

Here are some common potential problems in Critical Reasoning passages:

- **Shifts of scope:** The argument suddenly introduces a new term or idea that wasn't mentioned before and isn't connected to the rest of the argument.
- **Mistaking correlation for causation:** Just because two things happen at the same time doesn't mean that one caused the other.
- **Plans and predictions:** Could there be something inherently self-defeating about a proposed course of action? Any unintended consequences? Any important factors unaccounted for? The GMAT asks many questions about plans and predictions because they are like miniature business plans.

Consider the argument about the library again. Seems pretty reasonable at first glance—good lighting and working emergency exits are pretty important for a public building. But the critical reader might think, "Wait a second—I've got a lot of information about the problems but no information about the codes. Do the codes apply to flickering lights, for example?"

Since part of what you're called on to do here is to evaluate arguments, don't let yourself fall into the bad habits of the passive reader—reading solely for the purpose of getting through the stimulus. Those who read this way invariably find themselves having to read stimuli two or even three times. Then they're caught short on time. Read the stimulus right the first time—with a critical eye and an active mind.

Answer the Question Being Asked

One of the most disheartening experiences in Critical Reasoning is to understand the author's argument fully but then supply an answer to a question that wasn't asked.

The classic example of this error occurs on Strengthen/Weaken questions, one of the common CR question types we will cover in this chapter. When you're asked to strengthen or weaken an argument, you can be sure that there will be at least one answer choice that does the opposite of what's asked. Choosing such a wrong choice is less a matter of failing to understand the argument than of failing to remember the task at hand.

The question stem will always ask for something very specific. It's your job to follow the test makers' line of reasoning to the credited response.

Also, as you read the question stem, be on the lookout for words such as *not* and *except*. These little words are easy to miss, but they entirely change the kind of statement you're looking for among the choices.

Try to Predict an Answer

This principle, which is really an extension of the last one, is crucial. You must approach the answer choices with at least a faint idea of what the answer should look like. That is, predict the answer in your own mind before looking at the choices. This isn't to say you should ponder the question for minutes—it's still a multiple-choice test, so the right answer is on the screen. Just get in the habit of framing an answer in your head.

Once you have made a prediction, scan the choices. Sure, the correct choice on the exam will be worded differently and may be more fleshed out than your prediction. But if it matches your thought, you'll know it in a second. And you'll find that there's no more satisfying feeling in Critical Reasoning than predicting correctly and then finding the correct answer quickly and confidently.

Continuing with the library situation, suppose you were asked this question:

> The author's argument depends on which of the following assumptions about the new building codes?

Having hunted for potential problems and realized that the argument gave no information about whether the codes applied to the problems in the library, you could quickly predict that the answer must say something like *The new building codes apply in this situation*. Then an answer like this one would jump off the screen as clearly correct:

O   The new codes apply to existing buildings, as well as to buildings under construction.

Alternatively, the correct answer could be worded like this:

O   The new codes require that all buildings have stable electrical systems as well as clearly marked, easily accessible emergency exits.

The most effective predictions are general enough to fit with unexpected ideas (such as "existing buildings" in the example above) but specific enough about the scope of the argument to allow you to eliminate most wrong answers.

Keep the Scope of the Stimulus in Mind

When you're at the point of selecting one of the answer choices, focus on the scope of the stimulus. Most of the wrong choices for CR questions are wrong because they are irrelevant or unsupported. In other words, the wrong answer choices contain elements that don't match the author's ideas or that go beyond the context of the stimulus.

Some answer choices are too narrow or too broad, or they have nothing to do with the author's points. Others are too extreme to match the scope—they're usually signaled by such words as *all, always, never, none,* and so on. For arguments that are moderate in tone, correct answers are more qualified and contain such words as *usually, sometimes,* and *probably.*

To illustrate the concept of scope, let's look again at the question mentioned above:

> The author's argument depends on which of the following assumptions about the new building codes?

Let's say one of the answer choices reads as follows:

> ○   The new building codes are far too stringent.

Knowing the scope of the argument would help you to eliminate this choice very quickly. You know that this argument is just a claim about what the new codes will require: that the library be rehabilitated. It's not an argument about whether the requirements of the new codes are good, or justifiable, or ridiculously strict. That kind of value judgment is irrelevant to this argument.

Recognizing scope problems is a great way to eliminate wrong answers quickly. However, don't jump to eliminate an answer choice simply because it introduces a new term into discussion. A common error is to think that scope is purely about terminology. It's much more about the impact of the ideas in the answer choice on the ideas in the stimulus. If it has the right impact, the answer is relevant, regardless of its terminology. This fact reinforces the importance of using your Paraphrasing skills to see how the ideas in a stimulus relate to one another.

THE KAPLAN METHOD FOR CRITICAL REASONING

Now it's time to learn how to orchestrate all of these basic principles into a consistent protocol for approaching Critical Reasoning questions. Kaplan has developed a Method for Critical Reasoning that you can use to attack each and every CR question.

The Kaplan Method for Critical Reasoning

1. **Identify the question type.**

2. **Untangle the stimulus.**

3. **Predict the answer.**

4. **Evaluate the choices.**

STEP 1: IDENTIFY THE QUESTION TYPE

As you read in the introduction of basic Critical Reasoning principles, reading the question stem first is the best way to focus your reading of the stimulus. Determine the question type, and you'll know exactly what you're looking for. The majority of the rest of this chapter is devoted to a thorough analysis of each type of CR question, including practice questions for each type. There may also be other important information in the question stem—possibly the conclusion of the argument or a particular aspect of the stimulus that you will need to focus on.

STEP 2: UNTANGLE THE STIMULUS

With the question stem in mind, read the stimulus. Read actively, paraphrasing to make sure you understand the construction of the stimulus and hunting for any potential problems. Even though over 70 percent of CR stimuli contain arguments, other types of stimuli will not contain arguments. Depending on the type of question that you identified in Step 1 of the Method, you will look to gather different information from the stimulus.

STEP 3: PREDICT THE ANSWER

Form an idea of what the right answer choice should say or do. How you form your prediction will vary depending on the specific question type. For some question types, it can be difficult to form a specific prediction of what the correct answer choice will say, but based on your analysis in Steps 1 and 2, you will always know at least what function the correct answer will accomplish. On the next page is a chart that summarizes how to predict answers for different question types; you will learn about and practice all of these in depth later in this chapter.

STEP 4: EVALUATE THE CHOICES

Attack each answer choice critically. Keep your prediction in mind and see whether the answer choices match it. If you don't find a "clear winner," read through the answers that you haven't eliminated yet. You know what you *like* about each; now focus on what might be *wrong*.

STEPS 3 AND 4, BY QUESTION TYPE

You will look for different things in Steps 3 and 4 of the Method, depending on the question type.

- **Assumption:** Identify the argument's central assumption and hunt for the answer choice that matches your prediction. If that fails, use the Denial Test on each answer choice.
- **Strengthen/Weaken:** Identify the argument's central assumption and predict an answer explaining why that assumption is more (for a Strengthen question) or less (for a Weaken question) likely to be true.
- **Evaluation:** Identify the argument's central assumption and hunt for the answer choice that identifies missing information that would help assess the validity of that assumption.
- **Flaw:** Identify the argument's central assumption and predict the error in the argument's reasoning.
- **Explain:** Predict the answer that explains how two seemingly discrepant facts can both be true. If it's difficult to form a specific prediction, work through the answers one by one, eliminating choices that are clearly wrong, until you find the one that reconciles both parts of the supposed paradox.
- **Inference:** It's often difficult to form a prediction beyond "the right answer *must be true* based on what the stimulus states." Work through the answers one by one, eliminating choices that are clearly wrong.
- **Bolded Statement:** Predict an answer based on the logic and structure of the stimulus.

Now let's apply the Kaplan Method to the Critical Reasoning question you saw at the beginning of the chapter:

> A study of 20 overweight men revealed that each man experienced significant weight loss after adding SlimDown, an artificial food supplement, to his daily diet. For three months, each man consumed one SlimDown portion every morning after exercising, then followed his normal diet for the rest of the day. Clearly, anyone who consumes one portion of SlimDown every day for at least three months will lose weight and will look and feel his best.

Which one of the following is an assumption on which the argument depends?

- ○ The men in the study will gain back the weight if they discontinue the SlimDown program.
- ○ No other dietary supplement will have the same effect on overweight men.
- ○ The daily exercise regimen was not responsible for the effects noted in the study.
- ○ Women won't experience similar weight reductions if they adhere to the SlimDown program for three months.
- ○ Overweight men will achieve only partial weight loss if they don't remain on the SlimDown program for a full three months.

Step 1: Identify the Question Type

The question stem indicates directly that this is an Assumption question. Don't worry if you don't yet know much about Assumption questions; we will cover them in depth later in this chapter. For now, just focus on applying each step of the Method. You know from the mention of an "assumption" in this question stem that the argument in the stimulus will be missing a link in the chain of reasoning—some piece of support that the author takes for granted without which the conclusion wouldn't be valid. You will now turn to the stimulus, ready to find that link.

Step 2: Untangle the Stimulus

Sentence 1 introduces a study of 20 men who used a certain food supplement product. All 20 lost weight. Sentence 2 describes how they used it: once a day, for three months, after morning exercise. So far so good; it feels as if the argument is building up to something. The keyword *clearly* usually indicates that some sort of conclusion follows, and that's the case here: in sentence 3, the author predicts that anyone who has one portion of the product daily for three months will lose weight, too.

You might paraphrase the argument like this:

> Each of 20 overweight men lost weight after taking SlimDown every morning after exercise (but otherwise eating normally). So anyone who consumes SlimDown will lose weight.

Reading strategically, do you see any scope shifts or other potential problems? Sure—what happened to the exercise? It's in the evidence as part of the study regimen but is totally dropped from the conclusion. That's a pretty significant change in scope, and you can use that scope shift as the basis for your prediction in Step 3.

You could also look at the argument even more abstractly:

> A bunch of guys did *A* and *B* and had *X* result. So if someone does *A*, they'll get *X* result too.

This argument structure seems pretty weak: Who says *A* (SlimDown) caused *X* (weight loss)? Why couldn't *B* (exercise) have been the cause? The argument asserts that there could only be one cause for a certain effect even though other causes might, in reality, be possible. This kind of sloppy thinking about causality is a common GMAT pattern that you can use to help form your paraphrase.

You can use this insight to make a prediction in Step 3, too. No matter how abstract or concrete your prediction is, you arrive at the same basic issue—that the author isn't accounting for the exercise. There's rarely one "perfect way" to figure out the right answer; as long as you read critically, you'll be moving in the right direction.

Step 3: Predict the Answer

You've realized that the argument forgot to consider the exercise. So you might predict something like *The author assumes exercise doesn't matter.* That's it. There's no need to paraphrase with something fancy or complicated. A simple paraphrase, as long as it reflects the scope of the stimulus, is enough to help you find the right answer.

Step 4: Evaluate the Choices

Judge the answer choices based on how well they fulfill the requirements of your prediction. Sure enough, only **(C)** even mentions the exercise regimen. Reading it closely, you see it fits the prediction perfectly, clearing up the question of whether the exercise caused the weight loss.

Since the difficulty of Critical Reasoning is often in the answer choices (rather than the stimulus), you can't let them make you indecisive. Predicting the answer lets you know exactly what you're looking for, so you'll know it when you see it. You can choose **(C)** with confidence and move on.

CRITICAL REASONING QUESTION TYPES

Now that you're familiar with the basic principles of Critical Reasoning and the Kaplan Method, let's look at the most common types of questions. Certain question types appear again and again on the GMAT, so it pays to understand them beforehand.

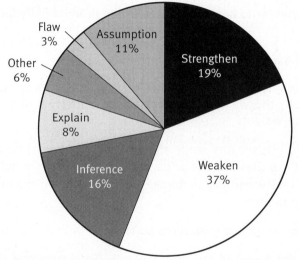

The Approximate Distribution of GMAT Critical Reasoning Questions

You have seen many references to arguments so far in this chapter, and indeed analyzing arguments is the most important—though not the only—skill you need possess for Critical Reasoning on the GMAT. Of the question types listed in the pie chart above, Assumption, Strengthen, Weaken, and Flaw questions are based on arguments. Another question type, Evaluation, is also based on arguments, but these questions are rare and are included in the "Other" category in the pie chart. For these five question types based on arguments, the way you will analyze the argument is quite similar. In all cases, the correct answer will depend on identifying and understanding the argument's conclusion, evidence, and central assumption.

GMAT ARGUMENTS

- GMAT arguments (given in the stimuli) are usually two to four sentences long.
- GMAT arguments vary in soundness: some are (intentionally) flawed.
- To untangle the stimulus, find the conclusion, evidence, and the author's central assumption.

Let's examine in depth Kaplan's strategies for the different types of CR questions based on arguments, starting with Assumption questions.

ASSUMPTION QUESTIONS

Assumption questions ask you for a piece of support that isn't explicitly stated but is necessary for the argument to remain valid. When a question asks you for what's missing from the argument or what the argument depends on, then it's asking you to find the author's necessary assumption.

Untangling the Stimulus for Assumption Questions

By first analyzing the question stem, you'll know what to look for in the stimulus. For Assumption questions—and all questions based on arguments—untangling the stimulus consists of identifying the three parts of a GMAT argument: conclusion, evidence, and assumption.

CONCLUSION

The conclusion is the main point of the author's argument. It's the thing that the author is seeking to convince you of. There are three ways to identify the conclusions of arguments:

- **Conclusion keywords or phrases:** As you learned in the Verbal Section Overview chapter of this book, keywords are clues to the structure of a passage or argument. They tell you how the author's ideas relate to one another. Keywords and phrases that signal an argument's conclusion include the following: *thus, therefore, so, hence, consequently, in conclusion, clearly, for this reason.*

- **The one-sentence test:** You can also identify the author's conclusion by asking, "If the author had to boil this entire argument down to one sentence that expresses the main point, which sentence would it be?"

- **Fact vs. opinion:** The conclusion of the argument is always a reflection of the author's opinion. This opinion can take several forms; it could be the author's plan, proposal, prediction, or value judgment or simply her interpretation or analysis of the evidence. Whereas the conclusion is always an opinion, the evidence is usually (but not always) factual in nature.

EVIDENCE

Evidence is provided to support the conclusion. GMAT arguments usually have little filler, so what isn't the conclusion is typically evidence. Evidence can take the form of data, such as statistics, surveys, polls, or historical facts. Sometimes, however, the evidence is merely a conjecture or an opinion. The best way to identify an argument's evidence is by examining its function within the argument: any material in the stimulus that provides support for the author's conclusion is evidence.

ASSUMPTION

All GMAT arguments contain one or more assumptions; identifying the assumptions is the most essential step when answering any Critical Reasoning question based on an argument. An assumption is the unstated evidence necessary to make the argument work. It bridges the gap between two pieces of the argument, usually between conclusion and evidence but occasionally between two unconnected pieces of evidence. Without the assumption, the argument falls apart. You can think of it as something the author *must* believe but doesn't directly state.

You can visualize the relationship between the various parts of an argument as follows:

Evidence + Assumption(s) → Conclusion

Predicting the Answer for Assumption Questions

As you saw in the question about SlimDown diet supplement earlier in this chapter, you can usually predict an answer to an Assumption question. Your prediction is simply the argument's assumption, which you've already identified when you untangled the stimulus during Step 2 of the Kaplan Method.

Let's practice the whole process of untangling the stimulus and predicting the answer using this simple stimulus:

> Allyson plays volleyball for Central High School. Therefore, Allyson must be over 6 feet tall.

The conclusion is the second sentence (signaled by the keyword *therefore*), and the evidence is the first. Is there a gap, or assumption, in this argument? Well, who's to say that all high school volleyball players have to be over 6 feet tall? So you can confidently predict that the answer to an Assumption question would say something like this:

> All volleyball players at Central High School are over 6 feet tall.

But what if the assumption doesn't just jump out at you? How can you track it down? One of the most common ways the GMAT uses assumptions is to cover over a scope shift in the argument. Notice how the argument above starts by talking about playing volleyball and then all of a sudden is talking about being over 6 feet tall. Look closely at the terms in each part of the argument. Could the scope of the evidence be slightly different than that of the conclusion?

Consider this seemingly solid argument:

> Candidate A won the presidential election, carrying 40 out of 50 states. Clearly, Candidate A has a strong mandate to push for her legislative agenda.

At first glance, this sounds pretty good. But take a close look at the terms of the argument. The evidence is a win representing a sizeable majority of states. The conclusion is about a strong mandate for an agenda. Even if you don't notice the subtle difference between these two things, you could still make a prediction like this: *Candidate A's big victory means she has a mandate for her agenda.* You'd be much more likely to recognize the right answer between these two possibilities:

○ No other candidate in the last 24 years has won as many states as did Candidate A.

○ Most of the people who voted for Candidate A support her legislative agenda.

The first answer choice doesn't deal with Candidate A's agenda at all. The second one shows a connection between her victory and her agenda, so it must be the right answer.

But what if you still aren't sure that your answer choice is correct? Or what if the assumption is so subtle that you can't predict the answer at all? In those cases, you can use the Denial Test.

The Denial Test

An assumption must be true in order for the conclusion to follow logically from the evidence. Therefore, in an Assumption question, you can test each answer choice by negating it—in other words, imagining that the information given in the answer choice is false. If this negation makes the author's argument fall apart, then the answer choice is a necessary assumption.

If the argument is unaffected, then the choice is wrong. Let's look at what you predicted earlier as the assumption in the volleyball argument:

All volleyball players at Central High School are over 6 feet tall.

Now let's negate it:

Some volleyball players at Central High School are not over 6 feet tall.

Would Allyson still have to be over 6 feet tall? Not anymore. That's why that prediction would be a necessary assumption. Keep in mind not to be too extreme when negating answer choices. The denial of *hot* isn't *cold* but rather *not hot*. Similarly, the denial of *all are* isn't *none are* but rather *some aren't*.

Now let's take another look at the answer choices for the question about Candidate A:

- ○ No other candidate in the last 24 years has won as many states as did Candidate A.
- ○ Most of the people who voted for Candidate A support her legislative agenda.

And now we'll negate them:

- ○ Some candidates in the last 24 years have won as many states as did Candidate A.

Could Candidate A still enjoy a strong mandate? Definitely. Just because others in the past were as popular doesn't mean that she doesn't enjoy support for her agenda as well.

- ○ A majority of those who voted for Candidate A do not actually support her legislative agenda.

Now can Candidate A claim a mandate for her agenda? No, she can't. That's why the second choice is the correct answer for this Assumption question.

Give the Denial Test a try on your own using the following argument. Negate each answer choice and then ask yourself, "Can the evidence still lead to the conclusion?"

I live in the city of Corpus Christi, so I also live in Texas.

The argument assumes which of the following:

- ○ Corpus Christi is the only city in Texas.
- ○ The only city named Corpus Christi is located in Texas.
- ○ If you have not been to Corpus Christi, you have not been to Texas.

The argument here is short and sweet, but it has all the essential elements of any GMAT argument. The conclusion is signaled by the keyword *so*: the author lives in Texas. The author's evidence is the claim in the first part of the sentence: he lives in Corpus Christi.

Rather than predict the correct answer right away, let's test the answer choice statements using the Denial Test.

Negation of statement (A): Corpus Christi is not the only city in Texas.

Does that threaten the argument? No. There could be other cities in Texas, and it could still be valid to say that living in Corpus Christi proves that the author lives in Texas. The evidence could still lead to the conclusion, so choice **(A)** is not the assumption.

Negation of statement (B): There is at least one other city named Corpus Christi that is not located in Texas.

If this is true, does the conclusion still follow logically from the evidence? No. In this case, if there is another town named Corpus Christi located in, say, California or Florida, it would no longer be logically valid to say that the author must live in Texas because he lives in Corpus Christi. Choice **(B)** is a necessary assumption for the argument.

Negation of statement (C): If you have not been to Corpus Christi, you still could have been to Texas.

Note that when you are denying an if/then statement, you should deny the "then," or result, portion of the statement. What impact does this negation have on the argument? None. Someone else could visit other cities in Texas, and still it may or may not be valid for the author to say, "I live in Texas because I live in Corpus Christi." Choice **(C)** is not the necessary assumption.

Argument Analysis Exercise

Answers are on the following page.

Now it's time to put all these skills together and practice breaking down some arguments. First find the conclusion, then identify the evidence that supports that conclusion, and finally determine the central assumption(s). Once you've identified the assumption, try the Denial Test to confirm that the assumption you've identified is necessary for the argument to hold:

1. Over the past 10 years, some businesses located in country X have moved manufacturing or assembly operations to country Y. But a proposed change to the laws of country Y would raise the minimum per-hour wage in country Y to approximately the same level as the equivalent rate in country X. Hence, if the change were to come into effect, very few businesses in country X would move manufacturing or assembly operations to country Y.

Conclusion:

Evidence:

Assumption(s):

2. In percentage terms, the total population of the United States grew faster from 1790 until 1890 than it did from 1890 to 1990. In 1890, the Census Bureau declared that the continental United States was settled to an extent that a frontier line could not be marked on a map. So, it seems safe to say that the existence of extensive space for an expansion of agricultural settlement is necessary for increases in national population.

Conclusion:

Evidence:

Assumption(s):

Argument Analysis Exercise: Answers

1. **Conclusion:** Country X businesses aren't likely to move to country Y.

   Evidence: Country Y is proposing to raise its minimum wage.

   Assumption: The only, or primary, reason for businesses to relocate to country Y is cheaper labor.

2. **Conclusion:** Countries need space for more agriculture in order to have national population growth.

   Evidence: The U.S. population grew more slowly after the frontier was closed.

   Assumptions: (In this case, the author is taking several things for granted.) Frontier space was primarily used for agriculture; agriculture is the reason for the population growth from 1790 to 1890. The example of the United States is representative of other countries, and there are no examples elsewhere that contradict this argument. Statements about rates of growth translate to statements about absolute growth.

Sample Question Stems

There are many ways to write a Critical Reasoning question. Any wording that suggests that you need to find a missing but vital piece of information indicates an Assumption question. Assumption questions are worded in some of the following ways:

- Which one of the following is assumed by the author?
- Upon which one of the following assumptions does the author rely?
- The argument depends on the assumption that...
- Which one of the following, if added to the passage, would make the conclusion logical?
- The validity of the argument depends on which one of the following?
- The argument presupposes which one of the following?

APPLYING THE KAPLAN METHOD: ASSUMPTION QUESTIONS

Now let's use the Kaplan Method for Critical Reasoning to solve an Assumption question:

When unemployment rates are high, people with full-time jobs tend to take fewer and shorter vacations. When unemployment rates are low, people tend to vacation more often and go away for longer periods of time. Thus, it can be concluded that full-time workers' perceptions of their own job security influence the frequency and duration of their vacations.

The argument above assumes that

- O the people who take the longest vacations when unemployment rates are low have no fear of losing their jobs
- O travel costs are lower during times of low unemployment
- O most people prefer to work full-time jobs
- O workers' perceptions of their own job security are in some way related to the unemployment rate
- O workers' fears of losing their jobs have increased recently

Step 1: Identify the Question Type

The word "assumes" in the question stem is a clear indication of an Assumption question.

Step 2: Untangle the Stimulus

"Thus" signals the argument's conclusion. You could paraphrase it as follows: *how much vacation time full-time workers take depends on how secure they feel in their jobs.* The author's evidence for this conclusion is the relationship between vacations and unemployment. When unemployment is high, workers take fewer and shorter vacations; when unemployment is low, the opposite happens.

Step 3: Predict the Answer

To find the central assumption, use Critical Thinking to link the terms in the evidence with the terms in the conclusion. If the evidence centers on employment levels and vacations, and if the conclusion centers on job security and vacations, then the central assumption must center on the connection between employment levels and job security.

Step 4: Evaluate the Choices

Choice **(D)** matches this prediction perfectly by bridging the terms of the evidence with the terms of the conclusion. The Denial Test can help confirm **(D)** as the correct answer; if there were no relationship between workers' perceptions of job security and the unemployment rate, then it would no longer make sense for the author to use evidence about the unemployment rate to support a conclusion about workers' perceptions of job security. **(D)** is an assumption necessary for the argument to hold.

The other choices are all incorrect in some definable way. It's great practice to identify exactly why each wrong choice is wrong. Doing so will help you develop your Pattern Recognition skills so you can identify common wrong answer types on Test Day. **(A)** is too extreme ("*no fear of losing their jobs*") to be the necessary assumption. **(B)** introduces the idea of travel costs, which have no necessary connection to job security in the conclusion. **(C)** is incorrect because whether those people who work full-time jobs prefer to work them is irrelevant. **(E)** tells us that workers' perceptions of their job security have deteriorated lately, but that has no necessary connection to the unemployment rate. Remember that the assumption must successfully link the evidence to the conclusion.

TAKEAWAYS: ASSUMPTION QUESTIONS

- On Assumption questions, identify the argument's conclusion and evidence, determine the central assumption, and predict the answer. Evaluate the answer choices and select the one that matches your prediction.
- If you read the answer choices and can't find your prediction, try eliminating choices by asking whether they are necessary for the argument to hold.
- The Denial Test discriminates between right and wrong answers; when you deny the correct answer to an Assumption question, the argument falls apart.

PRACTICE SET: ASSUMPTION QUESTIONS

Answers and explanations are at the end of the chapter.

1. Burger Land, a nationwide fast-food chain, recently announced a special promotion dramatically reducing the price of its most popular burger, the Big and Beefy. This development has provoked a strong response by the nation's nutritionists. Citing the extremely high levels of cholesterol in the Big and Beefy, they predict that the price reduction will have a negative impact on the health of our citizens.

    The nutritionists' argument assumes which of the following?

    O   Some consumers induced by the price reduction to purchase the Big and Beefy would otherwise have consumed food lower in cholesterol than the Big and Beefy.

    O   Reducing fat consumption is the most important factor in improving one's diet.

    O   Burger Land could not have increased sales of the Big and Beefy by reducing its cholesterol content and appealing to health-conscious consumers.

    O   Other fast-food companies will not respond to Burger Land's announcement by reducing the price of their own high-cholesterol burgers.

    O   Lost revenue due to the price reduction in the Big and Beefy will be offset by an increase in the number of burgers sold.

2. In Country X, all citizens eligible to vote must do so or face stiff fines. Because voting in Country X is mandatory, over 99 percent of the eligible voters voted in the last election. Thus, the winner of the last election is truly the people's choice.

    Which of the following identifies an assumption in the author's argument?

    O   In Country X, voters are allowed to vote for a candidate of their choice.

    O   If Country X did not make voting mandatory, few people would vote.

    O   Only in countries where voting is mandatory do people vote the way they wish to vote.

    O   Country X is a true democracy, despite the fact that all people are forced to vote.

    O   Only in countries where voting is not mandatory do the winners of elections truly reflect the people's choice.

3. In the next four years, the number of doctors, nurses, and other health care workers will increase significantly worldwide. Even so, the average compensation received by such professionals will not decline but rather is likely to increase. This is due, at least partly, to the fact that the median age of the world's population will increase steadily in this same period of time.

    The argument above depends logically upon which of the following assumptions?

    O   The increase in the number of health care workers will be responsible for the increase in the average life span.

    O   The compensation of doctors and physical therapists who treat the elderly will increase more than that of other health care workers.

    O   As a group, older people receive more attention from health care workers than do younger people.

    O   Geriatrics, a branch of medicine focusing on the health problems of older people, is the most expensive element of American health care.

    O   Increase in the median age of the population will occur in all regions of the world.

STRENGTHEN AND WEAKEN QUESTIONS

Determining an argument's necessary assumption, as you've just seen, is required to answer an Assumption question. But it also is required to answer two other common types of question: Strengthen and Weaken.

In the real world, we can weaken someone's argument by attacking her evidence. But the GMAT is testing not your ability simply to find evidence but rather your ability to analyze how that evidence is used. The right answer to a Weaken question on the GMAT will always weaken the connection between the evidence and the conclusion—in other words, the assumption.

The answer to many Weaken questions is the one that reveals an author's assumption to be unreasonable or untrue; conversely, the answer to many Strengthen questions provides additional support for the argument by affirming the truth of an assumption.

Let's return to a stimulus we've seen before and consider it in the context of Strengthen and Weaken questions:

> Allyson plays volleyball for Central High School. Therefore, Allyson must be over 6 feet tall.

Remember which assumption holds this argument together? It is that all volleyball players for Central High are over 6 feet tall. That assumption makes or breaks the argument. So if you're asked to weaken the argument, you'll want to attack that assumption:

> Which one of the following, if true, would most weaken the argument?

Prediction: Not all volleyball players at Central High School are over 6 feet tall.

Correct Answer:

> O   Some volleyball players at Central High School are under 6 feet tall.

Notice that we don't have to prove the conclusion wrong, just make it less likely. We've called into doubt the author's basic assumption, thus damaging the argument. Allyson still *could* be over 6 feet tall, but now she doesn't have to be.

What if the question asked you to strengthen the argument? Again, the key would be the necessary assumption:

> Which one of the following, if true, would most strengthen the argument?

Prediction: All volleyball players at Central High School are over 6 feet tall.

Correct Answer:

> O   No member of the Central High School volleyball team is under 6'2".

Here, by confirming the author's assumption, you've in effect bolstered the argument.

TAKEAWAYS: STRENGTHEN AND WEAKEN QUESTIONS

- The first steps to answering Strengthen and Weaken questions are the same as those for Assumption questions.
- Strengtheners make the conclusion more likely to follow from the evidence, while weakeners make it less so.

Strengthening and Weakening Arguments Exercise

Answers are on the following page.

Now it's time to put all these skills together and practice analyzing arguments and identifying possible strengtheners and weakeners. Find the conclusion, evidence, and assumption(s) for each of the following arguments. Then predict what a correct answer choice might contain for a Strengthen question and for a Weaken question.

1. Mountain biking on trails is soaring in popularity in the United States. The number of mountain bikes sold in the United States has increased 133 percent over the past four years. In addition, bike stores in the United States last year reported that mountain bikes accounted for more than 65 percent of their total sales, far more than in previous years, even though sales of other bikes have been strong.

Conclusion:

Evidence:

Assumption(s):

Predict strengtheners:

Predict weakeners:

2. A shoe manufacturer developed a man-made material that looked and felt just like natural leather. Over the course of a year, the manufacturer made its entire shoe line in both natural leather and man-made leather. During the year when both lines were sold, the man-made leather shoes outsold the natural leather shoes. The shoe manufacturer concluded that its customers prefer man-made leather to natural leather.

Conclusion:

Evidence:

Assumption(s):

Predict strengtheners:

Predict weakeners:

3. According to a recent study, the majority of people in a large city believe that most homeless people are drug addicts who could get jobs if they wanted to work. However, the public is misinformed. The city's Coalition for the Homeless estimates that over 85 percent of the homeless population is moderately to severely mentally ill.

Conclusion:

Evidence:

Assumption(s):

Predict strengtheners:

Predict weakeners:

Strengthening and Weakening Arguments Exercise: Answers

1. **Conclusion:** Mountain biking on trails is getting a lot more popular.

   Evidence: Stores are selling more mountain bikes, and mountain bikes are a greater proportion of their overall bike sales.

   Assumption: The people who are buying mountain bikes must be using them on trails.

   Possible strengthener: Most of the people who are driving the increase in mountain bike sales are involved in trail cycling.

   Possible weakener: People who buy mountain bikes tend to use them in urban or suburban settings, rather than on trails.

2. **Conclusion:** Customers prefer man-made leather to natural leather.

   Evidence: A shoe company made their full line of shoes in both natural and man-made, and the man-made outsold the real.

   Assumption: People are buying man-made leather because they prefer it, not for some other reason.

   Possible strengthener: There were not other reasons (i.e., price, availability, lack of adequate labeling in the store) for the customers to purchase the man-made instead of the natural leather.

   Possible weakener: There were other reasons (i.e., price, availability, lack of adequate labeling in the store) for the customers to purchase the man-made instead of the natural leather.

3. **Conclusion:** The public is misinformed in its belief that the homeless are drug addicts who don't want to work.

   Evidence: An estimate from Coalition for the Homeless that says the vast majority of homeless people are mentally ill.

   Assumption: If a homeless person is severely mentally ill, he is not a drug addict who is able to work.

   Possible strengthener: Moderate to severe mental illness makes it impossible to obtain or maintain employment.

   Possible weakener: Even the mentally ill are capable of maintaining employment if they want to.

Sample Stems

The stems associated with these two question types may use the word *weaken* or *strengthen*, or they may use other phrasing. Here's a list of some you can expect to see on Test Day.

Weaken:

- Which one of the following, if true, would most weaken the argument above?
- Which one of the following, if true, would most seriously damage the argument above?
- Which one of the following, if true, casts the most doubt on the argument above?
- Which of the following, if true, would most seriously call into question the plan outlined above?

Strengthen:

- Which one of the following, if true, would most strengthen the argument?
- Which one of the following, if true, would provide the most support for the conclusion in the argument above?
- The argument above would be more persuasive if which one of the following were found to be true?

It's also common for the question stem to refer explicitly to part of the argument. You might, for example, see something like this:

> Which of the following, if true, casts the most doubt on the author's conclusion that the Brookdale Public Library does not meet the requirements of the new building codes?

A Strengthen question may ask you to fill in the blank at the end of an argument, where the blank is preceded by a keyword signaling evidence, such as *since*. As with other Strengthen questions, you must choose the answer that supplies evidence that supports the author's conclusion.

When you identify the question type during Step 1 of the Method, make sure you understand what effect the correct answer will have on the argument. Wrong answers that have the opposite of the desired effect are called 180s, and they're extremely common on Strengthen and Weaken questions. If you're asked to weaken an argument, watch out for wrong answers that would strengthen it. Asked to strengthen? Be wary of weakeners. Pay close attention to what the question asks so you can avoid this trap.

APPLYING THE KAPLAN METHOD: STRENGTHEN AND WEAKEN QUESTIONS

Now let's use the Kaplan Method for Critical Reasoning to solve a Strengthen or Weaken question:

> Due to recent success, Lawton, a contractor, can be more selective than in the past regarding the types of clients he chooses to service. If he restricts his business to commercial clients and only those residential clients requiring $10,000 of work or more, he would cease doing most of the kind of residential work he currently does, which would allow him to earn a higher average profit margin per job.
>
> Which of the following, if true, would most strengthen the conclusion that limiting his service in the manner cited would increase Lawton's average profit margin per job?

- O   Lawton's recent success is due primarily to an upsurge in the number of residential clients he services.
- O   Lawton's commercial clients would prefer that he focus more of his time and energy on their projects and less on the concerns of his residential clients.
- O   Residential work for which Lawton cannot bill more than $10,000 comprises a significant proportion of his low-profit-margin work.
- O   Due to the use of a more efficient cost-accounting system, Lawton's average profit margin per job has increased in each of the last three years.
- O   Commercial jobs typically take longer to complete than residential jobs.

Step 1: Identify the Question Type

In addition to containing the telltale word "strengthen," the question stem helps you by identifying the conclusion. When the GMAT gives you a gift like this, accept it!

Step 2: Untangle the Stimulus

The conclusion has been handed to you by the question stem: by restricting his work to commercial projects and expensive ($10,000+) residential projects, Lawton will increase his average profit margin. The only evidence is the first sentence, which informs you that due to recent success, Lawton can restrict his work to certain clients if he chooses.

Step 3: Predict the Answer

The evidence proves that Lawton can be selective. However, it does not establish that restricting his business will actually improve his profit margin. The author's claim depends on an assumption: inexpensive residential jobs have lower profit margins than do commercial jobs and pricey residential jobs.

Step 4: Evaluate the Choices

Choice **(C)** supports the assumption, thereby strengthening the argument, and is the correct answer.

Wrong answer choices on Strengthen and Weaken questions commonly provide facts that are irrelevant to the argument; since such choices have no direct bearing on the argument presented, there's no way they could strengthen or weaken it. **(A)** is incorrect because the source of Lawton's recent success is irrelevant and has no connection to higher profit margins. **(B)** discusses the preferences of Lawton's commercial clients, which are also irrelevant. **(D)** credits a new accounting system with an increase in Lawton's profit margin per job. This statement doesn't tell us whether expensive jobs have a higher profit margin than do small residential jobs, so it doesn't help the argument. Furthermore, **(D)** focuses on past improvements, which have no bearing on whether his future plans will be successful. **(E)** tells us that commercial jobs will take longer to complete, but the profit margin of the jobs, not their duration, is what matters in this argument.

TAKEAWAYS: STRENGTHEN AND WEAKEN QUESTIONS

- On Strengthen and Weaken questions, determine the argument's conclusion, evidence, and assumption. Predict the strengthening or weakening answer based on the assumption.

- Weakening an argument is not the same as disproving a conclusion—and strengthening is not the same as proving it. A weakener tips the scale toward doubting the conclusion, while a strengthener tips the scale toward believing in the validity of the conclusion.

- The words "if true" in the question stem remind you that the correct answers should be treated as facts that can make the argument more or less likely to be true.

- Some Critical Reasoning questions provide the conclusion in the stem; use such cases to your advantage.

- Common wrong answers in Critical Reasoning include irrelevant choices and 180s.

PRACTICE SET: STRENGTHEN AND WEAKEN QUESTIONS

Answers and explanations are at the end of the chapter.

4. The threatened prosecution of businesses flying 20-by-38-foot garrison flags, which are traditionally to be flown on national holidays, instead of the smaller post flags, which can be flown at any time, is unconscionable. Legal technicalities of this sort should never restrict patriotic expression.

   Which of the following, if true, would most seriously weaken the argument above?

   O   Many people find the garrison flags' size to be distracting and ill suited to neighborhood aesthetics.

   O   The businesses that are flying garrison flags do so primarily to attract customers.

   O   The raising and lowering of different-sized flags on the correct days of the year is a laborious and time-consuming procedure.

   O   The regulations that govern the correct display of the nation's flags are part of an old and time-honored tradition.

   O   The symbolic significance of a flag's size is not generally understood by most of the customers patronizing these businesses.

5. Any college football player who uses steroids should be banned from competition. The national agency with the responsibility to preserve the natural competitive balance between players enforces rules specifically mandating that no player be allowed to use drugs to gain a competitive advantage. Studies show that steroid users tend to have much greater strength and weight than non-users.

   Which of the following statements, if true, would most strengthen the argument?

   O   Users of steroids often suffer from acne, extreme nervousness, and reduced sexual potency.

   O   Increased strength is more useful than increased weight to college football players.

   O   Superior strength and weight give college football players a significant competitive advantage.

   O   Steroid use is much more prevalent in college football than in college baseball.

   O   Random drug testing of athletes has been shown to be effective in the detection of drug use by athletes.

6. Since the 1960s, most drinking water provided by public water systems has had fluoride added, because research has demonstrated that adding fluoride to drinking water significantly reduces the occurrence of dental cavities in the populations served by those systems. However, manufacturers now add fluoride to toothpaste in amounts sufficient to provide the same level of protection against dental cavities as that provided by fluoridated water. Therefore, public water systems could now save the money formerly spent on water fluoridation without impacting the rate of occurrence of dental cavities in the communities they serve.

    Which of the following, if true, would most weaken the argument?

    O   The savings realized by public water systems would not be passed on to their customers but would be used for maintenance of and improvements to the system.

    O   The cost of adding fluoride to toothpaste is much less than the cost of adding fluoride to the water produced by public water systems.

    O   Fluoride is a commodity traded throughout the world, and the availability and price of fluoride can vary substantially due to economic and political events.

    O   Fluoride toothpaste has been widely available since 1980, and recent studies have found higher levels of dental cavities in communities with unfluoridated water than in communities with fluoridated water.

    O   Fluoride is colorless, odorless, and tasteless when added to water, but flavorings are added to fluoride toothpaste to deliver a taste that most people describe as pleasant.

7. Public interest law focuses on the legal issues that affect the entire community or involve broad areas of public concern, such as illegal discrimination, environmental protection, child welfare, and domestic violence. A particular nonprofit agency focusing on public interest law is woefully understaffed; many lawyers are urgently needed to continue its important work providing low-cost legal services to residents who are unable to afford a private attorney. In order to fill these vacancies as efficiently as possible, the agency should advertise the jobs to students in this year's graduating class at the local law school to encourage them to enter the field of public interest law.

    Each of the following, if true, weakens the recommendation above EXCEPT:

    O   Positions in corporate law that are advertised at the local law school have higher average salaries than do legal positions at nonprofit agencies.

    O   The local law school maintains an active placement service for its graduates and publicizes job openings in the community to its graduating class.

    O   The open positions at the nonprofit agency require several years of prior experience in the practice of law.

    O   Several lawyers recently left the nonprofit agency because the agency's salaries did not enable the lawyers to make their student loan payments.

    O   The local law school is ranked third highest in the country, and graduates of the school aspire to work for large, highly rated law firms located in major cities.

EVALUATION QUESTIONS

Evaluation is a rare Critical Reasoning question type. An Evaluation question asks you to identify information that would help you assess an argument's strength. The correct answer won't strengthen or weaken the author's reasoning or supply a missing assumption. Instead, the right answer will specify the kind of evidence that would help you judge the validity of the author's argument.

Since the needed information will usually fill a gap in the argument, the correct answer to an Evaluation question typically relates in some way to the assumption. For example, whereas a Weaken answer choice might state, "Businesses relocate their operations to country Y primarily to reduce labor costs," an Evaluation answer choice would instead claim that it would be most useful to know "whether factors besides labor costs affect the decisions of certain businesses to relocate their operations to country Y." Incorrect Evaluation answer choices are often irrelevant; the information they ask for would have little or no effect on the argument.

Sample Stems

Here are some example question stems that indicate an Evaluation question:

- Which of the following would it be most useful to know in order to evaluate the argument?
- The answer to which of the following questions would be most important in evaluating the proposal?
- To assess the likelihood that the plan will achieve its objective, it would be most useful to determine which of the following?
- To evaluate the author's reasoning, it would be most useful to compare...
- Which of the following must be studied in order to evaluate the argument presented above?

APPLYING THE KAPLAN METHOD: EVALUATION QUESTIONS

Now let's use the Kaplan Method for Critical Reasoning to solve an Evaluation question:

> Mullein has been employed as an expectorant for centuries and is still greatly praised for this purpose by herbalists. However, mullein roots and seeds are believed to contain rotenone, a compound that is used as an insecticide and fish toxin and that has been shown to be a causative factor in Parkinson's disease. Therefore, the use of mullein leaf tea for the treatment of dry coughs is not as safe as has previously been believed.
>
> Which of the following would be most useful to know in order to evaluate the truth of the argument's conclusion?
>
> O   Whether mullein roots and seeds are effective as pesticides
> O   Whether mullein roots and seeds contain other toxic chemicals besides rotenone
> O   Whether there are other agents besides rotenone involved in the etiology of Parkinson's disease
> O   Whether there are safer herbs that are effective expectorants
> O   Whether mullein leaves contain rotenone in sufficient quantities to contribute to Parkinson's disease

Step 1: Identify the Question Type

The word "evaluate" signals that this is an Evaluation question. Evaluation questions are similar to Strengthen/Weaken questions: you must find the answer choice that impacts the validity of the argument's conclusion.

Step 2: Untangle the Stimulus

Like Strengthen/Weaken questions, Evaluation questions are built around an argument's central assumption, so you should, as usual, begin by identifying the conclusion and evidence. The conclusion is the last sentence: using mullein leaf tea for coughs is not as safe as was once thought. The evidence is that mullein roots and seeds are believed to contain rotenone, a substance that causes Parkinson's disease. This argument contains a scope shift: the evidence is about "mullein roots and seeds," while the conclusion is about "mullein leaf tea." The scope shift signals the central assumption: a compound contained in the roots and seeds of the mullein plant must also be contained in its leaves.

Step 3: Predict the Answer

In order to evaluate whether the conclusion is strong or weak, you would need to know whether the assumption that mullein leaves contain rotenone is true. Specifically, you would need to know whether mullein leaves contain enough rotenone to cause Parkinson's disease.

Step 4: Evaluate the Choices

(E) matches this prediction and is the correct answer. **(A)** and **(B)** are incorrect because the toxicity of mullein roots and seeds is beside the point. The argument's conclusion concerns the leaves of the mullein plant, not the roots and seeds. **(C)** is incorrect because other chemicals that cause Parkinson's disease are irrelevant to the argument, which concludes that mullein leaves are unsafe due to their assumed rotenone content. Finally, the "safer herbs" mentioned in **(D)** are again irrelevant. The argument is about mullein; other herbs are irrelevant.

TAKEAWAYS: EVALUATION QUESTIONS

- Evaluation questions ask you to determine what information would most help to evaluate the argument.
- Untangle the stimulus the same way you do for other argument-based questions: identify the conclusion, evidence, and assumption(s).
- Choose the answer choice that would best fill in the gap in logic created by the central assumption.

PRACTICE SET: EVALUATION QUESTIONS

Answers and explanations are at the end of the chapter.

8. Herbed Wellness, a manufacturer of herbal products, wants its new headache remedy to be as effective as possible while using only natural ingredients. A controlled study has found that 58 percent of headache sufferers obtain complete headache relief from a dose of caffeine equivalent to that typically found in a cup of coffee. Therefore, even though the vast majority of its customers are health-conscious avoiders of coffee, Herbed Wellness should add caffeine to its new herbal headache treatment; doing so will prove both efficacious and cost-effective.

    The answer to which of the following questions would be most useful in evaluating the claim that caffeine will be efficacious in relieving headaches among Herbed Wellness customers?

    O   Is the headache relief provided by caffeine as long-lasting as that provided by over-the-counter drugs such as aspirin?

    O   What percentage of the study participants were regular coffee drinkers who suffer from caffeine-withdrawal headaches?

    O   Is caffeine less expensive per dose than the individual herbs used in the headache formulation?

    O   Does synthetic caffeine qualify as a natural substance?

    O   What percentage of Herbed Wellness customers will shun the new headache remedy if it contains caffeine?

9. A study of more than 5,000 people showed that those who lived at high latitudes, where UV exposure is minimal, had higher cancer rates than did those who lived near the equator, where UV exposure is, on average, far greater. One of the effects of UV radiation on humans is that it stimulates vitamin D manufacture in exposed skin. These results are consistent with other studies demonstrating that cancer patients often have lower than average vitamin D levels. Therefore, high blood levels of vitamin D reduce the risk of cancer in humans.

    The answer to which of the following questions would be most useful to know in order to evaluate the validity of the argument's conclusion?

    O   Does seasonal affective disorder, experienced more frequently by those living at high latitudes than by those living at the equator, predispose its sufferers to cancer?

    O   Do high blood levels of vitamin D reduce the incidence of the common cold?

    O   Can blood levels of vitamin D be raised through supplementation, thus reducing the risk of sunburn due to UV exposure?

    O   Does exposure to UV radiation prevent cancer in other mammals, such as laboratory rats?

    O   Are wintertime low vitamin D levels responsible for the flu season phenomenon?

FLAW QUESTIONS

Flaw questions are the final question type that is based on stimuli that consist of arguments. These questions are similar to Weaken questions, but instead of asking you for some new fact that, if true, would make the argument questionable, Flaw questions ask what's already wrong with the argument. So your prediction should focus on reasoning errors the author makes.

The good news is that the GMAT uses a handful of common flaws over and over:

- Confusing correlation and causation
- Confusing percent and actual value
- Unsupportable scope shifts between evidence and conclusion
- Inappropriate analogies (comparing things that aren't comparable)
- Overlooked alternatives
- Inappropriate conflation/distinction of terms

More important than memorizing all the items on this list, however, is understanding what unites them. All of these flaws center on the author's assumption, so you should handle them similarly to how you've handled all the other argument-based questions so far: by identifying the conclusion, evidence, and assumption. The correct answer to a Flaw question will describe the logical flaw inherent in the argument's assumption.

Sample Stems

Here are some example question stems that indicate a Flaw question:

- Which of the following is a flaw in the reasoning above?
- The argument above is vulnerable to which of the following criticisms?

APPLYING THE KAPLAN METHOD: FLAW QUESTIONS

Now let's use the Kaplan Method for Critical Reasoning to solve a Flaw question:

> The public service advertising campaign promoting the use of helmets has improved bicycle safety dramatically. Over the past 12 months, the number of serious bicycling injuries has been reduced by nearly 70 percent. Unfortunately, helmet usage has not reduced the number of all types of bike injuries. While serious head trauma has decreased by nearly 85 percent, broken bones now represent 20 percent of all reported bicycling injuries. This is a significant increase from last year's 14 percent.

> The reasoning in the argument is flawed because the argument does which of the following?

○ It fails to include information about any types of bicycle injuries other than head trauma and broken bones.

○ It implies that the same conclusion can result from two different sets of causes.

○ It fails to take into account any possible increase in the number of people riding bicycles over the past 12 months.

○ It presumes that an increase in the percentage of injuries involving broken bones precludes a decrease in the actual number of such injuries.

○ It ignores the fact that a 70 percent overall decrease in injuries would not allow for an 85 percent decrease in one specific type of injury.

Step 1: Identify the Question Type

The question stem alerts you to the idea that this argument is flawed, so Flaw is definitely the question type here.

Step 2: Untangle the Stimulus

The author concludes that the number of broken-bone bicycle injuries has gone up from last year to this year. The evidence for this is that broken bones made up 20 percent of this year's total bicycle-related injuries but were only 14 percent of last year's total.

Step 3: Predict the Answer

As soon as you see both percentages and numbers mentioned in the stimulus for a Flaw question, beware. In the Quantitative section, you will learn, if you have not already, that you must be careful when working with percentages. Twenty percent is guaranteed to equal a higher number than 14 percent only if those percentages are of the same total. And since the total number of injuries is much lower this year than last year, 20 percent of a much lower total could actually equal a lower number than 14 percent of last year's higher total.

If you're having trouble seeing this, you can use the Quant strategy of Picking Numbers. Suppose there were 100 bicycle injuries last year. That means that 14 percent, or 14 total, of those injuries involved broken bones. You know that this year, injuries have been reduced by 70 percent. In this example, that means there were a total of 30 bicycle injuries this year. Twenty percent of the new, lower total is 6 broken-bone injuries, a significantly lower number than last year's 14. The flaw here is the author's assumption that an increase in percentage cannot be consistent with a decrease in actual number.

Step 4: Evaluate the Choices

Only **(D)** accurately captures the logical flaw in this argument—confusing percent and actual value. **(D)** is the correct answer.

The fact that the author mentions only two types of injuries, as **(A)** says, is not a flaw in the argument, which concerns only whether or not the number of broken bones has been reduced. Other types of injuries are irrelevant. Since two sets of causes aren't discussed, you can rule out **(B)**. Causation does figure in many GMAT flaws, but not this one. **(C)** might seem tempting, since it does relate to the "percentage versus actual number" issue, but if the total number of bicyclists increased over the past year, the reduction in the number of total injuries would actually be greater. And since a 70 percent overall decrease in injuries could, in fact, allow for an 85 percent decrease in one specific type of injury, **(E)** can be ruled out as well.

TAKEAWAYS: FLAW QUESTIONS

- Flaw questions ask you to describe how the author's reasoning has gone awry. Identifying the author's assumption will reveal the flawed thinking.
- Some classic flaws include mistaking correlation for causation and confusing actual value with percent.
- On Flaw questions, determine the conclusion, evidence, and central assumption(s). Then predict an answer describing the reasoning error in the author's assumption.

PRACTICE SET: FLAW QUESTIONS

Answers and explanations are at the end of the chapter.

10. Our legislature is considering passing legislation to ban skateboarding on city streets, citing safety concerns. However, a review of public health records reveals that the legislature's concern is misplaced. Each year, many more people are injured while jogging than are injured while skateboarding. So in fact, skateboarding is safer than jogging.

    Which of the following indicates a flaw in the reasoning above?

    ○ It fails to distinguish professional skateboarders who attempt very dangerous maneuvers from amateurs who are comparatively cautious.

    ○ It assumes without warrant that no one who skateboards also jogs.

    ○ It fails to consider the number of people who skateboard as compared with the number of people who jog.

    ○ It ignores the possibility that other activities cause even more injuries than either skateboarding or jogging.

    ○ It fails to address the issue and instead attacks the character of the legislature.

11. Solo concert pianists, by convention, are not permitted to use musical scores during their performances. However, most members of chamber groups and orchestras are permitted to use sheet music during performances and perform well as a result. Therefore, all solo concert pianists should also be allowed to consult their musical scores during performances.

    The argument is most vulnerable to criticism on which of these grounds?

    ○ It overlooks the possibility that some solo concert pianists prefer performing without consulting musical scores.

    ○ It takes for granted that members of a chamber group or orchestra are less skilled than solo musicians and thus have more need for musical scores.

    ○ It overlooks the possibility that some solo concert pianists have broken with tradition and used musical scores during their performances.

    ○ It takes for granted that a solo concert pianist would use a musical score in the same way as does a member of a chamber group or orchestra.

    ○ It overlooks the possibility that performing in an orchestra is difficult despite the ability to use a musical score during the performance.

EXPLAIN QUESTIONS

Questions based on arguments (Assumption, Strengthen, Weaken, Evaluation, and Flaw) make up over 70 percent of all Critical Reasoning questions, but you will likely run into other question types on Test Day that are not necessarily based on arguments.

Explain question stimuli are not argumentative. Rather, they present a seeming discrepancy and ask you to find an explanation for the paradox. Your Paraphrasing skills and Attention to the Right Detail are the key to this question type—in your own simple but accurate words, restate not only the details in the stimulus but also the nature of the apparent contradiction. Once you've summed up the nature of the discrepancy, look for an answer choice that explains how the apparently contradictory facts in the stimulus could both be true.

It's sometimes difficult to predict exactly what the correct answer will contain, since an apparent contradiction can often be resolved in a number of different ways. On questions for which there could be multiple ways for the test maker to phrase the correct answer, predictions must be in the form of characterizing what the right answer will mean or do, not the words it will use. Again, Paraphrasing is crucial.

Sample Stems

Here are some example question stems that indicate an Explain question:

- Which of the following, if true, would best explain the discrepancy between customer satisfaction and sales?
- Which of the following, if true, would best resolve the paradox described above?

APPLYING THE KAPLAN METHOD: EXPLAIN QUESTIONS

Now let's use the Kaplan Method for Critical Reasoning to solve an Explain question:

> A series of experiments was conducted in which rats of various ages were placed in a series of mazes and timed to see how long it took them to find their way out. In the first set of runs, the younger rats made their way out of the mazes an average of 30 percent faster than the older rats. Three days later, however, when the same rats were placed in the same mazes, the older rats were faster than the younger rats by nearly 40 percent.
>
> Which of the following hypotheses best accounts for the findings of the experiment?
>
> O   A rat's sense of smell becomes less acute as it gets older.
> O   The older rats had been used in earlier experiments.
> O   Older rats have a better-developed sensory memory, which allows them to remember the mazes three days later.
> O   Younger rats become frustrated when faced with repeated dead ends in a maze, while older rats do not.
> O   Older rats tire more easily than younger rats.

Step 1: Identify the Question Type

The wording of this stem is less direct than most question stems, but any question that asks you to account for a certain set of potentially contradictory findings is an Explain question.

Step 2: Untangle the Stimulus

When untangling the stimulus, paraphrase the given information and make sure you understand the paradox. Indeed, the findings of the experiments described in this stimulus seem to be contradictory: at first it seems that younger rats are capable of completing mazes more quickly, and then it appears that older ones are.

Step 3: Predict the Answer

There could be a couple of reasons why this happened, so it's difficult to predict the exact answer here. But no matter how the right answer is phrased, you know that it will probably be something about older rats that allows them to perform better the second time around.

Step 4: Evaluate the Choices

If rats develop sensory memories as they get older, this would explain how the older rats, which were initially slower, were later able to complete the mazes more quickly: They "remembered" the route. This is what **(C)** indicates, so it's the correct answer.

Remember that for an answer choice to be correct, it must relate logically to *both* parts of the seeming contradiction in the stimulus. All the incorrect choices here explain only one side of the story or the other; in other words, they fail to resolve the paradox. If rats use their sense of smell to negotiate mazes, then **(A)** might explain why the older rats were slower initially, but it would not explain why they completed the mazes faster three days later. **(B)** might explain why the older rats finished the mazes faster in the later runs (assuming that the earlier experiments also involved mazes), but it wouldn't explain why they initially took longer than the younger ones. If **(D)** were true, you would expect older, more patient rats to finish more quickly every time. **(E)** might explain why the older rats took longer the first time, but it wouldn't explain why they finished more quickly the second time.

TAKEAWAYS: EXPLAIN QUESTIONS

- Explain questions require test takers to choose an answer choice that best explains why all the information in the stimulus is true.
- In many instances, the Explain question stimulus contains a paradox or discrepancy. The correct answer reconciles the information in the stimulus without contradicting it.
- On Explain questions, identify the seeming paradox and predict an answer that addresses the paradox but does not contradict the evidence at hand.

PRACTICE SET: EXPLAIN QUESTIONS

Answers and explanations are at the end of the chapter.

12. At a large manufacturing corporation, the ratio of the annual job-related injury insurance premium per employee to average employee annual net pay increased between 1978 and 2003. Yet, the annual number of job-related injuries per employee during that time decreased by more than 30 percent.

    Which of the following, if true, best explains the discrepancy outlined above?

    ○   From 1978 to 2003, the severity of job-related injuries at the corporation decreased significantly due to compliance with new workplace safety rules.

    ○   The number of employees at the corporation decreased between 1978 and 2003.

    ○   During the 1978–2003 period, inflation significantly eroded the purchasing power of the dollar.

    ○   The corporation did not change its insurance provider during the 1978–2003 period.

    ○   Between 1978 and 2003, health care costs per job-related injury rose sharply, pressuring insurance providers to raise premiums.

13. A certain town's pizza shop initiated an advertising campaign to bring in new customers and increase sales in December. The advertising campaign consisted of sending emails that promoted a two-for-one deal on sheet pizzas. Even though the pizza shop sent out thousands of these email advertisements, sales remained about the same in December as they had been in previous months.

    Which of the following, if true, most helps to explain the apparent discrepancy between the volume of advertisements and the volume of sales?

    ○   The emails did not list every type of pizza on the pizza shop's menu.

    ○   In December, a new coffee shop opened in the same neighborhood as the pizza shop.

    ○   Not every resident in the pizza shop's delivery area had an email address.

    ○   The pizza shop had email addresses only for customers who were members of its rewards club, which offers members weekly specials.

    ○   The other two pizza shops in town specialize in gourmet pizzas, which are more expensive on average than items on this pizza shop's menu.

INFERENCE QUESTIONS

A question type common to both Critical Reasoning and Reading Comprehension is the Inference question. The process of inferring is a matter of considering one or more statements as evidence and then drawing a conclusion from them. A valid inference is something that must be true if the statements in the stimulus are true—not *might* be true, not *probably* is true, but *must* be true.

Think of an inference as a conclusion that you draw based on the information, or evidence, given. It is your job on these questions to choose the inference that requires no assumption whatsoever; the correct answer will follow directly from the stimulus. But the answer to an Inference question is just as likely to be drawn from only one or two details as it is to take into account the stimulus as a whole. For this reason, it can be very difficult to predict an exact answer. Nevertheless, you can make a general prediction: the answer is the one that *must* be true based on the facts in the stimulus. You can use this prediction to help eliminate choices answer by answer, ruling out options that clearly don't match the facts as you paraphrased them. This is the beauty of a multiple-choice test—find four wrong answers, and you've also found the right one!

Let's examine a somewhat expanded version of the volleyball team argument:

> Allyson plays volleyball for Central High School, despite the team's rule against participation by nonstudents. Therefore, Allyson must be over 6 feet tall.

Wrong answer:

○   Allyson is the best player on the Central High School volleyball team.

Certainly Allyson *might* be the best player on the team. It's tempting to think that this would *probably* be true—otherwise the team would not risk whatever penalties violating the rule might entail. But *must* it be true? No. Allyson could be the second best. Or the third best. Or perhaps the coach owed Allyson's dad a favor. We have no support for the idea that she's the best on the team, so we can't infer this answer choice from the stimulus.

Valid inference:

○   Allyson is not a student at Central High School.

Clearly, if Allyson plays volleyball *despite* the team's rule against participation by nonstudents, she must not be a student. Otherwise, she wouldn't be playing despite the rule; she'd be playing in accordance with the rule. But note that this inference is not a necessary assumption of the argument because the conclusion about Allyson's height doesn't depend on it.

So be careful: unlike an assumption, an inference need not have anything to do with the author's conclusion. In fact, many Inference stimuli don't have conclusions at all—they consist not of arguments but of a series of facts. Make sure you are prepared for Inference questions, as they require a different approach than do other Critical Reasoning questions. Remember, everything that you need will be contained in the stimulus, so focus on the information as it's presented and avoid answers that twist the facts (or make up new ones).

Sample Stems

Inference questions probably have the most varied wording of all the Critical Reasoning question stems. Some question stems denote inference fairly obviously. Others are more subtle, and still others may look like other question types entirely. The bottom line is that if a question asks you to take the stimulus as fact and find something based on it, then you're looking at an Inference question. Here's a quick rundown of various Inference question stems that you may see on your test:

- Which one of the following can be inferred from the argument above?
- Which one of the following is implied by the argument above?
- The author suggests that _____.
- If all the statements above are true, which one of the following must also be true?
- The statements above, if true, support which of the following?
- Which of the following is best supported by the statements above?
- Which of the following is the conclusion toward which the author is probably moving?
- The statements above best support which of the following conclusions?

APPLYING THE KAPLAN METHOD: INFERENCE QUESTIONS

Now let's use the Kaplan Method for Critical Reasoning to solve an Inference question:

> A new electronic security system will only allow a single person at a time to pass through a secure door. A computer decides whether or not to unlock a secure door on the basis of visual clues, which it uses to identify people with proper clearance. The shape of the head, the shape and color of the eyes, the shape and color of the lips, and other characteristics of a person's head and face are analyzed to determine his or her identity. Only if the person trying to open a secure door has the required clearance will the door unlock. Because this new system never fails, an unauthorized person can never enter a secure door equipped with the system.
>
> If the statements above are true, which of the following conclusions can be most properly drawn?
>
> O   The new system is sure to be enormously successful and revolutionize the entire security industry.
> O   The new system can differentiate between people who are seeking to open a secure door and people passing by a secure door.
> O   No two people have any facial features that are identical, for example, identical lips.
> O   High costs will not make the new security system economically unviable.
> O   The new computer system is able to identify some slight facial differences between people who look very similar, such as identical twins.

Step 1: Identify the Question Type

Since the stem asks you to accept the statements as true and draw a conclusion on the basis of them, this is an Inference question.

Step 2: Untangle the Stimulus

When untangling the stimulus of an Inference question, briefly paraphrase the important facts to ensure you understand them. The stimulus tells you that a new electronic security system is completely fail-safe and will never allow an unauthorized person through a door equipped with the system. The system allows an authorized person to enter solely on the basis of the person's appearance and facial features.

Step 3: Predict the Answer

Attempting to predict the correct inference is difficult here, but on the GMAT, remember that an inference is something that must be true, not just something that could or might be true. It's crucial to approach the answer choices with this definition in mind.

Step 4: Evaluate the Choices

(A) is unsupported. There is no evidence of how the security industry is going to respond to the new system, so you can't say that this statement must be true based on what the stimulus states. **(B)** also doesn't need to be true. The new system doesn't need to differentiate between people passing by the door and people trying to enter, so long as it lets authorized people in and keeps unauthorized people out. **(C)** is too extreme. According to the stimulus, the security system examines multiple facial features to determine identity. You don't know that any *one* feature cannot be the same. All you know is that *all* of the features can't be the same. As for **(D)**, the stimulus only discusses the likelihood that unauthorized people will be able to get past the security system and through a secure door; there is no support for a statement about costs.

That means the correct inference must be **(E)**: if one twin is authorized and the other isn't, you know the system must be able to tell them apart, because the stimulus states that the security system never fails.

TAKEAWAYS: INFERENCE QUESTIONS

- Inference stimuli seldom contain complete arguments. Rather, they contain statements from which you must make a deduction.
- On an Inference question, you want the choice that *must* follow from the stimulus—not a choice that *might* or *could* follow.
- On Inference questions, determine which answer choice must be true, based on the stimulus.
- An inference need not be based on the entire stimulus. An inference may follow from a single sentence or fact.
- Some Inference question stems require you to complete a train of thought.

PRACTICE SET: INFERENCE QUESTIONS

Answers and explanations are at the end of the chapter.

14. The number of wild tigers living in India dropped from an estimated 40,000 at the turn of the century to 2,000 in 1970. Although determined conservation efforts have halted the precipitous decline, the survival of the wild tiger in India is uncertain even now. Still, it is beyond doubt that if the tiger is to survive in the wild at all, its best chance is in India.

    The statements above, if true, support which of the following?

    ○   There are now more than 2,000 wild tigers surviving in India.

    ○   There are fewer than 2,000 wild tigers living in the wild outside of India.

    ○   If tigers fail to survive in the wild in India, the species will become extinct.

    ○   It is impossible for a tiger raised in captivity to ever successfully adapt to life in the wild.

    ○   The survival of the wild tiger in countries other than India is also endangered.

15. A local department store hires college students for one month every spring to audit its unsold inventory. It costs the department store 20 percent less to pay wages to students than it would cost to hire outside auditors from a temporary service. Even after factoring in the costs of training and insuring the students against work-related injury, the department store spends less money by hiring its own auditors than it would by hiring auditors from the temporary service.

    The statements above, if true, best support which of the following assertions?

    ○   The amount spent on insurance for college-student auditors is more than 20 percent of the cost of paying the college students' basic wages.

    ○   It takes 20 percent less time for the college students to audit the unsold inventory than it does for the outside auditors.

    ○   The department store pays its college-student auditors 20 percent less than the temporary service pays its auditors.

    ○   By hiring college students, the department store will cause 20 percent of the auditors at the temporary service to lose their jobs.

    ○   The cost of training its own college-student auditors is less than 20 percent of the cost of hiring auditors from the temporary service.

16. For many years, polls have shown that most American taxpayers fear the fines and late fees that can follow an Internal Revenue Service (IRS) audit. The move to fashion a friendlier public image for the IRS in order to increase the operating efficiency of the agency may be counterproductive because _____.

○ many taxpayers are only concerned with receiving their refund checks

○ a friendlier public image for the IRS will increase voluntary compliance with tax laws

○ the timely collection of taxes could not be maintained if most taxpayers did not have a respectful fear of the IRS

○ fewer taxpayers fear the IRS today than feared it 10 years ago

○ collecting delinquent taxes does not necessarily cost the government more than collecting taxes on time

BOLDED STATEMENT QUESTIONS

Bolded Statement questions are usually based on stimuli that contain arguments, but the way you will analyze these arguments is different from what you have learned for other argument-based questions. Bolded Statement questions focus more on the structure than the substance of the stimulus.

A Bolded Statement question asks for the role that specific sentences play in an argument. The relevant sentences are, as the name implies, written in bold font. The answers to these questions will be abstract, using language such as "The first provides a counterexample to an opinion, while the second reaffirms that opinion by dismissing the counterexample." This technical language can make these questions seem intimidating.

Fortunately, these questions appear only occasionally. Moreover, if you do see any of these questions on Test Day, they shouldn't be nearly as difficult as they look. Remind yourself that Bolded Statement questions test the same core skill as much of the rest of the Critical Reasoning section: the ability to identify the evidence and the conclusion of an argument.

One caution: Unlike most GMAT stimuli, Bolded Statement questions often contain multiple arguments. Make sure that you note not only which parts of the argument are evidence and which are conclusions but also which evidence is connected to which conclusion. In addition, use keywords in the stimulus to identify which conclusion (if any) the author agrees with. Once you've done so, you should be able to make a prediction about the role of the bolded statements. Then you can turn these difficult questions into points.

Sample Stem

Bolded Statement question stems can't really avoid referring directly to the part(s) of the argument in bold type, so these stems are among the easiest to identify. A Bolded Statement question stem will look something like this example:

- The portions of the argument in boldface play which of the following roles?

APPLYING THE KAPLAN METHOD: BOLDED STATEMENT QUESTIONS

Now let's use the Kaplan Method for Critical Reasoning to solve a Bolded Statement question:

> Auto Manufacturer: For the past three years, the Micro has been our best-selling car. This year, however, sales of the Micro have been down for two consecutive quarters. Therefore, we are going to make certain features, like leather seats and CD players, standard on the Micro, rather than require buyers to pay extra for them. **This will make the Micro more attractive to buyers, thus stimulating sales.**
>
> Auto Dealer: Most people who buy the Micro do so because of its low cost. **Adding new standard features will raise the base price of the Micro,** costing us sales.
>
> In the argument above, the two statements in **bold** play which of the following roles?
>
> O The first is a conclusion; the second suggests that this conclusion is based on evidence that is irrelevant to the issue at hand.
>
> O The first presents a hypothesis; the second casts doubt on the evidence on which that hypothesis is based.
>
> O The first provides a conclusion; the second weakens the assumption on which that conclusion relies.
>
> O The first offers evidence that is disproved by the second.
>
> O The first presents a conclusion; the second supports the conclusion but offers a different interpretation of how it will impact the speakers' business.

Step 1: Identify the Question Type

This stem offers standard language for a Bolded Statement question—it asks you to determine the roles played in the arguments by each of the boldface statements.

Step 2: Untangle the Stimulus

The stimulus is organized as a dialogue. This is a rare stimulus format, but it does occasionally turn up on the GMAT. Here, the manufacturer has devised a solution to revive flagging sales of the Micro: to make certain features standard that used to cost buyers extra. The auto dealer, on the other hand, posits that adding new standard features will increase the price of the Micro, thereby hurting sales.

Step 3: Predict the Answer

Predict the answer by identifying the function of each of the bolded statements within the context of the argument-counterargument structure. The first bolded statement is a prediction that serves as the auto manufacturer's conclusion: adding more standard features to the Micro will stimulate sales. The manufacturer's conclusion relies on one of two assumptions: either that the added features will not result in an increase to the Micro's base price or that car buyers interested in the Micro are willing and able to pay more for a version of the car with added features. However, as the auto dealer states, people who buy the Micro do so primarily because of its low price. Because the addition of more standard features will result in an increase in price, the manufacturer's proposal will actually lower sales. The second bolded statement, therefore, weakens the manufacturer's prediction by challenging her assumption.

Step 4: Evaluate the Choices

Only **(C)** matches this analysis of the arguments and is correct. **(A)** begins correctly, but the second bolded statement does not challenge any of the manufacturer's evidence (that the Micro was the best-selling model for three years, that sales of the Micro have been down for two quarters, and that the company is planning to add new standard features to the Micro). **(B)** can also be eliminated for this reason. **(D)** is incorrect because the first bolded statement is not the manufacturer's evidence but her conclusion. **(E)** might also have appealed to you, since the auto dealer does offer a different point of view on how these new standard features will affect sales of the Micro. However, the dealer's point of view is actually the opposite of the manufacturer's conclusion, so saying that the second statement "supports the conclusion" of the first is incorrect.

TAKEAWAYS: BOLDED STATEMENT QUESTIONS

- Bolded Statement questions commonly ask test takers to choose the answer that describes a connection between the two parts of the stimulus that are in boldface.

- Predicting will help you deal with the wordy and difficult answer choices.

- On Bolded Statement questions, identify the purpose of every sentence in the stimulus and select the answer that matches your description of the bolded statements.

- The most challenging questions may present multiple points of view, often an argument and a counterargument.

PRACTICE SET: BOLDED STATEMENT QUESTIONS

Answers and explanations are at the end of the chapter.

17. An increased number of candidates running for a political position, one opinion says, is likely to raise the percentage of voters. **The larger the number of candidates who run for a given position, the better the chances that a voter will find a candidate that adequately represents his or her political opinions.** In the reality of the political world, however, the opposite is likely to be the case. **As more candidates enter the election process, the differences between their declared positions on political matters tend to become less obvious.**

In the argument given, the two portions in **boldface** play which of the following roles?

○ The first explains an opinion that was raised, and the second further supports that opinion by elaborating on the explanation.

○ The first raises an opinion, and the second raises another opinion contrary to the first opinion.

○ The first explains an opinion that was raised, and the second raises another opinion contrary to the first opinion.

○ The first raises an opinion, and the second supplies evidence that supports that opinion.

○ The first explains an opinion that was raised, and the second undermines that opinion by contradicting the explanation.

18. Social worker: Typically, physicians in the United States who promote specialized services do not charge as much as do physicians who do not promote their services at all. **Every time physicians are allowed to promote without restriction, the number of physicians promoting their specialty service has gone up, and patients have paid less for these consultations.** Recent changes in regulations of such promotions have lifted the requirement that the amount charged for a consultation appear on the promotion. An effect of this change will be that physicians will no longer be inclined to reduce their fees when they start to promote, and **many physicians who promote their services will increase their charges to patients.**

In the above argument, the two parts in **boldface** play which of the following roles?

O   The first makes a general claim that the social worker takes to be the truth; the second is proposed as an outcome resulting from the general claim's truth.

O   The first supplies an action and a consequence that the social worker argues will be replicated; the second recognizes a situation that would cause the action and consequence to fall apart.

O   The first supplies an action and a consequence that the social worker perceives will no longer hold true; the second gives an explanation to support that perception.

O   The first provides clarification that the social worker presents in advocacy of a prediction; the second is that prediction.

O   The first recognizes a perspective that opposes the point that the social worker advocates; the second is that point.

ADVANCED STRATEGIES: THREE SPECIAL CASES

Throughout this chapter, you have learned about the standard Critical Reasoning question types on the GMAT. Recognizing these formulaic question types enables you to read strategically—that is, to read for the details that make the difference between right and wrong answers. But the arguments in CR stimuli follow patterns as well. Recognizing common argument structures will allow you to analyze stimuli and predict correct answers more efficiently.

These advanced techniques are no substitute for knowing how to identify the conclusion, evidence, and assumptions in arguments—the ability to break down arguments into their component parts remains essential—but the three special cases we are about to discuss can help you zero in on the author's central assumption with speed and accuracy. When you understand the kind of argument an author is making, you can anticipate what kind of assumptions he or she is likely to make.

The three special cases are Causality; Representativeness; and Plans, Proposals, and Predictions. Causality and Representativeness are classic argument structures, and Plans, Proposals, and Predictions are classic argument conclusions that function in predictable ways.

Let's begin by discussing how to identify a causal argument and use that knowledge to your advantage on Critical Reasoning questions.

CAUSALITY

A causal argument is an assertion that a certain cause produced a certain effect. In other words, *X* caused *Y*, *X* made *Y* happen, or *Y* is the result of *X*. The author's assertion of causality may be explicit (e.g., "The drought led to large-scale crop failures," or "The new city plan is responsible for these underdeveloped downtown blocks") or implicit (e.g., "Since the introduction of the new radiator design, brand X cars have seen an 8 percent increase in incidents of overheating. Customer dissatisfaction will remain high until we announce a redesign"). Examine the following example of a conclusion that contains a claim of causality:

> Married people have been shown in several important studies to have higher levels of happiness than single people. Therefore, marriage causes happiness.

This argument draws its validity from a stated cause-effect relationship (namely, that marriage causes happiness). A conclusion that *X* caused *Y* relies on certain assumptions: (1) that nothing else—*A*, *B*, *C*, etc.—could have caused *Y*; (2) that *Y* was not the cause of *X*; and (3) that the apparent relationship between *X* and *Y* wasn't just a coincidence. An author who makes any of these assumptions may be confusing correlation and causation.

Causal conclusions often appear in Weaken stimuli. There are three ways to weaken causal arguments based on the assumptions listed above. Let's try them out with the following cause-effect statement:

"Marriage causes happiness."

X = cause (marriage); *Y* = effect (happiness)

Consider the following patterns when asked to weaken a causal argument:

>   **Alternative explanation:** It wasn't *X* that caused *Y*; it was actually *Z* that caused *Y*.
>
>   "Marriage doesn't cause happiness; in fact, financial security (which correlates strongly with marriage) was the real cause of the happiness reported in the surveys."
>
>   **Causality reversed:** It wasn't *X* that caused *Y*; it was actually *Y* that caused *X*.
>
>   "Marriage doesn't cause happiness; in fact, people who are already happy are significantly more likely to marry."
>
>   **Coincidence:** It wasn't *X* that caused *Y*; any correlation between *X* and *Y* is a coincidence, since they have no direct relationship.
>
>   "Marriage doesn't cause happiness; other studies that looked at the same group of people over time found that people reported similar levels of happiness before and after getting married. Any seeming correlation between marriage and happiness is coincidental or based on other factors."

In Weaken questions involving causality, the first of these three weakeners (alternative explanation) is the most common. It can be difficult to predict the specific alternative cause that will appear in the correct answer. You do know, however, that the right answer will provide a plausible explanation other than the one the author assumes to be true. The introduction of a plausible alternative cause undermines the author's conclusion.

APPLYING THE KAPLAN METHOD: CAUSALITY

Now let's use the Kaplan Method for Critical Reasoning to solve a question involving causality:

>   For the past year, a network television talk-show host has been making fun of the name of a particular brand of chainsaw, the Tree Toppler. The ridicule is obviously taking its toll: in the past 12 months, sales of the Tree Toppler have declined by 15 percent, while the sales of other chainsaws have increased.
>
>   Which of the following, if true, casts the most serious doubt on the conclusion drawn above?
>
>   O   The talk-show host who is ridiculing the Tree Toppler name actually owns a Tree Toppler.
>
>   O   The number of product complaints from owners of the Tree Toppler has not increased in the past year.
>
>   O   The average price of all chainsaws has increased by 10 percent in the past year.
>
>   O   The number of stores that sell the Tree Toppler has remained steady for the past year.
>
>   O   A year ago, a leading consumer magazine rated the Tree Toppler as "intolerably unsafe."

Step 1: Identify the Question Type

Because this stem asks you to "cast doubt" on the conclusion, this is a Weaken question.

Step 2: Untangle the Stimulus

For the last year, a talk-show host has been ridiculing Tree Toppler chainsaws. Over that time, Tree Toppler sales have fallen while other chainsaws' sales have risen. The author concludes that the talk-show host's jokes must have caused the declining Tree Toppler sales.

Step 3: Predict the Answer

To weaken an argument in which X is claimed to have caused Y, consider whether Y might actually have caused X (i.e., reversal) or whether something else might have caused Y (i.e., alternative cause). In this case, it seems unlikely that the decline in sales caused the on-air ridicule; the host is making fun of the chainsaw's name, not its declining sales. Therefore, the correct answer to this Weaken question will probably offer some alternative explanation for the decline in Tree Toppler sales.

Step 4: Evaluate the Choices

(E) provides that alternative explanation. If a prominent magazine rates a chainsaw as unsafe, that could certainly deter people from purchasing it, and a subsequent decline in sales would be reasonable to expect. **(E)** matches the prediction and is the correct answer.

If you hadn't immediately recognized **(E)** as a match for your prediction, you could still find the right answer by eliminating answer choices that miss the mark. Even if the talk-show host actually owns a Tree Toppler, as **(A)** says, the decline in sales could still be caused by the host's on-air ridicule; **(A)** is irrelevant. **(B)** is a 180 because it actually strengthens the argument by eliminating a potential alternative explanation for the decline in sales. **(C)** might be tempting, but the argument actually mentions that sales of other chainsaws have increased, so an increase in the purchase price of *all* chainsaws is not a reasonable alternative explanation. **(D)** also strengthens the argument by eliminating another alternative explanation for the decline in sales (that fewer stores are carrying the Tree Toppler).

Note that relevant alternative explanations for a causal relationship may, at first glance, appear to have no bearing on the argument. But this is precisely because the author failed to recognize that there was an alternative possibility. Before you move to the answer choices, come up with two or three specific alternative explanations. Focus on the *effect* each answer choice has on the alleged causal relationship. By weakening the causal relationship, the correct answer choice will undermine the logic of the argument.

TAKEAWAYS: CAUSALITY

When a GMAT argument uses evidence of a correlation to support a conclusion of causation ($X \rightarrow Y$), consider whether:

1. Something else is the cause of one or both of the correlated items ($Z \rightarrow Y$; or $Z \rightarrow X$ and Y).
2. Causality is reversed; the purported effect is actually the cause ($Y \rightarrow X$).
3. The correlation is mere coincidence (X and Y are unrelated).

PRACTICE SET: CAUSALITY

19. Our architecture schools must be doing something wrong. Almost monthly we hear of domes and walkways collapsing in public places, causing serious injuries. In their pursuit of some dubious aesthetic, architects design buildings that sway, crumble, and even shed windows into our cities' streets. This kind of incompetence will disappear only when the curricula of our architecture schools devote less time to so-called artistic considerations and more time to the basics of good design.

Which of the following, if true, would most seriously weaken the argument above?

   O   All architecture students are given training in basic physics and mechanics.

   O   Most of the problems with modern buildings stem from poor construction rather than poor design.

   O   Less than 50 percent of the curriculum at most architecture schools is devoted to aesthetics.

   O   Most buildings manage to stay in place well past their projected life expectancies.

   O   Architects study as long and as intensively as most other professionals.

20. Studies have shown that the number of books read in elementary school is correlated with later academic success. In the past year, local elementary students have read an average of 10 fewer books than the nationwide elementary student average of 35 books per year, while 90 percent of those local students report playing sports at least twice a week. If these students participated less in sports, they would read more books.

Which of the following, if true, would most effectively weaken the argument?

   O   A nationwide survey of middle school students determined that if given a choice between reading a book and playing a sport, most of these students would choose reading a book.

   O   Participating in sports in elementary school has been shown to be as highly correlated as reading books to later academic success.

   O   The attention spans of elementary school students do not allow these children to read for as long as older students and adults are expected to read.

   O   The local elementary school is in a rural area in which there is no bookstore or public library and Internet service is unreliable.

   O   Some local elementary school students who used to enjoy reading have said they no longer choose to read books, preferring to play sports at least twice a week.

21. Attempts to blame the mayor's policies for the growing inequality of wages are misguided. The sharp growth in the gap in earnings between college and high school graduates in this city during the past decade resulted from overall technological trends that favored the skills of more educated workers. The mayor's response to this problem cannot be criticized, as it would hardly be reasonable to expect him to attempt to slow the forces of technology.

Which of the following, if true, casts the most serious doubt on the conclusion drawn in the last sentence above?

- O The mayor could have initiated policies that would have made it easier for less-educated workers to receive the education necessary for better-paying jobs.

- O Rather than cutting the education budget, the mayor could have increased the amount of staff and funding devoted to locating employment for graduating high school seniors.

- O The mayor could have attempted to generate more demand for products from industries that paid high blue-collar wages.

- O Instead of reducing the tax rate on the wealthiest earners, the mayor could have ensured that they shouldered a greater share of the total tax burden.

- O The mayor could have attempted to protect the earnings of city workers by instituting policies designed to reduce competition from foreign industries.

REPRESENTATIVENESS

When GMAT arguments include evidence in the form of surveys, studies, polls, anecdotes, or experiments, a key issue is often the representativeness of the group used as evidence. You may be familiar with the idea of representativeness from a statistics or research methods class. This concept is no different on the GMAT. In order to be representative, a sample must be large enough, the survey length must have covered an adequate amount of time, and the population surveyed cannot be biased in some flawed way.

In GMAT arguments, the author always believes that her evidence leads to her conclusion. Therefore, the author who uses statistical evidence always assumes the data are relevant to the conclusion. But in order for this to be the case, the sample used in the evidence must be representative of the group to which the conclusion is applied. Oftentimes on GMAT questions, the sample will fail to provide sufficient evidence to fully support the conclusion.

APPLYING THE KAPLAN METHOD: REPRESENTATIVENESS

Now let's use the Kaplan Method for Critical Reasoning to solve a question involving representativeness:

> Candidate A was widely believed to be the favorite in her state's gubernatorial race. Candidate B, the incumbent governor, had figured prominently in a corruption scandal during the previous year. Although he was ultimately never charged with a crime, Candidate B received very negative coverage in local and national media. A poll of registered voters in the state showed that a majority supported Candidate A and would vote for her. In fact, election day "exit polls" of those who voted showed that most had voted for Candidate A, so she was expected to win. However, once the votes were counted, Candidate B was shown to have won a narrow victory. Clearly, respondents to the polls were not being honest when they claimed to have supported Candidate A.
>
> The argument above depends on which of the following assumptions?
>
> ○   It is difficult to predict the degree to which an incumbent candidate's support will be affected by negative media coverage.
>
> ○   The negative media coverage made supporters of Candidate B reluctant to express their views in public, and so they claimed to support Candidate A when they actually had voted for Candidate B.
>
> ○   No voter ever changes his or her mind about whom to vote for.
>
> ○   Candidate B successfully used the fact that he had not been charged with a crime to restore his good image with the voting public.
>
> ○   The sample of voters surveyed in the exit poll was representative of those who voted in the election.

Step 1: Identify the Question Type

This question directs you to find an assumption on which the argument depends, so this is definitely an Assumption question.

Step 2: Untangle the Stimulus

The argument concludes that respondents to recent election exit polls and preelection polls were not being honest when they claimed to have supported Candidate A for governor. The evidence for this is that despite a strong showing in these polls, Candidate A still lost the election.

Step 3: Predict the Answer

This conclusion is based in part on the results of two polls, so those polls need to have been conducted with representative samples in order for the conclusion to be valid. After all, what if the polls had both been conducted outside campaign rallies for Candidate A or in Candidate A's hometown? The sample group for the polls needs to be an adequate cross section of the voting population, and since this argument stakes its conclusion on the polls, the author of the argument must be assuming that the sample is indeed representative.

This question shows you that Kaplan's strategy for representativeness is not restricted to Strengthen and Weaken questions. On Test Day, if you're asked an Assumption question and you notice that the stimulus focuses on a study, survey, poll, or experiment, know that a choice that essentially says, "The sample was representative" is likely to be correct.

Step 4: Evaluate the Choices

(E) matches this prediction perfectly and is the correct answer. If you used the Denial Test to negate **(E)**, by stating that the poll's sample group was *not* representative, then the author's conclusion that voters must have lied can no longer be valid. If the people who participated in the polls were not representative of the larger voting population, then there would be no particular reason to expect the poll and voting results to be similar. **(E)** is therefore a necessary assumption of the argument.

(A) is not necessary to the argument because the author doesn't base her conclusion on a prediction drawn from the press coverage. Rather, the author bases her conclusion on a prediction drawn from the polling data. **(B)**, if true, would strengthen the argument, but this isn't a Strengthen question; the right answer to an Assumption question must be something upon which the argument relies. While the argument asserts that people polled lied about whom they voted for, it does not depend on any particular reason why they did so. **(C)** is far too extreme; the argument's point that the polls' respondents lied is not undone if one or two people simply changed their minds. As for **(D)**, the author doesn't necessarily assume anything about *how* Candidate B was able to eke out a victory.

TAKEAWAY: REPRESENTATIVENESS

When you see an argument based on the findings of a study, survey, experiment, or analogy, compare the population of the evidence with that of the conclusion.

PRACTICE SET: REPRESENTATIVENESS

Answers and explanations are at the end of the chapter.

22. Loneliness is commonly reported in elderly populations. A study of elderly people found that those who owned dogs reported feeling less lonely than those who did not own dogs. Clearly, an elderly person who adopts a pet will be less likely to suffer feelings of loneliness than an elderly person without a pet.

    Which of the following, if true, would most strengthen the argument above?

    O   Owning a pet has been linked to several health benefits, including lower blood pressure.

    O   Some people feel that cats do not engage socially with their owners as much as dogs do.

    O   The number of elderly people who own pets is projected to rise in the coming years.

    O   A large percentage of elderly dog owners report taking their dogs for walks and to dog parks.

    O   Pets other than dogs provide the same benefits of companionship as do dogs.

23. A social worker surveyed 200 women, each of whom had recently given birth to her first child. Half of the women surveyed had chosen to give birth in a hospital or obstetrics clinic; the other half had chosen to give birth at home under the care of certified midwives. Of the 100 births that occurred at home, only 5 presented substantial complications, whereas 17 of the hospital births presented substantial complications. The social worker concluded from the survey that the home is actually a safer environment in which to give birth than a hospital or clinic.

    Which of the following, if true, most seriously calls the social worker's conclusion into question?

    O   Women who give birth in hospitals and clinics often have shorter periods of labor than do women who give birth at home.

    O   Many obstetricians discourage patients from giving birth at home.

    O   All of the women in the study who had been diagnosed as having a high possibility of delivery complications elected to give birth in a hospital.

    O   Women who give birth at home tend to experience less stress during labor than women who deliver in hospitals.

    O   Pregnant doctors prefer giving birth in a hospital.

24. A team of pediatricians recently announced that pet birds are more likely to bite children under age 13 than people of any other age group. The team's finding was based on a study showing that the majority of all bird bites requiring medical attention involved children under 13. The study also found that the birds most likely to bite are cockatiels and parakeets.

Which of the following, if true, would most weaken the pediatricians' conclusion that birds are more likely to bite children under age 13 than people of any other age group?

- More than half of bird bites not requiring medical attention, which exceed the number requiring such attention, involve people aged 13 and older.
- The majority of bird bites resulting in the death of the bitten person involve people aged 65 and older.
- Many serious bird bites affecting children under age 13 are inflicted by birds other than cockatiels and parakeets.
- Most bird bites in children under age 13 that require medical attention are far less serious than they initially appear.
- Most parents can learn to treat bird bites effectively if they avail themselves of a small amount of medical information.

PLANS, PROPOSALS, AND PREDICTIONS

Once you start identifying plans, proposals, and predictions in Critical Reasoning stimuli, you'll realize that many arguments contain conclusions in these forms. All three have a future orientation and indicate the author's opinion.

Plans and proposals are found in conclusions that begin, "Thus, we should..." or "It's in the company's best interest to..." When a conclusion takes the form of a plan or proposal, the author is likely assuming that the plan or proposal is helpful and practical under the current circumstances. GMAT questions often test whether we realize that it may not be helpful or currently practical.

Critical Reasoning stimuli involving plans or proposals almost invariably offer only one reason for the plan or proposal. In other words, because of *X*, we should do *Y*.

So, what must the author be assuming about that evidence? That it's the only, or at least the most important, factor to consider. Thus, any answer that introduces an alternative and competing consideration weakens the argument. Any answer that rules out a possible alternative consideration strengthens it.

Think about how you might weaken the following proposal:

> Sam often oversleeps because he reaches over and turns off the alarm before he's fully awake. To fix this problem, Sam proposes buying a second alarm clock.

Sam's proposal is inherently flawed because it fails to consider some important factors: Sam might put the second clock right next to the first one and just shut it off, too. Alternatively, Sam might have to plug the second clock in too far from his bed. Then, he won't hear it, so it won't be of any help. Either way, there's an intervening consideration that suggests the plan will fail or will be self-defeating.

This happens in the business world all the time. For example, a sales manager might say, "Let's do *X* and increase sales. That will make us profitable." The operations manager might then respond, "Doing *X* would cost too much; this plan will lose money." The problem is not that the sales manager is unreasonable in claiming that proposal *X* would increase sales—it might, in fact, do so. However, the operations manager raises another concern, one that the sales manager overlooked, that could undermine proposal *X*'s chance of success.

Predictions are no different in CR questions than they are in real life; they use the future tense: "So-and-so will win the Oscar," "The economy will show modest growth," or "We will not be able to meet the production deadline." GMAT authors base their predictions on past and current trends or situations. In order to weaken such an argument, you want to find an answer choice that says that the trend will change. To strengthen it, look for an answer choice that says, "Future events will unfold as expected."

APPLYING THE KAPLAN METHOD: PLANS, PROPOSALS, AND PREDICTIONS

Now let's use the Kaplan Method for Critical Reasoning to solve a question involving a plan, proposal, or prediction:

> Several people have died while canoeing during high water on a nearby river in recent years. The local police have proposed a ban on canoeing when the river reaches flood stage. Opponents of the ban argue that the government should ban an activity only if it harms people other than those who willingly participate in the activity, and they therefore conclude that the proposed ban on high-water canoeing is unwarranted.
>
> Which of the following, if true, most seriously weakens the opponents' conclusion?
>
> O   Sailboats are not allowed on a nearby lake when winds exceed 50 miles per hour.
>
> O   Several other local governments have imposed similar bans on other rivers.
>
> O   Several police officers have been seriously injured while trying to rescue canoeists who were stranded on the river while attempting to canoe during high water.
>
> O   More canoeists drown while canoeing rivers at normal water levels than while canoeing rivers at high water levels.
>
> O   Statistics provided by the U.S. National Park Service show that fewer people drown on rivers with high-water canoeing bans than on rivers without such bans.

Step 1: Identify the Question Type

The stem contains the obvious keyword "weakens," but it also asks you to weaken the opponents' conclusion in particular. Keep this information in mind—there may be more than one argument in the stimulus.

Step 2: Untangle the Stimulus

The government shouldn't ban an activity that poses no risk to people who don't voluntarily participate. Therefore, the opponents argue, the government should not ban high-water canoeing.

Step 3: Predict the Answer

To weaken the argument, you need an answer choice that explains why the opponents' proposal should, on its own terms, be rejected. Here, the opponents assume that high-water canoeing does not harm anyone who does not willingly participate in the canoeing. To weaken the conclusion, look for an answer choice suggesting that canoeing during flood stage does in fact threaten people other than those who have chosen to canoe.

Step 4: Evaluate the Choices

(C) offers such a suggestion by stating that police officers, none of whom consented to expose themselves to the dangers of canoeing in high water, were in fact harmed as a result of such canoeing. **(C)** is the correct answer.

(A) has no bearing on the argument; it isn't clear how sailing on a lake during high wind is relevant to canoeing on a river during high water. This statement tells us nothing about whether high-water canoeing poses risks to non-canoers. And just because, as **(B)** says, other governments have also enacted the bans, that doesn't mean that the bans are necessarily reasonable. The opponents might still have a valid argument. Therefore, **(B)** is also irrelevant. **(D)** offers an irrelevant comparison: that more canoeists drown while the river is at normal levels may simply be due to the fact that there are more canoeists at that time to begin with. That has no bearing on whether canoeing should be banned at high water levels. And **(E)** might be tempting, but it doesn't show that the opponents' proposal to abolish the ban won't work *on its own terms*. **(E)** doesn't give an example of non-canoeists harmed by the canoeing.

TAKEAWAYS: PLANS, PROPOSALS, AND PREDICTIONS

When you see a question regarding a statement about the future, identify assumptions about the feasibility, usefulness, and relevance of the future conditions.

- To weaken an argument whose conclusion is a plan or proposal, show that the plan or proposal, on its own terms, will not work.
- To weaken an argument whose conclusion is a prediction, show why the prediction is unlikely to come to pass.
- To weaken an objection to a plan, proposal, or prediction, seek evidence that it *will* work or come true.

PRACTICE SET: PLANS, PROPOSALS, AND PREDICTIONS

Answers and explanations are at the end of the chapter.

25. A team of researchers at a university hospital has developed a chemical test that detects breast tumors in the early stages of development. In order to save lives, the researchers want to make the test a routine part of examinations at the hospital. However, a spokesperson for the hospital argued that because virtually all breast tumors are detectable by self-examination, the chemical test would have little impact on the breast cancer death rate.

    Which of the following, if true, would most seriously weaken the hospital spokesperson's argument?

    O   Fatal breast tumors are often not revealed by self-examination until it is too late for effective treatment.

    O   Breast tumors are usually discovered at an earlier stage of development than are lung tumors.

    O   Mammograms are currently in wide use as a breast cancer test and cost much less than the chemical test.

    O   Because men are not typically victims of breast cancer, the new test would benefit only half of the population.

    O   Most women learn how to check for signs of breast cancer from magazines and not from doctors.

26. Occupational safety advocate: Logging is one of the most dangerous occupations in the United States. A company has developed a chainsaw that will instantly shut off if there is kickback of the chain, which studies have shown to be the most common cause of chainsaw injuries. The logging industry should adopt this new chainsaw as standard equipment in order to prevent most of the logging-related deaths that occur each year.

    Which of the following statements, if true, most seriously weakens the occupational safety advocate's argument?

    O   Loggers are sometimes killed by problems with chainsaws other than the kickback of the chain.

    O   Injuries from falling trees cause the vast majority of deaths in the logging industry.

    O   The new chainsaw is inexpensive and easy to learn how to use.

    O   There are other, equally safe chainsaws available, but the logging industry has not adopted them.

    O   The chainsaw manufacturer's claims about its product are supported by a study conducted by a government agency.

27. According to a recent study, advertisements in medical journals often contain misleading information about the effectiveness and safety of new prescription drugs. The medical researchers who wrote the study concluded that the advertisements could result in doctors' prescribing inappropriate drugs to their patients.

    The researchers' conclusion would be most strengthened if which of the following were true?

    O   Advertisements for new prescription drugs are an important source of revenue for medical journals.

    O   Editors of medical journals are often unable to evaluate the claims made in advertisements for new prescription drugs.

    O   Doctors rely on the advertisements as a source of information about new prescription drugs.

    O   Advertisements for new prescription drugs are typically less accurate than medical journal articles evaluating those same drugs.

    O   The Food and Drug Administration, the government agency responsible for drug regulation, reviews advertisements for new drugs only after the ads have already been printed.

CRITICAL REASONING QUIZ

Answers and explanations are at the end of the chapter.

28. To avoid the appearance of conflicts of interest, the board of a major U.S. stock exchange is considering a new policy that would ban former top executives of the exchange from taking positions at publicly traded companies for a period of two years after leaving the stock exchange. Critics of the plan say the policy is unfair because it would likely prevent former top executives of the exchange from earning a decent living.

    Which of the following statements, if true, would most strengthen the prediction made by the critics of the proposed company policy?

    ○ The labor union that represents most of the stock exchange's employees has made public statements that threaten a strike if the policy is adopted.

    ○ Former employees of the exchange most often work for publicly traded companies after leaving the exchange.

    ○ Low-level managers at the exchange have an average tenure of 13 years, one of the longest in the industry.

    ○ Low-level managers at the exchange most often leave their jobs for positions with the state or federal government.

    ○ Former top executives of the exchange have a particular set of skills such that they are usually only able to find work with publicly traded companies.

29. The increase in taxes on cigarettes next month will not limit the use of addictive tobacco products to the extent that health advocates hope. Many cigarette smokers will shift their spending to cigars and chewing tobacco when the law takes effect.

    Which of the following, if true, would most strongly weaken the argument above?

    ○ Cigars and chewing tobacco can satisfy the nicotine cravings of most cigarette smokers.

    ○ The taste, smell, and texture of cigars and chewing tobacco are sufficiently different from those of cigarettes to deter cigarette smokers from using them.

    ○ Many health advocates themselves use tobacco products.

    ○ The government might also impose significant taxes on cigars and chewing tobacco over the course of two years.

    ○ Cigars and chewing tobacco are often more expensive than cigarettes.

30. The percentage of local businesses with more than 10 employees is higher in Grandview City than in any other city in the state. However, the percentage of local businesses with 15 employees or more is higher in Lakeshore City, which is in the same state, than in any other city in the state.

    If the statements above are true, then which of the following must also be true?

    ○ The percentage of local businesses with more than 18 employees is higher in Lakeshore City than in any other city in the state.

    ○ The state has more local businesses with more than 10 employees than any other state in the country.

    ○ The number of local businesses with 15 or more employees is greater in Lakeshore City than in Grandview City.

    ○ Some local businesses in Grandview City have 11 to 14 employees.

    ○ The average number of employees per business is higher in Lakeshore City than in Grandview City.

31. It appears that the number of people employed by a typical American software firm decreased in the 1980s and 1990s. This trend is borne out by two studies, conducted 20 years apart. In a large 1980 sample of randomly chosen American software firms, the median size of the firms' workforce populations was 65. When those same firms were studied again in 2000, the median size was 57.

    Which of the following points to the most serious logical flaw in the reasoning above?

    ○ The median number of employees in American firms in many industries decreased during the 1980s and 1990s.

    ○ During the 1980s and 1990s, many software firms increased the extent to which they relied on subcontractors to write code.

    ○ The data in the studies refer only to companies that existed in 1980.

    ○ The studies focused on the number of employees, but there are many ways of judging a firm's size, such as revenues and profits.

    ○ The median number of employees is not as sound a measure of the number of employees employed in an industry as is the mean number of employees, which accounts for the vast size of the few large firms that dominate most industries.

32. The Ministry of Tourism in country X began an expensive television advertising campaign in country Y two years ago. Since that time, the number of visitors to country X from country Y has increased by more than 8 percent. Clearly, the Ministry of Tourism's campaign is responsible for the increase.

    Which of the following, if true, would most weaken the argument above?

    ○ The advertisements sponsored by the Ministry of Tourism in country X were panned by the country Y media for lack of imagination.

    ○ A devaluation of the currency in country X two years ago made travel there more affordable for residents of country Y.

    ○ Increasing political turmoil in country X will lead to a decrease in visitors from country Y next year.

    ○ The number of visitors from country Y to country Z increased by more than 8 percent over the past two years.

    ○ Over the past two years, the advertisement campaign launched by the Ministry of Tourism in country X cost more money than residents of country Y spent traveling in country X.

33. A corporation's recent financial report indicates that customers in its Quarx stores, which play upbeat music through an in-store audio system, spend on average 25 percent more per shopping trip than customers in its Cubix stores, which advertise specials over the audio system. Clearly, hearing music has a greater impact than hearing advertisements on how much money customers spend when shopping.

    Which of the following, if true, would most strengthen the argument above?

    ○ A study conducted by a psychologist found that hearing music makes shoppers feel financially secure, so they are more likely to make impulse purchases.

    ○ Customers who hear advertisements for things they dislike form a negative association between their shopping experience and what they heard, making them less likely to return to the store where they heard the advertisement.

    ○ Stores that play music tend to carry products that are essential to daily life, while those that advertise specials often stock unessential, fun items that the stores hope consumers will decide to buy on a whim if offered a special price.

    ○ An economist who studied consumer shopping habits found that about half the population likes to listen to music while shopping, while the other half reports either disliking music or not noticing that music is playing.

    ○ According to a recent sociological study, customers say that hearing specials announced while they are shopping is irritating, but they often take advantage of the discounts offered in those announcements.

34. <u>Cable Television Executive</u>: **Our service and reliability have increased dramatically over the past year.** Our customer service line is receiving 30 percent fewer reports of interrupted service, and the number of subscribers canceling their accounts is barely half of what it was last year.

    <u>Cable Television Customer</u>: That doesn't mean your service and reliability have improved. **It's possible that customers don't bother to call your customer service line to report problems because they never get any assistance when they do.** And the drop-off in the number of canceled accounts could reflect the fact that nearly all of your dissatisfied customers have already canceled their accounts.

    In the argument above, the two portions in boldface play which of the following roles?

    O   The first is evidence designed to lead to a conclusion; the second offers further evidence in support of that conclusion.

    O   The first is evidence designed to lead to a conclusion; the second offers evidence designed to cast doubt on that conclusion.

    O   The first is a conclusion; the second offers evidence in support of that conclusion.

    O   The first is a conclusion; the second offers evidence designed to cast doubt on that conclusion.

    O   The first is a conclusion; the second is an alternative conclusion based on the same evidence.

35. Opponents of the laws prohibiting nonprescription narcotic drugs argue that in a free society, people have the right to take risks as long as the risks do not constitute a harm to others who have not elected to take such risks. These opponents conclude that it should be each person's decision whether or not to use narcotic drugs.

    Which of the following, if true, most seriously weakens the conclusion drawn above?

    O   Some narcotic drugs have been shown to have medicinal qualities.

    O   There are laws that govern the use of prescription drugs.

    O   Studies have shown that people who use nonprescription drugs are much more likely to perpetrate a violent crime when intoxicated than when sober.

    O   People who use narcotic drugs are twice as likely to die of an overdose as of natural causes.

    O   The rate of drug overdoses is higher in countries that do not have laws governing the use of narcotic drugs than in countries that do have such laws.

36. In a survey of undergraduates, two-fifths admitted to having cheated on an exam at least once during their education. However, the survey may underestimate the proportion of undergraduates who have cheated, because _____.

Which of the following best completes the passage above?

○ some undergraduates who have cheated at least once might have claimed on the survey never to have cheated

○ some undergraduates who have never cheated might have claimed on the survey to have cheated

○ some undergraduates who claimed on the survey to have cheated at least once may have cheated on multiple occasions throughout their education

○ some undergraduates who claimed on the survey to have cheated at least once may have been answering honestly

○ some students who are not undergraduates have probably cheated at least once during their education

37. During the last 18 years, the number of people who live or work in the Dry River Valley, which is prone to flash flooding, has continually increased, as has traffic on local roads and bridges. However, the number of people caught in flash floods has decreased, even though the annual number of floods has increased slightly.

Which of the following, if true, best explains the decrease described above?

○ Flash floods are more likely to happen in the first hour of a rainstorm than afterward.

○ Flash floods killed some people in the Dry River Valley in every one of the last 18 years.

○ Better meteorological technology, combined with a better understanding of the conditions conducive to flash flooding, has improved local authorities' ability to predict when and where flash floods will occur.

○ Many people work in the Dry River Valley but live elsewhere.

○ A law that went into effect 18 years ago mandated that all new homes built in the valley be built on raised foundations, making those homes much less susceptible to flood damage.

38. Colleges in Tycho City have failed to prepare their students for the business world. A recent study revealed that the majority of college graduates in Tycho City could not write a simple business letter.

    Which of the following, if true, would provide additional evidence in support of the claim above?

    ○ A majority of students attending colleges in Tycho City are business majors.

    ○ The state college in neighboring Twyla Township has recently improved its business program by adding courses in business writing.

    ○ Most Tycho City college graduates move outside the Tycho City area after they graduate.

    ○ Most Tycho City college students live in on-campus dormitories.

    ○ The majority of college graduates living in Tycho City received their college degrees from institutions located in Tycho City.

ANSWERS AND EXPLANATIONS

1.	A	14.	E	27.	C
2.	A	15.	E	28.	E
3.	C	16.	C	29.	B
4.	B	17.	E	30.	D
5.	C	18.	C	31.	C
6.	D	19.	B	32.	B
7.	A	20.	D	33.	A
8.	B	21.	A	34.	D
9.	A	22.	E	35.	C
10.	C	23.	C	36.	A
11.	D	24.	A	37.	C
12.	E	25.	A	38.	E
13.	D	26.	B		

1. **(A)**

    Burger Land, a nationwide fast-food chain, recently announced a special promotion dramatically reducing the price of its most popular burger, the Big and Beefy. This development has provoked a strong response by the nation's nutritionists. Citing the extremely high levels of cholesterol in the Big and Beefy, they predict that the price reduction will have a negative impact on the health of our citizens.

    The nutritionists' argument assumes which of the following?

    ○   Some consumers induced by the price reduction to purchase the Big and Beefy would otherwise have consumed food lower in cholesterol than the Big and Beefy.

    ○   Reducing fat consumption is the most important factor in improving one's diet.

    ○   Burger Land could not have increased sales of the Big and Beefy by reducing its cholesterol content and appealing to health-conscious consumers.

    ○   Other fast-food companies will not respond to Burger Land's announcement by reducing the price of their own high-cholesterol burgers.

    ○   Lost revenue due to the price reduction in the Big and Beefy will be offset by an increase in the number of burgers sold.

Step 1: Identify the Question Type

The word "assumes" in the question stem signals that this is an Assumption question. You're looking for an unstated piece of information that links the evidence to the conclusion. The stem also tells you that you should focus on the nutritionists' argument.

Step 2: Untangle the Stimulus

In Assumption questions, you first need to find the argument's conclusion and evidence. The conclusion is the nutritionists' prediction: cheaper Big and Beefy burgers will negatively impact citizens' health. The evidence is that the Big and Beefy is extremely high in cholesterol and that Burger Land plans to significantly lower the price of the Big and Beefy.

Step 3: Predict the Answer

This stimulus contains a scope shift, or change in topic between evidence and conclusion. To spot scope shifts, look for a brand-new term or idea that appears for the first time in the conclusion without having been mentioned in the evidence. Here, the conclusion introduces the idea of citizens' health being harmed, so you need to figure out why, given the evidence, the author thinks a negative impact on the population's health is likely. The author makes two assumptions: (1) that eating a lot of cholesterol is bad for one's health and (2) that the drop in price will entice people to purchase Big and Beefy burgers instead of lower-cholesterol food they would otherwise have eaten. (For this author's argument to work, it's not enough that Big and Beefy burgers are unhealthy; they've got to be less healthy than the foods they replace.) An answer choice that states either of these assumptions will be correct.

Step 4: Evaluate the Choices

(A) matches the second of the predictions: the reduced price will cause at least some people to purchase the Big and Beefy rather than other lower-cholesterol foods. This is the correct answer. **(B)** is irrelevant to the argument, which is concerned not with "fat consumption" but with the very high levels of cholesterol the burgers contain. **(C)** is incorrect because other approaches the burger chain could have taken are irrelevant. The argument is concerned only with the potential consequences of the move it actually made, which was to reduce the price of one particular burger. **(D)** is incorrect because other fast-food companies have no bearing on the argument. You're interested specifically in Burger Land. Finally, **(E)** is incorrect because lost revenues at Burger Land are irrelevant. What is important is the health impact of one specific burger that the company produces, not the company's finances.

2.   **(A)**

In Country X, all citizens eligible to vote must do so or face stiff fines. Because voting in Country X is mandatory, over 99 percent of the eligible voters voted in the last election. Thus, the winner of the last election is truly the people's choice.

Which of the following identifies an assumption in the author's argument?

○   In Country X, voters are allowed to vote for a candidate of their choice.

○   If Country X did not make voting mandatory, few people would vote.

○   Only in countries where voting is mandatory do people vote the way they wish to vote.

○   Country X is a true democracy, despite the fact that all people are forced to vote.

○   Only in countries where voting is not mandatory do the winners of elections truly reflect the people's choice.

Step 1: Identify the Question Type

The question stem contains the classic telltale word "assumption," so you can be confident that this is an Assumption question.

Step 2: Untangle the Stimulus

The argument concludes that the winner of the election is the people's choice. This is based on the evidence that nearly every eligible voter voted in the election and that voting is mandatory in Country X.

Step 3: Predict the Answer

But just because everyone voted doesn't mean that the winner is truly the people's choice. In fact, if voting is compulsory, people might be forced to vote in an election in which they don't prefer *any* of the candidates. The author's claim about the election depends on the assumptions that citizens of Country X are able to vote for whomever they like, that their votes express their preference, and that their votes will be tallied honestly and accurately.

Step 4: Evaluate the Choices

(A) is the correct answer and reflects the prediction nearly verbatim. **(B)** tells you that Country X may be justified in requiring its citizens to vote, but that does nothing to prove that the winner of the election is the people's choice. As for **(C)**, even if people vote for candidates of their choice in countries where voting is *not* mandatory, this argument could still be made. **(C)** also doesn't demonstrate anything about Country X specifically, so it's not the assumption you're looking for. **(D)** is tempting—but it requires the assumption that a "true democracy" is one in which the winner of any election is "the people's choice." Because the term "true democracy" is not defined in the answer choice or in the stimulus, **(D)** is irrelevant. **(E)** is the exact opposite of what you're seeking, because it would suggest that the winner of the election in Country X would *not* be the people's choice.

3. (C)

In the next four years, the number of doctors, nurses, and other health care workers will increase significantly worldwide. Even so, the average compensation received by such professionals will not decline but rather is likely to increase. This is due, at least partly, to the fact that the median age of the world's population will increase steadily in this same period of time.

The argument above depends logically upon which of the following assumptions?

- ○ The increase in the number of health care workers will be responsible for the increase in the average life span.
- ○ The compensation of doctors and physical therapists who treat the elderly will increase more than that of other health care workers.
- ○ As a group, older people receive more attention from health care workers than do younger people.
- ○ Geriatrics, a branch of medicine focusing on the health problems of older people, is the most expensive element of American health care.
- ○ Increase in the median age of the population will occur in all regions of the world.

Step 1: Identify the Question Type

The question stem instructs you to seek an assumption on which the argument depends.

Step 2: Untangle the Stimulus

First identify the conclusion: the number of health care workers is about to rise, as is the average compensation of those workers. Next, find the evidence: the median age of the world and, by extension, the number of elderly people are increasing.

Step 3: Predict the Answer

To find the central assumption, link the terms of the evidence with the terms of the conclusion. The conclusion centers on more workers who'll get more money. The evidence centers on more elderly. The assumption, which links the evidence and the conclusion, must center on the idea that the elderly are especially likely to require the services of health care workers.

Step 4: Evaluate the Choices

(C) is a match for the prediction and, thus, the correct answer. **(A)** gets the cause-and-effect relationship from the argument in the wrong order, since the author argues that the increase in life span will be responsible for an increase in the number of health care workers. **(B)** draws an irrelevant comparison; the author argues that the average compensation received by all health care workers will increase. **(D)** doesn't have to be true—the conclusion could still follow from the evidence even if there are elements of American health care that are more expensive than geriatrics. **(E)** is extreme. It need not be true that the median age of the population will increase in every corner of the globe.

4. **(B)**

The threatened prosecution of businesses flying 20-by-38-foot garrison flags, which are traditionally to be flown on national holidays, instead of the smaller post flags, which can be flown at any time, is unconscionable. Legal technicalities of this sort should never restrict patriotic expression.

Which of the following, if true, would most seriously weaken the argument above?

O   Many people find the garrison flags' size to be distracting and ill suited to neighborhood aesthetics.

O   The businesses that are flying garrison flags do so primarily to attract customers.

O   The raising and lowering of different-sized flags on the correct days of the year is a laborious and time-consuming procedure.

O   The regulations that govern the correct display of the nation's flags are part of an old and time-honored tradition.

O   The symbolic significance of a flag's size is not generally understood by most of the customers patronizing these businesses.

Step 1: Identify the Question Type

The word "weaken" in the question stem signals that this is a Weaken question. You need the answer choice that makes the argument's conclusion less likely to be true.

Step 2: Untangle the Stimulus

Start by finding the conclusion, evidence, and assumption. The conclusion is the first sentence, which states that businesses should not be prosecuted for flying large garrison flags rather than smaller post flags. The evidence is the second sentence: legal technicalities should not restrict patriotic expression. The author of this argument assumes that businesses are flying the garrison flags out of a sense of patriotism, rather than for some other reason.

Step 3: Predict the Answer

Because this is a Weaken question, the correct answer will make the central assumption less likely to be true. Look for a choice stating that businesses fly the larger flags for some reason other than patriotism.

Step 4: Evaluate the Choices

(B) is correct and matches the prediction: if businesses are flying large garrison flags to attract customers, they are not doing so out of a sense of patriotism. Because the argument's evidence hinges on "patriotic expression," the conclusion that these businesses should not be prosecuted is thus greatly weakened. This is the correct answer. **(A)** is incorrect because it is irrelevant to the argument, which is concerned not with "neighborhood aesthetics" but with the permissibility of flying the larger flags. **(C)** is incorrect because it is a slight strengthener, not a weakener. The fact that abiding by the proper flag calendar and switching back and forth between the larger and smaller flags is "laborious and time-consuming" could be cited as an additional reason businesses should not be prosecuted for sticking to the larger flags. **(D)** is irrelevant. It, like **(A)**, provides a reason that businesses should perhaps not be allowed to fly whichever flag they like with impunity, but this reason—long-standing tradition—has nothing to do with the scope of the argument, which focuses on patriotic expression. **(E)** is irrelevant. Whether or not business patrons understand the "symbolic significance" of a flag's size has no effect on the conclusion that business owners ought not to be prosecuted for flying the larger flags.

5. **(C)**

Any college football player who uses steroids should be banned from competition. The national agency with the responsibility to preserve the natural competitive balance between players enforces rules specifically mandating that no player be allowed to use drugs to gain a competitive advantage. Studies show that steroid users tend to have much greater strength and weight than non-users.

Which of the following statements, if true, would most strengthen the argument?

- ○ Users of steroids often suffer from acne, extreme nervousness, and reduced sexual potency.
- ○ Increased strength is more useful than increased weight to college football players.
- ○ Superior strength and weight give college football players a significant competitive advantage.
- ○ Steroid use is much more prevalent in college football than in college baseball.
- ○ Random drug testing of athletes has been shown to be effective in the detection of drug use by athletes.

Step 1: Identify the Question Type

The word "strengthen" gives this one away as a Strengthen question.

Step 2: Untangle the Stimulus

A Strengthen question is built around the argument's assumption. "Strengthen the argument" means "strengthen the conclusion," but you'll be strengthening the argument's conclusion specifically by affirming its central assumption.

The author concludes that steroid users should be banned from college football. The evidence comes in two parts. First, the rules forbid football players to use drugs to obtain a "competitive advantage." The second piece of evidence is that steroids cause big increases in strength and weight.

Step 3: Predict the Answer

The author's conclusion depends on the assumption that having "greater strength and weight" provides athletes with a "competitive advantage." (It's possible that added bulk could be a drawback for a college player; perhaps speed and flexibility are more important.) To strengthen the argument, look for an answer choice that suggests that players derive a benefit from the extra size and strength that steroids provide.

Step 4: Evaluate the Choices

(C) matches the prediction perfectly and is the correct answer. **(A)** introduces several negative side effects of steroids, all of which are irrelevant to the argument. **(B)** offers an irrelevant comparison between increased strength and increased weight. It doesn't matter which of these two qualities is more important to a college football player; it only matters whether these qualities provide a competitive advantage. **(D)** is another irrelevant comparison, this time between college football and college baseball. The argument is about steroid use among football players, so baseball is beside the point. The "prevalence" of steroid use is also irrelevant. **(E)** is incorrect because methods of drug detection have no bearing on the argument. It doesn't matter how players are caught.

6. **(D)**

Since the 1960s, most drinking water provided by public water systems has had fluoride added, because research has demonstrated that adding fluoride to drinking water significantly reduces the occurrence of dental cavities in the populations served by those systems. However, manufacturers now add fluoride to toothpaste in amounts sufficient to provide the same level of protection against dental cavities as that provided by fluoridated water. Therefore, public water systems could now save the money formerly spent on water fluoridation without impacting the rate of occurrence of dental cavities in the communities they serve.

Which of the following, if true, would most weaken the argument?

O   The savings realized by public water systems would not be passed on to their customers but would be used for maintenance of and improvements to the system.

O   The cost of adding fluoride to toothpaste is much less than the cost of adding fluoride to the water produced by public water systems.

O   Fluoride is a commodity traded throughout the world, and the availability and price of fluoride can vary substantially due to economic and political events.

O   Fluoride toothpaste has been widely available since 1980, and recent studies have found higher levels of dental cavities in communities with unfluoridated water than in communities with fluoridated water.

O   Fluoride is colorless, odorless, and tasteless when added to water, but flavorings are added to fluoride toothpaste to deliver a taste that most people describe as pleasant.

Step 1: Identify the Question Type

From the question stem, you know that you are to weaken the argument.

Step 2: Untangle the Stimulus

The conclusion of the argument, identified by the keyword "[t]herefore," states that public water systems can save the money they spend adding fluoride to water without causing an increase in the rate of cavities. The evidence is that manufacturers are now adding fluoride to toothpaste.

Step 3: Predict the Answer

The argument assumes that the fluoride in toothpaste will be as effective as the fluoride added to water. To weaken the argument, find a statement that suggests the two methods of delivering the fluoride differ in their ability to prevent cavities.

Step 4: Evaluate the Choices

In **(D)**, if fluoride toothpaste is widely available, but the people who consume fluoridated water have a lower rate of cavities than people without such water, then the toothpaste is likely not a wholly effective substitute for fluoridated water. By suggesting that the toothpaste may not work as well as the fluoridated water, **(D)** matches the prediction and is correct. **(A)** describes how the money that is saved will be used, but that is irrelevant. The argument is about dental health, not about how saving money might benefit public water systems. **(B)** and **(C)** talk about the cost of fluoride, but that has no bearing on what the argument is concerned with, which is comparing the results of two methods of delivering the fluoride. **(E)** is a subtle strengthener. If the fluoride toothpaste has a pleasant taste, that may make it more likely that people would use more of it, thereby supporting the idea that the fluoride in the water supply is unnecessary.

7. (A)

Public interest law focuses on the legal issues that affect the entire community or involve broad areas of public concern, such as illegal discrimination, environmental protection, child welfare, and domestic violence. A particular nonprofit agency focusing on public interest law is woefully understaffed; many lawyers are urgently needed to continue its important work providing low-cost legal services to residents who are unable to afford a private attorney. In order to fill these vacancies as efficiently as possible, the agency should advertise the jobs to students in this year's graduating class at the local law school to encourage them to enter the field of public interest law.

Each of the following, if true, weakens the recommendation above EXCEPT:

- ○ Positions in corporate law that are advertised at the local law school have higher average salaries than do legal positions at nonprofit agencies.
- ○ The local law school maintains an active placement service for its graduates and publicizes job openings in the community to its graduating class.
- ○ The open positions at the nonprofit agency require several years of prior experience in the practice of law.
- ○ Several lawyers recently left the nonprofit agency because the agency's salaries did not enable the lawyers to make their student loan payments.
- ○ The local law school is ranked third highest in the country, and graduates of the school aspire to work for large, highly rated law firms located in major cities.

Step 1: Identify the Question Type

This is a Weaken EXCEPT question. Look for an answer that strengthens the argument or that simply has no effect on the argument.

Step 2: Untangle the Stimulus

The recommendation is the final sentence, identified by the keyword "should." The conclusion states that "the agency should advertise" the available jobs to "this year's graduating class at the local law school" and that this is the most efficient way to fill the vacancies. The evidence is that "many lawyers are urgently needed" to fill open positions at the agency.

Step 3: Predict the Answer

In this argument, the central assumption is that advertising to the local law school's current graduating class is the most efficient way to fill the agency's vacancies. The four incorrect answers will make the assumption less likely, thus weakening the recommendation. The one correct answer will either make it more likely that advertising in the recommended way will be the most efficient way to fill the vacancies or will be irrelevant to the conclusion.

Step 4: Evaluate the Choices

(A) has no effect on the assumption and is correct. The agency doesn't need to attract every or even many graduates for advertising at the law school to be the most effective strategy to fill its positions. **(B)** points out that the local law school is already providing information about the positions to its graduating class, making it less likely that the advertising will have any effect. **(C)** suggests that the graduating students would not be qualified to fill the positions at the agency and thus weakens the argument. **(D)** states that several of the agency's vacancies are due to lawyers leaving the agency because of low pay, making it more likely that salaries, not advertising, are the issue. **(E)** makes it less likely that the agency's advertising will have a receptive audience.

8. **(B)**

Herbed Wellness, a manufacturer of herbal products, wants its new headache remedy to be as effective as possible while using only natural ingredients. A controlled study has found that 58 percent of headache sufferers obtain complete headache relief from a dose of caffeine equivalent to that typically found in a cup of coffee. Therefore, even though the vast majority of its customers are health-conscious avoiders of coffee, Herbed Wellness should add caffeine to its new herbal headache treatment; doing so will prove both efficacious and cost-effective.

The answer to which of the following questions would be most useful in evaluating the claim that caffeine will be efficacious in relieving headaches among Herbed Wellness customers?

O   Is the headache relief provided by caffeine as long-lasting as that provided by over-the-counter drugs such as aspirin?

O   What percentage of the study participants were regular coffee drinkers who suffer from caffeine-withdrawal headaches?

O   Is caffeine less expensive per dose than the individual herbs used in the headache formulation?

O   Does synthetic caffeine qualify as a natural substance?

O   What percentage of Herbed Wellness customers will shun the new headache remedy if it contains caffeine?

Step 1: Identify the Question Type

The phrase "most useful in evaluating the claim" tells you that this is an Evaluation question. Evaluation questions are very similar to Strengthen/Weaken questions: you must find the answer choice that impacts the validity of the argument's conclusion. This question specifically asks you to evaluate the claim that caffeine will be effective in relieving headaches among Herbed Wellness customers.

Step 2: Untangle the Stimulus

Evaluation questions are argument-based questions, so begin by identifying the conclusion and evidence. The conclusion of this argument is the rather lengthy last sentence, but the question stem directs you to a specific piece of that sentence: you are supposed to examine the claim that caffeine will provide effective headache relief to Herbed Wellness customers. The evidence for caffeine's effectiveness as a headache remedy is the study demonstrating that 58 percent of participants obtained headache relief from an amount of caffeine typically found in a cup of coffee.

Step 3: Predict the Answer

Whenever an argument contains a study or a sample, check to be certain that the sample is representative of the group it is supposed to shed light on. In this argument, the question becomes whether the study participants are representative of Herbed Wellness customers. The only bit of information you have about those customers is that they tend to avoid coffee. Did the study participants also habitually avoid coffee, then? If they did not, their behavior differs from that of Herbed Wellness customers, and the study does not provide a proper sample from which to draw a conclusion. It follows that in order to determine whether caffeine will indeed be an effective remedy for Herbed Wellness customers, you need to know whether or not the study participants also habitually avoided coffee.

Step 4: Evaluate the Choices

(B) matches the prediction and is the correct answer. If the study participants are habitual coffee drinkers, they are not representative of Herbed Wellness customers and the argument is weakened; thus, this information is important to know. **(A)** is incorrect because how long the headache relief provided by caffeine lasts is irrelevant to the argument, as are other headache remedies besides caffeine. **(C)** is incorrect because the question stem directs you to evaluate the claim of caffeine's efficacy, not its cost-effectiveness. **(D)** is incorrect because whether the caffeine the company uses is considered "natural" has no bearing on whether it is effective in relieving headaches. Finally, **(E)** is incorrect because whether customers actually buy the new headache remedy has no impact on its potential effectiveness in relieving their headaches.

9. **(A)**

A study of more than 5,000 people showed that those who lived at high latitudes, where UV exposure is minimal, had higher cancer rates than did those who lived near the equator, where UV exposure is, on average, far greater. One of the effects of UV radiation on humans is that it stimulates vitamin D manufacture in exposed skin. These results are consistent with other studies demonstrating that cancer patients often have lower than average vitamin D levels. Therefore, high blood levels of vitamin D reduce the risk of cancer in humans.

The answer to which of the following questions would be most useful to know in order to evaluate the validity of the argument's conclusion?

O   Does seasonal affective disorder, experienced more frequently by those living at high latitudes than by those living at the equator, predispose its sufferers to cancer?

O   Do high blood levels of vitamin D reduce the incidence of the common cold?

O   Can blood levels of vitamin D be raised through supplementation, thus reducing the risk of sunburn due to UV exposure?

O   Does exposure to UV radiation prevent cancer in other mammals, such as laboratory rats?

O   Are wintertime low vitamin D levels responsible for the flu season phenomenon?

Step 1: Identify the Question Type

The word "evaluate" indicates that this is an Evaluation question. The correct answer will contain a question relevant to the strength of the conclusion. Like Assumption, Strengthen, Weaken, and Flaw questions, Evaluation questions are built around assumptions in the stimuli.

Step 2: Untangle the Stimulus

Begin by identifying the conclusion, evidence, and assumption(s). The conclusion is signaled by the word "[t]herefore": high vitamin D levels reduce human cancer risk. The evidence comes in two main parts. First, the sun stimulates vitamin D production. People who live near the equator, where it's sunny, have lower cancer rates than do people who live in high latitudes and get less sun. Second, people suffering from cancer have unusually low vitamin D levels.

The author makes several assumptions here. One is that people living at higher latitudes have lower blood vitamin D levels. You know that people at high latitudes get less sun—but it's possible that their UV-related vitamin D deficit is offset by some other factor. The next assumption is that differing vitamin D levels, if in fact they do differ between people at high and low latitudes, contribute to the differing cancer rates in these populations. Third, the author assumes that the low vitamin D levels observed in cancer patients are not an effect of the cancer or of treatment for the cancer. Finally, the author assumes that there are no other differences between people in high latitudes and people in low latitudes that could affect their cancer risk.

Step 3: Predict the Answer

Whenever an argument includes a causal conclusion (*X* caused *Y*), consider two possibilities: an alternative cause (*Z* caused *Y*) or a reversal of causality (*Y* caused *X*). In this case, both possibilities could be relevant. To assess the strength of the argument, you would want to know, first, whether some factor unrelated to vitamin D could account for the difference in cancer rates between people at high and low latitudes (that's an alternative cause). Second, you would want to know whether the low levels of vitamin D observed in cancer sufferers were a cause of the cancer, as opposed to an effect of the cancer (that's a reversal of causality). An answer choice that addresses either of these two issues is correct.

Step 4: Evaluate the Choices

(A) matches the prediction and is the correct answer. If seasonal affective disorder does predispose humans to cancer, the conclusion that a low vitamin D level is responsible is greatly weakened. On the other hand, if seasonal affective disorder has no impact on cancer rates, then an alternative cause is ruled out, and the conclusion that vitamin D controls cancer risk is strengthened. **(B)** is irrelevant to the argument, which concerns cancer risk, not the risk of contracting a common cold. The method of raising vitamin D levels mentioned in **(C)** is likewise irrelevant, as are the "other mammals" mentioned in **(D)** and the "flu season phenomenon" mentioned in **(E)**.

10. (C)

Our legislature is considering passing legislation to ban skateboarding on city streets, citing safety concerns. However, a review of public health records reveals that the legislature's concern is misplaced. Each year, many more people are injured while jogging than are injured while skateboarding. So in fact, skateboarding is safer than jogging.

Which of the following indicates a flaw in the reasoning above?

O   It fails to distinguish professional skateboarders who attempt very dangerous maneuvers from amateurs who are comparatively cautious.

O   It assumes without warrant that no one who skateboards also jogs.

O   It fails to consider the number of people who skateboard as compared with the number of people who jog.

O   It ignores the possibility that other activities cause even more injuries than either skateboarding or jogging.

O   It fails to address the issue and instead attacks the character of the legislature.

Step 1: Identify the Question Type

The word "flaw" in the question stem indicates that this is a Flaw question. You'll be looking for the argument's faulty assumption.

Step 2: Untangle the Stimulus

In Flaw questions, just as in Assumption questions, you need to identify the argument's conclusion and evidence. In this argument, the conclusion is the final sentence: skateboarding is safer than jogging. The evidence is that more people are injured while jogging than while skateboarding.

Step 3: Predict the Answer

In Flaw questions, expect that the conclusion will not follow logically from the evidence because the author makes an inappropriate assumption. Here, the author incorrectly assumes that a higher number of people injured means a higher percentage of people injured, which is not necessarily the case. Picking numbers clarifies the issue. Let's say that 100 people skateboard in a given city, while 10,000 people jog. In that case, if 200 people are injured by jogging while only 10 are injured by skateboarding, jogging would actually be the far safer sport because 2 percent of joggers but 10 percent of skateboarders have sustained injuries. The flaw in the argument, then, is that it fails to provide you with the relative numbers of joggers versus skateboarders.

Step 4: Evaluate the Choices

(C) matches the prediction and is correct. **(A)** is an irrelevant comparison between professional and amateur skateboarders. **(B)** is incorrect because the evidence explicitly states that more people are hurt while jogging than while skateboarding. Even if some people do engage in both activities, the conclusion is based on evidence about which activity they were doing when they were injured, so it makes no difference whether there is any overlap between joggers and skateboarders. **(D)** is incorrect because activities other than jogging and skateboarding are irrelevant to the stimulus. **(E)** is incorrect because there is no attack on anybody's character in the argument.

11. **(D)**

Solo concert pianists, by convention, are not permitted to use musical scores during their performances. However, most members of chamber groups and orchestras are permitted to use sheet music during performances and perform well as a result. Therefore, all solo concert pianists should also be allowed to consult their musical scores during performances.

The argument is most vulnerable to criticism on which of these grounds?

○ It overlooks the possibility that some solo concert pianists prefer performing without consulting musical scores.

○ It takes for granted that members of a chamber group or orchestra are less skilled than solo musicians and thus have more need for musical scores.

○ It overlooks the possibility that some solo concert pianists have broken with tradition and used musical scores during their performances.

○ It takes for granted that a solo concert pianist would use a musical score in the same way as does a member of a chamber group or orchestra.

○ It overlooks the possibility that performing in an orchestra is difficult despite the ability to use a musical score during the performance.

Step 1: Identify the Question Type

The question asks how the argument is "vulnerable to criticism," so this is a Flaw question.

Step 2: Untangle the Stimulus

The author concludes that solo concert pianists should be allowed to use musical scores during their performances. The author supports this conclusion by drawing an analogy: members of chamber groups and orchestras are allowed to consult musical scores during their performances and perform well as a result.

Step 3: Predict the Answer

Flaws in arguments arise from an author's faulty assumptions. In an argument that relies on an analogy, such as this one, the assumption is that the two things being compared are sufficiently alike. Predict that the correct answer will state that the author has overlooked a relevant difference between solo pianists and performers in ensembles.

Step 4: Evaluate the Choices

(D) reflects the prediction and is correct. If a pianist would not use a score in the same way as, say, a violinist in an orchestra, then the analogy the argument relies on is not valid. As for **(A)**, it doesn't matter to the argument whether or not solo concert pianists prefer using musical scores; the author's argument states that they should be allowed to use them because they would perform better if they did. **(B)** is an irrelevant comparison; the argument does not rely on the relative skill levels of the two kinds of musicians. If anything, the author would take for granted that solo pianists are less skilled, since that might explain why they should be allowed to use sheet music. **(C)** mentions that some solo concert pianists may have used musical scores even though they're not supposed to; however, the author is arguing that these musicians *should* be allowed to perform with a score in front of them. **(E)** is incorrect because the author's assumption is that performing is less difficult with scores than without, not that it is easy.

12. (E)

At a large manufacturing corporation, the ratio of the annual job-related injury insurance premium per employee to average employee annual net pay increased between 1978 and 2003. Yet, the annual number of job-related injuries per employee during that time decreased by more than 30 percent.

Which of the following, if true, best explains the discrepancy outlined above?

O   From 1978 to 2003, the severity of job-related injuries at the corporation decreased significantly due to compliance with new workplace safety rules.

O   The number of employees at the corporation decreased between 1978 and 2003.

O   During the 1978–2003 period, inflation significantly eroded the purchasing power of the dollar.

O   The corporation did not change its insurance provider during the 1978–2003 period.

O   Between 1978 and 2003, health care costs per job-related injury rose sharply, pressuring insurance providers to raise premiums.

Step 1: Identify the Question Type

The phrase "explain the discrepancy" indicates that this is an Explain question. Your task will be to resolve an apparent contradiction in the stimulus.

Step 2: Untangle the Stimulus

Explain questions typically do not involve arguments. Rather, the stimulus will present you with two seemingly contradictory statements. Your job is to reconcile them without changing any of the information you are given. Here, the apparent contradiction is that, between 1978 and 2003, the cost of insurance premiums came to represent a greater proportion of workers' net pay. Over that same period, the number of job-related injuries per employee decreased. You would expect premiums to drop as the risk of injury drops; you need to explain the fact that they instead went up. It may also be the case that wages went down, while insurance premiums stayed the same, causing the ratio of insurance premiums to net pay to be higher.

Step 3: Predict the Answer

There must be some reason, unrelated to the number of workplace injuries, for the increase in the ratio of insurance premiums to net pay. Insurance premiums are typically tied to health care costs. So it may be that those job-related injuries that occurred in 2003 were more expensive to treat than those that occurred in 1978, either because those that occurred in 2003 were more severe or because diagnostic or other medical costs per injury increased during the stated time period.

Step 4: Evaluate the Choices

(E) matches the prediction exactly: the cost of treating an average workplace injury went way up. This would cause premiums to rise even if fewer workers were getting hurt on the job. (E) is the correct answer. (A) is incorrect because it is the opposite of what you want, or a 180. If the severity as well as the number of injuries decreased, then you would expect treatment costs, and thus insurance premiums, to decrease as well. (B) is incorrect because you're given the insurance premium per employee as well as the injury rate per employee. You don't have to calculate either of those numbers, so the actual number of workers employed by the manufacturing corporation is not relevant. (C) may sound tempting because inflation could certainly cause insurance premiums to increase, but it should also cause wages to increase at a similar rate. Therefore, since what is increasing is the ratio of the insurance premium to net pay, inflation is irrelevant. **(D)** is incorrect because, like **(A)**, it is the opposite of what you need. If the company had changed its insurance provider, that might account for the increased premiums. But if the company retained the same provider, you would expect the premiums to remain the same.

13. (D)

A certain town's pizza shop initiated an advertising campaign to bring in new customers and increase sales in December. The advertising campaign consisted of sending emails that promoted a two-for-one deal on sheet pizzas. Even though the pizza shop sent out thousands of these email advertisements, sales remained about the same in December as they had been in previous months.

Which of the following, if true, most helps to explain the apparent discrepancy between the volume of advertisements and the volume of sales?

- ○ The emails did not list every type of pizza on the pizza shop's menu.
- ○ In December, a new coffee shop opened in the same neighborhood as the pizza shop.
- ○ Not every resident in the pizza shop's delivery area had an email address.
- ○ The pizza shop had email addresses only for customers who were members of its rewards club, which offers members weekly specials.
- ○ The other two pizza shops in town specialize in gourmet pizzas, which are more expensive on average than items on this pizza shop's menu.

Step 1: Identify the Question Type

The question stem asks you to "explain the apparent discrepancy," so this is an Explain question. Furthermore, you know from the question stem that the mystery will involve advertisements and sales.

Step 2: Untangle the Stimulus

The stimulus should be viewed as a set of statements that present an apparent contradiction. The keywords "Even though" in the stimulus indicate a contrast or discrepancy. The discrepancy here is that pizza sales in December did not increase despite an increase in the number of emailed advertisements.

Step 3: Predict the Answer

The correct answer must explain why sales remained flat despite the fact that thousands of people were offered a two-for-one deal on sheet pizzas. There may be some reason this deal was unappealing to the people who received the emails. Alternatively, perhaps many people who took advantage of the sale would normally have bought pizzas at full price, so overall revenues did not increase.

Step 4: Evaluate the Choices

(D) states that the emails were sent only to customers who were already loyal customers and already getting special deals on pizza. This explains why they did not increase their pizza purchases and is the correct answer. **(A)** does not account for the advertisement's lack of effect on sales because the emails promoted a special price and not the variety of pizzas available. **(B)** mentions that a new coffee shop opened nearby, but because it's a very different kind of restaurant, it would not be a direct competitor to the pizza shop. Therefore, its presence does not explain the lack of appeal of two-for-one pizzas. The fact that some people in the area don't have email doesn't explain why the advertisement failed to attract those who do have email, so **(C)** doesn't explain the mystery. **(E)** mentions that the two other pizza shops in town offer more expensive gourmet pizzas. This would explain why not everyone would buy pizza at this pizza shop, but it doesn't explain why emails offering a special deal failed to attract more business from people who don't want more expensive pizza.

14. (E)

The number of wild tigers living in India dropped from an estimated 40,000 at the turn of the century to 2,000 in 1970. Although determined conservation efforts have halted the precipitous decline, the survival of the wild tiger in India is uncertain even now. Still, it is beyond doubt that if the tiger is to survive in the wild at all, its best chance is in India.

The statements above, if true, support which of the following?

○   There are now more than 2,000 wild tigers surviving in India.

○   There are fewer than 2,000 wild tigers living in the wild outside of India.

○   If tigers fail to survive in the wild in India, the species will become extinct.

○   It is impossible for a tiger raised in captivity to ever successfully adapt to life in the wild.

○   The survival of the wild tiger in countries other than India is also endangered.

Step 1: Identify the Question Type

Whenever you are asked to make a deduction based on the stimulus, you have an Inference question.

Step 2: Untangle the Stimulus

Instead of looking for evidence and conclusion, take the statements in the stimulus at face value and paraphrase them to make sure you understand the situation they describe. Here you're told that conservation efforts have stopped the decline of wild tigers in India, the number of which decreased from 40,000 in 1900 to 2,000 in 1970. Moreover, while tigers are still endangered in India, that country is nonetheless the wild tiger's best chance for survival.

Step 3: Predict the Answer

The answer to an Inference question is often difficult to predict because there are any number of deductions you might make from the stimulus. Instead, you must go through the answer choices, carefully checking each against the information in the stimulus, until you find the one that must be true based only on the information you are given.

Step 4: Evaluate the Choices

Because **(E)** states a deduction you can draw from the stimulus, it is correct. Indeed, the stimulus tells you that the wild tiger's best chance of survival is in India, even though it is endangered there. It follows that it must be endangered elsewhere as well. **(A)** cannot be the correct answer because the stimulus mentions nothing about the number of wild tigers existing in India at the present time; you only have numbers for 1900 and 1970. **(B)** is also incorrect because it mentions the number of tigers living outside India, about which you have no information. You cannot glean an inference this precise from this stimulus. For example, it's possible that Malaysia and Thailand each have 900 wild tigers, but it's also possible that Thailand has 3,000 but is losing 500 a year. You can't infer the statement in **(B)** without bringing in imagined outside information. **(C)** is too extreme. The stimulus does say that India is the best chance of the wild tiger's survival, but it does not go so far as to say that the species will go "extinct" if it doesn't survive in the wild; perhaps tigers could be bred in zoos. **(D)** is incorrect because the stimulus gives no information about tigers raised in captivity.

15. **(E)**

A local department store hires college students for one month every spring to audit its unsold inventory. It costs the department store 20 percent less to pay wages to students than it would cost to hire outside auditors from a temporary service. Even after factoring in the costs of training and insuring the students against work-related injury, the department store spends less money by hiring its own auditors than it would by hiring auditors from the temporary service.

The statements above, if true, best support which of the following assertions?

O   The amount spent on insurance for college-student auditors is more than 20 percent of the cost of paying the college students' basic wages.

O   It takes 20 percent less time for the college students to audit the unsold inventory than it does for the outside auditors.

O   The department store pays its college-student auditors 20 percent less than the temporary service pays its auditors.

O   By hiring college students, the department store will cause 20 percent of the auditors at the temporary service to lose their jobs.

O   The cost of training its own college-student auditors is less than 20 percent of the cost of hiring auditors from the temporary service.

Step 1: Identify the Question Type

Since the question stem is asking you to make an assertion supported by the statements in the stimulus, this is an Inference question.

Step 2: Untangle the Stimulus

Sometimes Critical Reasoning questions look like math word problems. Any time you see numbers and statistics, you need to pay close attention, especially to the distinction between actual numbers and percentages. For this question, the stimulus confirms that what the department store pays student auditors in wages is 20 percent less than the cost of hiring outside auditors. You also know that even after you add the costs of training and insuring the students (costs not involved with hiring outside auditors), the cost to the store is still less than hiring the outside auditors.

Step 3: Predict the Answer

Based on the statements here, it must be true that the costs of training and insuring the students are not more than 20 percent of the cost of hiring the outside auditors. If they were, then the 20 percent savings in wages would be outweighed by those extra costs, and hiring outside auditors would be cheaper.

Step 4: Evaluate the Choices

(E) matches the prediction and is the correct answer. **(A)** mentions the relationship between the students' wages and the cost of their insurance, but this relationship is not mentioned in the stimulus, so you can't infer anything about it. By the same token, **(B)** can be eliminated because it discusses the amount of time the employees take to audit the inventory, when the stimulus only concerns the cost to the department store. **(C)** distorts the 20 percent statistic from the stimulus. That statistic compares what the department store spends on student employees to what the store spends on outside auditors. What the temp service pays the auditors is totally irrelevant. **(D)** is yet another distortion of the 20 percent statistic. You can't say for sure that *any* of the outside auditors will lose their jobs if they are not hired by the department store.

16. **(C)**

For many years, polls have shown that most American taxpayers fear the fines and late fees that can follow an Internal Revenue Service (IRS) audit. The move to fashion a friendlier public image for the IRS in order to increase the operating efficiency of the agency may be counterproductive because _____.

- ○ many taxpayers are only concerned with receiving their refund checks
- ○ a friendlier public image for the IRS will increase voluntary compliance with tax laws
- ○ the timely collection of taxes could not be maintained if most taxpayers did not have a respectful fear of the IRS
- ○ fewer taxpayers fear the IRS today than feared it 10 years ago
- ○ collecting delinquent taxes does not necessarily cost the government more than collecting taxes on time

Step 1: Identify the Question Type

Questions that ask you to fill in a blank in a stimulus can be considered Inference questions, since you must complete the author's line of reasoning based on the information given.

Step 2: Untangle the Stimulus

In this stimulus, the author asserts that the IRS's attempt to be friendlier in order to increase its operating efficiency may be counterproductive. The author also cites polls indicating that a majority of taxpayers fear the fines and fees accompanying an IRS audit. The blank is preceded by the word "because," so what follows must be evidence that supports the author's opinion. Thus, you can also treat this question as a Strengthen question.

Step 3: Predict the Answer

The word "counterproductive" should make you look for an answer that shows why the new program will not work. Given what the author has already said, think about what reason the author is likely to give for why being friendlier could compromise the IRS's operating efficiency rather than enhance it. Perhaps taxpayers won't be as scared as the author describes them in the first sentence.

Step 4: Evaluate the Choices

(C) tells you that in order to ensure the timely collection of taxes, taxpayers need to have some fear of the IRS. If the IRS becomes too friendly and taxpayers no longer fear the IRS, then the timely collection of taxes will suffer. And that of course would defeat the IRS's stated goal of increasing its operating efficiency. Therefore, **(C)** is correct. **(A)** introduces the idea of refund checks, which has no bearing on an argument about the IRS being able to collect taxes efficiently. **(B)** suggests that the IRS wouldn't have to audit quite as much, since more people will cooperate. This would make the IRS's plan successful, not counterproductive. As for **(D)**, it's irrelevant whether or not more people feared the IRS 10 years ago. If people still fear the IRS, then becoming friendlier may still be productive. **(E)** suggests that becoming friendlier wouldn't necessarily help the IRS save money and efficiency, but it certainly doesn't suggest that becoming friendlier might cost the agency anything, either.

17. **(E)**

An increased number of candidates running for a political position, one opinion says, is likely to raise the percentage of voters. **The larger the number of candidates who run for a given position, the better the chances that a voter will find a candidate that adequately represents his or her political opinions.** In the reality of the political world, however, the opposite is likely to be the case. **As more candidates enter the election process, the differences between their declared positions on political matters tend to become less obvious.**

In the argument given, the two portions in **boldface** play which of the following roles?

- O The first explains an opinion that was raised, and the second further supports that opinion by elaborating on the explanation.

- O The first raises an opinion, and the second raises another opinion contrary to the first opinion.

- O The first explains an opinion that was raised, and the second raises another opinion contrary to the first opinion.

- O The first raises an opinion, and the second supplies evidence that supports that opinion.

- O The first explains an opinion that was raised, and the second undermines that opinion by contradicting the explanation.

Step 1: Identify the Question Type

Any question that asks you to identify the roles played by statements in boldface is a Bolded Statement question. Your task is to find the structure of the stimulus and to determine the structural functions of the statements in bold type.

Step 2: Untangle the Stimulus

This stimulus includes two contradictory opinions: the author's opinion, stated in the third sentence, and the "one opinion" the author is arguing against (call this the opponent's opinion), stated in the first sentence. The opponent believes that the more candidates there are running for office, the more voters will turn out at the polls. The first bolded statement serves as the opponent's evidence: more voters will turn out because the more candidates there are, the more likely voters are to find one they like and consequently want to vote for. The author counters the opponent, implying that in actual practice, the more candidates there are, the fewer voters will turn out. The second bolded statement serves as the author's evidence: the more candidates there are, the more alike they all look to voters.

Step 3: Predict the Answer

Both bolded statements, then, are evidence—the first for the opponent's position and the second for the author's.

Step 4: Evaluate the Choices

(E) matches the prediction and is correct, though the wording of this choice makes it a bit tricky. The first bolded statement definitely explains why the opponent holds the position he does. So far, so good. You know that the second bolded statement is the author's evidence. Because the author is contradicting the opponent, the author's evidence does in fact serve to "undermine" the opponent's view. Finally, the second bolded statement directly contradicts the first bolded statement. The first says that the more candidates there are, the more likely a voter will be to find one she likes. The second says that the more candidates there are, the more similar they start to seem, which implies that it will be more difficult for voters to find candidates they like. It follows that the final piece of **(E)**, "by contradicting [the first bolded statement]," is also correct. **(A)** is incorrect because the second bolded statement supports the author's view, not the opponent's. **(B)** is incorrect because both bolded statements are evidence for an opinion, not the opinion itself. **(C)** is incorrect because the second statement is, again, evidence for an opinion, not the opinion itself. **(D)** is incorrect because the first bolded statement is evidence, and the second is evidence for the author, not the opponent.

18. **(C)**

Social worker: Typically, physicians in the United States who promote specialized services do not charge as much as do physicians who do not promote their services at all. **Every time physicians are allowed to promote without restriction, the number of physicians promoting their specialty service has gone up, and patients have paid less for these consultations.** Recent changes in regulations of such promotions have lifted the requirement that the amount charged for a consultation appear on the promotion. An effect of this change will be that physicians will no longer be inclined to reduce their fees when they start to promote, and **many physicians who promote their services will increase their charges to patients.**

In the above argument, the two parts in **boldface** play which of the following roles?

○ The first makes a general claim that the social worker takes to be the truth; the second is proposed as an outcome resulting from the general claim's truth.

○ The first supplies an action and a consequence that the social worker argues will be replicated; the second recognizes a situation that would cause the action and consequence to fall apart.

○ The first supplies an action and a consequence that the social worker perceives will no longer hold true; the second gives an explanation to support that perception.

○ The first provides clarification that the social worker presents in advocacy of a prediction; the second is that prediction.

○ The first recognizes a perspective that opposes the point that the social worker advocates; the second is that point.

Step 1: Identify the Question Type

This is definitely a Bolded Statement question since it asks you to identify the roles played in the argument by the statements in boldface.

Step 2: Untangle the Stimulus

The social worker begins by stating that patients pay less for consultations with doctors who promote their specialties. Whenever doctors have been allowed to promote without restriction, more doctors have promoted, and patients have paid less. But under the new laws, the ads no longer have to say how much consultations cost. The social worker thinks this change means patients will pay more for care. The social worker asserts that doctors who promote their specialties will raise their fees and overall costs for patients will rise.

Step 3: Predict the Answer

The first boldface statement describes a cause-and-effect relationship that has existed in the past, but will no longer exist. The second statement shows why this relationship is unlikely to exist in the future.

Step 4: Evaluate the Choices

According to **(C)**, the first of the two bolded statements "supplies an action and a consequence"—i.e., a cause and an effect—that the author believes "will no longer hold true" in the future. **(C)** says that the second bolded statement provides evidence that this cause-effect relationship will not continue. This matches the prediction straight down the line, making **(C)** correct. **(A)** is incorrect because the second bolded statement does not describe "an outcome resulting from" the truth of the first bolded statement. **(B)** mischaracterizes the first bolded statement; the social worker does not believe that the cause-effect relationship "will be replicated." **(D)** inaccurately states that the first statement is evidence in support of the second statement. And **(E)** doesn't work, since nobody is arguing against the social worker's position.

19. (B)

Our architecture schools must be doing something wrong. Almost monthly we hear of domes and walkways collapsing in public places, causing serious injuries. In their pursuit of some dubious aesthetic, architects design buildings that sway, crumble, and even shed windows into our cities' streets. This kind of incompetence will disappear only when the curricula of our architecture schools devote less time to so-called artistic considerations and more time to the basics of good design.

Which of the following, if true, would most seriously weaken the argument above?

- ○ All architecture students are given training in basic physics and mechanics.
- ○ Most of the problems with modern buildings stem from poor construction rather than poor design.
- ○ Less than 50 percent of the curriculum at most architecture schools is devoted to aesthetics.
- ○ Most buildings manage to stay in place well past their projected life expectancies.
- ○ Architects study as long and as intensively as most other professionals.

Step 1: Identify the Question Type

The phrase "most seriously weaken" in the question stem tells you that you have a Weaken question.

Step 2: Untangle the Stimulus

The stimulus will contain an argument; you need to pick out the conclusion, evidence, and assumption. The conclusion is the last sentence, which states that a shift away from aesthetics in architecture schools' curricula is necessary for buildings to be more soundly constructed. The evidence is the frequency with which parts of buildings collapse. Note that this is a causal argument: the author assumes that architecture schools' artistic considerations, rather than something else, are directly responsible for the crumbling buildings because the time devoted to them prevents architects from learning good design principles.

Step 3: Predict the Answer

The correct answer for this Weaken question will contradict the assumption that aesthetic considerations are causing buildings to be poorly designed and thus to crumble. Simply scan the choices for one that provides an alternate cause for the decay of the city's buildings.

Step 4: Evaluate the Choices

(B) provides an alternate cause, poor building construction, and is thus the correct answer. **(A)** is irrelevant. Even if students are currently instructed in basic physics and mechanics, they may not be spending enough time learning good design principles. **(C)** is incorrect because you have no information to indicate how great a percentage of time spent studying aesthetics the author of this argument would consider too much. Perhaps "less than 50 percent" is still too much. **(D)** is incorrect because it fails to provide any new and relevant information. The author merely complains that some buildings are collapsing. The fact that "most" are not collapsing does not take away the fact that some are falling down. Finally, **(E)** is an irrelevant comparison between architects and other professionals.

20. (D)

Studies have shown that the number of books read in elementary school is correlated with later academic success. In the past year, local elementary students have read an average of 10 fewer books than the nationwide elementary student average of 35 books per year, while 90 percent of those local students report playing sports at least twice a week. If these students participated less in sports, they would read more books.

Which of the following, if true, would most effectively weaken the argument?

○ A nationwide survey of middle school students determined that if given a choice between reading a book and playing a sport, most of these students would choose reading a book.

○ Participating in sports in elementary school has been shown to be as highly correlated as reading books to later academic success.

○ The attention spans of elementary school students do not allow these children to read for as long as older students and adults are expected to read.

○ The local elementary school is in a rural area in which there is no bookstore or public library and Internet service is unreliable.

○ Some local elementary school students who used to enjoy reading have said they no longer choose to read books, preferring to play sports at least twice a week.

Step 1: Identify the Question Type

Since the word "weaken" appears in the question stem, this is a Weaken question.

Step 2: Untangle the Stimulus

The conclusion is that if the local elementary school students played sports less, they would read more books. The evidence is that almost all of these students play sports two or more times a week, while the average number of books they read is lower than the national average. The author assumes that playing sports is causing students to read relatively fewer books. Note that the first sentence of the stimulus functions as background information rather than as evidence; it tells you why reading books might be important, but it is not used to support the claim that the students would read more books if they played sports less.

Step 3: Predict the Answer

Whenever you're asked to weaken a causal argument, consider the three classic alternative explanations: (1) cause and effect may be reversed ("reading fewer books leads to playing sports more often"), (2) there may be an alternative cause of the effect ("many local students have little access to books"), or (3) the apparent link between two events is coincidental ("whatever the cause of reading fewer books, it isn't playing sports"). You don't know exactly what the right answer will say, but you can expect it to fall into one of these three categories.

Step 4: Evaluate the Choices

(D) weakens the argument by proposing another reason local children don't read books and do play sports. Since books are hard to get, if the children weren't allowed to play sports, they might just be bored rather than read more. Thus, **(D)** is correct. **(A)** is irrelevant because the argument is concerned with local elementary school students, not middle school students from across the country. The author's conclusion is about what would cause students to read more books, not about the effect their not reading books will eventually have, so **(B)** does not weaken the argument. **(C)** presents an irrelevant comparison. The argument specifically compares local elementary school students to a national population of elementary school students, so how younger children compare to older readers is irrelevant. **(E)** is a 180. It strengthens the argument, suggesting that indeed playing sports caused these students to read fewer books.

EXPLANATIONS

21. (A)

Attempts to blame the mayor's policies for the growing inequality of wages are misguided. The sharp growth in the gap in earnings between college and high school graduates in this city during the past decade resulted from overall technological trends that favored the skills of more educated workers. The mayor's response to this problem cannot be criticized, as it would hardly be reasonable to expect him to attempt to slow the forces of technology.

Which of the following, if true, casts the most serious doubt on the conclusion drawn in the last sentence above?

O   The mayor could have initiated policies that would have made it easier for less-educated workers to receive the education necessary for better-paying jobs.

O   Rather than cutting the education budget, the mayor could have increased the amount of staff and funding devoted to locating employment for graduating high school seniors.

O   The mayor could have attempted to generate more demand for products from industries that paid high blue-collar wages.

O   Instead of reducing the tax rate on the wealthiest earners, the mayor could have ensured that they shouldered a greater share of the total tax burden.

O   The mayor could have attempted to protect the earnings of city workers by instituting policies designed to reduce competition from foreign industries.

Step 1: Identify the Question Type

When you're asked to "cast doubt" on an argument, you're being asked to weaken it.

Step 2: Untangle the Stimulus

The argument concludes that the mayor's policies are not responsible for the growing inequality of wages in the city. The argument instead attempts to blame overall technological trends that favored the skills of more educated workers and thus enabled college graduates to earn more money than high school grads.

Step 3: Predict the Answer

To weaken an argument in which an author says that *X* did *not* cause *Y*, think about strengthening the idea that *X did* cause *Y*. Since the author is attempting to blame technological trends and not the mayor's policies, try to find an answer indicating that the mayor's policies did play a role.

Step 4: Evaluate the Choices

This is exactly what **(A)** does, making **(A)** the correct answer. If the mayor's policies neglected to even the playing field between better-educated workers and their less-educated counterparts, then the mayor does share some of the responsibility for the wage gap, and the author's argument is severely impaired. **(B)** misses the point. The point is not that the less-educated workers are unemployed; it's that the jobs they do have don't pay as much as those of better-educated workers. **(C)** takes too many leaps to be correct. In order to choose **(C)**, you'd have to assume that less-educated workers were all concentrated in blue-collar jobs, and you'd also have to assume that creating more demand for products from those blue-collar industries would result in higher wages for blue-collar employees. **(D)** introduces the tax rate, which is irrelevant to the argument, and **(E)** deals with city workers, which doesn't help or hurt the argument because city workers aren't necessarily better or less educated than other workers, so you don't know whether city workers are even a part of the wage gap problem.

22. (E)

Loneliness is commonly reported in elderly populations. A study of elderly people found that those who owned dogs reported feeling less lonely than those who did not own dogs. Clearly, an elderly person who adopts a pet will be less likely to suffer feelings of loneliness than an elderly person without a pet.

Which of the following, if true, would most strengthen the argument above?

○ Owning a pet has been linked to several health benefits, including lower blood pressure.

○ Some people feel that cats do not engage socially with their owners as much as dogs do.

○ The number of elderly people who own pets is projected to rise in the coming years.

○ A large percentage of elderly dog owners report taking their dogs for walks and to dog parks.

○ Pets other than dogs provide the same benefits of companionship as do dogs.

Step 1: Identify the Question Type

The word "strengthen" indicates that you should read to identify the author's conclusion and evidence, then think about what additional evidence would support the argument's conclusion, making its central assumption more likely to be true.

Step 2: Untangle the Stimulus

The conclusion is signaled by the keyword "Clearly" in the last sentence: an elderly person with a pet is less likely to be lonely than one without a pet. The evidence is a study that found less loneliness in elderly dog owners than in elderly non–dog owners.

Step 3: Predict the Answer

Whenever an argument references a sample or a study, suspect a representativeness issue. The heart of representativeness is the assumption that a group mentioned in the evidence is representative of the group mentioned in the conclusion. In this argument, the author is assuming that the benefit conferred by dogs upon elderly owners—namely the easing of loneliness—is representative of the benefit conferred on elderly owners by pets of any kind. To strengthen the argument, look for the answer choice that supports this assumption.

Step 4: Evaluate the Choices

(E) matches the prediction and is correct. **(A)** is incorrect because the argument is only about whether owning a pet will help with loneliness; other benefits of owning pets are irrelevant. If **(B)** said that cats actually don't engage socially with their owners as much as dogs, this choice would weaken the argument (not strengthen it) by providing evidence that not all pets are as good as dogs at alleviating loneliness. Since it talks only about how some people perceive cats, it has no effect on the argument; since it does not strengthen the argument, it can be eliminated. **(C)** is incorrect because ownership projections are irrelevant to the assumption. Finally, **(D)** provides more evidence for the utility of dogs as companion animals and possible facilitators of companionship (one might conceivably meet other people while walking the dog or at the dog park), but it does not support the conclusion about the efficacy of pets in general.

23. (C)

A social worker surveyed 200 women, each of whom had recently given birth to her first child. Half of the women surveyed had chosen to give birth in a hospital or obstetrics clinic; the other half had chosen to give birth at home under the care of certified midwives. Of the 100 births that occurred at home, only 5 presented substantial complications, whereas 17 of the hospital births presented substantial complications. The social worker concluded from the survey that the home is actually a safer environment in which to give birth than a hospital or clinic.

Which of the following, if true, most seriously calls the social worker's conclusion into question?

O   Women who give birth in hospitals and clinics often have shorter periods of labor than do women who give birth at home.

O   Many obstetricians discourage patients from giving birth at home.

O   All of the women in the study who had been diagnosed as having a high possibility of delivery complications elected to give birth in a hospital.

O   Women who give birth at home tend to experience less stress during labor than women who deliver in hospitals.

O   Pregnant doctors prefer giving birth in a hospital.

Step 1: Identify the Question Type

Since you need to call the social worker's conclusion into question, you need to weaken it.

Step 2: Untangle the Stimulus

The social worker's conclusion is that it is safer to give birth at home than at a hospital or clinic. The evidence for this is a survey in which some women chose to give birth at a hospital and others chose home birth. Overall, the hospital births presented more substantial medical complications than did the home births.

Step 3: Predict the Answer

You can successfully undermine the social worker's conclusion if you undermine the evidence on which it's based, namely, the study. If you find an answer choice that tells you that the survey is invalid or that the sample studied in the survey is unrepresentative, then any conclusion based on the survey would be in doubt.

Step 4: Evaluate the Choices

(C) tells you that the hospital births presented more complications simply because the women who chose to give birth at the hospital were predisposed to complications. This suggests that these women would have had complications no matter where they gave birth, which undermines the conclusion that a hospital is less safe than a home as a place to give birth. Thus, **(C)** is the correct answer. **(A)** is irrelevant. A shorter labor can still be more dangerous, so this isn't a valid weakener. Just because obstetricians discourage home birth, as **(B)** says, doesn't mean that the home is more or less safe than a hospital; there could be plenty of reasons why the obstetricians would discourage home birth. **(D)** strengthens the argument by telling you that women who give birth at home experience less stress, which could potentially make their births go more smoothly. **(E)** also has no bearing on the argument. Pregnant doctors might prefer to give birth in a hospital simply because they are more familiar with the hospital environment, not because a hospital is necessarily safer.

24. (A)

A team of pediatricians recently announced that pet birds are more likely to bite children under age 13 than people of any other age group. The team's finding was based on a study showing that the majority of all bird bites requiring medical attention involved children under 13. The study also found that the birds most likely to bite are cockatiels and parakeets.

Which of the following, if true, would most weaken the pediatricians' conclusion that birds are more likely to bite children under age 13 than people of any other age group?

○ More than half of bird bites not requiring medical attention, which exceed the number requiring such attention, involve people aged 13 and older.

○ The majority of bird bites resulting in the death of the bitten person involve people aged 65 and older.

○ Many serious bird bites affecting children under age 13 are inflicted by birds other than cockatiels and parakeets.

○ Most bird bites in children under age 13 that require medical attention are far less serious than they initially appear.

○ Most parents can learn to treat bird bites effectively if they avail themselves of a small amount of medical information.

Step 1: Identify the Question Type

This stem contains a wealth of helpful information. Not only do you see the telltale keyword "weaken" indicating the question type, but the conclusion of the argument is stated directly in the stem. Part of your job is already done.

Step 2: Untangle the Stimulus

The conclusion of the pediatricians is that pet birds are more likely to bite young children than bite older people. The evidence for this is a study, which should ring alarm bells for representativeness issues. The study indicates that most bird-bite injuries that required medical attention were to young children.

Step 3: Predict the Answer

But not all bird bites necessarily require medical attention, so in order for this study's results to prove that birds are more likely to bite young children *overall*, you need proof that the bird bites requiring medical attention are representative of all bird bites. So to weaken this argument, find a choice that essentially says, "Bites that require medical attention are *not* representative of bites in general."

Step 4: Evaluate the Choices

You'll then be drawn to **(A)**: looking at *all* bird-bite injuries reveals that most of them don't require medical attention, and of those that don't, more than half of them are suffered by people over the age of 13. **(A)** indicates that birds are just as likely, if not more likely, to bite people over the age of 13 as to bite younger children. Thus, **(A)** is the correct answer. Just because senior citizens are more likely to die from bird bites, as **(B)** says, doesn't mean that they're more likely to be bitten in the first place. **(C)** improperly seizes on the last sentence of the argument, which is a tangential statement that has no bearing on the overall conclusion. **(D)** is off base because the argument deals with the likelihood that a bird will bite someone, not with the likelihood that the bite is serious. **(E)** commits a similar error by dealing with treatment; this argument is only concerned with the relative frequency of bird bites occurring in the first place and not with the treatment plans for bites that have already occurred.

25. (A)

A team of researchers at a university hospital has developed a chemical test that detects breast tumors in the early stages of development. In order to save lives, the researchers want to make the test a routine part of examinations at the hospital. However, a spokesperson for the hospital argued that because virtually all breast tumors are detectable by self-examination, the chemical test would have little impact on the breast cancer death rate.

Which of the following, if true, would most seriously weaken the hospital spokesperson's argument?

○ Fatal breast tumors are often not revealed by self-examination until it is too late for effective treatment.

○ Breast tumors are usually discovered at an earlier stage of development than are lung tumors.

○ Mammograms are currently in wide use as a breast cancer test and cost much less than the chemical test.

○ Because men are not typically victims of breast cancer, the new test would benefit only half of the population.

○ Most women learn how to check for signs of breast cancer from magazines and not from doctors.

Step 1: Identify the Question Type

In addition to using the word "weaken" to signal the question type, this question stem points you to the "spokesperson's argument."

Step 2: Untangle the Stimulus

The spokesperson's conclusion is a prediction that the chemical test will have little impact on the breast cancer death rate. The spokesperson's evidence is that virtually all breast tumors are detectable by self-examination.

Step 3: Predict the Answer

The spokesperson assumes that the chemical test has no advantage over self-examination. Because this is a Weaken question, you need the answer choice that contradicts this assumption—so scan for a choice that cites an advantage of the chemical test.

Step 4: Evaluate the Choices

(A) suggests a possible advantage of the chemical test and is the correct answer. The stimulus states that the chemical test "detects breast tumors in the early stages of development." If it is true that self-examination reveals those same tumors too late for effective treatment, then the chemical test might in fact have an impact on the breast cancer death rate, and the conclusion is weakened. **(B)** is an irrelevant comparison between breast tumors and lung tumors. **(C)** introduces a different diagnostic tool, mammograms, which are irrelevant to the question of whether the chemical test would have any positive impact relative to self-examination. **(D)** is incorrect because the fact that men typically do not contract breast cancer is irrelevant to the question of whether the chemical test would positively impact the breast cancer death rate. **(E)** is again irrelevant. Where women learn to do breast exams has no bearing on the assumption that the chemical test has no advantage over those exams.

26. **(B)**

Occupational safety advocate: Logging is one of the most dangerous occupations in the United States. A company has developed a chainsaw that will instantly shut off if there is kickback of the chain, which studies have shown to be the most common cause of chainsaw injuries. The logging industry should adopt this new chainsaw as standard equipment in order to prevent most of the logging-related deaths that occur each year.

Which of the following statements, if true, most seriously weakens the occupational safety advocate's argument?

- ○ Loggers are sometimes killed by problems with chainsaws other than the kickback of the chain.
- ○ Injuries from falling trees cause the vast majority of deaths in the logging industry.
- ○ The new chainsaw is inexpensive and easy to learn how to use.
- ○ There are other, equally safe chainsaws available, but the logging industry has not adopted them.
- ○ The chainsaw manufacturer's claims about its product are supported by a study conducted by a government agency.

Step 1: Identify the Question Type

The word "weakens" in the question stem tells you this is a Weaken question.

Step 2: Untangle the Stimulus

The argument you're asked to weaken claims that the logging industry should adopt a new chainsaw to prevent most of the logging-related deaths each year. The author's evidence is that this chainsaw shuts off if there is a kickback, thus preventing injuries. The author assumes that chainsaw injuries cause the majority of logging-related deaths.

Step 3: Predict the Answer

The word "should" means this conclusion is a proposal, so think about common problems with proposals on the GMAT. The author must assume that the proposed solution to the problem will work. However, if at least half of deaths in the logging industry are caused by something other than chainsaws, then greater chainsaw safety won't eliminate most logging industry deaths. Look in the choices for evidence that most deaths are not chainsaw related.

Step 4: Evaluate the Choices

(B) is a match for the prediction and is correct. If most deaths are caused by falling trees, not chainsaws, then safer chainsaws won't prevent the majority of deaths. Just the fact that fatal injuries are *sometimes* caused by something other than kickbacks isn't enough to say that the new chainsaw will not prevent *most* deaths. It might be that 99% of logging fatalities are the result of chainsaw kickbacks, in which case the argument is still valid. If anything, **(C)** might strengthen the argument. If the new chainsaw is cheap and easy to use, the industry might be more willing to embrace it, and then chainsaw injuries would decrease. Even so, this statement fails to connect chainsaw injuries to logging deaths. **(D)** is irrelevant, as the argument is not about any chainsaw other than the new one. And finally, **(E)** is similar to **(C)** in that it potentially strengthens the argument for adopting the chainsaw but still does not show that chainsaws cause deaths among loggers.

27. (C)

According to a recent study, advertisements in medical journals often contain misleading information about the effectiveness and safety of new prescription drugs. The medical researchers who wrote the study concluded that the advertisements could result in doctors' prescribing inappropriate drugs to their patients.

The researchers' conclusion would be most strengthened if which of the following were true?

O   Advertisements for new prescription drugs are an important source of revenue for medical journals.

O   Editors of medical journals are often unable to evaluate the claims made in advertisements for new prescription drugs.

O   Doctors rely on the advertisements as a source of information about new prescription drugs.

O   Advertisements for new prescription drugs are typically less accurate than medical journal articles evaluating those same drugs.

O   The Food and Drug Administration, the government agency responsible for drug regulation, reviews advertisements for new drugs only after the ads have already been printed.

Step 1: Identify the Question Type

The phrase "most strengthened" tells you that this is a Strengthen question.

Step 2: Untangle the Stimulus

The researchers' argument concludes with a prediction: doctors will prescribe inappropriate drugs to their patients. This is apparently because advertisements in medical journals often contain misleading information about certain drugs.

Step 3: Predict the Answer

To strengthen this argument, you want a choice that gives a reason or reasons why the prediction will come to pass. What circumstances would lead to inappropriate prescriptions? Since the inaccurate information comes from medical journals, doctors will probably be more likely to prescribe inappropriate drugs if they base their decisions on what they read in the journals.

Step 4: Evaluate the Choices

If doctors rely on the ads in medical journals to learn about new drugs, as **(C)** suggests, then inaccurate information could very well lead to faulty prescriptions. So, **(C)** is correct. **(A)** tells you why the journals carry the ads, but it doesn't strengthen the idea that doctors will use them to make inappropriate prescriptions. **(B)** could explain why the ads are published despite the inaccurate and misleading information contained in them, but like **(A)**, **(B)** does not provide a bridge to doctors' inappropriate prescriptions. **(D)** makes an irrelevant comparison between the accuracy of ads and that of articles. **(E)**, like **(B)**, explains how an ad can make it to print with inaccurate information, but **(E)** doesn't tell you how an inaccurate ad necessarily translates to a faulty prescription by a doctor, so **(E)** can't strengthen the researchers' prediction.

28. (E)

To avoid the appearance of conflicts of interest, the board of a major U.S. stock exchange is considering a new policy that would ban former top executives of the exchange from taking positions at publicly traded companies for a period of two years after leaving the stock exchange. Critics of the plan say the policy is unfair because it would likely prevent former top executives of the exchange from earning a decent living.

Which of the following statements, if true, would most strengthen the prediction made by the critics of the proposed company policy?

- ○ The labor union that represents most of the stock exchange's employees has made public statements that threaten a strike if the policy is adopted.
- ○ Former employees of the exchange most often work for publicly traded companies after leaving the exchange.
- ○ Low-level managers at the exchange have an average tenure of 13 years, one of the longest in the industry.
- ○ Low-level managers at the exchange most often leave their jobs for positions with the state or federal government.
- ○ Former top executives of the exchange have a particular set of skills such that they are usually only able to find work with publicly traded companies.

Step 1: Identify the Question Type

You're looking to strengthen the argument here—specifically the prediction made by the critics of a policy. So as you examine the stimulus, the critics' argument will be most helpful.

Step 2: Untangle the Stimulus

A new policy would ban former top executives of a major stock exchange from working for publicly traded companies for two years after leaving the exchange. Critics of the policy contend that the policy will prevent the top executives from earning a decent living.

Step 3: Predict the Answer

Since you're strengthening the prediction, look for an answer choice that makes it more likely that the former top execs can't earn a decent living. A good prediction is "something that explains why top executives must work at publicly traded companies in order to make a decent living."

Step 4: Evaluate the Choices

Choose **(E)**, which states that former top executives of the firm can usually only find work at publicly traded companies because of their particular skill set. If this were true, then a two-year ban on working for publicly traded companies would mean no work for most former top executives (and by extension, no decent living), thus strengthening the prediction stated by critics of the plan. Whether or not the union strikes has no bearing on the effect the new policy would have on the former executives if enacted; thus, **(A)** is incorrect. **(B)** simply states that most former employees of the exchange work for publicly traded companies; it does not tell you that they could not make a decent living elsewhere if need be. **(C)** and **(D)** refer to low-level managers, and the prediction only discusses top executives; thus, both choices are irrelevant and incorrect.

29. (B)

The increase in taxes on cigarettes next month will not limit the use of addictive tobacco products to the extent that health advocates hope. Many cigarette smokers will shift their spending to cigars and chewing tobacco when the law takes effect.

Which of the following, if true, would most strongly weaken the argument above?

○ Cigars and chewing tobacco can satisfy the nicotine cravings of most cigarette smokers.

○ The taste, smell, and texture of cigars and chewing tobacco are sufficiently different from those of cigarettes to deter cigarette smokers from using them.

○ Many health advocates themselves use tobacco products.

○ The government might also impose significant taxes on cigars and chewing tobacco over the course of two years.

○ Cigars and chewing tobacco are often more expensive than cigarettes.

Step 1: Identify the Question Type

The wording is a little strange ("most strongly weaken"), but this is ultimately a Weaken question.

Step 2: Untangle the Stimulus

The conclusion in this argument is a prediction. According to the conclusion, many current cigarette smokers will shift their spending to cigars and chewing tobacco because of an impending increase in taxes on cigarettes. You could also look at this as a causality argument, as it asserts that the price of cigarettes affects smoking behavior.

Step 3: Predict the Answer

If you are using the plan/proposal/prediction approach, your prediction would be "something that explains why cigarette smokers won't use cigars or chewing tobacco, even though taxes on cigarettes will increase." And if you are approaching this argument focusing on causality, your prediction would likely be "another factor that affects smoking behavior." (The other two ways of weakening causality aren't very reasonable here—smoking behavior doesn't affect the price one pays for cigarettes, and you know from the stimulus that the price of cigarettes isn't set by coincidence.)

Step 4: Evaluate the Choices

(B) effectively weakens the author's prediction: if the differences in taste, smell, and texture will deter smokers from using cigars and chewing tobacco, then it is unlikely that cigarette smokers will shift their spending to them even if taxes are raised. They may find cigarette smoking prohibitively expensive, but they won't be likely to switch to other tobacco products, no matter how much cheaper those products are. And if you were looking for a new factor that affects smoking behavior, here there are three: taste, smell, and texture. **(A)** is a 180. It strengthens the author's prediction in the last sentence: if cigars and chewing tobacco satisfy the same nicotine cravings as cigarettes, then it is likely that cigarette smokers will buy them instead if taxes on cigarettes are raised. **(C)** is incorrect because the personal habits of health advocates have no bearing on the author's prediction. **(D)** is similarly irrelevant: the author's prediction is concerned only with the spending of consumers next month, not in two years. **(E)** is tempting at first glance, but it doesn't provide enough information to weaken the argument. Will cigars and chewing tobacco still be more expensive than cigarettes after the tax increase? Without more specific information, **(E)** doesn't weaken the argument.

30. **(D)**

The percentage of local businesses with more than 10 employees is higher in Grandview City than in any other city in the state. However, the percentage of local businesses with 15 employees or more is higher in Lakeshore City, which is in the same state, than in any other city in the state.

If the statements above are true, then which of the following must also be true?

○ The percentage of local businesses with more than 18 employees is higher in Lakeshore City than in any other city in the state.

○ The state has more local businesses with more than 10 employees than any other state in the country.

○ The number of local businesses with 15 or more employees is greater in Lakeshore City than in Grandview City.

○ Some local businesses in Grandview City have 11 to 14 employees.

○ The average number of employees per business is higher in Lakeshore City than in Grandview City.

Step 1: Identify the Question Type

This question asks you to choose the answer that makes a valid deduction from the stimulus, so it is an Inference question.

Step 2: Untangle the Stimulus

Usually, the stimulus of an Inference question will not include an argument. You just need to read and understand the statements in the stimulus and take note of any connections between them. This stimulus really just provides two related pieces of information: Grandview has the highest percentage of businesses with 11+ employees, while Lakeshore has the highest percentage with 15+.

Step 3: Predict the Answer

Grandview has the highest percentage of businesses with 11+ employees, but not the highest percentage with 15+. The only way that's possible is if Grandview has at least a few businesses with 11–14 employees. You might use picking numbers to make this deduction more obvious. For instance, say that both Grandview and Lakeshore have 100 businesses. If Grandview has 25 businesses with 11+ employees, and Lakeshore has 20 businesses with 15+ employees, Lakeshore could still have the higher percentage of 15+ employee businesses if Grandview has more than 5 businesses with 11–14 employees. What "must be true" is that Grandview has at least a few businesses with 11–14 employees. You'll be looking for an answer choice that says so.

Step 4: Evaluate the Choices

(D) matches the prediction and is the correct answer. **(A)** is incorrect because businesses with more than 18 employees have no bearing on the stimulus. **(B)** introduces an irrelevant comparison between states. You're only interested in two specific cities within one state, not in any other states. **(C)** is a bit tricky, but the actual number of businesses is irrelevant; you're concerned only with percentages, not raw numbers. Finally, **(E)** introduces another irrelevant point. You care only about businesses with very specific numbers of employees, not about the average number of employees per business.

EXPLANATIONS

31. (C)

It appears that the number of people employed by a typical American software firm decreased in the 1980s and 1990s. This trend is borne out by two studies, conducted 20 years apart. In a large 1980 sample of randomly chosen American software firms, the median size of the firms' workforce populations was 65. When those same firms were studied again in 2000, the median size was 57.

Which of the following points to the most serious logical flaw in the reasoning above?

○   The median number of employees in American firms in many industries decreased during the 1980s and 1990s.

○   During the 1980s and 1990s, many software firms increased the extent to which they relied on subcontractors to write code.

○   The data in the studies refer only to companies that existed in 1980.

○   The studies focused on the number of employees, but there are many ways of judging a firm's size, such as revenues and profits.

○   The median number of employees is not as sound a measure of the number of employees employed in an industry as is the mean number of employees, which accounts for the vast size of the few large firms that dominate most industries.

Step 1: Identify the Question Type

Since the question stem asks for a "logical flaw," you're dealing with a Flaw question here.

Step 2: Untangle the Stimulus

The argument concludes that the typical American software firm employs fewer people in the 2000s than it did in the 1980s and 1990s. This conclusion is supported by two studies; in order for the conclusion to be valid, both studies need to be representative.

Step 3: Predict the Answer

The sample in the 1980 study seems legitimate: it was large and randomly chosen. However, notice the problem with the 2000 study: it uses the same firms as in the 1980 study. The firms are no longer randomly chosen, nor does the sample size account for the many software firms that presumably sprang up between 1980 and 2000. In other words, the sample in the second survey was not representative of all American software firms.

Step 4: Evaluate the Choices

This prediction matches **(C)**, which pinpoints a problem with the representativeness of the 2000 survey. If the firms surveyed included only those that also existed 20 years ago, then no information is included about firms that have come into existence since then. If the survey is not based on information about all American software firms, including those that have come into existence over the last 20 years, then the survey is not representative, and any conclusions drawn from those results are called into question. **(A)**'s focus on many industries is irrelevant to the argument, which is concerned only with the number of people employed by a typical American software firm. **(B)** gives a plausible explanation of why the median size of firms is decreasing, but it fails to describe a flaw in the argument. **(D)** is irrelevant: the survey is concerned with the firm's size in terms of workforce population. All other measures of a firm's size are irrelevant. Finally, **(E)** is not a flaw in this argument. While it may be true that the mean is a better measure for total workforce population in an industry, this argument concerns the number of employees in *a typical firm* in one industry, not across the industry as a whole.

32. (B)

The Ministry of Tourism in country X began an expensive television advertising campaign in country Y two years ago. Since that time, the number of visitors to country X from country Y has increased by more than 8 percent. Clearly, the Ministry of Tourism's campaign is responsible for the increase.

Which of the following, if true, would most weaken the argument above?

- ○ The advertisements sponsored by the Ministry of Tourism in country X were panned by the country Y media for lack of imagination.
- ○ A devaluation of the currency in country X two years ago made travel there more affordable for residents of country Y.
- ○ Increasing political turmoil in country X will lead to a decrease in visitors from country Y next year.
- ○ The number of visitors from country Y to country Z increased by more than 8 percent over the past two years.
- ○ Over the past two years, the advertisement campaign launched by the Ministry of Tourism in country X cost more money than residents of country Y spent traveling in country X.

Step 1: Identify the Question Type

The question stem clearly indicates that this is a Weaken question.

Step 2: Untangle the Stimulus

The conclusion is that the Ministry of Tourism's ad campaign is responsible for the increase in the number of visitors from country Y to country X. The evidence is that since the ad campaign began running, the number of visitors from country Y to country X has gone up by more than 8 percent.

Step 3: Predict the Answer

This is a very straightforward causal argument. While there are three classic alternatives to a causal argument (reverse cause and effect, find an alternative cause, or suggest coincidence), the most common way of weakening a causal argument is to exploit the second alternative—citing another possible cause for the phenomenon. So look for an answer choice that offers another explanation for the increase of tourism from country Y.

Step 4: Evaluate the Choices

And **(B)** offers that alternative explanation, making it the correct answer. If travel to country X became more affordable at the same time that tourism to country X increased, it is possible that the devaluation in currency is responsible for this increase rather than the Ministry of Tourism's ad campaign. While it does not *disprove* that the ad campaign was the cause of the increase, it certainly weakens the author's argument by presenting another potential cause of the increase. **(A)** does not effectively weaken the argument. Just because the media panned the ads does not mean they could not have spurred the increase in tourism. The prediction in **(C)** is irrelevant to the author's argument about the past efficacy of the Ministry of Tourism's ad campaign. **(D)** brings up tourism in country Z, which has no bearing on the argument. And **(E)** is likewise irrelevant: the author is only concerned with establishing a causal relationship between the ad campaign and increased tourism, not with whether the campaign was cost-effective.

33. (A)

A corporation's recent financial report indicates that customers in its Quarx stores, which play upbeat music through an in-store audio system, spend on average 25 percent more per shopping trip than customers in its Cubix stores, which advertise specials over the audio system. Clearly, hearing music has a greater impact than hearing advertisements on how much money customers spend when shopping.

Which of the following, if true, would most strengthen the argument above?

○ A study conducted by a psychologist found that hearing music makes shoppers feel financially secure, so they are more likely to make impulse purchases.

○ Customers who hear advertisements for things they dislike form a negative association between their shopping experience and what they heard, making them less likely to return to the store where they heard the advertisement.

○ Stores that play music tend to carry products that are essential to daily life, while those that advertise specials often stock unessential, fun items that the stores hope consumers will decide to buy on a whim if offered a special price.

○ An economist who studied consumer shopping habits found that about half the population likes to listen to music while shopping, while the other half reports either disliking music or not noticing that music is playing.

○ According to a recent sociological study, customers say that hearing specials announced while they are shopping is irritating, but they often take advantage of the discounts offered in those announcements.

Step 1: Identify the Question Type

The question stem asks for the answer choice that will most strengthen the argument, making this a Strengthen question.

Step 2: Untangle the Stimulus

This is a causality argument. It concludes that playing music increases customer spending more than advertising specials over an in-store audio system. The evidence given is a report on two chains of stores. According to the report, Quarx stores play music on their audio systems and saw customers buy 25% more, on average, than customers at Cubix stores, which advertise specials on their audio systems.

Step 3: Predict the Answer

The correct answer will either make it more likely that hearing music causes customers to increase their spending or make it less likely that some other factor caused Quarx customers to outspend Cubix customers.

Step 4: Evaluate the Choices

(A) strengthens the conclusion. The study found a direct link between how music makes customers feel and their willingness to spend more than they initially planned, supporting the conclusion that music increases how much money is spent. **(B)** does not say anything about how much is spent at the time the ads are heard. Since the argument is about what is spent on a particular shopping trip, future shopping trips are irrelevant. **(C)** does not strengthen (or weaken) the conclusion because it doesn't link this information about product selection to how much money customers spend. **(D)** does not provide any information about the impact customers' opinions of hearing music while shopping has on how much money customers spend. Finally, **(E)** also fails to establish any connection to how much is spent. Furthermore, it fails to mention music at all.

34. (D)

Cable Television Executive: **Our service and reliability have increased dramatically over the past year.** Our customer service line is receiving 30 percent fewer reports of interrupted service, and the number of subscribers canceling their accounts is barely half of what it was last year.

Cable Television Customer: That doesn't mean your service and reliability have improved. **It's possible that customers don't bother to call your customer service line to report problems because they never get any assistance when they do.** And the drop-off in the number of canceled accounts could reflect the fact that nearly all of your dissatisfied customers have already canceled their accounts.

In the argument above, the two portions in boldface play which of the following roles?

○ The first is evidence designed to lead to a conclusion; the second offers further evidence in support of that conclusion.

○ The first is evidence designed to lead to a conclusion; the second offers evidence designed to cast doubt on that conclusion.

○ The first is a conclusion; the second offers evidence in support of that conclusion.

○ The first is a conclusion; the second offers evidence designed to cast doubt on that conclusion.

○ The first is a conclusion; the second is an alternative conclusion based on the same evidence.

Step 1: Identify the Question Type

This stem offers standard language for a Bolded Statement question—it asks you to determine the roles played in the arguments by each of the boldface statements.

Step 2: Untangle the Stimulus

The cable television executive uses evidence of fewer customer complaints and cancellations to conclude that the cable company's service has improved over the past year. The customer disagrees, providing an alternative explanation for the executive's evidence. According to the customer, there are fewer cancellations because all the dissatisfied customers have already canceled their accounts; the decreased number of complaints indicates that frustrated customers have simply given up.

Step 3: Predict the Answer

The first bolded statement is the cable executive's conclusion, and the second bolded statement is evidence from the customer that would support a contradictory conclusion.

Step 4: Evaluate the Choices

(D) is correct; the second statement is designed to cast doubt on the validity of the conclusion in the first. Since the first bolded statement represents the executive's conclusion, you can eliminate **(A)** and **(B)**, which characterize this statement as evidence. The customer clearly disagrees with the executive, so you can eliminate **(C)**. **(E)** may be tempting; the second statement does provide an alternate explanation of some of the evidence, but the second statement is not a conclusion, merely a possible interpretation. Always read diligently so that you can avoid half-right, half-wrong answer choices.

35. (C)

Opponents of the laws prohibiting nonprescription narcotic drugs argue that in a free society, people have the right to take risks as long as the risks do not constitute a harm to others who have not elected to take such risks. These opponents conclude that it should be each person's decision whether or not to use narcotic drugs.

Which of the following, if true, most seriously weakens the conclusion drawn above?

- ○ Some narcotic drugs have been shown to have medicinal qualities.
- ○ There are laws that govern the use of prescription drugs.
- ○ Studies have shown that people who use nonprescription drugs are much more likely to perpetrate a violent crime when intoxicated than when sober.
- ○ People who use narcotic drugs are twice as likely to die of an overdose as of natural causes.
- ○ The rate of drug overdoses is higher in countries that do not have laws governing the use of narcotic drugs than in countries that do have such laws.

Step 1: Identify the Question Type

The phrase "weakens the conclusion" in the question stem announces that this is a Weaken question.

Step 2: Untangle the Stimulus

As in all argument-based questions, you need to find the conclusion and evidence. The conclusion is the last sentence: use of nonprescription narcotic drugs should be everyone's personal decision. The evidence is that people have the right to take risks as long as taking those risks doesn't hurt anyone besides themselves.

Step 3: Predict the Answer

In a Weaken question, the correct answer will challenge the argument's central assumption. The opponents assume that nonprescription narcotics pose risks only to the people who use them. If narcotics could harm non-users, however, then narcotic use would not be a permissible risk; individuals would no longer have the right to use those drugs. Because this is a Weaken question, look for an answer choice that says that taking narcotics *can* in fact harm others besides the drug users themselves.

Step 4: Evaluate the Choices

(C) does the job perfectly. If people are more likely to commit violent crimes while under the influence of drugs, then others are at risk from the drug use, and the conclusion that it is everyone's personal right to choose whether to use drugs is greatly weakened. **(A)** is incorrect because it introduces the idea of medicinal qualities, which is irrelevant to the argument. The prescription drugs in **(B)** are likewise irrelevant to the argument, which is concerned only with nonprescription drugs. **(D)** has no bearing on the argument since it describes only a risk to the user of the drug, rather than a risk to others. Finally, **(E)** is an irrelevant comparison between two different sets of countries. The laws of those countries have no bearing on the argument because rates of overdose only indicate personal risk, not risk to others.

36. (A)

In a survey of undergraduates, two-fifths admitted to having cheated on an exam at least once during their education. However, the survey may underestimate the proportion of undergraduates who have cheated, because _____.

Which of the following best completes the passage above?

○ some undergraduates who have cheated at least once might have claimed on the survey never to have cheated

○ some undergraduates who have never cheated might have claimed on the survey to have cheated

○ some undergraduates who claimed on the survey to have cheated at least once may have cheated on multiple occasions throughout their education

○ some undergraduates who claimed on the survey to have cheated at least once may have been answering honestly

○ some students who are not undergraduates have probably cheated at least once during their education

Step 1: Identify the Question Type

Here, you have an Inference question that asks you to complete the final sentence of a brief argument.

Step 2: Untangle the Stimulus

The portion of the sentence you need to complete begins with the keyword "because." That tells you that whatever is to fill in the blank must provide evidence for what came before it in the sentence. Thus, you can treat this as a Strengthen question, keeping in mind the direction of the author's thinking. The author's conclusion is that the survey may have underestimated the proportion of undergraduates who cheated. You know from the first sentence that two-fifths of the students *reported* having cheated at least once. The author implies that there are additional, unreported cheaters out there.

Step 3: Predict the Answer

The one correct answer will provide a reason to think that there are additional, unreported cheaters among the undergraduate population.

Step 4: Evaluate the Choices

(A) is a match for the prediction and is correct: some undergrads may have cheated but lied about it on the survey. If you were looking for a reason why the survey might *overestimate* the proportion of undergrads cheating, **(B)** would be correct. **(C)** refers to multiple cases of cheating per student; the survey is only dealing with the proportion of students who have cheated at least once. **(D)** gives a reason why the survey might be accurate, which is the opposite of what you want, and **(E)** introduces students who are not undergrads, which is out of the scope of the survey.

37. (C)

During the last 18 years, the number of people who live or work in the Dry River Valley, which is prone to flash flooding, has continually increased, as has traffic on local roads and bridges. However, the number of people caught in flash floods has decreased, even though the annual number of floods has increased slightly.

Which of the following, if true, best explains the decrease described above?

○ Flash floods are more likely to happen in the first hour of a rainstorm than afterward.

○ Flash floods killed some people in the Dry River Valley in every one of the last 18 years.

○ Better meteorological technology, combined with a better understanding of the conditions conducive to flash flooding, has improved local authorities' ability to predict when and where flash floods will occur.

○ Many people work in the Dry River Valley but live elsewhere.

○ A law that went into effect 18 years ago mandated that all new homes built in the valley be built on raised foundations, making those homes much less susceptible to flood damage.

Step 1: Identify the Question Type

This is an Explain question. You can anticipate seeing a paradox or unusual coincidence described in the stimulus. Your task is to resolve the seemingly disparate pieces of information in order to explain the anomalous result.

Step 2: Untangle the Stimulus

The stimulus tells you about two increases—the number of people and the number of flash floods—in the Dry River Valley. The keyword "[h]owever" signals the seeming discrepancy: despite those increases, the number of people caught in flash floods has gone down. Think critically about how you can reconcile these facts.

Step 3: Predict the Answer

The stimulus involves numbers (of residents, floods, and flood victims), but it doesn't state any actual values. Picking numbers can help you visualize the situation in the stimulus.

Pick numbers that are permissible and manageable. Say that 18 years ago, there were 1,000 people, 10 floods, and 100 flood victims in the valley. Following the information in the stimulus, say there are now 2,000 people, 20 floods, and 50 victims.

	18 years ago	Now
People	1,000	2,000
Floods	10	20
People caught in floods	100	50

This shows that the floods are now less dangerous.

	18 years ago	**Now**
Proportion of people caught in floods	1 in 10	1 in 40
People caught per flood	10	2.5

The correct answer will explain this change. It will provide a reason why the floods have been less dangerous.

Step 4: Evaluate the Choices

(C) gives you the explanation you need and is correct: more accurate advance notice of floods allows local authorities to better prevent people from getting caught. **(A)** may be true of flash flooding in general, but it doesn't give you any difference between the floods now and those 18 years ago. **(B)** is irrelevant to the argument, which deals with people *caught* in the floods, not people killed by them. **(D)** doesn't explain the difference either, as there's no reason to think that flash floods somehow selectively avoid commuters. **(E)** is also irrelevant, since the argument does not focus on property damage.

38. (E)

Colleges in Tycho City have failed to prepare their students for the business world. A recent study revealed that the majority of college graduates in Tycho City could not write a simple business letter.

Which of the following, if true, would provide additional evidence in support of the claim above?

○   A majority of students attending colleges in Tycho City are business majors.

○   The state college in neighboring Twyla Township has recently improved its business program by adding courses in business writing.

○   Most Tycho City college graduates move outside the Tycho City area after they graduate.

○   Most Tycho City college students live in on-campus dormitories.

○   The majority of college graduates living in Tycho City received their college degrees from institutions located in Tycho City.

Step 1: Identify the Question Type

To "provide additional evidence in support" of an argument is to strengthen it, so this is a Strengthen question.

Step 2: Untangle the Stimulus

The argument concludes that colleges in Tycho City don't do a good job of preparing their grads for the business world, because the majority of college grads living in Tycho City couldn't write a simple business letter. Since this argument is based on a study, there is likely a representativeness problem.

Step 3: Predict the Answer

In this argument, the author makes a scope shift between the evidence and the conclusion: wthe evidence is based on "college graduates in Tycho City," while the conclusion refers to the supposed failings of "colleges in Tycho City." In order for the conclusion to hold, it must be true that the college grads in the study are representative of colleges in Tycho City—that is, that those people actually attended school in Tycho City. Look for an answer that bolsters that assumption.

Step 4: Evaluate the Choices

(E) properly strengthens the argument by reinforcing the assumption. In other words, **(E)** demonstrates that the sample studied is actually representative of colleges in Tycho City. **(A)** has no effect on the argument. While the argument concerns whether students are prepared for the business world, it is not relevant what the students are majoring in. **(B)** is irrelevant. What some other college is doing does not affect an argument about the effectiveness of Tycho City college programs. **(C)** actually weakens the argument. If most Tycho City college graduates leave the Tycho City area after graduation, then it is unlikely that a study of graduates in Tycho City is representative of graduates of Tycho City colleges. Be careful of 180 answers in Strengthen/Weaken questions. Finally, **(D)** is irrelevant, since where the students live has no effect on whether or not they're adequately prepared for the business world.

GMAT BY THE NUMBERS: CRITICAL REASONING

Now that you've learned how to approach Critical Reasoning questions on the GMAT, let's add one more dimension to your understanding of how they work.

Take a moment to try this question. Following is performance data from thousands of people who have studied with Kaplan over the decades. Through analyzing this data, we will show you how to approach questions like this one most effectively and how to avoid similarly tempting wrong answer choice types on Test Day.

> Wunderlich Park has a strict regulation that requires mountain bicyclists to wear helmets. Recently, a group of bicyclists acknowledged that helmets may prevent injuries to the wearer but protested, claiming the park should only regulate activities that may hurt a third party. Hence, the bicyclists argued that they should have the right to refrain from wearing helmets.
>
> Which of the following, if true, most seriously weakens the conclusion in the passage?
>
> ○ Ninety percent of bicyclists who use Wunderlich Park prefer to wear a helmet to protect themselves in case of an accident.
>
> ○ Lawyers for Wunderlich Park have warned that the repeal of the helmet regulation would lead to an increase in general admission park entrance fees to cover the legal expenses associated with personal injury lawsuits.
>
> ○ Motorcyclists in a neighboring county are required to wear a helmet while on the road.
>
> ○ Parks that require the use of helmets have a lower percentage of accidents resulting in deaths than parks that don't require the use of helmets.
>
> ○ More bicyclists who do not wear helmets are seriously injured in accidents than bicyclists who do wear helmets.

EXPLANATION

The argument's conclusion is presented in the final sentence, introduced by the keyword "[h]ence": the bicyclists claim that they shouldn't have to wear helmets in the park. But despite the wording of the question, it isn't really the *conclusion* itself that the test maker wants you to weaken—rather, you must weaken the *logic supporting that conclusion*. According to this argument, the reason why cyclists shouldn't be made to wear helmets is that the park should not restrict an activity that doesn't harm others. The right answer, therefore, will show how not wearing a helmet actually does harm someone else.

The correct answer—**(B)**—does just that; it shows how cyclists' not wearing helmets would in fact harm noncyclists: the harm would be financial.

QUESTION STATISTICS

10% of test takers choose (A)

46% of test takers choose (B)

2% of test takers choose (C)

23% of test takers choose (D)

19% of test takers choose (E)

Sample size = 3,132

The three most commonly selected wrong answers are wrong because they do not address the entire argument, only the general sense of the conclusion. **(D)** and **(E)** both give good reasons to wear a helmet, but they suggest that only the cyclist is at risk, not someone else. **(A)** discusses cyclists' preferences, but the argument about when to permit regulation has to do only with whether others would be harmed, not with personal preference. You can see that answers that ignore an argument's reasoning are popular, and as such are very common. Learn to avoid them, and you'll go a long way to improving your GMAT score.

MORE GMAT BY THE NUMBERS...

To see more questions with answer choice statistics, be sure to review the full-length CATs in your online resources.

GO ONLINE

kaptest.com/login

CHAPTER 7

Reading Comprehension

> It can be inferred from the passage that supporters of the Alvarez and Courtillot theories would hold which of the following views in common?
>
> ○ The KT boundary was formed over many thousands of years.
> ○ Large animals such as the dinosaurs died out gradually over millions of years.
> ○ Mass extinction occurred as an indirect result of debris saturating the atmosphere.
> ○ It is unlikely that the specific cause of the Cretaceous extinctions will ever be determined.
> ○ Volcanic activity may have been triggered by shock waves from the impact of an asteroid.

Above is a typical Reading Comprehension question. For now, don't worry that we haven't given you the passage this question refers to. In this chapter, we'll look at how to apply the Kaplan Method to this question, discuss the types of questions the GMAT asks about reading passages, and go over the basic principles and strategies that you want to keep in mind on every Reading Comprehension question. But before you move on, take a minute to think about what you see in the structure of this question and answer some questions about how you think it works:

- What does it mean to draw an inference from a GMAT passage?

- How much are you expected to know about the subject matter of the passages before you take the test?

- What can you expect to see in a GMAT passage that discusses two related theories?

- What GMAT Core Competencies are most essential to success on this question?

PREVIEWING READING COMPREHENSION

WHAT DOES IT MEAN TO DRAW AN INFERENCE FROM A GMAT PASSAGE?

You may remember from the Critical Reasoning chapter the definition of an "inference" on the GMAT: an inference is something that *must* be true, based on the information provided. There are two important parts to this definition:

(1) A valid GMAT inference *must* be true. This sets a high standard for what you consider a valid inference. It is sometimes difficult to determine whether a statement in an answer choice must always be true, but you can also approach these questions by eliminating the four answer choices that *could* be false. Keep both of these tactics in mind for questions that ask for an inference.

(2) A valid GMAT inference is based on the passage. By definition, an inference won't be explicitly stated in the passage; you will have to understand the passage well enough to read between the lines. But just because it isn't directly stated doesn't mean an inference could be anything under the sun. On the GMAT, any inference you draw will be unambiguously supported by something that is stated in the passage. It may take some Critical Thinking to figure out, but you will always be able to pinpoint exactly why a valid inference must be true.

HOW MUCH ARE YOU EXPECTED TO KNOW ABOUT THE SUBJECT MATTER OF THE PASSAGES BEFORE YOU TAKE THE TEST?

Familiarity with the subject matter is not required. GMAT passages contain everything you need to answer GMAT questions. In fact, many Reading Comp questions contain wrong answer choices based on information that is actually true but not mentioned in the passage. So if you know the subject, be careful not to let your prior knowledge influence your answer. And if you don't know the subject, be happy—some wrong answer traps won't be tempting to you!

Reading Comprehension is designed to test not your prior knowledge but your critical reading skills. Among other things, it tests whether you can do the following:

- Summarize the main idea of a passage
- Understand logical relationships between facts and concepts
- Make inferences based on information in a text
- Analyze the logical structure of a passage
- Deduce the author's tone and attitude about a topic from the text

Note that none of these objectives relies on anything other than your ability to understand and apply ideas found in the passage. This should be a comforting thought: everything you need is right there in front of you. In this chapter, you will learn strategic approaches to help you make the best use of the information the test makers provide.

WHAT CAN YOU EXPECT TO SEE IN A GMAT PASSAGE THAT DISCUSSES TWO RELATED THEORIES?

Because the GMAT cannot ask you purely factual questions that might reward or punish you for your outside knowledge, it tends to focus its questions on the opinions or analyses contained in the passages. Since this question asks you what Alvarez's and Courtillot's theories have in common, this means that they must agree on at least one thing. You can anticipate, however, that the two theories are largely *not* in agreement with each other.

This is a common structure for a GMAT passage: the author discusses more than one explanation of the same phenomenon, describing each in turn or perhaps comparing them directly, usually summarizing the relevant evidence and explaining why disagreement exists among the explanations' proponents. When a passage contains multiple opinions, keep track of who is making each assertion and how the assertion relates to the other opinions in the passage: does it contradict, agree with, or expand upon what came before? Another important thing to note is whether the author takes a side—does the author prefer one viewpoint to another? Does he offer his own competing argument?

WHAT GMAT CORE COMPETENCIES ARE MOST ESSENTIAL TO SUCCESS ON THIS QUESTION?

Since the GMAT constructs Reading Comprehension passages in similar ways and asks questions that conform to predictable "types," you can learn to anticipate how an author will express her ideas and what the GMAT test makers will ask you about a passage. The more you practice and the more you focus on structure as you read, the stronger your Pattern Recognition skills will become.

Critical Thinking is also essential. As you read, you should ask yourself why the author is including certain details and what the author's choice of transitional keywords implies about how the ideas in the passage are related.

The best test takers learn how to pay Attention to the Right Detail. Reading Comp passages are typically filled with more details than you could reasonably memorize—and more, in fact, than you will ever need to answer the questions. Since time is limited, you must prioritize the information you assimilate from the passage, focusing on the big picture but allowing yourself to return to the passage to research details as needed.

Practice Paraphrasing constantly as you read, both to keep yourself engaged and to make sure you understand what's being discussed. Developing this habit will make taking notes much easier, since you've already distilled and summarized the most important information in your head. You'll learn later in this chapter how to take concise and well-organized notes in the form of a passage map.

Here are the main topics we'll cover in this chapter:

- Question Format and Structure
- The Basic Principles of Reading Comprehension
- The Kaplan Method for Reading Comprehension
- Reading Comprehension Question Types

QUESTION FORMAT AND STRUCTURE

The directions for Reading Comprehension questions look like this:

> **Directions:** The questions in this group are based on the content of a passage. After reading the passage, choose the best answer to each question. Base your answers only on what is stated or implied in the text.

In Reading Comp, you are presented with a reading passage (in an area of business, social science, biological science, or physical science) and then asked three or four questions about that text. You are not expected to be familiar with any topic beforehand—all the information you need is contained in the text in front of you. In fact, if you happen to have some previous knowledge about a given topic, it is important that you not let that knowledge affect your answers. Naturally, some passages will be easier to understand than others, though each will present a challenge. The passages will have the tone and content that one might expect from a scholarly journal.

You will see four Reading Comp passages—most likely two shorter passages with 3 questions each and two longer passages with 4 questions each, for a total of approximately 14 questions. However, as is usual for the computer-adaptive GMAT, you will see only one question at a time on the screen, and you will have to answer each question before you can see the next question. The passage will appear on the left side of the screen. It will remain there until you've answered all of the questions that relate to it. If the text is longer than the available space, you'll be given a scroll bar to move through it. Plan to take no longer than 4 minutes to read and make notes on the passage and a little less than 1.5 minutes to answer each question associated with the passage.

TAKEAWAYS: QUESTION FORMAT AND STRUCTURE

- GMAT passages consist of one to five paragraphs and are up to 350 words in length.
- You will usually see two shorter and two longer passages in the Verbal section.
- Usually, you will get three questions on a shorter passage and four questions on a longer passage. You can answer only one at a time and can't go back to previous questions.
- The passages usually have the tone and content that one might expect from a scholarly journal.
- You are not expected to have prior knowledge of the subject matter in the passage.
- The passage stays on the screen for all questions that pertain to it.
- You should spend 4 minutes per passage and a little less than 1.5 minutes per question.

THE BASIC PRINCIPLES OF READING COMPREHENSION

In daily life, most people read to learn something or to pass the time pleasantly. Neither of these goals has much to do with the GMAT. On Test Day, you have a very specific goal—to get as many right answers as you can. So your reading needs to be tailored to that goal. There are really only two things a Reading Comp question can ask you about: the "big picture" of the passage or its "little details."

Since the passage is right there on the screen, you don't need to worry much about the little details as you read. (In fact, doing so may hinder your ability to answer questions, as you'll soon see.) So your main goal as you read is to prepare yourself to get the big-picture questions right, while leaving yourself as much time as possible to find the answers to the little-detail questions.

Here are the four basic principles you need to follow to accomplish this goal.

LOOK FOR THE TOPIC AND SCOPE OF THE PASSAGE

Think of the topic as the first big idea that comes along. Almost always, it will be right there in the first sentence. It will be something broad, far too big to discuss in the 150–350 words that most GMAT passages contain. Here's an example of how a passage might begin:

> The great migration of European intellectuals to the United States in the second quarter of the 20th century prompted a transmutation in the character of Western social thought.

What's the topic? The migration of European intellectuals to the United States in the second quarter of the 20th century. It would also be okay to say that the topic is the effects of that migration on Western social thought. Topic is a very broad concept, so you really don't need to worry about how exactly you word it. You just need to get a good idea of what the passage is talking about so you feel more comfortable reading.

Now consider scope. Think of scope as a narrowing of the topic. You're looking for an idea that the author might reasonably focus on for the length of a GMAT passage. If the topic is "the migration of European intellectuals to the United States in the second quarter of the 20th century," then perhaps the scope will be "some of the effects of that migration upon Western social thought." It will likely be even more specific: "one aspect of Western social thought affected by the migration." But perhaps something unexpected will come along. Might the passage compare two different migrations? Or contrast two different effects? Think critically about what's coming and look for clues in the text that let you know on what specific subject(s) the author intends to focus.

Finding the scope is critically important to doing well on Reading Comp. Many Reading Comp wrong answers are wrong because the information that would be needed to support them is simply not present in the passage. It's highly unlikely that there will be a topic sentence that lays out plainly what the author intends to write about—but the first paragraph probably will give some indication of the focus of the rest of the passage.

Note that some passages are only one paragraph long. In these cases, the topic can still appear in the first sentence. The passage will probably (but not necessarily) narrow in scope somewhere in the first third of the paragraph, as the author doesn't have much text to work with and needs to get down to business quickly.

GET THE GIST OF EACH PARAGRAPH AND ITS STRUCTURAL ROLE IN THE PASSAGE

The paragraph is the main structural unit of any passage. At first, you don't yet know the topic or scope, so you have to read the first paragraph pretty closely. But once you get a sense of where the passage is going, all you need to do is understand what role each new paragraph plays. Ask yourself the following:

- Why did the author include this paragraph?
- What's discussed here that's different from the content of the paragraph before?
- What bearing does this paragraph have on the author's main idea?
- What role do the details play?

Notice that last question—don't ask yourself, "What does this mean?" but rather, "Why is it here?" Many GMAT passages try to swamp you with tedious, dense, and sometimes confusing details. Consider this paragraph, which might appear as part of a difficult science-based passage:

> The Burgess Shale yielded a surprisingly varied array of fossils. Early chordates were very rare, but there were prodigious numbers of complex forms not seen since. *Hallucigenia*, so named for a structure so bizarre that scientists did not know which was the dorsal and which the ventral side, had fourteen legs. *Opabinia* had five eyes and a long proboscis. This amazing diversity led Gould to believe that it was highly unlikely that the eventual success of chordates was a predictable outcome.

This is pretty dense stuff. But if you don't worry about understanding all of the science jargon and instead focus on the gist of the paragraph and *why* the details are there, things get easier. The first sentence isn't that bad:

> The Burgess Shale yielded a surprisingly varied array of fossils.

A quick paraphrase is that the "Burgess Shale," whatever that is, had a lot of different kinds of fossils. The passage continues:

> Early chordates were very rare, but there were prodigious numbers of complex forms not seen since. *Hallucigenia*, so named for a structure so bizarre that scientists did not know which was the dorsal and which the ventral side, had fourteen legs. *Opabinia* had five eyes and a long proboscis.

When you read this part of the passage strategically, asking what its purpose is in context, you see that this is just a list of the different kinds of fossils and some facts about them. There were not a lot of "chordates," whatever they are, but there was lots of other stuff.

> This amazing diversity led Gould to believe that it was highly unlikely that the eventual success of chordates was a predictable outcome.

Notice that the beginning of this sentence tells us *why* those intimidatingly dense details are there; they are the facts that led Gould to a belief—namely that the rise of "chordates" couldn't have been predicted. So, on your noteboard, you'd jot down something like this:

Evidence for Gould's belief—chordate success not predictable.

Notice that you don't have to know what any of these scientific terms mean in order to know why the author brings them up. Taking apart every paragraph like this allows you to create a map of the passage's overall structure. We'll call this a *passage map* from here on—we'll discuss passage mapping in detail later in this chapter. Making a passage map will help you acquire a clear understanding of the big picture. It will give you a sense of mastery over the passage, even when it deals with a subject you don't know anything about.

To break down paragraphs and understand the structural function of each part, look for keywords, or structural words or phrases that link ideas to one another. You got an overview of the categories of keywords in the Verbal Section Overview chapter of this book. Let's now dig a little deeper into how keywords can help you distinguish the important things (such as opinions) from the unimportant (such as supporting examples) and to understand why the author wrote each sentence.

Types of keywords:

- **Contrast** keywords such as *but, however, nevertheless,* and *on the other hand* tell you that a change or disagreement is coming.

- **Continuation** keywords such as *moreover, also,* and *furthermore* tell you that the author is continuing on the same track or general idea.

- **Logic** keywords, which you've seen to be very important in Critical Reasoning stimuli, alert you to an author's reasoning. **Evidence** keywords let you know that something is being offered in support of a particular idea. The specifics of the support are usually unimportant for the first big-picture read, but you do want to know what the idea is. Examples of evidence keywords are *since, because,* and *as.* **Conclusion** keywords such as *therefore* and *hence* are usually *not* associated with the author's main point in Reading Comp. Rather, they indicate that the next phrase is a logical consequence of the sentence(s) that came before.

- **Illustration** keywords let you know that what follows is an example of a broader point. One example, of course, is *example. For instance* is another favorite in GMAT passages.

- **Sequence/Timing** is a broader category of keywords. These are any words that delineate lists or groupings. *First, second,* and *third* are obvious examples. But you could also get a chronological sequence (*17th century, 18th century,* and *today*). Science passages may also group complicated phenomena using simpler sequence keywords (*at a high temperature* and *at a low temperature,* for example).

- **Emphasis** and **Opinion** keywords can be subtler than those in the other categories, but these are perhaps the most important keywords of all. Emphasis keywords are used when the author wants to call attention to a specific point. These come in two varieties: generic emphasis keywords, such as *very* and *critical,* and charged emphasis keywords, such as *beneficial* or *dead end.* Opinion keywords point to the ideas in a passage; these opinions are frequently the focus of GMAT questions. Be sure to distinguish between the author's opinions and those of others. Others' opinions are easier to spot and will be triggered by words such as *believe, theory,* or *hypothesis.* The author's opinion is more likely to reveal itself in words that imply a value judgment, such as *valid* or *unsupported.* (If the passage expresses something in the first person, such as *I disagree,* that's also a clear sign.)

As you might have guessed, reading the passage strategically doesn't mean simply going on a scavenger hunt for keywords. Rather, it means using those keywords to identify the important parts of the passage—its opinions and structure—so you can focus on them and not on little details. Keywords also help you predict the function of the text that follows. Let's see how this works by taking a look at a simple example. Say you saw a passage with the following structure on Test Day. What kinds of details can you anticipate would fill each of the blanks?

Bob is very excited to go to East Main State Business School because _____ _____. Furthermore, _____ _____. Moreover, _____ _____. However, _____.

You learn about Bob's attitude toward East Main State Business School through the word *excited,* which is an emphasis keyword. After *because* (a logic keyword) will be a reason that East Main State is a great place to go to school or some reason it's special to Bob. After *furthermore* and *moreover* (continuation keywords) will be additional reasons or elaborations of the reason in the first sentence. After *however* will come some drawback or counterexample that undermines the previous string of good things about East Main State. You may not be able to predict the exact content of the details that fill the blanks, but you can predict the tone and purpose of the details. Reading this way is valuable because the GMAT test makers are more likely to ask you why the author put the details in, not what's true about them.

Reading for keywords seems straightforward when the passage deals with subject matter that's familiar or easy to understand. But what if you were to see the following passage about a less familiar topic? How can you decode the structure of the following paragraph?

> Recent studies suggest that mirror neurons play an important role in the learning
>
> process because _____. Furthermore, _____
>
> _____. Moreover, _____
>
> _____. However, _____.

Here the emphasis keyword *important* lets you know why the author cares about mirror neurons: they're important for learning. The details that would fill these blanks are probably dense and intimidating for the non-neurologist, but the strategic reader will still be able to understand the passage well enough to answer the questions correctly. Notice that the structure is identical to the paragraph about Bob, so the details that fill the blanks will serve the same purpose as those you predicted previously. You can anticipate what they will be and why the author is including them. Reading strategically allows you to take control of the passage; you will know where the author is going and what the GMAT will consider important, even if you know nothing about the subject matter of the passage.

LOOK FOR OPINIONS, THEORIES, AND POINTS OF VIEW—ESPECIALLY THE AUTHOR'S

An important part of strategic reading is distinguishing between factual assertions and opinions or interpretations. It's the opinions and interpretations that Reading Comp questions are most often based on, so you should pay the most attention to them. Let's say you come upon a paragraph that reads:

> The coral polyps secrete calcareous exoskeletons, which cement themselves into an underlayer of rock, while the algae deposit still more calcium carbonate, which reacts with sea salt to create an even tougher limestone layer. All of this accounts for the amazing renewability of the coral reefs despite the endless erosion caused by wave activity.

In a sense, this is just like the Burgess Shale paragraph; it begins with a lot of scientific jargon and later tells us why that jargon is there. In this case, it shows us how coral reefs renew themselves. But notice a big difference—the author doesn't tell us how someone else interprets these facts. He could have written "scientists believe that these polyps account for... ," but he didn't. This is the author's own interpretation.

It's important to differentiate between the author's own voice and other people's opinions. GMAT authors may disagree with other people but won't contradict themselves. So the author of the Burgess Shale passage might well disagree with Gould in the next paragraph. But the author of the Coral Reef passage has laid his cards on the table—he definitely thinks that coral polyps and algae are responsible for the renewability of coral reefs.

Spotting the opinions and theories also helps you to accomplish the goal of reading for structure. Once you spot an idea, you can step back from the barrage of words and use Critical Thinking to dissect the passage, asking, "Why is the author citing this opinion? Where's the support for this idea? Does the author agree or disagree?"

Consider how you would read the following paragraph strategically:

> Abraham Lincoln is traditionally viewed as an advocate of freedom because he issued the Emancipation Proclamation and championed the Thirteenth Amendment, which ended legal slavery in the United States. And indeed this achievement cannot be denied. But he also set uncomfortable precedents for the curtailing of civil liberties.

A strategic reader will zero in on the passage's keywords and analyze what each one reveals about the structure of the passage and the author's point of view. Here the keyword *traditionally* lets you know how people usually think about Lincoln. You might already anticipate that the author is setting up a contrast between the traditional view and her own. Sure enough, the keyword *but* makes the contrast clear: the author asserts that despite his other accomplishments, Lincoln in fact restricted civil liberties. And the word *uncomfortable* is an opinion keyword indicating that the author is not at all pleased with Lincoln because of it. However, the author already tempered her criticism with the phrase *this achievement cannot be denied*, meaning that she won't go so far as to say that Lincoln was an enemy of freedom.

At this point, the strategic reader can anticipate where the passage's structure will lead, just as you did on the earlier passages dealing with Bob at East Main State and mirror neurons. Given how this opening paragraph ends, you can predict that the author will spend at least one paragraph describing these "uncomfortable precedents" and how they restricted civil liberties. It might even be possible, since she uses the word *precedents*, that she goes on to describe how later governments or leaders used Lincoln's actions as justification for their own restrictions.

This is the power of predictive, strategic reading: by using keywords to anticipate where the author is heading, you will not only stay more engaged as you read, but you'll also develop a better understanding of the structure of the passage and the author's point of view—the very things that pay off in a higher GMAT score.

Put together, the passage's structure and the opinions and theories it contains will lead you to understand the author's primary purpose in writing the passage. This is critical, as most GMAT passages have a question that directly asks for that purpose. For the Lincoln passage, you might get a question like this:

> Which of the following best represents the main idea of the passage?
>
> O The Emancipation Proclamation had both positive and negative effects.
> O Lincoln's presidency laid the groundwork for future restrictions of personal freedoms.
> O The traditional image of Lincoln as a national hero must be overturned.
> O Lincoln used military pressure to influence state legislatures.
> O Abraham Lincoln was an advocate of freedom.

Just from a strategic reading of the first few sentences, you could eliminate **(A)** as being a distortion of the first and third sentences, **(C)** as being too extreme because of the *cannot be denied* phrase, **(D)** as irrelevant—either too narrow or just not present in the passage at all, and **(E)** as missing the author's big point—that Lincoln helped restrict civil liberties. And just like that, you can choose **(B)** as the right answer and increase your score.

DON'T OBSESS OVER DETAILS

On the GMAT, you'll need to read only for short-term—as opposed to long-term—retention. When you finish the questions about a certain passage, that passage is over and done with. You're promptly free to forget everything about it.

What's more, there's certainly no need to memorize—or even fully comprehend—details. You *do* need to know why they are there so that you can answer big-picture questions, but you can always go back and reread them in greater depth if you're asked a question that hinges on a detail. And you'll find that if you have a good sense of the passage's scope and structure, the ideas and opinions in the passage, and the author's purpose, then you'll have little problem navigating through the text as the need arises.

Furthermore, you can even hurt your score by reading the details too closely. Here's how:

- **Wasted time.** Remember, there will only be three or four questions per passage. The test makers can't possibly ask you about all the little details. So don't waste your valuable time by focusing on minutiae you will likely not need to know. If you do, you won't have nearly enough time to deal with the questions.
- **Tempting wrong answers.** Attempting to read and understand fully every last detail can cause your mind to jumble all the details—relevant and irrelevant alike—together in a confusing mess. Since most of the wrong answers in GMAT Reading Comp are simply distortions of details from the passage, they will sound familiar and therefore be tempting to uncritical readers. The strategic reader doesn't give those details undue importance and thus isn't tempted by answer choices that focus on them. Instead, he takes advantage of the open-book nature of the test to research specific details only when asked.
- **Losing the big picture.** It's very easy to miss the forest for the trees. If you get too drawn into the small stuff, you can pass right by the emphasis and opinion keywords that you'll need to understand the author's main purpose.

Here's a great trick for cutting through confusing, detail-laden sentences: focus on the subjects and verbs first, throwing away modifying phrases, and don't worry about fancy terminology. Let's revisit some dense text from before:

> The coral polyps secrete calcareous exoskeletons, which cement themselves into an underlayer of rock, while the algae deposit still more calcium carbonate, which reacts with sea salt to create an even tougher limestone layer. All of this accounts for the amazing renewability of the coral reefs despite the endless erosion caused by wave activity.

Now look at what happens if you paraphrase these sentences, distilling them to main subjects and verbs, ignoring modifiers, and not worrying about words you don't understand:

> Coral polyps (whatever they are) secrete something...and algae deposit something. This accounts for the amazing renewability of the coral reefs.

The structure of this paragraph has suddenly become a lot more transparent. Now the bulkiness of that first sentence won't slow you down, so you can understand its role in the big picture.

TAKEAWAYS: THE BASIC PRINCIPLES OF READING COMPREHENSION

The basic principles of Reading Comprehension are the following:

- Look for the topic and scope of the passage.
- Get the gist of each paragraph and its structural role in the passage.
- Look for opinions, theories, and points of view—especially the author's.
- Don't obsess over details.

Let's now put all these basic principles together to analyze a passage similar to one you may see on Test Day. However, unlike passages you'll see on Test Day, the following text has been formatted to approximate the way a strategic reader might see it—important keywords and phrases are in bold, the main ideas are in normal type, and the supporting details are grayed out. Take a moment to read only the bold and regular text: identify what the keywords tell you about the structure, paraphrase the crucial text, and practice predicting what the grayed-out portions contain.

The United States National Park Service (NPS) is in the **unenviable** position of being charged with two missions that are **frequently at odds with one another**. Created by an act of Congress in 1916, the NPS is mandated to maintain the country's national parks in "absolutely unimpaired" condition, while somehow
5 ensuring that these lands are available for "the use...and pleasure of the people." As the system of properties (known as units) managed by the NPS has grown over the years—a system now encompassing seashores, battlefields, and parkways—so has its popularity with the vacationing public. **Unfortunately**, the maintenance of the system has not kept pace with the record number of visits, and many of the
10 properties are in **serious** disrepair.

Several paths can be taken, perhaps simultaneously, to **alleviate the deterioration** of the properties within the system. Adopting tougher requirements for admission could reduce the number of additional units that the NPS manages. Congress has on occasion added properties without any input from the NPS itself.
15 It is debatable whether all of these properties, which may be of importance to the constituents of individual representatives of Congress, pass the test of "national significance." **Furthermore**, some of the units now in the NPS (there are close to 400) receive few visitors, and there is no reason to think that this trend will reverse itself. These units can be removed from the system, and their fates can
20 be decided by local public and private concerns. The liberated federal funds could then be rerouted to areas of greater need within the system.

Another approach would be to attack the root causes of the deterioration. Sadly, a great deal of the dilapidated condition of our national parks and park lands can be attributed not to overuse, but to misuse. Visitors should be educated about
25 responsible use of a site. Violators of these rules must be held accountable and fined harshly. There are, of course, already guidelines and penalties set in place, but studies strongly indicate that enforcement is lax.

From the first sentence, you can already tell a lot about this passage. The Park Service has an "unenviable" (opinion keyword) dilemma. You can predict that the author will state (in the grayed-out text of the first paragraph) what that dilemma is.

You get more opinion from the author in the final sentence of paragraph 1. "Unfortunately," (opinion keyword), the Park Service can't maintain the parks with so many visitors. The problem is apparently "serious" (emphasis keyword). On Test Day, you would jot some brief notes on your noteboard about the main idea of the first paragraph:

¶1: NPS problem: lots of visitors = hard to maintain lands

From the first sentence of the second paragraph, where do you anticipate that this passage will go? The phrase "alleviate the deterioration" indicates that the author will discuss some possible solutions to the Park Service's problem. Now is a good time to ask yourself whether this author is likely to express a preference for one of those solutions in particular. It seems that this author will probably describe the solutions without supporting one over the others, since she says there are "several" and that they might work at the same time. In the middle of the second paragraph, the word "Furthermore" is a continuation keyword, signaling that the paragraph continues to describe a proposed solution and why it might be effective. This is all you need to know about this paragraph from your initial read-through. Take down some notes for later reference:

¶2: Possible solutions; details about the first

Right off the bat, the third paragraph indicates that the author will describe "another approach." If you need to know details about this other approach, you can always return to the passage to research the answer to a question.

¶3: 2nd solution details

Just from this quick analysis, notice how much you already understand about the structure of the passage and the author's point of view. You effectively know what the grayed-out parts of the passage accomplish, even though you can't recite the details they contain. You are now in a strong position to approach the questions that accompany this passage, knowing that you can always return to the passage to clarify your understanding of any relevant details. Let's look at this first question:

Which of the following best describes the organization of the passage as a whole?

○ The author mentions a problem, and opposing solutions are then described.
○ The various factors that led to a problem are considered, and one factor is named the root cause.
○ A historical survey is made of an institution, followed by a discussion of the problem of management of the institution.
○ A problem is described, and two possibly compatible methods for reducing the problem are then outlined.
○ A description of a plan and the flaws of the plan are delineated.

This question asks for the organization of the entire passage. Fortunately, you already have the passage structure in your notes, so there's no need to go back to the passage itself to answer this question. The author begins by introducing a problem, then advances two potential solutions to that problem. The solutions are complementary, as the author states in line 11 that they can be undertaken "simultaneously." **(D)** matches this prediction and is the correct answer.

If you weren't sure about the answer, you could always eliminate incorrect answer choices by finding the specific faults they contain. **(A)** cannot be correct because it calls the two solutions "opposing."

(B) is incorrect because the focus of the passage is not on the "factors" leading to the problem but rather on solutions to the problem. **(C)** is incorrect because the passage gives no "historical survey" of the National Park Service; the only bit of historical data given is the date of its founding (1916). Finally, **(E)** is incorrect because the passage does not focus on the strengths and drawbacks of a single proposed plan of action; instead, it considers several different suggestions. Moreover, the passage never discusses the flaws of any of these possible solutions.

Let's now look at one more question about this passage:

> The author is primarily concerned with
>
> O   analyzing the various problems that beset the NPS
> O   summarizing the causes of deterioration of NPS properties
> O   criticizing the NPS's maintenance of its properties
> O   encouraging support for increased funding for the NPS
> O   discussing possible solutions for NPS properties' deterioration

This question asks for the author's purpose in writing the passage. As was the case in the previous question, you've already thought through the author's purpose as you read the passage strategically. Again, this question does not require specific research beyond the notes you've already taken.

The author is concerned with advancing two possible solutions to the dilemma faced by the National Park Service. **(E)** matches your prediction perfectly and is correct.

(A) is incorrect because only one problem is discussed, not "various" problems. **(B)** is incorrect because it is the solutions, not the causes, of the National Park Service's problem that are the focus of the passage. **(C)** is incorrect because the author is not critical of the NPS. Indeed, the word "unenviable" in the first sentence actually signals sympathy with the NPS's plight. **(D)** is incorrect because there is no discussion of funding in the passage.

THE KAPLAN METHOD FOR READING COMPREHENSION

Many test takers read the entire passage closely from beginning to end, taking detailed notes and making sure that they understand everything, and then try to answer the questions from memory. But this is *not* what the best test takers do.

The best test takers attack the passages and questions critically in the sort of aggressive, energetic, and goal-oriented way you've learned earlier. Working this way pays off because it's the kind of pragmatic and efficient approach that the GMAT rewards—the same type of approach that business schools like their students to take when faced with an intellectual challenge.

To help this strategic approach become second nature to you, Kaplan has developed a Method that you can use to attack each and every Reading Comp passage and question.

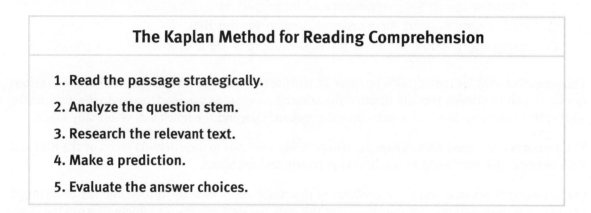

The Kaplan Method for Reading Comprehension

1. **Read the passage strategically.**

2. **Analyze the question stem.**

3. **Research the relevant text.**

4. **Make a prediction.**

5. **Evaluate the answer choices.**

STEP 1: READ THE PASSAGE STRATEGICALLY

Like most sophisticated writing, the prose you will see on the GMAT doesn't explicitly reveal its secrets. Baldly laying out the *why* and *how* of a passage up front isn't a hallmark of GMAT Reading Comprehension passages. And even more important (as far as the test makers are concerned), if the ideas were blatantly laid out, the test makers couldn't ask probing questions about them. So to set up the questions—to test how you think about the prose you read—the GMAT uses passages in which authors hide or disguise their reasons for writing and challenge you to extract them.

This is why it's essential to start by reading the passage strategically, staying on the lookout for structural keywords and phrases. With this strategic analysis as a guide, you should construct a passage map—a brief summary of each paragraph and its function in the passage's structure. You should also note the author's topic, scope, and purpose. Start by identifying the topic and then hunt for scope, trying to get a sense of where the passage is going, what the author is going to focus on, and what role the first paragraph is playing. As you finish reading each paragraph, jot down a short note about its structure and the role it plays in the passage. This process is similar to how you took notes on each paragraph of the National Park Service passage. When you finish reading the passage, double-check that you got the topic and scope right (sometimes passages can take unexpected turns) and note the author's overall purpose.

The topic will be the first big, broad idea that comes along. Almost always, it will be right there in the first sentence. There's no need to obsess over exactly how you word the topic; you just want a general idea of what the author is writing about so the passage gets easier to understand.

The scope is the narrow part of the topic that the author focuses on. If the author expresses his own opinion, then the thing he has an opinion about is the scope. Your statement of the scope should be as narrow as possible while still reflecting the passage as a whole. Your scope statement should also answer the question "What about this topic interests the author?" Identifying the scope is crucial because many wrong answers are unsupported by the facts the author has actually chosen to provide. Remember that even though the first paragraph usually narrows the topic down to the scope, there probably won't be a "topic sentence" in the traditional sense.

The purpose is what the author is seeking to accomplish by writing the passage. You'll serve yourself well by picking an active verb for the purpose. Doing so helps not only by setting you up to find the right answer—many answer choices contain active verbs—but also by forcing you to consider the author's opinion. Here are some verbs that describe the purpose of a neutral author: *describe, explain, compare.* Here are some verbs for an opinionated author: *advocate, argue, rebut, analyze.*

After you finish reading, your passage map should look something like this example:

¶1: NPS problem: lots of visitors = hard to maintain lands

¶2: Possible solutions; details about the first

¶3: 2nd solution details

Topic: National Park Service Dilemma

Scope: Reasons and possible solutions ⟶

Purpose: Describe two ⟶

You don't want to take any more than 4 minutes to read and write your passage map. After all, you get points for answering questions, not for creating nicely detailed passage maps. The more time you can spend working on the questions, the better your score will be. But creating a passage map and identifying the topic, scope, and purpose will prepare you to handle those questions efficiently and accurately.

It generally works best to create your passage map paragraph by paragraph. Don't write while you're reading, since you'll be tempted to write too much. But it's also not a good idea to wait until you've read the whole passage before writing anything, since it will be more difficult for you to recall what you've read. Analyze the structure as you read and take a few moments after you finish each paragraph to summarize the main points. Include details that are provided as evidence only when keywords indicate their importance. A line or two of paraphrase is generally enough to summarize a paragraph.

Your passage map can be as elaborate or as brief as you need it to be. Don't waste time trying to write out entire sentences if fragments and abbreviations will do. And notice in the above example how effective arrows can be. For example, there's no sense writing out the purpose as "Describe two solutions to the National Park Service's dilemma resulting from the dual imperative to keep lands unimpaired and also to allow for their recreational use," when some simple notes with arrows are just as helpful to you.

STEP 2: ANALYZE THE QUESTION STEM

Only once you have read the passage strategically and jotted down your passage map should you read the first question stem. The second step of the Kaplan Method is to identify the question type; the most common question types are Global, Detail, Inference, and Logic. We will cover each of these question types in detail later in this chapter. For now, know that you will use this step to ask yourself, "What should I do on this question? What is being asked?" Here are some guidelines for identifying each of the main question types:

- **Global.** These question stems contain language that refers to the passage as a whole, such as "primary purpose," "main idea," or "appropriate title for the passage."
- **Detail.** These question stems contain direct language such as "according to the author," "the passage states explicitly," or "is mentioned in the passage."
- **Inference.** These question stems contain indirect language such as "most likely agree," "suggests," or "implies."
- **Logic.** These question stems ask for the purpose of a detail or paragraph and contain language such as "in order to," "purpose of the second paragraph," or "for which of the following reasons."

In addition to identifying the question type, be sure to focus on *exactly* what the question is asking. Let's say you see this question:

> The passage states which of the following about the uses of fixed nitrogen?

Don't look for what the passage says about "nitrogen" in general. Don't even look for "fixed nitrogen" alone. Look for the *uses* of fixed nitrogen. (And be aware that the GMAT may ask you to recognize that *application* is a synonym of *use*.)

Finally, the GMAT occasionally asks questions that do not fall into one of the four major categories. These outliers make up only about 8 percent of GMAT Reading Comp questions, so you will probably see only one such question or maybe none at all. If you do see one, don't worry. These rare question types usually involve paraphrasing or analyzing specific points of reasoning in the passage. Often they are extremely similar to question types you know from GMAT Critical Reasoning. Because you can use your passage map to understand the passage's structure and Kaplan's strategies for Critical Reasoning to deconstruct the author's reasoning, you will be prepared to handle even these rare question types.

STEP 3: RESEARCH THE RELEVANT TEXT

Since there just isn't enough time to memorize the whole passage, you shouldn't rely on your memory to answer questions. Treat the GMAT like an open-book test, knowing you can return to the passage as needed. However, don't let that fact make you overreliant on research in the passage. Doing so could lead to lots of rereading and wasted time. For some question types, you are just as likely to find all the information you need to answer the question correctly using only your passage map. Here is how you should focus your research for each question type:

- **Global.** The answer will deal with the passage as a whole, so you should review your passage map and the topic, scope, and purpose you noted.
- **Detail.** Use the specific reference in the question stem to research the text. Look for the detail to be associated with a keyword.
- **Inference.** For questions that include specific references, research the passage based on the clues in the question stem. For open-ended questions, refer to your topic, scope, and purpose; you may need to research in the passage as you evaluate each answer choice.
- **Logic.** Use the specific reference in the question stem to research the text. Use keywords to understand the passage's structure. Refer to your passage map for the purpose of a specific paragraph.

STEP 4: MAKE A PREDICTION

As you have seen in the Critical Reasoning chapter of this book, predicting the answer before you look at the answer choices is a powerful strategy to increase your efficiency and accuracy. The same is true for GMAT Reading Comp. Making a prediction allows you to know what you're looking for before you consider the answer choices. Doing so will help the right answer jump off the screen at you. It will also help you avoid wrong answer choices that might otherwise be tempting. Here is how you should form your prediction for each question type:

- **Global.** Use your passage map and topic, scope, and purpose as the basis of your prediction.
- **Detail.** Predict an answer based on what the context tells you about the detail.
- **Inference.** Remember that the right answer *must* be true based on the passage. (Since many valid inferences could be drawn from even one detail, it's often best not to make your prediction more specific than that.)
- **Logic.** Predict an answer that focuses on *why* the paragraph or detail was used, not on *what* it says.

STEP 5: EVALUATE THE ANSWER CHOICES

Hunt for the answer choice that matches your prediction. If only one choice matches, it's the right answer.

If you can't find a match for your prediction, if more than one choice seems to fit your prediction, or if you weren't able to form a prediction at all (this happens for some open-ended Inference questions), then you'll need to evaluate each answer choice, looking for errors. If you can prove four answers wrong, then you can confidently select the one that remains, even if you aren't completely sure what you think about it. This is the beauty of a multiple-choice test—knowing how to eliminate the four wrong answers is as good as knowing how to identify the correct one.

Here are some common wrong answer traps to look out for:

- **Global.** Answers that misrepresent the scope or purpose of the passage and answers that focus too heavily on details from one part of the passage
- **Detail.** Answers that distort the context or focus on the wrong details entirely
- **Inference.** Answers that include extreme language or exaggerations of the author's statements, distortions of the passage's meaning, or the exact opposite of what might be inferred
- **Logic.** Answers that get the specifics right but the purpose wrong

Look out for unsupported answer choices and for "half-right/half-wrong" choices, which are fine at the beginning but then take a wrong turn. Some answer choices are very tempting because they have the correct details and the right scope, but they have a *not, doesn't,* or other twist that flips their meanings to the opposite of what the question asks for. Watch out for these "180s."

Now let's apply the Kaplan Method to an actual GMAT-length passage and some of its questions. One of the following questions is the same one you saw at the beginning of the chapter. Read the passage strategically and practice making a passage map. You can try your hand at the questions and then compare your analysis to ours, or you can let our analysis below guide you through the steps of the Kaplan Method. For now, don't worry if you're not quite sure how to identify the question types; we will cover those thoroughly later in this chapter. For now, concentrate on analyzing what the question asks of you and using the Method to take the most efficient path from question to correct answer.

Questions 1–2 are based on the following passage.

Since 1980, the notion that mass extinctions at the end of the Cretaceous period 65 million years ago resulted from a sudden event has slowly gathered support, although even today there is no scientific consensus. In the Alvarez scenario, an asteroid struck the earth, creating a gigantic crater. Beyond the immediate effects
5 of fire, flood, and storm, dust darkened the atmosphere, cutting off plant life. Many animal species disappeared as the food chain was snapped at its base.

Alvarez's main evidence is an abundance of iridium in the KT boundary, a thin stratum dividing Cretaceous rocks from rocks of the Tertiary period. Iridium normally accompanies the slow fall of interplanetary debris, but in KT boundary
10 strata, iridium is 10–100 times more abundant, suggesting a rapid, massive deposition. Coincident with the boundary, whole species of small organisms vanish from the fossil record. Boundary samples also yield osmium isotopes, basaltic sphericles, and deformed quartz grains, all of which could have resulted from high-velocity impact.

15 Paleontologists initially dismissed the theory, arguing that existing dinosaur records showed a decline lasting millions of years. But recent studies in North America, aimed at a comprehensive collection of fossil remnants rather than rare or well-preserved specimens, indicate large dinosaur populations existing immediately prior to the KT boundary. Since these discoveries, doubts about
20 theories of mass extinction have lessened significantly.

Given the lack of a known impact crater of the necessary age and size to fit the Alvarez scenario, some scientists have proposed alternatives. Courtillot, citing huge volcanic flows in India coincident with the KT boundary, speculates that eruptions lasting many thousands of years produced enough atmospheric debris to cause
25 global devastation. His analyses also conclude that iridium in the KT boundary was deposited over a period of 10,000–100,000 years. Alvarez and Asaro reply that the shock of an asteroidal impact could conceivably have triggered extensive volcanic activity. Meanwhile, exploration at a large geologic formation in Yucatan, found in 1978 but unstudied until 1990, has shown a composition consistent with
30 extraterrestrial impact. But evidence that the formation is indeed the hypothesized impact site remains inconclusive.

1. It can be inferred from the passage that supporters of the Alvarez and Courtillot theories would hold which of the following views in common?

   O The KT boundary was formed over many thousands of years.

   O Large animals such as the dinosaurs died out gradually over millions of years.

   O Mass extinction occurred as an indirect result of debris saturating the atmosphere.

   O It is unlikely that the specific cause of the Cretaceous extinctions will ever be determined.

   O Volcanic activity may have been triggered by shock waves from the impact of an asteroid.

2. The author mentions "recent studies in North America" (lines 16–17) primarily in order to

○ point out the benefits of using field research to validate scientific theories

○ suggest that the asteroid impact theory is not consistent with fossil evidence

○ describe alternative methods of collecting and interpreting fossils

○ summarize the evidence that led to wider acceptance of catastrophic scenarios of mass extinction

○ show that dinosaurs survived until the end of the Cretaceous period

Step 1: Read the Passage Strategically

Here's an example of how the passage should be analyzed. We've reprinted the passage as seen through the lens of strategic reading. On the left is the passage as you might read it, with keywords and important points in bold. On the right is what you might be thinking as you read.

PASSAGE

...**the notion** that mass extinctions at the end of the Cretaceous period 65 million years ago resulted from a sudden event **has slowly gathered support, although** even today there is **no** scientific **consensus**. In the **Alvarez scenario**, [bunch of details about an asteroid]

ANALYSIS

The first sentence is rich with information for the strategic reader. Not only do you get the topic (*mass extinctions at the end of the Cretaceous period*—whatever that is), but you also get an idea (*the notion that [the mass extinction] resulted from a sudden event*), the fact that some people agree with it (*slowly gathered support*), and the fact that not everyone does (*no scientific consensus*). You can predict that the passage will go on to talk not only about the support but also about why not everyone agrees. You also get one specific theory (*the Alvarez scenario*) and an elaborate description of what that is—it seems to involve an asteroid.

Alvarez's main evidence is [lots of detail]

The keywords are pretty clear—here's some evidence in support of one "sudden event" theory.

You don't need to focus too much on what the evidence is until there's a question about it.

Paleontologists initially dismissed the theory, arguing that [something] last[ed] **millions of years. But** recent studies...**doubts** about theories of mass extinction **have lessened significantly**.

With *dismissed the theory*, it's clear that this paragraph shows why some would oppose the "sudden event" idea (just as you predicted). Note that *millions of years*, not normally a keyword, creates contrast with "sudden event." Then the keyword *But* announces a change in direction: the recent studies lend support for the "sudden event" theory, so *doubts have lessened significantly*.

Given the **lack** of [evidence] to **fit the Alvarez scenario, some scientists have proposed alternatives. Courtillot,** citing [evidence], **speculates** that eruptions...cause[d] global devastation. **His analyses also conclude** [something about iridium]. **Alvarez and Asaro reply...But evidence...remains inconclusive.**

Alvarez lacks some evidence still, so there are some other theories. Courtillot says something about volcanoes and iridium. It looks like Alvarez makes a counterargument to Courtillot, too. But there isn't enough evidence either way, so the author doesn't pick a "winner."

Your passage map would look something like this:

¶1: Mass ext. & sudden event—Alvarez/asteroid

¶2: Alvarez evidence

¶3: Initial disagreement, recent studies, now less doubt

¶4: Courtillot/volcanoes; Alvarez reply; not enough evidence to choose

Topic: Mass extinctions at end of Cret. period

Scope: Theories about ⤴

Purpose: Describe two "sudden event" theories

This isn't the only way to word the passage map, of course. Anything along these lines would work—so long as you note that there are two theories and that the author doesn't ultimately prefer one to the other.

Step 2: Analyze the Question Stem

Now it's time to move to the questions and identify the question type. **Question 1** is what you will learn to call an Inference question: it uses the phrase *can be inferred*. Luckily, this Inference question contains clues that point you to a specific part of the passage. This will save you a lot of time. **Question 2** is a Logic question. The phrase *in order to* indicates that you're asked to identify *why* the author includes this detail.

Step 3: Research the Relevant Text

Question 1 asks you to find something that must be true according to both the Alvarez and the Courtillot theories. Our passage map shows that the Alvarez theory takes all of paragraph 2 and some of paragraph 4. That's too much to reread closely. But the Courtillot theory is mentioned only once, in paragraph 4 lines 22–26. Probably the most efficient way to research this question is to read through those two sentences and then deal with paragraph 2, doing focused research on each answer choice as needed.

Question 2 refers to lines 16–17, which are in paragraph 3. Since this is a Logic question, it's best to begin your research with the passage map. Here's what the map has to say about paragraph 3:

¶3: Initial disagreement, recent studies, now less doubt

So the "recent studies in North America" are either part of the initial disagreement or a reason that theories of mass extinction are less doubted now. Already, the word *recent* suggests the latter. But if you weren't confident about that, you could read the context of lines 16–17. The keywords *initially dismissed the theory* [*of mass extinction*] from the sentence before and from the sentence after (*Since these discoveries, doubts about theories of mass extinctions have lessened significantly*) seal the deal.

Step 4: Make a Prediction

The answer to **Question 1**, as you know, must be consistent with both theories. Since you researched Courtillot's theory, you can quickly eliminate any answer choice that disagrees with it.

Question 2 asks *why* the "recent studies in North America" were mentioned. Your research shows you that they provide the evidence that reduces doubt about theories of mass extinction. So an easy prediction would be something like "reasons why theories of mass extinction are doubted less than they used to be."

Step 5: Evaluate the Answer Choices

Question 1—**(A)** says that the KT boundary was formed over thousands of years, and that's consistent with Courtillot (line 26). What about Alvarez? Scanning through paragraph 2 for anything about "KT boundary" and time, you read in lines 9–11: "KT boundary...rapid, massive deposition." The word *rapid* is the only time signal at all, and it hardly fits with *many thousands of years*. Eliminate **(A)**. Perhaps you could eliminate **(B)** right away if you remembered that both theories are in the "sudden event" camp. But if not, your passage map saves the day—*dinosaurs died out gradually over millions of years* fits with *dinosaur records showed a decline lasting millions of years* in paragraph 3. But your map shows that to be evidence *against* Alvarez, not in support. So **(B)** is gone.

Debris saturating the atmosphere is consistent with Courtillot (line 24). What about Alvarez? Line 9 says *slow fall of interplanetary debris*. So both theories involve *debris*. Does it saturate the atmosphere? Not explicitly. But this is an Inference question, and you shouldn't expect to see things repeated explicitly from the passage. You do see that there was a *massive deposition*...and *massive* would suggest that there's a lot of this debris, so it's plausible that it saturated the atmosphere. There's not enough evidence to rule out **(C)**, so you can leave it alone for now.

(D) is the opposite of what Courtillot (as well as Alvarez) is trying to do, so this is a quick big-picture elimination. **(E)** is consistent with Alvarez's reply (lines 26–28). But this is a reply to Courtillot's theory—not his theory itself. The passage gives no indication of whether Courtillot would agree with this claim, so **(E)** is eliminated. Only **(C)** is left standing, so it must be right.

Note that you can prove **(C)** to be the right answer without proving *why* it's right. To prove why **(C)** is correct, you'd not only have to connect all the dots in paragraph 2, you'd have to tie it all to *mass extinctions* by going back to details from paragraph 1. It's much more efficient to eliminate **(A)**, **(B)**, **(D)**, and **(E)**.

Question 2—Your predicted answer from Step 4 ("reasons why theories of mass extinction are doubted less than they used to be") leads directly to **(D)**, the correct answer.

(A) sounds nice on its own, but the context has nothing to do with the benefits of field research in a specific way. **(B)** is the opposite of why those studies are introduced—it is in fact the old belief that these studies dispel. **(C)** and **(E)** focus on the details in lines 16–17 themselves—**(C)** in a distorted way—but not on *why* those details are there.

READING COMPREHENSION QUESTION TYPES

Though you might be inclined to classify Reading Comp according to the kinds of passages that appear—business, social science, biological science, or physical science—it's more effective to do so by question type. While passages differ in their content, you can read them in essentially the same way, employing the same strategic reading techniques for each.

Now that you're familiar with the basic principles of Critical Reasoning and the Kaplan Method, let's look at the most common types of questions. Certain question types appear again and again on the GMAT, so it pays to understand them beforehand.

The four main question types on GMAT Reading Comp are **Global**, **Detail**, **Inference**, and **Logic**. Let's walk through each of these question types in turn, focusing on what they ask and how you can approach them most effectively.

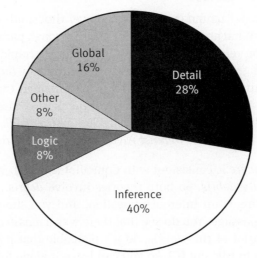

The Approximate Distribution of GMAT Reading Comprehension Questions

GLOBAL QUESTIONS

Any question that explicitly asks you to consider the passage as a whole is a Global question. Here are some examples:

- Which of the following best expresses the main idea of the passage?
- The author's primary purpose is to...
- Which of the following best describes the organization of the passage?
- Which of the following would be an appropriate title for this passage?

The correct answer will be consistent with the passage's topic, scope, purpose, and structure. If you've jotted these down on your noteboard (and you should!), then it will only take a few seconds to select the right answer.

The GMAT will probably word the answer choices rather formally, so by "few seconds," we mean closer to 45 than to 10. But that's still significantly under your average time per question, meaning that you can spend more time dealing with the trickier Inference questions.

Most wrong answers will either get the scope wrong (too narrow or too broad) or misrepresent the author's point of view. Be wary of Global answer choices that are based on details from the first or last paragraph. These are usually traps laid for those who wrongly assume that GMAT passages are traditional essays with "topic sentences" and "concluding sentences."

Often answer choices to Global questions asking about the author's purpose will begin with verbs; in this case, the most efficient approach is to scan vertically to eliminate choices with verbs that are inconsistent with the author's purpose. Common wrong answers misrepresent a neutral author by using verbs that indicate an opinionated stance.

TAKEAWAYS: GLOBAL QUESTIONS

- Step 1 of the Kaplan Method provides you with the information you need to predict the answer to Global questions.
- Use your passage map, topic, scope, and purpose to predict an answer. Then search the answer choices.
- If you can't find your prediction among the answer choices, eliminate wrong answer choices that misrepresent the scope.
- When all of the answer choices start with a verb, try a vertical scan, looking for choices that match your prediction or looking to eliminate choices that misrepresent the author's purpose.

DETAIL QUESTIONS

Detail questions ask you to identify what the passage explicitly says. Here are some sample Detail question stems:

- According to the passage, which of the following is true of X?
- The author states that...
- The author mentions which of the following in support of X?

It would be impossible to keep track of all of the details in a passage as you read through it the first time. Fortunately, Detail stems will always give you clues about where to look to find the information you need. Many Detail stems include specific words or phrases that you can easily locate in the passage. A Detail stem might even highlight a sentence or phrase in the passage itself. Using these clues, you can selectively reread parts of the passage to quickly zero in on the answer— a more efficient approach than memorization.

So between highlighting, references to specific words or phrases, and your passage map, locating the detail that the GMAT is asking about is usually not much of a challenge. What, then, could these questions possibly be testing? They are testing whether you understand that detail *in the context of the passage.* The best strategic approach, then, is to read not only the sentence that the question stem sends you to but also the sentences before and after it. Consider the following question stem:

> According to the passage, which of the following is true of the guinea pigs discussed in the highlighted portion of the passage?

Let's say that the highlighted portion of the passage goes like this:

> ...a greater percentage of the guinea pigs that lived in the crowded, indoor, heated area survived than did the guinea pigs in the outdoor cages.

If you don't read for context, you might think that something like this could be the right answer choice:

O   Guinea pigs survive better indoors.

But what if you read the full context, starting one sentence before?

> Until recently, scientists had no evidence to support the hypothesis that low temperature alone, and not other factors such as people crowding indoors, is responsible for the greater incidence and severity of influenza in the late fall and early winter. Last year, however, researchers uncovered several experiment logs from a research facility whose population of guinea pigs suffered an influenza outbreak in the winter of 1945; these logs documented that a greater percentage of the guinea pigs that lived in the indoor, heated area survived than did the guinea pigs in the outdoor cages.

Now you could identify this as the right answer:

O   Researchers discovered that some guinea pigs survived better indoors than outdoors during a flu outbreak.

By reading not just the highlighted portion of the passage but the information before it, you realize that it's not necessarily true that guinea pigs always survive better indoors; only a specific subset did. If you had picked an answer that matched the first prediction, you would be distorting the facts—you need to understand the information *in context.*

Make sure that you read entire sentences when answering Detail questions. Notice here that the question stem sends you to the end of the last sentence, but it's the "no evidence" and "however" at the *beginning* of the sentences that form the support for the right answer.

TAKEAWAYS: DETAIL QUESTIONS

- On Detail questions, use your passage map to locate the relevant text in the passage. If necessary, read that portion of the passage again. Then predict an answer.
- On Detail questions, never pick an answer choice just because it sounds familiar. Wrong answer choices on Detail questions are often distortions of actual details in the passage.
- All of the information needed to answer Detail questions is in the passage.

INFERENCE QUESTIONS

Reading Comp Inference questions, like Critical Reasoning Inference questions, ask you to find something that must be true based on the passage but is not mentioned *explicitly* in the passage. In other words, you need to read "between the lines." Here are some sample Inference question stems:

- Which of the following is suggested about X?
- Which of the following can be most reasonably inferred from the passage?
- The author would most likely agree that...

Inference questions come in two types. The first uses key phrases or highlighting to refer to a specific part of the passage. To solve this kind of question, find the relevant detail in the passage and consider it in the context of the material surrounding it. Then make a flexible prediction about what the correct answer will state.

Consider the following Inference question, once again asking about the guinea pigs we discussed earlier:

> Which of the following is implied about the guinea pigs mentioned in the highlighted portion of the passage?

Just like last time, you want to review the context around the highlighted portion. Doing so, you'll find that "until recently," there was "no evidence" that temperature affected the flu; "however," last year these guinea pig records appeared. The logical inference is not explicitly stated, but you can easily put the information from the two sentences together. The answer will be something like this:

○ Their deaths provided new evidence that influenza may be more dangerous in lower temperatures.

Other Inference questions make no specific references, instead asking what can be inferred from the passage as a whole or what opinion the author might hold. Valid inferences can be drawn from anything in the passage, from big-picture issues like the author's opinion to any of the little details. But you will probably be able to eliminate a few answers quickly because they contradict the big picture.

Then you'll investigate the remaining answers choice by choice, looking to put each answer in one of three categories—(1) proved right, (2) proved wrong, or (3) not proved right but not proved wrong either. It's distinguishing between the second and third categories that will lead to success on Inference questions. Don't throw away an answer because you aren't sure about it or "don't like it."

If you can't find material in the passage that proves an answer choice wrong, don't eliminate it. Since the correct answer to an Inference question is something that *must* be true based on the passage, you can often find your way to the correct answer by eliminating the four choices that *could* be false.

TAKEAWAYS: INFERENCE QUESTIONS

- On Inference questions, search for the answer choice that follows from the passage.
- When it's difficult to predict a specific answer to an Inference question, you still know that "the right answer *must* be true based on the passage."
- Wrong answer choices on Inference questions often use extreme language, or they exaggerate views expressed in the passage.

LOGIC QUESTIONS

Logic questions ask why the author does something—why he cites a source, why he includes a certain detail, why he puts one paragraph before another, and so forth. Another way of thinking of Logic questions is that they ask not for the purpose of the passage as a whole but for the purpose of a part of the passage. As a result, any answer choice that focuses on the actual content of a detail will be wrong.

Here are some sample Logic question stems:

- The author mentions X most probably in order to...
- Which of the following best describes the relationship of the second paragraph to the rest of the passage?
- What is the primary purpose of the third paragraph?

Most Logic questions can be answered correctly from your passage map—your written summary of each paragraph and the passage's overall topic, scope, and purpose. If the question references a detail, as does the first sample question stem above, then you should read the context in which that detail appears as well—just as you should for any Detail or Inference question that references a specific detail.

TAKEAWAYS: LOGIC QUESTIONS

- On Logic questions, predict the correct answer using the author's purpose and your passage map.
- Answer choices that focus too heavily on specifics are usually wrong—it's not content that's key in Logic questions but the author's motivation for including the content.

"OTHER" QUESTIONS

As you saw from the pie chart earlier, approximately 8 percent of Reading Comp questions will not fall neatly into the four main categories described above. On such questions, strategic reading of the question stem becomes even more important, since you'll need to define precisely what the question is asking you to do, and you may not be able to identify any specific pattern that the question falls into. But even within these rare "Other" question types, you can prepare yourself to see questions of the following varieties.

"Critical Reasoning" Questions

Occasionally in Reading Comp, you might find a question that seems more like one of the common Critical Reasoning question types, such as an **Assumption**, **Strengthen**, **Weaken**, or **Flaw** question. These questions refer to arguments, just as they do in Critical Reasoning—although unlike in Critical Reasoning, a particular argument will usually be confined to just one paragraph or portion of the Reading Comp passage, rather than the entire passage focusing on a single argument.

When you see questions like this, you should research the portion of the passage that includes the argument referenced by the question stem. Just as you would in Critical Reasoning, identify the conclusion and relevant evidence; then use the central assumption to form a prediction for the right answer.

Parallelism Questions

These questions ask you to take the ideas in a passage and apply them through analogy to a new situation. For example, a passage might describe a chain of economic events that are related causally, such as reduced customer spending leading to a slowdown of industrial production, which in turn leads to the elimination of industrial jobs. A Parallelism question might then ask you the following:

> Which of the following situations is most comparable to the economic scenario described the passage?

In this case, the correct answer will describe a scenario that is logically similar to the one in the passage. Don't look for a choice that deals with the same subject matter as the passage, as such choices are often traps. Parallelism questions are more concerned with structure than substance, so the correct answer will provide a chain of causally connected events, such as water pollution from a factory causing the death of a certain type of algae, which in turn causes a decline in the fish population that relied on that type of algae as its primary food source.

Application Questions

Application questions ask you to identify an example or application of something described in the passage. For instance, if the passage describes a process for realigning a company's management structure, an Application question could give you five answer choices, each of which describes the structure of a given company. Only the correct answer choice will accurately reflect the process described in the passage.

Application questions function similarly to Parallelism questions, except that whereas Parallelism questions ask you to identify an analogous logical situation (irrespective of subject matter), Application questions ask you to apply information or ideas directly, within the same subject area (rather than by analogy or metaphor).

Question Type Identification Exercise

Answers are on the page following this exercise.

Identifying the question type during Step 2 of the Kaplan Method for Reading Comprehension is a chance for you to put yourself in control of the entire process that follows: how to research, what to predict, and, thus, how to evaluate answer choices. Use the Core Competency of Pattern Recognition to analyze keywords in the question stem and determine what the question is asking you to do. Based on this analysis, choose the correct question type from the list of choices.

1. The passage implies which of the following about XXXXXXX?

   O   Global

   O   Detail

   O   Inference

   O   Logic

   O   Other

2. According to the passage, each of the following is true of XXXXXXX EXCEPT

   O   Global

   O   Detail

   O   Inference

   O   Logic

   O   Other

3. The author mentions XXXXXXX in order to

   O   Global

   O   Detail

   O   Inference

   O   Logic

   O   Other

4. The author's primary objective in the passage is to

   ○ Global
   ○ Detail
   ○ Inference
   ○ Logic
   ○ Other

5. The author makes which of the following statements concerning XXXXXXX?

   ○ Global
   ○ Detail
   ○ Inference
   ○ Logic
   ○ Other

6. An appropriate title for the passage would be

   ○ Global
   ○ Detail
   ○ Inference
   ○ Logic
   ○ Other

7. Which of the following statements about XXXXXXX can be inferred from the passage?

   O   Global
   O   Detail
   O   Inference
   O   Logic
   O   Other

8. Which of the following, if true, would most weaken the theory proposed by XXXXXXX?

   O   Global
   O   Detail
   O   Inference
   O   Logic
   O   Other

9. Which of the following best states the central idea of the passage?

   O   Global
   O   Detail
   O   Inference
   O   Logic
   O   Other

10. Which of the following situations is most comparable to XXXXXXX as it is presented in the passage?

    ○ Global
    ○ Detail
    ○ Inference
    ○ Logic
    ○ Other

11. The passage provides support for which of the following assertions about XXXXXXX?

    ○ Global
    ○ Detail
    ○ Inference
    ○ Logic
    ○ Other

12. The author indicates explicitly that which of the following has been XXXXXXX?

    ○ Global
    ○ Detail
    ○ Inference
    ○ Logic
    ○ Other

13. The author would most likely agree with which of the following?

   O   Global
   O   Detail
   O   Inference
   O   Logic
   O   Other

14. The author refers to XXXXXXX most probably in order to

   O   Global
   O   Detail
   O   Inference
   O   Logic
   O   Other

15. Which of the following represents the clearest application of XXXXXXX's theory as described in the passage?

   O   Global
   O   Detail
   O   Inference
   O   Logic
   O   Other

16. The passage is primarily concerned with

  ○   Global

  ○   Detail

  ○   Inference

  ○   Logic

  ○   Other

Question Type Identification Exercise: Answers

1. C

When you see "implies" or "suggests," know that you're facing an Inference question.

2. B

When you see direct, categorical language like "according to the passage," know that you're facing a Detail question.

3. D

The phrase "in order to" means that this is a Logic question. Logic questions deal with the author's motivations. If a question asks you why the author includes a paragraph, brings up a detail, or cites a source, know that you are facing a Logic question.

4. A

The phrase "primary objective" means that this is a Global question.

5. B

The phrase "makes which of the following statements" signals that this is a Detail question.

6. A

The phrase "title for the passage" means that we must base our answer on the whole passage, so this is a Global question.

7. C

The word "inferred" means that this is an Inference question.

8. E (Weaken)

The word "weaken" means that this is a Weaken question, one of the rarer question types in Reading Comp.

9. A

The phrase "central idea of the passage" means that this is a Global question.

10. E (Parallelism)

The phrase "most comparable to" means that this is a Parallelism question.

11. C

The phrase "passage provides support for" means that this is an Inference question.

12. B

The phrase "indicates explicitly" means that this is a Detail question.

13. C

The phrase "most likely agree" signals an Inference question.

14. D

The phrase "in order to" means that this is a Logic question.

15. E (Application)

The phrase "represents the clearest application of" means that this is an Application question. Application questions ask you to find the answer choice that is most consistent with a description, theory, or process described in the passage.

16. A

The phrase "passage is primarily concerned" means that this is a Global question.

READING COMPREHENSION QUIZ

Answers and explanations are at the end of the chapter.

Now it's time to apply the skills you've learned in this chapter to the following Reading Comprehension Quiz. Follow the Kaplan Method consistently so this strategic approach can become second nature by Test Day.

Note that the GMAT will give you three or four questions per passage, drawing those questions adaptively from a larger pool of up to six to eight problems. (The computer considers both your current score level and the distribution of question types you've seen so far.) For several passages on this quiz, we've given you more than four questions so that you can see the full range of questions the GMAT might ask about a given passage. But remember that on Test Day, you'll see only three or four.

Furthermore, remember that on Test Day, you can't take notes on the computer screen or skip forward and back between questions. So challenge yourself now not to take notes in this book (use separate scratch paper or a wet-erase noteboard like the one you'll use at the testing center) and to do the questions in order.

Questions 1–3 refer to the following passage.

Due to the laws and mechanics of the American presidential election system, the plurality winner of a state's popular vote generally gains that state's entire electoral vote. Thus, the winner of the national election is not necessarily the most popular candidate. In the 30 presidential elections from 1880 to 2000, there were two

5 occasions in which the winner of the presidential election did not win a plurality of the popular votes and ten occasions in which the president chosen by this system did not receive the majority of votes cast. Some critics believe that the electoral process should be replaced by a system that might better choose a president who is the most popular candidate among voters. Proposed alternatives include multiple

10 rounds of elections, "approval voting," and "rank voting."

In the approval voting system, each voter can cast votes for as many candidates as he or she wishes. A voter can select one candidate whom he or she favors, or a voter who disapproves of certain candidates can vote for every candidate except the ones whom he or she opposes. The Secretary General of the United Nations is elected using approval

15 voting, and, in a 1990 statewide referendum using the approval voting system, Oregon voters chose from five options for school financing. The approval voting system, however, can be confusing, and it can, theoretically, work against candidates who take strong stands on the issues and therefore attract disapproval.

Rank voting is known more formally as "Borda voting" after its first known

20 proponent, Jean Charles Borda. In this scheme, each voter can rank candidates from first to last. Depending on the number of candidates, each position would represent a number of points. For instance, if there were five candidates, the candidate ranked first would get five points, the candidate ranked second would get four points, and so on. The candidate with the most points in the end would be the winner. Rank voting

25 is used in the United States by the Associated Press to choose the best college sports teams, and a variant is used in most Australian elections. The rank system is advocated by a number of noted scholars, but it is criticized by some because the candidate ranked first by a majority of voters can still lose. For example, a

candidate who is ranked second by 80 percent of the voters could end up with more
30 points than one who is ranked first by 52 percent of the voters.

Although alternative voting systems offer noteworthy alternatives to the current process, there is not enough support for an alternative system in the United States to make its adoption likely in the near future on a national scale.

1. Which of the following best describes the main function of the first paragraph?

    O   To lament the nondemocratic nature of the U.S. presidential election system, and to provide alternatives to elections as a means of selecting presidents

    O   To show that the winner of a U.S. presidential election isn't necessarily the most popular candidate, and to explain that some critics suggest modifying the system

    O   To describe alternatives for the current U.S. presidential election system, and to advocate the acceptance of one alternative

    O   To attack the results of U.S. presidential elections, and to warn of the dangers of not adopting an alternative election system

    O   To advocate a sweeping reform of the U.S. presidential election system, and to provide evidentiary support for such a reform

2. It can be inferred from the passage that in a U.S. presidential election, the selection of the candidate most popular among the voters

    O   is more important than the other results that might be generated from the use of a particular election system

    O   would be attained through the use of the approval system for presidential elections

    O   has occurred in only a minority of U.S. presidential elections since 1880

    O   is critical to the maintenance of democratic institutions in the United States

    O   might be achieved through multiple rounds of elections

3. The primary purpose of the passage as a whole is to

    O   advocate a new system for electing presidents in the United States

    O   explain how the winner of the popular vote can lose the electoral vote

    O   argue that the current electoral system should be replaced with a rank voting system

    O   describe alternatives to the current U.S. presidential election system

    O   demonstrate that the current system of electing U.S. presidents is out-of-date

Questions 4–6 refer to the following passage.

The informal sector of the economy involves activities that, in both developed and underdeveloped countries, are outside the arena of the normal, regulated economy and thus escape official record-keeping. These activities, which include such practices as off-the-books hiring and cash payments, occur mainly in service
5 industries like construction, hotels, and restaurants. Many economists think that the informal sector is an insignificant supplement to the larger formal economy. They base this belief on three assumptions that have been derived from theories of industrial development. But empirical evidence suggests that these assumptions are not valid.

10 All three assumptions are, essentially, hypotheses about the character of the labor process at different levels of development. The first is that informal activities are transitory, being a consequence of the imperfect penetration of modern capitalism into less developed regions, and are thus destined to disappear with the advance of industrialization. The second is that the principal reason for the
15 continuing existence of an informal sector is to keep a redundant segment of the labor force alive through jobs invented to fit in the interstices of the modern economy. The third is that the informal sector is primarily a feature of peripheral economies such as those of Latin America, Africa, and most of Asia.

Data collected from both developed and underdeveloped countries, however,
20 reveal that the informal sector is neither disappearing with industrialization, limited in function to being an employment alternative of last resort, nor exclusively or particularly a Third World phenomenon. Informal sector employment rates in many countries have remained constant in the postwar era. Moreover, if the informal economy were exclusively a refuge from destitution, two facts would logically follow:
25 first, average income levels among the informally employed would be significantly lower than among workers in formal activities; second, those who found employment in formal activities would never leave voluntarily in order to move into the informal economy. But neither of these predictions is supported by data.

4. The primary purpose of this passage is to

O   compare the economies of developed and underdeveloped countries

O   suggest that economists should develop a new framework for studying the global economy

O   criticize the notion that the informal economy is primarily a Third World phenomenon

O   dispute a widely held view of the relationship between the formal and informal sectors of the world economy

O   argue that workers in the informal economy are almost as well paid as those in the formal economy

5. From the passage, which of the following can be inferred about employment opportunities in the informal economy?

   O   Workers employed in the informal economy generally receive much lower wages than do workers in the formal economy.

   O   Some workers have purposely chosen to work in the informal economy rather than in the formal economy.

   O   The number of workers employed in the informal economy has remained stable over the last few centuries.

   O   Employment opportunities in the informal economy will decline as agriculture is displaced by industry.

   O   The informal economy has created no employment for workers who would otherwise be unemployable.

6. The author states which of the following about activities in the informal economy?

   O   They are an insignificant aspect of the global economy.

   O   They provide income for workers who are unemployable in the formal economy.

   O   They are a consequence of capitalist penetration of less developed economies.

   O   They thrive mainly in underdeveloped countries in Asia, Africa, and Latin America.

   O   They consist of such unregulated practices as off-the-books hiring and cash payments.

Questions 7–12 refer to the following passage.

The Big Bang model posits that the universe was created in a primordial
fireball between 10 and 20 billion years ago. The model attempts to reconstruct
the behavior of the early universe using only the rules of general relativity,
elementary particle physics, and basic thermodynamics. Matching these claims with
5 observations of the universe today shows its validity.

The Big Bang produced a universe made almost entirely of hydrogen and helium.
For the first few seconds of the universe's existence, its temperature was so
high—over 10 billion degrees—and energetic electrons, neutrinos, and positrons so
abundant that subatomic particles such as neutrons and protons were constantly
10 transmuted into one another. As the universe cooled, these transmutations ceased.
Most of the matter took the form of the most stable particle, the proton, leaving a
universe where the ratio of protons to neutrons was about seven to one.

After a few minutes, the temperature of the universe fell to about 1 billion
degrees, cool enough for these protons and neutrons to bond and form nuclei.
15 Deuterons were formed as each neutron found a proton partner. Most deuterons
then joined another deuteron to form a helium nucleus. As the universe continued
to expand and cool, its density became too low to allow further fusion into heavier
elements, and so almost all the neutrons were incorporated into helium. Only
0.01 percent of the deuterons formed remained unpaired, and an even smaller
20 percentage had fused into elements heavier than helium, such as lithium.

Because only one neutron was formed for every seven protons, six-sevenths of all protons remained isolated. These remaining protons formed hydrogen nuclei containing one proton each. The Big Bang model predicts that about three-quarters of the total mass of the universe will be hydrogen and the remaining quarter

25   helium. This simple prediction matches observations very well.

7.   The author is primarily concerned with

○   explaining how the evolution of the universe is incompatible with the implications of the Big Bang model

○   chronicling the events that followed the creation of matter by the Big Bang

○   explaining how helium was formed in the early life of the universe

○   illustrating specific propositions of a model and showing how they have been supported by observation

○   showing how the ratios of protons to neutrons created in the Big Bang dictated the final ratio of hydrogen to helium in the universe

8.   In the fourth paragraph, the author introduces information about the Big Bang model's prediction for the molecular composition of the universe in order to

○   obviate the claim that six-sevenths of all protons remained isolated

○   show that the remaining quarter of the total mass of the universe must be helium

○   provide evidence for the veracity of the Big Bang model

○   describe the means by which remaining protons formed hydrogen nuclei

○   predict the results of a Big Bang

9.   According to the passage, which of the following was true during the first few seconds of the universe's existence?

   I.   The great majority of neutrons were incorporated into helium molecules.

   II. The temperature was not high enough to allow for the formation of deuterons.

   III. Vast numbers of subatomic particles rapidly metamorphosed into other types of particles.

○   None

○   I only

○   III only

○   II and III only

○   I, II, and III

10. The author uses the first paragraph to introduce

    O a scientific model that the passage will show to be supported by modern evidence

    O a theory of the origin of the universe that the passage will describe and attempt to refute

    O a description of the theoretical basis for a scientific model and the modern evidence undermining it

    O an attempt to use recent evidence to revive a discarded scientific model

    O a detailed description of an appealing but unsupported theoretical model

11. The author would most likely agree with the position that

    O models of the creation of the universe that were made before the Big Bang model was created failed because they did not take into account the behavior of subatomic particles

    O no credence can be given to a scientific model unless it is possible to produce supporting data through a series of controlled experiments

    O the Big Bang was part of a cycle of expansion and contraction in the universe

    O it is beneficial to use the statistical evidence at hand when judging the veracity of scientific models for which the process cannot be repeated in a laboratory

    O the simplicity of the Big Bang theory accounts for its accuracy

12. According to the passage, a helium nucleus

    O could only be created early in the universe's history

    O has a low density due to the cooling and expansion of the universe

    O is more stable than a lithium nucleus

    O has four times the mass of a hydrogen nucleus

    O consists of exactly two neutrons and two protons

Questions 13–17 refer to the following passage.

Parfleche is the French name for the Plains peoples' *hoemskot 'eo*—an envelope- shaped rawhide container for storing clothes, food, and personal items. The *parfleche* served not only as a practical and durable storage solution, but also as a decorative object of spiritual significance. Among certain tribes, most notably the Cheyenne and Arapaho, *parfleches*
5   were decorated by the women's painting society, whose members among the Cheyenne were known as *moneneheo*, the Selected Ones. Although similar in their economic and social importance to craftsmen's guilds in medieval and Renaissance Western Europe, the painting society also had a spiritual or religious nature. The shamanistic society required application for admission and held its members to high artistic and moral standards.
10 The society further displayed its importance by defining aspects of Cheyenne wealth and status.

Painting on rawhide was fraught with challenges. If painting was attempted while the prepared hide was too moist, the applied paint bled, but if the hide was too dry, the skin did not absorb the pigments. This restricted the time frame in which painting could best
15 be completed, which meant that designs had to be visualized fully before the work started.

Moreover, every aspect of creating a *parfleche* was a sacred act. Each design element, for instance, was a syntagma—a linguistic or visual unit intended to convey meaning—freighted with symbolic referents. For example, diamond shapes represented the *ha 'kot*, the grasshopper, an abundant grass eater itself symbolic of the bison, the sacred
20 source of food, shelter, tools, and clothing. The tools used were also symbolic: the shape of the "flesher" used to prepare the hide represented lightning bolts—emblematic of the masculine essence of spirit. The flesher removed the flesh from the hide, transforming it into a spiritual container that would hold earthly matter (the people's material goods).

Even the position of the *parfleche* in the lodge held symbolic significance. It was stored
25 beneath the bed of older women, not only because they were careful guardians, but also because they were closer to Grandmother Earth, from whose union with the lightning spirit the animals and plants of the middle world came to provide food and shelter. The symbolism of every aspect of the *parfleche,* therefore, from the interpretable design work on its outside to its storage place within the lodge, reflects the Cheyenne belief in a
30 complementary worldview: the blending of the masculine spirit and the feminine physical matter.

13. According to the passage, one reason why there was a limited time frame in which to paint a prepared rawhide was that

   O   the pigments dried quickly and thus had to be applied with speed to avoid cracking
   O   if the hide was too dry, it absorbed too much paint
   O   if the hide was too moist, it rejected the pigments
   O   the designs had to be fully visualized before painting was started
   O   if the hide was too moist, the paint bled

14. The main purpose of the passage is to

   O   describe a tool used among Native Americans when working with rawhide
   O   rebut a commonly held view about the symbolism of the *parfleche* for the Plains peoples
   O   analyze the societies of the Cheyenne and Arapaho people
   O   propose a new method for analyzing the use of symbolism in Native American art
   O   discuss the spiritual and symbolic importance of a rawhide container and its decorations to several Plains tribes

15. According to the author, the Cheyenne women's painting society was unlike Western European guilds of the Middle Ages and the Renaissance in that

   O   application for membership was required
   O   the group had significant economic standing in the community
   O   the group had significant social standing in the community
   O   the women's painting society was religious in nature
   O   the society had an influence on social standing and material valuation

16. You can most reasonably conclude that the Cheyenne definition of the term *moneneheo* (line 6) reflects

    ○ the high status some women enjoyed as artists in Cheyenne culture

    ○ the shamanistic spiritual origins of the women's painting society

    ○ the notion that artists were chosen by the gods to perform their tasks

    ○ the self-restrictive nature of the women's painting society

    ○ a woman's skill in using rawhide tools such as the "flesher"

17. The author describes the symbolic meanings of the diamond shape most likely in order to

    ○ indicate how precious the completed *parfleche* was to its owner

    ○ prove that the grasshopper was superior to the bison in Cheyenne religion

    ○ illustrate the visual complexity of the abstract forms used in creating a *parfleche*

    ○ provide an example of the many layers of symbolism involved in creating a *parfleche*

    ○ demonstrate the relationship between the symbolic shapes of the tools and the abstract designs used in creating a *parfleche*

Questions 18–23 refer to the following passage.

A one-child policy was implemented in China in 1979, and for nearly 40 years, until the policy was amended to allow two children in 2015, some Han Chinese families could legally only have one child. This rule was implemented in an attempt to slow continued growth of a population that had almost doubled since 1949. The Chinese
5   government claimed that the policy prevented 400 million births, though some have suggested that the decline may be at least partly due to economic reasons, not legal ones.

One result of the policy seems to be the birth and survival of significantly more boys than girls. One study found that China had 33 million more boys than girls under the age of
10 20, and it is believed that by 2030, 25 percent of Chinese men in their late 30s will never have been married. Research has shown that an excess of men of marriageable age is linked to higher rates of psychological problems, as it creates a marginalized underclass, and history would suggest such situations may correlate with increased aggression and violence, both inside and outside a country's borders.

15 Economist Amartya Sen wrote in 1990 of the phenomenon of "missing women" in population data, noting that in China, "the survival prospects of female children clearly have been unfavorably affected by restrictions on the size of the family." In a society that has traditionally strongly favored sons, it has been suggested that sex-specific pregnancy terminations and infanticide account for the discrepancy in numbers. But
20 others have countered this argument, believing that disease might better explain the phenomenon, either by making women more likely to give birth to male children or by making it more likely that female children will die prenatally or when very young. For at least some of the missing girls, however, a less sinister explanation may prove the

correct one: parents who already had a child, or who wanted to be able to have another
25   in an attempt to have a son, simply never registered their daughters with government
officials. A recent study found evidence that as many as 25 million girls were not
registered at birth, some of them officially "existing" only many years later and others
perhaps never officially existing at all.

18. The primary purpose of the passage is to

   O   criticize the accepted explanation for missing girls in China since the
       implementation of the one-child policy

   O   show why the expected population decline in China due to the one-child
       policy was not due to a decrease in the number of males

   O   demonstrate how China's one-child policy has influenced past and future
       birth rates

   O   explore the phenomenon of missing girls in China during the years of the
       one-child policy

   O   argue that the expected population decline in China due to the one-child
       policy was due entirely to a decrease in the number of women

19. According to the passage, which of the following is true of societies in which there
    are not enough female partners for men of marriageable age?

   O   They occurred historically but are not known to occur in the modern day.

   O   They may be at increased risk of international conflict.

   O   They are more likely to develop when a significant proportion of the
       population is psychologically damaged.

   O   They are not known to have occurred prior to the modern day.

   O   They can result in the disappearance of women from official records.

20. The last paragraph in the passage serves primarily to

   O   present multiple potential explanations for a phenomenon described in the
       second paragraph

   O   offer a critique of explanations put forward for the outcome of the policy in
       which the author is primarily interested

   O   demonstrate that the least sinister explanation of a troubling phenomenon is
       the correct one

   O   explain fully the phenomenon described in the second paragraph

   O   outline why social attitudes may explain the result of the policy that is the
       topic of the passage

21. According to the passage, each of the following is a possible reason for missing girls in China EXCEPT:

    O   Disease may cause more boys to be born than girls.

    O   The one-child policy does not require girls to be registered.

    O   Disease may cause more girls to die prenatally than boys.

    O   Infanticide of female children occurs because families prefer sons.

    O   Some girls are not registered so that parents can have another child.

22. Based on information in the passage, which of the following outcomes would have been most likely to occur if a Han Chinese family had a baby daughter prior to 2015?

    O   The parents are eventually pleased to have had a daughter, because there are so many marriageable men.

    O   Because disease may kill the daughter, the parents have another child in hopes of having a son.

    O   The parents appeal to the authorities to approve an exception to the number of children allowed.

    O   Because a pregnancy is more likely to result in a son than a daughter, the parents have another child.

    O   The parents fail to officially register the daughter, and they have another child.

23. The author mentions a "marginalized underclass" (line 12) most likely in order to

    O   show one potential societal risk of the one-child policy

    O   give an example of why there are more men than women in China

    O   demonstrate that men are inherently more violent than women

    O   argue that widespread poverty may cause people to value boys more than girls

    O   illustrate the effect of the one-child policy on average family income

Questions 24–29 refer to the following passage.

Generally, interspecific matings represent an evolutionary dead end, producing sterile offspring, if any at all. For some species of birds, however, such pairings may indeed bring evolutionary advantages to the participants. In the case of the female collared flycatchers of Gotland, three distinct factors may work to make interspecific
5   pairings with pied flycatcher males reproductively beneficial.

In many instances, female collared flycatchers nest with male pied flycatchers while continuing to mate with other collared flycatchers, in effect parasitizing the pied flycatchers, who invest in rearing and fledging any offspring. Often, more than half of the offspring raised by interspecific flycatcher pairs are, in fact, not hybrids.
10 Furthermore, an estimated 65 percent of the hybrid offspring of the resident pied flycatcher male are male. Because hybrid females are sterile and males are not, this male bias minimizes the primary disadvantage of interspecific matings: sterile offspring. Habitat specialization may be a third mechanism: these pairings tend to occur in the late spring when the coniferous woods favored by the pied flycatcher
15 provide a greater availability of food than the deciduous woods where the collared flycatchers tend to live. Together, these factors form a mechanism to improve substantially the reproductive success of female collared flycatchers beyond what would be expected of interspecific mating with pied flycatcher males.

Although all three of these mechanisms appear to act in concert to form a single
20 elaborate mechanism specifically evolved to circumvent the usual disadvantages of interspecific mating, studies have shown similar motivations for the behavior of female collared flycatchers mating within the species. According to Professor Siever Rohwer, collared flycatcher females will choose to nest with subordinate collared flycatcher males that inhabit good territory because collared flycatcher females
25 must pair-bond in order to be successful in raising offspring. To engender the best offspring, however, the females will continue to copulate with higher-quality collared males with whom they are not paired. Thus, females seem to be nesting with males of any species with the best territories available at the time, but they will continue to mate with more attractive males outside of their pair bonds.

30 A highly unusual behavior, interspecific mating seems to provide certain reproductive advantages to the collared flycatcher female. However, it remains unclear whether the mating behavior of female collared flycatchers evolved to circumvent the usual problems with interspecific mating or whether the behavior is simply an extension of how female collared flycatchers behave when mating within
35 their own species.

24. The author's primary purpose is to

   O   criticize the basis of a scientific theory
   O   defend a hypothesis concerning bird-mating behaviors
   O   point out the need for further study of female collared flycatchers
   O   describe two possible explanations for the interspecific mating behavior of
       female collared flycatchers
   O   defend an unpopular view of a natural phenomenon

25. According to the passage, female collared flycatchers' mating with male pied flycatchers could be explained by any of the following reasons EXCEPT:

    ○   Food is more available in pied flycatcher territories during the mating season.

    ○   Male pied flycatchers can help raise offspring successfully, even if the offspring are not theirs.

    ○   Male pied flycatchers sire more female offspring than do collared flycatcher males, increasing the reproductive success of the female collared flycatcher.

    ○   Females are known to nest with subordinate males while pursuing extra-pair copulation with higher-quality males.

    ○   Females enjoy greater reproductive success by pair-bonding with an inferior male than by not pair-bonding at all.

26. The bias toward male offspring resulting from the mating of collared flycatcher females and pied flycatcher males is presented as evidence that

    ○   collared flycatcher females that mate with pied flycatcher males have more dominant male offspring

    ○   the offspring from extra-pair matings with collared flycatcher males are more frequently male

    ○   female flycatchers are not deterred from interspecific pairing by the likelihood of sterile hybrid offspring

    ○   males are produced to reduce interspecific inbreeding in future generations

    ○   interspecific breeding is normal in all varieties of flycatchers

27. It can be inferred from the passage that

    ○   food resources are an important determinant of success in raising offspring

    ○   having 50 percent male offspring is not optimal for collared flycatcher pairs

    ○   flycatchers generally mate for life

    ○   males do not vary in the benefits they provide to their offspring

    ○   over half of all females engage in extra-pair matings

28. Professor Rohwer would most likely agree with which of the following statements?

    ○ All traits related to particular functions have evolved only for those particular functions.

    ○ Flycatchers represent the best population for studies of bird-mating behavior.

    ○ Behaviors may appear functional even under conditions other than those under which the behaviors evolved.

    ○ Evolution has played no role in shaping the behavior of interspecifically paired flycatchers.

    ○ Hybridization is generally beneficial.

29. The mating behavior of female collared flycatchers paired with subordinate male flycatchers is offered as

    ○ an unwarranted assumption behind the adaptive explanation of interspecific matings

    ○ an alternative explanation for pair matings of collared females with pied males

    ○ evidence supporting the hypothesis of adaption for interspecific breeding

    ○ a discredited mainstream explanation for why hybridization is a dead end

    ○ proof in support of the theory that collared and pied flycatchers are separate species

Questions 30–35 refer to the following passage.

Rainbows have long been a part of religion and mythology in cultures around the globe, appearing as bridges between the heavens and the earth, as messages from the gods, or as weapons wielded by divine powers. Some cultures have viewed rainbows themselves as deities, or even as demonic beings from which to hide children. But in the early
5   fourteenth century, Theodoric of Freiburg, a German friar, and Kamal al-Din al-Farisi, a Persian scientist, independently turned a scientific eye to the study of rainbows.

Theodoric and al-Farisi were thousands of miles apart, but both had studied Ibn al-Haytham's *Book of Optics*. Each concluded that a rainbow's appearance is the result of sunlight refracting and reflecting through water droplets left after a rainfall. They
10   conducted experiments to provide support for their conclusions, successfully re-creating the conditions necessary to make a rainbow appear; al-Farisi used a sphere and a camera obscura, while Theodoric used flasks and globes.

Both scholars were, as modern physics has shown, correct in their assessments. When light hits a water droplet, the water causes the light's speed to decrease. Furthermore,
15   the light refracts—or changes direction—upon entering the droplet, and some of the light reflects off the back of the droplet, refracting again as it exits. The angle of refraction depends on the wavelength of the light; thus, refraction "breaks" white light into multiple wavelengths—a phenomenon called dispersion—which appear as different colors.

But for a rainbow to fill the sky with color, more is needed. A single droplet of water will
20   disperse the entire visible light spectrum, with each wavelength leaving at a different angle, but it alone cannot create a rainbow. Only a little of the light from a particular

droplet reaches the eye of the human observer, striking the eye from a particular angle. For the observer to perceive the rainbow's characteristic banded arc of different colors, a multitude of droplets suspended in the air, refracting and dispersing light, are needed,

25 with the shorter wavelengths and shallower angles of indigo and violet appearing to the observer at the bottom and the longer wavelengths and steeper angles of red and orange appearing at the top.

30. The author mentions the angle at which light leaves water droplets (lines 19–21) primarily in order to

   ○   describe how refraction causes light to disperse as it leaves a water droplet

   ○   show that indigo and violet appear at the bottom of rainbows because those colors have shallower angles

   ○   illustrate that a change in the angle of light changes the wavelength of the light

   ○   explain that the human eye perceives a rainbow only when light is refracted from multiple points

   ○   introduce evidence that may help solve a longstanding mystery about the physics of refraction

31. Based on the passage, it can be inferred that the rainbow's middle colors of yellow, green, and blue

   ○   are not broken into separate bands by the dispersion of light leaving a droplet of water

   ○   have longer wavelengths than do the red and orange light at the top of the rainbow

   ○   have wavelengths that all strike the eye of a human observer at the same angle

   ○   have wavelengths that are refracted at shallower angles than the wavelengths of indigo and violet light

   ○   have wavelengths that are shorter than those of red and orange light and longer than those of indigo and violet light

32. According to the passage, the refraction of light upon entering and leaving a water droplet

   ○   changes the angle at which light leaves the water droplet, thereby altering the light's wavelength

   ○   causes the light to be reflected and thus intensify, becoming more visible to the human observer

   ○   disperses white light, allowing it to be seen as its different component colors

   ○   causes the light to slow and thus more readily disperse according to its different wavelengths

   ○   alters the light's wavelengths so they fall within the visible spectrum

33. The primary purpose of the passage is to

   ○   explain why rainbows are a relatively rare phenomenon

   ○   describe religious and scientific explanations for the appearance of rainbows

   ○   raise doubts about a historical explanation for the appearance of rainbows

   ○   explore the reasons that the refraction of light causes it to appear as different colors

   ○   examine the physics underlying the appearance of rainbows to the human observer

34. It can be inferred that the author of the passage would most likely agree with which of the following statements about the study of rainbows?

   ○   Scientific experiments performed hundreds of years ago sometimes provided accurate results.

   ○   Cultures that associate rainbows with divinity do not approve of scientific inquiry into the nature of rainbows.

   ○   The experiments of Theodoric and al-Farisi established that refraction of light occurs in water droplets but did not examine larger volumes of water.

   ○   In societies in which the results of scientific studies of rainbows are widely accepted, rainbows are no longer associated with spiritual meaning.

   ○   Studies such as Theodoric's and al-Farisi's now have no value because modern science has shown them to be simplistic.

35. The primary function of the second paragraph is to

   ○   discuss a challenge to the conception of rainbows as a religious symbol

   ○   evaluate two historical methods for observing rainbows

   ○   describe the difficulties early scholars overcame in their attempts to understand rainbows

   ○   support the idea that medieval science is similar in value to modern science

   ○   outline historical attempts to understand the scientific basis of rainbows

ANSWERS AND EXPLANATIONS BEGIN ON NEXT PAGE

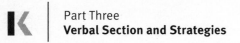

ANSWERS AND EXPLANATIONS

1.	B	10.	A	19.	B	28.	C
2.	E	11.	D	20.	A	29.	B
3.	D	12.	E	21.	B	30.	D
4.	D	13.	E	22.	E	31.	E
5.	B	14.	E	23.	A	32.	C
6.	E	15.	D	24.	D	33.	B
7.	D	16.	A	25.	C	34.	A
8.	C	17.	D	26.	C	35.	E
9.	C	18.	D	27.	A		

EXPLANATIONS

On the left, we've shown how keywords help you to identify the major elements of the passage and its structure and what you could skim over. On the right, we've shown what you might be thinking as you read the passage strategically.

Passage for Questions 1–3

PASSAGE

Due to the laws and mechanics of the **American presidential election system**, the plurality winner of a state's popular vote generally gains that state's entire electoral vote. **Thus**, the winner of the national election is not necessarily the most popular candidate. In the 30 presidential elections from 1880 to 2000, there were two occasions in which the winner of the presidential election did not win a plurality of the popular votes and ten occasions in which the president chosen by this system did not receive the majority of votes cast. **Some critics believe** that the electoral process should be replaced by a system that might better choose a president who is the most popular candidate among voters. **Proposed alternatives** include multiple rounds of elections, "approval voting," and "rank voting."

In the **approval voting system**, each voter can cast votes for as many candidates as he or she wishes. A voter can select one candidate whom he or she favors, or a voter who disapproves of certain candidates can vote for every candidate except the ones whom he or she opposes. The Secretary General of the United Nations is elected using approval voting, and, in a 1990 statewide referendum using the approval voting system, Oregon voters chose from five options for school financing. The approval voting system, **however**, can be confusing, and it can, theoretically, work against candidates who take strong stands on the issues and therefore attract disapproval.

ANALYSIS

The topic, the American presidential election system, is announced in the first sentence.

A quirky effect of the current system: the winner isn't necessarily the most popular candidate. This leads the critics to suggest that a different system might be better.

Because the author enumerates the possible alternative systems at the end of the opening paragraph, expect to see at least some of them discussed in later paragraphs.

Indeed, here's the first alternative the author will discuss: approval voting, which seems to be a system allowing voters to cast votes for multiple candidates they approve of.

The author gives a couple of examples of elections run according to approval voting.

The word "however" indicates contrast. Although approval voting is in use, the author believes that it has a couple of drawbacks.

Rank voting is known more formally as "Borda voting" after its first known proponent, Jean Charles Borda. **In this scheme**, each voter can rank candidates from first to last. Depending on the number of candidates, each position would represent a number of points. **For instance**, if there were five candidates, the candidate ranked first would get five points, the candidate ranked second would get four points, and so on. The candidate with the most points in the end would be the winner. Rank voting is used in the United States by the Associated Press to choose the best college sports teams, and a variant is used in most Australian elections. The rank system is **advocated** by a number of noted scholars, **but it is criticized** by some because the candidate ranked first by a majority of voters can still lose. **For example**, a candidate who is ranked second by 80 percent of the voters could end up with more points than one who is ranked first by 52 percent of the voters.

Although alternative voting systems offer **noteworthy alternatives** to the current process, there is **not enough support** for an alternative system in the United States to make its adoption likely in the near future on a national scale.

Now the author proceeds to discuss a second alternative: rank voting. The words "in this scheme" indicate that you're about to be given a description of the rank voting method.

Here the author gives specific examples of elections using rank voting.

Like approval voting, rank voting apparently has its pros and cons.

The keyword "Although" signals a contrast: the author thinks there are "noteworthy" methods that could replace the current one, but they aren't likely to be put into use anytime soon.

Passage Map

¶1: American presidential election system = electoral system

Problem: candidate with most popular vote can lose

Critics favor alternatives

¶2: Approval voting: can vote for several candidates

Drawback: can be confusing

¶3: Rank voting: voters rank choices

Drawback: candidate ranked 1st by majority could still lose

¶4: Author likes alternatives, but they probably won't be adopted soon

Topic: American presidential election system

Scope: Problem with, and alternatives to, the current system

Purpose: Describe problem with current electoral system and two potential alternatives

1.   **(B)**

Which of the following best describes the main function of the first paragraph?

○   To lament the nondemocratic nature of the U.S. presidential election system, and to provide alternatives to elections as a means of selecting presidents

○   To show that the winner of a U.S. presidential election isn't necessarily the most popular candidate, and to explain that some critics suggest modifying the system

○   To describe alternatives for the current U.S. presidential election system, and to advocate the acceptance of one alternative

○   To attack the results of U.S. presidential elections, and to warn of the dangers of not adopting an alternative election system

○   To advocate a sweeping reform of the U.S. presidential election system, and to provide evidentiary support for such a reform

Step 2: Analyze the Question Stem

Because you are asked for the function of a chunk of the passage, this is a Logic question. Specifically, you are asked to deduce the role played by the first paragraph.

Step 3: Research the Relevant Text

A glance at your passage map will suffice in this case. You shouldn't have to go back to the passage text itself.

Step 4: Make a Prediction

The first paragraph, as noted in the passage map, describes the American presidential election system, states that there is a problem with the current system that has caused it to receive some criticism, and lists several proposed alternatives.

Step 5: Evaluate the Answer Choices

(B) matches the prediction and is the correct answer. The fact that the winner of a U.S. presidential election isn't necessarily the most popular candidate is the "problem" recorded in the passage map. **(A)** is incorrect because the author takes a very neutral tone. The initial verb, "to lament," is sufficient to throw this one out. Moreover, the author never describes the U.S. presidential election system as "nondemocratic." **(C)** is incorrect because the author does not "advocate" for either of the proposed alternatives. **(D)** is incorrect because the author does not "attack" election results. **(E)** is similar to **(C)**; again, the author does not "advocate" making a change to the current system.

2. **(E)**

It can be inferred from the passage that in a U.S. presidential election, the selection of the candidate most popular among the voters

- ○ is more important than the other results that might be generated from the use of a particular election system
- ○ would be attained through the use of the approval system for presidential elections
- ○ has occurred in only a minority of U.S. presidential elections since 1880
- ○ is critical to the maintenance of democratic institutions in the United States
- ○ might be achieved through multiple rounds of elections

Step 2: Analyze the Question Stem

The word "inferred" signals that this is an Inference questions. The correct answer must be true based only on information in the passage. Note that the question asks specifically about the selection of the most popular candidate in U.S. presidential elections.

Step 3: Research the Relevant Text

Use your passage map to confirm that the question stem points to the first paragraph, where the author discusses the current practice used in American presidential elections. You read that under the current system, the winner of the popular vote is not necessarily the winner of an election and that critics have proposed alternative systems that would make the winner more likely to be the popular favorite, including multiple rounds of elections, approval voting, and rank voting.

Step 4: Make a Prediction

While it is difficult to make a specific prediction because the sentence in the question stem could be completed in multiple ways, the correct answer will be in accord with the information you have gleaned from the first paragraph about the U.S. presidential election system.

Step 5: Evaluate the Answer Choices

(E) is supported by the passage and is correct. It is true, according to the last few lines of the first paragraph, that selecting the most popular candidate "might" be achieved through multiple rounds of elections. **(A)** cannot be correct because there is nothing in the first paragraph to indicate that electing the most popular candidate is "more important" than any other result of a particular election system. **(B)** might be tempting, because you read about the possibility of using approval voting in the last sentence of the first paragraph. However, you can throw out this choice as extreme. The author merely states that approval voting is one of the systems that the critics believe "might" better choose the most popular candidate; there is no indication that the approval voting system would definitely have this effect. **(C)** cannot be correct according to the numbers given in the first paragraph. In 20 of 30 presidential elections, the winner has received the majority of votes cast, and in 28 of 30, the winner has received the plurality of votes cast. Either way, that's the majority of elections since 1880. **(D)** is unsupported. There is no mention of anything being "critical to the maintenance of democratic institutions."

3.   **(D)**

The primary purpose of the passage as a whole is to

○   advocate a new system for electing presidents in the United States
○   explain how the winner of the popular vote can lose the electoral vote
○   argue that the current electoral system should be replaced with a rank voting system
○   describe alternatives to the current U.S. presidential election system
○   demonstrate that the current system of electing U.S. presidents is out-of-date

Step 2: Analyze the Question Stem

The phrase "primary purpose" indicates that this is a Global question. You need to ascertain the author's purpose in writing the passage.

Step 3: Research the Relevant Text

The only research you'll need to do will be to consult your statements of topic, scope, and purpose.

Step 4: Make a Prediction

As stated in the passage map, the author's purpose is to describe a problem with the current U.S. electoral system, as well as two alternatives that have been proposed.

Step 5: Evaluate the Answer Choices

(D) matches the prediction and is the correct answer. **(A)** is incorrect because the author isn't "advocating" for anything. The tone of the passage is fairly neutral. **(B)** is a classic wrong answer type called "faulty use of detail." The passage definitely discusses how the winner of the popular vote can lose the electoral vote, but it goes on to discuss the two proposed alternative election systems. Watch out for answer choices that, like this one, provide you with only part of the passage when you're looking for a choice that encompasses the entire thing. **(C)** is incorrect because the author does not make any recommendations. **(E)** is incorrect because the passage makes no mention of the idea that the current electoral system is "out-of-date."

On the left, we've shown how keywords help you to identify the major elements of the passage and its structure and what you could skim over. On the right, we've shown what you might be thinking as you read the passage strategically.

Passage for Questions 4–6

PASSAGE

The **informal sector of the economy** involves activities that, in both developed and underdeveloped countries, are outside the arena of the normal, regulated economy and thus escape official record-keeping. These activities, which include such practices as off-the-books hiring and cash payments, **occur mainly** in service industries like construction, hotels, and restaurants. **Many economists** think that the informal sector is an insignificant supplement to the larger formal economy. They base this belief on three assumptions that have been derived from theories of industrial development. **But** empirical evidence suggests that these assumptions are **not valid**.

All three assumptions are, essentially, hypotheses about the character of the labor process at different levels of development. The **first** is that informal activities are transitory, being a consequence of the imperfect penetration of modern capitalism into less developed regions, and are thus destined to disappear with the advance of industrialization. The **second** is that the principal reason for the continuing existence of an informal sector is to keep a redundant segment of the labor force alive through jobs invented to fit in the interstices of the modern economy. The **third** is that the informal sector is primarily a feature of peripheral economies such as those of Latin America, Africa, and most of Asia.

ANALYSIS

The author begins by describing the informal sector of the economy, which will be the topic of the passage.

Economists think the informal sector is not important, based on three assumptions.

The author of the passage disagrees with the economists' assumptions, citing evidence to the contrary.

The second paragraph outlines the three assumptions made by the economists mentioned above.

The author's opinion doesn't figure into this paragraph—it only identifies the three assumptions.

Data collected from both developed and underdeveloped countries, **however**, reveal that the informal sector is neither disappearing with industrialization, limited in function to being an employment alternative of last resort, nor exclusively or particularly a Third World phenomenon. Informal sector employment rates in many countries have remained constant in the postwar era. **Moreover**, if the informal economy were exclusively a refuge from destitution, two facts would logically follow: first, average income levels among the informally employed would be significantly lower than among workers in formal activities; second, those who found employment in formal activities would never leave voluntarily in order to move into the informal economy. **But** neither of these predictions is supported by data.

Here the author discusses how the "data" refute the first of the economists' assumptions (transitory)...

and the second (redundant)...

and the third (peripheral).

The author further develops the rebuttal.

Passage Map

¶1: Description of informal sector

  Economists think it's unimportant, due to three assumptions

¶2: Economists' assumptions about the informal sector:

  (1) transitory

  (2) created for those who cannot find jobs within the formal economy (redundant)

  (3) a feature of developing economies (peripheral)

¶3: Economists' assumptions are all incorrect

  Reasons given to refute the first two

Topic: Informal sector of the economy

Scope: Economists' belief and assumptions about the informal sector

Purpose: To show the economists are incorrect in their assumptions and thus in their belief that the informal sector is insignificant

4. **(D)**

The primary purpose of this passage is to

O   compare the economies of developed and underdeveloped countries

O   suggest that economists should develop a new framework for studying the global economy

O   criticize the notion that the informal economy is primarily a Third World phenomenon

O   dispute a widely held view of the relationship between the formal and informal sectors of the world economy

O   argue that workers in the informal economy are almost as well paid as those in the formal economy

Step 2: Analyze the Question Stem

The phrase "primary purpose" signals that this is a Global question. You need the author's reason for writing the passage.

Step 3: Research the Relevant Text

For this question, simply consult your notes on topic, scope, and purpose. You shouldn't have to go back to the passage itself.

Step 4: Make a Prediction

As noted in the passage map, the author's purpose in writing the passage is to demonstrate that the economists are wrong in thinking the informal sector of the economy to be "insignificant" compared to the formal sector.

Step 5: Evaluate the Answer Choices

(D) matches the prediction and is correct. The "widely held view" is that of the economists. **(A)** is unsupported by the passage, which focuses on the economists' assumptions about the informal sector of the economy. **(B)** is again unsupported. The author makes no recommendation as to what the economists "should" do. **(C)** is a classic faulty use of detail. The idea that the informal sector is a Third World phenomenon is certainly mentioned and criticized in the passage (specifically, in paragraph 3), but this isn't the purpose of the entire passage. **(E)** is another faulty use of detail. The pay rates of informal- and formal-sector workers are mentioned in the third paragraph, but again, this doesn't constitute the purpose of the entire passage.

5. (B)

From the passage, which of the following can be inferred about employment opportunities in the informal economy?

- ○ Workers employed in the informal economy generally receive much lower wages than do workers in the formal economy.
- ○ Some workers have purposely chosen to work in the informal economy rather than in the formal economy.
- ○ The number of workers employed in the informal economy has remained stable over the last few centuries.
- ○ Employment opportunities in the informal economy will decline as agriculture is displaced by industry.
- ○ The informal economy has created no employment for workers who would otherwise be unemployable.

Step 2: Analyze the Question Stem

The word "inferred" signals an Inference question. This question stem provides a context clue: "employment opportunities in the informal economy."

Step 3: Research the Relevant Text

Unless a question specifically mentions a different point of view, it is asking for the author's perspective. You can safely confine your research to the first and third paragraphs and leave out the second, which describes the economists' assumptions. In the first paragraph, you learn that informal sector occupations are typically service jobs such as construction, hotel, or restaurant jobs. In the third paragraph, you learn that informal sector jobs are not jobs "of last resort," because they don't necessarily pay a great deal less than formal sector jobs and because some workers actually move "voluntarily" from the formal to the informal sector.

Step 4: Make a Prediction

While it is difficult to make a precise prediction for this question, the correct answer will follow from your research. Check the answer choices against it one at a time.

Step 5: Evaluate the Answer Choices

(B) paraphrases the last couple of lines of the passage: data support the idea that some workers do voluntarily move from formal sector employment to informal sector employment. This is the correct answer. **(A)** states the opposite of the wage information found in the third paragraph. **(C)** is too extreme. You learn in the third paragraph that "informal sector employment rates in many countries have remained constant in the postwar era," but you have no support for the idea that such employment has remained stable for "centuries." **(C)** also confuses employment rates (which are percentages) with the number employed. **(D)** restates one of the economists' assumptions. It is the economists, not the author, who believe that the informal sector will disappear with increasing industrialization. **(E)** is extreme. While the author debunks the economists' assumption that the informal sector is "limited in function to being an employment alternative of last resort," she never goes so far as to say that not a single job for an otherwise unemployable person has been created in the informal sector.

6. **(E)**

The author states which of the following about activities in the informal economy?

○ They are an insignificant aspect of the global economy.

○ They provide income for workers who are unemployable in the formal economy.

○ They are a consequence of capitalist penetration of less developed economies.

○ They thrive mainly in underdeveloped countries in Asia, Africa, and Latin America.

○ They consist of such unregulated practices as off-the-books hiring and cash payments.

Step 2: Analyze the Question Stem

This Detail question asks for something the author "states" explicitly. All you need to do is go back to the passage and look up the "activities in the informal economy."

Step 3: Research the Relevant Text

The "activities" that take place in the informal economy are mentioned at the beginning of the first paragraph. You learn that they are typically "off-the-books" and that they include hiring and cash payments in the construction, hotel, and restaurant industries.

Step 4: Make a Prediction

Look for an answer choice that mentions any of the details gleaned from your research. Remember that for a Detail question, the correct answer has to come from the passage nearly verbatim.

Step 5: Evaluate the Answer Choices

(E) restates what you read in the first paragraph and is the correct answer. **(A)** is incorrect because it is the economists, not the author, who believe that informal sector activities are "insignificant." **(B)** is incorrect because, again, it states one of the economists' assumptions, not the author's opinion. Similarly, **(C)** and **(D)** are incorrect because they present the economists' beliefs, not the author's.

On the left, we've shown how keywords help you to identify the major elements of the passage and its structure and what you could skim over. On the right, we've shown what you might be thinking as you read the passage strategically.

Passage for Questions 7–12

PASSAGE

The Big Bang model **posits** that the universe was created in a primordial fireball between 10 and 20 billion years ago. The model **attempts** to reconstruct the behavior of the early universe using only the rules of general relativity, elementary particle physics, and basic thermodynamics. Matching these claims with observations of the universe **today shows its validity**.

The Big Bang produced a universe made almost entirely of hydrogen and helium. For the **first few seconds** of the universe's existence, its temperature was so **high**— over 10 billion degrees—and energetic electrons, neutrinos, and positrons **so abundant** that subatomic particles such as neutrons and protons were constantly transmuted into one another. As the universe **cooled**, these transmutations ceased. Most of the matter took the form of the most stable particle, the proton, leaving a universe where the ratio of protons to neutrons was about seven to one.

After a few minutes, the **temperature** of the universe **fell** to about 1 billion degrees, **cool enough** for these protons and neutrons to bond and form nuclei. Deuterons were formed as each neutron found a proton partner. Most deuterons then joined another deuteron to form a helium nucleus. As the universe **continued to** expand and **cool**, its density became too low to allow further fusion into heavier elements, and so almost all the neutrons were incorporated into helium. Only 0.01 percent of the deuterons formed remained unpaired, and an even smaller percentage had fused into elements heavier than helium, such as lithium.

ANALYSIS

The topic appears right away: the Big Bang model.

The word "attempts" begs the question of whether the model succeeds.

Aha! Indeed, the Big Bang model succeeded. And current observations demonstrate this.

Lots of details about the Big Bang. Since you don't want to read details too closely, you could try to get away just with saying "details about the Big Bang" in your map, but then paragraph 3 would be the same thing. So, you have to find some way of grouping these details. The passage gives two sequences that let you do so easily: time ("first few seconds") or temperature ("so high" and "cooled").

Once again, a ton of details about the Big Bang. If you're using the time sequence, then this is the next "few minutes." If you're using the temperature sequence, then the universe continues to "cool." Happily, you don't need to understand a thing about particle physics to understand the basic structure of the passage!

EXPLANATIONS

Because only one neutron was formed for every seven protons, six-sevenths of all protons remained isolated. These remaining protons formed hydrogen nuclei containing one proton each. The Big Bang model **predicts** that about three-quarters of the total mass of the universe will be hydrogen and the remaining quarter helium. This simple **prediction matches** observations **very well**.

Still more details! These focus on the fact that the model's predictions match observations, which (as noted from paragraph 1) is why the model can be said to be valid.

Passage Map

¶1: *Introduce Big Bang model (BBM) of the universe's creation; it is valid*

¶2: *First seconds: temperature and energy high*

¶3: *After a few minutes: cooler, more stable*

¶4: *Observation confirms BBM*

Topic: *Big Bang model*

Scope: *Validity of (BBM)*

Purpose: *Demonstrate (the validity of the BBM)*

EXPLANATIONS

7. **(D)**

The author is primarily concerned with

○ explaining how the evolution of the universe is incompatible with the implications of the Big Bang model

○ chronicling the events that followed the creation of matter by the Big Bang

○ explaining how helium was formed in the early life of the universe

○ illustrating specific propositions of a model and showing how they have been supported by observation

○ showing how the ratios of protons to neutrons created in the Big Bang dictated the final ratio of hydrogen to helium in the universe

Step 2: Analyze the Question Stem

The phrase "primarily concerned" in the question stem lets you know that this is a Global question.

Step 3: Research the Relevant Text

Using your passage map—particularly the topic, scope, and purpose—you should be able to predict the correct answer without having to reread any of the passage.

Step 4: Make a Prediction

From your scope and purpose notes, you can predict that the correct answer will say that the author is "demonstrating the Big Bang model's validity."

Step 5: Evaluate the Answer Choices

(D) is the only choice to mention that the passage addresses how observation supports the model's propositions. **(D)** is the correct answer. **(A)** is a 180 trap; it claims that the Big Bang model isn't valid. Change *incompatible* to *compatible*, and it would be correct. **(B)** focuses on the details from paragraphs 2 and 3 but does not address how those details fit within the passage as a whole. **(C)** claims that the passage is focused mainly on helium; the word *helium* certainly shows up a bit in paragraphs 3 and 4, but it isn't the scope of the passage as a whole. **(E)** distorts details given in the passage. The author of the passage uses the ratios of hydrogen and helium to show how well the Big Bang model matches observations.

8. **(C)**

In the fourth paragraph, the author introduces information about the Big Bang model's prediction for the molecular composition of the universe in order to

○ obviate the claim that six-sevenths of all protons remained isolated

○ show that the remaining quarter of the total mass of the universe must be helium

○ provide evidence for the veracity of the Big Bang model

○ describe the means by which remaining protons formed hydrogen nuclei

○ predict the results of a Big Bang

Step 2: Analyze the Question Stem

This is a Logic question, because you are asked why the author used a specific piece of information. The question stem gives you a perfect reference—"the Big Bang model's prediction for the molecular composition of the universe"—to guide your research.

Step 3: Research the Relevant Text

The reference from the question stem leads to paragraph 4. The passage map paraphrased paragraph 4 as showing that observation confirms the Big Bang model. Note that by doing research in the passage map first, you save yourself from spending time rereading unnecessarily.

Step 4: Make a Prediction

From your research you can predict that the correct answer will say that the author included the details of the paragraph in order to "show us why the Big Bang model is valid."

Step 5: Evaluate the Answer Choices

The prediction matches very nicely with **(C)**; this is the correct answer. The word *obviate* in **(A)** means "to avoid or eliminate." The author believes it's true that six-sevenths of all protons remained isolated, so **(A)** doesn't make sense. **(B)** mixes things up; the author isn't using the Big Bang model to prove that the universe is made up of certain kinds of molecules; instead, the author is using the molecular makeup of the universe to argue that the Big Bang model is valid. **(D)** incorrectly states that the author's objective in this paragraph is to explain the *how* of hydrogen nucleus formation. The details of nucleus formation are discussed only to help the author make the case that the Big Bang theory is sound. **(E)** is wrong because the author, in the fourth paragraph, is not out to predict the results of a Big Bang, but rather to validate the Big Bang model's predictions.

EXPLANATIONS

9. (C)

According to the passage, which of the following was true during the first few seconds of the universe's existence?

  I. The great majority of neutrons were incorporated into helium molecules.
 II. The temperature was not high enough to allow for the formation of deuterons.
III. Vast numbers of subatomic particles rapidly metamorphosed into other types of particles.

O   None
O   I only
O   III only
O   II and III only
O   I, II, and III

Step 2: Analyze the Question Stem

The phrase "according to" in the stem signals a Detail question. So the right answer must be something that the author explicitly states. Also notice that you're looking for something that "was true during the first few seconds" of the universe.

Step 3: Research the Relevant Text

The passage map focuses your research on paragraph 2, specifically lines 7–10. Notice that this sentence emphasizes temperatures that are "so high" and particles "so abundant" that constant change was the order of the day (or, at least, its first few seconds).

Step 4: Make a Prediction

The correct answer will agree with the ideas expressed in lines 7–10. Anything else must be incorrect because that's the only place you learn about the "first few seconds."

Step 5: Evaluate the Answer Choices

(C) is the correct answer. For Roman numeral questions, start with the statement that appears most frequently in the answer choices, which in this case is III. Lines 8–10 provide support for Statement III. Each phrase and idea in Statement III matches directly with a phrase or idea from the passage: "vast numbers" matches with "so abundant," "rapidly metamorphosed" matches with "constantly transmuted," and "subatomic particles" matches with, well, "subatomic particles." Since Statement III is correct, eliminate **(A)** and **(B)**. Next evaluate Statement II, as it appears in two of the remaining three choices. Researching line 7 shows that the temperature was "high" during the first few seconds of the universe's existence. So, the phrase "not high enough" kills Statement II. That eliminates **(D)** and **(E)**, leaving only **(C)**.

Note that both Statements I and II refer to details from paragraph 3, which the time/sequence keywords show to describe not the first few seconds of the universe's existence but rather the few minutes thereafter.

10. (A)

The author uses the first paragraph to introduce

○ a scientific model that the passage will show to be supported by modern evidence

○ a theory of the origin of the universe that the passage will describe and attempt to refute

○ a description of the theoretical basis for a scientific model and the modern evidence undermining it

○ an attempt to use recent evidence to revive a discarded scientific model

○ a detailed description of an appealing but unsupported theoretical model

Step 2: Analyze the Question Stem

This question stem asks for the purpose not of the whole passage, but of one of its parts. That makes this a Logic question. The stem makes clear reference to the first paragraph.

Step 3: Research the Relevant Text

As the question focuses on the whole of the first paragraph, your research can be focused on the passage map. It states that paragraph 1 tells what the Big Bang model is and that it's valid, supported by observation of the universe.

Step 4: Make a Prediction

A reasonable prediction would be something like this: the author uses the first paragraph to introduce the Big Bang model and claim that it's valid.

Step 5: Evaluate the Answer Choices

(A) matches the prediction perfectly and is correct. Every other answer choice gets the detail right ("theory" or "model") but the purpose wrong: "refute," "undermining," "discarded," and "unsupported" are all negative terms, while the author's only purpose is to be positive.

11. (D)

The author would most likely agree with the position that

○ models of the creation of the universe that were made before the Big Bang model was created failed because they did not take into account the behavior of subatomic particles

○ no credence can be given to a scientific model unless it is possible to produce supporting data through a series of controlled experiments

○ the Big Bang was part of a cycle of expansion and contraction in the universe

○ it is beneficial to use the statistical evidence at hand when judging the veracity of scientific models for which the process cannot be repeated in a laboratory

○ the simplicity of the Big Bang theory accounts for its accuracy

Step 2: Analyze the Question Stem

The word "agree" makes this an Inference question, so the right answer *must* be true based on the passage but is likely not mentioned explicitly. This stem contains no reference to a particular detail or paragraph.

Step 3: Research the Relevant Text

When the test asks you an Inference question without providing a particular reference to guide your research, prepare yourself to evaluate the answers by refreshing your memory on the topic, scope, and purpose.

Step 4: Make a Prediction

You cannot anticipate the exact wording of the correct answer, but since you are asked what the author would agree with, you know the right answer will be in line with "The Big Bang model corresponds well with the observed universe; the model seems valid."

Step 5: Evaluate the Answer Choices

According to paragraphs 1 and 4, it is the model's match with observation that demonstrates its validity, as described in **(D)**. The wording of this choice is convoluted and dense, but the passage supports everything here: "statistical evidence at hand" could well refer to "0.01 percent," "six-sevenths," or "three-quarters." The author is indeed "judging the veracity of a scientific model." The passage discusses the creation of the universe and its behavior, a "process which cannot be repeated in a laboratory." But, more important than any of that is the fact that if the author *didn't* believe **(D)**, there's no way he could say that the Big Bang model is valid. **(D)** is correct. **(A)** can be eliminated for two reasons. First, the passage only mentions the Big Bang model, not any others. So there's no way you can state with confidence why any of those other models failed. Second, the author only ever uses *positive* opinion keywords, such as "validity." So an answer about why something "failed" can't be correct. **(B)** is a 180 wrong answer trap. The author gives credence to the Big Bang model, not by "a series of controlled experiments," but by "matching...claims with observations." **(C)** is incorrect because although the passage does mention "expansion" in line 17, there is no support for "contraction" or for "a cycle." (Here is a case of something that is generally believed to be true in the world outside the GMAT but that is not actually supported by the passage.) **(E)** is a distortion of the last sentence. The author may agree that the Big Bang model is simple but not that this is what "accounts for its accuracy."

12. (E)

According to the passage, a helium nucleus

○ could only be created early in the universe's history
○ has a low density due to the cooling and expansion of the universe
○ is more stable than a lithium nucleus
○ has four times the mass of a hydrogen nucleus
○ consists of exactly two neutrons and two protons

Step 2: Analyze the Question Stem

The phrase "according to" announces this as a Detail question, and the question gives a clear reference for your research: "helium nucleus."

Step 3: Research the Relevant Text

You know that the passage grows increasingly detail oriented in the third and fourth paragraphs. A quick scan reveals mention of the helium nucleus in line 16. The key to researching a detail is its context. Here, the sentence on the helium nucleus (lines 15–16) tells you that it is formed of two deuterons. And the sentence right before that tells you that deuterons are made up of one neutron and one proton.

Step 4: Make a Prediction

Your research shows that a good prediction for the correct answer choice is one that says the helium nucleus is made up of two deuterons or two protons and two neutrons.

Step 5: Evaluate the Answer Choices

The correct answer, **(E)**, uses almost exactly the language of the prediction. **(A)** is too extreme. The passage does say that fusion stopped after the first few minutes. But it doesn't say that fusion could *never* happen under *any* other circumstance. Moreover, **(A)** distorts the passage, which claims that "fusion *into heavier elements*" stopped—not that fusion into helium itself stopped. **(B)** is a tricky distortion. The sentence following the reference to the helium nucleus says, "As the universe continued to expand and cool, its density became too low..." But "its" refers to the universe, not the helium nucleus. Both **(C)** and **(D)** are mentioned nowhere in the passage. **(D)**, interestingly, happens to be a fact—you may recall from high school chemistry that a helium nucleus has four times the mass of a hydrogen nucleus. However, that fact is not mentioned in this passage, and it is not the correct response to a question asking for what's true "according to the passage." This answer is a good example of why it's important not to answer questions based on outside knowledge.

On the left, we've shown how keywords help you to identify the major elements of the passage and its structure and what you could skim over. On the right, we've shown what you might be thinking as you read the passage strategically.

Passage for Questions 13–17

PASSAGE

Parfleche is the French name for **the Plains peoples'** *hoemskot 'eo*—an envelope-shaped rawhide container for storing clothes, food, and personal items. The *parfleche* served **not only** as a **practical** and durable storage solution, **but also** as a decorative object of **spiritual significance**. Among certain tribes, **most notably** the Cheyenne and Arapaho, *parfleches* were decorated by the women's painting society, whose members among the Cheyenne were known as *moneneheo*, the Selected Ones. **Although similar** in their **economic and social** importance to craftsmen's guilds in medieval and Renaissance Western Europe, the painting society **also** had a **spiritual or religious** nature. The shamanistic society required application for admission and held its members to **high artistic and moral standards**. The society **further** displayed its importance by defining aspects of Cheyenne wealth and status.

Painting on rawhide was **fraught with challenges**. If painting was attempted while the prepared hide was too moist, the applied paint bled, but if the hide was too dry, the skin did not absorb the pigments. This restricted the time frame in which painting could best be completed, which meant that designs had to be visualized fully before the work started. **Moreover, every aspect** of creating a *parfleche* was a **sacred** act. Each design element, **for instance**, was a syntagma—a linguistic or visual unit intended to convey meaning—freighted with symbolic referents. **For example**, diamond shapes represented the *ha 'kot*, the grasshopper, an abundant grass eater itself symbolic of the bison, the sacred source of food, shelter, tools, and clothing. The tools used were **also symbolic**: the shape of the "flesher" used to prepare the hide represented lightning bolts—emblematic of the masculine essence of spirit. The flesher removed the flesh from the hide, transforming it into a spiritual container that would hold earthly matter (the people's material goods).

ANALYSIS

The topic, the *parfleche*, is addressed and defined in the first sentence.

The "not only … but also" structure indicates that the author will focus on the spiritual significance of the *parfleche*.

Another contrast: the group that made *parfleche* was economic/social "but also" spiritual/religious.

Making of *parfleche*: difficult; highly symbolic; even tools symbolic.

EXPLANATIONS

Even the **position** of the *parfleche* in the lodge held symbolic significance. It was stored beneath the bed of older women, **not only** because they were careful guardians, **but also because** they were closer to Grandmother Earth, from whose union with the lightning spirit the animals and plants of the middle world came to provide food and shelter. The symbolism of every aspect of the *parfleche*, **therefore**, from the interpretable design work on its outside to its storage place within the lodge, reflects the Cheyenne belief in a complementary worldview: the blending of the masculine spirit and the feminine physical matter.

Parfleche kept by mature women (considered spiritual people). Conclusion: *parfleche* reflects masculine/feminine blend.

Passage Map

¶1: Intro to the parfleche and the people who created it

¶2: The process and symbolism involved in making the parfleche

¶3: The parfleche as a symbol of the Cheyenne worldview

Topic: The parfleche

Scope: The spiritual significance of the production, decoration, and use of the parfleche

Purpose: To explain the cultural and spiritual significance of the parfleche to the Plains peoples

EXPLANATIONS

13. **(E)**

According to the passage, one reason why there was a limited time frame in which to paint a prepared rawhide was that

- ○ the pigments dried quickly and thus had to be applied with speed to avoid cracking
- ○ if the hide was too dry, it absorbed too much paint
- ○ if the hide was too moist, it rejected the pigments
- ○ the designs had to be fully visualized before painting was started
- ○ if the hide was too moist, the paint bled

Step 2: Analyze the Question Stem

The phrase "According to the passage…" indicates that this is a Detail question. The stem gives you a clear reference for your research: "limited time frame in which to paint a prepared rawhide."

Step 3: Research the Relevant Text

Using your passage map, you can refer to the second sentence of the second paragraph, where the author was discussing the difficulties in creating the *parfleche.*

Step 4: Make a Prediction

The second sentence of paragraph 2 provides everything you need for a prediction of the correct answer: "If painting was attempted while the prepared hide was too moist, the applied paint bled, but if the hide was too dry, the skin did not absorb the pigments."

Step 5: Evaluate the Answer Choices

(E) agrees perfectly with the first half of this statement and is correct. **(A)** is unsupported by the passage. **(B)** and **(C)** are both 180 wrong answer traps, since the sentence actually said that when the hides are too dry, they would not absorb paint. **(D)** is a distortion; it reverses the cause-and-effect relationship described in the passage. The reason that the designs had to be visualized in advance was the limited time during which the hides could be painted, not the other way around.

14. (E)

The main purpose of the passage is to

○ describe a tool used among Native Americans when working with rawhide

○ rebut a commonly held view about the symbolism of the *parfleche* for the Plains peoples

○ analyze the societies of the Cheyenne and Arapaho people

○ propose a new method for analyzing the use of symbolism in Native American art

○ discuss the spiritual and symbolic importance of a rawhide container and its decorations to several Plains tribes

Step 2: Analyze the Question Stem

The wording here—"main purpose of the passage"—makes this one of the most common Global question stems that appear on the GMAT.

Step 3: Research the Relevant Text

Since you paraphrased the author's purpose while creating your passage map, you can simply refer to that; there is no need to go back to the passage itself.

Step 4: Make a Prediction

The passage map tells you that the author wrote this passage to explain the *parfleche* and its "spiritual significance" to certain Indian tribes.

Step 5: Evaluate the Answer Choices

(E) best summarizes this and properly reflects the author's tone. **(E)** is the correct answer. Notice that **(E)** doesn't use the word *"parfleche"* but rather its definition. Looking for the right words in Reading Comp answer choices is misguided; always look for the answer choice that matches the meaning or idea that you've predicted. **(A)** is too narrow in scope; it reflects only one detail from the text instead of the passage as a whole. **(C)** is too broad in scope; the author is focused on one aspect of Cheyenne culture. **(B)** and **(D)** are not correct because the author of this passage does not take a stand on or disagree with anyone about the symbolism of the *parfleche* or the methods used for studying it.

EXPLANATIONS

15. (D)

According to the author, the Cheyenne women's painting society was unlike Western European guilds of the Middle Ages and the Renaissance in that

○ application for membership was required

○ the group had significant economic standing in the community

○ the group had significant social standing in the community

○ the women's painting society was religious in nature

○ the society had an influence on social standing and material valuation

Step 2: Analyze the Question Stem

This is another Detail question, again with a clear reference point for research during the upcoming Step 3. Here, you are asked what, in the author's words, distinguished the Cheyenne women's society that made the *parfleche* from medieval guilds.

Step 3: Research the Relevant Text

As expected, the contrast is highlighted by a keyword—in this case "Although"—in the passage. The Cheyenne group was similar to guilds in economic and social importance, but different because the Cheyenne painters' group was "spiritual or religious."

Step 4: Make a Prediction

The correct answer will highlight the Cheyenne groups' spiritual side.

Step 5: Evaluate the Answer Choices

Thus, **(D)** is the correct answer choice. **(A)** is unsupported by this passage, since while you know that the women's painting society required application for membership, you do not know that the guilds were any different in their requirements. **(B)**, **(C)**, and **(E)** all describe ways in which the women's painting society was similar to the Western European guilds.

16. **(A)**

You can most reasonably conclude that the Cheyenne definition of the term *moneneheo* (line 6) reflects

- ○ the high status some women enjoyed as artists in Cheyenne culture
- ○ the shamanistic spiritual origins of the women's painting society
- ○ the notion that artists were chosen by the gods to perform their tasks
- ○ the self-restrictive nature of the women's painting society
- ○ a woman's skill in using rawhide tools such as the "flesher"

Step 2: Analyze the Question Stem

The wording of this question stem is a bit unusual, but a moment's reflection tells you that this is an Inference question. Inference questions ask what must be true based on the passage. In this case, the passage gives you information indicating why the Cheyenne would refer to the women's painting society members as *moneneheo*. The question simply wants you to paraphrase that information accurately.

Step 3: Research the Relevant Text

The question stem refers to the word *moneneheo* in line 6, where the author tells you that it refers to the members of the women's painting society and translates as "the Selected Ones." The author goes on to explain the society's high importance and the "high artistic and moral standards" required for admission and membership.

Step 4: Make a Prediction

Predicting an answer to the question, say that the Cheyenne term reflects respect for the society member's status, talent, importance, etc. Remember, you aren't trying to predict the *words* of the answer but, rather, its meaning.

Step 5: Evaluate the Answer Choices

(A), with its emphasis on status, matches the prediction nicely and is correct. Although you are told that the *moneneheo* is a shamanistic organization, you learn nothing about its origins, so **(B)** is unsupported. **(C)** requires a leap from the use of "selected" to the notion that the gods do the selecting. Nothing the author writes supports this leap. The author mentions no sense in which the term *moneneheo* refers to anything "self-restrictive" on the part of the women's painting society; **(D)** is unsupported. The author draws no association between the term and the skinning tool or "flesher" (which is, in any case, not mentioned until the end of paragraph 2); thus, **(E)** is also unsupported.

17. (D)

The author describes the symbolic meanings of the diamond shape most likely in order to

○ indicate how precious the completed *parfleche* was to its owner

○ prove that the grasshopper was superior to the bison in Cheyenne religion

○ illustrate the visual complexity of the abstract forms used in creating a *parfleche*

○ provide an example of the many layers of symbolism involved in creating a *parfleche*

○ demonstrate the relationship between the symbolic shapes of the tools and the abstract designs used in creating a *parfleche*

Step 2: Analyze the Question Stem

This is an archetypal GMAT Logic question. You are referred to a detail—here, the "diamond shape"—and asked why the author includes it in the passage. Notice that the wording of the question, ending with "in order to…" means that the answer choices must begin with verbs.

Step 3: Research the Relevant Text

The diamond shape was among the symbols mentioned in the second paragraph. It is located in a sentence that begins with the illustration keywords "For example." The sentence goes on to tell you that the diamond represents the grasshopper, which in turn represents the bison, which in turn is sacred, and so on.

Step 4: Make a Prediction

Your research tells you that this answer must begin with a verb meaning "illustrate" or "give an example of" and continue by saying something about the symbolic meanings of the *parfleche*.

Step 5: Evaluate the Answer Choices

(D) matches the prediction and is correct. Given the verbs that begin each answer choice, only **(C)** and **(D)** are really in the running. **(C)** distorts the purpose of the diamond-shape example beyond what you read in the passage. Closer reading shows answers **(A)**, **(B)**, and **(E)**, already suspect for having the wrong purpose verbs, to be even worse. **(A)** addresses the value of the *parfleche* to its owner, a topic touched on nowhere in the passage. **(B)** suggests an unsupported, and rather ridiculous, comparison between the grasshopper and bison as characterized in Cheyenne culture. **(E)** tries to apply the diamond-shape example to the tool-use example that comes later in the paragraph.

On the left, we've shown how keywords help you to identify the major elements of the passage and its structure and what you could skim over. On the right, we've shown what you might be thinking as you read the passage strategically.

Passage for Questions 18–23

PASSAGE

A **one-child policy** was implemented in China...an **attempt** to slow continued growth in a population...[G]overnment **claimed** that the policy prevented 400 million births, **though** some have suggested that the decline may be at least partly due to economic reasons, **not** legal ones.

One result of the policy **seems** to be...more boys than girls. [Numbers]. **Research has shown**...higher rates of psychological problems...**and history would suggest**...may correlate with increased aggression and violence...

"[M]issing women" in population data...**suggested** that sex-specific pregnancy terminations and female infanticide account for the discrepancy...**But** others have **countered** this argument, believing that disease might better explain...For **at least some**...a **less sinister** explanation...simply never registered their daughters with government officials. A **recent study** found evidence...

ANALYSIS

The first sentence announces the topic: the one-child policy in China.

"Claimed" is a flag that there may be a dispute, and "though" signals another point of view or evidence to the contrary. Government claims one thing, "some" claim another explanation.

A result of the one-child policy: more boys born/survive than girls.

Research links this to psychological problems.

History shows excess male population correlates with increased violence, but this seems more speculative.

There are "missing women." Some believe this is due to deliberate actions.

Others believe there is a natural explanation.

Third possible explanation: not registering with government officials, per a recent study.

Author takes no stance on any of the theories.

Passage Map

¶1: *China's one-child policy*

¶2: *Result of policy: more boys born/survive than girls; potential negative results*

¶3: *Three theories about why: deliberate (prefer son), natural (disease), lack of government registration*

Topic: *China's one-child policy*

Scope: *Result of the policy = missing girls?*

Purpose: *Examine one apparent result of the one-child policy and three potential explanations for it*

18. (D)

The primary purpose of the passage is to

- ○ criticize the accepted explanation for missing girls in China since the implementation of the one-child policy
- ○ show why the expected population decline in China due to the one-child policy was not due to a decrease in the number of males
- ○ demonstrate how China's one-child policy has influenced past and future birth rates
- ○ explore the phenomenon of missing girls in China during the years of the one-child policy
- ○ argue that the expected population decline in China due to the one-child policy was due entirely to a decrease in the number of women

Step 2: Analyze the Question Stem

This Global question asks for the primary purpose of the passage as a whole.

Step 3: Research the Relevant Text

There's no need to go back to the passage itself. Review the purpose in the passage map.

Step 4: Make a Prediction

The author discussed one result of the one-child policy (missing girls) and three potential explanations for that result. The correct answer will reflect this.

Step 5: Evaluate the Answer Choices

(D), while phrased in broader terms than the purpose in the passage map, nonetheless encapsulates the passage as a whole and is the correct answer. The author does not criticize any of the potential explanations for the missing girls, so **(A)** is out. While the author does discuss the fact that more boys than girls apparently are born and survive (lines 8–9), nothing is said about whether the population of males declined. That population may have declined just as predicted, or even more than predicted; all that is known based on the passage is that the policy appears to have impacted women more than men. Eliminate **(B)**. The author does not discuss future birth rates, so eliminate **(C)**. **(E)** is extreme and has a similar problem as **(B)**: based on the information in the passage, it cannot be said that population decline occurred *only* because there were fewer women. Moreover, the author is neutral rather than making an argument. So **(E)**, too, can be eliminated.

19. (B)

According to the passage, which of the following is true of societies in which there are not enough female partners for men of marriageable age?

○ They occurred historically but are not known to occur in the modern day.

○ They may be at increased risk of international conflict.

○ They are more likely to develop when a significant proportion of the population is psychologically damaged.

○ They are not known to have occurred prior to the modern day.

○ They can result in the disappearance of women from official records.

Step 2: Analyze the Question Stem

This is a Detail question. The correct answer will be something discussed in the passage.

Step 3: Research the Relevant Text

The question stem refers to a gender imbalance, which is one result of the one-child policy. According to the passage map, results are discussed in the second paragraph, so research the answer there. The author says that having more men than women of marriageable age is " linked to higher rates of psychological problems" and "increased aggression and violence, both inside and outside a country's borders."

Step 4: Make a Prediction

Based on the research, the correct answer will be about psychological problems or increased conflict, or both.

Step 5: Evaluate the Answer Choices

While the author says there is only historical evidence of a correlation between international violence ("violence...outside a country's borders") and a society with more men than women, such conflict is a possibility. The qualified language of **(B)** ("may be") is a match to the text, and this choice is correct. The passage is discussing a potential modern-day example of such a society, proving such societies did not exist only in the past, so **(A)** can be eliminated. **(C)** confuses cause and effect. The passage indicates that the psychological damage occurs as a result of the society, not that the society develops as a result of psychological damage. **(D)** is the reverse of **(A)** and is also incorrect. While the author is primarily discussing a possible modern example of such a society, potential historical occurrences are also mentioned and so are not unknown. **(E)** is not supported by the passage. If women disappear from official records, their absence would create the appearance of a society in which men outnumber women, but in no way does such a society cause women to disappear.

20. (A)

The last paragraph in the passage serves primarily to

○ present multiple potential explanations for a phenomenon described in the second paragraph

○ offer a critique of explanations put forward for the outcome of the policy in which the author is primarily interested

○ demonstrate that the least sinister explanation of a troubling phenomenon is the correct one

○ explain fully the phenomenon described in the second paragraph

○ outline why social attitudes may explain the result of the policy that is the topic of the passage

Step 2: Analyze the Question Stem

This question asks you for the function of the final paragraph and is thus a Logic question. Think of it as being similar to a Global question about the author's purpose, but on a smaller scale. Instead of asking for the primary purpose of the passage as a whole, it asks for the purpose of one paragraph. Keep in mind that each paragraph supports the fulfillment of the author's overall purpose in writing.

Step 3: Research the Relevant Text

Rather than reviewing the entire paragraph, review the passage map for a summary. The final paragraph discusses theories about why there are fewer girls than boys in China. The missing girls are initially discussed in the second paragraph.

Step 4: Make a Prediction

The correct answer will summarize that the last paragraph provides explanations without evaluating their relative merits.

Step 5: Evaluate the Answer Choices

(A) matches the prediction and is correct. The "phenomenon described in the second paragraph" is the fact that in China, the number of boys who are born and survive seems to exceed the number of girls. "Present" matches the author's neutral tone. **(B)**, with "offer a critique," misses the mark, as the author of the passage doesn't evaluate the various explanations other people have put forward. While the author does describe the last explanation given as "less sinister," nowhere is it implied that this makes it more likely to be correct, so **(C)** is incorrect. The function of the final paragraph is to present several explanations offered by other people that may account for some or all of the missing girls, not to "fully explain" their absence as in **(D)**. Finally, **(E)** paraphrases one reason discussed in the last paragraph, a strong preference for sons, but the purpose of the paragraph is to offer several reasons, not just this one.

21. (B)

According to the passage, each of the following is a possible reason for missing girls in China EXCEPT:

O   Disease may cause more boys to be born than girls.

O   The one-child policy does not require girls to be registered.

O   Disease may cause more girls to die prenatally than boys.

O   Infanticide of female children occurs because families prefer sons.

O   Some girls are not registered so that parents can have another child.

Step 2: Analyze the Question Stem

"According to the passage" indicates that this is a Detail question. The "EXCEPT" means that each incorrect answer will be found in the passage, while the correct answer will not.

Step 3: Research the Relevant Text

The third paragraph gives possible reasons for the missing girls: societal preference for boys, disease, or parents' failure to register the births of girls.

Step 4: Make a Prediction

For an EXCEPT question, you can't predict what the correct answer will be, but you can predict the incorrect answers. In this case, the incorrect answers that you'll eliminate will reflect the reasons identified in Step 2.

Step 5: Evaluate the Answer Choices

(B) is not mentioned in the passage. While the final paragraph says that it is possible some of the missing girls are not registered, it suggests that parents avoid registering children to deceive the government and thus that parents are in fact supposed to register their daughters. Thus, **(B)** is the correct answer. **(A)**, **(C)**, **(D)**, and **(E)** are all stated in the passage and so are incorrect.

22. (E)

Based on information in the passage, which of the following outcomes would have been most likely to occur if a Han Chinese family had a baby daughter prior to 2015?

O   The parents are eventually pleased to have had a daughter, because there are so many marriageable men.

O   Because disease may kill the daughter, the parents have another child in hopes of having a son.

O   The parents appeal to the authorities to approve an exception to the number of children allowed.

O   Because a pregnancy is more likely to result in a son than a daughter, the parents have another child.

O   The parents fail to officially register the daughter, and they have another child.

Step 2: Analyze the Question Stem

This question presents a hypothetical situation and asks you to apply information from the passage to select the most likely outcome from those listed. Thus, this is an Application question. The words "[b]ased on information in the passage" are key: do not imagine what might be true but instead choose an outcome that the passage discusses.

Step 3: Research the Relevant Text

Han Chinese are mentioned in the first paragraph, where the author says that before 2015, some were allowed to have only one child. The rest of the passage discusses various consequences of this law, and actions that parents might take are mentioned in the third paragraph.

Step 4: Make a Prediction

As no exact prediction can be made, be prepared to research each choice individually, knowing that the correct answer will most likely be supported by information in the last paragraph.

Step 5: Evaluate the Answer Choices

(E) is supported by the final paragraph, which suggests that some parents indeed fail to register girls in order to have another child. This is the correct choice. The passage never discusses how parents come to feel about their children after the passage of time or whether a dearth of marriageable men is changing attitudes toward having daughters. Therefore, **(A)** is unsupported and incorrect. **(B)** is also unsupported, as the passage gives disease as a possible reason for a smaller than expected number of female children, but it does not imply that fear a daughter might die would lead parents to having another child. **(C)** can be eliminated because the passage provides no information about whether parents may appeal for an exception. **(D)** distorts the information that disease may cause more boys than girls to be born; it's never suggested that this phenomenon, if it is true, motivates parents to have a second child.

23. (A)

The author mentions a "marginalized underclass" (line 12) most likely in order to

- ○ show one potential societal risk of the one-child policy
- ○ give an example of why there are more men than women in China
- ○ demonstrate that men are inherently more violent than women
- ○ argue that widespread poverty may cause people to value boys more than girls
- ○ illustrate the effect of the one-child policy on average family income

Step 2: Analyze the Question Stem

The phrase "in order to" indicates that this is a Logic question. Specifically, the question asks *why* the author mentions a "marginalized underclass."

Step 3: Research the Relevant Text

The question stem refers to line 12, but the preceding line is also part of the relevant text: "Research has shown that an excess of men of marriageable age is linked to higher rates of psychological problems, as it creates a marginalized underclass…"

Step 4: Make a Prediction

The phrase appears as part of the evidence of the potential negative impact of having significantly more men than women.

Step 5: Evaluate the Answer Choices

(A) matches the prediction and is the correct answer. For **(B)**, while the passage says that more boys are being born/surviving than girls, it doesn't mention a "marginalized underclass" as a reason for this. This underclass does not cause, but may be caused by, the population discrepancy. **(C)** is a distortion. The passage says it is possible that violence will rise if there are significantly more men of marriageable age than women, but not that men are innately more violent. Regardless, violence is listed alongside the psychological issues that are caused by a "marginalized underclass" and so is not the reason the author uses that phrase. For **(D)**, the author is not attempting to make an argument at all; the passage is neutral in presentation. At any rate, there is no indication that attitudes toward boys and girls are caused by poverty. **(E)** is incorrect because while the one-child policy may result in unmarried and thus marginalized men, nothing is said about "average household income" across China.

On the left, we've shown how keywords help you to identify the major elements of the passage and its structure and what you could skim over. On the right, we've shown what you might be thinking as you read the passage strategically.

Passage for Questions 24–29

PASSAGE

Generally, interspecific matings represent an evolutionary **dead end**, producing sterile offspring, if any at all. For some species of birds, **however**, such pairings may indeed bring evolutionary advantages to the participants. **In the case of** the female collared flycatchers of Gotland, **three distinct factors** may work to make interspecific pairings with pied flycatcher males reproductively **beneficial**.

In many instances, female collared flycatchers nest with male pied flycatchers while continuing to mate with other collared flycatchers, in effect parasitizing the pied flycatchers, who invest in rearing and fledging any offspring. **Often**, more than half of the offspring raised by interspecific flycatcher pairs are, **in fact**, not hybrids. **Furthermore**, an estimated 65 percent of the hybrid offspring of the resident pied flycatcher male are male. **Because** hybrid females are sterile and males are not, this male bias minimizes the primary disadvantage of interspecific matings: sterile offspring. Habitat specialization may be **a third mechanism**: these pairings tend to occur in the late spring when the coniferous woods favored by the pied flycatcher provide a greater availability of food than the deciduous woods where the collared flycatchers tend to live. **Together**, these factors form a mechanism to **improve substantially** the reproductive success of female collared flycatchers beyond what would be expected of interspecific mating with pied flycatcher males.

ANALYSIS

"Generally" implies that there will be an exception. Usually, interspecific mating doesn't work.

The female collared flycatcher is the exception. You're going to see three reasons why.

Why interspecific mating works for female collared flycatchers:

1. They get pied flycatchers to raise their collared flycatcher offspring.

2. The offspring aren't all sterile.

3. Pied flycatchers live where the food is.

These factors seem to work together.

Although all three of these mechanisms appear to act in concert to form a single elaborate mechanism specifically evolved to circumvent the usual disadvantages of interspecific mating, **studies have shown similar motivations** for the behavior of female collared flycatchers mating within the species. **According to** Professor Siever Rohwer, collared flycatcher females will choose to nest with subordinate collared flycatcher males that inhabit good territory **because** collared flycatcher females must pair-bond in order to be successful in raising offspring. To engender the best offspring, **however**, the females will continue to copulate with higher-quality collared males with whom they are not paired. **Thus**, females **seem to** be nesting with males of any species with the best territories available at the time, **but they will** continue to mate with more attractive males outside of their pair bonds.

"Although…similar motivations": female collared flycatchers act the same way when mating with male collared flycatchers.

Pair with males that have good nests; mate with others, too.

A **highly unusual** behavior, interspecific mating **seems to provide** certain reproductive **advantages** to the collared flycatcher female. **However**, it **remains unclear** whether the mating behavior of female collared flycatchers evolved to circumvent the usual problems with interspecific mating or whether the behavior is simply an extension of how female collared flycatchers behave when mating within their own species.

The author is wrapping up.

"However" shows the central unanswered question: did female collared flycatchers evolve this way because of interspecific mating or just because they act this way generally?

Passage Map

¶1: Interspecific mating—usually evolutionary dead end/sterile offspring; FCF is exception

¶2: 3 advantages of interspecific mating for FCF

¶3: FCF nests/mates same way intraspecifically, too. Same advantages

¶4: Question—did FCF evolve this way for interspecific mating or just in general?

Topic: Interspecific mating—female collared flycatcher exception

Scope: FCF's interspecific and intraspecific mating behaviors and their evolutionary advantages

Purpose: Describe FCF's mating/nesting behavior and pose an unanswered question about its origins

24. **(D)**

The author's primary purpose is to

○ criticize the basis of a scientific theory

○ defend a hypothesis concerning bird-mating behaviors

○ point out the need for further study of female collared flycatchers

○ describe two possible explanations for the interspecific mating behavior of female collared flycatchers

○ defend an unpopular view of a natural phenomenon

Step 2: Analyze the Question Stem

"Primary purpose" signals that this is a Global question.

Step 3: Research the Relevant Text

No research within the passage is required. You just need to consult the passage map, specifically the statement of the author's purpose.

Step 4: Make a Prediction

The statement of the author's purpose said that the author was describing the mating behavior of the female collared flycatcher and posing a question about it. Two possible explanations are presented: (1) interspecies mating brings distinct benefits, and (2) interspecies mating is just an extension of normal behavior. With that background, you're more than ready to assess the choices.

Step 5: Evaluate the Answer Choices

(D) summarizes the author's purpose and is correct. **(A)** is incorrect because the author never takes a stand on either explanation and so does not "criticize" anything. Similarly, **(B)** and **(E)** are wrong because the author does not "defend" anything. The author never calls for further research, so **(C)** is not correct either.

25. (C)

According to the passage, female collared flycatchers' mating with male pied flycatchers could be explained by any of the following reasons EXCEPT:

- ○ Food is more available in pied flycatcher territories during the mating season.
- ○ Male pied flycatchers can help raise offspring successfully, even if the offspring are not theirs.
- ○ Male pied flycatchers sire more female offspring than do collared flycatcher males, increasing the reproductive success of the female collared flycatcher.
- ○ Females are known to nest with subordinate males while pursuing extra-pair copulation with higher-quality males.
- ○ Females enjoy greater reproductive success by pair-bonding with an inferior male than by not pair-bonding at all.

Step 2: Analyze the Question Stem

"According to the passage" is a clear indication that this is a Detail question. Just make sure you didn't miss the "EXCEPT" at the end of the stem. Here, the four wrong answers will all have been cited in the text. The correct answer will not. Remember, the correct answer to a Detail EXCEPT question may contradict the text or not be mentioned in the passage. The right answer might also repeat a piece of information that appears in the text but that has no relevance to the question posed in the stem (i.e., make a faulty use of detail). Here, the wrong answers will give possible explanations for the female collared flycatcher's unusual mating behavior.

Step 3: Research the Relevant Text

The female collared flycatcher's nesting and mating behaviors are explained in the second and third paragraphs. While the question asks specifically about explanations for the interspecific mating behaviors, remember that the third paragraph told you that the motivations for intraspecific mating behaviors were similar.

Step 4: Make a Prediction

You cannot predict what the correct answer will say, but the four wrong answers will be supported by text from paragraphs 2 or 3. Be prepared to eliminate these; what's left will be correct.

Step 5: Evaluate the Answer Choices

The passage says that pied males mating with collared females father more males than females. Thus, **(C)** directly contradicts paragraph 2, making **(C)** the correct answer. The coniferous forests where the pied flycatchers live are indeed richer in food late in the season, as **(A)** suggests. Females may use the pied males for their help in rearing young—including those sired by other males—as **(B)** says. **(D)** and **(E)** are both supported by paragraph 3.

26. (C)

The bias toward male offspring resulting from the mating of collared flycatcher females and pied flycatcher males is presented as evidence that

- ○ collared flycatcher females that mate with pied flycatcher males have more dominant male offspring
- ○ the offspring from extra-pair matings with collared flycatcher males are more frequently male
- ○ female flycatchers are not deterred from interspecific pairing by the likelihood of sterile hybrid offspring
- ○ males are produced to reduce interspecific inbreeding in future generations
- ○ interspecific breeding is normal in all varieties of flycatchers

Step 2: Analyze the Question Stem

The language of the question stem indicates that this is a Logic question. This stem goes out of its way to be helpful, though, by telling you that the detail at issue—the predominance of male offspring from male pied and female collared flycatcher mates—is presented as evidence. Your job will simply be to research what it is used as evidence for.

Step 3: Research the Relevant Text

The reference to the offspring of male pied and female collared flycatcher mates leads you to paragraph 2. You're told that the male offspring are not sterile, thus minimizing a typical downside to interspecies mating.

Step 4: Make a Prediction

The correct answer will tell you that the male offspring bias is evidence that a typical disadvantage—sterile offspring—of interspecies mating is not present when female collared flycatchers and male pied flycatchers mate.

Step 5: Evaluate the Answer Choices

(C) matches the prediction nicely. It is correct. **(A)** is simply not mentioned in the passage; the dominance of offspring is not discussed. **(B)** is a distortion; it is the interspecific hybrids, not pure collared flycatchers, that show a male bias in their offspring. **(D)** is incorrect because no argument is ever made about future generations of interspecific breeding. And **(E)** is incorrect because the passage does not comment on the regularity of interspecific breeding by any bird other than the female collared flycatcher.

27. (A)

It can be inferred from the passage that

○   food resources are an important determinant of success in raising offspring

○   having 50 percent male offspring is not optimal for collared flycatcher pairs

○   flycatchers generally mate for life

○   males do not vary in the benefits they provide to their offspring

○   over half of all females engage in extra-pair matings

Step 2: Analyze the Question Stem

Here's an open-ended Inference question. The stem references no specific detail or part of the passage. Begin your evaluation of the answers with reference to what you know about the topic, scope, and purpose overall.

Step 3: Research the Relevant Text

Given that there is no reference to guide your research within the passage, simply review your topic, scope, and purpose summaries. You may have to do further research choice by choice.

Step 4: Make a Prediction

Lacking a point of reference in the passage, you cannot make a prediction beyond saying that the correct answer will follow from the passage and agree with the author. That should be enough to help you find the correct answer or, at least, eliminate one or more of the wrong ones.

Step 5: Evaluate the Answer Choices

The second paragraph points out that the greater abundance of food in pied flycatcher habitats late in the mating season is a mechanism that makes interspecies pairings reproductively beneficial. If food were not relevant to the success of raising offspring, it could not be a mechanism to make interspecific mating reproductively beneficial. So **(A)** is true based on the passage; this is the exact criterion for the correct answer in an Inference question.

All four wrong answers are either unsupported by anything addressed by the passage or out-and-out contradict the passage. **(B)** is not mentioned—the percentage of male offspring is discussed only in relation to interspecific pairs. Mating for life is never mentioned either, so **(C)** is incorrect. The fact that females *do* choose males on the basis of reproductive benefits makes **(D)** incorrect; it contradicts what the passage implies. Lastly, you have no basis for knowing the proportion of females that engage in extra-pair matings, so **(E)** is unsupported.

E X P L A N A T I O N S

28. (C)

Professor Rohwer would most likely agree with which of the following statements?

- ○ All traits related to particular functions have evolved only for those particular functions.
- ○ Flycatchers represent the best population for studies of bird-mating behavior.
- ○ Behaviors may appear functional even under conditions other than those under which the behaviors evolved.
- ○ Evolution has played no role in shaping the behavior of interspecifically paired flycatchers.
- ○ Hybridization is generally beneficial.

Step 2: Analyze the Question Stem

This is also an Inference question, as signaled by the phrase "most likely agree with…" The key is to spot that it is Professor Rowher's opinion that you are drawing your inference from.

Step 3: Research the Relevant Text

Rohwer's opinion is discussed in the third paragraph, where the passage demonstrates the similarities between the female collared flycatcher's interspecies and intraspecies mating behavior. Rowher's point is that pair-bonding is essential to the female collared flycatcher's success in rearing young. The implication is that the female collared flycatcher will nest with one male and mate with others regardless of whether she is engaged in intra- or interspecies mating.

Step 4: Make a Prediction

The correct answer will have to address the context in which the author cites Rowher. The point is that it may be the necessity of pair-bonding, rather than an adaptation that favors interspecific mating, that drives the birds' behavior.

Step 5: Evaluate the Answer Choices

The prediction supports **(C)** as the correct answer. **(B)** and **(E)** are unsupported: the relative benefits of studying flycatchers rather than other birds is not discussed, nor is Rowher's opinion on the benefits of hybridization. **(A)** and **(D)** contradict, at least by implication, the message of the passage; they also include the phrases "*all* traits" and "played *no* role," which flag extreme statements.

29. (B)

The mating behavior of female collared flycatchers paired with subordinate male flycatchers is offered as

○ an unwarranted assumption behind the adaptive explanation of interspecific matings

○ an alternative explanation for pair matings of collared females with pied males

○ evidence supporting the hypothesis of adaption for interspecific breeding

○ a discredited mainstream explanation for why hybridization is a dead end

○ proof in support of the theory that collared and pied flycatchers are separate species

Step 2: Analyze the Question Stem

Here is another Logic question. Like all Logic stems, this one gives you a clear reference to guide your research. The female collared flycatchers that pair with subordinates are mentioned in the third paragraph. Remember that Logic questions ask *why* the author included the detail, not *what* she said about it.

Step 3: Research the Relevant Text

The third paragraph is about the female collared flycatcher's intraspecies nesting and mating behaviors. The specific fact highlighted by the author was that the female collared flycatcher behaves similarly when mating with male collared flycatchers as it does when mating with pied males. The author's point is that the female collared flycatcher's behavior may not have evolved exclusively in support of interspecies mating.

Step 4: Make a Prediction

While you don't know the wording that the correct answer will use, you can anticipate that it will address the position that the female collared flycatcher's behavior is possibly explained by more than just adaptation to interspecific mating.

Step 5: Evaluate the Answer Choices

The prediction leads to **(B)**, which is the correct answer. Paragraph 2 had explained how the female collared flycatcher's behavior is well adapted to the special problems of interspecies mating, so paragraph 3 qualifies as an "alternative explanation." Stated evidence can never be an assumption (which is unstated), so **(A)** is incorrect. The evidence in question does not support the adaptive explanation for interspecies breeding—in fact, it does just the opposite—so **(C)** is a wrong answer choice. This evidence is also not an explanation for why hybridization is a dead end; thus, **(D)** is wrong. Lastly, that the collared and pied flycatchers are separate species is a given in the passage; otherwise, the pairing of pied males and collared females could not be called interspecific. Moreover, this evidence has nothing to do with this issue, making **(E)** incorrect.

On the left, we've shown how keywords help you to identify the major elements of the passage and its structure and what you could skim over. On the right, we've shown what you might be thinking as you read the passage strategically.

Passage for Questions 30–35

PASSAGE	ANALYSIS
Rainbows have long been a part of religion and mythology in cultures around the globe.... **But** in the early fourteenth century, Theodoric...and al-Farisi...independently turned a **scientific** eye to the study of rainbows.	The topic of the passage is rainbows. Presence in religion/mythology; scientific study
Theodoric and al-Farisi were thousands of miles apart, **but both** had studied Ibn al-Haytham's *Book of Optics*. **Each** concluded that a rainbow's appearance . . .They conducted experiments to provide **support for their conclusions**...re-creating the conditions necessary to make a rainbow appear....	14th-c studies: very far apart, but both men reached same conclusion about rainbows, and both were able to re-create a rainbow in experiments
Both scholars were, as **modern physics** has shown, **correct**...When light hits a water droplet...the light **refracts...refracting again** as it exits. Refraction "breaks" white light into multiple wavelengths...called **dispersion**...which appear as different colors.	Jump to modern knowledge Refraction = light waves change direction. Dispersion = light breaks into separate wavelengths (colors).

EXPLANATIONS

A **single droplet** of water will disperse... **but** it alone cannot create a rainbow. **Only** a little of the light... reaches the... observer, striking the eye **from a particular angle**... a **multitude** of droplets... are needed... with the shorter wavelengths... at the bottom and the longer wavelengths... at the top.

Just refraction and dispersion aren't enough; angle also important. Rainbow = many drops refracting/reflecting light.

Passage Map

¶1: Rainbows in religion/myth & 14th-c. science

¶2: Medieval studies of rainbows by Theodoric/al-Farisi—different methods, same conclusion

¶3: Physics of rainbows confirms T & al-F's thinking; refraction/dispersion

¶4: More physics of rainbows (angle of observation); many droplets needed for rainbow

Topic: Rainbows

Scope: Explanations of rainbows in myth & science

Purpose: To describe supernatural and scientific explanations of rainbows

30. (D)

The author mentions the angle at which light leaves water droplets (lines 19–21) primarily in order to

- ○ describe how refraction causes light to disperse as it leaves a water droplet
- ○ show that indigo and violet appear at the bottom of rainbows because those colors have shallower angles
- ○ illustrate that a change in the angle of light changes the wavelength of the light
- ○ explain that the human eye perceives a rainbow only when light is refracted from multiple points
- ○ introduce evidence that may help solve a longstanding mystery about the physics of refraction

Step 2: Analyze the Question Stem

This is a Logic question that asks why the author included information about the angle of light leaving water droplets.

Step 3: Research the Relevant Text

The cited lines are in the last paragraph. First consult the passage map to review the main point of the paragraph, which is to explain why lots of droplets are needed for someone to see a rainbow. Then review the text, including a little above and below the cited lines. The author says that light emerges from a droplet at various angles, but light from that droplet only strikes the human eye at one angle, and this is why light from many droplets is needed for a rainbow to appear.

Step 4: Make a Prediction

The correct answer will associate the information about angles with the way light is perceived by the human observer.

Step 5: Evaluate the Answer Choices

(D) matches the prediction and is thus the correct answer. **(A)** relates to the discussion of refraction in the third paragraph, and dispersion of light is associated with the angles at which light leaves the water droplet. However, describing refraction is not why the author mentions the angle of light in the fourth paragraph. **(B)** is also found in the passage: later in the same paragraph, the author says that different angles of light are associated with different colors of the rainbow, but showing this to be true is not why the author discusses the angle of light in the cited lines. **(C)** misstates information in the passage; light's wavelength affects its angle of refraction, not the other way around. As for **(E)**, based on the passage, refraction is well understood, but even if it weren't, nothing in the passage implies that the angle of light is the key to understanding refraction.

31. (E)

Based on the passage, it can be inferred that the rainbow's middle colors of yellow, green, and blue

- ○ are not broken into separate bands by the dispersion of light leaving a droplet of water
- ○ have longer wavelengths than do the red and orange light at the top of the rainbow
- ○ have wavelengths that all strike the eye of a human observer at the same angle
- ○ have wavelengths that are refracted at shallower angles than the wavelengths of indigo and violet light
- ○ have wavelengths that are shorter than those of red and orange light and longer than those of indigo and violet light

Step 2: Analyze the Question Stem

This is an Inference question asking what you can reasonably conclude, based on the passage, about the three middle colors of the rainbow.

Step 3: Research the Relevant Text

The middle colors of yellow, green, and blue are not directly mentioned in the passage, but what colors *are* mentioned? The final sentence says that red and orange have the longest wavelengths and refract at the sharpest angles, and they appear at the top of the rainbow; by contrast, indigo and violet have the shortest wavelengths and refract at the shallowest angles, and they appear at the bottom of the rainbow.

Step 4: Make a Prediction

Based on the research, you can infer that the colors in the middle of the rainbow are also in the middle when it comes to wavelengths and angles of refraction. The correct answer should include one or both of these ideas.

Step 5: Evaluate the Answer Choices

(E) matches the prediction and is correct: the three middle colors can be inferred to have wavelengths that are shorter than those of orange and red and longer than those of indigo and violet. **(A)** is not supported by the passage, which never indicates that some colors' wavelengths do not disperse. **(B)** is a 180. The passage indicates that longer wavelengths are associated with higher positions on the rainbow, so the middle colors cannot have longer wavelengths than do red or orange. **(C)** also contradicts what the passage implies, which is that light of different colors refracts at different angles. **(D)**, like **(B)**, is a 180. The passage indicates that shallower angles are associated with lower positions on the rainbow, so the middle colors cannot have shallower angles than do indigo and violet.

32. (C)

According to the passage, the refraction of light upon entering and leaving a water droplet

- ○ changes the angle at which light leaves the water droplet, thereby altering the light's wavelength
- ○ causes the light to be reflected and thus intensify, becoming more visible to the human observer
- ○ disperses white light, allowing it to be seen as its different component colors
- ○ causes the light to slow and thus more readily disperse according to its different wavelengths
- ○ alters the light's wavelengths so they fall within the visible spectrum

Step 2: Analyze the Question Stem

The phrase "[a]ccording to the passage" indicates this is a Detail question. Here you are asked for something the passage says about refraction.

Step 3: Research the Relevant Text

Refraction is defined in the third paragraph as the changing of direction of a light wave upon entering or leaving a droplet of water. How much the light changes direction depends on its wavelength. White light consists of different wavelengths, so it is broken up, or dispersed, by refraction, and light at different wavelengths is seen as different colors.

Step 4: Make a Prediction

As discovered in Step 3, the passage presents several facts about refraction, and the correct answer will match one or more of these.

Step 5: Evaluate the Answer Choices

(C) paraphrases the last sentence of the third paragraph and is correct. **(A)** is half right, but it says that refraction changes the light's wavelength. In fact, the light's wavelength affects the angle of refraction, so **(A)** can be eliminated. Some light is reflected in the droplet, and while this allows the light to be refracted a second time, it is not caused by refraction, nor is anything said about "intensifying" the light. Eliminate **(B)**. As for **(D)**, the light wave does slow down when it hits a water droplet, and this is also when refraction occurs, but it's not said whether one causes the other. And finally, while refraction separates light according to its wavelengths, nothing is said about wavelengths being altered, and certainly refraction is not said to make invisible light visible. Eliminate **(E)**.

33. (B)

The primary purpose of the passage is to

○ explain why rainbows are a relatively rare phenomenon
○ describe religious and scientific explanations for the appearance of rainbows
○ raise doubts about a historical explanation for the appearance of rainbows
○ explore the reasons that the refraction of light causes it to appear as different colors
○ examine the physics underlying the appearance of rainbows to the human observer

Step 2: Analyze the Question Stem

This is a Global question, asking for the primary purpose of the passage as a whole.

Step 3: Research the Relevant Text

There's no need to review the whole passage. Use the passage map to find the purpose: "To describe explanations for rainbows (mythology/science)."

Step 4: Make a Prediction

The correct answer will reflect the purpose in your passage map.

Step 5: Evaluate the Answer Choices

(B) matches the prediction and is correct. Whether or not rainbows are rare is not mentioned in the passage, so **(A)** is incorrect. **(C)** is a 180, as the author confirms that the two historical explanations discussed are borne out by modern physics. **(D)** can be eliminated because this is merely a detail from the passage; the author is interested in explaining rainbows, not the refraction of light. Finally, **(E)** only addresses the last two paragraphs and is not the purpose of the passage as a whole.

34. **(A)**

It can be inferred that the author of the passage would most likely agree with which of the following statements about the study of rainbows?

- ○ Scientific experiments performed hundreds of years ago sometimes provided accurate results.
- ○ Cultures that associate rainbows with divinity do not approve of scientific inquiry into the nature of rainbows.
- ○ The experiments of Theodoric and al-Farisi established that refraction of light occurs in water droplets but did not examine larger volumes of water.
- ○ In societies in which the results of scientific studies of rainbows are widely accepted, rainbows are no longer associated with spiritual meaning.
- ○ Studies such as Theodoric's and al-Farisi's now have no value because modern science has shown them to be simplistic.

Step 2: Analyze the Question Stem

This is an Inference question, asking for the statement with which the author would most likely agree.

Step 3: Research the Relevant Text

Since most of the passage is about the study of rainbows, review the passage map to have the structure of the passage fresh in your mind as you review the answer choices. Plan to research each choice as needed to accept or eliminate it.

Step 4: Make a Prediction

No precise prediction of the correct answer is possible here. However, based on the passage map, you know that humans have observed rainbows for a long time and come up with various ideas about them, at least two medieval scholars conducted scientific experiments to understand rainbows, and modern physics—which explains rainbows in terms of light wavelengths and their refraction—validates the medieval research. The correct answer will align with one or more of these key ideas.

Step 5: Evaluate the Answer Choices

(A) is supported by the passage and is correct. Fourteenth-century science is first mentioned in the first paragraph and elaborated on in the second. Then, at the beginning of the third paragraph, the author says that modern physics has shown the findings of Theodoric and al-Farisi to be accurate. Thus, the author would agree that some experiments performed hundreds of years ago produced accurate results.

(B) can be researched in the first paragraph, where such cultures are discussed. While some of the ideas seem unscientific, the author never says that such peoples did not approve of scientific studies. **(C)** is not supported. The passage only discusses these researchers' work with water droplets, so whether they studied larger volumes of water is unknown. **(D)** is similar to **(B)** in that the author never implies that a scientific understanding of rainbows voids a belief in their spiritual significance. **(E)** is a 180. The author specifically mentions the accuracy of Theodoric and al-Farisi's work, thereby implying its value.

35. (E)

The primary function of the second paragraph is to

○ discuss a challenge to the conception of rainbows as a religious symbol

○ evaluate two historical methods for observing rainbows

○ describe the difficulties early scholars overcame in their attempts to understand rainbows

○ support the idea that medieval science is similar in value to modern science

○ outline historical attempts to understand the scientific basis of rainbows

Step 2: Analyze the Question Stem

This Logic question asks for the purpose of the second paragraph.

Step 3: Research the Relevant Text

Since the question asks about the second paragraph, review it in the passage map. The second paragraph is concerned with "medieval studies of rainbows by Theodoric & al-Farisi—different methods/same conclusion."

Step 4: Make a Prediction

The correct answer will align with the summary of the second paragraph in the passage map.

Step 5: Evaluate the Answer Choices

(E) matches the prediction and is the correct answer. **(A)** might be a tempting choice, since Theodoric and al-Farisi and their scientific approach to rainbows are introduced in the first paragraph with the contrast keyword "[b]ut." However, while the author indicates their approach differed from a religious or mythological approach, the passage never goes so far as to imply they sought to purge the use of rainbows as a symbol in their religions. The author does evaluate the two scholars' methods in a general way but at the beginning of the third paragraph, which states that the researchers' findings agree with those of modern physics. This is not the function of the second paragraph, so eliminate **(B)**. Nothing is said about any difficulties Theodoric or al-Farisi may have faced, so **(C)** can be eliminated. **(D)** is extreme. While the author indicates that in this case, findings from the fourteenth century agree with those of modern physicists, the passage in no way implies that medieval science as a whole is similar in value to modern science.

GMAT BY THE NUMBERS: READING COMPREHENSION

Now that you've learned how to approach Reading Comprehension questions on the GMAT, let's add one more dimension to your understanding of how they work.

Take a few minutes to read this passage and try the questions associated with it. Following the questions is performance data from thousands of people who have studied with Kaplan over the decades. Through analyzing this data, we will show you how to approach questions like these most effectively and how to avoid similarly tempting wrong answer choice types on Test Day.

Introduced in 1978, video optical discs were technologically more advanced than video cassettes—they offered better picture quality without degradation over time—yet video cassettes and recorders were far more successful commercially, at least in part because relatively few movies were ever released on optical discs. As this example illustrates, superior technology is no guarantee of success in the home audio and video market.

In home audio, vinyl records were the dominant format until the 1970s, when audio cassette tapes were introduced. Cassette tapes offered no better sound quality than vinyl records (in fact, some believed they offered lower quality), yet this format became widely successful for reasons having little to do with technical advancements in sound quality. Cassettes were more portable than records, and the ability to record from records onto cassettes made the two formats complementary. In addition to buying prerecorded records and tapes, consumers could now make copies of vinyl records and listen to them outside the home. Thus, cassette tape sales grew even as vinyl remained a popular format.

The rise of audio compact discs (CDs) was quite different. Introduced in 1983, CDs clearly offered higher sound quality than records or cassettes, yet they were not an immediate success. However, CDs were persistently and aggressively marketed by the industry, and by the 1990s they had become the most popular audio format. The dominant position of CDs was further cemented later in the 1990s by the advent of new technology that allowed consumers to create their own CDs at home—thus combining one of the best features of audio cassettes with the higher sound quality of CDs.

In home video, after the failure of optical discs, video cassettes remained the dominant format until the advent of digital video discs (DVDs). Introduced in 1997, DVDs quickly gained widespread popularity. These discs were based on a technology similar to that of optical discs and offered several clear advantages over video cassettes, including better picture quality and better search features. Yet perhaps the real key to their rapid rise was the fact that manufacturers quickly made many titles available on DVD. This combination of better technology and smart marketing helped the DVD avoid the fate of the optical disc.

1. The passage is primarily concerned with which of the following?

    ○   Contrasting the success of DVDs with the failure of optical discs

    ○   Describing the crucial role played by technology in the home audio and video market

    ○   Questioning the wisdom of introducing new audio or video formats

    ○   Illustrating that there is more than one path to success in the home audio and video market

    ○   Proving that good marketing is the only way to guarantee success in the home audio and video market

2. The author of this passage would most likely agree that

    ○   better technology alone will never cause the success of a new audio or video format

    ○   a combination of better technology and good marketing is the best way to ensure success when introducing a new format

    ○   there is no perfectly reliable way to predict the success or failure of new audio and video formats

    ○   companies in the home audio or video industry should invest less in product research and development than in marketing

    ○   consumer behavior is inherently irrational

3. According to the passage, which strategy is LEAST likely to produce a successful media format?

   ○   Aggressively marketing a brand-new format

   ○   Cautiously testing the market by releasing titles sparingly

   ○   Relying on word-of-mouth advertising

   ○   Creating a new format based on earlier technology

   ○   Introducing a product that works with existing products

EXPLANATION: QUESTION 1

It is crucial not to get lost in the details of a Reading Comprehension passage but to keep your eyes focused on the author's main idea. The last sentence of the first paragraph makes it clear that the passage will focus on how superior technology does not guarantee commercial success. Each body paragraph contains an example to support this point of view. The paragraphs describe many technical details but also provide other reasons for commercial success: flexibility of use (cassettes), aggressive marketing (CDs), wide availability (DVDs). The correct answer—**(D)**—reflects the idea that success is determined by several factors.

QUESTION STATISTICS

8% of test takers choose **(A)**

19% of test takers choose **(B)**

2% of test takers choose **(C)**

64% of test takers choose **(D)**

7% of test takers choose **(E)**

Sample size = 2,163

Many test takers focus too much on what the details say, rather than what idea the details support. The test makers understand this tendency, and they craft answer choices that reflect only the details. You can see how the most tempting wrong answer—**(B)**—accurately describes the details but misses the overall point that factors other than technology have an important influence. Also note how the second- and third-most popular wrong answers also miss the overall point by focusing on individual paragraphs instead of the entire passage: **(A)** focuses only on the fourth paragraph and **(E)** on the third. Although not a commonly selected wrong answer on this question, **(C)** is also wrong because it misconstrues the main idea, claiming that improved formats are not a good idea rather than simply insufficient for success.

EXPLANATION: QUESTION 2

Despite the vague wording of this question stem, the GMAT has a very specific standard for what defines the correct answer to Inference questions such as this one—and knowing that standard allows you to successfully avoid the common traps. From the test maker's point of view, an inference is valid only if it unambiguously *must* be true. So the right answer will be something that the author *must* agree with. If there's any room for doubt, or if it's possible that the author might not agree, the choice is wrong.

QUESTION STATISTICS

29% of test takers choose **(A)**

46% of test takers choose **(B)**

23% of test takers choose **(C)**

1% of test takers choose **(D)**

1% of test takers choose **(E)**

Sample size = 2,150

It's easy to see why unpopular choices **(D)** and **(E)** are wrong. The author neither makes directives to companies nor casts aspersions on consumers. But why are the two most commonly selected answers wrong? The reason is that they are too extreme.

It's very easy for an all-or-nothing statement to be possibly false. **(A)** claims that better technology will never cause the success of a new format. But the author only says that better technology "is no guarantee of success." A lack of a guarantee doesn't mean that something will *never* happen, so **(A)** is incorrect. **(B)** also goes too far by claiming that superior technology and good marketing is the *best* way to ensure success. The author clearly thinks that combining good technology with good marketing is better than having good technology alone. But this doesn't rule out the possibility that some other approach might be better still. In fact, marketing is not mentioned as part of the reason for the success of audio cassettes.

Notice how **(C)** uses more cautious wording, saying that no formula for success is "perfectly reliable." Given that the author mentions three different ways that new formats succeeded (flexibility of use, aggressive marketing, wide availability of titles), it makes sense for the author to agree that there's no one perfect way. That's why **(C)** is correct. Learn to avoid extreme language like "never" and "best" and to embrace hedged language like "no perfectly reliable," and you'll be well ahead of your competition and well on the way to a higher GMAT score.

EXPLANATION: QUESTION 3

Notice that the question explicitly tells you to base your answer on the content of the passage. Many test takers let their own opinions cloud their analysis and thus wander into traps. This question asks you to find the strategy most likely to fail. The first and fourth paragraphs both mention that the optical disc probably failed because not enough titles were available. That makes a cautious, slow release of titles a recipe for failure, which is why **(B)** is correct.

QUESTION STATISTICS

3% of test takers choose **(A)**

70% of test takers choose **(B)**

18% of test takers choose **(C)**

6% of test takers choose **(D)**

3% of test takers choose **(E)**

Sample size = 2,122

(A) and **(E)** are mentioned in the passage as reasons that new formats succeeded—CDs were aggressively marketed, and cassettes complemented vinyl—so it's no wonder that few test takers choose those answers. Neither **(C)** nor **(D)** is mentioned in the passage, which is why these choices are wrong—there's no support for either. But you can see from the question statistics that **(C)** is a popular choice. That is because you might look at "word-of-mouth advertising" and think that it isn't a sufficiently "aggressive" marketing strategy. This may be true in the real world (although if you're a savvy buzz marketer, you might disagree), but there is nothing *in the passage* to suggest that a word-of-mouth marketing campaign couldn't be aggressive. Stick with what's supported by the passage, and you'll be successful on Test Day.

MORE GMAT BY THE NUMBERS...

To see more questions with answer choice statistics, be sure to review the full-length CATs in your online resources.

GO ONLINE

kaptest.com/login

CHAPTER 8

Sentence Correction

Several consumer protection agencies have filed suit, seeking to bar distributors from advertising treatments for baldness <u>that brings no discernible improvement and may even result in potential harm.</u>

- ○ that brings no discernible improvement and may even result in potential harm
- ○ that bring no discernible improvement and may even prove harmful
- ○ bringing no discernible improvement and even being harmful
- ○ that brings no discernible improvement and may even potentially result in harm being done
- ○ that bring no discernible improvement, maybe even resulting in harm

Above is a typical Sentence Correction question. In this chapter, we'll look at how to apply the Kaplan Method to this question, discuss the grammar rules being tested, and go over the basic principles and strategies that you want to keep in mind on every Sentence Correction question. But before you move on, take a minute to think about what you see in this question and answer some questions about how you think it works:

- What skills and concepts does this question test?

- How does answer choice **(A)** relate to the given sentence?

- What other patterns do you notice in the answer choices?

- What GMAT Core Competencies are most essential to success on this question?

PREVIEWING SENTENCE CORRECTION

WHAT SKILLS AND CONCEPTS DOES THIS QUESTION TEST?

Many students, upon seeing Sentence Correction questions for the first time, think of them as "grammar" questions. It's true that correct answers often fix grammar mistakes, but you don't need to know the names of grammar rules or of different verb conjugations. What is it that you're being asked to do on Sentence Correction questions? These questions ask you to pick the answer that most clearly, correctly, or effectively gets across the idea of the sentence.

Sentence Correction questions cover a range of grammatical errors, some of which are so obscure that even good writers commit them. However, you don't have to be a grammar expert to do well on this section. All you need is a mode of attack and some knowledge about what does—and does not—constitute good GMAT grammar. Most of this chapter focuses on these common errors and how you can identify the answer choice that the GMAT considers correct.

Another key element in GMAT Sentence Correction is style, or what the directions for this question type call "effectiveness of expression." That means English that is clear and exact and without awkwardness, ambiguity, or redundancy. (Note that it doesn't have to be interesting. In fact, the test is set up to see whether you get worn down by difficult, often boring prose or whether you rise above that to stay involved—and awake.)

HOW DOES ANSWER CHOICE (A) RELATE TO THE GIVEN SENTENCE?

Each Sentence Correction sentence will contain an underlined portion and ask you which of the choices best fits in place of that underlined portion. Answer choice **(A)** will always repeat exactly that underlined part of the sentence. So, choice **(A)** is correct when there's no error. Recognizing this pattern means that you never need to spend any time reading choice **(A)** once you've read the original sentence. Given the statistically random distribution of correct answers across the five choices, you can anticipate that choice **(A)**—the sentence is correct as written—will be correct approximately 20 percent of the time.

WHAT OTHER PATTERNS DO YOU NOTICE IN THE ANSWER CHOICES?

Spotting patterns in how the answer choices are presented is the bedrock of the Kaplan Method for Sentence Correction. As you scan through these answer choices, you'll see that they tend to split easily into groups based on the varying ways they handle the grammatical issues in the sentence. Two of the choices start with *that bring*, two with *that brings*, and one with *bringing*.

We will return to analyze this particular question fully once we've learned the Kaplan Method, but for now just know that we call this phenomenon a "split"—certain patterns in how the answer choices are constructed allow us to place them into groups, sometimes even eliminating two or three answer choices solely on the basis of this categorization. Most Sentence Correction questions have a 3-2 or 2-2-1 split. This strategic, pattern-oriented approach will allow you to narrow the choices down to the one correct answer with the confidence and speed of an expert.

WHAT GMAT CORE COMPETENCIES ARE MOST ESSENTIAL TO SUCCESS ON THIS QUESTION?

Pattern Recognition and Attention to the Right Detail are the Core Competencies central to Sentence Correction questions. The typical Sentence Correction question contains two or more errors. The test makers reward you for being able to quickly spot and correct these problems that impair effective communication. Time is of the essence with these questions; the sentences vary in length and complexity, so you'll have to move considerably faster on the short ones to leave time for the long ones. Knowing the main types of grammatical errors that show up repeatedly on Sentence Correction questions and being able to analyze the patterns in how the answer choices are presented will help you move through these questions efficiently and accurately.

Here are the main topics we'll cover in this chapter:

- Question Format and Structure
- The Kaplan Method for Sentence Correction
- Commonly Tested Grammar on the GMAT

QUESTION FORMAT AND STRUCTURE

The GMAT Verbal Reasoning section includes about 13 Sentence Correction questions, which are mixed in with Critical Reasoning and Reading Comprehension.

The directions for Sentence Correction questions look like this:

> **Directions:** Each Sentence Correction question presents a sentence, part or all of which is underlined. Below each sentence you will find five ways to phrase the underlined portion. The first answer choice repeats the original version, while the other four choices are different. If the original seems best, choose the first answer choice. If not, choose one of the revisions.
>
> In choosing an answer, follow the norms of standard written English: grammar, word choice, and sentence construction. Choose the answer that produces the most effective sentence, aiming to eliminate awkwardness, ambiguity, redundancy, and grammatical error.

Sentence Correction tests your command of standard written English—the rather formal language that is used in textbooks and scholarly periodicals. It's the language that's used to convey complex information precisely, as opposed to the casual language that we use for everyday communication. The good news is that you do *not* need to know every grammar rule for these questions. Errors reflecting certain rules show up repeatedly on the GMAT. Focus on mastering these commonly tested rules—that's how to get the biggest bang for your study-time buck.

THE KAPLAN METHOD FOR SENTENCE CORRECTION

Now it's time to learn how to bring together all of the strategies you read about above into a consistent protocol for approaching Sentence Correction questions. Kaplan has developed a Method for Sentence Correction that you can use to attack each and every Sentence Correction question. Through regular practice, this method will become second nature by Test Day.

The Kaplan Method for Sentence Correction

1. **Read the original sentence carefully, looking for errors.**

2. **Scan and group the answer choices.**

3. **Eliminate choices until only one remains.**

Step 1: Read the Original Sentence Carefully, Looking for Errors

Read the sentence. Look for things that sound wrong but also keep your eyes peeled for signs of the classic errors that the GMAT loves to repeat. If you spot an error, eliminate **(A)** immediately. If you don't spot an error the first time through, don't bother rereading. You're no more likely to spot a problem the second time around—especially because there may not be an error at all! Instead, move straight to Step 2.

Step 2: Scan and Group the Answer Choices

Instead of wasting time reading each answer choice individually, quickly scan and compare the answers with one other. If you spotted an error in Step 1, sort the answer choices into two groups: those that do not fix the error (which you can eliminate) and those that appear to fix it.

If you *didn't* spot an error, try to zero in on a grammatical or stylistic difference that splits the answer choices into distinct groups. This will let you identify one of the issues that the question is testing. Once you know what is being tested, you can apply your knowledge of English grammar to determine which group is correct—thereby eliminating multiple answers at once.

Step 3: Eliminate Choices Until Only One Remains

If more than one choice remains, go back to Step 2 and scan again to find another difference. Then eliminate accordingly. Repeat this process until only one answer remains.

Important Pacing Tip: If more than one choice remains after you have eliminated all of the answers that you are sure are wrong, just go with your best guess. If you don't know the rule by Test Day, you probably won't successfully teach it to yourself while taking the exam. You'll get a much higher score by investing that time in other questions. If you are working on a quiz or a practice test, of course, reading the answer explanation closely will help you to learn the important rules so you can use them successfully on Test Day.

Now let's apply the Kaplan Method to the Sentence Correction question you saw earlier:

> Several consumer protection agencies have filed suit, seeking to bar distributors from advertising treatments for baldness <u>that brings no discernible improvement and may even result in potential harm</u>.
>
> O   that brings no discernible improvement and may even result in potential harm
> O   that bring no discernible improvement and may even prove harmful
> O   bringing no discernible improvement and even being harmful
> O   that brings no discernible improvement and may even potentially result in harm being done
> O   that bring no discernible improvement, maybe even resulting in harm

Step 1: Read the Original Sentence Carefully, Looking for Errors

The underlined phrase is a clause that is describing something in the first part of the sentence. (The use of the word *that* is a good clue that you are working with a clause.) What in the first part of the sentence "brings no discernible improvement" and may cause harm? *Treatments.* But you can't say *treatments brings.*

You've found a problem with this sentence (subject-verb agreement), so **(A)**, the original structure, can't be correct. The correct answer will fix the subject-verb agreement problem without introducing other errors.

Step 2: Scan and Group the Answer Choices

Now you'd quickly scan the choices, looking for any that repeat the error. That's **(D)**.

If you didn't spot the error at first, you'd look for the main differences among the choices. Here, you have a 2-2-1 split: two say *brings*, two say *bring*, and one says *bringing*. Which is correct?

Step 3: Eliminate Choices Until Only One Remains

If you spotted the error, you eliminated **(A)** and **(D)** as wrong, which leaves *bring* and *bringing*.

If you didn't spot the error, you'd now look at your groups of answer choices. Two answer choices say *brings*, two say *bring*—one is plural, the other singular. This is very likely about subject-verb agreement, one of the test makers' favorite types of errors. So what *brings* no improvement? Is it *baldness*? There's a *for* before *baldness*, so *baldness* can't be the subject. Plus "Baldness brings no discernible improvement" just doesn't make sense. It has to be *treatments*. You'd eliminate **(A)** and **(D)** and turn your attention to *bring/bringing*.

You'd eliminate *bringing*, either because you recognize that the continuous tense is awkward and unnecessary here or because you know that on the GMAT, *–ing* forms are almost always wrong in verb questions. Plus, only one answer choice uses *bringing*, so eliminate it and move on.

Scanning between **(B)** and **(E)**, you spot a difference at the end: *and may even prove harmful* versus *maybe even resulting in harm. Prove* is parallel with *bring*, and *resulting* is not. Eliminate **(E)**. That leaves only one answer, **(B)**.

TAKEAWAYS: THE KAPLAN METHOD FOR SENTENCE CORRECTION

- If you don't spot an error in the sentence, immediately scan the answer choices for differences. Focus on one error at a time. Usually you will find a 3-2 or 2-2-1 split somewhere in the wording.

- Some differences will provide an easier basis by which to eliminate than others. If you see a difference but can't determine which alternative is better, see if there are other differences that you can use.

- Knowing how to spot the differences in the answer choices is only half the battle. Learning the test makers' favorite errors, so that you can figure out which version is correct, is the other half.

PRACTICE SET: THE KAPLAN METHOD FOR SENTENCE CORRECTION

Answers and explanations are at the end of the chapter.

1. The rise in the number of new housing starts in the final two quarters of last year <u>suggest that the sluggish economy should continue its recovery into the first quarter of this year, but</u> weak job growth in the private sector continues to worry some economists.

   ○ suggest that the sluggish economy should continue its recovery into the first quarter of this year, but

   ○ suggest that the sluggish economy will continue to recover in the first quarter of this year, but that

   ○ suggest that the sluggish economy is continuing to recover in the first quarter of this year, but

   ○ suggests that the sluggish economy should continue its recovery into the first quarter of this year, but that

   ○ suggests that the sluggish economy will continue to recover in the first quarter of this year, but

2. The green flash, an atmospheric refractive phenomenon whereby the top edge of a setting sun will momentarily turn green, rarely is seen by the naked eye, primarily <u>on account of requiring</u> specific favorable conditions to occur.

   ○ on account of requiring

   ○ on account of their requiring

   ○ because they require

   ○ because it requires

   ○ because of requiring

3. A new study has found that college students <u>had been more involved in on-campus political activities during the last few years than at any time</u> in the past two decades.

   ○ had been more involved in on-campus political activities during the last few years than at any time

   ○ had been more involved in on-campus political activities during the last few years than at any other time

   ○ have been more involved in on-campus political activities during the last few years than at any other time

   ○ have been more involved in on-campus political activities during the last few years than at any time

   ○ are more involved in on-campus political activities during the last few years as compared to any other time

4. Fitness experts say that the weighted barbell squat or the weighted hip thrust, each part of a family of training maneuvers called compound movements, <u>is one of the best exercises for isolating and building the gluteal muscles</u>.

    ○   is one of the best exercises for isolating and building the gluteal muscles
    ○   are among the best exercises to isolate and for building the gluteal muscles
    ○   is one of the best exercises for isolating and to build the gluteal muscles
    ○   are among the best exercises for isolating and building the gluteal muscles
    ○   is one of the best exercises to isolate and for building the gluteal muscles

5. Noting that <u>its revenues had fallen due to a recent</u> prolonged slump in CD sales, the music-store chain announced that it would be forced to raise prices at all of its outlets.

    ○   its revenues had fallen due to a recent
    ○   its revenues have fallen due to a recently
    ○   its revenues are falling due to a recently
    ○   their revenues are falling due to a recent
    ○   their revenues had fallen due to a recent

COMMONLY TESTED GRAMMAR ON THE GMAT

Doing well on Sentence Correction questions begins with knowing how to approach them and then learning the errors that appear most frequently. Test takers who learn the most commonly tested patterns on GMAT Sentence Correction will be able to answer these questions confidently and efficiently. In this section, we'll look at the seven most commonly tested areas of grammar and usage:

- Verbs
- Pronouns
- Modification
- Parallel Structure
- Comparisons
- Usage/Idioms
- Miscellaneous Errors

It's important to master these areas of grammar and usage, but keep in mind that many questions, particularly those of higher difficulty, will test multiple concepts. Many questions contain more than one error. Using the Kaplan Method for Sentence Correction will give you an efficient way to focus on one error at a time. With both knowledge of these commonly tested areas and mastery of the Kaplan Method, you'll be able to handle all, even the toughest, Sentence Correction questions.

VERBS

Subject-Verb Agreement

A sentence is defined as an independent sequence of words that contains a subject and a verb. Verbs must agree with their subjects. Singular subjects have singular verbs, and plural subjects have plural verbs. If you're a native English speaker, this is probably so automatic that you may wonder why the GMAT tests it at all. But the test makers craftily separate subject and verb with lots of text to make it harder to recognize whether the subject and verb agree. Also, it is sometimes hard to tell whether the subject is singular or plural. You should look out for the following common subject-verb agreement issues:

- Long modifying phrases or clauses following the subject
- Phrases and clauses in commas between the subject and the verb
- Subjects joined by *either/or* and *neither/nor*
- Sentences in which the verb precedes the subject
- Collective nouns, such as *majority, committee, audience, team, group, flock, family*, especially when followed by a prepositional phrase containing a plural noun ("the group of legislators"):
  - Collective nouns take a singular verb when the members of the collective act as a unit ("the flock of geese is flying south") or are uncountable ("a lot of water was spilled").
  - When the members of the collective act as individuals, the collective noun takes a plural verb ("the majority of voters favor the proposal"; "a number of solutions are possible").

Subject-Verb Agreement Exercise

Answers are on the following page.

Correct each of the following subject-verb errors.

1. The depletion of natural resources, in addition to the rapid increase in utilization of these resources, have encouraged many nations to conserve energy.

2. There is, without a doubt, many good reasons to exercise.

3. Among the many problems plaguing suburbanites is the ubiquity of shopping malls, the increasing cost of gasoline, and the unavailability of mortgages.

4. The neighbors told police investigators that neither Annette nor her brother are capable of telling the truth.

5. The assembly of delegates intend to scrutinize the governor's policy decisions.

Subject-Verb Agreement Exercise: Answers

1. *Depletion* is the subject. Correct by changing *have* to *has* or by changing *in addition to* to *and*.

2. There *are* many good reasons. A good strategy for checking subject-verb agreement is to ignore, temporarily, any parts of the sentence that are set off by commas.

3. If the sentence ended at *malls*, *is* would be correct. But because there is more than one problem listed, *are* is the correct verb here.

4. "Neither Annette nor her brother is capable." In *or/nor* constructions, the verb agrees with the subject to which it is closest. So if it were "Neither Annette nor her friends," *are* would be called for.

5. Even though *delegates* is plural, the subject of the sentence, *assembly*, is a singular noun referring collectively to the group. *Assembly* therefore takes a singular verb: "The assembly *intends* to scrutinize."

Verb Tense

A verb tense indicates the order in which separate actions or events occur. Deciding which verb tense is appropriate in a given situation isn't just a matter of grammar; it's also a question of logic. Many GMAT sentences are long and complicated, involving or implying several different actions. The correct tenses make the sequence of events clear.

To determine whether the verbs in a sentence are in the proper tenses, pick one event as a standard and measure every other event against it. Ask yourself whether the other events are supposed to have happened before the standard event took place, after it took place, or while it took place. Those aren't mutually exclusive options, by the way: it is possible in English to have one action start before a second action and continue during that second action.

A frequent GMAT verb error is the inappropriate use of *–ing* forms: "I am going, I was going, I had been going," and so on. As far as the GMAT is concerned, the only reason to use an *–ing* form is to emphasize that an action is continuing or that two actions are occurring simultaneously. To remember this rule, think of the word *during* and its *–ing* ending. Other than that, pick a simpler tense—one that doesn't use the *–ing* form. In other words, avoid *–ing* forms as much as possible.

Most Commonly Tested Verb Tenses

- **Simple Present**—*I am*—Used for an action happening now, with no contextual information about when it started.

- **Simple Past**—*I was*—Used for an action that happened at a specified time in the past.

- **Simple Future**—*I will*—Used for an action that will happen in the future.

- **Past Perfect**—*I had been*—Used for an action that happened *before* another past action (e.g., "I had been on the subway for 30 minutes before I realized that I was going the wrong direction.").

- **Present Perfect**—*I have been*—Used for an action that started in the past but is still continuing now (e.g., "I have been on the subway for two hours now, and I still don't know where I'm going!") or for past events that happened at an unspecified time (e.g., "He has read *Don Quixote* seven times.").

There are other verb tenses in the English language, but these are the ones that are tested most often on the GMAT.

Verb Tense Exercise

Answers are on the following page.

Correct the verb tenses in each sentence.

1. The criminal escaped from custody and is believed to flee the country.

2. Some archaeologists believe that the Minoans of 3,700 years ago had practiced a religion that involved human sacrifice.

3. If the experiment works, it will be representing a quantum leap forward for pharmaceutical chemistry.

4. He had seen that movie recently, so he doesn't want to see it tonight.

5. By the time she retires, she will save enough money to allow her to live comfortably.

6. She already closed the door behind her when it occurred to her that she wasn't able to get back in later.

Verb Tense Exercise: Answers

1. The *criminal escaped* correctly uses simple past tense to refer to an event that happened at a specific time. The believing happens now, so simple present *is believed* is correct. However, the fleeing happened at an unknown and unspecified time in the past, so the present perfect should be used: "...is believed to have fled the country."

2. Here, there's no indication the Minoans practiced human sacrifice for a while and then did something else. So use the simple past *practiced* instead of the past perfect *had practiced*.

3. The experiment won't *be representing* a quantum leap; it will *represent* a quantum leap.

4. *Had* plus a past tense verb is used to indicate which of two things that went on in the past occurred earlier. That's not necessary in this sentence. "He saw that movie recently, so he doesn't want to see it tonight." ("He had seen the movie recently, so he didn't want to see it tonight," also works, although it changes the meaning of the sentence to indicate that the desire happened earlier tonight instead of happening now.)

5. Here, we're indicating an action that began in the past but will end in the future. Think of it this way: at some future time, what will have happened? "...she will have saved enough money."

6. *Closed, occurred*, and *wasn't able to get back in* are all in the simple past tense. But you need to indicate that she first closed the door and then something occurred to her—namely, that she wouldn't be able to do something in the future. "She had already closed the door behind her when it occurred to her that she wouldn't be able to get back in later."

APPLYING THE KAPLAN METHOD: VERBS

Now let's use the Kaplan Method on a Sentence Correction question dealing with verbs:

The governor's approval ratings <u>has been extremely high until</u> a series of corruption scandals rocked his administration last year.

- O has been extremely high until
- O have been extremely high until
- O had been extremely high until
- O were extremely high as
- O had been extremely high as

Step 1: Read the Original Sentence Carefully, Looking for Errors

Whenever a sentence contains an underlined verb, you need to make sure that it agrees with its subject and is in the correct tense. Here, the underlined portion contains a singular verb, "has been," that disagrees with the plural subject, "ratings." The verb is also in the wrong tense—"has been" indicates that the ratings are still high, but the sentence contradicts that. You can eliminate answer choice **(A)** immediately.

Step 2: Scan and Group the Answer Choices

Now it's time to look for a split in the answer choices. You see that the choices begin with many different verb forms: two "had been," one "were," one "have been," and one "has been." That's not a very helpful split. If you don't find a split at the beginnings of the answer choices, look for a split at the ends. Answer choices **(A)**, **(B)**, and **(C)** end with "until," whereas **(D)** and **(E)** end with "as"; this is a 3-2 split.

Step 3: Eliminate Choices Until Only One Remains

You eliminated answer choice **(A)** because the subject, "ratings," is plural, so the singular verb, "has been," cannot be correct. But verb tense is also at issue here. The correct verb tense is "had been extremely high," because the past perfect tense is used to indicate that something had already happened in the past before something else happened in the past. Here, the governor's ratings *had been* high, until scandals *rocked* his administration. This eliminates **(B)** and **(D)**. And **(E)** can be eliminated, since changing the preposition from "until" to "as" loses the sense that the scandals occurred before, and led to, the reversal in the governor's approval ratings. For the record, note that **(D)** also contains this error. The GMAT will often give you multiple opportunities to eliminate answer choices. This leaves **(C)** as the only flawless answer.

TAKEAWAYS: VERBS

- A complete sentence consists, at minimum, of a subject and a verb.
- The verb must agree with the subject of the sentence; plural subjects take plural verbs and singular subjects take singular verbs.
- The verb tense must match the meaning of the sentence as a whole.
- Don't fall for needlessly complicated verb tenses. Go for the simplest verb tense that makes sense given the time frame of the sentence.
- Use the past perfect tense (*had done, had seen*) to indicate something that happened prior to another past event.
- Use the present perfect tense for an action that happened at an unspecified time in the past (*have read, has said*) or an action that started in the past and has continued until the present time (*have lived, has been, have had*).
- Use the present perfect continuous tense (*have been studying, has been waiting*) for an action that started in the past and is still continuing now.

PRACTICE SET: VERBS

Answers and explanations are at the end of the chapter.

6. After all the research that has been conducted in the last 30 years, it is readily apparent that <u>there are, without question, a wealth of good reasons to do aerobic exercise regularly</u>.

    O   there are, without question, a wealth of good reasons to do aerobic exercise regularly

    O   there are, without question, a wealth of good reasons to exercise aerobically regularly

    O   there are, without question, a wealth of good reasons to engage regularly in aerobic exercise

    O   there is, without question, a wealth of good reasons to engage regularly in aerobic exercise

    O   there is, without question, a wealth of good reasons to do regular aerobic exercises

7. As state governments <u>become less and less able to support higher education in the coming years, universities have been becoming</u> more and more dependent on alumni networks, corporate sponsorships, and philanthropists.

    O   become less and less able to support higher education in the coming years, universities have been becoming

    O   are becoming less and less able to support higher education in the coming years, universities have become

    O   become less and less able to support higher education in the coming years, universities will become

    O   become less and less able to support higher education in the coming years, universities have become

    O   are becoming less and less able to support higher education in the coming years, universities will become

8. The most common breed of rabbit, *Oryctolagus cuniculus,* <u>is native to Europe but was accidentally introduced into the Australian continent in the 1850s, causing</u> decades of habitat destruction and crop devastation before its numbers were finally brought under control by bounty hunters.

- ○ is native to Europe but was accidentally introduced into the Australian continent in the 1850s, causing

- ○ is a native of Europe but was accidentally introduced into the Australian continent in the 1850s, which caused

- ○ was a native of Europe but was accidentally introduced into the Australian continent in the 1850s, causing

- ○ had been native to Europe but was accidentally introduced into the Australian continent in the 1850s, which caused

- ○ had been a native of Europe but was accidentally introduced into the Australian continent in the 1850s, causing

9. A recent spate of news reports questioning the long-term health benefits of high-fat diets <u>have done little to convince its practitioners that they should follow more traditional weight-loss plans</u>.

- ○ have done little to convince its practitioners that they should follow more traditional weight-loss plans

- ○ have done little to convince their practitioners to follow more traditional weight-loss plans

- ○ has done little to convince its practitioners to follow more traditional weight-loss plans

- ○ has done little to convince practitioners of these diets to follow more traditional weight-loss plans

- ○ has done little to convince practitioners of these diets they should follow more traditional weight-loss plans

ADVANCED PRACTICE SET: VERBS

Answers and explanations are at the end of the chapter.

10. Some economists contend that the way markets react to financial news <u>are based as much on irrational fears and expectations than on</u> sound fiscal analyses.

    ○ are based as much on irrational fears and expectations than on

    ○ are based as much on their irrational fears and expectations as they are on

    ○ is based as much on irrational fears and expectations than on

    ○ is based as much on irrational fears and expectations as on

    ○ has been based on irrational fears and expectations as much as

11. The newspaper reported that <u>some homes that were destroyed and severely damaged in the hurricane last year were</u> built too close to the coastline.

    ○ some homes that were destroyed and severely damaged in the hurricane last year were

    ○ some homes that were destroyed or severely damaged in the hurricane last year had been

    ○ some homes the hurricane destroyed and severely damaged last year have been

    ○ last year the hurricane destroyed or severely damaged some homes that have been

    ○ last year some of the homes that were destroyed or severely damaged in the hurricane have been

12. The adverse health effects of high-impact football tackles, which <u>had been shown to harm football players' health by causing concussions and irreversible brain damage, have led parents and educators to engage in</u> spirited debates about whether football should be banned in high schools across the country.

    ○ had been shown to harm football players' health by causing concussions and irreversible brain damage, have led parents and educators to engage in

    ○ were shown to harm football players' health by causing concussions and irreversible brain damage, are leading parents and educators to engage in

    ○ have been shown to harm football players' health by causing concussions and irreversible brain damage, have led parents and educators to engage in

    ○ are being shown to harm football players' health by causing concussions and irreversible brain damage, lead parents and educators to engage in

    ○ will have been shown to harm football players' health by causing concussions and irreversible brain damage, have led parents and educators to engage in

Pronouns

Pronoun errors are one of the most common Sentence Correction issues on the GMAT. Luckily, the GMAT doesn't test every kind of pronoun error. Common errors fall into two categories: reference and agreement. Pronoun reference errors mean that a given pronoun does not refer to—or stand for—a specific noun or pronoun in the sentence (its antecedent). The pronouns that cause the most trouble on the GMAT are *it, its, they, their, them, which,* and *that.*

For pronoun agreement errors, it's a question of numbers: perhaps a pronoun that refers to a singular noun is not in singular form, or a pronoun that refers to a plural noun is not in plural form.

As usual, the GMAT presents camouflaged examples of these two mistakes. Whenever you see a pronoun in the underlined portion of a sentence, look out for the following:

- Pronouns, such as *it* and *they*, that are often misused on the GMAT (and in everyday life)
- Pronouns that don't clearly refer to a specific noun
- Pronouns that don't agree in number or gender with their antecedents

Pronoun Agreement Exercise

Answers are on the following page.

Correct the following common pronoun reference and agreement errors.

1. Beatrix Potter's stories depict animals in an unsentimental and humorous manner, and she illustrated them with delicate watercolor paintings.

2. There is no known cure for certain forms of hepatitis; they hope, though, that a cure will be found soon.

3. If the partners cannot resolve their differences, the courts may have to do it.

4. In order to boost their name recognition, the Green Party sent canvassers to a busy shopping mall.

5. It is now recognized that the dangers of nuclear war are much graver than that of conventional warfare.

6. One of the men complained about the noise in the hallway, and they don't want to identify themselves.

Pronoun Agreement Exercise: Answers

1. *She* is clearly intended to refer to *Beatrix Potter*, but notice that the proper noun *Beatrix Potter* doesn't appear anywhere in this sentence; a pronoun cannot refer to a modifier, even a possessive modifier such as *Beatrix Potter's*. There's a second problem as well: it's not clear whether the *them* that are illustrated are the stories or the animals. Here's a rewrite that solves all the problems: "Beatrix Potter not only wrote stories that depicted animals in an unsentimental and humorous manner, but also illustrated each story with delicate watercolor paintings."

2. It's unclear what *they* refers to. The only plural noun is *forms*, but it can't be the *forms of hepatitis* that are hoping for a cure. It must be *scientists* or some other group of people: "scientists hope to find a cure soon."

3. *It* is the unclear pronoun here. There's no singular noun in the sentence for *it* to refer to. The main clause should read: "...the courts may have to do so."

4. A pronoun or possessive should match the form of the noun it refers to. Use *its* and not *their* in place of the Green Party, because *party*, like *audience*, is a singular noun that stands for a collective group: "In order to boost its name recognition, the Green Party..."

5. *Dangers* is plural, so the pronoun *that* should be plural as well: "...than those of conventional warfare."

6. The antecedent of *they* and *themselves* is *one*, so the pronouns do not agree in number or gender with their antecedent. Because the gender of *one* is male ("one of the men"), the pronouns should be changed to *he* and *himself*, and the verb *don't* should be changed to the singular *doesn't*.

APPLYING THE KAPLAN METHOD: PRONOUNS

Now let's use the Kaplan Method on a Sentence Correction question dealing with pronouns:

Despite <u>the platform of the opposition party supporting the measure, they keep</u> voting against campaign finance reform in Congress.

- ○ the platform of the opposition party supporting the measure, they keep
- ○ the opposition party's platform supporting the measure, they keep
- ○ the opposition party's platform which supports the measure, it keeps
- ○ support of the measure being in the opposition party's platform, it keeps
- ○ the opposition party's platform supporting the measure, party members keep

Step 1: Read the Original Sentence Carefully, Looking for Errors

Pattern Recognition and Attention to the Right Detail are essential to spotting pronoun issues in Sentence Correction. Here, you should be paying attention to the word "they" in the underlined portion of the sentence. Colloquially, it's common to use "they" as a nebulous pronoun with no clear antecedent. On the GMAT, though, such usage is always wrong. In this sentence, it isn't clear who "they" refers to, so you know that's an issue that needs to be fixed by the correct answer.

Step 2: Scan and Group the Answer Choices

The beginnings of the answer choices don't yield much in the way of splits, but the ends definitely do: **(A)** and **(B)** end with "they," **(C)** and **(D)** end with "it," and **(E)** dispenses with pronouns entirely. You have a 2-2-1 split.

Step 3: Eliminate Choices Until Only One Remains

The pronoun use here is wrong, because the sentence does not contain an antecedent plural noun to which "they" could refer. So, **(A)** and **(B)** are incorrect. **(C)** and **(D)** contain the singular pronoun "it"—but once again, the pronoun reference is confusing and wrong. It's not the *party platform* that keeps voting against the measure, as these choices imply. Both **(C)** and **(D)** can be eliminated. Only **(E)**, which avoids faulty pronoun reference and makes it clear that *party members* keep voting against the measure, makes sense and is the correct answer.

TAKEAWAYS: PRONOUNS

- A pronoun is a word that stands for a noun.
- A pronoun must refer unambiguously to a specific noun, known as its *antecedent*.
- A pronoun must agree in number and gender with the noun it replaces.
- When you see a pronoun underlined in the original sentence, focus on that pronoun and determine whether it is being used correctly.
- The pronouns that cause the most trouble on the GMAT *are it, they, its, their, them, which*, and *that*.
- Never use *they* to refer to a third-person singular noun on the GMAT, even if you don't know or don't want to specify gender.

PRACTICE SET: PRONOUNS

Answers and explanations are at the end of the chapter.

13. The government <u>has imposed sanctions and restricted foreign aid to a renegade nation last month after it violated</u> the terms of a worldwide arms control treaty.

○ has imposed sanctions and restricted foreign aid to a renegade nation last month after it violated

○ has imposed sanctions on and restricted foreign aid to a renegade nation last month after it violated

○ imposed sanctions on and restricted foreign aid to a renegade nation last month after that nation violated

○ imposed sanctions and restricted foreign aid to a renegade nation last month after violating

○ had imposed sanctions and restricted foreign aid to a renegade nation last month after it had violated

14. Every one of the police reports <u>have been filed so that they can be located by their case number, the date they were created, or the victim's last name</u>.

○ have been filed so that they can be located by their case number, the date they were created, or the victim's last name

○ have been filed so that they can be located by their case numbers, the dates they were created, or by the victims' last names

○ has been filed so that they can be located by their case number, the date they were created, or the victim's last name

○ has been filed so that it can be located by its case number, the date it was created, or the victim's last name

○ has been filed so that it can be located by its case number, the date it was created, or by the victim's last name

15. <u>Although swimming can cause cramps in a swimmer's legs or feet, they</u> can usually be avoided if the swimmer avoids overexertion and performs stretching exercises before entering the pool.

    ○   Although swimming can cause cramps in a swimmer's legs or feet, they

    ○   Cramps in a swimmer's legs or feet caused by swimming

    ○   Swimming can cause cramps in a swimmer's legs or feet, which

    ○   The fact that swimming can cause cramps in a swimmer's legs or feet

    ○   Swimming can cause cramps in a swimmer's legs or feet, although they

16. Film critics often cite the example of Nicolas Cage's winning the Academy Award for Best Actor as a reason that <u>an actor should not automatically be classified as elite if they win an Academy Award</u>.

    ○   an actor should not automatically be classified as elite if they win an Academy Award

    ○   an actor automatically classified as elite because they won an Academy Award should not always be classified as such

    ○   actors automatically classified as elite because they won an Academy Award should not always be classified as such

    ○   actors should not automatically be classified as elite if they win an Academy Award

    ○   actors should not be classified as automatically elite if they win an Academy Award

ADVANCED PRACTICE SET: PRONOUNS

Answers and explanations are at the end of the chapter.

17. According to a recently enacted law, any organization that engages in lobbying activities is required either to notify <u>their members about the percentage of dues that are used for lobbying activities or</u> pay a proxy tax.

    ○ their members about the percentage of dues that are used for lobbying activities or

    ○ their members about the percentage of dues they use for lobbying activities or to

    ○ their members about the percentage of dues that are used for lobbying activities or they should

    ○ its members about the percentage of dues that are used for lobbying activities or it should

    ○ its members about the percentage of dues that is used for lobbying activities or to

18. The chief executive officer met with the board of directors to consider the possibility of a hostile takeover attempt by a competitor and <u>how they would have to respond to deal with them</u>.

    ○ how they would have to respond to deal with them

    ○ how to deal with them if action would become necessary

    ○ what action would be required for dealing with such an event

    ○ what action would be necessary to deal with such an event

    ○ the necessity of taking action in order to deal with it

19. Arguing that the dominance of an economic theory has more to do with the persuasive skills of <u>its expositors than with its</u> accuracy in predicting economic events, Professor McCloskey examines the rhetorical practices of economists.

    ○ its expositors than with its

    ○ these expositors than its

    ○ its expositors compared to its

    ○ the theory's expositors than their

    ○ its expositors than with their

MODIFICATION

A modifier is a word, phrase, or clause that describes another part of the sentence. It should be placed as close as possible to whatever it is modifying. Adjectives modify nouns; adverbs modify verbs, adjectives, or other adverbs. Modifiers describe the word that they are right next to. (The only exception is the case of two modifiers; one has to be first.) The GMAT often creates modification errors by making a modifier appear to describe a word that it actually doesn't. Use Pattern Recognition to help you spot modification errors on the GMAT.

The most common GMAT modification error is a long modifier at the beginning of the sentence. It should modify the subject of the sentence but will likely not do so properly. Another common modification error is a long modifier that appears in the middle or at the end of a sentence. Often such a modifier on the GMAT will logically describe something elsewhere in the sentence, but grammatically a modifying phrase must modify the word that comes immediately before or after it. The result of a misplaced modifier is a nonsensical sentence. Also look out for the following:

- Sentences beginning or ending with descriptive phrases
- *That/which* clauses, especially ones that come at the end of sentences

Modification Exercise

Answers are on the following page.

In each of the following sentences, first identify what each clause or phrase is modifying. Then, fix each error you find.

1. Upon landing at the airport, the hotel sent a limousine to pick us up.

2. Based on the most current data available, the company made plans to diversify its holdings.

3. Small and taciturn, Joan Didion's presence often goes unnoticed by those she will later write about.

4. I took several lessons to learn how to play tennis without getting the ball over the net even once.

5. The house overlooked the lake, which was set back from the shore.

Modification Exercise: Answers

1. The sentence seems to be saying that the *hotel* landed at the airport. Your common sense will tell you that *upon landing at the airport* really intends to modify the unnamed *we*, instead. So you could say, "Upon landing at the airport, we were met by a limousine the hotel had sent."

2. As written, it sounds as though the company was based on current data. *Based on the most current data available* modifies the subject *company*. Obviously, though, what was based on the data were the *plans*, not the company. "Based on the most current data available, plans were made to diversify the company's holdings."

3. It's Joan Didion—not her presence—who is small and taciturn. "Small and taciturn, Joan Didion often goes unnoticed..."

4. As written, *without getting the ball over the net* is describing *how to play tennis*. The intended meaning is much more likely to be "I took many tennis lessons before I could get the ball over the net even once."

5. The misplaced modifying clause produces an absurd image: a lake that's set back from its own shore. Of course, the *which* clause should follow *the house*: "The house, which was set back from the shore, overlooked the lake."

APPLYING THE KAPLAN METHOD: MODIFICATION

Now let's use the Kaplan Method on a Sentence Correction question dealing with modification:

<u>Subjects tend to be vividly but disturbingly portrayed in Egon Schiele's portraits, often his closest friends and relatives.</u>

○   Subjects tend to be vividly but disturbingly portrayed in Egon Schiele's portraits, often his closest friends and relatives.

○   Subjects tend to be vividly but disturbingly portrayed in Egon Schiele's portraits, who were often his closest friends and relatives.

○   Subjects of Egon Schiele's portraits, often his closest friends and relatives, tend to be vividly but disturbingly portrayed.

○   In Egon Schiele's portraits, the subjects, often his closest friends and relatives, tend to be vividly but disturbingly portrayed.

○   Vividly but disturbingly, the subjects portrayed in Egon Schiele's portraits tended to be his closest friends and relatives.

Step 1: Read the Original Sentence Carefully, Looking for Errors

The entire sentence is underlined, but don't let that intimidate you. Use the Kaplan Method as you normally would and look for common errors. In this case, the error is a misplaced modifier at the end of the sentence. (Keep in mind that misplaced modifiers can occur anywhere in a sentence, not just at the beginning.) Here, the modifier is the final phrase set off by a comma, "often his closest friends and relatives." This phrase should refer to "subjects," but it's placed right next to "portraits." Always ask yourself when you see a modifier, "What should this word or phrase refer to? Is it as close to that word or phrase as possible?"

Step 2: Scan and Group the Answer Choices

As you scan, be on the lookout for where the modifier is placed. In these answer choices, the modifying phrase appears in several different positions. Any choice placing it far from the word it modifies—"subjects"—should be eliminated. In **(B)**, the modifying clause, "who were often his closest friends and relatives," seems to refer to *portraits* rather than *subjects*. Choice **(B)** retains the same problem as **(A)**, so you can eliminate it. Choice **(D)** places the modifier immediately after "subjects," so this is likely to be your answer.

Step 3: Eliminate Choices Until Only One Remains

In choice **(C)**, "subjects of Egon Schiele's portraits" seems to be one syntactical unit, so the phrase "often his closest friends and relatives" appears correctly to modify *subjects*, even though it is not directly adjacent to *subjects*. However, **(C)** is wrong because it is unclear whether "tend to be vividly but disturbingly portrayed" refers to how these subjects are displayed in the portraits, or elsewhere; perhaps biographers of Schiele depict them in this manner.

Finally, choice **(E)** is incorrect because the adverbial phrase "Vividly but disturbingly" appears to refer to the verb "tended" rather than to the adjective "portrayed," making it seem as if the subjects' tendency to be Egon's friends is what's vivid and disturbing. Only choice **(D)** properly addresses this misplaced modifier problem; it is therefore your correct answer. Moreover, choice **(D)**, unlike **(C)**, makes it clear that the vivid but disturbing portrayal is in the portraits themselves.

TAKEAWAYS: MODIFICATION

- Adjectives modify nouns; adverbs modify verbs, adjectives, or other adverbs.
- A modifying phrase must clearly refer to what it modifies. It should be placed as close as possible to what it modifies.
- Many GMAT modification errors involve misplaced modifiers at the beginning of the sentence. When there is a modifying phrase at the beginning of the sentence, make sure that the subject of that phrase is what follows the comma.
- Misplaced modifiers can also occur at the middle and end of a sentence, and they may or may not be set off by commas.
- When a particular modifying word or phrase appears in many different positions in the answer choices, determine exactly what it is meant to modify and pick the choice that places it where it belongs.

PRACTICE SET: MODIFICATION

Answers and explanations are at the end of the chapter.

20. In an effort to determine whether changes in diet and exercise can reverse coronary heart disease, <u>1,800 elderly heart patients will participate in a Medicare program costing $12,960,000 over the next three years to reduce lifestyle-related risk factors</u>.

    O   1,800 elderly heart patients will participate in a Medicare program costing $12,960,000 over the next three years to reduce lifestyle-related risk factors

    O $12,960,000 will be spent by Medicare over the next three years in a program to reduce lifestyle-related risk factors in 1,800 elderly patients

    O   over the next three years $12,960,000 will be spent on 1,800 patients by Medicare on a program to reduce lifestyle-related risk factors

    O   Medicare is to spend $12,960,000 over the next three years on a program for reducing lifestyle-related risk factors in 1,800 elderly heart patients

    O   Medicare will spend $12,960,000 over the next three years on a program to reduce lifestyle-related risk factors in 1,800 elderly heart patients

21. Children often pick up on gender norms very early in life, as many parents discover when <u>their toddlers recoil at toys that have only been designed to appeal to toddlers of the opposite sex</u>.

    O   their toddlers recoil at toys that have only been designed to appeal to toddlers of the opposite sex

    O   only their toddlers recoil at toys that have been designed to appeal to toddlers of the opposite sex

    O   their toddlers recoil at toys that have been designed to appeal to toddlers of the opposite sex only

    O   toys that have only been designed to appeal to toddlers of the opposite sex cause their toddlers to recoil

    O   only toys that have been designed to appeal to toddlers of the opposite sex cause their toddlers to recoil

22. <u>Based on the candidates' performances in the televised debates</u>, many pundits predicted that the rival was likely to score an upset defeat over the incumbent senator.

   ○ Based on the candidates' performances in the televised debates

   ○ Basing it on the candidates' performances in the televised debates

   ○ Basing their assessments on the candidates' performances in the televised debates

   ○ With the candidates' performances in the televised debates used as a basis

   ○ By the assessments of the candidates' performances in the televised debates that they made

23. Hoping to avert another situation in which the candidate who won the popular vote could lose the electoral vote, <u>it was proposed by Congress</u> that the Electoral College be abolished.

   ○ it was proposed by Congress

   ○ there was a proposal by Congress

   ○ a proposal was made by Congress

   ○ Congress proposed

   ○ Congress will have proposed

ADVANCED PRACTICE SET: MODIFICATION

Answers and explanations are at the end of the chapter.

24. Cheered by better-than-expected opening week box office returns, <u>it was decided by the movie's producer to give bonuses to the entire cast</u>.

    ○   it was decided by the movie's producer to give bonuses to the entire cast

    ○   the entire cast was given bonuses by the movie's producer

    ○   the movie's producer decided to give the entire cast bonuses

    ○   the decision of the movie's producer was to give the entire cast bonuses

    ○   bonuses to the entire cast were given by the movie's producer

25. <u>The argument over who invented calculus by math historians</u> typically features extensive discussion of the merits of Isaac Newton's and Gottfried Leibniz's mathematical achievements.

    ○   The argument over who invented calculus by math historians

    ○   Math historians argue over who invented calculus; this argument

    ○   Math historians' arguments over the invention of calculus

    ○   Who invented calculus by math historians is an argument that

    ○   Math historians argue over who invented calculus, yet this argument

26. <u>Using a seismic survey, hydrocarbons can be located even though they are buried far beneath Earth's surface.</u>

    ○   Using a seismic survey, hydrocarbons can be located even though they are buried far beneath Earth's surface.

    ○   Hydrocarbons can be located even though they are buried far beneath Earth's surface, using a seismic survey.

    ○   Locating hydrocarbons that are buried far beneath Earth's surface, a geophysicist can use a seismic survey.

    ○   Buried far beneath Earth's surface, hydrocarbons can be detected using a seismic survey.

    ○   Using a seismic survey, a geophysicist can locate hydrocarbons even though they are buried far beneath Earth's surface.

PARALLELISM

The basic concept behind parallelism is pretty simple: ideas with the same importance and function—nouns, verbs, phrases, or whatever—should be expressed in the same grammatical form. There are two types of constructions that test parallel structure on the GMAT:

- Lists of items or a series of events
- Two-part constructions such as *from* X *to* Y, *both* X *and* Y, *either* X *or* Y, *prefer* X *to* Y, *not only* X *but also* Y, and *as much* X *as* Y

Prepositions, articles, and auxiliaries can begin a list without needing to be repeated throughout. But if they are repeated, they must be in every element of the list.

- Correct: "Will you travel by plane, car, or boat?"
- Also correct: "Will you travel by plane, by car, or by boat?"
- Incorrect: "Will you travel by plane, car, or by boat?"

Analogies, similes, and other comparisons all require parallel structure.

- He was as brazen as his brother was diffident.
- Seeing her smile was like feeling the warmth of the sun.

Parallelism Exercise

Answers are on the following page.

For each of the following sentences, put parallel items into the same form.

1. The city's decay stems from governmental mismanagement, increasing unemployment, and many businesses are relocating.

2. Tourists' images of France range from cosmopolitan to the pastoral.

3. Excited about visiting New York, Jasmine minded neither riding the subways nor to cope with the crowded sidewalks.

4. To visualize success is not the same as achieving it.

5. I remember my aunt making her own dandelion wine and that she played the fiddle.

6. In my favorite Armenian restaurant, the menu is fascinating and the entrées exquisite.

Parallelism Exercise: Answers

1. *Many businesses are relocating* should be written as *business relocation* to parallel *governmental mismanagement* and *increasing unemployment.*

2. If you say *the* pastoral, you have to say *the* cosmopolitan. Or you could say "...from cosmopolitan to pastoral."

3. To parallel *riding*, you need *coping*—not *to cope.*

4. *To visualize* should be *visualizing* to parallel *achieving.* Alternately, *achieving* could be written as *to achieve* to be in parallel with *to visualize.*

5. Change *my aunt making* to *that my aunt made* to be parallel with *that she played.* Another possibility is to change *that she played* to *playing* to match *making.*

6. *The menu* is singular, but *entrées* is plural, so you must say *are exquisite* to parallel the phrase *is fascinating.*

APPLYING THE KAPLAN METHOD: PARALLELISM

Now let's use the Kaplan Method on a Sentence Correction question dealing with parallelism:

Pablo Picasso's genius is only fully revealed when one considers the various facets of his work as they developed through many artistic phases, beginning with his Red <u>period, continuing through his Blue period, and finishing with his period of Cubism</u>.

- O period, continuing through his Blue period, and finishing with his period of Cubism
- O period, continuing through his Blue period, and finishing with his Cubist period
- O period, and continuing through his Blue period and his Cubist period
- O period phase, his Blue period phase, and his phase of Cubism
- O period, his Blue period, and his period of Cubism

Step 1: Read the Original Sentence Carefully, Looking for Errors

The original sentence contains a list, so your Pattern Recognition skills should tell you to check for parallel structure. Because the first two items in the list contain "Red period" and "Blue period," you should expect the third item in the list to follow the adjective-noun pattern and contain "Cubist period." Instead, this sentence ends with "period of Cubism," breaking the pattern and making choice **(A)** incorrect.

Step 2: Scan and Group the Answer Choices

Choices **(B)** and **(C)** end with "his Cubist period," while **(A)** and **(E)** reference "his period of Cubism" and **(D)** ends with the similar construction "his phase of Cubism." You have a 3-2 split.

Step 3: Eliminate Choices Until Only One Remains

You've established that **(A)** is incorrect, so eliminate **(D)** and **(E)** as well. This leaves only **(B)** and **(C)** with the correct parallel construction "cubist period." The list should also contain the parallel phrases, "beginning...continuing...and finishing." **(C)** is wrong because it drops "finishing," which alters the meaning and also destroys the parallel structure. Only **(B)** exhibits parallel structure throughout the list and is the correct answer.

TAKEAWAYS: PARALLELISM

- Items in a list must have parallel form.
- Many two-part constructions set up parallel elements. Examples: "not only A but also B," "from A to B," and "either A or B."
- The key to handling parallel structure questions is consistency.
- Analogies, metaphors, similes, and other comparisons all require parallel structure.

PRACTICE SET: PARALLELISM

Answers and explanations are at the end of the chapter.

27. <u>The creation of an independent treasury, establishing lower tariffs, and purchasing</u> the Oregon Territory, all credited to the presidency of James Knox Polk, are among the significant accomplishments that persuade historians to rank this former governor of Tennessee as an above-average president.

   O   The creation of an independent treasury, establishing lower tariffs, and purchasing

   O   The creation of an independent treasury, establishing lower tariffs, as well as purchasing

   O   The creation of an independent treasury, the establishment of lower tariffs, and the purchase of

   O   Creating an independent treasury, the establishment of lower tariffs, and purchasing

   O   Creating an independent treasury, the establishing of lower tariffs, and the purchasing of

28. The rapid-rail lines that were recently introduced in southern California have had positive effects: <u>not only have they lowered pollution levels, they have helped in decongesting</u> the region's freeway system, which had been operating far above its capacity.

   O   not only have they lowered pollution levels, they have helped in decongesting

   O   the lines have not only lowered pollution levels, but also helped to decongest

   O   not only have pollution levels been lowered, but they have helped to decongest

   O   lines have lowered pollution levels, but also helped in decongesting

   O   not only have they lowered pollution levels, but also have they helped decongest

29. By conducting a national study of opioid abuse on college campuses, researchers hope to determine where students purchase opioids, how frequently students abuse opioids on average, and <u>which college stressors most commonly contribute to opioid abuse among students</u>.

    ○ which college stressors most commonly contribute to opioid abuse among students

    ○ which are the college stressors common to students who are likely to be turning to opioid abuse

    ○ the common stressors of college that are likely to contribute to opioid abuse among students

    ○ the stressors of college common among students who turn to opioid abuse

    ○ the types of college stressors that are common to students who are likely to turn to opioid abuse

30. <u>Hearing Kenneth Branagh deliver the "St. Crispin's Day" speech in *Henry V* is to be mesmerized by a great performer, with seemingly</u> boundless emotional energy.

    ○ Hearing Kenneth Branagh deliver the "St. Crispin's Day" speech in *Henry V* is to be mesmerized by a great performer, with seemingly

    ○ Hearing Kenneth Branagh deliver the "St. Crispin's Day" speech in *Henry V* is to be mesmerized by a great performer, one with seeming

    ○ Hearing Kenneth Branagh deliver the "St. Crispin's Day" speech in *Henry V* is being mesmerized by a great performer, one with seeming

    ○ To hear Kenneth Branagh deliver the "St. Crispin's Day" speech in *Henry V* is being mesmerized by a great performer, with seemingly

    ○ To hear Kenneth Branagh deliver the "St. Crispin's Day" speech in *Henry V* is to be mesmerized by a great performer, one with seemingly

ADVANCED PRACTICE SET: PARALLELISM

Answers and explanations are at the end of the chapter.

31. By the time they completed their journey, the young explorers had overcome their fears, sharpened their survival <u>skills, and had developed a healthy respect</u> for nature's potential destructiveness.

    ○ skills, and had developed a healthy respect
    ○ skills, and developed a healthy respect
    ○ skills and a healthy respect developed
    ○ skills, developing a healthy respect
    ○ skills, all the while developing a healthy respect

32. <u>Doctors both espouse the benefits of the influenza vaccination and advocate its administration</u> to children starting at age six months.

    ○ Doctors both espouse the benefits of the influenza vaccination and advocate its administration
    ○ Doctors both espouse the benefits of the influenza vaccination and are advocating its administration
    ○ Doctors, espousing the benefits of the influenza vaccination, advocate their administration
    ○ Both espousing the benefits of the influenza vaccination, the doctors advocate its administration
    ○ Espousing the benefits of the influenza vaccination, its administration is advocated by doctors

33. South Pacific Vacations has a package tour to Sydney, Australia, for $999 per person, including airfare from Los Angeles, <u>spending five nights at the Mega Hotel, and to take a harbor cruise, and round-trip airfare from New York is</u> an additional $400.

    ○ spending five nights at the Mega Hotel, and to take a harbor cruise, and round-trip airfare from New York is
    ○ spending five nights at the Mega Hotel, and taking a harbor cruise; and in addition round-trip airfare from New York is
    ○ five nights at the Mega Hotel, and a harbor cruise; round-trip airfare from New York is
    ○ with five nights at the Mega Hotel, and a harbor cruise, with round-trip airfare from New York being
    ○ to spend five nights at the Mega Hotel, and to take a harbor cruise; round-trip airfare from New York is

COMPARISONS

Faulty comparisons account for a significant number of errors in GMAT Sentence Correction questions. Most relate to the very simple idea that you can't compare apples to oranges. Of course, you want to compare things that are grammatically similar, but you also want to compare things that are logically similar. You can't logically compare, say, a person to a quality or an item to a group. You have to compare one individual to another, one quality to another, one group to another.

Use Attention to the Right Detail and Pattern Recognition to keep an eye out for the following:

- Key comparison words such as *like, as, compared to, less than, more than, other, that of*, and *those of*
- Long modifying phrases between compared elements. Don't be distracted! Ignore the modifying phrase at first so you can see the compared elements clearly.

Compared items must be parallel in terms of construction. If a preposition, article, or auxiliary is in one compared item, it needs to be in the other:

- Incorrect: I would do anything for my mother but not my boss.
- Correct: I would do anything for my mother but not for my boss.

Comparisons Exercise

Answers are on the following page.

Fix the comparisons in the sentences below.

1. Like a black bear that I once saw in the Buenos Aires Zoo, the Central Park Zoo polar bear's personality strikes me as being sadly neurotic.

2. The article questioned the popularity of jazz compared to classical music.

3. The challenger weighed 20 pounds less than that of the defender.

4. The Boston office contributes less to total national sales than any other U.S. branch.

5. The host paid more attention to his celebrity guest than the others.

Comparisons Exercise: Answers

1. *Like* creates a comparison, and you can compare only similar things. Here, you have to compare bears to bears or personalities to personalities. "Like a black bear I once saw in the Buenos Aires Zoo, the Central Park Zoo polar bear strikes me as being sadly neurotic."

2. "The article questioned the popularity of jazz compared to *that of* classical music."

3. "The challenger weighed 20 pounds less than the defender did," or "The challenger's weight was 20 pounds less than that of the defender."

4. There are two ways to read this sentence as it's written. We could be comparing the Boston office's contribution to national sales and other branches' contributions, but we also could be comparing the Boston office's contribution to national sales and the Boston office's contribution to those other branches. The former comparison is more logical, so we clarify: "…than any other U.S. branch *does*."

5. A similar problem—you need to repeat the verb after *than* ("than *he paid* to the others") or refer to the verb by placing *to* after *than* ("than *to* the others").

APPLYING THE KAPLAN METHOD: COMPARISONS

Now let's use the Kaplan Method on a Sentence Correction question dealing with comparisons:

<u>Like most other marsupial species and all other kangaroo species, the diet of the swamp wallaby consists</u> of leaves and other sorts of vegetation.

- ○ Like most other marsupial species and all other kangaroo species, the diet of the swamp wallaby consists

- ○ Like those of most other marsupial species and all other kangaroo species, the diets of the swamp wallaby consists

- ○ Just like the diet of most other marsupial species and all other kangaroo species, the diet of the swamp wallaby consists

- ○ Similar to the diets of most other marsupial species and all other kangaroo species, the swamp wallabies have a diet which consists

- ○ Like most other marsupial species and all other kangaroo species, the swamp wallaby has a diet consisting

Step 1: Read the Original Sentence Carefully, Looking for Errors

This sentence begins with the word "Like," which signals that you have a comparison to check. Look at the items being compared and make sure they are comparable. In the original sentence, *species* are compared to a *diet*. That's an incorrect comparison.

Step 2: Scan and Group the Answer Choices

All the answer choices contain "like" or "similar to," so they all contain comparisons. As you examine each choice, look to ensure that it makes a proper comparison. Notice how Attention to the Right Detail—to the words that signal a comparison—has helped you to quickly form a strategy for this question.

Step 3: Eliminate Choices Until Only One Remains

The incorrect comparison in the original sentence means that you would automatically eliminate **(A)**. Aside from sounding awkward, **(B)** contains a subject/verb agreement problem—the plural noun "diets" takes the singular verb "consists," which is incorrect. **(C)** should be eliminated because in the introductory phrase "diet" should be plural; also, there's no reason to use "Just like" rather than "Like." In addition, "Like" is preferable to "Similar to" in **(D)**, which also incorrectly compares *diets* to *wallabies*. Only **(E)** correctly compares the swamp wallaby to other species.

TAKEAWAYS: COMPARISONS

- Items being compared must be both grammatically and logically comparable.
- Compared items must have parallel form.
- The key to handling comparison questions is to make sure that the comparisons are correct and avoid any possibility of ambiguity.
- Don't let intervening phrases or clauses distract you from what is being compared.

PRACTICE SET: COMPARISONS

Answers and explanations are at the end of the chapter.

34. Recent surveys indicate that, contrary to popular belief, total abstinence from alcohol does not correlate <u>as strongly with good health as with moderate drinking</u>.

    ○ as strongly with good health as with moderate drinking

    ○ strongly with good health, like moderate drinking does

    ○ as strongly with good health as does moderately drinking

    ○ as strongly with good health as does moderate drinking

    ○ as strongly with good health as moderate drinking

35. Unlike <u>its fellow Baltic nations, Latvia and Lithuania, the economy of Estonia grew at an astonishing rate in the late 1990s, and at the end of the decade it was placed</u> on the fast track to join the European Union.

    ○ its fellow Baltic nations, Latvia and Lithuania, the economy of Estonia grew at an astonishing rate in the late 1990s, and at the end of the decade it was placed

    ○ its fellow Baltic nations, Latvia and Lithuania, Estonia grew at an astonishing rate economically in the late 1990s, and at the end of the decade earned itself a place

    ○ its fellow Baltic nations, Latvia and Lithuania, Estonia's economy grew at an astonishing rate in the late 1990s, and at the end of the decade they were placed

    ○ Latvia and Lithuania, its fellow Baltic nations, the economy of Estonia grew at an astonishing rate in the late 1990s, and at the end of the decade it was placed

    ○ its fellow Baltic nations, Latvia and Lithuania, Estonia experienced economic growth at an astonishing rate in the late 1990s, and at the end of the decade it earned a place

36. <u>No less significant than</u> international pressures are the constraints that domestic culture and ideology impose on decision making by national political figures.

    ○ No less significant than

    ○ The things that are just as significant as

    ○ Just like the significant

    ○ Not lesser than the significance of

    ○ What are as significant as

37. Golden and Labrador retrievers have enjoyed wide popularity as guide dogs because their dispositions are more suited to companion work <u>than</u> most other breeds.

    ○ than

    ○ than is true of

    ○ than are those of

    ○ in comparison to

    ○ as compared to

ADVANCED PRACTICE SET: COMPARISONS

Answers and explanations are at the end of the chapter.

38. Unlike doctors of allopathic medicine, who focus on the diagnosis and treatment of human diseases, <u>the focus of doctors of osteopathic medicine is on</u> alternative therapies, holistic medicine, and disease prevention.

    O   the focus of doctors of osteopathic medicine is on
    O   the things that doctors of osteopathic medicine focus on are
    O   doctors of osteopathic medicine differ a great deal because of their focus on
    O   doctors of osteopathic medicine focus on
    O   the focus of doctors of osteopathic medicine consists of

39. The legal considerations that have forced some universities to revise their affirmative action admissions programs are similar to <u>the revisions that certain large businesses have recently made to their affirmative action hiring practices</u>.

    O   the revisions that certain large businesses have recently made to their affirmative action hiring practices
    O   the affirmative action hiring practices that certain large businesses recently have revised
    O   those that have recently forced certain large businesses to revise their affirmative action hiring practices
    O   those recent revisions that have been made by certain large businesses to their affirmative action hiring practices
    O   what certain large businesses have done to their affirmative action hiring practices in the recent past

40. During the Civil War, nearly three times as many Americans lost their lives from infections that could have been prevented with antiseptic techniques <u>than</u> were killed on the battlefield.

    O   than
    O   than those who
    O   than the number who
    O   as the number who
    O   as

Idioms and Usage

The frequently tested principle of idioms concerns forms of expression that have established themselves in standard English as the "right" way to say things. There's no grammar rule that applies here; it's just that these particular expressions are generally agreed upon as correct by English speakers.

If you're a native English speaker, you probably know most idioms already. You'll hear them and be able to instinctively tell what's "right" and what's not. For example, if someone were to say to you, "I am aware about these problems, because I saw the newscast yesterday," you'd pick up on the error right away. The correct idiom is "aware *of*," not "aware *about*." But some idioms are commonly, through incorrectly, used in informal English. For example, your brother says to you, "Here's a tip—Mom prefers platinum over gold." Did you spot the error? The correct idiom is "prefers X *to* Y." So it's a good idea to review idioms and to keep a list of those you encounter but don't know.

If you're a nonnative English speaker, you'll likely know fewer idioms. Jot down all the idioms that you come across and make sure you know all the correct forms. Also, look out for the following:

- Prepositions (*to, from, at, over,* etc.) in the underlined portion of the sentence. Their usage is often dictated by idiomatic rules.
- Verbs whose idiomatic usage you've seen frequently tested. Common examples are *prefer, require,* and *regard.*

You will also need to know how to correct problems with usage and style. As tested on the GMAT, usage and style questions reward students for correcting both the syntax and diction of sentences. The GMAT will always prefer active voice and clear, direct style. Look out for the following:

- Unnecessary passive voice: "John wrote the letter" is better than "The letter was written by John."
- Unnecessary wording and redundancy. For example, the word "because" is better than the phrase "in view of the fact that."
- Awkward, choppy, or clunky phrasing: use your "ear" to help you identify sentences and phrases that simply don't read well.

Idioms and Usage Exercise, Part I

Answers are on the page following the exercises.

Fill in the blank with the correct word or phrase that completes the idiom correctly in the sentence. In some cases, the correct idiom may not require any additional words.

1. He modestly *attributed* his business's success _____ good luck.

2. My dictionary *defines* "idiom" _____ the usual way in which the words of a particular language are joined together.

3. Alexander Graham Bell is *credited* _____ inventing the telephone.

4. Some color-blind people cannot *distinguish* red _____ green.

5. Other color-blind people cannot *distinguish* _____ yellow _____ blue.

6. Although his story seems incredible, I *believe* it _____ the truth.

7. She is *regarded* _____ an expert on public health policy.

8. He is *considered* _____ a close friend of the president.

9. I like to *contrast* my plaid pants _____ a lovely paisley jacket.

10. According to Aristotle, contentment is *different* _____ happiness.

11. The oldest rocks on Earth are *estimated* _____ 4.6 billion years old.

12. Louisiana's legal system is *modeled* _____ the Napoleonic code.

13. I don't mean for my comments to be *perceived* _____ criticism.

14. Cigarette ads *aimed* _____ children have been banned by the FDA.

15. The mass extinction of dinosaurs has been *linked* _____ a large meteor impact.

16. Don't *worry* _____ all GMAT idioms; just memorize the ones that your ear doesn't recognize.

Idioms and Usage Exercise, Part II

Answers are on the page following the exercises.

Fill in the blank with the correct word or phrase that completes the idiom correctly in the sentence. In some cases, choose the option that correctly completes the idiom.

1. I sold more glasses of lemonade _____ my neighbor sold.

2. She sold as many glasses of lemonade _____ she could.

3. The bigger they come, _____ they fall, or so it is said.

4. According to my diet, I can have either cake <u>or/and</u> ice cream, but not both.

5. Given my choice, I would have both cake _____ ice cream.

6. I must decide between one _____ the other.

7. Neither the coach _____ the players <u>was/were</u> happy with the team's performance.

8. I couldn't decide <u>if/whether</u> he was kidding or not.

9. <u>Between/Among</u> the three candidates, he has the <u>more/most</u> impressive record.

10. There are <u>less/fewer</u> students in class today than there were yesterday.

11. However, the <u>amount/number</u> of students enrolled in this class has increased.

12. People are forbidden <u>from entering/to enter</u> the park at night.

13. The ruling prohibits the defendant <u>from discussing/to discuss</u> the case.

14. Most politicians do not want to be seen associating <u>with/among</u> convicted felons.

15. We should treat others <u>as/like</u> we would want them to treat us.

16. I would prefer a salty treat <u>like/such as</u> potato chips <u>over/to</u> a candy bar.

17. Scores on the GMAT range from 200 _____ 800.

18. Most local residents view the monument _____ an eyesore.

19. In the United States, there is less opposition _____ the use of genetically modified foods than in Europe.

20. Stress can lower one's resistance _____ cold and flu viruses.

21. The rise in inflation has become so significant _____ constitute a threat to the economic recovery.

22. The actress's performance was so poignant _____ the entire audience was moved to tears.

23. Just try _____ do as well as you can on the test.

Idioms and Usage Exercise, Part I: Answers

1. He modestly *attributed* his business's success **to** good luck.

2. My dictionary *defines* "idiom" **as** the usual way in which the words of a particular language are joined together.

3. Alexander Graham Bell is *credited* **with** inventing the telephone.

4. Some color-blind people cannot *distinguish* red **from** green.

5. Other color-blind people cannot *distinguish* **between** yellow **and** blue.

6. Although his story seems incredible, I *believe* it **to be** the truth.

7. She is *regarded* **as** an expert on public health policy.

8. He is *considered* a close friend of the president. **[This blank takes nothing.]**

9. I like to *contrast* my plaid pants **with** a lovely paisley jacket.

10. According to Aristotle, contentment is *different* **from** happiness.

11. The oldest rocks on Earth are *estimated* **to be** 4.6 billion years old.

12. Louisiana's legal system is *modeled* **after** the Napoleonic code.

13. I don't mean for my comments to be *perceived* **as** criticism.

14. Cigarette ads *aimed* **at** children have been banned by the FDA.

15. The mass extinction of dinosaurs has been *linked* **to** a large meteor impact.

16. Don't *worry* **about** all GMAT idioms; just memorize the ones that your ear doesn't recognize.

Idioms and Usage Exercise, Part II: Answers

1. I sold more glasses of lemonade **than** my neighbor sold.

2. She sold as many glasses of lemonade **as** she could.

3. The bigger they come, **the harder** they fall, or so it is said.

4. According to my diet, I can have either cake **or** ice cream, but not both.

5. Given my choice, I would have both cake **and** ice cream.

6. I must decide between one **and** the other.

7. Neither the coach **nor** the players **were** happy with the team's performance.

8. I couldn't decide **whether** he was kidding or not.

9. **Among** the three candidates, he has the **most** impressive record.

10. There are **fewer** students in class today than there were yesterday.

11. However, the **number** of students enrolled in this class has increased.

12. People are forbidden **to enter** the park at night.

13. The ruling prohibits the defendant **from discussing** the case.

14. Most politicians do not want to be seen associating **with** convicted felons.

15. We should treat others **as** we would want them to treat us.

16. I would prefer a salty treat **such as** potato chips **to** a candy bar.

17. Scores on the GMAT range from 200 **to** 800.

18. Most local residents view the monument **as** an eyesore.

19. In the United States, there is less opposition **to** the use of genetically modified foods than in Europe.

20. Stress can lower one's resistance ***to*** cold and flu viruses.

21. The rise in inflation has become so significant ***as to*** constitute a threat to the economic recovery.

22. The actress's performance was so poignant ***that*** the entire audience was moved to tears.

23. Just try ***to*** do as well as you can on the test.

APPLYING THE KAPLAN METHOD: IDIOMS AND USAGE

Now let's use the Kaplan Method on a Sentence Correction question dealing with idioms and usage:

> Growth in the industry is at an all-time low, with total employment <u>at less than 68,000 people and fewer</u> companies in the field than there have been during any of the past ten years.

- ○ at less than 68,000 people and fewer
- ○ at fewer than 68,000 people and fewer
- ○ lesser than 68,000 people and fewer
- ○ fewer than 68,000 people and less
- ○ at less than 68,000 people and there are less

Step 1: Read the Original Sentence Carefully, Looking for Errors

Notice that the underlined portion of the sentence contains the words "less" and "fewer." These words are often tested on the GMAT because they are often used incorrectly, so be sure to pay attention to them. Doing so will save you valuable time. "Less" can only refer to non-countable items, such as soup or confidence. "Fewer" must refer to countable items, such as chairs or peanuts. In this sentence, since "people" and "companies" can both be counted, "fewer" is appropriate.

Step 2: Scan and Group the Answer Choices

Even if that didn't occur to you as the issue in the sentence, you should note that some of the choices use "less" (or "lesser") and others use "fewer" and group accordingly into a 3-2 split.

Step 3: Eliminate Choices Until Only One Remains

You would eliminate choice **(A)** because the original sentence uses the non-countable adjective "less" to describe the countable noun "people." Choices **(C)** and **(E)** make similar errors (and choice **(C)**'s "lesser than" is thoroughly unidiomatic), so eliminate them as well. Choice **(D)** uses "less" to describe the countable noun "companies," so it is incorrect. Only in choice **(B)** are both countable nouns modified by the countable adjective "fewer," making it the correct answer.

TAKEAWAYS: IDIOMS AND USAGE

- Avoid verbosity and redundancy.
- Avoid passive verbs wherever possible.
- Avoid clunky, choppy, or awkward-sounding sentences.
- Use the correct idioms.
- There really are no rules when it comes to idioms, which are simply word combinations that, based on common usage, have established themselves as correct in standard written English. Many GMAT idiom questions require you to use the right prepositions.

PRACTICE SET: IDIOMS AND USAGE

Answers and explanations are at the end of the chapter.

41. <u>When a product costs more, be it</u> a bottle of wine or a handbag, the more likely it is to be esteemed by consumers.

    ○   When a product costs more, be it

    ○   When a product costs more, whether it is

    ○   As a product becomes more and more costly, like

    ○   The more a product costs, like

    ○   The more a product costs, whether it is

42. Mary Shelley is widely credited <u>for the invention of a new literary genre; many scholars consider her first and only novel, *Frankenstein*, to be</u> the first science fiction story.

    ○   for the invention of a new literary genre; many scholars consider her first and only novel, *Frankenstein*, to be

    ○   for inventing a new literary genre; many scholars consider her first and only novel, *Frankenstein*, as being

    ○   to have invented a new literary genre; many scholars regard her first and only novel, *Frankenstein*, to be

    ○   with the invention of a new literary genre; many scholars regard her first and only novel, *Frankenstein*, to be

    ○   with the invention of a new literary genre; many scholars consider her first and only novel, *Frankenstein*,

43. <u>The percentage of people aged 25–44 living alone increased abruptly between 1990 and 1995 and</u> continued to rise more slowly over the next five years.

    ○   The percentage of people aged 25–44 living alone increased abruptly between 1990 and 1995 and

    ○   There was an abruptly increased percentage of people aged 25–44 who lived alone between 1990 and 1995, and they

    ○   The percentage of people aged 25–44 who lived alone increased abruptly between 1990 and 1995 and has

    ○   There has been an abrupt increase in the percentage of people aged 25–44 living alone between 1990 and 1995, and it

    ○   Between 1990 and 1995, there was an abrupt increase in the percentage of people aged 25–44 who lived alone, which

ADVANCED PRACTICE SET: IDIOMS AND USAGE

Answers and explanations are at the end of the chapter.

44. The macabre nature of *Macbeth*, together with the widespread belief that real-life tragedies have accompanied many productions, <u>has made the name of the play so dreaded that not even the least superstitious members of most casts dare</u> utter it.

  ○ has made the name of the play so dreaded that not even the least superstitious members of most casts dare

  ○ have made the name of the play so dreaded, even the least superstitious members of most casts will not dare to

  ○ have made the play's name sufficiently dreaded, so that even the less superstitious members of most casts will not dare to

  ○ have made the name of the play sufficiently dreaded, so that not even the least superstitious members of most casts dare

  ○ has made the name of the play is dreaded, so that even the least superstitious members of most casts dare not

45. The university's board of trustees, <u>being worried over declining student enrollments and their failing</u> to secure additional funding from the state, has formed a committee to determine what cuts need to be made to staff and programs.

  ○ being worried over declining student enrollments and their failing

  ○ worrying over declining student enrollments and also the failure

  ○ worried about declining student enrollments and the failure

  ○ in that they are worried about the decline in student enrollments and the failure

  ○ because of its worry concerning the decline of student enrollments and, as well as concerning the failure

MISCELLANEOUS ERRORS

Most Sentence Correction errors fall into the categories we've just reviewed. Through our research, we've seen three other types of errors that show up with enough frequency on the GMAT to merit a word here.

Which, Where, When

The GMAT likes to test your understanding of the use of the relative pronouns *which*, *where*, and *when*. While the usage of these words may be flexible in informal speech, there are specific rules for how they are used on the GMAT:

- On the GMAT, *which* needs to be preceded by a comma and refer to the noun just before the comma, or else its use is wrong (except when it follows a preposition, as in the phrase "in which").
- On the GMAT, *where* must refer to an actual location, or else its use is wrong.
- On the GMAT, *when* must refer to an actual time or else its use is wrong.

Subjunctive Mood

The subjunctive mood is the form of a verb used to describe a situation that is contrary to fact. You will see the subjunctive mood used in sentences that describe an order or recommendation. The subjunctive mood is also used in sentences that present hypothetical situations. Here are the rules to keep in mind when you see one of these types of sentences:

- **Orders and recommendations:** With verbs such as *order*, *recommend*, *demand*, *insist*, etc., what follows the verb should be *that*, a new subject, and the infinitive form of a verb but without the *to*. Example: He *demanded* that the door *be* opened.
- **Hypothetical situations:** When contemplating hypothetical or contrary-to-fact situations, use *were* and *would*. Example: If I *were* rich, I *would* quit my job.

Clauses and Connectors

The GMAT uses compound and complex sentences to test your knowledge of clauses and connectors. Recall that a clause is a group of words that contains a subject and a verb. When two clauses appear in a sentence, the clauses should be connected by one, and only one, connector (*because*, *although*, *as*, *but*, etc.). The connector used should make sense with the rest of the sentence.

Miscellaneous Errors Exercise

Answers are on the following page.

For each of the following sentences, correct the error related to one of the three listed categories of miscellaneous errors.

1. After the mediation session, the victim said he was now in a state where he could forgive the offender.

2. The order from the vice president was that all employees will work through the weekend to finish the project.

3. If she was more competent, she would be promoted more quickly.

4. Many citizens agree that austerity measures are necessary, few are happy about the ones that were enacted.

5. She invited me to join her at the sushi restaurant which just opened next to Carlotta's Bistro on Main Street.

Miscellaneous Errors Exercise: Answers

1. "Where" can only refer to a place, and "a state (of mind)" is not a place. Use "in which" instead.

2. The verb in an order should be in the infinitive form, without the "to," so "to work" simply becomes "work"; there is no need for the "will": *The order from the vice president was that all employees work through the weekend to finish the project.*

3. Use "were" and "would" with hypothetical situations: *If she were more competent, she would be promoted more quickly.*

4. The two clauses in this sentence need to be related by a connector: *Many citizens agree that austerity measures are necessary, although few are happy about the ones that were enacted.*

5. "Which" is only correct when it appears immediately after a comma or as part of a phrase like "in which." "That" is the correct word in this case: *She invited me to join her at the sushi restaurant that just opened next to Carlotta's Bistro on Main Street.*

APPLYING THE KAPLAN METHOD: MISCELLANEOUS ERRORS

Now let's use the Kaplan Method on a Sentence Correction question dealing with miscellaneous errors:

More and more couples wait before trying to start a family, the average age of first-time parents is increasing.

- O   More and more couples wait before trying to start
- O   As more and more couples wait before trying to start
- O   As more and more couples wait before trying and starting
- O   Although more and more couples wait before trying to start
- O   Being that more and more couples are waiting before trying to start

Step 1: Read the Original Sentence Carefully, Looking for Errors

This sentence contains two complete clauses, each with its own subject and verb. The subject of "wait" is "couples," and the subject of "is increasing" is "age." Two complete clauses should be joined with a conjunction, but this sentence has no conjunction and is thus a run-on. The correct answer will provide the sentence with a conjunction. Choice **(A)** is incorrect.

Step 2: Scan and Group the Answer Choices

Choices **(B)** and **(C)** introduce "As" at the beginning of the sentence. Choice **(D)** substitutes "Although," and **(E)** uses "Being that."

Step 3: Eliminate Choices Until Only One Remains

The GMAT test makers consider "Being that" to be awkward and wordy, and an answer choice containing it will invariably be wrong. Recognizing this pattern makes choice **(E)** easy to eliminate. Choice **(D)** adds the conjunction "Although," which certainly sounds better than "Being that" but which indicates a contrast and therefore doesn't make logical sense. "Because" would be a more appropriate connector than "Although." **(B)** and **(C)** both start with "As," which does make logical sense as a conjunction for this sentence. **(C)** changes "trying to start" to "trying and starting," which is an idiomatically incorrect construction. The correct answer is **(B)**, which adds an appropriate conjunction and does not create any new errors.

TAKEAWAYS: MISCELLANEOUS ERRORS

- Memorize the rules for *which*, *where*, and *when* and apply them with rigor on Test Day.
- Memorize the situations in which the subjunctive is used and the rules for how to handle them.
- Clauses and connectors must be used correctly on the GMAT. Avoid missing or redundant connectors.

PRACTICE SET: MISCELLANEOUS ERRORS

Answers and explanations are at the end of the chapter.

46. The United States' trade deficit with China rose in 2003 to $123 billion, <u>which is 17 percent more than the previous year</u> and more than ten times the U.S.-China trade deficit in 1998.

    ○ which is 17 percent more than the previous year

    ○ which is 17 percent higher than it was the previous year

    ○ 17 percent higher than the previous year's figure was

    ○ an amount that is 17 percent more than the previous year was

    ○ an amount that is 17 percent higher than the previous year's figure

47. The two-party political system is one <u>where the electorate gives its votes largely to only two major parties and where</u> one or the other party can usually win a majority in the legislature.

    ○ where the electorate gives its votes largely to only two major parties and where

    ○ in which the electorate largely gives only its votes to two major parties and where

    ○ where the electorate gives largely its votes to only two major parties and in which

    ○ in which the electorate gives its votes largely to only two major parties and in which

    ○ in which the electorate largely gives only its votes to two major parties and in which

48. Most financial advisers <u>recommend that stock portfolios should be reviewed</u> at least once a year, if only to make sure that changes do not need to be made.

    ○ recommend that stock portfolios should be reviewed

    ○ recommend you to review your stock portfolio

    ○ recommend that stock portfolios be reviewed

    ○ are recommending that stock portfolios are reviewed

    ○ have a recommendation to review stock portfolios

49. The United States <u>would achieve a 10 percent reduction in gasoline consumption,</u> <u>if Congress will raise</u> fuel economy standards to 31.3 miles per gallon for passenger cars and to 24.5 mpg for light trucks.

    ○   would achieve a 10 percent reduction in gasoline consumption, if Congress will raise

    ○   will achieve a 10 percent reduction in gasoline consumption, if Congress were to raise

    ○   will have achieved a 10 percent reduction in gasoline consumption, if Congress will raise

    ○   would achieve a 10 percent reduction in gasoline consumption, if Congress were to raise

    ○   would achieve a 10 percent reduction in gasoline consumption, if Congress were raising

50. Because the moon's distance from Earth varies, <u>so the gravitational pull between</u> <u>the two bodies differ</u>, as do the size and times of oceanic tides.

    ○   so the gravitational pull between the two bodies differ

    ○   so the gravitational pull between the two bodies differs

    ○   the gravitational pull between the two bodies differs

    ○   therefore the gravitational pull between the two bodies differ

    ○   therefore the gravitational pull between the two bodies differs

SENTENCE CORRECTION QUIZ

Answers and explanations are at the end of the chapter.

51. With a height of 7'7" and a wingspan of over 8'6", <u>Manute Bol is often considered one of the most physically imposing players in the history of professional basketball</u>, and he also gave generously of his time and money to help refugees from his native Sudan.

    O   Manute Bol is often considered one of the most physically imposing players in the history of professional basketball

    O   Manute Bol is often considered in the history of professional basketball the player who was most physically imposing

    O   one of the most physically imposing players in the history of professional basketball is often considered Manute Bol

    O   Manute Bol's place in the history of professional basketball is that of one of the most physically imposing players

    O   one of the most often considered, physically imposing players in the history of professional basketball was Manute Bol

52. At more than 800 pages in length, the <u>novelist's life stands revealed in the new biography, which sets the standard for research</u>.

    O   novelist's life stands revealed in the new biography, which sets the standard for research

    O   new biography is setting standards of research on the novelist's life

    O   standard for research has been set by a new biography on the novelist

    O   new biography about the novelist sets the standard for research

    O   novelist's life is revealed in a standard-setting new biography

53. Because customers at Jim's restaurant frequently failed to leave the expected tips for the waitstaff, <u>they are now</u> automatically factored into the price of each menu item.

    O   they are now

    O   tips are now being

    O   the tipping of money is now

    O   tips are now

    O   it is now

54. Although the British were responsible for the early European settlement <u>of both Australia and the United States, Australia is having much closer political and cultural links with Britain than the United States is having</u>.

   O   of both Australia and the United States, Australia is having much closer political and cultural links with Britain than the United States is having

   O   in both Australia and the United States, they are closer in their political and cultural links in Australia than in the United States

   O   of both nations, Australia has much closer political and cultural links to Britain than the United States has

   O   in both nations, Australia is politically and culturally linked to Britain in a much closer fashion than the United States

   O   of both Australia and the United States, they have much closer political and cultural links to it than the United States has

55. <u>Each of the major setbacks the Germans suffered in June 1944—the fall of Rome, the collapse of Army Group Center on the Eastern Front, and the breaching of the Atlantic Wall at Normandy—were powerful shocks</u> signaling the inability of the German war machine to compete on multiple fronts.

   O   Each of the major setbacks the Germans suffered in June 1944—the fall of Rome, the collapse of Army Group Center on the Eastern Front, and the breaching of the Atlantic Wall at Normandy—were powerful shocks

   O   The fall of Rome, the collapse of Army Group Center on the Eastern Front, and the breaching of the Atlantic Wall at Normandy—each of them major setbacks the Germans suffered in June 1944—were powerful shocks

   O   Powerful shocks—the fall of Rome, the collapse of Army Group Center on the Eastern Front, and the breaching of the Atlantic Wall at Normandy—each a major setback for the Germans in June 1944, was such

   O   The major setbacks suffered by the Germans in June 1944—the fall of Rome, the collapse of Army Group Center on the Eastern Front, and the breaching of the Atlantic Wall at Normandy—each were powerful shocks

   O   Each of the major setbacks the Germans suffered in June 1944—the fall of Rome, the collapse of Army Group Center on the Eastern Front, and the breach of the Atlantic Wall at Normandy—was a powerful shock

56. Adult pelicans store fish in a deep, expandable pouch below the lower mandible, <u>of which the young feed</u>.

  ○ of which the young feed
  ○ being for the feeding of the young
  ○ from which the young feed
  ○ that it feeds the young from
  ○ young feed from

57. Anthony Trollope, one of the most famous English novelists of the nineteenth century, also <u>wrote travel books, some based on his undertaking of journeys</u> while an employee of the postal service.

  ○ wrote travel books, some based on his undertaking of journeys
  ○ wrote travel books, some based on journeys he undertook
  ○ undertook journeys, having based travel books on them
  ○ based travel books on journeys undertaken
  ○ wrote travel books, some based on journeys which he was to undertake

58. A federal government survey taken in 1997 showed that during the 12 months preceding the survey, 36 percent of the U.S. population had tried marijuana, cocaine, or other illicit drugs, 71 percent of the population <u>were smoking cigarettes, and 82 percent</u> tried alcoholic beverages.

  ○ were smoking cigarettes, and 82 percent
  ○ had smoked cigarettes, and 82 percent had
  ○ smoked cigarettes, and that 82 percent
  ○ smoked cigarettes, and 82 percent had
  ○ will be smoking cigarettes, and 82 percent

59. Like Art Nouveau jewelry designers, the <u>Art Deco movement used art materials suitable for expressing</u> the new stylistic language of the 1920s, one dominated by an interplay of geometric forms.

   O   Art Deco movement used art materials suitable for expressing

   O   Art Deco movement was expressed through the use of materials suitable for the

   O   artists of the Art Deco movement used materials suitable for expressing

   O   Art Deco movement's materials were used by artists to suitably express

   O   artists of the Art Deco movement also used suitable materials for the expression of

60. Amtrak, a government-owned corporation, schedules passenger rail service, <u>payments to privately owned firms to run trains, and bears all administrative costs, such as</u> those incurred by the purchase of new equipment and by the sale of tickets.

   O   payments to privately owned firms to run trains, and bears all administrative costs, such as

   O   pays privately owned firms to run trains, and is bearing all administrative costs, such as

   O   pays privately owned firms to run trains, and bears all administrative costs, such as

   O   pays privately owned firms to run trains, and bears all administrative costs, being inclusive of

   O   pays privately owned firms to run trains, and the bearer of all costs of administration, for example

61. In feudal Korea, <u>cattle were traditionally used as beasts of burden, rather than as a food source, and fish were</u> the primary source of protein in the typical diet.

   O   cattle were traditionally used as beasts of burden, rather than as a food source, and fish were

   O   cattle were being used as beasts of burden, rather than as a food source, and fish were providing

   O   cattle were traditionally used as beasts of burden, rather than a food source, with fish being

   O   the traditional use of cattle was as beasts of burden, rather than for the provision of food, and fish were

   O   cattle were traditionally used for beasts of burden, rather than for a food source, and fish were

62. The term "support staff" is often used to describe employees <u>that perform lower-level tasks but also are providing</u> essential administrative duties for executive-level managers.

    O   that perform lower-level tasks but also are providing
    O   performing lower-level tasks but also providing
    O   who perform lower-level tasks, but are also providing
    O   that performs lower-level tasks but also provide
    O   who perform lower-level tasks but also provide

63. National Women's History Month <u>began as a single week and as a local event when, in 1978, Sonoma County, California, sponsored</u> a women's history week to promote the teaching of women's history—a neglected subject in elementary and high school curricula at that time.

    O   began as a single week and as a local event when, in 1978, Sonoma County, California, sponsored
    O   began as a single week local event sponsoring, in Sonoma County, California,
    O   begins with a single week in 1978 sponsoring the local Sonoma County, California, of
    O   will have began in 1978 as a single week local event when Sonoma County, California, was in sponsorship of
    O   was begun in 1978 when, in Sonoma County, California, there was to be a sponsorship of

64. <u>By examining sets of identical twins in recent studies, mental disorders such as schizophrenia and autism have been found to be</u> the results of variations in gene expression and not simply a matter of genetic inheritance.

    ○   By examining sets of identical twins in recent studies, mental disorders such as schizophrenia and autism have been found to be

    ○   By examining sets of identical twins in recent studies, mental disorders such as schizophrenia and autism were found as being

    ○   Mental disorders such as schizophrenia and autism were examined in sets of identical twins in recent studies and has been found to be

    ○   Recent studies that examined sets of identical twins have shown that mental disorders such as schizophrenia and autism are

    ○   Recent studies that examined sets of identical twins has shown that mental disorders such as schizophrenia and autism are

65. Working with musician Stevie Wonder as a musical adviser, Ray Kurzweil developed what is now the preferred medium for creating nearly all music for today's commercial albums, films, and television: a computer-based instrument capable of <u>reproducing musical sounds of a quality once thought to be</u> possible only on grand pianos and other acoustic instruments.

    ○   reproducing musical sounds of a quality once thought to be

    ○   reproducing musical sounds with a quality as were once thought to be

    ○   reproducing in musical sounds a quality that was once thought to be

    ○   reproduction of musical sounds whose quality is the same as what were once thought to be

    ○   reproduction of musical sounds at a quality once thought of as

66. Twenty years ago, only 6 percent of students at Dunmore College who intended to major in chemistry were women; today that figure is <u>at least as high as 40 percent</u>.

    ○   at least as high as 40 percent

    ○   higher than at least 40 percent

    ○   higher by 40 percent at the least

    ○   40 percent high or more

    ○   more higher than 40 percent

ANSWERS AND EXPLANATIONS

1.	E	18.	D	35.	E	52.	D
2.	D	19.	A	36.	A	53.	D
3.	C	20.	E	37.	C	54.	C
4.	A	21.	C	38.	D	55.	E
5.	A	22.	C	39.	C	56.	C
6.	D	23.	D	40.	E	57.	B
7.	C	24.	C	41.	E	58.	B
8.	A	25.	B	42.	E	59.	C
9.	D	26.	E	43.	A	60.	C
10.	D	27.	C	44.	A	61.	A
11.	B	28.	B	45.	C	62.	E
12.	C	29.	A	46.	E	63.	A
13.	C	30.	E	47.	D	64.	D
14.	D	31.	B	48.	C	65.	A
15.	B	32.	A	49.	D	66.	A
16.	D	33.	C	50.	C		
17.	E	34.	D	51.	A		

1. **(E)**

    The rise in the number of new housing starts in the final two quarters of last year <u>suggest that the sluggish economy should continue its recovery into the first quarter of this year, but</u> weak job growth in the private sector continues to worry some economists.

    O   suggest that the sluggish economy should continue its recovery into the first quarter of this year, but

    O   suggest that the sluggish economy will continue to recover in the first quarter of this year, but that

    O   suggest that the sluggish economy is continuing to recover in the first quarter of this year, but

    O   suggests that the sluggish economy should continue its recovery into the first quarter of this year, but that

    O   suggests that the sluggish economy will continue to recover in the first quarter of this year, but

Step 1: Read the Original Sentence Carefully, Looking for Errors

Whenever the subject or predicate verb of a sentence is underlined, we need to check for subject-verb agreement. In this sentence, the predicate verb, "suggest," is underlined. The subject of that verb is "rise," which is singular, so we need a singular verb. However, "suggest" is plural. We've discovered a subject-verb agreement error, and the right answer will correct it.

Step 2: Scan and Group the Answer Choices

(A), **(B)**, and **(C)** retain the error; all use "suggest." **(D)** and **(E)** change the verb to "suggests."

Step 3: Eliminate Choices Until Only One Remains

Because **(A)**, **(B)**, and **(C)** all make the same subject-verb agreement mistake, you can eliminate them. The answer will be either **(D)** or **(E)**. **(D)** adds the word "that" to the end of the underlined part of the sentence, which changes the meaning. According to the original sentence, the only thing suggested by the rise in housing starts is that the sluggish economy will continue to recover. Adding the word "that" makes it sound as if the rise in housing starts also suggests that weak job growth continues to worry some economists, which is not what the original sentence implied. Because the correct choice will retain the meaning of the original sentence, **(D)** is incorrect, and **(E)** is the correct answer.

2. **(D)**

The green flash, an atmospheric refractive phenomenon whereby the top edge of a setting sun will momentarily turn green, rarely is seen by the naked eye, primarily <u>on account of requiring</u> specific favorable conditions to occur.

- ○ on account of requiring
- ○ on account of their requiring
- ○ because they require
- ○ because it requires
- ○ because of requiring

Step 1: Read the Original Sentence Carefully, Looking for Errors

The GMAT prefers concise constructions. This underlined piece sounds awkward. Moreover, *–ing* constructions such as "of requiring" are generally suspect on the GMAT. Seek an answer choice that is less wordy and that removes the phrase "of requiring."

Step 2: Scan and Group the Answer Choices

(A) and **(B)** keep "on account of." **(C)**, **(D)**, and **(E)** all use "because."

Step 3: Eliminate Choices Until Only One Remains

"Because" is certainly shorter and more concise than "on account of," so eliminate **(A)** and **(B)**. **(C)** uses the pronoun "they," but it refers to the "green flash," so the pronoun should be singular. Hence, **(C)** cannot be correct. **(D)** uses the pronoun "it," which agrees with its antecedent, the "green flash." This choice is concise and grammatically correct and is thus the correct answer. **(E)** is incorrect because it uses the phrase "of requiring," which sounds awkward in the original sentence. **(D)** is the correct answer.

3. **(C)**

A new study has found that college students <u>had been more involved in on-campus political activities during the last few years than at any time</u> in the past two decades.

○ had been more involved in on-campus political activities during the last few years than at any time

○ had been more involved in on-campus political activities during the last few years than at any other time

○ have been more involved in on-campus political activities during the last few years than at any other time

○ have been more involved in on-campus political activities during the last few years than at any time

○ are more involved in on-campus political activities during the last few years as compared to any other time

Step 1: Read the Original Sentence Carefully, Looking for Errors

This sentence contains an underlined verb, so that's a good place to start your investigation. There is no difference between the singular and plural forms of "had been," so there is no subject-verb agreement error. However, the verb tense does not match the meaning of the sentence. The past perfect tense, indicated by the use of the helping verb "had," is only appropriate when there are two past events, with one having occurred before the other. In that situation, the past perfect would be used for the earlier of the two events. In the underlined clause of this sentence, though, there is only a single, continuous action—involvement in on-campus political activities. So there should be no use of the past perfect, and the use of the word "had" needs to be corrected.

Step 2: Scan and Group the Answer Choices

(A) and **(B)** retain the verb "had been involved." **(C)** and **(D)** both use "have been involved," while **(E)** uses "are involved."

Step 3: Eliminate Choices Until Only One Remains

"Had been involved" is an incorrect verb tense, so eliminate **(A)** and **(B)**. **(E)** uses the present tense, but the action being described has been happening "during the last few years," so you have another inappropriate tense and can eliminate **(E)** as well. That leaves **(C)** and **(D)**. Both use the correct tense, the present perfect, to describe an action that occurred in the past over the course of several years. The only difference between them is that **(C)** adds the word "other" to the phrase "at any time," while **(D)** does not. You'll need to look carefully at the intended meaning of the original sentence to see which is correct. The "last few years" are included in the "past two decades," so the author of the sentence is really trying to compare the "last few years" to any "other" time during the past two decades. **(C)** adds this subtle but proper comparative adjective and is therefore the correct answer.

4. **(A)**

Fitness experts say that the weighted barbell squat or the weighted hip thrust, each part of a family of training maneuvers called compound movements, <u>is one of the best exercises for isolating and building the gluteal muscles</u>.

- ○ is one of the best exercises for isolating and building the gluteal muscles
- ○ are among the best exercises to isolate and for building the gluteal muscles
- ○ is one of the best exercises for isolating and to build the gluteal muscles
- ○ are among the best exercises for isolating and building the gluteal muscles
- ○ is one of the best exercises to isolate and for building the gluteal muscles

Step 1: Read the Original Sentence Carefully, Looking for Errors

Whenever a sentence contains an underlined verb, look for subject-verb agreement. In this sentence, the verb "is" is singular. The subject of the sentence is composed of the names of two exercises, connected by the conjunction "or." When a compound subject is connected by "or" and the last noun in the subject is singular, it takes a singular verb, meaning that "is" is correct. The rest of the sentence proceeds logically and without error.

Step 2: Scan and Group the Answer Choices

(A), **(C)**, and **(E)** retain the verb "is." **(B)** and **(D)** contain the verb "are."

Step 3: Eliminate Choices Until Only One Remains

Since "is" is the correct verb, eliminate **(B)** and **(D)**. Of the remaining choices, **(C)** and **(E)** do not use a parallel structure in the phrase at the end, using "for isolating and to build" and "to isolate and for building," respectively. That leaves **(A)** as the correct answer.

5. (A)

Noting that <u>its revenues had fallen due to a recent</u> prolonged slump in CD sales, the music-store chain announced that it would be forced to raise prices at all of its outlets.

- ○ its revenues had fallen due to a recent
- ○ its revenues have fallen due to a recently
- ○ its revenues are falling due to a recently
- ○ their revenues are falling due to a recent
- ○ their revenues had fallen due to a recent

Step 1: Read the Original Sentence Carefully, Looking for Errors

This sentence contains an underlined verb and a pronoun, so check both. The verb, "had fallen," agrees with its plural subject, "revenues." It is in the past perfect tense, which is appropriate because the revenues fell before the announcement was made. Whenever there are two past events, with one occurring before the other, the chronologically earlier event should be in the past perfect tense. The verb "had fallen," then, is correct. The singular pronoun "its" refers unambiguously to "the music-store chain," which is also singular, so the pronoun is correct as well. Chances are that the answer will be **(A)**, but check the other choices as well to make sure you haven't overlooked anything.

Step 2: Scan and Group the Answer Choices

(A), **(B)**, and **(C)** retain the pronoun "its." **(D)** and **(E)** change the pronoun to "their." There is a second 3-2 split: **(A)**, **(D)**, and **(E)** keep the adjective "recent," while **(B)** and **(C)** change "recent" to "recently."

Step 3: Eliminate Choices Until Only One Remains

(D) and **(E)** can be eliminated because they use a plural pronoun, "their," to refer to a singular subject, "the music-store chain." Of the remaining choices, **(B)** and **(C)** change the last underlined word from "recent" to "recently." The original sentence referred to a "prolonged slump" that happened in a "recent" time frame. If the adjective "recent" is changed to the adverb "recently," this word can no longer describe the noun "slump" (only adjectives can describe nouns). Instead, the adverb "recently" must describe the adjective "prolonged" (i.e., the slump was "recently prolonged"), thereby changing the meaning of the sentence. The correct answer to a Sentence Correction question must match the intended meaning of the original sentence. You can thus throw out **(B)** and **(C)**. The correct answer remains **(A)**.

EXPLANATIONS

6. **(D)**

After all the research that has been conducted in the last 30 years, it is readily apparent that <u>there are, without question, a wealth of good reasons to do aerobic exercise regularly</u>.

- ○ there are, without question, a wealth of good reasons to do aerobic exercise regularly
- ○ there are, without question, a wealth of good reasons to exercise aerobically regularly
- ○ there are, without question, a wealth of good reasons to engage regularly in aerobic exercise
- ○ there is, without question, a wealth of good reasons to engage regularly in aerobic exercise
- ○ there is, without question, a wealth of good reasons to do regular aerobic exercises

Step 1: Read the Original Sentence Carefully, Looking for Errors

Sometimes the subject of a clause will appear after the verb, as is the case in this sentence. In the underlined subordinate clause, the subject is "a wealth" and the verb is "are"—and both are underlined, so you must check for agreement. (The noun "reasons" cannot be the subject because it is part of the prepositional phrase "of good reasons," which modifies the subject.) "Wealth" is a singular noun, so you need a singular verb; "are" is plural, so you have a subject-verb agreement error.

Step 2: Scan and Group the Answer Choices

(A), **(B)**, and **(C)** retain the verb "are." **(D)** and **(E)** both change the verb to "is."

Step 3: Eliminate Choices Until Only One Remains

You know that "are" is incorrect, so eliminate **(A)**, **(B)**, and **(C)**. **(E)** changes "do aerobic exercise regularly" to "do regular aerobic exercises," which alters the meaning of the sentence in an illogical way. Here you want the adverb "regularly," which modifies how often a person should engage in exercise, not the adjective "regular," which modifies the noun "exercises," indicating that the exercises themselves should be "regular" or "normal." Because the correct answer must fix any existing errors without changing the meaning of the original sentence, **(E)** is incorrect, and **(D)** is the correct answer.

7. **(C)**

As state governments <u>become less and less able to support higher education in the coming years, universities have been becoming</u> more and more dependent on alumni networks, corporate sponsorships, and philanthropists.

- ○ become less and less able to support higher education in the coming years, universities have been becoming
- ○ are becoming less and less able to support higher education in the coming years, universities have become
- ○ become less and less able to support higher education in the coming years, universities will become
- ○ become less and less able to support higher education in the coming years, universities have become
- ○ are becoming less and less able to support higher education in the coming years, universities will become

Step 1: Read the Original Sentence Carefully, Looking for Errors

This sentence contains two underlined verbs. The first, "become," is plural, and agrees with its subject, "state governments," which is also plural. The second verb, "have been becoming," also agrees with its subject, "universities." However, universities' increasing dependence on alumni networks will take place "in the coming years," so you need the future tense, "will become." You can rule out **(A)**.

Step 2: Scan and Group the Answer Choices

Because you have identified a tense error in the second verb, you'll use that verb to split the answer choices. **(C)** and **(E)** use the future tense, "will become." **(A)**, **(B)**, and **(D)** retain some version of a past tense.

Step 3: Eliminate Choices Until Only One Remains

You definitely need the second verb to be in the future tense, so throw out **(A)**, **(B)**, and **(D)**. Of the remaining choices, **(C)** keeps the first verb, "become," while **(E)** changes the first verb to "are becoming." In general, the GMAT test makers prefer the simplest and most concise constructions. "As state governments become less and less able…in the coming years" makes sense, so there is no need to complicate the verb tense. **(C)** is the correct answer.

EXPLANATIONS

8. **(A)**

The most common breed of rabbit, *Oryctolagus cuniculus*, <u>is native to Europe but was accidentally introduced into the Australian continent in the 1850s, causing</u> decades of habitat destruction and crop devastation before its numbers were finally brought under control by bounty hunters.

○ is native to Europe but was accidentally introduced into the Australian continent in the 1850s, causing

○ is a native of Europe but was accidentally introduced into the Australian continent in the 1850s, which caused

○ was a native of Europe but was accidentally introduced into the Australian continent in the 1850s, causing

○ had been native to Europe but was accidentally introduced into the Australian continent in the 1850s, which caused

○ had been a native of Europe but was accidentally introduced into the Australian continent in the 1850s, causing

Step 1: Read the Original Sentence Carefully, Looking for Errors

Note the verbs "is" and "was accidentally introduced," as well as "causing" at the end of the underlined portion. Always pay attention to verbs in the underlined portion of a GMAT Sentence Correction question. Also pay attention to how the underlined portion ends, because that will likely be a source of variation among the answer choices.

Step 2: Scan and Group the Answer Choices

Conducting a quick survey of the beginnings and ends of the answer choices, note the 2-2-1 split among "is," "had been," and "was." Also, **(A)**, **(C)**, and **(E)** all end with "causing," while **(B)** and **(D)** end with "which caused."

Step 3: Eliminate Choices Until Only One Remains

First, tackle the verb issue. The rabbit breed *is* native to Europe; the status of its origins is immutable and does not change because it was introduced into the Australian continent in the 1850s. Therefore, the present tense is correct, making **(C)**, **(D)**, and **(E)** wrong. And **(B)** is wrong because the correct idiom to describe a species is "native to" rather than "a native of." My uncle is *a native of* Australia; the kangaroo is *native to* Australia. The sentence is correct as written, making **(A)** the answer. The author's use of "causing" is just fine here.

9. **(D)**

A recent spate of news reports questioning the long-term health benefits of high-fat diets <u>have done little to convince its practitioners that they should follow more traditional weight-loss plans</u>.

○   have done little to convince its practitioners that they should follow more traditional weight-loss plans

○   have done little to convince their practitioners to follow more traditional weight-loss plans

○   has done little to convince its practitioners to follow more traditional weight-loss plans

○   has done little to convince practitioners of these diets to follow more traditional weight-loss plans

○   has done little to convince practitioners of these diets they should follow more traditional weight-loss plans

Step 1: Read the Original Sentence Carefully, Looking for Errors

Note the verb in the beginning of the underlined portion. Here the GMAT is testing a common error in a classic way: the test is assessing your ability to determine correct subject-verb agreement by placing the subject as far as possible from the verb to disguise the error. The singular subject of the sentence, "spate," does not agree with the plural verb "have."

Step 2: Scan and Group the Answer Choices

Even if you didn't notice the subject-verb error, seeing the 3-2 split between "has" and "have," you should get the sense that subject-verb agreement is at issue here.

Step 3: Eliminate Choices Until Only One Remains

The actual subject of the sentence is "spate," which is singular, so **(A)** and **(B)** are out. Reading further, **(C)** is wrong because "its" is singular while the pronoun's antecedent, "diets," is plural. **(D)** is the correct answer because "convince practitioners...to follow" is idiomatically correct, whereas "convince practitioners...they should follow" is not. If **(D)** sounded better to you than **(E)**, you should learn to trust your ear on GMAT Sentence Correction questions.

10. (D)

Some economists contend that the way markets react to financial news <u>are based as much on irrational fears and expectations than on</u> sound fiscal analyses.

- ○ are based as much on irrational fears and expectations than on
- ○ are based as much on their irrational fears and expectations as they are on
- ○ is based as much on irrational fears and expectations than on
- ○ is based as much on irrational fears and expectations as on
- ○ has been based on irrational fears and expectations as much as

Step 1: Read the Original Sentence Carefully, Looking for Errors

Whenever a sentence contains an underlined verb, you must be sure to check whether it agrees with its subject. In this sentence, the verb "are based" is plural, but its subject, "way," is singular, so you have a subject-verb agreement error. Moreover, the words "as much" are part of the idiomatic phrase "as much…as," but this sentence instead uses "as much…than." The correct answer will fix both mistakes without introducing any new errors.

Step 2: Scan and Group the Answer Choices

(A) and **(B)** retain the plural verb phrase "are based." **(C)** and **(D)** instead use the singular "is based." **(E)** uses "has been based."

Step 3: Eliminate Choices Until Only One Remains

You can eliminate **(A)** and **(B)** because the plural verb is incorrect. **(E)** has a singular verb, but it changes the tense and therefore the meaning of the sentence, so you can rule out **(E)** as well. **(C)** and **(D)** both correctly use the present tense singular "is based." However, **(C)** does not correct the "as much…than" error. The correct answer is **(D)**, which corrects "as much…than" to "as much…as" and also uses the correct verb form.

11. **(B)**

The newspaper reported that <u>some homes that were destroyed and severely damaged in the hurricane last year were</u> built too close to the coastline.

○ some homes that were destroyed and severely damaged in the hurricane last year were

○ some homes that were destroyed or severely damaged in the hurricane last year had been

○ some homes the hurricane destroyed and severely damaged last year have been

○ last year the hurricane destroyed or severely damaged some homes that have been

○ last year some of the homes that were destroyed or severely damaged in the hurricane have been

Step 1: Read the Original Sentence Carefully, Looking for Errors

This underlined portion contains a lot of verbs. The homes "were destroyed and severely damaged" and "were built" too close to the coast. Did you notice the erroneous "and" in the underlined portion? It's actually not possible for homes to be destroyed and severely damaged. Homes are either destroyed *or* severely damaged, not both.

Step 2: Scan and Group the Answer Choices

(A) and **(C)** use "and," while the remaining choices use "or." Note also that the ends of the answer choices present a variety of verb tenses: "were," "had been," and "have been."

Step 3: Eliminate Choices Until Only One Remains

Because "and" is an inappropriate conjunction to use, **(A)** is out, as is **(C)**, which repeats the error. Since the homes were built first and then destroyed or damaged, the past perfect tense, "had been built," is appropriate to use here, making **(B)** the correct answer. **(D)** and **(E)** use the present perfect tense, "have been built," which doesn't make sense given the sequence of events in the sentence.

12. **(C)**

The adverse health effects of high-impact football tackles, which <u>had been shown to harm football players' health by causing concussions and irreversible brain damage, have led parents and educators to engage in</u> spirited debates about whether football should be banned in high schools across the country.

- ○ had been shown to harm football players' health by causing concussions and irreversible brain damage, have led parents and educators to engage in

- ○ were shown to harm football players' health by causing concussions and irreversible brain damage, are leading parents and educators to engage in

- ○ have been shown to harm football players' health by causing concussions and irreversible brain damage, have led parents and educators to engage in

- ○ are being shown to harm football players' health by causing concussions and irreversible brain damage, lead parents and educators to engage in

- ○ will have been shown to harm football players' health by causing concussions and irreversible brain damage, have led parents and educators to engage in

Step 1: Read the Original Sentence Carefully, Looking for Errors

The underlined portion of the sentence begins with a relatively complicated verb tense in "had been shown." For this past perfect verb tense to be correct, this action must have occurred before some other past action. The underlined portion contains two actions, one in the clause between commas ("had been shown") and the other in the main clause, which picks up again after the comma-enclosed text ("have led"). Since the tackles "have led" parents and educators to do something, the tackles must have been shown to have adverse effects at some point in the past, and logically these effects are still demonstrated (the brain damage will not have disappeared). Likewise, the parents and educators started having debates in the past and must still be debating the matter, since it is not resolved. Therefore, both actions take place in the same time frame, one that started in the past and is ongoing in the present, and "had been shown" is incorrect.

Step 2: Scan and Group the Answer Choices

Each choice starts with a different verb tense, so grouping choices by this verb is not possible. However, three choices, **(A)**, **(C)**, and **(E)**, use the present perfect "have led" after the comma. **(B)** uses "are leading," and **(D)** uses the simple present "lead."

Step 3: Eliminate Choices Until Only One Remains

As discussed in Step 1, both actions in this sentence started in the past and are still ongoing in the present. Therefore, the present perfect "have led" after the comma is correct; eliminate **(B)** and **(D)**. Eliminate **(A)** for the reason discussed in Step 1. Now compare **(C)** and **(E)**. **(E)** begins with the future tense "will have been shown," indicating that this action has not been completed yet. This is illogical, so **(C)**, with "have been shown" and "have led," is correct.

13. (C)

The government <u>has imposed sanctions and restricted foreign aid to a renegade</u> <u>nation last month after it violated</u> the terms of a worldwide arms control treaty.

- ○ has imposed sanctions and restricted foreign aid to a renegade nation last month after it violated
- ○ has imposed sanctions on and restricted foreign aid to a renegade nation last month after it violated
- ○ imposed sanctions on and restricted foreign aid to a renegade nation last month after that nation violated
- ○ imposed sanctions and restricted foreign aid to a renegade nation last month after violating
- ○ had imposed sanctions and restricted foreign aid to a renegade nation last month after it had violated

Step 1: Read the Original Sentence Carefully, Looking for Errors

This sentence contains three errors. First, the underlined pronoun "it" is ambiguous; grammatically, "it" could refer to the "government" or to the "renegade nation," though logically it should refer to the latter. Second, while the predicate verb "has imposed" agrees with its subject, "the government," the verb tense is incorrect. It makes no sense to say that "the government has imposed sanctions last month." To describe a single past event that occurred at a specific point in time, use the simple past tense: "The government imposed sanctions last month." Third, the phrase "imposed sanctions" must be followed by the preposition "on" instead of "to" as written. The correct answer must fix the ambiguous pronoun, the faulty verb tense, and the idiomatic phrase "imposed sanctions on" without introducing any new errors.

Step 2: Scan and Group the Answer Choices

(A), **(B)**, and **(E)** retain the pronoun ambiguity. **(C)** changes "it" to "that nation," while **(D)** removes the pronoun altogether. You find the same 3-2 split for the verb error: **(A)**, **(B)**, and **(E)** use "has imposed," while **(C)** and **(D)** use "imposed." There is also a 3-2 split following "imposed sanctions": **(B)** and **(C)** add the word "on," while **(A)**, **(D)**, and **(E)** do not.

Step 3: Eliminate Choices Until Only One Remains

Eliminate **(A)**, **(B)**, and **(E)** because all three commit the pronoun and verb tense errors noted in the original sentence. Of the remaining choices, **(D)** attempts to fix the ambiguous pronoun by simply leaving it out: "The government imposed sanctions...after violating..." This construction makes it sound as if the same government that imposed the sanctions violated the treaty, which doesn't make much logical sense. **(C)** fixes the pronoun ambiguity and also conveys the more logical meaning: "That nation" (i.e., the renegade nation) violated the treaty. Because **(C)** also fixes the verb tense error by changing "has imposed" to "imposed" and adds the preposition "on" after "imposed sanctions," it is the correct answer.

E X P L A N A T I O N S

14. (D)

Every one of the police reports <u>have been filed so that they can be located by their case number, the date they were created, or the victim's last name</u>.

- ○ have been filed so that they can be located by their case number, the date they were created, or the victim's last name

- ○ have been filed so that they can be located by their case numbers, the dates they were created, or by the victims' last names

- ○ has been filed so that they can be located by their case number, the date they were created, or the victim's last name

- ○ has been filed so that it can be located by its case number, the date it was created, or the victim's last name

- ○ has been filed so that it can be located by its case number, the date it was created, or by the victim's last name

Step 1: Read the Original Sentence Carefully, Looking for Errors

The subject of this sentence, "Every one," is singular. However, the verbs and pronouns in the underlined segment are all plural, so there are multiple errors: "Have" should be "has," "they" and "their" should be "it" and "its," and "were" should be "was." Note that the test maker is trying to trick you into thinking that the subject is "the police reports." Always remember to mentally bracket out prepositional phrases when searching for the subject of a sentence. The "police reports" are, in fact, the object of the preposition "of" and therefore cannot be the subject of the sentence.

Step 2: Scan and Group the Answer Choices

(A), **(B)**, and **(C)** keep the plural pronouns, while **(D)** and **(E)** change "they" and "their" to "it" and "its." There is a second split among the answer choices with regard to the predicate verb. **(A)** and **(B)** retain the plural form "have been," while **(C)**, **(D)**, and **(E)** change the predicate verb to the singular "has been."

Step 3: Eliminate Choices Until Only One Remains

You can throw out **(A)**, **(B)**, and **(C)** because all three use the incorrect plural pronouns. **(D)** and **(E)** both use the singular verb and singular pronouns, so look for some other difference between them. **(E)** introduces the word "by" into the last phrase: "or by the victim's last name." This addition creates a parallelism error. The original sentence contains a list of three different ways to locate a report, and the word "by" is used only once, before the first item in the list. Introducing "by" before the third term makes the second and third terms structurally different from each other so that the items in the list are no longer parallel. Because **(D)** is the only choice that fixes the errors in the original sentence without introducing any new mistakes, it is the correct answer.

15. (B)

<u>Although swimming can cause cramps in a swimmer's legs or feet, they</u> can usually be avoided if the swimmer avoids overexertion and performs stretching exercises before entering the pool.

- ○ Although swimming can cause cramps in a swimmer's legs or feet, they
- ○ Cramps in a swimmer's legs or feet caused by swimming
- ○ Swimming can cause cramps in a swimmer's legs or feet, which
- ○ The fact that swimming can cause cramps in a swimmer's legs or feet
- ○ Swimming can cause cramps in a swimmer's legs or feet, although they

Step 1: Read the Original Sentence Carefully, Looking for Errors

It's not enough to have a good sense of which noun an underlined pronoun refers to; the sentence has to be 100 percent clear about it. As you were reading, you might have instinctively assumed that "they" refers to "cramps," but this isn't good enough on the GMAT. Because "they" could also refer to "legs" or "feet," its use here is wrong.

Step 2: Scan and Group the Answer Choices

An initial scan doesn't yield much in the way of splits, but it's important to scan for the ways in which the answer choices will deal with the all too common "they" problem.

Step 3: Eliminate Choices Until Only One Remains

(A) is incorrect because the pronoun "they" here is ambiguous; "they" could refer to "cramps," "legs," or "feet." Likewise, **(E)** is wrong, as is **(C)**, although here the ambiguous pronoun is "which." What does "which" refer to in **(C)**: the legs or feet, the cramps, or the entire preceding clause? **(D)** is also wrong; a *fact* cannot be avoided. "The fact that" is another phrase that almost always signals a wrong answer choice on GMAT Sentence Correction questions. Finally, **(B)** is correct because it avoids pronoun reference problems and makes it clear that "cramps" can be avoided.

16. (D)

Film critics often cite the example of Nicolas Cage's winning the Academy Award for Best Actor as a reason that <u>an actor should not automatically be classified as elite if they win an Academy Award</u>.

- ○ an actor should not automatically be classified as elite if they win an Academy Award
- ○ an actor automatically classified as elite because they won an Academy Award should not always be classified as such
- ○ actors automatically classified as elite because they won an Academy Award should not always be classified as such
- ○ actors should not automatically be classified as elite if they win an Academy Award
- ○ actors should not be classified as automatically elite if they win an Academy Award

Step 1: Read the Original Sentence Carefully, Looking for Errors

Whenever a sentence contains an underlined pronoun, you should assess pronoun-antecedent agreement. This sentence contains the underlined pronoun "they," which is plural. Since the plural pronoun "they" refers to "an actor," which is a singular noun, the lack of agreement between the pronoun and its antecedent is an error in the sentence.

Step 2: Scan and Group the Answer Choices

All of the answer choices contain "they," so for the pronoun and antecedent to agree, the antecedent must be changed to something plural, such as "actors." **(A)** and **(B)** start with "an actor," while **(C)**, **(D)**, and **(E)** begin with "actors."

Step 3: Eliminate Choices Until Only One Remains

Eliminate **(A)** and **(B)** for the pronoun agreement error discussed above. Examining the remaining choices, note that **(C)** is wordy and subtly distorts the meaning of the original sentence; the original talks about how any actor should (not) be classified, while this choice limits the discussion to actors already classified as elite. **(E)** must be eliminated, because "automatically" should modify "should...be classified," not "elite." This leaves **(D)** as the correct answer; it fixes the pronoun agreement error and introduces no new errors.

17. **(E)**

According to a recently enacted law, any organization that engages in lobbying activities is required either to notify <u>their members about the percentage of dues that are used for lobbying activities or</u> pay a proxy tax.

- ○ their members about the percentage of dues that are used for lobbying activities or
- ○ their members about the percentage of dues they use for lobbying activities or to
- ○ their members about the percentage of dues that are used for lobbying activities or they should
- ○ its members about the percentage of dues that are used for lobbying activities or it should
- ○ its members about the percentage of dues that is used for lobbying activities or to

Step 1: Read the Original Sentence Carefully, Looking for Errors

This sentence contains several errors. For one thing, the plural pronoun "their" refers to the singular noun "organization." Pronouns must agree with their antecedents in number, so you need the singular pronoun "its." There is also a subject-verb agreement issue: "Percentage" is a collective noun referring to a sum of money being spent as a single unit, so it needs a singular verb. However, the verb phrase "are used" is plural. Finally, there is a parallelism error. The word "either" signals a list of two actions, "to notify" and "to pay." Both actions should be in parallel structure, but the sentence omits the second "to."

Step 2: Scan and Group the Answer Choices

Use the pronoun at the beginning of the underlined segment to split the choices because it's the easiest split to see. **(A)**, **(B)**, and **(C)** retain the plural pronoun "their." **(D)** and **(E)** use the singular pronoun "its."

Step 3: Eliminate Choices Until Only One Remains

(A), **(B)**, and **(C)** are out because they use the plural pronoun, which you know to be incorrect. You can also eliminate **(D)**, which does not correct the subject-verb agreement error. That leaves **(E)**, which corrects "are used" to "is used." Moreover, **(E)** fixes the parallelism error by inserting the word "to," so that you now have the correct construction "either to notify…or to pay." **(E)** is the correct answer.

18. **(D)**

The chief executive officer met with the board of directors to consider the possibility of a hostile takeover attempt by a competitor and <u>how they would have to respond to deal with them</u>.

- ○ how they would have to respond to deal with them
- ○ how to deal with them if action would become necessary
- ○ what action would be required for dealing with such an event
- ○ what action would be necessary to deal with such an event
- ○ the necessity of taking action in order to deal with it

Step 1: Read the Original Sentence Carefully, Looking for Errors

The sentence as written is wrong because "they" and "them" have no clear antecedent nouns. On the GMAT, any hint of pronoun ambiguity indicates an incorrect answer choice.

Step 2: Scan and Group the Answer Choices

Sniff out pronouns in the choices. **(A)** and **(B)** use "them," and **(E)** uses "it."

Step 3: Eliminate Choices Until Only One Remains

Because of their ambiguous use of "them," **(A)** and **(B)** are wrong. **(C)** contains the unidiomatic construction "required for dealing," and likewise **(E)** contains the unidiomatic construction "necessity of taking." Only **(D)** is idiomatically correct and avoids misused pronouns.

19. **(A)**

Arguing that the dominance of an economic theory has more to do with the persuasive skills of <u>its expositors than with its</u> accuracy in predicting economic events, Professor McCloskey examines the rhetorical practices of economists.

- ○ its expositors than with its
- ○ these expositors than its
- ○ its expositors compared to its
- ○ the theory's expositors than their
- ○ its expositors than with their

Step 1: Read the Original Sentence Carefully, Looking for Errors

There are no obvious problems with the original sentence. The underlined portion uses the pronoun "its" twice, though, so you should ensure that the pronouns agree in number with their antecedents and are not being used ambiguously.

Step 2: Scan and Group the Answer Choices

(A), **(B)**, and **(C)** use "its" exclusively, while **(D)** and **(E)** introduce "their."

Step 3: Eliminate Choices Until Only One Remains

The sentence is correct as written. Here the pronoun "its" clearly refers to "theory," so the use is correct. Eliminate **(D)** and **(E)**, which use "their." Also, **(A)** is the only choice that maintains correct parallel structure in the two-part construction "more to do with…than with…" Thus, **(A)** is the correct answer. Eliminate **(B)** and **(C)** because they violate the parallel structure.

20. **(E)**

In an effort to determine whether changes in diet and exercise can reverse coronary heart disease, <u>1,800 elderly heart patients will participate in a Medicare program costing $12,960,000 over the next three years to reduce lifestyle-related risk factors</u>.

- ○ 1,800 elderly heart patients will participate in a Medicare program costing $12,960,000 over the next three years to reduce lifestyle-related risk factors

- ○ $12,960,000 will be spent by Medicare over the next three years in a program to reduce lifestyle-related risk factors in 1,800 elderly patients

- ○ over the next three years $12,960,000 will be spent on 1,800 patients by Medicare on a program to reduce lifestyle-related risk factors

- ○ Medicare is to spend $12,960,000 over the next three years on a program for reducing lifestyle-related risk factors in 1,800 elderly heart patients

- ○ Medicare will spend $12,960,000 over the next three years on a program to reduce lifestyle-related risk factors in 1,800 elderly heart patients

Step 1: Read the Original Sentence Carefully, Looking for Errors

The intended meaning of this sentence is clear enough: Medicare is making an effort to determine whether lifestyle changes can reverse coronary heart disease. However, the modifying phrase at the beginning of the sentence that describes this effort is followed by the subject of the sentence, "1,800 elderly heart patients." Grammatically, a modifying phrase modifies whatever is nearest to it in the sentence. So, according to the grammar of this sentence as written, it is the heart patients who are trying to figure out whether lifestyle changes can reverse coronary heart disease—but that's not the intended meaning. The correct answer would have to either place "Medicare" next to the opening modifying phrase or use a different construction.

Step 2: Scan and Group the Answer Choices

(A), **(B)**, and **(C)** place something other than "Medicare" next to the opening modifying phrase. **(D)** and **(E)** start with "Medicare."

Step 3: Eliminate Choices Until Only One Remains

(A), **(B)**, and **(C)** can be eliminated because none of them fixes the misplaced modifier. The only difference between **(D)** and **(E)** is the verb phrase: "is to spend" versus "will spend." Because the program will occur over "the next three years," you need the future tense, and "will spend" is correct. That makes **(E)** the correct answer.

21. (C)

Children often pick up on gender norms very early in life, as many parents discover when <u>their toddlers recoil at toys that have only been designed to appeal to toddlers of the opposite sex</u>.

- ○ their toddlers recoil at toys that have only been designed to appeal to toddlers of the opposite sex
- ○ only their toddlers recoil at toys that have been designed to appeal to toddlers of the opposite sex
- ○ their toddlers recoil at toys that have been designed to appeal to toddlers of the opposite sex only
- ○ toys that have only been designed to appeal to toddlers of the opposite sex cause their toddlers to recoil
- ○ only toys that have been designed to appeal to toddlers of the opposite sex cause their toddlers to recoil

Step 1: Read the Original Sentence Carefully, Looking for Errors

As written, this sentence is illogical. No toy would be designed "only…to appeal to toddlers of the opposite sex." Toys are designed with lots of functions in mind—entertainment, safety, etc. The modifier "only" is in the wrong place. It should be modifying "toddlers of the opposite sex." The correct answer will place it properly.

Step 2: Scan and Group the Answer Choices

The choices place the word "only" in a variety of different places. Because this is the only error spotted and "only" should go toward the end of the sentence, expect that the correct answer will still start the same way as the underlined part of the original sentence. Split the choices along these lines. **(A)** and **(C)** retain "their toddlers" at the beginning of the underlined segment; choices **(B)**, **(D)**, and **(E)** do not.

Step 3: Eliminate Choices Until Only One Remains

You know that **(A)** is incorrect, and chances are that **(B)**, **(D)**, and **(E)** make erroneous changes, so start by checking **(C)**. Here, "only" falls at the very end of the sentence and correctly modifies "toddlers of the opposite sex." This is the correct answer. For the record: **(B)** uses "only" to modify "their toddlers," so the sentence now excludes any other toddlers. That's not the intended meaning of the original sentence, so **(B)** is incorrect. **(D)** rephrases the underlined segment, but the word "only" still modifies the verb "designed," so the original error is preserved. **(E)** uses "only" to modify "toys," so that the sentence now indicates that nothing besides toys can cause toddlers to recoil. This is again not the intended meaning of the original sentence, so it is also incorrect. **(C)** is the correct answer.

22. (C)

<u>Based on the candidates' performances in the televised debates</u>, many pundits predicted that the rival was likely to score an upset defeat over the incumbent senator.

○ Based on the candidates' performances in the televised debates

○ Basing it on the candidates' performances in the televised debates

○ Basing their assessments on the candidates' performances in the televised debates

○ With the candidates' performances in the televised debates used as a basis

○ By the assessments of the candidates' performances in the televised debates that they made

Step 1: Read the Original Sentence Carefully, Looking for Errors

When a modifying phrase at the beginning of the sentence is underlined, your job is to make sure that the subject of the phrase is what follows the comma. If you read this sentence aloud, you might not have noticed anything because this is a very common error in spoken English. But the subject following the comma is "pundits," and the modifying phrase "Based on the candidates' performances in the televised debates" refers not to the pundits but to their predictions. This is a big error.

Step 2: Scan and Group the Answer Choices

There aren't many obvious splits here, but the opening phrase followed by a comma tells you to eliminate choices based on how they handle the modification error.

Step 3: Eliminate Choices Until Only One Remains

(A) should be eliminated because of the modification error just mentioned. **(B)** is wrong because the pronoun "it" is misused here, as the reference is unclear and the number should be plural. **(D)** and **(E)** are awkward and unidiomatic. **(E)** is also wrong because it is not clear what "they" refers to. Only **(C)** is correct, because the subject of the phrase is "pundits," as it should be, and this choice also avoids pronoun reference problems.

23. (D)

Hoping to avert another situation in which the candidate who won the popular vote could lose the electoral vote, <u>it was proposed by Congress</u> that the Electoral College be abolished.

- ○ it was proposed by Congress
- ○ there was a proposal by Congress
- ○ a proposal was made by Congress
- ○ Congress proposed
- ○ Congress will have proposed

Step 1: Read the Original Sentence Carefully, Looking for Errors

See that opening phrase followed by a comma? Since that phrase is not underlined, you cannot change it. Instead, you need to make the rest of the sentence align with it. So ask yourself, "Who in the sentence was hoping to avert the situation?" The answer, Congress, should come right after that comma. Anything else is wrong.

Step 2: Scan and Group the Answer Choices

(A), **(B)**, and **(C)** all begin by talking about the proposal, whereas **(D)** and **(E)** begin by talking about Congress.

Step 3: Eliminate Choices Until Only One Remains

Since Congress hoped to avert the situation in the sentence, Congress needs to be placed at the beginning of the underlined portion. This eliminates **(A)**, **(B)**, and **(C)**. Between **(D)** and **(E)**, the difference lies in verb tense. **(E)**'s "will have proposed" doesn't make sense; you would need specific clues in the sentence that require the use of the future perfect tense, and no such clues exist. The simple past, "proposed," works perfectly well, making **(D)** the correct answer.

EXPLANATIONS

24. (C)

Cheered by better-than-expected opening week box office returns, <u>it was decided by the movie's producer to give bonuses to the entire cast</u>.

○ it was decided by the movie's producer to give bonuses to the entire cast

○ the entire cast was given bonuses by the movie's producer

○ the movie's producer decided to give the entire cast bonuses

○ the decision of the movie's producer was to give the entire cast bonuses

○ bonuses to the entire cast were given by the movie's producer

Step 1: Read the Original Sentence Carefully, Looking for Errors

When a sentence starts with a modifying phrase, as this one does, be on the alert for misplaced modifiers. The modifying phrase should be placed right next to whatever it logically modifies. In this case, the logic of the sentence dictates that it is the producer who felt "cheered" by the great box office returns. Therefore, "the movie's producer" should immediately follow the comma. **(A)** cannot be the correct answer.

Step 2: Scan and Group the Answer Choices

Only **(C)** places "the movie's producer" immediately after the comma that follows the modifying phrase. In **(B)**, "the entire cast" follows the comma, while **(D)** and **(E)** start out with "the decision" and "bonuses," respectively.

Step 3: Eliminate Choices Until Only One Remains

You cannot change anything in the part of the sentence that is not underlined, so the opening phrase has to stay where it is. Because you can only rearrange the underlined segment, the only way to fix the modification error is to place "the movie's producer" right at the beginning of the answer choice. **(C)** is therefore the correct answer. For the record: **(D)** and **(E)** place inanimate things after the comma, which makes no logical sense. A "decision" cannot feel "cheered," nor can "bonuses." As for **(B)**, while it may be true that the "entire cast" felt happy about the box office returns, the logical cause-and-effect relationship indicated by the sentence needs to be reflected in its grammar. The producer feels "cheered" and therefore awards the cast bonuses. No matter how the cast feels about the box office returns, the sentence's initial phrase logically refers to "the movie's producer." **(C)** is correct.

25. (B)

The argument over who invented calculus by math historians typically features extensive discussion of the merits of Isaac Newton's and Gottfried Leibniz's mathematical achievements.

- ○ The argument over who invented calculus by math historians
- ○ Math historians argue over who invented calculus; this argument
- ○ Math historians' arguments over the invention of calculus
- ○ Who invented calculus by math historians is an argument that
- ○ Math historians argue over who invented calculus, yet this argument

Step 1: Read the Original Sentence Carefully, Looking for Errors

The sentence is incorrect as written. The phrase "who invented calculus by math historians" suggests that historians invented calculus when, in fact, they merely debate aspects of its creation.

Step 2: Scan and Group the Answer Choices

(A) and **(D)** retain the phrase "who invented calculus by math historians." **(B)** and **(E)** begin the sentence with "Math historians." **(C)** begins with "Math historians' arguments."

Step 3: Eliminate Choices Until Only One Remains

As well as **(A)**, the original sentence, **(D)** should be eliminated because it contains the incorrect phrase "who invented calculus by math historians." **(C)** can be eliminated because it introduces a subject-verb agreement error; "arguments" is a plural subject and should be matched with the verb "feature," not "features." **(E)** fixes the modifier error, but it introduces a new error by using the contrast word "yet" as a connector when the sentence does not contrast two ideas. **(B)** is the correct answer.

26. (E)

Using a seismic survey, hydrocarbons can be located even though they are buried far beneath Earth's surface.

- ○ Using a seismic survey, hydrocarbons can be located even though they are buried far beneath Earth's surface.
- ○ Hydrocarbons can be located even though they are buried far beneath Earth's surface, using a seismic survey.
- ○ Locating hydrocarbons that are buried far beneath Earth's surface, a geophysicist can use a seismic survey.
- ○ Buried far beneath Earth's surface, hydrocarbons can be detected using a seismic survey.
- ○ Using a seismic survey, a geophysicist can locate hydrocarbons even though they are buried far beneath Earth's surface.

Step 1: Read the Original Sentence Carefully, Looking for Errors

The original sentence is wrong because it begins with the modifying phrase "using a seismic survey," so what follows the phrase should be its subject, which is definitely not "hydrocarbons" (it wouldn't make any sense for hydrocarbons to use a seismic survey).

Step 2: Scan and Group the Answer Choices

These choices don't scan easily, but since you are dealing with an error with the modifying phrase "using a seismic survey," you can group choices based on what subject that phrase modifies. **(C)** and **(E)** both have the subject "a geophysicist," which makes sense. **(B)** and **(D)** are both vague at best about the subject, but in any case, it's not someone who'd use a seismic survey.

Step 3: Eliminate Choices Until Only One Remains

The modification error disqualifies **(A)**. **(B)** likewise contains the same misplaced modifying phrase, although here it can be found at the end of the sentence rather than the beginning. **(C)** sounds awkward and changes the meaning of the sentence, because the seismic survey is precisely what the geophysicist uses to locate the hydrocarbons in the first place. **(D)** uses a passive verb and never explains who is using the seismic survey. Only **(E)** correctly places the phrase "Using a seismic survey" next to the subject of the phrase, "a geophysicist." Thus, **(E)** is the correct answer.

27. (C)

The creation of an independent treasury, establishing lower tariffs, and purchasing the Oregon Territory, all credited to the presidency of James Knox Polk, are among the significant accomplishments that persuade historians to rank this former governor of Tennessee as an above-average president.

○ The creation of an independent treasury, establishing lower tariffs, and purchasing

○ The creation of an independent treasury, establishing lower tariffs, as well as purchasing

○ The creation of an independent treasury, the establishment of lower tariffs, and the purchase of

○ Creating an independent treasury, the establishment of lower tariffs, and purchasing

○ Creating an independent treasury, the establishing of lower tariffs, and the purchasing of

Step 1: Read the Original Sentence Carefully, Looking for Errors

The underlined segment of this sentence contains a list of three accomplishments of Polk's presidency. Items in a list must have parallel form, but these do not: the first term in the list is a noun, "creation," but the second and third terms are *-ing* verb forms. The correct answer will either change "The creation of" to "Creating," or it will change "establishing" and "purchasing" to "the establishment of" and "the purchase of," respectively.

Step 2: Scan and Group the Answer Choices

(A), **(B)**, and **(C)** keep the noun "creation" at the beginning of the sentence, while **(D)** and **(E)** change "creation" to "creating."

Step 3: Eliminate Choices Until Only One Remains

(A) is definitely incorrect due to the parallelism issue. You'll need to check each of the other choices for proper parallel structure. **(B)** and **(C)** begin with the word "creation," so the remaining two items on the list should both be nouns. **(B)** still has the two gerund forms, "establishing" and "purchasing," so it does not have the correct parallel structure and cannot be correct. **(C)**, though, gets it right: the three items here are "creation," "establishment," and "purchase." This is the correct answer. A quick look at **(D)** and **(E)** reveals that neither has parallel structure. In **(D)**, the middle term is different from the first and third. **(E)** uses three gerund forms, but there is still a parallelism error. The second and third terms are in the same form, "the establishing of" and "the purchasing of," but the first term lacks the words "the" and "of." **(C)** is correct.

28. (B)

The rapid-rail lines that were recently introduced in southern California have had positive effects: <u>not only have they lowered pollution levels, they have helped in decongesting</u> the region's freeway system, which had been operating far above its capacity.

- ○ not only have they lowered pollution levels, they have helped in decongesting
- ○ the lines have not only lowered pollution levels, but also helped to decongest
- ○ not only have pollution levels been lowered, but they have helped to decongest
- ○ lines have lowered pollution levels, but also helped in decongesting
- ○ not only have they lowered pollution levels, but also have they helped decongest

Step 1: Read the Original Sentence Carefully, Looking for Errors

The underlined part of this sentence contains the phrase "not only." That means that the words "but also" should appear elsewhere in the sentence, but those words are absent. Additionally, the sentence includes the phrase "helped in decongesting" where "helped to decongest" would be more idiomatic. Therefore, eliminate **(A)**. The correct answer will fix these problems without introducing any new errors.

Step 2: Scan and Group the Answer Choices

(B), **(D)**, and **(E)** add the "but also" construction; **(C)** does not, though it adds the word "but."

Step 3: Eliminate Choices Until Only One Remains

(C) adds "but," but it leaves out "also." **(E)** has both halves of the proper construction, but the verb phrase at the end, "have they helped decongest," sounds like a question and is awkward at best. **(D)** adds "but also" but removes the "not only," so it only has half the construction. Moreover, **(D)** omits the article "the" at the beginning, such that the second half of the sentence now seems to refer to "lines" generally, rather than to the new Californian rapid rail lines specifically. That leaves **(B)**, which provides both parts of the "not only…but also" construction. Additionally, **(B)** uses the idiomatically correct form "helped to decongest." **(B)** is the correct answer.

29. (A)

By conducting a national study of opioid abuse on college campuses, researchers hope to determine where students purchase opioids, how frequently students abuse opioids on average, and <u>which college stressors most commonly contribute to opioid abuse among students</u>.

○ which college stressors most commonly contribute to opioid abuse among students

○ which are the college stressors common to students who are likely to be turning to opioid abuse

○ the common stressors of college that are likely to contribute to opioid abuse among students

○ the stressors of college common among students who turn to opioid abuse

○ the types of college stressors that are common to students who are likely to turn to opioid abuse

Step 1: Read the Original Sentence Carefully, Looking for Errors

Because this sentence has a list in the underlined portion, determine whether that list has a parallel structure. The list is "where students purchase…how frequently students…and which college stressors…" As written, the list has parallel structure, with each item beginning with a word—"where," "how," and "which"—that could begin a question (an interrogative adverb, if you're curious) followed by a noun—"students," "students," and "college stressors," respectively. Other elements worth checking are the modifying words "most commonly" before the verb "contribute" and the idiomatic usage of "contribute to." All are correct.

Step 2: Scan and Group the Answer Choices

(A) and **(B)** begin with "which," which is parallel to "where" and "how." The remaining choices begin with elements that break the parallel structure.

Step 3: Eliminate Choices Until Only One Remains

(C), **(D)**, and **(E)** are incorrect because they begin with a word that breaks the parallel structure of the list. **(B)** is wrong because it is unnecessarily wordy. The sentence here is correct as written, so **(A)** is the answer.

30. (E)

Hearing Kenneth Branagh deliver the "St. Crispin's Day" speech in *Henry V* is to be mesmerized by a great performer, with seemingly boundless emotional energy.

O   Hearing Kenneth Branagh deliver the "St. Crispin's Day" speech in *Henry V* is to be mesmerized by a great performer, with seemingly

O   Hearing Kenneth Branagh deliver the "St. Crispin's Day" speech in *Henry V* is to be mesmerized by a great performer, one with seeming

O   Hearing Kenneth Branagh deliver the "St. Crispin's Day" speech in *Henry V* is being mesmerized by a great performer, one with seeming

O   To hear Kenneth Branagh deliver the "St. Crispin's Day" speech in *Henry V* is being mesmerized by a great performer, with seemingly

O   To hear Kenneth Branagh deliver the "St. Crispin's Day" speech in *Henry V* is to be mesmerized by a great performer, one with seemingly

Step 1: Read the Original Sentence Carefully, Looking for Errors

Elements in a comparison or analogy, like items in a list, must exhibit parallel structure. Here, the original sentence is incorrect because the analogy states that "Hearing...is to be mesmerized..." The two ideas compared should both be either gerunds ending in *–ing* or infinitives. Because the GMAT is not particularly fond of gerunds, expect the right answer to change "hearing" to "to hear."

Step 2: Scan and Group the Answer Choices

The first three answer choices all begin with "hearing," while the last two begin with "to hear."

Step 3: Eliminate Choices Until Only One Remains

Because the elements in the comparison in the original sentence are not parallel, eliminate **(A)**. **(B)** should be eliminated because it contains the same parallel structure error. **(D)** also contains a parallel structure error: "To hear...is being mesmerized . . ." **(C)** may seem a bit more parallel, but it still sounds awkward: "Hearing is being mesmerized..." (You should usually avoid answer choices that contain "being" on GMAT Sentence Corrections.) Moreover, **(C)** contains an adverb/adjective error: the adjective form "seeming" is incorrect because it modifies the adjective "boundless," and thus the correct form is the adverb "seemingly." Finally, **(E)** is correct because it exhibits parallel structure and uses the correct adverbial form, "seemingly."

31. (B)

By the time they completed their journey, the young explorers had overcome their fears, sharpened their survival <u>skills, and had developed a healthy respect</u> for nature's potential destructiveness.

- ○ skills, and had developed a healthy respect
- ○ skills, and developed a healthy respect
- ○ skills and a healthy respect developed
- ○ skills, developing a healthy respect
- ○ skills, all the while developing a healthy respect

Step 1: Read the Original Sentence Carefully, Looking for Errors

This sentence contains an underlined verb, which means that you must check for subject-verb agreement and correct tense. The verb phrase "had developed" agrees with its subject, "the young explorers." Because the young explorers' actions precede the completion of their journey, the use of the past perfect tense is correct. However, the phrase "had developed a healthy respect" is part of a list of three things the young explorers did during their journey, so you must also check for parallel structure. Here there is an error, as the second and third items on the list do not have the same structure. The second verb on the list, "sharpened," does not repeat the helping verb, "had," that is used at the beginning of the list to indicate the past perfect tense. But the third verb, "had developed," does repeat the word "had." You can rule out **(A)**.

Step 2: Scan and Group the Answer Choices

Of the remaining choices, **(B)** simply removes "had" but leaves the rest of the underlined segment alone, while **(D)** and **(E)** change the verb to "developing." Like **(B)**, **(C)** uses "developed," but changes the word order.

Step 3: Eliminate Choices Until Only One Remains

Because you cannot change anything in the sentence except the underlined part, you cannot correct the parallelism error by changing "sharpened" to "had sharpened." Your only recourse is to change "had developed" to "developed." **(B)** does just that without changing anything else, and this will likely turn out to be the correct answer. A quick look at **(C)** reveals that in changing the word order, it destroys the parallelism of the list of three actions completely. As for **(D)** and **(E)**, changing "developed" to "developing" changes the tense and again destroys the list's parallel structure. **(B)** remains the correct answer.

32. (A)

Doctors both espouse the benefits of the influenza vaccination and advocate its administration to children starting at age six months.

- ○ Doctors both espouse the benefits of the influenza vaccination and advocate its administration
- ○ Doctors both espouse the benefits of the influenza vaccination and are advocating its administration
- ○ Doctors, espousing the benefits of the influenza vaccination, advocate their administration
- ○ Both espousing the benefits of the influenza vaccination, the doctors advocate its administration
- ○ Espousing the benefits of the influenza vaccination, its administration is advocated by doctors

Step 1: Read the Original Sentence Carefully, Looking for Errors

The leading words of this sentence, "Doctors both espouse," set up a *both...and* construction. Look for the second part of this construction and determine whether it is parallel. As written, "Doctors both espouse...and advocate" maintains parallel structure. It's also worth noting the pronoun here: the singular "its" refers to the singular "vaccination" and is correct.

Step 2: Scan and Group the Answer Choices

(A) and **(B)** start with "Doctors both espouse." **(C)** begins with "Doctors" but places the "espousing" in a modifying phrase, followed by a single verb. **(D)** and **(E)** begin with a modifying phrase.

Step 3: Eliminate Choices Until Only One Remains

Eliminate **(B)** because "espouse" and "are advocating" are not in parallel form. **(C)** could be an acceptable rearrangement of the grammatical elements, but it replaces "its" with the plural "their." This would refer to the plural "benefits," but it is the vaccine, not the benefits the vaccine confers, that doctors want to administer. By starting the modifying phrase with "Both" and not pairing this word with "and," **(D)** makes a statement about just two doctors, but the original sentence is talking about doctors in general. **(E)** commits a modification error, saying that the administration of the vaccine espouses the vaccine's benefits. Thus, **(A)** is the correct answer.

33. (C)

South Pacific Vacations has a package tour to Sydney, Australia, for $999 per person, including airfare from Los Angeles, <u>spending five nights at the Mega Hotel, and to take a harbor cruise, and round-trip airfare from New York is</u> an additional $400.

- ○ spending five nights at the Mega Hotel, and to take a harbor cruise, and round-trip airfare from New York is

- ○ spending five nights at the Mega Hotel, and taking a harbor cruise; and in addition round-trip airfare from New York is

- ○ five nights at the Mega Hotel, and a harbor cruise; round-trip airfare from New York is

- ○ with five nights at the Mega Hotel, and a harbor cruise, with round-trip airfare from New York being

- ○ to spend five nights at the Mega Hotel, and to take a harbor cruise; round-trip airfare from New York is

Step 1: Read the Original Sentence Carefully, Looking for Errors

Note that the sentence makes a list of items included in the package tour, so that list should be in parallel form. But each of the three items is in a different form: "Airfare," "spending five nights," and "to take a harbor cruise" are about as far from parallel as you can get. Expect the right answer to rectify this by making the other items parallel to "airfare," since that's the one item you can't change.

Step 2: Scan and Group the Answer Choices

(A) and **(B)** don't change the form of the second item in the list ("spending five nights"), while **(C)**, **(D)**, and **(E)** change it in various ways.

Step 3: Eliminate Choices Until Only One Remains

Since the noun "airfare," the first item in the list, is not underlined, the other items in the list must be changed to agree with this form. The only choice that turns the second item, "spending five nights," into a simple noun is **(C)**. Each of the other choices fails to exhibit truly parallel structure and should be eliminated on that basis. As a side note, **(C)** also changes the conjunction "and" before "round-trip airfare" to a semicolon, which is preferable because this part of the sentence starts a new thought.

34. (D)

Recent surveys indicate that, contrary to popular belief, total abstinence from alcohol does not correlate <u>as strongly with good health as with moderate drinking</u>.

○   as strongly with good health as with moderate drinking

○   strongly with good health, like moderate drinking does

○   as strongly with good health as does moderately drinking

○   as strongly with good health as does moderate drinking

○   as strongly with good health as moderate drinking

Step 1: Read the Original Sentence Carefully, Looking for Errors

This sentence contains an illogical comparison. The sentence is trying to say that abstinence does not correlate as strongly with good health as moderate drinking does. In other words, it is trying to compare abstinence to moderate drinking in terms of health impact. However, the word "with" before "moderate drinking" creates the rather bizarre comparison between good health and moderate drinking; what the sentence actually says is that abstinence correlates better with moderate drinking than it does with good health, which makes no logical sense. Rule out **(A)** and proceed to split the remaining choices.

Step 2: Scan and Group the Answer Choices

(C), **(D)**, and **(E)** retain the comparison, "as strongly," while **(B)** uses the comparison word "like" instead of "as."

Step 3: Eliminate Choices Until Only One Remains

Eliminate **(B)** because it uses the wrong word, "like," to make a comparison between clauses (subject + verb), whereas "like" should be used only to compare nouns. **(B)** also alters the meaning of the sentence: rather than comparing how strongly total abstinence and moderate drinking correlate with good health, **(B)** states that only one of the two behaviors correlates strongly with good health. **(C)** corrects the comparison, but "drinking" is a gerund—a verb being used as a noun—and should therefore be modified by an adjective, not the adverb "moderately." While **(E)** leaves out the word "with," it still commits the same illogical comparison as does the original sentence. **(D)**, like **(C)**, fixes the comparison, this time without introducing any new mistakes. **(D)** is the correct answer.

35. (E)

Unlike <u>its fellow Baltic nations, Latvia and Lithuania, the economy of Estonia grew at an astonishing rate in the late 1990s, and at the end of the decade it was placed</u> on the fast track to join the European Union.

○ its fellow Baltic nations, Latvia and Lithuania, the economy of Estonia grew at an astonishing rate in the late 1990s, and at the end of the decade it was placed

○ its fellow Baltic nations, Latvia and Lithuania, Estonia grew at an astonishing rate economically in the late 1990s, and at the end of the decade earned itself a place

○ its fellow Baltic nations, Latvia and Lithuania, Estonia's economy grew at an astonishing rate in the late 1990s, and at the end of the decade they were placed

○ Latvia and Lithuania, its fellow Baltic nations, the economy of Estonia grew at an astonishing rate in the late 1990s, and at the end of the decade it was placed

○ its fellow Baltic nations, Latvia and Lithuania, Estonia experienced economic growth at an astonishing rate in the late 1990s, and at the end of the decade it earned a place

Step 1: Read the Original Sentence Carefully, Looking for Errors

"Unlike" signals that this sentence will contain a comparison, so you'll need to check whether that comparison is logical. In this sentence, it is not: Latvia and Lithuania are being compared to Estonia's economy. Countries can only be compared to other countries, not to economies. The correct answer will fix this illogical comparison.

Step 2: Scan and Group the Answer Choices

(A) and **(D)** compare Latvia and Lithuania to "the economy of Estonia." **(C)** compares Latvia and Lithuania to "Estonia's economy." **(B)** and **(E)** compare Latvia and Lithuania to "Estonia."

Step 3: Eliminate Choices Until Only One Remains

(A), **(C)**, and **(D)** all commit the error of comparing a country to a country's economy, so all are incorrect. **(B)** correctly compares Latvia and Lithuania to Estonia, but it unnecessarily employs a reflexive pronoun, "itself," and its use of the word "economically" sounds rather awkward. **(E)** also correctly compares Latvia and Lithuania to Estonia, this time without resorting to unnecessary or awkward constructions. **(E)** is the correct answer.

EXPLANATIONS

36. **(A)**

<u>No less significant than</u> international pressures are the constraints that domestic culture and ideology impose on decision making by national political figures.

- ○ No less significant than
- ○ The things that are just as significant as
- ○ Just like the significant
- ○ Not lesser than the significance of
- ○ What are as significant as

Step 1: Read the Original Sentence Carefully, Looking for Errors

Because a comparison is made, check whether the comparison is valid. The original sentence contains a slightly unusual construction, but it is correct.

Step 2: Scan and Group the Answer Choices

There are no splits here, but be on the lookout for answer choices that alter the comparison in any way.

Step 3: Eliminate Choices Until Only One Remains

The original sentence appears to make a valid comparison between "international pressures" and "constraints," so **(A)** is correct. Eliminate **(B)** and **(E)** for being unnecessarily wordy. Eliminate **(C)** because it changes the meaning of the sentence slightly by leaving out the idea that the constraints are equally significant. Finally, eliminate **(D)** because it compares "significance" with "constraints."

37. (C)

Golden and Labrador retrievers have enjoyed wide popularity as guide dogs because their dispositions are more suited to companion work <u>than</u> most other breeds.

- ○ than
- ○ than is true of
- ○ than are those of
- ○ in comparison to
- ○ as compared to

Step 1: Read the Original Sentence Carefully, Looking for Errors

Even though your ear may not catch the error in this sentence the first time you read it, the comparison in the sentence needs to compare two logically comparable things in order to be correct. Here, "dispositions" are being compared to "breeds," which is an illogical comparison.

Step 2: Scan and Group the Answer Choices

(A), **(B)**, and **(C)** begin with "than," while **(D)** and **(E)** use lengthier constructions. Note that the only way one of these can be correct is if one of them corrects the error, and none of the shorter answer choices does.

Step 3: Eliminate Choices Until Only One Remains

Because the sentence needs to compare the dispositions of golden and Labrador retrievers with the dispositions of other breeds, you can eliminate **(A)**, **(B)**, **(D)**, and **(E)** as none of them makes the proper comparison. Only the correct answer, **(C)**, offers a logical comparison.

EXPLANATIONS

38. **(D)**

Unlike doctors of allopathic medicine, who focus on the diagnosis and treatment of human diseases, <u>the focus of doctors of osteopathic medicine is on</u> alternative therapies, holistic medicine, and disease prevention.

- ○ the focus of doctors of osteopathic medicine is on
- ○ the things that doctors of osteopathic medicine focus on are
- ○ doctors of osteopathic medicine differ a great deal because of their focus on
- ○ doctors of osteopathic medicine focus on
- ○ the focus of doctors of osteopathic medicine consists of

Step 1: Read the Original Sentence Carefully, Looking for Errors

The word "Unlike" at the beginning of the sentence indicates that a comparison is involved in this sentence. The comparison should make logical sense and be in parallel form. In this sentence, it would be logical to compare doctors of allopathic medicine to doctors of osteopathic medicine; however, as written, the sentence seems to be comparing *doctors* of allopathic medicine to the *focus* of doctors of osteopathic medicine.

Step 2: Scan and Group the Answer Choices

(E), as well as **(A)**, begins with "the focus." **(B)** compares "doctors of allopathic medicine" to "the things," while **(C)** and **(D)** compare "doctors of allopathic medicine" to "doctors of osteopathic medicine."

Step 3: Eliminate Choices Until Only One Remains

(A) has already been deemed incorrect in Step 1, and **(E)** must be eliminated because it commits the same illogical comparison as **(A)**. **(B)** illogically compares "doctors of allopathic medicine" to "the things that doctors...focus on." **(C)** and **(D)** both make a logical comparison between "doctors of allopathic medicine" and "doctors of osteopathic medicine," but **(C)** makes the comparison about the notion that osteopaths "differ a great deal." This would make sense if allopaths differed only a little from [something] and the author's point was that osteopaths are unlike allopaths because they differ a great deal from [something]. However, the point is they differ *from each other* in terms of their focus. **(D)** fixes the error in the original sentence in a clear and concise fashion and is correct.

39. (C)

The legal considerations that have forced some universities to revise their affirmative action admissions programs are similar to <u>the revisions that certain large businesses have recently made to their affirmative action hiring practices</u>.

○ the revisions that certain large businesses have recently made to their affirmative action hiring practices

○ the affirmative action hiring practices that certain large businesses recently have revised

○ those that have recently forced certain large businesses to revise their affirmative action hiring practices

○ those recent revisions that have been made by certain large businesses to their affirmative action hiring practices

○ what certain large businesses have done to their affirmative action hiring practices in the recent past

Step 1: Read the Original Sentence Carefully, Looking for Errors

"Are similar to" in the original sentence indicates a comparison, so you have to make sure that similar elements are being compared. Whenever you recognize a comparison, cut through the filler until you've assessed whether the elements being compared are logically and grammatically similar. This sentence begins with "legal considerations…are similar to…" so what follows should also be "legal considerations."

Step 2: Scan and Group the Answer Choices

(A) begins with "revisions." **(B)** begins with "…hiring practices." **(C)** and **(D)** begin with "those," a word that could refer to "legal considerations." **(E)** begins with "what certain large businesses have done."

Step 3: Eliminate Choices Until Only One Remains

"Revisions" and "practices" aren't comparable to "legal considerations," so eliminate **(A)** and **(B)**. **(D)** begins with "those," but if you read further, you'll notice that **(D)** uses "those recent revisions," which are not comparable to "legal considerations," so eliminate **(D)**. Finally, **(E)** is unclear and doesn't provide a specific noun to compare to "legal considerations." Only **(C)** makes logical sense and corrects the comparison error.

40. **(E)**

During the Civil War, nearly three times as many Americans lost their lives from infections that could have been prevented with antiseptic techniques <u>than</u> were killed on the battlefield.

- ○ than
- ○ than those who
- ○ than the number who
- ○ as the number who
- ○ as

Step 1: Read the Original Sentence Carefully, Looking for Errors

The underlined portion here is only one word: "than." Note that in the beginning of the sentence, the phrase "nearly three times as many" indicates a comparison. Comparisons require parallel construction. If you remove the intervening words "Americans...antiseptic techniques," the sentence would read, "nearly three times as many than." That's an incorrect construction.

Step 2: Scan and Group the Answer Choices

One choice here is between "than" in **(A)**, **(B)**, and **(C)** and "as" in **(D)** and **(E)**, so you would have to decide which one is correct even if you didn't spot the error while completing Step 1 of the Kaplan Method.

Step 3: Eliminate Choices Until Only One Remains

The correct word is "as," to complete the construction "as many...as..." Thus, **(A)**, **(B)**, and **(C)** are all out. But the comparison also requires parallel structure to "Americans lost their lives..." "The number" is not parallel to "Americans." So **(D)** needs to be eliminated in favor of **(E)**. **(E)** is the correct answer.

41. (E)

<u>When a product costs more, be it</u> a bottle of wine or a handbag, the more likely it is to be esteemed by consumers.

- ○ When a product costs more, be it
- ○ When a product costs more, whether it is
- ○ As a product becomes more and more costly, like
- ○ The more a product costs, like
- ○ The more a product costs, whether it is

Step 1: Read the Original Sentence Carefully, Looking for Errors

The underlined segment of this sentence gives you the first half of a comparison: "A product costs more" than something. Unfortunately, the sentence fails to state what the product is being compared to. It costs more than…what? Half a comparison is definitely an error that the correct answer will have to fix. You get a clue as to the proper construction you need from the second half of the sentence. The construction "the more likely" is part of a two-part construction, similar to "not only…but also." The correct construction is "the more…the more." This sentence should read, "The more a product costs…the more likely it is to be esteemed by consumers."

Step 2: Scan and Group the Answer Choices

(A) and **(B)** retain the partial comparison. **(C)** gets rid of the comparison with the phrase, "more and more costly." **(D)** and **(E)** use the construction you're looking for: "The more a product costs…"

Step 3: Eliminate Choices Until Only One Remains

(A) and **(B)** are incorrect because both contain the partial comparison that was flagged as an error. Eliminate **(C)** because while it attempts a statement of proportionality, it does not use the correct grammatical construction; the sentence needs to start with the phrase "The more." Both remaining choices use "The more," so one of them will be the correct answer. **(D)** uses "like" in place of the original "be it." The original meaning of the sentence is that it doesn't matter whether the product in question is a bottle of wine or a handbag (or something else). The use of the word "like" in **(D)** changes the meaning of the sentence. On the GMAT, "like" is used to mean "similar to," so this answer choice causes the sentence to refer only to items that are similar to wine and handbags. An answer choice that changes the meaning of the sentence cannot be correct, so the answer must be **(E)**. Indeed, **(E)** substitutes "whether it is" for "be it" so that the idea that the identity of the product makes no difference is preserved. **(E)** is the correct answer.

42. (E)

Mary Shelley is widely credited <u>for the invention of a new literary genre; many scholars consider her first and only novel, *Frankenstein*, to be</u> the first science fiction story.

○ for the invention of a new literary genre; many scholars consider her first and only novel, *Frankenstein*, to be

○ for inventing a new literary genre; many scholars consider her first and only novel, *Frankenstein*, as being

○ to have invented a new literary genre; many scholars regard her first and only novel, *Frankenstein*, to be

○ with the invention of a new literary genre; many scholars regard her first and only novel, *Frankenstein*, to be

○ with the invention of a new literary genre; many scholars consider her first and only novel, *Frankenstein*,

Step 1: Read the Original Sentence Carefully, Looking for Errors

The original sentence contains an idiom error—two, in fact. The sentence says Shelley is "credited for" inventing a genre and that her book is "consider[ed]...to be" the first science fiction book.

Step 2: Scan and Group the Answer Choices

The choices have a 2-2-1 split: **(A)** and **(B)** begin with "for," **(C)** begins with "to have," and **(D)** and **(E)** begin with "with."

Step 3: Eliminate Choices Until Only One Remains

The correct idiomatic expression is "*credited* with," so **(A)**, **(B)**, and **(C)** are all wrong. Also, you should note that, although many grammarians have no problem using "consider" with "to be," on the GMAT the correct answer choice will always use "consider" without the "to be." **(D)** is wrong because the correct idiomatic expression is "regard *as*," not "regard *to be*." Only **(E)** is idiomatically correct.

43. (A)

<u>The percentage of people aged 25–44 living alone increased abruptly between 1990 and 1995 and</u> continued to rise more slowly over the next five years.

- ○ The percentage of people aged 25–44 living alone increased abruptly between 1990 and 1995 and
- ○ There was an abruptly increased percentage of people aged 25–44 who lived alone between 1990 and 1995, and they
- ○ The percentage of people aged 25–44 who lived alone increased abruptly between 1990 and 1995 and has
- ○ There has been an abrupt increase in the percentage of people aged 25–44 living alone between 1990 and 1995, and it
- ○ Between 1990 and 1995, there was an abrupt increase in the percentage of people aged 25–44 who lived alone, which

Step 1: Read the Original Sentence Carefully, Looking for Errors

The original sentence sounds correct and exhibits parallel structure: "increased abruptly...and continued to rise more slowly..." But check out the other choices to see whether you may have missed something.

Step 2: Scan and Group the Answer Choices

Note that **(B)**, **(D)**, and **(E)** contain "there was" or "there has been." This type of construction is rarely correct on the GMAT. Unless the other choices commit grievous errors, be prepared to eliminate these.

Step 3: Eliminate Choices Until Only One Remains

You can eliminate **(B)**, **(D)**, and **(E)** because "there" constructions ("there was," "there has been," etc.) should generally be avoided; these constructions are wordy and often turn verbs into passive voice. **(C)** is wrong here because the present perfect tense, "has continued," indicates that the action began in the past but continues into the present. Because the sentence is discussing what happened between 1995 and 2000, the simple past tense is correct. Therefore, **(A)** is in fact correct.

44. **(A)**

The macabre nature of *Macbeth*, together with the widespread belief that real-life tragedies have accompanied many productions, <u>has made the name of the play so dreaded that not even the least superstitious members of most casts dare</u> utter it.

○ has made the name of the play so dreaded that not even the least superstitious members of most casts dare

○ have made the name of the play so dreaded, even the least superstitious members of most casts will not dare to

○ have made the play's name sufficiently dreaded, so that even the less superstitious members of most casts will not dare to

○ have made the name of the play sufficiently dreaded, so that not even the least superstitious members of most casts dare

○ has made the name of the play is dreaded, so that even the least superstitious members of most casts dare not

Step 1: Read the Original Sentence Carefully, Looking for Errors

Learn to ignore long phrases between commas when you first read the sentence. If you do that here, you'll see that the subject of the sentence, "nature," is singular, so the verb should be singular too, and "has made" fits that bill.

Step 2: Scan and Group the Answer Choices

One split here is between "has" in **(A)** and **(E)** and "have" in **(B)**, **(C)**, and **(D)**. Use that split to begin eliminating answer choices.

Step 3: Eliminate Choices Until Only One Remains

Because "has made" is the correct verb for a singular subject, eliminate **(B)**, **(C)**, and **(D)**. Eliminate **(E)** because it contains an extra verb, "is," that makes the sentence unclear. **(A)** is the only choice left, which means the sentence must be correct as written. Note that **(A)** also contains the correct construction "so dreaded...that."

45. (C)

The university's board of trustees, <u>being worried over declining student enrollments and their failing</u> to secure additional funding from the state, has formed a committee to determine what cuts need to be made to staff and programs.

- ○ being worried over declining student enrollments and their failing
- ○ worrying over declining student enrollments and also the failure
- ○ worried about declining student enrollments and the failure
- ○ in that they are worried about the decline in student enrollments and the failure
- ○ because of its worry concerning the decline of student enrollments and, as well as concerning the failure

Step 1: Read the Original Sentence Carefully, Looking for Errors

The sentence as written is wrong because the underlined portion begins with the suspicious and unnecessary "being," which is rarely correct on the GMAT. Another thing to notice is that the underlined portion contains a two-part list, so you should check for parallel structure. As written, the board is worried over (1) "declining student enrollments" and (2) "their failing to secure..." This is not parallel. Finally, notice the original sentence's improper use of the pronoun "their." The antecedent is "board," and the members of the board are acting as a unit, so the correct pronoun would be "its." (And notice, by the way, that the non-underlined part of the sentence includes the singular verb "has." This alerts you that the plural pronoun "their" is not correct here.)

Step 2: Scan and Group the Answer Choices

All four of the viable answer choices, **(B)**, **(C)**, **(D)**, and **(E)**, correct the pronoun error and the parallel structure error—the original sentence's "their failing" is replaced in each of these choices by "the failure"—so you can turn your focus to the first part of each choice. The options are "worrying," "worried," "in that they are worried," and "because of its worry." **(D)**'s "in that they are worried" is verbose and introduces another *it/they* pronoun error, so you can eliminate it right away. Now you must decide which of the three remaining choices, **(B)**, **(C)**, and **(E)**, is the most economical and idiomatic.

Step 3: Eliminate Choices Until Only One Remains

(E)'s phrase "because of its worry" is needlessly wordy, so you can strike it out. **(B)**'s phrase "worrying over" is not idiomatic. Notice, too, that **(B)** adds a superfluous word: "also." **(C)** contains the correct idiom "worried about" and does not add any excess verbiage. **(C)** is the correct answer.

46. (E)

The United States' trade deficit with China rose in 2003 to $123 billion, <u>which is 17 percent more than the previous year</u> and more than ten times the U.S.-China trade deficit in 1998.

- ○ which is 17 percent more than the previous year
- ○ which is 17 percent higher than it was the previous year
- ○ 17 percent higher than the previous year's figure was
- ○ an amount that is 17 percent more than the previous year was
- ○ an amount that is 17 percent higher than the previous year's figure

Step 1: Read the Original Sentence Carefully, Looking for Errors

Because the relative pronoun "which" refers to the noun that comes immediately before it, this means the underlined segment illogically compares a sum of money, "$123 billion," to "the previous year." The correct answer must compare a sum and a sum, not a sum and a year.

Step 2: Scan and Group the Answer Choices

(A) and **(B)** both start with "which." **(C)** leaves out "which," while **(D)** and **(E)** substitute "an amount that" for "which."

Step 3: Eliminate Choices Until Only One Remains

You can eliminate **(A)** because of its illogical comparison. **(B)** also bungles the comparison, thanks to its careless use of the slippery pronoun "it." Because "which" refers to "123 billion," **(B)** seems to say, nonsensically, that $123 billion is 17 percent higher than $123 billion was the previous year. **(D)** also fails to fix the illogical comparison; it compares "an amount" to "the previous year." That leaves only **(C)** and **(E)**. Both of these choices correctly compare two amounts of money. However, **(C)** adds "was" at the end, which is unnecessary and not parallel with the last part of the sentence, which does not use the verb. **(E)**, which introduces no new errors, is the correct answer.

47. (D)

The two-party political system is one <u>where the electorate gives its votes largely to only two major parties and where</u> one or the other party can usually win a majority in the legislature.

- ○ where the electorate gives its votes largely to only two major parties and where
- ○ in which the electorate largely gives only its votes to two major parties and where
- ○ where the electorate gives largely its votes to only two major parties and in which
- ○ in which the electorate gives its votes largely to only two major parties and in which
- ○ in which the electorate largely gives only its votes to two major parties and in which

Step 1: Read the Original Sentence Carefully, Looking for Errors

The underlined part of this sentence contains two incorrect uses of "where." On the GMAT, "where" is used correctly only if it refers to location. (For instance, "this is the café where we had lunch last week.") In the original sentence, "where" refers, both times, to the "two-party political system." A system is not a location, so you have an error, and you know that **(A)** is incorrect.

Step 2: Scan and Group the Answer Choices

Of the remaining choices, **(B)** substitutes "in which" for the first "where," but it retains the second "where." **(C)** keeps the first "where" and substitutes "in which" for the second. **(D)** and **(E)** substitute "in which" for both uses of "where" in the original sentence.

Step 3: Eliminate Choices Until Only One Remains

You can eliminate **(B)** and **(C)** because each still contains an incorrect usage of "where" to refer to something other than a location. That leaves **(D)** and **(E)** as the remaining contestants. The difference between them is that **(E)** moves the placement of "only," so instead of "gives its votes largely to only two major parties," the sentence now reads, "gives only its votes to two major parties." It's a small change, but it alters the meaning of the sentence dramatically. **(E)** makes it sound as if the electorate had other things besides its votes to give to the parties, which is not a meaning implied by the original sentence. You're left with **(D)** as the correct answer, since it fixes the original mistake without introducing any new errors and without changing the meaning of the original sentence.

48. (C)

Most financial advisers <u>recommend that stock portfolios should be reviewed</u> at least once a year, if only to make sure that changes do not need to be made.

- ○ recommend that stock portfolios should be reviewed
- ○ recommend you to review your stock portfolio
- ○ recommend that stock portfolios be reviewed
- ○ are recommending that stock portfolios are reviewed
- ○ have a recommendation to review stock portfolios

Step 1: Read the Original Sentence Carefully, Looking for Errors

Underlined verbs are worth your attention. The subject of "recommend" is "advisers." Subject and verb are both plural, so there is no subject-verb agreement error. However, verbs describing orders and recommendations must be followed by "that," a new subject, and another verb in the infinitive, but without the "to." In this sentence, the phrase that follows "recommend" contains the extra, unnecessary word "should." **(A)** will not be the correct answer.

Step 2: Scan and Group the Answer Choices

Of the remaining choices, **(C)** and **(D)** preserve "that," while **(B)** and **(E)** leave it out.

Step 3: Eliminate Choices Until Only One Remains

You can eliminate **(B)** and **(E)** because orders and recommendations must be followed by "that." Moreover, "have a recommendation" in **(E)** is wordy and awkward. **(D)** uses "that," but it introduces a new error: instead of "be," it uses "are." Only **(C)** remains and must be correct. Indeed, **(C)** has exactly the right grammatical structure for a recommendation: "that...be reviewed."

49. (D)

The United States <u>would achieve a 10 percent reduction in gasoline consumption, if Congress will raise</u> fuel economy standards to 31.3 miles per gallon for passenger cars and to 24.5 mpg for light trucks.

- ○ would achieve a 10 percent reduction in gasoline consumption, if Congress will raise
- ○ will achieve a 10 percent reduction in gasoline consumption, if Congress were to raise
- ○ will have achieved a 10 percent reduction in gasoline consumption, if Congress will raise
- ○ would achieve a 10 percent reduction in gasoline consumption, if Congress were to raise
- ○ would achieve a 10 percent reduction in gasoline consumption, if Congress were raising

Step 1: Read the Original Sentence Carefully, Looking for Errors

The word "if" in the underlined part of this sentence signals a hypothetical situation, so you need the subjunctive mood; you must use "were" and "would." "Would achieve" is correct, but "will raise" is not. Rule out **(A)**.

Step 2: Scan and Group the Answer Choices

(B) and **(C)** start with "will." **(D)** and **(E)** start with "would."

Step 3: Eliminate Choices Until Only One Remains

(B) is incorrect because "will achieve" is ordinary future tense, not subjunctive. Similarly, **(C)** is incorrect because "will have achieved" is also not subjunctive. **(D)** and **(E)** both use "would achieve," which is the proper subjunctive mood. The difference between them comes at the end. **(D)** uses "if Congress were to raise," while **(E)** has "if Congress were raising." The final phrase in **(E)** sounds a bit odd and is in fact grammatically incorrect. The proper subjunctive construction calls for the verb that follows "were" to be in the infinitive, not the *–ing* form. **(E)** is thus incorrect, and **(D)**, which contains the proper "were"-plus-infinitive construction, is the correct answer.

50. (C)

Because the moon's distance from Earth varies, <u>so the gravitational pull between the two bodies differ</u>, as do the size and times of oceanic tides.

○ so the gravitational pull between the two bodies differ

○ so the gravitational pull between the two bodies differs

○ the gravitational pull between the two bodies differs

○ therefore the gravitational pull between the two bodies differ

○ therefore the gravitational pull between the two bodies differs

Step 1: Read the Original Sentence Carefully, Looking for Errors

Two clauses need to be connected by one, and only one, conjunction. This sentence connects its introductory clause to its main clause with two conjunctions, "because" and "so." That's one conjunction too many. Moreover, this sentence contains a subject-verb agreement error. The subject of "differ" is "gravitational pull," which is singular. The verb should be "differs." The correct answer will fix both these mistakes without introducing any new ones.

Step 2: Scan and Group the Answer Choices

The choices group naturally with respect to the conjunction. **(A)** and **(B)** retain "so." **(D)** and **(E)** substitute "therefore," while **(C)** eliminates the conjunction entirely.

Step 3: Eliminate Choices Until Only One Remains

You've already determined that "Because" at the beginning of the sentence is the only conjunction you need to connect the first and second clauses of this sentence. **(A)**, **(B)**, **(D)**, and **(E)** all have an extra conjunction and are therefore all incorrect. Only **(C)** eliminates the superfluous conjunction. It also changes "differ" to "differs," so it fixes both mistakes and is the correct answer.

51. (A)

With a height of 7′7″ and a wingspan of over 8′6″, <u>Manute Bol is often considered one of the most physically imposing players in the history of professional basketball,</u> and he also gave generously of his time and money to help refugees from his native Sudan.

- ○ Manute Bol is often considered one of the most physically imposing players in the history of professional basketball
- ○ Manute Bol is often considered in the history of professional basketball the player who was most physically imposing
- ○ one of the most physically imposing players in the history of professional basketball is often considered Manute Bol
- ○ Manute Bol's place in the history of professional basketball is that of one of the most physically imposing players
- ○ one of the most often considered, physically imposing players in the history of professional basketball was Manute Bol

Step 1: Read the Original Sentence Carefully, Looking for Errors

The introductory phrase followed by a comma indicates that this question is testing your understanding of modifiers. The subject that is modified should be placed as close as possible to the modifier, "With a height…and a wingspan of 8′6″." It is Manute Bol who had these characteristics, and "Manute Bol" follows immediately after the comma. Another element in the sentence worth examining is the verb "considered," which idiomatically does not take *to be* after it. "Manute Bol is often considered one of the…" shows correct usage. The comparison word "most" is right, as a superlative is appropriate when more than two nouns are being compared (and there are more than two professional basketball players). Finally, the series of modifying prepositional phrases in the underlined portion proceed logically: "of the most physically imposing players" modifies the preceding "one"; "in the history" says which players are being talked about; "of professional basketball" tells which history is meant.

Step 2: Scan and Group the Answer Choices

(A) and **(B)** begin with "Manute Bol," **(D)** begins with "Manute Bol's place," and **(C)** and **(E)** begin with "one of the most."

Step 3: Eliminate Choices Until Only One Remains

(C) and **(E)** should be eliminated, since they inappropriately place the subject being modified, Manute Bol, far from the modifying phrase. **(B)** puts "Manute Bol" in the right place but moves "in the history of professional basketball" directly after "considered." However, the *considering* is not part of basketball history; Bol's imposing presence was. Thus, this choice commits a modification error. Also, eliminate **(D)**, which makes it sound as though the height and wingspan are characteristics of Bol's place in basketball history, rather than qualities of Bol himself. Since the sentence is correct as written, **(A)** is the correct answer.

52. (D)

At more than 800 pages in length, the <u>novelist's life stands revealed in the new biography, which sets the standard for research</u>.

- ○ novelist's life stands revealed in the new biography, which sets the standard for research
- ○ new biography is setting standards of research on the novelist's life
- ○ standard for research has been set by a new biography on the novelist
- ○ new biography about the novelist sets the standard for research
- ○ novelist's life is revealed in a standard-setting new biography

Step 1: Read the Original Sentence Carefully, Looking for Errors

The opening phrase of this sentence is a modifier, and modifiers on the GMAT always need to be placed as close to what they modify as possible. When you see such opening phrases, ask yourself, "What in the sentence is this phrase describing?" Here, the only thing in the sentence that could be more than 800 pages in length is "the new biography," so that should come right after the comma.

Step 2: Scan and Group the Answer Choices

In GMAT sentences that open with a modifying phrase set off by a comma, what comes after the comma is crucial. **(A)** and **(E)** begin with the "novelist's life," **(B)** and **(D)** begin with the "new biography," and **(C)** begins with the "standard for research…"

Step 3: Eliminate Choices Until Only One Remains

Get rid of **(A)**, **(C)**, and **(E)**, because none of them has the correct subject for the modifier. Only **(B)** and **(D)** use the correct subject after the phrase. But the verb tense in **(B)** changes the original sense of the sentence ("is setting" would indicate that the process of setting the standard hasn't yet been completed, which doesn't make sense). Only **(D)** has the correct subject and the correct tense.

53. (D)

Because customers at Jim's restaurant frequently failed to leave the expected tips for the waitstaff, <u>they are now</u> automatically factored into the price of each menu item.

- O   they are now
- O   tips are now being
- O   the tipping of money is now
- O   tips are now
- O   it is now

Step 1: Read the Original Sentence Carefully, Looking for Errors

The pronoun "they" is often used ambiguously in everyday speech but must have a clear antecedent on the GMAT. The problem with this sentence is that the pronoun "they" could refer to "customers," "waitstaff," or "tips." From the sentence's context, you may deduce that "they" refers to the tips, but the structure of the sentence does not clearly express this meaning.

Step 2: Scan and Group the Answer Choices

(A) uses "they," while **(E)** uses "it." **(B)**, **(C)**, and **(D)** avoid using a pronoun, instead using the noun "tips" or "the tipping."

Step 3: Eliminate Choices Until Only One Remains

Because "they" is ambiguous in the original sentence, eliminate **(A)**. By replacing "they" with "it," **(E)** not only fails to correct the pronoun ambiguity error but also introduces disagreement in number between the plural noun "tips" and the singular pronoun. Eliminate **(C)** because tips by definition involve money, so the phrase "of money" is redundant. Also, it's not the act of "tipping" that's included in the prices but the tips themselves. Now for the choices that start with "tips": **(B)** overly complicates the verb tense with the use of "being," an often-problematic word on the GMAT; the simple present "are" is correct. Only **(D)** clears up the ambiguous pronoun in a correct, concise way.

54. (C)

Although the British were responsible for the early European settlement <u>of both Australia and the United States, Australia is having much closer political and cultural links with Britain than the United States is having</u>.

○ of both Australia and the United States, Australia is having much closer political and cultural links with Britain than the United States is having

○ in both Australia and the United States, they are closer in their political and cultural links in Australia than in the United States

○ of both nations, Australia has much closer political and cultural links to Britain than the United States has

○ in both nations, Australia is politically and culturally linked to Britain in a much closer fashion than the United States

○ of both Australia and the United States, they have much closer political and cultural links to it than the United States has

Step 1: Read the Original Sentence Carefully, Looking for Errors

Note the strange verb tense—present progressive—used in the underlined portion. The –*ing* tense is usually wrong on the GMAT and is certainly not correct if the intention is to express a permanent state of affairs, as is the case here. Also, in most cases, the present progressive can be ditched in favor of the more concise present tense. (Why use "is having" when you can use "has"?) The only time that the GMAT tends to use the progressive tense in the correct answer is when doing so changes a misplaced modifier to a verb. (Example: "The dog walked down the street, which was carrying a stick." should actually be "the dog walked down the street, carrying a stick.") Here, there's no good reason for the verb construction "is having," so it's incorrect.

Step 2: Scan and Group the Answer Choices

As you scan, you might notice that the sentence is also testing an idiom issue. **(A)**, **(C)**, and **(E)** all begin with "of," while **(B)** and **(D)** begin with "in." This difference forces you to decide which one is correct, even if you hadn't thought of it while reading the original sentence.

Step 3: Eliminate Choices Until Only One Remains

The correct idiom is "settlement of," not "settlement in," so eliminate **(B)** and **(D)**. The odd choice of verb tense in the original sentence disqualifies **(A)**. Finally, **(E)** can be eliminated because it includes the pronouns "it" and "they," which make the sentence ambiguous. Only **(C)** corrects the verb tense and does so in a clear, concise manner.

55. **(E)**

Each of the major setbacks the Germans suffered in June 1944—the fall of Rome, the collapse of Army Group Center on the Eastern Front, and the breaching of the Atlantic Wall at Normandy—were powerful shocks signaling the inability of the German war machine to compete on multiple fronts.

- ○ Each of the major setbacks the Germans suffered in June 1944—the fall of Rome, the collapse of Army Group Center on the Eastern Front, and the breaching of the Atlantic Wall at Normandy—were powerful shocks

- ○ The fall of Rome, the collapse of Army Group Center on the Eastern Front, and the breaching of the Atlantic Wall at Normandy—each of them major setbacks the Germans suffered in June 1944—were powerful shocks

- ○ Powerful shocks—the fall of Rome, the collapse of Army Group Center on the Eastern Front, and the breaching of the Atlantic Wall at Normandy—each a major setback for the Germans in June 1944, was such

- ○ The major setbacks suffered by the Germans in June 1944—the fall of Rome, the collapse of Army Group Center on the Eastern Front, and the breaching of the Atlantic Wall at Normandy—each were powerful shocks

- ○ Each of the major setbacks the Germans suffered in June 1944—the fall of Rome, the collapse of Army Group Center on the Eastern Front, and the breach of the Atlantic Wall at Normandy—was a powerful shock

Step 1: Read the Original Sentence Carefully, Looking for Errors

Note that this question is testing two classic GMAT Sentence Correction concepts. The first, parallel structure, was probably easier to spot since the sentence uses dashes to set off a list of the setbacks that the Germans faced. Those elements—(1) "the fall," (2) "the collapse," and (3) "the breaching"—are not parallel, since "breaching" is a gerund. Also, the use of a lengthy phrase between dashes should signal this sentence's attempt to disguise a subject-verb agreement error. The subject of the sentence is not "setbacks" but "each," which is singular, so the verb "were" doesn't agree in number with this subject. (The subject of a sentence will never appear in a prepositional phrase, as "setbacks" does.)

Step 2: Scan and Group the Answer Choices

Because of the verb issue, see if you can scan the choices quickly to note the verb each uses. **(B)** and **(D)**, like the original sentence, use "were," so unless one of these choices changes the subject of the sentence to something plural, these can probably be eliminated.

Step 3: Eliminate Choices Until Only One Remains

Get rid of **(A)** right away because of both errors present there. **(B)**, **(C)**, and **(D)** all fail to correct the parallelism error, so they can all be eliminated. (Note that **(D)** also continues to use "each...were" and **(C)** is incredibly confusing and poorly constructed. Often the GMAT will put multiple errors in an underlined portion to give you more than one opportunity to eliminate wrong answers.) Only **(E)** has parallel structure and uses the singular verb "was." Thus, **(E)** is the correct answer.

56. (C)

Adult pelicans store fish in a deep, expandable pouch below the lower mandible, <u>of which the young feed</u>.

- ○   of which the young feed
- ○   being for the feeding of the young
- ○   from which the young feed
- ○   that it feeds the young from
- ○   young feed from

Step 1: Read the Original Sentence Carefully, Looking for Errors

This underlined portion is quite short, but a quick reading indicates that this question is testing idiomatic usage. Young pelicans do not feed "of" something, as the original sentence says. They feed "from" something.

Step 2: Scan and Group the Answer Choices

As you scan the choices, try to spot constructions and individual words that are not likely to be correct, such as "being" in **(B)**.

Step 3: Eliminate Choices Until Only One Remains

To "feed of" something is incorrect, so **(A)** is out. Eliminate **(B)** because it is way too wordy and uses the disfavored "being" construction. Eliminate **(D)** and **(E)** because "from" is left dangling at the end of the sentence, and it is considered poor form on the GMAT to end a sentence with a preposition. Furthermore, **(D)** uses the singular pronoun "it" to stand in for plural "pelicans," and **(E)** hardly makes sense as written; it merely tacks on a separate clause with no conjunction to connect it to the rest of the sentence. Only **(C)** is both idiomatically and grammatically correct.

57. (B)

Anthony Trollope, one of the most famous English novelists of the nineteenth century, also <u>wrote travel books, some based on his undertaking of journeys</u> while an employee of the postal service.

- ○ wrote travel books, some based on his undertaking of journeys
- ○ wrote travel books, some based on journeys he undertook
- ○ undertook journeys, having based travel books on them
- ○ based travel books on journeys undertaken
- ○ wrote travel books, some based on journeys which he was to undertake

Step 1: Read the Original Sentence Carefully, Looking for Errors

The beginning of the underlined portion contains the verb "wrote," which is correct here given the appropriateness of the simple past tense. The problem with this sentence is one of usage and style. As you have seen, the GMAT disfavors –*ing* constructions. The phrase "based on his undertaking" is needlessly awkward.

Step 2: Scan and Group the Answer Choices

There are no discernible splits here. Since "wrote" is correct, though, be suspicious of **(C)** and **(D)**, which change the verb to something different.

Step 3: Eliminate Choices Until Only One Remains

Because of the awkward construction in the original sentence, eliminate **(A)**. Eliminate **(C)**, which makes it sound as though Trollope based the travel books on the journeys before he took the journeys. Similarly, eliminate **(E)** because the travel books were based on journeys he had already undertaken, not on journeys he would undertake in the future. Eliminate **(D)**, which makes it unclear who is actually undertaking the journeys. Only **(B)** keeps the meaning of the sentence intact while adhering to GMAT style. Thus, **(B)** is the correct answer.

58. **(B)**

A federal government survey taken in 1997 showed that during the 12 months preceding the survey, 36 percent of the U.S. population had tried marijuana, cocaine, or other illicit drugs, 71 percent of the population <u>were smoking cigarettes, and 82 percent</u> tried alcoholic beverages.

- ○ were smoking cigarettes, and 82 percent
- ○ had smoked cigarettes, and 82 percent had
- ○ smoked cigarettes, and that 82 percent
- ○ smoked cigarettes, and 82 percent had
- ○ will be smoking cigarettes, and 82 percent

Step 1: Read the Original Sentence Carefully, Looking for Errors

This question is testing parallel structure: similar elements must be in a similar form. Here you have three statistics being compared, and the one that is not underlined reads "36 percent…had…" Therefore, the other two statistics must be in the same form.

Step 2: Scan and Group the Answer Choices

Note the variety of verb tenses: **(A)** uses "were smoking," **(B)** uses "had smoked," **(C)** and **(D)** use "smoked," and **(E)** uses "will be smoking."

Step 3: Eliminate Choices Until Only One Remains

"Had smoked" is correct for two reasons. First of all, it's the past perfect tense, which should always be used to describe actions occurring before other actions in the past. Here, before the survey was *taken* in 1997, people *had used* drugs, cigarettes, and alcohol. Second, "had smoked" is parallel to the elements of the sentence that are not underlined and that therefore cannot be changed. Eliminate **(A)**, **(C)**, **(D)**, and **(E)** because they use tenses that don't make sense given the sequence of events in the sentence and because they do not put similar elements in a similar form. Only **(B)** corrects both problems.

59. (C)

Like Art Nouveau jewelry designers, the <u>Art Deco movement used art materials suitable for expressing</u> the new stylistic language of the 1920s, one dominated by an interplay of geometric forms.

○ Art Deco movement used art materials suitable for expressing

○ Art Deco movement was expressed through the use of materials suitable for the

○ artists of the Art Deco movement used materials suitable for expressing

○ Art Deco movement's materials were used by artists to suitably express

○ artists of the Art Deco movement also used suitable materials for the expression of

Step 1: Read the Original Sentence Carefully, Looking for Errors

As soon as you see "like" at the beginning of the sentence, know that a comparison is being made. The GMAT is fond of testing your ability to distinguish between logical and illogical comparisons. As written, the sentence compares "Art Nouveau jewelry designers" to "the Art Deco movement," which is an illogical comparison. The beginning of the underlined portion will need to be changed to something more comparable to "jewelry designers."

Step 2: Scan and Group the Answer Choices

(A) and **(B)** begin with "Art Deco movement," **(C)** and **(E)** begin with "artists of the Art Deco movement," and **(D)** begins with "Art Deco movement's materials." Only one of these beginnings will be correct.

Step 3: Eliminate Choices Until Only One Remains

"Artists of the Art Deco movement" is correct, since "artists" can properly be compared to "jewelry designers" in the beginning of the sentence. Therefore, eliminate **(A)**, **(B)**, and **(D)**. Then eliminate **(E)** because "also" here is redundant (since the sentence already begins with "like") and because it is less concise than **(C)**, which is the only choice that remains.

60. (C)

Amtrak, a government-owned corporation, schedules passenger rail service, <u>payments to privately owned firms to run trains, and bears all administrative costs, such as</u> those incurred by the purchase of new equipment and by the sale of tickets.

- O   payments to privately owned firms to run trains, and bears all administrative costs, such as
- O   pays privately owned firms to run trains, and is bearing all administrative costs, such as
- O   pays privately owned firms to run trains, and bears all administrative costs, such as
- O   pays privately owned firms to run trains, and bears all administrative costs, being inclusive of
- O   pays privately owned firms to run trains, and the bearer of all costs of administration, for example

Step 1: Read the Original Sentence Carefully, Looking for Errors

The sentence presents a list of Amtrak's responsibilities. The first one is a verb in the present tense, "schedules," and this verb isn't underlined, so the other two elements in the list must be parallel to this form. As it stands, "payments" is not parallel with "schedules" and "bears."

Step 2: Scan and Group the Answer Choices

Every choice except for **(A)** uses "pays." Furthermore, **(A)**, **(C)**, and **(D)** use "bears," while **(B)** uses "is bearing" and **(E)** uses "the bearer."

Step 3: Eliminate Choices Until Only One Remains

Because of the original parallelism error, eliminate **(A)**. Eliminate **(B)** and **(E)** because they change the verb tense in the second part of the clause from "bears" to a non-parallel construction. Finally, eliminate **(D)** because "being inclusive of" is wordy and awkward and contains the often incorrect "being." **(C)** has all elements parallel and, thus, is the correct answer.

61. **(A)**

In feudal Korea, <u>cattle were traditionally used as beasts of burden, rather than as a food source, and fish were</u> the primary source of protein in the typical diet.

- ○ cattle were traditionally used as beasts of burden, rather than as a food source, and fish were
- ○ cattle were being used as beasts of burden, rather than as a food source, and fish were providing
- ○ cattle were traditionally used as beasts of burden, rather than a food source, with fish being
- ○ the traditional use of cattle was as beasts of burden, rather than for the provision of food, and fish were
- ○ cattle were traditionally used for beasts of burden, rather than for a food source, and fish were

Step 1: Read the Original Sentence Carefully, Looking for Errors

When reading the sentence, you may have noticed that the sentence uses passive voice in the beginning of the underlined portion ("cattle were…used"). Normally, the GMAT does not prefer to use passive voice because it is wordier and takes the focus off the person/thing completing the action of the sentence. In order to select a better alternative, though, you'll need to pinpoint the specific people who used the cattle as beasts of burden.

Step 2: Scan and Group the Answer Choices

(A), **(B)**, **(C)**, and **(E)** all continue to use passive voice in the beginning of the underlined portion. **(D)** avoids this in favor of the wordy "the traditional use of cattle was as…" None of the sentences actually make clear who is completing the action described. Without a clear way to eliminate using passive voice to group the answer choices, you must evaluate them one by one, eliminating those that contain identifiable flaws.

Step 3: Eliminate Choices Until Only One Remains

Because the sentence discusses traditional uses, all verbs should be in the past tense. Eliminate **(B)** and **(C)** because they use the incorrect –*ing* verb tense in the second part of the sentence; **(B)** uses "were providing" at the end, which is awkward, and **(C)** contains "being," which is rarely correct on the GMAT. Eliminate **(D)** because it is overly wordy; whenever there is some other answer choice that expresses the same idea just as correctly but with fewer words, select that answer. Eliminate **(E)** because it incorrectly substitutes "used for" for "used as." The sentence is correct as written, making **(A)** the correct answer.

62. **(E)**

The term "support staff" is often used to describe employees <u>that perform lower-level tasks but also are providing</u> essential administrative duties for executive-level managers.

- ○ that perform lower-level tasks but also are providing
- ○ performing lower-level tasks but also providing
- ○ who perform lower-level tasks, but are also providing
- ○ that performs lower-level tasks but also provide
- ○ who perform lower-level tasks but also provide

Step 1: Read the Original Sentence Carefully, Looking for Errors

Always pay close attention to the beginnings of underlined portions—these beginnings are not chosen at random. The underlined portion of this sentence begins with "that." Looking at what comes before, you should notice that the previous word, "employees," requires the pronoun "who" on the GMAT, since the noun "employees" refers to people. Also, the verb tenses of the elements that are being compared should be the same, and here, "perform" doesn't match "are providing."

Step 2: Scan and Group the Answer Choices

(A) and **(D)** begin with "that." **(C)** and **(E)** begin with "who." **(B)** gets rid of the pronoun altogether and begins with "performing."

Step 3: Eliminate Choices Until Only One Remains

The modifier should begin with "who" rather than "that," so **(A)** and **(D)** should be eliminated. Get rid of **(B)** because there is no need to use the progressive verb tense ("performing" and "providing") when the simple present tense conveys the idea clearly. Eliminate **(C)** because the verb forms are not parallel. **(E)** is correct because it uses the pronoun "who" and the verbs are parallel, both using the simple present tense.

63. **(A)**

National Women's History Month <u>began as a single week and as a local event when, in 1978, Sonoma County, California, sponsored</u> a women's history week to promote the teaching of women's history—a neglected subject in elementary and high school curricula at that time.

- ○ began as a single week and as a local event when, in 1978, Sonoma County, California, sponsored
- ○ began as a single week local event sponsoring, in Sonoma County, California,
- ○ begins with a single week in 1978 sponsoring the local Sonoma County, California, of
- ○ will have began in 1978 as a single week local event when Sonoma County, California, was in sponsorship of
- ○ was begun in 1978 when, in Sonoma County, California, there was to be a sponsorship of

Step 1: Read the Original Sentence Carefully, Looking for Errors

From the beginning of the underlined portion, you can tell that this question tests verb tenses and clarity. Since the sentence discusses something that happened in 1978, all verbs should be in the past tense, and the structure of the sentence should reflect the facts that National Women's History Month was both a single week and a local event and that it was sponsored by Sonoma County. All of that information is clearly reflected in the question stem, so it is most likely correct. However, check all the answer choices to make sure that none of them is more concise, especially in such a long sentence.

Step 2: Scan and Group the Answer Choices

The most obvious difference in the answer choices is in their beginnings. **(A)** and **(B)** use "began," while the remaining choices use a variety of tenses ranging from present in **(C)** to future perfect in **(D)** to a passive construction in **(E)**.

Step 3: Eliminate Choices Until Only One Remains

Eliminate **(B)** because it does not make it clear that Sonoma County sponsored the event. Eliminate **(C)** both because it uses the incorrect verb tense and because it suggests that the single week sponsors Sonoma County. Eliminate **(D)** because it uses the incorrect verb tense. Eliminate **(E)** because it also introduces a subject-verb agreement error; the subject "mental disorders" is plural, while the verb "has" is singular. By process of elimination, **(A)** is indeed the correct answer.

64. **(D)**

By examining sets of identical twins in recent studies, mental disorders such as schizophrenia and autism have been found to be the results of variations in gene expression and not simply a matter of genetic inheritance.

- ○ By examining sets of identical twins in recent studies, mental disorders such as schizophrenia and autism have been found to be
- ○ By examining sets of identical twins in recent studies, mental disorders such as schizophrenia and autism were found as being
- ○ Mental disorders such as schizophrenia and autism were examined in sets of identical twins in recent studies and has been found to be
- ○ Recent studies that examined sets of identical twins have shown that mental disorders such as schizophrenia and autism are
- ○ Recent studies that examined sets of identical twins has shown that mental disorders such as schizophrenia and autism are

Step 1: Read the Original Sentence Carefully, Looking for Errors

The original sentence begins with a modifying phrase, so ensure that the phrase is correctly placed. The word or phrase that follows the comma should be the thing described by the phrase. Here, the author has followed "[b]y examining sets of identical twins in recent studies" with "mental disorders," making it sound as though the mental disorders examined the twins—an illogical meaning.

Step 2: Scan and Group the Answer Choices

Scanning and grouping the answers in this question is difficult because the answer choices show a good deal of variety in sentence structure. Instead, evaluating each choice in order is the better approach. Pay particular attention to the relationship between the "mental disorders" and the studies of twins, since this is the error in the original sentence.

Step 3: Eliminate Choices Until Only One Remains

Eliminate **(A)** for the reason discussed in Step 1. Eliminate **(B)** because it commits the same error as **(A)**. **(C)** and **(E)** fix the modifier error, but both use the singular verb "has" with the plural subjects "mental disorders" and "studies," respectively, committing subject-verb agreement errors. Only **(D)** correctly fixes the modifier error while introducing no new errors.

65. (A)

Working with musician Stevie Wonder as a musical adviser, Ray Kurzweil developed what is now the preferred medium for creating nearly all music for today's commercial albums, films, and television: a computer-based instrument capable of <u>reproducing musical sounds of a quality once thought to be</u> possible only on grand pianos and other acoustic instruments.

- ○ reproducing musical sounds of a quality once thought to be
- ○ reproducing musical sounds with a quality as were once thought to be
- ○ reproducing in musical sounds a quality that was once thought to be
- ○ reproduction of musical sounds whose quality is the same as what were once thought to be
- ○ reproduction of musical sounds at a quality once thought of as

Step 1: Read the Original Sentence Carefully, Looking for Errors

This is a long sentence, but the colon indicates that what comes after the colon is simply going to explain more about what comes before the colon, so let's just focus on what comes after the colon, since that's where the underlined portion is. The original sentence may have sounded just fine to you. Before selecting **(A)**, though, make sure none of the other choices expresses the idea more clearly and concisely.

Step 2: Scan and Group the Answer Choices

(A) and **(B)** begin with "reproducing musical sounds," **(C)** begins with "reproducing in musical sounds," and **(D)** and **(E)** begin with "reproduction of musical sounds." It appears that this sentence is testing idiomatic constructions.

Step 3: Eliminate Choices Until Only One Remains

In **(B)**, "with a quality" changes the sentence to mean that the instrument possesses the "quality," when it's the quality of the sounds that's discussed here; furthermore, "as were once" is unidiomatic in the sentence. **(C)** unnecessarily introduces "in" and "that was." Extraneous words are a sign of an incorrect answer in GMAT Sentence Correction questions. **(D)** and **(E)** introduce the awkward construction "capable of reproduction of." **(D)** is also extremely wordy, and **(E)** also includes the unidiomatic "at a quality" and "once thought of as." The original sentence is correct as written, making **(A)** the correct answer. It contains the correct constructions: "capable of reproducing...sounds of a quality once thought to be possible..."

66. (A)

Twenty years ago, only 6 percent of students at Dunmore College who intended to major in chemistry were women; today that figure is <u>at least as high as 40 percent</u>.

○   at least as high as 40 percent
○   higher than at least 40 percent
○   higher by 40 percent at the least
○   40 percent high or more
○   more higher than 40 percent

Step 1: Read the Original Sentence Carefully, Looking for Errors

Comparisons are being tested in this sentence (your hint is the use of the words "at least as high" and the words "higher" and "more" throughout the answer choices). Here you are looking for the construction that makes the comparison as clear and correct as possible. This sentence compares the previous figure, or "6 percent," with today's figure, so you want something that is as similar in structure as possible to "6 percent."

Step 2: Scan and Group the Answer Choices

The comparison sounds good as is, but scan the choices for the ways in which the choices use other comparative words like "higher" (as in **(B)**, **(C)**, and **(E)**) and "more" (as in **(D)** and **(E)**).

Step 3: Eliminate Choices Until Only One Remains

(B) is awkward and redundant; it doesn't make sense to have both "higher than" and "at least" next to each other. **(C)** changes the meaning of the sentence by saying "higher by 40 percent," which means something different from "higher than 40 percent." **(D)** introduces the awkward and confusing "40 percent high," which is hard to decipher. Finally, **(E)** uses the egregious construction "more higher." The correct choice is **(A)**, "at least as high as 40 percent."

GMAT BY THE NUMBERS: SENTENCE CORRECTION

Now that you've learned how to approach Sentence Correction questions on the GMAT, let's add one more dimension to your understanding of how they work.

Take a moment to try this question. Following is performance data from thousands of people who have studied with Kaplan over the decades. Through analyzing this data, we will show you how to approach questions like this one most effectively and how to avoid similarly tempting wrong answer choice types on Test Day.

> The European Union announced that cod and mackerel are the only fish
> that <u>exceeds their new requirements for dioxin level and that they allow</u>
> fishermen to catch.
>
> ○   exceeds their new requirements for dioxin level and that they allow
> ○   exceed its new requirements for dioxin level and that they allow
> ○   exceeds its new requirements for dioxin level and that it allows
> ○   exceed its new requirements for dioxin level and that it allows
> ○   exceed their new requirements for dioxin level and that they allow

EXPLANATION

Attention to the Right Detail and Pattern Recognition are both essential to success on Sentence Correction questions. You want to check the sentence very carefully for errors, giving special consideration to the recurring patterns that the GMAT test maker is so fond of. In this sentence, there are two underlined pronouns plus an underlined verb. Both underlined pronouns, "their" and "they," refer to the European Union, which is a singular noun. These pronouns are therefore incorrect; the sentence should use "its" and "it," respectively. Only **(C)** and **(D)** get both pronouns right, so one of these choices has to be the correct answer. The difference between **(C)** and **(D)** is the use of "exceeds" versus "exceed." Since there are two kinds of fish, "cod and mackerel," you need the plural verb. Choice **(D)** is correct.

QUESTION STATISTICS

2% of test takers choose **(A)**

6% of test takers choose **(B)**

14% of test takers choose **(C)**

56% of test takers choose **(D)**

22% of test takers choose **(E)**

Sample size = 4,437

Note that the two most popular wrong choices, **(C)** and **(E)**, each correct one of the two errors in the sentence but not both. Many test takers will spot an answer choice that fixes the one mistake they were scanning for and think, "Aha—that's the answer!" and move on without actually reading the answer back into the sentence. The test maker is aware of this tendency. So beware of trap answers that correct just one of two or more errors, as well as trap answers that fix one mistake but introduce another. Always read your choice back into the sentence. It only takes a few seconds and prevents careless mistakes.

MORE GMAT BY THE NUMBERS...

To see more questions with answer choice statistics, be sure to review the full-length CATs in your online resources.

GO ONLINE

kaptest.com/login

PART FOUR

Quantitative Section and Strategies

CHAPTER 9

Quantitative Section Overview

- Composition of the Quantitative Section
- What the Quantitative Section Tests
- Pacing on the Quantitative Section
- How the Quantitative Section Is Scored
- Core Competencies on the Quantitative Section

COMPOSITION OF THE QUANTITATIVE SECTION

Slightly fewer than half of the multiple-choice questions that count toward your overall score appear in the Quantitative (math) section. You'll have 62 minutes to answer 31 Quantitative questions in two formats: Problem Solving and Data Sufficiency. These two types of questions are mingled throughout the Quantitative section, so you never know what's coming next. Here's what you can expect to see:

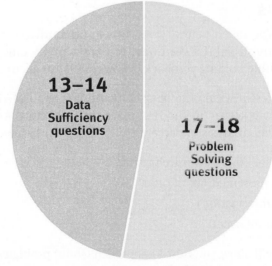

13–14
Data
Sufficiency
questions

17–18
Problem
Solving
questions

The Approximate Mix of Questions on the GMAT Quantitative Section

You may see more of one question type and fewer of the other due to the test's somewhat random selection of questions.

WHAT THE QUANTITATIVE SECTION TESTS

MATH CONTENT KNOWLEDGE

Of course, the GMAT tests your math skills. So you will have to work with concepts that you may not have used for the last few years. Calculator use is not permitted on the Quantitative section, and even if you use math all the time, it's probably been a while since you were unable to use a calculator or computer to perform computations. So refreshing your fundamental math skills is definitely a crucial part of your prep.

But the range of math topics tested is actually fairly limited. The GMAT covers only the math that U.S. students usually see during or before their first two years of high school. No trigonometry, no advanced algebra, no calculus. As you progress in your GMAT prep, you'll see that the same concepts are tested again and again in remarkably similar ways.

Areas of math content tested on the GMAT include the following: algebra, arithmetic, number properties, proportions, basic statistics, certain specific math formulas, and geometry. Algebra and arithmetic are the most commonly tested topics—they are tested either directly or indirectly on a majority of GMAT Quantitative questions. Geometry questions account for fewer than one-sixth of all GMAT math questions, but they can often be among the most challenging for test takers, so you may benefit from thorough review and practice with these concepts.

A large part of what makes the GMAT Quantitative section so challenging, however, is not the math content itself, but rather how the test makers combine the different areas of math to make questions more challenging. Rare is the question that tests a single concept; more commonly, you will be asked to integrate multiple skills to solve a question. For instance, a question that asks you about triangles could also require you to solve a formula algebraically and apply your understanding of ratios to find the correct answer.

QUANTITATIVE ANALYSIS

Most of the math tests you've taken before—even other standardized tests like the SAT and the ACT—ask questions in a fairly straightforward way. You know pretty quickly how you should solve the problem, and the only thing holding you back is how quickly or accurately you can do the math.

But the GMAT is a little different. Often the most difficult part of a GMAT Quantitative problem is figuring out which math skills to use in the first place. In fact, the GMAT's hardest Quantitative problems are about 95 percent analysis, 5 percent calculation. You'll have to do the following:

- Understand complicated or awkward phrasing
- Process information presented out of order
- Analyze incomplete information
- Simplify complicated information

In the next few chapters, we'll show you how to approach Quant problems strategically so you can do the analysis that will lead you to efficient solutions, correct answers, and a high score. But first, let's look at some techniques for managing the Quantitative section as a whole.

PACING ON THE QUANTITATIVE SECTION

The best way to attack the computer-adaptive GMAT is to exploit the way it determines your score. Here's what you're dealing with:

- **Penalties:** If you run out of time at the end of the section, you receive a penalty that's about twice what you'd have received if you got all those answers wrong. *And* there's an extra penalty for long strings of wrong answers at the end.

- **No review:** There is no going back to check your work. You cannot move backward to double-check your earlier answers or skip past a question that's puzzling and return to try it again later. So if you finish early, you won't be able to use that remaining time.

- **Difficulty level adjustment:** Questions get harder or easier, depending on your performance. Difficult questions raise your score more when you get them right and hurt your score less when you get them wrong. Easier questions are the opposite—getting them right helps your score less, and getting them wrong hurts your score more.

Obviously, the best of both worlds is being able to get the early questions mostly right, while taking less than *two minutes per question on average* so that you have a little extra time to think about those harder questions later on. To achieve that goal, you need to do three things:

1. **Know your math basics cold.** Don't waste valuable time on Test Day sweating over how to add fractions, reverse-FOIL quadratic equations, or use the rate formula. When you do math, you want to feel right at home.

2. **Look for strategic approaches.** Most GMAT problems are susceptible to multiple possible approaches. So the test makers deliberately build in shortcuts to reward critical thinkers by allowing them to move quickly through the question, leaving them with extra time. We'll show you how to find these most efficient approaches.

3. **Practice, practice, practice.** Do lots of practice problems so that you get as familiar as possible with the GMAT's most common analytical puzzles. That way you can handle them quickly (and correctly!) when you see them on Test Day. We've got tons in the upcoming chapters.

If you follow this advice, you'll do more than just set yourself up to manage your pacing well. You'll also ensure that most of the questions fall into a difficulty range that's right for you. If you struggle on a few hard questions and are sent back down to the midrange questions, that's OK! You'll get them correct, which will send you right back up to the high-value hard questions again.

During the test, do your best not to fall behind early on. Don't rush, but don't linger. Those first 5 questions shouldn't take more than 10 minutes total, and the first 10 questions shouldn't take more than 20 minutes. Pay attention to your timing as you move through the section. If you notice that you are falling behind, try to solve some questions more quickly (or if you're stuck, make strategic guesses) to catch up.

STRATEGIC GUESSING

Since missing hard questions doesn't hurt your score very much but not finishing definitely does, making a few guesses on the hardest questions will give you the chance to finish on time and earn your highest possible score.

Occasionally, you'll find that you have to make a guess, but don't guess at random. Narrowing down the answer choices first is imperative. Otherwise, your odds of getting the right answer will be pretty slim. Follow this plan when you guess:

1. **Eliminate answer choices you know are wrong.** You can often identify wrong answer choices after a little calculation. For instance, on Data Sufficiency questions, you can eliminate at least two answer choices by determining the sufficiency of just one statement.

2. **Avoid answer choices that make you suspicious.** You can get rid of these without doing any work on the problem! These answer choices either don't make logical sense with the problem, or they conform to common wrong-answer types. For example, if only one of the answer choices in a Problem Solving question is negative, chances are that it will be incorrect.

3. **Choose one of the remaining answer choices.** The fewer options you have to choose from, the higher your chances of selecting the right answer. You can often identify the correct answer using estimation, especially if the answer choices are spaced widely apart.

EXPERIMENTAL QUESTIONS

Some questions on the GMAT are experimental. These questions are not factored into your score. They are questions that the test maker is evaluating for possible use on future tests. To get good data, the test makers have to test each question against the whole range of test takers—that is, high and low scorers. Therefore, you could be on your way to an 800 and suddenly come across a question that feels out of line with how you think you are doing.

Don't panic; just do your best and keep on going. The difficulty level of the experimental questions you see has little to do with how you're currently scoring. Remember, there is no way for you to know for sure whether a question is experimental or not, so approach every question as if it were scored.

Keep in mind that it's hard to judge the true difficulty level of a question. A question that seems easy to you may simply be playing to your personal strengths and be very difficult for other test takers. So treat every question as if it counts. Don't waste time trying to speculate about the difficulty of the questions you're seeing and what that implies about your performance. Rather, focus your energy on answering the question in front of you as efficiently as possible.

HOW THE QUANTITATIVE SECTION IS SCORED

The Quantitative section of the GMAT is quite different from the math sections of paper-and-pencil tests you may have taken. The major difference between the test formats is that the GMAT computer-adaptive test (CAT) adapts to your performance. Each test taker is given a different mix of questions, depending on how well he or she is doing on the test. In other words, the questions get harder or easier depending on whether you answer them correctly or incorrectly. Your GMAT score is not determined by the number of questions you get right but rather by the difficulty level of the questions you get right.

When you begin a section, the computer

- assumes you have an average score (500), and
- gives you a medium-difficulty question. About half the people who take the test will get this question right, and half will get it wrong. What happens next depends on whether you answer the question correctly.

If you answer the question correctly,

- your score goes up, and
- you are given a slightly harder question.

If you answer the question incorrectly,

- your score goes down, and
- you are given a slightly easier question.

This pattern continues for the rest of the section. As you get questions right, the computer raises your score and gives you harder questions. As you get questions wrong, the computer lowers your score and gives you easier questions. In this way, the computer homes in on your score.

If you feel like you're struggling at the end of the section, don't worry! Because the CAT adapts to find the outer edge of your abilities, the test will feel hard; it's designed to be difficult for everyone, even the highest scorers.

CORE COMPETENCIES ON THE QUANTITATIVE SECTION

Unlike most subject-specific tests you have taken throughout your academic career, the scope of knowledge that the GMAT requires of you is fairly limited. In fact, you don't need any background knowledge or expertise beyond fundamental math and verbal skills. While mastering those fundamentals is essential to your success on the GMAT—and this book is concerned in part with helping you develop or refresh those skills—the GMAT does *not* primarily seek to reward test takers for content-specific knowledge. Rather, the GMAT is a test of high-level thinking and reasoning abilities; it uses math and verbal subject matter as a platform to build questions that test your critical thinking and problem solving capabilities. As you prepare for the GMAT, you will notice that similar analytical skills come into play across the various question types and sections of the test.

Kaplan has adopted the term "Core Competencies" to refer to the four bedrock thinking skills rewarded by the GMAT: Critical Thinking, Pattern Recognition, Paraphrasing, and Attention to the Right Detail. The Kaplan Methods and strategies presented throughout this book will help you demonstrate these all-important skills. Let's dig into each of the Core Competencies in turn and discuss how each applies to the Quantitative section.

CRITICAL THINKING

Most potential MBA students are adept at creative problem solving, and the GMAT offers many opportunities to demonstrate this skill. You probably already have experience assessing situations to see when data are inadequate; synthesizing information into valid deductions; finding creative solutions to complex problems; and avoiding unnecessary, redundant labor.

In GMAT terms, a critical thinker is a creative problem solver who engages in critical inquiry. One of the traits of successful test takers is their skill at asking the right questions. GMAT critical thinkers first consider what they're being asked to do, then study the given information and ask the right questions, especially, "How can I get the answer in the most direct way?" and "How can I use the question format to my advantage?"

For instance, the answer choices in a GMAT Problem Solving question often give clues to the solution. Use them. As you examine a Problem Solving question, you'll ask the test maker: "What are you really looking for in this math problem?" or "Why have you set things up in this way?" You might even discover opportunities to find the answer to a difficult question by plugging the answer choices into the information in the question—a strategy Kaplan calls "backsolving."

Likewise, as you examine a Data Sufficiency question, you'll learn to ask: "What information will I need to answer this question?" or "How can I determine whether more than one solution is possible?"

Those test takers who learn to ask the right questions become creative problem solvers—and GMAT champs. Let's see how to apply the GMAT Core Competency of Critical Thinking to a sample Problem Solving question:

1. If the perimeter of a rectangular property is 46 meters, and the area of the property is 76 square meters, what is the length of each of the shorter sides?

   ○ 4
   ○ 6
   ○ 9
   ○ 18
   ○ 23

This question is a perfect example of one that can be answered with minimal calculations, provided the test taker understands how to use the test format to his advantage.

Here you are asked for the shorter sides of a rectangle. Recalling the formula for the area of a rectangle ($Area = Length \times Width$) may help you see a shorter path to the solution here. Rather than set up a complicated system of equations, remember that the property is 76 square meters in size. Since you're looking for the shorter side, you're looking for the smaller number that, when multiplied by a larger number, yields 76. You can immediately eliminate 9, 18, and 23 as possible answers, since multiplying any of those numbers by something larger than itself will give a result bigger than 76. Out of the two remaining choices, 4 divides evenly into 76. If the shorter sides measure 4, the larger sides would measure 19. And if the dimensions of the rectangle are 4 and 19, then the perimeter does equal 46. Therefore, choice **(A)** is correct.

This isn't to say that all questions are amenable to such amazing shortcuts. But it is true that almost every question on the Quantitative section of the GMAT could be solved using more than one approach. The time constraints on the GMAT are designed to reward those test takers who, through Critical Thinking and practice, have honed their ability to identify and execute the most efficient approach to every problem they might see on Test Day.

PATTERN RECOGNITION

Most people fail to appreciate the level of constraint that standardization places on test makers. Because the test makers must give reliable, valid, and comparable scores to many thousands of students each year, they're forced to reward the same skills on every test. They do so by repeating the same kinds of questions with the same traps and pitfalls, which are susceptible to the same strategic solutions.

Inexperienced test takers treat every problem as if it were a brand-new task, whereas the GMAT rewards those who spot the patterns and use them to their advantage. Of course Pattern Recognition is a key business skill in its own right: executives who recognize familiar situations and apply proven solutions to them will outperform those who reinvent the wheel every time.

Even the smartest test taker will struggle if she approaches each GMAT question as a novel exercise. But the GMAT features nothing novel—just repeated patterns. Kaplan knows this test inside and out, and we'll show you which patterns you will encounter on Test Day. You will know the test better than your competition does. Let's see how to apply the GMAT Core Competency of Pattern Recognition to a sample Problem Solving question:

2. If $x > 7$, which of the following is equal to $\dfrac{x^2 + 8x + 16}{x^2 - 16}$?

- ○ $\dfrac{x + 4}{4(x - 4)}$

- ○ $\dfrac{x - 4}{x + 4}$

- ○ $\dfrac{x - 2}{x + 4}$

- ○ $\dfrac{x + 4}{x - 4}$

- ○ $\dfrac{x - 8}{x - 4}$

This question features one of the many patterns that is repeated over and over in the Quantitative section. The Kaplan-trained test taker looks at this problem and sees two "classic quadratics": the square of a binomial in the numerator and the difference of squares in the denominator. Factoring these expressions allows you to rewrite them as follows:

$$\frac{(x + 4)(x + 4)}{(x + 4)(x - 4)}$$

You can then cancel an $(x + 4)$ on the top and bottom and choose the correct answer, choice **(D)**. As you practice with more and more GMAT questions, stay attuned to patterns you see; certain math concepts appear regularly enough on the GMAT to warrant memorization.

PARAPHRASING

The third Core Competency is Paraphrasing: the GMAT rewards those who can reduce difficult, abstract, or polysyllabic prose to simple terms. Paraphrasing is, of course, an essential business skill: executives must be able to define clear tasks based on complicated requirements and accurately summarize mountains of detail.

In the Quantitative section of the GMAT, you will often be asked to paraphrase English as "math" or to simplify complicated equations using arithmetic or algebraic properties. Let's see how to apply the GMAT Core Competency of Paraphrasing to a sample Problem Solving question:

3. A basketball team plays games only against the other five teams in its league and always in the following order: Croton, Darby, Englewood, Fiennes, and Garvin. If the team's final game of the season is against Fiennes, which of the following could be the number of games in the team's schedule?

    ○   18
    ○   24
    ○   56
    ○   72
    ○   81

Rather than become intimidated by the complicated wording of this question, a smart test taker will ask, "How might I rephrase this question more simply?" A good paraphrase looks something like this: a team plays five other teams over and over in the same order, but the season stops at Fiennes. This is the fourth game of the sequence; what could the total number of games be?

With this paraphrase in hand, it's time to employ some Critical Thinking. Suppose the team plays a full round, and the next round is interrupted after the fourth game—what will the total number of games be? $5 + 4 = 9$. Suppose there are two full rounds before the interruption? $5 + 5 + 4 = 14$. Three rounds? $5 + 5 + 5 + 4 = 19$. Thinking through these scenarios causes the pattern to emerge: the answer must end in 4 or 9. The correct choice is **(B)**, which represents four full rounds plus a set of four games ending with Fiennes.

Notice how this convoluted word problem becomes manageable once paraphrased. Putting GMAT prose into your own words helps you get a handle on the situation being described and know what to do next.

ATTENTION TO THE RIGHT DETAIL

Details present a dilemma: missing them can cost you points. But if you try to absorb every fact in a complicated word problem all at once, you may find yourself swamped, delayed, and still unable to determine the best approach, because you haven't sorted through the information to determine what's most important. Throughout this book, you will learn how to discern the essential details from those that can slow you down or confuse you. The GMAT test makers reward examinees for paying attention to "the right details"—the ones that make the difference between right and wrong answers.

Attention to the Right Detail distinguishes great administrators from poor ones in the business world as well. Just ask anyone who's had a boss who had the wrong priorities or who was so bogged down in minutiae that the department stopped functioning.

Not all details are created equal, and there are mountains of them on the test. Learn to target only what will turn into correct answers. Let's see how to apply the GMAT Core Competency of Attention to the Right Detail to a sample Problem Solving question:

4. A drought decreased the amount of water in city X's reservoirs from 118 million gallons to 96 million gallons. If the reservoirs were at 79 percent of total capacity before the drought began, approximately how many million gallons were the reservoirs below total capacity after the drought?

    ○ 67
    ○ 58
    ○ 54
    ○ 46
    ○ 32

There are a lot of words in this problem, but there's one that's more important than all the others. Recognizing the word "approximately" is crucial to being able to take a strategic approach to this question.

Attention to the Right Detail on the Quantitative section also means defining precisely what the question is asking you to solve for. Here you need the current (post-drought) difference between capacity and holdings. Identifying up front what you need to solve for is important on the GMAT because the answer choices will often include options that represent "the right answer to the wrong question": the value you might come up with if you did all the math correctly but solved accidentally for a different unknown in the problem (for instance, the number of gallons below capacity the reservoir was *before* the drought).

This question gives information on the pre- and post-drought holdings, as well as on the pre-drought percentage of capacity. Use that info to approximate the current shortage. To start, figure out the total capacity before the drought. You know that 118 million was 79 percent of capacity. Because approximation is perfectly fine in this case, you can round these numbers to 120 million and 80 percent, respectively, to make the math easier. Then use the percent formula:

$$120 = 0.80(\text{Total capacity})$$
$$120 = \frac{4}{5}(\text{Total capacity})$$
$$120\left(\frac{5}{4}\right) = \text{Total capacity}$$
$$150 = \text{Total capacity}$$

The question states that the current volume is 96 million gallons, which is 54 million gallons under capacity. Choice **(C)** is correct.

Think of how much time you saved by noticing that the question asked for an approximate value, thereby allowing you to avoid precise calculation with unwieldy numbers. Moreover, Attention to the Right Detail ensured that you did not select a trap answer choice: if you had accidentally solved for the total capacity and then subtracted 118 (the amount of water originally in the reservoir), you would have selected incorrect choice **(E)**.

CHAPTER 10

Problem Solving

George's drawer has 10 loose black socks, 15 loose blue socks, and 8 loose white socks. If George takes socks out of the drawer at random, how many would he need to take out to be sure that the removed socks include at least one matching pair?

○ 3

○ 4

○ 9

○ 15

○ 31

Above is a typical Problem Solving question. In this chapter, we'll look at how to apply the Kaplan Method to this question, discuss the math concepts being tested, and go over the basic principles and strategies that you want to keep in mind on every Problem Solving question. But before you move on, take a minute to think about what you see in this question and answer some questions about how you think it works:

- What mathematical concepts are being tested in this question?

- How is this different from a typical math question you may have seen in high school?

- How can you use the answer choices to your advantage?

- What GMAT Core Competencies are most essential to success on this question?

PREVIEWING PROBLEM SOLVING

WHAT MATHEMATICAL CONCEPTS ARE BEING TESTED IN THIS QUESTION?

At first, this question appears to be setting up a situation involving probability. George is randomly selecting socks from a drawer whose contents are described in the question. But then the question takes an unexpected turn—rather than asking for the probability of choosing a certain combination of socks, it instead asks for the minimum number of socks George would need to draw in order to be sure of having a matching pair. There's no formula to follow here or algebraic equation to solve. This question is testing your ability to reason through the situation and choose the correct answer.

Problem Solving questions test basic math skills and an understanding of some elementary mathematical concepts—ones such as algebra, arithmetic, and geometry that most U.S. students have learned by 10th grade. Most importantly, they test the ability to reason quantitatively. All GMAT Quantitative questions depend at least as much on logical analysis as on math skills. Most rely more on logic than on math. Some, like this one, rely purely on logic and require no math skills beyond the ability to count.

Think about it this way: if business schools wanted to know how much math you knew, they could easily look at your college transcript to see what math classes you took and how you fared in them. So why require the GMAT? Because they want to look at something else. In business school, you will be given *a lot* of information, especially in the form of case studies. One of the biggest challenges you'll face will be figuring out how to think about all that information—deciding how it fits together, what deductions you can make from it, and how it pertains to business challenges.

So the Quantitative section presents you with microcosms of that task—mathematical puzzles in which the data are often presented in a confusing or misleading way, demanding that you first figure out how you can solve the puzzles before beginning any calculations. Hence the name "Problem Solving" instead of just "Math."

The most advanced questions rarely involve math that is much more difficult than the math used in intermediate-range questions. Rather, the task of analyzing the problem to figure out what math to use becomes harder.

HOW IS THIS DIFFERENT FROM A TYPICAL MATH QUESTION YOU MAY HAVE SEEN IN HIGH SCHOOL?

Besides the emphasis on logic mentioned above, there's another important characteristic of GMAT Problem Solving that distinguishes it from the math you have likely been required to do on exams throughout your educational career: all that the GMAT requires is that you choose the correct answer. There's no math teacher looking over your shoulder to verify that you are completing each step precisely and showing your work fully. There is no extra or partial credit for finding a mathematically elegant solution. It may seem obvious, but it bears emphasizing: the sole goal on a Problem Solving question is getting the question correct and earning your points.

What that means for the savvy test taker is that a range of paths to the solution are available. Of course, you can do the straightforward math, but you can also use other strategies such as the ones you will learn in this chapter. The value of a strategic approach is that you can often get to the answer more quickly and accurately than if you had relied on classroom math.

The challenge is that the classroom math approach has probably been so impressed upon you throughout school that you are likely to favor that approach automatically, even when it's not the best way to a solution. So as you practice, one of the best things you can do for your ultimate success on Test Day is get into the habit of Critical Thinking: always ask yourself what approaches are available to you and which one will work best on that particular question. Since the GMAT is a timed test and the adaptive format ensures that you will see questions you will find difficult, finding opportunities to increase your efficiency is of paramount importance to your score.

How Can You Use the Answer Choices to Your Advantage?

One of the big advantages you have on Problem Solving questions is the presence of the five answer choices, one of which *must* be correct. Especially when those answers are simple numbers, as they are in this question, you can often find your way to the correct answer by plugging the answer choices back into the situation described in the problem to see which one works. This is a strategy called backsolving, and you will learn later in this chapter how to apply it.

In this question, you can't literally substitute the answer choices back into the problem, since there's very little math to do here. But in this case, you can use the answer choices to help think through the basic scenario you are given. For instance, try choice **(A)** on for size: if George has three types of sock, is he guaranteed to pull out a matching pair when he draws only three socks? No, of course not; he could end up drawing one sock of each color. At the other end of the spectrum, what about choice **(E)**? If he pulls out 31 of his 33 socks, will he end up with a matching pair? Surely he will; in fact, he'll have many matching pairs. So the correct answer will be smaller than 31. If you aren't sure at first how to approach a question, thinking through the answer choices you are given will often guide you toward a game plan.

What GMAT Core Competencies Are Most Essential to Success on This Question?

The first step of the Kaplan Method for Problem Solving is to analyze the question. This analysis up front helps you find the most efficient approach to the question.

Attention to the Right Detail comes into play in Step 2 of the Method when you identify the task that the question requires of you. It's all too easy to be in a hurry and solve for a value other than what the question asks for. The GMAT test makers know this and include such trap answers among the answer choices.

Pattern Recognition is essential to determining what math topic a question is testing and recognizing what formulas or rules will get you to the answer. Since the GMAT structures questions similarly from test to test, you'll become familiar with the common tasks and traps as you practice. Remember that the goal of your practice is never simply to find the correct answer. You won't see your practice questions on Test Day, but you will likely see questions very similar to them; if you keep your eyes open to patterns, you will feel prepared for any question the GMAT can throw at you.

Finally, you will benefit from Paraphrasing the information given to you by Problem Solving questions. Sometimes the given information is complicated or presented in a less-than-helpful order. Other times, the information is in the form of a word problem that must be "translated" into math. In all cases, you will distill the given information into scratchwork, which should be simple, accurate, and well organized.

Here are the main topics we'll cover in this chapter:

- Question Format and Structure
- The Kaplan Method for Problem Solving
- The Basic Principles of Problem Solving
- Problem Solving Strategy
  - Picking Numbers
  - Backsolving
  - Strategic Guessing

QUESTION FORMAT AND STRUCTURE

The instructions for the Problem Solving questions look like this:

Directions: Solve the problems and choose the best answer.

Note: Unless otherwise indicated, the figures accompanying questions have been drawn as accurately as possible and may be used as sources of information for answering the questions.

All figures lie in a plane except where noted.

All numbers used are real numbers.

There are about 17 Problem Solving questions on each GMAT Quantitative section. Happily, the format of the questions is simple enough: each Problem Solving question consists of the question stem—which gives you information and defines your task—and five answer choices. To answer a question, select the choice that correctly answers the question.

The directions indicate that some diagrams on the GMAT are drawn to scale, which means that you can use them to estimate measurements and size relationships. Other diagrams are labeled "Not drawn to scale," so you can't eyeball them. In fact, when a diagram says "Not drawn to scale," working past the confusing picture is often the key to the problem.

The directions also let you know that you won't have to deal with imaginary numbers, such as $\sqrt{-1}$, and that you'll be dealing with flat figures, such as squares and circles, unless a particular question says otherwise.

THE KAPLAN METHOD FOR PROBLEM SOLVING

Now that you've seen how Problem Solving questions are constructed, let's look at how to handle them. Kaplan has developed a Method for Problem Solving that you can use to attack each and every question of this type.

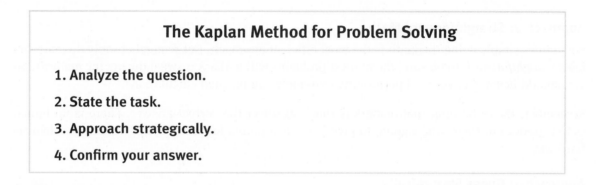

The Kaplan Method for Problem Solving

1. Analyze the question.

2. State the task.

3. Approach strategically.

4. Confirm your answer.

STEP 1: ANALYZE THE QUESTION

Begin your analysis of the problem by getting an overview. If it's a word problem, what's the basic situation? Or is this an algebra problem? An overlapping sets problem? A permutations problem? Getting a general idea of what's going on will help you to organize your thinking and know which rules or formulas you'll have to use.

If there's anything that can be quickly simplified, do so—but don't start solving yet. For example, if a question stem gives you the classic quadratic $x^2 - y^2 = 64$, it would be fine to rewrite it immediately in your scratchwork as $(x + y)(x - y) = 64$. But you wouldn't want to start solving for values just yet; doing so would likely cause you to miss an important aspect of the problem or to overlook an efficient alternative solution.

Also, make sure to glance at the answer choices. Can they help you choose an approach? If they are variable expressions, you can use picking numbers (a strategy we'll cover later in this chapter). If they are widely spread, you can estimate. If they are numerical values, you might be able to plug them back into the question, a strategy we call backsolving. Looking at the choices may trigger an important strategic insight for you.

STEP 2: STATE THE TASK

Before you choose your approach, make sure you know what you're solving for. The most common wrong answer trap in Problem Solving is the right answer—but to the wrong question. And perhaps you won't have to do as much work as you might think—you may be able to solve for what you need without calculating the value of every single variable involved in the problem.

STEP 3: APPROACH STRATEGICALLY

The operative word here is *strategically*. Resist the temptation to hammer away at the problem, hoping for something to work. Use your analysis from Steps 1 and 2 to find the most straightforward approach that allows you to make sense of the problem.

There is rarely a single "right approach." Choose the easiest for you given the current problem. Broadly speaking, there are three basic approaches.

Approach 1: A Kaplan Strategy

Frequently there will be a more efficient strategic approach to the math for those who analyze the problem carefully. Consider picking numbers or backsolving, which you will learn about later in this chapter. These approaches can simplify some tough problems and should always be on your mind as possible alternatives.

Approach 2: Straightforward Math

Sometimes simply doing the math is the most efficient approach. But remember, only do math that feels *straightforward*. To be sure, the hardest problems will make you sweat during the *analysis*, but you should never find yourself performing extremely complicated calculations.

Remember, the only thing that matters is that you select the correct answer. There is no human GMAT grader out there who's going to give you extra points for working out a math problem the hard way.

Approach 3: Guess Strategically

If you notice that estimation or simple logic will get you the answer, use those guessing techniques. They will often be faster than doing the math. If you have spent 60 to 90 seconds analyzing the problem and still haven't found a straightforward path to a solution, make a guess. You only have an average of 2 minutes per question, so you need to keep moving.

And if you have fallen behind pace, you need to guess strategically to get back on track. Hunt actively for good guessing situations and guess quickly on them (within 20–30 seconds). Don't wait until you fall so far behind that you are forced into random guesses or forced to guess on questions that you could otherwise have easily solved. Never try to make up time by rushing!

STEP 4: CONFIRM YOUR ANSWER

Because the GMAT is adaptive, you aren't able to return to questions you've already seen to check your work, so you need to build that step into your process on each question. The most efficient way to do this is to reread the question stem as you select your answer. If you notice a wrinkle in the problem that you missed earlier, you should redo the problem (if you have time) or change your answer. If you got everything right the first time, move on to the next problem with confidence.

Now, let's apply the Kaplan Method for Problem Solving to the question you saw at the beginning of this chapter:

> George's drawer has 10 loose black socks, 15 loose blue socks, and 8 loose white socks. If George takes socks out of the drawer at random, how many would he need to take out to be sure that the removed socks include at least one matching pair?
>
> ○   3
> ○   4
> ○   9
> ○   15
> ○   31

Step 1: Analyze the Question

George has a bunch of unpaired socks and is pulling them out at random. This doesn't sound like the best way to get dressed, but that's the situation the question gives you.

Step 2: State the Task

What's the smallest number of socks George has to remove to be sure of getting a matching pair? In other words, how many socks does George need to pick before he is guaranteed to have 2 matching socks? The question doesn't specify which color, so any matching color will do.

Step 3: Approach Strategically

There's no equation to set up here. Despite the fact that the question starts off sounding like a probability question, you're not asked to calculate probabilities directly.

So think logically. Obviously, George can't have a matching pair of socks if he only removes 1 sock. You need at least 2 for a pair. So what if George removes 2 socks? He *could* get a pair, of course; there's nothing stopping him from randomly drawing, for example, 2 blue socks. But he also *could* get an unmatched pair—1 blue and 1 black, perhaps—so removing 2 socks doesn't *guarantee* a matching pair.

What if he takes 3 socks? Again, he *could* match a color—1 blue and 2 whites, for example. But could he still have no match with 3 socks? Yes, as it's possible (and happily you are not asked to calculate exactly *how* possible) for him to get 1 of each color—1 white, 1 blue, and 1 black.

But after that, he's guaranteed to match 1 of the colors. After all, there are only 3 colors. So even if he didn't have a match after taking out 3 (1 white, 1 blue, and 1 black), he's guaranteed to have a pair when he selects a 4th sock. You can't know whether that pair will be white, blue, or black, but the question didn't ask you to get a specific color...any one will do. The correct answer is **(B)**.

Step 4: Confirm Your Answer

Reread the question stem, making sure that you didn't miss anything about the problem or give the right answer to the wrong question—a common GMAT trap. For example, **(E)** is what you would have selected if you solved for the total number of socks minus 1 pair.

TAKEAWAYS: THE KAPLAN METHOD FOR PROBLEM SOLVING

- The Kaplan Method is a tested, proven way to approach Problem Solving questions consistently, efficiently, and confidently.
- Through practice, the Kaplan Method will become second nature by Test Day.
- Always be on the lookout for the most strategic approach; some Problem Solving questions require more logical analysis than mathematical calculation.

PRACTICE SET: THE KAPLAN METHOD FOR PROBLEM SOLVING

1. Youssef lives x blocks from his office. It takes him 1 minute per block to walk to work and 20 seconds per block to ride his bicycle to work. If it takes him exactly 10 minutes more to walk to work than to ride his bicycle, then x equals

    ◯ 4
    ◯ 7
    ◯ 10
    ◯ 15
    ◯ 20

2. A book club rented the party room of a local restaurant to meet and discuss its current novel over dinner. The total charge, including food and service, was $867.50. If each member of the club paid at least $42, then what is the greatest possible number of members in the club?

    ◯ 19
    ◯ 20
    ◯ 21
    ◯ 23
    ◯ 25

3. A machine manufactures notebooks in a series of five colors: red, blue, black, white, and yellow. After producing a notebook of one color from that series, it produces a notebook of the next color. Once five are produced, the machine repeats the same pattern. If the machine began a day producing a red notebook and completed the day by producing a black notebook, how many notebooks could have been produced that day?

    ◯ 27
    ◯ 34
    ◯ 50
    ◯ 61
    ◯ 78

THE BASIC PRINCIPLES OF PROBLEM SOLVING

By adopting a methodical approach to Problem Solving, you will have a clear, strategic way to think through your way to a response. You won't waste time by attacking a question in a tentative or haphazard manner, nor will you get stuck doing inefficient math. A systematic approach will ensure that you find the most efficient solution to the problem and that you make as few careless and unnecessary errors as possible. Here are some ways you can optimize your Problem Solving performance by employing the Method in conjunction with the Core Competencies.

ANALYZE AND SIMPLIFY BEFORE SOLVING

The biggest mistake test takers make on GMAT Problem Solving is doing the math right after reading the problem (or even more dangerously, *while* still reading the problem). Problem Solving questions are written to be confusing, and the approach that the question might seem to be talking you into may not be the most efficient. Consider this problem:

> At a certain diner, Joe ordered 3 doughnuts and a cup of coffee and was charged $2.25. Stella ordered 2 doughnuts and a cup of coffee and was charged $1.70. What is the price of 2 doughnuts?
>
> ○ $0.55
> ○ $1.00
> ○ $1.10
> ○ $1.30
> ○ $1.80

If you started doing math right away, you might immediately jot down something like $J = 3d + c$, thereby making the problem a lot tougher by introducing a variable, J, that really doesn't need to be part of the solution. If you used x and y instead of d and c, you would make your job even harder, as a part of your brain that could be used to solve the problem would be taken up remembering whether x stood for doughnuts or coffee.

However, if you analyzed the question before getting into math, you would realize that the orders are very similar. In fact, they differ by only 1 doughnut. So the price of a doughnut could be calculated simply by subtracting the prices of the orders. Instead of wasting time writing out $S = 2d + c$, you have almost completely solved the problem. Time invested in analysis usually pays off in a much more efficient solution and in less time spent on the question overall.

Here's another example of the benefit of analysis and simplification:

> What is the product of all the possible values of x if $x^2(x + 2) + 7x(x + 2) + 6(x + 2) = 0$?
>
> ○ −29
> ○ −12
> ○ 12
> ○ 29
> ○ 168

If you did math before any analysis, you'd distribute the multiplication and get $x^3 + 9x^2 + 20x + 12 = 0$. You might then be stuck not knowing what to do next to simplify this equation.

But if you analyzed first, you'd realize that distribution would lead to a complicated cubic equation. Looking for an easier way, you might notice that if the multiple occurrences of $(x + 2)$ were gone, you'd have a normal quadratic. You could factor out the occurrences of $(x + 2)$ and be on your way to solving:

$$x^2(x+2) + 7x(x+2) + 6(x+2) = 0$$

Factor: $$(x+2)(x^2+7x+6) = 0$$

Reverse-FOIL: $$(x+2)(x+6)(x+1) = 0$$

Solve for x: $$x = -2 \text{ or } -6 \text{ or } -1$$

Multiply: $$-2 \times -6 \times -1 = -12$$

FOCUS ON WHAT'S ASKED

Go back to the problem with the doughnuts and the coffee. Did you spot the trap? The question doesn't ask for the price of a doughnut but rather for the price of *two* doughnuts. Sure enough, one of the answer choices gives the cost of only one.

Focusing on what's asked will also help you to choose an efficient approach. Consider this question:

> If $4x + y = 8$ and $y - 3x = 7$, then what is the value of $x + 2y$?
>
> ○ $\dfrac{1}{7}$
>
> ○ 3
>
> ○ 15
>
> ○ $\dfrac{52}{7}$
>
> ○ $\dfrac{60}{7}$

You might just rush into solving for x and y and then plug them in, but focus on what you are being asked for: not x or y individually but rather $x + 2y$. How could you solve for *that*? Looking at the equations, you might notice that one equation has $4x$ and the other $-3x$, and together, that's x. Each has one y, so together you have $2y$. You can add the equations together.

Rearrange $y - 3x = 7$ to $-3x + y = 7$ so things line up nicely. Then combine the equations:

$$
\begin{aligned}
4x + y &= 8 \\
+[-3x + y &= 7] \\
\hline
x + 2y &= 15
\end{aligned}
$$

In the end, the math was quick because you focused on what the question asked.

Note that in this question, answer choices **(A)** and **(D)** represent the values of the individual variables. Right answers to the wrong questions are the most common wrong answer type in Problem Solving, so it pays to define the task in Step 2 of the Kaplan Method.

CONSIDER ALTERNATIVE APPROACHES

You just saw three questions that were all most easily solved in a manner other than the math that might first occur to you. You added equations in the $x + 2y$ problem, factored instead of multiplied in the $(x + 2)$ problem, and realized that all you needed to do on the diner problem was find the difference in cost between the two orders.

The takeaway from these examples: it pays to *think* about what you're doing before diving into math. Most problems can be solved many different ways, some easy and some not so easy. The GMAT test maker writes the questions in such a way that the first approaches that occur to you are usually of the not-so-easy variety. So turn the problem over in your mind until you find an approach that will work. Trust your intuition—if you're thinking of a solution that involves lots of difficult math, then look for a different approach.

Here's how you might approach a more difficult question, considering different approaches until you find one that works:

$$\begin{array}{r} AB \\ +BA \\ \hline 121 \end{array}$$

In the addition problem above, *A* and *B* represent digits in two different two-digit numbers. What is the sum of *A* and *B*?

- ○ 6
- ○ 8
- ○ 9
- ○ 11
- ○ 14

This question may seem intimidating, so approach it calmly and methodically. Start as always by analyzing the question stem. You are told that *A* and *B* represent digits in two different two-digit numbers. Recall that a digit is any of the integers 0 through 9 and that a two-digit number is a number that has digits in the tens place and the units place, like 42 or 11. This means that *AB* is a two-digit number with *A* in the tens place and *B* in the units place. For example, if *A* is 3 and *B* is 5, then *AB* is 35.

Now, how do you solve for *A* and *B*? You could just experiment with different possibilities, plugging different combinations of digits in until you get $AB + BA = 121$. But since there are 10 digits, there'd be something like 100 different possible combinations. You don't have time for that. And, you know that when you find yourself beginning a drawn-out, tedious process like this, there's usually an easier way to solve the problem.

This is where Critical Thinking can help. You know that you can sometimes solve for an expression without figuring out the individual variables. The sum of *A* and *B* is $A + B$, and that is in fact what you are being asked to solve for. Look back at the question stem, and see if you can find $A + B$:

$$
\begin{array}{r}
AB \\
+BA \\
\hline
121
\end{array}
$$

$A + B$ is the sum of the digits in the tens place. Is the answer 12? You know that it can't be, because 12 isn't an answer choice. It's possible that the $A + B$ in the tens column is getting spillover from the $B + A$ in the units column, which would mean $A + B$ is less than 12, but you can't know the amount. At the very least, though, you've established that choice **(E)** is too large, since the answer is either 12 or something less.

By now, or before now, you've realized that $B + A$ is the same as $A + B$. So the answer is also the sum of the digits in the units places:

$$
\begin{array}{r}
AB \\
+BA \\
\hline
121
\end{array}
$$

So the units digit of the answer has to be 1. Having recognized this pattern, you can look at the answer choices and see that only **(D)** has a 1 in the units place. The answer has to be **(D)**.

Note that you didn't need the exact values of A and B to solve this problem. In fact, many different pairs of digits would satisfy this equation.

Don't be put off by the challenging presentation of a problem, even when you're not sure at first how you're going to solve it. As with this problem, separate what you know from what you don't, so you don't feel overwhelmed. Always consider multiple possible approaches, reevaluating them if they get too hard to follow or seem not to be working. Use what you know about the GMAT to help you, and look everywhere for clues to the solution—both in the question stem and in the answer choices.

APPLYING THE KAPLAN METHOD: THE BASIC PRINCIPLES OF PROBLEM SOLVING

Now let's use the Kaplan Method and the strategic principles of Problem Solving to answer a sample question:

In a certain town, there are four times as many people who were born in the town's state as there are people who were born in another state or country. The ratio of those residents born in the town's state to the town's total population is

○ 1 to 4
○ 1 to 3
○ 1 to 2
○ 3 to 4
○ 4 to 5

Step 1: Analyze the Question

The phrase "total population" near the end of the question stem should stand out as key. One of the classic tricks used by the GMAT test makers is to give you a part-to-part ratio and ask for an answer expressed as a part-to-whole ratio.

Step 2: State the Task

You need to use the ratio of those born in state to those born out of state to determine the ratio of those born in state to the total population.

Step 3: Approach Strategically

Having four times as many people born in state as out of state means a ratio of 4:1. You are looking for the ratio of those born in the state to the total. You are told that 4 is the part of the ratio for those who were born in the state. You can find the total by adding the two parts, in state (4) and out of state (1), getting 5. The part-to-whole ratio is then 4:5, choice **(E)**.

Step 4: Confirm Your Answer

A good natural-language paraphrase of the information is "Four of every five residents were born in-state." That matches choice **(E)**. You need to avoid traps that restate or distort the part-to-part information. Be wary of answer choice **(A)**, which is just a distortion of the original ratio.

TAKEAWAY: THE BASIC PRINCIPLES OF PROBLEM SOLVING

- Most GMAT word problems do not present the information in the most straightforward way. You will need to read strategically to understand the problem.
- Focusing on the question first
  - helps you understand what to look for in the problem.
  - allows you to avoid solving for "the right answer to the wrong question"—a common GMAT mistake.

PRACTICE SET: THE BASIC PRINCIPLES OF PROBLEM SOLVING

4. A team won 50 percent of its first 60 games in a particular season and 80 percent of its remaining games. If the team won a total of 60 percent of its games that season, what was the total number of games that the team played?

   ○   180

   ○   120

   ○   90

   ○   85

   ○   30

5. A local restaurant recently renovated its dining space, purchasing new tables and chairs to use in addition to the original tables and chairs. The new tables each seat 6 customers, while the original tables each seat 4 customers. Altogether, the restaurant now has 40 tables and is capable of seating 220 customers. How many more new tables than original tables does the restaurant have?

   ○   10

   ○   20

   ○   30

   ○   34

   ○   36

PROBLEM SOLVING STRATEGY

In the previous section, you learned about the attitude that all great GMAT test takers share: that there must be a straightforward way to solve and there's no need to panic if you don't find it right away. And even if you don't use the algebra-based approach that your high school math teacher would have preferred, you will get the right answer and you will raise your score.

Identifying a more efficient alternative approach involves staying open to possibilities that might not occur to you immediately. Two such approaches—picking numbers and backsolving—are so straightforward, can eliminate so much math, and can be used so often that they deserve special mention.

PICKING NUMBERS

Picking numbers is a powerful alternative to solving problems by brute force. Rather than trying to work with unknown variables, you pick concrete values for the variables. In essence, you're transforming algebra or abstract math rules into basic arithmetic, giving yourself a much simpler task. Pick numbers to stand in for the variables or unknowns.

How does picking numbers work?

- Pick **permissible** numbers. Some problems have explicit rules such as "x is odd." Other problems have implicit rules. For example, if a word problem says, "Betty is five years older than Tim," don't pick $b = -2$ and $t = -7$; these numbers wouldn't work in the problem.
- Pick **manageable** numbers. Some numbers are simply easier to work with than others. $d = 2$ will probably be a more successful choice than will $d = 492\sqrt{\pi}$, for example. The problems themselves will tell you what's manageable. For instance, $d = 2$ wouldn't be a great pick if an answer choice were $\frac{d}{12}$. (The number 12, 24, or even 120 would be much better in that case, since each is divisible by 12.)
- Once you've picked numbers to substitute for unknowns, approach the problem as basic arithmetic instead of algebra or number properties.
- Test every answer choice—sometimes certain numbers will yield a "false positive" in which a wrong answer looks right. If you get more than one "right answer," just pick a new set of numbers. The truly correct answer must work for all permissible numbers.

Note that it's just fine to pick the numbers 0 or 1 for most questions. True, the special properties of 0 and 1 do sometimes cause "false positives," but so do other numbers. The GMAT sometimes writes questions based on those special properties, so if you aren't considering 0 and 1, you won't get the right answer to those questions. Furthermore, they are the most manageable numbers in all of math. Imagine picking numbers for the following problem with anything other than $b = 0$ or $b = 1$:

$$7^b + 7^b + 7^b + 7^b + 7^b + 7^b + 7^b =$$

- 7^b
- 7^{b+1}
- 7^{7b}
- 8^b
- 49^b

The occasional inconvenience of repicking numbers is far outweighed by the advantages that 0 and 1 provide.

Picking $b = 1$:

$$= 7^b + 7^b + 7^b + 7^b + 7^b + 7^b + 7^b$$
$$= 7^1 + 7^1 + 7^1 + 7^1 + 7^1 + 7^1 + 7^1$$
$$= 7 + 7 + 7 + 7 + 7 + 7 + 7$$
$$= 49$$

Plugging $b = 1$ into the answer choices yields

(A) $7^b = 7^1 = 7$

(B) $7^{b+1} = 7^{1+1} = 7^2 = 49$

(C) $7^{7b} = 7^7$ Whatever that is, it's a lot bigger than 49.

(D) $8^b = 8^1 = 8$

(E) $49^b = 49^1 = 49$

Two answer choices match the desired result of 49, so you need to pick a new number. Try $b = 0$. First, plug it into the stem.

$$= 7^b + 7^b + 7^b + 7^b + 7^b + 7^b + 7^b$$
$$= 7^0 + 7^0 + 7^0 + 7^0 + 7^0 + 7^0 + 7^0$$
$$= 1 + 1 + 1 + 1 + 1 + 1 + 1$$
$$= 7$$

Now you only need to plug $b = 0$ into **(B)** and **(E)**, the only two answer choices that worked when $b = 1$. Doing so yields

(B) $7^{b+1} = 7^{0+1} = 7^1 = 7$

(E) $49^b = 49^0 = 1$

The answer is **(B)**.

PICKING NUMBERS

There are four signals that picking numbers will be a possible approach to the problem:

1. Variables in the Question Stem
2. Percents in the Answer Choices
3. Variables in the Answer Choices
4. Must Be/Could Be/Cannot Be

These aren't in any particular order. You'll see many instances of each case on Test Day. We'll start with the first.

PICKING NUMBERS WITH VARIABLES IN THE QUESTION STEM

If you see a question that has variables in the question stem or asks about a fraction of an unknown whole, pick numbers to represent the unknown(s) in the question stem and walk through the arithmetic of the problem. Look in the question stem and the answer choices for clues about what the most manageable numbers might be.

Example:

> Carol spends $\frac{1}{4}$ of her savings on a stereo and $\frac{1}{3}$ less than she spent on the stereo for a television. What fraction of her savings did she spend on the stereo and television?

> ○ $\frac{1}{4}$
>
> ○ $\frac{2}{7}$
>
> ○ $\frac{5}{12}$
>
> ○ $\frac{1}{2}$
>
> ○ $\frac{7}{12}$

Lowest common denominators of fractions in the question stem are good choices for numbers to pick. So are numbers that appear frequently as denominators in the answer choices. In this case, the common denominator of the fractions in the stem is 12, so let the number 12 represent Carol's total savings (12 dollars).

That means she spends $\frac{1}{4} \times 12$ dollars, or 3 dollars, on her stereo and $\frac{2}{3} \times 3$ dollars, or 2 dollars, on her television. That comes out to be $3 + 2 = 5$ dollars; that's how much she spent on the stereo and television combined. You're asked what *fraction* of her savings she spent. Because her total savings was 12 dollars, she spent $\frac{5}{12}$ of her savings; **(C)** is correct. Notice how picking a common denominator for the variable (Carol's savings) made it easy to convert each of the fractions $\left(\frac{1}{4} \text{ and } \frac{2}{3} \times \frac{1}{4} \text{ of her savings}\right)$ to a simple integer.

A tricky part of this question is understanding how to determine the price of the television. The television does not cost $\frac{1}{3}$ of her savings. It costs $\frac{1}{3}$ *less* than the stereo; that is, it costs $\frac{2}{3}$ as much as the stereo.

By the way, some of these answers could have been eliminated quickly using basic logic. **(A)** is too small; the stereo alone costs $\frac{1}{4}$ of her savings. **(D)** and **(E)** are too large. The television costs *less* than the stereo, so the two together must cost less than $2 \times \frac{1}{4}$, or half, of Carol's savings. We'll look more at using logic to eliminate answers later in this chapter.

APPLYING THE KAPLAN METHOD: PICKING NUMBERS WITH VARIABLES IN THE QUESTION STEM

Now let's use the Kaplan Method on a Problem Solving question that involves picking numbers with variables in the question stem:

If $w > x > y > z$ on the number line, y is halfway between x and z, and x is halfway between w and z, then $\frac{y-x}{y-w} =$

○ $\frac{1}{4}$

○ $\frac{1}{3}$

○ $\frac{1}{2}$

○ $\frac{3}{4}$

○ 1

Step 1: Analyze the Question

This question presents a very complicated relationship among four variables. Since there are multiple variables in the problem, picking numbers is a possible approach. The answer choices are all numbers, so you won't have to test each answer choice—you'd just plug numbers into the question. Since the phrase *number line* appears, you may want to consider drawing a number line to help visualize the situation:

Step 2: State the Task

The question asks you to evaluate a rather complicated fraction: $\frac{y-x}{y-w}$. The question stem gives you no actual values for the variables, but the answer choices are numbers. This means that the value of the fractional expression must always be the same, as long as the values of the variables follow the rules described in the question stem.

Step 3: Approach Strategically

The math seems like it would be difficult and time-consuming. You'd have to translate each rule that states a relationship between variables into a separate algebraic equation and then somehow combine them to solve for the fraction in the stem. Picking numbers, on the other hand, will be much more straightforward.

The rules are pretty complicated, so pick numbers one at a time, making sure the numbers you pick are permissible (follow the rules in the stem) and manageable (easy to work with). x and z each appear twice in the rules, so starting with those two numbers would seem to make sense.

Let's go with $z = 1$ and $x = 3$ to leave room for y.

y is halfway between 3 and 1, so $y = 2$.

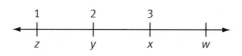

x, or 3, is halfway between w and 1, so $w = 5$.

Once you've picked a set of permissible numbers, it's time to plug these numbers into the expression in the stem:

$$\frac{y-x}{y-w} = \frac{2-3}{2-5} = \frac{-1}{-3} = \frac{1}{3}$$

The answer is **(B)**. Picking numbers can often take you to the correct answer much more directly than algebra.

Step 4: Confirm Your Answer

Look back at the question stem and make sure you understood all the rules and picked permissible numbers. "y is halfway between x and z." Check. "x is halfway between w and z." Check. Another potential error would have been to make w the smallest variable instead of the largest. (Did you notice how the question stem puts w on the left of the inequality statement, even though it belongs on the right-hand side of the number line?) That's another potential mistake you could catch in this step.

TAKEAWAYS: PICKING NUMBERS WITH VARIABLES IN THE QUESTION STEM

- Most people find it easier to perform calculations with numbers than to perform calculations with variables.
- Variables may be letters (n, x, t, etc.) or unspecified values (e.g., "a factory produces some number of units of a product each month").
- When picking numbers, be sure that the numbers are permissible and manageable.

PRACTICE SET: PICKING NUMBERS WITH VARIABLES IN THE QUESTION STEM

6. If $\dfrac{c-a}{c-b} = 2$, then $\dfrac{5b-5a}{c-a} =$

   ○ 0.5

   ○ 1

   ○ 1.5

   ○ 2

   ○ 2.5

7. Company Z spent $\frac{1}{4}$ of its revenues last year on marketing and $\frac{1}{7}$ of the remainder on maintenance of its facilities. What fraction of last year's original revenues did Company Z have left after its marketing and maintenance expenditures?

   ○ $\dfrac{5}{14}$

   ○ $\dfrac{1}{2}$

   ○ $\dfrac{17}{28}$

   ○ $\dfrac{9}{14}$

   ○ $\dfrac{9}{11}$

8. During a sale, a store sells 20 percent of its remaining stock each day, without replenishment. After 4 days, what fraction of its original stock has it sold?

   ○ $\dfrac{1}{625}$

   ○ $\dfrac{256}{625}$

   ○ $\dfrac{61}{125}$

   ○ $\dfrac{64}{125}$

   ○ $\dfrac{369}{625}$

PICKING NUMBERS WITH PERCENTS IN THE ANSWER CHOICES

Picking numbers also works well on Problem Solving questions for which the answer choices are given in percents. When the answers are in percents, 100 will almost always be the most manageable number to pick. Using 100 not only makes your calculations easier, but it also simplifies the task of expressing the final value as a percent of the original.

Example:

> The manufacturer of Sleep-EZ mattresses is offering a 10 percent discount on the price of its king-size mattress. Some retailers are offering additional discounts. If a retailer offers an additional 20 percent discount, then what is the total discount available at that retailer?
>
> ○   10%
> ○   25%
> ○   28%
> ○   30%
> ○   35%

Since the answers are in percents, pick $100 as the original price of the mattress. (Remember, realism is irrelevant—only permissibility and manageability matter.) The manufacturer offers a 10% discount: 10% of $100 is $10. So now the mattress costs $90.

Then the retailer offers an additional 20% discount. Since the price has fallen to $90, that 20% is taken off the $90 price. A 20% discount is now a reduction of $18. The final price of the mattress is $90 − $18, or $72.

The mattress has been reduced to $72 from an original price of $100. That's a $28 reduction. Since you started with $100, you can easily calculate that $28 is 28% of the original price. Choice **(C)** is correct.

Notice that choice **(D)** commits the error of simply adding the two percents given in the question stem. An answer choice like **(D)** will never be correct on a question that gives you information about multiple percent changes.

APPLYING THE KAPLAN METHOD: PICKING NUMBERS WITH PERCENTS IN THE ANSWER CHOICES

Now let's use the Kaplan Method on a Problem Solving question that involves picking numbers with percents in the answer choices:

> In 1998, the profits of Company N were 10 percent of revenues. In 1999, the revenues of Company N fell by 20 percent, but profits were 15 percent of revenues. The profits in 1999 were what percent of the profits in 1998?
>
> ○   80%
> ○   105%
> ○   120%
> ○   124.2%
> ○   138%

Step 1: Analyze the Question

Profits and revenues are both changing over time. Since the answer choices are percents, picking 100 is a good idea.

Step 2: State the Task

The profits in 1999 were what percent of the profits in 1998?

You'll have to compare the profits of the two years. The year 1998 is the basis of the comparison. You're not solving for the increase or decrease, just the relative amount.

In other words, you want this fraction, $\frac{1999 \text{ profits}}{1998 \text{ profits}}$, expressed as a percent.

Step 3: Approach Strategically

You should start with the original profits, since the question presents its 1999 information as a change from the 1998 information. You read this about 1998 profits: "In 1998, the profits of Company N were 10 percent of revenues." So you'll know profits if you know revenues. You're given no information about revenue at all, so just pick a number. Given the percents in the answer choices, pick $100. That makes profits in 1998 equal to $10.

Now, what about 1999 profits? You read, "In 1999...profits were 15% of revenues." So you have to know revenues in 1999 to know profits. What does the question say about 1999's revenues? "In 1999, the revenues of Company N fell by 20 percent." Revenues were $100, so they fell $20 to $80. Profits, then, were 15% of $80, or 0.15($80) = $12.

By the way, you don't have to calculate that directly. You can use Critical Thinking and say:

15% of 80 = 10% of 80 + 5% of 80

15% of 80 = 10% of 80 + half of (10% of 80)

15% of 80 = 8 + half of 8

15% of 80 = 8 + 4

15% of 80 = 12

Plugging your results back into the question yields $\frac{1999 \text{ profits}}{1998 \text{ profits}} = \frac{12}{10} = 1.2$.

Just multiply by 100% to convert to percent: $1.2 \times 100\% = 120\%$. Choice **(C)** is correct.

Step 4: Confirm Your Answer

Make sure to reread the question stem to confirm that you interpreted the relationships correctly.

TAKEAWAYS: PICKING NUMBERS WITH PERCENTS IN THE ANSWER CHOICES

- On a question involving multiple changes in percent, one of the trap answers will most likely involve simply adding or subtracting the percents.
- When you see a percent question with unspecified values, pick 100 for the unknown value. Doing so will make the calculations much easier.

PRACTICE SET: PICKING NUMBERS WITH PERCENTS IN THE ANSWER CHOICES

9. If a bicyclist in motion increases his speed by 30 percent and then increases this speed by 10 percent, what percent of the original speed is the total increase in speed?

    ○   10%
    ○   40%
    ○   43%
    ○   64%
    ○   140%

10. Jane makes toy bears. When she works with an assistant, she makes 80 percent more bears per week and works 10 percent fewer hours each week. Having an assistant increases Jane's output of toy bears per hour by what percent?

    ○   20%
    ○   80%
    ○   100%
    ○   180%
    ○   200%

11. Crystal made a budget for her vacation. If she traveled by plane, airfare would be 40 percent of the total budget, meals and lodging would be 50 percent, and miscellaneous expenses would be 10 percent. If she drove, transportation would cost 10 percent less than flying, and miscellaneous expenses would be the same. If Crystal wanted to travel by car and spend no more in total than if she flew, what is the maximum percentage by which she could increase the budget for meals and lodging?

    ○   4%
    ○   8%
    ○   10%
    ○   12%
    ○   40%

PICKING NUMBERS WITH VARIABLES IN THE ANSWER CHOICES

Whenever the answer choices contain variables, you should consider picking numbers. The correct answer choice is the one that yields the result that you got when you plugged the same number(s) into the question stem. Make sure that you test each answer choice, just in case more than one answer choice produces the desired result. In such a case, you will need to pick a new set of numbers and repeat the process only for the answer choices that worked out the first time.

Example:

If $a > 1$, which of the following is equal to $\dfrac{2a + 6}{a^2 + 2a - 3}$?

- ○ a
- ○ $a + 3$
- ○ $\dfrac{2}{a - 1}$
- ○ $\dfrac{2a}{a - 3}$
- ○ $\dfrac{a - 1}{2}$

The question says that $a > 1$, so the most manageable permissible number will probably be 2. Then $\dfrac{2(2) + 6}{2^2 + 2(2) - 3} = \dfrac{4 + 6}{4 + 4 - 3} = \dfrac{10}{5} = 2$.

Now substitute 2 for a in each answer choice, looking for choices that equal 2 when $a = 2$. Eliminate choices that do not equal 2 when $a = 2$.

Choice **(A)**: $a = 2$. Choice **(A)** is possibly correct.

Choice **(B)**: $a + 3 = 2 + 3 = 5$. This is not 2. Discard.

Choice **(C)**: $\dfrac{2}{a - 1} = \dfrac{2}{2 - 1} = \dfrac{2}{1} = 2$. Possibly correct.

Choice **(D)**: $\dfrac{2a}{a - 3} = \dfrac{2(2)}{2 - 3} = \dfrac{4}{-1} = -4$. This is not 2. Discard.

Choice **(E)**: $\dfrac{a - 1}{2} = \dfrac{2 - 1}{2} = \dfrac{1}{2}$. This is not 2. Discard.

You're down to **(A)** and **(C)**. When more than one answer choice remains, you must pick another number. Try $a = 3$. Then $\dfrac{2(3) + 6}{3^2 + 2(3) - 3} = \dfrac{6 + 6}{9 + 6 - 3} = \dfrac{12}{12} = 1$.

Now work with the remaining answer choices.

Choice **(A)**: $a = 3$. This is not 1. Discard.

Now that all four incorrect answer choices have been eliminated, you know that **(C)** must be correct. Check to see whether it equals 1 when $a = 3$.

Choice **(C)**: $\dfrac{2}{a - 1} = \dfrac{2}{3 - 1} = \dfrac{2}{2} = 1$. Choice **(C)** does equal 1 when $a = 3$.

This approach to picking numbers also applies to many confusing word problems on the GMAT. Picking numbers can resolve a lot of that confusion. The key to picking numbers in word problems is to reread the question stem after you've picked numbers, substituting the numbers in place of the variables.

Example:

> A car rental company charges for mileage as follows: x dollars per mile for the first n miles and $x + 1$ dollars per mile for each mile over n miles. How much will the mileage charge be, in dollars, for a journey of d miles, where $d > n$?
>
> ○ $d(x + 1) - n$
> ○ $xn + d$
> ○ $xn + d(x + 1)$
> ○ $x(n + d) - d$
> ○ $(x + 1)(d - n)$

Suppose that you pick $x = 4$, $n = 3$, and $d = 5$. Now the problem would read like this:

A car rental company charges for mileage as follows: $4 per mile for each of the first 3 miles and $5 per mile for each mile over 3 miles. How much will the mileage charge be, in dollars, for a journey of 5 miles?

All of a sudden, the problem has gotten much more straightforward. The first 3 miles are charged at $4/mile. So that's $4 + $4 + $4, or $12. There are 2 miles remaining, and each one costs $5. So that's $5 + $5, for a total of $10. If the first 3 miles cost $12 and the next 2 cost $10, then the total charge is $12 + $10, which is $22.

Plugging $x = 4$, $n = 3$, and $d = 5$ into the answer choices, you get

(A) $d(x + 1) - n = 5(4 + 1) - 3 = 22$

(B) $xn + d = 4 \times 3 + 5 = 17$

(C) $xn + d(x + 1) = 4 \times 3 + 5(4 + 1) = 37$

(D) $x(n + d) - d = 4(3 + 5) - 5 = 27$

(E) $(x + 1)(d - n) = (4 + 1)(5 - 3) = 10$

Only **(A)** yields the same number you got when you plugged these numbers into the question stem, so **(A)** is the answer. No need for algebra at all.

APPLYING THE KAPLAN METHOD: PICKING NUMBERS WITH VARIABLES IN THE ANSWER CHOICES

Now let's use the Kaplan Method on a Problem Solving question that involves picking numbers with variables in the answer choices:

> Cindy paddles her kayak upstream at m kilometers per hour, and then returns downstream the same distance at n kilometers per hour. How many kilometers upstream did she travel if she spent a total of p hours for the round trip?

○ mnp

○ $\dfrac{mn}{p}$

○ $\dfrac{m + n}{p}$

○ $\dfrac{mnp}{m + n}$

○ $\dfrac{pm}{n} - \dfrac{pn}{m}$

Step 1: Analyze the Question

Cindy is going upstream and then the same distance back downstream. Notice that the answer choices contain variables. Whenever the answer choices have variable(s), consider picking numbers as an approach.

Step 2: State the Task

The question asks, "How many kilometers upstream did she travel if she spent a total of p hours for the round trip?" You're solving not for the total distance of her round trip, just one leg of it.

Step 3: Approach Strategically

It will be hard to pick all the variables at once, so don't try to do so. You can always go one variable at a time. It's often easiest to start with the variable that appears most often, as that value often has the greatest influence over what numbers will be manageable. In this problem, that's the distance upstream (it appears twice, since she goes the same distance downstream). So if you picked that distance to be, say 6 kilometers, you could then easily pick manageable numbers for m and n.

But for the sake of argument, let's say you didn't see that you needed to pick distance. That's OK. If you start by picking two manageable numbers for m and n—for example, $m = 2$ and $n = 3$—then the question becomes this:

> Cindy paddles her kayak upstream at 2 kilometers per hour, and then returns downstream the same distance at 3 kilometers per hour. How many kilometers upstream did she travel if she spent a total of p hours for the round trip?

To figure out the time, you'd need the distance. As none is given, you can pick one. If the speeds are 2 kph and 3 kph, a distance of 6 kilometers works nicely. Now the question is this:

> Cindy paddles her kayak 6 kilometers upstream at 2 kilometers per hour, and then returns downstream 6 kilometers at 3 kilometers per hour. How many kilometers upstream did she travel if she spent a total of p hours for the round trip?

Now the time is very straightforward to calculate. Six kilometers upstream at 2 kilometers per hour means a total of 3 hours. Six kilometers downstream at 3 kilometers per hour means a total of 2 hours. That's $3 + 2 = 5$ hours for the round trip.

Now plug $m = 2$, $n = 3$, and $p = 5$ into the answer choices to see which yields 6 for the number of kilometers traveled upstream.

(A) $mnp = 2 \times 3 \times 5 = 30$. Eliminate.

(B) $\dfrac{mn}{p} = \dfrac{(2 \times 3)}{5} = \dfrac{6}{5}$. Eliminate.

(C) $\dfrac{m+n}{p} = \dfrac{(3+2)}{5} = \dfrac{5}{5} = 1$. Eliminate.

(D) $\dfrac{mnp}{m+n} = \dfrac{(2 \times 3 \times 5)}{(2+3)} = \dfrac{(2 \times 3 \times 5)}{5} = 2 \times 3 = 6$. **(D)** could be right, but you need to test **(E)** to make sure.

(E) $\dfrac{pm}{n} - \dfrac{pn}{m} = \dfrac{5 \times 2}{3} - \dfrac{5 \times 3}{2} = \dfrac{10}{3} - \dfrac{15}{2} = \dfrac{20}{6} - \dfrac{45}{6} = -\dfrac{25}{6}$. Eliminate.

Only choice **(D)** remains, so it is correct.

Step 4: Confirm Your Answer

Make sure to reread the question stem to confirm that you interpreted the information correctly.

Picking numbers can make word problems much easier to understand, so it's important that you don't hastily start writing down equations. Were you to immediately start writing down algebraic equations for this question, you'd wind up with six variables: speed upstream, speed downstream, time upstream, time downstream, distance for each leg of the trip, and total time. That's a lot to deal with. See how picking numbers simplifies things.

TAKEAWAYS: PICKING NUMBERS WITH VARIABLES IN THE ANSWER CHOICES

- Questions with variables in the answer choices comprise the majority of situations in which test takers should consider picking numbers.
- After picking numbers, reread the question stem, substituting your number(s) for the variable(s).
- When picking numbers with variables in the answer choices, check each answer choice to make sure the numbers you picked don't happen to work for more than one choice.
  - Exception: For "could be" questions (e.g., "Which of the following could be odd?"), you can safely choose the first answer choice that works.

PRACTICE SET: PICKING NUMBERS WITH VARIABLES IN THE ANSWER CHOICES

12. If $n \neq 1$, $j \neq 0$, $k \neq 0$, and $m \neq 0$ and if $n = \dfrac{jkm}{jk + jm + km}$, then $\dfrac{1}{n-1} =$

○ $\dfrac{1}{j} + \dfrac{1}{k} + \dfrac{1}{m}$

○ $\dfrac{jk + jm + km}{jkm - jk - jm - km}$

○ $\dfrac{jk + jm + km}{jkm}$

○ $\dfrac{jkm - jk - jm - km}{jk + jm + km}$

○ $j + k + m$

13. The positive difference between Sam and Lucy's ages is a, and the sum of their ages is z. If Lucy is older than Sam, then which of the following represents Lucy's age?

○ $\dfrac{z - a}{2}$

○ $a - \dfrac{z}{2}$

○ $2a + z$

○ $\dfrac{z + a}{2}$

○ $\dfrac{a - z}{2}$

14. In order to fulfill a local school's request for x cakes, B parents agreed to each bake an equal number of cakes. If p of the parents did not bake any cakes, which of the following represents the additional number of cakes that each of the other parents had to bake in order for the school's request for x cakes to be fulfilled?

○ $\dfrac{px}{B}$

○ $\dfrac{px}{B(B - p)}$

○ $\dfrac{x}{B - p}$

○ $\dfrac{p}{B - px}$

○ $\dfrac{p}{B(B - p)}$

Chapter 10
Problem Solving $\sqrt{X}$

PICKING NUMBERS ON MUST BE/COULD BE/CANNOT BE QUESTIONS

This is a slightly different style of question that asks things like "Which of the following must be an even integer?" or "Which of the following CANNOT be true?" These questions are usually based not on algebra or arithmetic but rather on the properties of the numbers themselves. Some of these questions can be very abstract, so picking numbers really helps. Just as with word problems, making a number properties question concrete helps you to understand it.

Example:

If a and b are odd integers, which of the following must be an even integer?

○ $a(b - 2)$

○ $ab + 4$

○ $(a + 2)(b - 4)$

○ $3a + 5b$

○ $a(a + 6)$

You can run through the answer choices quite quickly using the picking numbers strategy. Try $a = 1$, $b = 3$. Only **(D)**, $3 + 15 = 18$, is even.

Another approach that works well for many "must be"/"could be"/"cannot be" problems is to pick different numbers for each answer choice, looking to eliminate the wrong answers. The principle of focusing on what's asked is particularly important here, as you need a clear idea of what you're looking for in a wrong answer. Always characterize what you're looking for among the answer choices before you dive in and start testing them. For instance, in the example you just saw, any expression that comes back even may be the correct answer, but any expression that comes back odd must certainly be incorrect and should be eliminated.

Knowing how to test the answer choices on must be/could be/cannot be questions is essential to your success on these questions. As you just saw, on a "must be" question, it's not enough to stop when you reach the first answer choice that works with the numbers you picked. If an answer choice works, that only proves that it *could* be true, not that it *must* be true every time. To be sure you're choosing the right answer to a "must be" or "cannot be" question, pick numbers to eliminate all four incorrect answers. However, for a "could be" question (e.g., "Which of the following could be odd?"), you can safely choose the first answer choice that works. If none of the answer choices work using the numbers you picked, you will need to pick another set of numbers and test the choices again. Always think critically about what the question stem is asking and *how* to pick numbers to find the answer most efficiently.

Roman numeral questions often feature must be/could be/cannot be language in their question stems. Let's look at how to handle one of these questions.

Example:

If integers x and y are distinct factors of 24, then which of the following CANNOT be a factor of 24?

I. $(x + y)^2$

II. $x^2 - y^2$

III. $xy + y^2$

○ I only

○ I and II

○ II and III

○ II only

○ III only

Roman numeral questions are rare but can be big time wasters if you don't work strategically. Evaluate statements one at a time, eliminating answer choices as you go. Usually you should start with the statement that appears most frequently in the answer choices.

This question asks you to figure out which statement or statements can never be a factor of 24. That means you can eliminate a statement if it could ever possibly equal a factor of 24. If you pick some numbers that don't yield a factor of 24, all that means is that the statement *might* be part of the right answer. But if you pick numbers that do yield a factor of 24, you know that any answer choice that includes that statement can be eliminated. It's much more straightforward, therefore, to prove answers wrong rather than to prove them right.

Since the question involves factors of 24, it's a good idea to list these factors out. Anytime a question deals with a small set of specific numbers, write them down. You'll find keeping track of the options to be much easier:

$$1, 2, 3, 4, 6, 8, 12, 24$$

Statement II appears three times among the answer choices, so if you can eliminate it, you'll be down to two choices right away. Squaring something large like 24 or 12 is going to produce a large number, which wouldn't be a factor of 24. So choose smaller numbers instead: $x = 4$ and $y = 2$, perhaps. Then $x^2 - y^2$ would equal $16 - 4$, or 12. Because 12 is a factor of 24, you can eliminate any answer choice containing statement II. That leaves only **(A)** and **(E)**.

Look at statement III next. Not only are you squaring and multiplying, but you're also adding, so this number is going to get big fast. To keep it in your target range, pick the smallest numbers on your list, $x = 1$ and $y = 2$. Then $xy + y^2$ would equal $1(2) + 4$, or 6. That's a factor of 24, so **(E)** is eliminated. You know that **(A)** is the right answer without ever having to evaluate statement I.

APPLYING THE KAPLAN METHOD: PICKING NUMBERS ON MUST BE/COULD BE/CANNOT BE QUESTIONS

Now let's use the Kaplan Method on a Problem Solving question that involves picking numbers with must be/could be/cannot be questions:

If j and k are integers, and $2j + k = 15$, which of the following must be true?

O $j + k$ is odd.
O $j + k$ is even.
O j is odd.
O k is odd.
O $k > j$

Step 1: Analyze the Question

You're given the equation $2j + k = 15$ and told that j and k are integers. Those two variables also show up in the answer choices. Whenever the answer choices contain variables, consider picking numbers.

Step 2: State the Task

You're looking for an answer that MUST be true. Since you know to characterize the answer choices on must be/could be/cannot be problems, you know to remind yourself that if an answer choice could be false, even in one case, it can be eliminated.

Step 3: Approach Strategically

Pretend for a moment that you weren't able to confidently pick different numbers, trying to see whether each answer could be false and thus eliminated. You'd have to pick one set of numbers and plug them into all the choices.

Let's say that you start with $j = 4$ and $k = 7$.

(A) $4 + 7$ is odd. True. Can't be eliminated.

(B) $4 + 7$ is even. False. Eliminate.

(C) 4 is odd. False. Eliminate.

(D) 7 is odd. True. Can't be eliminated.

(E) $7 > 4$. True. Can't be eliminated.

Now you'd have to try a different set of numbers, hoping to eliminate some more. **(E)** looks like the easiest one to target, as you just have to think of a j that's greater than or equal to k. You could choose $j = 5$ and $k = 5$. There's no need to test **(C)** or **(B)**, as they've already been eliminated.

(A) $5 + 5$ is odd. False. Eliminate.

(D) 5 is odd. True. Can't be eliminated.

(E) $5 > 5$. False. Eliminate.

Only **(D)** wasn't eliminated, so it must be the correct answer.

Step 4: Confirm Your Answer

Make sure to reread the question stem to confirm that you interpreted the stem correctly.

TAKEAWAYS: PICKING NUMBERS ON MUST BE/COULD BE/CANNOT BE QUESTIONS

- On these questions, you can pick numbers and plug them into every answer choice…
- …or you can pick different numbers for each answer choice, trying either to eliminate it or to confirm it.
- Characterizing what you're looking for in the answer choices will help you to pick numbers.
- On Roman numeral questions, test the options that appear most often in the available choices to try to eliminate answer choices.

PRACTICE SET: PICKING NUMBERS ON MUST BE/ COULD BE/CANNOT BE QUESTIONS

15. If integers a and b are distinct factors of 30, which of the following CANNOT be a factor of 30?

      I. $ab + b^2$

     II. $(a + b)^2$

    III. $a + b$

  ○ I only

  ○ II only

  ○ III only

  ○ I and II only

  ○ I, II, and III

16. The integer a is less than -1, b is greater than -1, c is less than 1, and the integer d is greater than 1. If b is negative and c is positive, then of the following, which must be the greatest negative number?

  ○ $b - a$

  ○ $b - c$

  ○ $b - d$

  ○ $c - a$

  ○ $c - d$

17. In the set S of consecutive integers from 1 to 10, inclusive, D is the subset of all odd numbers, M is the subset of all prime numbers, and Q is the subset of all numbers whose positive square root is also a member of set S. If d is an element of D, m is an element of M, and q is an element of Q, which of the following could be true?

  ○ $d = \sqrt{mq}$

  ○ $d = \dfrac{q}{m}$

  ○ $m = q$

  ○ $q = \dfrac{m}{d^2}$

  ○ $q = \sqrt{dm}$

BACKSOLVING

Backsolving is just like picking numbers, except instead of coming up with the number yourself, you use the numbers in the answer choices. You'll literally work backward through the problem, looking for the answer choice that agrees with the information in the question stem. This is a good approach whenever the task of plugging a choice into the question would allow you to confirm its details in a straightforward way.

You want to backsolve systematically, not randomly. Start with either **(B)** or **(D)**. If the choice you pick isn't correct, you'll often be able to figure out whether you need to try a number that's larger or one that's smaller. Since numerical answer choices will always be in ascending or descending order, you'll be able to eliminate several choices at once.

Backsolving can save you a great deal of time. It is also an exceptional approach when you have no idea how to begin a problem.

Example:

> Ron begins reading a book at 4:30 p.m. and reads at a steady pace of 30 pages per hour. Michelle begins reading a copy of the same book at 6:00 p.m. If Michelle started 5 pages behind the page that Ron started on and reads at an average pace of 50 pages per hour, at what time would Ron and Michelle be reading the same page?

- ○ 7:00 p.m.
- ○ 7:30 p.m.
- ○ 7:45 p.m.
- ○ 8:00 p.m.
- ○ 8:30 p.m.

You could perhaps set up a complex system of equations to solve this problem. Even if you knew exactly what those equations would be and how to solve them, that's not a very efficient use of your time. Backsolving will work better here. Pick an answer choice and see whether Michelle and Ron are on the same page at that time. There's no compelling reason to prefer one choice to another. So just quickly choose **(B)** or **(D)**.

Let's say you choose **(B)**. On what page is Ron at 7:30 p.m.? He started reading at 4:30 p.m., so he's been reading for 3 hours. His pace is 30 pages per hour. So he's read 30 × 3, or 90 pages. Since Michelle started 5 pages behind Ron, she'd need to read 95 pages to be at the same place. She's been reading since 6:00 p.m., so she's read for 1.5 hours. At 50 pages per hour, she's read 75 pages. That's 20 short of what she needs. So **(B)** is not the right answer.

Since Michelle is reading faster than Ron, she'll catch up to him with more time. Therefore, they'll be on the same page sometime later than 7:30 p.m., so you should try an answer choice that gives a later time. The most strategic answer choice to turn to at this point is choice **(D)**. If **(D)** ends up being correct, you can choose it and move on. If **(D)** is too late, then **(C)** must be the answer. If **(D)** is too early, then the correct choice must be **(E)**.

Let's try out **(D)**. At 8:00 p.m., Ron has read for 3.5 hours. At a pace of 30 pages per hour, he's read 30 × 3.5, or 105 pages. Since Michelle started 5 pages behind, she'd need to read 110 pages to be at the same place. She's been reading for 2 hours at this point; at 50 pages per hour, she's read 100 pages. That's still 10 short of what she needs to catch up. So **(D)** is also not the right answer, and you need a later time than 8:00 p.m.—choice **(E)** must be correct.

When you start with either **(B)** or **(D)**, you'll have picked the right answer 20 percent of the time. Another 20 percent of the time, you'll know the right answer by process of elimination without ever having to test another choice.

Sometimes you may have to test more than one choice. But as you saw above, you should never have to test more than two answer choices. Stick to **(B)** or **(D)**, and you'll save valuable time and worry.

Example:

A crate of apples contains 1 bruised apple for every 30 apples in the crate. Three out of every 4 bruised apples are considered not fit to sell, and every apple that is not fit to sell is bruised. If there are 12 apples not fit to sell in the crate, how many apples are there in the crate?

- ○ 270
- ○ 360
- ○ 480
- ○ 600
- ○ 840

Start backsolving with choice **(B)**. Suppose that there are 360 apples in the crate. Then $\frac{360}{30}$ apples, or 12 apples, are bruised. Then $\frac{3}{4}$ of those 12 apples, or 9 apples, are unsalable. This is too few unsalable apples. So **(B)** is too small. The answer must be larger than 360, so **(A)** and **(B)** are eliminated. Regardless of what you might suspect the answer to be, you should next test **(D)**. If **(D)** is not right, you'll know whether it's too large—in which case **(C)** would be correct—or too small—in which case **(E)** would be correct. No matter what, you'll only have to test one more choice.

Testing **(D)**, suppose that there are 600 apples in the crate. Then $\frac{600}{30}$ apples, or 20 apples, are bruised. Of those 20, $\frac{3}{4}$, or 15, are unsalable. That's too many. So **(D)** and **(E)** are both out, proving that **(C)** is correct.

Backsolving works for more than just word problems. You can use it whenever you're solving for a single variable in the question stem.

Example:

What is the value of x if $\frac{x+1}{x-3} - \frac{x+2}{x-4} = 0$?

- ○ −2
- ○ −1
- ○ 0
- ○ 1
- ○ 2

Since **(D)** looks easier to work with than **(B)**, start with that choice.

$$\frac{1+1}{1-3} - \frac{1+2}{1-4} = \frac{2}{-2} - \frac{3}{-3} = -1 - (-1) = 0$$

Therefore, **(D)** is correct, and you don't have to test any more choices.

APPLYING THE KAPLAN METHOD: BACKSOLVING

Now let's use the Kaplan Method on a Problem Solving question that lends itself to backsolving:

> At a certain zoo, the ratio of sea lions to penguins is 4 to 11. If there are 84 more penguins than sea lions at the zoo, how many sea lions are there?
>
> ○ 24
> ○ 36
> ○ 48
> ○ 72
> ○ 132

Step 1: Analyze the Question

A zoo has more penguins than sea lions, and you're given both a ratio and a numerical difference between them.

Step 2: State the Task

You need to figure out the number of sea lions. You should jot this down in your scratchwork to help you keep track of the task.

Step 3: Approach Strategically

Backsolving is an option whenever you can manageably plug an answer choice into the question stem. After doing so, you merely confirm whether that value is consistent with the other values given in the stem.

Let's say you start by backsolving answer choice **(B)**. You're pretending that there are, in fact, 36 sea lions. So "the ratio of sea lions to penguins is 4 to 11" becomes "the ratio of 36 to penguins is 4 to 11," or 36:*penguins* is 4:11. If you don't see the number of penguins right away, consider rewriting the ratio vertically:

sea lions : penguins

4 : 11

36 : penguins

You multiply the proportional value (4) by 9 to get the actual value (36). So the actual number of penguins is $11 \times 9 = 99$.

Is that consistent with the rest of the information? There should be 84 more penguins than sea lions, but $99 - 36 = 63$. If **(B)** were correct, there would be only 63 more penguins. You can eliminate **(B)**. Do you need more or fewer sea lions? Well, you need to increase the difference between them. Since the animals are in a ratio of 4:11, every time you remove 4 sea lions, you'd remove 11 penguins, *shrinking* the difference between them by 7. So you definitely need *more* sea lions—every time you add 4 sea lions, you add 11 penguins, increasing the difference by 7. Eliminate **(A)** as well and test **(D)**.

sea lions : penguins

4 : 11

72 : penguins

You multiply the proportional value (4) by 18 to get the actual value (72). So the actual number of penguins is 11 × 18 = 198. (Or you could more simply say that since you've doubled the number of sea lions from what you had in choice **(B)**, you must double the number of penguins as well.)

Is that consistent with the rest of the information? There should be 84 more penguins than sea lions. But 198 − 72 = 126. If **(D)** were correct, there would be 126 more penguins. That's too many more, so **(D)** is eliminated. You need a smaller difference, which means you need a smaller number of sea lions. The answer must be **(C)**.

Step 4: Confirm Your Answer

If you had accidentally answered **(E)**, which is the number of penguins, this step would save you from a wrong answer.

Did you start this problem by adding 84 to the number of sea lions in one of the answer choices and then checking whether it was consistent with the given ratio? That's fine too. If you had trouble figuring out whether you needed to increase or decrease the number of sea lions, you could have either checked all five answer choices, stopping when you found the right ratio, or changed your approach to the question.

TAKEAWAYS: BACKSOLVING

- Like picking numbers, backsolving allows you to plug numbers into the problem. In this case, the numbers are those in the answer choices.
- To backsolve, plug in a value from an answer choice and solve the problem arithmetically. If your calculations are consistent with the question stem, then the answer is correct.
- The most efficient way to backsolve is to plug in either **(B)** or **(D)** first. If your first choice isn't correct, consider whether the correct answer is larger or smaller.
- Testing the answer choices strategically allows you to find the answer after testing, at most, two answer choices.

PRACTICE SET: BACKSOLVING

18. A teacher grades students' tests by subtracting twice the number of incorrect responses from the number of correct responses. If Student A answers each of the 100 questions on her test and receives a score of 73, how many questions did Student A answer correctly?

   ○ 55
   ○ 60
   ○ 73
   ○ 82
   ○ 91

19. If $\left(\frac{1}{64}\right)^x = 4{,}096$, $x =$

   ○ $-\frac{1}{3}$
   ○ $-\frac{1}{2}$
   ○ $-\sqrt{2}$
   ○ -2
   ○ -3

20. One used-car salesperson receives a commission of $200 plus 4 percent of $1,000 less than the car's final sale price. Another car salesperson earns a straight commission of 6 percent of the car's final sale price. What is the final sale price of a car if both salespeople would earn the same commission for selling it?

   ○ $5,000
   ○ $6,000
   ○ $8,000
   ○ $10,000
   ○ $12,000

STRATEGIC GUESSING

A well-placed guess can sometimes be the best thing you can do on a problem. Because of the severe penalty exacted on those who fail to finish a section, you need to stay on a steady pace. If you fall behind, it's a good idea to guess on the hardest problems. That way you'll get back lost time instead of falling further behind. And while you shouldn't be afraid to guess, you *should* be afraid to rush! The GMAT builds in twists and writes problems in complicated ways; rushing almost always leads to a misperception of the problem. The test makers base many wrong answers on the most common misperceptions. So rushing through a problem virtually guarantees a wrong answer. It's far better to guess as needed than to rush through an entire section.

Sometimes you just have no idea how to approach a problem. Instead of throwing away 3 or 4 minutes getting frustrated, make a guess. If you didn't know how to approach the problem, you weren't likely to choose the right answer in any case, and you can use the time you save to solve other problems that you stand a better chance of answering correctly.

Lastly, there are some problems that are *best* solved using guessing techniques. The two keys to good guessing are (1) elimination of likely wrong answers by using your knowledge of the problem and of the GMAT's tendencies and (2) maintaining your focus on the "big picture"—remembering that your performance on the section as a whole matters much more than your performance on two or three questions. Better to make a guess in 1 minute and be done with a hard problem than spend 6 minutes before guessing; the extra time will pay off.

Also, keep in mind that the hardest questions are the ones you'll be most likely to need to guess on—and are also the ones that will hurt your score the *least* when you get them wrong. So don't be afraid to guess!

There are six guessing strategies that you can apply to Problem Solving:

1. Use Critical Thinking
2. Estimate the Answer
3. Eliminate Numbers Appearing in the Question Stem
4. Eliminate the Oddball
5. Eliminate Uncritical Solutions
6. On "Which of the Following" Questions, Favor **(D)** and **(E)**

You won't be able to use all of these strategies on every problem. But if you run through the "checklist" and eliminate what you can, you'll make your best possible guess in the least possible amount of time. Let's look at the strategies.

Use Critical Thinking

Some answers are simply logically impossible. By analyzing and simplifying before attempting to solve, you may learn enough about the problem to eliminate many wrong answer choices. Consider this problem:

> A container holding 12 ounces of a solution that is 1 part alcohol to 2 parts water is added to a container holding 8 ounces of a solution that is 1 part alcohol to 3 parts water. What is the ratio of alcohol to water in the resulting solution?
>
> O   2:5
> O   3:7
> O   3:5
> O   4:7
> O   7:3

It seems a challenging problem at first glance. But the simplified version of the problem is that you're adding a 1:2 solution to a 1:3 solution. So logically, the right answer has to be between 1:3 (or $\frac{1}{3}$, or 0.333...) and 1:2 (or $\frac{1}{2}$, or 0.5). **(A)** and **(B)** are both in that range, but all the others are above 1:2. So you can make a guess—with 50 percent odds of being right—just by analyzing the problem logically.

In case you were curious, the answer is **(B)**. The 12-ounce solution has 4 oz alcohol and 8 oz water. The 8 oz solution has 2 oz alcohol and 6 oz water. Add the amounts of alcohol and water to get 6 oz alcohol and 14 oz water for a ratio of 3:7 alcohol to water.

Also, note that Roman numeral questions are good candidates for logic-based guessing. If you can evaluate only one statement, you can still logically eliminate several answers.

Estimate the Answer

The GMAT asks some questions that are intended to be solved via estimation. When a question stem includes a word like *approximately*, that's a clear signal that estimation is the best approach you can take.

Example:

> The product of all positive even numbers less than or equal to 20 is closest to which of the following?
>
> O 10^6
> O 10^7
> O 10^8
> O 10^9
> O 10^{10}

If you had a calculator on the Quant section, you could quickly figure out that the product in question is 3,715,891,200. But with no calculator, what can you do? The keys to the solution are the word *closest* and the big spread of values in the answer choices—each is 10 times the nearest value. This problem has "estimation" written all over it.

Jot down the numbers in question:

$$2 \times 4 \times 6 \times 8 \times 10 \times 12 \times 14 \times 16 \times 18 \times 20$$

Now, how to estimate these values? Since each answer is a power of 10, you should estimate each value in a way that easily relates to 10:

$$2 \times 4 \times 6 \times 8 \times 10 \times 12 \times 14 \times 16 \times 18 \times 20$$

$$2 \times 4 \times 6 \times 10 \times 10 \times 10 \times 10 \times 20 \times 20 \times 20$$

What about the small ones? $2 \times 4 \times 6 = 48$, which is very close to 50.

$$50 \times 10 \times 10 \times 10 \times 10 \times 20 \times 20 \times 20$$

Continuing to look for tens:

$$(5 \times 10) \times 10 \times 10 \times 10 \times 10 \times (2 \times 10) \times (2 \times 10) \times (2 \times 10)$$

That's eight 10s, one 5, and three 2s:

$$2 \times 2 \times 2 \times 5 \times 10^8$$

$$(2 \times 2) \times (2 \times 5) \times 10^8$$

$$4 \times 10 \times 10^8$$

$$4 \times 10^9$$

That's closer to 10^9 than to 10^{10}, so **(D)** is the correct answer. No calculator needed, just the willingness to estimate!

Eliminate Numbers Appearing in the Question Stem

The test makers lay psychological traps as well as mathematical ones, and this guessing principle helps you to stay out of them. It's part of human psychology to deal with being lost by looking for familiar things. When you get lost in a problem, you tend to grab hold of familiar numbers, such as those you've just seen in the question stem. The GMAT doesn't like to reward people who get lost with right answers, so such numbers tend to be wrong.

Eliminate the Oddball

This is psychology again. Our eyes are attracted to difference. (Next time you watch a movie or a TV show, notice how often no one else is dressed in the same color as the main character—it's a subtle trick to keep your attention where the director wants it.) Random guessers, then, will be attracted to uniqueness. As the GMAT does not like to reward random guessing, the "oddballs" should be eliminated.

A word of warning about this technique: the GMAT also uses a little reverse psychology. The test makers know that people tend to be afraid of answers that seem *too* out of line with the others. These outlying values, then, will sometimes be *correct*. What Kaplan means by an "oddball," then, is *not* a number that's notably bigger or smaller but an answer choice that is structurally unique—the only fraction or the only negative number, for example.

Look at these five answer choices, for example:

○ $\sqrt{2}$
○ 2
○ 4
○ 16
○ 2,056

In this case, the answer choice 2,056 is *not* an oddball and should not be eliminated. But $\sqrt{2}$ is and should be.

Eliminate Uncritical Solutions

Because the GMAT is a test of critical thinking, answers that you'd get just by mashing numbers together are usually wrong. Consider this question:

> A bag holds 2 red marbles and 3 green marbles. If you removed 2 randomly selected marbles from the bag, without replacement, what is the probability that both would be red?

○ $\dfrac{1}{10}$

○ $\dfrac{1}{5}$

○ $\dfrac{3}{10}$

○ $\dfrac{2}{5}$

○ $\dfrac{1}{2}$

It's true that you want 2 of the 5 marbles in the bag. But GMAT questions usually require a little more math than just that, so $\frac{2}{5}$ isn't likely to be correct. (In fact, it's the odds of getting *1* red marble when selecting 1; the probability of getting 2 red when selecting 2 is actually $\frac{1}{10}$.)

On "Which of the Following" Questions, Favor (D) and (E)

When Problem Solving questions include the phrase "which of the following," the answer is about 60 percent likely to be either **(D)** or **(E)**. The reason for this is that questions that ask "which of the following" are generally set up in such a way that the only way to solve for the answer is to test the answer choices one by one. On such questions, the test makers "hide" the correct answers at the end of the set of choices disproportionately often. So if you haven't eliminated both **(D)** and **(E)** for other reasons, the odds are in your favor if you guess one of those two choices. (Note that this is only true for Problem Solving in the Quantitative section, not for any questions in the Verbal section.)

Furthermore, if you do plan to solve the question rather than take a strategic guess, it's a good idea to start by testing choice **(E)** and work your way up through the answer choices, since doing so will often enable you to find the correct answer sooner and avoid spending time testing more choices than necessary.

Stay Alert for Guessing Opportunities

Believe it or not, there are some GMAT problems for which a guessing strategy—most notably Logic or Estimation—is the best approach you could take. Remember that the test makers aren't trying to judge your math skills alone; they are also testing your ability to find efficient solutions to problems. Every so often, they give you a set of choices with only one logically possible answer. Make sure to look at the answer choices before you choose your approach. Otherwise, you might not realize that you can estimate.

Example:

> If a store owner increases a product's price by 20 percent and then increases this price by another 15 percent, what percent of the original price is the total price increase?
>
> O   20%
> O   35%
> O   38%
> O   65%
> O   135%

It's true that you could pick the original price to be $100, but you can do better here by thinking logically about the question and the answer choices. The price goes up 20% and then up another 15%. That 15% increase is being applied not to the original price but to the price after the first increase. If it were 15% of the original, then the total increase would be 20% + 15% = 35% (that's the "uncritical solution"). But since the second increase is based on a higher starting price, the total increase will be a little more than 35%. Only one answer, choice **(C)**, fits the bill, so it must be correct.

If applied strategically, guessing will be a great tool for you on Test Day. It will help keep you out of time management trouble, help you to feel confident and in charge of the test, and occasionally reward you with a very quick right answer.

ANSWERS AND EXPLANATIONS

1.	D	8.	E	15.	B
2.	B	9.	C	16.	B
3.	E	10.	C	17.	B
4.	C	11.	B	18.	E
5.	B	12.	B	19.	D
6.	E	13.	D	20.	C
7.	D	14.	B		

1.   **(D)**

Youssef lives x blocks from his office. It takes him 1 minute per block to walk to work and 20 seconds per block to ride his bicycle to work. If it takes him exactly 10 minutes more to walk to work than to ride his bicycle, then x equals

- ○   4
- ○   7
- ○   10
- ○   15
- ○   20

Step 1: Analyze the Question

Youssef walks a block in 1 minute and bikes a block in 20 seconds. As the answer choices are all in minutes, convert the bike rate to 3 blocks per minute. It takes Youssef 10 minutes longer to walk x blocks than to bike x blocks. Such a setup implies the need for algebra, but that might not be the best way to solve.

Step 2: State the Task

Find the value of x, which is the number of blocks Youssef walks in the scenario.

Step 3: Approach Strategically

Setting up the algebra will get complicated quickly, but the answer choices are whole numbers that represent the number of blocks Youssef might have traveled to work, so backsolving is the best approach. Backsolving is an option whenever you can manageably plug an answer choice into the question stem.

As it takes Youssef 10 more minutes to walk than bike, start with **(D)**. If Youssef lives 15 blocks from his office, it would take him 15 minutes to walk (at 1 block per minute) and 5 minutes to bike (at 3 blocks per minute). That's a difference of $15 - 5 = 10$ minutes. A 10-minute difference is exactly what you were looking for, so **(D)** is the correct answer.

Step 4: Confirm Your Answer

Walking takes Youssef 10 minutes longer than biking. Since it takes Youssef a minute to walk each block, the correct answer must be greater than 10. That allows you to quickly eliminate **(A)**, **(B)**, and **(C)**. **(E)** results in a biking time that isn't a whole number of minutes, which would lead to an answer choice that isn't a whole number. You can therefore confirm that **(D)** is correct.

2. (B)

A book club rented the party room of a local restaurant to meet and discuss its current novel over dinner. The total charge, including food and service, was $867.50. If each member of the club paid at least $42, then what is the greatest possible number of members in the club?

- ○ 19
- ○ 20
- ○ 21
- ○ 23
- ○ 25

Step 1: Analyze the Question

For word problems, you need to get a logical sense of the situation so that you can understand how the information fits together. This question tells you that some unknown number of people split a bill of $867.50 and that each person paid at least $42—meaning that some could have paid more than $42 but no one could have paid less.

Step 2: State the Task

Figure out the greatest possible number of club members. The phrase "greatest possible" tells you that there's probably no way to calculate the exact number, but there is some way to set an upper limit on the number.

Step 3: Approach Strategically

Since you're asked about the number of club members, see what the question stem tells you about club members. You're only told that each one paid a minimum of $42. So you'll know something about the total number of members if you learn something about the total amount paid. The question tells you that the total paid was $867.50.

The bigger the number of members, the less each one would have to pay to cover the tab (e.g., if there were 868 members, each would pay a little less than $1). The least each member can pay is $42. So if you split the total of $867.50 into portions of $42, you'll figure out how many members you need to have to cover those portions.

You can do this calculation with a few easy steps: $42 × 10 yields $420. Twice that is $42 × 20 = $840. One more $42, or $42 × 21, yields $882. That's too much money. If there were 21 members, and each paid no less than the minimum of $42, then they'd have paid more than the question stem says they did. So there can be at most 20 members (some will have to pay a little more than $42 to meet the bill, but the question allows for that).

Since you have numbers in the answer choices, backsolving is also a great strategy to use here. Start with **(B)**, since 20 is a nice round number. You have 20 members, each of whom pays a minimum of $42, and in total they pay a minimum of $42 × 20 = $840. If there were one more member paying the minimum of $42, then together they all would have paid $840 + $42 = $882, which is too much. So **(B)** is the right answer.

Step 4: Confirm Your Answer

Reread the question stem, making sure that you didn't miss anything about the problem. For example, if you misread the question stem to think that each member paid exactly $42, you may not have selected **(B)**. But then when you reread, you'd see the "at least" and realize that you had to rethink your answer choice.

3. **(E)**

A machine manufactures notebooks in a series of five colors: red, blue, black, white, and yellow. After producing a notebook of one color from that series, it produces a notebook of the next color. Once five are produced, the machine repeats the same pattern. If the machine began a day producing a red notebook and completed the day by producing a black notebook, how many notebooks could have been produced that day?

- ○ 27
- ○ 34
- ○ 50
- ○ 61
- ○ 78

Step 1: Analyze the Question

A machine makes notebooks in 5 colors, following a repeating pattern: red, blue, black, white, and yellow. You might abbreviate this in your scratchwork as R, Blu, Bla, W, Y. The machine starts on R and ends on Bla.

Step 2: State the Task

How many notebooks could the machine have made? The question makes it clear that there's more than one possible number of notebooks produced, but since this is a multiple-choice question, you know that the answer choices contain only one possible value and four impossible values.

Step 3: Approach Strategically

So, what do you know about what's possible or impossible for this machine?

The numerical answers are so high that it would probably take a long time to count each notebook one by one. Instead, look for a pattern or rule that tells you what kinds of numbers are possible or impossible answers.

The machine always follows the same pattern: R, Blu, Bla, W, Y. Since it starts on R, the third notebook will be Bla. Sadly, 3 is not an answer. The machine will make 2 more (W and Y) before the pattern is set to repeat. Then, as before, 3 new notebooks are made before you get Bla. So after the first 3, the machine needs to make 5 more to get another Bla. Since the pattern repeats, it does the same thing over and over again. So while you don't know exactly how many times the pattern repeats, you know that each time it does, 5 notebooks get made.

In other words, you've reconceptualized the pattern from "repeat {R, Blu, Bla, W, Y}" to "R, Blu, Bla + repeat {W, Y, R, Blu, Bla}."

To get a Bla notebook, then, make 3 notebooks and then any repetition of 5 notebooks. So the correct answer will be "some multiple of 5" + 3. This means the correct answer will end in either a 3 or an 8. Only **(E)**, 78, which is 75 + 3, is possible.

Step 4: Confirm Your Answer

Reread the question stem, making sure that you didn't miss anything about the problem. For example, if the machine had started on a W notebook, then the answer would have been "some multiple of 5" without the "plus 3."

4. (C)

A team won 50 percent of its first 60 games in a particular season and 80 percent of its remaining games. If the team won a total of 60 percent of its games that season, what was the total number of games that the team played?

○ 180

○ 120

○ 90

○ 85

○ 30

Step 1: Analyze the Question

You are given many different pieces of information about a team. First, the team won 50% of its first 60 games, for a total of 30 wins. Then you are told that the team won 80% of the remaining games after the initial 60. Finally, you know that the team won 60% of its games overall.

Step 2: State the Task

What was the total number of games the team played throughout the entire season?

Step 3: Approach Strategically

The quickest way to solve this problem is to use backsolving. Start with **(B)**. If the total number of games is equal to 120, you know that the team played 60 more games after the initial 60. They won 80% of the latter 60 games, for a total of 48 games. Adding the initial 30 games won to the 48 games won in the second part of the season, you get 78 games won out of a total of 120 games. You are told the winning percentage is 60% overall, but $\frac{78}{120} = 0.65$, or 65%. This number is too high, so you can eliminate **(B)**.

Think strategically about which answer choice to try next. The first portion of games has a 50% winning average, while the second portion has an 80% winning average. Since the percentage you calculated for **(B)** was too high and the second portion of games has the higher winning percentage, **(B)** has too much weight on the later portion of games. You need fewer games in the second portion and therefore fewer games total. Eliminate both **(A)** and **(B)**.

(D) gives a total number of games equaling 85. You have already accounted for the first 60 games, so focus on the remaining 25. If the team won 80% of those games, they won 20 more games. In total, the team would have won $\frac{50}{85} \approx 0.59$, or 59%. Since **(D)** is too small (less than 60%) and **(B)** is too big (greater than 60%), you know without calculating that the correct answer is **(C)**.

Step 4: Confirm Your Answer

To confirm your answer, backsolve for **(C)**. If there are 90 total games, then there are 30 games in the second portion of the season. The team won 80% of those games, or 24 games. In total, the team would have won $\frac{54}{90} = 0.6$, or 60%.

5. (B)

A local restaurant recently renovated its dining space, purchasing new tables and chairs to use in addition to the original tables and chairs. The new tables each seat 6 customers, while the original tables each seat 4 customers. Altogether, the restaurant now has 40 tables and is capable of seating 220 customers. How many more new tables than original tables does the restaurant have?

O   10
O   20
O   30
O   34
O   36

Step 1: Analyze the Question

This is an algebra word problem with two variables. You should also note that you are told that the restaurant has more new tables than old and that the correct answer will represent the difference between those two numbers.

Step 2: State the Task

Your task is to determine the difference between the number of new tables and the number of old tables. You will need to find the number of each and then subtract.

Step 3: Approach Strategically

You could solve this problem by translating the information directly into equations and then combining or substituting the variables to determine the number of each type of table. But backsolving provides a more efficient route to the correct answer here. When backsolving, begin with **(B)** or **(D)**, since this will require checking at most two answers. Remembering that we have a total of 40 tables, begin with **(D)**. A difference of 34 would mean that the restaurant has 37 new tables and 3 old tables. With 37 tables seating 6 diners each ($37 \times 6 = 222$), you are already over the seating capacity of 220. That means you need fewer of the new tables in the mix. Try **(B)**. A difference of 20 means 30 new tables and 10 original tables: $30 \times 6 = 180$ and $10 \times 4 = 40$. Adding 180 and 40 gives you 220, the seating capacity indicated in the question stem. **(B)** is correct.

Step 4: Confirm Your Answer

The easiest way to go wrong in a problem like this one is to solve for the wrong thing. Both the number of new tables (30) and the number of old tables (10) are present in an answer choice. A quick check of the question to confirm that the correct answer represents the *difference* between the table types is worthwhile before selecting the answer and moving on.

6. (E)

If $\dfrac{c-a}{c-b} = 2$, then $\dfrac{5b-5a}{c-a} =$

○ 0.5
○ 1
○ 1.5
○ 2
○ 2.5

Step 1: Analyze the Question

There isn't much to analyze here, as you are given one algebraic expression set equal to 2 and asked to solve for another.

Step 2: State the Task

Determine the value of the second expression.

Step 3: Approach Strategically

You are given an initial equation with three variables and asked to solve for a second expression that uses the same variables. Rather than trying to isolate variables or use substitution (which could get complicated with three variables), try picking numbers. Make sure that the numbers are permissible, meaning that they fit the given equation.

Start by choosing a value for c, since it appears twice in the initial equation. By setting $c = 4$ and $a = 2$, the numerator becomes 2. Since the numerator is 2 and the entire expression must be equal to 2, the denominator must be equal to 1. You need to choose $b = 3$. Once you have chosen your numbers, plug them into the second expression. Once you do so, the expression becomes $\dfrac{5b-5a}{c-a} = \dfrac{5(3)-5(2)}{4-2} = \dfrac{5}{2} = 2.5$. This corresponds to **(E)**.

Step 4: Confirm Your Answer

To confirm your answer, go back through your math. Check that when the numbers are substituted into the initial equation, you get 2, and that when they are substituted into the second equation, you get 2.5. Since both of these are true, the answer is confirmed.

7. **(D)**

Company Z spent $\frac{1}{4}$ of its revenues last year on marketing and $\frac{1}{7}$ of the remainder on maintenance of its facilities. What fraction of last year's original revenues did Company Z have left after its marketing and maintenance expenditures?

○ $\frac{5}{14}$

○ $\frac{1}{2}$

○ $\frac{17}{28}$

○ $\frac{9}{14}$

○ $\frac{9}{11}$

Step 1: Analyze the Question

Company Z spends portions of its revenues on two things. It's also important to note that the answer choices are fractions, not dollar values and not variable expressions.

Step 2: State the Task

Determine the fraction of last year's revenues that Company Z had left after the expenses.

Notice that you are given absolutely no way to know how much revenue Company Z received last year. But the answer choices don't contain any variables at all. Somehow, then, the variable that would represent the unknown revenue gets canceled out along the way.

Step 3: Approach Strategically

Whenever variables cancel, leaving only numbers in the answer choices, picking numbers is an approach you should consider. Be sure to pick a permissible and manageable number for Company Z's revenue. Since you have to take $\frac{1}{4}$ and $\frac{1}{7}$ of the revenue, a number divisible by both 4 and 7 will be most manageable. Make the calculations even easier by picking the smallest such number, 28.

Now, "Company Z spent $\frac{1}{4}$ of its revenues last year on marketing," becomes "Company Z spent $7 last year on marketing."

The next sentence mentions "the remainder," so you need to know what that is. Because $28 − $7 = $21, "Company Z spent $\frac{1}{7}$ ... of the remainder on maintenance" means "Company Z spent...$3 on maintenance."

What's left from $28 after Company Z spent $7 and then $3 is $18. So the answer is $\frac{18}{28}$. A common factor of 2 can be canceled from both the numerator and the denominator, leaving $\frac{9}{14}$. **(D)** is correct.

Step 4: Confirm Your Answer

Had you accidentally answered how much Company Z spent, which is **(A)**, this step would save you from a wrong answer.

8. (E)

During a sale, a store sells 20 percent of its remaining stock each day, without replenishment. After 4 days, what fraction of its original stock has it sold?

○ $\dfrac{1}{625}$

○ $\dfrac{256}{625}$

○ $\dfrac{61}{125}$

○ $\dfrac{64}{125}$

○ $\dfrac{369}{625}$

Step 1: Analyze the Question

For 4 days, a store sells the same percentage of its remaining stock each day. In other words, it's not selling the same amount each day but the same proportion of each day's stock.

We're given no way to know exactly how much stock the store starts with. But the answer choices don't have any variables. Whenever variables cancel, leaving only numbers in the answer choices, picking numbers is an approach you should consider. Note that the answers are fractions. So despite the word "percent" in the question stem, 100 might not be as safe a choice when picking numbers as would a common denominator.

Step 2: State the Task

Determine the fraction of its original stock the store has sold after 4 days.

Step 3: Approach Strategically

Instead of picking 100 for the stock, pick a common denominator. A good choice seems to be 625. Not only is it the denominator of three of the answer choices, but the number in the other two denominators (125) is a factor of 625.

There's a lot to keep track of—starting stock, stock sold, stock remaining for the next day, all on 4 different days—so jotting down a chart on your scratch paper would not be a bad idea:

Day	Start	Sold	Remains
1	625	125	500
2	500	100	400
3	400	80	320
4	320	64	256

You can calculate the total amount sold either by adding $125 + 100 + 80 + 64$ or by subtracting the eventual remains from the original amount ($625 - 256$). Whichever approach you take, 369 is the result.

The store sold $\frac{369}{625}$ of its original stock, so **(E)** is correct.

Step 4: Confirm Your Answer

Had you accidentally answered **(B)**, which is how much stock remained, or **(D)**, which resembles how much was sold on the fourth day, this step would save you from a wrong answer.

9. **(C)**

If a bicyclist in motion increases his speed by 30 percent and then increases this speed by 10 percent, what percent of the original speed is the total increase in speed?

○ 10%
○ 40%
○ 43%
○ 64%
○ 140%

Step 1: Analyze the Question

The question gives you information about two increases to the speed of a bicyclist.

Step 2: State the Task

Determine the total percent increase.

Step 3: Approach Strategically

When faced with percentages in the question stem and in the answer choices, use the strategy of picking numbers and pick 100. If the bicyclist is initially riding at 100 (the units aren't mentioned in this problem, and in any case, your numbers don't need to be realistic—just permissible and manageable) and then increases his speed by 30%, he is now riding at 130. To increase 130 by 10%, find 10% of 130, which is 13, and add it to 130, making his final speed 143. That is an increase of 43 over his original speed of 100. Since you chose 100 as your initial number, 43 is simply 43% of the original, **(C)**.

Step 4: Confirm Your Answer

When confirming the answer for questions that ask about multiple percent changes, make sure that you calculated the percent changes appropriately and didn't simply add the percentages given in the question, as **(B)** does. Also, check to make sure that you solved for the correct value, the increase in speed as a percentage of the original speed. **(E)** is a trap answer because it makes the same mistake as **(B)** but is close to the final speed of 143.

10. (C)

Jane makes toy bears. When she works with an assistant, she makes 80 percent more bears per week and works 10 percent fewer hours each week. Having an assistant increases Jane's output of toy bears per hour by what percent?

- ○ 20%
- ○ 80%
- ○ 100%
- ○ 180%
- ○ 200%

Step 1: Analyze the Question

Jane seems to work faster with an assistant. Since the answer choices are percents, picking 100 is a good idea.

It's also worth noting that the answer choices are widely spaced—**(A)** has no answer close to it, and **(B)** and **(C)** are much smaller than **(D)** and **(E)**. When answers are spread out, estimation and logic are also great approaches.

Step 2: State the Task

Determine how much having an assistant increases Jane's output of toy bears per hour.

"Percent increase" is not the same thing as "what percent of the old value is the new value." Make sure you solve for the *increase*, not just for the new value.

Step 3: Approach Strategically

Search the question stem for information about "output of toy bears" or "hours." For the former, you find this: "When she works with an assistant, she makes 80 percent more bears per week." To make things easy, say that Jane alone makes 100 bears. With the assistant, she makes 180.

Looking for hours, you find this: "When she works with an assistant, she...works 10 percent fewer hours each week." So say that she initially works 100 hours per week by herself. With an assistant, she works 10 fewer hours, or 90 in total.

Your task is to find the increase in bears/hour. Her rate used to be $\frac{100 \text{ bears}}{100 \text{ hours}}$, or 1 bear per hour. With an assistant, it's $\frac{180 \text{ bears}}{90 \text{ hours}}$, or 2 bears per hour. She has increased from 1 bear per hour to 2 bears per hour. You're solving for the increase, which is $2 - 1$, or 1. That's 100% of the original value.

However, look at how your work could have been simpler had you started just by thinking logically about the answers: An 80% increase in bears produced in the same number of hours would mean an 80% increase in bears per hour. But the number of hours does change—it is reduced by 10%. So 80% more bears are made in a little less time than before, so her per-hour output must be a little higher than 80%. Only one answer choice, **(C)**, is a little higher than 80%. So **(C)** must be correct.

Step 4: Confirm Your Answer

Had you chosen **(E)**, which is Jane's new output rate as a percentage of her old rate, confirming your answer would have uncovered that error.

11. (B)

Crystal made a budget for her vacation. If she traveled by plane, airfare would be 40 percent of the total budget, meals and lodging would be 50 percent, and miscellaneous expenses would be 10 percent. If she drove, transportation would cost 10 percent less than flying, and miscellaneous expenses would be the same. If Crystal wanted to travel by car and spend no more in total than if she flew, what is the maximum percentage by which she could increase the budget for meals and lodging?

- ○ 4%
- ○ 8%
- ○ 10%
- ○ 12%
- ○ 40%

Step 1: Analyze the Question

The percentage breakdown of a budget is given for transportation, meals and lodging, and miscellaneous expenses. If transportation costs 10% less, more can be spent on meals and lodging while keeping total expenses the same. Since no amounts of money are given and the answer choices are percents, pick $100 for the total budget.

Step 2: State the Task

Determine by what percent the amount budgeted for meals and lodging can be increased to bring total expenses up to what they would be if Crystal flew.

Step 3: Approach Strategically

If the total budget is $100, then the amount allocated to airfare would be $0.40 \times \$100 = \$40$, and the amount for meals and lodging would be $0.50 \times \$100 = \$50$. A 10% reduction in the first amount would be $0.10 \times \$40 = \$4$. Reallocating that part of the budget to meals and lodging would allow for $\$50 + \$4 = \$54$ to be spent on that category. An increase of $4 from an original amount of $50 is $\frac{4}{50} \times 100\% = 8\%$. Therefore, **(B)** is correct.

Step 4: Confirm Your Answer

Check your calculations and your logic. If you divided the increase of 4 by the total budget of 100 instead of the portion originally allocated for meals and lodging, you would have selected **(A)**, 4%. If you had assumed that a 10% reduction in one expense automatically meant a 10% increase in the other, you would have chosen **(C)**, 10%.

12. **(B)**

If $n \neq 1$, $j \neq 0$, $k \neq 0$, and $m \neq 0$ and if $n = \dfrac{jkm}{jk + jm + km}$, then $\dfrac{1}{n-1} =$

○ $\dfrac{1}{j} + \dfrac{1}{k} + \dfrac{1}{m}$

○ $\dfrac{jk + jm + km}{jkm - jk - jm - km}$

○ $\dfrac{jk + jm + km}{jkm}$

○ $\dfrac{jkm - jk - jm - km}{jk + jm + km}$

○ $j + k + m$

Step 1: Analyze the Question

The question stem states that the variable n equals a fraction containing various combinations of three other variables: j, k, and m. The answer choices are other expressions with these three variables. The restrictions on the variables avoid division by zero. Furthermore, you can deduce that since n doesn't equal 1, the numerator and denominator of the fraction are not equal ($jkm \neq jk + jm + km$).

Step 2: State the Task

Use the given equation to determine the value of $\frac{1}{n-1}$ in terms of j, k, and m.

Step 3: Approach Strategically

The algebraic manipulation here is daunting and difficult to accomplish within the time constraints of the GMAT, so consider picking numbers for j, k, and m. Choose manageable numbers that don't break the question's rules. For example, if $j = 2$, $k = 2$, and $m = 2$, all three variables are not equal to 0 and $(2)(2)(2) \neq 2(2) + 2(2) + 2(2)$, meaning that n does not equal 1.

Substituting 2 for j, k, and m yields $n = \dfrac{jkm}{jk + jm + km} = \dfrac{(2)(2)(2)}{2(2) + 2(2) + 2(2)} = \dfrac{8}{12} = \dfrac{2}{3}$. So, $n - 1 = -\dfrac{1}{3}$ and $\dfrac{1}{n-1} = \dfrac{1}{-\frac{1}{3}} = -3$. Test each answer choice, looking for those that produce a value of -3 when 2 is plugged in for j, k, and m. As soon as you determine the value is not -3, stop calculating and move on.

(A) $\dfrac{1}{2} + \dfrac{1}{2} + \dfrac{1}{2} \neq -3$; eliminate **(A)**.

(B) $\dfrac{(2)(2) + (2)(2) + (2)(2)}{(2)(2)(2) - (2)(2) - (2)(2) - (2)(2)} = \dfrac{12}{8 - 12} = -\dfrac{12}{4} = -3$. This value is a match, but test the remaining choices to make sure no others also equal -3.

(C)   This fraction is just the reciprocal of that in the question stem, so **(C)** is $\dfrac{1}{n}$ or $\dfrac{3}{2}$ with your picked numbers; eliminate **(C)**.

(D)   This fraction is the reciprocal of that in **(B)**, so its value with your picked numbers is $-\dfrac{1}{3}$; eliminate **(D)**.

(E) $j + k + m = 2 + 2 + 2 \neq -3$, so eliminate **(E)**.

The correct answer is **(B)**.

Step 4: Confirm Your Answer

Ensure that you determined the value of $\frac{1}{n-1}$, not of n, $n-1$, $\frac{1}{n}$, or something else.

13. (D)

The positive difference between Sam and Lucy's ages is a, and the sum of their ages is z. If Lucy is older than Sam, then which of the following represents Lucy's age?

○ $\dfrac{z - a}{2}$

○ $a - \dfrac{z}{2}$

○ $2a + z$

○ $\dfrac{z + a}{2}$

○ $\dfrac{a - z}{2}$

Step 1: Analyze the Question

There are two people—Sam and Lucy—whose ages are related in some way, and Lucy is the older of the two. You don't need to translate to algebra in this step.

Notice that the answer choices contain variables. Whenever this is the case, consider picking numbers.

Step 2: State the Task

Solve for Lucy's age. Be careful not to answer with Sam's age, as that's likely to be one of the wrong answers.

Step 3: Approach Strategically

It's easy enough to pick two numbers for a and z. But then you still have to backtrack from those to calculate the two ages. So you still have to do algebra. If this happens, consider reevaluating your approach. Are there other variables you could pick first that would make things easier?

If you pick numbers for Lucy's and Sam's ages, then all you need to do to figure out the values of a and z is simple arithmetic. Say that Lucy is 5 years old and Sam is 3 years old. That makes a, their difference, equal to 2. And z, their sum, is equal to 8.

Plug in $a = 2$ and $z = 8$ to see which choices yield Lucy's age of 5.

(A)   is $\dfrac{8 - 2}{2} = \dfrac{6}{2} = 3$. Eliminate.

(B)   is $2 - \dfrac{8}{2} = 2 - 4 = -2$. Eliminate.

(C)   is $2(2) + 8 = 4 + 8 = 12$. Eliminate.

(D)   is $\dfrac{8 + 2}{2} = \dfrac{10}{2} = 5$. Possibly right.

(E)   is $\dfrac{2 - 8}{2} = \dfrac{-6}{2} = -3$. Eliminate.

As the only possible answer, **(D)** is correct.

Step 4: Confirm Your Answer

Make sure to reread the question stem to confirm that you interpreted the information correctly.

14. (B)

In order to fulfill a local school's request for x cakes, B parents agreed to each bake an equal number of cakes. If p of the parents did not bake any cakes, which of the following represents the additional number of cakes that each of the other parents had to bake in order for the school's request for x cakes to be fulfilled?

○ $\dfrac{px}{B}$

○ $\dfrac{px}{B(B-p)}$

○ $\dfrac{x}{B-p}$

○ $\dfrac{p}{B-px}$

○ $\dfrac{p}{B(B-p)}$

Step 1: Analyze the Question

Remember, don't translate word problems into algebra right away—focus on the logic of the situation first. Some parents are baking cakes for a school, but a couple of them don't follow through, leaving the other parents to pick up the slack.

Notice that the answer choices contain variables. Whenever this is the case, consider picking numbers.

Step 2: State the Task

Solve for the number of extra cakes to be baked by each of the parents who didn't abandon the project.

Step 3: Approach Strategically

Pick some numbers for x, B, and p, making sure that the numbers you pick are manageable and permissible (if p is bigger than B, you'll be left with a negative number of parents trying to bake cakes!).

Say that you started with 10 parents, so $B = 10$. Now say that 4 don't bake any cakes, so $p = 4$. That leaves 6 parents left to bake the cakes. You're going to want to pick x so that it can be divided evenly both by 10 (the original parents) and 6 (the ones who stay on the project). $x = 30$ will do nicely.

Now the question reads:

In order to fulfill a local school's request for *30 cakes, 10 parents* agreed to each bake an equal number of cakes. If *4 of the parents did not bake any cakes*, which of the following represents the additional number of cakes that each of the *6 other parents* had to bake in order for the school's request for *30 cakes* to be fulfilled?

Now the math is much easier to see. If 10 parents agreed to bake an equal number of cakes, totaling 30 cakes, that's 3 cakes for each parent. When 4 of the parents drop out, that leaves 6 parents baking an equal number of cakes, totaling 30 cakes. That's 5 cakes for each parent.

The extra number of cakes each parent needs to bake is 2. Now plug $x = 30$, $B = 10$, and $p = 4$ into the answer choices and see which ones equal 2:

(A) is $\dfrac{4 \times 30}{10} = \dfrac{120}{10} = 12$. Eliminate.

(B) is $\dfrac{4 \times 30}{10(10-4)} = \dfrac{120}{10 \times 6} = \dfrac{120}{60} = 2$. Possibly correct.

(C) is $\dfrac{30}{10-4} = \dfrac{30}{6} = 5$. Eliminate.

(D) is $\dfrac{4}{10-(4 \times 30)} = \dfrac{4}{10-120} = \dfrac{4}{-110} =$ definitely not 2. Eliminate.

(E) is $\dfrac{4}{10(10-4)} = \dfrac{4}{10 \times 6} = \dfrac{4}{60} =$ definitely not 2. Eliminate.

Only **(B)** remains as a possible answer, and it must therefore be correct.

Step 4: Confirm Your Answer

Make sure to reread the question stem to confirm that you interpreted the information correctly.

15. (B)

If integers a and b are distinct factors of 30, which of the following CANNOT be a factor of 30?

      I. $ab + b^2$

     II. $(a + b)^2$

    III. $a + b$

- ○   I only
- ○   II only
- ○   III only
- ○   I and II only
- ○   I, II, and III

Step 1: Analyze the Question

You are given two integers, a and b, and are then told that they are distinct factors of 30. This means that a cannot equal b. Before working out the problem, jot down the factors of 30: 1, 2, 3, 5, 6, 10, 15, 30.

Step 2: State the Task

Determine which of the Roman numeral statements cannot be a factor of 30.

Step 3: Approach Strategically

Start with Statement I, not because it is first but because it appears in the most answer choices. Since variables in the expression are multiplied together or squared, the value could get quite large; you should therefore pick small numbers for a and b. Let's choose $a = 1$ and $b = 2$. Substituting into the equation, you get $1(2) + 2^2 = 2 + 4 = 6$. Since 6 is a factor of 30, Statement I can be a factor of 30. Because you are looking for the choice that CANNOT be a factor of 30, you can eliminate any answer choice containing Statement I: **(A)**, **(D)**, and **(E)** cannot be correct.

Since Statements II and III each appear once in the remaining answer choices, pick the easier expression to evaluate, Statement III. If you again pick $a = 1$ and $b = 2$, you will get $1 + 2 = 3$. Because 3 is a factor of 30, you can eliminate **(C)**. Without even needing to evaluate Statement II, you know the correct answer is **(B)**.

Step 4: Confirm Your Answer

You can check your answer by reviewing your substitutions and checking that all expressions were solved correctly.

Alternatively, you can verify that Statement II CANNOT be a factor of 30 by picking numbers. If $a = 1$ and $b = 2$, you get $(1 + 2)^2 = 3^2 = 9$, which is not a factor of 30. However, one instance of not being a factor of 30 doesn't mean this expression can never equal a factor of 30. Try the next smallest possible set of numbers that would produce a distinct result: $a = 1$ and $b = 3$. Plugging these in, you get $(1 + 3)^2 = 4^2 = 16$, also not a factor of 30. Trying a third set, $a = 2$ and $b = 3$, you get $(2 + 3)^2 = 5^2 = 25$. Again, this is not a factor of 30. One more set is all you need here; if $a = 1$ and $b = 5$, you get $(1 + 5)^2 = 6^2 = 36$. Since this is higher than 30, any other number combination you plug in will also be higher than 30 and therefore not a factor. You have confirmed that **(B)** is correct.

16. (B)

The integer a is less than -1, b is greater than -1, c is less than 1, and the integer d is greater than 1. If b is negative and c is positive, then of the following, which must be the greatest negative number?

- ○ $b - a$
- ○ $b - c$
- ○ $b - d$
- ○ $c - a$
- ○ $c - d$

Step 1: Analyze the Question

The question provides quite a bit of information, so translating that information into a simpler form can be helpful: "a is an integer that is less than -1, b is greater than -1" becomes $a < -1 < b$; and "c is less than 1, and d is an integer that is greater than 1" becomes $c < 1 < d$. Combining these two statements with "b is negative, and c is positive," yields the following single statement: $a < -1 < b < 0 < c < 1 < d$, in which a and d are integers.

Step 2: State the Task

Determine which answer choice must be the greatest negative number, meaning the negative number that is closest to 0 on the number line.

Step 3: Approach Strategically

Consider picking numbers. An example of permissible and manageable numbers to pick would be $a = -2$, $b = -0.5$, $c = 0.5$, and $d = 2$.

Substitute your numbers into the choices to see which is the largest negative number. Note that the only difference among **(A)**, **(B)**, and **(C)** is which number is subtracted from b, so you might compare those choices first:

(A) $b - a = -0.5 - (-2) = 1.5$

(B) $b - c = -0.5 - 0.5 = -1$

(C) $b - d = -0.5 - 2 = -2.5$

The greatest negative value among these three choices is **(B)**. Now test **(D)** and **(E)**.

(D) $c - a = 0.5 - (-2) = 2.5$

(E) $c - d = 0.5 - 2 = -1.5$

(D) is positive, so eliminate it. Compare **(B)** and **(E)**: since **(B)** is both negative and larger than **(E)**, **(B)** is the correct answer.

You may be wondering why it is unnecessary to pick a second set of numbers to show that **(B)** *must* be true. Failing with any set of permissible values is enough to fail the "must be true" test. Since you've eliminated four choices, the remaining choice must be the right one.

Step 4: Confirm Your Answer

Ensure that you answered the right question, finding the expression that represents the greatest negative number, which is the negative number closest to zero. A common error would be to choose the negative number with the greatest magnitude (absolute value), which is actually the smallest number.

17. (B)

In the set S of consecutive integers from 1 to 10, inclusive, D is the subset of all odd numbers, M is the subset of all prime numbers, and Q is the subset of all numbers whose positive square root is also a member of set S. If d is an element of D, m is an element of M, and q is an element of Q, which of the following could be true?

○ $d = \sqrt{mq}$

○ $d = \dfrac{q}{m}$

○ $m = q$

○ $q = \dfrac{m}{d^2}$

○ $q = \sqrt{dm}$

Step 1: Analyze the Question

The information in the question stem can be summarized as follows: the set of consecutive integers is $\{1, 2, 3, \ldots, 9, 10\}$; subsets include $D = \{1, 3, 5, 7, 9\}$, $M = \{2, 3, 5, 7\}$, and $Q = \{1, 4, 9\}$. (Subset Q consists of integers from 1 to 10 whose positive square roots are integers from 1 to 10—in other words, perfect squares.) The answer choices are equations relating members of these subsets.

Step 2: State the Task

Determine which of the statements in the answer choices *could* be true. The implication here is that, once you have found a choice that works, you can select it without having to concern yourself with any of the others; each of those is *never* true.

Step 3: Approach Strategically

Since there are variables in both the question stem and choices and the choices don't lend themselves to efficient analysis using number properties rules, consider picking numbers to test only as many choices as needed to find one equation that can be true. Pick numbers for d, m, and q that are members of the variables' respective subsets.

(A) Since this choice states that the square root of mq is an integer d, mq must be a perfect square that equals d^2. However, there is no m-value that, when multiplied by any q-value, results in a perfect square. For example, if $m = 2$, then $2 \times 1 = 2$, $2 \times 4 = 8$, and $2 \times 9 = 18$, none of which is a perfect square. Run through the remaining possible pairs of m and d in the same way and eliminate **(A)**, since it cannot be true.

(B) This choice says that when q is divided by m, the result is an integer d, so m must be a factor of q. Start with $m = 2$ and look at subset Q: it contains 4, which is a multiple of 2, so the equation would be $d = \frac{4}{2} = 2$, but that value is not in D. However, if $m = 3$ and $q = 9$, then $d = \frac{9}{3} = 3$, and that value is in D. **(B)** is thus the correct answer.

While there is no need to test the remaining choices, here is what you would have found:

(C) This choice indicates that a term from M equals a term from Q. However, no such match exists, so **(C)** cannot be true; eliminate it.

(D) Since q is an integer, for this equation to be true, d^2 must be a factor of m. Check $d = 1$: $d^2 = 1$. Any value m divided by 1 is unchanged, and no values of m are in q, so $q \neq \frac{m}{1^2}$ and d cannot equal 1. Then check $d = 3$: $3^2 = 9$, which is greater than any possible value of m, so d cannot equal 3 or any larger value. Since **(D)** cannot be true, eliminate it.

(E) This choice is similar to **(A)** in that the product of two numbers must be a perfect square. In this choice, dm must be a perfect square that equals q^2. Although it is possible to create a perfect square from one member of D and one member of M (i.e., 3^2, 5^2, and 7^2), none of these perfect squares matches the square of any element of Q. Since **(E)** cannot be true, eliminate it.

Step 4: Confirm Your Answer

Make sure that you found the choice that could be true, not that must be false! Also, make sure that you plugged in numbers from the right subset for each variable when testing the choices.

18. (E)

A teacher grades students' tests by subtracting twice the number of incorrect responses from the number of correct responses. If Student A answers each of the 100 questions on her test and receives a score of 73, how many questions did Student A answer correctly?

- ○ 55
- ○ 60
- ○ 73
- ○ 82
- ○ 91

Step 1: Analyze the Question

Student A received a score of 73 for answering 100 questions. Her score is computed by subtracting twice the number of incorrect answers from the number of correct answers.

Step 2: State the Task

Find the number of questions Student A answered correctly.

Step 3: Approach Strategically

You could solve this problem algebraically, but seeing whole numbers in the answer choices is a clue that it might be easier to backsolve this one instead. Backsolving is an option whenever you can manageably plug an answer choice into the question stem.

A penalty equal to twice the number of incorrect answers is rather harsh, so a student would have to answer many questions correctly to receive a decent score. Therefore, begin by testing **(D)**. If Student A answered 82 questions out of 100 correctly, she must have gotten $100 - 82 = 18$ incorrect. On Test Day, do not actually calculate $82 - 2(18) = 82 - 36 = 46$. Instead, get into the habit of realizing that 82 minus such a large penalty will definitely result in a number that's smaller than 73. As **(D)** is too small, the correct answer choice must be **(E)**.

Step 4: Confirm Your Answer

If Student A got 91 questions right, she would have gotten $100 - 91 = 9$ questions wrong. That would result in a score of $91 - 2(9) = 91 - 18 = 73$, the exact score you are looking for. The astute test taker will notice that a score of 73 on such a punishing scale allows one to eliminate **(A)**, **(B)**, and **(C)** before even beginning; this student must have answered more than 73 questions correctly to receive that score.

19. **(D)**

If $\left(\dfrac{1}{64}\right)^x = 4{,}096$, $x =$

○ $-\dfrac{1}{3}$

○ $-\dfrac{1}{2}$

○ $-\sqrt{2}$

○ -2

○ -3

Step 1: Analyze the Question

The question stem provides an equation containing a fraction that is raised to an unknown number x. The choices, each of which is a number, represent potential values of x.

Step 2: State the Task

Determine the value of x.

Step 3: Approach Strategically

Each choice is a negative value, so you are really raising the number 64 to the positive version of each (e.g., $\left(\dfrac{1}{64}\right)^{-\frac{1}{3}} = \dfrac{1}{\left(\frac{1}{64}\right)^{\frac{1}{3}}} = 64^{\frac{1}{3}}$). Since raising a positive integer to a fractional exponent does not result in a larger number, eliminate **(A)** and **(B)**. Also, since raising an integer to $\sqrt{2}$ results in a non-integer, eliminate **(C)**.

Now, since the remaining choices **(D)** and **(E)** are small integers, consider using the backsolving strategy. You'll need to test only one of these two choices to arrive at the correct answer. Since 2 is a smaller number than 3 and thus makes for easier math, test **(D)**: $\left(\dfrac{1}{64}\right)^{-2} = 64^2 = 64(64) = 4{,}096$. This outcome matches that in the question stem, so you have found the correct answer: **(D)**.

Step 4: Confirm Your Answer

Ensure that you did not make any careless math errors in testing the answer choices.

20. (C)

One used-car salesperson receives a commission of $200 plus 4 percent of $1,000 less than the car's final sale price. Another car salesperson earns a straight commission of 6 percent of the car's final sale price. What is the final sale price of a car if both salespeople would earn the same commission for selling it?

- ○ $5,000
- ○ $6,000
- ○ $8,000
- ○ $10,000
- ○ $12,000

Step 1: Analyze the Question

This question presents you with two salespeople, each with different commission rules. Don't jump to translating the information algebraically, as that might not be the most strategic solution.

Step 2: State the Task

Your task is to find the price of a car for which the two salespeople would earn an equal commission.

Step 3: Approach Strategically

Since you could just pick a price from the answer choices and see whether the salespeople earn the same commission, backsolving is a good choice. Backsolving is an option whenever you can manageably plug an answer choice into the question stem.

Let's say that you started with **(D)**, the $10,000 car. Salesperson 1 earns $200 + 4% of $9,000. That's $200 + $360 = $560. Salesperson 2 earns 6% of $10,000, or $600. They aren't earning the same commission, so you can eliminate **(D)**.

How does the price of the car need to change? If you have trouble figuring out abstractly whether you need a larger or smaller value, consider what would happen with extremely large or extremely small values. With a $10,000 car, you saw that Salesperson 2 earns just $40 more. But if the car cost $10 billion, then that extra 2% earned by Salesperson 2 would be so large as to make the extra $200 earned by Salesperson 1 meaningless. So, as the car gets more expensive, Salesperson 2 gets more money relative to Salesperson 1. Therefore, the correct answer must be less than $10,000. Eliminate **(E)** and test **(B)**.

If the car were $6,000, then Salesperson 1 would earn $200 + 4% of $5,000. That's $200 + $200 = $400. Salesperson 2 would earn 6% of $6,000, or $360. Now the car is too cheap. So **(C)** must be the answer.

Step 4: Confirm Your Answer

Reread the question, making sure you didn't miss anything. For example, if you overlooked the "$1,000 less than" phrase, you'd have selected **(D)**. This step would save you from the wrong answer.

GMAT BY THE NUMBERS: PROBLEM SOLVING

Now that you've learned how to approach Problem Solving questions on the GMAT, let's add one more dimension to your understanding of how they work.

Take a moment to try this question. Following is performance data from thousands of people who have studied with Kaplan over the decades. Through analyzing this data, we will show you how to approach questions like this one most effectively and how to avoid similarly tempting wrong answer choice types on Test Day.

> The number x of cars sold each week varies with the price y in dollars according to the equation $x = 800,000 - 50y$, where $y \leq 16,000$. What would be the total weekly revenue, in dollars, from the sale of cars priced at $15,000?

- ○ 50,000
- ○ 750,000
- ○ 850,000
- ○ 7,500,000
- ○ 750,000,000

EXPLANATION

The first—and in many ways most important—step in Problem Solving is to understand what you're solving for. This problem gives you an equation: $x = 800{,}000 - 50y$, with x representing the number of cars sold and y representing their price. You're given the price, so $y = 15{,}000$. But you aren't solving for x. Rather, you're solving for the total revenue. You'll therefore find the number of cars sold (x), then multiply by their price ($\$15{,}000$).

Substituting 15,000 for y in the equation, you get:

$$x = 800{,}000 - 50y$$

$$x = 800{,}000 - 50(15{,}000)$$

$$x = 800{,}000 - 750{,}000$$

$$x = 50{,}000$$

Multiplying 50,000 cars by $\$15{,}000$ yields revenue of $\$750{,}000{,}000$. **(E)** is correct.

QUESTION STATISTICS

30% of test takers choose **(A)**

18% of test takers choose **(B)**

3% of test takers choose **(C)**

5% of test takers choose **(D)**

44% of test takers choose **(E)**

Sample size = 4,464

Notice that the math involved here is not extremely challenging, yet fewer than half of test takers select the right answer. That's because two wrong answers are actually right answers—but to the wrong questions. **(A)**, the most popular incorrect choice, is the value of x. It's easy to assume that you're solving for a variable given by the problem, but often you won't be. **(B)**, the other commonly selected wrong answer, is the value of $50y$. These "intermediate values" that you generated on your way to the right answer make for very tempting wrong answers—so tempting in this problem that more test takers choose them than the right answer! Be clear about what you need to solve for, and you'll avoid the biggest Problem Solving pitfall.

MORE GMAT BY THE NUMBERS...

To see more questions with answer choice statistics, be sure to review the full-length CATs in your online resources.

GO ONLINE

kaptest.com/login

CHAPTER 11

Data Sufficiency

Is the product of x, y, and z equal to 1?

(1) $x + y + z = 3$
(2) x, y, and z are each greater than 0.

○ Statement (1) ALONE is sufficient, but statement (2) is not sufficient.
○ Statement (2) ALONE is sufficient, but statement (1) is not sufficient.
○ BOTH statements TOGETHER are sufficient, but NEITHER statement ALONE is sufficient.
○ EACH statement ALONE is sufficient.
○ Statements (1) and (2) TOGETHER are NOT sufficient.

Above is a typical Data Sufficiency question. In this chapter, we'll look at how to apply the Kaplan Method to this question, discuss how to tackle this question type, and go over the basic principles and strategies that you want to keep in mind on every Data Sufficiency question. But before you move on, take a minute to think about what you see in this question and answer some questions about how you think it works:

- How is the structure of this question different from that of a typical math question?

- What mathematical concepts are tested in this question?

- How can you use the answer choices to your advantage?

- What GMAT Core Competencies are most essential to success on this question?

PREVIEWING DATA SUFFICIENCY

HOW IS THE STRUCTURE OF THIS QUESTION DIFFERENT FROM THAT OF A TYPICAL MATH QUESTION?

The problem starts off with the question stem, which asks whether the product of x, y, and z equals the value of 1. But then there's no other information in the question stem. So how are you supposed to answer the question? A Data Sufficiency question stem will never give you enough information to solve for an answer, which is very different from typical math problems. You're probably used to having a lot of information presented up front, followed by the actual question. But Data Sufficiency works differently: the other data are presented *after* the initial question; these are called the "statements." Your goal in a Data Sufficiency question is to determine whether the data in the statements are enough to allow you to answer the question.

Sound unusual? Absolutely. Data Sufficiency is unique to the GMAT—no other standardized test presents questions in this format. Confusing? It doesn't have to be. As just noted, all you need to do is determine whether the data are sufficient to be able to answer the question. What is *not* your goal? To do a lot of time-consuming calculations. Business schools don't care about how many advanced math classes you took. They care about something else: they want to know that you're able to assimilate a lot of information and make deductions from that information. Many Data Sufficiency questions can be solved without finding the specific answer to the question presented in the stem.

WHAT MATHEMATICAL CONCEPTS ARE TESTED IN THIS QUESTION?

At first, it appears that this question tests only some fairly basic arithmetic concepts: namely, multiplication (in the question stem), addition (in the first statement), and inequalities (in the second statement). But as is often the case on GMAT Quantitative questions, what's *not* stated is also important. This is not merely an arithmetic question. It's testing number properties: how numbers with certain characteristics behave in predictable ways. A careless test taker might take for granted that x, y, and z are integers. But unless the question stem says so, never assume that variables must be integers—or even positive numbers, for that matter. Training your mind to think like this on the GMAT will take time and practice, but using the Kaplan Method for Data Sufficiency and remembering how to apply the Core Competencies will help you through even the toughest Data Sufficiency questions.

HOW CAN YOU USE THE ANSWER CHOICES TO YOUR ADVANTAGE?

Earlier you read that Data Sufficiency questions don't necessarily require you to solve the problem. This is because the answer choices are in a fixed format. All five of the answer choices have to do with the "sufficiency" or "insufficiency" of the statements. In other words, does one of the statements alone provide enough information to answer the question? Do both of them? Do both of them, but only when combined? Or is there just not enough information? Again, the answer choices will never give you actual values or expressions, such as "35,612" or "$4x^3 - 15y$." We'll show you how to use this fixed format to your advantage.

WHAT GMAT CORE COMPETENCIES ARE MOST ESSENTIAL TO SUCCESS ON THIS QUESTION?

For all Data Sufficiency questions, Critical Thinking is crucial. Mastering the format and structure will put you at an advantage over your competition, since Data Sufficiency is notoriously one of the greatest challenges for most GMAT test takers. By understanding how these questions are constructed and what the potential traps are, you will know how to get at the heart of what the test makers are asking you to do.

Attention to the Right Detail is also key to your success on Data Sufficiency. Most importantly, don't fail to consider the details that *aren't* mentioned or the restrictions that *don't* exist. Never assume anything in a Data Sufficiency question.

Here are the main topics we'll cover in this chapter:

- Question Format and Structure
- The Kaplan Method for Data Sufficiency
- The Basic Principles of Data Sufficiency
- Data Sufficiency Strategy
  - Picking Numbers in Data Sufficiency
  - Combining Statements
  - Strategic Guessing

QUESTION FORMAT AND STRUCTURE

The instructions for the Data Sufficiency section on the GMAT look like this:

Directions: In each of the problems, a question is followed by two statements containing certain data. You are to determine whether the data provided by the statements are sufficient to answer the question. Choose the correct answer based upon the statements' data, your knowledge of mathematics, and your familiarity with everyday facts (such as the number of minutes in an hour or cents in a dollar). You must indicate whether:

- ○ Statement (1) ALONE is sufficient, but statement (2) is not sufficient.
- ○ Statement (2) ALONE is sufficient, but statement (1) is not sufficient.
- ○ BOTH statements TOGETHER are sufficient, but NEITHER statement ALONE is sufficient.
- ○ EACH statement ALONE is sufficient.
- ○ Statements (1) and (2) TOGETHER are NOT sufficient.

Note: Diagrams accompanying problems agree with information given in the question but may not agree with additional information given in statements (1) and (2).

All numbers used are real numbers.

The GMAT is the only test featuring Data Sufficiency questions, and beginners often misunderstand the format. On the Quantitative section, you'll see about 14 Data Sufficiency questions, which ask you to assess whether certain statements provide enough information to answer a question. Often the question requires little or no mathematical work. The key to solving the question is understanding how the question type is structured and using that knowledge to work efficiently.

The directions may seem confusing at first, but they become clear with use. Let's walk through a simple example:

$$A \quad\quad B \quad\quad C$$

What is the length of segment *AC*?

(1) *B* is the midpoint of *AC*.

(2) *AB* = 5

O   Statement (1) ALONE is sufficient, but statement (2) is not sufficient.

O   Statement (2) ALONE is sufficient, but statement (1) is not sufficient.

O   BOTH statements TOGETHER are sufficient, but NEITHER statement ALONE is sufficient.

O   EACH statement ALONE is sufficient.

O   Statements (1) and (2) TOGETHER are NOT sufficient.

The diagram tells you that there is a line segment *AC* with point *B* somewhere between *A* and *C*. You're asked to figure out the length of *AC*.

Statement (1) tells you that *B* is the midpoint of *AC*, so $AB = BC$ and $AC = 2AB = 2BC$. Since Statement (1) does not give an actual value for *AB* or *BC*, you cannot answer the question using Statement (1) alone.

Statement (2) says that $AB = 5$. Since Statement (2) does not give you any information about *BC*, the question cannot be answered using Statement (2) alone.

Using both of the statements together, you can find a value for both *AB* and *BC*; therefore, you can solve for the length of *AC*, and the answer to the question is choice **(C)**.

THE KAPLAN METHOD FOR DATA SUFFICIENCY

This Method is the essential systematic approach to mastering Data Sufficiency. Use this approach for every Data Sufficiency question. It will allow you to answer questions quickly and will guarantee that you avoid the common Data Sufficiency mistake of subconsciously combining the statements instead of considering them separately at first.

The Kaplan Method for Data Sufficiency

1. **Analyze the question stem.**

   • Determine Value or Yes/No.

   • Simplify.

   • Identify what is needed to answer the question.

2. **Evaluate the statements using 12TEN.**

STEP 1: ANALYZE THE QUESTION STEM

There are three things you should accomplish in this step:

- **Determine Value or Yes/No.** Which type of Data Sufficiency question is this? Depending on whether the question is a Value question or a Yes/No question, the rules for sufficiency are a little different. If you treat the two types the same way, you probably won't get the right answer. Later in this chapter, you'll learn the critical differences between these two types.

- **Simplify.** If the given information is an equation that can be simplified, you should do so up front. Likewise, any word problems should be translated into math or otherwise paraphrased in your scratchwork. When a question asks for the value of a specific variable and gives you a multi-variable equation, isolate the variable being asked for so you can more clearly see what kind of information you need in order to solve.

- **Identify What Is Needed to Answer the Question.** What kind of information would get you the answer to the question? The more you think up front about what information would be sufficient, the better you'll be able to evaluate the statements.

Don't rush through this step, even for seemingly simple questions. The more you glean from the question stem, the easier it will be to find the right answer.

STEP 2: EVALUATE THE STATEMENTS USING 12TEN

Since the answer choices depend on considering each statement alone, don't let the information you learn from one statement carry over into your analysis of the other. Consider each statement separately, in conjunction with the question stem. Remember that each statement is always true. Don't waste time verifying the statements; just evaluate whether this information lets you answer the question.

On Test Day, you don't want to spend even a second reading the answer choices or thinking about which answer choice is which. They will never change, so you will save yourself much time and confusion by memorizing what the answer choices mean and working with them until you've fully internalized them.

A helpful way to remember how the answer choices are structured is to use the acronym **1-2-TEN**.

1 Only Statement **(1)** is sufficient.

2 Only Statement **(2)** is sufficient.

T You must put the statements **together** for them to be sufficient.

E **Either** statement alone is sufficient.

N **Neither** separately nor together are the statements sufficient.

In fact, it's so important to memorize the answer choices that after this initial sample question, we will no longer print the choices along with the questions. For each practice question, you should follow the routine you will use on Test Day: write 12TEN in your scratchwork for each question and cross out the incorrect answer choices as you eliminate them. We'll teach you patterns for eliminating answer choices later in this chapter.

Now, let's apply the Kaplan Method for Data Sufficiency to the question you saw at the beginning of this chapter:

Is the product of x, y, and z equal to 1?

(1) $x + y + z = 3$

(2) x, y, and z are each greater than 0.

○ Statement (1) ALONE is sufficient, but statement (2) is not sufficient.

○ Statement (2) ALONE is sufficient, but statement (1) is not sufficient.

○ BOTH statements TOGETHER are sufficient, but NEITHER statement ALONE is sufficient.

○ EACH statement ALONE is sufficient.

○ Statements (1) and (2) TOGETHER are NOT sufficient.

Step 1: Analyze the Question Stem

This is a Yes/No question. If $xyz = 1$, then the answer is "yes." If $xyz \neq 1$, then the answer is "no." Either answer—yes or no—would be sufficient. There's nothing that needs to be simplified in this step; all variables are in their simplest terms, and there are no common variables to combine. It's often worth thinking about how you could get the yes or no that you're looking for. For instance, if x, y, and z all equal 1, you would get an answer of yes. But is this the only way? This question is short but definitely not simple, since there may be many other possibilities to consider.

Step 2: Evaluate the Statements Using 12TEN

Picking numbers for Statement (1), you can readily see how to get a yes: $x = 1$, $y = 1$, and $z = 1$. Can you pick numbers in such a way that the sum is 3 but the product is not 1? Not if you only consider positive integers. But if you consider different kinds of numbers, you can easily find some. Zero doesn't alter a sum, but it forces a product to be 0. So $x = 3$, $y = 0$, and $z = 0$, while they follow the restrictions given in Statement (1), will give you an answer of "no" to the original question. Since you can get both a yes and a no, Statement (1) is insufficient. Eliminate **(A)** and **(D)**—or choices "1" and "E," if you've written 12TEN in your scratchwork.

Now that you've reached a verdict on Statement (1) on its own, completely put Statement (1) out of your mind as you evaluate Statement (2) independently. Statement (2) rules out the possibility of using 0 but not the possibility of using fractions or decimals. So $x = 1$, $y = 1$, and $z = 1$ is also permissible here, but so is something like $x = 100$, $y = 100$, and $z = 100$. So xyz could equal 1, but it could also equal 1,000,000. So you can get both a yes and a no here, as well. Statement (2) is also insufficient, so you can eliminate **(B)**—which is the "2" of 12TEN.

Since each statement is insufficient on its own, you need to consider them together. Can you pick numbers that add to 3 and are all positive? Again, $x = 1$, $y = 1$, and $z = 1$ makes the cut and answers the question with a yes. Can you think of numbers that *don't* multiply to 1 that also are consistent with both statements? Once again, you have to expand your thinking to include other types of numbers besides positive integers. Fractions and decimals make things bigger when added but smaller when multiplied. For example, $x = 2.8$, $y = 0.1$, and $z = 0.1$ fit the bill. They are all positive and sum to 3. Their product is $2.8(0.1)(0.1) = 0.028$; this answers the question with a no. Since you can get both a yes and a no answer, the statements are insufficient to answer the question even when combined. The answer is **(E)**—which corresponds to the "N" of 12TEN.

Now take a few minutes and answer the questions in the following practice set. Don't worry if they're challenging at first; you're only getting started working with this unique question type. For now, do not concentrate on speed—or even on getting the correct answer in the end—but rather on building your technique for approaching Data Sufficiency questions systematically using the Method. You'll get much more practice with these questions throughout the chapter.

PRACTICE SET: THE KAPLAN METHOD FOR DATA SUFFICIENCY

1. If $x > 0$, what is the value of x?

    (1) $x > 5$
    (2) $40 - x^2 = 4$

2. The nth term of a sequence of distinct positive integers is determined by $a_n = (k^{a_{n-2}})(a_{n-1})$, where $n \geq 3$ and k is a constant. If $a_2 = 4$, and $a_3 = 36$, what is the value of a_5?

    (1) $a_1 = 2$
    (2) $k = 3$

3. Team X won 40 basketball games. What percent of its basketball games did Team X win?

    (1) Team X played the same number of basketball games as Team Y.

    (2) Team Y won 45 games, representing 2.5 percent of the basketball games it played.

4. If $3b - |a| = 27$, what is the value of b?

    (1) $a^2 = 81$

    (2) $a^3 > 0$

5. A certain company produces exactly three products: X, Y, and Z. In 1990, what was the total income for the company from the sale of its products?

    (1) In 1990, the company sold 8,000 units of product X, 10,000 units of product Y, and 16,000 units of product Z.

    (2) In 1990, the company charged $28 per unit for product X and twice as much for product Z.

THE BASIC PRINCIPLES OF DATA SUFFICIENCY

Especially because this question type is more abstract than Problem Solving, it's essential to have a strategic approach to every Data Sufficiency question. Don't waste time or mental energy doing unnecessary calculations. A systematic approach will ensure that you find the most efficient solution to the problem and that you make as few careless and avoidable errors as possible. Here are some ways you can optimize your Data Sufficiency performance by using the Kaplan Method.

KNOW HOW TO ELIMINATE DATA SUFFICIENCY ANSWER CHOICES

As you've already learned, the directions and answer choices for Data Sufficiency questions never change, so it's to your advantage to memorize them. But you can take this approach one step further by learning how to eliminate answer choices as you work through Data Sufficiency problems.

As you evaluate the two statements, use your noteboard to keep track of which answer choices you have ruled out as incorrect. Use the following patterns to guide your elimination:

>   If Statement (1) is sufficient, the answer could only be **(A)** or **(D)**. *Eliminate* **(B)**, **(C)**, *and* **(E)**.

>   If Statement (1) is insufficient, the answer could only be **(B)**, **(C)**, or **(E)**. *Eliminate* **(A)** *and* **(D)**.

>   If Statement (2) is sufficient, the answer could only be **(B)** or **(D)**. *Eliminate* **(A)**, **(C)**, *and* **(E)**.

>   If Statement (2) is insufficient, the answer could only be **(A)**, **(C)**, or **(E)**. *Eliminate* **(B)** *and* **(D)**.

Using the mnemonic device 12TEN will help you keep track of these answer choices, allowing you to attack the question more efficiently and avoid considering an answer choice you've already ruled out.

You also want to avoid a common mistake on Data Sufficiency: choosing **(C)** when the answer is actually **(A)**, **(B)**, or **(D)**. Remember: if either statement *by itself* is sufficient, then of course the two statements *together* will also be sufficient, since the statements are always true and never contradict each other. But **(C)** can be correct *only* when each statement alone is insufficient and combining the statements is necessary to obtain sufficiency.

You should consider the statements together only if each is insufficient on its own. When you evaluate the statements together, keep in mind that each statement is true. So if you're picking numbers to evaluate the statements combined, you must choose values that are permitted by *both* statements.

KNOW THE TWO TYPES OF DATA SUFFICIENCY QUESTIONS

There are two broad types of Data Sufficiency questions, and they play by slightly different rules. The two types are Value questions and Yes/No questions. During Step 1 of the Kaplan Method for Data Sufficiency, you need to determine which type of question you're dealing with, since this will determine your approach.

Value Questions

A Value question will ask you for the exact value of something. If a statement narrows the possibilities down to exactly one number, then it is sufficient. Otherwise, it is not. Of the Data Sufficiency questions you'll see on Test Day, approximately two-thirds will be Value questions.

Let's take a closer look at how this question type functions using a sample question:

Example:

What is the value of x?

(1) $x^2 - 7x + 6 = 0$

(2) $5x = 30$

Step 1: Analyze the Question Stem

This is a Value question, meaning you need to find the value of x to obtain sufficiency. There's nothing that needs to be simplified in this step, since there's just one variable: x. Before you evaluate the statements, remember that sufficiency is obtained when you can identify one, and *only* one, possible value for x.

Step 2: Evaluate the Statements Using 12TEN

Statement (1) can be reverse-FOILed to $(x - 1)(x - 6) = 0$, which means that there are two possible values for x, either 1 or 6. But you don't even need to calculate these two values; once you know there is more than one possible value, you know that Statement (1) must be insufficient.

Statement (2) is a linear equation, containing a single variable. Therefore, there can only be one possible result (in this case, $x = 6$), and it is sufficient.

Since Statement (1) is insufficient and Statement (2) is sufficient by itself, the answer is **(B)**.

PRACTICE SET: VALUE QUESTIONS

6. What is the value of $4n - 5m$?

    (1) $\dfrac{n}{5} = \dfrac{m}{4}$

    (2) $\dfrac{n}{4} = \dfrac{m}{5}$

7. What is the value of $\dfrac{st}{u}$?

    (1) $s = \dfrac{3t}{4}$ and $u = 2t$.

    (2) $s = u - 10$ and $u = s + t + 2$.

8. If z is an integer, what is the units digit of z^3?

    (1) z is a multiple of 5.

    (2) $\sqrt{z}$ is an integer.

9. If d is the product of exactly two distinct prime factors, what is the value of the larger of those prime factors?

    (1) $100 \le d \le 120$

    (2) d is an even number.

Yes/No Questions

Yes/No questions are, simply put, questions that call for a "yes" or a "no" answer. A key difference between Value questions and Yes/No questions is that a range of values can establish sufficiency for Yes/No questions. For example, if a question asks, "Is $x > 10$?" a statement saying $x < 9$ will be sufficient.

Note that in this example, the answer to the question in the stem is, "No, x is never greater than 10." Don't confuse an answer of yes to the question "Is Statement (1) sufficient?" with a yes to the question in the stem; they are not the same. This mistake is the most common pitfall test takers face on Yes/No questions. You can avoid this pitfall by remembering that any answer of "ALWAYS yes" or "ALWAYS no" is sufficient; only "sometimes yes, sometimes no" answers are insufficient. The definitiveness of your answer to the stem question is more important in determining sufficiency than whether the answer itself happens to be yes or no.

Sometimes Yes/No questions don't appear to call for a yes or no answer. Suppose a Data Sufficiency question asks which employee, Jane or Sam, earned more in 2017. Ask yourself, "Do I really need to know the specific earnings of Jane and Sam?" As it turns out, you don't. You should handle this question the same way as you would a Yes/No question that asked, "Did Jane earn more than Sam last year?" In both cases, you have sufficient information when you determine that only one answer is possible—Jane or Sam—even if you don't know a precise value for either Jane's earnings or Sam's earnings. Again, you can determine sufficiency knowing only ranges of values (for example, it's sufficient to know that Jane earned more than $20,000 and that Sam earned less than $16,000).

Let's take a closer look at how this question type functions using a sample question:

Example:

If x is an integer, and $0 < x < 4$, is x prime?

(1) $x > 1$
(2) x is even.

Step 1: Analyze the Question Stem

This is a Yes/No question, meaning you need to determine whether x is prime or not. According to the question stem, x could be 1, 2, or 3. You know that 2 and 3 are prime but 1 is not. In order to attain a definite yes answer, x must be either 2 or 3, and to obtain a definite no answer, x must be equal to 1. In other words, you could restate the question as "Does x equal 2 or 3?"

Step 2: Evaluate the Statements Using 12TEN

Start with Statement (1). Knowing that x is greater than 1 rules out 1, leaving only 2 and 3 as possible values of x. Since both 2 and 3 are prime, you have an answer: definitely yes. This statement is sufficient. Notice that you don't know which of those two values x equals, but for a Yes/No question, knowing a precise value is irrelevant; you can still have sufficiency as long as you know the answer is "always yes" or "always no." Eliminate choices **(B)**, **(C)**, and **(E)**.

Now set aside Statement (1) and move on to Statement (2). Of the possible values of x—1, 2, and 3—only one of them is even. You've determined that x must be 2. Because 2 is prime, the statement gives you a definite yes. Statement (2) is also sufficient, so the answer is **(D)**.

PRACTICE SET: YES/NO QUESTIONS

10. Is $4 + \dfrac{n}{6}$ an integer?

    (1) n is a multiple of 3.

    (2) n divided by 6 has a remainder of 0.

11. If x and y are prime numbers, is $y(x - 3)$ odd?

    (1) $x > 10$

    (2) $y < 3$

12. Is $0 < \dfrac{a}{b} < 1$?

    (1) $ab > 1$

    (2) $a - b < 1$

13. If the integer $y > 6$, is $x^3y > 56$?

    (1) $4 < x^2 \leq 9$

    (2) $x^3 + x > x^3$

THE STATEMENTS ARE ALWAYS TRUE

The statements are new pieces of data that apply to the problem and are always true. Don't waste time trying to verify a statement.

The fact that the statements are always true has an important corollary that will help you catch careless errors: the statements will never contradict each other. Although they won't always be sufficient to answer the question, they'll never be mutually exclusive. If it appears that two statements are in disagreement with each other, you should recheck your work, because you have made an error.

Example:

What is the value of t?

(1) $t^2 = t$
(2) $t + 6 = 6$

This is a straightforward Value question for which you need a value of t. Let's say that you made an error in your analysis of Statement (1) and thought that t had to equal 1. You'd think that Statement (1) was sufficient.

Then you'd look at Statement (2). Simplifying, you'd learn that t equals 0. That's also sufficient. So you'd think that the answer would be **(D)**. However, according to your analysis, the statements contradict each other:

(1) $t = 1$
(2) $t = 0$

That isn't possible. So you'd know to go back and recheck your work. Statement (2) pretty obviously says that $t = 0$, so you would recheck your work on Statement (1). Is 1 the only number that equals itself when squared? Substitute the 0 from Statement (2) and you get $0^2 = 0 \times 0 = 0$. So Statement (1) actually permits *two* values and is therefore insufficient.

(1) $t = 0$ or 1
(2) $t = 0$

The correct answer is **(B)**, not **(D)**.

IT'S ALL ABOUT THE QUESTION STEM

On Data Sufficiency questions, if you rush past the question and dive into the statements, you risk doing a whole bunch of unnecessary—and possibly misleading—math. It's essential that you understand the question stem before you analyze the statements. For one thing, there's a huge difference between a Value question and a Yes/No question. Consider this identical pair of statements:

(1) $x^3 = x$ (1) $x^3 = x$
(2) $x^2 = x$ (2) $x^2 = x$

Here's how they evaluate:

(1) $x = -1$, 0, or 1   (1) $x = -1$, 0, or 1
(2) $x = 0$ or 1   (2) $x = 0$ or 1

But you still have no idea what the answers are without seeing the question stems:

What is the value of x?   Is $x < -1$?

(1) $x = -1$, 0, or 1   (1) $x = -1$, 0, or 1

(2) $x = 0$ or 1   (2) $x = 0$ or 1

For the question on the left, a Value question, Statement (1) is insufficient because there are three possible values of x. Statement (2) is also insufficient because it permits two possible values. Even when the statements are considered together, x could be either 0 or 1. That's two values, which is insufficient for a Value question. The answer is **(E)**.

But the question on the right is a Yes/No question, so you will need to evaluate it differently. This question asks whether x is less than -1. First, look at Statement (1). Is $-1 < -1$? No. Is $0 < -1$? No. Is $1 < -1$? No. Always no: this statement is sufficient. The same for Statement (2): Both values answer the question with a no, so it's sufficient, as well. The answer is **(D)**.

That's as different as two Data Sufficiency answers can be, and it had *nothing* to do with the statements, which were identical. It's all about the question stem.

But during Step 1 of the Kaplan Method, you want to look for more than just whether the question is a Value or a Yes/No question. You saw how Problem Solving questions get much easier with some analysis and simplification before an approach is chosen. So too with Data Sufficiency.

Example:

If $w \neq x$, $w \neq z$, and $x \neq y$, is $\dfrac{(x-y)^3(w-z)^3}{(w-z)^2(x-y)(w-x)^2} > 0$?

(1) $x > y$

(2) $w > z$

This is a Yes/No question that asks about a fraction containing multiple variable expressions as factors. At first glance, this may look like a scary question stem. But take a closer look at that fraction. There are a lot of shared terms in the numerator and the denominator. Using the laws of exponents, you can cancel the $(w-z)^2$ and the $(x-y)$ in the denominator:

If $w \neq x$, $w \neq z$, and $x \neq y$, is $\dfrac{(x-y)^{3^2}(w-z)^{3^1}}{(w-z)^2(x-y)(w-x)^2} > 0$?

That simplifies the question to this:

If $w \neq x$, $w \neq z$, and $x \neq y$, is $\dfrac{(x-y)^2(w-z)}{(w-x)^2} > 0$?

This is looking better already. You can simplify even further by thinking logically about the question. You aren't asked for the value of anything, just whether this complicated fraction is positive. Without knowing anything about the values of w, x, y, and z, what can you already know about the answer to this question stem? Well, for one thing, you know that a squared term cannot be negative. So there's no way that $(x-y)^2$ or $(w-x)^2$ is negative. In fact, since $w \neq x$ and $x \neq y$, they can't be zero, either. So those two terms are both positive, which is the only thing that matters to the question. You can simplify the question even further, to this:

Is $\dfrac{(\text{positive})(w-z)}{\text{positive}} > 0$?

Since multiplying and/or dividing $(w - z)$ by anything positive will not change its sign, you have this:

Is $w - z > 0$?

Now *that's* a much simpler question. Look at how much easier the statements have become to evaluate:

(1) $x > y$
(2) $w > z$

Statement (1) is totally irrelevant to whether $w - z > 0$. This statement is insufficient.

Statement (2) tells you that w is bigger than z, so $w - z$ must be positive. (Subtract z from both sides of the inequality, and you get $w - z > 0$.) That's a definite yes. This is sufficient, so the answer is **(B)**.

The more analysis and simplification you do with the question stem, the easier dealing with the statements will become.

Think About Sufficiency, Not Calculation

Get into the habit of thinking about what's needed for *sufficiency*, rather than doing arithmetic calculations. One of the ways that the GMAT makes a Data Sufficiency question harder is to make the numbers scarier. But if you aren't worrying about arithmetic, you won't be fazed by this. Let's take a look at two important math concepts that can help you avoid number crunching in Data Sufficiency.

The "*N*-Variables, *N*-Equations" Rule

Perhaps one of the most powerful tools to evaluate sufficiency is the *n*-variables, *n*-equations rule. If you have at least as many distinct, linear equations as you have variables, you will be able to solve for the unique numerical values of all the variables. If there are two variables, you need at least two equations to solve for all the values. If you have three variables, you need at least three equations. If you have four variables, you need at least four equations, and so on.

Note that when you apply the *n*-variables, *n*-equations rule, you must be alert to the exact definition of the word "distinct": each equation must provide new, different information. For instance, even though the equations $x + 3y = 5$ and $2x + 6y = 10$ look different, they are not in fact distinct—the second equation is merely the first equation multiplied by 2. Another example is the following system of equations: $x + 2y - 3z = 8$, $2y + 6z = 2$, and $x + 4y + 3z = 10$. These may also initially seem to be distinct, but a closer look reveals that the third equation is merely the sum of the first two. It therefore adds no new information, so this system of equations cannot be solved for unique numerical values for each variable.

Example:

A souvenir shop made $2,400 in revenue selling postcards. If a large postcard costs twice as much as a small postcard, the shop sold 950 large postcards, and it sold no other type of postcard besides these two sizes, then how many small postcards did it sell?

(1) A large postcard costs $2.
(2) If the shop had sold 20% fewer small postcards, its revenue would have been reduced by $4\frac{1}{6}\%$.

There are four factors that affect the outcome of this problem: (1) the price of a small postcard, (2) the price of a large postcard, (3) the number of small postcards sold, and (4) the number of large postcards sold. That's four variables, so four distinct, linear equations would enable you to solve for any of the variables. How many equations do you have already? Well, something-or-other equals $2,400 (that's one), there's a relationship between the prices (that's two), and you get the number of large postcards (that's three). With three equations for four variables, *any new equation* will be sufficient, as long as it is distinct and it doesn't introduce a new variable.

Statement (1) is a new equation and is therefore sufficient. Statement (2) is a more complicated equation, and it would likely be time-consuming to calculate. But it is still a new, distinct equation, and it is therefore sufficient. The answer is **(D)**.

Imagine how much time it would take to work through these equations. Using the *n*-variables, *n*-equations rule, it need take no longer than a minute.

One word of caution, though: having the same number of distinct, linear equations guarantees sufficiency, but having fewer does *not* guarantee insufficiency. The GMAT will set up equations so that you can sometimes solve for what's asked even though you can't solve for every variable individually.

Example:

> A fruit stand sells apples, pears, and oranges. If oranges cost $0.50 each, then what is the cost of 5 oranges, 4 apples, and 3 pears?
>
> (1) The cost of 1 apple is $0.30.
> (2) The cost of 8 apples and 6 pears is $3.90.

There are three variables in this problem (the cost of an orange, the cost of an apple, and the cost of a pear), so three distinct equations could solve for everything. You're given only one (the exact price of an orange). So two additional distinct equations will guarantee sufficiency. But you should keep your eyes open for a way to answer your question with fewer. Since you already know the price of an orange, the only thing you'd need to answer your question is the price of 4 apples and 3 pears.

Statement (1) is insufficient, as you still do not know anything about the price of a pear. Statement (2) is only one equation, but if you divided it by 2, you'd get the cost of 4 apples and 3 pears, which is exactly what you need. This statement is sufficient, so the correct answer is **(B)**.

Proportions

Another common way that the GMAT allows you to get sufficiency without knowing all the individual values is to ask questions based on proportions (ratios, percents, averages, rates/speed, etc.). The goal of the following exercise is to get you to think about what kind of information can be sufficient to answer a question, even though you can't calculate the exact value of every variable involved. Read the question stem and each of the following statements, asking yourself whether it gives you enough information to answer. Don't waste time trying to come up with the actual value.

What was the percent increase in profits for Company X between 1991 and 1993?

Do the following statements provide sufficient information?

(1) The company earned 20% less profit in 1991 than in 1993.

(2) The average annual profit from 1991 to 1993 was 12.5% higher than the profit in 1991.

(3) The average of the annual profits of 1991 and 1993 was 12.5% higher than the profit in 1991.

(4) In 1991, the profit was $4.5 million less than in 1993.

Let's evaluate each statement on its own:

Statement (1) is sufficient. You could "reverse" the math and figure out percent increase from the given decrease. Let the 1993 profit equal P_{1993} and the 1991 profit equal P_{1991}. The statement can be translated to $P_{1991} = 0.8\,(P_{1993})$, which is $P_{1991} = \frac{4}{5}(P_{1993})$. That means $P_{1993} = \frac{5}{4}P_{1991} = 1.25\,(P_{1991})$. That's 125% of 1991, or a 25% increase.

Statement (2) is insufficient because you don't know anything about the profit in 1992, and this information would be necessary to set up the calculation.

Statement (3) is sufficient because you are given a proportional relationship between the two years' profits: $\left(\frac{P_{1991} + P_{1993}}{2} = 1.125(P_{1991})\right)$. The question asks you for a proportional relationship, so this is exactly what you need.

Statement (4) is insufficient because you aren't given the total; you don't know what percentage a $4.5 million difference represents.

TAKEAWAYS: THE BASIC PRINCIPLES OF DATA SUFFICIENCY

The basic principles of Data Sufficiency are the following:

- Know the Data Sufficiency answer choices cold.
- Know the two types of Data Sufficiency questions.
- The statements are always true.
- It's all about the question stem.
- Think about sufficiency, not calculation.

DATA SUFFICIENCY STRATEGY

Now that you're familiar with how Data Sufficiency questions are constructed, let's look at two important strategic approaches to these questions. The first you're already familiar with from the Problem Solving chapter: we'll start by looking at how to effectively utilize the Picking Numbers strategy. After that, we'll discuss in greater detail how to most effectively combine statements.

PICKING NUMBERS IN DATA SUFFICIENCY

You've already seen the power of the Kaplan strategy of picking numbers for Problem Solving questions. You can also use this strategy for many Data Sufficiency questions that contain variables, unknown quantities, or percents of an unknown whole. When using this strategy, you always pick at least two different sets of numbers, trying to prove that the statements are *insufficient* by producing two different results. It's usually easier to prove insufficiency than sufficiency. But as you practice this strategy, the Core Competency of Pattern Recognition will also come into play. You will become adept at recognizing the types of numbers that can produce different results: positives vs. negatives, fractions vs. integers, odds vs. evens, and so on. Also, don't hesitate to use the numbers 0 and 1, as they have unique properties that make them great candidates for the picking numbers strategy.

APPLYING THE KAPLAN METHOD: PICKING NUMBERS IN DATA SUFFICIENCY

Now let's use the Kaplan Method on a Data Sufficiency question that involves picking numbers:

> If $a + b = 20$, then what is the value of $c - d$?
>
> (1) $ac - bd + bc - ad = 60$
> (2) $d = 4$

Step 1: Analyze the Question Stem

Here's a Value question, so you need one, and *only* one, value for the expression $c - d$. There's nothing much to simplify here, but keep in mind that you are given a value for another expression, $a + b$. To obtain sufficiency, you'll need values for both c and d or a way to relate the equation $a + b = 20$ to the expression $c - d$.

Step 2: Evaluate the Statements Using 12TEN

As always, think strategically. Since the GMAT doesn't present the statements in any particular order, it's sometimes wise to start by evaluating Statement (2) if it looks easier to evaluate than Statement (1). Here, Statement (2) gives you a value for d but not for c. There's also no way to relate the equation $a + b = 20$ to the expression $c - d$. Eliminate **(B)** and **(D)**. Notice that you've eliminated 50 percent of the wrong answer choices very quickly.

Now let's tackle Statement (1), remembering to use the information it provides in conjunction with the question stem. You're given $a + b = 20$, so let's use picking numbers here. Pick $a = 10$ and $b = 10$.

Now, Statement (1) reads: $10c - 10d + 10c - 10d = 60$

Combine the like terms: $20c - 20d = 60$

Factor out the 20: $20(c - d) = 60$

Divide out the 20: $c - d = 3$

So, the expression $c - d$ can equal 3. But you're not finished yet. You have to pick a different set of numbers to see whether you can produce a different answer.

What permissible numbers might be likely to produce a different answer? Since Statement (1) involves subtraction, try negative numbers. Try $a = 25$ and $b = -5$.

Now Statement (1) reads:	$25c - (-5)d + (-5)c - 25d = 60$
Move the common terms next to each other:	$25c + (-5)c - (-5)d - 25d = 60$
Simplify the positive and negative signs:	$25c - 5c + 5d - 25d = 60$
Combine like terms:	$20c - 20d = 60$
Factor out the 20:	$20(c - d) = 60$
Divide out the 20:	$c - d = 3$

After picking two sets of numbers that have different properties and receiving the same result, you can say with reasonable confidence that Statement (1) is sufficient. Eliminate **(C)** and **(E)**. The correct answer is **(A)**.

TAKEAWAYS: PICKING NUMBERS IN DATA SUFFICIENCY

- To evaluate a statement (or the statements combined), you must pick at least two sets of numbers.
- When picking the second set of numbers, try to produce a different answer than that given by the first set.

PRACTICE SET: PICKING NUMBERS IN DATA SUFFICIENCY

14. If x is an integer with n distinct prime factors, is n greater than or equal to 3?

    (1) x is divisible by 6.
    (2) x is divisible by 10.

15. If $x^3 < x$, is $x > x^2$?

    (1) $x > -5$
    (2) $x < -2$

16. Is $|15 - m| + |m - 15| > 15$?

    (1) $m > 6$
    (2) $m < 7$

COMBINING STATEMENTS

If—and *only* if—each statement on its own is insufficient, you must then consider the statements together. The best way to do this is to think of the statements as one long sentence. At this stage, you can essentially approach the question as you would a Problem Solving question, using all the information you're given to answer the question. The main difference is that, since this is still Data Sufficiency, you will stop solving as soon as you know that you *can* solve. The time saved by avoiding unnecessary calculations is better spent on questions later in the section.

As you've learned earlier in this chapter, information is always consistent between the statements. The statements never contradict each other. For example, you'll never see a question in which Statement (1) says that x must be negative and Statement (2) says that x is positive. You might, however, learn from Statement (1) that x is greater than -5 and learn from Statement (2) that it's positive. Learning to recognize how one statement does or does not limit the information in the other is the key in deciding between choices **(C)** and **(E)**.

Combining Statements Exercise

Answers are on the following page.

The following exercise contains a single question stem—"What is the value of x?"— and many sets of sample statements, which have already been simplified and evaluated for you. Imagine that you had analyzed the statements and gotten the possible values for x listed below: Which statements, either separately or combined, are sufficient to answer the question? Choose the appropriate Data Sufficiency answer choice—**(A)**, **(B)**, **(C)**, **(D)**, or **(E)**—for each pair of statements.

What is the value of x?

1. (1) $x = -1, 0, 1$ 4. (1) $x = -1, 1$ 7. (1) $x = -1, 1$

    (2) $x = 0, 1$ (2) $x = 1, 2$ (2) $x = -1$

2. (1) $x < 3$ 5. (1) $x < 4$ 8. (1) $x \geq 2$

    (2) $x > 1$ (2) $x < 2$ (2) $x \leq 2$

3. (1) $x = -1, 0$ 6. (1) $x = -1, 0$ 9. (1) x is even.

    (2) $x < 0$ (2) $x = -1, 0$ (2) x is prime.

Combining Statements Exercise: Answers

1. **(E)**; x could be 0 or 1.

2. **(E)**; x could be any number between (but not including) 1 and 3. Don't assume that variables are integers.

3. **(C)**; $x = -1$.

4. **(C)**; $x = 1$.

5. **(E)**; x could be any number smaller than 2.

6. **(E)**; x could be 0 or -1. Statements that give redundant information are never sufficient when combined.

7. **(B)**; Statement (2) is sufficient. Note that you would never combine statements in this case.

8. **(C)**; $x = 2$.

9. **(C)**; $x = 2$.

APPLYING THE KAPLAN METHOD: COMBINING STATEMENTS

Now let's use the Kaplan Method on a Data Sufficiency question that involves picking numbers:

If x and y are positive integers, is $\frac{2x}{y}$ an integer?

(1) Some factors of y are also factors of x.

(2) All distinct prime factors of y are also prime factors of x.

Step 1: Analyze the Question Stem

First, this is a Yes/No question. Any statement that gives you a "sometimes yes; sometimes no" answer is insufficient. Now, how can you paraphrase the question in the stem? You can say either, "Is $2x$ a multiple of y?" or "Does $2x$ divide evenly by y?"

Step 2: Evaluate the Statements Using 12TEN

Use the Kaplan strategy of picking numbers. Pick permissible, manageable numbers. If you pick $x = 5$ and $y = 5$, that will give you a yes to the original question, since $2x$, or 10, divided by y, or 5, will yield an integer. But if you pick a different set of numbers, say $x = 2$ and $y = 42$, that will yield a fraction. Statement (1) is insufficient; eliminate **(A)** and **(D)**.

Pick numbers for Statement (2), making sure they're permissible. For example, 36 and 6 have the same distinct prime factors: 2 and 3. Picking the numbers $x = 36$ and $y = 6$ gives you an integer; choosing $x = 6$ and $y = 36$, on the other hand, gives you a fraction. Therefore, Statement (2) is insufficient; eliminate **(B)**.

Now, combining the statements, you will notice something interesting. Statement (2) is more restrictive than Statement (1). So as you combine the statements, ask yourself, "Will any numbers that satisfy Statement (2) also satisfy Statement (1)?" Yes, they will. For instance, $x = 36$ and $y = 6$, which you picked for Statement (2), also work for Statement (1): these numbers will again yield a yes answer. And $x = 6$ and $y = 36$ also work for Statement (1), yielding a no answer. Since combining the statements didn't add any new information and the information presented was insufficient, the answer must be **(E)**. Even combined, you get a "sometimes yes, sometimes no" answer to the question in the stem.

TAKEAWAYS: COMBINING STATEMENTS

- Each data statement is true. Therefore, when combining statements, look for values that are permitted by both statements.
- Treat combined statements as one long statement.
- Never combine statements unless each statement is insufficient on its own.

PRACTICE SET: COMBINING STATEMENTS

17. If a and b are positive, what is the value of $a - b$?

    (1) $a^2 + 2ab + b^2 = 36$

    (2) $a^2 - b^2 = 12$

18. Is $y^2 < 1$?

    (1) $y > -1$

    (2) $y < 1$

19. A taqueria has exactly two items on its menu, a taco and a burrito. On a particular day, it sold 600 items, exactly half of which were tacos. What was the taqueria's revenue on that day?

    (1) The average price of an item on the menu is $4.50.

    (2) A burrito costs twice as much as a taco.

STRATEGIC GUESSING

When you run into a very complicated question, like the following, don't forget to use a sound Data Sufficiency guessing strategy. That means perhaps skipping a statement that looks too daunting and trying to eliminate some answer choices by looking at the easier statement. Try your hand at the difficult question below. Don't try to solve it; instead, see if you can narrow down the possibilities quickly.

Example:

What was the maximum temperature in City A on Saturday, May 14?

(1) The average (arithmetic mean) of the maximum daily temperatures in City A from Sunday, May 8, to Saturday, May 14, was 72 degrees, which was 2 degrees less than the average (arithmetic mean) of the maximum daily temperatures in City A from Monday, May 9, to Friday, May 13.

(2) The maximum temperature in City A on Saturday, May 14, was 5 degrees greater than the maximum temperature in City A on Sunday, May 8.

Step 1: Analyze the Question Stem

This is a Value question. To obtain sufficiency, you need an exact maximum temperature.

Step 2: Evaluate the Statements Using 12TEN

Statement (1) is long and complicated. Skip it and go straight to Statement (2); it's much easier.

Statement (2) tells you that the value you're looking for is 5 degrees more than the temperature on some other day. Without knowing the temperature on that other day, you don't have the information you need. This statement is insufficient. You can eliminate **(B)** and **(D)** and give yourself a one-in-three chance to get the right answer without even evaluating Statement (1).

Perhaps you feel comfortable evaluating Statement (1). Perhaps you don't. But let's pretend for a moment that you aren't sure how to evaluate Statement (1). Keep in mind that on the GMAT, complicated or hard-to-evaluate statements are more likely to be sufficient than insufficient. For this reason, you should avoid **(E)** and lean toward **(A)**, unless you have a logical reason to suspect that Statement (1) alone is insufficient. Of course, this doesn't guarantee you a correct answer, but if you're falling behind on time, it will help you move through the Quantitative section most efficiently. Remember, no one particular question will make or break your GMAT score, but spending too much time on one question and having to rush through several others just to make up for the lost time will hurt your score. As it turns out, **(C)** is the right answer to this particular problem.

Fortunately, you're unlikely to run into anything as complicated as Statement (1) on Test Day. The point of this exercise is to show you that even if you do encounter something this difficult, you're still in control. If you work the odds and look for the strategic approach, you will increase your likelihood of picking up the points even for questions you're not sure how to solve.

For the record, let's analyze Statement (1). If the average maximum temperature from May 8 to May 14 was 72 degrees, then the sum of the maximum temperatures of those days is $7 \times 72 = 504$ degrees. If the average maximum temperature from May 9 to May 13 was $72 + 2$, or 74 degrees, then the sum of the maximum temperatures of those days was $5 \times 74 = 370$ degrees.

The difference between those two sums is simply the sum of the maximum temperature on May 8, which you can call x, and the maximum temperature on May 14, which you can call y (since these two days were left out of the second time period). So $x + y = 504 - 370 = 134$. Statement (1) by itself is insufficient. But Statement (2) tells you that $y - x = 5$. You have the two distinct linear equations, $x + y = 134$ and $y - x = 5$. These equations can be solved for a single value for y, so the statements taken together are sufficient: choice **(C)**.

This example demonstrates how guessing can be a good alternative approach for certain questions. By looking at only one statement, you can narrow down the possibilities to two or three choices. This can be a great help, particularly on difficult or time-consuming problems for which you think you might have to guess. But you must be sure you know the rules for eliminating answer choices absolutely cold by Test Day.

ANSWERS AND EXPLANATIONS

1.	B	8.	E	15.	B
2.	D	9.	E	16.	B
3.	C	10.	B	17.	C
4.	A	11.	D	18.	C
5.	E	12.	E	19.	A
6.	A	13.	C		
7.	C	14.	C		

1. **(B)**

    If $x > 0$, what is the value of x?

    (1) $x > 5$
    (2) $40 - x^2 = 4$

Step 1: Analyze the Question Stem

In this Value question, sufficiency means finding one and only one value for x. You are told that x must be greater than 0.

Step 2: Evaluate the Statements Using 12TEN

Statement (1) tells you that $x > 5$. While that certainly narrows down the options for x, there is no way to figure out one and only one value for x from that information alone, so this statement is insufficient. Eliminate **(A)** and **(D)**.

Statement (2) provides an equation that allows you to determine the value of x^2. Every positive number has two square roots, one positive and one negative, so this statement narrows the options down to two values for x. This would normally not be sufficient. However, the question stem states that $x > 0$, which eliminates the negative square root, leaving one and only one value for x. Statement (2) alone is sufficient, so **(B)** is correct.

2. **(D)**

The nth term of a sequence of distinct positive integers is determined by $a_n = (k^{a_{n-2}})(a_{n-1})$, where $n \geq 3$ and k is a constant. If $a_2 = 4$, and $a_3 = 36$, what is the value of a_5?

(1) $a_1 = 2$

(2) $k = 3$

Step 1: Analyze the Question Stem

The question stem defines a sequence by providing a relationship among three consecutive terms $(a_{n-2}, a_{n-1},$ and $a_n)$, and it asks for the value of a_5, or the fifth number in the sequence. Since this is not Problem Solving, do not be overly concerned with interpreting the sequence notation to solve for a value. Just know that the subscript represents a value's position in the sequence, so to solve for the fifth term, you'd use the equation $a_5 = (k^{a_3})(a_4)$. You are given the values of the second and third terms, so knowing the value of k would allow you to solve for the fourth term. Then you would know the values of the third and fourth terms and k, and you'd be able to solve.

Simplify the given information to make it easier to see what is needed to determine k's value:

$$a_3 = (k^{a_1})(a_2)$$

$$36 = (k^{a_1})(4)$$

$$k^{a_1} = 9$$

If you know the value of a_1, you can solve for k.

Step 2: Evaluate the Statements Using 12TEN

Statement (1) tells you the value of the first term in the sequence. From that value, you could determine the value of k. Then, as described in Step 1, you could determine the value of a_4 and then of a_5. Since this is a Data Sufficiency question, knowing that you could determine the value of a_5 is enough—don't spend precious time actually calculating it! Eliminate **(B)**, **(C)**, and **(E)**.

Statement (2) tells you the value of k. This would allow calculation of a_4 and then a_5. This statement is also sufficient.

Since either statement on its own provides enough information to determine the value of a_5, the correct choice is **(D)**.

3. **(C)**

Team X won 40 basketball games. What percent of its basketball games did Team X win?

(1) Team X played the same number of basketball games as Team Y.

(2) Team Y won 45 games, representing 2.5 percent of the basketball games it played.

Step 1: Analyze the Question Stem

In this Value question, the stem gives the number of games won by Team X and asks for the percentage of games the team won. For sufficiency, you need to be able to determine the number of games Team X played. From that, you can determine Team X's winning percentage.

Step 2: Evaluate the Statements Using 12TEN

Statement (1) tells you that Team X played the same number of games as Team Y, but you know nothing of Team Y. This statement is insufficient, so eliminate **(A)** and **(D)**.

Statement (2) tells you how many games Team Y won and gives enough information to calculate how many total games Team Y played. Because you do not know the relevance of Team Y's performance from this statement (remember not to combine the statements yet), the statement is insufficient. You can eliminate **(B)**.

Because each of the statements is insufficient alone, combine the statements. From Statement (2), you could determine the number of games that Team Y played, and from Statement (1), you know that this is equal to the number of games that Team X played. Together, the statements are sufficient, so the correct answer choice is **(C)**.

4. (A)

If $3b - |a| = 27$, what is the value of b?

(1) $a^2 = 81$

(2) $a^3 > 0$

Step 1: Analyze the Question Stem

This is a Value question, which means that sufficiency requires one and only one value for b. A value for $|a|$ is needed in order to solve for b. Since absolute value is always positive, only the magnitude of a is needed, not its sign.

Step 2: Evaluate the Statements Using 12TEN

Statement (1) gives a value for a^2; although a itself could be either positive or negative, taking the absolute value of either will have the same result. Therefore, this statement is sufficient, eliminating **(B)**, **(C)**, and **(E)**.

Statement (2) indicates that a^3 is positive. Since a negative number or zero raised to an odd exponent would not be positive, this shows that a is positive, but many values of a are still possible. This is insufficient, eliminating **(D)**.

Therefore, Statement (1) alone is sufficient, and the correct choice is **(A)**.

Note that using the Kaplan Method will keep you from falling into a trap laid by the test maker. If you thought from the first statement that having two possible values—one positive and one negative—for a meant that the information was insufficient to get one value, you might have thought you needed the information in Statement (2) to get one value for a. However, by determining what you need for sufficiency before looking at the statements, you realized that it does not matter whether you have the positive or negative value of a, as either allows solving for one and only one value for b.

5. (E)

A certain company produces exactly three products: X, Y, and Z. In 1990, what was the total income for the company from the sale of its products?

(1) In 1990, the company sold 8,000 units of product X, 10,000 units of product Y, and 16,000 units of product Z.

(2) In 1990, the company charged $28 per unit for product X and twice as much for product Z.

Step 1: Analyze the Question Stem

In this Value question, you are told that a company makes three products and are asked to find the total income from the sale of these products. For sufficiency, you need to be able to determine the quantities and prices of all three products.

Step 2: Evaluate the Statements Using 12TEN

Statement (1) gives you quantity information, by product, for each of the three products. Because it has no pricing information, the statement is insufficient. Eliminate **(A)** and **(D)**.

Statement (2) gives you pricing information for one product and information to calculate the price of a second product. However, it has no quantity information and nothing about the pricing of the third product. The statement is therefore insufficient, and you can eliminate **(B)**.

Because each of the statements is insufficient, combine the statements. When combined, you have quantity information for all three products but only have pricing information for two of them. Therefore, the two statements combined are insufficient to answer the question. **(E)** is correct.

6. (A)

What is the value of $4n - 5m$?

(1) $\dfrac{n}{5} = \dfrac{m}{4}$

(2) $\dfrac{n}{4} = \dfrac{m}{5}$

Step 1: Analyze the Question Stem

This Value question requires one and only one value for the expression $4n - 5m$. You will either need to find the value for that expression or find the values of n and m individually.

Step 2: Evaluate the Statements Using 12TEN

Statement (1) may not look like much help at first, but cross multiplying results in the equation $4n = 5m$. Subtract $5m$ from both sides to find that $4n - 5m = 0$. This is one and only one value for the expression in the question stem, so this statement is sufficient. Eliminate **(B)**, **(C)**, and **(E)**.

Statement (2) looks very similar to Statement (1), but cross multiplying here results in the equation $5n = 4m$. From this, there is no way to figure out the values of n or m (you would need two distinct equations to do that, given that there are two variables) and no way to isolate $4n - 5m$. Statement (2) is therefore insufficient, so you can eliminate **(D)**.

Statement (1) alone is sufficient, so the correct answer is **(A)**.

7. **(C)**

What is the value of $\frac{st}{u}$?

(1) $s = \frac{3t}{4}$ and $u = 2t$.

(2) $s = u - 10$ and $u = s + t + 2$.

Step 1: Analyze the Question Stem

This is a Value question. The stem for this item includes three variables. Specific values for each of the variables would be sufficient to get one value for the entire expression.

Step 2: Evaluate the Statements Using 12TEN

Statement (1) gives you restatements of two of the variables—s and u—in terms of the third variable, t. If you take the expression in the stem and replace s and u with the expressions given in the statement, you can see that the variable t is not eliminated:

$$\frac{st}{u} = \frac{\left(\frac{3t}{4}\right)t}{2t} = \frac{\frac{3t^2}{4}}{2t} = \frac{3t^2}{4} \times \frac{1}{2t} \times \frac{3t^2}{8t} = \frac{3}{8}t$$

Therefore, Statement (1) is insufficient, and you can eliminate **(A)** and **(D)**.

At first glance, Statement (2) appears to invite a similar conclusion to the one for Statement (1). However, further analysis of the information is worth a try. You are told that $s = u - 10$ and also that $u = s + t + 2$. Substituting $u - 10$ for s in the second equation, you find that

$$u = u - 10 + t + 2$$
$$8 = t$$

Substitute the value of 8 for t and substitute $u - 10$ for s:

$$\frac{st}{u} = \frac{(u - 10)(8)}{u} = \frac{8u - 80}{u}$$

Unfortunately, this still doesn't eliminate the variable u, so Statement (2) is insufficient and you can eliminate **(B)**.

Combining the statements, you determined from Statement (1) that the expression $\frac{st}{u} = \frac{3}{8}t$. If you substitute the value of 8 for the variable t—from Statement (2)—you see that you can get one value, even without actually solving the math.

Therefore, the correct answer is **(C)**: Neither statement alone is sufficient, but the statements combined are sufficient.

8. (E)

If z is an integer, what is the units digit of z^3?

(1) z is a multiple of 5.
(2) $\sqrt{z}$ is an integer.

Step 1: Analyze the Question Stem

In this Value question, to have sufficiency, you need to know either the value of integer z or something about z that would enable you to determine the units digit of its cube.

Step 2: Evaluate the Statements Using 12TEN

Statement (1) tells you that z is a multiple of 5. Multiples of 5 have units digits of either 0 or 5. Cubes of numbers with units digits of 0 or 5 keep the same units digit (e.g., the cube of 10 is 1,000; the cube of 5 is 125). The statement is insufficient because it gives you two possible answers to the question stem. Eliminate **(A)** and **(D)**.

Statement (2) tells you that the square root of z is an integer. This means that z is a perfect square. The statement is insufficient because there are perfect squares with many different units values. Eliminate **(B)**.

Because each of the statements is insufficient on its own, combine the statements. Combined, you know that z is both a multiple of 5 and a perfect square. If you can find examples for z that are perfect squares ending in each of the values from Statement (1), then the combined statements are insufficient. If $z = 25$, it is a multiple of 5 and its square root is an integer, and the answer to the question stem is 5. If $z = 100$, then both statements are true, and the answer to the question is 0. Since more than one answer to the question is possible, the two statements taken together are insufficient. Eliminate **(C)**. **(E)** is the correct answer.

EXPLANATIONS

9. (E)

If *d* is the product of exactly two distinct prime factors, what is the value of the larger of those prime factors?

(1) $100 \leq d \leq 120$

(2) *d* is an even number.

Step 1: Analyze the Question Stem

This is a Value question, so sufficiency will exist if there's enough information to determine one exact numeric value for *d*. Start with the question stem: since *d* is the product of *exactly* two distinct prime factors, *d* must be an integer whose only factors besides 1 and *d* are those two prime factors.

Step 2: Evaluate the Statements Using 12TEN

Statement (1) gives a range of possible values. Thus, you need to determine whether more than one of those values is the product of two prime factors. In fact, several are: $2 \times 53 = 106$, $5 \times 23 = 115$, and $7 \times 17 = 119$, to name a few. Thus, there are a number of different values within the range that are the product of two prime factors, and you can't establish a single value for the larger factor. Statement (1) is insufficient. Eliminate **(A)** and **(D)**.

Statement (2) only tells you that *d* is even. You know from the question stem that *d* is the product of two prime factors, so if *d* is even, one of those two prime factors must be 2 (because all other prime numbers are odd, and the product of any two odd numbers is odd, whereas the product of an even times an odd will always be even). However, there's no way to establish an exact value for *d*. Eliminate **(B)**.

Now consider the statements together. Treating (1) and (2) as one long statement, *d* has a value from 100 to 120, and it's even. Knowing that one of the prime factors of *d* is 2, you can reconsider the value range established by Statement (1) in terms of multiples of 2: $(2 \times 50) \leq d \leq (2 \times 60)$. List out the numbers between 50 and 60 and eliminate those that aren't prime: 50, 51, 52, 53, 54, 55, 56, 57, 58, 59, 60. Since no prime number besides 2 is even, you can cross off all of the even values, which leaves 51, 53, 55, 57, and 59. Eliminate 55, since it's a multiple of 5. Since 51 has digits that sum to a multiple of 3 ($5 + 1 = 6$), 51 is a multiple of 3. Eliminate it. That leaves 53, 57, and 59. All of these are prime (if you have the primes up to 100 memorized, you'll recognize this; if not, some testing will establish that all three are prime). Thus, any one of them might be the larger prime factor of *d*, so there's no way to establish a single value for this larger prime factor, and the two statements in combination are insufficient. The correct choice is **(E)**.

10. (B)

Is $4 + \dfrac{n}{6}$ an integer?

(1) n is a multiple of 3.

(2) n divided by 6 has a remainder of 0.

Step 1: Analyze the Question Stem

This Yes/No question asks whether $4 + \frac{n}{6}$ is an integer. Sufficiency means showing that the value of the expression is definitely an integer or definitely not an integer. As 4 is an integer and will therefore have no effect on whether the entire expression is equal to an integer, you simply need to consider whether $\frac{n}{6}$ is definitely an integer.

Step 2: Evaluate the Statements Using 12TEN

Statement (1) narrows the value of n to multiples of 3. Picking numbers can illustrate: if $n = 6$, $\frac{n}{6}$ is an integer, but if $n = 9$, $\frac{n}{6}$ is not an integer. There is no definite yes or no outcome for the given expression, so this statement is insufficient. Eliminate **(A)** and **(D)**.

Statement (2) restricts n to values that leave a remainder of 0 when divided by 6. These are, by definition, multiples of 6, and any multiple of 6 for n will always make $\frac{n}{6}$ an integer. This statement provides a definite yes answer, so it is sufficient. Eliminate **(C)** and **(E)**.

Statement (2) alone is sufficient, so the correct answer is **(B)**.

11. (D)

If x and y are prime numbers, is $y(x - 3)$ odd?

(1) $x > 10$
(2) $y < 3$

Step 1: Analyze the Question Stem

This is a Yes/No question. You are asked whether a particular expression is odd. For sufficiency, you need to be able to determine whether the solution to the expression is definitely odd or definitely even. Here, you should consider the rules of odds and evens: (odd × odd) = odd, (even × even) = even, and (odd × even) = even; (odd + odd) = even, (odd + even) = odd, and (even + even) = even. So if either y is even or if x is odd (making $x - 3$ even), you will be able to answer the question with a no. Note also that you're told that x and y are prime numbers. Seeing that you're asked about odd numbers, and seeing that you're dealing with primes, you should expect that the question involves the fact that 2 is the only even prime number.

Step 2: Evaluate the Statements Using 12TEN

Statement (1): If x is a prime number greater than 10, then it must be odd. Therefore, $x - 3$ must be even. The statement is sufficient to answer the question stem with a no, which eliminates **(B)**, **(C)**, and **(E)**.

Statement (2): If y is a prime number less than 3, y must equal 2, which is even. The statement is sufficient to answer the question stem with a no. That eliminates **(A)** and tells you that **(D)** is the correct answer.

Because at least one of the statements alone is sufficient to answer the question, do not evaluate the statements combined.

12. (E)

Is $0 < \dfrac{a}{b} < 1$?

(1) $ab > 1$

(2) $a - b < 1$

Step 1: Analyze the Question Stem

This is a Yes/No question. For sufficiency, a definite yes would show that $\frac{a}{b}$ is always a positive fraction less than 1, or a definite no would show that $\frac{a}{b}$ is always something other than a positive fraction less than 1. Picking numbers will help simplify this.

Step 2: Evaluate the Statements Using 12TEN

Statement (1) tells you that ab is greater than 1. That means either that a and b are both positive or that they are both negative. Pick some numbers to test out the possibilities:

Case 1:	a = −3, b = −2	(−3)(−2) > 1	Stem question: No
Case 2:	a = 2, b = 3	(2)(3) > 1	Stem question: Yes

Because you can pick numbers that follow the rules of the statement without giving a clear yes or no answer to the question stem, the statement is insufficient. Eliminate **(A)** and **(D)**.

Statement (2) tells you that $a - b$ is less than 1. The same pairs of numbers you tested for Statement (1) apply here as well, making the statement insufficient.

Case 1:	a = −3, b = −2	(−3) − (−2) < 1	Stem question: No
Case 2:	a = 2, b = 3	2 − 3 < 1	Stem question: Yes

Eliminate **(B)**.

Because each of the statements is insufficient on its own, combine the statements. Since the same cases applied to both statements, combining the statements adds no new information to the analysis, and the combined statements are therefore insufficient. The answer must be **(E)**.

13. (C)

If the integer $y > 6$, is $x^3y > 56$?

(1) $4 < x^2 \leq 9$

(2) $x^3 + x > x^3$

Step 1: Analyze the Question Stem

This is a Yes/No question. The stem tells you that y is an integer greater than 6, meaning its minimum value is 7, and it asks whether x^3y is greater than 56. Substituting 7 into the second expression reads, "Is $7x^3$ greater than 56?" Simplify further by dividing both sides by 7: "Is x^3 greater than 8?" And finally, take the cube root of both sides, "Is x greater than 2?" If you can answer this question for certain, with either a yes or a no, you'll have sufficiency.

Step 2: Evaluate the Statements Using 12TEN

Statement (1) says that $4 < x^2 \leq 9$. If you take the square root of all parts of this inequality, you get two possible value ranges for x: either $2 < x \leq 3$ or $-3 \leq x < -2$ (since you must consider negative as well as positive square roots). Since x itself might be either positive or negative, x^3 could be either positive or negative (because a negative number cubed remains negative). Therefore, x^3 could be greater than 8 but not greater than 27 *or* it could be less than -8 but not less than -27. Thus, you don't know whether x is greater than 2 and it's not possible to determine whether $x^3y > 56$; since y is positive, if x^3 is negative, x^3y will be negative, and if x^3 is positive, x^3y will be positive as well. Statement (1) is insufficient, so eliminate **(A)** and **(D)**.

Statement (2) tells you that $x^3 + x > x^3$. Remembering that the statements are always true, pick some positive and negative numbers here to see which are permissible. If $x = 3$, then $x^3 + x = 27 + 3 = 30$, and the statement is true, since $30 > 27$; therefore, x could equal 3. Not only that, but the sum of any positive number and the cube of that number will be greater than the cube alone. However, if $x = -3$, then $x^3 + x = -27 + (-3) = -30$, and the inequality is no longer true, since -30 is not greater than -27. This example demonstrates that adding a negative number to its cube results in a value smaller than the cube. Thus, Statement (2) establishes that x is a positive number. However, that's all it establishes about the value of x, which could be 3, or 100, or 0.005, or any other positive value. Therefore, this statement doesn't provide enough information to determine whether x^3y is greater than 56. Eliminate **(B)**.

Now consider the two statements together: Statement (1) establishes a pair of value ranges for x: $2 < x \leq 3$ or $-2 > x \geq -3$, and Statement (2) establishes that the range of values for x can only be positive. Thus, you know that $x > 2$, which is sufficient to answer the question. The correct choice is **(C)**.

14. (C)

If x is an integer with n distinct prime factors, is n greater than or equal to 3?

(1) x is divisible by 6.

(2) x is divisible by 10.

Step 1: Analyze the Question Stem

This is a Yes/No question, so you don't need to know the exact value of n, just whether $n \geq 3$.

There's nothing to simplify, but it's important to note the relationship between the variables: n is the number of distinct prime factors of x. (Every non-prime number can be rewritten as a series of prime numbers multiplied together; those are the number's prime factors.)

To answer the question, you'll need to know whether or not x has at least three distinct prime factors.

Step 2: Evaluate the Statements Using 12TEN

Let's say that you weren't sure how to evaluate the statements abstractly. Picking numbers allows you to evaluate a Data Sufficiency statement when you aren't comfortable with a more rules-based approach.

Statement (1): Pick the simplest number that's divisible by 6, namely $x = 6$ itself. You get $6 = 2 \times 3$. Since there are two prime factors, $n = 2$. Now test that number in the question: "Is $2 \geq 3$?" No, it isn't.

But your work on Statement (1) isn't done. You only know that Statement (1) *can* yield the answer no. You have no idea yet whether the answer is "definitely no," because other permissible numbers might yield different results. Always test at least two sets of numbers when picking numbers in Data Sufficiency so that you can differentiate between the *definite* answers and the *maybe* answers.

Since you already got a no answer, your task is to see whether you can get a yes, thus proving that Statement (1) does not provide one definite answer. Could you think of a value for x that has three or more prime factors? Since 2 and 3 showed up as prime factors already, you can think of a value for x that has a different prime factor: 5, perhaps. So pick x to be a multiple of 5 that is also divisible by 6 (otherwise it won't be permissible). You'll find that $x = 30$ fits the bill: $30 = 2 \times 3 \times 5$. That's three prime factors, so $n = 3$. Put that into the question: "Is $3 \geq 3$?" Yes, it is.

Because you've found both a yes and a no answer, Statement (1) answers the question "maybe yes, maybe no." That's not a definite answer, so Statement (1) is insufficient. Eliminate **(A)** and **(D)**.

Statement (2): Now pick the simplest number that's divisible by 10, namely $x = 10$ itself. You get $10 = 2 \times 5$. Since there are two prime factors, $n = 2$. Now test that number in the question: "Is $2 \geq 3$?" No, it isn't. See whether you can pick a number that yields a different answer. You've already seen a number that has three prime factors: 30. And it's divisible by 10, so it's permitted by Statement (2). You get $30 = 2 \times 3 \times 5$. That's three prime factors, so $n = 3$. Put that into the question: "Is $3 \geq 3$?" Yes, it is. As with Statement (1), you've produced a "maybe" answer, so Statement (2) is insufficient. Eliminate **(B)**.

(C) and **(E)** still remain, so now you have to consider the statements together. You have to pick values for x that are divisible both by 6 and by 10. Happily, you already know one from your earlier work. If $x = 30$, then the answer to the question is yes. Can you find a number that's divisible both by 6 and by 10 but has fewer than three prime factors? Try $x = 6 \times 10$, or $x = 60$. You get $60 = 6 \times 10 = 2 \times 3 \times 2 \times 5 = 2^2 \times 3 \times 5$. That's also three distinct prime factors. If you weren't at this point confident that any number that's divisible both by 6 and by 10 would have to have 2, 3, and 5 as prime factors (that's at least three!), quickly testing one or two other possibilities (e.g., $x = 90$, $x = 120$) would confirm it. No matter what permissible numbers you pick, you get the same answer: yes. So considering the statements together, the answer is "definitely yes." **(C)** is correct.

15. (B)

If $x^3 < x$, is $x > x^2$?

(1) $x > -5$

(2) $x < -2$

Step 1: Analyze the Question Stem

This is a Yes/No question, so you don't need to know the exact value of x, just whether x is definitely greater than x^2 or definitely *not* greater than x^2.

Is it possible to simplify the question? You're told that $x^3 < x$. When would a number be *greater* than its cube? Picking numbers can help you understand the question. If $x = 2$, then $x^3 = 8$; 8 is not less than 2, so $x = 2$ is not a permissible number according to the question stem. Neither is $x = 1$ nor $x = 0$, as in both cases $x^3 = x$. What about other kinds of numbers, like fractions less than 1 or negatives?

If $x = \frac{1}{2}$, then $x^3 = \left(\frac{1}{2}\right)^3 = \frac{1}{8}$. Because $\frac{1}{8}$ is less than $\frac{1}{2}$, x could be a fraction between 0 and 1. And if $x = -2$, then $x^3 = -8$; -8 is less than -2, so x could be a negative number less than -1.

How would these different possible values affect the question "Is $x > x^2$?" If $x = \frac{1}{2}$, then $x^2 = \left(\frac{1}{2}\right)^2 = \frac{1}{4}$; $\frac{1}{2}$ is greater than $\frac{1}{4}$. So if x is a fraction between 0 and 1, the answer to the question is yes. And if $x = -2$, then $x^2 = 4$; -2 is not greater than 4, so if x is negative, then the answer to the question is no.

To answer the question, you'll need to know definitely which of the two permitted types of number x is—a positive fraction or a number less than -1.

Step 2: Evaluate the Statements Using 12TEN

Statement (1) permits any number greater than -5. Certainly x could be negative. And since there's no upper limit provided on x, it could also be a positive fraction. You haven't gotten a definite yes or no answer to the question, so Statement (1) is insufficient. Eliminate **(A)** and **(D)**.

Statement (2) permits only negative numbers and excludes positive fractions. So now the answer to the question is definitely no. Statement (2) is sufficient, and **(B)** is correct.

16. (B)

Is $|15 - m| + |m - 15| > 15$?

(1) $m > 6$

(2) $m < 7$

Step 1: Analyze the Question Stem

In this Yes/No question, sufficiency means proving that $|15 - m| + |m - 15|$ is either definitely greater than 15 or definitely less than or equal to 15. As the question stem is dealing with a range, picking numbers will help in evaluating the statements.

Step 2: Evaluate the Statements Using 12TEN

Statement (1) restricts m to values greater than 6. When picking numbers to evaluate statements, remember to always pick at least two sets of numbers to see if you can get more than one possible answer to the question—in this case, pick one number near the start of the range and one much farther away. First try $m = 7$.

$$|15 - m| + |m - 15| = |15 - 7| + |7 - 15|$$
$$= |8| + |-8|$$
$$= 8 + 8$$
$$= 16$$

Since 16 is greater than 15, $m = 7$ results in a yes answer to the question. Now try $m = 15$.

$$|15 - m| + |m - 15| = |15 - 15| + |15 - 15|$$
$$= |0| + |0|$$
$$= 0 + 0$$
$$= 0$$

Since 0 is less than 15, $m = 15$ results in a no. As $m > 6$ sometimes means yes and sometimes means no, this statement is insufficient. Eliminate **(A)** and **(D)**.

Statement (2) restricts m to values less than 7. You'll need to pick at least two values once again, so start with $m = 6$.

$$|15 - m| + |m - 15| = |15 - 6| + |6 - 15|$$
$$= |9| + |-9|$$
$$= 9 + 9$$
$$= 18$$

Because 18 is greater than 15, that's a yes. Try $m = 0$.

$$|15 - m| + |m - 15| = |15 - 0| + |0 - 15|$$
$$= |15| + |-15|$$
$$= 15 + 15$$
$$= 30$$

Not only is that also a yes, but also the value is actually getting larger as m gets smaller, so this statement will always return an answer of yes to the question. Eliminate **(C)** and **(E)**.

Statement (2) alone is sufficient, so the correct answer is **(B)**.

17. (C)

If a and b are positive, what is the value of $a - b$?

(1) $a^2 + 2ab + b^2 = 36$
(2) $a^2 - b^2 = 12$

Step 1: Analyze the Question Stem

In this Value question, to have sufficiency, you must have enough information to find one and only one value for $a - b$. Note that this does not necessarily mean knowing the values of a and b individually. You're told that both variables are positive.

Step 2: Evaluate the Statements Using 12TEN

Statement (1) provides a classic quadratic form, $a^2 + 2ab + b^2 = 36$, which can be factored into the binomial form $(a + b)(a + b) = 36$. Thus, $(a + b)^2 = 36$ and, since a and b are positive, $a + b = 6$. While this establishes a value for $a + b$, there's no way to find $a - b$; it could be that $a = 5$ and $b = 1$, or that $a = 2$ and $b = 4$, or any other combination of positive values that sums to 6, and each would yield a different value for $a - b$. Therefore, this statement is insufficient. Eliminate **(A)** and **(D)**.

Statement (2) provides another classic quadratic, which can be translated into the factored form $(a + b)(a - b) = 12$. This again is not enough to determine exact values for a and b individually, or to find the value of $a - b$. Therefore, this statement is insufficient. Eliminate **(B)**.

Combining the statements tells you that $a + b = 6$ and $(a + b)(a - b) = 12$. Substituting 6 in for $(a + b)$ in the second equation yields $6(a - b) = 12$. Thus, $(a - b)$ must equal 2. Combining the statements creates sufficiency, so the correct answer is **(C)**.

18. (C)

Is $y^2 < 1$?

(1) $y > -1$

(2) $y < 1$

Step 1: Analyze the Question Stem

In this Yes/No question, sufficiency means determining that y^2 is either definitely less than 1 or definitely greater than or equal to 1. All squares are non-negative—so how could it be that y^2 is less than 1? The only way this could happen is if y fell somewhere between 1 and −1 on the number line. The square of $\frac{1}{2}$, for instance, is $\frac{1}{4}$; the square of $-\frac{1}{2}$ is also $\frac{1}{4}$. Likewise, the square of 0 is 0. So the question stem can be simplified to "Is y less than 1 and greater than −1?"

Step 2: Evaluate the Statements Using 12TEN

Statement (1) states that $y > -1$. Picking numbers will make this easier: $y = 0$ leads to a yes answer, as y^2 would be less than 1. However, $y = 2$ leads to an answer of no, as y^2 would be greater than 1. This statement is insufficient, so we can eliminate **(A)** and **(D)**.

Statement (2) states that $y < 1$. As we saw above, $y = 0$ leads to a yes answer. However, $y = -2$ would lead to a no answer, as y^2 would be greater than 1. This statement is insufficient, so eliminate **(B)**.

Combining the statements results in the inequality $-1 < y < 1$. That effectively limits the range of values for y to 0 and fractions whose absolute value is less than 1. Squaring any fraction whose absolute value is less than 1 will always result in a positive fraction less than 1, producing a yes answer, and you've already seen that $y = 0$ produces a yes answer. Therefore, combining the statements will produce a definite answer of yes to the question, and the correct answer is **(C)**.

19. (A)

A taqueria has exactly two items on its menu, a taco and a burrito. On a particular day, it sold 600 items, exactly half of which were tacos. What was the taqueria's revenue on that day?

(1) The average price of an item on the menu is $4.50.

(2) A burrito costs twice as much as a taco.

Step 1: Analyze the Question Stem

This is a Value question. Translate the English into math and set up an equation. The taqueria sells two menu items, and the question asks for the revenue on a day when equal numbers of the two items were sold, for a total of $600. If t represents the price of a taco and b the price of a burrito, then, since 300 of each were sold, the revenue would be given by the expression $300t + 300b$. Factor out the common term to get $300(t + b)$. Thus, to answer this question, either the individual prices or their sum is needed.

Step 2: Evaluate the Statements Using 12TEN

Statement (1) doesn't give enough to determine the individual price of each item, but remember that the average formula can be rearranged to Sum of the terms = Average × Number of terms. The average price ($4.50) and the number of items on the menu (2) are known, so the sum of the prices of the items can be determined. That sum can be plugged into the revenue expression to yield the answer, so Statement (1) is sufficient. Eliminate **(B)**, **(C)**, and **(E)**.

Statement (2) gives a ratio for the prices of the two menu items, but a number of different actual prices are possible that conform to this ratio, each one of which would give a different revenue total for the day. Statement (2) is insufficient, so eliminate **(D)**. The answer is **(A)**.

If you thought that you needed Statement (2) to determine the individual price of each item, you would have answered **(C)**. Since Statement (1) provides enough information by itself to answer the question, however, there is no need to combine statements.

GMAT BY THE NUMBERS: DATA SUFFICIENCY

Now that you've learned how to approach Data Sufficiency questions on the GMAT, let's add one more dimension to your understanding of how they work.

Take a moment to try this question. Following is performance data from thousands of people who have studied with Kaplan over the decades. Through analyzing this data, we will show you how to approach questions like this one most effectively and how to avoid similarly tempting wrong answer choice types on Test Day.

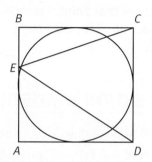

In the figure above, a circle is inscribed in square *ABCD*. What is the area of △*CDE*?

(1) The circle has a radius of length 3.

(2) *CDE* is isosceles.

○ Statement (1) ALONE is sufficient, but Statement (2) is not sufficient.

○ Statement (2) ALONE is sufficient, but Statement (1) is not sufficient.

○ BOTH statements TOGETHER are sufficient, but NEITHER statement ALONE is sufficient.

○ EACH statement ALONE is sufficient.

○ Statements (1) and (2) TOGETHER are NOT sufficient.

EXPLANATION

You're asked to find the area of triangle *CDE*. The area of a triangle is equal to $\frac{1}{2}$ Base $\times$ Height. You can use *CD* as a base, and the height would be the length of a perpendicular drawn from point *E* to *CD*. Since that perpendicular line would be equal in length to *BC*, you only need to learn the length of the sides of square *ABCD* to know the length of both the base (*CD*) and the height (equal to *BC*) of triangle *CDE*.

Statement (1) says that the radius of the inscribed circle is 3, so its diameter is 6. That diameter equals the length of the sides of the square, which is what you need to answer the question. So Statement (1) is sufficient. Statement (2) gives no measurements to work with. It does allow you to figure out that point *E* bisects *AB*, but that's irrelevant to the question. Statement (2) is insufficient. Since Statement (1) is sufficient but Statement (2) is not, the correct answer is **(A)**.

QUESTION STATISTICS

44% of test takers choose **(A)**

2% of test takers choose **(B)**

32% of test takers choose **(C)**

1% of test takers choose **(D)**

21% of test takers choose **(E)**

Sample size = 4,069

The question statistics reveal two very common habits that lead to wrong answers. Many test takers select **(C)**, believing that the statements are sufficient only when combined. Statement (1) alone does not tell you the placement of point *E*, but you don't need that information to find the triangle's area. You don't always need to know *everything* to be able to answer the question that's asked.

Also, some people struggle to relate the data about the circle to the square and then to the triangle. They look at Statement (1) and think, "I don't know how to solve with this," so they treat the statement as insufficient, leading in this question to **(E)**. But to do so is to equate "I don't know how to solve this" with "This can't be solved"—not the same thing at all! You can see from the question statistics that this is a common line of thinking—and not one that the GMAT likes to reward. Be wary of guessing that a statement is insufficient unless you can see exactly why it doesn't lead to a clear answer.

MORE GMAT BY THE NUMBERS...

To see more questions with answer choice statistics, be sure to review the full-length CATs in your online resources.

GO ONLINE

kaptest.com/login

CHAPTER 12

Algebra on the GMAT

If $x + y = 2$ and $x^2 - xy - 10 - 2y^2 = 0$, what does $x - 2y$ equal?

- ○ 0
- ○ 1
- ○ 2
- ○ 5
- ○ 10

Above is a typical Problem Solving algebra question. In this chapter, we'll look at how to apply the Kaplan Method to this question, discuss the algebra rules being tested, and go over the basic principles and strategies that you want to keep in mind on every Quantitative question involving algebra. But before you move on, take a minute to think about what you see in this question and answer some questions about how you think it works:

- What mathematical concepts are being tested in this question?

- What does the format of the answer choices tell you about this question?

- Do you need to know the exact values of *x* and *y* to answer this question?

- What GMAT Core Competencies are most essential to success on this question?

PREVIEWING ALGEBRA ON THE GMAT

There won't be that many problems that involve only algebra—maybe 20 percent of the Quantitative section. But a majority of the questions on the Quantitative section will involve algebra in some way. This makes algebra a necessary skill on the GMAT—mastering some frequently tested algebra concepts could yield large improvements on your Quant score. This chapter will guide you through the basics and give you practice applying algebra concepts to GMAT questions ranging from the simple to the most advanced.

WHAT MATHEMATICAL CONCEPTS ARE BEING TESTED IN THIS QUESTION?

For those who find algebra intimidating, this question can seem complicated and abstract at first. Unlike a word problem, which gives you a story to relate to, this question directly measures your ability to use algebraic rules to manipulate unknown terms, or variables. The first step of the Kaplan Method for Problem Solving is to analyze the question stem, and often the best way to start is to "inventory" the question to determine which math skills you will have to use to solve it.

In the question that opens this chapter, you see two algebraic equations, one of which has variables raised to the second power. If you recognized that factoring quadratic equations will be important here, congratulations! If not, don't worry—you will learn and practice those topics later in this chapter. You are being asked to solve for the algebraic expression $x - 2y$, so you can anticipate that you will manipulate these two equations to isolate (in other words, put by itself on one side of the equal sign) the expression $x - 2y$.

WHAT DOES THE FORMAT OF THE ANSWER CHOICES TELL YOU ABOUT THIS QUESTION?

This may seem like a somewhat obvious deduction, but it's a crucial—and potentially reassuring—one: the answer choices here are all numbers, so this means it *is* possible to solve for a single numerical value for $x - 2y$. The GMAT can't ask you a trick question, so you can rest assured that there must be a way to use combination or substitution on these two equations to answer the question. You can think of it like a puzzle, and the test makers have given you all the pieces; it's up to you to put them together.

DO YOU NEED TO KNOW THE EXACT VALUES OF *x* AND *y* TO ANSWER THIS QUESTION?

A common mistake that test takers make in approaching a question like this one is to think they need to solve for exact values of x and y. While it's true that values for those two variables would enable you to solve for the expression $x - 2y$, they are not necessary—in fact, they may be time-consuming or even impossible to solve for. For instance, if $x = 8$ and $y = 3$, you would come up with the same value for the expression ($x - 2y = 2$) as you would if $x = -10$ and $y = -6$. An infinite number of values are possible for x and y that would all yield the same result for this expression. Stay focused on the specific task and keep an open mind about how you can use the given information to find the correct answer; often the best path to the solution won't be the most obvious one.

WHAT GMAT CORE COMPETENCIES ARE MOST ESSENTIAL TO SUCCESS ON THIS QUESTION?

Here the test maker rewards Pattern Recognition; certain algebraic concepts are tested over and over on the GMAT, and you will learn and practice the most important ones in this chapter. On this question, the test taker who recognizes the opportunity to factor the quadratic equation will answer this question efficiently and accurately. Those test takers who are not as comfortable with the algebraic structures that appear frequently on the GMAT could spend a long time with a question like this one just figuring out where to begin.

Here are the main topics we'll cover in this chapter:

- Translating Words into Expressions and Equations
- Isolating a Variable
- Quadratic Equations
- Systems of Linear Equations
- Special Cases in Systems of Linear Equations
- Functions and Symbolism

HANDLING GMAT ALGEBRA

Now let's apply the Kaplan Method to the algebra question you saw earlier:

If $x + y = 2$ and $x^2 - xy - 10 - 2y^2 = 0$, what does $x - 2y$ equal?

○ 0
○ 1
○ 2
○ 5
○ 10

Let's use the Kaplan Method for Problem Solving to find the most efficient approach to this problem. Don't worry if the math is unfamiliar to you; you will have an opportunity to learn it later in the chapter. For now, focus on the basics of applying the Kaplan Method to a GMAT algebra problem.

Step 1: Analyze the Question

The GMAT will reward you for recognizing patterns. Here, you are given two variables and two equations, one of which is not linear. When you see an equation that resembles one of the quadratic patterns you know, try factoring it using reverse-FOIL. Odds are the problem will be greatly simplified.

Step 2: State the Task

You need to solve for $x - 2y$. Notice that you are asked for the value of an expression, not an individual variable. Don't waste time solving for all the variables individually if it's not necessary.

Step 3: Approach Strategically

If you add 10 to both sides of the second equation, you get $x^2 - xy - 2y^2 = 10$. Now the left side looks like an expression that you can factor with reverse-FOIL. Since you could get the x^2 term by multiplying x and x, you know both factors will contain x:

$$(x\quad)(x\quad) = 10$$

Next, determine what two factors multiplied together will equal $-2y^2$. You need either $-2y$ and y or $2y$ and $-y$. Since the coefficient of the xy term is negative, choose $-2y$ and y. Then the sum of the outer and inner products will give you $-xy$. Thus, the factorization of $x^2 - xy - 2y^2$ is

$$(x + y)(x - 2y)$$

Now, notice that both factors of $x^2 - xy - 2y^2$ appear in the question stem. You are told that $x + y = 2$, and you are asked to find the value of $x - 2y$.

You can find the value of $x - 2y$ by returning to the equation you've already factored. You know that $(x + y)(x - 2y) = 10$. Since $x + y = 2$, you can replace $(x + y)$ with 2, giving you $2(x - 2y) = 10$, or $(x - 2y) = 5$. So **(D)** is the correct answer.

Did you get to $2(x - 2y) = 10$ and then go further to $2x - 4y = 10$ or to $x = 5 + 2y$? If so, you lost sight of what was asked. You may find it helpful to write down what's asked on your noteboard so it's always in your line of sight.

Step 4: Confirm Your Answer

Reread the question stem to check that you have answered the right question. Here, confirm that you have solved for $x - 2y$ and not x or y. When you have done that, you can move on.

Now let's look at each of the six most important algebra topics that show up on the GMAT Quantitative section, starting with translating words into expressions and equations.

TRANSLATING WORDS INTO EXPRESSIONS AND EQUATIONS

Often the most frustrating aspect of word problems is the odd way in which information is presented. Don't get frustrated. Just break down the information into small pieces and take things one step at a time. Word problems can usually be translated from left to right, but not always. Say you see this sentence: "There are twice as many dollars in George's wallet as the amount that is 5 dollars less than the amount in Bill's wallet." Instead of trying to translate it into math all in one go, approach it piecemeal.

Whenever possible, choose letters for your variables that make sense in the context of the problem. You could start by calling the amount in George's wallet G and the amount in Bill's wallet B. Now, think about the relationship between the two amounts: G is not compared to B but to 5 dollars less than B, or $(B - 5)$. You can now say that G is twice as large as $(B - 5)$. So if you were to set them *equal* to each other, you'd have to multiply $(B - 5)$ by 2. The equation is $G = 2(B - 5)$.

If you had tried to translate it in the order it's written, you might have come up with something like $2G = 5 - B$, and you can be sure that there'd be a wrong answer choice waiting to take advantage of that. So think carefully before you translate.

The hardest part of word problems is the process of taking the English sentences and extracting the math from them. The actual math in word problems tends to be the easiest part. The following translation table should help you start dealing with English-to-math translation.

Word Problems Translation Table	
English	**Math**
equals, is, was, will be, has, costs, adds up to, the same as, as much as	=
times, of, multiplied by, product of, twice, double, by	×
divided by, per, out of, each, ratio	÷
plus, added to, and, sum, combined	+
minus, subtracted from, smaller than, less than, fewer, decreased by, difference between	−
a number, how much, how many, what	x, n, etc.

Take a look at the following example:

Beatrice's wage **is** **3 dollars more than** **twice Alan's wage**
    ↓   ↓   ↓   ↓
    B = $3 +$ $2A$

Start by breaking the problem down into smaller, more manageable pieces:

- Define the variables: B for Beatrice, A for Alan.
- Break the sentence into shorter phrases: the information about Beatrice and the information about Alan.
- Translate each phrase into an expression: B for Beatrice's wage, $3 + 2A$ for three more than twice Alan's wage.
- Put the expressions together to form an equation: $B = 3 + 2A$.

Always take the time to make sure you are translating the problem correctly. Improper translation will cost you points.

Translation Exercise

Answers are on the following page.

Translate the following sentences into algebra. When names are used, use the first letter of each person's name as the appropriate variable.

1. w is x less than y.
2. The ratio of $3x$ to $8y$ is 5 to 7.
3. The product of x decreased by y and one-half the sum of x and twice y.
4. Mike's score on his geometry test was twice Lidia's score.
5. Samantha is 4 years older than Jeannette.
6. Jamie is 5 years older than Charlie was 3 years ago.
7. Giuseppa's weight is 75 pounds more than twice Jovanna's weight.
8. Luigi has 17 fewer dollars than Sean has.
9. In 5 years, Sandy will be 4 years younger than twice Tina's age.
10. The sum of Richard's age and Cindy's age in years is 17 more than the amount by which Tim's age is greater than Kathy's age.
11. If Mack's salary were increased by \$5,000, then the combined salaries of Mack and Andrea would be equal to three times what Mack's salary would be if it were increased by one-half of itself.

Translation Exercise: Answers

1. $w = y - x$

2. $\dfrac{3x}{8y} = \dfrac{5}{7}$

3. $(x - y)\left[\dfrac{1}{2}(x + 2y)\right]$

4. $M = 2L$

5. $S = J + 4$

6. $J = (C - 3) + 5$

7. $G = 2J + 75$

8. $L = S - 17$

9. $S + 5 = 2(T + 5) - 4$

10. $R + C = (T - K) + 17$

11. $(M + 5{,}000) + A = 3\left(M + \dfrac{1}{2}M\right)$

IN-FORMAT QUESTION: TRANSLATING WORDS INTO EXPRESSIONS AND EQUATIONS ON THE GMAT

Now let's use the Kaplan Method on a Problem Solving question dealing with translating words into expressions and equations:

> Charles's and Sarah's current ages are C years and S years, respectively. If 6 years from now, Charles will be at least as old as Sarah was 2 years ago, which of the following must be true?
>
> ○ $C + 6 < S - 2$
>
> ○ $C + 6 \leq S + 2$
>
> ○ $C + 6 = S - 2$
>
> ○ $C + 6 > S - 2$
>
> ○ $C + 6 \geq S - 2$

Step 1: Analyze the Question

This problem may look complicated at first, but it's really just asking you to translate the English sentence into math. Once the word problem has been translated, you can apply basic algebra to simplify the statement to match the correct answer choice.

Step 2: State the Task

You need to translate the word problem into math.

Step 3: Approach Strategically

Look at the word problem and work from left to right to extract your algebraic statements. Rather than picking x and y for your variables, use C for Charles's age and S for Sarah's age:

Six years from now, Charles's age will be $C + 6$.

Two years ago, Sarah's age was $S - 2$.

Now connect these two algebraic statements. You are told that in 6 years, Charles will be at least as old as Sarah was 2 years ago. The phrase "will be at least as old as" implies that Charles could be exactly the same age as Sarah 2 years ago, or he could be older. Therefore, use the "greater than or equal to" sign between the two statements:

$$C + 6 \geq S - 2$$

The correct answer is **(E)**.

Step 4: Confirm Your Answer

This translation directly matches **(E)**, but be careful to check that the variables are in the correct order and that you have used the correct inequality sign.

TAKEAWAYS: TRANSLATING WORDS INTO EXPRESSIONS AND EQUATIONS

- Word problems can be translated into math, usually one phrase at a time and from left to right.
- Don't automatically choose x and y for everything. Pick letters (or groups of letters) whose meaning will be clear at a glance.

PRACTICE SET: TRANSLATING WORDS INTO EXPRESSIONS AND EQUATIONS ON THE GMAT

1. Machine A produces r paperclips per hour. Machine B produces s paperclips per hour. If s is 30 greater than r, which expression represents the number of paperclips the two machines working together produce in t hours?

    ○ $r + s + 30$
    ○ $t(r + s) + 30$
    ○ $t(r + s + 30)$
    ○ $t(2s + 30)$
    ○ $t(2r + 30)$

2. The youngest of 4 children has siblings who are 3, 5, and 8 years older than she is. If the average (arithmetic mean) age of the 4 siblings is 21, what is the age of the youngest sibling?

    ○   17
    ○   18
    ○   19
    ○   21
    ○   22

ISOLATING A VARIABLE

A **term** is a numerical constant or the product of a numerical constant and one or more variables. Examples of terms are 5, $3x$, $4x^2yz$, and $2ac$.

An **algebraic expression** is a combination of one or more terms. Terms in an expression are separated by either $+$ or $-$ signs. Examples of expressions are $3xy$, $4ab + 5cd$, and $x^2 - 1$.

In the term $3xy$, the numerical constant 3 is called a **coefficient**. In a simple term such as z, 1 is the coefficient. A number without any variables is called a **constant term**. An expression with one term, such as $3xy$, is called a **monomial**; one with two terms, such as $4a + 2d$, is a **binomial**; one with three terms, such as $xy + z - a$, is a **trinomial**. The general name for expressions with more than one term is **polynomial**.

SUBSTITUTION

Substitution is a method that you can employ to evaluate an algebraic expression or to express an algebraic expression in terms of other variables.

Example: Evaluate $3x^2 - 4x$ when $x = 2$.

Replace every x in the expression with 2 and then carry out the designated operations. Remember to follow the order of operations (PEMDAS):

$$\begin{aligned}
\textbf{P} &= \text{Parentheses} \\
\textbf{E} &= \text{Exponents} \\
\textbf{M} &= \text{Multiplication} \\
\textbf{D} &= \text{Division}
\end{aligned}\quad \Big\} \quad \text{in order from left to right}$$

$$\begin{aligned}
\textbf{A} &= \text{Addition} \\
\textbf{S} &= \text{Subtraction}
\end{aligned}\quad \Big\} \quad \text{in order from left to right}$$

$$3x^2 - 4x$$
$$= 3(2)^2 - 4(2)$$
$$= 3 \times 4 - 4 \times 2$$
$$= 12 - 8$$
$$= 4$$

Example: Express $\dfrac{a}{b-a}$ in terms of x and y if $a = 2x$ and $b = 3y$.

Here, replace every a with $2x$ and every b with $3y$:

$$\frac{a}{b-a} = \frac{2x}{3y - 2x}$$

Operations with Polynomials

All of the laws of arithmetic operations, such as the commutative, associative, and distributive laws, are also applicable to polynomials.

Commutative Law

$$2x + 5y = 5y + 2x$$

$$5a \times 3b = 3b \times 5a = 15ab$$

Associative Law

$$2x - 3x + 5y + 2y = (2x - 3x) + (5y + 2y) = -x + 7y$$

$$(-2x)\left(\tfrac{1}{2}x\right)(3y)(-2y) = (-x^2)(-6y^2) = 6x^2y^2$$

Note that the process of simplifying an expression by subtracting or adding together those terms with the same variable component is called **combining like terms**.

Distributive Law

$$3a(2b - 5c) = (3a \times 2b) - (3a \times 5c) = 6ab - 15ac$$

The product of two binomials can be calculated by applying the distributive law twice.

Example: $(y + 5)(y - 2)$

$$= y(y - 2) + 5(y - 2)$$

$$= (y \times y) + (y \times -2) + (5 \times y) + (5 \times -2)$$

$$= y^2 - 2y + 5y - 10$$

$$= y^2 + 3y - 10$$

You multiply the First terms first, then the Outer terms, then the Inner terms, and finally the Last terms. A simple mnemonic for this is the word **FOIL**.

Factoring Algebraic Expressions

Factoring a polynomial means expressing it as a product of two or more simpler expressions.

Common Monomial Factor

When there is a monomial factor common to every term in the polynomial, it can be factored out by using the distributive law.

Example: $2a + 6ac = 2a(1 + 3c)$

Here, $2a$ is the greatest common factor of $2a$ and $6ac$.

Making problems look more complicated than they are by distributing a common factor is a classic GMAT trick. Whenever algebra looks scary, check whether common factors could be factored out.

Equations

An **equation** is an algebraic sentence that says that two expressions are equal to each other. The two expressions consist of numbers, variables, and arithmetic operations to be performed on these numbers and variables.

Solving Equations

To solve for some variable, you can manipulate the equation until you have isolated that variable on one side of the equal sign, leaving any numbers or other variables on the other side. Of course, you must be careful to manipulate the equation only in accordance with the equality postulate: *whenever you perform an operation on one side of the equation, you must perform the same operation on the other side.* Otherwise, the two sides of the equation will no longer be equal.

The steps for isolating a variable are as follows:

1. Eliminate any **fractions** by multiplying both sides by the least common denominator.
2. Put all terms with the variable you're solving for on one **side** by adding or subtracting on both sides.
3. **Combine** like terms.
4. **Factor** out the desired variable.
5. **Divide** to leave the desired variable by itself.

Linear, or First-Degree, Equations

These are equations in which all the variables are raised to the first power (there are no squares or cubes). To solve such an equation, you'll need to perform operations on both sides of the equation in order to get the variable you're solving for alone on one side. The operations you can perform without upsetting the balance of the equation are addition and subtraction, as well as multiplication or division by a number other than 0. At each step in the process, you'll need to use the reverse of the operation that's being applied to the variable in order to isolate the variable.

Example: If $4x - 7 = 2x + 5$, what is x?

1. Put all the terms with the variable on one side of the equation. Put all constant terms on the other side of the equation.

$$4x - 7 = 2x + 5$$
$$4x - 2x - 7 + 7 = 2x - 2x + 5 + 7$$
$$4x - 2x = 5 + 7$$

2. Combine like terms.

$$2x = 12$$

3. Divide to leave the desired variable by itself.

$$\frac{2x}{2} = \frac{12}{2}$$
$$x = 6$$

You can easily check your work when solving this kind of equation. The answer you arrive at represents the value of the variable that makes the equation hold true. Therefore, to check that it's correct, you can just substitute this value for the variable in the original equation. If the equation holds true, you've found the correct answer. In the previous example, you got a value of 6 for x. Replacing x with 6 in your original equation results in $4(6) - 7 = 2(6) + 5$, or $24 - 7 = 12 + 5$, which simplifies to $17 = 17$. That's a true statement, so 6 is indeed the correct value for x.

Equations with Fractions

The GMAT loves to make algebra problems look harder than they need to be by using fractions. Whenever you see a fraction in an algebra question, always get rid of the fraction as your first step. Let's see how to solve such a problem.

Example: Solve $\dfrac{x-2}{3} + \dfrac{x-4}{10} = \dfrac{x}{2}$

1. Eliminate fractions by multiplying both sides of the equation by the least common denominator (LCD). Here the LCD is 30.

$$30\left(\frac{x-2}{3}\right) + 30\left(\frac{x-4}{10}\right) = 30\left(\frac{x}{2}\right)$$
$$10(x-2) + 3(x-4) = 15(x)$$
$$10x - 20 + 3x - 12 = 15x$$

2. Put all terms with the variable on one side by adding or subtracting on both sides. Put all constant terms on the other side of the equation.

$$-20 - 12 = 15x - 10x - 3x$$

3. Combine like terms.

$$-32 = 2x$$

4. Divide to leave the desired variable by itself.

$$x = \frac{-32}{2}$$
$$x = -16$$

Literal Equations

On some problems involving more than one variable, you cannot find a specific value for a variable; you can only solve for one variable in terms of the others. To do this, try to get the desired variable alone on one side and all the other variables on the other side.

Example: In the formula $V = \dfrac{PN}{R + NT}$ solve for N in terms of P, R, T, and V.

1. Eliminate fractions by cross multiplying.

$$\frac{V}{1} = \frac{PN}{R + NT}$$
$$V(R + NT) = PN$$

2. Remove parentheses by distributing.

$$VR + VNT = PN$$

3. Put all terms containing N on one side and all other terms on the other side.

$$VNT - PN = -VR$$

4. Factor out the common factor N.

$$N(VT - P) = -VR$$

5. Divide by $(VT - P)$ to get N alone.

$$N = \frac{-VR}{VT - P}$$

Note: You can reduce the number of negative terms in the answer by multiplying both the numerator and the denominator of the fraction on the right-hand side by -1.

$$N = \frac{VR}{P - VT}$$

In-Format Question: Isolating a Variable on the GMAT

Now let's use the Kaplan Method on a Problem Solving question dealing with isolating a variable:

If $\dfrac{5}{2+\dfrac{3}{n}} = 2$, then $n =$

- ○ $\dfrac{1}{2}$
- ○ 1
- ○ $\dfrac{3}{2}$
- ○ 3
- ○ 6

Step 1: Analyze the Question

Follow the steps for isolating a variable carefully and methodically. In this question, the variable you need to isolate is buried under two fractions. When working with fractions, you can often simplify the work by one of two strategies: (1) multiplying by a common denominator or (2) cross multiplying the equation. For this question, use cross multiplication to isolate n.

Step 2: State the Task

Your task is to bring the variable n to one side of the equation and the rest of the terms to the other side.

Step 3: Approach Strategically

Begin by cross multiplying the equation, which results in this equation:

$$5(1) = 2\left(2 + \frac{3}{n}\right)$$

Now simplify the equation:

$$5 = 2(2) + 2\left(\frac{3}{n}\right)$$

$$5 = 4 + \frac{6}{n}$$

Combine like terms:

$$5 - 4 = \frac{6}{n}$$

$$1 = \frac{6}{n}$$

$$n = 6$$

The correct answer is **(E)**.

Step 4: Confirm Your Answer

You can check your calculations by simply plugging $n = 6$ into the original equation. If the expression on the left side is equal to 2, the calculations are correct. You could have also used backsolving, but since there isn't an easy way to know whether you must select an answer choice that is larger or smaller than the one you started with, algebra is the most efficient way to get the answer here.

TAKEAWAYS: ISOLATING A VARIABLE

- Simplify equations with fractions by first eliminating the fractions.
- To solve for a variable, isolate that variable on one side of the equation and put all constants on the other side of the equation.
- If a problem involves more than one variable, put the desired variable alone on one side of the equation and all the other variables and constants on the other side.

PRACTICE SET: ISOLATING A VARIABLE ON THE GMAT

3. If $b \neq 1$ and if $\dfrac{ab}{a - b} = 1$, what is the value of a in terms of b?

   ○ $\dfrac{b}{1 - b}$

   ○ $\dfrac{b - 1}{b}$

   ○ $\dfrac{b}{b + 1}$

   ○ $\dfrac{b + 1}{b}$

   ○ $\dfrac{1 - b}{b}$

4. If $x \neq 0$ and $x - \dfrac{2 - x^2}{x} = \dfrac{y}{x}$, then $y =$

   ○ $-2 - 3x^2$

   ○ $x^2 - 2$

   ○ $2x^2 - 2$

   ○ $x - 2 - x^2$

   ○ $x - 2 + x^2$

5. Susan weighs m pounds more than Anna does, and together they weigh a total of n pounds. Which of the following represents Anna's weight in pounds?

   ○ $\dfrac{n - m}{2}$

   ○ $\dfrac{n + m}{2}$

   ○ $\dfrac{n}{2} - m$

   ○ $2n - m$

   ○ $n - 2m$

QUADRATIC EQUATIONS

The term *quadratic* refers to a mathematical expression in the form $ax^2 + bx + c$, where a, b, and c are constants and a does not equal zero. The algebraic rules you learned for solving a linear equation still apply to quadratics, but there are also some specific things to know about handling quadratic equations. On the GMAT, you will find that questions dealing with quadratics use the same patterns over and over.

FACTORING QUADRATIC EXPRESSIONS

Earlier in this chapter, you learned that two binomials can be multiplied together by applying the distributive law twice; in other words, you use FOIL (multiplying the First terms first, then the Outer terms, then the Inner terms, and finally the Last terms) to "expand" the expression. The result is often a quadratic expression in the form $ax^2 + bx + c$.

Example: $(y + 5)(y - 2)$

$$= y(y - 2) + 5(y - 2)$$
$$= (y \times y) + (y \times -2) + (5 \times y) + (5 \times -2)$$
$$= y^2 - 2y + 5y - 10$$
$$= y^2 + 3y - 10$$

Factoring is the reverse of this process of expanding the expression. Factoring can be thought of as applying the FOIL method backward, or using "reverse-FOIL." Below you will learn how to factor the most common forms of quadratic expression on the GMAT.

Polynomials of the Form $x^2 + bx + c$

Many quadratic polynomials can be factored into a product of two binomials. The product of the first term in each binomial must equal the first term of the polynomial. The product of the last term of each binomial must equal the last term of the polynomial. The sum of the remaining products must equal the second term of the polynomial.

Example: $x^2 - 3x + 2$

Using reverse-FOIL, you can factor this into two binomials, each containing an x term. Start by writing down what you know.

$$x^2 - 3x + 2 = (x\ )(x\ )$$

In each binomial on the right, you need to fill in the missing term. The product of the two missing terms will be the last term in the polynomial: 2. The sum of the two missing terms will be the coefficient of the second term of the polynomial: -3. Try the possible factors of 2 until you get a pair that adds up to -3. There are two possibilities: 1 and 2 or -1 and -2. Since $(-1) + (-2) = -3$, you can fill -1 and -2 into the empty spaces.

Thus, $x^2 - 3x + 2 = (x - 1)(x - 2)$.

If the coefficient of the constant (the last term) is negative, then your binomials will have different signs (one + and one −). If the coefficient of the constant is positive, then your binomials will both have the same sign as the coefficient in the middle term (two +'s or two −'s). Check out the previous example: both binomials have a minus sign because of the −3 coefficient of the term −3x.

Note: Whenever you factor a polynomial, you can check your answer by using FOIL to obtain the original polynomial.

CLASSIC QUADRATICS

The process of reverse-FOIL works on the quadratics you will find on the GMAT. However, there also exist some patterns called "classic quadratics," which you can factor more quickly by recognizing the pattern than by using reverse-FOIL.

Difference of Two Perfect Squares

The difference of two squares can be factored into the product of two binomials: $a^2 - b^2 = (a + b)(a - b)$.

In the case of equations written as the difference of two squares, you don't need to go through all the steps of factoring using reverse-FOIL; just recognize the pattern.

Example: $d^2 - 16 = (d + 4)(d - 4)$

Polynomials of the Form $a^2 + 2ab + b^2$

This type of polynomial is also a pattern that appears frequently enough on the GMAT to warrant memorization. Any polynomial of this form is equivalent to the square of a binomial. Notice that according to FOIL, $(a + b)^2 = a^2 + 2ab + b^2$.

Factoring such a polynomial using reverse-FOIL is just reversing this procedure.

Example: $x^2 + 6x + 9 = (x)^2 + 2(x)(3) + (3)^2 = (x + 3)^2$

Polynomials of the Form $a^2 - 2ab + b^2$

Any polynomial of this form is equivalent to the square of a binomial as in the previous example. Here though, the binomial is the difference of two terms: $(a - b)^2 = a^2 - 2ab + b^2$.

Example: $x^2 - 10x + 25 = (x)^2 - 2(x)(5) + (5)^2 = (x - 5)^2$

The GMAT uses these three "classic quadratics" over and over. Review them thoroughly and look out for them as you practice. Notice that all the forms begin and end in a perfect square:

$$a^2 - b^2$$
$$a^2 + 2ab + b^2$$
$$a^2 - 2ab + b^2$$

Picking up on these patterns will save you lots of work, especially in the difficult questions. Imagine seeing this expression show up on the test:

$$4x^2 + 52x^2 + 169$$

This may look daunting at first glance. But if you realize that 169 is 13^2, and $4x^2$ is $(2x)^2$, you can then make the educated guess that this polynomial factors as $(2x + 13)^2$. You then only have to confirm that $52x^2 = 2 \times 2x^2 \times 13$ (which it is) to start making the problem easier.

SOLVING QUADRATIC EQUATIONS

If the expression $ax^2 + bx + c$ is set equal to zero, there is a special name for it: a quadratic equation. Since it is an equation, you can find the value or values for x that make the equation work. You can do so by using the factored form of the equation obtained through reverse-FOIL.

Example: $x^2 - 3x + 2 = 0$

To find the solutions, or **roots**, start by factoring using reverse-FOIL. Factor $x^2 - 3x + 2$ into $(x - 1)$ $(x - 2)$, making the quadratic equation

$$(x - 1)(x - 2) = 0$$

You now have a product of two binomials that is equal to zero. When does a product of two terms equal zero? The only time that happens is when at least one of the terms is zero. If the product of $(x - 1)$ and $(x - 2)$ is equal to zero, that means either the first term equals zero or the second term equals zero. So to find the roots, you just need to set the two binomials equal to zero. That gives you

$$x - 1 = 0 \text{ or } x - 2 = 0$$

Solving for x, you get $x = 1$ or $x = 2$. As a check, you can plug in 1 and 2 into the equation $x^2 - 3x + 2 = 0$, and you'll see that either value makes the equation work.

IN-FORMAT QUESTION: QUADRATIC EQUATIONS ON THE GMAT

Now let's use the Kaplan Method on a Problem Solving question dealing with quadratic equations:

If $(a - 3)^2 = 5 - 10a$, then which of the following is the value of a?

- ○ -3
- ○ -2
- ○ 0
- ○ 2
- ○ 3

Step 1: Analyze the Question

When you are asked to solve for a variable that is squared, the most efficient solution is typically to factor the equation into two binomials. Remember that in order to factor the equation, you must bring all of the terms to one side of the equation and have only zero on the other side.

Step 2: State the Task

You need to solve for the value of a. To do this, you'll need to first simplify the equation in the question stem to fit the standard quadratic equation format needed to factor $(ax^2 + bx + c = 0)$; then determine the factors for the equation.

Step 3: Approach Strategically

You are given the equation in the form $(a - 3)^2 = 5 - 10a$.

You can simplify the equation by subtracting 5 from both sides and adding 10a to both sides:

$$(a - 3)^2 - 5 + 10a = 0$$

Next, multiply out the far left expression using FOIL and simplify:

$$(a - 3)(a - 3) - 5 + 10a = 0$$
$$a^2 - 3a - 3a + 9 - 5 + 10a = 0$$
$$a^2 - 6a + 9 - 5 + 10a = 0$$
$$a^2 + 4a + 4 = 0$$

Now use reverse-FOIL to factor the quadratic expression on the left:

$$(a + 2)(a + 2) = 0$$

To solve for a, set each of the binomials equal to zero. In this case, there is only one binomial, so $a + 2 = 0$, and $a = -2$. Choice **(B)** is correct.

You can also use backsolving, although this may not be the most efficient solution, since it would be difficult to know after testing an incorrect answer choice whether the right answer should be larger or smaller, and you could end up testing several choices before finding the correct one. Even in such situations, backsolving can still help you find the right answer when you aren't sure how to solve algebraically. Let's say you start with choice **(B)**.

$$(-2 - 3)^2 = 5 - 10(-2)$$
$$(-5)^2 = 5 - (-20)$$
$$25 = 25$$

In this case, you got lucky and found the correct answer on the first try. If you hadn't, you could then proceed to test the other choices (in order of their manageability) until you found one that works.

Step 4: Confirm Your Answer

You can plug your calculated value for a into the equation in the question stem to confirm that the calculations are correct.

TAKEAWAYS: QUADRATIC EQUATIONS

- FOIL = **F**irst, **O**uter, **I**nner, **L**ast
  - $(a + b)(c + d) = ac + ad + bc + bd$
- To solve a quadratic equation, rewrite the equation in the form $ax^2 + bx + c = 0$, then perform reverse-FOIL.
- Following are three classic quadratics that often appear on the GMAT. Recognize them to avoid spending time performing FOIL or reverse-FOIL on Test Day.
  - $a^2 - b^2 = (a + b)(a - b)$
  - $(a + b)^2 = (a + b)(a + b) = a^2 + 2ab + b^2$
  - $(a - b)^2 = (a - b)(a - b) = a^2 - 2ab + b^2$
- Quadratic equations usually have two roots (solutions). Suppose the quadratic equation has been written so that the right side is zero. If both factors involving a variable on the left side are the same (see classic quadratics 2 and 3 above), then there is only one distinct root.

Practice Set: Quadratic Equations on the GMAT

6. Is n negative?

   (1) $n^2 + n - 6 = 0$
   (2) $n^2 + 6n + 9 = 0$

7. Which of the following expressions CANNOT be equal to 0 when $x^2 - 2x = 3$?

   ○ $x^2 - 6x + 9$
   ○ $x^2 - 4x + 3$
   ○ $x^2 - x - 2$
   ○ $x^2 - 7x + 6$
   ○ $x^2 - 9$

8. If $x^2 - 2x - 15 = (x + r)(x + s)$ for all values of x, and if r and s are constants, then which of the following is a possible value of $r - s$?

   ○ 8
   ○ 2
   ○ −2
   ○ −3
   ○ −5

SYSTEMS OF LINEAR EQUATIONS

In general, if a problem has multiple variables and you want to find unique numerical values for all of the variables, you will need as many distinct equations as you have variables. If you are given two distinct equations with two variables, you can combine the equations to obtain a unique solution set. Don't be intimidated by calculating values, since usually—though not always—the GMAT will give integer answers for the variables. Focus instead on looking for opportunities to combine equations. The GMAT rewards those who find clever combinations with quick solutions.

Note that the word "distinct" means that each equation must provide new, different information. In other words, each additional equation must contain information you couldn't have derived using the equation(s) you already have.

Approach 1

Isolate one variable in one equation. Then plug the expression that it equals into its place in the other equation.

Example: Find the values of m and n if $m = 4n + 2$ and $3m + 2n = 20$.

1. You know that $m = 4n + 2$. Substitute $4n + 2$ for m in the second equation.

$$3(4n + 2) + 2n = 20$$

2. Solve for n.

$$12n + 6 + 2n = 20$$
$$14n + 6 = 20$$
$$14n = 14$$
$$n = \frac{14}{14} = 1$$

3. To find the value of m, substitute 1 for n in the first equation and solve.

$$m = 4n + 2$$
$$m = 4(1) + 2$$
$$m = 4 + 2 = 6$$

Approach 2

Add or subtract whole equations from each other to eliminate a variable.

Example: Find the values of x and y if $4x + 3y = 27$ and $3x - 6y = -21$.

There's no obvious isolation/substitution to be done, since all variables have coefficients. But if you multiplied the first equation by 2, you'd be able to get rid of the y's.

$$2(4x + 3y) = 2(27)$$

Distribute: $$8x + 6y = 54$$

Now add the new equation to the second equation, carefully lining them up to combine like terms:

$$
\begin{array}{r}
8x + 6y = 54 \\
+ [3x - 6y = -21] \\
\hline
11x = 33
\end{array}
$$

Divide by 11: $x = 3$

This value can now be substituted back into either equation to yield the other value.

$$4x + 3y = 27$$
$$4(3) + 3y = 27$$
$$12 + 3y = 27$$
$$3y = 15$$
$$y = 5$$

IN-FORMAT QUESTION: SYSTEMS OF LINEAR EQUATIONS ON THE GMAT

Now let's use the Kaplan Method on a Problem Solving question dealing with systems of linear equations:

If $x + y = 5y - 13$ and $x - y = 5$, then $x =$

- ○ 11
- ○ 12
- ○ 13
- ○ 14
- ○ 15

Step 1: Analyze the Question

You have two distinct linear equations and two variables, so you will be able to solve for x. Remember that there are two techniques for solving distinct linear equations: (1) substitution and (2) combination. Since these equations look easy to simplify, substituting one equation into the other will be the most efficient approach here.

Step 2: State the Task

Substitute one linear equation into the other to eliminate y and solve for x.

Step 3: Approach Strategically

Simplify the first equation:

$$x + y = 5y - 13$$
$$x - 4y = -13$$

Simplify the second equation:

$$x - y = 5$$
$$-y = 5 - x$$
$$y = x - 5$$

Substitute the second equation into the first and solve for x:

$$x - 4(x - 5) = -13$$
$$x - 4x + 20 = -13$$
$$-3x = -33$$
$$x = 11$$

Choice **(A)** is correct.

Step 4: Confirm Your Answer

You can confirm your work by substituting $x = 11$ into either equation to find a value for y. This value for y can then be substituted into the other equation to ensure that $x = 11$.

TAKEAWAYS: SYSTEMS OF LINEAR EQUATIONS

- In a system of equations with n distinct variables, you must have at least n distinct linear equations to be able to solve for each variable.
- Use one of the following two ways to solve a system of linear equations:
  - Substitution: Solve one equation for one of the variables and substitute that value into the other equation.
  - Combination: Add or subtract one equation from the other to cancel out one of the variables.

Practice Set: Systems of Linear Equations on the GMAT

9. A theater charges $12 for seats in the orchestra and $8 for seats in the balcony. On a certain night, a total of 350 tickets were sold for a total cost of $3,320. How many more tickets were sold that night for seats in the balcony than for seats in the orchestra?

   O   90
   O   110
   O   120
   O   130
   O   220

10. Hallie has only nickels, dimes, and quarters in her pocket. Nickels are worth $0.05, dimes are worth $0.10, and quarters are worth $0.25. If she has at least 1 of each kind of coin and has a total of $2.75 in change, how many nickels does she have?

   (1) She has a total of 21 coins, with twice as many dimes as nickels.
   (2) She has $1.50 in quarters.

11. Jacob is now 12 years younger than Michael. If 9 years from now Michael will be twice as old as Jacob, how old will Jacob be in 4 years?

   O   3
   O   5
   O   7
   O   15
   O   19

SPECIAL CASES IN SYSTEMS OF LINEAR EQUATIONS

On the GMAT, it is not always necessary to solve for each variable to answer a question. Some questions will ask you to solve for a sum, difference, or other relationship between variables rather than for the variables themselves. In such a case, rather than attempting to solve for both x and y, you will solve for values for expressions such as $(x + y)$ or $(x - y)$, the average of x and y, or the ratio between the two variables. Questions involving special cases reward test takers who seek out opportunities to use Critical Thinking and Pattern Recognition in GMAT questions.

Special cases in systems of linear equations appear most frequently in problems involving sums, differences, averages, and ratios. You will see them appear more often in Data Sufficiency questions than in Problem Solving questions, because Data Sufficiency questions require you to recognize whether you have enough information to determine a relationship. Don't assume that you can't answer a question just because there are more variables present than there are equations. By simplifying the equation, you may be able to cancel out one or more variables entirely.

IN-FORMAT QUESTION: SPECIAL CASES IN SYSTEMS OF LINEAR EQUATIONS ON THE GMAT

Let's look at a Data Sufficiency question that involves special cases in systems of linear equations.

> What is the value of $x - y$?
>
> (1) $3x + 3y = 31$
> (2) $3x - 3y = 13$

Step 1: Analyze the Question Stem

First, look at your question stem and recognize that this is a special situation. You are not asked for the value of x or y; rather, you are asked for the value of $x - y$. Next, determine whether there is enough information to find the value of $x - y$. Keep in mind that you do not have to know the values of each of the variables x and y to be able to find the value of $x - y$. Because the question stem does not provide any information for finding the value of $x - y$, look at the statements.

Step 2: Evaluate the Statements Using 12TEN

Statement (1) is $3x + 3y = 31$. There is no way to rearrange this equation to find the value of $x - y$. Therefore, Statement (1) is insufficient. You can eliminate **(A)** and **(D)**.

Statement (2) is $3x - 3y = 13$. Factoring 3 from the left side of this equation, you have $3(x - y) = 13$. Dividing both sides of this equation by 3, you have $x - y = \frac{13}{3}$, and Statement (2) is sufficient to find the value of $x - y$. Choice **(B)** is correct.

TAKEAWAYS: SPECIAL CASES IN SYSTEMS OF LINEAR EQUATIONS

- Use Critical Thinking and Pattern Recognition to solve problems involving special cases in systems of linear equations.

- When you are asked to solve for the sum/difference/product/quotient of variables, you may not need to solve for each variable. Don't assume that you can't answer a question just because there are more variables present than there are equations.

- Make sure to cancel out or combine variables before you determine that there are more variables than equations.

Practice Set: Special Cases in Systems of Linear Equations on the GMAT

12. If the average (arithmetic mean) of x and y is 30 and $3y + z = 180$, what is the value of $\frac{z}{x}$?

   ○ $\frac{1}{6}$

   ○ $\frac{1}{3}$

   ○ 1

   ○ 3

   ○ 6

13. What is the value of b?

   (1) $5b - a = 3b + 5a$

   (2) $4(b - a) = 12 - 4a$

14. What is the value of $a + b$?

   (1) $5a + 2b = 22$

   (2) $3b = 30 - 6a$

FUNCTIONS AND SYMBOLISM

The GMAT uses classic function notation that you may recall from your later high school algebra classes. It also uses some untraditional notation, such as ◇, ♠, or ⊗. Both types boil down to substitution.

The basic idea is that these questions ask you to substitute values or operations in a unique way described by the problem. Here's a classic function problem.

Example: What is the minimum value of the function $f(x) = x^2 - 1$?

What this problem is telling you is that whatever number is between those parentheses gets substituted in place of x in $x^2 - 1$. For instance, $f(2) = 2^2 - 1 = 3$.

A strategic way to solve would be to substitute whatever answer choices the GMAT gives you as the answer to the function. Some may not be possible; some will be. For example, $x^2 = -4$ isn't possible, since the GMAT uses only "real" numbers, and the square of a real number must be non-negative. The smallest of the possible answer choices would be the correct response.

You could solve this question logically, too. The value of the function will be smallest when x^2 is smallest. Squaring a negative number produces a positive number, so x^2 can never be negative. The smallest result you could get is $x^2 = 0$. So the smallest $x^2 - 1$ can be is $0 - 1$, or -1.

Some questions offer strange symbols but work basically the same way—as rules for how to substitute.

Example: If $x \spadesuit y = 3x - y^2$, then what is the value of $8 \spadesuit 2$?

The given equation is really just a rule for substitution. Whatever is to the left of the ♠ symbol is x and should be substituted in place of x in $3x - y^2$. Similarly, anything to the right of ♠ is y and should be substituted for y.

$$x \spadesuit y = 3x - y^2$$
$$8 \spadesuit 2 = 3(8) - (2)^2$$
$$8 \spadesuit 2 = 24 - 4$$
$$8 \spadesuit 2 = 20$$

For the most part, symbols on the GMAT define operations (i.e., the process that one or more numbers must be put through). Occasionally, the GMAT will use symbols to stand in for digits, but this isn't as common.

IN-FORMAT QUESTION: FUNCTIONS AND SYMBOLISM ON THE GMAT

Now let's use the Kaplan Method on a Data Sufficiency question dealing with functions and symbolism:

The symbol ♣ represents one of the following operations: addition, subtraction, multiplication, or division. What is the value of 6 ♣ 2?

(1) 0 ♣ 3 = 0
(2) 2 ♣ 1 = 2

Step 1: Analyze the Question Stem

You need to determine whether there is sufficient information to find the value of 6 ♣ 2, and you are told that the symbol ♣ can stand for any one of the four operations of addition, subtraction, multiplication, or division.

Now, since there is no further information in the question stem, look at the statements.

Step 2: Evaluate the Statements Using 12TEN

Statement (1) tells you that 0 ♣ 3 = 0. The potential operations that yield this value are:

$$\text{Multiplication: } 0 \times 3 = 0$$
$$\text{Division: } 0 \div 3 = 0$$

So ♣ could stand for multiplication or division. However, $6 \times 2 = 12$ and $6 \div 2 = 3$, so there is more than one possible answer to the question. Statement (1) is insufficient. Eliminate **(A)** and **(D)**.

Statement (2) tells you that 2 ♣ 1 = 2. The potential operations that yield this value are:

$$\text{Multiplication: } 2 \times 1 = 2$$
$$\text{Division: } 2 \div 1 = 2$$

So again, ♣ could be multiplication or division; as you saw in evaluating the first statement, the value of 6 ♣ 2 changes depending on whether the symbol represents multiplication or division. More than one answer is possible for the question, so Statement (2) is insufficient. Eliminate **(B)**.

Taking the statements together, you still know only that ♣ could be multiplication or division. However, since each of these operations yields a different value, the two statements taken together are insufficient. Therefore, **(E)** is correct.

TAKEAWAYS: FUNCTIONS AND SYMBOLISM

- GMAT symbolism questions define symbols and then ask test takers to apply those definitions.
- The definitions given in a GMAT symbolism question apply only to the particular GMAT question at hand.
- Symbolism questions are usually solved by substitution.
- In most GMAT symbolism questions, symbols represent operations, but in some GMAT symbolism questions, symbols represent numbers.

PRACTICE SET: FUNCTIONS AND SYMBOLISM ON THE GMAT

15. Let $\boxed{x} = \dfrac{x^2 + 1}{2}$ and $\bigcirc{y} = \dfrac{3y}{2}$, for all integers x and y. If $m = 2$, $\boxed{\bigcirc{m}}$ is equal to which of the following?

   ○ $\dfrac{13}{8}$
   ○ 3
   ○ $\dfrac{15}{4}$
   ○ 5
   ○ $\dfrac{37}{2}$

$$\times \begin{array}{c} \diamond \\ \underline{\triangle} \\ \bullet \end{array}$$

16. In the multiplication problem above, each of the symbols ◇, △, and • represents a positive digit. If ◇ > △, what is the value of ◇?

   (1) △ = 1
   (2) • = 9

17. For all positive numbers x and y, the operation $x \blacklozenge y$ is defined by $x \blacklozenge y = \dfrac{x^2 - x}{2xy}$. If $x \blacklozenge 5 = 2$, then $x =$

   ○ 1
   ○ 5
   ○ 11
   ○ 20
   ○ 21

18. The operation $\flat\, x$ is defined by the equation $\flat\, x = ax - b(x - 1) + c$, where a, b, and c are constants that are positive integers. The value of $\flat\, 0$ is 7. What is the value of b?

   (1) $a = 3$
   (2) $c = 5$

ANSWERS AND EXPLANATIONS BEGIN ON NEXT PAGE

ANSWERS AND EXPLANATIONS

1.	E	7.	D	13.	B
2.	A	8.	A	14.	C
3.	A	9.	A	15.	D
4.	C	10.	A	16.	B
5.	A	11.	C	17.	E
6.	B	12.	D	18.	B

1. **(E)**

Machine A produces r paperclips per hour. Machine B produces s paperclips per hour. If s is 30 greater than r, which expression represents the number of paperclips the two machines working together produce in t hours?

- ○ $r + s + 30$
- ○ $t(r + s) + 30$
- ○ $t(r + s + 30)$
- ○ $t(2s + 30)$
- ○ $t(2r + 30)$

Step 1: Analyze the Question

The sentences in this word problem can be translated into algebraic statements to determine the total number of paperclips produced by both machines over a given number of hours. Alternatively, numbers could be picked for r and t and arithmetic could be done, but algebra is the more efficient approach if you are comfortable with it.

Step 2: State the Task

Find the expression that represents the number of paperclips both machines working together produce in t hours.

Step 3: Approach Strategically

Translate the phrase "s is 30 greater than r" as $s = r + 30$. Thus, the two machines produce $r + r + 30 = 2r + 30$ paperclips in each hour. In t hours, that would be $t(2r + 30)$. That's **(E)**.

Step 4: Confirm Your Answer

If you solve using algebra, you could pick numbers to confirm: say $r = 10$, then $s = 10 + 30 = 40$. Together, the machines produce $10 + 40 = 50$ paperclips each hour. If $t = 2$, then the machines produce $50 \times 2 = 100$ paperclips in 2 hours. When you plug the numbers you picked into the answer choices, only **(E)** equals 100.

EXPLANATIONS

2.   **(A)**

The youngest of 4 children has siblings who are 3, 5, and 8 years older than she is. If the average (arithmetic mean) age of the 4 siblings is 21, what is the age of the youngest sibling?

- ○   17
- ○   18
- ○   19
- ○   21
- ○   22

Step 1: Analyze the Question

You can apply the translation rules to this word problem to convert the question into a manageable algebraic equation.

Step 2: State the Task

Once the word problem has been translated, apply basic algebra to simplify the statement to match the correct answer choice.

Step 3: Approach Strategically

Let x be the age of the youngest sibling in years. Then the ages of the other siblings, who are 3, 5, and 8 years older than the youngest sibling, are $x + 3$, $x + 5$, and $x + 8$, respectively. The average age of the four siblings is 21. Therefore, the average of x, $x + 3$, $x + 5$, and $x + 8$ is 21.

The average formula is $\text{Average} = \frac{\text{Sum of the terms}}{\text{Number of terms}}$. So you can write the equation $\frac{x + (x + 3) + (x + 5) + (x + 8)}{4} = 21$.
Solve the equation for x:

$$\frac{x + (x + 3) + (x + 5) + (x + 8)}{4} = 21$$

$$\frac{x + x + 3 + x + 5 + x + 8}{4} = 21$$

$$\frac{4x + 16}{4} = 21$$

$$4x + 16 = 84$$

$$4x = 68$$

$$x = \frac{68}{4} = 17$$

The correct answer is **(A)**.

Step 4: Confirm Your Answer

For Average questions, an easy way to confirm your answer is to plug your value for x into the average formula and see if the same answer comes out on both sides. If not, go back over your calculations.

3. (A)

If $b \neq 1$ and if $\dfrac{ab}{a-b} = 1$, what is the value of a in terms of b?

○ $\dfrac{b}{1-b}$

○ $\dfrac{b-1}{b}$

○ $\dfrac{b}{b+1}$

○ $\dfrac{b+1}{b}$

○ $\dfrac{1-b}{b}$

Step 1: Analyze the Question

You are provided with two pieces of information: $b \neq 1$ and $\dfrac{ab}{a-b} = 1$.

Step 2: State the Task

Find the value of a in terms of b.

Step 3: Approach Strategically

Isolate the variable a:

$$\frac{ab}{a-b} = 1$$
$$ab = a - b$$
$$ab - a = -b$$
$$a(b-1) = -b$$
$$a = \frac{-b}{b-1}$$

The final expression doesn't seem to match any of the answer choices, but multiplying the expression on the right by $\dfrac{-1}{-1}$ yields the expression $\dfrac{b}{1-b}$, which matches **(A)**.

Step 4: Confirm Your Answer

Check your answer by plugging $\dfrac{b}{1-b}$ for a back into $\dfrac{ab}{a-b} = 1$. When doing so, remember that $1 - b = -1(b-1)$:

$$\frac{ab}{a-b} = 1$$
$$ab = a - b$$
$$ab - a = -b$$
$$a(b-1) = -b$$
$$\left(\frac{b}{1-b}\right)\left(b-1\right) = -b$$
$$-b = -b$$

The equality holds, so you've confirmed that **(A)** is correct.

4. **(C)**

If $x \neq 0$ and $x - \dfrac{2 - x^2}{x} = \dfrac{y}{x}$, then $y =$

○ $-2 - 3x^2$

○ $x^2 - 2$

○ $2x^2 - 2$

○ $x - 2 - x^2$

○ $x - 2 + x^2$

Step 1: Analyze the Question

For this question, you must isolate the variable y on one side of the equation. Note that when there are fractions in an equation, it is best to multiply the entire equation by a common denominator to remove the fractions.

Step 2: State the Task

Move y to one side of the equation and everything else to the other side.

Step 3: Approach Strategically

Both of the fractions in the equation have a common denominator of x. If you multiply both sides of the equation by x, all the denominators will be eliminated. Be careful on this step to multiply every term in the equation by x:

$$x\left[x - \frac{2 - x^2}{x}\right] = x\left[\frac{y}{x}\right]$$

$$x(x) - x\left[\frac{2 - x^2}{x}\right] = x\left[\frac{y}{x}\right]$$

$$x^2 - 2 + x^2 = y$$

$$y = 2x^2 - 2$$

The correct answer is **(C)**.

Step 4: Confirm Your Answer

When checking your calculations here, confirm that you applied the common denominator to all terms in the equation and that any negative signs were correctly transferred across the parentheses.

5.   (A)

Susan weighs m pounds more than Anna does, and together they weigh a total of n pounds. Which of the following represents Anna's weight in pounds?

○ $\dfrac{n-m}{2}$

○ $\dfrac{n+m}{2}$

○ $\dfrac{n}{2} - m$

○ $2n - m$

○ $n - 2m$

Step 1: Analyze the Question

In this question, you must determine the relationship between Susan and Anna's weights. Notice that even though there are variables in the answer choices, it will be difficult to apply the picking numbers strategy here, because without the actual weights of the girls, you are still left with algebraic equations to solve. You must instead directly apply algebra to solve this question.

Step 2: State the Task

First translate the words into equations. Then isolate Anna's weight on one side of the equation.

Step 3: Approach Strategically

Call Anna's weight A pounds.

Because Susan weighs m pounds more than Anna, Susan's weight is $A + m$ pounds.

Because the sum of Anna's weight and Susan's weight is n pounds, you have the equation $A + (A + m) = n$.

You can now solve this equation for A:

$$A + (A + m) = n$$
$$A + A + m = n$$
$$2A + m = n$$
$$2A = n - m$$
$$A = \frac{n-m}{2}$$

The correct answer is **(A)**.

Step 4: Confirm Your Answer

When confirming your answer, make sure that the original phrases were correctly translated and make sense.

6. **(B)**

Is n negative?

(1) $n^2 + n - 6 = 0$

(2) $n^2 + 6n + 9 = 0$

Step 1: Analyze the Question Stem

In this Yes/No question, sufficiency means determining that n is either definitely negative or definitely non-negative (zero or positive).

Step 2: Evaluate the Statements Using 12TEN

Statement (1) provides a quadratic equation in which the sign of the constant term (-6) is negative. A negative sign in this position of a quadratic equation guarantees that the quadratic has two roots—one positive and one negative. This statement is therefore insufficient. Eliminate **(A)** and **(D)**.

Statement (2) provides a quadratic equation in which the sign of the constant term (9) is positive. A plus sign here means the quadratic may have one (if the quadratic is a perfect square) or two roots. In the case of two roots, the roots would either be both positive or both negative. The plus sign before the middle term ($6n$) indicates that the roots will both be negative. This statement is therefore sufficient to provide a definite yes answer to the question. Eliminate **(C)** and **(E)**.

Statement (2) alone is sufficient, so the correct answer is **(B)**.

7. **(D)**

Which of the following expressions CANNOT be equal to 0 when $x^2 - 2x = 3$?

- ○ $x^2 - 6x + 9$
- ○ $x^2 - 4x + 3$
- ○ $x^2 - x - 2$
- ○ $x^2 - 7x + 6$
- ○ $x^2 - 9$

Step 1: Analyze the Question

Pay special attention to the language used in this question stem. You must determine which of the answer choices cannot be equal to zero if the equation $x^2 - 2x = 3$ is true. Another way to interpret this would be to eliminate the answer choices that share common factors with the equation in the question stem.

Step 2: State the Task

First factor the equation in the question stem. Then factor the equations in the answer choices until you find an equation that does not share a factor with the stem equation.

Step 3: Approach Strategically

Factoring the question stem:

You need to get all the terms on one side of the equation and zero on the other. Subtract 3 from both sides of $x^2 - 2x = 3$ to get $x^2 - 2x - 3 = 0$.

This factors to $(x - 3)(x + 1) = 0$.

Now, check to see which answer choice has either of these factors and eliminate those that do. Because this is a "which of the following" question, start with **(E)**.

(E) is $x^2 - 9 = (x + 3)(x - 3)$. Eliminate.

(D) is $x^2 - 7x + 6 = (x - 6)(x - 1)$. Correct.

Since there can be only one correct answer to this question, you can stop here, confident that each of the other answer choices will share at least one factor with the equation in the question stem. For the record, testing the other answer choices yields the following:

(C) is $x^2 - x - 2 = (x - 2)(x + 1)$. Eliminate.

(B) is $x^2 - 4x + 3 = (x - 3)(x - 1)$. Eliminate.

(A) is $x^2 - 6x + 9 = (x - 3)(x - 3)$. Eliminate.

(D) is the only answer choice without either factor, so it is correct.

Step 4: Confirm Your Answer

When factoring equations, an easy way to check your work is to expand the binomials back into the original equation by applying the FOIL technique. Be sure to do this for every equation you factor, time permitting, to avoid calculation errors.

8. **(A)**

If $x^2 - 2x - 15 = (x + r)(x + s)$ for all values of x, and if r and s are constants, then which of the following is a possible value of $r - s$?

○ 8

○ 2

○ −2

○ −3

○ −5

Step 1: Analyze the Question

At first glance, this question appears very abstract, but if you look a little deeper, you are really only asked to factor the expression on the left side of the equation and compare the binomials with the variables on the right.

Step 2: State the Task

Factor the expression on the left side of the equation.

Step 3: Approach Strategically

Factor the expression $x^2 - 2x - 15$. You have $x^2 - 2x - 15 = (x - 5)(x + 3)$.

So $(x - 5)(x + 3) = (x + r)(x + s)$.

So either (1) $r = -5$ and $s = 3$ or (2) $r = 3$ and $s = -5$.

If $r = -5$ and $s = 3$, then $r - s = -5 - 3 = -8$.

If $r = 3$ and $s = -5$, then $r - s = 3 - (-5) = 3 + 5 = 8$.

The possible values of $r - s$ are -8 and 8. Only 8 appears among the answer choices. **(A)** is correct.

Step 4: Confirm Your Answer

When factoring equations, an easy way to check your work is to expand the binomials back into the original equation by applying the FOIL technique. Be sure to do this for every equation you factor to avoid simple calculation errors.

9. **(A)**

A theater charges $12 for seats in the orchestra and $8 for seats in the balcony. On a certain night, a total of 350 tickets were sold for a total cost of $3,320. How many more tickets were sold that night for seats in the balcony than for seats in the orchestra?

○ 90

○ 110

○ 120

○ 130

○ 220

Step 1: Analyze the Question

A theater sells $12 seats in the orchestra and $8 seats in the balcony. A total of 350 seats were sold for $3,320 on a certain night.

Step 2: State the Task

Find the difference in the number of tickets sold between the balcony and the orchestra.

Step 3: Approach Strategically

With two variables to solve for and enough information to set up two distinct equations, the best approach is to set up a system of linear equations. If R = orchestra seats and B = balcony seats, then you can set up the two equations $12R + 8B = 3,320$ and $R + B = 350$. Given the relative simplicity of the second equation, substitution is the preferred approach. Solving for B in the second equation yields $B = 350 - R$. Substitute this value for B into the first equation and solve for R:

$$12R + 8B = 3,320$$
$$12R + 8(350 - R) = 3,320$$
$$12R + 2,800 - 8R = 3,320$$
$$4R = 520$$
$$R = 130$$

Since $R + B = 350$ and $R = 130$, B must be $350 - 130 = 220$. Watch out for trap answers **(D)** and **(E)**, as the problem isn't asking for the number of orchestra or balcony tickets. You need the difference between the two, which is $220 - 130 = 90$. The correct answer is **(A)**.

Step 4: Confirm Your Answer

Confirm your answer by trying combination. Multiplying the second equation by 8 gives $8R + 8B = 2,800$. Subtracting this equation from the first gives $4R = 520$, or $R = 130$. Combination provides the same value for R and will, by extension, provide the same value for B. You've confirmed that **(A)** is correct.

10. (A)

Hallie has only nickels, dimes, and quarters in her pocket. Nickels are worth $0.05, dimes are worth $0.10, and quarters are worth $0.25. If she has at least 1 of each kind of coin and has a total of $2.75 in change, how many nickels does she have?

(1) She has a total of 21 coins, with twice as many dimes as nickels.

(2) She has $1.50 in quarters.

Step 1: Analyze the Question Stem

Translate the information in the question stem into the equation $0.05N + 0.10D + 0.25Q = 2.75$, where N, D, and Q are the numbers of nickels, dimes, and quarters, respectively. To solve for N, you need two more distinct equations containing those variables (or else some more direct information about N or $0.10D + 0.25Q$).

Step 2: Evaluate the Statements Using 12TEN

Statement (1) can be translated into the equations $N + D + Q = 21$ and $D = 2N$. This gives you a total of three distinct equations and is, therefore, enough information to solve for N. You can eliminate **(B)**, **(C)**, and **(E)**.

Statement (2) can be translated into the equation $0.25Q = 1.50$, which simplifies to $Q = 6$. With Statement (2) and the question stem, you only have two distinct equations (and no special case), so you cannot answer the question.

Since Statement (2) is not sufficient, the correct answer is **(A)**.

11. **(C)**

Jacob is now 12 years younger than Michael. If 9 years from now Michael will be twice as old as Jacob, how old will Jacob be in 4 years?

○ 3

○ 5

○ 7

○ 15

○ 19

Step 1: Analyze the Question

You must first translate the question into algebraic equations and then apply the techniques of combination or substitution to solve for Jacob's age.

Step 2: State the Task

Translate the question stem; then solve for Jacob's age using substitution.

Step 3: Approach Strategically

Equation for Michael's and Jacob's current ages: $M = J + 12$.

Equation for Michael's and Jacob's ages 9 years from now: $M + 9 = 2(J + 9)$.

You now have two distinct equations with two unknowns that you can solve. You can substitute the first equation into the second for M, yielding this equation:

$$(J + 12) + 9 = 2(J + 9)$$
$$J + 12 + 9 = 2J + 18$$
$$J + 21 = 2J + 18$$
$$3 = J$$

Thus, $J = 3$. So if Jacob is 3 years old now, then in 4 years, he will be 7 years old. **(C)** is correct.

Step 4: Confirm Your Answer

You can plug $J = 3$ into the original question stem to confirm your answer. Be careful with your calculations, since **(A)** is a trap for those who don't add 4 years to his current age.

12. **(D)**

If the average (arithmetic mean) of x and y is 30 and $3y + z = 180$, what is the value of $\frac{z}{x}$?

- $\frac{1}{6}$
- $\frac{1}{3}$
- 1
- 3
- 6

Step 1: Analyze the Question

You're given the average of x and y and the value of $3y + z$. There are two equations and three variables, so look for a way to eliminate y, which is not part of the value you're solving for.

Step 2: State the Task

Find the value of $\frac{z}{x}$.

Step 3: Approach Strategically

Translate "the average of x and y is 30" as $\frac{x+y}{2} = 30$. Multiply both sides by 2 to find that $x + y = 60$. Since you need the value of $\frac{z}{x}$, isolate each of these variables: $x + y = 60$, so $x = 60 - y$, and $3y + z = 180$, so $z = 180 - 3y$. Therefore, $\frac{z}{x} = \frac{180 - 3y}{60 - y}$. Factoring out a 3 from the numerator yields $\frac{z}{x} = \frac{3(60 - y)}{60 - y} = 3$. The correct choice is **(D)**.

Here's another approach. After getting $x + y = 60$, multiply this equation by 3 to get $3x + 3y = 180$. Since $3y + z = 180$, you can set the two equations equal to each other: $3x + 3y = 3y + z$. Subtract $3y$ from both sides to find $3x = z$. Now divide both sides by x: $3 = \frac{z}{x}$.

Step 4: Confirm Your Answer

Confirm that you've found $\frac{z}{x}$ and not $\frac{x}{z}$, which is **(B)**. You can also pick numbers to confirm: Since the average of x and y is 30, choose $x = 30$ and $y = 30$. Then $3y = 90$, so since $z = 180 - 3y$, $z = 90$. Then $\frac{z}{x} = \frac{90}{30} = 3$.

EXPLANATIONS

13. (B)

What is the value of b?

(1) $5b - a = 3b + 5a$
(2) $4(b - a) = 12 - 4a$

Step 1: Analyze the Question Stem

This Value question stem gives no information about b. Thus, move on to the statements. For sufficiency, a statement must supply information that would allow you to calculate a single value for b.

Step 2: Evaluate the Statements Using 12TEN

Statement (1) is $5b - a = 3b + 5a$. Simplifying this equation yields $2b = 6a$, which is $b = 3a$, but neither variable cancels out. Thus, you have one equation with two variables, and you can't solve for the value of either variable. Therefore, there is not enough information to find the value of b. Statement (1) is insufficient. Eliminate **(A)** and **(D)**.

Statement (2) is $4(b - a) = 12 - 4a$. Simplify this equation to see whether a variable cancels out. Multiplying out the left side of the equation gives $4b - 4a = 12 - 4a$. Adding $4a$ to both sides yields $4b = 12$, so the variable a cancels out in the simplification, leaving you with one linear equation containing only one variable, b, which you could solve for. Thus, Statement (2) is sufficient, and **(B)** is correct.

If you see a question like this one on Test Day, don't be too quick to assume that you need two equations to solve for the value of either variable—be sure to simplify the equation first.

14. (C)

What is the value of $a + b$?

(1) $5a + 2b = 22$
(2) $3b = 30 - 6a$

Step 1: Analyze the Question Stem

In this Value question, you must determine whether there is sufficient information to determine the value of $a + b$. Note that this may not require finding the individual values of a and b; solving for the value of the entire expression would suffice. Because no information is given in the question stem, move on to the statements.

Step 2: Evaluate the Statements Using 12TEN

Statement (1) provides one equation with two variables, $5a + 2b = 22$. Because the number of variables is greater than the number of different equations, there's no way to solve for the values of a and b. Moreover, there's no way to isolate $a + b$ on one side. Thus, Statement (1) is insufficient. Eliminate **(A)** and **(D)**.

Statement (2) gives $3b = 30 - 6a$, which is one equation with the two variables a and b. Rearranging this gives $6a + 3b = 30$; dividing each term by 3 yields $2a + b = 10$. Again, because the number of variables is greater than the number of different equations, and because there's no way to simplify for the value of $a + b$, Statement (2) is insufficient. Eliminate **(B)**.

Now look at the statements together. You have two distinct linear equations and two variables, so you can solve for their values. Therefore, the two statements taken together are sufficient, and **(C)** is correct. For the record, here's the math: if you rearrange the equation in Statement (2) by adding $6a$ to both sides, you get $6a + 3b = 30$. Now use combination, subtracting one equation from the other, to solve for $a + b$ in one step:

$$
\begin{array}{r}
6a + 3b = 30 \\
- [5a + 2b = 22] \\
\hline
a + b = 8
\end{array}
$$

EXPLANATIONS

15. **(D)**

Let $\boxed{x} = \dfrac{x^2 + 1}{2}$ and $\textcircled{y} = \dfrac{3y}{2}$, for all integers x and y. If $m = 2$, $\boxed{\textcircled{m}}$ is equal to which of the following?

- ○ $\dfrac{13}{8}$
- ○ 3
- ○ $\dfrac{15}{4}$
- ○ 5
- ○ $\dfrac{37}{2}$

Step 1: Analyze the Question

This is a symbolism problem containing two definitions and a nested function. You will need to begin with the innermost function and work your way outward.

Step 2: State the Task

Find the value of $\boxed{\textcircled{m}}$.

Step 3: Approach Strategically

Symbolism problems may look frighteningly complicated, so it's important to remember that they are nothing more than dressed-up equations for which you are asked to plug in a value. In this question, you are given two definition equations and a nested function (a function within a function). You're also told that $m = 2$. With nested functions, you start with the innermost equation and work outward, so begin by plugging 2 in for the variable in the circle equation: $\dfrac{3y}{2} = \dfrac{3(2)}{2} = 3$. Now take the result, 3, and plug that into the square equation:

$$\frac{x^2 + 1}{2} = \frac{3^2 + 1}{2}$$

$$= \frac{9 + 1}{2}$$

$$= \frac{10}{2}$$

$$= 5$$

The value of $\boxed{\textcircled{m}}$ is 5, so the correct answer is **(D)**.

Step 4: Confirm Your Answer

When working with nested functions, remember to always work from the inside out. Doing so allows you to avoid trap choices like **(C)**, which is the result of working from the outside in.

16. (B)

$$\begin{array}{r} \diamond \\ \times\; \underline{\triangle} \\ \bullet \end{array}$$

In the multiplication problem above, each of the symbols $\diamond$, $\triangle$, and $\bullet$ represents a positive digit. If $\diamond > \triangle$, what is the value of $\diamond$?

(1) $\triangle = 1$
(2) $\bullet = 9$

Step 1: Analyze the Question Stem

Before beginning the solution, note for clarity that a positive digit is one of the integers 1, 2, 3, 4, 5, 6, 7, 8, and 9. You are given in the question stem that the product of the digits $\diamond$ and $\triangle$ is $\bullet$ and that $\diamond > \triangle$. You want to know if there is sufficient information to determine the value of the digit $\diamond$.

Step 2: Evaluate the Statements Using 12TEN

Statement (1) says that $\triangle = 1$. So the product of $\diamond$ and 1 is $\bullet$. Because the product of any number and 1 is that number, the product of $\diamond$ and 1 is $\diamond$. So $\diamond = \bullet$. You know from the question stem that $\diamond > \triangle$, and because Statement (1) says that $\triangle = 1$, you have $\diamond > 1$. However, you do not know the value of the digit. So $\diamond$ could be any of the eight remaining positive digits 2, 3, 4, 5, 6, 7, 8, and 9. Because there is more than one possible value for $\diamond$, Statement (1) is insufficient. Eliminate **(A)** and **(D)**.

Statement (2) says that $\bullet = 9$. So the product of $\diamond$ and $\triangle$ is 9. There are two ways to write 9 as the product of two digits, 9×1 and 3×3. Because $\diamond \times \triangle = 9$ and you must have $\diamond > \triangle$, it must be the case that $\diamond = 9$ and $\triangle = 1$. So $\diamond$ has only one possible value, 9. Statement (2) is sufficient. **(B)** is correct.

17. (E)

For all positive numbers x and y, the operation $x \blacklozenge y$ is defined by $x \blacklozenge y = \frac{x^2 - x}{2xy}$.
If $x \blacklozenge 5 = 2$, then $x =$

- ○ 1
- ○ 5
- ○ 11
- ○ 20
- ○ 21

Step 1: Analyze the Question

You're told that $x \blacklozenge y$ is defined by the expression $\frac{x^2 - x}{2xy}$. Translated into English, this means that when you "diamond" two numbers, you square the first number, then subtract the first number from this square, and divide the result by 2 times the product of the first and second numbers. You also know that when y (the second number) equals 5 in this expression, the result is 2.

Step 2: State the Task

Determine the value of x based on the definition.

Step 3: Approach Strategically

Because you know that $x \blacklozenge 5 = 2$, replace y with 5 in the defining equation and set it equal to 2:
$\frac{x^2 - x}{(2x)5} = 2$. Combine factors in the denominator: $\frac{x^2 - x}{10x} = 2$. Next, multiply both sides by 10x: $x^2 - x = 20x$.
Subtract 20x from both sides to yield $x^2 - 21x = 0$. Now factor out an x from each term on the left: $x(x - 21) = 0$. Thus, either $x = 21$ or $x = 0$. The question stem specifies that x is positive, so you're left with $x = 21$. The correct choice is **(E)**.

Step 4: Confirm Your Answer

Check that you substituted numbers correctly into the definition and verify your calculations, making sure you solve for the value of x and not y. If you plugged in 5 for x and solved for y, you probably chose **(A)**.

18. (B)

The operation ♩ x is defined by the equation ♩ $x = ax - b(x - 1) + c$, where a, b, and c are constants that are positive integers. The value of ♩ 0 is 7. What is the value of b?

(1) $a = 3$
(2) $c = 5$

Step 1: Analyze the Question Stem

The stem describes an operation performed on the variable x as ♩ $x = ax - b(x - 1) + c$, where a, b, and c are positive integers. The additional information that ♩ $0 = 7$ is provided. Therefore, substitute 0 for x into the function and set it equal to 7: $a(0) - b(0 - 1) + c = 7$; this simplifies to $b + c = 7$.

Simplified, the question stem provides two variables but only one equation. Each additional value for ♩ x would enable you to create an equation in terms of a, b, and c, just as you did when you translated ♩ $0 = 7$ into $b + c = 7$. So, two more values for ♩ x or some other information that enables you to determine a value for c would be sufficient.

Step 2: Evaluate the Statements Using 12TEN

Statement (1) says that $a = 3$. This information, unlike a value for ♩ x, does not enable you to write another equation, nor does a appear in the equation $b + c = 7$. Thus, Statement (1) is insufficient. Eliminate **(A)** and **(D)**.

Statement (2) informs you that $c = 5$. This information also does not enable you to write another equation, so you do not have enough information to determine the value of *all* the variables. However, you can plug this value into $b + c = 7$ to get the value of b. Therefore, Statement (2) is sufficient to solve for the value of b, and **(B)** is correct.

GMAT BY THE NUMBERS: ALGEBRA

Now that you've learned how to approach algebra questions on the GMAT, let's add one more dimension to your understanding of how they work.

Take a moment to try this question. Following is performance data from thousands of people who have studied with Kaplan over the decades. Through analyzing this data, we will show you how to approach questions like this one most effectively and how to avoid similarly tempting wrong answer choice types on Test Day.

What is the value of g?

(1) $f + g = 9$

(2) $3f - 27 = -3g$

○ Statement (1) ALONE is sufficient, but statement (2) is not sufficient.

○ Statement (2) ALONE is sufficient, but statement (1) is not sufficient.

○ BOTH statements TOGETHER are sufficient, but NEITHER statement ALONE is sufficient.

○ EACH statement ALONE is sufficient.

○ Statements (1) and (2) TOGETHER are NOT sufficient.

EXPLANATION

This question asks you to find the value of *g*. Neither statement by itself can give you that value, since each contains the variable *f* as well.

QUESTION STATISTICS

0% of test takers choose **(A)**

2% of test takers choose **(B)**

25% of test takers choose **(C)**

1% of test takers choose **(D)**

72% of test takers choose **(E)**

Sample size = 4,242

It's tempting to think as one-fourth of test takers did: the statements together will be sufficient because you can rewrite Statement (1) as $f = 9 - g$, substitute into Statement (2), and then solve for *g*. But that's only tempting to a test taker who doesn't first simplify Statement (2):

$$3f - 27 = -3g$$

$$3f + 3g = 27$$

$$f + g = 9$$

This is the same equation as Statement (1), so it doesn't add any new information. Knowing that $f + g = 9$ isn't enough to know the value of *g*, so the statements are insufficient even when combined. Choice **(E)** is correct.

GMAT questions rarely give you algebraic statements in their most useful form. It's a safe bet that you'll need to simplify or reexpress almost all the algebra you see on Test Day. Doing so will help you steer clear of common wrong answers and keep you on the road to a higher score.

MORE GMAT BY THE NUMBERS...

To see more questions with answer choice statistics, be sure to review the full-length CATs in your online resources.

 GO ONLINE

kaptest.com/login

CHAPTER 13

Arithmetic on the GMAT

If x is a number such that $-2 \leq x \leq 2$, which of the following has the largest possible absolute value?

- ○ $3x - 1$
- ○ $x^2 - x$
- ○ $3 - x$
- ○ $x - 3$
- ○ $x^2 + 1$

Above is a typical Problem Solving arithmetic question. In this chapter, we'll look at how to apply the Kaplan Method to this question, discuss the arithmetic rules being tested, and go over the basic principles and strategies that you want to keep in mind on every Quantitative question involving arithmetic. But before you move on, take a minute to think about what you see in this question and answer some questions about how you think it works:

- What mathematical concepts are being tested in this question?

- What do you notice about the answer choices?

- How do the math concepts in the question relate to the answer choices?

- What GMAT Core Competencies are most essential to success on this question?

PREVIEWING ARITHMETIC ON THE GMAT

Most of the Quantitative questions you will see on the GMAT involve arithmetic to some extent. The GMAT frequently increases the difficulty level of questions by combining various topics, such as absolute value, inequalities, exponents, and fractions, and often incorporating these topics into questions that involve algebra, geometry, or proportions. You will be in a much stronger position on Test Day if you have these definitions and operations down cold, freeing up your brain to focus on the more complex critical thinking tasks these difficult and often abstract questions require. This chapter will guide you through the basics and give you practice applying arithmetic concepts to GMAT questions ranging from the simple to the most advanced.

WHAT MATHEMATICAL CONCEPTS ARE BEING TESTED IN THIS QUESTION?

As is often the case with GMAT Quantitative questions, a couple of different yet related concepts are involved within this single question. Here, the question gives a range of possible values of x. So you're looking at inequalities, dealing with both positive and negative numbers. The question itself asks about absolute value, a different topic, but very much related to inequalities, as you'll see later in this chapter.

WHAT DO YOU NOTICE ABOUT THE ANSWER CHOICES?

Each answer choice contains one variable, x, which makes the question seem a little more straight-forward. However, note that a few of the answer choices contain x^2, which introduces more complexity, in that you must understand the behavior of exponential expressions.

HOW DO THE MATH CONCEPTS IN THE QUESTION
RELATE TO THE ANSWER CHOICES?

Absolute value is the measure of a number's distance from zero on the number line. (Because 5 and −5 are the same distance from zero—5 units—both numbers have the same absolute value: 5.) When squaring a term, the result will always be non-negative. So even though the possible values of x are both positive and negative, certain answer choices will test your ability to recognize this property of terms raised to even exponents.

WHAT CORE COMPETENCIES ARE MOST ESSENTIAL
TO SUCCESS ON THIS QUESTION?

Here, the test maker rewards those who understand how paying Attention to the Right Detail is important to answering the question correctly. Despite the basic nature of some of the math topics, the GMAT ultimately rewards test takers who not only know the rules but can apply them to answer questions most efficiently.

Here are the main topics we'll cover in this chapter:

- Arithmetic Basics
- Fractions and Decimals
- Exponents
- Radicals
- Absolute Value
- Inequalities

Handling GMAT Arithmetic

Now let's apply the Kaplan Method to the arithmetic question you saw earlier:

> If x is a number such that $-2 \leq x \leq 2$, which of the following has the largest possible absolute value?
>
> - ○ $3x - 1$
> - ○ $x^2 - x$
> - ○ $3 - x$
> - ○ $x - 3$
> - ○ $x^2 + 1$

Step 1: Analyze the Question

This is an abstract question for which the answer choices contain variables, so picking numbers will be a very efficient strategy to use. Since you are asked to find the answer choice that yields the largest absolute value, you should pick numbers at the ends of the range of possible values for x. You will need to check all of the answer choices, so even though this is a "which of the following" question, there is no benefit to starting with **(E)**.

Step 2: State the Task

Evaluate each answer choice, using both $x = 2$ or $x = -2$ (the values for x with the greatest possible absolute value), in order to determine which choice will produce the largest absolute value.

Step 3: Approach Strategically

You'll need to plug in those values of x, but first notice choices **(C)** and **(D)**. $3 - x$ and $x - 3$ are negatives of each other, which means they have the same absolute value. Since the question asks for the choice that has the largest possible absolute value, you can eliminate both of these choices. Notice also that with choice **(E)**, the absolute value will be the same if using 2 or -2, since squaring the x-term will give the same value.

Since the question tests absolute value, plug in -2 first for x in each of the remaining answer choices. Choice **(A)** gives $3(-2) - 1$, which equals -7. The absolute value of -7 is equal to 7. Choice **(B)** gives $(-2)^2 - (-2) = 4 - (-2) = 6$, which has an absolute value of 6. Choice **(E)** gives $(-2)^2 + 1 = 4 + 1 = 5$, which has an absolute value of 5. You already know that choice **(E)** will yield the same absolute value when $x = 2$, so eliminate choice **(E)**; you already found that choices **(A)** and **(B)** give a larger possible absolute value.

Try $x = 2$ with the remaining two answer choices. In choice **(A)**, $3(2) - 1 = 6 - 1 = 5$, and the absolute value of 5 is equal to 5. For choice **(B)**, $(2)^2 - 2 = 4 - 2 = 2$, and the absolute value of 2 is equal to 2. The largest absolute value you found was for choice **(A)**, when $x = -2$. Therefore, **(A)** is correct.

Step 4: Confirm Your Answer

Confirm that your calculations are correct and that your answer makes sense.

ARITHMETIC BASICS

ORDER OF OPERATIONS

$$\mathbf{P} = \text{Parentheses}$$
$$\mathbf{E} = \text{Exponents}$$
$$\mathbf{M} = \text{Multiplication}$$
$$\mathbf{D} = \text{Division}$$
$\left.\right\}$ in order from left to right
$$\mathbf{A} = \text{Addition}$$
$$\mathbf{S} = \text{Subtraction}$$
$\left.\right\}$ in order from left to right

If an expression has parentheses within parentheses, work from the innermost out. This mnemonic will help you remember the order of operations: Please Excuse My Dear Aunt Sally (PEMDAS).

Example: $30 - 5 \times 4 + (7 - 3)^2 \div 8$

First, perform any operations within **parentheses**.	$30 - 5 \times 4 + 4^2 \div 8$
Next, raise to any powers indicated by **exponents**.	$30 - 5 \times 4 + 16 \div 8$
Then, do all **multiplication** and **division** in order from left to right.	$30 - 20 + 2$
Last, do all **addition** and **subtraction** in order from left to right.	$10 + 2$
Answer:	12

LAWS OF OPERATIONS

These laws will not be tested directly on the GMAT (you won't need to define what each law is). Focus rather on understanding how to manipulate numbers using the various laws listed below.

Commutative Law

It doesn't matter in what order the operation is performed. Addition and multiplication are both commutative, while division and subtraction are not commutative.

Example:
$$5 + 8 = 8 + 5$$
$$2 \times 6 = 6 \times 2$$
$$3 - 2 \neq 2 - 3$$
$$6 \div 2 \neq 2 \div 6$$

Associative Law

The terms can be regrouped without changing the result. Addition and multiplication are also associative, while division and subtraction are not.

Example:
$$(a + b) + c = a + (b + c) \qquad (a \times b) \times c = a \times (b \times c)$$
$$(3 + 5) + 8 = 3 + (5 + 8) \qquad (4 \times 5) \times 6 = 4 \times (5 \times 8)$$
$$8 + 8 = 3 + 13 \qquad\qquad\quad 20 \times 6 = 4 \times 30$$
$$16 = 16 \qquad\qquad\qquad\quad 120 = 120$$

Distributive Law

The distributive law allows you to "distribute" a factor among the terms being added or subtracted. In general, $a(b + c) = ab + ac$.

Example: $4(3 + 7) = 4 \times 3 + 4 \times 7$
$$4 \times 10 = 12 + 28$$
$$40 = 40$$

Division can be distributed in a similar way.

Example: $\dfrac{4 + 6}{2} = \dfrac{4}{2} + \dfrac{6}{2}$
$$\dfrac{10}{2} = 2 + 3$$
$$5 = 5$$

However, when the sum or difference is in the **denominator**, no distribution is possible.

Example: $\dfrac{9}{4 + 5}$ is *not* equal to $\dfrac{9}{4} + \dfrac{9}{5}$.

Factoring

The technique called *factoring* uses the distributive law in its reverse form. You can factor to simplify some calculations.

Example: $11 + 22 + 33 + 44$

$(11 \times 1) + (11 \times 2) + (11 \times 3) + (11 \times 4)$

$11 \times (1 + 2 + 3 + 4)$

11×10

110

FRACTIONS AND DECIMALS

FRACTIONS

$4 \leftarrow$ numerator (also known as the *dividend*)

$— \leftarrow$ fraction bar (means *divided by*)

$5 \leftarrow$ denominator (also known as the *divisor*)

Equivalent Fractions

When you multiply the numerator and denominator by the same number (any number other than zero), the fraction is unchanged. You simply get an equivalent fraction.

Example: $\dfrac{1}{2} = \dfrac{1 \times 2}{2 \times 2} = \dfrac{2}{4}$

Similarly, dividing the top and bottom by the same nonzero number leaves the fraction unchanged.

Example: $\dfrac{5}{10} = \dfrac{5 \div 5}{10 \div 5} = \dfrac{1}{2}$

The GMAT often uses this technique to change the form of fractions that have radicals in the denominator.

Example: $\dfrac{9}{\sqrt{2}} = \dfrac{9 \times \sqrt{2}}{\sqrt{2} \times \sqrt{2}} = \dfrac{9\sqrt{2}}{2}$

Canceling and Reducing Fractions

Generally speaking, when you work with fractions on the GMAT, you'll need to put them in the **lowest terms**. That means that the numerator and the denominator are not divisible by any common integer greater than 1.

Example: The fraction $\dfrac{1}{2}$ is in lowest terms, but the fraction $\dfrac{3}{6}$ is not, since 3 and 6 are both divisible by 3.

The method you use to take a fraction and put it in lowest terms is called **reducing**. That simply means to factor and divide out any **common multiples** from both the numerator and denominator. This process is also commonly called **canceling**. Canceling is particularly useful to avoid time-consuming calculation.

Example: Reduce $\dfrac{15}{35}$ to lowest terms.

First, determine the largest common factor of the numerator and denominator. Then, divide the top and bottom by that number to reduce.

$$\dfrac{15}{35} = \dfrac{3 \times 5}{7 \times 5} = \dfrac{3 \times \cancel{5}}{7 \times \cancel{5}} = \dfrac{3}{7}$$

Adding and Subtracting Fractions

We can't add or subtract two fractions directly unless they have the same, or a *common*, denominator.

A common denominator is just a **common multiple** of the denominators of the fractions. The **least common denominator** (LCD) is the **least common multiple** (LCM): the smallest positive number that is a multiple of all the terms.

Example: $\dfrac{3}{5} + \dfrac{2}{3} - \dfrac{1}{2}$

Denominators are 5, 3, 2.

Least common denominator (LCD) = 30.

For each fraction, divide the LCD by the denominator.

$$30 \div 5 = 6$$
$$30 \div 3 = 10$$
$$30 \div 2 = 15$$

Then, multiply the numerator and denominator by that result.

$$\left(\frac{3}{5} \times \frac{6}{6}\right) + \left(\frac{2}{3} \times \frac{10}{10}\right) - \left(\frac{1}{2} \times \frac{15}{15}\right)$$

$$= \frac{18}{30} + \frac{20}{30} - \frac{15}{30}$$

Combine the numerators by adding or subtracting and keep the LCD as the denominator.

$$= \frac{18 + 20 - 15}{30} = \frac{23}{30}$$

Multiplying Fractions

To multiply fractions, simply multiply the numerators together and the denominators together. Often this process can be sped up by canceling common factors before you multiply.

Example: $\frac{10}{9} \times \frac{3}{4} \times \frac{8}{15}$

First, reduce (cancel) diagonally and vertically.

$$\frac{{}^{2}\cancel{10}}{{}_{3}\cancel{9}} \times \frac{{}^{1}\cancel{3}}{{}_{1}\cancel{4}} \times \frac{\cancel{8}^{2}}{\cancel{15}_{3}}$$

In this case, divide both 10 in the numerator and 15 in the denominator by their common factor 5. Likewise, 3 in the numerator and 9 in the denominator can be reduced by factoring out a 3. Finally, 8 in the numerator and 4 in the denominator can be divided by the common factor 4.

Then multiply the numerators together and the denominators together.

$$\frac{2 \times 1 \times 2}{3 \times 1 \times 3} = \frac{4}{9}$$

Dividing Fractions

To divide one fraction by another, you actually multiply the first fraction by the **reciprocal** of the divisor (the second fraction).

To get the reciprocal of a fraction, invert it. Simply switch around the numerator and the denominator. For example, the reciprocal of the fraction $\frac{3}{7}$ is $\frac{7}{3}$.

Example: $\frac{4}{3} \div \frac{4}{9}$

Invert the divisor, then multiply as usual.

$$\frac{4}{3} \div \frac{4}{9}$$

$$= \frac{4}{3} \times \frac{9}{4}$$

$$= \frac{{}^{1}\cancel{4}}{{}_{1}\cancel{3}} \times \frac{\cancel{8}^{3}}{\cancel{4}_{1}}$$

$$= \frac{1 \times 3}{1 \times 1} = \frac{3}{1}$$

$$= 3$$

Complex Fractions

A complex fraction is a fraction that contains one or more fractions in its numerator or denominator. There are two methods for simplifying complex fractions.

Method I: Use the distributive law. Find the least common multiple of all the denominators and multiply all the terms in the top and bottom of the complex fraction by the LCM. This will eliminate all the denominators, greatly simplifying the calculation.

Example:

$$\dfrac{\dfrac{7}{9}-\dfrac{1}{6}}{\dfrac{1}{3}+\dfrac{1}{2}}$$

The LCM of all the denominators is 18.

$$=\dfrac{18\times\left(\dfrac{7}{9}-\dfrac{7}{6}\right)}{18\times\left(\dfrac{1}{3}+\dfrac{1}{2}\right)}$$

$$=\dfrac{\dfrac{^{2}\cancel{18}}{1}\times\dfrac{7}{\cancel{9}_{1}}-\dfrac{^{3}\cancel{18}}{1}\times\dfrac{1}{\cancel{6}_{1}}}{\dfrac{^{6}\cancel{18}}{1}\times\dfrac{1}{\cancel{3}_{1}}+\dfrac{^{9}\cancel{18}}{1}\times\dfrac{1}{\cancel{2}_{1}}}$$

$$=\dfrac{2\times7-3\times1}{6\times1+9\times1}$$

$$=\dfrac{14-3}{6+9}$$

$$=\dfrac{11}{15}$$

Method II: Treat the numerator and denominator separately. Combine the terms in each to get a single fraction on top and a single fraction on bottom. You are left with the division of two fractions, which you perform by multiplying the top fraction by the reciprocal of the bottom one. This method is preferable when it is difficult to get an LCM for all of the denominators.

Example:

$$\dfrac{\dfrac{5}{11}-\dfrac{5}{22}}{\dfrac{7}{16}+\dfrac{3}{8}}$$

The LCM of the numerator is 22.

The LCM of the denominator is 16.

$$=\dfrac{\dfrac{10}{22}-\dfrac{5}{22}}{\dfrac{7}{16}+\dfrac{6}{16}}=\dfrac{\dfrac{5}{22}}{\dfrac{13}{16}}=\dfrac{5}{^{11}\cancel{22}}\times\dfrac{\cancel{16}^{8}}{13}=\dfrac{40}{143}$$

Comparing Positive Fractions

If the numerators are the same, the fraction with the smaller denominator will have the larger value, since the numerator is divided into a smaller number of parts.

Example: $\dfrac{4}{5} > \dfrac{4}{7}$

If the denominators are the same, the fraction with the larger numerator will have the larger value.

Example: $\dfrac{5}{8} > \dfrac{3}{8}$

If neither the numerators nor the denominators are the same, express all of the fractions in terms of some common denominator. The fraction with the largest numerator will be the largest.

One version of this method is to multiply the numerator of the left fraction by the denominator of the right fraction and vice versa (similar to cross multiplying). Then compare the products obtained this way. If the left product is greater, then the left fraction was greater to start with.

Example: Compare $\dfrac{5}{7}$ and $\dfrac{9}{11}$.

Compare 5×11 and 9×7.

Because $55 < 63$, $\dfrac{5}{7} < \dfrac{9}{11}$.

Example: Compare $\dfrac{22}{9}$ and $\dfrac{11}{9}$.

As before, the comparison can be made by cross multiplying.

Compare 22×9 and 11×19.

Because $198 < 209$, $\dfrac{22}{19} < \dfrac{11}{9}$.

You can also convert the fractions to percents or decimals for easy comparison. This technique is especially useful when finding a common denominator seems time-consuming.

Example: Compare $\dfrac{5}{8}$, $\dfrac{2}{3}$, and $\dfrac{7}{11}$.

$\dfrac{5}{8} = 0.625$, $\dfrac{2}{3} = 0.66666\ldots$, and $\dfrac{7}{11} = 0.636363\ldots$

Because $0.625 < 0.636363\ldots < 0.66666\ldots$, $\dfrac{5}{8} < \dfrac{7}{11} < \dfrac{2}{3}$.

Converting fractions to decimals or percents frequently comes up on the GMAT. Often the problem gives you fractions in the question but percents in the answer choices. It's a good idea to memorize the common fraction-to-decimal equivalencies for Test Day.

Another way to compare fractions is to find a "benchmark value" against which the fractions can be compared, particularly when dealing with large numbers.

Example: Compare $\frac{13}{24}$ and $\frac{33}{68}$.

Both are very close to $\frac{1}{2}$.

$\frac{1}{2} = \frac{12}{24}$ and $\frac{1}{2} = \frac{34}{68}$.

Because $\frac{13}{24} > \frac{1}{2}$ and $\frac{33}{68} < \frac{1}{2}$, $\frac{13}{24} > \frac{33}{68}$.

Mixed Numbers

Fractions whose numerators are greater than their denominators may be converted into mixed numbers and vice versa. Mixed numbers consist of an integer and a fraction. For example, $3\frac{1}{4}$, $12\frac{2}{5}$, and $5\frac{7}{8}$ are all mixed numbers.

Example: Convert $\frac{23}{4}$ to a mixed number.

$$\frac{23}{4} = \frac{20}{4} + \frac{3}{4}$$
$$= 5\frac{3}{4}$$

Example: Convert $2\frac{3}{7}$ to a fraction.

$$2\frac{3}{7} = 2 + \frac{3}{7}$$
$$= \frac{14}{7} + \frac{3}{7}$$
$$= \frac{17}{7}$$

DECIMALS

Decimals can be converted to common fractions with a power of 10 in the denominator.

Example: $0.053 = \frac{53}{10^3} = \frac{53}{1,000}$

Numbers are made up of **digits** in specific **places**. The GMAT occasionally asks questions using the terms *digit* and *place*, so you should be familiar with the naming convention:

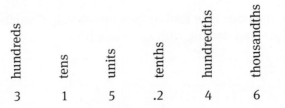

When a GMAT question specifies that a variable is a digit, the only possible values are the integers between 0 and 9, inclusive.

Comparing Decimals

To compare decimals, add zeros after the last digit to the right of the decimal point until all the decimals have the same number of digits. Doing this will make all the denominators of the fractions the same. Therefore, comparing the numerators will determine the order of values.

Example: Arrange in order from smallest to largest: 0.7, 0.77, 0.07, 0.707, and 0.077.

$$0.7 = 0.700 = \frac{700}{1,000}$$

$$0.77 = 0.770 = \frac{770}{1,000}$$

$$0.07 = 0.070 = \frac{70}{1,000}$$

$$0.707 = 0.707 = \frac{707}{1,000}$$

$$0.077 = 0.077 = \frac{77}{1,000}$$

Because $70 < 77 < 700 < 707 < 770$, $0.07 < 0.077 < 0.7 < 0.707 < 0.77$.

Adding and Subtracting Decimals

When adding or subtracting decimals, make sure that the decimal points are lined up, one under the other. This will ensure that the corresponding places are added: that is, tenths are added to tenths, hundredths to hundredths, etc.

Example: $0.5 + 0.05 + 0.005 =$

0.5	(1 decimal place)
0.05	(2 decimal places)
+ 0.005	+ (3 decimal places)
0.555	(3 decimal places)

Multiplying and Dividing Decimals

To multiply two decimals, initially multiply them as you would integers and ignore the decimal places. The number of decimal places in the product will be the sum of the number of decimal places in the factors that are multiplied together.

Example: $0.675 \times 0.42 =$

0.675	(3 decimal places)
× 0.42	+ (2 decimal places)
1350	
+ 27000	
0.28350	(5 decimal places)

Division—Method I: When dividing a decimal by another decimal, multiply each by a power of 10 such that the divisor becomes an integer; that is, move the decimal point of each the same number of places. (This doesn't change the value of the quotient.) Then carry out the division as you would with integers, placing the decimal point in the quotient directly above the decimal point in the dividend.

Example: $0.675 \div 0.25 =$ Move the decimal point over two places to the right to make 0.25 an integer.

$67.5 \div 25 =$

$$
\begin{array}{r}
2.7 \\
25\overline{)67.5} \\
\underline{50} \\
175 \\
\underline{175} \\
0
\end{array}
$$

Division—Method II: Turn the division problem into a fraction. It is best when the numbers have common factors. Move the decimal point in the numerator and the denominator an equivalent number of places to make both numbers integers. Then, cancel common factors.

Example: $0.675 \div 0.25$

$$\frac{0.675}{0.25}$$

$$\frac{675}{250}$$

$$\frac{\cancel{675}^{135}}{\cancel{250}_{50}} = \frac{\cancel{135}^{27}}{\cancel{50}_{10}} = \frac{27}{10} = 2.7$$

In-Format Question: Fractions and Decimals on the GMAT

Now let's use the Kaplan Method on a Problem Solving question dealing with fractions:

$$\frac{1}{3} + \left(\frac{2}{3}\right)^2 =$$

○ $\dfrac{5}{12}$

○ $\dfrac{17}{27}$

○ $\dfrac{7}{9}$

○ 1

○ $\dfrac{5}{3}$

Step 1: Analyze the Question

You're given an expression with two fractions, one of which is raised to an exponent. Attention to the Right Detail is important here; in this case, note the use of the parentheses around only one of the fractions.

Step 2: State the Task

Follow the order of operations (PEMDAS); start with the parentheses, then add the fractions by finding a common denominator.

Step 3: Approach Strategically

First, square both the numerator and denominator of $\frac{2}{3}$, giving a value of $\frac{4}{9}$. Then find a common denominator for the two fractions $\frac{1}{3}$ and $\frac{4}{9}$. Multiply the numerator and denominator of $\frac{1}{3}$ by 3, which yields $\frac{3}{9}$. Now that the denominators are the same, you can add the two fractions $\frac{3}{9} + \frac{4}{9}$, which gives you the answer, $\frac{7}{9}$, choice **(C)**.

Step 4: Confirm Your Answer

Take a moment to verify your math, particularly making sure you followed the order of operations and accurately converted fractions into forms that have a common denominator. Note that **(D)** would be a tempting wrong answer if you had first added the two fractions and then squared the result.

TAKEAWAYS: FRACTIONS AND DECIMALS

- When adding or subtracting fractions, you must have a common denominator.
- $\frac{a}{b} \times \frac{c}{d} = \frac{ac}{bd}$

- $\dfrac{\left(\dfrac{a}{b}\right)}{\left(\dfrac{c}{d}\right)} = \dfrac{a}{b} \times \dfrac{d}{c} = \dfrac{ad}{bc}$

- Knowing common fraction-to-decimal equivalencies will help save you time on Test Day.

PRACTICE SET: FRACTIONS AND DECIMALS ON THE GMAT

1. If z is equal to one of the numbers $\frac{3}{5}$, $\frac{5}{8}$, or $\frac{2}{3}$, what is the value of z?

    (1) $\frac{1}{2} < z < \frac{2}{3}$

    (2) $\frac{5}{9} < z < \frac{5}{6}$

2. The equation $\frac{5a}{2b} + \frac{10}{3} = 5$ is equivalent to each of the following EXCEPT:

    O $3a = 2b$

    O $5a - 2b = \frac{4b}{3}$

    O $\frac{5a}{2b} + 1 = \frac{8}{3}$

    O $3a + 2b - 1 = 2a + 3b$

    O $\frac{a}{2b} = \frac{1}{3}$

3. If $xy \neq 0$, is the reciprocal of $\frac{x}{y}$ greater than $\frac{x}{y}$?

    (1) $x > y$

    (2) $xy > 0$

EXPONENTS

RULES OF OPERATIONS WITH EXPONENTS

In the term $3x^2$, 3 is the **coefficient**, x is the **base**, and 2 is the **exponent**. The exponent refers to the number of times the base is multiplied by itself. For instance, in 4^3, you multiply 4 by itself 3 times: $4^3 = 4 \times 4 \times 4 = 64$.

Accurately distinguishing among these elements is important. For instance, in the expression $3x^2$, only the x is being squared (x is the base), not the 3 (3 is the coefficient). In other words, $3x^2 = 3(x^2)$. If you wanted to square the 3 as well, you would need to rewrite the term as $(3x)^2$ to make 3 part of the base. Remember that in the order of operations, you raise to a power *before* you multiply, so in $3x^2$, you square x and *then* multiply by 3.

A number multiplied by itself twice is called the **square** of that number (e.g., 5^2 is 5 squared).

A number multiplied by itself three times is called the **cube** of that number (e.g., 4^3 is 4 cubed).

To multiply two terms with the same base, keep the base and add the exponents.

Example: $\quad 2^2 \times 2^3 = 2^{2+3}$
$$= 2^5$$

To divide two terms with the same base, keep the base and subtract the exponent of the denominator from the exponent of the numerator.

Example: $\quad \dfrac{4^4}{4^2} = 4^{4-2}$
$$= 4^2$$

To raise a power to another power, multiply the exponents.

Example: $\quad \left(3^2\right)^4 = 3^{2 \times 4}$
$$= 3^8$$

To multiply two terms with the same exponent but different bases, multiply the bases together and keep the exponent.

Example: $\quad (2^3)(3^3) = (2 \times 3)^3$
$$= 6^3$$

Any number raised to the first power equals itself: $a^1 = a$.

Any number except zero that is raised to the zero power is equal to 1: $a^0 = 1$. The exception to this rule is when the base is also equal to zero (0^0 is undefined).

A negative exponent indicates a reciprocal. To arrive at an equivalent expression, take the reciprocal of the base and change the sign of the exponent.

$$a^{-n} = \frac{1}{a_n} \text{ or } \left(\frac{1}{a}\right)^n$$

Example: $2^{-3} = \dfrac{1}{2^3} = \dfrac{1}{8}$

When raising a fraction to an exponent, you can solve in one of two ways: either by raising the numerator and the denominator to the exponent separately, or by multiplying the whole fraction by itself the number of times indicated by the exponent. Either approach yields the same result.

Example: $\left(\dfrac{2}{3}\right)^2 = \dfrac{2^2}{3^2} = \dfrac{4}{9}$

$\left(\dfrac{2}{3}\right)^2 = \dfrac{2}{3} \times \dfrac{2}{3} = \dfrac{2 \times 2}{3 \times 3} = \dfrac{4}{9}$

Note that the squared value here, $\frac{4}{9}$, is less than the base, $\frac{2}{3}$. Raising a positive fraction less than 1 to a positive exponent greater than 1 results in a smaller value. The higher the exponent, the smaller the result.

BASES OF 10

The exponent of a base of 10 tells you how many zeros the number would contain if written out.

Example: $10^6 = 1,000,000$ (6 zeros), since 10 multiplied by itself 6 times is equal to 1,000,000.

When multiplying a number by a power of 10, move the decimal point to the right the same number of places as in the exponent; that is, the number of zeros in that power of 10.

When dividing by a power of 10, move the decimal point the corresponding number of places to the left. (Note that dividing by 10^4 is the same as multiplying by 10^{-4}.)

IN-FORMAT QUESTION: EXPONENTS ON THE GMAT

Now let's use the Kaplan Method on a Data Sufficiency question dealing with exponents:

Does $a = b$?

(1) $a^2 - b^2 = 0$

(2) $1 - \dfrac{a^3}{b^3} = 0$

Step 1: Analyze the Question Stem

This is a Yes/No question. You need to determine whether there is enough information to answer the question "Does $a = b$?" There is no information provided in the question stem, so look at the statements.

Step 2: Evaluate the Statements Using 12TEN

Statement (1) says that $a^2 - b^2 = 0$, which is the same as saying $a^2 = b^2$. Now if $a^2 = b^2$, then either $a = b$ or $a = -b$. You can test a few cases by picking numbers. If $a = 5$ and $b = 5$, then $a^2 = b^2$, so Statement (1) is true and $a = b$. The answer to the question is yes.

If $a = 5$ and $b = -5$, then $a^2 = b^2$ because $5^2 = (-5)^2 = 25$, so Statement (1) is true and a is not equal to b. The answer to the question is no. Because more than one answer to the question is possible, Statement (1) is insufficient. You can eliminate **(A)** and **(D)**.

Statement (2) tells you that $1 - \frac{a^3}{b^3} = 0$, which can be simplified as $1 - \frac{a^3}{b^3}$ or $a^3 = b^3$. In the equation $a^3 = b^3$, both a and b are raised to the same odd exponent. Remembering the rules governing exponents, you know that when raised to an odd power, positive numbers yield positive results and negative numbers yield negative results. So, if $a^3 = b^3$ you can now conclude that $a = b$. The answer to the question is always yes, and Statement (2) is sufficient. The correct answer is **(B)**.

If you weren't sure about the rules of exponents, you could use picking numbers to evaluate Statement (2). In order for a^3 to equal b^3, a and b must have the same value. For instance, if $a = -5$ and $b = -5$, then $a^3 = b^3$ because $(-5)^3 = (-5)^3 = -125$. You cannot pick numbers such as $a = 5$ and $b = -5$, since $5^3 = 125 \neq (-5)^3 = -125$. Since it's impossible to pick different numbers for a and b, the answer to the question is always yes, and you can choose **(B)**.

Note how the Core Competency of Attention to the Right Detail plays a big role in answering the question correctly. It's easy to be misled into thinking that if $a^2 = b^2$, then a must be equal to b. Pay attention to whether exponents are even or odd when confronted with a similar problem.

TAKEAWAYS: EXPONENTS

- Exponents count the number of times something is multiplied by itself.
- $a^b \times a^c = a^{b+c}$
- $\dfrac{a^b}{a^c} = a^{b-c}$
- $\left(a^b\right)^c = a^{b \times c}$
- $\left(a^b\right)\left(c^b\right) = \left(a \times c\right)^b$
- $a^{-b} = \dfrac{1}{a^b}$
- Raising a positive fraction less than 1 to a positive exponent greater than 1 results in a smaller value. The higher the exponent, the smaller the result.
- When a negative number is raised to an even exponent, the result is positive. When a negative number is raised to an odd exponent, the result is negative.
- When multiplying a number by a power of 10, the exponent just represents the number of places to move the decimal.

PRACTICE SET: EXPONENTS ON THE GMAT

4. At Car Part Corporation, there is a machine that produces brake pads. As the machine works, a wheel assembly turns. After the wheel assembly turns 4.09×10^6 times, the machine needs maintenance. Since being installed, the machine has received maintenance 30 times. Approximately how many total turns had the wheel assembly made when the machine last received maintenance?

    O 1.3×10^5
    O 1.2×10^7
    O 1.2×10^8
    O 4.1×10^7
    O 7.0×10^8

5. If $4^{2x+2} = 16^{3x-1}$, what is the value of x?

    O   0
    O   1
    O   2
    O   3
    O   4

6. If a is a positive integer, then $2^a + 2^{a+1} =$

    O 3^{a+1}
    O 2^{a+1}
    O $2a$
    O $2a^{a+1}$
    O $3(2^a)$

RADICALS

FRACTIONS AS EXPONENTS

A fractional exponent indicates a root. So $(a)^{\frac{1}{n}} = \sqrt[n]{a}$ (read "the *n*th root of *a*"). If no specific *n* is present, the radical sign means a square root. If the numerator in the fractional exponent is a different integer, raise the resulting term to that exponent.

Example: $8^{\frac{1}{3}} = \sqrt[3]{8} = 2$

Example: $8^{\frac{2}{3}} = \left(\sqrt[3]{8}\right)^2 = 2^2 = 4$

RULES OF OPERATIONS WITH RADICAL SYMBOLS

By convention, the symbol $\sqrt{}$ (called *radical*) means the *positive* square root only. Even though there are two different numbers whose square is 9 (both 3 and −3), when you see $\sqrt{9}$ on the GMAT, it refers to the positive number 3 only.

Example: $\sqrt{9} = +3;\ -\sqrt{9} = -3$

When it comes to the four basic arithmetic operations, you treat radicals in much the same way you would treat variables.

Addition and Subtraction

Only like radicals can be added to or subtracted from one another.

Example: $2\sqrt{3} + 4\sqrt{2} - \sqrt{2} - 3\sqrt{3} = \left(4\sqrt{2} - \sqrt{2}\right) + \left(2\sqrt{3} - 3\sqrt{3}\right)$ [Note: $\sqrt{2} = 1\sqrt{2}$]

$$= 3\sqrt{2} + \left(-\sqrt{3}\right)$$

$$= 3\sqrt{2} - \sqrt{3}$$

Multiplication and Division

To multiply or divide one radical by another, multiply or divide the numbers outside the radical signs, then the numbers inside the radical signs.

Example: $\left(6\sqrt{3}\right) \times \left(2\sqrt{5}\right) = (6 \times 2) \times \left(\sqrt{3} \times \sqrt{5}\right) = 12\sqrt{3 \times 5} = 12\sqrt{15}$

Example: $12\sqrt{15} \div 2\sqrt{5} = (12 \div 2) \times \left(\sqrt{15} \div \sqrt{5}\right) = 6\sqrt{\frac{15}{5}} = 6\sqrt{3}$

Example: $\dfrac{4\sqrt{18}}{2\sqrt{6}} = \left(\dfrac{4}{2}\right)\left(\dfrac{\sqrt{18}}{\sqrt{6}}\right) = 2\sqrt{\dfrac{18}{6}} = 2\sqrt{3}$

If the number inside the radical is a multiple of a perfect square, the expression can be simplified by factoring out the perfect square.

Example: $\sqrt{72} = \sqrt{36 \times 2} = \sqrt{36} \times \sqrt{2} = 6\sqrt{2}$

Warning: You *cannot* "split up" addition underneath a radical sign, although the GMAT will try to trick you into thinking you can.

Example: $\sqrt{100} = 10$

$\sqrt{100} = \sqrt{36 + 64}$

$\sqrt{100} \neq \sqrt{36} + \sqrt{64}$

$\sqrt{100} \neq 6 + 8$

$\sqrt{100} \neq 14$

EXPONENTS AND POWERS OF 10 WITH RADICALS

If an exponent is under the square root sign, just divide the exponent by 2. If an exponent is under a cube root sign, divide it by 3.

Example: $\sqrt{13^4} = 13^2$

$\sqrt[3]{7^6} = 7^2$

If a decimal is under a square root sign, take the square root of the number and divide the number of decimal places by 2. Likewise, if a decimal is under a cube root sign, take the cube root of the number and divide the number of decimal places by 3.

Example: $\sqrt{0.0009} = 0.03$

$\sqrt[3]{0.000125} = 0.05$

IN-FORMAT QUESTION: RADICALS ON THE GMAT

Now let's use the Kaplan Method on a Problem Solving question dealing with radicals:

$$(\sqrt{3} + \sqrt{7})(\sqrt{3} - \sqrt{7}) =$$

○ $-7 - 2\sqrt{3}$

○ -4

○ 3

○ $2\sqrt{7} + 3$

○ $7 + 2\sqrt{3}$

Step 1: Analyze the Question

You have to multiply two expressions with square roots in the terms. Note that the numbers under the radical signs are the same; this may be a signal to look at the question more strategically.

Step 2: State the Task

To begin, recall that $\sqrt{a} + \sqrt{b}$ does *not* equal $\sqrt{a + b}$. Also, $\sqrt{a} - \sqrt{b}$ does not equal $\sqrt{a - b}$. Thus, in this question, you cannot combine the radicals inside the parentheses; instead, you need to multiply the expressions $\sqrt{3} + \sqrt{7}$ and $\sqrt{3} - \sqrt{7}$ using FOIL.

Step 3: Approach Strategically

If you've memorized the classic quadratic equations, you might recognize the expression in the stem as the factors of the difference of two squares. Recognizing this pattern will save you time, since you can avoid going through the entire process of applying FOIL.

Remember that $(a + b)(a - b) = a^2 - b^2$.

Substitute $\sqrt{3}$ for a, and $\sqrt{7}$ for b. Then you have $\sqrt{3}^2 - \sqrt{7}^2$, or $3 - 7$, which equals -4.

If you hadn't noticed the shortcut, you could have applied FOIL:

$$\left(\sqrt{3} + \sqrt{7}\right)\left(\sqrt{3} - \sqrt{7}\right) = \left(\sqrt{3}\right)\left(\sqrt{3}\right) - \left(\sqrt{3}\right)\left(\sqrt{7}\right) + \left(\sqrt{7}\right)\left(\sqrt{3}\right) - \left(\sqrt{7}\right)\left(\sqrt{7}\right)$$

Now, $\left(\sqrt{3}\right)\left(\sqrt{3}\right) = 3$ and $\left(\sqrt{7}\right)\left(\sqrt{7}\right) = 7$, so you are left with $3 - 0 - 7 = -4$.

Either way, **(B)** is correct.

Step 4: Confirm Your Answer

Quickly double-check the last calculation step, and you're done.

TAKEAWAYS: RADICALS

- Radicals follow the same rules as exponents.
- $\sqrt{ab} = \sqrt{a} \times \sqrt{b}$
- $\sqrt{\dfrac{a}{b}} = \dfrac{\sqrt{a}}{\sqrt{b}}$
- $\sqrt{a + b} \neq \sqrt{a} + \sqrt{b}$
- $\sqrt{a - b} \neq \sqrt{a} - \sqrt{b}$
- $\left(\sqrt{a}\right)^2 = a$
- $\sqrt{a^2} = |a|$
- $a^{\frac{1}{2}} = \sqrt{a}$
- $a^{\frac{b}{c}} = \left(\sqrt[c]{a}\right)^b$

PRACTICE SET: RADICALS ON THE GMAT

7. $\sqrt{\dfrac{4 \times 9 + 9 \times 16}{25}} =$

- ○ $\dfrac{6\sqrt{5}}{5}$

- ○ $\dfrac{2\sqrt{3}}{5}$

- ○ $\dfrac{3\sqrt{26}}{5}$

- ○ $\dfrac{12\sqrt{5}}{5}$

- ○ $\dfrac{18}{5}$

8. What positive number, when squared, is equal to the cube of the positive square root of 16?

- ○ 64
- ○ 32
- ○ 8
- ○ 4
- ○ 2

9. If $r > 0$, is $\sqrt{r}$ an integer?

(1) r^2 is an integer.

(2) $r = m^2$, where m is an integer.

ABSOLUTE VALUE

The **absolute value** of a number is the number's distance from zero on the number line. It is denoted by two vertical lines. Since absolute value is a distance, it is always non-negative. For instance, both $+3$ and -3 are 3 units from zero, so their absolute values are both 3.

Example: $|-3| = 3$
$|+3| = 3$

The GMAT will increase the difficulty of an absolute value question (and therefore the benefit of getting it right) by using variables.

Example: $|z| = 3$

You don't know what z equals. Since z is 3 units from 0, you can deduce that it either equals $+3$ or -3.

So you can rewrite this one equation as two:

$$z = 3 \text{ OR } z = -3$$

Another way to conceptualize this is as follows:

$$|z| = 3$$
$$\pm z = 3$$
$$+z = 3 \text{ OR } -z = 3$$
$$z = 3 \text{ OR } z = -3$$

These problems are fairly straightforward when only one number is involved. But what about expressions? Treat the absolute value bars as parentheses and figure out the value of what's inside *before* you perform the operation. Needless to say, the GMAT will base wrong answers on performing these operations in the wrong order.

INCORRECT: $|-3| + |5| = |-3 + 5| = |2| = 2$

CORRECT: $|-3| + |5| = 3 + 5 = 8$

Now, let's look at what happens when you are given expressions with variables.

Example: $|x - 3| = 3$

Believe it or not, this isn't any different from the earlier example:

$$|z| = 3$$
$$z = 3 \text{ OR } z = -3$$

Think of it this way:

$$|<<chunk>>| = 3$$
$$<<chunk>> = 3 \text{ OR } <<chunk>> = -3$$

Since the $<<chunk>>$ here is $x - 3$, that gives you the following:

$$|x - 3| = 3$$
$$x - 3 = 3 \text{ OR } x - 3 = -3$$
$$x = 6 \text{ OR } x = 0$$

The GMAT sometimes adds another layer of complexity to absolute value questions by including inequalities. The key is to remember that *when considering the possible negative value, the inequality sign changes direction*:

$$|x - z| > 3$$
$$x - z > 3 \text{ OR } x - z < -3$$

Don't worry if that concept seems a little strange to you right now. We'll explore this idea further when we discuss inequalities later in this chapter.

IN-FORMAT QUESTION: ABSOLUTE VALUE ON THE GMAT

Now let's use the Kaplan Method on a Problem Solving question dealing with absolute value:

How many possible integer values are there for x, if $|4x - 3| < 6$?

- O   One
- O   Two
- O   Three
- O   Four
- O   Five

Step 1: Analyze the Question

You're asked for the number of integers that could satisfy an inequality. The inequality includes an expression with an absolute value.

Step 2: State the Task

You'll have to evaluate the inequality, find the range of x on the number line, and then count the number of integers that could be acceptable values of x. Remember that the correct answer is not any particular value of x but the number of possible integer values.

Step 3: Approach Strategically

Since you have an absolute value in an expression, you have to consider two possibilities: either $4x - 3 < 6$ or $-(4x - 3) < 6$. Multiply both sides of the second inequality by -1, remembering to reverse the inequality sign: the second inequality can be written as $4x - 3 > -6$. Combine these two statements to analyze the expression more quickly: $-6 < 4x - 3 < 6$. Adding 3 to each of the three members, you have $-3 < 4x < 9$. Dividing each of the three members by 4 gives you $-\frac{3}{4} < x < \frac{9}{4}$. The possible integer values of x such that $-\frac{3}{4} < x < \frac{9}{4}$ are 0, 1, and 2. There are three such values, and **(C)** is correct.

Step 4: Confirm Your Answer

Confirm that your calculations are correct. Quickly sketch the range of x on a number line to confirm your count of the number of possible integer values of x.

TAKEAWAYS: ABSOLUTE VALUE

- Use these three tools to solve absolute value problems:
    1. Interpret absolute value as the expression's distance from zero on the number line.
    2. Draw a number line.
    3. Write two equations for every equation with an absolute value; one or the other of these new equations must be true.
- When there is an absolute value sign, there is a high likelihood of a trap answer for those who assume the quantity inside can only be positive.

PRACTICE SET: ABSOLUTE VALUE ON THE GMAT

10. Which of the following could be the value of x, if $|4x - 2| = 10$?

  ○ −3

  ○ −2

  ○ 1

  ○ 2

  ○ 4

11. What is the value of p?

  (1) $-|p| = -2$

  (2) $p^2 - 4 = 0$

12. If $\left|\dfrac{m}{5}\right| > 1$, then which of the following must be true?

  ○ $m > 5$

  ○ $m < 5$

  ○ $m = 5$

  ○ $m \neq 5$

  ○ $m < -5$

INEQUALITIES

INEQUALITY SYMBOLS

> greater than **Example:** $x > 4$ means x is greater than 4.

< less than **Example:** $x < 0$ means x is less than zero (x is a negative number).

$\geq$ greater than or equal to **Example:** $x \geq -2$ means x can be -2 or any number greater than -2.

$\leq$ less than or equal to **Example:** $x \leq \frac{1}{2}$ means x can be $\frac{1}{2}$ or any number less than $\frac{1}{2}$.

A range of values is often expressed on a number line. Two ranges are shown below.

(a) represents the set of all numbers between -4 and 0, excluding the endpoints -4 and 0, or $-4 < x < 0$.

(b) represents the set of all numbers greater than -1, up to and *including* 3, or $-1 < x \leq 3$.

Sketching a number line is a great way to help yourself to visualize inequalities on Test Day.

SOLVING INEQUALITIES

To solve inequalities, you use the same methods as used in solving equations with one exception: *if the inequality is multiplied or divided by a negative number, the direction of the inequality is reversed.*

If the inequality $-3x < 2$ is multiplied by -1, the resulting inequality is $3x > -2$.

Example: Solve for x and represent the solution set on a number line: $3 - \frac{x}{4} \geq 2$

1. Multiply both sides by 4. $\qquad\qquad\qquad\qquad\qquad 12 - x \geq 8$
2. Subtract 12 from both sides. $\qquad\qquad\qquad\qquad -x \geq -4$
3. Divide both sides by -1 and change the direction of the sign. $\qquad x \leq 4$

Note that the solution set to an inequality is not a single value but a range of possible values. Here, the values include 4 and all numbers less than 4.

Example: Describe the possible values for x if $|2x - 5| < 3$.

With an absolute value, you must split the inequality into two: one with a positive number and one with a negative number. But you *must reverse the direction of the inequality sign in the negative case*:

$$|2x - 5| < 3$$
$$2x - 5 < 3 \quad \text{AND} \quad 2x - 5 > -3$$
$$2x < 8 \quad \text{AND} \quad 2x > 2$$
$$x < 4 \quad \text{AND} \quad x > 1$$
$$1 < x < 4$$

You also need to watch out for this possibility when multiplying or dividing by variables.

Example: Simplify $3b < 2b^2$.

$$3b < 2b^2$$

Divide both sides by b: Before you can do so, you must know whether b is negative.

Write down both possibilities: if b is neg.   OR   if b is pos.
$$3 > 2b \quad \text{OR} \quad 3 < 2b$$

Divide by 2: $\frac{3}{2} > b \quad \text{OR} \quad \frac{3}{2} < b$

All negative numbers are less than $\frac{3}{2}$, so b could equal any negative number at all or any positive number greater than $\frac{3}{2}$.

$$b < 0 \quad \text{OR} \quad \frac{3}{2} < b$$

THREE-PART INEQUALITIES

If you are given a three-part inequality, you can still perform calculations on it. But instead of saying, "What I do to one side, I must also do to the other," you say, "What I do to one part, I must do to *all* parts."

Example: Simplify $-11 < 2x - 5 < 1$.

$$-11 < 2x - 5 < 1$$

add 5 to all parts: $-11 + 5 < 2x - 5 + 5 < 1 + 5$

combine like terms: $-6 < 2x < 6$

divide all parts by 2: $-3 < x < 3$

IN-FORMAT QUESTION: INEQUALITIES ON THE GMAT

Now let's use the Kaplan Method to solve a Problem Solving question dealing with inequalities:

> If $x > 4$ and $3x - 2y = 0$, then which of the following must be true?
>
> ○ $y < -6$
> ○ $y < -4$
> ○ $y = 6$
> ○ $y < 6$
> ○ $y > 6$

Step 1: Analyze the Question

You're given an equation with two variables and an inequality giving you a range of values for one of the variables. Using this information, and scanning the answer choices, you need to determine what will always be true of y for the equation and the inequality to be true.

Step 2: State the Task

Solve the equation for x in terms of y, then substitute the resulting expression for x into the inequality. Finally, evaluate the answer choices and determine which must be true.

Step 3: Approach Strategically

You should start by solving the equation for x as follows:

$$3x - 2y = 0$$
$$3x = 2y$$
$$x = \frac{2}{3}y$$

Because you know that $x > 4$, you can replace x with the value of the equation, so $\frac{2}{3}y > 4$. You can plow through with the calculations here, but by applying Critical Thinking, you can actually get the right answer now. Since multiplying y by a proper fraction must be larger than 4, then y itself must be larger than 4 as well. Since there's no other limitation, find the answer choice that gives you a range of results that are all larger than 4. The only choice that does that is choice **(E)**.

Step 4: Confirm Your Answer

You can confirm your answer using traditional math: multiply both sides of the inequality $\frac{2}{3}y > 4$ by 3. So, $2y > 12$. Next, divide both sides of this inequality by 2, which leads to the conclusion that $y > 6$. Answer choice **(E)** is correct.

TAKEAWAYS: INEQUALITIES

Inequalities should be treated exactly as equations, with two exceptions:

1. When you multiply or divide an inequality by a negative number, you must reverse the direction of the inequality sign.
2. Single-variable equations are usually solved for a specific value, whereas inequalities can only be solved for a range of values.

PRACTICE SET: INEQUALITIES ON THE GMAT

13. Is $a > 5$?

   (1) $8a \geq 40$

   (2) $4a + 6 \leq 25$

14. How many integer values are there for x such that $1 < 3x + 5 < 17$?

   ○ Two
   ○ Three
   ○ Four
   ○ Five
   ○ Six

15. If $b \neq 0$ and $a > b$, is $a > c$?

   (1) $\dfrac{a}{b} > \dfrac{c}{b}$

   (2) $5ab > 6bc$

ANSWERS AND EXPLANATIONS BEGIN ON NEXT PAGE

ANSWERS AND EXPLANATIONS

1.	E	6.	E	11.	E
2.	D	7.	A	12.	D
3.	E	8.	C	13.	B
4.	C	9.	B	14.	D
5.	B	10.	B	15.	E

1. **(E)**

If z is equal to one of the numbers $\frac{3}{5}$, $\frac{5}{8}$, or $\frac{2}{3}$, what is the value of z?

(1) $\frac{1}{2} < z < \frac{2}{3}$

(2) $\frac{5}{9} < z < \frac{5}{6}$

Step 1: Analyze the Question Stem

This is a Value question. The question stem restricts the value of z to three possible fractions. For sufficiency, you need to narrow this list down to one and only one fraction. It can be hard to compare fractions that have different denominators, so it helps to know the fraction-to-decimal equivalents. Convert the three fractions in the question stem before proceeding: $\frac{3}{5} = 0.6$, $\frac{5}{8} = 0.625$, and $\frac{2}{3} = 0.\overline{6}$.

Step 2: Evaluate the Statements Using 12TEN

Statement (1) places z somewhere between 0.5 and $0.\overline{6}$. That removes $\frac{2}{3}$ from the list of possibilities but still leaves $\frac{3}{5}$ and $\frac{5}{8}$ in the running, so this statement is insufficient. Eliminate **(A)** and **(D)**.

Statement (2) places z somewhere between $\frac{5}{9}$ and $\frac{5}{6}$. The decimal equivalent of $\frac{5}{9}$ may not be a familiar one, but dividing 9 into 5 gives you 0.5 followed by something, so $\frac{5}{9}$ is definitely less than $\frac{3}{5}$. As $\frac{2}{3} = \frac{4}{6} < \frac{5}{6}$, this statement does not actually narrow down the given list of fractions at all and is therefore insufficient. Eliminate **(B)**.

Combining the statements does no good because Statement (2) gave us no useful information that wasn't provided in Statement (1). Eliminate **(C)**.

The statements even when combined are insufficient, so the correct answer is **(E)**.

2. **(D)**

The equation $\frac{5a}{2b} + \frac{10}{3} = 5$ is equivalent to each of the following EXCEPT:

○ $3a = 2b$

○ $5a - 2b = \frac{4b}{3}$

○ $\frac{5a}{2b} + 1 = \frac{8}{3}$

○ $3a + 2b - 1 = 2a + 3b$

○ $\frac{a}{2b} = \frac{1}{3}$

Step 1: Analyze the Question

The question states that four of the answer choices are equivalent to $\frac{5a}{2b} + \frac{10}{3} = 5$ and one isn't. Simplify that equation to make it easier to compare to the choices. There are a couple of routes you might take. You might first subtract $\frac{10}{3}$ from both sides: $\frac{5a}{2b} + \frac{10}{3} - \frac{10}{3} = \frac{15}{3} - \frac{10}{3}$. So, $\frac{5a}{2b} = \frac{5}{3}$. Cross multiply to get $15a = 10b$. Then divide by 5 so that $3a = 2b$.

Alternatively, you might have cleared the fractions first by multiplying each term by $(2b)(3)$:

$$\frac{5a\,(2b)\,(3)}{2b} + \frac{10(2b)\,(3)}{3} = 5(2b)(3)$$

$$15a + 20b = 30b$$

$$15a = 10b$$

$$3a = 2b$$

Step 2: State the Task

Determine which of the answer choices is *not* equivalent to the given equation. This means that the same values that produce an equality in the stated equation do *not* produce an equality for the correct choice.

Step 3: Approach Strategically

Rearranging the given equation in lots of different ways until you've satisfied yourself that it's equivalent to four of the choices could be time-consuming. Fortunately, picking numbers will be an efficient approach. Since $3a = 2b$, $a = 2$ and $b = 3$ would be good choices.

Because you've already simplified the given equation to $3a = 2b$, you know that **(A)** is equivalent and is not the correct choice.

(B): Since $5a - 2b = 5(2) - 2(3) = 10 - 6 = 4$ and $\frac{4b}{3} = \frac{4(3)}{3} = 4$, this choice is equivalent to the original. Eliminate.

(C): Plug the numbers into this equation: $\frac{5(2)}{2(3)} + 1 = \frac{10}{6} + \frac{6}{6} = \frac{16}{6} = \frac{8}{3}$. This also works. Eliminate.

(D): $3a + 2b - 1 = 3(2) + 2(3) - 1 = 11$, but $2a + 3b = 2(2) + 3(3) = 13$. This is not a valid equation, so **(D)** is correct.

Since this is an EXCEPT question, there is no need to check **(E)**. For the record, $\frac{2}{2(3)} = \frac{2}{6} = \frac{1}{3}$.

Step 4: Confirm Your Answer

Confirm that your calculations for **(D)** are correct and that you chose an answer that is *not* a valid equation.

3. (E)

If $xy \neq 0$, is the reciprocal of $\frac{x}{y}$ greater than $\frac{x}{y}$?

(1) $x > y$

(2) $xy > 0$

Step 1: Analyze the Question Stem

This is a Yes/No question. The question stem only says that the product of the two variables is not equal to zero, so you know that neither variable is equal to zero. Next you want to rephrase the question in a simpler format: Is $\frac{y}{x} > \frac{x}{y}$?

Step 2: Evaluate the Statements Using 12TEN

Statement (1) says that $x > y$. Picking positive numbers, if $x = 3$ and $y = 2$, you find that $\frac{2}{3}$ is not greater than $\frac{3}{2}$ and the answer to the question is no. Picking negative numbers, if $x = -1$ and $y = -2$, you find that $\frac{-2}{-1}$ is greater than $\frac{-1}{-2}$ and the answer to the question is yes. Statement (1) is insufficient. Eliminate **(A)** and **(D)**.

Statement (2) says that the product of x and y is positive, so you know that x and y are either both positive or both negative. Because the numbers picked for Statement (1) already fall into that category, you can immediately tell that Statement (2) is also insufficient. Eliminate **(B)**.

As the numbers picked could be used for either Statement (1) or (2), they can still be used when you combine the information from both statements. Therefore, even when the statements are taken together, it is still not possible to get a definite answer. **(E)** is correct.

4. (C)

At Car Part Corporation, there is a machine that produces brake pads. As the machine works, a wheel assembly turns. After the wheel assembly turns 4.09×10^6 times, the machine needs maintenance. Since being installed, the machine has received maintenance 30 times. Approximately how many total turns had the wheel assembly made when the machine last received maintenance?

○ 1.3×10^5
○ 1.2×10^7
○ 1.2×10^8
○ 4.1×10^7
○ 7.0×10^8

Step 1: Analyze the Question

This question states that after a machine's wheel assembly turns 4.09×10^6 times, the machine needs maintenance. The machine has received maintenance 30 times.

Step 2: State the Task

Find the approximate total number of turns that the wheel assembly had made at the time of its last maintenance.

Step 3: Approach Strategically

Because the machine received maintenance 30 times, the total turns must be 30 times 4.09×10^6. Since the question asks for an approximate value, round 4.09 to 4. Notice that the answer choices are written in terms of powers of 10. Therefore, rewrite 30 as 3×10. Then calculate:

$$3 \times 10^1 \times 4 \times 10^6$$

$$3 \times 4 \times 10^1 \times 10^6$$

$$12 \times 10^7$$

Looking at the answer choices, notice that the leading value 12 is not among the options. However, 12 can be rewritten as 1.2×10, giving $1.2 \times 10^1 \times 10^7 = 1.2 \times 10^8$. **(C)** is correct.

Step 4: Confirm Your Answer

Reread the question stem, making sure that you translated the scenario correctly into math. For example, dividing 4.09×10^6 by 30 would result in **(A)**. Also, make sure you accurately kept track of the exponent and the decimal places in your answer.

5. (B)

If $4^{2x+2} = 16^{3x-1}$, what is the value of x?

○ 0
○ 1
○ 2
○ 3
○ 4

Step 1: Analyze the Question

You need to solve for x in an equation with exponents. The bases of the two terms with exponents are not the same, but notice that one of the bases, 16, is equal to the other one, 4, squared.

Step 2: State the Task

Because there are manageable numbers in the answer choices, approach this question algebraically or by backsolving.

Step 3: Approach Strategically

Although it would be difficult to know after testing an incorrect answer choice whether the right answer should be larger or smaller, backsolving may still be the most efficient solution, since the answer choices are all small, manageable integers. Unless you've been able to eliminate choices, start backsolving with **(B)** or **(D)**. In **(B)**, $x = 1$, which is an easy value to test. Substituting 1 for x will give you $4^{2(1)+2} = 16^{3(1)-1}$, $4^{2+2} = 16^{3-1}$, and $4^4 = 16^2$. Replacing 16 with 4^2, you get $4^4 = (4^2)^2$, or $4^4 = 4^4$, which is true. **(B)** is correct.

You could also solve the question algebraically. Having noticed that $16 = 4^2$, you can replace the 16 with 4^2 on the right side of the equation, as 4 is the base on the left side of the equation. Then $4^{2x+2} = (4^2)^{3x-1}$. When a power is raised to an exponent, take the product of the exponents and keep the same base. (Algebraically, $(a^b)^c = a^{bc}$.) So using this rule on the right side of the equation $4^{2x+2} = (4^2)^{3x-1}$, you get $4^{2x+2} = 4^{2(3x-1)}$.

When equal powers have the same base, where that same base is not 1, 0, or −1, the exponents must be equal. So $2x + 2 = 2(3x - 1)$. Solve this equation for x:

$$2x + 2 = 2(3x - 1)$$
$$2x + 2 = 6x - 2$$
$$4 = 4x$$
$$x = 1$$

Step 4: Confirm Your Answer

If you used backsolving, confirm that your calculations for **(B)** are correct. If you chose to solve algebraically, confirm by quickly substituting 1 for x in the question stem.

6. (E)

If a is a positive integer, then $2^a + 2^{a+1} =$

○ 3^{a+1}

○ 2^{a+1}

○ $2a$

○ $2a^{a+1}$

○ $3(2^a)$

Step 1: Analyze the Question

You have to evaluate an expression with exponents. Notice the bases of the two terms are equal, but you're adding the terms, not multiplying them. You'll have to use a strategy or think critically in applying the exponent rules.

Step 2: State the Task

You have variables in the answer choices, so you can approach this question algebraically or by picking numbers.

Step 3: Approach Strategically

You can solve this question algebraically. To evaluate 2^{a+1}, recall that when multiplying two numbers with the same base, you add the exponents. So $2^{a+1} = 2^a(2^1)$, and the original expression $2^a + 2^{a+1} = 2^a + 2^a(2^1) = 2^a(1 + 2) = 2^a(3) = 3(2^a)$. **(E)** is correct.

You could also use the picking numbers strategy. For a question with variables in the answer choices, all four incorrect choices must be eliminated because sometimes one or more incorrect choices will work for the particular value that you choose.

Use $a = 1$. Then $2^a + 2^{a+1} = 2^1 + 2^{1+1} = 2^1 + 2^2 = 2 + 4 = 6$.

Now substitute 1 for a into each answer choice. Any answer choice that does not equal 6 when $a = 1$ can be eliminated.

(A) is $3^{a+1} = 3^2 = 9$. This is not 6, so you can eliminate **(A)**.

(B) is $2^{a+1} = 2^{1+1} = 2^2 = 4$. This is not 6, so you can eliminate **(B)**.

(C) is $2a = 2(1) = 2$. This is not 6, so you can eliminate **(C)**.

(D) is $2a^{a+1} = 2(1^{1+1}) = 2(1^2) = 2$. This is not 6, so you can eliminate **(D)**.

Now that all four incorrect answer choices have been eliminated, you know that **(E)** must be correct.

Step 4: Confirm Your Answer

If you chose to pick numbers, you can confirm your answer by checking **(E)**: $3(2^a) = 3(2^1) = 3(2) = 6$. **(E)** does work. If you chose to solve algebraically, confirm that your application of the exponent rules and your calculations are correct.

7. **(A)**

$$\sqrt{\frac{4 \times 9 + 9 \times 16}{25}} =$$

○ $\dfrac{6\sqrt{5}}{5}$

○ $\dfrac{2\sqrt{3}}{5}$

○ $\dfrac{3\sqrt{26}}{5}$

○ $\dfrac{12\sqrt{5}}{5}$

○ $\dfrac{18}{5}$

Step 1: Analyze the Question

You are given a radical expression to simplify.

Step 2: State the Task

Use the rules of radicals to simplify the given expression.

Step 3: Approach Strategically

Straightforward math is the best approach here. Make sure you remember the rules for performing operations on radicals and when you can and cannot combine them. You should also look for common factors so that you can avoid unnecessary calculations.

$$\sqrt{\frac{4 \times 9 + 9 \times 16}{25}} = \frac{\sqrt{9(4 + 16)}}{\sqrt{25}}$$

$$= \frac{\sqrt{(9)(4)(1 + 4)}}{5}$$

$$= \frac{\sqrt{9}\,\sqrt{4}\,\sqrt{5}}{5}$$

$$= \frac{3 \times 2\,\sqrt{5}}{5}$$

$$= \frac{6\sqrt{5}}{5}$$

The correct answer is **(A)**.

Step 4: Confirm Your Answer

With arithmetic, remember to follow PEMDAS, the order of operations. On this problem, be sure to do all of the multiplication before any of the addition in the numerator.

8. **(C)**

What positive number, when squared, is equal to the cube of the positive square root of 16?

- ○ 64
- ○ 32
- ○ 8
- ○ 4
- ○ 2

Step 1: Analyze the Question

You need to find a number that meets the requirements of the question stem.

Step 2: State the Task

Translate the information in the question stem into algebra so you can solve for the answer.

Step 3: Approach Strategically

Call the positive number the question is asking for n. When this number is squared, you obtain n^2. You are told that n^2 is equal to the cube of the positive square root of 16. Start with the number you're given and work step-by-step. The positive square root of 16 is 4. The cube of the positive square root of 16 is the cube of 4: 4^3 is $4 \times 4 \times 4 = 64$. Therefore, $n^2 = 64$. Because $n > 0$, n is the positive square root of 64. So $n = 8$. **(C)** is correct.

Step 4: Confirm Your Answer

Reread the question stem and confirm that your translations and calculations are correct.

9.   (B)

If $r > 0$, is $\sqrt{r}$ an integer?

(1) r^2 is an integer.

(2) $r = m^2$, where m is an integer.

Step 1: Analyze the Question Stem

This is a Yes/No question. Here you are given that r is positive, and you need to find out whether you have sufficient information to determine whether $\sqrt{r}$ is an integer. There is no information in the question stem that you can use to determine whether or not $\sqrt{r}$ is an integer, so look at the statements.

Step 2: Evaluate the Statements Using 12TEN

Statement (1) says that r^2 is an integer. If $r = 4$, then $r^2 = 4^2 = 16$ is an integer, so Statement (1) is true. In this case, $\sqrt{r} = \sqrt{4} = 2$ is an integer, and the answer to the question is yes. If $r = 5$, then $r^2 = 5^2 = 25$ is an integer, so Statement (1) is true. In this case, $\sqrt{r} = \sqrt{5}$ is not an integer, and the answer to the question is no. Because different answers to the question are possible, this statement is insufficient. You can eliminate **(A)** and **(D)**.

Now look at Statement (2). If $r = m^2$, where m is an integer, then $\sqrt{r} = \sqrt{m^2} = |m|$. Thus, $\sqrt{r}$ must always be an integer, since you are told that m is an integer. Statement (2) is sufficient, so **(B)** is correct.

10. **(B)**

Which of the following could be the value of x, if $|4x - 2| = 10$?

- ○ -3
- ○ -2
- ○ 1
- ○ 2
- ○ 4

Step 1: Analyze the Question

You are given the equation $|4x - 2| = 10$.

Step 2: State the Task

Find the possible value of x.

Step 3: Approach Strategically

If $|4x - 2| = 10$, the quantity inside the absolute value signs must equal either 10 or -10, so you should solve for x by breaking the equation into $4x - 2 = 10$ and $4x - 2 = -10$.

If $4x - 2 = 10$, then $4x = 12$ and $x = 3$.

If $4x - 2 = -10$, then $4x = -8$ and $x = -2$.

Only one of these values will show up in the answer choices (since only one answer is correct), and that's -2, which is **(B)**.

Step 4: Confirm Your Answer

To confirm your answer, you can backsolve, plugging -2 in for x in the original equation: $|4(-2) -2| = |-8 - 2| = |-10| = 10$. **(B)** is confirmed as correct.

11. (E)

What is the value of p?

(1) $-|p| = -2$
(2) $p^2 - 4 = 0$

Step 1: Analyze the Question Stem

This is a Value question. You need to be able to determine a single value for p. There is no information in the question stem that you can use to determine p, so look at the statements.

Step 2: Evaluate the Statements Using 12TEN

Statement (1) tells you that p can equal either -2 or 2, so it is not sufficient to determine a single value for p. Eliminate **(A)** and **(D)**.

Statement (2) tells you that $p^2 = 4$, so p equals either -2 or 2; this too is insufficient. Eliminate **(B)**.

When you combine the statements, you still have the same two possible values, so even together, the statements are insufficient. **(E)** is correct.

12. **(D)**

If $\left|\dfrac{m}{5}\right| > 1$, then which of the following must be true?

- ○ $m > 5$
- ○ $m < 5$
- ○ $m = 5$
- ○ $m \neq 5$
- ○ $m < -5$

Step 1: Analyze the Question

You have to evaluate an inequality and then determine which of the answer choices is always true. The inequality contains an expression with absolute value signs.

Step 2: State the Task

Evaluate the inequality, find the range of m on the number line, and then evaluate the answer choices.

Step 3: Approach Strategically

When you have an absolute value in an expression, you have to consider both possibilities:

Either $\dfrac{m}{5} > 1$ OR $\dfrac{m}{5} < -1$.

So $m > 5$ OR $m < -5$.

Remember that when you multiplied by -5 in the second possibility, you changed the direction of the inequality sign.

Now you're ready to evaluate the choices. Remember, you're looking for the choice that is always true. Each of choices **(A)**, **(B)**, and **(E)** could be true but does not have to be. **(C)** is never true given the question stem. **(D)** is the only choice that *must* be true.

Step 4: Confirm Your Answer

Confirm that your calculations are correct. A quick sketch of the range of m on a number line shows **(D)** is correct.

13. (B)

Is $a > 5$?

(1) $8a \geq 40$

(2) $4a + 6 \leq 25$

Step 1: Analyze the Question Stem

In this Yes/No question, sufficiency means demonstrating that a is either definitely greater than 5 or that a is definitely less than or equal to 5.

Step 2: Evaluate the Statements Using 12TEN

Simplify Statement (1). If $8a \geq 40$, then $a \geq 5$. This means that a can be greater than 5 or equal to 5, so this statement is insufficient. Eliminate **(A)** and **(D)**.

Statement (2) says that $4a + 6 \leq 25$, which simplifies to $4a \leq 19$ and $a \leq (19 \div 4)$. Since $19 \div 4 < 5$, a must be less than 5. This means that the answer to the stem question is unequivocally no, so Statement (2) alone is sufficient. **(B)** is correct.

14. (D)

How many integer values are there for x such that $1 < 3x + 5 < 17$?

○ Two
○ Three
○ Four
○ Five
○ Six

Step 1: Analyze the Question

You're asked for the number of integers that could satisfy an inequality.

Step 2: State the Task

You'll have to evaluate the inequality, find the range of x on the number line, and then count the number of integers that could be acceptable values of x.

Step 3: Approach Strategically

You can solve for the range of values that satisfy this inequality by isolating x, the same way you would for an equation. You must, however, do the same thing to all three parts. Subtracting 5 from all three parts, you get $-4 < 3x < 12$. Then divide all three parts by 3 to get $-\frac{4}{3} < x < 4$.

The integer values that satisfy this inequality are -1, 0, 1, 2, and 3. Therefore, there are five integer values, and the correct answer is **(D)**.

Step 4: Confirm Your Answer

Confirm that your calculations are correct. Quickly sketch the range of x on a number line to confirm your count of the number of possible integer values of x.

15. (E)

If $b \neq 0$ and $a > b$, is $a > c$?

(1) $\dfrac{a}{b} > \dfrac{c}{b}$

(2) $5ab > 6bc$

Step 1: Analyze the Question Stem

This is a Yes/No question. The question stem tells you that $b \neq 0$ and $a > b$. You want to find out whether there is sufficient information to determine whether $a > c$. There is no information in the question stem that you can use to determine whether or not $a > c$, so look at the statements.

Step 2: Evaluate the Statements Using 12TEN

Both of the statements are inequalities, so remember that when you multiply both sides of an inequality by a positive number, the direction of the inequality sign stays the same, but when you multiply both sides of an inequality by a negative number, the direction of the inequality sign is reversed. Keeping this in mind, look at the statements.

Begin with Statement (1), $\frac{a}{b} > \frac{c}{b}$. If b is positive, then multiplying both sides by b gives you $a > c$. But if b is negative, then multiplying both sides by b gives you $a < c$, since the sign of the inequality must be reversed. Therefore, Statement (1) does not tell you whether or not a is greater than c. Eliminate **(A)** and **(D)**.

You can use the same logic when approaching Statement (2), $5ab > 6bc$. If b is positive, then dividing both sides by b gives you $5a > 6c$. If only 5 pieces of a is more than 6 pieces of c, a itself must be greater than c. However, if b is negative, then dividing by b gives you $5a < 6c$. In this instance, a could be less than c, but it could also be greater than c. Thus, Statement (2) is insufficient. Eliminate **(B)**.

When putting the two statements together, it is still necessary to know whether b is positive or negative in order to answer the question. Since you do not have this information, the statements taken together are insufficient, and the correct answer is **(E)**.

GMAT BY THE NUMBERS: ARITHMETIC

Now that you've learned how to approach arithmetic questions on the GMAT, let's add one more dimension to your understanding of how they work.

Take a moment to try this question. Following is performance data from thousands of people who have studied with Kaplan over the decades. Through analyzing this data, we will show you how to approach questions like this one most effectively and how to avoid similarly tempting wrong answer choice types on Test Day.

What is the value of integer n?

(1) $n = n^4$

(2) $1^n \neq n$

- ○ Statement (1) ALONE is sufficient, but statement (2) is not sufficient.
- ○ Statement (2) ALONE is sufficient, but statement (1) is not sufficient.
- ○ BOTH statements TOGETHER are sufficient, but NEITHER statement ALONE is sufficient.
- ○ EACH statement ALONE is sufficient.
- ○ Statements (1) and (2) TOGETHER are NOT sufficient.

EXPLANATION

This question asks for the value of n and tells you only that it's an integer. This leaves *all* integers as possible values—an important observation because some integers behave differently in certain arithmetic operations than others. The values 1, 0, and negative numbers all have special properties that are often crucial to consider.

QUESTION STATISTICS

19% of test takers choose **(A)**

9% of test takers choose **(B)**

48% of test takers choose **(C)**

3% of test takers choose **(D)**

21% of test takers choose **(E)**

Sample size = 4,200

Statement (1) tells you that $n = n^4$. It may be tempting to think that n must equal 1, but 0 also equals its own fourth power: 0. The question statistics reveal that test takers often overlook this possibility, choosing **(A)**, so it's no surprise that the test maker creates questions that exploit this error. Since n could equal either 1 or 0, Statement (1) is insufficient.

Statement (2) tells you only that $1^n \neq n$. No matter what exponent 1 is raised to, the value will remain 1. For example, $1^2 = 1$, as do 1^3 and 1^4. So the only value of n that Statement (2) excludes is $n = 1$. Alone, this statement is certainly insufficient. But when combined with Statement (1), you have an answer. Statement (1) permits only $n = 1$ and $n = 0$. Statement (2) removes $n = 1$ from consideration, leaving $n = 0$ as the only possibility. The correct answer is **(C)**.

Considering different values, such as 0, will help you to avoid traps. Also noteworthy is how many test takers select **(E)** on this problem. Such a response reflects a common error on difficult Data Sufficiency questions: these two statements are abstract, so many test takers—unsure of how to handle them—decide that they are insufficient. Correct these common assumptions—that values are positive integers and that abstract statements don't contain useful information—and you'll see a much higher score on Test Day.

MORE GMAT BY THE NUMBERS...

To see more questions with answer choice statistics, be sure to review the full-length CATs in your online resources.

GO ONLINE

kaptest.com/login

CHAPTER 14

Number Properties on the GMAT

> Each of the 600 elements of Set *X* is a distinct integer. How many of the integers in Set *X* are positive odd integers?
>
> (1) Set *X* contains 150 even integers.
> (2) 70% of the odd integers in Set *X* are positive.

Above is a typical Data Sufficiency question dealing with number properties. In this chapter, we'll look at how to apply the Kaplan Method to this question, discuss the number properties rules being tested, and go over the basic principles and strategies that you want to keep in mind on every Quantitative question involving number properties. But before you move on, take a minute to think about what you see in this question and answer some questions about how you think it works:

- What does it mean that each of the elements is a distinct integer?

- How are integers related to even and odd numbers?

- How are positive integers different from non-negative integers?

- What GMAT Core Competencies are most essential to success on this question?

PREVIEWING NUMBER PROPERTIES ON THE GMAT

Number properties are all about categories and rules. Certain kinds of numbers behave the same ways in all cases. When discussing number properties, don't assume that they apply exclusively to integers. Integers are one subset of numbers: namely, positive and negative whole numbers and zero. The concept of number properties is perfect fodder for the GMAT test makers because it allows them to reward you for using the Core Competencies of Pattern Recognition and Critical Thinking to draw inferences about how numbers behave, based on certain characteristics they possess. That's why number properties questions appear on the Quant section with greater frequency than other topics: these questions constitute approximately 20 percent of GMAT Problem Solving questions and nearly 30 percent of Data Sufficiency questions.

WHAT DOES IT MEAN THAT EACH OF THE ELEMENTS IS A DISTINCT INTEGER?

Distinct simply means "different." So in this question, all 600 integers are different—there are no integers that show up more than once in the set. Don't assume that a set of integers always contains only distinct integers. This concept often comes into play with questions dealing with variables. Just because *x* and *y* are different letters does not necessarily mean that they represent different values.

HOW ARE INTEGERS RELATED TO EVEN AND ODD NUMBERS?

All integers are either odd or even. Students often forget that 0 is an even number. All integers ending with the digit 0, 2, 4, 6, or 8 are considered "even numbers," and all integers ending with the digit 1, 3, 5, 7, or 9 are considered "odd numbers." When a number is classified as even or odd, it must also be an integer; non-integers are not considered odd or even.

HOW ARE POSITIVE INTEGERS DIFFERENT FROM NON-NEGATIVE INTEGERS?

Basically, the only difference is the number zero. Zero is the only number that is neither positive nor negative. This is a great example of how number properties questions test your Attention to the Right Detail. A question that asks about negative numbers does not include zero as a possibility, but a question that asks for non-positive numbers does include zero. You can bet that considering zero when it shouldn't be considered, or vice versa, can lead to a wrong answer on Test Day.

WHAT GMAT CORE COMPETENCIES ARE MOST ESSENTIAL TO SUCCESS ON THIS QUESTION?

As mentioned earlier, because number properties deal with the expected behavior of numbers based on certain rules, Pattern Recognition is an essential Core Competency for these questions. Also, you should use Critical Thinking in two ways: by remembering the abstract rules of number properties and by using the Kaplan strategy of picking numbers to make those properties more concrete in your mind on Test Day.

Here are the main topics we'll cover in this chapter:

- Integers and Non-Integers
- Odds and Evens
- Positives and Negatives
- Factors and Multiples
- Remainders and Primes
- Sequences

Handling GMAT Number Properties

Now let's apply the Kaplan Method to the number properties question you saw earlier:

Each of the 600 elements of Set X is a distinct integer. How many of the integers in Set X are positive odd integers?

(1) Set X contains 150 even integers.
(2) 70% of the odd integers in Set X are positive.

Step 1: Analyze the Question Stem

This is a Value question. To have sufficiency, you need a single value for the number of positive odd integers in Set X. The question stem tells you that the total number of integers in the set is 600 and that they are all distinct, or different from each other.

Step 2: Evaluate the Statements Using 12TEN

Once you are sure you understand the information in the question stem, move on to the statements. Statement (1) tells you the number of even integers in Set X, from which you could determine the number of odd integers in Set X. But you don't know the number of these odd integers that are positive. Statement (1) is insufficient. Eliminate **(A)** and **(D)**.

Statement (2) tells you the percentage of the odd integers in Set X that are positive. But Statement (2) tells you nothing about the number of odd or even integers in Set X. Statement (2) is insufficient. Eliminate **(B)**.

Now combine the statements. From the two statements together, you could determine the number of odd integers and the percentage of those odd integers that are positive. Together, the two statements are sufficient. Choice **(C)** is correct.

Now let's look at each of the six areas of number properties that show up on the GMAT Quantitative section, starting with integers and non-integers.

INTEGERS AND NON-INTEGERS

Integers are a particularly useful number properties category for the GMAT test makers, since questions that focus on the rules governing integers force test takers to discriminate between different categories of numbers (whole numbers versus fractions or decimals) and since integers include positives, negatives, and zero. Additionally, integers can be easily combined with other number properties to make more difficult questions (e.g., saying that the square root of a number is an integer means that the number is a perfect square, or saying that the quotient of two numbers is an integer means that the numbers are multiples/factors of one another).

These questions also contain an important trap that you must learn to avoid: never assume a number is an integer unless you're told that it is. The absence of information in a GMAT question can be just as important as its inclusion.

Real Numbers

All numbers on the number line. All of the numbers on the GMAT are real.

Integers

All of the numbers with no fractional or decimal parts: in other words, all multiples of 1. Negative numbers and 0 are also integers.

Rational Numbers

All of the numbers that can be expressed as the ratio of two integers (all integers and fractions).

Irrational Numbers

All real numbers that are not rational, both positive and negative (e.g., π, $-\sqrt{3}$).

On the GMAT, it's highly unlikely that you'll get a question that uses the terms **rational** or **irrational**, but you will see many questions that use the term **integer**. Both positive and negative whole numbers are integers. Zero is also an integer. Keep in mind that if a question doesn't say a number is an integer, then the number could be a fraction. Some Data Sufficiency answers depend upon this possibility.

Two rules are important to remember when performing operations with integers:

- When an integer is added to, subtracted from, or multiplied by another integer, the result is an integer.
- An integer divided by an integer may or may not result in an integer.

As with all number properties questions, picking numbers for questions about integers and non-integers can make them easier to tackle.

IN-FORMAT QUESTION: INTEGERS AND NON-INTEGERS ON THE GMAT

Now let's use the Kaplan Method on a Data Sufficiency question dealing with integers and non-integers:

> Is z an integer?
>
> (1) $2z$ is an even integer.
> (2) $4z$ is an even integer.

Step 1: Analyze the Question Stem

This is a Yes/No question, so remember that either "always yes" or "always no" is required for sufficiency. The stem asks you whether z is an integer. It doesn't provide any other information, so move on to the statements.

Step 2: Evaluate the Statements Using 12TEN

Statement (1): If $2z$ is an even number, z must be an integer because all even numbers can be evenly divided by 2. You can use picking numbers to test this. For instance, if $2z = 2$, then $z = 1$. If $2z = -122$, then $z = -61$. You can pick any even integer for $2z$ and always find that z is an integer, so Statement (1) is sufficient. Eliminate **(B)**, **(C)**, and **(E)**.

Statement (2) looks similar to Statement (1), but you can use picking numbers to be sure. If $4z = 4$, then $z = 1$, which is an integer. But if $4z = 6$, then $z = 1.5$, which is *not* an integer. So you can't say that z is always or never an integer. Statement (2) is insufficient, and **(A)** is correct.

TAKEAWAYS: INTEGERS AND NON-INTEGERS

- The term *integer* refers to positive whole numbers, zero, and negative whole numbers.
- When an integer is added to, subtracted from, or multiplied by another integer, the result is an integer. An integer divided by an integer may or may not result in an integer.
- When *integer* is a central word in a question, you have a number properties question. Take note of whether you are using rules or picking numbers.

PRACTICE SET: INTEGERS AND NON-INTEGERS ON THE GMAT

1. Is z an integer?

    (1) $\frac{z}{3}$ is an integer.

    (2) $\frac{z}{2}$ is NOT an integer.

2. If f and g are positive integers, is $\frac{f + g}{f}$ an integer?

    (1) $g = 5f - 4$

    (2) $f = \frac{1}{3}g$

3. If d is a positive integer, is $\sqrt{d}$ an integer?

    (1) $\sqrt{9d}$ is an integer.

    (2) $\sqrt{10d}$ is NOT an integer.

ODDS AND EVENS

The terms **odd** and **even** apply only to integers. Even numbers are integers that are divisible by 2, and odd numbers are integers that are not. Odd and even numbers may be negative; 0 is even. A number needs just a single factor of 2 to be even, so the product of an even number and any integer will always be even.

The GMAT tests the same odds and evens rules over and over. The rules are simple, and putting a little effort into memorizing them now will save you precious time on Test Day.

Rules for Odds and Evens

Odd $\pm$ Odd = Even	Odd $\times$ Odd = Odd
Even $\pm$ Even = Even	Even $\times$ Even = Even
Odd $\pm$ Even = Odd	Odd $\times$ Even = Even

Applying these rules, we notice some important implications for odd and even numbers raised to exponents:

Exponent Rules for Odds and Evens

$$Odd^{\text{any positive integer}} = Odd$$

$$Even^{\text{any positive integer}} = Even$$

Knowing these rules cold will free up your mind so you can strategize when answering questions. As with all number properties questions, picking numbers is a useful strategy to use for questions that deal with odds and evens.

IN-FORMAT QUESTION: ODDS AND EVENS ON THE GMAT

Now let's use the Kaplan Method on a Data Sufficiency question dealing with odds and evens:

> If x is an integer, is x odd?
>
> (1) $x + 4$ is an odd integer.
>
> (2) $\frac{x}{3}$ is NOT an even integer.

Step 1: Analyze the Question Stem

This is a Yes/No question. You are told that x is an integer. You want to determine whether there is enough information to answer the question "Is x odd?" Now look at the statements.

Step 2: Evaluate the Statements Using 12TEN

Statement (1) says that $x + 4$ is an odd integer. So x is equal to an odd integer minus 4. Because 4 is an even integer, x is an odd integer minus an even integer. Because an odd minus an even is odd, x must be odd. Statement (1) is sufficient. You can eliminate **(B)**, **(C)**, and **(E)**.

Statement (2) says that $\frac{x}{3}$ is not an even integer. To determine sufficiency, pick a number for x.

If $x = 3$, then $\frac{x}{3} = \frac{3}{3} = 1$ is an odd integer, so $\frac{x}{3}$ is not an even integer, and Statement (2) is true. In this case, $x = 3$ is odd, so the answer to the question is yes.

If $x = 2$, then $\frac{x}{3} = \frac{2}{3}$ is not an even integer; in fact, it is not an integer at all. And that is fine, because nowhere in the question does it state that $\frac{x}{3}$ is an integer. So Statement (2) is true. In this case, $x = 2$ is even, not odd, and the answer to the question is no.

Because more than one answer to the question is possible, Statement (2) is insufficient. Choice **(A)** is correct.

TAKEAWAYS: ODDS AND EVENS

- Most questions about odd and even numbers can be solved by using a few simple rules:

Odd $\pm$ Odd = Even	Odd $\times$ Odd = Odd
Even $\pm$ Even = Even	Even $\times$ Even = Even
Odd $\pm$ Even = Odd	Odd $\times$ Even = Even

PRACTICE SET: ODDS AND EVENS ON THE GMAT

4. If z is an integer, is z even?

    (1) $\dfrac{z+7}{3} = 2m + 1$, where m is an integer.

    (2) z^3 is even.

5. The set S contains n integers. Is the sum of all the elements of set S odd?

    (1) All the elements of S are prime numbers.

    (2) $n = 2$

6. If m is an odd number and p is a prime number, which of the following must be odd?

    ○ mp

    ○ $m(m + p)$

    ○ $m - p$

    ○ $m^2 + 2p^2 + 1$

    ○ $m^2(m + 2p)$

POSITIVES AND NEGATIVES

Some GMAT questions hinge on whether the numbers involved are positive or negative. These properties are especially important to keep in mind when picking numbers on a Data Sufficiency question. If both positives and negatives are permissible for a given question, make sure you test both possibilities, since doing so will often yield noteworthy results. Take the same approach that you've been learning to use for other number properties: spend some time memorizing the rules but always keep your eye out for strategic opportunities.

Properties of Zero

Adding or subtracting zero from a number does not change the number.

Examples: $2 + 0 = 2$
$4 - 0 = 4$

Any number multiplied by zero equals zero.

Example: $12 \times 0 = 0$

Division by zero is **undefined**. When given an algebraic expression, be sure that the denominator is not zero. The fraction $\frac{0}{0}$ is likewise undefined.

Properties of 1 and −1

Multiplying or dividing a number by 1 does not change the number.

Examples: $4 \times 1 = 4$
$-3 \div 1 = -3$

Multiplying or dividing a number by −1 changes the sign, but not the absolute value.

Examples: $6 \times (-1) = -6$
$-2 \div (-1) = -(-2) = 2$

Note: The sum of a number and −1 times that number is equal to zero.

The **reciprocal** of a number is 1 divided by the number. The product of a number and its reciprocal is 1. Zero has no reciprocal, since $\frac{1}{0}$ is undefined.

Properties of Numbers between −1 and 1

The reciprocal of a number between 0 and 1 is greater than the number itself.

Example: The reciprocal of $\frac{2}{3}$ is $\frac{1}{\frac{2}{3}}$.

$$\frac{1}{\frac{2}{3}} = 1 \div \frac{2}{3} = 1 \times \frac{3}{2} = \frac{3}{2}$$

$$\frac{3}{2} > \frac{2}{3}$$

(You can also easily get the reciprocal of a fraction by switching the numerator and denominator. The result will be the same. For example, the reciprocal of $\frac{2}{3}$ is $\frac{3}{2}$.)

The reciprocal of a number between −1 and 0 is less than the number itself.

Example: The reciprocal of $-\frac{2}{3}$ is $\dfrac{1}{-\frac{2}{3}}$.

$$\frac{1}{-\frac{2}{3}} = 1 \div -\frac{2}{3} = 1 \times -\frac{3}{2} = -\frac{3}{2}$$

$$-\frac{3}{2} < -\frac{2}{3}$$

The square of a number between 0 and 1 is less than the number itself.

Example: $\left(\frac{1}{2}\right)^2 = \frac{1}{2} \times \frac{1}{2} = \frac{1}{4}$, which is less than $\frac{1}{2}$.

Multiplying any positive number by a fraction between 0 and 1 gives a product smaller than the original number.

Example: $6 \times \frac{1}{4} = \frac{6}{4} = \frac{3}{2}$, which is less than 6.

Multiplying any negative number by a fraction between 0 and 1 gives a product greater than the original number.

Example: $-3 \times \frac{1}{6} = -\frac{3}{6} = -\frac{1}{2}$, which is greater than −3.

The special properties of −1, 0, and 1 make them important numbers to consider when you are picking numbers for Data Sufficiency questions, as well as for the "could be/must be" kinds of Problem Solving questions. Because numbers between −1 and 1 can make things larger or smaller in different ways than do other numbers, they are good numbers to pick when testing whether one expression always has to be less than or greater than another.

All these properties can best be seen by observation rather than by memorization.

OPERATIONS WITH POSITIVES AND NEGATIVES

Addition

With like signs: Add the absolute values and keep the same sign. Adding a negative number is the same as subtracting a positive number.

Example: $(-6) + (-3) = -9$

With unlike signs: Take the difference of the absolute values and keep the sign of the number with the larger absolute value.

Example: $(-7) + (+3) = -4$

Subtraction

Subtraction is the inverse operation of addition, so subtracting a negative number is the same as adding a positive number.

Example:
$$(-5)-(-10)$$
$$=(-5)+(+10)$$
$$=5$$

Multiplication and Division

The product or the quotient of two numbers with the same sign is positive.

Examples: $(-2) \times (-5) = +10$ and $\dfrac{-50}{-5} = +10$

The product or the quotient of two numbers with opposite signs is negative.

Examples: $(-2) \times (+3) = -6$ and $\dfrac{-6}{2} = -3$

Keep in mind that it doesn't matter whether the negative sign is in the numerator or in the denominator. The fraction $\dfrac{-6}{2}$ is the same as $\dfrac{6}{-2}$ and $-\dfrac{6}{2}$.

In-Format Question: Positives and Negatives on the GMAT

Now let's use the Kaplan Method on a Data Sufficiency question dealing with positives and negatives:

> Is $x - 2y + z$ greater than $x + y - z$?
>
> (1) y is positive.
> (2) z is negative.

Step 1: Analyze the Question Stem

This is a Yes/No question. The question stem asks, "Is $x - 2y + z > x + y - z$?" Don't miss an opportunity to use Critical Thinking to find a more efficient solution to this problem. You can simplify this inequality to make it easier to work with:

$$x - 2y + z > x + y - z$$
$$-2y + z > y - z$$
$$z > 3y - z$$
$$2z > 3y$$

This simplified inequality is equivalent to the original inequality. Now you can work with the equivalent question stem, "Is $2z > 3y$?" Look at the statements next.

Step 2: Evaluate the Statements Using 12TEN

Statement (1) says that y is positive. However, you're given no information about z, so this statement is insufficient. You can test this by picking numbers. For example, if $y = 1$ and $z = 5$, then y is positive, so Statement (1) is true. You have $2z = 2(5) = 10$ while $3y = 3(1) = 3$. In this case, $2z$ is greater than $3y$, and the answer to the question is yes.

However, if $y = 1$ and $z = -4$, then y is positive, so Statement (1) is true. You have $2z = 2(-4) = -8$ while $3y = 3(1) = 3$. In this case, $2z$ is less than $3y$, and the answer to the question is no.

Because more than one answer to the question is possible, Statement (1) is insufficient. You can eliminate **(A)** and **(D)**.

Statement (2) says that z is negative. However, you have no information about y, so this statement is insufficient. For example, if you pick numbers so that $y = -4$ and $z = -1$, then z is negative, so Statement (2) is true. You have $2z = 2(-1) = -2$, while $3y = 3(-4) = -12$. In this case, $2z$ is greater than $3y$, and the answer to the question is yes.

However, if $y = 1$ and $z = -4$, which are the values that you worked with when you considered Statement (1), then z is negative, so Statement (2) is true. Again, $2z = 2(-4) = -8$ while $3y = 3(1) = 3$, so in this case, $2z$ is less than $3y$, and the answer to the question is no. Because more than one answer to the question is possible, Statement (2) is insufficient. You can eliminate **(B)**.

Taking the statements together, as y is positive, $3y$ is positive. Because z is negative, $2z$ is negative. Because $2z$ is negative and $3y$ is positive, $2z$ is less than $3y$. It is not true that $2z > 3y$. You can answer the question with a definite no. The two statements taken together are sufficient. **(C)** is correct.

TAKEAWAYS: POSITIVES AND NEGATIVES

- When multiplying or dividing numbers with the same sign, the result is always positive. When multiplying or dividing two numbers with different signs, the result is always negative.
- Subtracting a negative number is the same as adding a positive number.

PRACTICE SET: POSITIVES AND NEGATIVES ON THE GMAT

7. If $x - y = 8$, which of the following must be true?

   I. Both x and y are positive.
   II. If x is positive, y must be positive.
   III. If x is negative, y must be negative.

   ○ I only
   ○ II only
   ○ III only
   ○ I and II
   ○ II and III

8. If x and y are integers such that $x > y$, which of the following CANNOT be a positive integer?

   I. $y(y - x)$
   II. $y(x - y)$
   III. $\dfrac{x - y}{y - x}$

   ○ I only
   ○ II only
   ○ III only
   ○ I and II only
   ○ II and III only

9. Is $x > y$?

   (1) $9x = 4y$
   (2) $x > -y$

FACTORS AND MULTIPLES

Factors and multiples are relatively simple concepts used to make some fairly difficult GMAT problems. Multiples—the products of a given integer and other integers—boil down to the numbers you list when "counting by" a certain number. For example, the multiples of 5 are 5, 10, 15, 20, and so on. Factors—those integers that divide another integer without leaving a remainder—are a little trickier, but this section and the next, on remainders and primes, will show you some ways to determine the factors of a number on Test Day.

Multiples

A **multiple** is the product of a given integer and another integer. An integer that is divisible by another integer without a remainder is a multiple of that integer.

Example: 12 is a multiple of 3, since 12 is divisible by 3.

Factors

The **factors**, or **divisors**, of a number are the positive integers that divide into that number without a remainder (or a remainder of 0).

Example: The number 36 has nine positive factors: 1, 2, 3, 4, 6, 9, 12, 18, and 36.

You can group these factors in pairs: $1 \times 36 = 2 \times 18 = 3 \times 12 = 4 \times 9 = 6 \times 6$.

These rules can be synthesized into one: $\dfrac{\text{Multiple}}{\text{Factor}} = \text{Integer}$.

The **greatest common factor**, or **greatest common divisor**, of a pair of numbers is the largest factor shared by the two numbers.

As with all number properties questions, picking numbers is a useful strategy to use with questions about factors and multiples. When picking numbers, keep in mind the following:

- Every number is both a factor and a multiple of itself.
- 1 is a factor of every number.
- 0 is a multiple of every number.

IN-FORMAT QUESTION: FACTORS AND MULTIPLES ON THE GMAT

Now let's use the Kaplan Method on a Problem Solving question dealing with factors and multiples:

If p, q, and r are positive integers such that q is a factor of r, and r is a multiple of p, which of the following must be an integer?

○ $\dfrac{p + q}{r}$

○ $\dfrac{r + p}{q}$

○ $\dfrac{p}{q}$

○ $\dfrac{pq}{r}$

○ $\dfrac{r(p + q)}{pq}$

Step 1: Analyze the Question

You are given the information that q is a factor of r, so you know that r is a multiple of q. The question stem also says that r is a multiple of p. Thus, r is a multiple of both p and q. This question is very abstract, so picking numbers that are permissible will help you make quick work of the answer choices.

Step 2: State the Task

You need to pick numbers for p, q, and r and apply them to the answer choices. Pay Attention to the Right Detail: you are looking for the answer choice that is an integer. Eliminate any answer choices that do not yield an integer.

Step 3: Approach Strategically

Based on work in Step 1, you know that r is a multiple of both p and q. So if $p = 2$ and $q = 3$, then $r = 12$ meets the criteria stated in the question stem.

You can now substitute these values into the answer choices. Because this is a "which of the following" question, begin with **(E)**.

Choice **(E)**: $\dfrac{r(p + q)}{pq} = \dfrac{12(2 + 3)}{2(3)} = \dfrac{12(5)}{6} = 10$. The answer is an integer, so possibly correct.

Choice **(D)**: $\dfrac{pq}{r} = \dfrac{2(3)}{12} = \dfrac{6}{12}$. Not an integer. Eliminate.

Choice **(C)**: $\dfrac{p}{q} = \dfrac{2}{3}$. Not an integer. Eliminate.

Choice **(B)**: $\dfrac{r+p}{q} = \dfrac{12+2}{3} = \dfrac{14}{3}$. Not an integer. Eliminate.

Choice **(A)**: $\dfrac{p+q}{r} = \dfrac{2+3}{12} = \dfrac{5}{12}$. Not an integer. Eliminate.

Step 4: Confirm Your Answer

If all other four answer choices can give non-integers, **(E)** must be the answer. Note that if you had originally picked different numbers, you may have ended up with more than one answer choice that produced an integer value. Whenever this is the case, you would need to pick a new set of numbers and test only the answer choices that worked out the first time.

(E) also makes logical sense because it equals $\dfrac{rp+rq}{pq} = \dfrac{rp}{pq} + \dfrac{rq}{pq} = \dfrac{r}{q} + \dfrac{r}{p}$, and according to the question stem, q and p are both factors of r, so $\dfrac{r}{q}$ and $\dfrac{r}{p}$ are both integers. Therefore, their sum must also be an integer.

TAKEAWAYS: FACTORS AND MULTIPLES

- A *multiple* is the product of a given integer and another integer.
- A *factor* is an integer that divides another integer without leaving a remainder.

PRACTICE SET: FACTORS AND MULTIPLES ON THE GMAT

10. How many positive integers less than 50 are multiples of 4 but NOT multiples of 6?

    ○ 4
    ○ 6
    ○ 8
    ○ 10
    ○ 12

11. If a certain number is divisible by 12 and 10, it is NOT necessarily divisible by which of the following?

    ○ 4
    ○ 6
    ○ 15
    ○ 20
    ○ 24

12. What is the greatest positive integer x such that 9^{6x} is a factor of 81^{10+x}?

    ○ 2
    ○ 4
    ○ 5
    ○ 6
    ○ 15

REMAINDERS AND PRIMES

These two topics—remainders and prime numbers—are math concepts that you may not use a lot in day-to-day life. Although you may be rusty on these concepts, there's no need to be intimidated. The most important thing for you to understand is what a remainder is and how it differs from a quotient. In most areas of life and work, you likely perform division using a calculator, which automatically calculates the decimal places. Remainders are tested on the GMAT, in part, because they are distinctly *not* what calculators give you.

Remainders

The **remainder** is what is left over in a division problem. A remainder is always smaller than the number you are dividing by.

Example: 17 divided by 3 is 5 with a remainder of 2.

The GMAT sometimes asks questions that require you to identify numbers that when divided by a given number produce a certain remainder. For example, "*n* is a number that when divided by 7 has a remainder of 2." Most GMAT remainder problems like this one are best solved by the strategy of picking numbers.

Prime Numbers

A **prime** number is an integer greater than 1 that has only two positive factors, 1 and itself. The number 1 is not considered a prime. The number 2 is the first prime number and the only even prime. (Do you see why? Any other even number has 2 as a factor and, therefore, is not prime.) The GMAT expects test takers to recognize the prime numbers up to 50. They are 2, 3, 5, 7, 11, 13, 17, 19, 23, 29, 31, 37, 41, 43, and 47.

Prime Factorization

The **prime factorization** of a number is the expression of the number as the product of its prime factors. No matter how you factor a number, its prime factors will always be the same.

Example: $36 = 6 \times 6 = 2 \times 3 \times 2 \times 3 = 2^2 \times 3^2$

Example: $480 = 48 \times 10 = 8 \times 6 \times 2 \times 5$

$$= 4 \times 2 \times 2 \times 3 \times 2 \times 5$$

$$= 2 \times 2 \times 2 \times 2 \times 3 \times 2 \times 5$$

$$= 2^5 \times 3 \times 5$$

The easiest way to determine a number's prime factorization is to figure out a pair of factors of the number and then determine their factors, continuing the process until you're left with only prime numbers. Those primes will be the prime factorization.

Example: Find the prime factorization of 1,050.

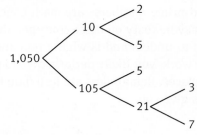

So the prime factorization of 1,050 is $2 \times 3 \times 5^2 \times 7$.

Prime factorization is one of the most valuable tools for the entire Quantitative section. Any question about multiples or factors is really, at its heart, a question about prime factors. Quickly jotting down the prime factorizations of the numbers in such questions can provide the key to the solution. Prime factorization is often the key to dealing with scary exponents as well. If a GMAT problem gives you 35^8, rewriting it as $(5 \times 7)^8 = 5^8 \times 7^8$ is almost certainly the way to go.

Distinct Prime Factors

The GMAT asks not only about prime factors, but also about distinct prime factors. *Distinct* simply means "different." Thus, $1,050 = 2 \times 3 \times 5 \times 5 \times 7$, five numbers with 5 repeating once; it has five prime factors, but only four distinct ones.

Divisibility Tests

Several tests can quickly determine whether a given number is a multiple of 2, 3, 4, 5, 7, 8, 9, 10, and 11.

A number is divisible by 2 if its units digit is even.

> 138 is divisible by 2 because 8 is even.

> 177 is not divisible by 2 because 7 is not even.

A number is divisible by 3 if the sum of its digits is divisible by 3.

> 4,317 is divisible by 3 because $4 + 3 + 1 + 7 = 15$ and 15 is divisible by 3.

> 32,872 is not divisible by 3 because $3 + 2 + 8 + 7 + 2 = 22$ and 22 is not divisible by 3.

A number is divisible by 4 if its last two digits compose a two-digit number that is itself divisible by 4.

> 1,732 is divisible by 4 because 32 is divisible by 4.

> 1,746 is not divisible by 4 because 46 is not divisible by 4.

A number is divisible by 5 if its units digit is either a 5 or a 0.

> 26,985 is divisible by 5.

> 55,783 is not divisible by 5.

A number is divisible by 7 if the difference between its units digit multiplied by 2 and the rest of the number is a multiple of 7.

> 147 is divisible by 7 because $14 - 7(2) = 0$, which is divisible by 7.

> 682 is not divisible by 7 because $68 - 2(2) = 64$, which is not divisible by 7.

A number is divisible by 8 if its last three digits compose a three-digit number that is itself divisible by 8.

76,848 is divisible by 8 because 848 is divisible by 8.

65,102 is not divisible by 8 because 102 is not divisible by 8.

A number is divisible by 9 if the sum of its digits is divisible by 9.

16,956 is divisible by 9 because $1 + 6 + 9 + 5 + 6 = 27$, and 27 is divisible by 9.

4,317 is not divisible by 9 because $4 + 3 + 1 + 7 = 15$, and 15 is not divisible by 9.

A number is divisible by 10 if its units digit is zero.

67,890 is divisible by 10.

56,432 is not divisible by 10.

A number is divisible by 11 if the difference between the sum of its odd-placed digits and the sum of its even-placed digits is divisible by 11.

5,181 is divisible by 11 because $(5 + 8) - (1 + 1) = 11$, which is divisible by 11.

5,577 is a multiple of 11 because $(5 + 7) - (5 + 7) = 0$, which is divisible by 11.

827 is not divisible by 11 because $(8 + 7) - 2 = 13$, which is not divisible by 11.

Bonus rule for 11: If the digit in the tens place of a three-digit number is equal to the sum of the digits in that number's hundreds and units places, then that number is divisible by 11.

Furthermore, the quotient of the number divided by 11 will be a two-digit number composed of the digits in the original number's hundreds and units places. Divisibility by 11 shows up with surprising regularity in the GMAT's tougher Quantitative problems.

341 is divisible by 11 because $3 + 1 = 4$. Furthermore, $341 = 31 \times 11$.

792 is divisible by 11 because $7 + 2 = 9$. Furthermore, $792 = 72 \times 11$.

This rule *cannot* be used to rule out divisibility, only to rule it in:

715 is divisible by 11, even though $7 + 5 \neq 1$ ($715 = 65 \times 11$).

You can combine these rules above with factorization to figure out whether a number is divisible by other numbers.

To be divisible by 6, a number must pass the divisibility tests for both 2 and 3, since $6 = 2 \times 3$.

534 is divisible by 6 because 4 is divisible by 2 *and* $5 + 3 + 4 = 12$, which is divisible by 3.

To be divisible by 44, a number must pass the divisibility tests for both 4 and 11, since $44 = 4 \times 11$.

1,848 is divisible by 44 because 48 is divisible by 4 *and* $(1 + 4) - (8 + 8) = -11$, which is divisible by 11.

Note that combining rules to test divisibility only works when the separate numbers you are testing do not have any factors in common (as is the case with 2 and 3 and with 4 and 11 above).

In-Format Question: Remainders and Primes on the GMAT

Now let's use the Kaplan Method on a Problem Solving question dealing with remainders and primes:

> If a and b are prime numbers, which of the following CANNOT be the value of ab?
>
> ○ 9
> ○ 14
> ○ 21
> ○ 23
> ○ 25

Step 1: Analyze the Question

Given that a and b are prime numbers, you are looking for the one answer choice that cannot be the product of two prime numbers. Note though that when the question is testing prime numbers, remember to test the special case of the number 2, since 2 is both the smallest prime number and also the only even prime number.

Step 2: State the Task

Pick numbers that are permissible and systematically apply the numbers to the answer choices. Eliminate answer choices that cannot be the product of the two prime numbers.

Step 3: Approach Strategically

This is a "which of the following" question, so you can start with **(E)** and test the choices.

Choice **(E)**: The product is 25, which can be created by multiplying 5×5. Because 5 is a prime number, 25 can be the product of two primes and, thus, cannot be the correct choice. Notice that the question stem requires only that a and b be prime numbers, not that they be distinct prime numbers. Eliminate.

Choice **(D)**: The number 23 is prime; its only factors are 1 and 23. Because 1 is not a prime number, 23 cannot be the product of two prime numbers. Therefore, **(D)** is correct.

Step 4: Confirm Your Answer

Use Critical Thinking to check your work. Logically, it makes sense that the correct answer would be a prime number, since a and b, as prime numbers, must both be greater than 1, making it impossible for ab to be a prime number.

TAKEAWAYS: REMAINDERS AND PRIMES

- A *remainder* is the number left over when one integer is divided by another.
- A *prime number* is a positive integer greater than 1 that is divisible only by 1 and itself.

PRACTICE SET: REMAINDERS AND PRIMES ON THE GMAT

13. If *n* is a positive integer greater than 16, is *n* a prime number?

    (1) *n* is odd.
    (2) The remainder when *n* is divided by 3 is 1, and the remainder when *n* is divided by 7 is 1.

14. If $a = 5m + 2$ and $b = 5n + 13$, and *m* and *n* are positive integers, what is the remainder when $a + b$ is divided by 5?

    ○ 0
    ○ 1
    ○ 2
    ○ 3
    ○ 4

15. If $a = 105$ and $a^3 = 21 \times 25 \times 45 \times b$, what is the value of *b*?

    ○ 35
    ○ 42
    ○ 45
    ○ 49
    ○ 54

SEQUENCES

A sequence is an ordered list of numbers a_{n-1}, a_n, a_{n+1}, where n denotes where in the sequence the number is located. Sequence-based questions on the GMAT can look complicated, but once you learn to break down the notation, they're not that tricky.

Example: If $n = 2$, a_2 is the 2nd number,

$a_{2+1} = a_3$ is the 3rd number,

$a_{2-1} = a_1$ is the 1st number, and so on.

Before you dive into statement and answer evaluation, make sure you understand what you are looking for. Use Paraphrasing to state the information in the question in your own words. Then apply Critical Thinking to identify the pattern in the sequence you're given. (Since this is the GMAT, there will always be a discernible pattern to the sequence even if it isn't transparent immediately.)

Once you have a thorough understanding of the question stem and the sequence, look at the statements and answers. Picking numbers is a useful strategy if you're not given concrete values for the terms in a sequence.

With a little patience and a strategic approach, you can attack even the most intimidating sequence questions effectively.

In-Format Question: Sequences on the GMAT

Now let's use the Kaplan Method on a Problem Solving question dealing with sequences:

> In an increasing sequence of 8 consecutive even integers, the sum of the first 4 integers is 268. What is the sum of all the integers in the sequence?

- ○   552
- ○   568
- ○   574
- ○   586
- ○   590

Step 1: Analyze the Question Stem

You are asked to determine the sum of all the integers in the sequence, and you are given the sum of the first 4 of 8 integers. As discussed in the Statistics chapter of this book, half of the numbers in a consecutive sequence with an even number of terms must be greater than and half must be less than the mean.

Step 2: State the Task

Since you are given the sum of the first half of the sequence, you can use the average formula to solve this strategically.

Step 3: Approach Strategically

Since the sum of 4 terms is 268, the average is $268 \div 4 = 67$, which means the 4 even integers must be 64, 66, 68, and 70. This means that the next 4 must be 72, 74, 76, and 78. The sum of all 8 is 568, and that's your answer. You could also apply Critical Thinking and realize that since the numbers in the sequence are consecutive even integers, the first term in the second group will be 8 larger than the first term in the first group, the second term in the second group 8 larger than the second term in the first group, and so on. This means that the final 4 numbers add up to 268 + (8 + 8 + 8 + 8), or 300. Then 268 + 300 = 568. Choice **(B)** is correct.

Step 4: Confirm Your Answer

The numbers in the answer choices here are not very spread out, so estimation is not likely to be very helpful. A quick double-check, especially using the alternative method above, will confirm that you didn't make any mistakes.

TAKEAWAY: SEQUENCES

- Sequences can look complicated, and their descriptions can be confusingly worded. Paraphrase, simplify, and stay attuned to the patterns.

Practice Set: Sequences on the GMAT

$$l, m, n, o, p$$

16. An arithmetic sequence is a sequence in which each term after the first is equal to the sum of the preceding term and a constant. If the list of letters shown above is an arithmetic sequence, which of the following must also be an arithmetic sequence?

    I. $3l$, $3m$, $3n$, $3o$, $3p$
    II. l^2, m^2, n^2, o^2, p^2
    III. $l - 5$, $m - 5$, $n - 5$, $o - 5$, $p - 5$

    ○ I only
    ○ II only
    ○ III only
    ○ I and III
    ○ II and III

17. In a certain sequence of positive integers, the term t_n is given by the formula $t_n = 3(t_{n-2}) + 2(t_{n-1}) - 1$ for all $n \geq 1$. If $t_6 = 152$ and $t_5 = 51$, what is the value of t_2?

    ○ 1
    ○ 2
    ○ 3
    ○ 6
    ○ 17

18. In the infinite sequence S, each term S_n after S_2 is equal to the sum of the two terms S_{n-1} and S_{n-2}. If S_1 is 4, what is the value of S_2?

    (1) $S_3 = 7$
    (2) $S_4 = 10$

ANSWERS AND EXPLANATIONS BEGIN ON NEXT PAGE

ANSWERS AND EXPLANATIONS

1.	A	7.	C	13.	E
2.	B	8.	C	14.	A
3.	A	9.	C	15.	D
4.	D	10.	C	16.	D
5.	E	11.	E	17.	B
6.	E	12.	C	18.	D

1.   **(A)**

Is z an integer?

(1) $\frac{z}{3}$ is an integer.

(2) $\frac{z}{2}$ is NOT an integer.

Step 1: Analyze the Question Stem

In this Yes/No question, sufficiency means demonstrating that z is either definitely an integer or definitely not an integer.

Step 2: Evaluate the Statements Using 12TEN

Statement (1) states that $\frac{z}{3}$ is an integer, so z must be a multiple of 3. As every multiple of 3 is an integer, this statement is sufficient. Eliminate **(B)**, **(C)**, and **(E)**.

Statement (2) states that $\frac{z}{2}$ is not an integer. There are two ways for this to be true: either z is an odd integer, in which case it would still be an integer, or z is not an integer. There is no definite answer to the question, so this statement is insufficient. Eliminate **(D)**.

Statement (1) alone is sufficient, so the correct answer is **(A)**.

2. **(B)**

If f and g are positive integers, is $\dfrac{f + g}{f}$ an integer?

(1) $g = 5f - 4$

(2) $f = \dfrac{1}{3}g$

Step 1: Analyze the Question Stem

This Yes/No question states that f and g are positive integers and asks whether the fraction $\dfrac{f+g}{f}$ is an integer. While multiplication, addition, and subtraction of integers all result in an integer, when an integer is divided by an integer, the numerator must be a multiple of the denominator for the result to be an integer. Thus, you need enough information to determine whether $f + g$ is a multiple of f.

Step 2: Evaluate the Statements Using 12TEN

Statement (1) informs you that $g = 5f - 4$. Substitute that into the fraction in the question stem to get $\dfrac{f + 5f - 4}{f} = \dfrac{6f - 4}{f} = 6 - \dfrac{4}{f}$. This is an integer only if 4 is a multiple of f. There is not enough information to determine whether that is true, so eliminate **(A)** and **(D)**.

Statement (2), $f = \dfrac{1}{3}g$, can be rearranged as $3f = g$. Substitute that into the fraction to get $\dfrac{f + 3f}{f} = \dfrac{4f}{f} = 4$. This is, indeed, an integer, so **(B)** is correct.

3. (A)

If d is a positive integer, is $\sqrt{d}$ an integer?

(1) $\sqrt{9d}$ is an integer.

(2) $\sqrt{10d}$ is NOT an integer.

Step 1: Analyze the Question Stem

This is a Yes/No question. You are told that d is a positive integer. You need to determine whether there is enough information to answer the question "Is $\sqrt{d}$ an integer?" You can use Paraphrasing to restate the question stem as "Is d a perfect square?" Now look at the statements.

Step 2: Evaluate the Statements Using 12TEN

Because number properties are involved in the statements, it may be easiest to use picking numbers.

Statement (1) tells you that $\sqrt{9d}$ is an integer. This means that $9d$ is a perfect square. So some permissible values for d are 1, 4, and 9, which all have integer square roots. Statement (1) is sufficient to answer the question yes. Eliminate **(B)**, **(C)**, and **(E)**.

To evaluate Statement (1) algebraically, use the rules for radicals to simplify it. You know that $\sqrt{9d}$ is an integer, so $\sqrt{9}(\sqrt{d})$ is an integer and $3\sqrt{d}$ is an integer. Your integer result must be a multiple of 3, and $\sqrt{d}$ must be a factor of that number and itself an integer. You can also analyze this statement by using Paraphrasing and restating it as "$9d$ is a perfect square." Since 9 itself is a perfect square, d alone must also be a perfect square, and the answer to the question stem is always yes.

Statement (2) tells you that $\sqrt{10d}$ is not an integer. Again picking numbers to evaluate this statement, choose $d = 1$. You know that $\sqrt{10}$ is not an integer, so 1 is an acceptable value of d, and $\sqrt{1} = 1$, an integer, so the answer to the question is yes. But if you choose $d = 2$, $\sqrt{10(2)} = \sqrt{20}$. This is not an integer, so 2 is an acceptable value for d and $\sqrt{2}$ is not an integer, and the answer to the question is no. Because more than one answer to the question is possible, Statement (2) is insufficient. Eliminate **(D)**, and the correct answer is **(A)**.

4. **(D)**

If z is an integer, is z even?

(1) $\dfrac{z+7}{3} = 2m + 1$, where m is an integer.

(2) z^3 is even.

Step 1: Analyze the Question Stem

In this Yes/No question, you are told that z is an integer. Sufficiency means showing that z is either definitely even or definitely odd.

Step 2: Evaluate the Statements Using 12TEN

Statement (1) provides an equation involving the integer m. Investigate by simplifying the equation:

$$\frac{z+7}{3} = 2m + 1$$

$$z + 7 = 3(2m + 1)$$

$$z + 7 = 6m + 3$$

$$z = 6m - 4$$

So z is $6m - 4$. You can use number properties rules to determine whether z is even. Because 6 is even, $6m$ is even. Then 4 is even, and subtracting an even integer from an even integer results in an even integer. Thus, z is always even, and this statement is sufficiency. You could also pick numbers for m to determine whether z must be even. If $m = 0$ (an even number), then $z = -4$. If $m = 1$ (an odd number), then $z = 6 - 4 = 2$. Whether m is odd or even, z ends up being even. Again, Statement (1) is sufficient. Eliminate **(B)**, **(C)**, and **(E)**.

Statement (2) tells you that z^3 is even. If you know your odds and evens rules, you know this means that z is even, but if you don't remember that rule, or if you want to double-check, use picking numbers. Pick some different numbers for z: $1^3 = 1$, $2^3 = 8$, $3^3 = 27$, $4^3 = 64$. Only even numbers raised to the third power end up even, so this statement is sufficient. Eliminate **(A)**.

Each statement alone is sufficient to answer the question, so **(D)** is the correct answer.

5. (E)

The set S contains n integers. Is the sum of all the elements of set S odd?

(1) All the elements of S are prime numbers.

(2) $n = 2$

Step 1: Analyze the Question Stem

This is a Yes/No question. You want to determine whether the sum of all the elements of set S is odd. The only information that the question stem gives you is that S contains n integers, so look at the statements.

Step 2: Evaluate the Statements Using 12TEN

Statement (1) says that all the elements of S are prime numbers. Remember that there is one even prime number, the integer 2. All other prime numbers are odd.

If $S = \{2, 3\}$, then the sum of all the elements of S is $2 + 3 = 5$, which is odd. In this case, the answer to the question is yes. If $S = \{3, 5\}$, then the sum of all the elements of S is $3 + 5 = 8$, which is even. In this case, the answer to the question is no. Because there is more than one possible answer to the question, Statement (1) is insufficient. You can eliminate **(A)** and **(D)**.

Statement (2) says that $n = 2$; that is, there are two integers in set S. If $S = \{2, 3\}$, then Statement (2) is true, and the answer to the question is yes because $2 + 3$ is odd. If $S = \{3, 5\}$, then Statement (2) is true, and the answer to the question is no because $3 + 5$ is not odd. Because there is more than one possible answer to the question, Statement (2) is insufficient. Eliminate **(B)**.

Now take the statements together. If $S = \{2, 3\}$, then both statements are true, and the answer to the question is yes. If $S = \{3, 5\}$, then both statements are true, and the answer to the question is no. Because there is more than one possible answer to the question when both statements are taken together, the two statements taken together are insufficient. **(E)** is correct.

6. (E)

If m is an odd number and p is a prime number, which of the following must be odd?

○ mp
○ $m(m + p)$
○ $m - p$
○ $m^2 + 2p^2 + 1$
○ $m^2(m + 2p)$

Step 1: Analyze the Question

In this abstract number properties question, m must be an odd number and p must be a prime number. A prime number is a positive integer with exactly two factors: 1 and itself. Examples of prime numbers include 2, 3, 5, and 7. Note that 2 is even (2 is the only even prime number), so p may be even or odd.

Step 2: State the Task

Determine which answer choice must always be odd or, in other words, eliminate any answer choices that can be even.

Step 3: Approach Strategically

For some number properties questions, picking numbers is an efficient strategy.

Since m is an odd number, let m be a small, easy-to-manage value such as 1. While 1 can be a poor choice for picking numbers in a Problem Solving question where you are solving for a numeric value, it is a fine choice when you are finding an expression with a particular number property, since 1 behaves the same way as any other odd number. Since p is a prime number, 5 is a good choice. Evaluate each answer choice by plugging in these values and eliminating any choice that produces an even value.

(A) $mp = (1)(5) = 5$. Keep **(A)**.

(B) $m(m + p) = 1(1 + 5) = 1(6) = 6$. Eliminate **(B)**.

(C) $m - p = 1 - 5 = -4$. Eliminate **(C)**.

(D) $m^2 + 2p^2 + 1 = 1^2 + 2(5)^2 + 1 = 1 + 50 + 1 = 52$. Eliminate **(D)**.

(E) $m^2(m + 2p) = 1^2(1 + 2 \times 5) = 1(1 + 10) = 1(11) = 11$. Keep **(E)**.

Since both **(A)** and **(E)** produced odd values, they both can be odd. But *must* they be odd? Pick numbers one more time. Pick 2 for p to test an even number for this variable. Keep $m = 1$ since all other permissible values for m are also odd and will not affect the result.

(A) $mp = (1)(2) = 6$. Eliminate **(A)**.

Therefore, **(E)** is correct.

Step 4: Confirm Your Answer

You can verify that **(E)** is correct: $m^2(m + 2p) = 1^2(1 + 2 \times 2) = 1(1 + 4) = 1(5) = 5$. Also, you can check **(E)** by applying the rules for odds and evens. Since m^2 is an odd value squared, this is an odd $\times$ odd, which is always odd. Then $2p$ is even for any p value, and $m + 2p$ is then an odd + even, which is odd. Lastly, multiplying two odd values, m^2 and $m + 2p$, yields an odd product.

7. (C)

If $x - y = 8$, which of the following must be true?

    I. Both x and y are positive.
   II. If x is positive, y must be positive.
  III. If x is negative, y must be negative.

- ○ I only
- ○ II only
- ○ III only
- ○ I and II
- ○ II and III

Step 1: Analyze the Question

You know that $x - y = 8$. As this is a Roman numeral question with variables, expect to use picking numbers and don't forget to check the Roman numeral statements in the most efficient order. In this question, begin with Statement II, as it shows up the most in the answer choices.

Step 2: State the Task

Determine which of the Roman numeral statements are true.

Step 3: Approach Strategically

Statement II: If x is positive, y must be positive. To test whether this statement needs to be true, try to pick some numbers for x and y where the result is false. The key is to pick numbers such that the condition is true but the result is false. If $x = 6$ and $y = -2$, then $x - y$ does equal 8. The condition is true, yet you were able to make the result false, so Statement II does not need to be true. Eliminate **(B)**, **(D)**, and **(E)**.

Of the remaining statements, Statement I (Both x and y are positive) is the easier one to test because the numbers picked for x and y can be used to invalidate this statement as well. Eliminate **(A)**.

Therefore, the correct answer is **(C)**.

Step 4: Confirm Your Answer

Confirm the answer by checking Statement III: If x is negative, y must be negative. In the equation $x - y = 8$, if x is negative and y is positive, then the result would simply get more negative. The only way to arrive at a positive answer when x is negative is for y to also be negative. Choice **(C)** is confirmed.

8. **(C)**

If x and y are integers such that $x > y$, which of the following CANNOT be a positive integer?

     I. $y(y - x)$

    II. $y(x - y)$

    III. $\dfrac{x - y}{y - x}$

- ○ I only
- ○ II only
- ○ III only
- ○ I and II only
- ○ II and III only

Step 1: Analyze the Question

As with most number properties questions, the most efficient strategy to solving this question will be to pick some numbers for the variables that are manageable and permissible. Also, since this is a Roman numeral question, you should determine which Roman numeral appears in the answer choices most frequently and assess that one first. In this question, the most frequently appearing Roman numeral is II.

Step 2: State the Task

Pick numbers for the variables x and y and eliminate the statements that can yield a positive integer.

Step 3: Approach Strategically

Statement II: $y(x - y)$. Since $x > y$, you can pick $x = 2$ and $y = 1$. Then $y(x - y) = (1)(2 - 1) = (1)(1) = 1$. So if y is also positive, then $y(x - y)$ is a positive times a positive, which is positive. Because Statement II can be a positive integer, this option will not be part of the correct answer. You can eliminate **(B)**, **(D)**, and **(E)** because these choices contain Statement II.

Statement I: $y(y - x)$. Test the negative case. If $x = -3$ and $y = -4$, then $y(y - x) = (-4)[-4 - (-3)] = (-4)(-4 + 3) = (-4)(-1) = 4$. Because Statement I can be a positive integer, this option will not be part of the correct answer. Eliminate **(A)** (and **(D)**, if you didn't do so already).

You have now eliminated all four incorrect answer choices, so the correct answer must be **(C)**.

Step 4: Confirm Your Answer

Just to be sure, check **(C)**. If you use picking numbers, you will always find that $\frac{x-y}{y-x} = -1$, which is negative. This is because the numerator $x - y$ is the negative of the denominator $y - x$. So $\frac{x-y}{y-x} = \frac{-(y-x)}{y-x} = -1$ (cancel a factor of $y - x$ from the numerator and denominator to obtain -1). Because Statement III is always -1, it cannot ever be a positive integer.

9. (C)

Is $x > y$?

(1) $9x = 4y$

(2) $x > -y$

Step 1: Analyze the Question Stem

This is a Yes/No question. The stem does not give you much information, so go directly to the statements, looking for information about the relationship between x and y.

Step 2: Evaluate the Statements Using 12TEN

Rewrite Statement (1) as $\frac{9x}{4} = y$. Now you can use picking numbers. If $x = 4$, then $y = 9$, so x is *not* greater than y in this case. But x could also be negative. If $x = -4$, then $y = -9$, and now x *is* greater than y. Different answers to the question are possible, so Statement (1) is insufficient. Eliminate **(A)** and **(D)**.

If x is any positive number, then Statement (2) will be true for any non-negative value of y, which means that x may or may not be greater than y. For example, if $x = 5$, y could be 1 or y could be 10. Either value of y works, but in one case x is greater than y and in the other x is less than y. So Statement (2) is also insufficient. Eliminate **(B)**.

To evaluate the two statements together, you can combine the equation in Statement (1) with the inequality from Statement (2). Because $\frac{9x}{4} = y$, you can replace y in the Statement (2) inequality with $\frac{9x}{4}$. This gives you $x > \frac{9x}{4}$, or $x + \frac{9x}{4} > 0$. Rewriting x as $\frac{4x}{4}$, you have $\frac{4x}{4} + \frac{9x}{4} > 0$, or $\frac{13x}{4} > 0$, so x must be positive.

Now return to $\frac{9x}{4} = y$. If x must be greater than zero, then any value you pick for x will make y larger than x. For example, if $x = 4$, $y = 9$. So x can never be greater than y. The answer to the question stem is always no, meaning that the two statements together are sufficient. The correct answer is **(C)**.

10. (C)

How many positive integers less than 50 are multiples of 4 but NOT multiples of 6?

○ 4
○ 6
○ 8
○ 10
○ 12

Step 1: Analyze the Question

This question involves multiples of 4 and multiples of 6. When dealing with such problems, remember that prime factorization can often provide a much faster solution than doing things the hard way.

Step 2: State the Task

Find the number of multiples of 4 less than 50 that aren't also multiples of 6.

Step 3: Approach Strategically

The prime factorization of 4 and 6 is 2×2 and 2×3, respectively. This shows that you need a minimum of two 2s and one 3 to "make" either a 4 or a 6 (not both at once), so a number that is a multiple of both 4 and 6 is a multiple of $2 \times 2 \times 3 = 12$. To find the number of multiples of 4 that aren't also multiples of 6, you should find the number of multiples of 4 under 50 and subtract the number of multiples of 12 under 50.

Dividing 4 into 50 yields 12 and a remainder. Dividing 12 into 50 yields 4 and a remainder. That means there are 12 multiples of 4 that are less than 50 and 4 multiples of 12 that are less than 50. (Note: Had either one not yielded a remainder, you would need to subtract 1 from that count since these are "less than 50" and not "50 or less.") Therefore, there are $12 - 4 = 8$ multiples of 4 under 50 that aren't also a multiple of 6. **(C)** is correct.

Step 4: Confirm Your Answer

To confirm the answer, write out all of the multiples of 4 under 50, then cross out any that are multiples of 6. The multiples of 4 under 50 are 4, 8, 12, 16, 20, 24, 28, 32, 36, 40, 44, and 48. Of these, 12, 24, 36, and 48 are multiples of 6. Crossing those out leaves eight numbers, so **(C)** is confirmed.

11. (E)

If a certain number is divisible by 12 and 10, it is NOT necessarily divisible by which of the following?

○ 4
○ 6
○ 15
○ 20
○ 24

Step 1: Analyze the Question Stem

You are asked to consider common multiples of 10 and 12 and determine which answer choice may not also be a factor of their common multiples.

Step 2: State the Task

To determine the least common multiple of two numbers, use the prime factorization of those numbers.

Step 3: Approach Strategically

Begin by finding the least common multiple of 10 and 12. You know 10 has two prime factors: 2 and 5. And 12 has three prime factors: 2, 2, and 3. Combining those, you find that the least common multiple of 10 and 12 is $2 \times 2 \times 3 \times 5 = 60$. Likewise, 120, 180, 240, etc. will also be multiples of 10 and 12. Checking the answer choices, notice that 4, 6, 15, and 20 are all factors of 60 but **(E)**, 24, is not. **(E)** is the correct choice.

Step 4: Confirm Your Answer

The test maker sets several traps here. The easiest trap to fall into is to miss the NOT in the question stem and pick an answer that *is* a factor of 60. On Test Day, you never want to lose a point for which you did all of the math correctly and then answered the wrong question. Another potential pitfall is to pick just one multiple of 10 and 12—say 240—and dismiss **(E)** because 24 is a factor of 240. The wording in the question stem says that the correct answer is *not necessarily* a factor of a multiple of both 10 and 12. This is one reason that finding the least common multiple is a good rule of thumb in questions like this one.

12. (C)

What is the greatest positive integer x such that 9^{6x} is a factor of 81^{10+x}?

○   2

○   4

○   5

○   6

○   15

Step 1: Analyze the Question

This question states that 9^{6x} can be a factor of 81^{10+x}. Because x is a positive integer, both exponent terms are positive integers. The answer choices are possible values of x.

Step 2: State the Task

Use the rules of exponents and an understanding of factors and multiples to find the largest possible exponent x that will make 9^{6x} a factor of 81^{10+x}.

Step 3: Approach Strategically

First, to work more easily with the two exponent terms, give them the same base. Since 81 is 9^2, 81^{10+x} is $(9^2)^{10+x} = 9^{20+2x}$.

Now the task is to find the largest x such that 9^{6x} is a factor of 9^{20+2x}. Recall that the largest factor of a positive integer is that integer (e.g., the greatest factor of 5 is 5, and the greatest factor of 100 is 100). So the largest factor of 81^{10+x} is a value equivalent to 81^{10+x}. Therefore, find the x value that makes 9^{6x} equal to 9^{20+2x}. Since the bases are the same, set the exponents equal to each other and solve for x.

$$6x = 20 + 2x$$

$$4x = 20$$

$$x = 5$$

When $x = 5$, 9^{6x} equals 81^{10+x} and is its greatest possible factor. **(C)** is correct.

Step 4: Confirm Your Answer

Plugging 5 back in for x shows that the two exponent terms are equal. You get $9^{6\times5}$ and 81^{10+5}, or 9^{30} and 81^{15}. Because $81 = 9^2$, $81^{15} = (9^2)^{15} = 9^{30}$. The two values are equal, and 9^{6x} is as large as it can be to still be a factor of 81^{10+x}; x can't be any greater than 5.

13. (E)

If n is a positive integer greater than 16, is n a prime number?

(1) n is odd.

(2) The remainder when n is divided by 3 is 1, and the remainder when n is divided by 7 is 1.

Step 1: Analyze the Question Stem

In this Yes/No question, you are told that n is a positive integer greater than 16. Sufficiency means showing that n is either definitely prime or definitely not prime.

Step 2: Evaluate the Statements Using 12TEN

Statement (1) notes that n is odd. While prime numbers above 16 are certainly all odd, there are some odd numbers—for example, odd multiples of 3 or 5—that are not prime. This statement is insufficient. Eliminate **(A)** and **(D)**.

Statement (2) notes that n divided by 3 and n divided by 7 both yield a remainder of 1. As 3 and 7 do not have any factors in common, this is equivalent to saying that n divided by $3 \times 7 = 21$ yields a remainder of 1. That means n can be $21 + 1 = 22$, $2(21) + 1 = 43$, $3(21) + 1 = 64$, or $4(21) + 1 = 85$, just to name the first four possibilities. Of these four, 43 is prime but the other three are not, so this statement is insufficient. Eliminate **(B)**.

Combining the statements reveals that n is odd and 1 more than a multiple of 21. This too is insufficient because the first two possible values of n are 43 and 85 and 43 is prime while 85 is not. Eliminate **(C)**.

The statements, even when combined, are insufficient, so the correct answer is **(E)**.

EXPLANATIONS

14. (A)

If $a = 5m + 2$ and $b = 5n + 13$, and m and n are positive integers, what is the remainder when $a + b$ is divided by 5?

○ 0
○ 1
○ 2
○ 3
○ 4

Step 1: Analyze the Question

This question tests your ability to think critically about the characteristics of remainders in division.

Step 2: State the Task

Use the two equations given to find the remainder when $a + b$ is divided by 5.

Step 3: Approach Strategically

Start by determining the value of $a + b$ by adding the two given equations: $a + b = 5m + 2 + 5n + 13 = 5m + 5n + 15$. Notice that all three terms have a common factor of 5, so $a + b = 5(m + n + 3)$. Thus, $(a + b) \div 5 = m + n + 3$. Since m and n are integers, $m + n + 3$ must be an integer. So, when $a + b$ is divided by 5, the result is an integer; this means that $a + b$ is a multiple of 5. Since $a + b$ is a multiple of 5, there is no remainder when $a + b$ is divided by 5, and **(A)** is correct.

Step 4: Confirm Your Answer

To double-check your work, you could pick numbers. Using 2 for m and n will make the arithmetic easy. Now $a = 5(2) + 2 = 12$ and $b = 5(2) + 13 = 23$. Thus, $a + b = 12 + 23 = 25$, which is evenly divisible by 5.

15. (D)

If $a = 105$ and $a^3 = 21 \times 25 \times 45 \times b$, what is the value of b?

- ○ 35
- ○ 42
- ○ 45
- ○ 49
- ○ 54

Step 1: Analyze the Question

You are told that $a = 105$ and that $a^3 = 21 \times 25 \times 45 \times b$. You want to determine the value of b. This question is a great candidate for prime factorization, since you need to factor a large product to determine the unknown factor b.

Step 2: State the Task

Determine the prime factors of each term in the product and then cancel out all of the common terms. Those that remain will be the prime factors of b.

Step 3: Approach Strategically

Find the prime factorization of each term:

$$105 = 3 \times 35 = 3 \times 5 \times 7$$

$$21 = 3 \times 7$$

$$25 = 5 \times 5$$

$$45 = 5 \times 9 = 5 \times 3 \times 3$$

Now plug the prime factors as products into the equation from the question stem and solve for b:

$$a^3 = 21 \times 25 \times 45 \times b$$

$$105 \times 105 \times 105 = 21 \times 25 \times 45 \times b$$

$$b = \frac{105 \times 105 \times 105}{21 \times 25 \times 45}$$

$$b = \frac{(3 \times 5 \times 7)(3 \times 5 \times 7)(3 \times 5 \times 7)}{(3 \times 7)(5 \times 5)(3 \times 3 \times 5)}$$

$$= 7 \times 7$$

$$= 49$$

(D) is the correct answer.

Step 4: Confirm Your Answer

When using prime factorization, be careful to list all of the prime factors, including ones that repeat, such as 3×3 or 5×5.

16. **(D)**

An arithmetic sequence is a sequence in which each term after the first is equal to the sum of the preceding term and a constant. If the list of letters shown above is an arithmetic sequence, which of the following must also be an arithmetic sequence?

    I. $3l$, $3m$, $3n$, $3o$, $3p$

    II. l^2, m^2, n^2, o^2, p^2

    III. $l - 5$, $m - 5$, $n - 5$, $o - 5$, $p - 5$

○ I only
○ II only
○ III only
○ I and III
○ II and III

Step 1: Analyze the Question

You are provided with the definition of an arithmetic sequence and told that l, m, n, o, p is one such sequence. As this is a Roman numeral question with variables, expect to use picking numbers and don't forget to check the Roman numeral statements in the most efficient order. In this question, you will want to begin with Statement III, as it shows up the most in the answer choices.

Step 2: State the Task

Determine which of the Roman numeral statements are true.

Step 3: Approach Strategically

Statement III: To test this statement, say the original arithmetic sequence is 6, 9, 12, 1 5, 18 (adding a constant of 3 each time). Statement III would have you subtract 5 from each term, which results in the sequence 1, 4, 7, 10, 13. This is still an arithmetic sequence as each term is exactly 3 more than its preceding term, so Statement III is a true statement. Eliminate **(A)** and **(B)**.

Of the remaining statements, Statement I is easier to test. Using the same original sequence you had above, Statement I would have you multiply each term by 3. Doing so results in the sequence 18, 27, 36, 45, 54. This is still an arithmetic sequence as each term is exactly 9 more than its preceding term, so Statement I is a true statement. Eliminate **(C)** and **(E)**.

Therefore, the correct answer is **(D)**.

Step 4: Confirm Your Answer

To confirm the answer, test Statement II: Using the same original sequence picked above, Statement II would have you square each term. The larger numbers can make this time-consuming, but just squaring the first three terms (36, 81, 144) should be enough to show you that Statement II does not result in an arithmetic sequence. **(D)** is confirmed.

17. **(B)**

In a certain sequence of positive integers, the term t_n is given by the formula $t_n = 3(t_{n-2}) + 2(t_{n-1}) - 1$ for all $n \geq 1$. If $t_6 = 152$ and $t_5 = 51$, what is the value of t_2?

- ○ 1
- ○ 2
- ○ 3
- ○ 6
- ○ 17

Step 1: Analyze the Question

The question stem provides the formula for a sequence and the values for the fifth and sixth terms in the sequence, t_5 and t_6.

Step 2: State the Task

Determine the value of the second term in the sequence, t_2.

Step 3: Approach Strategically

Work "backward" from the known values until you get to t_2. For t_6, the t_{n-2} term is t_4 and the t_{n-1} term is t_5. Plug the two known values into the formula for the series to get $152 = 3(t_4) + 2(51) - 1$. This simplifies to $3(t_4) = 51$, so $t_4 = 17$. For t_5, the formula is $51 = 3(t_3) + 2(17) - 1$. Thus, $3(t_3) = 18$ and $t_3 = 6$. One more to go! For t_4, $17 = 3(t_2) + 2(6) - 1$. So, $3(t_2) = 6$ and $t_2 = 2$, which is **(B)**.

Step 4: Confirm Your Answer

(D) is t_3 and **(E)** is t_4. Checking your scratchwork to make sure you've calculated through to the correct number in the sequence will help you avoid these wrong answer traps.

18. (D)

In the infinite sequence S, each term S_n after S_2 is equal to the sum of the two terms S_{n-1} and S_{n-2}. If S_1 is 4, what is the value of S_2?

(1) $S_3 = 7$
(2) $S_4 = 10$

Step 1: Analyze the Question Stem

This is a Value question. You must determine what information is needed to solve directly for the term S_2. The question stem says that if S_n is the nth term of the sequence, then for $n > 2$, you have $S_n = S_{n-1} + S_{n-2}$. That is, after the second term in the sequence, the next term is equal to the sum of the two previous terms. For example, the third term is equal to the sum of the first and second terms.

You also know that S_1 is 4. Because $S_3 = S_2 + S_1$, $S_3 = S_2 + 4$. So, you have one linear equation with two variables, S_3 and S_2. To find the value of S_2, you need more information that will lead to a single possible value for S_2.

You could find the value of S_2 if you were given the value of S_3. You could also find the value of S_2 if you were given another linear equation with the variables S_3 and S_2 that is different from the first equation. Look at the statements.

Step 2: Evaluate the Statements Using 12TEN

Statement (1) says that $S_3 = 7$. Because $S_3 = S_2 + 4$, you have the equation $7 = S_2 + 4$. From this equation, you can find the single possible value of S_2. Statement (1) is sufficient. Eliminate **(B)**, **(C)**, and **(E)**.

Statement (2) says that $S_4 = 10$. Because $S_4 = S_3 + S_2$, you have the equation $S_3 + S_2 = 10$. This is another linear equation containing the terms S_2 and S_3. Because the two equations are distinct, you have enough information to determine the values for both S_3 and S_2. Statement (2) is sufficient. **(D)** is correct.

GMAT BY THE NUMBERS: NUMBER PROPERTIES

Now that you've learned how to approach number properties questions on the GMAT, let's add one more dimension to your understanding of how they work.

Take a moment to try this question. Following is performance data from thousands of people who have studied with Kaplan over the decades. Through analyzing this data, we will show you how to approach questions like this one most effectively and how to avoid similarly tempting wrong answer choice types on Test Day.

If a and b are positive integers, is $3a^2b$ divisible by 60?

(1) a is divisible by 10.

(2) b is divisible by 18.

○ Statement (1) ALONE is sufficient, but statement (2) is not sufficient.

○ Statement (2) ALONE is sufficient, but statement (1) is not sufficient.

○ BOTH statements TOGETHER are sufficient, but NEITHER statement ALONE is sufficient.

○ EACH statement ALONE is sufficient.

○ Statements (1) and (2) TOGETHER are NOT sufficient.

EXPLANATION

This Yes/No question asks whether $3a^2b$ is divisible by 60. In other words, it asks whether $\frac{3a^2b}{60}$ is an integer. The 3 in the numerator cancels out a factor of 3 from the denominator, so it's really asking whether $\frac{a^2b}{20}$ is an integer. For this expression to be an integer, the remaining factors in the denominator will have to be canceled out by the numerator. Since $20 = 2 \times 2 \times 5$, you're really being asked whether a^2b contains two 2s and one 5 among its factors.

Statement (1) says that a is divisible by 10. Since $10 = 2 \times 5$, you know that a contains at least one 2 and at least one 5 among its factors. Therefore, the a^2 in the numerator must have at least two 2s and at least two 5s. It doesn't matter what factors b contains, since a^2 alone provides all the factors needed to cancel out the 20. Statement (1) is therefore sufficient.

Since $18 = 2 \times 3 \times 3$, Statement (2) tells you that b has at least one 2 and at least two 3s among its factors. By itself, b does not guarantee two factors of 2, let alone any factor of 5. Therefore, Statement (2) is insufficient.

Since Statement (1) alone is sufficient but Statement (2) is not, **(A)** is correct.

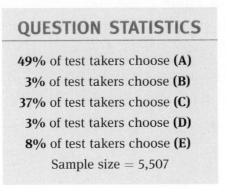

QUESTION STATISTICS

49% of test takers choose **(A)**

3% of test takers choose **(B)**

37% of test takers choose **(C)**

3% of test takers choose **(D)**

8% of test takers choose **(E)**

Sample size = 5,507

As the question statistics reveal, many test takers automatically assume that they need information about every variable in order to answer a question. Knowing this, the test maker often writes statements that provide sufficient information despite not telling you about each variable. Don't automatically think that you need information on all the variables—analyze the question stem carefully to see what you *really* need, and you'll put yourself well ahead of your competition.

MORE GMAT BY THE NUMBERS...

To see more questions with answer choice statistics, be sure to review the full-length CATs in your online resources.

GO ONLINE

kaptest.com/login

CHAPTER 15

Proportions on the GMAT

A baseball team won 45 percent of the first 80 games it played. How many of the remaining 82 games will the team have to win in order to have won exactly 50 percent of all the games it played?

- ○ 36
- ○ 45
- ○ 50
- ○ 55
- ○ 81

Above is a typical Problem Solving proportions question. In this chapter, we'll look at how to apply the Kaplan Method to this question, discuss the proportions rules being tested, and go over the basic principles and strategies that you want to keep in mind on every Quantitative question involving proportions. But before you move on, take a minute to think about what you see in this question and answer some questions about how you think it works:

- What are the various ways you can express 45 percent (as a decimal, fraction, or ratio)?

- What are two different ways to solve this question? Which one is most efficient?

- What trap answer choices might the test makers include for those who misread the question?

- What GMAT Core Competencies are most essential to success on this question?

PREVIEWING PROPORTIONS ON THE GMAT

Proportions show up on the GMAT in the form of fractions, ratios, decimals, and percents. Fundamentally, proportions represent relationships. You deal with proportions somehow every day, even if you might not realize it. Rates and speeds, for example, are expressed as proportions: a car travels 30 miles per hour, or a worker earns \$80 per task. You can use these proportional relationships to determine how many miles a car travels at this speed over a given length of time, or how many tasks a worker must complete in order to earn a given amount of money. Prices are also proportions: a certain item costs \$4.50, so how much would 24 of the same item cost? But proportions can exist between any values: the ratio of gerbils to parrots in a pet store might be 2:3; in other words, you may not be given the exact number of gerbils or parrots, but you do know that for every 2 gerbils the store has, there are 3 parrots as well.

Often the GMAT tests proportions in the form of word problems, so the translation skills you learned in the Algebra chapter (a form of Paraphrasing) will continue to be valuable here as you cut through the seeming novelty of the given "story" to understand the underlying proportional relationships being described.

WHAT ARE THE VARIOUS WAYS YOU CAN EXPRESS 45 PERCENT (AS A DECIMAL, FRACTION, OR RATIO)?

One of the most important skills you can develop for dealing with proportions questions on the GMAT is the ability to convert quickly among percent, decimal, fractional, and ratio forms of the same value. This skill is so crucial because GMAT problems often mix these various formats within the same problem—getting all the values expressed in the same way will make them easier to handle. Also, certain values are just easier to work with in one format or another. For instance, you'd much rather perform arithmetic operations with the fraction $\frac{1}{7}$ than you would with the unwieldy decimal 0.1428571...

In this problem, you may choose to express 45 percent as a decimal (0.45); as a fraction ($\frac{45}{100}$, which reduces to $\frac{9}{20}$); or as a ratio (45:100, which reduces to 9:20), depending on which is easiest to work with at the time. Remembering that *percent* simply means "out of 100" is the key to making these conversions. Later in this chapter you will find a chart to help you memorize some of the common conversions you're most likely to need on Test Day.

WHAT ARE TWO DIFFERENT WAYS TO SOLVE THIS QUESTION? WHICH ONE IS MOST EFFICIENT?

A lot of information is given in this question, so it is especially important that you organize your scratchwork effectively. You are asked for the number of games a team still needs to win in order to achieve a certain winning percentage. You are given the team's winning percentage so far, the number of games it's played so far, and the number of games it still needs to play, so you have all the information you need to solve arithmetically.

As is usual on the GMAT, this question doesn't necessarily give you the information in the most convenient form, so you will have to do some calculating to figure out the actual number of games the team has won so far and the total number of games the team will have played, but these calculations are possible, so you can solve this question arithmetically. (We will return to this question and solve it using the Kaplan Method later this chapter.)

If that approach was the one that first occurred to you, that's fine—and you're not alone. You have likely been rewarded all your academic life for knowing how to do the "schoolroom math," and this approach can get you the correct answer on the GMAT as well. What might not have occurred to you initially is the other strategy you could use to solve this problem: backsolving. Whenever you are asked to solve for a single value (here, it's the number of games the team still needs to win) and the answer choices are all simple numerical values, it may be quicker and easier to answer the question by plugging the values in the answer choices into the scenario described in the question stem.

More guidance on backsolving is available in the Problem Solving chapter of this book; it's a highly efficient strategy, and it's well worth becoming comfortable with, even if you are generally expert at solving using "classroom math."

WHAT TRAP ANSWER CHOICES MIGHT THE TEST MAKERS INCLUDE FOR THOSE WHO MISREAD THE QUESTION?

There are various unknowns in this question that the unwary test taker might mistakenly choose as the correct answer—but to the wrong question. As you practice, never choose an answer choice simply because you recognize that number from your calculations; some of these choices are likely to be traps.

This question asks you for the number of additional games the team must win. Possible trap answers are the number of wins so far—choice **(A)**—and the total number of wins the team needs—choice **(E)**.

The final step of the Kaplan Method for Problem Solving is to confirm your answer; by double-checking that you are answering the question that was asked, you will avoid this all-too-common mistake.

WHAT GMAT CORE COMPETENCIES ARE MOST ESSENTIAL TO SUCCESS ON THIS QUESTION?

As you've seen throughout the Quant section, Critical Thinking is necessary for deciding on the most efficient strategic approach, and Attention to the Right Detail will ensure that you answer the question that is asked instead of falling for trap answers. Specifically on proportions questions, you will use your skill in Paraphrasing to convert ratios into the form that's easiest for that problem. You will also pay Attention to the Right Detail so that you don't confuse different types of ratios such as part-to-part and part-to-whole.

Here are the main topics we'll cover in this chapter:

- Applying Fractions to Proportions
- Ratios
- Percents with Specified Values
- Mixtures

HANDLING GMAT PROPORTIONS

Now let's apply the Kaplan Method to the proportions question you saw earlier:

> A baseball team won 45 percent of the first 80 games it played. How many of the remaining 82 games will the team have to win in order to have won exactly 50 percent of all the games it played?
>
> ○ 36
> ○ 45
> ○ 50
> ○ 55
> ○ 81

Step 1: Analyze the Question

You are given the percentage of games a team has won for the first 80 games and the number of games it has yet to play (82). You are asked to calculate how many more games the team needs to win to have a 50% win record.

Step 2: State the Task

You need to calculate the total number of games that will be played, then the total number of those that need to be won for a 50% record. Then calculate how many games have already been won and subtract that from the total number of wins needed.

Step 3: Approach Strategically

First, add the 80 games that have already been played to the number of remaining games to get the total games: $80 + 82 = 162$. To win 50% of the games, the team would need to win half of these, or 81. You can use the percentage given to calculate how many games the team has already won: 45% of 80.

The number of the games the team still needs to win is $81 - 36 = 45$. Choice **(B)** is correct. 45% can be expressed as $\frac{45}{100} = \frac{9}{20}$. Use this fraction when multiplying: $\frac{9}{20} \times 80 = 9 \times 4 = 36$.

The answer choices are small, manageable numbers, so you may want to use backsolving, especially if you're not sure how to set up the arithmetic. If you choose to backsolve, remember to think about exactly what the answer choices represent: the number of additional games the team needs to win. Start with choice **(B)**, 45 games. Calculate the games already won, 45% of $80 = \frac{9}{20} \times 80 = 36$, and add the 45 additional games: $36 + 45 = 81$.

Now you can ask yourself, is 81 half (or 50%) of all the games? The team's already played 80, and there are 82 left to play, so $80 + 82 = 162$ and, yes, choice **(B)** is 50% of 162.

If you had instead backsolved starting with **(D)**, you would have ended up with too high a proportion of games won (91 of 162) and known that you need a smaller number of wins during the second part of the season in order to end up with a winning percentage of 50%.

Step 4: Confirm Your Answer

Review your calculations to be sure they're correct. You can also verify that your answer is logical using Critical Thinking: the team would need more than 40 additional wins to make up for the fact that it won less than 50% of its first 80 games.

Now let's look at each of the areas of proportions that show up on the GMAT Quantitative section, starting with applying fractions to proportions.

APPLYING FRACTIONS TO PROPORTIONS

The GMAT will frequently ask you to deal with proportional relationships by working with fractions used to represent ratios. We will deal more specifically with how ratios are tested on the GMAT later in this chapter, but in the meantime, let's look at how to apply the skills you learned in the Arithmetic chapter for dealing with fractions to questions that ask about proportions.

A proportion is a comparison of two ratios. Usually, a proportion consists of an equation in which two ratios (expressed as fractions) are set equal to each other. You can set up proportions whenever you are given a relationship between more than one fraction or ratio and are asked to solve for the missing part. Fractions in proportions represent part-to-part or part-to-whole relationships. When dealing with proportions, pay close attention to what something is a proportion of. A common "twist" is to use different denominators in the same problem.

In the proportion $\frac{a}{b} = \frac{c}{d}$, a and d are identified as the **extremes**, and c and b are identified as the **means**. These terms stem from the alternate notation for these ratios, $a:b = c:d$, in which the extremes occupy the end positions of the equation. But despite that terminology, it's usually easier to express proportions as fractions when solving GMAT problems.

To solve a proportion, use cross multiplication to multiply the numerator from the first ratio by the denominator from the second ratio, then the denominator from the first ratio by the numerator of the second ratio, and set the values equal to each other. In other words, set the product of the means equal to the product of the extremes. After this step, divide both sides of this new equation to isolate the variable you're solving for.

Example: Solve for m: $\frac{6}{11} = \frac{m}{33}$.

Using cross multiplication, the equation becomes $6 \times 33 = m \times 11$. Before you spend time multiplying out 6×33, notice that you can instead divide both sides of the equation by 11. This simplifies to $6 \times 3 = m$. Thus, $m = 18$.

In word problems, set up the proportions so that units of the same type are either one above the other or directly across from one another.

Example: The ratio of T-shirts to sweaters in a closet is 4:5. If there are 12 T-shirts in the closet, how many sweaters are there?

Set up a proportion to solve this question, being careful to line up the units. There are different ways you can approach this problem to get the correct answer. One possible proportion would be $\frac{4 \text{ T-shirts}}{5 \text{ sweaters}} = \frac{12 \text{ T-shirts}}{x \text{ sweaters}}$. Note that the label of T-shirts appears in both numerators and the label of sweaters appears in both denominators. Another possible proportion would be $\frac{4 \text{ T-shirts}}{12 \text{ T-shirts}} = \frac{5 \text{ sweaters}}{x \text{ sweaters}}$, where the numbers corresponding with T-shirts appear on the left side and the values corresponding with sweaters appear on the right side. Either way, cross multiplying the means and the extremes results in the equation $4x = 60$. Therefore, $x = 15$. There are 15 sweaters in the closet.

IN-FORMAT QUESTION: APPLYING FRACTIONS TO PROPORTIONS ON THE GMAT

Now let's use the Kaplan Method on a Data Sufficiency question that involves applying fractions to proportions:

> After 360 liters of fuel were added to a container, the amount of fuel in the container was $\frac{5}{8}$ of the tank's capacity. What is the capacity of the container?
>
> (1) After the 360 liters were added, the container had 108 liters less than $\frac{3}{4}$ of the tank's capacity.
> (2) Before the 360 liters were added, there were 180 liters of fuel in the container.

Step 1: Analyze the Question Stem

First, recognize that this is a Value question. You need an exact value of the capacity of the container after 360 liters of fuel are added to it. Next, take control of the question by setting up an equation. Call the capacity of the container C liters and say that before the 360 liters of fuel were added, there were N liters of fuel in the container. Since after the 360 liters of fuel were added, the amount of fuel in the container was $\frac{5}{8}$ of the tank's capacity, write the equation $N + 360 = \frac{5}{8}C$. Now look at the statements.

Step 2: Evaluate the Statements Using 12TEN

Start with Statement (2), which looks like the more straightforward of the two. Statement (2) says that before the 360 liters were added, there were 180 liters of fuel in the container. After the 360 liters were added, there were $180 + 360 = 540$ liters. Since after the 360 liters were added, the amount of fuel in the container was $\frac{5}{8}$ of the tank's capacity, you can write the equation $540 = \frac{5}{8}C$. This is a first-degree equation, so it must lead to exactly one value for C. Don't waste time calculating to find the exact value. All you need to know is that Statement (2) is sufficient. Eliminate **(A)**, **(C)**, and **(E)**.

Now look at Statement (1). Statement (1) says that after the 360 liters were added, the container had 108 liters less than $\frac{3}{4}$ of the tank's capacity. You can translate this as $N + 360 = \frac{3}{4}C - 108$. Since you know from the question stem that $N + 360 = \frac{5}{8}C$, you can say that $\frac{5}{8}C = \frac{3}{4}C - 108$. This is a first-degree equation, so it must lead to exactly one value for C. Statement (1) is sufficient. Eliminate choice **(B)**.

If you want to check your work, you can solve the equation $\frac{5}{8}C = \frac{3}{4}C - 108$ for C to be sure that there is just one solution. Multiplying both sides by 8, you have $8\left(\frac{5}{8}C\right) = 8\left(\frac{3}{4}C - 108\right)$, $5C = 8\left(\frac{3}{4}C\right) - 8(108)$, and $864 = C$. You see that there is indeed just one solution. This statement is sufficient.

Either statement is sufficient, making **(D)** the correct answer.

Notice that both statements lead to the same capacity of 864 liters for the container. The statements in a Data Sufficiency question will never contradict one another, so if each statement alone is sufficient, the two statements will always answer the question in the same exact way. You can use this fact to double-check whether you are applying the statements correctly.

TAKEAWAYS: APPLYING FRACTIONS TO PROPORTIONS

- Fractions in proportions represent the part-to-part or part-to-whole relationships in a question.
- To solve a question that asks for the missing part of a ratio, set up a proportion by setting two equivalent fractions equal to each other; then use cross multiplication to solve for the missing piece.

PRACTICE SET: APPLYING FRACTIONS TO PROPORTIONS ON THE GMAT

1. The cost of Brand V paper is proportional to the weight. If 18 ounces of Brand V paper cost $3.06, what is the cost of 24 ounces of Brand V paper?

    ○ $4.08
    ○ $5.58
    ○ $6.12
    ○ $7.31
    ○ $7.59

2. The volume of a certain substance is always directly proportional to its weight. If 48 cubic inches of the substance weigh 112 ounces, what is the volume, in cubic inches, of 63 ounces of this substance?

    ○   27
    ○   36
    ○   42
    ○   64
    ○   147

3. There are chips of four different colors distributed in stacks as follows: $\frac{1}{2}$ are white, $\frac{1}{6}$ are green, $\frac{1}{5}$ are blue, and the remaining 12 chips are red. What is the total number of chips in the four stacks?

    ○   60
    ○   75
    ○   90
    ○   100
    ○   125

RATIOS

A ratio is a comparison of two quantities by division. Ratios may be written with a fraction bar $\left(\frac{x}{y}\right)$, with a colon ($x{:}y$), or in English ("the ratio of x to y"). Ratios can (and in most cases, should) be reduced to lowest terms, just as fractions are reduced.

Example: Joe is 16 years old and Mary is 12. The ratio of Joe's age to Mary's age is 16 to 12.

$$\frac{16}{12} = \frac{4}{3} \text{ or } 4{:}3$$

In a ratio of two numbers, the numerator is often associated with the word *of* and the denominator with the word *to*.

$$\text{Ratio} = \frac{\text{Of} \ldots}{\text{To} \ldots}$$

Example: In a box of doughnuts, 12 are sugar and 18 are chocolate. What is the ratio of sugar doughnuts to chocolate doughnuts?

$$\text{Ratio} = \frac{\text{Of sugar}}{\text{To chocolate}} = \frac{12}{18} = \frac{2}{3}$$

PART-TO-PART RATIOS AND PART-TO-WHOLE RATIOS

A ratio represents the proportional relationship between quantities or numbers. A ratio can compare either a part to another part or a part to a whole. One type of ratio can readily be converted to the other only if all the parts together equal the whole and there is no overlap among the parts (that is, if the whole is equal to the sum of its parts).

Example: The ratio of domestic sales to foreign sales of a certain product is 3:5. What fraction of the total sales are the domestic sales?

> First note that this is the same as asking for the ratio of the amount of domestic sales to the amount of total sales.

> In this case, the whole (total sales) is equal to the sum of the parts (domestic and foreign sales). You can convert from a part : part ratio to a part : whole ratio. For every 8 sales of the product, 3 are domestic and 5 are foreign. The ratio of domestic sales to total sales is then $\frac{3}{8}$ or 3:8.

Example: The ratio of domestic to European sales of a certain product is 3:5. What is the ratio of domestic sales to total sales?

> Here you cannot convert from a part : part ratio (domestic sales : European sales) to a part : whole ratio (domestic sales : total sales) because you don't know whether there are any other sales besides domestic and European sales. The question doesn't say that the product is sold only domestically and in Europe, so you cannot assume there are no other sales. The ratio asked for here cannot be determined.

RATIOS WITH MORE THAN TWO TERMS

Some GMAT questions deal with ratios that have three or more terms. Always represent them with colons (e.g., *x*:*y*:*z*).

Even though they convey information about more relationships, ratios involving more than two terms are governed by the same principles as two-term ratios. Ratios involving more than two terms are usually ratios of various parts, and it is usually the case that the sum of these parts equals the whole, making it possible to find part-to-whole ratios as well.

Example: Given that the ratio of men to women to children in a room is 4:3:2, what other ratios can be determined?

> The whole here is the number of people in the room, and since every person is either a man, a woman, or a child, you can determine part : whole ratios for each of these parts. Of every nine ($4 + 3 + 2 = 9$) people in the room, 4 are men, 3 are women, and 2 are children. This gives you three part : whole ratios:
>
> Ratio of men : total people $= 4:9$ or $\frac{4}{9}$.
>
> Ratio of women : total people $= 3:9 = 1:3$ or $\frac{1}{3}$.
>
> Ratio of children : total people $= 2:9$ or $\frac{2}{9}$.
>
> In addition, from any ratio of more than two terms, you can determine various two-term ratios among the parts.
>
> Ratio of women : men $= 3:4$ or $\frac{3}{4}$.
>
> Ratio of men : children $= 4:2 = 2:1$ or $\frac{2}{1}$.
>
> Ratio of children : women $= 2:3$ or $\frac{2}{3}$.
>
> And finally, if you were asked to establish a relationship between the number of adults and the number of children in the room, this would also be possible. For every 2 children, there are 4 men and 3 women, which is $4 + 3 = 7$ adults. Thus,
>
> Ratio of children : adults $= 2:7$ or $\frac{2}{7}$.
>
> Ratio of adults : children $= 7:2$ or $\frac{7}{2}$.

Naturally, a GMAT question will require you to determine only one or at most two of these ratios, but knowing how much information is contained within a given ratio will help you to determine quickly which questions are solvable and which, if any, are not.

RATIOS VERSUS ACTUAL NUMBERS

Ratios are always reduced to simplest form. If a team's ratio of wins to losses is 5:3, this does not necessarily mean that the team has won exactly 5 games and lost exactly 3. For instance, if a team has won 30 games and lost 18, its ratio is still 5:3. Unless you know the actual number of games played (or the actual number won or lost), you can't know the actual values of the parts in the ratio.

Example: In a classroom of 30 students, the ratio of the boys in the class to students in the class is 2:5. How many students are boys?

You are given a part-to-whole ratio (boys : students). This ratio can also be expressed as a fraction. Multiplying this fraction by the actual whole gives the value of the corresponding part. There are 30 students, and $\frac{2}{5}$ of them are boys, so the number of boys must be $\frac{2}{5} \times 30$. (Note: It's usually most helpful to set up ratio scratchwork in columns so you see the relationships clearly.)

$$\frac{2 \text{ boys}}{{}_1\cancel{5} \text{ students}} \times \cancel{30}^{6} \text{ students} = 2 \times 6 \text{ boys} = 12 \text{ boys}$$

You can make some deductions about the actual values, though, even when you aren't given a total directly. Often, this is the key to solving a challenging proportions question.

Let's say that a car dealership has used and new cars in stock in a ratio of 2:5. You don't know the actual number. You know that if there are 2 used cars, there will be 5 new cars. And if there are 4 (or 2×2) used cars, there will be 10 (or 5×2) new cars. If there are 6 used cars (2×3), then there are 15 new cars (5×3). In other words, the actual numbers will always equal the figures in the ratio multiplied by the same (unknown) factor.

You can translate from ratios into algebra:

$$\text{used} : \text{new} = 2:5$$

$$\text{used} = 2x; \text{ new} = 5x$$

Example: A homecoming party at College Y is initially attended by students and alumni in a ratio of 1 to 5. But after two hours, 36 more students arrive, changing the ratio of students to alumni to 1 to 2. If the number of alumni did not change over those two hours, how many people were at the party when it began?

Besides the 36 additional students who arrive, nowhere are actual numbers referred to directly. But you can jot down the two ratios you're given in a slightly more useable form:

$$S : A \qquad s + 36 : A$$

$$1{:}5 \qquad\qquad 1{:}2$$

Translate into algebra. Let x be the number of students initially at the party.

$$S : A \qquad s + 36{:}A$$

$$1{:}5 \qquad\qquad 1{:}2$$

$$x : 5x \qquad x + 36 : 2(x + 36)$$

Now you've got some equations to work with:

$$A = 5x$$

$$A = 2x + 72$$

You now have two different expressions for A that are equal. Thus,

$$5x = 2x + 72$$

$$3x = 72$$

$$x = 24$$

Now you know that there were 24 students initially.

Substitute 24 for x to solve for alumni:

$$A = 5 \times 24$$

$$A = 120$$

The party started with 24 students and 120 alumni, for a total of 144 people.

GUESSING WITH RATIOS

You may have noticed that many GMAT ratio problems involve things like students, women, children, cars, and so forth—things that cannot really exist as non-integer values. (You can't have $43\frac{1}{5}$ people at a party, for instance!)

There's a valuable deduction to be made here—if the entities in a problem cannot logically be non-integers, then the factor by which the ratio is multiplied must be an integer. Therefore, *the actual number of something must be a multiple of its value in the ratio.*

Example:

A movie buff stores movies on the Internet and on her personal computer in a ratio of 7:2. If she purchases 6 new movies and downloads them to her personal computer, that ratio would change to 11:4. If she stores movies in no other locations, what was the original number of movies she owned before the purchase of new movies?

- ○ 22
- ○ 28
- ○ 77
- ○ 99
- ○ 105

The question asks for the whole of the ratio for which you are initially given only two parts. The question specifies that there are no other parts to the whole, so you can add the two parts together:

Internet : Computer : Total

7:2:9

There's no such thing as "a fraction of a movie," so the common factor by which you'd multiply 7, 2, and 9 to find the actual numbers must be an integer. That means the number of movies stored on the Internet is a multiple of 7, the number of movies stored on the computer is a multiple of 2, and the total—what you're looking for—must be a multiple of 9.

Take a look at the answers—only **(D)** is a multiple of 9, so there's no need to do any more math; **(D)** must be the answer.

IN-FORMAT QUESTION: RATIOS ON THE GMAT

Now let's use the Kaplan Method on a Problem Solving question dealing with ratios:

> The ratio of two quantities is 2:3. If each of the quantities is increased by 6, what is the ratio of the new quantities?
>
> ○   2:3
> ○   6:7
> ○   8:9
> ○   8:3
> ○   It cannot be determined from the information given.

Step 1: Analyze the Question

For ratio questions, keep careful track of which values are ratios and which are actual quantities. You are told that the ratio of quantities is 2:3. So the smallest value for quantity A is 2 and for quantity B is 3. You could also have any multiple of this ratio, so you could have quantity A = 4 and quantity B = 6, for example.

Step 2: State the Task

Now that you have a clear picture of the information, pay Attention to the Right Detail. You are given the ratio of the two quantities, not the exact number of each. Without the actual total value or one of the quantities' values, you can't determine the new values. The correct answer is **(E)**.

If you weren't able to apply this rule so directly, you could solve this question by picking numbers for the possible quantities.

Step 3: Approach Strategically

First test the smallest possible quantities, since these will be the most manageable: quantity A = 2 and quantity B = 3. Adding 6 to each quantity, you get the following new values: quantity A = 8 and quantity B = 9. The new ratio would be 8:9.

Before you select **(C)**, however, you must test a second case. If quantity A = 4 and quantity B = 6, then after adding 6 to each quantity, you get the following new values: quantity A = 10 and quantity B = 12. The new ratio would be 10:12, or 5:6.

You can get two distinct results depending on the original values you choose for the actual quantities, so the correct answer must be **(E)**.

Step 4: Confirm Your Answer

In ratio questions, if you change the actual quantities through multiplication or division, the resulting ratio will be the same, regardless of the starting values of the quantities. However, the same ratio may not be preserved if you add or subtract from the quantities. Knowing this rule is a great way to confirm your answer. Note, by the way, that while this was a Problem Solving question, the GMAT likes to test your understanding of this rule with Data Sufficiency questions in which you need to determine whether you have enough information to solve.

TAKEAWAYS: RATIOS

- A ratio represents the proportional relationship between quantities or numbers.
- If you are given the number of each item, you can determine the ratio.
- If you are given a ratio and the actual number of items that corresponds to one element of the ratio, you can determine the number of items represented by each of the other elements of the ratio.
- The GMAT can describe ratios in various forms. For example, "the ratio of x to y" $= \frac{x}{y} = x{:}y$.

PRACTICE SET: RATIOS ON THE GMAT

4. Three investors, A, B, and C, divide the profits from a business enterprise in the ratio of 5:7:8, respectively. If Investor A earned $3,500, how much money did Investors B and C earn in total?

    ○ $4,000
    ○ $4,900
    ○ $5,600
    ○ $9,500
    ○ $10,500

5. If $\frac{a}{b} = \frac{c}{d}$, what is the numerical ratio of b to d?

    (1) $\frac{a}{b} = \frac{3c}{2b}$

    (2) $a = 2$ and $d = 4$.

6. If the ratio of a to b is 4 to 3 and the ratio of b to c is 1 to 5, what is the ratio of a to c?

    ○ $\frac{4}{5}$

    ○ $\frac{1}{3}$

    ○ $\frac{2}{5}$

    ○ $\frac{4}{5}$

    ○ $\frac{7}{6}$

PERCENTS WITH SPECIFIED VALUES

In the Problem Solving chapter of this book, you learned how to use the picking numbers strategy to deal with questions that involve taking percents of unspecified values. Questions that specify the exact values are often more straightforward, but they require your familiarity with several formulas for dealing with fractions and percents.

Key to these questions is the fact that *percent* is just another word for "per one hundred."

Therefore, 19% (or 19 percent) means 19 hundredths

or $\dfrac{19}{100}$

or 0.19

or 19 out of every 100 things

or 19 parts out of a whole of 100 parts.

CONVERTING PERCENTS, FRACTIONS, AND DECIMALS

GMAT questions will often require that you convert among percents, decimals, fractions, and ratios. Below you will learn the process for making each of these conversions, but they all boil down to using the percent formula:

$$\text{Percent} = \frac{\text{Part}}{\text{Whole}} \times 100\%$$

Plug in the information you have and solve for the missing pieces.

To make a percent from a decimal or fraction, multiply by 100%. Since 100% means 100 hundredths, or 1, multiplying by 100% will not change the number.

Example: $0.17 = 0.17 \times 100\% = 17\%$

Example: $\dfrac{1}{4} = \dfrac{1}{4} \times 100\% = 25\%$

To drop a percent, divide by 100%. Once again, dividing by 100%, which is equivalent to 1, will not change the number.

Example: $32\% = \dfrac{32\%}{100\%} = \dfrac{32}{100} = \dfrac{8}{25}$

Example: $\dfrac{1}{2}\% = \dfrac{\frac{1}{2}\%}{100\%} = \dfrac{1}{200}$

To change a percent to a decimal, just drop the percent sign and move the decimal point two places to the left. (This is the same as dividing by 100%.)

Example: $0.8\% = 0.008$

Being familiar with the following fraction-to-percent equivalents can save you a lot of time on questions that require you to perform such conversions.

COMMON FRACTION-TO-PERCENT EQUIVALENTS

$$\frac{1}{20} = 5\% \qquad \frac{1}{11} = 9\frac{1}{11}\% \qquad \frac{1}{10} = 10\% \qquad \frac{1}{9} = 11\frac{1}{9}\% \qquad \frac{1}{8} = 12\frac{1}{2}\%$$

$$\frac{1}{6} = 16\frac{2}{3}\% \qquad \frac{1}{5} = 20\% \qquad \frac{1}{4} = 25\% \qquad \frac{1}{3} = 33\frac{1}{3}\% \qquad \frac{1}{2} = 50\%$$

$$10\% = \frac{1}{10} \qquad\qquad 12\frac{1}{2}\% = \frac{1}{8} \qquad\qquad 16\frac{2}{3}\% = \frac{1}{6}$$

$$20\% = \frac{2}{10} = \frac{1}{5} \qquad 25\% = \frac{2}{8} = \frac{1}{4} \qquad 33\frac{1}{3}\% = \frac{2}{6} = \frac{1}{3}$$

$$30\% = \frac{3}{10} \qquad\qquad 37\frac{1}{2}\% = \frac{3}{8} \qquad\qquad 50\% = \frac{3}{6} = \frac{1}{2}$$

$$40\% = \frac{4}{10} = \frac{2}{5} \qquad 50\% = \frac{4}{8} = \frac{2}{4} = \frac{1}{2} \qquad 66\frac{2}{3}\% = \frac{4}{6} = \frac{2}{3}$$

$$50\% = \frac{5}{10} = \frac{1}{2} \qquad 62\frac{1}{2}\% = \frac{5}{8} \qquad\qquad 83\frac{1}{3}\% = \frac{5}{6}$$

$$60\% = \frac{6}{10} = \frac{3}{5} \qquad 75\% = \frac{6}{8} = \frac{3}{4}$$

$$70\% = \frac{7}{10} \qquad\qquad 87\frac{1}{2}\% = \frac{7}{8}$$

$$80\% = \frac{8}{10} = \frac{4}{5}$$

$$90\% = \frac{9}{10}$$

$$100\% = \frac{10}{10} = 1$$

PERCENT PROBLEMS

Percent problems will usually give you two of the terms from the formula below and ask for the third. It is usually easiest to change the percent to a common fraction before performing the calculation. Most percent problems can be solved by plugging into a variant of the percent formula:

$$\text{Percent} \times \text{Whole} = \text{Part}$$

In percent problems, the whole generally will be associated with the word *of*, and the part will be associated with the word *is*. The percent can be represented as the ratio of the part to the whole, or the *is* to the *of*.

Example: What is 25% of 36?

Here you are given the percent and the whole. To find the part, change the percent to a fraction, then multiply. Use the following formula:

$$x\% \text{ of } y = \frac{x}{100} \times y$$

Since $25\% = \frac{1}{4}$, you are really being asked what one-fourth of 36 is.

$$\frac{1}{4} \times 36 = 9$$

Example: 13 is $33\frac{1}{3}\%$ of what number?

Recall that

$$33\frac{1}{2} = \frac{1}{3}$$

$$13 = \frac{1}{3}n$$

$$39 = n$$

Example: 18 is what percent of 3?

$$m \times 3 = 18$$

$$m = 6$$

$$6 \times 100\% = 600\%$$

Other problems will ask you to calculate "percent greater than" or "percent less than." In these cases, it is the number that follows the word *than* to which the percentage is applied.

You may find it faster to convert *percent greater/less than* to *percent of*. "*x*% greater than" becomes "$(100 + x)\%$ of." "*x*% less than" becomes "$(100 - x)\%$ of."

Example: What number is 15% less than 60?

$$n = 60 - (15\% \times 60)$$

$$n = 60 - \left(\frac{15}{100} \times 60\right)$$

$$n = 60 - 9$$

$$n = 51$$

Example: What is the price of a television that costs 28% more than a $50 radio?

Let t equal the price of the television and r equal the price of the radio.

$$t = r + (28\% \times r)$$

$$t = 50 + \left(\frac{28}{100} \times 50\right)$$

$$t = 50 + \frac{28}{2}$$

$$t = 50 + 14$$

$$t = \$64$$

PERCENT INCREASE AND DECREASE

$$\text{Percent decrease} = \frac{\text{Amount of decrease}}{\text{Original whole}} \times 100\%$$

$$\text{Percent decrease} = \frac{\text{Amount of decrease}}{\text{Original whole}} \times 100\%$$

$$\text{New whole} = \text{Original whole} \pm \text{Amount of change}$$

When dealing with percent increase and percent decrease, always be careful to put the amount of increase or decrease over the *original* whole, not over the new whole.

Example: If a dress is offered for a discounted price of $120, what is the percent discount if the regular price is $150?

$$\text{Percent decrease} = \frac{\text{Amount of decrease}}{\text{Original whole}} \times 100\%$$

You're asked to calculate the discount, so you'll use the regular selling price of $150 as the original whole. The difference in prices is $150 − $120, or $30.

$$\text{Percent discount} = \frac{\$30}{\$150} \times 100\%$$

$$\text{Percent discount} = \frac{1}{5} \times 100\% = 20\%$$

Combining Percents: On some problems, you'll need to find more than one percent, or a percent of a percent. Be careful: you can't just add percents, unless the percents are of the same whole. Let's look at an example.

Example: The price of an antique is reduced by 20 percent, and then this discount price is further reduced by 10 percent. If the antique originally cost $200, what is its final price?

First, you know that the price is reduced by 20%. That's the same thing as saying that the price becomes (100% − 20%), or 80% of what it originally was. Eighty percent of $200 is equal to $\frac{8}{10} \times \$200$ or $160. Then, *this price* is reduced by 10%. So 10% × $160 = $16, and the final price of the antique is $160 − $16 = $144.

A common error in this kind of problem is to assume that the final price is simply a 30 percent reduction of the original price. That would mean that the final price is 70 percent of the original, or 70% × $200 = $140. But, as you've just seen, this is *not* correct. Adding or subtracting percents directly only works if those percents are being taken of the same whole. In this example, since you took 20% of the original price, and then 10% of the reduced price, you can't just add the percents together.

Note that in this example, a 20% reduction followed by a 10% reduction does not equal a 30% reduction but rather one of 28%. This will always happen—two decreases cause a total percent decrease of less than the sum of the two individual percents. This is because the second percent decrease is taken from a smaller starting value. Likewise, two increases cause a total increase of more than the sum of the two individually, since the second percent increase is calculated based on a higher starting point. You can use this fact to estimate an answer quickly.

IN-FORMAT QUESTION: PERCENTS WITH SPECIFIED VALUES ON THE GMAT

Now let's use the Kaplan Method on a Problem Solving question that involves percents with specified values:

> A pet store regularly sells pet food at a discount of 10 percent to 30 percent from the manufacturer's suggested retail price. If during a sale, the store discounts an additional 20 percent from the discount price, what would be the lowest possible price of a container of pet food that had a manufacturer's suggested retail price of $20.00?
>
> ○ $10.00
> ○ $11.20
> ○ $14.40
> ○ $16.00
> ○ $18.00

Step 1: Analyze the Question

This question is asking for the lowest possible price of pet food that has been marked down twice. Another way to phrase the question is that you want the maximum possible discount. So you'll take the maximum discount at each stage of the markdown to determine the lowest price.

Since the question gives you an actual starting value for the price, you cannot pick numbers to make the calculations easier. Notice that you could backsolve this question, since the answer choices are all numbers, but since this question involves multiple discounts, backsolving could result in lots of calculation. The more efficient approach here is to use what you know about percent decrease.

Step 2: State the Task

Using the starting value of $20, you must apply the two maximum discounts, one after the other.

Step 3: Approach Strategically

The original price for the pet food was $20, and the maximum reduction the store gives is 30%. You can approach the reduction calculation in two ways:

1. You could determine 30% of $20 and then subtract this amount from $20:

$$\$20 \times 0.3 = \$6; \$20 - \$6 = \$14$$

2. You can find the new price directly. Since $100\% - 30\% = 70\%$, the new price is 70% of $20:

$$\$20 \times 0.7 = \$14$$

Regardless of the approach, you find that the first reduced price is $14.

Now, you need to take the 20% discount off this reduced price. Again, you could apply either approach to calculate this value, but the second approach is more efficient: $14 \times 0.8 = \$11.20$. **(B)** is correct.

Step 4: Confirm Your Answer

Since there wasn't much arithmetic, you can quickly check for any careless errors. Also, reread the question stem to make sure that you didn't misinterpret anything and that you solved for the correct value.

TAKEAWAYS: PERCENTS WITH SPECIFIED VALUES

- $x\% = \dfrac{x}{100}$

- $x\%$ of $y = \dfrac{x}{100} \times y$

- $\text{Percent} = \dfrac{\text{Part}}{\text{Whole}} \times 100\%$

- $\text{Final as percent of original} = \dfrac{\text{Final}}{\text{Original}} \times 100\%$

- $\text{Percent change} = \dfrac{\text{Difference}}{\text{Original}} \times 100\%$

PRACTICE SET: PERCENTS WITH SPECIFIED VALUES ON THE GMAT

7. Each employee of Company X is a member of precisely 1 of 3 shifts of employees. Among the 60 members of the first shift, 20 percent participate in the pension program; among the 50 members of the second shift, 40 percent participate in the pension program; and among the 40 members of the third shift, 10 percent participate in the pension program. What percent of the workers at Company X participate in the pension program?

○ 20%

○ 24%

○ 36%

○ 37.5%

○ 70%

8. In 2010, a basketball team won 30 percent of its 20 basketball games. In 2011, the team won 28 percent of its 25 basketball games. What was the percent increase from 2010 to 2011 in the number of basketball games the team won?

○ 5%

○ $14\frac{2}{7}$%

○ $16\frac{2}{3}$%

○ $23\frac{1}{3}$%

○ 60%

Survey of Student Preferences

No Preference
10%

Art Museum
30%

Science Museum
60%

9. The administration of a certain school surveys all 120 students to plan a field trip. Each student can express a preference for only one destination: the science museum, the art museum, or neither. The results of the student survey are shown above. Assuming that the maximum number of students who are allowed to visit their preferred museum visit that museum for the field trip, how many students who have a preference do <u>not</u> visit their preferred museum?

   (1) Due to transportation constraints, the maximum number of students who can take a field trip to the science museum is 55.

   (2) Due to high demand, the art museum can accommodate a maximum of 50 students.

MIXTURES

Problems involving mixtures may appear intimidating, with their intimations of chemistry, but really they are just proportion, ratio, and percentage problems in disguise. Most mixture questions will ask you to combine two portions that are themselves subdivided into portions. At other times, the question stem may prescribe the ratio of elements in a mixture and then add or remove some or all of one of those portions, asking you to recalculate the new ratio that results. Recognize the familiar patterns at work and you will be a step ahead on the GMAT.

Mixtures on the GMAT are most commonly mixtures of liquids.

Example: You currently have 10 ounces of a solution that is 14 percent alcohol and the rest water. How much water would you have to add to the solution to make the alcohol content equal to 10 percent?

If the solution is 14% alcohol now, that means there are 10 oz $\times \frac{14}{100} = 1.4$ oz of alcohol in the initial solution. The rest of the solution is water.

Think critically about this situation, since it's one that occurs often in mixtures problems: When water is added, the amount of alcohol in the mixture remains constant at 1.4 oz. However, you are told that this same amount of alcohol represents 10% of the resulting mixture.

Since 1.4 is 10% of 14, the final mixture must have a total volume of 14 oz. The difference in volume between the old and new mixtures is accounted for solely by the addition of water, so you'd need to add $14 - 10 = 4$ oz of water to make a 10% alcohol solution.

Notice that the only real difference between this and a lot of the proportion or ratio questions that you've seen so far in this chapter is that it deals with a liquid, rather than with cars, students, adults, or children. Mixture problems involve many of the same skills you use on other ratio problems, except they require you to keep track of amounts rather than numbers.

In-Format Question: Mixtures on the GMAT

Now let's use the Kaplan Method on a Problem Solving question dealing with mixtures:

Two brands of detergent are to be combined. Detergent X contains 20 percent bleach and 80 percent soap, while Detergent Y contains 45 percent bleach and 55 percent soap. If the combined mixture is to be 35 percent bleach, what percent of the final mixture should be Detergent X?

- ○   10%
- ○ $32\frac{1}{2}\%$
- ○   35%
- ○   40%
- ○   60%

Step 1: Analyze the Question

This is a complex question, but there is a straightforward solution. You are creating a new mixture from two others, X and Y. X is 20% bleach, and Y is 45% bleach. The new mixture is to be 35% bleach.

In other words, some amount of a 20% bleach mixture plus some amount of a 45% bleach mixture will balance each other out to form a 35% bleach mixture.

Step 2: State the Task

Because this question involves finding a particular balance between Detergents X and Y, you can use the balanced average approach to solve. You could also use algebra or backsolving, but the balanced average approach will be the most efficient. This will let you calculate the proportion of Detergent X in the final mixture.

Step 3: Approach Strategically

The question does not state how many parts of Detergent X are used, so call this x. And the question does not state how many parts of Y are used, so call this y. Here's how it balances:

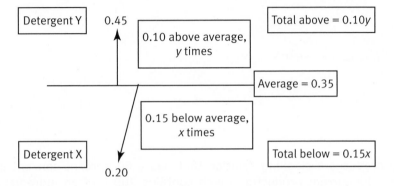

Since the amount above the average has to equal the amount below the average, $0.10y = 0.15x$. To solve for a proportional amount, you can view this as a ratio. Divide both sides by y and by 0.15 to get the ratio of x to y:

$$0.10y = 0.15x$$

$$\frac{0.10}{0.15} = \frac{x}{y}$$

$$\frac{10}{15} = \frac{x}{y}$$

$$\frac{2}{3} = \frac{x}{y}$$

So $x{:}y$ is 2:3. Add the total to the ratio to determine how x relates to the total: $x{:}y{:}\text{total} = 2{:}3{:}5$.

Thus, $x{:}\text{total} = 2{:}5$. That means x makes up $\frac{2}{5}$, or 40%, of the total mixture. Choice **(D)** is correct.

Step 4: Confirm Your Answer

Review your calculations for this question. Also, confirm that your answer choice makes sense in the context of the question.

TAKEAWAYS: MIXTURES

- For mixture problems, translate the given information into ratios.
- For questions that involve altering a given mixture, identify whether any of the amounts remain constant between the old and new mixtures.

Practice Set: Mixtures on the GMAT

10. How many liters of water must be evaporated from 50 liters of a 3 percent sugar solution to get a 5 percent sugar solution?

    ○ 2
    ○ 4
    ○ 6
    ○ 10
    ○ 20

11. A company produces a cleaning solution that has a 60 percent concentration of Chemical K. The current production batch contains 200 L of an ingredient with a 30 percent concentration of Chemical K and 150 L of an ingredient with a 40 percent concentration of Chemical K. How much pure Chemical K must be added to the batch to attain the correct concentration of Chemical K?

    ○ 150 L
    ○ 175 L
    ○ 200 L
    ○ 225 L
    ○ 250 L

12. A display case contains a certain number of donuts, some chocolate, some jelly filled, and the rest plain. One-sixth of the donuts are chocolate. How many chocolate donuts must be added so that one-fourth of the total donuts are chocolate?

    (1) There are 40 plain donuts in the case.
    (2) The ratio of plain donuts to jelly-filled donuts is 2:1.

ANSWERS AND EXPLANATIONS BEGIN ON NEXT PAGE

ANSWERS AND EXPLANATIONS

1.	A	5.	A	9.	C
2.	A	6.	A	10.	E
3.	C	7.	B	11.	D
4.	E	8.	C	12.	C

1. **(A)**

The cost of Brand V paper is proportional to the weight. If 18 ounces of Brand V paper cost $3.06, what is the cost of 24 ounces of Brand V paper?

O $4.08
O $5.58
O $6.12
O $7.31
O $7.59

Step 1: Analyze the Question

You know two things—the cost of Brand V paper is proportional to its weight, and 18 ounces of this paper costs $3.06.

Step 2: State the Task

Calculate the cost of 24 ounces of Brand V paper.

Step 3: Approach Strategically

Let x = the cost of 24 ounces of Brand V paper. The paper cost is proportional to its weight, and you are given three parts of a proportion, so set up the proportion and solve:

$$\frac{18}{\$3.06} = \frac{24}{x}$$

$$\frac{6}{\$1.02} = \frac{24}{x}$$

The numerator on the right is now 4 times the numerator on the left, so x must be 4 times the simplified denominator, or $1.02 \times 4 = $4.08. **(A)** is correct.

Step 4: Confirm Your Answer

The answer choices are fairly spread out, so estimation is a great way to confirm our answer. Because 24 is less than one-and-a-half times 18, we need an answer that is also less than one-and-a-half times $3.06. Only **(A)** comes close.

2. **(A)**

The volume of a certain substance is always directly proportional to its weight. If 48 cubic inches of the substance weigh 112 ounces, what is the volume, in cubic inches, of 63 ounces of this substance?

- ○ 27
- ○ 36
- ○ 42
- ○ 64
- ○ 147

Step 1: Analyze the Question

The language in the first sentence is asking you to translate the question stem into algebra. You can set up an equation relating the volume of an object to its weight.

Step 2: State the Task

Set up the equations from the question stem and solve for the volume of the substance.

Step 3: Approach Strategically

Say that the volume is v cubic inches. Then 48 cubic inches is to 112 ounces as v cubic inches is to 63 ounces. Then $\frac{48}{112} = \frac{v}{63}$. Simplifying the left side, you have this:

$$\frac{48 \div 4}{112 \div 4} = \frac{v}{63}$$

$$\frac{12}{28} = \frac{v}{63}$$

$$\frac{12 \div 4}{28 \div 4} = \frac{v}{63}$$

$$\frac{3}{7} = \frac{v}{63}$$

To solve for x, you can cross multiply:

$$3 \times 63 = 7 \times v$$

$$3 \times 9 = v$$

$$v = 27$$

(A) is correct.

Step 4: Confirm Your Answer

You can plug your calculated value for v back into the original equation from the question stem to confirm that your answer makes sense. You can also use estimation to check your work: 63 is slightly more than half of 112, so you need a value for v that is slightly more than half of 48. Among the answer choices, only 27 is a possibility.

3. (C)

There are chips of four different colors distributed in stacks as follows: $\frac{1}{2}$ are white, $\frac{1}{6}$ are green, $\frac{1}{5}$ are blue, and the remaining 12 chips are red. What is the total number of chips in the four stacks?

○   60
○   75
○   90
○   100
○   125

Step 1: Analyze the Question

This question presents colored chips as parts that make up a whole. Most of the parts are identified as fractions of the whole, while one part is identified as a specific quantity. If you note that the actual number of each color of chips as well as the total number of chips must be integers, this insight will help you backsolve efficiently. (Things that normally come whole, such as chips, people, pets, etc., will never be broken into pieces in proportions questions on the GMAT.)

Step 2: State the Task

Use the information given about chips of different colors to determine the total number of chips.

Step 3: Approach Strategically

There is more than one way to approach this question. One strategy is to determine what fraction of the total are the 12 red chips and then use that information to calculate the total number. Convert the three given fractions to the common denominator of 30 and add those rewritten fractions:

$$\left(\frac{15}{15}\right)\left(\frac{1}{2}\right)+\left(\frac{5}{5}\right)\left(\frac{1}{6}\right)+\left(\frac{6}{6}\right)\left(\frac{1}{5}\right)=\frac{15}{30}+\frac{5}{30}+\frac{6}{30}=\frac{26}{30}$$

So, the rest of the chips, $\frac{30}{30}-\frac{26}{30}=\frac{4}{30}=\frac{2}{15}$, are the 12 red ones. Solve for the total number of chips, x, by setting up the proportion of part-to-whole ratios, $\frac{12}{x}=\frac{2}{15}$. Cross multiply: $2x = 180$. Thus, $x = 90$, and **(C)** is correct.

Alternatively, you could backsolve. Since $\frac{1}{2}$, $\frac{1}{6}$, and $\frac{1}{5}$ of the chips are integers, the total number of chips must be divisible by 2, 5, and 6. Thus, the total is divisible by the least common multiple of 2, 5, and 6, which is 30. Since the total number of chips must be divisible by 30, eliminate **(B)**, **(D)**, and **(E)**. Select one of the two remaining choices to backsolve. For **(A)**, 60, there would be $\frac{1}{2}\times 60 = 30$ white chips, $\frac{1}{6}\times 60 = 10$ green chips, and $\frac{1}{5}\times 60 = 12$ blue chips. Thus, $60 - 30 - 10 - 12 = 8$ chips would be red if 60 were the correct total. Since there are actually 12 red chips, the correct choice must be **(C)**, 90.

Step 4: Confirm Your Answer

As a quick check that you determined the correct total, use the fact that when a fraction is taken of a whole, the fraction is multiplied by the whole. Thus, multiply the fractions given in the question stem by 90 and then sum those values along with the 12 red chips. The result should equal 90:

$$\frac{1}{2}(90)+\frac{1}{6}(90)+\frac{1}{5}(90)+12=45+15+18+12=90$$

4.   **(E)**

Three investors, A, B, and C, divide the profits from a business enterprise in the ratio of 5:7:8, respectively. If Investor A earned $3,500, how much money did Investors B and C earn in total?

   O $4,000
   O $4,900
   O $5,600
   O $9,500
   O $10,500

Step 1: Analyze the Question

Three investors, A, B, and C, divide profits in the ratio of 5:7:8, and Investor A receives $3,500 in profits.

Step 2: State the Task

Find the amount earned by Investors B and C combined.

Step 3: Approach Strategically

The easiest way to visualize this problem is to consider the profits in terms of equal shares. Investors A, B, and C divide profits in the ratio of 5:7:8, so there are a total of $5 + 7 + 8 = 20$ "shares" of profits. Investor A has 5 of these shares, which leaves Investors B and C with $20 - 5 = 15$ profit shares. Because 15 is 3 times 5, Investors B and C combined must have earned 3 times what Investor A earned, or $3,500 \times 3 = \$10,500$. **(E)** is correct.

Step 4: Confirm Your Answer

When dealing with ratios, be sure to match the given part to the correct part of the ratio.

5.   (A)

If $\dfrac{a}{b} = \dfrac{c}{d}$, what is the numerical ratio of b to d?

(1) $\dfrac{a}{b} = \dfrac{3c}{2b}$

(2) $a = 2$ and $d = 4$.

Step 1: Analyze the Question Stem

This Value question stem provides a proportion with four variables and asks for a numerical value of the ratio of b to d. Rearranging the proportion to put b over d on one side may help you visualize what is needed: cross multiply to get $ad = bc$; divide both sides by d to get $a = \dfrac{bc}{d}$, and divide both sides by c to get $\dfrac{a}{c} = \dfrac{b}{d}$. Therefore, you need the ratio of a to c in order to determine the ratio of b to d.

Step 2: Evaluate the Statements Using 12TEN

Statement (1) says that $\dfrac{a}{b} = \dfrac{3c}{2b}$. Cross multiply to find that $2ab = 3bc$. Divide both sides by b: $2a = 3c$. This means that $\dfrac{a}{c} = \dfrac{3}{2}$. You've already determined that this is also the ratio of $\dfrac{b}{d}$. This statement is sufficient, so eliminate **(B)**, **(C)**, and **(E)**.

Plug the values in Statement (2) into the equation: $\dfrac{2}{b} = \dfrac{c}{4}$. Cross multiplying results in $bc = 8$. Although the statement provides a value for d, you can't determine the value of b, so this statement is insufficient. **(A)** is correct.

6. **(A)**

If the ratio of a to b is 4 to 3 and the ratio of b to c is 1 to 5, what is the ratio of a to c?

○ $\dfrac{4}{5}$

○ $\dfrac{1}{3}$

○ $\dfrac{2}{5}$

○ $\dfrac{4}{5}$

○ $\dfrac{7}{6}$

Step 1: Analyze the Question

You are given two ratios, a to b and b to c, and are asked to solve for the ratio of a to c.

Step 2: State the Task

Produce the ratio a to c. You can do so by picking numbers or by translating the given information into equations and combining them.

Step 3: Approach Strategically

Translating the first equation, you have $\frac{a}{b} = \frac{4}{3}$.

Translating the second equation, you have $\frac{b}{c} = \frac{1}{5}$.

You can calculate $\frac{a}{c}$ by multiplying $\frac{a}{b}$ by $\frac{b}{c}$:

$$\frac{a}{c} = \left(\frac{a}{b}\right)\left(\frac{b}{c}\right) = \left(\frac{4}{3}\right)\left(\frac{1}{5}\right) = \frac{4}{15}$$

(A) is correct.

Had you used picking numbers, the most straightforward values to choose are $a = 4$ and $b = 3$. If $b = 3$, then the only permissible value of c is 15. That makes the ratio of a to c equal to $\frac{4}{15}$.

Step 4: Confirm Your Answer

When you are given two ratios, their product or quotient will always produce a third ratio. Be sure to confirm the order of the words in the question stem ratios to ensure that you have translated the ratios correctly.

7. (B)

Each employee of Company X is a member of precisely 1 of 3 shifts of employees. Among the 60 members of the first shift, 20 percent participate in the pension program; among the 50 members of the second shift, 40 percent participate in the pension program; and among the 40 members of the third shift, 10 percent participate in the pension program. What percent of the workers at Company X participate in the pension program?

- ○ 20%
- ○ 24%
- ○ 36%
- ○ 37.5%
- ○ 70%

Step 1: Analyze the Question

This is a complex percents problem with multiple pieces. You'll need to take things one at a time to avoid getting overwhelmed.

Step 2: State the Task

Find the percentage of Company X workers who participate in the pension program.

Step 3: Approach Strategically

There are three shifts of workers, and a different percentage of each participates in the pension program, so you'll need to calculate each piece separately before combining them to get your answer.

First shift: 20% of the 60 workers participate, or $60 \times 0.2 = 12$ first-shift workers participate. Second shift: 40% of the 50 workers participate, or $50 \times 0.4 = 20$ second-shift workers participate. Third shift: 10% of the 40 workers participate, or $40 \times 0.1 = 4$ third-shift workers participate. That's a total of $12 + 20 + 4 = 36$ workers who participate in the pension program out of the overall $60 + 50 + 40 = 150$ workers at Company X.

Now you can plug these totals into the ratio the question asks for: $\frac{36}{150} = \frac{12}{50} = \frac{24}{100} = 24\%$. **(B)** is correct.

Step 4: Confirm Your Answer

If you are pressed for time, you can use estimation on this question. Notice that the two shifts with the most employees have 20% and 40%, respectively, participating in the pension program. Of the two, the 20% is from the larger group, so a rough estimate of these two groups alone puts the answer south of 30% (which would be the midpoint of 20% and 40%). Coupled with the fact that the remaining shift only has a paltry 10% participation rate, you have enough to immediately eliminate **(C)**, **(D)**, and **(E)**.

8. (C)

In 2010, a basketball team won 30 percent of its 20 basketball games. In 2011, the team won 28 percent of its 25 basketball games. What was the percent increase from 2010 to 2011 in the number of basketball games the team won?

- ○ 5%
- ○ $14\frac{2}{7}\%$
- ○ $16\frac{2}{3}\%$
- ○ $23\frac{1}{3}\%$
- ○ 60%

Step 1: Analyze the Question

This question stem contains a lot of information, which you must translate carefully to solve the question. You are asked to calculate the percent increase in the number of games won by the basketball team from 2010 to 2011. To determine this value, you need the actual number of games won in 2010 and won in 2011.

Now that you know what information you need, the first two sentences make sense. You can calculate the number of games won in each year from those two statements.

Step 2: State the Task

Translate the question stem into three equations to determine (1) number of games won in 2010, (2) number of games won in 2011, and (3) percent increase in the number of games won.

Step 3: Approach Strategically

Translating the first sentence (2010), you have 30% × 20 games = 0.30 × 20 games = 6 games.

Translating the second sentence (2011), you have 28% × 25 games = 0.28 × 25 games = 7 games.

The percent increase formula is very important to memorize for Test Day. It is

$$\text{Percent increase} = \frac{\text{Difference in values}}{\text{Original value}} \times 100\%$$

$$\text{Percent increase} = \frac{7-6}{6} \times 100\% = \frac{1}{6} \times 100\% = 16\frac{2}{3}\%$$

(C) is correct.

Step 4: Confirm Your Answer

There are a number of calculations in this solution, so be sure to double-check your work, especially in calculating the percent increase.

9.   **(C)**

Survey of Student Preferences

The administration of a certain school surveys all 120 students to plan a field trip. Each student can express a preference for only one destination: the science museum, the art museum, or neither. The results of the student survey are shown above. Assuming that the maximum number of students who are allowed to visit their preferred museum visit that museum for the field trip, how many students who have a preference do <u>not</u> visit their preferred museum?

(1)   Due to transportation constraints, the maximum number of students who can take a field trip to the science museum is 55.

(2)   Due to high demand, the art museum can accommodate a maximum of 50 students.

Step 1: Analyze the Question Stem

This is a Value question. When presented with a chart, take a quick look at the information in it and consider the types of calculations that can be made using that information. This circle graph displays the results of the student survey. Since there are 120 students, the number of students who prefer the science museum is 120×0.60, the number of students who prefer the art museum is 120×0.30, and the number of students who prefer neither museum is 120×0.10.

The question stem asks how many students will *not* be able to visit their preferred museum. This question implies that there is some limitation on the number of students who can attend each museum. You can ignore the students who have no preference as they are irrelevant to this question.

Step 2: Evaluate the Statements Using 12TEN

Statement (1) indicates that no more than 55 students can visit the science museum for the field trip. Comparing 55 to the number of students who prefer the science museum would allow determination of how many of these students won't get their first choice. (If you're curious, $120 \times 0.60 = 72$ students would like to go, so $72 - 55 = 17$ students who don't get their first choice.) However, this statement alone provides no information about how many students who want to visit the art museum will be denied the opportunity to attend that museum. Eliminate **(A)** and **(D)**.

Statement (2) says that the limitation for the art museum is $3 \times 25 = 75$. Again, comparing 75 to the number of students who wish to visit the art museum would allow determination of the number thwarted in their desire. (The number who prefer the art museum is $120 \times 0.30 = 36$, so all these students get their first choice and the number denied is 0.) By itself, however, this statement provides no information about the students who want to visit the science museum, so eliminate **(B)**.

Together, the statements allow calculation of the number of students from the science museum group and the art museum group who will not get their preferred museum. All students who have expressed a preference are accounted for. Thus, **(C)** is correct.

10. (E)

How many liters of water must be evaporated from 50 liters of a 3 percent sugar solution to get a 5 percent sugar solution?

- ○ 2
- ○ 4
- ○ 6
- ○ 10
- ○ 20

Step 1: Analyze the Question

You have 50 liters of a 3% sugar solution, and the question tells you that some amount of water is evaporated from the solution.

Step 2: State the Task

Find the number of liters of water that must evaporate to get a 5% sugar solution.

Step 3: Approach Strategically

You can calculate that 50 liters of a 3% sugar solution has $50 \times 0.03 = 1.5$ liters of sugar. Since the only thing that changes from the old to the new solution is the amount of water, you know that the amount of sugar remains constant at 1.5 liters. A 5% sugar solution with the same 1.5 liters of sugar would have $\frac{1.5}{0.05} = 30$ liters of water. You must therefore evaporate $50 - 30 = 20$ liters of water. **(E)** is correct.

Step 4: Confirm Your Answer

The answer choices are spread widely apart, so estimation is a great way to confirm your answer. 3% to 5% is almost double the concentration of sugar, so you'll need to lose almost half of the water. Only **(E)** comes close.

11. **(D)**

A company produces a cleaning solution that has a 60 percent concentration of Chemical K. The current production batch contains 200 L of an ingredient with a 30 percent concentration of Chemical K and 150 L of an ingredient with a 40 percent concentration of Chemical K. How much pure Chemical K must be added to the batch to attain the correct concentration of Chemical K?

- ○ 150 L
- ○ 175 L
- ○ 200 L
- ○ 225 L
- ○ 250 L

Step 1: Analyze the Question

This question provides the amounts and percentage concentration of Chemical K for two of the three ingredients in a mixture and the final concentration after the third ingredient, which is pure Chemical K, is added. Logically, the concentration of pure Chemical K is 100%.

Step 2: State the Task

Determine how much pure Chemical K must be added to the two ingredients already in the batch to bring the final concentration of Chemical K up to 60%.

Step 3: Approach Strategically

You can approach this question in two ways: with the balance approach to averages and mixtures or with algebra.

To use the balance approach, compare the concentrations of the individual components to the final concentration of 60%. The concentration of the 30% component is $60\% - 30\% = 30\%$ below the final concentration. Since there are 200 L of this ingredient, "weight" the 30% shortfall by 200: $30 \times 200 = 6{,}000$. The 40% component is 20% under, and there are 150 L of this ingredient, so this contributes another $20 \times 150 = 3{,}000$ to the shortfall. The total shortfall is $6{,}000 + 3{,}000 = 9{,}000$. Thus, the amount of pure Chemical K added must produce an overage of 9,000. The pure Chemical K is 40% over the desired concentration. So, if k is the amount of this ingredient, then $40 \times k = 9{,}000$, and $k = 225$ L. **(D)** is correct.

Alternatively, you could use algebra to determine the amount of pure Chemical K needed. The amount of Chemical K in the first ingredient is $200 \times 0.30 = 60$ L, and the amount in the second ingredient is $150 \times 0.40 = 60$ L. Set the amount of pure Chemical K added to the mixture equal to k. The final concentration is the amount of Chemical K divided by the total volume of the ingredients: $\frac{60 + 60 + k}{200 + 150 + k} = \frac{120 + k}{350 + k}$. Set this equal to 0.60 and multiply both sides of the equation by $350 + k$: $(350 + k)\left(\frac{120 + k}{350 + k}\right) = (350 + k)(0.60)$, which simplifies to $120 + k = 210 + 0.6k$. Subtract 120 and $0.6k$ from both sides to yield $0.4k = 90$. That's $\frac{4}{10}k = 90$, so $k = 90 \times \frac{10}{4} = 225$. Thus, 225 L of pure Chemical K solution are needed, **(D)**.

Step 4: Confirm Your Answer

Check your calculations and be certain that you used the correct values from the question stem. This will be easiest if you have kept your scratchwork well organized.

12. **(C)**

A display case contains a certain number of donuts, some chocolate, some jelly filled, and the rest plain. One-sixth of the donuts are chocolate. How many chocolate donuts must be added so that one-fourth of the total donuts are chocolate?

(1) There are 40 plain donuts in the case.

(2) The ratio of plain donuts to jelly-filled donuts is 2:1.

Step 1: Analyze the Question Stem

For this Value question, your first step is to translate the words into math. Let c equal the number of chocolate donuts, j equal the number of jelly donuts, and p equal the number of plain donuts. If T is the total number of donuts, then $c + j + p = T$ and $c = \frac{1}{6}T$. You want to know how many more chocolate donuts (x) need to be added to make the case consist of one-quarter chocolate donuts. When x chocolate donuts are added, this also adds to the total number of donuts, so $c + x = \frac{1}{4}(T + x)$. Substituting $\frac{1}{6}T$ for c makes the equation $\frac{1}{6}T + x = \frac{1}{4}(T + x)$. Thus, if you had enough information to determine how many donuts are in the case (T), you could solve for x.

Step 2: Evaluate the Statements Using 12TEN

Statement (1): While this tells you the number of plain donuts in the case, the fact that $p = 40$ doesn't tell you how many donuts there are in total. Thus, Statement (1) is insufficient. Eliminate **(A)** and **(D)**.

Now evaluate Statement (2), which provides a ratio between plain donuts and jelly-filled donuts. This tells you how the $\frac{5}{6}$ of donuts that aren't chocolate are divvied up between plain and jelly, but since there is no actual number of any of the donut types, this statement does not allow calculation of T or c. Statement (2) is not sufficient. Eliminate **(B)**.

Now combining the statements, you can say that $p = 40$ and that $\frac{p}{j} = \frac{2}{1}$, so you can set up a proportion to determine how many jelly-filled donuts there are: $\frac{40}{j} = \frac{2}{1}$, so $40 = 2j$ and $j = 20$. Thus, there are $40 + 20 = 60$ non-chocolate donuts in the case. You know that $60 = \frac{5}{6}$ of the total donuts (because $\frac{1}{6}$ of the donuts are chocolate), so $T = 60 \div \frac{5}{6} = 60 \times \frac{6}{5} = 12 \times 6 = 72$. You've determined that finding this is enough to answer the question, so the statements together are sufficient, and the correct choice is **(C)**.

While you only need to know that you have sufficient information to find a value to answer a Data Sufficiency value question, if you're curious, here's what the math would look like. You're starting with 72 total donuts, so $T = 72$:

$$\frac{1}{6}T + x = \frac{1}{4}(T + x)$$

$$\frac{1}{6}(72) + x = \frac{1}{4}(72 + x)$$

$$12 + x = 18 + \frac{1}{4}x$$

$$\frac{3}{4}x = 6$$

$$x = 8$$

So you start with 72 total donuts, 12 of which are chocolate. Adding 8 chocolate donuts yields 20 chocolate donuts and 80 total donuts, and the number of chocolate donuts is now $\frac{1}{4}$ of the total.

EXPLANATIONS

GMAT BY THE NUMBERS: PROPORTIONS

Now that you've learned how to approach proportions questions on the GMAT, let's add one more dimension to your understanding of how they work.

Take a moment to try this question. Following is performance data from thousands of people who have studied with Kaplan over the decades. Through analyzing this data, we will show you how to approach questions like this one most effectively and how to avoid similarly tempting wrong answer choice types on Test Day.

The price of a certain car this year is $42,000, which is 25 percent greater than the cost of the car last year. What was the price of the car last year?

- ○ $27,000
- ○ $28,000
- ○ $31,500
- ○ $33,600
- ○ $34,500

EXPLANATION

The test makers often set up percentage problems to reward those who do two important things. The first is to be careful about what number the percentage is applied to. The second is to remember to look for ways to simplify calculations.

QUESTION STATISTICS

1% of test takers choose **(A)**
1% of test takers choose **(B)**
19% of test takers choose **(C)**
74% of test takers choose **(D)**
5% of test takers choose **(E)**
Sample size = 3,799

This problem tells you that an increase of 25% raises the price of a car to $42,000. Be careful to apply that 25% increase to the unknown original price, not the $42,000. Decreasing $42,000 by 25% yields $31,500, which is the most common wrong answer. Avoid that one error, and your odds of getting the right answer go up dramatically.

If you set up the arithmetic the way the GMAT presents it, you get:

$$\text{Original price} \times 1.25 = 42,000$$

This would have you dividing 42,000 by 1.25—a simple task for a calculator but a time-consuming one for a person. On the GMAT, you'll often have more success by converting percentages to fractions. An increase of 25% means an increase of $\frac{1}{4}$, bringing the total up to $\frac{5}{4}$ of the original:

$$\text{Original price} \times \frac{5}{4} = 42,000$$
$$\text{Original price} = 42,000 \times \frac{4}{5}$$
$$\text{Original price} = 8,400 \times 4$$
$$\text{Original price} = 33,600$$

Choice **(D)** is correct.

MORE GMAT BY THE NUMBERS...

To see more questions with answer choice statistics, be sure to review the full-length CATs in your online resources.

 GO ONLINE

kaptest.com/login

CHAPTER 16

Statistics on the GMAT

Tracy has 3 bags of marbles, each bag containing at least 1 blue marble, at least 1 red marble, and no marbles of another color. If Tracy selects 1 marble at random from each bag, what is the probability that all 3 marbles that she selects will be red?

(1) There is a total of 5 red marbles and 5 blue marbles in the 3 bags.
(2) The ratios of red to blue marbles in the 3 bags are 2:1, 1:1, and 1:2.

Above is a typical Data Sufficiency question dealing with probability, one of the categories of statistics that we will discuss in this chapter. In this chapter, we'll look at how to apply the Kaplan Method to this question, discuss the probability rules being tested, and go over the basic principles and strategies that you want to keep in mind on every Quantitative question involving statistics. But before you move on, take a minute to think about what you see in this question and answer some questions about how you think it works:

- What does probability measure?

- How can ratios help you calculate probability on this question?

- What Kaplan strategy can you use to solve this question?

- What GMAT Core Competencies are most essential to success on this question?

PREVIEWING STATISTICS ON THE GMAT

WHAT DOES PROBABILITY MEASURE?

Probability measures the likelihood of a certain event occurring. Probability can be expressed as a fraction or decimal between 0 and 1 or as a percentage between 0 percent and 100 percent. The lower the probability, the less likely that event is to occur. On the GMAT, the test makers often incorporate this concept into high-difficulty questions that ask about the probability of multiple events happening or not happening. In addition to learning the rules, operations, and formulas specific to probability, remember that the same rules you already know for proportions and fractions continue to apply.

HOW CAN RATIOS HELP YOU CALCULATE PROBABILITY ON THIS QUESTION?

In a situation like the one described in this question stem, the probability of a given outcome of random selection is equal to the ratio of the items from which the selection is being made. In other words, if a bag contains only 2 red marbles and 2 blue marbles, the probability of selecting a red marble from this bag is the same as the ratio of red marbles to total marbles in the bag, which is 2:4, or $\frac{1}{2}$.

WHAT KAPLAN STRATEGY CAN YOU USE TO SOLVE THIS QUESTION?

Since different scenarios are possible for how many marbles of each color are in each bag, picking numbers will help you test out the possible distributions of marbles among the bags and determine whether the information is sufficient to solve for a single answer to the question stem.

Remember that whenever you pick numbers for a Data Sufficiency question, the numbers you pick must be permissible—they must obey any rules or restrictions given in the stem and the statement you're testing. For example, if a statement tells you that there cannot be more than 6 marbles in each bag, you cannot pick the numbers red = 4 and blue = 5 for that bag.

WHAT GMAT CORE COMPETENCIES ARE MOST ESSENTIAL TO SUCCESS ON THIS QUESTION?

Critical Thinking will help you determine what information is necessary to calculate the desired probability: are ratios sufficient, or do you need actual numbers of the marbles? Do you need information on each bag individually, or is information about all three bags combined enough? Even though Data Sufficiency questions don't ask you to calculate an exact value for the answer to the question stem, you do need to know how you *would* calculate that answer if you needed to.

Pattern Recognition is crucial here, as it is on all statistics questions, since the GMAT often asks questions that hinge on the same concepts and formulas that you can memorize. Here, you need to remember the probability formula, as well as how to calculate the joint probability of independent events (Tracy's selection from each of the three bags).

Finally, Attention to the Right Detail is necessary whenever you work with probabilities, which are essentially fractions or ratios. You need to be clear whether you are dealing with part-to-part or part-to-whole ratios and keep track of which items are in the numerator and denominator.

Here are the main topics we'll cover in this chapter:

- Median, Mode, Range, and Standard Deviation
- Sequences of Integers
- Combinations and Permutations
- Probability

HANDLING GMAT STATISTICS

Now let's apply the Kaplan Method to the statistics question we saw earlier:

> Tracy has 3 bags of marbles, each bag containing at least 1 blue marble, at least 1 red marble, and no marbles of another color. If Tracy selects 1 marble at random from each bag, what is the probability that all 3 marbles that she selects will be red?
>
> (1) There is a total of 5 red marbles and 5 blue marbles in the 3 bags.
> (2) The ratios of red to blue marbles in the 3 bags are 2:1, 1:1, and 1:2.

Step 1: Analyze the Question Stem

This is a Value question. You are asked for the probability that when one marble is chosen at random from each of the three bags, each marble chosen is red. You know that each bag contains at least one blue marble, at least one red marble, and no other marbles of any other color. Now let's look at the statements.

Step 2: Evaluate the Statements Using 12TEN

Statement (1) tells you that a total of five red marbles and five blue marbles are distributed among the three bags. Because there are different ways to distribute the marbles among the bags, there are different possible probabilities and, therefore, different possible answers to the question.

You can use picking numbers to test out these different scenarios; if the different permissible scenarios result in different answers to the question stem, then the statement is insufficient.

For example, let's call the bags Bag 1, Bag 2, and Bag 3. If Bag 1 contains three blue marbles and three red marbles, while Bags 2 and 3 each contain one blue marble and one red marble, then the probability that all three marbles chosen are red can be calculated by multiplying together the individual probabilities of selecting a red marble from each of the three bags:

$$\frac{\text{Bag 1 red}}{\text{Bag 1 total}} \times \frac{\text{Bag 2 red}}{\text{Bag 2 total}} \times \frac{\text{Bag 3 red}}{\text{Bag 3 total}} = \frac{1}{2} \times \frac{1}{2} \times \frac{1}{2} = \frac{1}{8}$$

If, however, Bag 1 contains three blue marbles and one red marble, Bag 2 contains one blue marble and three red marbles, and Bag 3 contains one blue marble and one red marble, then the probability that all three marbles chosen are red is $\frac{1}{4} \times \frac{3}{4} \times \frac{1}{2} = \frac{3}{32}$.

Because different answers to the question are possible when you pick different permissible numbers, Statement (1) is insufficient. Eliminate choices **(A)** and **(D)**.

Now look at Statement (2). You are told the ratio of red to blue marbles in each bag. So you can say that the probability of picking a red marble from one bag is $\frac{2}{3}$, the probability of picking a red marble from another bag is $\frac{1}{2}$, and the probability of picking a marble from the remaining bag is $\frac{1}{3}$. The probability of picking a red marble from each of the three bags is $\frac{2}{3} \times \frac{1}{2} \times \frac{1}{3}$. You do not have to calculate the value of this expression. Just knowing that you *can* calculate this probability is enough. Statement (2) is sufficient, and **(B)** is correct.

Now let's look at each of the areas of statistics that show up on the GMAT Quantitative section, starting with median, mode, range, and standard deviation.

MEDIAN, MODE, RANGE, AND STANDARD DEVIATION

MEDIAN

If an odd group of numbers is arranged in numerical order, the median is the middle value.

Example: What is the median of 4, 5, 100, 1, and 6?

First, arrange the numbers in numerical order: 1, 4, 5, 6, and 100. The middle number (the median) is 5.

If a set has an even number of terms, then the median is the average (arithmetic mean) of the two middle terms after the terms are arranged in numerical order.

Example: What is the median value of 2, 9, 8, 17, 11, and 37?

Arrange the values in numerical order: 2, 8, 9, 11, 17, 37. The two middle numbers are 9 and 11. The median is the average of 9 and 11, that is, 10.

The median can be quite different from the average. For instance, in the first set of numbers above, {1, 4, 5, 6, 100}, the median is 5, but the average is $\frac{1+4+5+6+100}{5} = \frac{116}{5} = 23.2$.

MODE

The mode is the number that appears most frequently in a set. For example, in the set {1, 2, 2, 2, 3, 4, 4, 5, 6}, the mode is 2.

It is possible for a set to have more than one mode. For example, in the set {35, 42, 35, 57, 57, 19}, the two modes are 35 and 57.

RANGE

The range is the positive difference between the largest term in the set and the smallest term. For example, in the set {2, 4, 10, 20, 26}, the range is 24.

STANDARD DEVIATION

Standard deviation measures the dispersion of a set of numbers around the mean. If you've worked with the standard deviation formula in high school or college, you might remember that the formula looks like this:

$$\sqrt{\frac{1}{N}\left[(x_1 - \mu)^2 + (x_2 - \mu)^2 + \cdots + (x_N - \mu)^2\right]}$$

It can be intimidating, so let's paraphrase it in plain English. Calculating the standard deviation involves the following steps:

1. Find the average (arithmetic mean) of the set.
2. Subtract the average of the set from each term in that set.
3. Square each result.
4. Take the average of those squares.
5. Calculate the positive square root of that average.

Fortunately, the GMAT will only very rarely require you to apply this formula, and only on the most difficult questions. When standard deviation is tested, all you will generally need to understand is the basic concept: standard deviation represents how close or far the terms in a list are from the average.

Thus, {1, 2, 3} and {101, 102, 103} have the same standard deviation, since they both have one term on the average and two terms exactly one unit away from the average. A quickly sketched number line can confirm this:

The set {1, 3, 5} will have a smaller standard deviation than {0, 3, 6}. Both sets have an average of 3, but the first has terms 2, 0, and 2 units from the average while the second has terms 3, 0, and 3 units from the average. Again, you can confirm this with a quick sketch:

You could also calculate the standard deviation for the sets {1, 3, 5} and {0, 3, 6} to confirm:

{1, 3, 5}

mean = 3

$$\sqrt{\frac{1}{3}\left[(1-3)^2 + (3-3)^2 + (5-3)^2\right]}$$

$$\sqrt{\frac{1}{3}\left[(-2)^2 + 0^2 + 2^2\right]}$$

$$\sqrt{\frac{1}{3}(4+0+4)}$$

$$\sqrt{\frac{1}{3}(8)}$$

$$\sqrt{\frac{8}{3}}$$

{0, 3, 6}

mean = 3

$$\sqrt{\frac{1}{3}\left[(0-3)^2 + (3-3)^2 + (6-3)^2\right]}$$

$$\sqrt{\frac{1}{3}\left[(-3)^2 + 0^2 + 3^2\right]}$$

$$\sqrt{\frac{1}{3}(9+0+9)}$$

$$\sqrt{\frac{1}{3}(18)}$$

$$\sqrt{6}$$

Since 6 is larger than $\frac{8}{3}$, you can see that the standard deviation of the second, more widely spaced set of numbers is larger than that of the first set. However, you will save much time on Test Day by using your understanding of how standard deviation works to estimate rather than calculating the answers to questions such as these.

In other words, the GMAT test makers are more interested in whether you understand the concept of standard deviation and can apply Critical Thinking to situations that involve it than in whether you can perform complex mathematical calculations.

In-Format Question: Median, Mode, Range, and Standard Deviation on the GMAT

Now let's use the Kaplan Method on a Data Sufficiency question dealing with median, mode, range, and standard deviation:

> List L consists of 12, 8, 10, 14, and 6. If two numbers are removed from list L, what is the standard deviation of the new list?
>
> (1) The range of the new list is 8.
> (2) The median of the new list is 8.

Step 1: Analyze the Question Stem

This is a Value question. You know that two numbers are removed from the list 12, 8, 10, 14, 6. You want to determine the standard deviation of the new list. There is no other information given, so let's look at the statements.

Step 2: Evaluate the Statements Using 12TEN

Statement (1): You are told that the range of the new list is 8. The only way to have a range of 8 is for both 6 and 14 to appear in the new list, because any other pair of numbers in the original list will be closer to one another than 8. So the new list must contain 6 and 14.

The new list will also contain one of the numbers 8, 10, and 12. If, for example, the third number in the list is 10, then the list will be 6, 10, and 14. If the third number in the list is 12, then the numbers in the list will be 6, 12, and 14. The standard deviation of the list 6, 10, and 14 will be different from the standard deviation of the list 6, 12, and 14 because the two sets have different means and the numbers in the two lists are dispersed differently around the mean.

More than one standard deviation is possible, and therefore more than one answer to the question is possible. Statement (1) is insufficient. Eliminate choices **(A)** and **(D)**.

Statement (2) says that the median of the new set is 8. Because there will be an odd number (3) of members of the new list, 8 will have to appear in the list in order for 8 to be the median. Additionally, since 8 must be in the middle of the new list and there is only one possible value less than 8, you know that 6 must also be in the list. The new list could be 6, 8, 10, which has a median of 8, and the new list could also be 6, 8, 14, which also has a median of 8.

The standard deviation of the numbers in the list 6, 8, 10 is less than the standard deviation of the list 6, 8, 14. More than one standard deviation is possible, and therefore more than one answer to the question is possible. So Statement (2) is insufficient. You can eliminate choice **(B)**.

Now that you've determined that Statement (1) and Statement (2) are both insufficient on their own, look at the statements together: you know from Statement (1) that 6 and 14 must be in the list, and you know from Statement (2) that 6 and 8 must be in the list. The statements taken together tell you that the list must consist of 6, 8, and 14. Because there is only one possible list, there can only be one standard deviation. The statements taken together are sufficient. **(C)** is correct.

TAKEAWAYS: MEDIAN, MODE, RANGE, AND STANDARD DEVIATION

- In a list with an odd number of terms arranged in ascending or descending order, the median is the middle term.
- In a list with an even number of terms arranged in ascending or descending order, the median is the average of the two middle terms.
- The mode of a list of terms is the term(s) that appear(s) most frequently.
- The range is the positive difference between the largest term in the list and the smallest term.
- Standard deviation measures the dispersion of a set of numbers around the mean. The GMAT will hardly ever require you to apply the formula for standard deviation. Instead, use Critical Thinking and quick sketches of number lines to determine how close the terms in a list are from the average.

PRACTICE SET: MEDIAN, MODE, RANGE, AND STANDARD DEVIATION ON THE GMAT

1. Set S contains the elements $\{-4, x, 0, 17, 1\}$. What is the median of set S?

    (1) $x > 1$
    (2) $x < 2$

2. If the range of the eight numbers 17, 8, 14, 28, 9, 4, 11, and n is 25, what is the difference between the greatest possible value of n and the least possible value of n?

    ○   1
    ○   3
    ○   21
    ○   26
    ○   29

3. The range of the set $\{60, 120, -30, x, 0, 60\}$ is 210. If a is the median, b is the mode, and c is the average (arithmetic mean), is $a = b$?

    (1) $abc > 0$
    (2) $b = 60$

4. If $x \leq 4$ and $y \geq 10$, what is the range of the numbers in the set $\{5, 8, x, y\}$?

    (1) $3x + 5y = 72$
    (2) $-7x + 7y = 56$

SEQUENCES OF INTEGERS

AVERAGE AND MEDIAN OF CONSECUTIVE INTEGERS

The average, or mean, of a set of consecutive integers will equal its median.

Example: What is the average of 1, 2, 3, 4, and 5?

$$\frac{1+2+3+4+5}{5} = \frac{15}{5} = 3$$

For this set, 3 is both the mean and the median. This is always the case for sets of consecutive or evenly spaced integers.

There is another way to calculate the average of this set. The average of a series of consecutive or evenly spaced integers is also the same as the average of its first and last terms. For the last example, that works out to $\frac{1+5}{2} = \frac{6}{2} = 3$.

SUM OF NUMBERS

If you know the average of a group of numbers and how many numbers are in the group, you can find the sum of the numbers. You can think of it as if all the numbers in the group are equal to the average value.

Sum of values = Average value × Number of values

Example: What is the sum of all the integers between 1 and 66 inclusive?

Since this is a series of consecutive integers, you can find its average by averaging the first and last terms: $\frac{1+66}{2} = \frac{67}{2}$.

To find the number of terms in a set of consecutive integers, take the difference between the largest and the smallest numbers and add 1.

Sum of values = Average value × Number of values

$$\frac{67}{2} \times 66 = \frac{67}{\cancel{2}} \times \cancel{66}^{33} = 2{,}211$$

Granted, you still have to calculate 67 × 33, but that is much easier than adding all 66 numbers!

You may also have to find a sum in what might seem to be a normal average problem.

Example: The average daily temperature for the first week in January was 31 degrees. If the average temperature for the first six days was 30 degrees, what was the temperature on the seventh day?

The sum for all 7 days = 31 × 7 = 217 degrees.

The sum of the first 6 days = 30 × 6 = 180 degrees.

The temperature on the seventh day = 217 − 180 = 37 degrees.

IN-FORMAT QUESTION: SEQUENCES OF INTEGERS ON THE GMAT

Now let's use the Kaplan Method on a Problem Solving question dealing with sequences of integers:

In a new housing development, trees are to be planted in a straight line along a 166-foot stretch of sidewalk. Each tree will be planted in a square plot with sides measuring 1 foot. If there must be 14 feet between each plot, what is the maximum number of trees that can be planted?

- ○ 8
- ○ 9
- ○ 10
- ○ 11
- ○ 12

Step 1: Analyze the Question

Though this is not a geometry question, a quick sketch of the situation will help illustrate how to solve it.

So you know that the unit of one tree and one space is 1 foot + 14 feet = 15 feet.

Step 2: State the Task

To find how many trees can be planted, determine the feet required for a tree and the space between trees. Then divide the total length of the sidewalk by the unit of 1 tree and the space between trees.

Step 3: Approach Strategically

Each tree takes up 1 foot, and each space takes up 14 feet. Together they take up 15 feet. Now find how many times 15 goes into the total number of feet on one side of the sidewalk:

$$166 \div 15 = 11, \text{ with a remainder of 1 foot.}$$

You can plant 1 last tree in the remaining foot, bringing the total number of trees to 12. This means along the sidewalk, you can plant 12 trees with 11 spaces between them, as long as you start and end with a tree. **(E)** is correct.

Step 4: Confirm Your Answer

Make sure your answer makes sense in the context of the question. Did you take into account the remainder of the division? Will an entire tree fit in the remaining space? You can use these questions to confirm your work.

TAKEAWAYS: SEQUENCES OF INTEGERS

- In a sequence of consecutive or evenly spaced integers, the average, or mean, equals the median.
- To find the number of terms in a sequence of consecutive integers, take the difference between the largest and the smallest and add 1.
- To find the sum of a sequence of consecutive or evenly spaced integers, multiply the average of the largest and the smallest term by the number of terms.
- To find the sum of any set of numbers, multiply the average by the number of terms.

PRACTICE SET: SEQUENCES OF INTEGERS ON THE GMAT

5. What is the sum of the integers 45 through 175 inclusive?

    ○   12,295
    ○   13,000
    ○   14,300
    ○   14,410
    ○   28,820

6. What is the sum of the multiples of 4 between 13 and 125 inclusive?

    ○   1,890
    ○   1,960
    ○   2,200
    ○   3,780
    ○   4,400

7. If t is the sum of three consecutive positive integers, is t a multiple of 24?

    (1) The smallest of the three integers is even.
    (2) t is a multiple of 3.

8. The sum of a sequence of six consecutive positive integers is Z. The sum of terms in a different sequence of five consecutive integers is $Z - 5$. If the greatest term of the five-number sequence is 40, what is the difference between the median term of the five-number sequence and the least term of the six-number sequence?

    ○   5
    ○   7
    ○   8
    ○   9
    ○   10

COMBINATIONS AND PERMUTATIONS

Some GMAT questions ask you to count the number of possible ways to select a small subgroup from a larger group. If the selection is **unordered**, then it's a combinations question. But if the selection is **ordered**, it is a permutations question.

For example, if a question asks you to count the possible number of different slates of officers who could be elected to positions in class government, then order matters—President Bob and Vice President Thelma is a different slate than President Thelma and Vice President Bob. You would use the permutations formula in this scenario. But if you had to count the number of pairs of flavors of jelly beans, you are solving a combinations question; cherry and lemon is the same pair as lemon and cherry, so order does not matter (i.e., you wouldn't count those as two different pairs).

The very first thing you need to do is use Critical Thinking to figure out whether a given question calls for an ordered or an unordered selection—otherwise, you won't know which formula to use.

COMBINATIONS

The combinations formula is used when solving for the number of k unordered selections one can make from a group of n items, where $k \leq n$. This is usually referred to as $_nC_k$, which is often said as "n choose k." Not that the GMAT is an oral exam, of course, but it's helpful to say it that way to yourself because that's what making combinations is—an act of choosing small groups from a larger group.

Here's the formula, in which $n!$, or n-factorial, is the product of n and every positive integer smaller than n (for example, $5! = 5 \times 4 \times 3 \times 2 \times 1$), where n is a positive integer:

$$_nC_k = \frac{n!}{k!(n-k)!}$$

Example: A company is selecting 4 members of its board of directors to sit on an ethics subcommittee. If the board has 9 members, any of whom may serve on the subcommittee, how many different selections of members could the company make?

Since the order in which you select the members doesn't change the composition of the committee in any way, this is a combinations question. The size of the group from which you choose is n, and the size of the selected group is k. So $n = 9$ and $k = 4$.

$$_9C_4 = \frac{9!}{4!(9-4)!}$$

$$\frac{9!}{4!5!}$$

$$\frac{9 \times 8 \times 7 \times 6 \times 5 \times 4 \times 3 \times 2 \times 1}{4 \times 3 \times 2 \times 1 \times 5 \times 4 \times 3 \times 2 \times 1}$$

Save yourself some work. There's rarely a need to multiply out factorials, since many of the factors can quickly be canceled.

$$\frac{9 \times \cancel{8}^{2} \times 7 \times \cancel{6} \times \cancel{5 \times 4 \times 3 \times 2} \times 1}{\cancel{4} \times \cancel{3 \times 2} \times 1 \times \cancel{5 \times 4 \times 3 \times 2} \times 1}$$

$$9 \times 2 \times 7 = 126$$

Sometimes the problems will be more complicated and will require multiple iterations of the formula.

Example: County X holds an annual math competition, to which each county high school sends a team of 4 students. If School A has 6 boys and 7 girls whose math grades qualify them to be on their school's team, and competition rules stipulate that the team must consist of 2 boys and 2 girls, how many different teams might School A send to the competition?

The order of selection doesn't matter here, so you can use the combinations formula. But be careful: if you lump all the students together in a group of 13 and calculate $_{13}C_4$, you'd wind up including some all-boy teams and all-girl teams. The question explicitly says you can only select 2 boys and 2 girls. So you aren't really choosing 4 students from 13 but rather choosing 2 boys from 6 and 2 girls from 7.

$$_6C_2 \text{ and } _7C_2$$

$$\frac{6!}{2!4!} \times \frac{7!}{2!5!}$$

$$\frac{6 \times 5 \times 4 \times 3 \times 2 \times 1}{2 \times 1 \times 4 \times 3 \times 2 \times 1} \times \frac{7 \times 6 \times 5 \times 4 \times 3 \times 2 \times 1}{2 \times 1 \times 5 \times 4 \times 3 \times 2 \times 1}$$

$$\frac{\cancel{6}^{3} \times 5 \times \cancel{4 \times 3 \times 2 \times 1}}{2 \times 1 \times \cancel{4 \times 3 \times 2 \times 1}} \times \frac{7 \times \cancel{6}^{3} \times \cancel{5 \times 4 \times 3 \times 2 \times 1}}{\cancel{2} \times 1 \times \cancel{5 \times 4 \times 3 \times 2 \times 1}}$$

$3 \times 5 \times 7 \times 3 = 315$ possible teams consisting of 2 boys and 2 girls.

PERMUTATIONS

If the order of selection matters, you can use the permutation formulas:

Number of permutations (arrangements) of n items $= n!$

Number of permutations of k items selected from $n = {_nP_k} = \frac{n!}{(n-k)!}$

Example: How many ways are there to arrange the letters in the word ASCENT?

Clearly order matters here, since ASCENT is different from TNECSA. There are 6 letters in the word, so you must calculate the permutations of 6 items:

$$6! = 6 \times 5 \times 4 \times 3 \times 2 \times 1 = 720$$

Another way to solve is to draw a quick sketch of the problem with blanks for the arranged items. Then write in the number of possibilities for each blank in order. Finally, multiply the numbers together. Many high-difficulty GMAT permutation questions resist formulaic treatment but are easier to complete with the "draw blanks" approach.

Here's how you would use this technique to solve the ASCENT problem:

ASCENT has 6 letters, so you need 6 blanks:

$$\underline{} \times \underline{} \times \underline{} \times \underline{} \times \underline{} \times \underline{}$$

There are 6 letters you might place in the first blank (A, S, C, E, N, or T):

$$\underline{6} \times \underline{} \times \underline{} \times \underline{} \times \underline{} \times \underline{}$$

No matter which letter you placed there, there will be 5 possibilities for the next blank:

$$\underline{6} \times \underline{5} \times \underline{} \times \underline{} \times \underline{} \times \underline{}$$

There will be 4 for the next, 3 thereafter, 2 after that, and just 1 letter left for the last:

$$\underline{6} \times \underline{5} \times \underline{4} \times \underline{3} \times \underline{2} \times \underline{1} = 720$$

Notice that you wind up reproducing the arrangements formula, $n!$. It's quite possible to solve most permutation problems without figuring out the right formula ahead of time, although knowing the formulas can save you time on Test Day.

Example: There are 6 children at a family reunion, 3 boys and 3 girls. They will be lined up single-file for a photo, alternating genders. How many arrangements of the children are possible for this photo?

You may not be sure how to approach this with a formula, so draw a picture. You know you'll have 6 "blanks," but you don't know whether to begin with a boy or with a girl. It could be either one. So try both:

bgbgbg or *gbgbgb*

$$\underline{} \times \underline{} \times \underline{} \times \underline{} \times \underline{} \times \underline{} + \underline{} \times \underline{} \times \underline{} \times \underline{} \times \underline{} \times \underline{}$$

Any of the 3 boys could go in the first spot, and any of the 3 girls in the second:

$$\underline{3} \times \underline{3} \times \underline{} \times \underline{} \times \underline{} \times \underline{} + \underline{} \times \underline{} \times \underline{} \times \underline{} \times \underline{} \times \underline{}$$

The next spot can be filled with either of the remaining 2 boys; the one after by either of the 2 remaining girls. Then the last boy and the last girl take their places:

$$\underline{3} \times \underline{3} \times \underline{2} \times \underline{2} \times \underline{1} \times \underline{1} + \underline{} \times \underline{} \times \underline{} \times \underline{} \times \underline{} \times \underline{}$$

That's the boy-first possibility. The same numbers of boys and girls apply to the girl-first possibility, and so you get:

$$\underline{3} \times \underline{3} \times \underline{2} \times \underline{2} \times \underline{1} \times \underline{1} + \underline{3} \times \underline{3} \times \underline{2} \times \underline{2} \times \underline{1} \times \underline{1}$$

$$9 \times 4 \times 1 + 9 \times 4 \times 1$$

$36 + 36 = 72$ possible arrangements of 3 boys and 3 girls, alternating genders.

HYBRIDS OF COMBINATIONS AND PERMUTATIONS

Some questions involve elements of both ordered and unordered selection.

Example: How many ways are there to arrange the letters in the word ASSETS?

Earlier you saw that the rearrangement of ASCENT was a permutation. But what about ASSETS? The order of the E, the A, the T, and the S's matter... but the order of the three S's themselves does not.

Think about it this way: put a "tag" on the S's... $AS_1S_2ETS_3$. If you just calculated 6! again, you'd be counting $AS_1S_2ETS_3$ and $AS_3S_1ETS_2$ as different words, even though with the tags gone, you can clearly see that they aren't (ASSETS is the same as ASSETS). So you'll need to eliminate all the redundant arrangements from the 6! total.

Since there are 3 S's in the word ASSETS, there are 3! ways to rearrange those S's without changing the word. You need to count every group of 3! within the 6! total as only 1 arrangement.

So instead of 6! arrangements, as there were for ASCENT, the word ASSETS has $\frac{6!}{3!}$.

$$\frac{6!}{3!} = \frac{6 \times 5 \times 4 \times 3 \times 2 \times 1}{3 \times 2 \times 1} = 6 \times 5 \times 4 = 120$$

The same logic would apply to the arrangements of ASSESS: $\frac{6!}{4!}$.

And if two letters repeat, you need two corrections to eliminate the redundant arrangements. For instance, the number of arrangements of the letters in the word REASSESS is $\frac{8!}{4!2!}$.

Some tricky GMAT problems boil down to this "rearranging letters" problem.

Example: A restaurant is hanging 7 large tiles on its wall in a single row. How many arrangements of tiles are possible if there are 3 white tiles and 4 blue tiles?

This problem essentially asks for the arrangements of *WWWBBBB*. Remember that although there are 7 total tiles to arrange, all the white tiles are indistinguishable from one another, as are the blue tiles. Therefore, you will need to divide out the number of redundant arrangements from the 7! total arrangements:

$$\frac{7!}{3!4!} = \frac{7 \times 6 \times 5 \times 4 \times 3 \times 2 \times 1}{3 \times 2 \times 1 \times 4 \times 3 \times 2 \times 1}$$

Did you notice that $\frac{7!}{3!4!}$ is the same as $_7C_3$? Which is also the same as $_7C_4$, $\frac{7!}{4!3!}$?

Whether you think "rearrange *WWWBBBB*," "choose 4 of the 7 tiles to be blue (the rest will be white)," or "choose 3 of the 7 tiles to be white (the rest will be blue)," the result is the same. As you'll soon see, many probability questions involve just this kind of calculation.

In-Format Question: Combinations and Permutations on the GMAT

Now let's use the Kaplan Method on a Problem Solving question dealing with combinations and permutations:

Six children, Arya, Betsy, Chen, Daniel, Emily, and Franco, are to be seated in a single row of six chairs. If Betsy cannot sit next to Emily, how many different arrangements of the six children are possible?

- ○ 240
- ○ 480
- ○ 540
- ○ 720
- ○ 840

Step 1: Analyze the Question

You have to arrange 6 children in 6 chairs, but 2 of the children can't sit together. You're asked to calculate the number of different arrangements of children.

Step 2: State the Task

You need to calculate the total number of possible arrangements of the children. Then, you'll subtract the number of ways Betsy can sit next to Emily.

Step 3: Approach Strategically

The possible number of arrangements of 6 elements is $6! = 6 \times 5 \times 4 \times 3 \times 2 \times 1 = 720$.

Now you'll have to calculate the number of arrangements that would violate the question stem by putting Betsy next to Emily. If you number the seats from left to right, there are 5 ways they could sit together if Betsy is on the left and Emily is on the right:

Seats 1 & 2

Seats 2 & 3

Seats 3 & 4

Seats 4 & 5

Seats 5 & 6

And there are 5 more ways if Emily is on the left and Betsy is on the right, for a total of 10. Now, for any one of those 10 ways, the 4 remaining children can be seated in 4! ways: $4! = 4 \times 3 \times 2 \times 1 = 24$. So you need to subtract $24 \times 10 = 240$ ways that have Betsy and Emily sitting together from your original total of 720: $720 - 240 = 480$. The correct answer is **(B)**.

Step 4: Confirm Your Answer

You made several calculations for this problem, so review your work to confirm your calculations are correct.

TAKEAWAYS: COMBINATIONS AND PERMUTATIONS

- The combination formula, $_nC_k = \frac{n!}{k!(n-k)!}$, gives the number of **unordered** subgroups of k items that can be selected from a group of n different items, where $k \leq n$. If n is a positive integer, $n!$ is the product of the first n positive integers.

- The permutation formula, $_nP_k = \frac{n!}{(n-k)!}$, gives the number of **ordered** subgroups of k items that can be made from a set of n different items, where $k \leq n$.

- The number of possible arrangements of n different items is $n!$.

PRACTICE SET: COMBINATIONS AND PERMUTATIONS ON THE GMAT

9. Amanda goes to the toy store to buy 1 ball and 3 different board games. If the toy store is stocked with 3 types of balls and 6 types of board games, how many different selections of the 4 items can Amanda make?

   ○ 9
   ○ 12
   ○ 14
   ○ 15
   ○ 60

10. There are 6 identical chips, each of which has 1 red side and 1 blue side. How many more ways are there to arrange the chips with 3 red sides and 3 blue sides showing than there are to arrange the chips with 4 red sides and 2 blue sides showing?

    ○ 3
    ○ 5
    ○ 6
    ○ 15
    ○ 20

11. Each of the coins in a collection is distinct and is either silver or gold. In how many different ways could all of the coins be displayed in a row, if no 2 coins of the same color could be adjacent?

    (1) The display contains an equal number of gold and silver coins.
    (2) If only the silver coins were displayed, 5,040 different arrangements of the silver coins would be possible.

12. Of the 5 distinguishable wires that lead into an apartment, 2 are for cable television service and 3 are for telephone service. Using these wires, how many distinct combinations of 3 wires are there such that at least 1 of the wires is for cable television?

   ○   6
   ○   7
   ○   8
   ○   9
   ○   10

PROBABILITY

Probability is the likelihood that a desired outcome will occur.

$$\text{Probability} = \frac{\text{Number of desired outcomes}}{\text{Number of total possible outcomes}}$$

Example: If you have 12 shirts in a drawer and 9 of them are white, the probability of picking a white shirt at random is $\frac{9}{12} = \frac{3}{4}$. The probability can also be expressed as 0.75 or 75%.

To find the probability that one or another of mutually exclusive events occurs, add the probabilities of the events.

Example: Of the 12 shirts in a drawer, 4 are white, 5 are blue, and 3 are green. If you choose one shirt at random, what is the probability that the shirt you choose is either white or green?

If you choose only one shirt, that shirt cannot be more than one color. This is what the phrase "mutually exclusive events" means; the shirt you choose will either be white, or blue, or green. In this case, the desired outcomes are white and green. The probability of picking a white shirt at random is $\frac{4}{12}$. The probability of picking a green shirt at random is $\frac{3}{12}$. The probability that the chosen shirt is either white or green is therefore $\frac{4}{12} + \frac{3}{12} = \frac{7}{12}$.

Many hard probability questions involve finding the probability of a certain outcome after multiple repetitions of the same experiment or different experiments (a coin being tossed several times, etc.).

Broadly speaking, there are five approaches you can take to probability questions.

APPROACH 1

Multiply the probabilities of individual events.

This works best when you know the probability for each event and you need to find the probability of all the events occurring (e.g., the probability that the first flip of a coin lands heads up and the second flip lands tails up). Make sure to pay attention to what effect, if any, the outcome of the first event has on the second, the second on the third, and so on.

Example: If 3 students are chosen at random from a class with 6 girls and 4 boys, what is the probability that all 3 students chosen will be girls?

The probability that the first student chosen will be a girl is $\frac{6}{10}$, or $\frac{3}{5}$.

After that girl is chosen, there are 9 students remaining, 5 of whom are girls. So the probability of choosing a girl for the second student is $\frac{5}{9}$.

Finally, for the third pick, there are 8 total students remaining, 4 of whom are girls. The probability of choosing a girl for the third student is therefore $\frac{4}{8} = \frac{1}{2}$.

The probability that all 3 students chosen will be girls is $\frac{3}{5} \times \frac{5}{9} \times \frac{1}{2} = \frac{15}{90} = \frac{1}{6}$.

Approach 2

Subtract the probability of the *undesired* outcomes from the total.

This approach works best when you cannot readily calculate the probability of the desired outcomes but you can readily do so for the undesired ones. In probability, the total of all possible outcomes is always 1.

Example: If a fair coin is flipped 3 times, what is the probability of getting at least 1 tail?

Note that "fair" means that every outcome is equally possible. A fair coin will land heads up 50 percent of the time.

What's desired is 1 tail, 2 tails, or 3 tails in 3 flips. That's a lot to keep track of. But what's undesired is very clear—3 heads in a row.

Total − Undesired

$1 - HHH$

$1 - \frac{1}{2} \times \frac{1}{2} \times \frac{1}{2}$

$1 - \frac{1}{8}$

$\frac{7}{8}$

The "Total − Undesired" approach works well for many kinds of GMAT questions, not just for probability. For example, if a question presented a circle inscribed in a square, it's how you'd calculate the area of the parts of the figure that were inside the square but outside the circle—you'd subtract the area of the circle from the area of the square.

Approach 3

Solve for the probability of one possible desired outcome, then multiply by all the permutations of that outcome.

This works best when you need to know the probability that an event will occur a certain number of times, but the order of those occurrences doesn't matter.

Example: If a fair coin is flipped 5 times, what is the probability of getting exactly 3 heads?

It's clear what you desire—3 heads and 2 tails—but you don't have to get it in any particular order. *HTHTH* would be fine, as would *HHHTT*, *TTHHH*, and so forth. So Approach #1 wouldn't work well for this problem. But you can use Approach #1 to figure out the probability of *one* of these outcomes:

$$\frac{1}{2} \times \frac{1}{2} \times \frac{1}{2} \times \frac{1}{2} \times \frac{1}{2} = \frac{1}{32}$$

Now you can multiply this result by the number of ways you could get this outcome—in other words, by the number of ways you could rearrange the letters in *HHHTT*. You saw how to do this earlier, in our discussion of "hybrid combinations and permutations" problems a few pages ago.

Use the combinations formula to solve for the number of arrangements of *HHHTT* (which is the same as calculating the total number of arrangements, 5!, and dividing out the indistinguishable outcomes):

$$\frac{5!}{3!2!} = \frac{5 \times 4 \times 3 \times 2 \times 1}{3 \times 2 \times 1 \times 2 \times 1} = 5 \times 2 = 10$$

There are 10 different ways to get 3 heads and 2 tails. Each one of those outcomes has a probability of $\frac{1}{32}$.

The probability of getting exactly 3 heads in 5 coin flips is $\frac{1}{32} \times 10 = \frac{5}{16}$.

APPROACH 4

You could work with the numerator and denominator of the probability formula separately, then lump the results together into one calculation. You calculate the total number of possible outcomes and the total number of desired outcomes, then put them together in one big fraction (instead of multiplying lots of little fractions together).

Like Approach 3, this one also works best when what you want is very specific but the order in which it happens is not.

Example: A bag holds 4 red marbles, 5 blue marbles, and 2 green marbles. If 5 marbles are selected one after another without replacement, what is the probability of drawing 2 red marbles, 2 blue marbles, and 1 green marble?

$$\text{Probability} = \frac{\text{Number of desired outcomes}}{\text{Number of total possible outcomes}}$$

Start by thinking about the possible outcomes. You are reaching into a bag of 11 marbles and pulling out 5. (The fact that they are pulled out one by one doesn't change anything; in the end, you still have 5 marbles.) Quite literally, this is "11 choose 5," $_{11}C_5$.

$$\text{\# possible selections} = {_{11}C_5} = \frac{11!}{5!6!} = \frac{11 \times 10 \times 9 \times 8 \times 7 \times 6 \times 5 \times 4 \times 3 \times 2 \times 1}{5 \times 4 \times 3 \times 2 \times 1 \times 6 \times 5 \times 4 \times 3 \times 2 \times 1} = 11 \times 2 \times 3 \times 7$$

Save yourself some work: don't multiply out factors that may later cancel. You can leave the expression as $11 \times 2 \times 3 \times 7$ for now.

Now, what is desired? You want 2 of the 4 red marbles, literally "4 choose 2," or $_4C_2$. You also want 2 of the 5 blue marbles ($_5C_2$) and 1 of the 2 green marbles ($_2C_1$).

$$\text{\# desired selections} = {_4C_2} \text{ and } {_5C_2} \text{ and } {_2C_1}$$

$$\frac{4!}{2!2!} \times \frac{5!}{2!3!} \times \frac{2!}{1!1!}$$

$$\frac{4 \times 3 \times 2 \times 1}{2 \times 1 \times 2 \times 1} \times \frac{5 \times 4 \times 3 \times 2 \times 1}{2 \times 1 \times 3 \times 2 \times 1} \times \frac{2 \times 1}{1 \times 1}$$

$$6 \times 10 \times 2$$

Now put the fraction together:

$$\frac{\text{Number of desired outcomes}}{\text{Number of total possible outcomes}} = \frac{6 \times 10 \times 2}{11 \times 2 \times 3 \times 7} = \frac{10 \times 2}{11 \times 7} = \frac{20}{77}$$

APPROACH 5

Don't do any math at all. Just count the various outcomes.

This approach works best when the numbers involved are small. In this circumstance, there's really no need to waste time thinking of the right arithmetic calculation.

Example: If a fair coin is flipped 2 times, what is the probability of getting exactly 1 head?

Two coin flips aren't very much. List out the possible results:

HH, HT, TH, or *TT*

Of these 4 possibilities, 2 have exactly 1 head—*HT* and *TH*. So the probability of getting exactly 1 head in 2 flips is $\frac{2}{4}$, or $\frac{1}{2}$.

Take your time thinking probability questions through—often the hardest part is figuring out which approach you want to take.

IN-FORMAT QUESTION: PROBABILITY ON THE GMAT

Now let's use the Kaplan Method on a Problem Solving question dealing with probability:

Robert tossed a fair coin 3 times. What is the probability that the coin landed heads up exactly twice?

O   0.125
O   0.250
O   0.375
O   0.750
O   0.875

Step 1: Analyze the Question

As with any probability question, think carefully about your approach before you start any calculations. You know that each coin flip has a $\frac{1}{2}$ chance of being heads and a $\frac{1}{2}$ chance of being tails.

Step 2: State the Task

You need to calculate the probability of exactly 2 heads in 3 flips. There are many approaches you could take. But even if you didn't see a math-based one, the low number of flips means that you could just count possibilities.

Step 3: Approach Strategically

You can write out all the ways of flipping a coin 3 times and count how many result in exactly 2 heads. As long as you are systematic about it, so you don't miss anything, you can get the answer well within 2 minutes. *HHH, HHT, HTH, HTT, THH, THT, TTH, TTT.* That's 8 possible outcomes, 3 of which have exactly 2 heads: $\frac{3}{8}$, or 0.375, is the answer.

Of course, there are math-based solutions as well. One is to calculate the probability of one desired outcome, then multiply by the number of desired outcomes. *HHT* has a probability of $\frac{1}{2} \times \frac{1}{2} \times \frac{1}{2} = \frac{1}{8}$, or 0.125. The number of ways of arranging 2 *H*s and 1 *T* is calculated in the same manner as the rearranged letter problems. In this case, that's

$$\frac{3!}{2!1!} = 3$$

So the probability of getting exactly 2 heads in 3 flips is $0.125 \times 3 = 0.375$. The answer is **(C)**.

Step 4: Confirm Your Answer

Whichever method you chose, there weren't many calculations to make. Double-check your arithmetic so that you avoid careless errors and quickly reread the question stem, confirming that you answered the question that was asked.

TAKEAWAYS: PROBABILITY

$$\text{Probability} = \frac{\text{Number of desired outcomes}}{\text{Total number of outcomes}}$$

- The sum of the probabilities of a complete set of mutually exclusive possible outcomes is 1.
- To find the probability that one *or* another of two mutually exclusive events will occur, add the probabilities of the two events.
- To find the probability that one *and* another of two independent events will occur, multiply the probabilities of the two events.
- Sometimes it is easier to subtract the probability of an event *not* occurring from 1, rather than to find directly the probability of the event occurring.

PRACTICE SET: PROBABILITY ON THE GMAT

13. A bowl has only 5 apples and 5 bananas. If 1 piece of fruit is selected from the bowl at random, and a second piece is selected from the bowl without replacing the first, what is the probability that both pieces of fruit chosen are apples?

    ○ $\frac{1}{10}$

    ○ $\frac{1}{5}$

    ○ $\frac{2}{9}$

    ○ $\frac{2}{5}$

    ○ $\frac{1}{2}$

14. A fair coin is tossed 5 times. What is the probability that it lands heads up at least twice?

    ○ $\frac{1}{16}$

    ○ $\frac{3}{16}$

    ○ $\frac{2}{5}$

    ○ $\frac{13}{16}$

    ○ $\frac{27}{32}$

15. A student is entered in a college housing lottery for two consecutive years. What is the probability that the student receives housing through the lottery for at least one of these years?

    (1) Of the students in the lottery, 80 percent do not receive housing through the lottery in any given year.

    (2) Each year, 1 of 5 students receives housing through the lottery.

16. A bag contains 4 red marbles and 5 marbles of other colors. A second bag contains 3 red marbles and 6 marbles of other colors. If 1 marble is selected at random from each bag, what is the probability that exactly 1 of the marbles will be red?

    ○ $\dfrac{4}{27}$

    ○ $\dfrac{7}{18}$

    ○ $\dfrac{13}{27}$

    ○ $\dfrac{17}{27}$

    ○ $\dfrac{55}{81}$

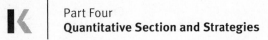
ANSWERS AND EXPLANATIONS

1.	A	7.	A	13.	C
2.	D	8.	C	14.	D
3.	E	9.	E	15.	D
4.	B	10.	B	16.	C
5.	D	11.	C		
6.	B	12.	D		

1. **(A)**

Set S contains the elements $\{-4, x, 0, 17, 1\}$. What is the median of set S?

(1) $x > 1$
(2) $x < 2$

Step 1: Analyze the Question Stem

In this Value question, you are asked to determine the median of Set S. The median of a set with an odd number of terms is the middle term when the terms are arranged in ascending or descending order. Sufficiency means being able to determine one and only one value for the median.

Step 2: Evaluate the Statements Using 12TEN

Statement (1) states that $x > 1$. This results in either the set $\{-4, 0, 1, x, 17\}$ or the set $\{-4, 0, 1, 17, x\}$. In either case, the median is 1, so this statement is sufficient. Eliminate **(B)**, **(C)**, and **(E)**.

Statement (2) states that $x < 2$. If $x < 0$, the set could be $\{x, -4, 0, 1, 17\}$ or $\{-4, x, 0, 1, 17\}$; either way, the median is 0. However, if $0 < x < 1$, the set is $\{-4, 0, x, 1, 17\}$ and the median is x. If $1 < x < 2$, the set is $\{-4, 0, 1, x, 17\}$ and the median is 1. This statement permits multiple possibilities for the median, so it is insufficient. Eliminate **(D)**.

Statement (1) alone is sufficient, so the correct answer is **(A)**.

2. **(D)**

If the range of the eight numbers 17, 8, 14, 28, 9, 4, 11, and n is 25, what is the difference between the greatest possible value of n and the least possible value of n?

- ○ 1
- ○ 3
- ○ 21
- ○ 26
- ○ 29

Step 1: Analyze the Question

By saying that the range of these eight numbers is 25, this question is saying that the difference between the largest and smallest value is 25. The range of the seven known numbers in the set is $28 - 4 = 24$. Thus, n must be either the largest number or the smallest number in the set.

Step 2: State the Task

Determine how far n can be from the smallest known value and the largest known value in the set and then find the difference between those distances.

Step 3: Approach Strategically

List the known numbers in order, leaving spaces to visualize where n might be in the list: __, 4, 8, 9, 11, 14, 17, 28, __. The largest known value is 28, so if that were the largest value of all eight numbers, n would have to be $28 - 25 = 3$. On the other hand, the smallest known value is 4, so if that were the smallest value, n would have to be $4 + 25 = 29$. Thus, n could either be 3 or 29. Therefore, the difference between the largest and smallest possible values of n is $29 - 3 = 26$. The correct answer is **(D)**.

Step 4: Confirm Your Answer

Review the order of numbers on your list and confirm your calculations. Finally, make sure you answered the question asked, which is not about a possible value of n—**(B)** and **(E)** represent n's possible values—but the difference between its possible values.

3. (E)

The range of the set {60, 120, −30, x, 0, 60} is 210. If a is the median, b is the mode, and c is the average (arithmetic mean), is a = b?

(1) abc > 0

(2) b = 60

Step 1: Analyze the Question Stem

In this Yes/No question, the range of the set {60, 120, −30, x, 0, 60} is 210. Write the given numbers of the list in increasing order and you have {−30, 0, 60, 60, 120}. Because no pair of numbers from −30, 0, 60, 60, and 120 differs by 210, you must have one of these possibilities:

If x < −30, then 120 − x = 210, in which case x = −90.

If x > 120, then x − (−30) = 210, in which case x = 180.

These are the only possible values of x. Your task is now much clearer. You must determine if x is equal to either of these values. Now look at the statements.

Step 2: Evaluate the Statements Using 12TEN

Statement (1): You are told that abc > 0. You can test your two possible values for x to determine whether this is sufficient.

If x = −90, then the members of the list written in increasing order are −90, −30, 0, 60, 60, 120. The median a is $\frac{0+60}{2}$ = 30, so the median is positive.

The mode b is 60, which is positive. The average c of the numbers is also positive. Statement (1) is true because abc is positive, and it is not true that a = b. In this case, the answer to the question is no.

If x = 180, then the members of the list written in increasing order are −30, 0, 60, 60, 120, and 180. Here, the median a is 60, so the median is positive.

The mode b is 60, which is positive. The average c of the numbers is also positive. So here, Statement (1) is true because abc is positive, and it is true that a = b. In this case, the answer to the question is yes.

Because different answers to the question are possible, Statement (1) is insufficient. Eliminate **(A)** and **(D)**.

Statement (2): From Statement (1), you have seen that if x = −90, then the members of the list written in increasing order are −90, −30, 0, 60, 60, and 120. Statement (2) is true because the mode b is 60. The median a is 30, which is not equal to the mode b. In this case, the answer to the question is no.

You have also seen that if x = 180, then the members of the list written in increasing order are −30, 0, 60, 60, 120, 180. Statement (2) is true because the mode b is 60. The median a is 60, which is equal to the mode b, which is 60. In this case, the answer to the question is yes.

Because different answers to the question are possible, Statement (2) is insufficient. Eliminate **(B)**.

Each statement permitted both x = 180 and x = −90. So when combined, both values are still possible. The statements together are insufficient, so **(E)** is correct.

4. (B)

If $x \leq 4$ and $y \geq 10$, what is the range of the numbers in the set $\{5, 8, x, y\}$?

(1) $3x + 5y = 72$

(2) $-7x + 7y = 56$

Step 1: Analyze the Question Stem

This is a Value question. You're asked for the range of numbers in a set that includes two variables, and you're given inequalities expressing the range of possible values for each of the variables. The inequalities allow you to arrange the numbers in the set from smallest to largest: $x, 5, 8, y$. Remembering that the definition of the range of a set of numbers is the difference between the largest and smallest value, there are two ways you'll be able to answer the question with a single value: get the individual values of x and y, or find the value of the expression $y - x$.

Step 2: Evaluate the Statements Using 12TEN

Picking numbers illustrates that Statement (1) is insufficient. If, for example, $x = 0$, you would get $3(0) + 5y = 72$. This is just the same as saying that $5y = 72$. Dividing each side by 5 leaves you with $y = 14.4$, so $y - x$ would equal 14.4. The exact calculation is unimportant. For a Value question, you just need to confirm that another permissible pair of numbers will yield a different result to know that the statement is insufficient. Try $x = 4$. This gives you $3(4) + 5y = 72$. Do the multiplication and subtract 12 from each side to get $5y = 60$. Divide each side by 5, and you have $y = 12$. In this case, $y - x$ would equal 8. Since two solutions are possible, Statement (1) is insufficient. Eliminate **(A)** and **(D)**.

Simplifying Statement (2) shows that it is sufficient. Start by rewriting the equation to read $7y - 7x = 56$. Now factor out the 7 to get $7(y - x) = 56$. Divide each side by 7, and you're left with $y - x = 8$. Since the expression $y - x$ has the same value as the range of numbers in the set, Statement (2) is sufficient. The correct answer is **(B)**.

5. (D)

What is the sum of the integers 45 through 175 inclusive?

○ 12,295
○ 13,000
○ 14,300
○ 14,410
○ 28,820

Step 1: Analyze the Question

You are asked to sum up a very large list of numbers. When the GMAT presents you with seemingly onerous calculations, it generally means there is a much easier way if you apply Critical Thinking.

Step 2: State the Task

Find the sum of all the integers from 45 to 175, inclusive.

Step 3: Approach Strategically

To find the sum of a series of consecutive integers, multiply the average of the largest and smallest terms (which is equal to the average of all the terms in the set) by the total number of terms. The largest and smallest terms in this sequence are 175 and 45, and their average is $\frac{175+45}{2} = \frac{220}{2} = 110$. There are $175 - 45 + 1 = 131$ terms in the set, so the sum of all the integers in the set is $110 \times 131 = 14,410$. The correct answer is **(D)**.

Step 4: Confirm Your Answer

Double-check your calculations to ensure that you haven't made any avoidable mistakes.

6.   **(B)**

What is the sum of the multiples of 4 between 13 and 125 inclusive?

○   1,890
○   1,960
○   2,200
○   3,780
○   4,400

Step 1: Analyze the Question

When working with consecutive sets, look for ways to save time and work by recognizing patterns and first and last terms in the set.

To find the sum of terms in a set of consecutive numbers, apply the average formula:

$$\text{Average} = \frac{\text{Sum of terms}}{\text{Number of terms}}$$

$$\text{Sum of terms} = (\text{Average})(\text{Number of terms})$$

Step 2: State the Task

You need to calculate the average of the terms in the set and the number of items in the set. To do so, you need to determine the smallest and largest terms in the sequence.

Step 3: Approach Strategically

Find the largest and smallest multiple of 4 between 13 and 125. In this range, the smallest multiple of 4 is 16, and the largest is 124.

The average of a consecutive set equals the average of the smallest and largest terms. The average of these two numbers is

$$\frac{16 + 124}{2} = \frac{140}{2} = 70$$

So the average of all terms in this set is 70.

Now find the number of multiples of 4 between 16 and 124 inclusive. You could simply list all of the terms in the sequence, but that would be time-consuming. A great shortcut to determine this value is to find the difference between the smallest and largest terms and add 1. Because the numbers in this set are multiples of 4, you must divide the difference by 4 before adding 1.

The number of terms in this set is

$$\frac{124 - 16}{4} + 1 = \frac{108}{4} + 1 = 27 + 1 = 28$$

There are 28 multiples of 4 between 16 and 124 inclusive.

So the average of the terms in the set is 70, and the number of terms in the set is 28. The sum of the terms in the set is simply the product of these two values:

$$28 \times 70 = 1,960$$

(B) is correct.

Step 4: Confirm Your Answer

Pay careful attention to the wording of this question stem. The set is inclusive, so confirm that you added 1 when you calculated the number of terms.

7. (A)

If t is the sum of three consecutive positive integers, is t a multiple of 24?

(1) The smallest of the three integers is even.

(2) t is a multiple of 3.

Step 1: Analyze the Question Stem

This is a Yes/No question. If t is the sum of three consecutive positive integers, you can call the smallest integer x and write the other 2 as $(x + 1)$ and $(x + 2)$, respectively. Therefore, the sum of the three consecutive integers is $x + (x + 1) + (x + 2)$ or, combining like terms, $3x + 3$. Finally, you can factor and get $3(x + 1)$.

So the question really asks, "Is $3(x + 1)$ a multiple of 24?"

Step 2: Evaluate the Statements Using 12TEN

Statement (1): You are told that x is an even number. If x is even, then $x + 1$ must be odd since an even plus an odd is always odd. Also, an odd times an odd is always odd; therefore, $3(x + 1)$ is odd. Since an odd number is never divisible by an even number, $3(x + 1)$ *cannot* be a multiple of 24. Hence, the answer is always no, and Statement (1) is sufficient. Eliminate **(B)**, **(C)**, and **(E)**.

8. (C)

The sum of a sequence of six consecutive positive integers is Z. The sum of terms in a different sequence of five consecutive integers is $Z - 5$. If the greatest term of the five-number sequence is 40, what is the difference between the median term of the five-number sequence and the least term of the six-number sequence?

- ○ 5
- ○ 7
- ○ 8
- ○ 9
- ○ 10

Step 1: Analyze the Question

There are two sequences of integers. The sum of the sequence with six consecutive integers is Z. The second sequence consists of five consecutive integers, the sum of which is $Z - 5$. The greatest integer in this latter sequence is 40.

Step 2: State the Task

Determine the difference between the median, or middle, term of the five-number sequence and the smallest term of the six-number sequence.

Step 3: Approach Strategically

If the greatest term in the five-number sequence is 40, that sequence must be 36, 37, 38, 39, 40. The sum of a sequence of integers is the average (arithmetic mean) times the number of terms. Since this sequence has an odd number of consecutive terms, the middle or median value, 38, is also the mean. Thus, the sum of terms in this sequence is $38 \times 5 = 190$. Since this sum is equivalent to $Z - 5$, $Z = 195$.

Since the sum of terms in the six-term sequence is 195, then using the formula $\text{Average} = \frac{\text{Sum of terms}}{\text{Number of terms}}$ yields $195 \div 6 = 32.5$. This sequence has an even number of terms, so the mean is the average of the two middle terms when all of the terms are arranged in numeric order. Therefore, the third and fourth terms in the sequence must be 32 and 33, and the entire sequence is 30, 31, 32, 33, 34, 35. Thus, the difference between the third term of the five-number sequence (38) and the smallest term of the six-number sequence (30) is 8, which is **(C)**.

Step 4: Confirm Your Answer

Go back over the question stem to make sure that you didn't misread anything. Then check your determination of the sequences to make sure you selected the correct values to compare.

9.   **(E)**

Amanda goes to the toy store to buy 1 ball and 3 different board games. If the toy store is stocked with 3 types of balls and 6 types of board games, how many different selections of the 4 items can Amanda make?

○   9
○   12
○   14
○   15
○   60

Step 1: Analyze the Question

Amanda is buying 1 ball and 3 different board games from a selection of 3 balls and 6 types of board games. Since you are solving for the number of different subgroups that can be chosen from a group, this appears to be a combinations or permutations question.

Step 2: State the Task

You need to find the number of different selections of 4 items that Amanda can make.

Step 3: Approach Strategically

Amanda is choosing 3 board games from a total of 6, so you can use the combination formula (since a different arrangement of the same board games is not considered a different selection) to find the number of combinations of board games:

$$_nC_k = \frac{n!}{k!(n-k)!}$$

$$_6C_3 = \frac{6!}{3!(6-3)!}$$

$$_6C_3 = \frac{\cancel{6} \times 5 \times 4 \times \cancel{3!}}{\cancel{3!} \times \cancel{3!}}$$

$$_6C_3 = 20$$

There are 20 ways for Amanda to choose 3 board games from a total of 6. For each of those 20 ways, Amanda can choose 1 of 3 balls, so there are $20 \times 3 = 60$ different ways for Amanda to choose 1 ball and 3 games from 3 balls and 6 games. **(E)** is correct.

Step 4: Confirm Your Answer

With combinations and permutations questions, check to ensure that you used the correct formula and that you didn't make a mistake when canceling out terms from the numerator and denominator.

10. **(B)**

There are 6 identical chips, each of which has 1 red side and 1 blue side. How many more ways are there to arrange the chips with 3 red sides and 3 blue sides showing than there are to arrange the chips with 4 red sides and 2 blue sides showing?

- ○ 3
- ○ 5
- ○ 6
- ○ 15
- ○ 20

Step 1: Analyze the Question

The question states that there are 6 identical chips, each with a red side and a blue side. Since the chips are identical, there is no way to distinguish among any chips with the same color showing.

Step 2: State the Task

Determine the difference between the number of ways that 3 red-sided and 3 blue-sided chips can be arranged and the number of ways 4 red-sided and 2 blue-sided chips can be arranged.

Step 3: Approach Strategically

If the chips were all different from each other, there would be 6! ways to arrange them. However, that number must be reduced by factors that represent the number of ways that the red sides can be arranged and the blue sides can be arranged, since all of these configurations are identical.

For 3 of each color, divide 6! by 3! twice to represent the indistinguishable arrangements of 3 blue and 3 red chips. Thus, the number of ways to arrange the chips is $\frac{6!}{3!(3!)} = \frac{6 \times 5 \times 4}{3 \times 2 \times 1} = 5 \times 4 = 20$. Similarly, the number of ways to arrange 4 reds and 2 blues is $\frac{6!}{4!(2!)} = \frac{6 \times 5}{2 \times 1} = 3 \times 5 = 15$. Since $20 - 15 = 5$, **(B)** is correct.

Step 4: Confirm Your Answer

Check that you answered the question that is actually asked. **(C)** is merely the number of chips, and **(D)** and **(E)** represent the number of arrangements for each of the 2 configurations.

11. **(C)**

Each of the coins in a collection is distinct and is either silver or gold. In how many different ways could all of the coins be displayed in a row, if no 2 coins of the same color could be adjacent?

(1) The display contains an equal number of gold and silver coins.

(2) If only the silver coins were displayed, 5,040 different arrangements of the silver coins would be possible.

Step 1: Analyze the Question Stem

This is a Value question. You know that all the coins are distinguishable from one another and that every coin is gold or silver. No gold coins can be adjacent, and no silver coins can be adjacent. The question asks whether you can determine how many arrangements are possible. If you are given information that will lead you to a single number of possible arrangements, then you have sufficiency. If the given information leads to more than one possible number of arrangements, then you have insufficiency. Now look at the statements.

Step 2: Evaluate the Statements Using 12TEN

Statement (1): You are told that the display contains an equal number of gold and silver coins. Because there are many more possible displays if there are 10 gold coins and 10 silver coins than if there are 3 gold coins and 3 silver coins, there is more than one possible answer to the question. Statement (1) is insufficient. Eliminate **(A)** and **(D)**.

Statement (2): You are told that 5,040 different arrangements of only the silver coins are possible. If you let n be the number of silver coins, then $n! = 5,040$. This will lead to a unique value for n. (Actually, $n = 7$, because $7! = 5,040$. However, you do not have to determine the value of n.)

From this, you could determine the number of possible arrangements of n silver coins and n gold. But what if there were $n + 1$ or $n - 1$ gold coins? You would then have a different number of possible arrangements while still obeying the restrictions in the question stem. You can eliminate **(B)**.

Combine statements: You know that equal numbers of gold and silver coins are to be displayed, and you can determine the number of silver coins to be displayed. Therefore, you also know the number of gold coins. Since you know the numbers of each kind of coin, you could calculate their arrangements. Happily, since this isn't Problem Solving, you don't actually have to do the calculation. The statements together are sufficient, so **(C)** is the answer.

12. (D)

Of the 5 distinguishable wires that lead into an apartment, 2 are for cable television service and 3 are for telephone service. Using these wires, how many distinct combinations of 3 wires are there such that at least 1 of the wires is for cable television?

- ○ 6
- ○ 7
- ○ 8
- ○ 9
- ○ 10

Step 1: Analyze the Question

For any question that asks you to make subsets or groups of a larger pool of items, pay careful attention to the wording of the question stem. You need to determine whether the order of the items in each subgroup matters. In this question, you are asked to make distinct combinations of 3 wires from a set of 5 wires. Because you want distinct combinations, the order of the wires will not matter, and you can apply the combinations formula to solve the question. Notice the phrase "at least" in the question stem. When questions use that phrase, solving for the total and then subtracting the undesired outcomes is usually a very efficient approach. The total is the number of ways one could select any 3 wires from 5. The undesired outcome is selecting only telephone wires.

Step 2: State the Task

Apply the combinations formula to determine how many subsets of 3 wires can be created from the pool of 5 wires. Then determine how many ways there are to select only 3 telephone wires and subtract.

Step 3: Approach Strategically

Use the combinations formula, $\frac{n!}{k!(n-k)!}$, to find the total number of ways to choose 3 wires out of 5. Substituting 5 for n and 3 for k, you find that the total number of ways to choose 3 wires out of 5 is

$$\frac{5!}{3!(5-3)!} = \frac{5!}{3!2!} = \frac{5(4)(3!)}{3!2!} = \frac{5(4)}{2} = 5(2) = 10$$

You now know that there are 10 subsets of 3 wires. Now turn your attention to what is undesired—selecting only telephone wires. Because there are only 3 telephone wires, there is only 1 possible way to choose 3 of the 5 wires such that all are telephone wires. Thus, there are $10 - 1 = 9$ ways to choose 3 wires such that at least 1 of the wires would be for cable. **(D)** is correct.

Step 4: Confirm Your Answer

Pay careful attention to exactly what the question stem is asking. Notice that **(E)** is a trap for the unwary test taker who simply calculates the total number of possible outcomes.

13. (C)

A bowl has only 5 apples and 5 bananas. If 1 piece of fruit is selected from the bowl at random, and a second piece is selected from the bowl without replacing the first, what is the probability that both pieces of fruit chosen are apples?

- ○ $\frac{1}{10}$
- ○ $\frac{1}{5}$
- ○ $\frac{2}{9}$
- ○ $\frac{2}{5}$
- ○ $\frac{1}{2}$

Step 1: Analyze the Question

Two pieces of fruit are randomly chosen, one at a time without replacement, from a bowl containing 5 apples and 5 bananas.

Step 2: State the Task

Find the probability of selecting 2 apples.

Step 3: Approach Strategically

There are 5 apples and 5 bananas in the bowl, so the probability of choosing the first apple is $\frac{5}{10} = \frac{1}{2}$. After removing the apple, there are now 4 apples and 5 bananas left, so the probability of selecting the second apple is $\frac{4}{9}$. To find the probability of both events happening, multiply the probabilities: $\frac{1}{\cancel{2}_1} + \frac{\cancel{4}^2}{9} = \frac{2}{9}$. **(C)** is correct.

Step 4: Confirm Your Answer

Reread the question stem to ensure that you understood the scenario correctly and double-check that you didn't make any avoidable mistakes in calculating the probabilities.

14. (D)

A fair coin is tossed 5 times. What is the probability that it lands heads up at least twice?

- ○ $\frac{1}{16}$
- ○ $\frac{3}{16}$
- ○ $\frac{2}{5}$
- ○ $\frac{13}{16}$
- ○ $\frac{27}{32}$

Step 1: Analyze the Question

In this question, you must analyze the various scenarios in which a coin lands heads up at least twice in 5 tosses. However, keep in mind that with many probability questions, it is sometimes easier to calculate the probability of the situation *not* occurring and subtract this probability from 1. As you think through the various scenarios that can occur, determine whether there are fewer scenarios that will not occur. If so, working out the undesired probabilities will save you time on Test Day.

Step 2: State the Task

Determine the probability of each undesired outcome, then subtract the sum of these values from 1 to calculate the probability the question stem asks for.

Step 3: Approach Strategically

To determine the probability of at least 2 heads in 5 tosses, you must calculate the sum of the following probabilities: exactly 2 heads, exactly 3 heads, exactly 4 heads, and exactly 5 heads.

On the other hand, the undesired outcome can occur in only 2 possible ways: exactly 1 head is tossed, or no heads are tossed. This will be much simpler to calculate.

No heads: since the probability of heads or tails is $\frac{1}{2}$ for a fair coin, the probability of no heads tossed, or all 5 tosses landing tails up, is $\frac{1}{2} \times \frac{1}{2} \times \frac{1}{2} \times \frac{1}{2} \times \frac{1}{2} = \frac{1}{32}$.

Exactly 1 head: if you let H represent heads and T represent tails, then in a sequence of 5 tosses, here are all the ways in which exactly 1 head can be tossed: *HTTTT, THTTT, TTHTT, TTTHT, TTTTH*.

Thus, in tossing a coin 5 times, the single toss of heads could occur on the first, second, third, fourth, or fifth toss. The probability of the sequence *HTTTT* occurring when a fair coin is tossed 5 times is

$$\frac{1}{2} \times \frac{1}{2} \times \frac{1}{2} \times \frac{1}{2} \times \frac{1}{2} = \frac{1}{32}$$

Now the probability of each of the sequences *HTTTT, THTTT, TTHTT, TTTHT,* and *TTTTH* is $\frac{1}{32}$, so the probability of tossing exactly 1 head is $5\left(\frac{1}{32}\right)$, which is $\frac{5}{32}$.

The probability of no heads is $\frac{1}{32}$, and the probability of exactly 1 head is $\frac{5}{32}$, so the probability of tossing fewer than 2 heads, which is the probability of tossing no heads or 1 head, is

$$\frac{1}{32} + \frac{5}{32} = \frac{6}{32} = \frac{3}{16}$$

Therefore, the probability of tossing at least 2 heads is $1 - \frac{3}{16} = \frac{13}{16}$. **(D)** is correct.

Step 4: Confirm Your Answer

While this approach is a much more efficient strategy, be careful to remember to subtract the calculated value from 1 at the end of your work. The undesired outcome is often a wrong answer trap, as seen in **(B)**.

15. **(D)**

A student is entered in a college housing lottery for two consecutive years. What is the probability that the student receives housing through the lottery for at least one of these years?

(1) Of the students in the lottery, 80 percent do not receive housing through the lottery in any given year.

(2) Each year, 1 of 5 students receives housing through the lottery.

Step 1: Analyze the Question Stem

This Value question asks for the probability that a student receives housing in at least one of two consecutive years. In order to calculate that probability, you would need to know the probability of getting housing in each year. (Another possibility that could be useful is the chance of *not* getting housing, since 1 − Undesired Probability = Desired Probability.)

Step 2: Evaluate the Statements Using 12TEN

Statement (1): This gives you the probability of *not* getting into housing. An 80% chance of not getting housing each year means a 20% chance of getting housing each year. The exact answer isn't something that you need to worry about, since this isn't Problem Solving. You know an answer can be calculated, so Statement (1) is sufficient. Eliminate choices **(B)**, **(C)**, and **(E)**.

Statement (2): This isn't given in percentage form, but any proportion will serve. This gives you the likelihood of getting housing in any given year. You now know that Statement (2), which gives you the same information that Statement (1) does, must be sufficient. **(D)** is correct.

16. (C)

A bag contains 4 red marbles and 5 marbles of other colors. A second bag contains 3 red marbles and 6 marbles of other colors. If 1 marble is selected at random from each bag, what is the probability that exactly 1 of the marbles will be red?

- $\frac{4}{27}$
- $\frac{7}{18}$
- $\frac{13}{27}$
- $\frac{17}{27}$
- $\frac{55}{81}$

Step 1: Analyze the Question

The question says that there are two different bags containing 9 marbles each. One bag contains 4 red marbles, and the other bag has 3 red marbles. A marble is selected randomly from each of the bags.

Step 2: State the Task

Determine the probability that exactly 1 of the 2 marbles that is drawn is red.

Step 3: Approach Strategically

There are two ways to select exactly 1 red marble. One way is to select a red marble from the first bag and a non-red marble from the second bag. The other way is to select a non-red marble from the first bag and a red marble from the second bag. Since the desired result can be attained in one manner or another, add these two probabilities to get the total probability of selecting exactly 1 red marble.

The probability that the red marble is chosen from the first bag is $\frac{4}{9}$, and the probability that a non-red marble is chosen from the second bag is $\frac{9-3}{9} = \frac{6}{9}$. Since both of these outcomes must occur, multiply their probabilities to get $\frac{4}{9} \times \frac{6}{9} = \frac{24}{81}$. There is no need to simplify at this point because you will be adding this to another fraction.

The probability that a non-red marble is chosen from the first bag is $\frac{9-4}{9}=\frac{5}{9}$, and the probability that a red marble is chosen from the second bag is $\frac{3}{9}$. Since both of these outcomes must occur, multiply their probabilities to get $\frac{5}{9}\times\frac{3}{9}=\frac{15}{81}$.

Now, add the probabilities of the two desired outcomes; the probability that exactly 1 of the chosen marbles is red is $\frac{24}{81}+\frac{15}{81}=\frac{39}{81}=\frac{13}{27}$. **(C)** is correct.

Step 4: Confirm Your Answer

Confirm that these two scenarios are the only two ways in which the desired outcome can occur. **(A)** is the probability that both marbles will be red, and **(D)** is the probability that one *or* both will be red.

GMAT BY THE NUMBERS: STATISTICS

Now that you've learned how to approach statistics questions on the GMAT, let's add one more dimension to your understanding of how they work.

Take a moment to try this question. Following is performance data from thousands of people who have studied with Kaplan over the decades. Through analyzing this data, we will show you how to approach questions like this one most effectively and how to avoid similarly tempting wrong answer choice types on Test Day.

A company plans to award prizes to its top 3 salespeople, with the largest prize going to the top salesperson, the next-largest prize to the next salesperson, and a smaller prize to the third-ranking salesperson. If the company has 12 salespeople on staff, how many different arrangements of winners are possible?

○   1,728
○   1,440
○   1,320
○   220
○   6

EXPLANATION

Questions that ask test takers to count possibilities are often the most frustrating. This is because most people try to shoehorn the problem into a preexisting arithmetic formula without first analyzing the problem to see whether the formula applies. Understand the question before you jump into solving.

This problem asks you to calculate the number of ways you can distribute first-, second-, and third-place prizes among 12 people. Many test takers try to apply the combinations formula here. But doing so is not appropriate because that formula counts the number of *unordered* selections one can make from a group. You're asked to *order* your selections into first-, second-, and third-place, so you need a different approach: simply count the number of possibilities for each prize.

Any of 12 people might win first place, leaving 11 possible choices for second. This leaves 10 possible winners for third. Hence, these prizes could be awarded $12 \times 11 \times 10 = 1,320$ possible ways. Choice **(C)** is correct.

QUESTION STATISTICS

3% of test takers choose **(A)**

4% of test takers choose **(B)**

58% of test takers choose **(C)**

33% of test takers choose **(D)**

2% of test takers choose **(E)**

Sample size = 5,473

Unsurprisingly, the only other commonly selected answer on this problem, choice **(D)**, is the result of erroneously applying the combinations formula to this problem. When solving a statistics question, understand the scenario before you start any arithmetic. You'll dramatically improve your odds of avoiding the common traps and selecting the right answer.

MORE GMAT BY THE NUMBERS...

To see more questions with answer choice statistics, be sure to review the full-length CATs in your online resources.

GO ONLINE

kaptest.com/login

CHAPTER 17

Math Formulas on the GMAT

If the average (arithmetic mean) of x, 25, y, and 30 is $x + y$, which of the following equals the value of x?

- ○ $18\frac{1}{3}y$

- ○ $18\frac{1}{3} + y$

- ○ $18 - \frac{3}{y}$

- ○ $y - 18\frac{1}{3}$

- ○ $18\frac{1}{3} - y$

Above is a typical Problem Solving question dealing with a commonly tested math formula. In this chapter, we'll look at how to apply the Kaplan Method to this question, discuss the common math formulas tested on the GMAT, and go over the basic principles and strategies that you want to keep in mind on every Quantitative question involving math formulas. But before you move on, take a minute to think about what you see in this question and answer some questions about how you think it works:

- What math formula is being tested in this question?

- What does the format of the answer choices tell you about your task?

- What can you infer about how the GMAT constructs questions based on common math formulas?

- What GMAT Core Competencies are most essential to success on this question?

PREVIEWING MATH FORMULAS ON THE GMAT

WHAT MATH FORMULA IS BEING TESTED IN THIS QUESTION?

This question tests your understanding of the formula to solve for the average, or arithmetic mean, of a group of values. In this case, you are told the average $(x + y)$ and are asked to solve for a missing term (x).

WHAT DOES THE FORMAT OF THE ANSWER CHOICES TELL YOU ABOUT YOUR TASK?

The answer choices are algebraic expressions, not numerical values, so you can infer that the question must not supply enough information to solve for the actual value of x. Rather, what you will solve for is x "in terms of y." All this means is that the actual value of x will vary depending on the value of y.

From the format of the answer choices, you can glean that your task on this question is to set up the average formula, plug in the information provided by the question stem into the appropriate positions in the formula, and use what you know about solving algebraic equations to isolate the variable x on one side and everything else on the other.

WHAT CAN YOU INFER ABOUT HOW THE GMAT CONSTRUCTS QUESTIONS BASED ON COMMON MATH FORMULAS?

The GMAT assumes that you have a working knowledge of several classic formulas. You should be comfortable using these so that you don't have to waste time trying to remember them on Test Day.

The GMAT tests these formulas by giving you some information that relates to a known formula and asking you for a different, missing piece of information that can be solved for using that formula.

Many of the formulas commonly tested on the GMAT have three parts. For example:

$$\text{Rate} = \frac{\text{Quantity A}}{\text{Quantity B}}$$

$$\text{Speed} = \frac{\text{Distance}}{\text{Time}}$$

$$\text{Average} = \frac{\text{Sum of terms}}{\text{Number of terms}}$$

This chapter will cover the formulas listed above, plus others. The important thing to remember is that when you are given two parts of any three-part formula, you can always solve for the missing part. Keep this in mind when you encounter a question that seems to have you stumped. Always start by figuring out what formula is at issue; then figure out what parts of the given information can be substituted into that formula. At this point, the path to the solution will usually become clear.

WHAT GMAT CORE COMPETENCIES ARE MOST ESSENTIAL TO SUCCESS ON THIS QUESTION?

As with all questions that hinge on standard mathematical formulas, you must first use your Pattern Recognition skills to identify the relevant formula. Once you've done so, Critical Thinking becomes important as you determine how the given information applies to the formula at hand. The GMAT often presents information in a less-than-intuitive way, forcing you to decode the meaning and relevance of that information to the solution.

Here are the main topics we'll cover in this chapter:

- Averages
- Rates and Speed—Converting Rates
- Rates and Speed—Multi-Part Journeys
- Combined Rates and Combined Work
- Interest Rates
- Overlapping Sets

HANDLING GMAT MATH FORMULAS

Now let's apply the Kaplan Method to the math formulas question you saw earlier:

If the average (arithmetic mean) of x, 25, y, and 30 is $x + y$, which of the following equals the value of x?

- ○ $18\frac{1}{3}y$
- ○ $18\frac{1}{3} + y$
- ○ $18 - \frac{3}{y}$
- ○ $y - 18\frac{1}{3}$
- ○ $18\frac{1}{3} - y$

Step 1: Analyze the Question

This question gives you a lot of information. You are told that the average of the four terms, x, 25, y, and 30, is $x + y$. A quick glance at the answer choices reveals that you are being asked to solve for x in terms of y.

Step 2: State the Task

You'll need to set up the average formula and then isolate x. But don't rush to the conclusion that you have to do a lot of algebra here.

Step 3: Approach Strategically

Think critically about how you can approach this problem to save time. Picking numbers is almost always a simple way to handle problems in which you need to solve for one variable in terms of another. Once you put the terms in the average formula, you can pick a number for x, solve the problem for y, and then plug that number into the answer choices to get the one that matches your choice for x. The average formula is the sum of terms divided by the number of terms. Here, that would look like this: $\frac{x + 25 + y + 30}{4} = x + y$. Multiplying both sides by 4 results in $x + 25 + y + 30 = 4(x + y)$. Distribute the 4 and you have $x + 25 + y + 30 = 4x + 4y$.

Now pick an easy number to substitute for x. Let's have $x = 1$. That gives you $1 + 25 + y + 30 = 4 + 4y$. Combine like terms, and you have $56 + y = 4 + 4y$. Doing the subtraction necessary to get y and the numbers on different sides of the equation leaves you with $52 = 3y$. Divide each side by 3, and you find that $y = 17\frac{1}{3}$. Since you chose 1 to stand in for x, all you need to do is substitute $17\frac{1}{3}$ in for y and find the answer choice that equals 1. That's choice **(E)**.

You could also have solved algebraically. Taking the equation above, $x + 25 + y + 30 = 4x + 4y$, you can continue to simplify by combining like terms until you get $55 = 3x + 3y$. Factoring out a 3 from the right side gives you $55 = 3(x + y)$, and dividing both sides by 3 results in $\frac{55}{3}$. Isolating x and converting $\frac{55}{3}$ to a mixed number results in $x = 18\frac{1}{3} - y$, which corresponds to choice **(E)**.

Step 4: Confirm Your Answer

Using picking numbers can save you valuable time on this problem. You can also solve it with pure algebra, of course, and that approach can be used to confirm your answer if you initially solve by picking numbers.

Now let's look at each of the common math formulas that show up on the GMAT Quantitative section, starting with averages.

AVERAGES

The average (arithmetic mean) of a group of numbers is defined as the sum of the values divided by the number of values.

$$\text{Average value} = \frac{\text{Sum of values}}{\text{Number of values}}$$

Example: Henry buys 3 items costing $2.00, $0.75, and $0.25. What is the average price?

$$\text{Average price} = \frac{\text{Sum of prices}}{\text{Number of prices}}$$

$$= \frac{\text{Total price}}{\text{Number of prices}}$$

$$= \frac{\$2.00 + \$0.75 + \$0.25}{3}$$

$$= \frac{\$3.00}{3}$$

$$= \$1.00$$

Balanced Average: You can save yourself a lot of laborious and error-prone calculation if you think of the average as a "balancing point" between the numbers in the series. That is, the difference between the average and every number below it will equal the difference between the average and every number above it. The "balanced average" approach dramatically reduces the difficulty of the arithmetic.

You've already seen that the average of $2.00, $0.75, and $0.25 is $1.00. Here's how that balances:

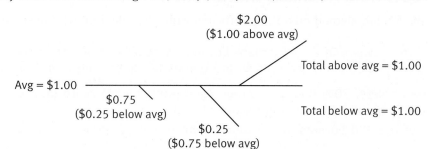

Now let's use this approach to solve a problem.

Example: The average of 43, 44, 45, and x is 45. What is the value of x?

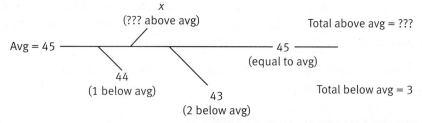

Since the amount above the average must equal the amount below the average, the amount above must be 3. Therefore, x is 3 above the average: $3 + 45 = 48$; $x = 48$.

Weighted Average: A further way to calculate averages on the GMAT is to use the "weighted average" formula:

Weighted average of n terms $=$ $(\text{Percent}_1)(\text{Average}_1) + (\text{Percent}_2)(\text{Average}_2) + \cdots + (\text{Percent}_n)(\text{Average}_n)$

Weighted averages are useful when you know the average of different portions of the whole. For example, if two-fifths of the students in a class have a GPA of 79 and the remaining three-fifths have an average of 84, you could set up the weighted average formula as follows:

$$\text{Weighted average} = (0.4)(79) + (0.6)(84)$$
$$= 31.6 + 50.4$$
$$= 82$$

Notice the average of the whole class comes out to be closer to 84 than to 79. This will always be the case when the portions of the whole are of different sizes. In fact, this is where the term "weighted average" comes from; the larger the portion of the whole, the more heavily "weighted" that portion is when calculating the overall average. Note that you can use the weighted average formula as long as you have averages for all portions adding up to 100 percent of the whole.

IN-FORMAT QUESTION: AVERAGES ON THE GMAT

Now let's use the Kaplan Method on a Data Sufficiency question dealing with averages:

> If each of the bowlers in a tournament bowled an equal number of games, what is the average (arithmetic mean) score of all the games bowled in the tournament?
>
> (1) Of the bowlers, 70% had an average (arithmetic mean) score of 120, and the other 30% had an average score of 140.
>
> (2) Each of the 350 bowlers in the tournament bowled 3 games.

Step 1: Analyze the Question Stem

First, determine the type of Data Sufficiency question you're dealing with. You need one exact value for the average score of the games, so this a Value question.

There's no direct simplification to be done, but the fact that you're asked for an average should alert you to the possibility that you can get the answer in a variety of ways—either through direct calculation of the scores or through a weighted average approach.

To answer the question, you'll need either the number of games and the total of the scores or some way to calculate a weighted average.

Step 2: Evaluate the Statements Using 12TEN

Statement (2) is very straightforward, so starting there makes sense. This tells you the number of games but nothing about the scores. Insufficient. Eliminate **(B)** and **(D)**.

Statement (1) doesn't allow you to figure out exactly the number of games or the exact sum of the scores. But since the proportions add up to 100% of the total, and since all the bowlers bowled the same number of games, you can calculate the overall average using the weighted average approach. Sufficient. The answer is **(A)**.

Remember, you don't actually want to calculate the average, just know that you could. That calculation would be: overall average $= 0.7(120) + 0.3(140)$.

The GMAT rewards those who think critically and find the most efficient approach to a problem. By using the weighted average approach, you avoided messy calculations and saved valuable time.

TAKEAWAYS: AVERAGES

- $\text{Average} = \dfrac{\text{Sum of the terms}}{\text{Number of terms}}$.
- Balanced average approach: the sum of the differences between each term and the average must be zero. You can solve some average questions using this fact alone.
- Weighted average of n terms $= (\text{Percent}_1)(\text{Average}_1) + (\text{Percent}_2)(\text{Average}_2) + \cdots + (\text{Percent}_n)(\text{Average}_n)$.

Practice Set: Averages on the GMAT

1. Jerry's average (arithmetic mean) score on the first 3 of 4 tests is 85. If Jerry wants to raise his average by 2 points, what score must he earn on the fourth test?

    ○ 87
    ○ 89
    ○ 90
    ○ 93
    ○ 95

2. The average (arithmetic mean) of all scores on a certain algebra test was 90. If the average of the 8 male students' grades was 87, and the average of the female students' grades was 92, how many female students took the test?

    ○ 8
    ○ 9
    ○ 10
    ○ 11
    ○ 12

3. An exam is given in a certain class. The average (arithmetic mean) of the highest score and the lowest score on the exam is equal to x. If the average score for the entire class is equal to y and there are z students in the class, where $z > 5$, then in terms of x, y, and z, what is the average score for the class, excluding the highest and lowest scores?

    ○ $\dfrac{zy - 2x}{z}$

    ○ $\dfrac{zy - 2}{z}$

    ○ $\dfrac{zx - y}{z - 2}$

    ○ $\dfrac{zy - 2x}{z - 2}$

    ○ $\dfrac{zy - x}{z + 2}$

4. The average price of Emily's 5 meals was $20. Meals with a price of $25 or more include a free dessert. How many of Emily's 5 meals included a free dessert?

    (1) The most expensive of the 5 meals had a price of $50.

    (2) The least expensive of the 5 meals had a price of $10.

RATES AND SPEED—CONVERTING RATES

You've seen this formula before:

$$\text{Speed} = \frac{\text{Distance}}{\text{Time}}$$

The most common rate is a speed—miles per hour—but anything with the word *per* is a rate: kilometers per second, miles per gallon, ounces of cheese per party guest, and so forth. A rate is any quantity of *A* per quantity of *B*.

$$\text{Rate } A \text{ per } B = \frac{\text{Quantity of } A}{\text{Quantity of } B}$$

Most rate problems involve conversions from one rate to another. These are best handled by multiplying the various rates so that measurements cancel. You may have to invert some of the rates to make the measurements cancel.

Example: If a car averages 25 miles per gallon and each gallon of gas costs $2.40, what's the value of the gas consumed in a trip of 175 miles?

$$\frac{\$2.40}{\text{gallon}} \times \frac{\text{gallon}}{25 \text{ miles}} \times 175 \text{ miles}$$

$$\frac{\$2.40}{\cancel{\text{gallon}}} \times \frac{\cancel{\text{gallon}}}{\cancel{25}^1 \cancel{\text{miles}}} \times \cancel{175}^7 \cancel{\text{miles}}$$

$$\$2.40 \times 7$$

$$\$16.80$$

Here's what a GMAT question might look like that gives you a rate that you must then convert. Follow along with this example:

> If José reads at a constant rate of 2 pages every 5 minutes, how many seconds will it take him to read *N* pages?
>
> ○ $\frac{2}{5}N$
> ○ $2N$
> ○ $\frac{5}{2}N$
> ○ $24N$
> ○ $150N$

There are two common ways of solving rate problems: algebraically and by using the picking numbers strategy. Let's try both for the problem above.

Algebraic Solution: You can call the number of seconds that you've been asked to find T. The first hurdle that you need to clear in this problem is that you're given a rate in minutes but asked to calculate the number of seconds. Change the rate you're given to seconds so you can get that aspect of the problem out of the way. There are 60 seconds to a minute. So you need to change the rate as follows:

$$\frac{2 \text{ pages}}{5 \text{ minutes}} \times \frac{1 \text{ minute}}{60 \text{ seconds}} = \frac{2 \text{ pages}}{300 \text{ seconds}} = \frac{1 \text{ page}}{150 \text{ seconds}}$$

Since the rates are the same, N and T will be in the same proportion as the rate you are given. So you can set up this equation:

$$\frac{1}{150} = \frac{N}{T}$$

Now cross multiply to solve for T: $T = 150N$. The answer is **(E)**.

Picking Numbers Solution: Since this question asks you to solve for the amount of time it takes José to read an unspecified number of pages, you can make the situation more concrete by picking a number for N. Keep the number simple, so that it's easy to work with: try $N = 2$, since José reads exactly 2 pages every 5 minutes, or 300 seconds (5×60 seconds $= 300$ seconds). Now look for the answer choices that yield 300 when $N = 2$. The only one that does so is **(E)**, so that must be the answer.

In-Format Question: Rates and Speed—Converting Rates on the GMAT

Now let's use the Kaplan Method on a Problem Solving question dealing with converting rates:

> If the city centers of New York and London are 3,471 miles apart, which of the following is closest to the distance between the city centers in inches? (There are 5,280 feet in a mile.)
>
> ○ 1.75×10^7
> ○ 1.83×10^7
> ○ 2.10×10^8
> ○ 2.10×10^9
> ○ 2.20×10^{10}

Step 1: Analyze the Question

There are some scary numbers in this question. Attention to the Right Detail can help you zero in on the most crucial piece of information: the words *closest to* let you know that you can afford to estimate, as does the fact that most answers are a whole power of 10 different from each other.

Step 2: State the Task

Your task is to convert 3,471 miles into inches.

Step 3: Approach Strategically

The problem gives you 5,280 feet per mile, allowing you to convert miles to feet. (The GMAT will expect you to know more common conversions, such as 12 inches per foot.)

So the calculation is $3,471 \text{ miles} \times \frac{5,280 \text{ feet}}{\text{mile}} \times \frac{12 \text{ inches}}{\text{foot}}$.

That's $3,471 \times 5,280 \times 12$. Happily, you can estimate, so save time by changing that to $3,500 \times 5,000 \times 10 = 175,000,000$, or 1.75×10^8. The only answer that's remotely close (within a power of 10) is **(C)**, so **(C)** is the answer.

Step 4: Confirm Your Answer

Reread the question stem, making sure that you didn't miss anything about the problem. For example, if you accidentally solved for feet instead of inches, you'd have chosen **(A)** or **(B)**. This step would save you from the error.

TAKEAWAYS: RATES AND SPEED—CONVERTING RATES

- Rate $= \dfrac{\text{Quantity of } A}{\text{Quantity of } B} = $ Quantity of A per Quantity of B

- Speed $= \dfrac{\text{Distance}}{\text{Time}}$

- When solving a conversion algebraically, set up the equation so that units cancel.

- Keep track of the units of measurement. Rate questions often involve converting minutes to hours or days to weeks.

PRACTICE SET: RATES AND SPEED—CONVERTING RATES ON THE GMAT

5. A truck owner will refuel his vehicle at a rate of 2 gallons of diesel fuel every 5 seconds. If diesel fuel costs $1.25 per gallon, how long will it take for the truck owner to refuel his vehicle with $40 worth of diesel fuel?

   O 20 seconds
   O 1 minute
   O 1 minute 20 seconds
   O 20 minutes
   O 1 hour 20 minutes

6. The moon revolves around the earth at a speed of approximately 1.02 kilometers per second. This approximate speed is how many kilometers per hour?

   O 60
   O 61.2
   O 62.5
   O 3,600
   O 3,672

7. Magnabulk Corp sells boxes holding *d* magnets each. The boxes are shipped in crates, each holding *b* boxes. What is the price charged per magnet, in cents, if Magnabulk charges *m* dollars for each crate?

○ $\dfrac{100bd}{m}$

○ $\dfrac{100m}{bd}$

○ $\dfrac{bd}{100m}$

○ $\dfrac{m}{bd}$

○ $\dfrac{bd}{m}$

RATES AND SPEED—MULTI-PART JOURNEYS

The GMAT often uses scenarios involving multi-part journeys in order to ask questions about "average rates." In such cases, the test makers will give you information that includes two or more different rates or speeds. So far in this chapter, you've learned about both averages and rates, so it's understandably tempting in this situation simply to average the different individual rates you're given.

Don't fall for this trap. Just as you cannot use the averages of two different portions of a group to determine the group's overall average (unless you know the weights of the portions), you also cannot find the average speed of a journey from the speeds of two parts unless you know the proportion of time spent or distance traveled in those parts. The GMAT's biggest trap with multi-part journeys or tasks is to offer an answer choice that fails to account for the weighting of the averages and simply splits the difference between the two portions. The GMAT writes its problems so that this is *never* the correct solution. Instead, you'll need to use the average rate formula.

Average Rate (Average *A* per *B*):

$$\text{Average } A \text{ per } B = \frac{\text{Total } A}{\text{Total } B}$$

Example: John travels 30 miles in 2 hours and then 60 miles in 3 hours. What is his average speed in miles per hour?

$$\text{Average miles per hour} = \frac{\text{Total miles}}{\text{Total hours}}$$

$$= \frac{(30+60) \text{ miles}}{(2+3) \text{ hours}} = \frac{90 \text{ miles}}{5 \text{ hours}} = 18 \text{ miles/hour}$$

Notice how you can check your work on this question by applying some Critical Thinking: John's first rate was 15 miles per hour, and his second rate was 20 miles per hour, so his average rate will fall somewhere between 15 and 20 miles per hour. You can estimate effectively on this question, as on most average rate questions, by identifying the rate at which John spent longer traveling. In this case, John spent more time traveling at 20 miles per hour, so his average rate should be closer to 20 than to 15. Indeed, 18 miles per hour is consistent with the direction in which the average rate should be weighted.

Average rate problems on the GMAT can become quite complex. If your paraphrase of the question stem is anything like "First this person moves at one speed, then at another," then you're dealing with a multi-part journey problem. There is frequently a lot of information to deal with.

To organize the data on complicated multi-part journey problems, try jotting down this chart on your noteboard:

	Rate	Time	Distance
Part 1 of trip			
Part 2 of trip			
Entire trip			

This chart folds many equations into one:

- Rate × Time = Distance; each row of boxes multiplies across.
- Time (part 1) + Time (part 2) = Time (entire trip); time boxes add down.
- Distance (part 1) + Distance (part 2) = Distance (entire trip); distance boxes add down.
- Rates *do not* add down; they are calculated by dividing distance by time. If you need to calculate the speed for the entire trip, use the average speed formula:

$$\text{Average speed} = \frac{\text{Total distance}}{\text{Total time}}$$

Let's go through a sample question, and you'll see how the chart helps you.

> A powerboat crosses a lake at 18 miles per hour and returns at 12 miles per hour. If the time taken turning the boat around was negligible and it returns by the same route, then what was the boat's average speed for the round trip, in miles per hour?

When you notice that you have a multi-part journey problem, jot down the chart, using a question mark to indicate the value that the question asks you for:

	Rate (mph)	Time (hr)	Distance (miles)
Part 1 of trip			
Part 2 of trip			
Entire trip	?		

Now fill in the data given by the problem:

	Rate (mph)	Time (hr)	Distance (miles)
Part 1 of trip	18		
Part 2 of trip	12		
Entire trip	?		

Now you clearly have to get some information about either the time or the distance to be able to solve for much of anything. The only other piece of information you have is that the boat traveled the same route both times. That means the distance must have been the same. You could use the variable *D*, but the math will get fairly complicated if you do. Instead, keep it simple and pick numbers. A number that's a multiple both of 18 and of 12 will make the math work out nicely, so let's say the lake was 36 miles across:

	Rate (mph)	Time (hr)	Distance (miles)
Part 1 of trip	18		36
Part 2 of trip	12		36
Entire trip	?		

Now you can solve for the times and the total distance:

	Rate (mph)	Time (hr)	Distance (miles)
Part 1 of trip	18	**2**	36
Part 2 of trip	12	**3**	36
Entire trip	?		**72**

And finally for total time:

	Rate (mph)	Time (hr)	Distance (miles)
Part 1 of trip	18	2	36
Part 2 of trip	12	3	36
Entire trip	?	**5**	72

Now you have what you need to solve for average rate. It's $\frac{\text{Total distance}}{\text{Total time}} = \frac{72}{5} = 14.4$ mph. This answer makes logical sense, since the two rates are 18 and 12 miles per hour and the boat spent more time traveling at the lower speed, so the average is closer to 12 than to 18.

IN-FORMAT QUESTION: RATES AND SPEED—MULTI-PART JOURNEYS ON THE GMAT

Now let's use the Kaplan Method on a Data Sufficiency question dealing with a multi-part journey:

What was the average speed of a runner in a race from Point X to Point Z?

(1) The runner's average speed from Point X to Point Y was 10 miles per hour.

(2) The runner's average speed from Point Y to Point Z was 8 miles per hour.

Step 1: Analyze the Question Stem

This is a Value question, so you need one exact speed for the trip from Point X to Point Z.

Use Critical Thinking: there's no direct simplification to be done, but since you can sometimes calculate exact speeds with unknown distance or time, there might be a way to solve for speed without knowing the exact distance and time.

To answer the question, you'll need either the exact distance and time or some information about distance or time that allows you to calculate speed.

Step 2: Evaluate the Statements Using 12TEN

Statement (1) gives you some data about the trip from X to Y but nothing about X to Z. Insufficient. Eliminate **(A)** and **(D)**. Likewise, Statement (2) gives you data about the trip from Y to Z but nothing about X to Z. Insufficient. Eliminate **(B)**.

Now you must combine. Notice that something crucial is missing—information relating either the times or the distances of the X-to-Y and the Y-to-Z leg. If the X-to-Y distance were 10 miles and the Y-to-Z distance were 10 inches, the average speed would be essentially 10 mph. And if it's the other way around, with the X-to-Y distance 10 inches and the Y-to-Z distance 10 miles, the average speed would be essentially 8 mph. The combined statements are insufficient, so the answer is **(E)**.

TAKEAWAYS: RATES AND SPEED—MULTI-PART JOURNEYS

- In average rate and average speed questions, one wrong answer choice involves not accounting for the weighting of the averages. To avoid this wrong answer, use the average rate and average speed formulas.

- Average speed $= \dfrac{\text{Total distance}}{\text{Total time}}$.

- For multi-part journeys, use a chart to organize data.

- In an average speed question, if you recognize the direction in which the speed should be weighted, you can rapidly eliminate incorrect answers.

PRACTICE SET: RATES AND SPEED—MULTI-PART JOURNEYS ON THE GMAT

8. A motorcyclist started riding at highway marker A, drove 120 miles to highway marker B, and then, without pausing, continued to highway marker C, where she stopped. The average speed of the motorcyclist, over the course of the entire trip, was 45 miles per hour. If the ride from marker A to marker B lasted 3 times as many hours as the rest of the ride, and the distance from marker B to marker C was half of the distance from marker A to marker B, what was the average speed, in miles per hour, of the motorcyclist while driving from marker B to marker C?

    O   40
    O   45
    O   50
    O   55
    O   60

9. A hiker walks three sections of a trail that are of equal length. The first section of the trail is flat, and on this section the hiker travels at 3 miles per hour for 1.5 hours. The second section is uphill, and on this section the hiker's pace slows by 25 percent. The third section is downhill, and here his speed doubles. What was the hiker's average speed for the entire three-section hike?

    O   1.5
    O   3
    O   3.25
    O   4.5
    O   9.75

10. A truck driver drove for 2 days. On the second day, he drove 3 hours longer and at an average speed of 15 miles per hour faster than he drove on the first day. If he drove a total of 1,020 miles and spent 21 hours driving during the 2 days, what was his average speed on the first day, in miles per hour?

   ○   25
   ○   30
   ○   35
   ○   40
   ○   45

11. Did Jon complete a journey of 40 kilometers in less time than it took Ann to complete the same journey?

   (1)   Jon traveled at an average speed of 30 kilometers per hour for the first 10 kilometers and then at an average speed of 15 kilometers per hour for the rest of the journey.

   (2)   Ann traveled at an average speed of 20 kilometers per hour for the entire journey.

COMBINED RATES AND COMBINED WORK

Combined work questions present you with information about different people or machines that can perform the same job in different amounts of time. Rates in combined work questions are expressed in a similar way to how you'll see them expressed in other rate questions:

$$\text{Rate} = \frac{\text{Number of tasks}}{\text{Time to complete tasks}}, \text{ or number of tasks } per \text{ amount of time}$$

Combined work questions would be much more straightforward if they provided you with the rates at which people or machines work; instead, the test makers make things more complicated by giving you the information in terms of how much time it takes for each individual to complete a given task. To calculate the total time needed for everyone working together to finish the job, use this formula:

The reciprocal of the time it takes everyone working together = The sum of the reciprocals of the times it would take each working individually. (The reciprocal of A is $\frac{1}{A}$.)

Written algebraically, this formula comes out as follows:

$\frac{1}{\text{Total time}} = \frac{1}{A} + \frac{1}{B} + \frac{1}{C} + \cdots + \frac{1}{N}$, where A, B, C, etc. represent the time it takes the individual people or machines to do the job by themselves.

You can use this general version of the formula with any number of people or machines working together.

If, however, the question presents you with only two people or machines working together, you will save time by using the following simplified version of the combined work formula:

$$\text{Total time } = \frac{AB}{A + B}$$

Again, A and B are the times it takes the two people working alone to finish the job. By solving for the total time directly instead of for its reciprocal, you'll avoid a common trap.

Example: Bob can clean a room in 3 hours, and George can clean the same room in 2 hours. How many hours does it take Bob and George to clean the room if they work together but independently?

$$\text{Total time } = \frac{AB}{A + B} = \frac{3 \times 2}{3 + 2}$$

Total time $= \frac{6}{5}$ hours, or 1 hour 12 minutes.

Attention to the Right Detail is crucial on combined work problems in which the GMAT can give you the needed information in various forms. The Critical Thinker will be rewarded by seeing what the question requires and choosing the most strategic approach.

Let's now look at a seemingly complicated GMAT work problem and see how the formula makes things much easier.

Working together, John, David, and Roger require $2\frac{1}{4}$ hours to complete a certain task, if each of them works at his respective constant rate. If John alone can complete the task in $4\frac{1}{2}$ hours and David alone can complete the task in 9 hours, how many hours would it take Roger to complete the task working alone?

- ○ $2\frac{1}{3}$

- ○ $4\frac{1}{2}$

- ○ $6\frac{3}{4}$

- ○ 9

- ○ 12

Combined Work Formula: Here's the solution, employing the combined work formula.

$$\frac{1}{T} = \frac{1}{J} + \frac{1}{D} + \frac{1}{R}$$

$$\frac{1}{2.25} = \frac{1}{4.5} + \frac{1}{9} + \frac{1}{R}$$

$$\frac{4}{9} = \frac{2}{9} + \frac{1}{9} + \frac{1}{R}$$

$$\frac{1}{9} = \frac{1}{R}$$

$$R = 9$$

Hour-by-Hour Approach: An alternative approach to this kind of problem that some find intuitive and quick is to break down the work on an hour-by-hour basis. Take David first. By himself, he could do the entire task in 9 hours. Therefore, during every single hour that these three people work together, David will complete $\frac{1}{9}$ of the task ($\frac{1}{9}$ is just the reciprocal of 9). In the second hour, he'll do another $\frac{1}{9}$. And in that extra $\frac{1}{4}$ hour, he'll do $\frac{1}{36}$ of the task. Add them up: David will be doing $\frac{1}{9} + \frac{1}{9} + \frac{1}{36} = \frac{9}{36} = \frac{1}{4}$ of the entire task during the period in question.

How about John? He's much faster than David. Working alone, he could complete the entire task in $4\frac{1}{2}$ hours (or $\frac{9}{2}$ hours). So during each hour he works, he'll do the reciprocal of $\frac{9}{2}$ (or $\frac{2}{9}$) of the task. Multiply that $\frac{2}{9}$ of a task per hour by the $2\frac{1}{4}$ hours the three men work, and you see that John himself will account for $\frac{2}{9} \times \frac{9}{4}$ or $\frac{1}{2}$ of the task.

With David and John accounting for $\frac{1}{4}$ and $\frac{1}{2}$ of the task respectively, that leaves exactly $\frac{1}{4}$ of the task to be performed by Roger. You can either see that this means that Roger and David work at the same rate—so it'll also take Roger 9 hours—or just divide $2\frac{1}{4}$ hours by $\frac{1}{4}$ task to get 9 hours per task, choice **(D)**.

Some harder work problems involve tasks left undone. In those cases, you'd need to use this hour-by-hour approach, so it's worthwhile to be familiar with it.

IN-FORMAT QUESTION: COMBINED RATES AND COMBINED WORK ON THE GMAT

Now let's use the Kaplan Method on a Problem Solving question dealing with combined rates and combined work:

Working alone, Machine X can manufacture 1,000 nails in 12 hours. Working together, Machines X and Y can manufacture 1,000 nails in 5 hours. How many hours does it take Machine Y to manufacture 1,000 nails working alone?

- ○ $3\frac{9}{17}$
- ○ $5\frac{1}{3}$
- ○ 7
- ○ $7\frac{1}{5}$
- ○ $8\frac{4}{7}$

Step 1: Analyze the Question

You have a choice of approaches for this combined work question. You can add the rates or solve with the times directly, whichever you find easier.

Step 2: State the Task

You're asked for the time it takes Machine Y to make 1,000 nails.

Step 3: Approach Strategically

Many combined work questions have answer choices that can be logically eliminated, and this is no different. Since the machines take 5 hours together, it's hardly reasonable to think that one machine would take *fewer* than 5 hours on its own. **(A)** can't be correct. Some estimation allows you to eliminate one more—**(B)** is very, very close to the combined time. Even though Machine X isn't very fast, it's not so slow that it would save only a third of an hour. You've just eliminated two answer choices through Critical Thinking.

Since you're given times and they are all for the same-sized task (manufacturing 1,000 nails), and the task is completed, the formula $T = \frac{AB}{A+B}$ will apply nicely.

$$5 = \frac{12Y}{12+Y}$$

$$5(12+Y) = 12Y$$

$$60 + 5Y = 12Y$$

$$60 = 7Y$$

$$\frac{60}{7} = Y$$

$$8\frac{4}{7} = Y$$

The answer is **(E)**.

You also could have solved this problem by adding the rates.

$$\text{Total rate} = \text{Rate } X + \text{Rate } Y$$

$$\text{Rate} = \frac{\text{Task}}{\text{Time}}$$

If the tasks are all the same, you can save yourself a lot of work by just giving one task the value of 1—in this problem, meaning "1 batch of 1,000 nails."

$$\frac{1}{5} = \frac{1}{12} + \frac{1}{Y}$$

$$\frac{12}{60} = \frac{5}{60} + \frac{1}{Y}$$

$$\frac{12}{60} - \frac{5}{60} = \frac{1}{Y}$$

$$\frac{7}{60} = \frac{1}{Y}$$

$$\frac{60}{7} = Y$$

$$8\frac{4}{7} = Y$$

Step 4: Confirm Your Answer

Reread the question stem, making sure that you didn't miss anything about the problem. More complicated combined work problems will shift the size of the task halfway through the question stem.

TAKEAWAYS: COMBINED RATES AND COMBINED WORK

- When using rates in a combined work question, $\dfrac{\text{Number of tasks}}{\text{Time to complete tasks}}$.

- The combined work formula for two workers is $\dfrac{AB}{A+B}$, where T equals the time both workers take to do the task when working together, and A and B equal the time needed by each worker to do the job on his or her own, respectively.

- If more than two workers work together, use the generic formula for combined work:

$$\frac{1}{T} = \frac{1}{A} + \frac{1}{B} + \frac{1}{C} + \cdots + \frac{1}{N}$$

PRACTICE SET: COMBINED RATES AND COMBINED WORK ON THE GMAT

12. Working at its usual constant rate, Pump A can empty a water storage tank in 3 hours. Pump B, also working at its usual constant rate, can empty half of the same tank in 4 hours. How many hours will it take both pumps working together at their usual respective constant rates to empty half of the tank?

   ○ $\dfrac{12}{11}$

   ○ $\dfrac{24}{11}$

   ○ $\dfrac{24}{7}$

   ○ $\dfrac{7}{2}$

   ○ $\dfrac{36}{7}$

13. Machine 1 and Machine 2 working together can produce 12,000 meters of steel cable per hour. Each machine works at a constant rate. Machine 1 by itself can produce 5,000 meters of cable per hour. How many hours would it Machine 2 working alone to produce 12,000 meters of cable?

   ○ $\dfrac{7}{12}$

   ○ $\dfrac{67}{40}$

   ○ $\dfrac{12}{7}$

   ○ $\dfrac{11}{5}$

   ○ $\dfrac{5}{2}$

14. Two trucks travel from Alphaburg to Betaville along the same route. The speed limit for the first 30 miles is 60 miles per hour (mph). The speed limit for the next 10 miles is 40 mph, and the limit for the final 60 miles is 55 mph. Truck F has a maximum speed of 70 mph, but Truck S has a speed-limiting governor installed to cap its maximum speed at 50 mph. Truck S departs Alphaburg 12 minutes before Truck F. If each truck travels at the lesser of the speed limit or the maximum speed of the truck, how far from Betaville is the point where Truck F catches up with Truck S?

○   5 miles

○   20 miles

○   55 miles

○   95 miles

○   Both trucks arrive at Betaville simultaneously.

INTEREST RATES

Interest rates are something that you might be acutely aware of in real life, especially as they apply to mortgages and credit cards, but unless you work directly in a field that touches on loans or mortgages, you probably don't think about the formulas used to calculate them.

Fortunately, you don't have to puzzle over calculating out the interest year-by-year or step-by-step. You can memorize and apply formulas to help you manage the information from the question stem much more efficiently and accurately than by simply applying brute force to the arithmetic.

Interest rate questions rely on three important pieces of information: (1) the principal, or the amount initially invested; (2) the interest rate, or the rate at which the investment grows; and (3) the time period during which the investment accrues interest.

Attention to the Right Detail is necessary even when applying the formulas—and no detail is more important to interest rate questions than whether the interest is simple or compound. Simple and compound interest use different formulas:

Simple interest is interest applied only to the principal, not to the interest that has already accrued. Use this formula:

> **(Total of principal and interest)** = **Principal** $\times$ **(1 + rt)**, where r equals the interest rate per time period expressed as a decimal and t equals the number of time periods

Example: If \$100 were invested at 12 percent simple annual interest, what would be the total value of the investment after 3 years?

$$\text{Total} = \$100 \times (1 + 0.12 \times 3) = \$100(1.36) = \$136$$

Compound interest is interest applied to the principal and any previously accrued interest. Use this formula:

> **(Total of principal and interest)** = **Principal** $\times$ **(1 + r)^t**, where r equals the interest rate per time period expressed as a decimal and t equals the number of time periods

Example: If $100 were invested at 12 percent interest compounded annually, what would be the total value of the investment after 3 years?

$$\text{Total} = \$100 \times (1 + 0.12)^3 = \$100(1.12)^3$$

Despite the GMAT's general preference for simplified values in the answer choices, you will often see answer choices for a compound interest rate problem written as expressions similar to the result above. You can be thankful that you won't have to calculate values such as 1.12^3, since you don't have the use of a calculator on the Quant section.

On Test Day you might also encounter a more difficult question that requires dealing with annual interest but payments not on an annual basis. In this case, r equals the annual rate divided by the number of times per year it is applied, and t equals the number of years multiplied by the number of times per year interest is applied.

Example: If $100 were invested at 12 percent annual interest, compounded quarterly, what would be the total value of the investment after 3 years?

$$\text{Total} = \$100 \times \left(1 + \frac{0.12}{4}\right)^{(3 \times 4)} = \$100(1.03)^{12}$$

IN-FORMAT QUESTION: INTEREST RATES ON THE GMAT

Now let's use the Kaplan Method on a Problem Solving question dealing with interest rates:

> The number of bacteria in a petri dish increased by 50 percent every 2 hours. If there were 108 million bacteria in the dish at 2:00 p.m., at what time were there 32 million bacteria in the dish?
>
> ○ 6:00 p.m.
> ○ 8:00 p.m.
> ○ 6:00 a.m.
> ○ 8:00 a.m.
> ○ 10:00 a.m.

Step 1: Analyze the Question

This may not look like an interest rate question at first glance, but interest rates are just percent increases applied multiple times. The number of bacteria increases 50% every 2 hours. You could think of this as 50% compounded interest applied once every 2 hours.

Step 2: State the Task

Instead of calculating forward, you have to calculate back—if there are 108 million in the dish at 2:00 p.m., when were there 32 million?

Step 3: Approach Strategically

This problem could be solved as a straightforward percent change, but let's look at it through the lens of interest rates:

$$108 = 32 \times (1.5)^t$$

$$\frac{108}{32} = (1.5)^t$$

$$\frac{27}{8} = (1.5)^t$$

$$\frac{27}{8} = \left(\frac{3}{2}\right)^t$$

$$\frac{27}{8} = \frac{3^t}{2^t}$$

$$\frac{3^3}{2^3} = \frac{3^t}{2^t}$$

Clearly, then $t = 3$. That's three 2-hour increases for a total of 6 hours. Since there were 108 million at 2:00 p.m., there were 32 million 6 hours earlier at 8:00 a.m.

The answer is **(D)**.

This is also an excellent backsolving question, as you could easily just try out a time for 32 million and see whether that's consistent with 108 million at 2:00 p.m.

Let's say you try **(B)** first:

Time	Millions of bacteria
8:00 p.m.	32
10:00 p.m.	48
Midnight	72
2:00 a.m.	108

That's either far too soon (12 hours too soon) or far too late (12 hours too late), depending on how you envision the day. Either way, **(B)** is wrong by a lot, and just shifting 2 hours to 6:00 p.m. won't help matters. Eliminate **(A)** as well.

Now let's try **(D)**:

Time	Millions of bacteria
8:00 a.m.	32
10:00 a.m.	48
Noon	72
2:00 p.m.	108

Exactly what it should be (you might also have seen that **(D)** would be correct when you noticed that **(B)**, 8:00 p.m., was off by exactly 12 hours). The answer is **(D)**.

Step 4: Confirm Your Answer

Reread the question stem, making sure that you didn't accidentally skip over any important aspects of the situation.

TAKEAWAYS: INTEREST RATES

- Simple interest:

  (**Total of principal and interest**) = **Principal** $\times$ (**1** + **rt**), where r equals the interest rate per time period expressed as a decimal and t equals the number of time periods.

- Compound interest:

  (**Total of principal and interest**) = **Principal** $\times$ (**1** + **r**)^t, where r equals the interest rate per time period expressed as a decimal and t equals the number of time periods.

PRACTICE SET: INTEREST RATES ON THE GMAT

15. Binh invested $1,000 in a certificate of deposit (CD) that matured in 4 years. The certificate paid 4 percent annual interest compounded quarterly for the original 4-year term and then 2 percent simple annual interest on the compounded amount after that until the CD was redeemed by the holder. If Binh held his CD for exactly 6 years, how much money did he receive when he redeemed it?

    ○ $1,000 \times (1.01)^{16} \times 1.04$

    ○ $1,000 \times (1.01)^{16} \times (1.02)^{2}$

    ○ $1,000 \times (1.04)^{6}$

    ○ $1,000 \times (1.01)^{24}$

    ○ $1,000 \times (1.04)^{16} \times (1.02)^{2}$

16. The amount of an investment will double in approximately $70/p$ years, where p is the percent interest, compounded annually. If Thelma invests $40,000 in a long-term CD that pays 5 percent interest, compounded annually, what will be the approximate total value of the investment when Thelma is ready to retire 42 years later?

    ○ $280,000

    ○ $320,000

    ○ $360,000

    ○ $450,000

    ○ $540,000

17. A certain account pays 1.5 percent compound interest every 3 months. A person invested an initial amount and did not invest any more money in the account after that. If after exactly 5 years, the amount of money in the account was T dollars, which of the following is an expression for the original number of dollars invested in the account?

    ○ $(1.015)^{4}T$

    ○ $(1.015)^{15}T$

    ○ $(1.015)^{20}T$

    ○ $\dfrac{T}{(1.015)^{15}}$

    ○ $\dfrac{T}{(1.015)^{20}}$

OVERLAPPING SETS

Another classic GMAT setup involves a large group that is subdivided into two potentially overlapping subgroups. For example, let's say that in a room of 20 people, there are 12 dog owners and 14 cat owners. Since 12 plus 14 is more than 20, the only way this situation makes any sense is if some people own both a dog and a cat. And it's possible that some own neither. Essentially, there are four different subgroups to consider: (1) those who own a dog but not a cat, (2) those who own a cat but not a dog, (3) those who own both a cat and a dog, and (4) those who own neither a cat nor a dog. You could also combine some of these groups to consider both the total number of dog owners and the total number of cat owners.

There are three ways to work these problems. Let's look at each.

Approach 1: Overlapping Sets Formula

Use the overlapping sets formula:

$$\text{Group 1} + \text{Group 2} - \text{Both} + \text{Neither} = \text{Total}$$

Example: An office manager orders 27 pizzas for a party. Of these, 15 have pepperoni, and 10 have mushrooms. If 4 pizzas have no toppings at all, and no other toppings are ordered, then how many pizzas were ordered with both pepperoni and mushrooms?

$$\text{Group 1} + \text{Group 2} - \text{Both} + \text{Neither} = \text{Total}$$
$$\text{Pepperoni} + \text{Mushrooms} - \text{Both} + \text{Neither} = \text{Total}$$
$$15 + 10 - \text{Both} + 4 = 27$$
$$29 - \text{Both} = 27$$
$$\text{Both} = 2$$

Approach 2: Venn Diagram

Organize the given information using a Venn diagram. This approach uses partially overlapping circles to represent the data visually:

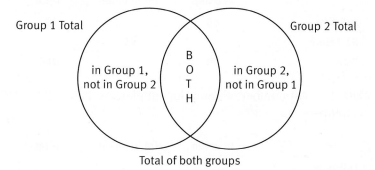

Example: All the students in a class study either Forensics or Statistics. There are 16 Forensics students, 3 of whom also study Statistics. How many Statistics students are in the class if the class has 25 students altogether?

Because 3 of the Forensics students also study Statistics, there must be 13 who study only Forensics. If the "Forensics only" and "Both" groups total 16 and there are 25 students in the class, then 25 − 16, or 9, students study only Statistics. Thus, 9 + 3 = 12, the total number of Statistics students. Putting all these numbers into the Venn diagram as you go helps you to see these relationships clearly:

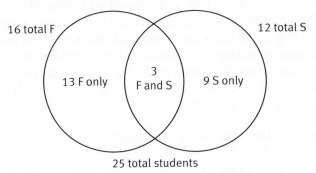

16 total F   12 total S

13 F only   3 F and S   9 S only

25 total students

Approach 3: Chart

Organize the given information using a chart. This way works best with complicated overlapping sets problems because it has a separate place for each of the nine data points you might be given. Take your time organizing the chart, and the problem will almost solve itself:

	In Group 1	Not in Group 1	Total
In Group 2			
Not in Group 2			
Total			

Example: A company has 200 employees, 90 of whom belong to a union. If there are 95 part-time nonunion employees and 80 full-time union employees, then how many full-time employees are in the company?

Start by putting the data into the chart, using a question mark to indicate the value that the question asks for:

	In union	Not in union	Total
Full-time	80		?
Part-time		95	
Total	90		200

Now you can calculate the total number of nonunion employees (200 − 90 = 110) and the number of part-time union employees (90 − 80 = 10):

	In union	Not in union	Total
Full-time	80		?
Part-time	10	95	
Total	90	110	200

And now either calculate full-time nonunion employees (110 − 95 = 15) or the total number of part-time employees (10 + 95 = 105):

	In union	Not in union	Total
Full-time	80	**15**	?
Part-time	10	95	**105**
Total	90	110	200

Either way, you can then calculate the total number of full-time employees (80 + 15 = 95 or 200 − 105 = 95):

	In union	Not in union	Total
Full-time	80	15	**95**
Part-time	10	95	105
Total	90	110	200

There are 95 full-time employees.

Each of the three approaches has its pluses and minuses. Your own personal thinking style will respond best to one of these over the others. Practice all of them so you get a sense of which approach you like with different problems.

Now try the following example on your own, using Critical Thinking to assess which of the three approaches will be most effective:

> A group of 25 children went to the circus, 60 percent of whom liked the clowns. If the number of preschool children who liked the clowns was 3 more than the number of preschool children who did not, and the number of preschool children was 1 larger than the number of school-age children, then how many school-age children did not like the clowns?

In your overview of the problem, you can see that there are some complex relationships going on; you shouldn't try to understand them all at once. But notice that there are two ways in which children can be classified: preschool or school-age, liked or didn't like the clowns. That makes this an overlapping sets problem.

The approach that offers the most flexibility, shows the most detail, and is therefore frequently the safest to use with this question type is this chart:

	In Group 1	Not in Group 1	Total
In Group 2			
Not in Group 2			
Total			

In this problem, the two groupings are preschool or school-age and likes clowns or doesn't like clowns. So here's the chart you'd use for this problem:

	Likes clowns	Doesn't like	Total
Preschool			
School-age			
Total			

Now enter the information from the question stem:

	Likes clowns	Doesn't like	Total
Preschool	$x + 3$	x	$s + 1$
School-age		?	s
Total	60% of 25		25

Two calculations can be done right away: 60% of 25 = (0.6)(25) = 15. Also, $(s + 1) + s = 25$. That means $2s + 1 = 25$, so $2s = 24$ and $s = 12$.

	Likes clowns	Doesn't like	Total
Preschool	$x + 3$	x	13
School-age		?	12
Total	15		25

The next two calculations suggested by the chart are the total number of children who don't like clowns, $25 - 15 = 10$, and the value of x. Use the equation $(x + 3) + x = 13$, or $2x + 3 = 13$. That means $2x = 10$, or $x = 5$. Then $x + 3 = 8$.

	Likes clowns	Doesn't like	Total
Preschool	8	5	13
School-age		?	12
Total	15	10	25

Now you know the answer to the question…the number of school-age children who didn't like the clowns is $10 - 5$, or 5. You can fill in the number of school-age children who like clowns, too, just for fun.

	Likes clowns	Doesn't like	Total
Preschool	8	5	13
School-age	7	<u>5</u>	12
Total	15	10	25

Because this chart shows all nine possible data points in these problems, it allows you to answer any question that might be asked. Fraction of school-age kids who liked the clowns? It's $\frac{7}{12}$. Percentage of children who didn't like the clowns who were also preschoolers? It's 50%. Ratio of school-age children who liked the clowns to preschoolers who didn't? It's 7:5.

When overlapping sets questions involve proportions, be very clear about what the basis of the proportion is. For example, the number of preschoolers who didn't like the clowns could be described as

20% (of the children), 50% (of the children who didn't like clowns), or 100% (as large as the number of school-age children who didn't like the clowns).

IN-FORMAT QUESTION: OVERLAPPING SETS ON THE GMAT

Now let's use the Kaplan Method on a Problem Solving question dealing with overlapping sets:

> A polling company surveyed a certain country, and it found that 35 percent of that country's registered voters had an unfavorable impression of both of that state's major political parties and that 20 percent had a favorable impression only of Party A.
> If 1 registered voter has a favorable impression of both parties for every 2 registered voters who have a favorable impression only of Party B, then what percentage of the country's registered voters have a favorable impression of both parties (assuming that respondents to the poll were given a choice between favorable and unfavorable impressions only)?
>
> ○ 15
> ○ 20
> ○ 30
> ○ 35
> ○ 45

Step 1: Analyze the Question

You're presented with a lot of information in this overlapping sets question. Don't try to digest it all at once. Notice that the total group (registered voters) can be separated into two major categories (those who like Party A and those who like Party B) and that those categories are not mutually exclusive (which means that someone could be in both categories—in this case, that someone could like both parties). That's the general setup for overlapping sets questions.

Use Critical Thinking to choose the best approach for this problem. This is a complicated question with many data points. The most powerful tool for understanding confusing or complicated overlapping sets is a chart:

	Favorable B	Not favorable B	Total
Favorable A	?		
Not favorable A			
Total			

Step 2: State the Task

You need to calculate the percentage of registered voters who like both parties; in other words, the value in the upper left-hand box.

Step 3: Approach Strategically

Start by putting the information into the chart. For simplicity's sake, pick 100 for the total number of voters.

	Favorable B	Not favorable B	Total
Favorable A	?	20	
Not favorable A		35	
Total			100

The other piece of data is "1 registered voter has a favorable impression of both parties for every 2 registered voters who have a favorable impression only of Party B." In other words, the ratio of "favorable A and favorable B" to "favorable B and not favorable A" is 1:2. So you have something else to put in the chart—let's call that x and $2x$.

	Favorable B	Not favorable B	Total
Favorable A	x(?)	20	
Not favorable A	$2x$	35	
Total			100

Since this chart adds down (and across), you can fill in the rest easily enough:

	Favorable B	Not favorable B	Total
Favorable A	x(?)	20	$20 + x$
Not favorable A	$2x$	35	$35 + 2x$
Total	$3x$	55	100

Whether you use the Total column or the Total row, you have the same equation to solve for x:

$$3x + 55 = 100$$
$$3x = 45$$
$$x = 15$$

The answer is **(A)**.

Step 4: Confirm Your Answer

Reread the question stem, making sure that you didn't accidentally misread anything.

TAKEAWAYS: OVERLAPPING SETS

- Overlapping sets questions on the GMAT require you to determine the elements in a set that do, or do not, overlap with elements of other sets.
- There are three approaches for overlapping sets questions:
  - Use the overlapping sets formula: Total = Group 1 + Group 2 − Both + Neither.
  - Draw a Venn diagram and use numbers to notate areas of overlap.
  - Jot a chart on your noteboard and solve. This way works best with complicated overlapping set problems.

PRACTICE SET: OVERLAPPING SETS ON THE GMAT

18. Of the 65 books released last year by a particular publishing house, 25 were no more than 200 pages. The publisher released 35 fiction books, of which 20 were more than 200 pages, and it also published nonfiction books. How many nonfiction books of no more than 200 pages did the publishing house release last year?

   ○ 5
   ○ 10
   ○ 20
   ○ 30
   ○ 35

19. Three hundred students at College Q study a foreign language. Of these, 110 of those students study French and 170 study Spanish. If at least 90 students who study a foreign language at College Q study neither French nor Spanish, then the number of students who study Spanish but not French could be any number from

   ○ 10 to 40
   ○ 40 to 100
   ○ 60 to 100
   ○ 60 to 110
   ○ 70 to 110

20. The *Financial News Daily* has 25 reporters covering Asia, 20 covering Europe, and 20 covering North America. Four reporters cover Asia and Europe but not North America, 6 reporters cover Asia and North America but not Europe, and 7 reporters cover Europe and North America but not Asia. How many reporters cover all of the 3 continents (Asia, Europe, and North America)?

   (1) The *Financial News Daily* has 38 reporters in total covering at least 1 of the following continents: Asia, Europe, and North America.

   (2) There are more *Financial News Daily* reporters covering only Asia than there are *Financial News Daily* reporters covering only North America.

ANSWERS AND EXPLANATIONS BEGIN ON NEXT PAGE

ANSWERS AND EXPLANATIONS

1.	D	8.	E	15.	A
2.	E	9.	B	16.	B
3.	D	10.	D	17.	E
4.	C	11.	C	18.	B
5.	C	12.	A	19.	C
6.	E	13.	C	20.	A
7.	B	14.	A		

1. **(D)**

Jerry's average (arithmetic mean) score on the first 3 of 4 tests is 85. If Jerry wants to raise his average by 2 points, what score must he earn on the fourth test?

○ 87
○ 89
○ 90
○ 93
○ 95

Step 1: Analyze the Question

Jerry has an 85 average after 3 exams. After his fourth exam, he wants an overall average of 87.

Step 2: State the Task

Find the score Jerry must earn on his fourth exam to achieve an overall average of 87.

Step 3: Approach Strategically

The quickest way to solve this problem is to use the "balanced average" approach. To earn an overall average of 87 on 4 exams, Jerry needs his fourth test to be an 87 plus the number of points that his other 3 tests were "deficient" with respect to this goal. You know that the average of the first 3 exams was a score of 85, so each of those 3 exams, on average, falls short by $87 - 85 = 2$ points. Therefore, Jerry needs a score of $87 + 2 + 2 + 2 = 93$ on his fourth exam. **(D)** is correct.

Step 4: Confirm Your Answer

To confirm your answer, you can backsolve by plugging **(D)** back into the question: if Jerry scores 85, 85, 85, and 93 on his 4 exams, that's an average of $\frac{85+85+85+93}{4} = \frac{348}{4} = 87$. This confirms that **(D)** is correct.

2. **(E)**

The average (arithmetic mean) of all scores on a certain algebra test was 90. If the average of the 8 male students' grades was 87, and the average of the female students' grades was 92, how many female students took the test?

○ 8
○ 9
○ 10
○ 11
○ 12

In most questions dealing with averages, you should consider picking numbers, setting each term in a group equal to the average of that group. You'll see in Step 3 how doing so allows you to perform efficient solutions.

Step 1: Analyze the Question

Eight male students take a test, and an unknown number of female students take the test. This question gives you lots of information about averages. Don't rush to set up algebra yet, as there may be a more efficient approach.

Step 2: State the Task

Figure out how many female students took the test. Call that number f.

Step 3: Approach Strategically

This would be a very straightforward backsolving question, as you could just test an answer choice and see whether it's consistent with the rest of the information in the question stem. But first, look at a quick math-based approach, taking advantage of the rapid calculations permitted by the balanced average approach.

The balanced average approach takes advantage of the fact that the sum of the differences between the terms and the average must be zero. Phrased another way, the total amount by which the terms above the average are larger than the average must equal the total amount by which the terms below the average are smaller than the average:

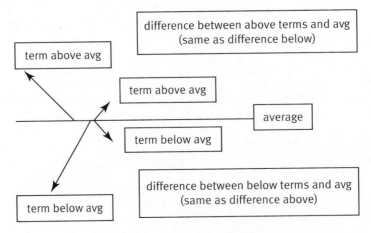

For this problem, here's how it works: since the only restrictions are that the male students' scores must average to 87 and that the female students' scores must average to 92, you can pick numbers and set all 8 male scores equal to 87 and all female scores equal to 92.

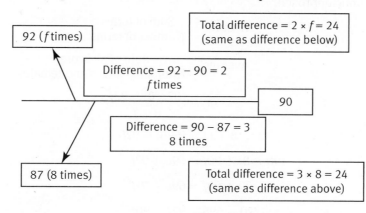

This approach gives you an equation to solve for f.

$$2f = 24$$

$$f = 12$$

The answer is **(E)**.

Now, try the question using backsolving. Say that you started with **(D)**. If there were 11 female students whose scores averaged 92, then

$$\text{Average} = \frac{\text{Sum of terms}}{\text{Number of terms}}$$

$$92 = \frac{\text{Sum of female scores}}{11}$$

$$92 \times 11 = \text{Sum of female scores}$$

$$1{,}012 = \text{Sum of female scores}$$

The men's scores are given:

$$87 = \frac{\text{Sum of male scores}}{8}$$

$$87 \times 8 = \text{Sum of male scores}$$

$$696 = \text{Sum of male scores}$$

You can set up the formula for the average of the whole group as follows:

$$\text{Average} = \frac{\text{Sum of terms}}{\text{Number of terms}}$$

$$\text{Average} = \frac{\text{Sum of all scores}}{\text{Number of males and females}}$$

$$\text{Average} = \frac{696 + 1{,}012}{8 + 11}$$

$$\text{Average} = \frac{1{,}708}{19}$$

$$\text{Average} = 89\frac{17}{19}$$

But the average is supposed to be 90. You're too low, so you need more female students' scores to pull the average up. **(E)** must be correct.

And here's the algebraic approach:

$$\text{Average} = \frac{\text{Sum of terms}}{\text{Number of terms}}$$

$$\text{Average} = \frac{\text{Sum of all scores}}{\text{Number of males and females}}$$

$$90 = \frac{(87 \times 8) + 92f}{8 + f}$$

$$90 \times (8 + f) = (696) + 92f$$

$$(90 \times 8) + 90f = 696 + 92f$$

$$720 + 90f = 696 + 92f$$

$$720 - 696 = 92f - 90f$$

$$24 = 2f$$

$$12 = f$$

The balanced average approach almost always permits fewer steps and easier calculations.

Step 4: Confirm Your Answer

Reread the question stem, making sure that you didn't miss any important information in the problem.

3.   **(D)**

An exam is given in a certain class. The average (arithmetic mean) of the highest score and the lowest score on the exam is equal to x. If the average score for the entire class is equal to y and there are z students in the class, where $z > 5$, then in terms of x, y, and z, what is the average score for the class, excluding the highest and lowest scores?

- ○ $\dfrac{zy - 2x}{z}$
- ○ $\dfrac{zy - 2}{z}$
- ○ $\dfrac{zx - y}{z - 2}$
- ○ $\dfrac{zy - 2x}{z - 2}$
- ○ $\dfrac{zy - x}{z + 2}$

Step 1: Analyze the Question

This is a very complicated word problem, with lots of variables, including variables in the answer choices. Whenever there are variables in the answer choices, consider picking numbers. When picking numbers in a question dealing with averages, pick all the numbers in a group to equal the average of that group.

Step 2: State the Task

Your task is to calculate the average of the class after excluding the highest and lowest scores. Before rushing into the math, think logically about what the task tells you about the correct answer. Since the total size of the class is z, there will be $(z - 2)$ scores after the high score and low scores are eliminated. Since an average is the sum divided by the number of terms, the correct answer must have $(z - 2)$ as a denominator. A quick check of the answer choices reveals that only **(C)** and **(D)** might possibly be correct. If you were falling behind on time or unsure of how to approach this question, you could make a 50/50 guess pretty quickly.

Many GMAT word problems have answer choices that can be eliminated without much math.

Step 3: Approach Strategically

See what you know about the class. The average of the whole class is y, and there are z students in the class. Now what about the high and low scores? You're told nothing about them, save that their average is x.

This is all pretty abstract, so simplify things by picking numbers. Start with the number of students. It must be greater than 5, so say that it's 6 ($z = 6$).

Now pick scores for the 6 students. You could pick all different scores, but the easiest approach of all is to let all 6 scores be equal to the average of those scores. Say that the class as a whole averages a score of 2. After all, "realism" doesn't matter when picking numbers, only permissibility and manageability. So $y = 2$.

scores (in order): 2, 2, 2, 2, 2, 2

Now, what are the highest and the lowest? Let's bold them below for emphasis:

scores (in order): **2**, 2, 2, 2, 2, **2**

Together, the high and low scores also average 2. We can calculate that so quickly because when all the terms in a group equal the same value, the average is also equal to that value. So $x = 2$.

Your task is to calculate the average of the class after excluding the high and low scores:

scores (in order): ~~2~~, 2, 2, 2, 2, ~~2~~

Looks like that average will be 2 as well. Now you just need to plug $z = 6$, $y = 2$, and $x = 2$ into the answer choices, looking for the result of 2:

(A) $\dfrac{(6 \times 2) - (2 \times 2)}{6} = \dfrac{12 - 4}{6} = \dfrac{8}{6} = \dfrac{4}{3}$. Eliminate.

(B) $\dfrac{(6 \times 2) - 2}{6} = \dfrac{12 - 2}{6} = \dfrac{10}{6} = \dfrac{5}{3}$. Eliminate.

(C) $\dfrac{(6 \times 2) - 2}{6 - 2} = \dfrac{12 - 2}{4} = \dfrac{10}{4} = \dfrac{5}{2}$. Eliminate.

(D) $\dfrac{(6 \times 2) - (2 \times 2)}{6 - 2} = \dfrac{12 - 4}{4} = \dfrac{8}{4} = 2$. Possibly correct.

(E) $\dfrac{(6 \times 2) - 2}{6 + 2} = \dfrac{12 - 2}{8} = \dfrac{10}{8} = \dfrac{5}{4}$. Eliminate.

The answer is **(D)**.

There is an algebraic solution, but you may find this approach more complicated and abstract:

$$\text{Average of non-excluded scores} = \frac{\text{Sum of non-excluded scores}}{\text{Number of non-excluded scores}}$$

$$\text{Number of non-excluded scores} = \text{Number of all scores} - \text{Number of excluded scores}$$

$$\text{Number of non-excluded scores} = z - 2$$

$$\text{Sum of non-excluded scores} = \text{Sum of all scores} - \text{Sum of excluded scores}$$

$$\text{Average of all scores} = \frac{\text{Sum of all scores}}{\text{Number of all scores}}$$

$$y = \frac{\text{Sum of all scores}}{z}$$

$$zy = \text{Sum of all scores}$$

$$\text{Average of excluded scores} = \frac{\text{Sum of excluded scores}}{\text{Number of excluded scores}}$$

$$x = \frac{\text{Sum of excluded scores}}{2}$$

$$2x = \text{Sum of excluded scores}$$

$$\text{Sum of non-excluded scores} = zy - 2x$$

$$\text{Average of non-excluded scores} = \frac{\text{Sum of non-excluded scores}}{\text{Number of non-excluded scores}}$$

$$\text{Average of non-excluded scores} = \frac{zy - 2x}{z - 2}$$

This expression matches **(D)**, which is the correct answer.

Picking numbers can reduce some of the most complicated average questions to very simple arithmetic.

Step 4: Confirm Your Answer

Reread the question stem, making sure that you didn't miss anything about the problem.

4. **(C)**

The average price of Emily's 5 meals was $20. Meals with a price of $25 or more include a free dessert. How many of Emily's 5 meals included a free dessert?

(1) The most expensive of the 5 meals had a price of $50.

(2) The least expensive of the 5 meals had a price of $10.

Step 1: Analyze the Question Stem

This is a Value question. Since the average price of Emily's 5 meals was $20, the sum of the prices of all 5 meals was 5 × $20 = $100. You're also told that meals with a price of $25 or more include a free dessert. You need to determine whether there's enough information to find how many of Emily's meals included a free dessert. Thus, you'll have sufficient information if you can determine the exact number of meals that had a price of at least $25.

Step 2: Evaluate the Statements Using 12TEN

Look at Statement (1). The most expensive meal had a price of $50, and the sum of all 5 prices was $100, so the prices of the other 4 meals must have had a sum of $100 − $50 = $50. However, there's no way to determine how that $50 was distributed among the remaining 4 meals; it could be that 1 of the meals was $25 or more and each of the other 3 was less than $25, or it could be that each of the 4 meals was less than $25. Because there's insufficient information in this statement to determine an exact number of meals costing $25 or more, eliminate **(A)** and **(D)**.

Statement (2) tells you that the least expensive of the 5 meals had a price of $10. Since the prices of the 5 meals sum to $100, the prices of the 4 most expensive meals sum to $90. Now, consider the possibilities: it could be that 3 of these 4 meals are $25 each and the fourth is $15, or that 1 meal is $45 and the other 3 are $15 each, or some other combination of prices that sum to $90. Since there is more than one possibility for the number of meals that cost at least $25, this statement is insufficient. Eliminate **(B)**.

Now, consider the statements together. If the most expensive meal were $50 and the least expensive meal were $10, then the sum of the remaining 3 meals was $100 − $50 − $10 = $40. How might this $40 be distributed among the remaining 3 meals? Since Emily's least expensive meal was $10, each of these 3 remaining meals must cost more than $10, so 2 of the 3 together must cost over $20; therefore, the third cannot be as much as $25 (for example, if 2 of these 3 remaining meals were $10.50 each, there would only be $40 − $10.50 − $10.50 = $19 left for the third meal). Therefore, it's only possible for 1 meal (the most expensive, $50 one) to have a price of at least $25. Thus, the two statements combined are sufficient to determine an exact number of meals that cost at least $25, and the correct choice is **(C)**.

5. **(C)**

A truck owner will refuel his vehicle at a rate of 2 gallons of diesel fuel every 5 seconds. If diesel fuel costs $1.25 per gallon, how long will it take for the truck owner to refuel his vehicle with $40 worth of diesel fuel?

- ○ 20 seconds
- ○ 1 minute
- ○ 1 minute 20 seconds
- ○ 20 minutes
- ○ 1 hour 20 minutes

Step 1: Analyze the Question

You are provided with two pieces of information: diesel fuel is $1.25 per gallon and the truck in question refuels at a rate of 2 gallons every 5 seconds. As the choices are in seconds, minutes, and hours, you need to be comfortable converting from one unit to another.

Step 2: State the Task

Find the amount of time it would take to add $40 of diesel fuel to the truck.

Step 3: Approach Strategically

There's a lot going on in this problem, so the key is to take things one step at a time. Begin by figuring out the amount of fuel you're looking to add. At a price of $1.25 per gallon, the truck owner is looking to refuel his vehicle with $\frac{\$40}{\$1.25 \text{ per gallon}} = 32$ gallons of fuel. Fuel enters the vehicle at 2 gallons every 5 seconds, so it would take $\frac{32}{2} \times 5$ seconds $= 80$ seconds to refuel the vehicle. Finally, 80 seconds is 1 minute and 20 seconds, which makes **(C)** the correct answer.

Step 4: Confirm Your Answer

When evaluating the choices for a question like this, be careful not to read them too quickly, as **(E)** is designed to look very similar to the correct answer at first glance.

EXPLANATIONS

6. (E)

The moon revolves around the earth at a speed of approximately 1.02 kilometers per second. This approximate speed is how many kilometers per hour?

- ○ 60
- ○ 61.2
- ○ 62.5
- ○ 3,600
- ○ 3,672

Step 1: Analyze the Question

You're given a rate, and it looks like you'll have to convert it. You'll have to pay close attention to the units (seconds, hours, minutes, etc.) so you make the right conversion.

Step 2: State the Task

Convert 1.02 kilometers per second into terms of kilometers per hour. In other words, you start with this:

$$\frac{1.02 \text{ kilometers}}{\text{second}}$$

And want to end up with this:

$$\frac{??? \text{ kilometers}}{\text{hour}}$$

Step 3: Approach Strategically

You don't want to change the "kilometers" term, but you do want to change "seconds" to "hours." There are 60 seconds per minute and 60 minutes per hour. In other words, the rates are:

$$\frac{60 \text{ seconds}}{\text{minute}} \text{ and } \frac{60 \text{ minutes}}{\text{hour}}$$

Then set up multiplication so that the seconds cancel, as do the minutes:

$$\frac{1.02 \text{ kilometers}}{\text{seconds}} \times \frac{60 \text{ seconds}}{\text{minute}} \times \frac{60 \text{ minutes}}{\text{hour}} =$$

$$\frac{1.02 \text{ kilometers}}{\cancel{\text{seconds}}} \times \frac{60 \cancel{\text{ seconds}}}{\cancel{\text{minute}}} \times \frac{60 \cancel{\text{ minutes}}}{\text{hour}} =$$

$$\frac{(1.02 \times 60 \times 60) \text{ kilometers}}{\text{hour}}$$

So your calculation is 1.02 × 60 × 60. That's 1.02 × 3,600. While this isn't the hardest calculation in the world, you don't have to perform it at all, as only **(E)** is larger than 3,600.

Step 4: Confirm Your Answer

Reread the question stem, making sure that you didn't miss anything about the problem. For example, if you solved for kilometers per minute, you'd have selected **(B)**. This step would save you from choosing the wrong answer.

7. (B)

Magnabulk Corp sells boxes holding d magnets each. The boxes are shipped in crates, each holding b boxes. What is the price charged per magnet, in cents, if Magnabulk charges m dollars for each crate?

- ○ $\dfrac{100bd}{m}$
- ○ $\dfrac{100m}{bd}$
- ○ $\dfrac{bd}{100m}$
- ○ $\dfrac{m}{bd}$
- ○ $\dfrac{bd}{m}$

Step 1: Analyze the Question

This question gives you a complicated setup, with several different variables. Picking numbers will probably be a safe approach.

Step 2: State the Task

Your task is to calculate the price per magnet. The word *per* signals a rate:

$$\frac{\text{cents}}{\text{magnet}}$$

Many GMAT word problems have wrong answers that can be eliminated logically, and this is no exception. Since the answer is the amount of money that each magnet costs, you can be sure that the more dollars charged per crate (m), the more money each magnet would cost. In other words, the right answer would have to get bigger as m gets bigger. **(A)**, **(C)**, and **(E)** all have m in the denominator, so those expressions would get smaller as m gets bigger. Those answers can be eliminated.

Step 3: Approach Strategically

You need to solve for "magnets" and "cents."

What do you know about the number of magnets? According to the question stem, "Magnabulk Corp sells boxes holding d magnets." That means d magnets per box:

$$\frac{d\,\text{magnets}}{\text{box}}$$

What do you know about boxes? "Boxes are shipped in crates, each holding b boxes." That's b boxes per crate:

$$\frac{b\,\text{boxes}}{\text{crate}}$$

What do you know about the crates? "Magnabulk charges m dollars for each crate." That's m dollars per crate:

$$\frac{m \text{ dollars}}{\text{crate}}$$

And, of course, dollars convert to cents at the rate of 100 cents per dollar:

$$\frac{100 \text{ cents}}{\text{dollar}}$$

Then set up multiplication such that cents are in the numerator, magnets in the denominator, and everything else cancels:

$$\frac{100 \text{ cents}}{\text{dollar}} \times \frac{m \text{ dollars}}{\text{crate}} \times \frac{\text{crate}}{b \text{ boxes}} \times \frac{\text{box}}{d \text{ magnets}} =$$

$$\frac{100 \text{ cents}}{\cancel{\text{dollar}}} \times \frac{m \cancel{\text{ dollars}}}{\cancel{\text{crate}}} \times \frac{\cancel{\text{crate}}}{b \cancel{\text{ boxes}}} \times \frac{\cancel{\text{box}}}{d \text{ magnets}} =$$

$$\frac{100 m \text{ cents}}{bd \text{ magnets}}$$

That's **(B)**.

Picking numbers will also work well. Just choose permissible and manageable numbers. Say $d = 2$, $b = 5$, and $m = 4$. With these numbers substituted, the question stem reads as follows:

Magnabulk Corp sells boxes of 2 magnets. The boxes are shipped in crates, each holding 5 boxes. What is the price charged per magnet, in cents, if Magnabulk charges $4 for each crate?

Each crate holds 10 magnets, so 400 cents for 10 magnets is 40 cents per magnet. Plugging in $d = 2$, $b = 5$, and $m = 4$:

(A) $\dfrac{(100 \times 5 \times 2)}{4} = 25 \times 10 = 250$. Eliminate.

(B) $\dfrac{(100 \times 4)}{(5 \times 2)} = \dfrac{400}{10} = 40$. Possibly correct.

(C) $\dfrac{(5 \times 2)}{(100 \times 4)} = \dfrac{10}{400} = \dfrac{1}{40}$. Eliminate.

(D) $\dfrac{4}{(5 \times 2)} = \dfrac{4}{10} = \dfrac{2}{5}$. Eliminate.

(E) $\dfrac{(5 \times 2)}{4} = \dfrac{10}{4} = \dfrac{5}{2}$. Eliminate.

Step 4: Confirm Your Answer

Reread the question stem, making sure that you didn't miss anything about the problem. For example, the problem uses m for dollars and d for magnets instead of vice versa.

8. **(E)**

A motorcyclist started riding at highway marker A, drove 120 miles to highway marker B, and then, without pausing, continued to highway marker C, where she stopped. The average speed of the motorcyclist, over the course of the entire trip, was 45 miles per hour. If the ride from marker A to marker B lasted 3 times as many hours as the rest of the ride, and the distance from marker B to marker C was half of the distance from marker A to marker B, what was the average speed, in miles per hour, of the motorcyclist while driving from marker B to marker C?

- ○ 40
- ○ 45
- ○ 50
- ○ 55
- ○ 60

Step 1: Analyze the Question

A motorcyclist rides from highway marker to highway marker for different distances and durations and at different speeds. With so many pieces of information given for this multi-stage journey, you should be prepared to track it all with a table.

Step 2: State the Task

Find the average speed, in miles per hour (mph), of the motorcyclist while driving from marker B to marker C.

Step 3: Approach Strategically

With so much information to keep track of, the best way to approach this problem is first to organize all of the given concrete information into a table:

	Rate (mph)	Time (hr)	Distance (miles)
Marker A to marker B			120
Marker B to marker C	?		
Total	45		

You're told that the ride from marker A to marker B took 3 times as long as the ride from marker B to marker C and that the distance from marker B to marker C is half the distance from marker A to marker B. Using *t* for the amount of time, in hours, that it took to ride from marker B to marker C, you can now fill in your table with the following:

	Rate (mph)	Time (hr)	Distance (miles)
Marker A to marker B		3*t*	120
Marker B to marker C	?	*t*	60
Total	45	4*t*	180

It took $4t$ hours to go 180 miles at 45 miles per hour, so t must equal 1. You can now finish the table:

	Rate (mph)	Time (hr)	Distance (miles)
Marker A to marker B	40	3	120
Marker B to marker C	60	1	60
Total	45	4	180

You're looking for the average speed from marker B to marker C, which, according to the table, is 60 miles per hour. The correct choice is **(E)**.

Step 4: Confirm Your Answer

When using a table to organize information, check to ensure that the given pieces of information are filled into the correct parts of the table. Also remember that unlike time and distance, for which the values in the columns sum to get the total, the only way to calculate rate is to divide the distance for that row by the corresponding time.

9. (B)

A hiker walks three sections of a trail that are of equal length. The first section of the trail is flat, and on this section the hiker travels at 3 miles per hour for 1.5 hours. The second section is uphill, and on this section the hiker's pace slows by 25 percent. The third section is downhill, and here his speed doubles. What was the hiker's average speed for the entire three-section hike?

- ○ 1.5
- ○ 3
- ○ 3.25
- ○ 4.5
- ○ 9.75

Step 1: Analyze the Question

A journey consists of three parts of equal distance, traveled at different speeds. You know both the speed and the time needed to cover the first section, so you can derive the distance of each section from this information. The speeds for the second and third parts of the journey are given in terms of the speed for the previous part.

Step 2: State the Task

Use the average rate formula to calculate the hiker's average speed for the entire journey.

Step 3: Approach Strategically

To find the average rate of speed for the entire journey, you'll need the total distance hiked and the total time the hike took.

To find the distance of the first section of the hike, use the distance formula: Distance = Rate × Time. In this case, that means distance = 3 mph × 1.5 hours = 4.5 miles. Since each section is the same length, each section of the hike is 4.5 miles, and the total hike is 3 × 4.5 miles.

Now calculate the time needed for the second section of the hike. This will be distance divided by speed. The hiker's speed on the second section is 25% less than the speed on the first section, which is 100 − 25% = 75% of the starting speed; calculate 0.75 × 3 mph = 2.25 mph. (Be careful here! You have to apply the percentage to the hiker's rate, not his time.) Thus, the time needed for the second section of the hike is 4.5 miles ÷ 2.25 mph = 2 hours.

For the third section, apply the same process: the hiker's rate is twice his rate on the second section, so that's 2 × 2.25 mph = 4.5 mph. Again the distance is 4.5 miles, so the time needed is 4.5 miles ÷ 4.5 mph = 1 hour. Therefore, the time for the entire hike is 1.5 hours + 2 hours + 1 hour = 4.5 hours.

Finally, calculate the average rate for the journey: $\dfrac{3 \times 4.5 \text{ miles}}{4.5 \text{ hours}} = 3$ mph.

You might find it helpful to organize the information in a table and fill in each piece of information as you find it:

	Rate (mph)	Time (hrs)	Distance (miles)
Part 1 of hike	3	1.5	**3 × 1.5 = 4.5**
Part 2 of hike			4.5
Part 3 of hike			4.5
Entire hike	?		

Now calculate the data for each cell:

	Rate (mph)	Time (hrs)	Distance (miles)
Part 1 of hike	3	1.5	3 × 1.5 = 4.5
Part 2 of hike	0.75 × 3 = 2.25	4.5 ÷ 2.25 = 2	4.5
Part 3 of hike	2 × 2.25 = 4.5	4.5 ÷ 4.5 = 1	4.5
Entire hike	?		3 × 4.5

Finally, find the time and then the rate for the entire trip:

	Rate (mph)	Time (hrs)	Distance (miles)
Part 1 of hike	3	1.5	3 × 1.5 = 4.5
Part 2 of hike	0.75 × 3 = 2.25	4.5 ÷ 2.25 = 2	4.5
Part 3 of hike	2 × 2.25 = 4.5	4.5 ÷ 4.5 = 1	4.5
Entire hike	(3 × 4.5) ÷ 4.5 = **3**	1.5 + 2 + 1 = 4.5	3 × 4.5

The correct choice is **(B)**.

Step 4: Confirm Your Answer

Be sure that you've properly applied the percent adjustments to the appropriate speeds for each section of the hike and that you used the correct formula, Average rate = Total distance ÷ Total time, to find the final answer.

10. **(D)**

A truck driver drove for 2 days. On the second day, he drove 3 hours longer and at an average speed of 15 miles per hour faster than he drove on the first day. If he drove a total of 1,020 miles and spent 21 hours driving during the 2 days, what was his average speed on the first day, in miles per hour?

○ 25
○ 30
○ 35
○ 40
○ 45

Step 1: Analyze the Question

This is another multi-stage journey question. So despite the intimidating presentation, you know that you will transfer the data from the question stem into this chart:

	Rate (mph)	Time (hr)	Distance (miles)
Day 1	?		
Day 2			
Entire trip			

Step 2: State the Task

Solve for speed on the first day, which is the top-left box of the chart.

Step 3: Approach Strategically

Before you get too worried about what your solution will be, plug the data into the chart to help organize your thinking. The first thing you read is "On the second day, he drove 3 hours longer... than he drove on the first day." You know the total time will be 21 hours, so you can't just pick a number. Use t for time on the first day. That makes time on the second day $t + 3$.

Similarly, "On the second day, he drove...at an average speed of 15 miles per hour faster than he drove on the first day" allows you to say that if r is speed on the first day, then $r + 15$ is speed on the second day. The rest of the data is simply numerical:

	Rate (mph)	Time (hr)	Distance (miles)
Day 1	r(?)	t	
Day 2	$r + 15$	$t + 3$	
Entire trip		21	1,020

Since the total of the two days' times will be the time for the entire trip, you can say:

$$t + (t + 3) = 21$$
$$2t + 3 = 21$$
$$2t = 18$$
$$t = 9$$

Put that into the chart:

	Rate (mph)	Time (hr)	Distance (miles)
Day 1	$r(?)$	**9**	
Day 2	$r + 15$	**12**	
Entire trip		21	1,020

That allows you to find distance for each day by multiplying (Rate × Time = Distance).

	Rate (mph)	Time (hr)	Distance (miles)
Day 1	$r(?)$	9	**9r**
Day 2	$r + 15$	12	**12(r + 15)**
Entire trip		21	1,020

Now you have an equation that will allow you to solve for r, which is what you're looking for—speed on Day 1. Since the total of the 2 days' distances will be the distance for the entire trip, you can say:

$$9r + 12(r + 15) = 1,020$$

$$9r + 12r + 180 = 1,020$$

$$21r = 840$$

$$r = 40$$

The answer is **(D)**.

Step 4: Confirm Your Answer

Reread the question stem, making sure that you didn't miss anything about the problem. For example, if you inverted some information about the 2 days, you could end up with **(A)**.

11. (C)

Did Jon complete a journey of 40 kilometers in less time than it took Ann to complete the same journey?

(1) Jon traveled at an average speed of 30 kilometers per hour for the first 10 kilometers and then at an average speed of 15 kilometers per hour for the rest of the journey.

(2) Ann traveled at an average speed of 20 kilometers per hour for the entire journey.

Step 1: Analyze the Question Stem

This is a Yes/No question. The stem asks you to compare the time it took two people to complete the same journey of 40 km. Remember that $\frac{Distance}{Time}$. Since you're given the distance in the question stem, you'll need information adequate to determine both travelers' rates of speed.

Step 2: Evaluate the Statements Using 12TEN

Statement (1) gives you Jon's speed. Together with the question stem, this is enough information to determine the time required by Jon to complete the journey. But you get no information about Ann. Statement (1) is insufficient. You can eliminate **(A)** and **(D)**.

Statement (2) and the question stem together give enough information to determine the time Ann took to complete the journey but nothing about Jon. Statement (2) is also insufficient. Eliminate **(B)**.

Combining the two statements, you have enough to determine both the time Jon took to complete the journey and the time Ann took to complete the journey. Note that you don't need to calculate their times; knowing that you could calculate them is enough. **(C)** is correct.

EXPLANATIONS

12. (A)

Working at its usual constant rate, Pump A can empty a water storage tank in 3 hours. Pump B, also working at its usual constant rate, can empty half of the same tank in 4 hours. How many hours will it take both pumps working together at their usual respective constant rates to empty half of the tank?

○ $\frac{12}{11}$

○ $\frac{24}{11}$

○ $\frac{24}{7}$

○ $\frac{7}{2}$

○ $\frac{36}{7}$

Step 1: Analyze the Question

Pump A takes 3 hours to empty a tank, and Pump B takes 4 hours to empty half of the same tank—that is, it would take Pump B 8 hours to empty the whole tank.

Step 2: State the Task

Use an understanding of combined rates to find the number of hours it would take both pumps, working together at their respective rates, to empty half the tank.

Step 3: Approach Strategically

While you could calculate this problem using the combined work formula, some critical thinking can go far here. Since Pump A by itself can empty the tank in 3 hours, it stands to reason that Pump A and Pump B working together must be able to empty the tank in fewer than 3 hours. Notice that **(C)**, **(D)**, and **(E)** are all greater than 3, so eliminate all of them. Furthermore, you're trying to find how long it would take the two pumps to empty only half of the tank, so logically, that must be less than half of 3 hours, or 1.5 hours. Since **(B)** is greater than 1.5, you can eliminate it as well. Thus, the correct answer is the only remaining choice, **(A)**.

Step 4: Confirm Your Answer

If you used the logical approach above, then to confirm your answer, use the combined work formula, $T = \frac{AB}{A+B}$. (If you used the formula in the first place, then check your answer against the logic of the situation.)

In this case, T is the time Pump A and Pump B take to empty the entire tank when working together, and A and B are the respective amounts of time that it takes each pump to empty the tank individually. Plug the given times into this formula and solve:

$$T = \frac{AB}{A+B}$$

$$T = \frac{3 \times 8}{3+8}$$

$$T = \frac{24}{11}$$

So it takes Pump A and Pump B working together $\frac{24}{11}$ hours to empty the whole tank. Since you need to find how long it would take to empty just half the tank, that's $\frac{24}{11} \div 2 = \frac{12}{11}$ hours.

13. (C)

Machine 1 and Machine 2 working together can produce 12,000 meters of steel cable per hour. Each machine works at a constant rate. Machine 1 by itself can produce 5,000 meters of cable per hour. How many hours would it Machine 2 working alone to produce 12,000 meters of cable?

- ○ $\dfrac{7}{12}$
- ○ $\dfrac{67}{40}$
- ○ $\dfrac{12}{7}$
- ○ $\dfrac{11}{5}$
- ○ $\dfrac{5}{2}$

Step 1: Analyze the Question

This is a combined work problem with a twist. Rather than being given the time each machine can complete the job separately, you're given the time it takes the two machines together to complete the job and the portion of the job one of the two machines can do in the same amount of time.

Step 2: State the Task

Find how long it will take the second machine, working alone, to complete the entire job.

Step 3: Approach Strategically

You can use the combined work formula, $T = \dfrac{AB}{A+B}$. In this formula, A and B are the times that each machine can do the job in time T. You're given that Machine 1 and Machine 2 together can produce 12,000 meters of cable in 1 hour, so in this scenario, $T = 1$.

You're also given that Machine 1 by itself can produce 5,000 meters of cable in 1 hour. From this, you can find how long it would take Machine 1 to complete the entire 12,000 meters: Machine 1 can complete $\dfrac{5,000}{12,000} = \dfrac{5}{12}$ of the job in 1 hour. Therefore, Machine 1 will take 1 hour $\div \dfrac{5}{12}$ hours/job $= \dfrac{12}{5}$ hours to complete the entire job.

Now plug this information into the combined work formula: $\dfrac{\frac{12}{5}B}{\frac{12}{5}+B} = 1$. Multiply both sides by the denominator to simplify: $\dfrac{12}{5}B = \dfrac{12}{5} + B$. Multiply each term by 5 to clear the fractions: $12B = 12 + 5B$. Then $7B = 12$, and $B = \dfrac{12}{7}$. This is the time it would take Machine 2 to make 12,000 meters of cable, and **(C)** is correct.

EXPLANATIONS

Step 4: Confirm Your Answer

You can confirm your answer with an alternative approach. Once you've determined that Machine 1 can do $\frac{5}{12}$ of the job (producing 12,000 meters of cable) in 1 hour, you can deduce that Machine 2 must be able to complete $\frac{12}{12} - \frac{5}{12} = \frac{7}{12}$ of the job in 1 hour. Set up a proportion of jobs to hours and solve for the hours for 1 job:

$$\frac{\text{jobs}}{\text{hours}} = \frac{\frac{7}{12}}{1} = \frac{1}{x}$$

Cross multiply: $\frac{7}{12}x = 1$, and $x = \frac{12}{7}$.

14. (A)

Two trucks travel from Alphaburg to Betaville along the same route. The speed limit for the first 30 miles is 60 miles per hour (mph). The speed limit for the next 10 miles is 40 mph, and the limit for the final 60 miles is 55 mph. Truck F has a maximum speed of 70 mph, but Truck S has a speed-limiting governor installed to cap its maximum speed at 50 mph. Truck S departs Alphaburg 12 minutes before Truck F. If each truck travels at the lesser of the speed limit or the maximum speed of the truck, how far from Betaville is the point where Truck F catches up with Truck S?

- ○ 5 miles
- ○ 20 miles
- ○ 55 miles
- ○ 95 miles
- ○ Both trucks arrive at Betaville simultaneously.

Step 1: Analyze the Question

Because two trucks are traveling the same route and the slower truck sets out on the journey before the faster truck, this is an overtaking problem. The relative speed of the two trucks is the *difference* between their speeds; this is the rate at which the faster truck catches up with the slower truck. There are limiting factors included in the question, including the speed limits on the roads and the maximum speeds of the trucks.

- For the first 30 miles, Truck F travels at 60 mph and Truck S at 50 mph, so F is gaining on S at the rate of 10 mph.
- Both trucks travel the next 10 miles at 40 mph.
- For the final 60 miles, Truck F travels at 55 mph and Truck S at 50 mph, so F is traveling 5 mph faster than S.

Step 2: State the Task

Determine the distance from Betaville to the point where Truck F overtakes Truck S.

Step 3: Approach Strategically

Since there are different speeds involved in the three segments of the journey, analyze this piece by piece. The first leg is 30 miles. Using the formula Distance = Rate × Time rearranged as Time = $\frac{\text{Distance}}{\text{Rate}}$, Truck S traverses this leg in $\frac{30}{50} = 0.6$ hours. Truck F starts 12 minutes later, or $\frac{12}{60} = \frac{1}{5} = 0.2$ hours later. It completes this leg in $\frac{30}{60} = 0.5$ hours, which is 0.1 hours less than the time for S. However, since Truck F started 0.2 hours after Truck S, Truck F arrives at the end of the 30-mile leg 0.2 − 0.1 = 0.1 hour after Truck S.

The trucks will complete the 10-mile segment in the same amount of time since they both are limited to 40 mph, so Truck F will begin the final 60-mile leg 0.1 hour after Truck S does.

For the last 60 miles, Truck F overtakes Truck S at a rate of 5 mph. Truck S starts this leg 0.1 hour before Truck F. Traveling at 50 mph, that is a 50 × 0.1 = 5-mile head start. So, given that F is traveling 5 mph faster, it would catch up with S in exactly an hour. The point at which this occurs would be 1 hour × 55 mph = 55 miles from the start of the leg. Because the entire segment is 60 miles long, this point is 60 − 55 = 5 miles from Betaville. **(A)** is correct.

Step 4: Confirm Your Answer

The tricky part of this question is all the details presented regarding distances and speeds. Reread the question stem, making sure that you used the correct values, and check your calculations. **(B)** is the distance the trucks traveled on the last leg before F catches up to S. **(D)** is the correct distance from Alphaburg rather than from Betaville.

15. (A)

Binh invested $1,000 in a certificate of deposit (CD) that matured in 4 years. The certificate paid 4 percent annual interest compounded quarterly for the original 4-year term and then 2 percent simple annual interest on the compounded amount after that until the CD was redeemed by the holder. If Binh held his CD for exactly 6 years, how much money did he receive when he redeemed it?

- ○ $1,000 \times (1.01)^{16} \times 1.04$
- ○ $1,000 \times (1.01)^{16} \times (1.02)^2$
- ○ $1,000 \times (1.04)^6$
- ○ $1,000 \times (1.01)^{24}$
- ○ $1,000 \times (1.04)^{16} \times (1.02)^2$

Step 1: Analyze the Question

A $1,000 certificate of deposit paid 4% annual interest compounded quarterly until it matured in 4 years, which means that 1% was added to the principal 4 times per year. Thereafter, the certificate paid 2% annual simple interest on the compounded amount. Binh purchased such a certificate and redeemed it after 6 years.

Step 2: State the Task

Determine which expression among the answer choices represents the value of the CD after 6 years.

Step 3: Approach Strategically

The formula for compound interest is Principal $\times (1 + r)^t$, where r is the interest rate per time period expressed as a decimal and t is the number of time periods. Since this CD had a 4% annual rate with interest compounded quarterly, $r = \frac{1}{4} \times 0.04 = 0.01$. Because the compounding occurred 4 times per year for 4 years, $t = 4 \times 4 = 16$. Thus, the value of the CD at the end of 4 years was $1,000 \times (1.01)^{16}$. This amount then amassed simple interest. The formula for simple interest is Principal $\times (1 + rt)$. In this case, the interest rate was 2%, so $r = 0.2$, and it accrued for 2 years, so $t = 2$. So Principal $\times (1 + 0.02(2)) = $ Principal $\times 1.04$. Thus, the total value after 6 years was $(1.01)^{16} \times 1.04$. **(A)** is correct.

Step 4: Confirm Your Answer

Whenever an interest problem involves compounding other than annually, be certain to adjust the interest rate per compounding period and the number of times that compounding occurs. Double-check these values in your solution.

16. (B)

The amount of an investment will double in approximately 70/*p* years, where *p* is the percent interest, compounded annually. If Thelma invests $40,000 in a long-term CD that pays 5 percent interest, compounded annually, what will be the approximate total value of the investment when Thelma is ready to retire 42 years later?

- ○ $280,000
- ○ $320,000
- ○ $360,000
- ○ $450,000
- ○ $540,000

Step 1: Analyze the Question

You're given a piece of information other than just interest rate and principal. How might it influence your solution? You may not be sure yet, but it's unlikely to be extraneous information. Also, the word *approximate* should make you happy: you may be able to estimate rather than calculate.

Step 2: State the Task

What is the approximate value in 42 years of a $40,000 investment that earns 5% compound annual interest?

Step 3: Approach Strategically

This problem is a great example of why strategic reading and logical analysis should precede any math. If you rush blindly into math, you'd get Total = $40,000 × $(1.05)^{42}$. There's no way to solve, even approximately, without a calculator.

But what if you approached the problem strategically? You're asked for "total value of the investment." Scan through the question stem looking for information related to total value, and you find "*the amount of an investment* will double in approximately $\frac{70}{p}$ years, where *p* is the percent interest."

Then search for the interest and discover that it is 5%. So you now know that the investment will double every $\frac{70}{5}$ years—or every 14 years.

Now look for how many years the money is invested and see that it's 42 years: 42 is 14 × 3, so 42 years means 3 doublings. The total value will be approximately $40,000 × 2 × 2 × 2 = $40,000 × 8 = $320,000.

The answer is **(B)**.

Step 4: Confirm Your Answer

Reread the question stem, making sure that you didn't accidentally skip over any important aspects of the situation.

17. (E)

A certain account pays 1.5 percent compound interest every 3 months. A person invested an initial amount and did not invest any more money in the account after that. If after exactly 5 years, the amount of money in the account was T dollars, which of the following is an expression for the original number of dollars invested in the account?

- ○ $(1.015)^4 T$
- ○ $(1.015)^{15} T$
- ○ $(1.015)^{20} T$
- ○ $\dfrac{T}{(1.015)^{15}}$
- ○ $\dfrac{T}{(1.015)^{20}}$

Step 1: Analyze the Question

The question addresses compound interest. It's worth noting that the interest is not annual interest but is compounded every 3 months. Since there are 12 months per year, the interest compounds 4 times per year.

Although there are variables in the answer choices, picking numbers probably won't be needed, as the answers are just various ways that the interest formula might be constructed.

Step 2: State the Task

Solve for the original amount in the account. Call it P for principal.

Step 3: Approach Strategically

Since the question seems all about whether you can properly construct the compound interest formula, make sure that you carefully set up each part. The general formula is this:

$$T = P(1 + r)^t$$

All of the answer choices use 1.015, so you know for certain—if you didn't already—that inside the parentheses must be 1.015:

$$T = P(1.015)^t$$

Since interest is compounded 4 times per year for 5 years, $t = 4 \times 5 = 20$.

$$T = P (1.015)^{20}$$
$$\frac{T}{(1.015)^{20}} = P$$

The answer is **(E)**.

Step 4: Confirm Your Answer

Reread the question stem, making sure that you didn't accidentally skip over any important aspects of the situation. For example, if you initially missed the "every 3 months" part of the stimulus, you would have been looking for an answer with an exponent of 4. This step gives you the chance to catch such errors.

18. **(B)**

Of the 65 books released last year by a particular publishing house, 25 were no more than 200 pages. The publisher released 35 fiction books, of which 20 were more than 200 pages, and it also published nonfiction books. How many nonfiction books of no more than 200 pages did the publishing house release last year?

- ○ 5
- ○ 10
- ○ 20
- ○ 30
- ○ 35

Step 1: Analyze the Question

This question provides you with information about a group of 65 books; every book is classified as either fiction or nonfiction and as either greater than 200 pages or less than or equal to 200 pages (to avoid having these irrelevant numbers in your head, you might paraphrase this as "long books and short books"). Plan on organizing the details in a table to keep track of them.

Step 2: State the Task

Find the total number of nonfiction books "of no more than 200 pages"—in other words, less than or equal to 200 pages, or short nonfiction books.

Step 3: Approach Strategically

Organize all of the given information into a table:

	Fiction	Nonfiction	Total
Short		?	25
Long	20		
Total	35		65

With everything organized, fill in the blanks. Once you have two entries in a row or column, you can fill in the third entry for that row or column. If the two known values are subtotals, add them to get the total; if one of the known values is a total, subtract the known subtotal from the total to get the other subtotal.

	Fiction	Nonfiction	Total
Short	15	**10**	25
Long	20	20	40
Total	35	30	65

Arrive at the correct answer either by subtracting 15 short fiction books from 25 total short books in the first row or by subtracting 20 long nonfiction books from 30 total nonfiction books in the second column. The number of short nonfiction books is 10. **(B)** is correct.

Step 4: Confirm Your Answer

When using a table, check to make sure that you answer with the right piece of information; three of the incorrect choices are numbers that fill in other cells in the table. Also, double-check that you answered the right question; for example, if you read the question as "How many nonfiction books of more than 200 pages" instead of "*no* more than 200 pages," you may have chosen **(C)**.

19. (C)

Three hundred students at College Q study a foreign language. Of these, 110 of those students study French and 170 study Spanish. If at least 90 students who study a foreign language at College Q study neither French nor Spanish, then the number of students who study Spanish but not French could be any number from

O   10 to 40

O   40 to 100

O   60 to 100

O   60 to 110

O   70 to 110

Step 1: Analyze the Question

Since students are split into two potentially overlapping sets—those who study Spanish and those who study French—this is an overlapping sets problem. To help organize the data, draw a table:

	French	Not French	Total
Spanish		?	
Not Spanish			
Total			

Step 2: State the Task

You need to find a valid range, with both an upper and lower limit, for those who are in the "Spanish and not French" category.

Step 3: Approach Strategically

You have a piece of data with a lower limit ("at least 90") but nothing with an upper limit. It's hard to know intuitively what that upper limit should be, so put in the data from the question stem so you can understand the problem more clearly:

	French	Not French	Total
Spanish		?	170
Not Spanish		at least 90	
Total	110		300

From this, you can figure out how many do *not* study each language:

	French	Not French	Total
Spanish		?	170
Not Spanish		at least 90	130
Total	110	190	300

Now that you have a clearer understanding of the situation, you can understand more about the limitations on the "at least 90" group. Since the total of the "not Spanish" row is 130, there could be no more than 130 in the "not Spanish and not French" category. (More than 130 would require a negative number of students in the "French and not Spanish" category.)

	French	Not French	Total
Spanish		?	170
Not Spanish		90 to 130	130
Total	110	190	300

The "Spanish and not French" category must add with "90 to 130" to yield 190. There could be as many as 100 (since $100 + 90 = 190$) or as few as 60 (since $60 + 130 = 190$).

The answer is **(C)**.

Step 4: Confirm Your Answer

Reread the question stem, making sure that you didn't accidentally misread anything. For example, **(E)** is the value of the "Spanish and French" category.

20. (A)

The *Financial News Daily* has 25 reporters covering Asia, 20 covering Europe, and 20 covering North America. Four reporters cover Asia and Europe but not North America, 6 reporters cover Asia and North America but not Europe, and 7 reporters cover Europe and North America but not Asia. How many reporters cover all of the 3 continents (Asia, Europe, and North America)?

(1) The *Financial News Daily* has 38 reporters in total covering at least 1 of the following continents: Asia, Europe, and North America.

(2) There are more *Financial News Daily* reporters covering only Asia than there are *Financial News Daily* reporters covering only North America.

Step 1: Analyze the Question Stem

This is a Value question. It is asking for the number of reporters who cover all three continents.

There's a lot of information, and it begs to be simplified. As the reporters may cover one, two, or three of the continents, this is an overlapping sets question. But with *three* sets, a chart-based approach would be too unwieldy. The best way to visualize three overlapping sets is with a Venn diagram. Take care to put the totals for each continent just outside the circles so that you don't lose the distinction between the number covering a continent and the number covering *only* that continent.

So that you know what you need, put an *x* in the "all three continents" space on the diagram.

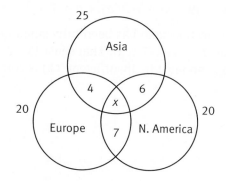

You can continue to analyze your information. A total of 25 reporters cover Asia, 6 of whom also cover only North America, 4 of whom also cover only Europe, and *x* of whom also cover both Europe and North America.

Therefore, $25 - (6 + 4 + x)$, or $15 - x$, cover only Asia.

Similarly, $20 - (4 + 7 + x)$, or $9 - x$, cover only Europe, and $20 - (7 + 6 + x)$, or $7 - x$, cover only North America.

Put that into your diagram:

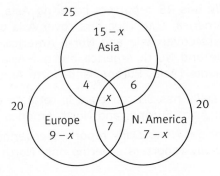

Many kinds of information, therefore, would allow you to figure out the number of reporters who cover all three continents. Any data that lets you make an equation with *x* would be sufficient.

Step 2: Evaluate the Statements Using 12TEN

Statement (1) says that the grand total of all the reporters is 38. In other words, if you added up all the various subcategories, you'd get 38. That's sufficient, as the only variable in that equation would be *x*. Eliminate **(B)**, **(C)**, and **(E)**.

Although you wouldn't want to set the whole thing up (you'd stop as soon as you knew that you *could* set up the equation), here's what it would be:

$$(15 - x) + (9 - x) + (7 - x) + 4 + 7 + 6 + x = 38$$

Once the information from the question stem has been fully simplified and analyzed, you see that Statement (2) is only saying that $(15 - x) > (7 - x)$. That's just $15 > 7$, which is hardly new information. Statement (2) adds nothing and must be insufficient. **(A)** is correct.

GMAT BY THE NUMBERS: MATH FORMULAS

Now that you've learned how to approach math formulas questions on the GMAT, let's add one more dimension to your understanding of how they work.

Take a moment to try this question. Following is performance data from thousands of people who have studied with Kaplan over the decades. Through analyzing this data, we will show you how to approach questions like this one most effectively and how to avoid similarly tempting wrong answer choice types on Test Day.

> In an election, candidate Smith won 52 percent of the total vote in Counties A and B. He won 61 percent of the vote in County A. If the ratio of people who voted in County A to County B is 3:1, what percent of the vote did candidate Smith win in County B?

- ○ 25%
- ○ 27%
- ○ 34%
- ○ 43%
- ○ 49%

EXPLANATION

QUESTION STATISTICS

57% of test takers choose **(A)**

16% of test takers choose **(B)**

10% of test takers choose **(C)**

12% of test takers choose **(D)**

5% of test takers choose **(E)**

Sample size = 5,221

The statistics above show that this is a hard question, as many test takers get it wrong. But no single wrong answer stands out as a common trap. This is the sign of a problem that is challenging because most test takers simply don't know how to approach it. However, this question doesn't have to be difficult.

The question demonstrates the pattern in which two entities, each with a different proportion or average, are combined to form a total with a new overall proportion or average. You can make quick work of this problem using the balance approach. Smith ends up at 52%, and County A is 9 points above this at 61%. Moreover, there are 3 people in County A for every 1 person in County B, so multiply A's 9-point surplus by 3 to get a 27-point surplus. To bring the vote percentage into balance at 52%, County B has to be 27 points below 52%, or 25%. **(A)** is correct.

Or you can use a formula that handles this problem:

(Proportion A)(Weight of A) + (Proportion B)(Weight of B) = (Total proportion)(Total weight)

You can represent the proportion of the vote Smith won in County B with the variable b. Then just plug the data into the formula and solve:

$$(0.61)(3) + (b)(1) = (0.52)(3 + 1)$$
$$1.83 + b = (0.52)(4)$$
$$1.83 + b = 2.08$$
$$b = 2.08 - 1.83$$
$$b = 0.25$$

By learning these classic formulas and problem-solving techniques, you'll find yourself comfortably handling problems that stump many other test takers.

MORE GMAT BY THE NUMBERS...

To see more questions with answer choice statistics, be sure to review the full-length CATs in your online resources.

GO ONLINE

kaptest.com/login

CHAPTER 18

Geometry on the GMAT

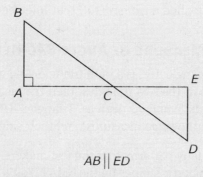

$AB \parallel ED$

Note: Figure not drawn to scale.

In the figure above, $ED = 1$, $CD = 2$, and $AE = 6\sqrt{3}$. What is the perimeter of $\triangle ABC$?

- ○ $3\sqrt{3}$
- ○ $10 + 5\sqrt{3}$
- ○ $10\sqrt{3}$
- ○ $15 + 5\sqrt{3}$
- ○ $25\sqrt{3}$

Above is a typical Problem Solving geometry question. In this chapter, we'll look at how to apply the Kaplan Method to this question, discuss the geometry rules being tested, and go over the basic principles and strategies that you want to keep in mind on every Quantitative question involving geometry. But before you move on, take a minute to think about what you see in this question and answer some questions about how you think it works:

- What types of shapes are presented in the figure?

- How does knowing that lines *AB* and *ED* are parallel help you?

- How does knowing the measure of angle *BAC* help you?

- What GMAT Core Competencies are most essential to success on this question?

PREVIEWING GEOMETRY ON THE GMAT

WHAT TYPES OF SHAPES ARE PRESENTED IN THE FIGURE?

The diagram contains two triangles. More importantly, note that since the triangles meet at a common point, the angles that meet at that point (in this case, angles *BCA* and *DCE*) must be equal as well.

HOW DOES KNOWING THAT LINES *AB* AND *ED* ARE PARALLEL HELP YOU?

You're given that sides *AB* and *ED* are parallel. This defines a relationship between angles *ABC* and *CDE*: they are equal. You'll see this mentioned later in this chapter, but these two are alternate interior angles, formed by a line (called a *transversal*) that intersects two parallel lines.

HOW DOES KNOWING THE MEASURE OF ANGLE *BAC* HELP YOU?

Since angle *BAC* is a right angle, triangle *ABC* is a right triangle. And given that *BA* and *ED* are parallel and two pairs of angles are equal in the two triangles, then the measure of angle *BAC* must also be equal to that of *CED*, and both must equal 90 degrees. Triangles *ABC* and *CDE* are therefore similar triangles—their three angles have the same measures, and their side lengths share the same ratio.

Because right triangles have so many patterns that the test makers can write questions about, they are the most frequently tested geometric shapes on the GMAT. You'll learn later in this chapter about the relationships certain right triangles display between their side lengths and angle measurements.

WHAT GMAT CORE COMPETENCIES ARE MOST ESSENTIAL TO SUCCESS ON THIS QUESTION?

Pattern Recognition will play a key role here, as we'll look at how the lengths of a right triangle can often give us more information about a triangle, such as angle measurements. Additionally, even though in this case you're not translating a word problem into an equation, your ability to apply the Core Competency of Paraphrasing is important, since you can use information about one part of the figure to draw inferences about other parts. In particular, knowing how to interpret the information about the parallel lines will be the key to answering this question efficiently.

Here are the main topics we'll cover in this chapter:

- Lines and Angles
- Triangles
- Polygons
- Circles
- Multiple Figures
- Solids
- Coordinate Geometry

HANDLING GMAT GEOMETRY

Now let's apply the Kaplan Method to the geometry question you saw earlier:

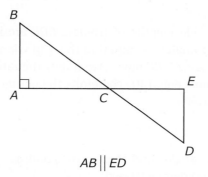

$AB \parallel ED$

Note: Figure not drawn to scale.

In the figure above, $ED = 1$, $CD = 2$, and $AE = 6\sqrt{3}$. What is the perimeter of $\triangle ABC$?

- ○ $3\sqrt{3}$
- ○ $10 + 5\sqrt{3}$
- ○ $10\sqrt{3}$
- ○ $15 + 5\sqrt{3}$
- ○ $25\sqrt{3}$

Step 1: Analyze the Question

You're given two triangles that meet at a certain point and are told that two of the line segments that form their sides are parallel. Additionally, you're given that angle *BAC* is a right angle, which makes triangle *ABC* a right triangle. Since *AB* and *ED* are parallel, angles *ABC* and *CDE* are equal, because they are alternate interior angles formed by two parallel lines cut by a transversal. Angles *BCA* and *DCE* are also equal, since these are vertical angles. And since the measure of all interior angles of a triangle must add up to a specific number, 180, then angles *BAC* and *CED* must also be equal.

Step 2: State the Task

You're asked to find the perimeter of triangle *ABC*. You'll need to use the information about triangle *CDE* to be able to figure out the side lengths of *ABC*. The last step will be to add up the side lengths.

Step 3: Approach Strategically

Since you know that *CDE* is a right triangle, you can use the Pythagorean theorem to first find the length of the missing side of triangle *CDE* by substituting the relevant values into the equation $(ED)^2 + (CE)^2 = (CD)^2$.

However, if you noticed that one side of the triangle, *ED*, is equal to 1 and the hypotenuse, *CD*, is equal to 2, then you may recognize that this is a special right triangle, specifically the 30-60-90 triangle. Recognizing this pattern will save you much time. If the hypotenuse is twice the length of one of the sides of the triangle, then the side lengths of the triangle will be in the ratio of $1:\sqrt{3}:2$. Therefore, side CE must have a length of $\sqrt{3}$. Since you are given that AE equals $6\sqrt{3}$, leg AC must equal $6\sqrt{3} - \sqrt{3} = 5\sqrt{3}$.

Since you established that the side lengths of triangle CDE are in the ratio of $1:\sqrt{3}:2$, and you identified that its corresponding angles are equal to those of triangle ABC, then the two triangles are similar, and the three sides $AB:AC:BC$ must also follow the ratio of $1:\sqrt{3}:2$. Because AC equals $5\sqrt{3}$, AB must equal 5, and BC must equal 10. Therefore, the perimeter of triangle ABC is $5\sqrt{3} + 5 + 10$, or $15 + 5\sqrt{3}$. Choice **(D)** is correct.

Step 4: Confirm Your Answer

Make sure you've paired up the angles and their corresponding side lengths correctly, using the ratio of side lengths of a 30-60-90 degree triangle.

Now let's look at each of the seven areas of geometry that show up on the GMAT Quantitative section, starting with lines and angles.

LINES AND ANGLES

LINES

A line is a one-dimensional abstraction—infinitely long with no width. Two points determine a straight line; given any two points, there is exactly one straight line that passes through them.

A line **segment** is a section of a straight line of finite length with two endpoints. A line segment is named for its endpoints, as in segment AB below. The **midpoint** is the point that divides a line segment into two equal parts.

Example:

In the figure above, A and B are the endpoints of the line segment AB, and M is the midpoint ($AM = MB$). What is the length of AB?

Since AM is 6, MB is also 6, so AB is $6 + 6$, or 12.

Two lines are **parallel** if they lie in the same plane and never intersect each other regardless of how far they are extended. If line ℓ_1 is parallel to line ℓ_2, you write $\ell_1 \parallel \ell_2$.

Two lines are **perpendicular** if they intersect at a 90° angle. The shortest distance from a point to a line is the line segment drawn from the point to the line such that it is perpendicular to the line. If line ℓ_1 is perpendicular to line ℓ_2, you write $\ell_1 \perp \ell_2$. If $\ell_1 \perp \ell_2$ and $\ell_2 \perp \ell_3$, then $\ell_1 \parallel \ell_3$.

ANGLES

An angle is formed by two lines or line segments intersecting at a point. The point of intersection is called the **vertex** of the angle. Angles are measured in degrees (°).

Angle x, $\angle ABC$, and $\angle B$ all denote the same angle shown in the diagram above.

Acute, Right, and Obtuse Angles

An **acute angle** is an angle whose degree measure is between 0° and 90°. A **right angle** is an angle whose degree measure is exactly 90°. An **obtuse angle** is an angle whose degree measure is between 90° and 180°. A **straight angle** is an angle whose degree measure is exactly 180° (half of a circle, which contains 360°).

acute	right	obtuse	straight
$(0 < x < 90)$	$(y = 90)$	$(90 < z < 180)$	$(w = 180)$

Sums of Angle Measures

The sum of the measures of the angles on one side of a straight line is 180°.

straight
$x + y + z = 180$

The sum of the measures of the angles around a point is 360°.

$a + b + c + d + e = 360$

Two angles are **supplementary** if together they make up a straight angle (i.e., if the sum of their measures is 180°). Two angles are **complementary** if together they make up a right angle (i.e., if the sum of their measures is 90°).

$c + d = 180$
supplementary

$a + b = 90$
complementary

A line or line segment **bisects** an angle if it splits the angle into two smaller, equal angles. Line segment BD below bisects $\angle ABC$, and $\angle ABD$ has the same measure as $\angle DBC$. The two smaller angles are each half the size of $\angle ABC$.

Vertical Angles

Vertical angles are a pair of opposite angles formed by two intersecting line segments. At the point of intersection, two pairs of vertical angles are formed. Angles a and c below are vertical angles, as are b and d.

The two angles in a pair of vertical angles have the same degree measure. In the previous diagram, $a = c$ and $b = d$. In addition, since ℓ_1 and line ℓ_2 are straight lines, $a + b = c + d = a + d = b + c = 180$.

In other words, each angle is supplementary to each of its two adjacent angles.

If two parallel lines intersect with a third line (called a *transversal*), the third line will intersect each of the parallel lines at the same angle. In the figure below, $a = e$ because the transversal intersects lines ℓ_1 and ℓ_2 at the same angle. Since a and e are equal, and $c = a$ and $e = g$ (vertical angles), you know that $a = c = e = g$. Similarly, $b = d = f = h$.

In other words, when two parallel lines intersect with a third line, all acute angles formed are equal, all obtuse angles formed are equal, and any acute angle is supplementary to any obtuse angle.

IN-FORMAT QUESTION: LINES AND ANGLES ON THE GMAT

Now let's use the Kaplan Method on a Problem Solving question dealing with lines and angles:

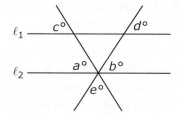

If ℓ_1 is parallel to ℓ_2 in the figure above, which of the following expressions must equal 180?

　　　I. $a + b$
　　II. $c + e$
　　III. $c + d + e$

- ○ I only
- ○ II only
- ○ III only
- ○ II and III only
- ○ I, II, and III

Step 1: Analyze the Question

When analyzing a geometry question that includes a figure, you'll want to consider the question stem and the figure together. Here, the question stem tells you that ℓ_1 and ℓ_2 are parallel. This is the time to use Critical Thinking to help you come to an efficient solution. Since ℓ_1 and ℓ_2 are parallel, you know that the corresponding angles created by the transversals (intersecting lines) will be of equal measure. Specifically, that means

$$a = c$$
$$b = d$$

Looking at the figure again, you see that angles a and b, plus that third angle between them, compose a straight line, which is 180°. Since angle e is the "vertical angle" of that third angle, their measures are the same. So you can deduce

$$a + b + e = 180$$

Step 2: State the Task

Your task is to determine which of the three Roman numeral statements are equal to 180. You just deduced $a + b + e = 180$, so if a statement is equal to $a + b + e$, then it will also be equal to 180.

Step 3: Approach Strategically

Which Roman numeral statement should you check first? You could start with Statement III, which looks similar to what you're after. It also appears in the most answer choices (tying Statement II), so that's another good reason to start with Statement III.

Does $c + d + e = a + b + e$? You figured out earlier that $a = c$ and $b = d$. Substituting a for c and b for d, you confirm that $c + d + e$ does in fact equal $a + b + e$, which means that it also equals 180. The right answer must contain Statement III, so you can eliminate **(A)** and **(B)**. (You can also use Critical Thinking to note that c, d, and e are vertical angles for the triangle in the middle of the picture; the angles in a triangle always sum to 180 degrees.)

Looking at the answers that remain, you see that Statement II appears twice, whereas Statement I appears only once. Evaluate Statement II next.

Does $c + e = a + b + e$? You deduced earlier that $c + d + e = a + b + e$. The only way, then, that $c + e$ would also equal $a + b + e$ is if $d = 0$. You have no idea what its value is, but it's definitely not 0. So Statement II is not part of the right answer. That lets you eliminate **(D)** and **(E)**, leaving only the correct answer, **(C)**.

You could also have solved by picking numbers. A Roman numeral statement will be part of the right answer only if it *must* equal 180. So if you can pick numbers to get a statement to equal something other than 180, you can eliminate it. Let's say that you pick $c = 30$ and $d = 40$. Since a and c are corresponding angles, $a = 30$. Similarly, $b = 40$. That means that the unnamed angle between a and b must equal $180 - (30 + 40)$, or 110. Since e has the same measure, $e = 110$. Quickly plugging those numbers into the Roman numeral statements gives the following:

I. $30 + 40 = 70$. Eliminate.

II. $30 + 110 = 140$. Eliminate.

III. $30 + 40 + 110 = 180$. Don't eliminate.

After you eliminate Statements I and II, only choice **(C)** is possible.

Step 4: Confirm Your Answer

Finally, reread the question stem, making sure that you didn't miss anything about the problem. You're looking for the angles in the figure that add up to 180. You've determined that $a + b + e = 180$ and that $a + b + e = c + d + e$. Therefore, $c + d + e = 180$, making **(C)** the only correct answer.

TAKEAWAYS: LINES AND ANGLES

- Vertical angles are equal.
- The sum of angles that form a straight line is 180°.
- When two parallel lines are intersected by a third line, the corresponding angles are equal.
- Sometimes it is possible to determine the relationship between angles without determining the degree measures of the angles.

PRACTICE SET: LINES AND ANGLES ON THE GMAT

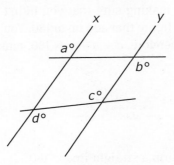

1. In the figure above, if lines x and y are parallel, what is the value of $a + c$?

    (1) $b - d = 20$

    (2) $b + d = 260$

2. In the figure above, the value of x is

    ○   30

    ○   60

    ○   75

    ○   100

    ○   120

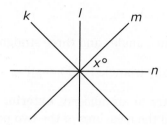

3. What is the value of x?

    (1) Lines k and m are perpendicular.

    (2) Lines l and n are perpendicular.

TRIANGLES

A triangle is a closed figure with three angles and three straight sides.

The sum of the **interior angles** of any triangle is 180 degrees.

Each interior angle is supplementary to an adjacent **exterior angle**. The degree measure of an exterior angle is equal to the sum of the measures of the two nonadjacent (remote) interior angles.

In the figure below, a, b, and c are interior angles. Therefore, $a + b + c = 180$. In addition, d is supplementary to c; therefore, $d + c = 180$. So $d + c = a + b + c$, and $d = a + b$. Thus, the exterior angle d is equal to the sum of the two remote interior angles a and b.

The **altitude** (or height) of a triangle is the perpendicular distance from a vertex to the side opposite the vertex. The altitude can fall inside the triangle, outside the triangle, or on one of the sides.

Altitude = AD   Altitude = EH   Altitude = IK

Sides and Angles

The length of any side of a triangle is less than the sum of the lengths of the other two sides, and it is greater than the positive difference of the lengths of the other two sides.

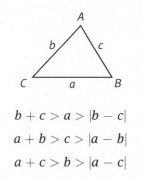

$$b + c > a > |b - c|$$
$$a + b > c > |a - b|$$
$$a + c > b > |a - c|$$

If the lengths of two sides of a triangle are unequal, the greater angle lies opposite the longer side and vice versa. In the figure above, if $\angle A > \angle B > \angle C$, then $a > b > c$.

Area of a Triangle

The formula for the area of a triangle is

$$\frac{1}{2} \times \text{base} \times \text{height}$$

Example:

In the diagram above, the base has length 4 and the altitude length 3, so you can write

$$A = \frac{1}{2}bh$$

$$= \frac{1}{2} \times 4 \times 3 = 6$$

Remember that the height (or altitude) is perpendicular to the base. Therefore, when two sides of a triangle are perpendicular to each other, the area is easy to find. In a right triangle, the two sides that form the 90° angle are called the **legs**. Then the area is one-half the product of the legs, or

$$A = \frac{1}{2}bh$$

$$= \frac{1}{2} \times l_1 \times l_2$$

Example:

In the triangle above, you could treat the hypotenuse as the base, since that is the way the figure is drawn. If you did this, you would need to know the distance from the hypotenuse to the opposite vertex to determine the area of the triangle. A more straightforward method is to notice that this is a right triangle with legs of lengths 6 and 8, which allows you to use the alternative formula for area:

$$A = \frac{1}{2} \times l_1 \times l_2$$

$$= \frac{1}{2} \times 6 \times 8$$

$$= 24$$

Perimeter of a Triangle

The perimeter of a triangle is the distance around the triangle. In other words, the perimeter is equal to the sum of the lengths of the sides.

Example:

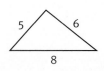

In the triangle above, the sides are of length 5, 6, and 8. Therefore, the perimeter is 5 + 6 + 8, or 19.

Isosceles Triangles

An isosceles triangle is a triangle that has two sides of equal length. The two equal sides are called **legs**, and the third side is called the **base**.

Since the two legs have the same length, the two angles opposite the legs must have the same measure. In the figure below, $PQ = PR$, and $\angle Q = \angle R$.

Equilateral Triangles

An equilateral triangle has three sides of equal length and three 60° angles.

Similar Triangles

Triangles are **similar** if corresponding angles have the same measure. For instance, any two triangles whose angles measure 30°, 60°, and 90° are similar. In similar triangles, corresponding side lengths are proportional to one another. Triangles are **congruent** if corresponding angles have the same measure and corresponding sides have the same length.

Example:

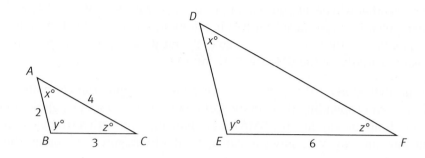

What is the perimeter of $\triangle DEF$ above?

Each triangle has an $x°$ angle, a $y°$ angle, and a $z°$ angle; therefore, the triangles are similar, and corresponding sides are proportional to one another. BC and EF are corresponding sides; each is opposite the $x°$ angle. Since EF is twice the length of BC, each side of $\triangle DEF$ will be twice the length of the corresponding side of $\triangle ABC$. Therefore, $DE = 2(AB)$ or 4, and $DF = 2(AC)$ or 8. The perimeter of $\triangle DEF$ is $4 + 6 + 8 = 18$.

The ratio of the areas of two similar triangles is the square of the ratio of corresponding lengths. For instance, in the example above, since each side of $\triangle DEF$ is 2 times the length of the corresponding side of $\triangle ABC$, $\triangle DEF$ must have 2^2 or 4 times the area of $\triangle ABC$.

$$\frac{\text{Area } \triangle DEF}{\text{Area } \triangle ABC} = \left(\frac{DE}{AB}\right)^2 = \left(\frac{2}{1}\right)^2 = 4$$

Right Triangles

A right triangle has one interior angle of $90°$, which is also the largest angle of the triangle. The longest side, which lies opposite the right angle, is called the **hypotenuse**. The other two sides are called the **legs**.

Pythagorean Theorem: The **Pythagorean theorem** holds for all right triangles and states that the square of the hypotenuse is equal to the sum of the squares of the legs.

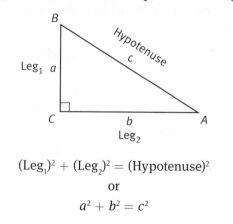

$$(\text{Leg}_1)^2 + (\text{Leg}_2)^2 = (\text{Hypotenuse})^2$$

or

$$a^2 + b^2 = c^2$$

Some sets of integers happen to satisfy the Pythagorean theorem. These sets of integers are commonly referred to as *Pythagorean triples*. One very common set that you might remember is 3, 4, and 5. Since $3^2 + 4^2 = 5^2$, you can have a right triangle with legs of lengths 3 and 4 and hypotenuse of length 5. This is the most common kind of right triangle on the GMAT. You should be familiar with the numbers so that whenever you see a right triangle with legs of 3 and 4, you will immediately know the hypotenuse must have length 5. In addition, any multiple of these lengths makes a Pythagorean triple; for instance, $6^2 + 8^2 = 10^2$, so 6, 8, and 10 also make a right triangle. One other triple that appears regularly on the GMAT is 5, 12, and 13.

Don't overuse the Pythagorean theorem. Easily recognizable right triangle patterns such as the triples allow you to avoid spending time on the formula when solving the majority of GMAT geometry problems. But from time to time the GMAT may challenge you with a triangle that doesn't offer any convenient shortcuts, so make sure you can apply the Pythagorean theorem when necessary.

Example: What is the length of the hypotenuse of a right triangle with legs of length 9 and 10?

Use the Pythagorean theorem: the square of the length of the hypotenuse equals the sum of the squares of the lengths of the legs. Here the legs are 9 and 10, so you have

$$\text{Hypotenuse}^2 = 9^2 + 10^2$$
$$= 81 + 100 = 181$$
$$\text{Hypotenuse} = \sqrt{181}$$

Special Right Triangles: You can always use the Pythagorean theorem to find the lengths of the sides in a right triangle. There are two special kinds of right triangles, though, that always have side lengths in the same ratios:

(for isosceles right triangles)   (for 30-60-90 triangles)

These two special right triangles appear frequently, and you are very likely to see them. However, the GMAT can hide them in unexpected ways. For example, the diagonal of a square creates two isosceles right triangles, also known as 45-45-90 triangles. And bisecting an equilateral triangle creates two 30-60-90 triangles:

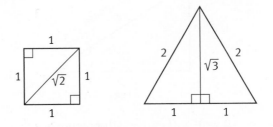

IN-FORMAT QUESTION: TRIANGLES ON THE GMAT

Now let's use the Kaplan Method on a Problem Solving question dealing with triangles:

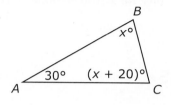

In $\triangle ABC$ above, $x =$

- ○ 30
- ○ 45
- ○ 60
- ○ 65
- ○ 75

Step 1: Analyze the Question

This is a straightforward triangle question that tests your knowledge of basic triangle properties. As with most questions in the Quantitative section, you can solve this one by using more than one approach. You could use algebra to solve for x, or you could backsolve, plugging the answer choices for x into the figure. With either method, you'll need to remember the fact that the angles of a triangle sum to 180°.

Step 2: State the Task

Your task is to solve for x. You could use either algebra or backsolving.

Step 3: Approach Strategically

If you solved with algebra, you'd use the fact that all the angles of a triangle sum to 180° to set up this equation:

$$30 + x + x + 20 = 180$$
$$2x + 50 = 180$$
$$2x = 130$$
$$x = 65$$

(D) is the correct answer.

If you backsolved, you could start with any answer choice, but as an example, let's say that you started with **(B)**. If you test $x = 45$, then the three angles of the triangle would be 30°, 45°, and 65°, which sum to 140°. You know triangles have 180°, so this answer choice is too small, and you can eliminate **(A)** and **(B)**. Testing **(D)** yields angles of 30°, 65°, and 85°. These angles sum to 180°, which proves that **(D)** is correct.

Step 4: Confirm Your Answer

Read back over the problem to confirm that your solution accurately follows from the information in the question. You were asked to solve for x. You've done so correctly, so you can move on to the next problem.

TAKEAWAYS: TRIANGLES

- Area $= \frac{1}{2}$ (base)(height).
- The interior angles of any triangle sum to 180°.
- Every external angle of a triangle equals the sum of the two remote interior angles.
- In any triangle, a side opposite a greater angle is longer than a side opposite a smaller angle, and sides opposite equal angles are equal.
- Every side of a triangle must be longer than the difference of the lengths of the other two sides and shorter than the sum of the lengths of the other two sides.
- Some special right triangles to recognize are those with sides in the proportions 3:4:5 and 5:12:13.
- Some special right triangles to recognize are those with angle measures 30-60-90 and 45-45-90. The side lengths of these triangles are $x:x\sqrt{3}:2x$ and $x:x:x\sqrt{2}$, respectively.
- Pythagorean theorem: in a right triangle, if the sides are a, b, and c, $a^2 + b^2 = c^2$.

PRACTICE SET: TRIANGLES ON THE GMAT

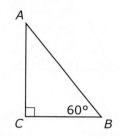

4. If the area of $\triangle ABC$ is $8\sqrt{3}$, what is the length of AB?

   ○ 4
   ○ 5
   ○ 6
   ○ 7
   ○ 8

5. What is the area of the triangle in the figure above?

   ○ $2 + 2\sqrt{3}$
   ○ $4\sqrt{3}$
   ○ 8
   ○ $8\sqrt{3}$
   ○ 12

6. In △*ABC* above, which of the following must be true?

    I. $x > 50$

    II. $AC < 10$

    III. $AB > 10$

    ○ I only
    ○ III only
    ○ I and II only
    ○ I and III only
    ○ I, II, and III

POLYGONS

A polygon is a closed figure whose sides are straight line segments.

The **perimeter** of a polygon is the distance around the polygon, or the sum of the lengths of the sides.

A **vertex** of a polygon is the point where two adjacent sides meet.

A **diagonal** of a polygon is a line segment connecting two nonadjacent vertices.

A **regular** polygon has sides of equal length and interior angles of equal measure.

The number of sides determines the specific name of the polygon. A **triangle** has three sides, a **quadrilateral** has four sides, a **pentagon** has five sides, and a **hexagon** has six sides. Triangles and quadrilaterals are by far the most important polygons on the GMAT.

INTERIOR AND EXTERIOR ANGLES

A polygon can be divided into triangles by drawing diagonals from a given vertex to all other non-adjacent vertices. For instance, the pentagon below can be divided into three triangles. Since the sum of the interior angles of each triangle is 180°, the sum of the interior angles of a pentagon is $3 \times 180° = 540°$.

Example:

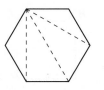

What is the measure of one interior angle of the regular hexagon above?

> You need to find the sum of the interior angles and divide by the number of interior angles, or 6. Since the hexagon is regular, all angles are equal, so each of them is equal to one-sixth of the sum. Since you can draw four triangles in a six-sided figure, the sum of the interior angles will be $4 \times 180°$, or 720°. Therefore, each of the six interior angles measures $\frac{720}{6}$ or 120°.

While splitting up polygons into triangles always works to find the sum of the interior angles, there is a formula you can memorize to speed up the process. The sum of the interior angle measures of a polygon with n sides is equal to $(n - 2)180°$. Therefore, in a regular polygon, the measure of each interior angle can be calculated using this formula: $\frac{(n-2)180°}{n}$.

QUADRILATERALS

The most important quadrilaterals to know for the GMAT are the rectangle and square. Anything could show up on the test, but concentrate on the most important figures and principles. The lesser-known properties can readily be deduced from the way the figure looks and from your knowledge of geometry.

Quadrilateral

A quadrilateral is a four-sided polygon. The sum of its four interior angles is 360°.

Rectangle

A rectangle is a quadrilateral with four equal angles, each a right angle.

The opposite sides of a rectangle are equal in length. Also, the diagonals of a rectangle have equal length and bisect each other.

Square

A square is a rectangle with four equal sides.

Areas of Quadrilaterals

To find the area of a rectangle, you multiply the lengths of any two adjacent sides, called the length and width.

Area of a rectangle = length × width = lw.

To find the area of a square, since length and width are equal, you say:

Area of a square = (side)^2 = s^2.

In the rare event that you have to find the area of a parallelogram (a quadrilateral with equal and parallel opposite sides), multiply the base and the height.

Area of a parallelogram = base × height = *bh*

The diagonals of a parallelogram do not necessarily have equal length, but they do bisect each other.

The area of a trapezoid—a quadrilateral with exactly one pair of parallel sides—can be calculated as follows:

Area of a trapezoid = $\frac{1}{2}$ (the sum of the bases)(height) = $\frac{1}{2}(b_1 + b_2)(h)$

IN-FORMAT QUESTION: POLYGONS ON THE GMAT

Now let's use the Kaplan Method on a Problem Solving question dealing with polygons:

What is the perimeter of the figure above?

- ○ 43
- ○ 44
- ○ 46
- ○ 47
- ○ 48

Step 1: Analyze the Question

If this were a simple square or triangle, your work would be quick. However, when given an unfamiliar shape on the GMAT, you can often split the figure into smaller, familiar shapes to calculate the needed sides or angles.

Step 2: State the Task

The task is to solve for the perimeter of the figure, or the sum of the length of its sides. To do this, you need to determine the length of the unlabeled side.

Step 3: Approach Strategically

Pattern Recognition helps you recognize that this polygon can be broken down into smaller, more manageable figures. In this case, you can break the shape into a rectangle and a right triangle. Drop a perpendicular from the left endpoint of the top horizontal side of length 10 to the bottom horizontal side of length 16.

This perpendicular will divide the quadrilateral into a right triangle and a rectangle. Because the lengths of the opposite sides of a rectangle are equal, the horizontal sides of the rectangle both have a length of 10. This means that the horizontal leg of the right triangle will have a length of 16 − 10, or 6.

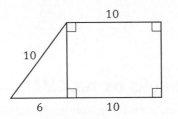

At this point, you might recognize that the right triangle is a special right triangle. It is a 3:4:5 right triangle, and each side of it is a member of the 3 to 4 to 5 ratio multiplied by 2. The leg of length 6 is 2×3, and the hypotenuse of length 10 is 2×5. So the length of the other leg is $2 \times 4 = 8$. Because opposite sides of a rectangle are equal, the vertical side of the rectangle at the right also has a length of 8.

Now you can find the perimeter of the quadrilateral. The sum of the length of the figure's sides is $16 + 10 + 10 + 8 = 44$. That's choice **(B)**.

If you were short on time for this question, you could use Critical Thinking to strategically eliminate a few of the answer choices. In any right triangle, the hypotenuse is always the longest side of the triangle. So in the figure, the side shared by the triangle and rectangle must be less than 10, since it makes up one of the legs of the right triangle.

If the short side of the rectangle were equal to 10, then the perimeter of the total quadrilateral would be 10 + 10 + 10 + 16 = 46. Since you know that one of the sides must be less than 10, the perimeter must be less than 46. This definitively eliminates **(C)**, **(D)**, and **(E)**, and you have a much better chance of picking the correct answer.

Step 4: Confirm Your Answer

Read back over the problem, confirming that your solution accurately follows the information in the question.

TAKEAWAYS: POLYGONS

- A polygon is a closed plane figure formed by three or more line segments.
  - Perimeter = sum of all sides.
- The sum of the interior angle measures of a polygon with n sides is equal to $(n - 2)180°$.
- Special case: parallelograms (quadrilaterals whose opposite sides are parallel)
  - Parallelograms include rectangles and squares.
  - Opposite sides are equal.
  - Opposite angles are equal.
  - Area = (base)(height).
  - The diagonals bisect each other.
- Special case: trapezoid
  - Area = $\frac{1}{2}$ (the sum of the bases)(height).

PRACTICE SET: POLYGONS ON THE GMAT

7. A frame 2 inches wide is placed around a rectangular picture with dimensions 8 inches by 12 inches. What is the area of the frame, in square inches?

    ○ 44
    ○ 96
    ○ 128
    ○ 144
    ○ 168

8. A square garden with an area of 36 square meters is enlarged into a rectangular garden, as shown in the figure above. What is the perimeter of the additional section of the garden, in meters?

    ○ 40
    ○ 52
    ○ 56
    ○ 124
    ○ 160

9. Is the length of a side of square S greater than the length of a side of equilateral triangle T?

    (1) The sum of the lengths of a side of S and a side of T is 22.

    (2) The ratio of the perimeter of square S to the perimeter of triangle T is 5 to 6.

CIRCLES

A circle is the set of all points in a plane at the same distance from a certain point. This point is called the **center** of the circle.

A circle is labeled by its center point: circle O means the circle with center point O. Two circles of different size with the same center are called **concentric**.

Diameter

A diameter is a line segment that connects two points on the circle and passes through the center of the circle. In circle O, AB is a diameter.

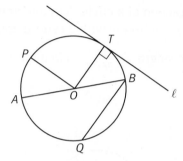

Radius

A radius is a line segment from the center of the circle to any point on the circle. The radius of a circle is one-half the length of the diameter. In circle O, OA, OB, OP, and OT are radii.

Chord

A chord is a line segment joining two points on the circle. In circle O, QB and AB are chords. A diameter of a circle is a longest chord of the circle.

Central Angle

A central angle is an angle formed by two radii. In circle O, $\angle AOP$, $\angle POB$, $\angle AOB$, along with others, are central angles.

Tangent

A line that touches only one point on the circumference of the circle is **tangent** to that circle. A line drawn tangent to a circle is perpendicular to the radius at the point of tangency. Line ℓ is tangent to circle O at point T.

Circumference and Arc Length

The distance around a circle is called the **circumference**. The number π ("pi") is the ratio of a circle's circumference to its diameter. The value of π is $3.14159265\ldots$, usually approximated as 3.14. For the GMAT, it is usually sufficient to remember that π is a little more than 3.

Since π equals the ratio of the circumference to the diameter, a formula for the circumference is

$$C = \pi d$$

or

$$C = 2\pi r$$

An **arc** is a portion of the circumference of a circle. In the figure below, *AB* is an arc of the circle that spans central angle *AOB*. The shorter distance between *A* and *B* along the circle is called the **minor arc**; the longer distance *AXB* is the **major arc**. An arc that is exactly half the circumference of the circle is called a **semicircle** (in other words, half a circle).

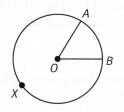

The length of an arc is the same fraction of a circle's circumference as its degree measure is of the degree measure of the circle (360°). For an arc with a central angle measuring *n* degrees,

$$\text{Arc length} = \left(\frac{n}{360}\right) \times \text{circumference}$$

$$= \frac{n}{360} \times 2\pi r$$

Example:

What is the length of arc *ABC* of the circle with center *O* above?

Since circumference $= 2\pi r$ and the radius is 6, the circumference is $2 \times \pi \times 6 = 12\pi$.

Since $\angle AOC$ measures 60°, the arc is $\frac{60}{360}$, or one-sixth, of the circumference.

Therefore, the length of the arc is $\frac{1}{6} \times 12\pi$, or 2π.

Inscribed Angle and Arc Length

An **inscribed angle** is one that opens up from the edge of a circle instead of its center. Here, angle *ABC* is inscribed.

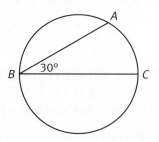

An inscribed angle also has a relationship with minor arc length. For an inscribed angle measuring n degrees,

$$\text{Arc length} = \left(\frac{n}{180}\right) \times \text{circumference}$$

In other words, an angle that's inscribed defines an arc twice as long as one defined by a central angle of equal angle measure.

Area of a Circle

The area of a circle is given by this formula:

$$\text{Area} = \pi r^2$$

A **sector** is a portion of the circle bounded by two radii and an arc. In the circle below with center O, OAB is a sector. To determine the area of a sector of a circle, use a similar method to the one you used to find the length of an arc: determine what fraction of $360°$ is in the degree measure of the central angle of the sector, then multiply that fraction by the area of the circle.

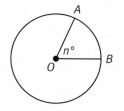

$$\text{Area of sector} = \left(\frac{n}{360}\right) \times (\text{Area of circle})$$

$$= \frac{n}{360} \times \pi r^2$$

Example:

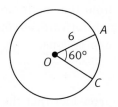

What is the area of sector AOC in the circle with center O above?

Since $\angle AOC$ measures $60°$, a $60°$ "slice" is $\frac{60}{360}$, or one-sixth, of the circle. So the sector has an area of $\frac{1}{6} \times \pi r^2 = \frac{1}{6} \times \pi(6)^2 = \frac{1}{6} \times 36\pi = 6\pi$.

IN-FORMAT QUESTION: CIRCLES ON THE GMAT

Now let's use the Kaplan Method on a Problem Solving question dealing with circles:

> If the diameter of a circle increases by 50 percent, by what percent will the area of the circle increase?

- ○ 25%
- ○ 50%
- ○ 100%
- ○ 125%
- ○ 225%

Step 1: Analyze the Question

For any geometry question without a figure, it is important to draw a quick sketch of the described figure to avoid simple mistakes on Test Day. So on your noteboard, you should draw two circles: (1) the original circle and (2) the circle with increased diameter.

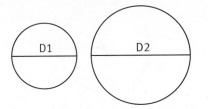

Now look at the question stem again. Notice that this is a percent question in disguise and that you are not given the original or final diameter. This is a great candidate for picking numbers.

Step 2: State the Task

You want the percent increase of area from the small circle to the large one. If you use picking numbers, the task will be much more straightforward, as you will be solving for the increase between two numbers rather than two algebraic expressions.

Step 3: Approach Strategically

To make your calculations manageable, consider that the area of a circle is given in terms of its radius and the radius is $\frac{1}{2}$ of the diameter. So you want the diameter to be a multiple of 2. Suppose that the original diameter is 4. Then the original radius is $\frac{1}{2}(4) = 2$. Therefore, the area of the original circle is

$$\pi r^2 = \pi(2)^2 = 4\pi$$

The diameter of 4 is increased by 50%, or $\frac{1}{2}$. The new diameter is $4 + \frac{1}{2}(4) = 4 + 2 = 6$. Therefore, the new radius is $\frac{1}{2}(6) = 3$. The area of the new circle is

$$\pi r^2 = \pi(3)^2 = 9\pi$$

To calculate the percent increase between the two circles, use the following equation:

$$\text{Percent increase} = \frac{\text{Difference}}{\text{Original}} \times 100\%$$

$$\text{Difference} = 9\pi - 4\pi = 5\pi$$

$$\text{Percent increase} = \frac{5\pi}{4\pi} \times 100\%$$

$$= \frac{5}{4} \times 100\%$$

$$= 1.25 \times 100\%$$

$$= 125\%$$

The correct answer is **(D)**.

Step 4: Confirm Your Answer

Be very careful how you apply the percent increase equation. A common error is to use the wrong value in the denominator. Another is to solve not for the percent difference but for how much one amount is as a percent of another. **(E)**, for example, is the answer to "The area of the circle after the increase is what percent of its original area?" Always take a moment to confirm that your answer choice makes sense logically.

TAKEAWAYS: CIRCLES

- Area $= \pi r^2$.
- Circumference $= 2\pi r$.
- The length of an arc as a fraction of a circle's circumference is equal to the degree measure of the corresponding central angle as a fraction of 360.
- The area of a sector as a fraction of a circle's area is equal to the degree measure of the corresponding central angle as a fraction of 360.
- A line that has exactly one point in common with a circle is tangent to the circle and perpendicular to the radius.

PRACTICE SET: CIRCLES ON THE GMAT

10. If the area of circle O is 16π, what is the length of an arc on the circle formed by a central angle measuring 45 degrees?

    ○ π

    ○ $\dfrac{3\pi}{2}$

    ○ 2π

    ○ $\dfrac{5\pi}{2}$

    ○ 8π

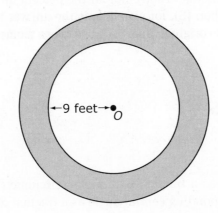

11. The figure above represents a circular garden, with center O, surrounded by a circular walkway that is 4 feet wide. What is the area of the walkway, in square feet?

    ○ 16π

    ○ 25π

    ○ 81π

    ○ 88π

    ○ 169π

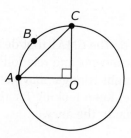

12. What is the area of the circle above with center O?

    (1) The area of $\triangle AOC$ is 18.

    (2) The length of arc ABC is 3π.

MULTIPLE FIGURES

You can expect to see some questions on the GMAT that deal with multiple figures. They test your understanding of various geometrical concepts and relationships, not just your ability to memorize a few formulas. The hypotenuse of a right triangle may be the side of a neighboring rectangle or the diameter of a circumscribed circle. Keep looking for the relationships between the different figures until you find one that leads you to the answer.

One common kind of multiple-figures question involves irregularly shaped regions formed by two or more overlapping figures, often with one region shaded. When you are asked to find the area of such a region, either or both of the following methods may work:

1. Break up that shaded area into smaller pieces you know the formula for; find the area of each using the proper formula; add those areas together.

2. Find the area of the whole figure and the area of the unshaded region and subtract the latter from the former.

Example:

Rectangle *ABCD* above has an area of 72 and is composed of 8 equal squares. Find the area of the shaded region.

For this problem, you can use either of the two approaches. First, divide 8 into 72 to get the area of each square, which is 9. Since the area of a square equals the length of its side squared, each side of the small squares must have length 3. Now you have a choice of methods.

1. You can break up the trapezoid into right triangle *DEH*, rectangle *EFGH*, and right triangle *FGC*. The area of triangle *DEH* is $\frac{1}{2} \times 6 \times 6$, or 18. The area of rectangle *EFGH* is 3×6, or 18. The area of triangle *FGC* is $\frac{1}{2} \times 6 \times 3$, or 9. The total area is $18 + 18 + 9$, or 45. You could also use the formula for the area of a trapezoid, $\frac{1}{2}(b_1 + b_2)(h)$, to get the same result: $\frac{1}{2}(3 + 12)(6) = \frac{1}{2}(15)(6) = 15 \times 3 = 45$.

2. The area of the whole rectangle *ABCD* is 72. The area of unshaded triangle *AED* is $\frac{1}{2} \times 6 \times 6$, or 18. The area of unshaded triangle *FBC* is $\frac{1}{2} \times 6 \times 3$, or 9. Therefore, the total unshaded area is $18 + 9 = 27$. The area of the shaded region is the area of the rectangle minus the unshaded area, or $72 - 27 = 45$.

Inscribed and Circumscribed Figures

A polygon is **inscribed** in a circle if all the vertices of the polygon lie on the circle. A polygon is **circumscribed** about a circle if all the sides of the polygon are tangent to the circle.

Square *ABCD* is inscribed in circle *O*. (We can also say that circle *O* is circumscribed about square *ABCD*.)

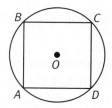

Square *PQRS* is circumscribed about circle *O*. (We can also say that circle *O* is inscribed in square *PQRS*.)

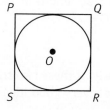

A triangle inscribed in a semicircle such that one side of the triangle coincides with the diameter of the semicircle is a right triangle.

IN-FORMAT QUESTION: MULTIPLE FIGURES ON THE GMAT

Now let's use the Kaplan Method on a Problem Solving question dealing with multiple figures:

What is the length of *BC* in the figure above?

- ○ 10
- ○ 16
- ○ 18
- ○ 20
- ○ 24

Step 1: Analyze the Question

As with any complicated shape on the GMAT, you can begin by breaking this figure into two simpler shapes: triangle ABC and triangle DBC. Analyze them separately first.

Triangle ABC: BC is one leg of this right triangle. The other leg, AC, is equal to the sum of $4x + 5x = 9x$. The hypotenuse is 30.

Triangle DBC: BC is also one leg of this right triangle. The other leg is $DC = 5x$, and the hypotenuse is 26.

Use your Pattern Recognition skills to note that the two hypotenuses are each consistent with special right triangles. The hypotenuse $BD = 26$, which is 13×2, so DBC might be a 5:12:13 right triangle. That would make the other sides $12 \times 2 = 24$ and $5 \times 2 = 10$.

The hypotenuse $BA = 30$, which is 5×6, so it might be part of a 3:4:5 triangle. That would make the other sides $3 \times 6 = 18$ and $4 \times 6 = 24$. If these are special right triangles, which you know the GMAT likes to use, then they'd share a side length of 24. The side they share is BC, so it would be reasonable to guess right now that $BC = 24$.

Step 2: State the Task

You are solving for BC. Since BC must be 24 if these two triangles are special right triangles (again, very common on the GMAT), it would be a very good idea to guess **(E)** if you were behind on time.

Step 3: Approach Strategically

Since you already suspect that $BC = 24$, that BDC is a 5:12:13 triangle, and that ABC is a 3:4:5 triangle, you should try to confirm it. Use the special triangle ratios to see what one triangle would be if $BC = 24$ and check whether that makes sense with the other triangle. If it does, BC is indeed 24.

If DBC is a 5:12:13, then DC would equal 10. So $5x$ may be 10, and x may be 2. If $x = 2$, then AC, which equals $9x$, would equal 18. That's exactly what it should equal if ABC is a 3:4:5 triangle, so everything in the figure works with $BC = 24$. The correct answer is **(E)**. In essence, this was a back-solving solution.

You could have solved with algebra, but it would have been much more time-consuming.

Applying the Pythagorean theorem to each triangle, you get this:

Triangle ABC:

$$(BC)^2 + (9x)^2 = (30)^2$$
$$(BC)^2 + 81x^2 = 900$$
$$(BC)^2 = 900 - 81x^2$$

Triangle DBC:

$$(BC)^2 + (5x)^2 = (26)^2$$
$$(BC)^2 + 25x^2 = 676$$
$$(BC)^2 = 676 - 25x^2$$

To solve for *BC*, you must first calculate *x*. To do so, you can set the two equations equal to one another:

$$900 - 81x^2 = 676 - 25x^2$$
$$56x^2 = 224$$
$$x^2 = \frac{224}{56} = 4$$
$$x = 2 \text{ or } x = -2$$

Remember that in the context of a geometry question, all side lengths must be positive, so *x* must equal 2.

Now you can plug this value for *x* into either of your original equations to find *BC*. *BC* = 24.

Triangle *ABC*: The length of leg *AC* is $9x = 9(2) = 18$.

Since $AC = 18 = 6 \times 3$, the hypotenuse $AB = 30 = 6 \times 5$, and $BC = 24 = 6 \times 4$, you've just proved that *ABC* is a 3:4:5 right triangle.

Triangle *DBC*: The length of leg *DC* is $5x = 5(2) = 10$.

Since $DC = 10 = 2 \times 5$, the hypotenuse $DB = 26 = 2 \times 13$, and $BC = 24 = 2 \times 12$, you've just proved that *DBC* is a 5:12:13 right triangle.

The correct answer is **(E)**.

Notice how the solution that doesn't rely on using the suspected Pythagorean triples is much more complex and time-consuming. Use Critical Thinking and Pattern Recognition to your advantage here. Special right triangles are immense time-savers, and the GMAT uses them all the time—two big reasons why it makes sense to use them whenever you suspect that they appear.

Step 4: Confirm Your Answer

Reread the question and the figure, making sure that you didn't misread anything or solve for the wrong measure. Beware of traps: if you'd solved for *AC*, you'd have selected **(C)**, and if you'd solved for *DC*, you'd have selected **(A)**.

TAKEAWAYS: MULTIPLE FIGURES

- Difficult geometry questions often contain complex figures. The key to answering these questions is to break the figures down into simpler figures.
- Look for measurements that are shared across figures so that you can take information about one figure and apply it to another.

PRACTICE SET: MULTIPLE FIGURES ON THE GMAT

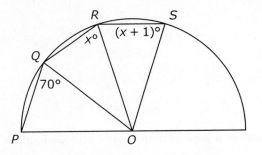

13. In the figure above, point O is the center of the semicircle, and PQ is parallel to OS. What is the measure of $\angle ROS$?

    ○ 34°
    ○ 36°
    ○ 54.5°
    ○ 72°
    ○ 73°

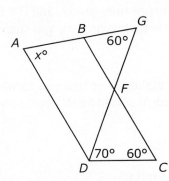

14. In the figure above, what is the value of x?

    (1) $AD \parallel BC$
    (2) $\angle GBC = 70°$

15. An isosceles triangle is inscribed in a circle such that one of the triangle's sides coincides with the circle's longest chord. If the measure of another side of the triangle is 5, what is the difference between the area of the circle and the area of the triangle?

○ $\dfrac{25}{2}(1 - \pi)$

○ $25(\pi - 1)$

○ $\dfrac{25}{2}(\pi + 1)$

○ $\dfrac{25}{2}(\pi - 1)$

○ $\dfrac{25}{4}(\pi - 1)$

SOLIDS

A **solid** is a three-dimensional figure (a figure having length, width, and height) and is, therefore, rather difficult to represent accurately on a two-dimensional page. Figures are drawn "in perspective," giving them the appearance of depth. If a diagram represents a three-dimensional figure, that fact will be specified in the accompanying text.

Fortunately, only a few types of solids appear with any frequency on the GMAT: rectangular solids (including cubes) and cylinders. These are both uniform solids (solids in which the measure of each dimension is constant through the entire object). Other types, such as spheres, may appear, but these questions typically will involve only understanding the solid's properties and not applying any special formula.

TERMINOLOGY

Here are the terms used to describe the common solids:

Vertex

The vertices of a solid are the points at its corners. For example, a cube has 8 vertices.

Edge

The edges of a solid are the line segments that connect the vertices and form the sides of each face of the solid. A cube has 12 edges.

Face

The faces of a solid are the polygons that are the boundaries of the solid. A cube has 6 faces, all squares.

Volume

The volume of a solid is the amount of space enclosed by that solid. The volume of any uniform solid is equal to the area of its base times its height.

Surface Area

In general, the surface area of a solid is equal to the sum of the areas of the solid's faces.

RECTANGULAR SOLID

A rectangular solid is a solid with six rectangular faces (all edges meet at right angles). Examples are cereal boxes, bricks, etc.

Volume = area of base × height = length × width × height.

$$V = l \times w \times h$$

Surface area = sum of areas of faces.

$$SA = 2lw + 2lh + 2wh$$

Diagonals in Rectangular Solids

It's common for difficult geometry questions to ask you to calculate the length of a rectangular solid's diagonal (one that runs from lower-front-left to upper-back-right, for example).

There's a simple formula to calculate the diagonal. It looks a lot like the Pythagorean theorem (in fact, it's derived using that theorem).

$$\text{Diagonal}^2 = \text{Length}^2 + \text{Width}^2 + \text{Height}^2$$

Cube

A cube is a special rectangular solid with all edges equal ($l = w = h$), such as a die or a sugar cube. All faces of a cube are squares.

Volume = Area of base × Height = Edge³.

$$V = l \times w \times h = e^3$$

Surface area = Sum of areas of faces = 6 × edge².

$$SA = 6e^2$$

CYLINDER

A cylinder is a uniform solid whose horizontal cross section is a circle, for example, a soup can. You need two pieces of information for a cylinder: the radius of the base and the height.

Volume = Area of base × Height.

$$V = \pi r^2 \times h$$

Lateral surface area (LSA) = Circumference of base × Height.

$$LSA = 2\pi r \times h$$

Total surface area = Areas of bases + LSA.

$$SA = 2\pi r^2 + 2\pi rh$$

You can think of the surface area of a cylinder as having two parts: one part is the top and bottom (the circles), and the other part is the lateral surface. In a can, for example, the area of either the top or the bottom is just the area of the circle, or lid, which represents the top; hence, πr^2 for the top and πr^2 for the bottom, yielding a total of $2\pi r^2$. For the lateral surface area, the area around the can, think of removing the can's label. When unrolled, it's actually in the shape of a rectangle. One side is the height of the can, and the other side is the distance around the circle, or circumference. Hence, its area is $h \times (2\pi r)$, or $2\pi rh$. Thus, the total surface area is $2\pi r^2 + 2\pi rh$.

SPHERE

A sphere is made up of all the points in space a certain distance from a center point; it's like a three-dimensional circle. The distance from the center to a point on the sphere is the radius of the sphere. A basketball is a good example of a sphere. A sphere is not a uniform solid; the cross sections are all circles, but they are of different sizes. (In other words, a slice of a basketball from the middle is bigger than a slice from the top.)

It is not important to know how to find the volume or surface area of a sphere, but occasionally a question might require you to understand what a sphere is.

IN-FORMAT QUESTION: SOLIDS ON THE GMAT

Now let's use the Kaplan Method on a Data Sufficiency question dealing with solids:

> A rectangular fish tank has uniform depth. How long does it take to fill the tank with water?
>
> (1) The tank is 4 feet wide and 10 feet long.
> (2) The tank is filled with water at a rate of 1.5 cubic feet per minute.

Step 1: Analyze the Question

This Value question requires you to determine if there is sufficient information to find how long it takes to fill a rectangular tank with a uniform depth with water. Not only do you need the volume of the tank, but you also need the rate at which the tank is being filled.

Step 2: Evaluate the Statements Using 12TEN

Statement (1) tells you that the tank is 4 feet wide and 10 feet long. Because you are not given any information about the depth, you cannot determine the volume of the tank. Furthermore, you are not given any information about the rate at which the tank is filled with water. This statement is insufficient. You can eliminate **(A)** and **(D)**.

Statement (2) tells you that the tank is being filled at a rate of 1.5 cubic feet per minute. You have no information with which to determine the volume of the tank, so you cannot determine how long it will take to fill the tank with water. Eliminate **(B)**.

Now you must combine statements. You know the length of the tank, the width of the tank, and the rate at which it is being filled. Because you do not know the depth of the tank, you cannot determine its volume. Because you cannot determine the volume of the tank, you cannot solve for how long it takes to fill the tank with water. The two statements taken together are insufficient, and **(E)** is correct.

TAKEAWAYS: SOLIDS

- Almost all solids on the GMAT are uniform solids (solids in which the measure of each dimension is constant through the entire object).
- To determine the volume of a uniform solid, multiply the area of the base by the height.
  - Volume of cylinder $= \pi r^2 h$.
  - Volume of rectangular solid $= l \times w \times h$.

PRACTICE SET: SOLIDS ON THE GMAT

16. A cylindrical tank with a height of 8 feet is completely full of gasoline. This gasoline is pumped into an empty cylindrical tank with a diameter of 24 feet and a height of 18 feet. If the gasoline reaches a height of 2 feet in this tank, what is the diameter, in feet, of the original tank?

   ○ 3
   ○ 6
   ○ 8
   ○ 10
   ○ 12

17. A rectangular solid has the dimensions 4, 5, and x. If the number of units in the solid's volume and the number of units in that solid's surface area are the same, what is the sum of the areas of the two largest faces of the solid?

   ○ 20
   ○ 40
   ○ 100
   ○ 200
   ○ 400

18. A cube with an edge length of 6 contains the largest possible sphere that completely fits inside of it. If the volume V of a sphere with radius r is given by the formula $V = \frac{4}{3}\pi r^3$, what is the volume of the empty space inside the cube?

    ○ $36(\pi^3 - 6)$

    ○ 36π

    ○ $36(6 - \pi)$

    ○ $36(\pi - 1)$

    ○ $36(4 - \pi)$

COORDINATE GEOMETRY

Slope

The slope of a line on a coordinate plane tells you how steeply that line goes up or down. If a line gets higher as you move to the right, it has a positive slope. If it goes down as you move to the right, it has a negative slope. To find the slope of a line, use the following formula:

$$\text{Slope} = \frac{\text{Rise}}{\text{Run}} = \frac{\text{Change in } y}{\text{Change in } x}$$

Rise means the difference between the y-coordinate values of the two points on the line, and *run* means the difference between the x-coordinate values.

Example: What is the slope of the line that contains the points $(1, 2)$ and $(4, -5)$?

$$\text{Slope} = \frac{-5 - 2}{4 - 1} = \frac{-7}{3} = -\frac{7}{3}$$

To determine the slope of a line from an equation, put the equation into slope-intercept form: $y = mx + b$, where the slope is m.

Example: What is the slope of the line given by the equation $3x + 2y = 4$?

$$3x + 2y = 4$$
$$2y = -3x + 4$$
$$y = -\frac{3}{2}x + 2, \text{ so } m \text{ is } -\frac{3}{2}$$

The word *intercept* in "slope-intercept form" is there because b is the value of the y-intercept—the point at which the line crosses the y-axis. Another way to think of that is that $(0, b)$ will be a point on the line.

Perpendicular lines have slopes that are negative reciprocals of one another. For the line in this example, with a slope of $-\frac{3}{2}$, a perpendicular line would have a slope of $\frac{2}{3}$.

Calculating Distance on the Coordinate Plane

To determine the distance between any two points on a coordinate plane, you can use the Pythagorean theorem.

Example: What is the length of *AB*?

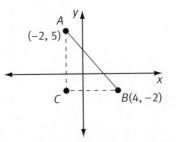

Sketch lines from points A and B parallel to the axes. They will form a right triangle, and the intersection will have the same x-coordinate as one point and the same y-coordinate as the other. Because the new lines aren't diagonal, their length is easy to figure out. In this example, the length of AC is 7 because the line drops down 5 from A to the x-axis and then another 2 to C. Similarly, the length of BC is 6.

Now you can use the Pythagorean theorem to calculate AB:

$$AB^2 = BC^2 + AC^2$$
$$AB^2 = 6^2 + 7^2$$
$$AB^2 = 36 + 49$$
$$AB^2 = 85$$
$$AB = \sqrt{85}$$

In-Format Question: Coordinate Geometry on the GMAT

Now let's use the Kaplan Method on a Data Sufficiency question dealing with coordinate geometry:

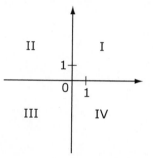

If $st > 0$, in which quadrant of the coordinate system above does the point (s, t) lie?

(1) $(s, -t)$ lies in quadrant II.

(2) s is negative.

Step 1: Analyze the Question

In this Value question, you are asked to determine which quadrant the point (s, t) is in. You are told in the question stem that $st > 0$, which means that s and t are either both positive or both negative. This is only true in quadrants I and III.

Step 2: Evaluate the Statements Using 12TEN

Statement (1): You know that $(s, -t)$ lies in quadrant II, which tells you that s is negative and $-t$ is positive, so t must be negative. Because s and t are both negative, (s, t) is in quadrant III, and the statement is sufficient. Eliminate **(B)**, **(C)**, and **(E)**.

Statement (2): You are told that s is negative, which is also sufficient, because you already deduced from the question stem that s and t have the same sign.

The correct answer is **(D)**.

TAKEAWAYS: COORDINATE GEOMETRY

- Slope of a line $= \dfrac{\text{Rise}}{\text{Run}} = \dfrac{\text{Change in } y}{\text{Change in } x}$.

- The equation of a non-vertical straight line in the two-dimensional coordinate plane is typically expressed in the form $y = mx + b$, where m is the slope and b is the point at which the line intercepts the y-axis.

- Be aware that difficult geometry questions may present lines in the form $x = cy + d$. In this equation, c is NOT the slope! You need to put the line in $y = mx + b$ form to find the slope.

- The slope of a line is the negative reciprocal of the slope of a perpendicular line.

- One way to find a distance in the coordinate plane is to use the Pythagorean theorem.

PRACTICE SET: COORDINATE GEOMETRY ON THE GMAT

19. Line ℓ_1 is given by the equation $y = mx + 3$, and line ℓ_2 is given by the equation $y = nx - 7$; m and n are constants. Is ℓ_1 parallel to ℓ_2?

    (1) $m^2 - n^2 = 0$

    (2) mn is positive.

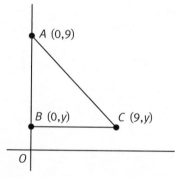

20. In the rectangular coordinate system above, triangle ABC has an area of 27 square units. Vertex A is at point $(0, 9)$, vertex B is at point $(0, y)$, and vertex C is at point $(9, y)$. What is the value of y?

    ○   1

    ○   2

    ○   3

    ○   4

    ○   6

21. In the *xy*-coordinate system, if (m, n) and $(m + 2, n + k)$ are two points on the line with the equation $x = 2y + 5$, then $k =$

   ○ $\frac{1}{2}$

   ○ 1

   ○ 2

   ○ $\frac{5}{2}$

   ○ 4

ANSWERS AND EXPLANATIONS BEGIN ON NEXT PAGE

ANSWERS AND EXPLANATIONS

1.	B	8.	B	15.	D
2.	D	9.	B	16.	B
3.	E	10.	A	17.	D
4.	E	11.	D	18.	C
5.	A	12.	D	19.	C
6.	C	13.	A	20.	C
7.	B	14.	A	21.	B

1. (B)

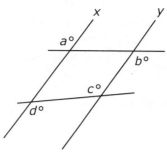

In the figure above, if lines x and y are parallel, what is the value of $a + c$?

(1) $b - d = 20$

(2) $b + d = 260$

Step 1: Analyze the Question Stem

This is a Value question. You're given a figure and told that lines x and y are parallel, which makes the other lines in the figure transversals. When a transversal intersects a pair of parallel lines, all acute angles formed by that transversal will be equal, and all obtuse angles formed will be equal. Therefore, since angle a and angle b are both obtuse angles on the same transversal, they're equal to each other. Likewise, because angle c and angle d are obtuse angles formed by the same transversal, they're equal to each other. Since you're looking for the value of $a + c$, you'll have sufficiency if you have enough information to find one angle on each transversal or some sum of angles between the two transversals.

Step 2: Evaluate the Statements Using 12TEN

Statement (1) indicates that $b - d = 20$. Since you've already determined that $b = a$ and $d = c$, you can rewrite this as $a - c = 20$. However, without having a value for either a or c, there's no way to determine the value of $a + c$, so this statement is insufficient. Eliminate **(A)** and **(D)**.

Statement (2) says that $b + d = 260$. Since you know that $b = a$ and $d = c$, you can rewrite this equation as $a + c = 260$. Thus, you have sufficiency. The correct choice is **(B)**.

2. **(D)**

In the figure above, the value of x is

- ○ 30
- ○ 60
- ○ 75
- ○ 100
- ○ 120

Step 1: Analyze the Question

There are many relationships that you could deduce from the diagram. There are two ways to relate y to x. Looking at angles that make straight lines, you can say the following:

$$2y + x + 20 = 180$$
$$2y + x = 160$$

Or, looking at vertical angles, you can say this:

$$4y = x + 20$$

Those two equations alone would be enough to set up a two-variable, two-equation system to solve for both x and y. But this problem gives you even more:

$$2y + 4y = 180$$
$$6y = 180$$
$$y = 30$$

Step 2: State the Task

The task is very straightforward: to solve for x. Given the deductions you made from the figure, you have your choice of equations in which to substitute 30 for y.

Step 3: Approach Strategically

If you use the first equation, you get this:

$$2y + x = 160$$
$$2(30) + x = 160$$
$$60 + x = 160$$
$$x = 100$$

The correct answer is **(D)**.

Or you could use the second equation:

$$4y = x + 20$$
$$4(30) = x + 20$$
$$120 = x + 20$$
$$100 = x$$

(D) is correct.

Alternatively, you could have backsolved. If you aren't comfortable with algebra, you might prefer this solution. Let's say that you started with **(B)**. If $x = 60$, then the angle on the bottom of the figure is 80°.

The angle on the left ($2y$) must make a straight line with that angle, so it must be 100°. If $2y = 100$, then $4y = 200$, so $2y + 4y = 300$. But since $2y$ and $4y$ combine to make a straight line, they need to add up to 180, so y in this scenario is too big. To make y smaller, you must make x bigger. You can eliminate **(A)** and **(B)**.

Testing **(D)**, the angle at the bottom of the figure is 120°, so the angle on the left must be 60°. So $2y = 60$, which makes $4y = 120$ and $2y + 4y = 180$. This is what you need, so the correct answer is **(D)**.

Step 4: Confirm Your Answer

Reread the question stem, making sure that you didn't miss anything about the problem.

3.   **(E)**

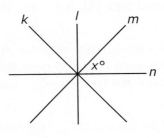

What is the value of *x*?

(1) Lines *k* and *m* are perpendicular.

(2) Lines *l* and *n* are perpendicular.

Step 1: Analyze the Question Stem

In the figure, you can observe that lines *k*, *l*, *m*, and *n* intersect at a central point and create eight angles. Note that you cannot assume that these angles are all equal, since you are not given any information explicitly stating this. Angle *x* is one of the 8 angles at this intersection. To solve for *x*, you need the values of at least three other angles that comprise a straight line with angle *x* or the value of the vertical angle across from *x*.

Step 2: Evaluate the Statements Using 12TEN

Statement (1) tells you that lines *k* and *m* are perpendicular to each other. This means that *x* is part of a 90-degree angle formed at the intersection of lines *k* and *m*. However, while you have narrowed down the range of values of *x* to less than 90 degrees, you cannot determine the specific value of *x* because you don't know the orientation of line *n* relative either to line *k* or to line *m*. It does look as though it divides the angle perfectly in half, but you cannot determine exact angle measures simply from eyeballing the figure. Statement (1) is not sufficient. Eliminate **(A)** and **(D)**.

Statement (2) is similar to Statement (1), and you can draw the same conclusion: *x* is less than 90 degrees, but since you do not know the orientation of line *m* relative to line *n* or to line *l*, you cannot determine a specific value for *x*, so Statement (2) is also not sufficient. Eliminate **(B)**.

Now you must combine statements. You know the orientation of lines *n* and *l* relative to each other and of lines *k* and *m* relative to each other. But there is no information relating either *n* or *l* to either *k* or *m*. Therefore, you can't determine the value of *x*. **(E)** is correct.

4. **(E)**

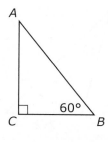

If the area of $\triangle ABC$ is $8\sqrt{3}$, what is the length of AB?

- ○ 4
- ○ 5
- ○ 6
- ○ 7
- ○ 8

Step 1: Analyze the Question

You are given a figure of a right triangle and are told that it has an area of $8\sqrt{3}$.

Step 2: State the Task

Find the length of AB, which is the triangle's hypotenuse. The answer choices all give simple integers for the length of AB, which is good news, because that means the $8\sqrt{3}$ will cancel out somehow.

Step 3: Approach Strategically

The triangle in the figure is a right triangle with a $60°$ angle, so the triangle is a 30-60-90 right triangle and its side lengths are in the proportion $x : x\sqrt{3} : 2x$. Plug this into the formula for the area of a triangle and solve for x:

$$\text{Area} = \frac{1}{2}bh$$
$$8\sqrt{3} = \frac{1}{2}(x)\left(x\sqrt{3}\right)$$
$$8\sqrt{3} = \frac{1}{2}x^2\sqrt{3}$$
$$8 = \frac{1}{2}x^2$$
$$16 = x^2$$
$$4 = x$$

You're looking for hypotenuse AB, which, in the above ratio, corresponds to $2x$. Since $x = 4$, the length of AB is $4 \times 2 = 8$. **(E)** is correct.

Step 4: Confirm Your Answer

Double-check the question stem to ensure that the chosen choice is the answer to the correct question. Here, you're looking for the length of AB and not the value of x.

5. (A)

What is the area of the triangle in the figure above?

- ○ $2 + 2\sqrt{3}$
- ○ $4\sqrt{3}$
- ○ 8
- ○ $8\sqrt{3}$
- ○ 12

Step 1: Analyze the Question

The question asks you to find the area of the triangle in the figure. To do so, you need to determine the base and height of the triangle. An angle measurement is missing from the diagram. Since all the angles in a triangle add to 180°, the missing angle must be $180° - (30° + 105°)$, or 45°. There are no more obvious deductions to be made from the diagram, but notice those two angle measurements: 30° and 45°. They are part of two of the GMAT's most commonly used shapes: the 30-60-90 triangle and the 45-45-90 triangle. If a special triangle appears in a GMAT problem, it will almost certainly be part of the solution.

Step 2: State the Task

You are trying to find the area, which involves a very straightforward formula: Area $= \frac{1}{2}$ (base) (height). You can divide the triangle into two small right triangles and use the classic triangle ratios mentioned above to determine the base and height of the triangle. After these two lengths are determined, calculate the area of the triangle.

Step 3: Approach Strategically

One possible base is already given in the figure: the bottom side of the triangle, which is labeled $2\sqrt{2}$. However, the height associated with this base would need to be drawn outside of the triangle, from the tip of the 30-degree angle to the base, and you do not have a quick way to determine this height. But you can use a different base and height. Because the line you drew to create the two special right triangles meets the long side in a right angle, it can serve as the height, with the long side being the base:

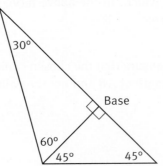

For the 45-45-90 triangle, the ratio of corresponding sides is $x:x:x\sqrt{2}$. Since the side across from the 90-degree angle is $2\sqrt{2}$, the other two sides must equal 2. That means that the height of the triangle is 2. This also means that the lower part of the base is equal to 2.

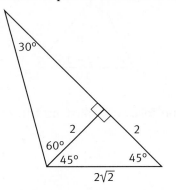

For the 30-60-90 triangle, the ratio of corresponding sides is $x:x\sqrt{3}:2x$. The side opposite the 30-degree angle is equal to 2, so $x = 2$. This means that the side opposite the 60-degree angle is $2\sqrt{3}$. Therefore, the final length of the base of this triangle is $2 + 2\sqrt{3}$.

Remember, the question asked for the area of this triangle. You now have all of the components needed to calculate this value. The area of a triangle is $\frac{1}{2}$(base)(height). So you have

$$\text{Area} = \frac{1}{2}\left(2 + 2\sqrt{3}\right)(2) = 2 + 2\sqrt{3}$$

(A) is correct.

Step 4: Confirm Your Answer
Reread the question stem, making sure that you didn't miss anything about the problem.

6.   (C)

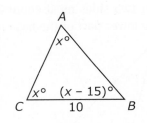

In △ABC above, which of the following must be true?

    I. $x > 50$
   II. $AC < 10$
  III. $AB > 10$

○ I only
○ III only
○ I and II only
○ I and III only
○ I, II, and III

Step 1: Analyze the Question

There are a number of observations you can make from the figure before you review the Roman numeral statements and answer choices. This step will save valuable time when evaluating the answer choices.

First, notice that two of the angles are the same, x. This means that their corresponding opposite side lengths are equal. Angle A is opposite side BC, which equals 10, so side AB also equals 10.

Next, note that all three angles within the triangle are defined in terms of one variable, x. You know that the sum of the angles within the triangle must equal 180, so if needed, you can calculate the exact value of each angle. You do not need to complete the calculation now, but it is useful to know you can do so if needed.

Finally, look at the relationship among the three angles in the triangle. Two angles are equal to x, and the third is defined as $x - 15$. This means that the third angle is smaller than the other two and, therefore, its corresponding opposite side is also smaller than the other two sides, or less than 10.

Step 2: State the Task

Evaluate each Roman numeral statement looking for what must be true. Using the deductions you made in Step 1 will help.

Step 3: Approach Strategically

Begin by evaluating Statement I because it appears most frequently in the answer choices.

Statement I: $x > 50$. One of the most efficient ways to determine this is to see what will happen if $x = 50$. This will tell you whether x needs to be larger or smaller.

If $x = 50$, the sum of the angles within the triangle will be $50 + 50 + (50 - 15) = 100 + 35 = 135$. You know that the sum of the angles must equal 180, so x must be larger than 50, and Statement I is true. Eliminate **(B)**. Notice that you did not solve for the actual value of x, though you could have if needed. Remember that on Test Day, you should only work out the calculations that are absolutely necessary so that you manage your time efficiently.

Statements II and III each appear twice in the remaining choices, and the deductions you made earlier help equally with both.

Statement III: $AB > 10$. From your analysis in Step 1, you know this cannot be true, because AB actually equals 10. Eliminate **(D)** and **(E)**.

Statement II: $AC < 10$. As with III, you know from your earlier analysis that this is indeed true, because the angle opposite side AC is smaller than the other two angles. Eliminate **(A)**. The correct answer is **(C)**.

Step 4: Confirm Your Answer

Keep careful track of which side corresponds to which angle. Confirm that your answer makes sense logically based on the analysis done in Step 1.

7. **(B)**

A frame 2 inches wide is placed around a rectangular picture with dimensions 8 inches by 12 inches. What is the area of the frame, in square inches?

- ○ 44
- ○ 96
- ○ 128
- ○ 144
- ○ 168

Step 1: Analyze the Question

A 2-inch frame is placed around a rectangular picture that measures 8 inches by 12 inches. The problem does not come with a figure, so be prepared to draw one.

Step 2: State the Task

Find the area of the frame, in square inches.

Step 3: Approach Strategically

Begin by drawing a figure:

To find the area of the frame (the shaded area), you'll need to find the total area—picture and frame together—and then subtract the area of the picture.

Including the 2-inch frame, the figure has dimensions of 12 by 16, for an area of $12 \times 16 = 192$. The picture itself has an area of $8 \times 12 = 96$. That means the frame alone has an area of $192 - 96 = 96$. **(B)** is correct.

Step 4: Confirm Your Answer

Double-check the figure to ensure that it accurately reflects the information in the question stem.

8. **(B)**

A square garden with an area of 36 square meters is enlarged into a rectangular garden, as shown in the figure above. What is the perimeter of the additional section of the garden, in meters?

○ 40
○ 52
○ 56
○ 124
○ 160

Step 1: Analyze the Question

You're told the area of the square garden, from which you can determine the length of each side of the square. You're also given the length that was added to the two sides of the square garden to form the larger rectangular garden. From this, you can determine the side lengths of the rectangle.

Step 2: State the Task

Find the perimeter of the added section of the garden; this is the sum of the lengths of its sides.

Step 3: Approach Strategically

The area of a square is the side length squared, so the side length can be found by finding the square root of the area. In this case, the side length is $\sqrt{36 \text{ meters}^2} = 6$ meters. Therefore, the width of the large rectangle is $6 + 4 = 10$ meters, and the length is $6 + 10 = 16$ meters.

At this point, you might be tempted to begin calculating the individual segment lengths that form the perimeter of the added section of the garden. However, since the "indented" section formed by the square has side lengths that are the two inner sides of the square, and because the outer two sides of the square sum to exactly the same length as the inner two sides, you can actually ignore this indent and just calculate the perimeter of the large rectangle. The perimeter of a rectangle is $(2 \times \text{length}) + (2 \times \text{width})$; here, that's $(2 \times 16) + (2 \times 10) = 32 + 20 = 52$ meters. Therefore, the perimeter of the added section of garden is 52 meters. **(B)** is correct.

Step 4: Confirm Your Answer

Make sure you found the perimeter of the added portion of the garden. If you found its area, you chose **(D)**. Furthermore, double-check that you accounted for the length of each side exactly once.

9. **(B)**

Is the length of a side of square S greater than the length of a side of equilateral triangle T?

(1) The sum of the lengths of a side of S and a side of T is 22.

(2) The ratio of the perimeter of square S to the perimeter of triangle T is 5 to 6.

Step 1: Analyze the Question Stem

This Yes/No question requires that you determine whether there is enough information to answer the question "Is the length of a side of square S greater than the length of a side of the equilateral triangle T?" Let a be the length of a side of square S and let b be the length of a side of equilateral triangle T. Then you can paraphrase the question as "Is $a > b$?" There is no information in the question stem that you can use to determine whether or not there is sufficiency, so look at the statements.

Step 2: Evaluate the Statements Using 12TEN

Statement (1) says that $a + b = 22$. Here, a could be greater, b could be greater, or a and b could be equal. If $a = 18$ and $b = 4$ (they have to be consistent with Statement (1), so they must total 22), then $a > b$, and the answer to the question is yes. However, if $a = 4$ and $b = 18$ (again, consistent with Statement (1), as they total 22), then $a < b$, and the answer to the question is no.

Because different answers to the question are possible, Statement (1) is insufficient. Eliminate **(A)** and **(D)**.

Statement (2): The ratio of the perimeter of the square to the perimeter of the triangle is 5 to 6. The perimeter of the square is $4a$. The perimeter of the equilateral triangle is $3b$. Thus, you can write the equation $\frac{4a}{3b} = \frac{5}{6}$. Since this equation gives a proportional relationship between a and b, you know that you could simplify this equation and answer the question with a definite yes or no. Because a and b are side lengths, a and b are both positive, so this equation will describe a consistent ratio between these values. Note that you don't have to solve for the ratio in order to know that Statement (2) is sufficient. **(B)** is correct.

10. (A)

If the area of circle O is 16π, what is the length of an arc on the circle formed by a central angle measuring 45 degrees?

○ π

○ $\dfrac{3\pi}{2}$

○ 2π

○ $\dfrac{5\pi}{2}$

○ 8π

Step 1: Analyze the Question

A given circle has an area of 16π.

Step 2: State the Task

Find the length of an arc formed by a $45°$ central angle. Even though arc length is related to circumference, not to area (the measurement given to you in the question stem), you can use the area to solve for the length of the radius and the radius to solve for the circumference.

Step 3: Approach Strategically

This problem seems complicated at first, but it is quite manageable if you take things step-by-step.

The area of a circle is πr^2, so a circle with an area of 16π has a radius of 4. The circumference of a circle is $2\pi r$, so the circumference of this circle is 8π. To find the length of the arc, set up a proportion that relates it to the central angle:

$$\frac{\text{Length of arc}}{\text{Circumference}} = \frac{\text{Central angle}}{360°}$$

$$\frac{\text{Length of arc}}{8\pi} = \frac{45°}{360°}$$

$$\frac{\text{Length of arc}}{8\pi} = \frac{1}{8}$$

$$\text{Length of arc} = \pi$$

(A) is correct.

Step 4: Confirm Your Answer

When setting up a proportion, ensure that the correct items are placed in the correct positions.

11. (D)

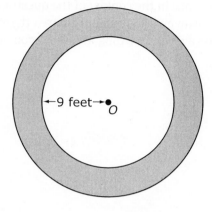

The figure above represents a circular garden, with center O, surrounded by a circular walkway that is 4 feet wide. What is the area of the walkway, in square feet?

○ 16π
○ 25π
○ 81π
○ 88π
○ 169π

Step 1: Analyze the Question

This is a classic GMAT geometry question. The figure contains one circle inside a larger circle. There are three components for any such question: (1) the area or perimeter of the inner shape, (2) the area or perimeter of the outer shape, and (3) the area or perimeter of the combined shape. Remember that oddly shaped figures are composed of combinations of simpler ones. In this case, the shaded region is the difference in area between the two circles.

Step 2: State the Task

Calculate the area of the walkway, or outer shape in the figure. The area of the walkway is equal to the area of the large circular region minus the area of the circular garden, so you must calculate these two values separately and then take their difference.

Step 3: Approach Strategically

First, find the area of the inner circle. The formula for the area of a circle is πr^2. From the figure, you know that $r = 9$, so the area of the inner circle is

$$\pi r^2 = \pi(9)^2 = 81\pi$$

Now solve for the area of the combined (larger) circle. The radius of the combined circle is the sum of the radius of the garden plus the width of the walkway. So the radius is $9 + 4 = 13$, and the area of the large circular region is

$$\pi r^2 = \pi(13)^2 = 169\pi$$

Now you can solve for the area of the walkway. This value is the difference of the two values you calculated above: $169\pi - 81\pi = 88\pi$. The correct answer is **(D)**.

Step 4: Confirm Your Answer

Confirm that your answer makes sense in the context of the question. Notice that you can eliminate **(E)** using logic, because the walkway must be smaller in area than the total combined area of the two circles. This step would also save you a wrong answer if you accidentally selected the area of the garden, **(C)**.

12. (D)

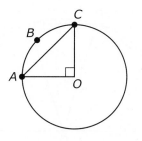

What is the area of the circle above with center O?

(1) The area of $\triangle AOC$ is 18.

(2) The length of arc ABC is 3π.

Step 1: Analyze the Question Stem

This is a Value question. For any circle question, you only need one defining parameter of a circle (area, circumference, diameter, or radius) in order to calculate any of the other parameters. Also, all radii of the same circle will have the same length. So $AO = CO$. That makes the triangle an isosceles right triangle (or 45-45-90) for which you know the ratio of the side lengths. Not only would the circle's area, circumference, diameter, or radius be sufficient, but information that gave you any side length of triangle AOC would also be sufficient, as it would give you the length of the radius.

Step 2: Evaluate the Statements Using 12TEN

Statement (1) gives you the area of the triangle, and you already know that the base and the height are equal. So if you call the radius of the circle r, then the area of the triangle is equal to

$$\frac{1}{2}(\text{base})(\text{height}) = \frac{1}{2}(r)(r) = \frac{1}{2}r^2 = 18$$

Remember that you are not asked to calculate the actual value of r. Because you have set up an equation with one variable, and you know in this case that r can only be positive since it is part of a geometry figure, you have enough information to determine the area of the circle (the solution would have been $r^2 = 36$, so $r = 6$).

Therefore, Statement (1) is sufficient. You can eliminate **(B)**, **(C)**, and **(E)**.

Statement (2): Because O is the center of the circle and angle AOC measures 90 degrees, you know that the length of arc ABC is one-fourth of the circumference. Because this statement allows you to solve for the circumference, it is sufficient.

The correct answer is **(D)**.

13. (A)

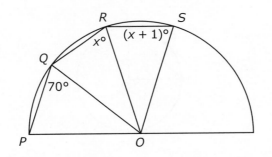

In the figure above, point O is the center of the semicircle, and PQ is parallel to OS. What is the measure of $\angle ROS$?

○ 34°
○ 36°
○ 54.5°
○ 72°
○ 73°

Step 1: Analyze the Question

This question presents you with a complex figure consisting of three triangles inscribed in a semi-circle. You are told that PQ is parallel to OS.

Step 2: State the Task

Find the measure of $\angle ROS$.

Step 3: Approach Strategically

The problem looks downright daunting, but the key, as with all geometry problems that involve complex figures, is to use any concrete information given to determine the starting point. With that in mind, begin by listing what you know from the figure:

1. Two of the three sides of each of the three inscribed triangles are radii of the semicircle. That means the three inscribed triangles are isosceles.

2. Since PQ is parallel to OS, QO is a transversal. When a transversal intersects with a pair of parallel lines, alternate interior angles are equal. In this case, since $\angle PQO = 70°$, $\angle QOS$ must also be 70°.

Add this information to your sketch of $\triangle QOR$ and $\triangle ROS$:

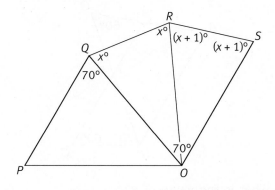

As you can't simply split angle $\angle QOS$ in half to find your answer (you can't make assumptions about the relative sizes of angles just from eyeballing the diagram), you'll instead need to solve for x. To do so, recall that a triangle's interior angles sum to $180°$. If you add up all six interior angles from $\triangle QOR$ and $\triangle ROS$, you'll have a sum of $360°$. You can now set up an equation to solve for the value of x.

$$x + x + (x + 1) + (x + 1) + 70 = 360$$
$$4x + 72 = 360$$
$$4x = 288$$
$$x = 75$$

Since $x = 72$, each of the two base angles in $\triangle ROS$ is $72 + 1 = 73°$. Therefore, the measure of $\angle ROS$ is $180 - 2(73) = 180 - 146 = 34°$. The correct answer is **(A)**.

Step 4: Confirm Your Answer

If you were pressed for time, a bit of Critical Thinking would reveal that isosceles triangles with base angles of approximately $70°$ cannot possibly allow a remaining angle as large as **(C)**, **(D)**, or **(E)** would indicate.

14. (A)

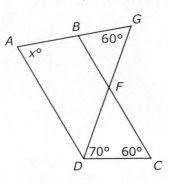

In the figure above, what is the value of *x*?

(1) *AD* ∥ *BC*

(2) ∠*GBC* = 70°

Step 1: Analyze the Question Stem

For this Value question, you can make the following observations from the figure:

In triangle *DFC*, the measure of angle *DFC* is 180° − 70° − 60° = 50°.

Angle *BFG* is vertical to angle *DFC*, so the measure of angle *BFG* is also 50°.

In triangle *FBG*, the measure of angle *GBF* is 180° − 50° − 60° = 70°.

Angle *ABF* completes a straight line with angle *GBF*, so the measure of angle *ABF* is 180° − 70° = 110°.

Angles *GFC* and *BFD* each complete a straight line with angle *DFC*, so the measure of each of these angles is 180° − 50° = 130°.

There are many things that would give you the value of *x*. You have two of the angles in quadrilateral *ABFD*, so getting the measure of angle *FDA* would give you the third and allow you to solve for *x* (all quadrilaterals have interior angles that sum to 360°). It's a complex figure, so there may be other ways to solve for *x* as well. You'll need to think carefully about any information you're given.

Step 2: Evaluate the Statements Using 12TEN

Statement (1) states that *AD* is parallel to *BC*. Therefore, angle *GBF* and the angle marked *x*° must be equal. Because the measure of angle *GBF* is 70°, the measure of the angle marked *x*° must be 70°. Thus, *x* = 70. Statement (1) is sufficient. You can eliminate **(B)**, **(C)**, and **(E)**.

Statement (2) tells you that ∠*GBC* = 70°. You already concluded that ∠*GBF* = 70° when you gathered information from the figure in Step 1. Because angle *GBF* is the same as angle *GBC*, this statement does not provide you with any new information and is therefore insufficient.

The correct answer is **(A)**.

15. (D)

An isosceles triangle is inscribed in a circle such that one of the triangle's sides coincides with the circle's longest chord. If the measure of another side of the triangle is 5, what is the difference between the area of the circle and the area of the triangle?

○ $\frac{25}{2}(1 - \pi)$

○ $25(\pi - 1)$

○ $\frac{25}{2}(\pi + 1)$

○ $\frac{25}{2}(\pi - 1)$

○ $\frac{25}{4}(\pi - 1)$

Step 1: Analyze the Question

"An isosceles triangle is inscribed in a circle" means that each vertex of a triangle with at least 2 sides of equal length is on the circumference of a circle. Furthermore, "one of the triangle's sides coincides with the circle's longest chord" means that one side of the triangle is a diameter of the circle. When a side of a triangle that's inscribed in a circle is a diameter of the circle, the vertex across from the diameter is a right angle, so the triangle is a right triangle and the side that coincides with the diameter is its hypotenuse. You're also told that the measure of another side of this triangle is 5. Since the triangle is isosceles, the third side must also have a length of 5, and the angles that are opposite those sides must also be of equal measure. Since one angle already measures 90°, each of the other two measures 45°. Thus, the inscribed figure is a 45°-45°-90° triangle.

Sketching a figure on your noteboard to visualize the figures will be helpful. Your sketch might look something like this:

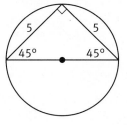

Step 2: State the Task

Determine the difference between the circle's area and the triangle's area, or $A_C - A_T$.

Step 3: Approach Strategically

You're given a measure of one of the triangle's sides, so start by finding the area of the triangle. Since it is a right triangle, one leg is the triangle's base, and the other leg is the height. Substitute those lengths into the formula for area of a triangle: $\frac{1}{2}bh = \frac{1}{2}(5)(5) = \frac{25}{2}$.

The formula for area of a circle is πr^2, so to find the area of the circle, you need to know the radius. In this figure, the radius of the circle is half the length of the triangle's hypotenuse. Because the triangle is a 45°-45°-90° triangle, the measures of the sides are in the ratio $1 : 1 : \sqrt{2}$. Thus, since each of the two legs measures 5, the hypotenuse measures $5\sqrt{2}$. This is also the circle's diameter, so the radius is half of $5\sqrt{2}$, or $\frac{5\sqrt{2}}{2}$. Thus, the circle's area is this:

$$\pi r^2 = \pi\left(\frac{5\sqrt{2}}{2}\right)^2 = \pi\left[\frac{(5)^2(\sqrt{2})^2}{(2)^2}\right] = \pi\left(\frac{25 \times \cancel{2}}{2^{\cancel{2}}}\right) = \frac{25\pi}{2}$$

Finally, the area of the circle minus the area of the triangle is $\frac{25\pi}{2} - \frac{25}{2} = \frac{25}{2}(\pi - 1)$, which matches **(D)**—the correct choice.

On Test Day, if you were behind on time and needed to make a strategic guess, you could note that **(A)** stands out as being the only choice whose binomial factor doesn't begin with π. Indeed, because π is greater than 1, $1 - \pi$ is negative. This choice is thus the product of a positive number and a negative number, which is negative. The difference between the area of a circle the area of a triangle inscribed within it must be positive, so you could eliminate **(A)** and guess from among the other choices.

Step 4: Confirm Your Answer

Ensure that you answered the question, which asks for the difference in areas between the circle and the triangle. Potential trap answers include **(A)**, which is the area of the triangle minus the area of the circle, and **(C)**, which is the sum of the two areas.

16. (B)

A cylindrical tank with a height of 8 feet is completely full of gasoline. This gasoline is pumped into an empty cylindrical tank with a diameter of 24 feet and a height of 18 feet. If the gasoline reaches a height of 2 feet in this tank, what is the diameter, in feet, of the original tank?

○   3
○   6
○   8
○   10
○   12

Step 1: Analyze the Question

There are two cylindrical tanks. The first is completely full of gasoline, which is all transferred to the second. The height of the first tank is given. Both the height and the diameter of the second tank are given, but that height is actually irrelevant since you're not finding the volume of the second tank; what is relevant is the height that the gasoline reaches in that second tank. The key to such a transference problem is noting that the volume of the gasoline in the original tank must equal the volume of the gasoline in the new tank.

Step 2: State the Task

Use the formula for volume of a cylinder to find the diameter of the original tank.

Step 3: Approach Strategically

The volume of any uniform solid is equal to the area of its base times that solid's height, so the volume of a right circular cylinder is $\pi r^2 h$. More information is given about the second cylinder, so start there. It has a diameter of 24 feet, so its radius must be 12 feet. The gasoline fills it to a height of 2 feet, so use 2 for the height. Thus, the volume of the gasoline in that tank is $\pi(12)^2(2) = 288\pi$ ft^3.

Now, plug this value back into the volume formula for the first cylinder to find its diameter: $288\pi = \pi r^2(8)$, so $r^2 = 36$ and $r = 6$ ft. The answer is **(B)**.

Step 4: Confirm Your Answer

As always, be sure to read the question stem carefully, noting the key details. Here, the diameter, not the radius, of the second tank's base was given and the gasoline did not reach the top of the second tank.

17. (D)

A rectangular solid has the dimensions 4, 5, and x. If the number of units in the solid's volume and the number of units in that solid's surface area are the same, what is the sum of the areas of the two largest faces of the solid?

- ○ 20
- ○ 40
- ○ 100
- ○ 200
- ○ 400

Step 1: Analyze the Question

The question stem tells you that the number of units in a rectangular solid's volume and the number of units in that solid's surface area are the same. Recall that the volume of a rectangular solid is Length $\times$ Height $\times$ Width and that the surface area is the sum of the areas of all 6 faces. You are also given specific values (4 and 5) for two of the three dimensions of the solid.

Step 2: State the Task

Determine the sum of the areas of the two largest faces of the solid.

Step 3: Approach Strategically

The solid's volume and surface area are equal values, so $\ell wh = 2\ell w + 2\ell h + 2wh$. Since you are not told which dimensions 4 and 5 represent, simply substitute those values into this equation in a consistent way, assigning x to the third dimension. If, say, $\ell = 4$ and $w = 5$, then $4(5)x = 2(4)(5) + 2(4)x + 2(5)x$. Now, solve for x:

$$20x = 2(4)(5) + 2(4)x + 2(5)x = 2[4(5) + 4x + 5x]$$
$$20x = 2(9x + 20)$$
$$10x = 9x + 20$$
$$x = 20$$

Because 20 is greater than 4 or 5, 20 is the largest dimension of the solid. Use that value and the second-largest dimension's measure to find the area of each of the largest faces of the solid: $20(5) = 100$. Finally, since opposite faces of a rectangular solid have the same area, double 100 to determine the sum of the areas of those two largest faces: $2(100) = 200$.

The correct choice is **(D)**.

Step 4: Confirm Your Answer

Ensure that you answered the question asked. For example, if you stopped working after solving for x, you might have selected **(A)**. If you forgot to double the area in the last step, **(C)** was waiting for you.

18. **(C)**

A cube with an edge length of 6 contains the largest possible sphere that completely fits inside of it. If the volume V of a sphere with radius r is given by the formula $V = \frac{4}{3}\pi r^3$, what is the volume of the empty space inside the cube?

○ $36(\pi^3 - 6)$

○ 36π

○ $36(6 - \pi)$

○ $36(\pi - 1)$

○ $36(4 - \pi)$

Step 1: Analyze the Question

The question stem tells you that a cube with edge 6 contains the largest possible sphere that completely fits inside of it. So the length of the sphere's diameter is the same as the length of the cube's side. There is also some empty space in the cube that is not occupied by the sphere; this is the three-dimensional equivalent of inscribing a circle in a square—there's some empty space in the corners. The formula for the volume of a sphere is given to you. Recall that the volume of a cube is the edge length cubed.

Step 2: State the Task

Determine the volume of the empty space in the cube, which is the difference between the cube's and sphere's volumes: $V_{\text{empty space}} = V_{\text{cube}} - V_{\text{sphere}} = (\text{edge})^3 - \frac{4}{3}\pi r^3$.

Step 3: Approach Strategically

You're given concrete information about the cube, so start by finding its volume: $V_{\text{cube}} = e^3 = 6^3 = 216$.

Now use the given formula to find the volume of the sphere. Since the length of the sphere's diameter is the same as the length of the cube's edge, the sphere's radius is half the length of the cube's edge: $r = \frac{1}{2}(6) = 3$. Plug this in for r in the formula: $V = \frac{4}{3}\pi r^3 = \frac{4}{3}(3^3)\pi = 4(3^2)\pi = 4(9)\pi = 36\pi$.

Now, determine the volume of the empty space in the cube: $V_{cube} - V_{sphere} = 216 - 36\pi$. This doesn't look like any of the answer choices, which all begin with a factor of 36. Factor 36 out of this expression to get $36(6 - \pi)$.

This matches **(C)**, which is the correct choice.

Step 4: Confirm Your Answer

Make sure you determined the difference between the volume of the cube and the volume of the sphere and not some other value, starting with confirming that you correctly derived the sphere's radius.

19. (C)

Line ℓ_1 is given by the equation $y = mx + 3$, and line ℓ_2 is given by the equation $y = nx - 7$; m and n are constants. Is ℓ_1 parallel to ℓ_2?

(1) $m^2 - n^2 = 0$

(2) mn is positive.

Step 1: Analyze the Question Stem

This is a Yes/No question asking whether two lines, each of which is represented by a unique equation, are parallel. Since two lines are parallel if they have the same slope, the statements are sufficient if they provide enough information to determine whether m and n, the slopes of lines ℓ_1 and ℓ_2, respectively, are equal.

Step 2: Evaluate the Statements Using 12TEN

Statement (1) says that $m^2 - n^2 = 0$. This is one of the "classic" quadratics; it factors to $(m + n)(m - n) = 0$. This means that $m = n$ or $-n$. In other words, m and n have the same magnitude, but they could have either the same sign or opposite signs. So, if they had the same sign, the slopes would be equal and the answer to the question would be yes, but if they had opposite signs, the slopes would not be equal and the answer would be no. Thus, this statement is insufficient; eliminate **(A)** and **(D)**.

Statement (2) says that the product of m and n is positive. This means that m and n have the same sign; they're either both positive or both negative. Without more information, though, there's no way to know whether they're equal, so this statement is insufficient. Eliminate **(B)**.

Now, combine the statements. According to (1), $m = n$ or $-n$, but according to (2), m and n must have the same sign. That leaves $m = n$ as the only possibility. Even though there's not enough information to determine what the slopes are, they must be equal to each other. Choose **(C)**.

20. (C)

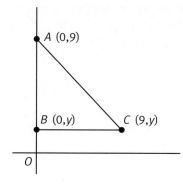

In the rectangular coordinate system above, triangle *ABC* has an area of 27 square units. Vertex *A* is at point (0, 9), vertex *B* is at point (0, *y*), and vertex *C* is at point (9, *y*). What is the value of *y*?

- ○   1
- ○   2
- ○   3
- ○   4
- ○   6

Step 1: Analyze the Question

You're given the *x*- and *y*-coordinates of one of the three vertices of triangle *ABC*, the *x*-coordinates of the remaining two vertices, and the area of the triangle. Since the *y*-coordinates of the two vertices not specified are both represented by *y*, they are the same, so the side *BC* of the triangle is parallel to the *x*-axis. Additionally, side *AB* lies on the *y*-axis, so this is a right triangle.

Step 2: State the Task

Determine the *y*-coordinate of points *B* and *C* on the graph.

Step 3: Approach Strategically

Since you are given the area of the triangle, use the formula for the area of a triangle to determine the missing coordinate:

The area of triangle $ABC = \left(\frac{1}{2}\right)(\text{base})(\text{height}) = 27$. Since the graph indicates that the base of the triangle extends from point (0, *y*) to point (9, *y*), the base has a length of 9, so $\left(\frac{1}{2}\right)(9)(\text{height}) = 27$. Simplifying yields $9 \times \text{height} = 54$, so $\text{height} = 54 \div 9 = 6$. Since vertex *A* lies at point (0, 9), the *y*-coordinate of vertex *B* must be $9 - 6 = 3$. Thus, $y = 3$. The correct choice is **(C)**.

Step 4: Confirm Your Answer

Use the height you've calculated from the *y*-coordinate you've found to check whether the area matches that in the question stem. Note also that 6 in **(E)** is a trap answer for the unwary test taker, since that's the height of the triangle, not the value of *y*.

21. (B)

In the *xy*-coordinate system, if (m, n) and $(m + 2, n + k)$ are two points on the line with the equation $x = 2y + 5$, then $k =$

○ $\dfrac{1}{2}$

○ 1

○ 2

○ $\dfrac{5}{2}$

○ 4

Step 1: Analyze the Question

For any question involving the equation of a line, a good place to start is the slope-intercept form of the line, $y = mx + b$. Remember that if you have two points on a line, you can derive the entire equation, and if you have an equation of the line, you can calculate any points on that line.

Step 2: State the Task

You must solve for k, which is the amount by which the *y*-coordinate increases when the *x*-coordinate increases by 2.

Step 3: Approach Strategically

The slope of a line is the ratio between the change in *y* and the change in *x*. In other words, every time the *x*-coordinate increases by 1, the *y*-coordinate increases by the amount of the slope.

The equation of the line in the question stem is defined as $x = 2y + 5$. You must isolate *y* to have slope-intercept form:

$$x = 2y + 5$$
$$x - 5 = 2y$$
$$\frac{x - 5}{2} = y$$
$$y = \frac{1}{2}x - \frac{5}{2}$$

So the slope of this line is $\frac{1}{2}$. This means that for every change of $+1$ in the *x* direction, there is a change of $+\frac{1}{2}$ in the *y* direction. Therefore, you know that, because there is an increase of 2 units in the *x* direction when moving from m to $m + 2$, there must be a change of 1 unit in the *y* direction when moving from n to $n + k$. So $k = 1$.

Since there are variables that eventually cancel (m and n are not part of the answer choices), you can use picking numbers. Say that you choose the *y*-coordinate of the point (m, n) to be 0 to allow for easier calculations. Using the equation you're given to relate *x*- and *y*-coordinates, you can calculate the *x*-coordinate:

$$x = 2y + 5$$
$$x = 2(0) + 5$$
$$x = 5$$

So (m, n) is the point $(5, 0)$.

Now you'll plug your values of m and n into the next point: $(m + 2, n + k)$. That yields $(7, k)$. All you have to do is plug an x-coordinate of 7 into the equation to solve for k, the y-coordinate:

$$x = 2y + 5$$
$$7 = 2k + 5$$
$$2 = 2k$$
$$1 = k$$

(B) is correct.

Step 4: Confirm Your Answer

Reread the question, making sure that you didn't miss anything. For example, if you thought that the original equation was $y = 2x + 5$, then you would have answered **(E)**. This step would help you to catch that error.

GMAT BY THE NUMBERS: GEOMETRY

Now that you've learned how to approach geometry questions on the GMAT, let's add one more dimension to your understanding of how they work.

Take a moment to try this question. Following is performance data from thousands of people who have studied with Kaplan over the decades. Through analyzing this data, we will show you how to approach questions like this one most effectively and how to avoid similarly tempting wrong answer choice types on Test Day.

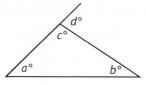

In the figure above, what is the value of *b*?

(1) $a + c + d = 225$

(2) $d - a = 55$

○ Statement (1) ALONE is sufficient, but statement (2) is not sufficient.

○ Statement (2) ALONE is sufficient, but statement (1) is not sufficient.

○ BOTH statements TOGETHER are sufficient, but NEITHER statement ALONE is sufficient.

○ EACH statement ALONE is sufficient.

○ Statements (1) and (2) TOGETHER are NOT sufficient.

EXPLANATION

The key to most GMAT geometry problems is to analyze the given figure before you worry too much about how you're going to solve. In this problem, you're given a triangle and a straight line, both of which have angles that add to 180°. Hence, you can create two equations:

$$a + b + c = 180 \quad \text{and} \quad d + c = 180$$

Since both $(a + b + c)$ and $(d + c)$ equal 180, you can set them equal to each other. And since you're solving for b, you'll want to first simplify the equation to isolate b:

$$a + b + c = d + c$$

$$a + b = d$$

$$b = d - a$$

To solve for b, you need only find a value for $d - a$. Having thus analyzed the question stem, you see that Statement (2) gives you exactly what you need and is sufficient and that Statement (1) does not and is insufficient. Hence, **(B)** is correct.

QUESTION STATISTICS

7% of test takers choose **(A)**

25% of test takers choose **(B)**

50% of test takers choose **(C)**

5% of test takers choose **(D)**

13% of test takers choose **(E)**

Sample size = 4,597

The question statistics reveal what the test maker already knows—that the vast majority of test takers don't do much up-front analysis, thereby making their task much harder and causing them to miss what could be straightforward solutions. Make sure to analyze figures before you solve, and you'll make GMAT geometry much easier.

MORE GMAT BY THE NUMBERS...

To see more questions with answer choice statistics, be sure to review the full-length CATs in your online resources.

GO ONLINE

kaptest.com/login

CHAPTER 19

Advanced Math Practice

In this chapter, you'll find two 20-question practice sets consisting entirely of questions most test takers find challenging. The first practice set contains Problem Solving questions; the second contains Data Sufficiency questions. Following each practice set, you'll find the answer key, as well as complete explanations for every question.

Use these question sets to hone your critical thinking skills if you are aiming for a very high GMAT score. If you are not yet comfortable with the practice questions in the preceding chapters of this book, then continue to review the arithmetic, algebra, geometry, and other topics presented there until you are able to find the correct answers to most of those practice questions. Then you'll be ready to tackle the tougher questions here.

As always, be sure to *review the explanation* to every problem you do in this chapter. Noting a different way to work through a problem, even if you got that problem right, is a powerful way to enhance your critical thinking skills—and it's ultimately those skills that you will be relying on in order to achieve a very high score on Test Day.

Ready to take your Quantitative score to the next level? Then turn the page and begin work!

ADVANCED PROBLEM SOLVING PRACTICE SET

1. The numbers m, n, and T are all positive, and $m > n$. A weekend farm stand sells only peaches. On Saturday, the farm stand has T peaches to sell, at a profit of m cents each. Any peaches remaining for sale on Sunday will be marked down and sold at a profit of $(m - n)$ cents each. If all peaches available for sale on Saturday morning are sold by Sunday evening, how many peaches, in terms of T, m, and n, does the stand need to sell on Saturday in order to make the same profit on each day?

   ○ $\dfrac{Tm}{m - n}$

   ○ $\dfrac{Tm}{n - m}$

   ○ $\dfrac{m(m - n)}{T}$

   ○ $\dfrac{T}{m - n}$

   ○ $\dfrac{T(m - n)}{2m - n}$

2. Set X consists of at least 2 members and is a set of consecutive odd integers with an average (arithmetic mean) of 37.

   Set Y consists of at least 10 members and is also a set of consecutive odd integers with an average (arithmetic mean) of 37.

   Set Z consists of all of the members of both set X and set Y.

   Which of the following statements must be true?

   I. The standard deviation of set Z is not equal to the standard deviation of set X.

   II. The standard deviation of set Z is equal to the standard deviation of set Y.

   III. The average (arithmetic mean) of set Z is 37.

   ○ I only
   ○ II only
   ○ III only
   ○ I and III
   ○ II and III

3. The number 10,010 has how many positive integer factors?

   ○ 31
   ○ 32
   ○ 33
   ○ 34
   ○ 35

4. A department of motor vehicles asks visitors to draw numbered tickets from a dispenser so that they can be served in order by number. Six friends have graduated from truck-driving school and go to the department to get commercial driving licenses. They draw tickets and find that their numbers are a set of evenly spaced integers with a range of 10. Which of the following could NOT be the sum of their numbers?

   ○ 1,254
   ○ 1,428
   ○ 3,972
   ○ 4,316
   ○ 8,010

5. For all values of x, y, and z, $x \diamond y \diamond z = x^2(y - 1)(z + 2)$.

   If $a < 0$, which of the following shows R, S, and T arranged in order from least to greatest?

   R: $1 \diamond a \diamond 3$

   S: $3 \diamond a \diamond 1$

   T: $a \diamond 3 \diamond 1$

   ○ R, S, T
   ○ T, S, R
   ○ R, T, S
   ○ T, R, S
   ○ S, R, T

6. If a and b are integers, and $2a + b = 17$, then $8a + b$ cannot equal which of the following?

   ○ -1
   ○ 33
   ○ 35
   ○ 65
   ○ 71

7. Two workers have different pay scales. Worker A receives $50 for any day worked plus $15 per hour. Worker B receives $27 per hour. Both workers may work for a fraction of an hour and be paid in proportion to their respective hourly rates. If Worker A arrives at 9:21 a.m. and receives the $50 upon arrival and Worker B arrives at 10:09 a.m., assuming both work continuously, at what time would their earnings be identical?

    ○   11:09 a.m.

    ○   12:01 p.m.

    ○   2:31 p.m.

    ○   3:19 p.m.

    ○   3:36 p.m.

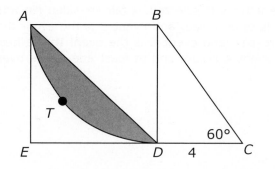

8. In the figure above, *ABDE* is a square, and arc *ATD* is part of a circle with center *B*. The measure of angle *BCD* is 60 degrees, and line segment *CD* has a length of 4. What is the area of the shaded region?

    ○ $16\pi - 32$

    ○ $12\pi - 24$

    ○ $12\pi - 48$

    ○ $48\pi - 24$

    ○ $48\pi - 48$

9. When the cube of a non-zero number y is subtracted from 35, the result is equal to the result of dividing 216 by the cube of that number y. What is the sum of all the possible values of y?

- ⭘ $\dfrac{5}{2}$
- ⭘ 5
- ⭘ 6
- ⭘ 10
- ⭘ 12

10. One letter is selected at random from the 5 letters V, W, X, Y, and Z, and event A is the event that the letter V is selected. A fair six-sided die with sides numbered 1, 2, 3, 4, 5, and 6 is to be rolled, and event B is the event that a 5 or a 6 shows. A fair coin is to be tossed, and event C is the event that a head shows. What is the probability that event A occurs and at least one of the events B and C occurs?

- ⭘ $\dfrac{1}{30}$
- ⭘ $\dfrac{1}{15}$
- ⭘ $\dfrac{1}{10}$
- ⭘ $\dfrac{2}{15}$
- ⭘ $\dfrac{1}{5}$

11. A car traveled from Town A to Town B. The car traveled the first $\frac{3}{8}$ of the distance from Town A to Town B at an average speed of x miles per hour, where $x > 0$. The car traveled the remaining distance at an average speed of y miles per hour, where $y > 0$. The car traveled the entire distance from Town A to Town B at an average speed of z miles per hour. Which of the following equations gives y in terms of x and z?

- ○ $y = \dfrac{3x + 5z}{8}$

- ○ $y = \dfrac{5xz}{8x + 3z}$

- ○ $y = \dfrac{8x - 3z}{5xz}$

- ○ $y = \dfrac{3xz}{8x - 5z}$

- ○ $y = \dfrac{5xz}{8x - 3z}$

12. An ornithologist has studied a particular population of starlings and discovered that their population has increased by 400 percent every 10 years starting in 1890. If the initial population in 1890 was 256 birds, how large was the population of starlings in 1970?

- ○ 102,400
- ○ 10,000,000
- ○ 16,777,216
- ○ 20,000,000
- ○ 100,000,000

13. If $(x^2 + 8)yz < 0$, $wz > 0$, and $xyz < 0$, then which of the following must be true?

     I. $x < 0$

    II. $wy < 0$

   III. $yz < 0$

- ○ II only
- ○ III only
- ○ I and III only
- ○ II and III only
- ○ I, II, and III

14. If $\dfrac{61^2 - 1}{h}$ is an integer, then h could be divisible by each of the following EXCEPT:

- ○ 8
- ○ 12
- ○ 15
- ○ 18
- ○ 31

15. If *a*, *b*, and *c* are integers such that $0 < a < b < c$, and *a* is even, *b* is prime, and *c* is odd, which of the following is a possible value for *abc*?

   ○ 5
   ○ 12
   ○ 16
   ○ 34
   ○ 54

16. A fair die with sides numbered 1, 2, 3, 4, 5, and 6 is to be rolled 4 times. What is the probability that on at least 1 roll the number showing will be less than 3?

   ○ $\frac{65}{81}$

   ○ $\frac{67}{81}$

   ○ $\frac{8}{9}$

   ○ $\frac{26}{27}$

   ○ $\frac{80}{81}$

17. There are 816 students in enrolled at a certain high school. Each of these students is taking at least one of the subjects economics, geography, and biology. The sum of the number of students taking exactly one of these subjects and the number of students taking all three of these subjects is 5 times the number of students taking exactly two of these subjects. The ratio of the number of students taking only the two subjects economics and geography to the number of students taking only the two subjects economics and biology to the number of students taking only the two subjects geography and biology is 3:6:8. How many of the students enrolled at this high school are taking only the two subjects geography and biology?

O   35

O   42

O   64

O   136

O   240

18. Working alone at a constant rate, Machine P produces a widgets in 3 hours. Working alone at a constant rate, Machine Q produces b widgets in 4 hours. If Machines P and Q work together for c hours, then in terms of a, b, and c, how many widgets will Machines P and Q produce?

O $\dfrac{3ac + 4bc}{12}$

O $\dfrac{4ac + 3bc}{12}$

O $\dfrac{4ac + 3bc}{6}$

O $4ac + 3bc$

O $\dfrac{ac + 2bc}{4}$

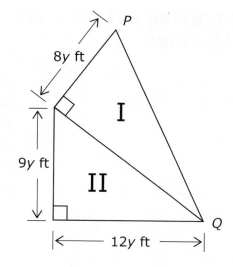

19. In the figure above, the perimeter of triangle I is 16 feet greater than the perimeter of triangle II. What is the length of *PQ*, in feet?

   ○ 27
   ○ 51
   ○ 68
   ○ 75
   ○ 85

20. If $x > 0$, $y > 0$, and $\dfrac{7x^2 + 72xy + 4y^2}{4x^2 + 12xy + 5y^2} = 4$, what is the value of $\dfrac{x + y}{y}$?

   ○ $\dfrac{3}{4}$

   ○ $\dfrac{4}{3}$

   ○ $\dfrac{10}{7}$

   ○ $\dfrac{7}{4}$

   ○ $\dfrac{7}{3}$

ADVANCED PROBLEM SOLVING PRACTICE SET: ANSWERS AND EXPLANATIONS

1.	E	8.	B	15.	E
2.	C	9.	B	16.	A
3.	B	10.	D	17.	C
4.	D	11.	E	18.	B
5.	E	12.	E	19.	C
6.	B	13.	D	20.	E
7.	D	14.	D		

1. **(E)**

The numbers m, n, and T are all positive, and $m > n$. A weekend farm stand sells only peaches. On Saturday, the farm stand has T peaches to sell, at a profit of m cents each. Any peaches remaining for sale on Sunday will be marked down and sold at a profit of $(m - n)$ cents each. If all peaches available for sale on Saturday morning are sold by Sunday evening, how many peaches, in terms of T, m, and n, does the stand need to sell on Saturday in order to make the same profit on each day?

○ $\dfrac{Tm}{m - n}$

○ $\dfrac{Tm}{n - m}$

○ $\dfrac{m(m - n)}{T}$

○ $\dfrac{T}{m - n}$

○ $\dfrac{T(m - n)}{2m - n}$

Step 1: Analyze the Question

There are a total of T peaches, all of which are to be sold during the course of the weekend. On Saturday, the profit for each peach is m cents. On Sunday, the profit for each peach is $(m - n)$ cents.

Step 2: State the Task

How many peaches must be sold on Saturday to make Saturday's profit equal Sunday's profit?

Step 3: Approach Strategically

Start by setting up expressions for Saturday's profit and Sunday's profit and then set those expressions equal. There's no variable given for the number of peaches sold on either day, so call the number of peaches to be sold on Saturday x. The total profit for Saturday will be (m cents per peach) times (x peaches), which is mx cents. On Sunday, there will be $(T - x)$ peaches left, each of which will bring a profit of $(m - n)$ cents. The total profit for Sunday will be [$(m - n)$ cents per peach] times [$(T - x)$ peaches], which is $(m - n)(T - x)$ cents. Saturday's profit must equal Sunday's profit: $mx = (m - n)(T - x)$. The question asks for the number of peaches to be sold on Saturday, so solve for x:

$$mx = (m - n)(T - x)$$

$$mx = mT - mx - nT + nx$$

$$2mx - nx = mT - nT$$

$$(2m - n)x = mT - nT$$

$$x = \frac{mT - nT}{2m - n}$$

None of the answer choices are written $\frac{mT - nT}{2m - n}$. However, $\frac{mT - nT}{2m - n} = \frac{T(m - n)}{2m - n}$.

(E) is correct.

Step 4: Confirm Your Answer

Confirm that your answer makes sense. Rewrite the denominator to test the size of the fraction: $\frac{m-n}{2m-n} = \frac{m-n}{2(m-n)+n}$. It should be fairly easy to see that this is less than $\frac{1}{2}$. So $\frac{T(m-n)}{2m-n}$, which equals $T\left(\frac{m-n}{2m-n}\right)$, must be less than $T\left(\frac{1}{2}\right)$, or $\frac{T}{2}$. It follows that the number of peaches sold on Saturday, which is $\frac{T(m-n)}{2m-n}$, is less than half of the total number of peaches sold. That makes sense because the profit per peach is lower on Sunday than on Saturday—so fewer than half the peaches would have to be sold on Saturday in order for both days' profits to be equal.

2. **(C)**

Set X consists of at least 2 members and is a set of consecutive odd integers with an average (arithmetic mean) of 37.

Set Y consists of at least 10 members and is also a set of consecutive odd integers with an average (arithmetic mean) of 37.

Set Z consists of all of the members of both set X and set Y.

Which of the following statements must be true?

  I. The standard deviation of set Z is not equal to the standard deviation of set X.
 II. The standard deviation of set Z is equal to the standard deviation of set Y.
III. The average (arithmetic mean) of set Z is 37.

- ○ I only
- ○ II only
- ○ III only
- ○ I and III
- ○ II and III

Step 1: Analyze the Question

Set X has at least 2 members and consists of consecutive odd integers that have a mean of 37. For any set of evenly spaced numbers, the mean equals the median, so the median of set X is 37. For a set of consecutive odd integers to have an average that is an odd integer, there must be an odd number of members. So set X must actually contain at least 3 members. Thus, set X could be, for example, $\{35, 37, 39\}$ or $\{33, 35, 37, 39, 41\}$.

Set Y has the same mean and median as set X. However, set Y has a greater minimum number of members. The question says that set Y has at least 10 members. But again, for a set of consecutive odd integers to have an average that is an odd integer, there must be an odd number of members, so set Y must contain at least 11 members. Note that although set Y has a higher minimum number of terms, neither set has a maximum. This means that it's possible for set X to have more members than set Y or even for the sets to be equal to one another.

Set Z contains all the members of both set X and set Y. When sets X and Y have different numbers of members, set Z equals either set X or set Y, whichever has the greater number of members. For example, if set $X = \{35, 37, 39\}$ and set $Y = \{27, 29, 31, 33, 35, 37, 39, 41, 43, 45, 47\}$, then set Z would be equal to set Y, as the entirety of set X is contained within set Y. When sets X and Y have the same number of members (and therefore are equal), set Z equals both sets X and Y.

Step 2: State the Task

Evaluate the three statements and determine which are always true about sets X, Y, and Z.

Step 3: Approach Strategically

Of the Roman numeral statements, III is the most frequently mentioned in the answer choices and, conveniently, also the easiest to consider. Set Z will always equal set X and/or Y, and both set X and set Y have a mean of 37. Therefore, set Z will also always have a mean of 37, and Statement III is part of the correct answer. Eliminate **(A)** and **(B)**.

The other two options involve the standard deviation of set *Z*. Recall that standard deviation refers to how spread out a set of numbers is. Like many GMAT questions involving standard deviation, this one does not require calculation of the actual value. Instead, recognize that sets of equally spaced integers will have different standard deviations depending on how many members are in the set. When two sets have equally spaced numbers and the spacing in both sets is the same, the set with the greater number of numbers has the greater standard deviation. While the standard deviation of set *Z* will always be equal to either (or both) the standard deviation of set *X* or *Y*, it is not necessarily different than the standard deviation of set *X*, nor is it necessarily equal to the standard deviation of set *Y*. This eliminates **(D)** and **(E)**, making **(C)** the correct answer.

Step 4: Confirm Your Answer

Quickly confirm by recognizing that when set *X* has more members than set *Y*, both Statements I and II are not true. Statement III is the only one that is true under all circumstances.

3. (B)

The number 10,010 has how many positive integer factors?

- ○ 31
- ○ 32
- ○ 33
- ○ 34
- ○ 35

Step 1: Analyze the Question

There's no information to catalogue in the question stem; there is just the number 10,010. However, the answer choices provide a clue: you need to find a way to count more than 30 factors.

Step 2: State the Task

The question asks for the total number of positive factors, not just prime factors.

Step 3: Approach Strategically

Making a chart of all factors of a number works well for two-digit numbers, but it would require a great deal of arithmetic in this case. Instead, start by finding the prime factorization of 10,010, and then use those prime factors to find the total number of factors. The number 10,010 ends in zero, so it's divisible by 10, or 2×5. So far, you have $2 \times 5 \times 1,001$. Now use divisibility rules to investigate the factor 1,001. This is not an even number, so it isn't divisible by 2. Its digits do not sum to 3, so it isn't divisible by 3. It doesn't end in 5 or 0, so 5 is also not a factor. What about 7? To check whether a given number is divisible by 7, multiply the units digit by 2, subtract the result from the remaining digits, and check if the result is divisible by 7. If yes, then the original number is also divisible by 7. The units digit of 1,001 is 1. Multiply by 2 and subtract from 100: $100 - 2 = 98$. Because 98 is divisible by 7 ($98 = 7 \times 14$), 1,001 is also divisible by 7. Do the long division to find that $1,001 \div 7 = 143$. Now again apply divisibility rules to 143. It's not divisible by 2, 3, 5, or 7. What about 11? A number is divisible by 11 if the difference between the sum of its even-placed digits and the sum of its odd-placed digits is divisible by 11 without leaving a remainder. In the case of 143, $(1 + 3) - 4 = 0$. Zero divided by 11 is 0 without any remainder, so 143 is divisible by 11. Do the division to find that $143 \div 11 = 13$.

The full prime factorization of 10,010, then, is as follows: $2 \times 5 \times 7 \times 11 \times 13$. Once you have its prime factorization, the fastest way to determine how many factors a number has is to add 1 to each exponent in the prime factorization and multiply the resulting values. You can write the prime factorization of 10,010 as $2^1 \times 5^1 \times 7^1 \times 11^1 \times 13^1$. Now add 1 to each exponent and multiply: $(1 + 1)(1 + 1)(1 + 1)(1 + 1)(1 + 1) = (2)(2)(2)(2)(2) = 32$. The correct answer is **(B)**.

Step 4: Confirm Your Answer

Do a quick check to make sure you included all the prime factors you discovered and check the exponents.

4. (D)

A department of motor vehicles asks visitors to draw numbered tickets from a dispenser so that they can be served in order by number. Six friends have graduated from truck-driving school and go to the department to get commercial driving licenses. They draw tickets and find that their numbers are a set of evenly spaced integers with a range of 10. Which of the following could NOT be the sum of their numbers?

- ○ 1,254
- ○ 1,428
- ○ 3,972
- ○ 4,316
- ○ 8,010

Step 1: Analyze the Question

Six people draw six evenly spaced integers with a range of 10. You could pick two numbers with a range of 10, such as 1 and 11 or 2 and 12, and experiment to see how six evenly spaced integers could fit in the range. Clearly, the integers must be 2 apart.

Alternatively, the formula for the number of members in a set of evenly spaced integers is this:

$$\text{\# of numbers} = \frac{\text{Range}}{\text{Interval}} + 1$$

In this case:

$$6 = \frac{10}{\text{Interval}} + 1$$

$$6(\text{Interval}) = 10 + 1(\text{Interval})$$

$$5(\text{Interval}) = 10$$

$$\text{Interval} = 2$$

Anytime the GMAT uses a small set of evenly spaced integers, remember that a single variable is sufficient to represent the series. Thus, x can represent the first integer, and the 6 integers can be written x, $x + 2$, $x + 4$, $x + 6$, $x + 8$, $x + 10$. The sum of these would be $6x + 30$, or $6(x + 5)$. While you do not know the value of this expression (since you do not know the value of x), you do know it is a multiple of 6.

Step 2: State the Task

You need to find the answer choice that *cannot* equal $6(x + 5)$. The correct answer is the one that is *not* a multiple of 6.

Step 3: Approach Strategically

Use the rule for divisibility by 6, which combines the rules for divisibility by 2 and 3. To be divisible by 2, the number must be even, and to be divisible by 3, the sum of the digits of the number must be divisible by 3.

All the answer choices are even, so use the rule for divisibility by 3.

(A): $1 + 2 + 5 + 4 = 12$. Eliminate.

(B): $1 + 4 + 2 + 8 = 15$. Eliminate.

(C): $3 + 9 + 7 + 2 = 21$. Eliminate.

(D): $4 + 3 + 1 + 6 = 14$, which is *not* divisible by 3. This is the correct answer.

For the record...

(E): $8 + 0 + 1 + 0 = 9$. Eliminate.

Step 4: Confirm Your Answer

If you divide 4,316 by 6, you get 719 with a remainder of 2. Therefore, 4,316 is not divisible by 6, and **(D)** is correct.

5. (E)

For all values of x, y, and z, $x \diamond y \diamond z = x^2(y - 1)(z + 2)$.

If $a < 0$, which of the following show R, S, and T arranged in order from least to greatest?

R: $1 \diamond a \diamond 3$

S: $3 \diamond a \diamond 1$

T: $a \diamond 3 \diamond 1$

○ R, S, T
○ T, S, R
○ R, T, S
○ T, R, S
○ S, R, T

Step 1: Analyze the Question

You are given a symbolic algebra equation that describes the relationship of variables x, y, and z. Using this symbolism as a function, substitute 1, 3, and a for x, y, and z in the various orders shown. Keep in mind that a is negative.

Step 2: State the Task

The question requires you to use the symbolic equation given and evaluate R, S, and T, placing them in order from smallest to largest.

Step 3: Approach Strategically

There are no obvious answer choices to eliminate, so calculate the values of R, S, and T and rank them in order from smallest to largest. Again, $x \diamond y \diamond z = x^2(y - 1)(z + 2)$.

$$R: 1 \diamond a \diamond 3 = 1^2(a - 1)(3 + 2)$$
$$= 1(a - 1)(5)$$
$$= 5(a - 1) = 5a - 5$$

$$S: 3 \diamond a \diamond 1 = 3^2(a - 1)(1 + 2)$$
$$= 9(a - 1)(3)$$
$$= 27(a - 1) = 27a - 27$$

$$T: a \diamond 3 \diamond 1 = a^2(3 - 1)(1 + 2)$$
$$= a^2(2)(3) = 6a^2$$

You know that T must be a positive value because the a is squared and multiplied by a positive number. Keeping in mind that a is negative, it should be clear that the expressions that result for R and S subtract a positive value from a negative value, making them both negative numbers. Therefore, T must be the greatest of the choices. Eliminate **(B)**, **(C)**, and **(D)**.

Next compare R and S. Both involve multiplying the negative value a by a constant and then subtracting a positive integer. However, both terms of S have a greater absolute value than those of R, making S less than R and **(E)** the correct answer.

Step 4: Confirm Your Answer

You could pick numbers for a to confirm your answer. For example, if $a = -1$, then $R = 5a - 5 = 5(-1) - 5 = -10$, $S = 27a - 27 = 27(-1) - 27 = -54$, and $T = 6(-1^2) = 6$. For any permissible value of a, S is always less than R and T is always positive, again making **(E)** the correct answer.

6. (B)

If a and b are integers, and $2a + b = 17$, then $8a + b$ cannot equal which of the following?

- ○ -1
- ○ 33
- ○ 35
- ○ 65
- ○ 71

Step 1: Analyze the Question

Because the question asks about what $8a + b$ *cannot* equal, try to find some rule about what the expression must equal and go from there. The correct answer will violate some property represented in the given information.

Step 2: State the Task

To find the value in the answer choices that would not work with the given information, use the equation $2a + b = 17$ in conjunction with the expression $8a + b$.

Step 3: Approach Strategically

Since you have only one equation, you can't solve for either variable, but you can still substitute and get one variable in the expression you're evaluating. Substituting for either variable would work, but it is easier to substitute for b, since all you have to do is put $2a$ on the other side of the equation. If $b = -2a + 17$, then the expression $8a + b$ becomes $8a + (-2a + 17)$, which simplifies to $6a + 17$. Because you know that a is an integer, $6a$ must be a multiple of 6. Then because you're adding 17 to a multiple of 6, the correct answer must be just that—the result of adding 17 to a multiple of 6. (If you notice that this is 1 less than a multiple of 6, evaluating the answer choices is even faster.)

(A): $-1 - 17 = -18$, a multiple of 6. Eliminate.

(B): $33 - 17 = 16$, which is not a multiple of 6. **(B)** is the correct answer.

For the record...

(C): $35 - 17 = 18$, a multiple of 6. Eliminate.

(D): $65 - 17 = 48$, a multiple of 6. Eliminate.

(E): $71 - 17 = 54$, a multiple of 6. Eliminate.

Step 4: Confirm Your Answer

Using substitution, you know that $8a + b = 6a + 17$. If $6a + 17 = 33$, then $6a = 16$ and $a = \frac{8}{3}$, which is not an integer. **(B)** is correct.

7.   **(D)**

Two workers have different pay scales. Worker A receives $50 for any day worked plus $15 per hour. Worker B receives $27 per hour. Both workers may work for a fraction of an hour and be paid in proportion to their respective hourly rates. If Worker A arrives at 9:21 a.m. and receives the $50 upon arrival and Worker B arrives at 10:09 a.m., assuming both work continuously, at what time would their earnings be identical?

   ○   11:09 a.m.
   ○   12:01 p.m.
   ○   2:31 p.m.
   ○   3:19 p.m.
   ○   3:36 p.m.

Step 1: Analyze the Question Stem

The stem gives you a lot of information. There are two workers, each with a different pay scale as well as time arrived. It would be worth writing down the basics on your noteboard, like this:

A: 9:21 $50 + 15/hr

B: 10:09 $27/hr

Step 2: State the Task

Even though this is about wages and money, it's a combined rates problem, just like a question that asks when two trains pass each other. The correct answer will be the time that the different rates produce the same sum of money.

Step 3: Approach Strategically

While it's possible to backsolve, it would be necessary to plug each time into two different formulas, making this approach both time-consuming and potentially error-prone. Furthermore, combining rates is usually very fast if done correctly. However, if combining the rates as described below seems too tricky and you feel confident with the arithmetic involved (and understand what result would indicate a time too late or too early), backsolving may be a good option.

Anytime the GMAT gives you different rates and asks you to find when or where they produce the same result, you can use four steps to get the answer—often in a minute or less.

The first step is to calculate any distance/work/earnings that one entity achieves when the other is not active. In this case, A works for 48 minutes before B begins, so you want to know how much money A has already made. In combined work problems, calculations are easiest if you state time as a fraction, and 48 minutes is $\frac{4}{5}$ of an hour. Thus, $15 \times \frac{4}{5} = 12 earned. Also, A gets $50 right off the bat, so A is $12 + $50 = $62 up when B begins working.

The second step is to combine rates. In this case, think about B catching up to A. Worker A makes $15 an hour and Worker B makes $27 an hour, so for each hour they both work, B gains on A by $12.

The third step is to divide the distance/work/earnings by the combined rate to get the time, so divide $62 by $12 per hour, and get $5\frac{2}{12}$ or $5\frac{1}{6}$ hours. A sixth of an hour is 10 minutes, so they are both working for 5 hours 10 minutes.

The last step is to add the time worked to the starting time. In this case, add 5 hours 10 minutes to the first time when both started working, 10:09 a.m., and get 3:19 p.m. **(D)** is the correct answer.

Step 4: Confirm Your Answer

When taking the four steps described above leads to an answer that exactly matches one of the choices, you can feel confident that you have solved correctly. However, to confirm, you could find that Worker A worked for 5 hours 58 minutes and so, at $15 an hour, made $89.50 + $50, or $139.50. Worker B worked for 5 hours 10 minutes at $27 an hour, which also yields $139.50. Again, **(D)** is correct.

8. (B)

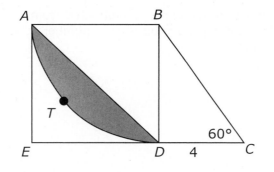

In the figure above, *ABDE* is a square, and arc *ATD* is part of a circle with center *B*. The measure of angle *BCD* is 60 degrees, and line segment *CD* has a length of 4. What is the area of the shaded region?

- ○ $16\pi - 32$
- ○ $12\pi - 24$
- ○ $12\pi - 48$
- ○ $48\pi - 24$
- ○ $48\pi - 48$

Step 1: Analyze the Question

In a shaded region question, it is important to recognize what shapes are interacting to produce the shaded region. In this case, the shaded region is the result of removing triangle *ABD*, whose area is half the area of square *ABDE*, from the sector of a circle. Additionally, you are given two important measurements for triangle *BCD*: angle *BCD* measures 60 degrees and side *CD* has a length of 4.

Step 2: State the Task

Subtract half the area of the square from the area of the circle sector to calculate the area of the shaded region.

Step 3: Approach Strategically

The area of a sector of a circle has the same proportional relationship to the area of the full circle as its central angle does to 360 degrees. This sector has a central angle which is interior angle *ABD* of the square. Since *B* is a vertex of a square, the measure of angle *ABD* is 90 degrees. Because 90 degrees is one-fourth of 360 degrees, the sector defined by arc *ATD* has an area one-fourth of that of the full circle. To calculate the area of both the half square and quarter circle, determine the length of *BD*, which is both a radius of the circle and a side of the square. Triangle *BCD* is a 30-60-90 triangle, and its sides therefore have the proportion $x:\sqrt{3}x:2x$. Side *CD* is opposite the 30-degree angle and is therefore represented by the *x* in this proportional relationship. Side *BD* thus has a length of $4\sqrt{3}$. The area of the square is $\left(4\sqrt{3}\right)^2 = 16 \times 3 = 48$, and the area of triangle *ABD* is 24. The area of the circle is $\pi\left(4\sqrt{3}\right)^2 = 48\pi$, and the quarter circle has an area of $\frac{1}{4}(48\pi) = 12\pi$. Therefore, the area of the shaded region is $12\pi - 24$, and the correct answer is **(B)**.

Step 4: Confirm Your Answer

Check that you correctly applied the 30-60-90 triangle side length ratio and performed the calculations accurately.

9.   **(B)**

When the cube of a non-zero number y is subtracted from 35, the result is equal to the result of dividing 216 by the cube of that number y. What is the sum of all the possible values of y?

○ $\dfrac{5}{2}$

○   5

○   6

○   10

○   12

Step 1: Analyze the Question

Start by translating the English into math. The cube of the number y is y^3. The result of subtracting the cube of the number y from 35 is $35 - y^3$. When the 216 is divided by y^3, the result is $\dfrac{216}{y^3}$. So $35 - y^3 = \dfrac{216}{y^3}$.

Step 2: State the Task

Solve for all possible values of y and add them.

Step 3: Approach Strategically

Solve the equation you've written for y.

$$35 - y^3 = \frac{216}{y^3}$$

Multiply both sides by y^3: $\qquad (35 - y^3)y^3 = \left(\dfrac{216}{y^3}\right)y^3$

Simplify both sides: $\qquad\qquad 35y^3 - y^6 = 216$

Subtract 216 from both sides: $\quad 35y^3 - y^6 - 216 = 0$

Multiply both sides by -1: $-35y^3 + y^6 + 216 = 0$

Rearrange the left side: $\quad y^6 - 35y^3 + 216 = 0$

Now simplify the equation $y^6 - 35y^3 + 216 = 0$. It helps to recognize that $y^6 = y^{3 \times 2} = (y^3)^2$. Replacing y^6 with $(y^3)^2$ in the equation $y^6 - 35y^3 + 216 = 0$ produces $(y^3)^2 - 35y^3 + 216 = 0$. Now notice that you have a quadratic equation if you consider y^3 to be the unknown. The equation $(y^3)^2 - 35y^3 + 216 = 0$ factors to $(y^3 - 8)(y^3 - 27) = 0$. So $y^3 = 8$ or $y^3 = 27$. Now $8 = 2^3$ and $27 = 3^3$. So if $y^3 = 8$, then $y = 2$, while if $y^3 = 27$, then $y = 3$. The possible values of y are 2 and 3. The sum of all the possible values of y is $2 + 3 = 5$.

(B) is correct.

Step 4: Confirm Your Answer

You can check that you have the correct values of y by plugging them into the equation $35 - y^3 = \dfrac{216}{y^3}$. If $y = 2$, you get $35 - 8 = \dfrac{216}{8}$, or $27 = 27$. If $y = 3$, you get $35 - 27 = \dfrac{216}{27}$, or $8 = 8$.

10. (D)

One letter is selected at random from the 5 letters V, W, X, Y, and Z, and event A is the event that the letter V is selected. A fair six-sided die with sides numbered 1, 2, 3, 4, 5, and 6 is to be rolled, and event B is the event that a 5 or a 6 shows. A fair coin is to be tossed, and event C is the event that a head shows. What is the probability that event A occurs and at least one of the events B and C occurs?

○ $\frac{1}{30}$

○ $\frac{1}{15}$

○ $\frac{1}{10}$

○ $\frac{2}{15}$

○ $\frac{1}{5}$

Step 1: Analyze the Question

This is a probability question with three separate and independent events.

Step 2: State the Task

You need to calculate the probability that event A will occur *and* that either *or* both events B and C will occur.

Step 3: Approach Strategically

The probability of an event is $\frac{\text{Number of desired outcomes}}{\text{Number of possible outcomes}}$. For event A, 1 letter is selected at random from the 5 letters V, W, X, Y, and Z, so the probability that event A occurs is $\frac{1}{5}$. For event B, a 5 or 6 must occur from the 6 possible outcomes 1, 2, 3, 4, 5, and 6, so the probability that event B occurs is $\frac{2}{6} = \frac{1}{3}$. For event C, a head comes up out of 2 possible outcomes, heads and tails, so the probability that event C occurs is $\frac{1}{2}$.

This can be written as $P(A) = \frac{1}{5}, P(B) = \frac{1}{3}$, and $P(C) = \frac{1}{2}$.

The probability that event A occurs and at least one of the events B and C occurs is $P(A) \times P(B \text{ or } C)$.

Find $P(B \text{ or } C)$: Applying the generalized formula for 2 events, $P(B \text{ or } C) = P(B) + P(C) - P(B \text{ and } C)$.

The events B and C are independent, so $P(B \text{ and } C) = P(B)P(C)$.

Replacing $P(B \text{ and } C)$ with $P(B)P(C)$, you have $P(B \text{ or } C) = P(B) + P(C) - P(B)P(C)$. Then substitute in $P(B) = \frac{1}{3}$ and $P(C) = \frac{1}{2}$:

$$P(B \text{ or } C) = \frac{1}{3} + \frac{1}{2} - \frac{1}{3} \times \frac{1}{2}$$

$$= \frac{2}{6} + \frac{3}{6} - \frac{1}{6}$$

$$= \frac{4}{6} = \frac{2}{3}$$

Now find the probability that event A occurs and at least one of the events B and C occurs:

$$P(A) \times P(B \text{ or } C) = \frac{1}{5} \times \frac{2}{3} = \frac{2}{15}$$

(D) is correct.

Step 4: Confirm Your Answer

You can check that you have calculated $P(B \text{ or } C)$ correctly by calculating the probability that neither B nor C occurs and subtracting from 1. $P(\sim B) = \frac{2}{3}$ and $P(\sim C) = \frac{1}{2}$, so $P(B \text{ or } C) = 1 - \frac{2}{3} \times \frac{1}{2} = 1 - \frac{1}{3} = \frac{2}{3}$.

11. (E)

A car traveled from Town A to Town B. The car traveled the first $\frac{3}{8}$ of the distance from Town A to Town B at an average speed of x miles per hour, where $x > 0$. The car traveled the remaining distance at an average speed of y miles per hour, where $y > 0$. The car traveled the entire distance from Town A to Town B at an average speed of z miles per hour. Which of the following equations gives y in terms of x and z?

○ $y = \dfrac{3x + 5z}{8}$

○ $y = \dfrac{5xz}{8x + 3z}$

○ $y = \dfrac{8x - 3z}{5xz}$

○ $y = \dfrac{3xz}{8x - 5z}$

○ $y = \dfrac{5xz}{8x - 3z}$

Step 1: Analyze the Question

The car moves at x mph for the first $\frac{3}{8}$ of the trip and y mph for the final $\frac{5}{8}$. Its average speed over the entire distance traveled is z mph.

Step 2: State the Task

You want y in terms of x and z.

Step 3: Approach Strategically

Remember that Distance = Speed × Time, and that Total Distance = Average Speed × Total Time. Call the distance from Town A to Town B d miles. Then the first $\frac{3}{8}$ of the distance from Town A to Town B is $\frac{3d}{8}$ miles. Since the car traveled the first $\frac{3d}{8}$ miles at an average speed of x miles per hour, the time that it took the car to travel the first $\frac{3d}{8}$ miles was $\dfrac{\left(\frac{3d}{8}\ \text{miles}\right)}{\left(x\ \frac{\text{miles}}{\text{hour}}\right)} = \dfrac{3d}{8x}$ hours. The remainder of the distance from Town A to Town B, in miles, was $\frac{5d}{8}$. Since the car traveled $\frac{5d}{8}$ miles at an average speed of y miles per hour, the time that it took the car to travel the remaining $\frac{5d}{8}$ miles was $\dfrac{\left(\frac{5d}{8}\ \text{miles}\right)}{\left(y\ \frac{\text{miles}}{\text{hour}}\right)} = \dfrac{5d}{8y}$ hours.

The total time for the trip was $\left(\frac{3d}{8x} + \frac{5d}{8y}\right)$ hours. Since the car traveled a distance of d miles in $\left(\frac{3d}{8x} + \frac{5d}{8y}\right)$ hours, the average speed of the car was $\dfrac{d\ \text{miles}}{\left(\frac{3d}{8x} + \frac{5d}{8y}\right)\text{hours}}$, or $\dfrac{d}{\left(\frac{3d}{8x} + \frac{5d}{8y}\right)}$ miles per hour. You know that the average speed of the car was z miles per hour. So $\dfrac{d}{\left(\frac{3d}{8x} + \frac{5d}{8y}\right)} = z$.

Now solve this equation for y in terms of x and z. The variable d is in the way, but it looks like this variable can be canceled. Factoring d out of the denominator in the left side of the equation $\dfrac{d}{\left(\frac{3d}{8x}+\frac{5d}{8y}\right)}=z$ yields $\dfrac{d}{d\left(\frac{3}{8x}+\frac{5}{8y}\right)}=z$. Canceling d from the numerator and denominator of the left side results in $\dfrac{1}{\left(\frac{3}{8x}+\frac{5}{8y}\right)}=z$. Multiplying both sides by the denominator $\frac{3}{8x}+\frac{5}{8y}$, you get $1=z\left(\frac{3}{8x}+\frac{5}{8y}\right)$. Multiplying out the right side produces $1=\frac{3z}{8x}+\frac{5z}{8y}$. Multiply both sides by the least common denominator on the right side, which is $8xy$, to get rid of the denominators: $8xy(1)=8xy\left(\frac{3z}{8x}+\frac{5z}{8y}\right)$, so $8xy=3yz+5xz$.

Since you are trying to solve for y in terms of x and z, get all the expressions involving y on one side of the equation, and all expressions not involving y on the other side of the equation. Subtracting $3yz$ from both sides yields $8xy-3yz=5xz$. Factoring y out of the left side, $y(8x-3z)=5xz$. Dividing both sides by $8x-3z$, $y=\frac{5xz}{8x-3z}$.

(E) is correct.

Step 4: Confirm Your Answer

Check to make sure you applied the average speed formula correctly and that you solved for the correct variable.

12. **(E)**

An ornithologist has studied a particular population of starlings and discovered that their population has increased by 400 percent every 10 years starting in 1890. If the initial population in 1890 was 256 birds, how large was the population of starlings in 1970?

- O   102,400
- O   10,000,000
- O   16,777,216
- O   20,000,000
- O   100,000,000

Step 1: Analyze the Question

You know that the initial population of starlings in 1890 is 256 and that the population increases by 400% every 10 years.

Step 2: State the Task

Find the size of the population of starlings in 1970.

Step 3: Approach Strategically

Although this question does not deal with money, it is useful to notice that the given facts fit the compound interest formula perfectly. The formula, as applied to money, is (Total of principal and interest) = Principal $\times (1 + r)^t$, where r is the interest rate per time period and t is the number of time periods. In this question, the total of "principal and interest" is the final population of starlings in 1970, the "principal" is the initial population (256), the "interest rate" is the population growth rate expressed as a decimal (4.00), and t is the number of 10-year periods from 1890 to 1970 (8). Thus, you have the following:

1970 population $= 256 \times (1 + 4)^8 = 256 \times 5^8$

At this point, you could do the arithmetic, but without a calculator, this approach would be time-consuming and potentially prone to errors. Remember that when seemingly complicated arithmetic arises on the GMAT, there is often a more strategic way to get to the answer. If you notice that 256 is a power of 2, you can use the exponent rules to make your task much simpler:

$256 \times 5^8 = 2^8 \times 5^8 = (2 \times 5)^8 = 10^8 = 100,000,000$

The correct answer is **(E)**.

Step 4: Confirm Your Answer

Confirm that you have applied the compound interest formula correctly.

13. (D)

If $(x^2 + 8)yz < 0$, $wz > 0$, and $xyz < 0$, then which of the following must be true?

  I. $x < 0$
  II. $wy < 0$
  III. $yz < 0$

○ II only
○ III only
○ I and III only
○ II and III only
○ I, II, and III

Step 1: Analyze the Question

This question concerns positive and negative number properties. Since $wz > 0$ and $xyz < 0$, each of the variables w, x, y, and z is non-zero. In the first inequality, which is $(x^2 + 8)yz < 0$, x^2 must be greater than zero because from the third inequality $xyz < 0$, you know that x is not zero. Since x^2 is positive and 8 is positive, $x^2 + 8$ is positive. Since $(x^2 + 8)yz < 0$, and since $x^2 + 8$ is positive, it must be that yz is negative. Thus, y and z have opposite signs. Since $wz > 0$, both w and z must have the same sign. Finally, in order for xyz to be negative, either 1 or all of the 3 variables x, y, and z must be negative.

Step 2: State the Task

Determine which of three inequalities must be true.

Step 3: Approach Strategically

Usually, the most efficient way to solve this type of question is to start with the Roman numeral statement that appears most often in the answer choices; in this case, that is Statement III, $yz < 0$. You already determined that y and z have opposite signs, so this statement must be true. You can eliminate **(A)**.

Look at Statement II next. You determined that w and z have the same sign. Therefore, if y times z is negative, then y times w must also be negative, and Statement II must be true. You can now eliminate **(B)** and **(C)**.

Finally, if xyz is negative and yz is also negative, then x must be positive. Eliminate **(E)**. **(D)** is correct.

Step 4: Confirm Your Answer

Check your reasoning to confirm that y has the opposite sign as w, that y has the opposite sign as z, and that x is positive.

14. **(D)**

If $\dfrac{61^2 - 1}{h}$ is an integer, then h could be divisible by each of the following EXCEPT:

- ○ 8
- ○ 12
- ○ 15
- ○ 18
- ○ 31

Step 1: Analyze the Question

Calculating the actual value of the numerator would be too time-consuming, but it's presented in the form of the difference of two perfect squares (61^2 and 1^2). This is one of the classic quadratics: $61^2 - 1^2 = (61 + 1)(61 - 1)$, or $(62)(60)$.

Step 2: State the Task

In order for $\dfrac{61^2 - 1}{h}$ to be an integer, $61^2 - 1^2$ must be a multiple of h. So the question essentially asks which factor of h would *not* divide evenly into the numerator. Four of the choices will divide evenly into the numerator; the correct answer will not.

Step 3: Approach Strategically

It would take far too much time to find the product of 60 and 62 and then divide that by each of the answer choices. Instead, remember that for h to divide evenly into the product of 60 and 62, h must share factors with 60 and/or 62. Moreover, the answer choices represent factors of h. Looking at the choices, 8 has factors of 2 and 4. Because 2 is a factor of 62 and 4 is a factor of 60, you can cross out **(A)**. Choices **(B)**, **(C)**, and **(E)** are a little more straightforward; since 12 itself is a factor of 60, 15 is also a factor of 60, and 31 is a factor of 62. The only choice that is not a factor of either number is 18. The correct answer is **(D)**.

Step 4: Confirm Your Answer

You can quickly check that 18 is not a factor of the product of 60 and 62 by breaking down 18, 60, and 62 into their prime factors: $\dfrac{60 \times 62}{18} = \dfrac{2 \times 2 \times 3 \times 5 \times 2 \times 31}{2 \times 3 \times 3}$. Notice that the 2 in the denominator will cancel out one of the 2s in the numerator, but only one of the 3s in the denominator will cancel out. So the denominator will have a 3 remaining that cannot be canceled out. Therefore, the product of 60 and 62 is *not* divisible by 18, and **(D)** is correct.

15. (E)

If a, b, and c are integers such that $0 < a < b < c$, and a is even, b is prime, and c is odd, which of the following is a possible value for abc?

- ○ 5
- ○ 12
- ○ 16
- ○ 34
- ○ 54

Step 1: Analyze the Question

You are told that a, b, and c are integers such that $0 < a < b < c$, and you know that a is even, b is prime, and c is odd.

Step 2: State the Task

Determine which of the answer choices is a *possible* value for abc. Note that this doesn't mean that the correct choice is the *only* possible value for abc.

Step 3: Approach Strategically

Given the structure of the problem, you will have to eliminate any answer choice that cannot be a possible value for abc rather than solve for a single value of abc. If you think of abc as $a \times bc$, then, regardless of the values of b and c, abc must be even since a is an even number. Eliminate **(A)**.

To deal with the remaining answer choices, since the question contains variables and the answer choices are numbers, picking numbers is a good approach. The least value possible for a is 2, the first even number greater than 0. The next largest prime number, 3, can be substituted for b. (Note that b is a prime number that has to be greater than a positive even number, meaning it can't be 2, the only even prime number.) The product of a and b would be 6, and this could be multiplied by 2 to make $abc = 12$. However, 2 is not a permissible value for c, so eliminate **(B)**. $2 \times 3 = 6$, $2 \times 5 = 10$, and $2 \times 7 = 14$ are not factors of 16, and moving up to the next even number, 4, makes the smallest possible value for ab 20, so eliminate **(C)**. Similarly, if a is 2, the only possible values of ab that are less than 34 are 6, 10, 14, 22, and 26. None of these are factors of 34, so you'll have to consider $a = 4$. Since $ab = 20$ and $ab = 28$ are not factors of 34, eliminate **(D)**. Since $6 \times 9 = 54$ and 9 is a valid value for c, 54 is indeed one possible value for abc, and **(E)** is correct.

Step 4: Confirm Your Answer

Check that you used permissible values when checking the answer choices.

16. (A)

A fair die with sides numbered 1, 2, 3, 4, 5, and 6 is to be rolled 4 times. What is the probability that on at least one roll the number showing will be less than 3?

- $\frac{65}{81}$
- $\frac{67}{81}$
- $\frac{8}{9}$
- $\frac{26}{27}$
- $\frac{80}{81}$

Step 1: Analyze the Question

Note that "less than 3" means a 1 or 2.

Step 2: State the Task

You need the probability that *at least* 1 roll is a 1 or 2. That means the probability that 1, 2, 3, or 4 rolls result in a 1 or 2.

Step 3: Approach Strategically

Instead of calculating all those probabilities separately and adding them together, it will be easier to find the probability that *no* rolls result in a 1 or 2, and then subtract that probability from 1. Start by finding the probability that each of the 4 rolls results in at least a 3. The probability formula is Probability $= \frac{\text{Number of desired outcomes}}{\text{Number of possible outcomes}}$. When rolling the die once, there are 4 desired outcomes, which are 3, 4, 5, and 6, and there are 6 possible outcomes, which are 1, 2, 3, 4, 5, and 6. The probability that when the die is rolled once, a number greater than or equal to 3 results is $\frac{4}{6} = \frac{2}{3}$. Since the results of the 4 rolls of the dice are independent of each other, the probability that all 4 rolls result in a number greater than or equal to 3 is $\frac{2}{3} \times \frac{2}{3} \times \frac{2}{3} \times \frac{2}{3} = \frac{2 \times 2 \times 2 \times 2}{3 \times 3 \times 3 \times 3} = \frac{16}{81}$. It follows that the probability that at least 1 roll results in a number less than 3 is $1 - \frac{16}{81} = \frac{81}{81} - \frac{16}{81} = \frac{81-16}{81} = \frac{65}{81}$.

(A) is correct.

Step 4: Confirm Your Answer

Check that you've calculated the probability of rolling a 3, 4, 5, or 6 correctly; check that you've accounted for 4 rolls; and check your subtraction.

17. (C)

There are 816 students in enrolled at a certain high school. Each of these students is taking at least one of the subjects economics, geography, and biology. The sum of the number of students taking exactly one of these subjects and the number of students taking all three of these subjects is 5 times the number of students taking exactly two of these subjects. The ratio of the number of students taking only the two subjects economics and geography to the number of students taking only the two subjects economics and biology to the number of students taking only the two subjects geography and biology is 3:6:8. How many of the students enrolled at this high school are taking only the two subjects geography and biology?

- ○ 35
- ○ 42
- ○ 64
- ○ 136
- ○ 240

Step 1: Analyze the Question

This is a tough overlapping sets question. You are given the total number of students (816), sufficient information to set up two equations about students taking one, two, and three of the subjects and ratios of the various two-subject combinations.

Step 2: State the Task

You need to find the number of students taking one particular two-subject combination: geography and biology.

Step 3: Approach Strategically

Start by setting up a couple of equations concerning students taking one, two, and three subjects. Say that the number of students taking exactly one of the subjects is x, say that the number of students taking exactly two of the subjects is y, and say that the number of students taking all three of the subjects is z. Since there are 816 students in the high school, $x + y + z = 816$. Since the sum of the number of students taking exactly one of the subjects and the number of students taking all three of the subjects is 5 times the number of students taking exactly two of the subjects, $x + z = 5y$. Now rewrite the equation $x + y + z = 816$ as $(x + z) + y = 816$. Substitute $5y$ for $x + z$ to find that $5y + y = 816$, $6y = 816$, and $y = \frac{816}{6} = 136$. Thus, the number of students taking exactly two of the subjects is 136.

Now make use of the ratios provided. The ratio of the number of students taking only economics and geography to the number of students taking only economics and biology to the number of students taking only geography and biology is 3:6:8, so the number of students taking only the two subjects geography and biology is $\frac{8}{3+6+8}(136) = \frac{8}{17}(136) = 8(8) = 64$. **(C)** is correct.

Step 4: Confirm Your Answer

One way to confirm your answer is to calculate how many students are taking the other two-subject combinations, and then add the 3 values to see if they in fact sum to 136: $\frac{3}{17}(136) = (3)(8) = 24$ and $\frac{6}{17}(136) = (6)(8) = 48$. It is in fact the case that $64 + 24 + 48 = 136$.

18. (B)

Working alone at a constant rate, machine P produces a widgets in 3 hours. Working alone at a constant rate, machine Q produces b widgets in 4 hours. If machines P and Q work together for c hours, then in terms of a, b, and c, how many widgets will machines P and Q produce?

○ $\dfrac{3ac + 4bc}{12}$

○ $\dfrac{4ac + 3bc}{12}$

○ $\dfrac{4ac + 3bc}{6}$

○ $4ac + 3bc$

○ $\dfrac{ac + 2bc}{4}$

Step 1: Analyze the Question

The question gives the production rates for three machines. The answer choices are given in algebraic terms.

Step 2: State the Task

Find the number of widgets produced by two of the three machines.

Step 3: Approach Strategically

Since Machine P produces a widgets in 3 hours, it produces widgets at the rate of $\frac{a}{3}$ widgets per hour. By the same logic, Machine P produces widgets at the rate of $\frac{b}{4}$ widgets per hour. So working together, Machine P and Machine Q produce widgets at the rate of $\frac{a}{3} + \frac{b}{4}$ widgets per hour. Recall that Work × Rate = Time. Thus, in c hours, working together, Machine P and Machine Q produce $\left[\left(\frac{a}{3} + \frac{b}{4}\right)\frac{\text{widgets}}{\text{hour}}\right] \times (c \text{ hours}) = c\left(\frac{a}{3} + \frac{b}{4}\right)$ widgets.

None of the answer choices is written as $c\left(\frac{a}{3} + \frac{b}{4}\right)$. So rewrite this expression:

$$c\left(\frac{a}{3} + \frac{b}{4}\right) = c\left(\frac{a \times 4}{3 \times 4} + \frac{b \times 3}{4 \times 3}\right)$$

$$= c\left(\frac{4a}{12} + \frac{3b}{12}\right) = c\left(\frac{4a + 3b}{12}\right) = \frac{4ac + 3bc}{12}$$

(B) is correct.

Step 4: Confirm Your Answer

Double-check your calculations to make sure your algebra is correct.

19. (C)

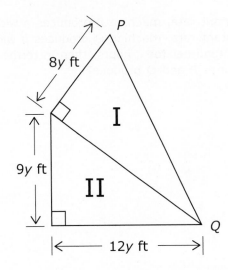

In the figure above, the perimeter of triangle I is 16 feet greater than the perimeter of triangle II. What is the length of PQ, in feet?

- ○ 27
- ○ 51
- ○ 68
- ○ 75
- ○ 85

Step 1: Analyze the Question

The question shows two right triangles arranged so that the hypotenuse of one triangle is also one of the legs of the other triangle. Dimensions of some of the sides are provided in terms of the variable y. The question also provides information about the difference between the perimeters of the two triangles. The answer choices are numbers, not expressed in terms of y.

Step 2: State the Task

Find the length of the unshared hypotenuse.

Step 3: Approach Strategically

Describe the lengths of the hypotenuses of right triangles I and II in terms of y and feet. Looking at right triangle II, you see that the leg of length $9y$ feet can be expressed as $3 \times (3y$ feet) and the leg of length $12y$ feet is $4 \times (3y$ feet). So right triangle II is a 3-4-5 right triangle with each member of the 3 to 4 to 5 ratio multiplied by $3y$ feet. That means the length of the hypotenuse of right triangle II is $5 \times (3y$ feet) $= 15y$ feet.

Now find the length of PQ. Triangle I is a right triangle with one leg of length $8y$ feet and the other leg (the hypotenuse of triangle II) of $15y$ feet. You may have the ratio 8:15:17 memorized, and if so, you know that PQ is $17y$ feet. Alternatively, you can use the Pythagorean theorem: $a^2 + b^2 = c^2$, or $8^2 + 15^2 = PQ^2$.

$$PQ^2 = (8y)^2 + (15y)^2$$

$$= 64y^2 + 225y^2$$

$$= (64 + 225)(y^2)$$

$$= 289y^2$$

$$PQ = \sqrt{289y^2} = 17y$$

You now know the lengths of all the sides of triangles I and II.

The perimeter of triangle I is $8y + 15y + 17y = 40y$.

The perimeter of triangle II is $9y + 12y + 15y = 36y$.

The perimeter of triangle I is 16 feet greater than the perimeter of triangle II. So $40y = 36y + 16$, $4y = 16$, and $y = 4$. The length of PQ, in feet, is $17y = 17(4) = 68$. **(C)** is correct.

Step 4: Confirm Your Answer

Since PQ is the hypotenuse of the triangle that has a leg that is the hypotenuse of the other triangle, PQ must be the longest side of either triangle. The greatest length of the other sides is $15y$, so $17y$ is a logical value.

20. (E)

If $x > 0$, $y > 0$, and $\dfrac{7x^2 + 72xy + 4y^2}{4x^2 + 12xy + 5y^2} = 4$, what is the value of $\dfrac{x + y}{y}$?

- ○ $\dfrac{3}{4}$
- ○ $\dfrac{4}{3}$
- ○ $\dfrac{10}{7}$
- ○ $\dfrac{7}{4}$
- ○ $\dfrac{7}{3}$

Step 1: Analyze the Question

The problem presents an equation in two variables, x and y, with quadratic expressions in both the numerator and denominator. The answer choices are in the form of fractions, with no variables.

Step 2: State the Task

Find the numeric value of an expression stated in terms of x and y.

Step 3: Approach Strategically

Begin by simplifying the equation $\frac{7x^2 + 72xy + 4y^2}{4x^2 + 12xy + 5y^2} = 4$.

$$7x^2 + 72xy + 4y^2 = 4(4x^2 + 12xy + 5y^2)$$
$$7x^2 + 72xy + 4y^2 = 16x^2 + 48xy + 20y^2$$
$$72xy + 4y^2 = 9x^2 + 48xy + 20y^2$$
$$24xy + 4y^2 = 9x^2 + 20y^2$$
$$24xy = 9x^2 + 16y^2$$
$$9x^2 - 24xy + 16y^2 = 0$$
$$(3x - 4y)(3x - 4y) = 0$$

Thus, $3x - 4y = 0$.

You are seeking the value of $\frac{x+y}{y}$. Rewrite this as $\frac{x+y}{y} = \frac{x}{y} + \frac{y}{y} = \frac{x}{y} + 1$.

Solve the equation $3x - 4y = 0$ for the value of $\frac{x}{y}$:

$$3x - 4y = 0$$
$$3x = 4y$$
$$\frac{3x}{y} = 4$$
$$\frac{x}{y} = \frac{4}{3}$$

Thus, $\frac{x+y}{y} = \frac{x}{y} + 1 = \frac{4}{3} + 1 = \frac{7}{3}$. **(E)** is correct.

Step 4: Confirm Your Answer

Unfortunately, there is no easy way to plug the solution back into the problem. Check the math used to derive your answer.

ADVANCED DATA SUFFICIENCY PRACTICE SET

1. If x and y are positive even integers, is $(40x)^x$ divisible by y?

   (1) $x = \dfrac{1}{128}y$

   (2) y is a multiple of 160.

2. If $a \neq 0$, $\dfrac{x}{y} = -\dfrac{1}{a}$, and $\dfrac{y}{z} = \dfrac{b}{3}$, is $\dfrac{x}{z} > \dfrac{1}{2}$?

   (1) $a^2 - 2a - 3 = 0$
   (2) $b^2 - 4b + 4 = 1$

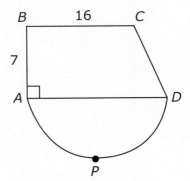

3. In the figure above, what is the area of semicircle DPA?

   (1) The area of quadrilateral $ABCD$ is 140.

   (2) The length of the line segment whose endpoints are B and D is 25.

4.   Is x divisible by 39?

   (1) x divided by 65 results in a remainder of 7.

   (2) x divided by 36 results in a remainder of 15.

5.   If a and b are positive integers with different units digits, and b is the square of an integer, is a also the square of an integer?

   (1) The units digit of $a + b$ is 8.

   (2) $b = 121$

6.   What is the value of $8x + y$?

   (1) $3x - 2y + z = 10$

   (2) $2(x + 3y) - (y + 2z) = -25$

7.   If b and c are two-digit positive integers and $b - c = 22d$, is d an integer?

   (1) The tens digit and the units digit of b are identical.

   (2) $\dfrac{b + c}{22} = x$, and x is an integer.

8. The integers x and y are positive, $x > y + 8$, and $y > 8$. What is the remainder when $x^2 - y^2$ is divided by 8?

    (1) The remainder when $x + y$ is divided by 8 is 7.

    (2) The remainder when $x - y$ is divided by 8 is 5.

9. If $x > y > 0$, does $3^{x+1} + 3(2^y) = 12v$?

    (1) $\dfrac{3^{2x} - 2^{2y}}{3^x - 2^y} = 4v$

    (2) $2(3^{x+2}) + 9(2^{y+1}) = 72v$

10. In the figure above, the measure of angle EAB in triangle ABE is 90 degrees, and $BCDE$ is a square. What is the length of AB?

    (1) The length of AE is 12, and the ratio of the area of triangle ABE to the area of square $BCDE$ is $\dfrac{6}{25}$.

    (2) The perimeter of square $BCDE$ is 80 and the ratio of the length of AE to the length of AB is 3 to 4.

11. In the sequence T, the first term is the non-zero number a, and each term after the first term is equal to the non-zero number r multiplied by the previous term. What is the value of the fourth term of the sequence?

    (1) The sum of the first two terms of the sequence is 16.

    (2) The 18th term of the sequence is 81 times the 14th term of the sequence.

12. A person is to be selected at random from the group T of people. What is the probability that the person selected is a member of club E?

    (1) The probability that a person selected at random from group T is not a member of club D and is not a member of club E is $\frac{1}{4}$.

    (2) The probability that a person selected at random from group T is a member of club D and not a member of club E is $\frac{5}{12}$.

13. The population of Town X on January 1, 2010, was 56 percent greater than the population of the same town on January 1, 2005. The population of Town X on January 1, 2015, was 75 percent greater than the population of the same town on January 1, 2010. What was the population of Town X on January 1, 2005?

    (1) The population of Town X on January 1, 2015, was 21,840.

    (2) The increase in the population of Town X from January 1, 2010, to January 1, 2015, was 4,880 greater than the increase in the population of Town X from January 1, 2005, to January 1, 2010.

14. What is the value of $x - 3z$?

    (1) $x + 4y = 3$

    (2) $x^2 + 4xy - 3xz - 12yz = 24$

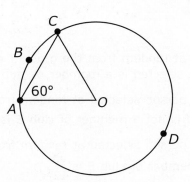

15. In the figure above, the center of the circle is O, and the measure of angle CAO is 60 degrees. What is the perimeter of triangle OAC?

    (1) The length of arc CDA is 16π greater than the length of arc ABC.

    (2) The area of triangle OAC is $36\sqrt{3}$.

16. If x and y are integers and $3x > 8y$, is $y > -18$?

    (1) $-9 < x < 20$

    (2) $y = \dfrac{(x - 42)}{5}$

17. Over the course of 5 days, Monday through Friday, Danny collects a total of 76 baseball cards. Each day, he collects a different number of cards. If Danny collects the largest number of cards on Friday and the second largest number of cards on Thursday, did Danny collect more than 8 cards on Thursday?

    (1) On Friday, Danny collected 49 cards.

    (2) On one of the first 3 days, Danny collected 6 cards.

18. If $y = x^2$, is the equation $(2^{5y})(4^{120}) = 16^{20x}$ true?

    (1) $(4 - x)(12 - x) = 0$

    (2) $(x - 4)(x - 8)(x - 24) = 0$

19. The ratio of the number of students in an auditorium who are seniors to the number of students in the auditorium who are not seniors is 7:5. How many students are there in the auditorium?

    (1) The ratio of the number of students who are seniors who are taking history to the number of students who are not seniors who are taking history is 21:5.

    (2) Of the students in the auditorium who are seniors, $\frac{3}{5}$ are taking history;

        of the students in the auditorium who are not seniors, $\frac{1}{5}$ are taking history;

        and the number of seniors in the auditorium who are taking history is 208 greater than the number of students in the auditorium who are not seniors and taking history.

20. If $y > 0$, is $\frac{x}{y} < 3$?

    (1) $x(x + y) - 4y(x + y) < 0$

    (2) $5(y + 8) < 20y - 3x + 40$

ANSWERS AND EXPLANATIONS BEGIN ON NEXT PAGE

ADVANCED DATA SUFFICIENCY PRACTICE SET: ANSWERS AND EXPLANATIONS

1. A
2. E
3. B
4. A
5. A
6. C
7. C

8. C
9. D
10. B
11. E
12. C
13. D
14. C

15. D
16. B
17. A
18. A
19. B
20. E

1. (A)

If x and y are positive even integers, is $(40x)^x$ divisible by y?

(1) $x = \dfrac{1}{128}y$

(2) y is a multiple of 160.

Step 1: Analyze the Question Stem

This is a Yes/No question. Essentially, the question asks whether $\dfrac{(40x)^x}{y}$ is an integer. Note that x and y are both even. Also note that because x is even and 40 is an integer, the expression $(40x)^x$ must be even. Finally, note that x is a factor of the base as well as the exponent.

To determine that y divides evenly into $(40x)^x$, you need to know that y has no prime factors that are not found in 40 or x and that it has no prime factor raised to an exponent that is greater than the number of times that prime number is a factor of $(40x)^x$. If a statement allows you to establish both these conditions, you can answer the question with a yes, and the statement is sufficient. If you can show that either of these conditions does not exist, then the statement allows you to answer the question with a no and is likewise sufficient.

Step 2: Evaluate the Statements Using 12TEN

Statement (1) tells you that $y = 128x$. Taking this statement into account, the question now becomes whether $\dfrac{(40x)^x}{128x}$ is an integer. The number 128 has only 2 as a prime factor, breaking down to 2^7. So focus on the number of times 2 is a factor of the expression $(40x)^x$. Remember that x is positive and even, so $x \geq 2$. Since x is the exponent in the expression $(40x)^x$, a greater value of x will make the number of times 2 is a factor of $(40x)^x$ greater. It follows that if $x = 2$ makes 128x a factor of $(40x)^x$, the answer to the question is definitively yes, and you have sufficiency. (Note that if $x > 2$, all other factors of x besides 2 will cancel in the denominator because there will be a greater number of them in the numerator due to the exponent. For instance, if $x = 6 = (2)(3)$, then there will be one factor of 3 in the denominator and six factors of 3 in the numerator.)

Substituting 2 for x yields:

$$\frac{(40x)^x}{128x} = \frac{(40 \times 2)^2}{128 \times 2} = \frac{(2^3 \times 5 \times 2)^2}{2^7 \times 2} = \frac{2^8 \times 5}{2^8} = 5$$

So $x = 2$ makes 128x a factor of $(40x)^x$, and Statement (1) is sufficient. Eliminate **(B)**, **(C)**, and **(E)**.

Statement (2) tells you that y is a multiple of 160 and thus has 2 and 5 as its distinct prime factors. While that may seem to align with the 40 in the exponent, y being a multiple of 160 means that it could be infinitely large and thus potentially too big to be a factor, given that you don't know the value of x. Statement (2) is insufficient.

(A) is the correct answer.

2. (E)

If $a \neq 0$, $\frac{x}{y} = -\frac{1}{a}$, and $\frac{y}{z} = \frac{b}{3}$, is $\frac{x}{z} > \frac{1}{2}$?

(1) $a^2 - 2a - 3 = 0$

(2) $b^2 - 4b + 4 = 1$

Step 1: Analyze the Question Stem

The question stem gives two equations and asks whether a third algebraic fraction is greater than a constant, making this a Yes/No question. You can simplify the given information by combining the two equations. Note that multiplying them together will make the y cancel out: $\left(\frac{x}{y}\right)\left(\frac{y}{z}\right) = \left(-\frac{1}{a}\right)\left(\frac{b}{3}\right)$ results in $\frac{x}{z} = -\frac{b}{3a}$. The question asks about $\frac{x}{z}$, so if you can find the values of a and b, you will have sufficiency. You will also have sufficiency if you can find the value of $\frac{b}{a}$. Since $\frac{a}{b}$ is the reciprocal of $\frac{b}{a}$, you will also have sufficiency if you can find the value of $\frac{a}{b}$. Finally, you will have sufficiency if you can find that, in some other way, there is only one answer to the question regarding $\frac{x}{z}$ and $\frac{1}{2}$.

Step 2: Evaluate the Statements Using 12TEN

Since each statement uses only one of the variables needed, **(A)**, **(B)**, and **(D)** can be crossed off immediately. The task then becomes determining whether the two statements taken together are sufficient or not.

Neither of the statements is simpler than the other, so begin by factoring either of them. In Statement (1), factoring the left side of the equation $a^2 - 2a - 3 = 0$ yields $(a + 1)(a - 3) = 0$, making $a = -1$ or 3. In Statement (2), subtract 1 from both sides, resulting in $b^2 - 4b + 3 = 0$. Factoring the left side of the equation $b^2 - 4b + 3 = 0$ produces $(b - 1)(b - 3) = 0$, making $b = 1$ or $b = 3$.

As noted in Step 1, in order to answer the question is $\frac{x}{z} > \frac{1}{2}$, you must know the values of a and b, or you must know the value $\frac{b}{a}$, or you must know the value $\frac{a}{b}$, or you must be able to compare $\frac{x}{z}$ and $\frac{1}{2}$ in some other way. The four possible combinations of a and b are these:

$a = -1$ and $b = 1$

$a = -1$ and $b = 3$

$a = 3$ and $b = 1$

$a = 3$ and $b = 3$

Test the first pair, as it is the easiest. If $a = -1$ and $b = 1$, then $\frac{x}{z} = -\frac{b}{3a} = -\frac{1}{3(-1)} = \frac{1}{3}$, which is *not* greater than $\frac{1}{2}$. In this case, the answer to the question is no.

To try to avoid having to test all four combinations, notice that with both a and b positive, $-\frac{b}{3a}$ will be negative, and the answer will still be no. So stay with $a = -1$. You can expect a greater value for $\frac{x}{z}$ when $b = 3$ than when $b = 1$, so test $b = 3$. If $a = -1$ and $b = 3$, $\frac{x}{z} = -\frac{b}{3a} = -\frac{3}{3(-1)} = 1$. In this case, $\frac{x}{z} > \frac{1}{2}$ and the answer to the question is yes.

One possibility gives you an answer of yes to the question and a different possibility gives you an answer of no to the question, making the statements taken together insufficient to answer the question definitively. The correct answer is **(E)**.

3. **(B)**

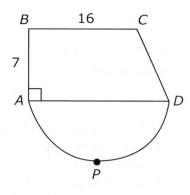

In the figure above, what is the area of semicircle *DPA*?

(1) The area of quadrilateral *ABCD* is 140.

(2) The length of the line segment whose endpoints are *B* and *D* is 25.

Step 1: Analyze the Question Stem

This is a Value question. The question stem contains a diagram with multiple figures, and you need to be able to find a single possible area of the semicircle *DPA* to have sufficiency. In order to do that, you would need to know the length of diameter *AD* of the semicircle. *AD* is also a side of quadrilateral *ABCD*. Because a semicircle has half the area of a circle with the same diameter, knowing the length of *AD* would allow you to calculate the area of semicircle *DPA*.

Step 2: Evaluate the Statements Using 12TEN

Statement (1) tells you that the area of the quadrilateral *ABCD* is 140. Using the formula for the area of a trapezoid, Area $= \frac{b_1 + b_2}{2} \times h$, it would appear that you could plug in the information you know from the diagram and Statement (1) (the area, the height, and b_1) to solve for b_2. However, it's important to remember that figures in Data Sufficiency questions are not necessarily drawn to scale. You are not given enough information to determine whether sides *AD* and *BC* are parallel; therefore, *ABCD* is not necessarily a trapezoid. Statement (1) is thus insufficient, and you can eliminate **(A)** and **(D)**.

Statement (2) tells you that the length of the line segment whose endpoints are *B* and *D* is 25. This line segment, if added to the figure, would be the hypotenuse of right triangle *ABD*. Since you now know two sides of a right triangle, it would be possible to calculate the length of the third side, *AD*, by using the Pythagorean theorem. As mentioned above, knowing the length of *AD* would allow you to calculate the area of the semicircle, and Statement (2) is sufficient. Therefore, the correct answer is **(B)**.

4. **(A)**

    Is *x* divisible by 39?

    (1) *x* divided by 65 results in a remainder of 7.

    (2) *x* divided by 36 results in a remainder of 15.

Step 1: Analyze the Question

This is a Yes/No question. Unlike other remainder questions in which you can pick numbers, the remainders in the statements would be very tedious and time-consuming to test multiple times individually, let alone to combine. Thus, there must be a simpler way to determine divisibility. Whenever the numbers given are unwieldy, the easiest and most efficient way to establish divisibility is to find the prime factors. In this case, 39 breaks down to 3×13, so for *x* to be divisible by 39, it must be divisible by both 3 and 13.

Step 2: Evaluate the Statements Using 12TEN

Statement (1) gives the number 65. Consider that 65 is 5×13; one of the prime factors of 39 is present. For *x* to be divisible by 13, the remainder itself must be a multiple of 13. The remainder 7 is not a multiple of 13, so it is impossible for *x* to be divisible by 13 or 39. This makes the answer to the question always no, and Statement (1) is sufficient. Eliminate choices **(B)**, **(C)**, and **(E)**.

In evaluating Statement (2), you can use the same principle. The number 36 is divisible by 3, one of the necessary primes, so the remainder must also be divisible by 3. The remainder 15 is divisible by 3, meaning that *x* is a multiple of 3. Since you don't know anything else about *x*, it's entirely possible that *x* is also divisible by 13, while there are certainly values that would make *x* not divisible by 13. Statement (2) is insufficient.

The correct answer is **(A)**.

5.   **(A)**

If *a* and *b* are positive integers with different units digits, and *b* is the square of an integer, is *a* also the square of an integer?

(1) The units digit of *a* + *b* is 8.

(2) *b* = 121

Step 1: Analyze the Question Stem

This is a Yes/No question. The given information provides a clue about the two numbers having different units digits and tells you that *b* is a perfect square. On advanced number properties questions, it's worth checking if two different types of clues work together. Units digits of certain groups of numbers often fall into consistent patterns, and squares certainly fit into that category. The units digits of the squares of 1–10 are {1, 4, 9, 6, 5, 6, 9, 4, 1, 0}, and this pattern will continue, since the units digits of 11–20, 21–30, and so on will be the same as those of 1–10. So a perfect square can only have one of six units digits: 0, 1, 4, 5, 6, or 9. For *a* to be a perfect square, its units digit must be one of those numbers.

Step 2: Evaluate the Statements Using 12TEN

Evaluating Statement (1), you see that the sum of the integers *a* and *b* has a units digit of 8. Work your way through the list of possible units digits of squares of integers. Again, that list is 0, 1, 4, 5, 6, and 9. If the units digit of *b* is 0, then the units digit of *a* is 8, and 8 is not on the list. If the units digit of *b* is 1, the units digit of *a* is 7, and 7 is also not on the list. If the units digit of *b* is 4, the units digit of *a* is 4, but this is not permitted because the units digits of *a* and *b* must be different. If the units digit of *b* is 5, the units digit of *a* is 3, and 3 is not on the list. If the units digit of *b* is 6, the units digit of *a* is 2, and 2 is not on the list. If the units digit of *b* is 9, the units digit of *a* is 9, but again, the units digits of *a* and *b* must be different. It follows that the units digit of *a* cannot be the units digit of the square of an integer, so *a* cannot be the square of an integer. The answer to the question is definitively no, and Statement (1) is sufficient. Eliminate **(B)**, **(C)**, and **(E)**.

Statement (2) precludes *a* from having 1 as its units digit, but it does nothing else, since the only relevant limitation is that the two numbers have different units digits. Statement (2) is insufficient.

The correct answer is **(A)**.

6. **(C)**

What is the value of $8x + y$?

(1) $3x - 2y + z = 10$

(2) $2(x + 3y) - (y + 2z) = -25$

Step 1: Analyze the Question Stem

This is a Value question: a statement that allows the calculation of a single value for $8x + y$ is sufficient. Simplify the equation in Statement (2):

$$2(x + 3y) - (y + 2z) = -25$$
$$2x + 6y - y - 2z = -25$$
$$2x + 5y - 2z = -25$$

Step 2: Evaluate the Statements Using 12TEN

Each of the two statements is an equation with the same three variables. As neither of these equations can be solved for $8x + y$, neither statement on its own is sufficient, and you can eliminate **(A)**, **(B)**, and **(D)**.

Taken together, the two statements represent a system of equations. To solve for each variable in a system of linear equations with three variables, three distinct equations are required. Since the statements provide only two equations, **(E)** may be tempting. However, even when there are fewer equations than variables, sometimes the value of a particular variable, or the value of an expression, can be found. When a question concerns solving a system of equations for an expression, consider whether multiplying one or both equations by a constant and combining them will allow you to solve. Multiplying the equation in Statement (1) by 2 results in $6x - 4y + 2z = 20$. Adding the corresponding sides of this equation and the simplified equation in Statement (2), $2x + 5y - 2z = -25$, gives $8x + y = -5$. Since both statements together allow the calculation of $8x + y$, the correct answer is **(C)**.

7.   **(C)**

If b and c are two-digit positive integers and $b - c = 22d$, is d an integer?

(1) The tens digit and the units digit of b are identical.

(2) $\dfrac{b + c}{22} = x$, and x is an integer.

Step 1: Analyze the Question Stem

This is a Yes/No question. The question stem tells you that the variables b and c are integers between 10 and 99 inclusive and asks whether $b - c$ is a multiple of 22.

Step 2: Evaluate the Statements Using 12TEN

Statement (1) merely tells you that the two digits of b are the same, so the value of b must be 11, 22, 33, etc. Since you are given no further information about c, Statement (1) by itself is insufficient, and answer **(A)** and **(D)** can be eliminated.

Statement (2) provides the information that $b + c$ is a multiple of 22, since $b + c = 22x$ and x is an integer. However, the question asks about $b - c$, not $b + c$, so this statement, too, is insufficient. If you were unsure, you could plug in some number pairs to verify that $b - c$ could be a multiple of 22 but need not be. Set $b = 12$ and $c = 10$; $b + c = 22$, which is divisible by 22, but $b - c = 2$, which clearly is not divisible by 22. Now try $b = 11$ and $c = 33$; $b + c = 44$ is divisible by 22, while $b - c = -22$ is divisible by 22 as well. Eliminate **(B)**.

Now look at both statements together along with the information in the question stem. Statement (1) says that the tens and units digits of b are the same, so b is a multiple of 11. From Statement (2), you know that $b + c$ is a multiple of 22. Every multiple of 22 is a multiple of 11, so $b + c$ is a multiple of 11. Since $b + c$ is a multiple of 11 and b is a multiple of 11, $(b + c) - b = c$, which is a multiple of 11. Since b and c are both multiples of 11, $b - c$ is also a multiple of 11. Since $b + c$ is a multiple of 22, $b + c$ is even. This means that both b and c are even or both b and c are odd. In either case, $b - c$ is even, or, in other words, $b - c$ is a multiple of 2. Since $b - c$ is a multiple of 11, $b - c$ is a multiple of 2, and the integers 2 and 11 have no common factor greater than 1, $b - c$ is a multiple of $11 \times 2 = 22$. The statements taken together are sufficient to answer the question definitively yes. **(C)** is correct.

8. **(C)**

The integers x and y are positive, $x > y + 8$, and $y > 8$. What is the remainder when $x^2 - y^2$ is divided by 8?

(1) The remainder when $x + y$ is divided by 8 is 7.

(2) The remainder when $x - y$ is divided by 8 is 5.

Step 1: Analyze the Question Stem

This is a Value question. You are given two positive integers. Since y is an integer and $y > 8$, the minimum value of y is 9. Since $x > y + 8$, and the minimum value of y is 9, x must be greater than $9 + 8 = 17$. Thus, $x > 17$. Since x is an integer, the minimum value of x is 18. The question asks for the remainder when the difference of the squares of the two numbers is divided by 8. You can factor the expression $x^2 - y^2$ to its equivalent $(x + y)(x - y)$.

Step 2: Evaluate the Statements Using 12TEN

Statement (1): Since the remainder when $x + y$ is divided by 8 is 7, you can represent $x + y$ as $8m + 7$, where m is an integer. Substituting this into the factored expression, $(8m + 7)(x - y)$ still doesn't tell you enough about $x - y$ to get a definite answer, so Statement (1) is insufficient. Eliminate **(A)** and **(D)**.

Statement (2): This time, you can substitute $8n + 5$ for $x - y$, where n is an integer, but now you don't know enough about $x + y$, so Statement (2) is also insufficient and you can eliminate **(B)**.

Combining the results above, can you determine with certainty the remainder when $(8m + 7)(8n + 5)$ is divided by 8?

Using FOIL, you can write the expression $(8m + 7)(8n + 5)$ as $64mn + 40m + 56n + 35$. Since the first three terms contain the coefficients 64, 40, and 56, respectively, and m and n are integers, each of these terms is evenly divisible by 8. Thus, the remainder resulting from dividing the expression $x^2 - y^2$ by 8 is the remainder when 35 is divided by 8, which is 3. So the statements together are sufficient, and **(C)** is correct.

9.   **(D)**

If $x > y > 0$, does $3x + 1 + 3(2y) = 12v$?

(1) $\dfrac{3^{2x} - 2^{2y}}{3^x - 2^y} = 4v$

(2) $2(3^{x+2}) + 9(2^{y+1}) = 72v$

Step 1: Analyze the Question Stem

This is a Yes/No question. A statement is sufficient if it allows you to answer the question with either a definite yes or a definite no.

Begin by simplifying the equation $3^{x+1} + 3(2^y) = 12v$. Using the law of exponents that says that $b^a b^c = b^{a+c}$, you can rewrite 3^{x+1} as $(3^x)(3^1) = 3(3^x)$. So replace 3^{x+1} with $3(3^x)$: $3(3^x) + 3(2^y) = 12v$. Now factor a 3 out of the left side to yield $3(3^x + 2^y) = 12v$. Dividing both sides of the equation by 3 results in $3^x + 2^y = 4v$. So the question stem is asking, "If $x > y > 0$, does $3^x + 2^y = 4v$?"

Step 2: Evaluate the Statements Using 12TEN

Statement (1): Rewrite the equation $\dfrac{3^{2x} - 2^{2y}}{3^x - 2^y} = 4v$ to evaluate it. There is a law of exponents that says that $(b^a)^c = b^{ac}$, so $3^{2x} = (3^x)^2$ and $2^{2y} = (2^y)^2$. It follows that $3^{2x} - 2^{2y} = (3^x)^2 - (2^y)^2$. This is one of the classic quadratics: $(3^x)^2 - (2^y)^2 = (3^x - 2^y)(3^x + 2^y)$. So Statement (1) can be written as $\dfrac{(3^x - 2^y)(3^x + 2^y)}{3^x - 2^y} = 4v$. Cancel a factor of $3^x - 2^y$ from the numerator and denominator of the left side of the equation to find that $3^x + 2^y = 4v$. Since $3^x + 2^y = 4v$ is equivalent to $3^{x+1} + 3(2^y) = 12v$, Statement (1) allows you to answer the question with a definite yes and is sufficient. Eliminate **(B)**, **(C)**, and **(E)**.

Statement (2): Because $b^a b^c = b^{a+c}$, $3^{x+2} = (3^x)(3^2) = (3^x)(9) = 9(3^x)$. Also, $2^{y+1} = (2^y)(2^1) = (2^y)(2) = 2(2^y)$. Thus, $2(3^{x+2}) + 9(2^{y+1}) = 72v$ can be written as $2[9(3^x)] + 9[2(2^y)] = 72v$, or $18(3^x) + 18(2^y) = 72v$. Factoring 18 out of the left side of the equation gives $18(3^x + 2^y) = 72v$. Divide both sides of the equation by 18: $3^x + 2^y = 4v$. Since this is the same equation shown to be sufficient for Statement (1), Statement (2) allows you to answer the question with a definite yes and is sufficient.

(D) is correct.

10. (B)

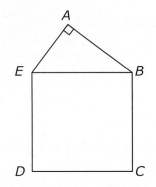

In the figure above, the measure of angle *EAB* in triangle *ABE* is 90 degrees, and *BCDE* is a square. What is the length of *AB*?

(1) The length of *AE* is 12, and the ratio of the area of triangle *ABE* to the area of square *BCDE* is $\frac{6}{25}$.

(2) The perimeter of square *BCDE* is 80 and the ratio of the length of *AE* to the length of *AB* is 3 to 4.

Step 1: Analyze the Question Stem

This is a Value question. The figure shows a right triangle whose hypotenuse is one side of a square, and a statement that is sufficient would allow you to find the length of side *AB*.

Step 2: Evaluate the Statements Using 12TEN

Statement (1): The area of right triangle *ABE* is $\frac{1}{2}(AE)(AB) = \frac{1}{2}(12)(AB) = 6(AB)$. Since triangle *ABE* is a right triangle, the Pythagorean theorem says that $(BE)^2 = (AB)^2 + 12^2 = (AB)^2 + 144$. Thus, $BE = \sqrt{(AB)^2 + 144}$. The area of square *BCDE* is $(BE)^2 = \sqrt{(AB)^2 + 144} \times \sqrt{(AB)^2 + 144} = (AB)^2 + 144$.

Since the ratio of the area of triangle *ABE* to the area of square *BCDE* is $\frac{6}{25}$, $\frac{6(AB)}{(AB)^2 + 144} = \frac{6}{25}$. Solve this equation for *AB*:

$$\frac{y}{y^2 + 144} = \frac{1}{25}$$
$$25y = y^2 + 144$$
$$y^2 - 25y + 144 = 0$$

Factor $y^2 - 25y + 144$. With some testing, you find that $y^2 - 25y + 144 = (y - 9)(y - 16)$. So $(y - 9)(y - 16) = 0$. Thus, it is possible that the length of *AB* is 9 or 16. Because more than one answer to the question is possible, Statement (1) is insufficient. Eliminate **(A)** and **(D)**.

Statement (2): The perimeter of square *ABCD* is 80, so the length of one side of the square is $\frac{80}{4} = 20$. Because the ratio of *AE* to *AB* is 3 to 4, right triangle *ABE* is a 3-4-5 right triangle. Knowing the ratios of the sides and the length of the hypotenuse, you could calculate the length of side *AB*. However, since this is a Data Sufficiency question, there is no need to perform the calculations. Statement (2) is sufficient. (For the record, right triangle *ABE* has side lengths of 12, 16, and 20. *AB* is the longer leg and equals 16.)

(B) is correct.

11. (E)

In the sequence *T*, the first term is the non-zero number *a*, and each term after the first term is equal to the non-zero number *r* multiplied by the previous term. What is the value of the fourth term of the sequence?

(1) The sum of the first two terms of the sequence is 16.

(2) The 18th term of the sequence is 81 times the 14th term of the sequence.

Step 1: Analyze the Question Stem

This is a Value question involving a geometric sequence. Each term after the first term is *r* times the previous term. So if the *n*th term is a_n, where *n* is an integer and $n \geq 1$, then $a_1 = a$, $a_2 = ar$, $a_3 = ar^2$, $a_4 = ar^3$, $a_5 = ar^4$, and so on. In general, if *n* is an integer and $n \geq 1$, then the *n*th term is the product of one factor of *a* and $n - 1$ factors of *r*, or $a_n = ar^{n-1}$.

Step 2: Evaluate the Statements Using 12TEN

Statement (1): The sum of the first two terms is 16. Thus, $a + ar = 16$. This is one equation with two variables, and there are many possible values for *a* and *r*. Statement (1) is insufficient. Eliminate **(A)** and **(D)**.

Statement (2): This statement says that $a_{18} = 81a_{14}$. You know the following:

$$a_{15} = a_{14}r$$
$$a_{16} = a_{15}r$$
$$a_{17} = a_{16}r$$
$$a_{18} = a_{17}r$$

So $a_{18} = a_{17}r = (a_{16}r)r = a_{16}r^2 = (a_{15}r)r^2 = a_{15}r^3 = (a_{14}r)r^3 = a_{14}r^4$.

Since $a_{18} = 81a_{14}$, $a_{14}r^4 = 81a_{14}$. According to the question stem, $a \neq 0$ and $r \neq 0$, so a_{14} does not equal 0. Divide by a_{14}: $r^4 = 81$. Now $81 = 3^4$ or $(-3)^4$, so $r = 3$ or $r = -3$. This statement provides two values for *r* and no information about *a*, so the fourth term cannot be calculated. For example, if $a = 4$ and $r = 3$, then $a_4 = 4(3^{4-1}) = 4(3^3) = 4(27) = 108$. But if $a = 2$ and $r = -3$, then $a_4 = 2(-3)^{4-1} = 2(-3)^3 = 2(-27) = -54$. Since different answers to the question are possible, Statement (2) is insufficient. Eliminate **(B)**.

The statements taken together: From Statement (1), which says that the sum of the first two terms is 16, you know that $a + ar = 16$. From Statement (2), which says that $a_{18} = 81a_{14}$, you know that $r = 3$ or $r = -3$.

Consider the case where $r = 3$. Substituting 3 for *r* into the equation $a + ar = 16$, $a + a(3) = 16$, $a + 3a = 16$, $4a = 16$, and $a = 4$. In this case, the fourth term is $ar^{4-1} = 4(3^{4-1}) = 4(3^3) = 4(27) = 108$. Now consider the case where $r = -3$. Substituting -3 for *r* into the equation $a + ar = 16$, $a + a(-3) = 16$, $a - 3a = 16$, $-2a = 16$, and $a = -8$. With these values of *r* and *a*, the fourth term is $(-8)(-3)^{4-1} = (-8)(-3)^3 = (-8)(-27) = 216$. Because there is more than one possible answer to the question, the statements taken together are insufficient.

(E) is correct.

12. (C)

A person is to be selected at random from the group T of people. What is the probability that the person selected is a member of club E?

(1) The probability that a person selected at random from group T is not a member of club D and is not a member of club E is $\frac{1}{4}$.

(2) The probability that a person selected at random from group T is a member of club D and not a member of club E is $\frac{5}{12}$.

Step 1: Analyze the Question Stem

This is a Value question involving the probability of a single event. A person is to be selected at random from group T, and the question asks for the probability that the person selected is a member of club E. The probability that the person selected is a member of club D can be written as $P(D)$ and the probability that the person is a member of club E as $P(E)$.

Step 2: Evaluate the Statements Using 12TEN

Statement (1): The probability that the person selected is not a member of either club is $\frac{1}{4}$. The probability that an event does not occur is equal to 1 minus the probability that the event does occur, so the probability that the person chosen is a member of at least one of the two clubs—that is, $P(D$ or $E)$—is $1 - \frac{1}{4} = \frac{3}{4}$. In general, $P(D$ or $E) = P(D) + P(E) - P(D$ and $E)$. (This formula is worth memorizing.) In this case, you can substitute $\frac{3}{4}$ for $P(D$ or $E)$, so $P(D) + P(E) - P(D$ and $E) = \frac{3}{4}$. However, without any other information about $P(D)$ or $P(D$ and $E)$, you cannot find $P(E)$. Statement (1) is insufficient. Eliminate **(A)** and **(D)**.

Statement (2): Because the probability that the chosen person is a member of club D and not club E is $\frac{5}{12}$, and $P(D$ and not $E) = \frac{5}{12}$. Since $P(D) = P(D$ and $E) + P(D$ and not $E)$, $P(D$ and not $E) = P(D) - P(D$ and $E)$. Thus, $P(D) - P(D$ and $E) = \frac{5}{12}$. There is no way to find $P(E)$ from this information. Statement (2) is insufficient, and **(B)** can be eliminated.

The statements taken together: from Statement (1), $P(D) + P(E) - P(D$ and $E) = \frac{3}{4}$. From Statement (2), $P(D) - P(D$ and $E) = \frac{5}{12}$. You can rearrange the equation from Statement (1): $P(D) - P(D$ and $E) + P(E) = \frac{3}{4}$. Using $P(D) - P(D$ and $E) = \frac{5}{12}$, substitute $\frac{5}{12}$ for $P(D) - P(D$ and $E)$ in $P(D) - P(D$ and $E) + P(E) = \frac{3}{4}$. Then $\frac{5}{12} + P(E) = \frac{3}{4}$, and you can solve for the probability that the person selected is a member of club E. There is no need to do the calculation, but for the record, it would be $P(E) = \frac{3}{4} - \frac{5}{12} = \frac{9}{12} - \frac{5}{12} = \frac{4}{12} = \frac{1}{3}$. The statements taken together are sufficient.

(C) is correct.

13. (D)

The population of Town X on January 1, 2010, was 56 percent greater than the population of the same town on January 1, 2005. The population of Town X on January 1, 2015, was 75 percent greater than the population of the same town on January 1, 2010. What was the population of Town X on January 1, 2005?

(1) The population of Town X on January 1, 2015, was 21,840.

(2) The increase in the population of Town X from January 1, 2010, to January 1, 2015, was 4,880 greater than the increase in the population of Town X from January 1, 2005, to January 1, 2010.

Step 1: Analyze the Question Stem

This is a Value question involving multiple percent increases. Say the population of Town X on January 1, 2005, was N. Because the population of Town X on January 1, 2010, was 56% greater than the population on January 1, 2005, the population in 2010 was $N + (56\%$ of $N) = N + 0.56N = 1.56N$. Then because the population on January 1, 2015, was 75% greater than the population on January 1, 2010, the population in 2015 can be written as follows:

$$1.56N + 0.75(1.56N) = 1.56N + \frac{3}{4}(1.56N)$$
$$= 1.56N + 3(0.39N)$$
$$= 1.56N + 1.17N$$
$$= 2.73N$$

Note that because you know the percent increase from each of the three named years to the next, a statement that provides the population for any of those three years will be sufficient.

Step 2: Evaluate the Statements Using 12TEN

Statement (1): Because the population on January 1, 2015, was $2.73N$, you can write the equation $2.73N = 21,840$. Then $N = \frac{21,840}{2.73}$. This equation produces just one value for N, so Statement (1) is sufficient. Eliminate **(B)**, **(C)**, and **(E)**.

Statement (2): The increase in the population from 2005 to 2010 can be written as $1.56N - N = 0.56N$. The increase in the population from 2010 to 2015 is $2.73N - 1.56N = 1.17N$. Because the increase from 2010 to 2015 was 4,880 greater than the increase from 2005 to 2010, you can write the equation $1.17N = 0.56N + 4,880$. There is one equation with one variable, so you could solve for N and Statement (2) is sufficient.

(D) is correct.

14. (C)

What is the value of $x - 3z$?

(1) $x + 4y = 3$
(2) $x^2 + 4xy - 3xz - 12yz = 24$

Step 1: Analyze the Question Stem

This is a Value question. Knowing the values of x and z separately would be sufficient to answer the question, as would knowing the value of the entire expression $x - 3z$.

Step 2: Evaluate the Statements Using 12TEN

Statement (1) is clearly insufficient, as the equation $x + 4y = 3$ does not include the variable z. Eliminate **(A)** and **(D)**.

Statement (2) provides one equation with three variables, so there will be different possible values for $x - 3z$. For example, if you let $x = 0$ and $y = 8$, then the equation $x^2 + 4xy - 3xz - 12yz = 24$ leads to $z = -\frac{1}{4}$. Plugging $x = 0$ and $z = -\frac{1}{4}$ into $x - 3z$, you have $x - 3z = 0 - 3\left(-\frac{1}{4}\right) = \frac{3}{4}$. In this case, the answer to the question is $\frac{3}{4}$. But if you let $x = 3$ and $y = 0$, the equation $x^2 + 4xy - 3xz - 12yz = 24$ leads to $z = -\frac{5}{3}$. Plugging $x = 3$ and $z = -\frac{5}{3}$ into $x - 3z$ gives you the following: $x - 3z = 3 - 3\left(-\frac{5}{3}\right) = 3 + 5 = 8$. In this case, the answer to the question is 8. Since different answers to the question are possible, Statement (2) is insufficient. Eliminate **(B)**.

To combine the statements, start by simplifying the left side of the equation in Statement (2):

$$x^2 + 4xy - 3xz - 12yz = x(x + 4y) - 3z(x + 4y) = (x + 4y)(x - 3z)$$

Thus, Statement (2) is equivalent to $(x + 4y)(x - 3z) = 24$. Statement (1) says that $x + 4y = 3$. Substitute 3 for $x + 4y$ in the equation $(x + 4y)(x - 3z) = 24$ to produce $3(x - 3z) = 24$. Dividing both sides by 3 yields $x - 3z = 8$. The statements together lead to a single possible value of 8 for $x - 3z$. The statements taken together are sufficient.

(C) is correct.

15. **(D)**

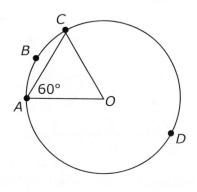

In the figure above, the center of the circle is O, and the measure of angle CAO is 60 degrees. What is the perimeter of triangle OAC?

(1) The length of arc CDA is 16π greater than the length of arc ABC.

(2) The area of triangle OAC is $36\sqrt{3}$.

Step 1: Analyze the Question Stem

This question asks for the perimeter of the triangle, so it is a Value question. Sides OA and OC of triangle OAC are both radii of the circle, so $OA = OC$, making the triangle isosceles, so that $\angle OCA$ must also equal $60°$. Because the three angles of a triangle must sum to $180°$, the central angle is also $60°$—in other words, triangle OAC is equilateral. So each of its three sides is equal to the circle's radius. If you can find the radius, you can find the perimeter of the triangle, and you have sufficiency.

Step 2: Evaluate the Statements Using 12TEN

Statement (1): In a circle with radius r, the length L of an arc intercepted by a central angle whose measure is n degrees is given by the formula $L = 2\pi r \times \frac{n}{360}$. Here, the central angle intercepting arc CDA has a measure of $360° - 60° = 300°$, and the central angle intercepting arc ABC has a measure of $60°$. So the length of arc CDA is $2\pi r \times \frac{300}{360} = 2\pi r \times \frac{5}{6} = \frac{5\pi r}{3}$, and the length of arc ABC is $2\pi r \times \frac{60}{360} = 2\pi r \times \frac{1}{6} = \frac{\pi r}{3}$. Since Statement (1) says that the length of arc CDA is 16π greater than the length of arc ABC, you know that $\frac{5\pi r}{3} = \frac{\pi r}{3} + 16\pi$. That's a single equation in one variable, so you can solve for r. Statement (1) is sufficient. (For the record, dividing both sides of this equation by π and multiplying both sides by 3 yields $5r = r + 48$, so $r = 12$, and the perimeter is $3(12) = 36$.) Eliminate **(B)**, **(C)**, and **(E)**.

Statement (2) says that the area of triangle OAC is $36\sqrt{2}$. Triangle OAC is equilateral. Call the length of each side of triangle OAC s.

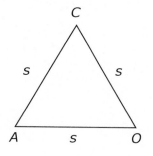

Drop an altitude from point C to side OA:

Altitude CD divides triangle OAC into two identical 30°-60°-90° right triangles.

$$AE = \frac{s}{2} \qquad EO = \frac{s}{2}$$

The 2 identical 30°-60°-90° right triangles are triangles ACE and OCE. The side lengths in a 30°-60°-90° right triangle are in a ratio of 1 to $\sqrt{3}$ to 2. Since the length of hypotenuse AC of right triangle ACE is s, the length of leg AE, which is opposite the 30° angle must be $\frac{s}{2}$, and the length of leg CE, which is opposite the 60° angle, must be $\frac{s}{2} \times \sqrt{3} = \frac{s\sqrt{3}}{2}$. You can now describe the area of triangle OAC in terms of s. The area of any triangle is $\frac{1}{2} b \times h$. Call the base OA and the height CE. Then $OA = s$ and $CE = \frac{s\sqrt{3}}{2}$. The area of triangle OAC is $\frac{1}{2} \times OA \times CE = \frac{1}{2} \times s \times \frac{s\sqrt{3}}{2} = \frac{s^2\sqrt{3}}{4}$. Since the area of triangle OAC is given in Statement (2) to be $36\sqrt{3}$, you can write the equation $\frac{s^2\sqrt{3}}{4} = 36\sqrt{3}$. That's again a single equation in one variable. It does have a squared term, but as negative lengths are disallowed, you can stop here and declare Statement (2) sufficient. (For the record: $\frac{s^2}{4} = 36$ so $s^2 = 144$ and $s = 12$. The perimeter is again $3(12) = 36$.)

(D) is correct.

16. (B)

If x and y are integers and $3x > 8y$, is $y > -18$?

(1) $-9 < x < 20$

(2) $y = \dfrac{(x - 42)}{5}$

Step 1: Analyze the Question Stem

This is a Yes/No question with two integer variables. Simplify the inequality given in the stem, $3x > 8y$, to get $y < \frac{3}{8}x$.

Step 2: Evaluate the Statements Using 12TEN

Statement (1): The possible values of x are limited by the range of this inequality, so examine the endpoints of the range. If $x > -9$, the least value that is permissible for x is -8. Since y is *less than* $\frac{3}{8}x$, it follows that $y < -3$. Some values of y could be > -18, but there is no lower limit for y, so it could also be < -18. There is no need to evaluate the upper boundary of x. Statement (1) is insufficient, so eliminate **(A)** and **(D)**.

Statement (2): Simplify the equation by multiplying both sides by 5 to get $5y = x - 42$. Add 42 to both sides and $x = 5y + 42$. Substitute this value for x into the inequality $3x > 8y$:

$$3(5y + 42) > 8y$$
$$15y + 126 > 8y$$
$$7y + 126 > 0$$
$$7y > -126$$
$$y > -18$$

Statement (2) is sufficient to answer definitively yes.

(B) is correct.

17. **(A)**

Over the course of 5 days, Monday through Friday, Danny collects a total of 76 baseball cards. Each day, he collects a different number of cards. If Danny collects the largest number of cards on Friday and the second largest number of cards on Thursday, did Danny collect more than 8 cards on Thursday?

(1) On Friday, Danny collected 49 cards.

(2) On one of the first 3 days, Danny collected 6 cards.

Step 1: Analyze the Question Stem

This is a Yes/No question that is packed with information in the stem. Danny collects a *different* number of cards each of the 5 days. He collects the *largest* number of cards on Friday and the *second largest* number on Thursday. The question asks if Danny collected *more* than 8 cards on Thursday.

Step 2: Evaluate the Statements Using 12TEN

Statement (1): The largest number of cards collected on Thursday that would result in a no answer to the question is 8. Since the number of cards collected Monday, Tuesday, and Wednesday is different each day and must be less than 8, the maximum numbers of cards he could collect on those days are 5, 6, and 7. Totaling up all the days, $5 + 6 + 7 + 8 + 49 = 75$. Collecting 8 cards on Thursday does not enable Danny to collect 76 cards in total given the constraints of the question, so the information in Statement (1) means that Danny must have collected more than 8 cards on Thursday. Statement (1) is sufficient to answer "always yes," so eliminate **(B)**, **(C)**, and **(E)**.

Statement (2): If Danny collects 6 cards on one of the first 3 days, the fewest cards he could have collected on those days would be $6 + 2 + 1 = 9$, leaving $76 - 9 = 67$ cards to be collected on Thursday and Friday. Danny could have collected 7 cards on Thursday and 60 on Friday, in which case the answer to the question is no. Alternatively, he could have collected as many as 33 cards on Thursday and 34 on Friday and the answer would be yes. Therefore, Statement (2) is insufficient.

(A) is correct.

18. (A)

If $y = x^2$, is the equation $(2^{5y})(4^{120}) = 16^{20x}$ true?

(1) $(4 - x)(12 - x) = 0$

(2) $(x - 4)(x - 8)(x - 24) = 0$

Step 1: Analyze the Question Stem

This question asks whether an equation is true, making it a Yes/No question. Start by simplifying the equation in the question stem. Notice that you can write all three powers with a base of 2, since $4 = 2^2$ and $16 = 2^4$. Substituting these values produces $(2^{5y})((2^2)^{120}) = (2^4)^{20x}$, which simplifies to $(2^{5y})(2^{2 \times 120}) = 2^{4 \times 20x}$, or $(2^{5y})(2^{240}) = 2^{80x}$. This, in turn, can be rewritten as $2^{5y + 240} = 2^{80x}$. When equal powers have the same base, the exponents must be equal. So $5y + 240 = 80x$. Remember that $y = x^2$, so you can substitute x^2 for y to yield $5x^2 + 240 = 80x$. Subtracting $80x$ from both sides, $5x^2 - 80x + 240 = 0$. Dividing both sides by 5, $x^2 - 16x + 48 = 0$. This factors to $(x - 4)(x - 12) = 0$. So $x - 4 = 0$ or $x - 12 = 0$, and $x = 4$ or $x = 12$.

So if $x = 4$ or $x = 12$, then the equation $(2^{5y})(4^{120}) = (16^{20x})$ is true, and the answer to the question is definitively yes. If x is neither of these values, the answer is definitively no. Either of these situations would be sufficient.

Step 2: Evaluate the Statements Using 12TEN

Statement (1) says that $(4 - x)(12 - x) = 0$. When the product of a group of numbers is 0, at least one of the numbers must be 0. So if $(4 - x)(12 - x) = 0$, then $4 - x = 0$ or $12 - x = 0$. If $4 - x = 0$, then $4 = x$, or $x = 4$. If $12 - x = 0$, then $12 = x$, or $x = 12$. You've already determined that the equation $(2^{5y})(4^{120}) = (16^{20x})$ is true when $x = 4$ or $x = 12$. Statement (1) is sufficient, as the answer to the question is always yes. Eliminate **(B)**, **(C)**, and **(E)**.

Statement (2) says that $(x - 4)(x - 8)(x - 24) = 0$. Again, when the product of a group of numbers is 0, at least one of the numbers must be 0. So in this case, $x - 4 = 0$, $x - 8 = 0$, or $x - 24 = 0$. If $x - 4 = 0$, then $x = 4$. If $x - 8 = 0$, then $x = 8$. If $x - 24 = 0$, then $x = 24$. The possible values of x are 4, 8, and 24. You know that the equation $(2^{5y})(4^{120}) = (16^{20x})$ is true when $x = 4$ or $x = 12$. If $x = 4$, then the answer to the question is yes. If $x = 8$, or if $x = 24$, the answer to the question is no. Since more than one answer to the question is possible, Statement (2) is insufficient.

(A) is correct.

19. (B)

The ratio of the number of students in an auditorium who are seniors to the number of students in the auditorium who are not seniors is 7:5. How many students are there in the auditorium?

(1) The ratio of the number of students who are seniors who are taking history to the number of students who are not seniors who are taking history is 21:5.

(2) Of the students in the auditorium who are seniors, $\frac{3}{5}$ are taking history;

of the students in the auditorium who are not seniors, $\frac{1}{5}$ are taking history;

and the number of seniors in the auditorium who are taking history is 208 greater than the number of students in the auditorium who are not seniors and taking history.

Step 1: Analyze the Question Stem

This is a Value question. Since the question asks for the total number of students, start by rewriting the part-to-part ratio in the question stem as a part-to-whole ratio. The ratio of seniors to non-seniors is 7:5, so the ratio of the students who are seniors to the total number of students is $\frac{7}{7+5} = \frac{7}{12}$, and the ratio of the students in the auditorium who are not seniors to the total number of students is $\frac{5}{7+5} = \frac{5}{12}$. Remember that there is a common multiplier in the numerator and denominator of every ratio, so you could write the ratio of seniors to total students as $\frac{7x}{12x}$ and the ratio of non-seniors to total students as $\frac{5x}{12x}$. If you can find the common multiplier x, you can find the total number of students, and you have sufficiency.

Step 2: Evaluate the Statements Using 12TEN

Statement (1): You are given the ratio of the number of students who are seniors who are taking history to the number of students who are not seniors who are taking history. There is no actual number of students given, and there's no way to calculate the common multiplier in the original ratio and thus calculate the total number of students. Statement (1) is insufficient. Eliminate **(A)** and **(D)**.

Statement (2): From the ratio given in the question stem, you know that there are $7x$ seniors, $5x$ non-seniors, and $12x$ total students present in the auditorium. From Statement (2), you know that of the $7x$ seniors, $\frac{3}{5}$ are taking history. In other words, $\frac{(7x)(3)}{5} = \frac{21x}{5}$ seniors are taking history. Similarly, $\frac{1}{5}$ of the $5x$ non-seniors are taking history, so $\frac{5x}{5} = x$ non-seniors are taking history. Furthermore, the number of seniors taking history is 208 greater than the number of non-seniors taking history, so you can write an equation to solve for x: $\frac{21x}{5} = x + 208$. This is a single equation in one variable, so you can stop here and declare Statement (2) to be sufficient. (For the record: $21x = 5x + 208(5)$, $16x = 208(5)$, $x = 13(5) = 65$. There are $12x = (12)(65) = 780$ total students.)

(B) is correct.

20. (E)

If $y > 0$, is $\dfrac{x}{y} < 3$?

(1) $x(x + y) - 4y(x + y) < 0$

(2) $5(y + 8) < 20y - 3x + 40$

Step 1: Analyze the Question Stem

Since y is positive, you can multiply both sides of the inequality $\dfrac{x}{y} < 3$ by the positive number y to obtain the equivalent inequality $x < 3y$. So the question is equivalent to "If $y > 0$, is $x < 3y$?"

Step 2: Evaluate the Statements Using 12TEN

Statement (1): Factor $x + y$ out of the left side of the inequality to yield $x(x + y) - 4y(x + y) = (x + y)$ $(x - 4y)$. So Statement (1) is equivalent to $(x + y)(x - 4y) < 0$. When the product of two quantities is negative, one of the quantities must be negative and the other quantity must be positive. So either (i) $x + y < 0$ and $x - 4y > 0$, or (ii) $x + y > 0$ and $x - 4y < 0$. (Keep in mind that y is positive.) In case (i), if $x + y < 0$, then $x < -y$. If $x - 4y > 0$, then $x > 4y$. So in case (i), $x < -y$ and $x > 4y$. Since y is positive, $x < -y$ means that x is less than $-y$, where $-y$ is a negative number. Since y is positive, $x > 4y$ means that x is greater than $4y$, where $4y$ is a positive number. So case (i) requires that x be less than the negative number $-y$ and also requires that x be greater than the positive number $4y$. This is impossible. So case (i), which is $x + y < 0$ and $x - 4y > 0$, cannot happen. On to case (ii), which is $x + y > 0$ and $x - 4y < 0$. (Again, keep in mind that $y > 0$.) If $x + y > 0$, then $x > -y$. If $x - 4y < 0$, then $x < 4y$. So this time, $x > -y$ and $x < 4y$. Since y is positive, $x > -y$ means that x is greater than the negative number $-y$. Since y is positive, $x < 4y$ means that x is less than the positive number $4y$. So case (ii), $x + y > 0$ and $x - 4y < 0$, is possible. In case (ii), you can conclude that $-y < x < 4y$. Because case (i) is impossible, Statement (1) is equivalent to $-y < x < 4y$. Since y is positive, $3y < 4y$. You know that $x < 4y$. However, you do not know whether or not $x < 3y$.

More than one answer to the question is possible, so Statement (1) is insufficient. Eliminate **(A)** and **(D)**.

Statement (2): Simplify the inequality $5(y + 8) < 20y - 3x + 40$.

$$5(y + 8) < 20y - 3x + 40$$
$$5y + 40 < 20y - 3x + 40$$
$$5y < 20y - 3x$$
$$3x < 15y$$
$$x < 5y$$

Statement (2) is equivalent to $x < 5y$. Since y is positive, $3y < 5y$. You know that $x < 5y$. However, you do not know whether or not $x < 3y$. Statement (2) is insufficient. Eliminate **(B)**.

The statements taken together: Statement (1) is equivalent to $-y < x < 4y$ and Statement (2) is equivalent to $x < 5y$. Because the question requires that $y > 0$, $4y < 5y$ and the range in Statement (1) is a subset of the range in Statement (2). Therefore, the statements taken together require that $-y < x < 4y$, which you have already determined to be insufficient.

(E) is correct.

PART FIVE

Analytical Writing and Integrated Reasoning Sections

CHAPTER 20

Analytical Writing Assessment

- Essay Format and Structure
- The Basic Principles of Analytical Writing
- How the AWA Is Scored
- The Kaplan Method for Analytical Writing
- Breakdown: Analysis of an Argument
- GMAT Style Checklist
- Practice Essays

The Analytical Writing Assessment (AWA) is either the first task or the last task on the GMAT, depending on which section order you choose. When the section begins, you will be presented with the Analysis of an Argument essay assignment. You will have 30 minutes to complete it.

For the essay, you will analyze a given topic and then type your essay into a simple word processing program. It allows you to do only the following basic functions:

- Insert text
- Delete text
- Cut and paste
- Undo the previous action
- Scroll up and down on the screen

Spell-check and grammar-check functions are not available in the program, so you will have to check those things carefully yourself. One or two spelling errors or a few minor grammatical errors will not lower your score. But many spelling errors can hurt your score, as can errors that are serious enough to obscure your intended meaning.

Thirty minutes is not enough time to produce the same kind of essay you've written for college classes. Nor is it enough time to do a lot of trial and error as you type. It is, however, enough time to write a "strong first draft" if you plan carefully, and that's what the essay graders are looking for.

ESSAY FORMAT AND STRUCTURE

If you are concerned that you do not type very fast, you should practice giving yourself 30 minutes to brainstorm and type AWA essays between now and Test Day. By doing so, you will get an idea of how much you can type in the time allotted; your typing speed might also improve with practice.

Your task for the Argument essay is to assess the logic and use of evidence in an argument. It doesn't matter whether you agree or disagree with the argument's conclusion. Rather, you need to explain the ways in which the author has failed to fully support that conclusion.

Let's take a look at a sample prompt:

> The following appeared in a memo from the CEO of My Pie, a chain of pizza restaurants.
>
> "Officials in the film industry report that over half of the films released last year targeted an age 14–22 audience. Moreover, national sales data indicate that pizza is a favorite food among this age group. Since Filmmax opened a theater in a local mall last year, pizza sales at our restaurant in that mall have been higher than at any other restaurant in our chain. Because watching movies seems to stimulate pizza sales, the best way to increase our profits is to expand by opening new My Pie restaurants near every Filmmax theater."
>
> Consider how logical you find this argument. In your essay, be sure to discuss the line of reasoning and the use of evidence in the argument. For example, you may need to consider what questionable assumptions underlie the thinking and what alternative explanations or counterpoints might weaken the conclusion. You may also discuss what types of evidence would strengthen or refute the argument, what changes in the argument would make it more logically sound, and what, if anything, would help you better evaluate its conclusion.

Where are the holes in the argument? In what ways does it fail to be completely convincing? Why might the plan fail? Not only do you have to identify its major weaknesses, you must also explain them.

THE BASIC PRINCIPLES OF ANALYTICAL WRITING

You aren't being evaluated solely on the strength of your ideas. Your score will also depend on how well you express them. If your writing style isn't clear, your ideas won't come across, no matter how brilliant they are.

Good essay writing isn't just grammatically correct. It is also clear and concise. The following principles will help you express your ideas in good GMAT style.

YOUR CONTROL OF LANGUAGE IS IMPORTANT

Writing that is grammatical, concise, direct, and persuasive displays the "superior control of language" (as the test maker terms it) that earns top GMAT Analytical Writing scores. To achieve effective GMAT style in your essays, you should pay attention to the following points.

Grammar

Your writing must follow the same general rules of standard written English that are tested by Sentence Correction questions. If you're not confident of your mastery of grammar, review the Sentence Correction chapter of this book.

Diction

Diction means word choice. Do you use the words *affect* and *effect* correctly? What about *its* and *it's*, *there* and *their*, *precede* and *proceed*, *principal* and *principle*, and *whose* and *who's*? In addition to avoiding errors of usage, you will need to demonstrate your ability to use language precisely and employ a formal, professional tone.

Syntax

Syntax refers to sentence structure. Do you construct your sentences so that your ideas are clear and understandable? Do you vary the length and structure of your sentences?

KEEP THINGS SIMPLE

Perhaps the single most important piece of advice to bear in mind when writing a GMAT essay is to keep everything simple. This rule applies to word choice, sentence structure, and organization. If you obsess about how to use or spell an unusual word, you can lose your way. The more complicated your sentences are, the more likely they'll be plagued by errors. The more complex your organization becomes, the more likely your argument will get bogged down in convoluted sentences that obscure your point.

Keep in mind that simple does not mean *simplistic*. A clear, straightforward approach can still be sophisticated and convey perceptive insights.

MINOR GRAMMATICAL FLAWS WON'T HARM YOUR SCORE

Many test takers mistakenly believe they'll lose points over a few mechanical errors. That's not the case. GMAT essays should be final first drafts. This means that a couple of misplaced commas, misspellings, or other minor glitches aren't going to affect your score. Occasional mistakes of this type are acceptable and inevitable, given that you have only 30 minutes to construct your essay. In fact, according to the scoring rubric, a top-scoring essay may well have a few minor grammatical flaws.

But if your essays are littered with misspellings and grammar mistakes, the graders may conclude that you have a serious communication problem. Keep in mind that sentence fragments are not acceptable, nor are informal structures such as bullet points or numerical enumeration (e.g., "(1)" instead of "first"). So be concise, forceful, and correct. An effective essay wastes no words; makes its point in a clear, direct way; and conforms to the generally accepted rules of grammar and style.

USE A LOGICAL STRUCTURE

Good essays have a straightforward, linear structure. The problem is that we rarely think in a straightforward, linear way. That's why it's so important to plan your response before you begin typing. If you type *while* planning, your essay will likely loop back on itself, contain redundancies, or fail to follow through on what it sets up.

Logical structure consists of three things:

Paragraph Unity

Paragraph unity means each paragraph discusses one thing and all the discussion of that one thing happens in that paragraph. Let's say that you're responding to the essay prompt we just saw and one of your points is that there may have been reasons for the success of the My Pie restaurant other than its proximity to the Filmmax theater. Your next paragraph should move on to another idea—perhaps something about the expense of opening a new My Pie restaurant near every Filmmax theater. If, in the middle of that next paragraph, you went back to your point about other possible reasons for the success of the My Pie restaurant, you'd be violating paragraph unity.

Train of Thought

This is similar to paragraph unity, but it applies to the whole essay. It's confusing to the reader when an essay keeps jumping back and forth between the different weaknesses of an argument. Discuss one point fully, and then address the next. Don't write another paragraph about a topic you've already discussed.

Flow

The basic idea of flow is that you should deliver on what you promise and not radically change the subject. If your introductory paragraph says that you will mention reasons why Hula burgers might be less popular among the 8- to 12-year-old demographic than regular hamburgers are, you need to make sure that you actually do so. Similarly, avoid suddenly expanding the scope of the essay in the last sentence.

TAKEAWAYS: THE BASIC PRINCIPLES OF ANALYTICAL WRITING

- Your control of language is important.
- Keep things simple.
- Minor grammatical flaws won't harm your score.
- Use a logical structure.

HOW THE AWA IS SCORED

Your essays will be graded on a scale from 0 to 6 (highest). You'll receive one score, which will be an average of the scores that you receive from each of the two graders, rounded up to the nearest half point. Your essay will be graded by a human grader as well as a computerized essay grader (the IntelliMetric™ system). The two grade completely independently of each other—IntelliMetric™ isn't told the human's score, nor is the human told the computer's.

If the two scores are identical, then that's your score. If the scores differ by one point, those scores are averaged. If they differ by more than one point, a second human will grade the essay to resolve any differences. IntelliMetric™ and the human grader agree on the same grade about 55 percent of the time and agree on identical or adjacent grades 97 percent of the time. (Only 3 percent of essays need rereading.) These figures are equivalent to how often two trained human graders agree.

IntelliMetric™ was designed to make the same judgments that a good human grader would. In fact, part of the Graduate Management Admission Council's (GMAC's) argument for the validity of IntelliMetric™ is that its performance is statistically indistinguishable from a human's. Still, you should remember that it is *not* a human and write accordingly.

IntelliMetric's™ grading algorithm was designed using 400 officially graded essays for each prompt. That's a huge sample of responses, so don't worry about whether IntelliMetric™ will understand your ideas—it's highly likely that someone out of those 400 responses made a similar point.

Before you begin to write, outline your essay. Good organization always counts, but with a computer grader, it's more important than ever. Use transitional phrases like *first*, *therefore*, *since*, and *for example* so that the computer can recognize structured arguments. The length of your essay is not a factor; the computer does not count the number of words in your response.

Furthermore, computers are not good judges of humor or creativity. (The human judges don't reward those either. The standard is business writing, and you shouldn't be making overly witty or irreverent remarks in, say, an email to a CEO.)

Though IntelliMetric™ doesn't grade spelling per se, it could give you a lower score if it can't understand you or thinks you used the wrong words.

Here's what your essay will be graded on:

- **Structure.** Does your essay have good paragraph unity, organization, and flow?
- **Evidence.** It's not enough simply to assert good points. Do you develop them well? How strong are the examples you provide?
- **Depth of Logic.** Do you take apart the argument and analyze its major weaknesses effectively?
- **Style.** The GMAC calls this "control of the elements of standard written English." How well do you express your ideas?

Now let's take a more in-depth look at the scoring scale so you get a sense of what to aim for. The following rubric shows how the GMAC will grade your essay based on the four categories of Structure, Evidence, Depth of Logic, and Style:

	1 Seriously Deficient	2 Substantially Flawed	3 Inadequate	4 Satisfactory	5 Good	6 Excellent
Structure	Lacks length and organization; *does not adhere* to topic.	Lacks length and organization; *unclear understanding* of topic.	Lacks length enough for real analysis; *strays from topic* or is partially unfocused.	Has *good basic organization* and sufficient paragraphing.	Has *well-developed paragraphs* and structure; stays on topic.	Has well-developed paragraphs and structure; *paragraphing works with examples*.
Evidence	Provides *few, if any, examples* to back up claims.	Provides *very sparse examples* to back up claims.	Provides *insufficient examples* to back up claims.	Provides *sufficient examples* to back up claims.	Provides *strong examples* to back up claims.	Provides *very strong examples* to back up claims.
Depth of Logic	Shows *very little understanding of the argument* and gives no analysis of/takes no position on it.	Presents the writer's views, but *fails to give any analytical critique.*	Analyzes somewhat, but *fails to show some key parts of the argument.*	Shows key parts of the argument adequately with *some analysis.*	Shows key parts of the argument and *analyzes them thoughtfully.*	Shows key parts of the argument and *analyzes them with great clarity.*
Style	Has *severe and persistent errors* in sentence structure and use of language; meaning is lost.	*Frequently uses language incorrectly* and sentence structure, grammar, and usage errors inhibit meaning.	*Uses language imprecisely* and is deficient in variety; some major errors or a number of small errors.	*Controls language adequately,* including syntax and diction; a few flaws.	*Controls language with clarity,* including variety of syntax and diction; may have a flaw here and there.	*Controls language extremely well,* including variety of syntax and diction; may have a small flaw here and there.

GMAC will grade your essay holistically based on the above rubric to arrive at your final score:

- **6: Excellent.** Essays that earn the top score must be insightful, well supported by evidence, logically organized, and skillfully written. A 6 need not be "perfect," just very good.

- **5: Good.** A 5 essay is well written and well supported but may not be as compellingly argued as a 6. There may also be more frequent or more serious writing errors than in a 6.

- **4: Satisfactory.** The important elements of the argument are addressed but not explained robustly. The organization is good, and the evidence provided is adequate. The writing may have some flaws but is generally acceptable.

- **3: Inadequate.** A 3 response misses important elements of the argument, has little or no evidence to support its ideas, and doesn't clearly express its meaning.

- **2: Substantially Flawed.** An essay scoring a 2 has some serious problems. It may not use any examples whatsoever or support its ideas in any way. Its writing will have many errors that interfere with the meaning of the sentences.

- **1: Seriously Deficient.** These essays are rare. A 1 score is reserved for essays that provide little or no evidence of the ability to analyze an argument or to develop ideas in any way. A 1 essay will have so many writing errors that the essay may be unintelligible.
- **0: No Score.** A score of 0 signifies an attempt to avoid addressing the prompt at all, either by writing only random or repeating characters or by copying the prompt. You could also score a 0 by not writing in English or by addressing a completely different topic.
- **NR: Blank.** This speaks for itself. This is what you get if you write no essay at all. Some schools will not consider your GMAT score if your essay receives an NR. By skipping the essay, you give yourself an unfair advantage—everyone else wrote an essay for 30 minutes *before* the other sections!

TAKEAWAYS: HOW THE AWA IS SCORED

- Your AWA score does not count toward the 200–800 score for the rest of the test.
- Business schools receive the text of your essay along with your score report.
- The essay grading is almost pass/fail in nature: there's a clear line between 1–3 (bad) and 4–6 (good).
- A writer with a solid plan should earn a score of 4 or higher on the AWA.

THE KAPLAN METHOD FOR ANALYTICAL WRITING

You have a limited amount of time to show the business school admissions officers that you can think logically and express yourself in clearly written English. They don't care how many syllables you can cram into a sentence or how fancy your phrases are. They care that you make sense. Whatever you do, don't hide beneath a lot of hefty words and abstract language. Make sure that everything you say is clearly written and relevant to the topic. Get in there, state your main points, back them up, and get out. The Kaplan Method for Analytical Writing—along with Kaplan's recommendations for how much time you should devote to each step of the Method—will help you produce the best essay you're capable of writing in 30 minutes.

The Kaplan Method for Analytical Writing

1. **Take apart the argument.**

2. **Select the points you will make.**

3. **Organize using Kaplan's essay template.**

4. **Write your essay.**

5. **Proofread your work.**

STEP 1: TAKE APART THE ARGUMENT

- Read through the prompt to get a sense of its scope.
- Identify the author's conclusion and the evidence used to support it.
- You can take about 2 minutes on this step.

STEP 2: SELECT THE POINTS YOU WILL MAKE

- Identify all the important gaps (assumptions) between the evidence and the conclusion.
- Think of how you'll explain or illustrate those gaps and under what circumstances the author's assumptions would not hold true.
- Think about how the author could remedy these weaknesses. This part of the Kaplan Method is very much like predicting the answer to a Critical Reasoning Strengthen or Weaken question.
- Step 2 should take about 5 minutes.

STEP 3: ORGANIZE USING KAPLAN'S ESSAY TEMPLATE

- Outline your essay.
- Lead with your best arguments.
- If you practice with the Kaplan template for the argument essay before Test Day, organizing the essay will go smoothly and predictably. Using the Kaplan template will help you turn vague thoughts about the prompt into organized, developed paragraphs.
- The organization process should take less than 1 minute.

ORGANIZING THE ARGUMENT ESSAY: THE KAPLAN TEMPLATE

PARAGRAPH 1:
SHOW that you understand the argument by putting it in your own words.

PARAGRAPH 2:
POINT OUT one flawed assumption in the author's reasoning; explain why it is questionable.

PARAGRAPH 3:
IDENTIFY another source of the author's faulty reasoning; explain why it is questionable.

ADDITIONAL PARAGRAPHS AS APPROPRIATE:
CONTINUE to bring in points of fault in the argument, as time permits.

Time Valve #1:
Skip to the next paragraph without adding any additional flaws.

SECOND-TO-LAST PARAGRAPH:
DESCRIBE evidence that would—if it were provided—strengthen the argument.

Time Valve #2:
Combine this paragraph with the last paragraph.

LAST PARAGRAPH:
CONCLUDE that without such evidence, you're not persuaded.

STEP 4: WRITE YOUR ESSAY

- Be direct.
- Use paragraph breaks to make your essay easier to read.
- Use transitions and structural keywords to link related ideas; they will help your writing flow.
- Finish strongly.
- You can afford no more than 20 minutes of typing. The other 10 minutes should be dedicated to planning and correcting.

STEP 5: PROOFREAD YOUR WORK

- Save enough time to read through the entire essay—2 minutes at minimum.
- Fix any spelling, grammar, syntax, or diction errors.
- Add any needed keywords to improve the flow of your ideas.
- Don't add any new ideas or change the structure of your essay. There just isn't time.

BREAKDOWN: ANALYSIS OF AN ARGUMENT

THE INSTRUCTIONS

Screen 1: General Instructions

The general instructions for the Argument essay will look like this:

**Analytical Writing Assessment Instructions
Analysis of an Argument Essay**

Time: 30 Minutes

In this part of the test, you will be asked to write a critical analysis of the argument in the prompt. You are not being asked to give your own views on the topic.

COMPOSING YOUR ESSAY: Before you begin to type, take a little time to look at the argument and plan your essay. Make sure your ideas are organized and clearly stated. Leave some time to read over your essay and make any changes you think are necessary. You will have 30 minutes to write your essay.

ESSAY ASSESSMENT: Qualified graders with varied backgrounds, including experience in business subject areas, will assess the overall quality of your analysis and composition. They will look at how well you:

- identify key elements of the argument and examine them;
- arrange your analysis of the argument presented;
- give appropriate examples and reasons for support; and
- master the components of written English.

The instructions on Screen 1 tell you to read the argument, plan your essay before writing it, and leave a little time at the end for review. Sound familiar? The Kaplan Method mirrors these steps. While the prompts for the essay vary, the general directions are always the same. Become familiar with the essay directions now so you don't waste valuable time reading them on Test Day.

Screen 2: Specific Prompt

The next screen you go to will contain the specific essay prompt.

> Read the argument and the directions that follow it, and write down any ideas that will be helpful in mapping out your essay. Begin writing your essay in the box at the bottom of this screen.

> "The problem of poorly trained teachers that has plagued the state public school system is bound to become a good deal less serious in the future. The state has initiated comprehensive guidelines that oblige state teachers to complete a number of required credits in education and educational psychology at the graduate level before being certified."

> Consider how logical you find this argument. In your essay, be sure to discuss the line of reasoning and the use of evidence in the argument. For example, you may need to consider what questionable assumptions underlie the thinking and what alternative explanations or counterpoints might weaken the conclusion. You may also discuss what types of evidence would strengthen or refute the argument, what changes in the argument would make it more logically sound, and what, if anything, would help you better evaluate its conclusion.

The only part of Screen 2 that will change is the specific prompt, which is in quotation marks. The instructions above and below it will stay the same. Again, practicing with these directions now will mean that you won't waste time reading them on Test Day.

THE STIMULUS

Analysis of an Argument topics will probably remind you of Critical Reasoning questions. The basic idea is similar. Just as in Critical Reasoning, the writer tries to persuade you of something—her conclusion—by citing some evidence. So look for these two basic components of an argument: a conclusion and supporting evidence. You should read the argument in the Analysis of an Argument topic in much the same way you read Critical Reasoning stimuli; be on the lookout for assumptions— the ways the writer makes the leap from evidence to conclusion.

THE QUESTION STEM

The question stem instructs you to decide how convincing you find the argument, explain why, and discuss what might improve the argument. Note that there is a right answer here: the argument *always* has some problems. You want to focus your efforts on finding them, explaining them, and fixing them.

Exactly what are you being asked to do here? Paraphrase the following sentences of the question stem.

> Consider how logical you find this argument. In your essay, be sure to discuss the line of reasoning and the use of evidence in the argument.

Translation: Critique the argument. Discuss the ways in which it is not convincing. How and why might the evidence not fully support the conclusion?

> For example, you may need to consider what questionable assumptions underlie the thinking and what alternative explanations or counterpoints might weaken the conclusion. You may also discuss what types of evidence would strengthen or refute the argument, what changes in the argument would make it more logically sound, and what, if anything, would help you better evaluate its conclusion.

Translation: Spot weak links in the argument and offer constructive modifications that would strengthen them.

Let's use the Kaplan Method for Analytical Writing on the Analysis of an Argument topic we saw before:

> "The problem of poorly trained teachers that has plagued the state public school system is bound to become a good deal less serious in the future. The state has initiated comprehensive guidelines that oblige state teachers to complete a number of required credits in education and educational psychology at the graduate level before being certified."

> Consider how logical you find this argument. In your essay, be sure to discuss the line of reasoning and the use of evidence in the argument. For example, you may need to consider what questionable assumptions underlie the thinking and what alternative explanations or counterpoints might weaken the conclusion. You may also discuss what types of evidence would strengthen or refute the argument, what changes in the argument would make it more logically sound, and what, if anything, would help you better evaluate its conclusion.

STEP 1: TAKE APART THE ARGUMENT

First, identify the conclusion—the point the argument is trying to make. Here, the conclusion is the first sentence:

> The problem of poorly trained teachers that has plagued the state public school system is bound to become a good deal less serious in the future.

Next, identify the evidence—the basis for the conclusion. Here, the evidence is the second sentence of the argument:

> The state has initiated comprehensive guidelines that oblige state teachers to complete a number of required credits in education and educational psychology at the graduate level before being certified.

Finally, paraphrase the argument in your own words: the problem of badly trained teachers will become less serious because new teachers will be required to take a certain number of graduate level classes.

If you aren't able to put the argument in your own words, you don't yet understand it well enough to analyze it sufficiently. Don't rush this step; you can afford a full 2 minutes if you need it.

STEP 2: SELECT THE POINTS YOU WILL MAKE

Now that you've found the conclusion and evidence, think about what assumptions the author is making or any reasoning flaws she commits. Also, think about any unaddressed questions that you feel would be relevant.

- She assumes that the courses will improve teachers' classroom performance.
- What about bad teachers who are already certified? Would they also be required to retrain?
- Have currently poor-performing teachers already had this training?
- Will this plan have any unintended negative consequences?

You also will need to explain how these assumptions could be false or how the questions reveal weaknesses in the author's argument. Add to your notes:

- She assumes that the courses will improve teachers' classroom performance. What if the problem is cultural? Or if it's a language barrier? Or if the teacher doesn't know the subject?
- What about bad teachers who are already certified? Would they also be required to retrain? If not, those bad teachers would still be in the system.
- Have currently poor-performing teachers already had this training? If so, this fact demonstrates that this training won't solve the problems.
- Will this plan have any unintended negative consequences? What does this training cost? If the state has to pay for it, will that mean there is less money available for other uses? If teachers have to pay for it, will good teachers leave the system?

Then think about evidence that would make the argument stronger or more logically sound:

- Evidence verifying that the training will make teachers better
- Evidence that currently bad teachers have not already received this training and that they either will soon receive it or will be removed from the classroom
- Evidence that the cost of the training is not prohibitive

STEP 3: ORGANIZE USING KAPLAN'S ESSAY TEMPLATE

Look over the notes you've jotted down. Select the strongest point to be first, the next-strongest to be second, and so on. Two criteria determine whether a point is strong. One is how well you can explain it. If, for example, you aren't sure how to explain potential negative consequences of an expensive training program, you should use that idea last—if at all. The other is how severe a problem the weakness poses to the argument's persuasiveness. If the training doesn't work, for example, the argument is in serious trouble.

Then decide how you'll arrange your points. Follow the Kaplan template. The following is an example of an effective shorthand outline like the one you will create on Test Day:

¶ Restate argument (conc: solve problem of poorly trained teachers; evid: courses in education and ed. psychology)

¶ Assump: courses = better performance. Culture? Language? Subject matter? Need: evid. of relevance

¶ Assump: current bad teachers not already trained. If they have, training doesn't work. Need: evid. of no training

¶ Assump: bad teachers will go if not trained. If not, will be bad until they retire. Need: everyone to be trained or leave

¶ Assump: not too $. If too $, other priorities suffer. Need: evid. of low $

¶ ways to strengthen arg. (needed evid.)

Remember, you may not have time to use all your points. Leaving your weakest for last means that if you run short on time, you'll leave out your weakest point instead of your best.

STEP 4: WRITE YOUR ESSAY

Begin typing your essay now. Keep in mind the basic principles of writing that we discussed earlier.

Keep your writing simple and clear. Choose words that you know how to use well. Avoid the temptation to make your writing "sound smarter" with overly complicated sentences or vocabulary that feels awkward.

Keep your eye on the clock and make sure that you don't run out of time to proofread. If you need to, leave out your last point or two. (Make sure that you include at least two main points.) Let's pretend that the writer of the following essay had only 6 minutes left on the clock after the third paragraph. She wisely chose neither to rush through her final paragraph nor to skip proofreading. Instead, she left out her point about cost and used the time valve in the template of combining the next-to-last and last paragraphs.

> The author concludes that the present problem of poorly trained teachers will become less severe in the future because of required credits in education and psychology. However, the conclusion relies on assumptions for which the author does not supply clear evidence.
>
> The author assumes that the required courses will produce better teachers. In fact, the courses might be entirely irrelevant to the teachers' failings. If, for example, the prevalent problem is cultural or linguistic gaps between teacher and student, graduate-level courses that do not address these specific issues probably won't do much good. The courses also would not be heplful for a teacher who does not know their subject matter.
>
> In addition, the author assumes that currently poor teachers have not already had this training. In fact, the author doesn't mention whether some or all of the poor teachers have had similar training. If they have, then the training seems not to have been effective and the plan should be rethought.
>
> Finally, the author assumes that poor teachers currently working will either stop teaching in the future or will receive training. The author provides no evidence, though, to indicate that this is the case. As the argument stands, it's highly possible that only brand-new teachers will be receiving the training and the bright future to which the author refers is decades away.
>
> To strengthen the argument, the author must provide several pieces of evidence to support his assumptions. First of all, the author's implicit claim that the courses will improve teachers could be strengthened by providing evidence that the training will be relevant to teachers' problems. The author could also make a stronger case by showing that currently poor teachers have not already had training comparable to the new requirements. Finally, the author's argument can only hold in the presence of evidence that all teachers in the system will receive the training—and will then change there teaching methods accordingly. In its current state, the argument relies too heavily on unsupported assumptions to be convincing.

STEP 5: PROOFREAD YOUR WORK

Save a few minutes to go back over your essay and catch any obvious errors. Look over the essay above. It has at least four grammatical errors and is missing at least one keyword. By leaving herself ample proofreading time, our author will be able to find them.

- **Paragraph 1:**
  - The phrase "because of required credits" is awkward and unclear. Change to "because the state will require teachers to complete credits."

- **Paragraph 2:**
  - Add a keyword to the beginning of the paragraph. Since it is the first assumption discussed, "The author assumes…" should be changed to "First, the author assumes…."
  - The last sentence could be improved: "The courses also would not be heplful for a teacher who does not know their subject matter." For one thing, "heplful" should be "helpful." For another, "a teacher" is singular, but "their" is plural. Change "their" to "his" or "her."

- **Paragraph 3:** no errors
- **Paragraph 4:**
  - There's an awkward phrase about halfway through: "only brand-new teachers will be receiving the training." There's no need for anything but simple future tense: "only brand-new teachers will receive the training."

- **Paragraph 5:**
  - In the next-to-last sentence, "there teaching methods" should be "their teaching methods."

The best way to improve your writing and proofreading skills is practice. When you practice responding to AWA prompts, do so on a computer—but to mimic test conditions, don't use the automatic spell check or grammar check. Write practice essays using the prompts at the end of this chapter, those provided by the test maker at **mba.com**, or those in the *Official Guide for GMAT Review*. The pool of prompts provided by the test maker contains the actual prompts from which the GMAT will select your essay topic on Test Day.

GMAT STYLE CHECKLIST

On the GMAT, there are three rules of thumb for successful writing: be concise, be forceful, and be correct. Following these rules is a sure way to improve your writing style—and your score. Let's look at each one in more depth.

BE CONCISE

- Cut out words, phrases, and sentences that don't add any information or serve a necessary purpose.
- Watch out for repetitive phrases such as "refer back" or "absolutely essential."
- Don't use conjunctions to join sentences that would be more effective as separate sentences.
- Don't use needless qualifiers such as "really" or "kind of."

Examples

Wordy: The agency is not prepared to undertake expansion at this point in time.
Concise: The agency is not ready to expand.

Redundant: All of these problems have combined together to create a serious crisis.
Concise: Combined, these problems create a crisis.

Too many qualifiers: Ferrara seems to be sort of a slow worker.
Concise: Ferrara works slowly.

BE FORCEFUL

- Don't refer to yourself needlessly. Avoid pointless phrases like "in my personal opinion"; even phrases such as "I agree" or "I think" are considered stylistically weak.
- Avoid jargon and pompous language; it won't impress anybody. For example, "a waste of time and money" is better than "a pointless expenditure of temporal and financial resources."
- Don't use the passive voice. Use active verbs whenever possible.
- Avoid clichés and overused terms or phrases (for example, "beyond the shadow of a doubt").
- Don't be vague. Avoid generalizations and abstractions when more specific words would be clearer.
- Don't use weak sentence openings. Be wary of sentences that begin with "there is" or "there are." For example, "There are several ways in which this sentence is awkward" should be rewritten as "This sentence is awkward in several ways."
- Don't be monotonous; vary sentence length and style.
- Use transitions to connect sentences and make your essay easy to follow.

Examples

Needlessly references self: Although I am no expert, I do not think privacy should be valued more than social concerns.
Speaks confidently: Privacy should not be valued more than social concerns.

Uses passive voice: The report was compiled by a number of field anthropologists and marriage experts.
Uses active voice: A number of field anthropologists and marriage experts compiled the report.

Opens weakly: It would be of no use to fight a drug war without waging a battle against demand for illicit substances.
Opens strongly: The government cannot fight a drug war effectively without waging a battle against the demand for illicit substances.

Uses cliché: A ballpark estimate of the number of fans in the stadium would be 120,000.
Employs plain English: About 120,000 fans were in the stadium.

BE CORRECT

- Observe the rules of standard written English. The most important rules are covered in the Sentence Correction chapter of this book.

Examples

Subject and verb disagree: Meredith, along with her associates, expect the sustainable energy proposal to pass.
Subject and verb agree: Meredith, along with her associates, expects the sustainable energy proposal to pass.

Uses faulty modification: Having worked in publishing for 10 years, Stokely's resume shows that he is well qualified.
Uses correct modification: Stokely, who has worked in publishing for 10 years, appears from his resume to be well qualified.

Uses pronouns incorrectly: A retirement community offers more activities than a private dwelling does, but it is cheaper.

Uses pronouns correctly: A retirement community offers more activities than a private dwelling does, but a private dwelling is cheaper.

Has unparallel structure: The dancer taught her understudy how to move, how to dress, and how to work with choreographers and deal with professional competition.

Has parallel structure: The dancer taught her understudy how to move, dress, work with choreographers, and deal with professional competition.

Fragmented sentence: There is time to invest in property. After one has established oneself in the business world, however.

Complete sentence: There is time to invest in property, but only after one has established oneself in the business world.

Run-on sentence: Antonio just joined the athletic club staff this year, however, because Barry has been with us since 1975, we would expect Barry to be more skilled with the weight-lifting equipment.

Correct sentence: Antonio joined the athletic club staff this year. However, because Barry has been with us since 1975, we would expect him to be more skilled with the weight-lifting equipment.

PRACTICE ESSAYS

Directions: Write an essay on each of the three topics below. The writing should be concise, forceful, and grammatically correct. After you have finished, proofread to catch any errors. Allow yourself 30 minutes to complete each essay. Practice writing under timed conditions so that you get a feel for how much you can afford to write while leaving enough time to proofread.

ESSAY 1

The following appeared in a memo from a staff member of a local health care clinic.

"Many lives might be saved if inoculations against cow flu were routinely administered to all people in areas where the disease is detected. However, since there is a small possibility that a person will die as a result of the inoculations, we cannot permit inoculations against cow flu to be routinely administered."

Consider how logical you find this argument. In your essay, be sure to discuss the line of reasoning and the use of evidence in the argument. For example, you may need to consider what questionable assumptions underlie the thinking and what alternative explanations or counterpoints might weaken the conclusion. You may also discuss what types of evidence would strengthen or refute the argument, what changes in the argument would make it more logically sound, and what, if anything, would help you better evaluate its conclusion.

After writing your essay, compare it to the sample responses that follow. Don't focus on length, as word count is not part of the grading criteria. Rather, focus on how logical the structure is and whether the essay makes its points in a clear and straightforward style.

Student Response 1 (as written, including original errors):

The writer argues that innoculations against cow flu shouldn't be administered because there is a possibility of a person dying from the innoculation. The flaw in this argument is suggested by the writer's use of the phrases "many lives" and "small possibility." These are vague words, but, they imply, that cow flu itself poses a greater risk to people in an area where the disease is present than the prevention against it. If this is the case, then the writer's argument is greatly weakened.

The writer could make the argument better by showing that the overall death rate from cow flu among those who haven't been innoculated in an area where cow flu has been detected is lower than the death rate from the vaccine among individuals who have been given the innoculation. This would show that the vaccine poses a greater risk than the disease itself. Also, it would be good to know whether some people are more likely to die from the innoculation than others and whether these people can be located. It's possible that those people who are most at risk from the innoculation are also most at risk from the disease itself, in which case the innoculation might do no greater harm than the disease would, and would also save the lives of many who were not in this high risk group. On the other hand, if those people who are most at risk from the vaccine are not at a very high risk from the disease, then maybe we can exempt them from the vaccine, but continue to administer it to those people who it will help.

Analysis 1:

Structure: The writer gives his evaluation of the argument in paragraph 1. However, the organization breaks down in paragraph 2, where the writer tries to cover too much. In this paragraph, the writer discusses ways of strengthening the argument, the need for more information, and alternative possibilities for the scenario. A better-written essay might have split paragraph 2 into several different paragraphs, each covering one topic.

Evidence: The writer does not fully support his position with specific examples. Rather, he writes vaguely of different possibilities. While this is not completely wrong, it's also not the type of concrete support that is needed here.

Depth of Logic: This is probably the weakest area in the essay. The writer fails to fully develop his ideas. He looks at the problem only through a cost-benefit lens—which way saves more lives?—as opposed to questioning whether any risk of death means that we shouldn't routinely inoculate.

Style: The writing style is flat and the first sentence in paragraph 2 is long and convoluted. The ideas in paragraph 2 seem strung together.

This essay would earn a score of 3. While the writer has some decent ideas and shows adequate writing ability, the structure of the essay is poor, the logic fails to show some parts of the author's argument, and the writer inadequately develops support for his own points. Had this student used the same ideas, but developed and organized them according to the Kaplan template, he would almost assuredly have earned a score of 4 or better.

Student Response 2 (as written, including original errors):

The argument above states that inoculations against cow flu could be useful in combating the disease, but, due to the risk of death from the inoculations themselves, the vaccines should not be widely administered. This argument relies on several unsupported assumptions and therefore fails to be persuasive.

The argument against widespread inoculations is rooted in the assumption that the risk of death from the inoculations is greater than the risk of death from cow flu. However, the author provides no evidence to support this key assumption. Without specific statistics regarding the death rates from inoculations and cow flu, we cannot assume that one outweighs the other: cow flu and the inoculations may be equally risky, or cow flu may in fact be riskier than the inoculations. In addition, the language of the argument appears to contradict its primary assumption. The author states that "many lives" could be saved by inoculations, but there is a "small possibility" of death from the inoculations. These terms suggest that the risk from cow flu is greater than that of the inoculations, further weakening the author's position that inoculations should not be routinely administered.

Additionally, the author takes an "all or nothing" position, suggesting that inoculations must be widely administered or not administered at all. This position ignores the possibility of variation in rates of infection and effects of the inoculation in different environments. The vaccine may pose a serious risk to those relatively unaffected by cow flu, while posing little risk to those most impacted by cow flu. In this case, vaccines administered to select portions of the population might save the most lives while putting the fewest lives in danger.

To make this argument persuasive, the author needs to present specific evidence to support the argument's assumptions. For instance, details regarding the number of deaths caused by cow flu and the vaccine would clarify the relative risks of the flu and the inoculations, allowing an accurate evaluation of the merits and risks of the vaccine. Also, a less extreme stance on inoculations—one that allowed for selective administration of the inoculations based upon an area's risk for the disease—would provide a more realistic solution to the challenge of balancing the dangers of cow flu and inoculations. Without such changes, the conclusion of this argument remains unconvincing.

Analysis 2:

Structure: The writer of this essay has clearly used the Kaplan template to her benefit. She frames the argument succinctly in the first paragraph. In each of the middle paragraphs, she lays out one major problem in the argument's reasoning and explains with clear support why it is a problem. In the final paragraph, the writer introduces evidence that would strengthen the argument and then draws her conclusion.

Evidence: The evidence is solid. The writer could have brought in counterexamples to support criticisms of the argument, but this is not a fatal flaw.

Depth of Logic: The logic in this essay is much stronger than in the last. The organization of the essay leaves few gaps in the reasoning.

Style: The writing style is superior, with fewer (although not zero) grammatical mistakes and much stronger flow.

This essay would receive a score of 6 from the GMAT graders. It is not perfect, but the graders do not expect perfection. The conclusion is somewhat clunky, and the writer missed one or two opportunities to strengthen her point. However, it is still a very strong essay in all four categories of evaluation, and it is a vast improvement over the earlier effort.

ESSAY 2

The following appeared in a memo from the regional manager of Luxe Spa, a chain of high-end salons.

"Over 75 percent of households in Parksboro have Jacuzzi bathtubs. In addition, the average family income in Parksboro is 50 percent higher than the national average, and a local store reports record-high sales of the most costly brands of hair and body care products. With so much being spent on personal care, Parksboro will be a profitable location for a new Luxe Spa—a salon that offers premium services at prices that are above average."

Consider how logical you find this argument. In your essay, be sure to discuss the line of reasoning and the use of evidence in the argument. For example, you may need to consider what questionable assumptions underlie the thinking and what alternative explanations or counterpoints might weaken the conclusion. You may also discuss what types of evidence would strengthen or refute the argument, what changes in the argument would make it more logically sound, and what, if anything, would help you better evaluate its conclusion.

After writing your essay, compare it to the sample response that follows.

Student Response (as written, including original errors):

Though it might seem at first glance that the regional manager of Luxe Spa has good reasons for suggesting that Parksboro would be a profitable location for a new spa, a closer examination of the arguments presented reveals numerous examples of leaps of faith, poor reasoning, and ill-defined terminology. In order to better support her claim, the manager would need to show a correlation between the figures she cites in reference to Parksboro's residents and a willingness to spend money at a spa with high prices.

The manager quotes specific statistics about the percentage of residents with Jacuzzis and the average income in Parksboro. She then uses these figures as evidence to support her argument. However, neither of these statistics as presented does much to bolster her claim. Just because 75% of homes have Jacuzzis doesn't mean those homeowners are more likely to go to a pricey spa. For instance, the presence of Jacuzzis in their houses may indicate a preference for pampering themselves at home. Parksboro could also be a planned development in the suburbs where all the houses are designed with Jacuzzis. If this is the case, than the mere ownership of a certain kind of bathtub should hardly be taken as a clear indication of a person's inclination to go to a spa. In addition, the fact that Parksboro's average family income is 50% higher than the national average is not enough on its own to predict the success or failure of a spa in the region. Parksboro may have a very small population, for instance, or a small number of wealthy people counterbalanced by a number of medium- to low-income families. We simply cannot tell from the information provided. In addition, the failure of the manager to provide the national average family income for comparison makes it unclear if earning 50% more would allow for a luxurious lifestyle or not.

The mention of a local store's record-high sales of expensive personal care items similarly provides scant evidence to support the manager's assertions. We are given no indication of what constitutes "record-high" sales for this particular store or what "most costly" means in this context. Perhaps this store usually sells very few personal care products and had one unusual month. Even if this one store sold a high volume of hair- and body-care products, it may not be representative of the Parksboro market as a whole. And perhaps "most costly" refers only to the most costly brands available in Parksboro, not to the most costly brands nationwide. The manager needs to provide much more specific information about residents' spending habits in order to provide compelling evidence that personal care ranks high among their priorities.

To make the case that Parksboro would be a profitable location for Luxe Spa, the regional manager should try to show that people there have a surplus of income and a tendency to spend it on indulging in spa treatments. Although an attempt is made to make this very argument, the lack of supporting information provided weakens rather than strengthens the memo. Information such as whether there are other high-end spas in the area and the presence of tourism in the town could also have been introduced as reinforcement. As it stands, Luxe Spa would be ill-advised to open a location in Parksboro based solely on the evidence provided here.

Analysis:

Structure: The use of the Kaplan template is evident here. In the first paragraph, the writer demonstrates his understanding of the argument and gives a summary of its flaws. Each paragraph that follows elaborates on one flaw in the author's reasoning. The final paragraph introduces evidence that, if provided, would strengthen the argument.

Evidence: The evidence is strong. The writer develops his points by providing examples to explain why the author's reasoning is questionable. Some minor flaws are evident, as in the second paragraph, when the writer misses an opportunity to point out that a small population might not be enough to support a spa.

Depth of Logic: Once again, the organization of the essay enhances its depth of logic. The writer takes apart the argument methodically and provides clear analysis of each part.

Style: The writing style is smooth and controlled, and grammar and syntax errors are minimal to nonexistent.

This essay would score a 6. The writer makes a very strong showing in all four categories of the grading rubric.

ESSAY 3

The following appeared in a document released by a community's arts bureau:

"In a recent county survey, 20 percent more county residents indicated that they watch TV programs dedicated to the arts than was reported eight years ago. The number of visitors to our county's museums and galleries over the past eight years has gone up by a comparable proportion. Now that the commercial funding public TV relies on is facing severe cuts, which will consequently limit arts programming, it is likely that attendance at our county's art museums will also go down. Therefore, public funds that are currently dedicated to the arts should be partially shifted to public television."

Consider how logical you find this argument. In your essay, be sure to discuss the line of reasoning and the use of evidence in the argument. For example, you may need to consider what questionable assumptions underlie the thinking and what alternative explanations or counterpoints might weaken the conclusion. You may also discuss what types of evidence would strengthen or refute the argument, what changes in the argument would make it more logically sound, and what, if anything, would help you better evaluate its conclusion.

After writing your essay, compare it to the sample response that follows.

Student Response (as written, including original errors):

In a time of threatened scarcity of funding, a community arts organization is asking to shift public arts funds partly to public television. The organization cites a recent survey of county residents that shows a 20 percent self-reported increase in arts TV-watching over the last eight years concomitant with a similar, documented increase in local museum and art gallery attendance. This earnest plea is understandable, but the underlying rationale for shifting funding is flawed and lacks sufficient substantiation.

First, the author may be confusing correlation with causation. Does the survey—even if we accept its findings as valid—really indicate that people went to museums as a result of seeing arts programming on television? Its quite possible that there are alternate reasons for the increase in attendance at museums, such as partnerships with schools, discount programs for senior citizens, introduction of IMAX theaters, or popular traveling exhibits. Alternatively, people may be watching more arts programming on television as a direct result of being lured into museum attendance for reasons that have nothing to do with television.

A second reason to be hesitant to adopt the recommended funding shift is that it assumes that there are only two viable sources of funding for public television: commercial and public. Before it resorts to diverting public funds from other arts organizations, public television has the option to pursue direct fundraising from viewers; these newly enthusiastic television arts program viewers may be delighted to support such programming directly. Public television has a unique opportunity to reach its audience in a way that is more elusive to smaller art museums. It is potentially in a superior position to recover from reduced corporate funding without needing to rely more heavily on public funds.

Conversely, it is possible that the author knows more than he has shared about a connection between public television watching and local museum attendance. For instance, there may have been some specific partnerships in the last eight years between local museums and local public television stations, including specific programming designed to tie in with current museum exhibitions. The recent survey to which the author alluded may have referenced direct ties between the television programming and museum attendance. Such data would make it more likely that increasing the public funding for public television would also directly benefit local museums.

Until more information is provided to us, however, we cannot accept the authors' argument for a shift in public funds to local public television as a way to support local art museums.

Analysis:

Structure: This essay is very well organized. The essayist's use of transitions is particularly strong here, as she leads the reader through the points of fault in the argument and describes evidence that could potentially strengthen the argument.

Evidence: The essayist provides multiple strong examples that strengthen her major points.

Depth of Logic: The essayist accurately identifies the assumptions inherent in the argument and develops her points by proposing plausible alternative explanations for the evidence the argument's author cites.

Style: The essayist has a few problems with misplaced apostrophes; otherwise, the grammar and syntax are strong.

This essay would score a 6. It is an excellent example of how following the Kaplan template will help you organize your ideas into a convincing essay. After the introduction, two paragraphs develop and support the author's two main points, followed by a paragraph describing how the argument could be strengthened and a clear conclusion.

Integrated Reasoning

The Integrated Reasoning section is either the second section or the next-to-last section of the GMAT, depending on which section order you choose. You'll have 30 minutes to complete the 12 questions it contains.

The Integrated Reasoning section consists of four unique question types. They are as follows:

- **Graphics Interpretation** questions contain two statements that must be completed using drop-down menus. The statements pertain to a graph, scatter plot, or other form of visual information.

- **Multi-Source Reasoning** questions provide given information in the form of text, charts, or tables spread across two or three tabbed pages. Some of the questions are traditional five-answer multiple-choice, while others consist of three true/false–style statements that must all be answered correctly in order to receive credit for the question.

- **Table Analysis** questions present information in the form of a sortable spreadsheet. Table Analysis questions feature the same true/false question format seen in Multi-Source Reasoning questions.

- **Two-Part Analysis** questions start out like an ordinary Quant or Verbal question, but instead of selecting one answer from five choices, you must select answers to two related questions from a common pool of six choices. The two answers can be the same.

SECTION FORMAT AND STRUCTURE

SCORING

The Integrated Reasoning section does not contribute to the total 200–800 GMAT score. Instead, it's scored on its own scale from 1 to 8, in whole-point increments.

With the exception of the occasional traditional multiple-choice question, every question in an Integrated Reasoning section requires two or three selections. There is no partial credit. Thus, getting two questions right and one question wrong on a three-part question in Table Analysis or

Multi-Source Reasoning is exactly the same as getting all three questions wrong. For more information about scoring, see Chapter 1: Introduction to the GMAT.

FORM AND CONTENT

Integrated Reasoning questions are designed to resemble the types of problems you will encounter in business school and in your business and management career. These questions focus on your ability to solve complex problems using data from multiple sources in a variety of formats.

In the Integrated Reasoning section, you must analyze different types of data (presented in graphs, tables, and passages, among other formats), synthesize data in verbal and graphical formats, and evaluate outcomes and trade-offs. Some of the data are presented in interactive formats, such as spreadsheets. You may need to sort data within columns to determine the answer or click on multiple tabbed pages to view additional information.

There are 12 questions in the Integrated Reasoning section, nearly all of which include multiple parts. For example, a single graph, discussion, or chart will be used as the basis for several parts of one question, and each question may measure a different skill set.

In this chapter, you will find two to three examples of each type of question set. You can practice with additional Integrated Reasoning questions, complete with answers and explanations, in the quizzes and practice tests in your online resources.

Because the questions in the Integrated Reasoning section vary greatly in form and content, flexibility will be key to success. Since Integrated Reasoning questions draw on many of the same skills you need for the Verbal and Quantitative sections, thorough practice with GMAT questions of all types is the best way to prepare for Integrated Reasoning.

LENGTH AND NAVIGATION

The new Integrated Reasoning section is 30 minutes long. Navigation on the Integrated Reasoning section, as on the rest of the GMAT, moves forward only. You may not skip questions and go back to them later, and you may not return to questions you have already answered. If you are unsure of the answer, you need to take your best guess and keep going.

Unlike the Quantitative and Verbal sections of the GMAT, the Integrated Reasoning section is not computer adaptive. Your performance on one question will not determine the difficulty of the one that follows.

USER INTERFACE

The Integrated Reasoning section looks very different from the rest of the GMAT. Because hands-on experience is the best way to learn the user interface, it is recommended that you practice with these question types in your Kaplan online resources.

In the Integrated Reasoning section, you will see question formats other than multiple choice. You may be required to select your answer from drop-down menus or true/false options. The new formats are straightforward and easy to use but look very different from the multiple-choice questions used in the Quantitative and Verbal sections and require some different techniques.

You will also need to understand how to navigate through spreadsheets and tabbed pages. Table Analysis questions present you with a table of data that can be sorted using a drop-down menu. Pay close attention to how the drop-down menu operates and make sure to consider all your sorting options. Multi-Source Reasoning questions require you to integrate information from several tabbed pages.

You have the use of an onscreen calculator for the Integrated Reasoning section *only*. You are not allowed to bring your own calculator into the exam. The calculator performs basic functions and can be accessed by clicking an icon on the screen. A calculator screen will then pop up over the question. The calculator looks like this:

Use caution when using the calculator. You run the risk of entering information incorrectly, resulting in a wrong answer; moreover, rounding and estimation are often much faster than the time-consuming process of entering multiple large numbers. Use the calculator only when necessary.

THE INTEGRATED REASONING QUESTION TYPES

Now that you have an idea of what to expect in the Integrated Reasoning section, let's examine each of the four question types.

GRAPHICS INTERPRETATION

Graphics Interpretation questions test your ability to interpret and analyze data presented visually in graphs or graphical images. For each question, you will see a graph with accompanying text and two questions.

As with a Reading Comprehension passage, you do not need to absorb every bit of information on the graph to answer the questions. What you *do* need to do is get the gist of the graph and what it contains so that you can efficiently find the information you need. You will then read the question stem, view the answer choices, and use the information in the graph to select the correct answer.

Graphics Interpretation questions feature many different types of graphs, including line graphs, scatter plots, Venn diagrams, and even geological timelines. Both examples in this chapter happen to focus on scatter plots, but don't take this as a sign that scatter plots are more important than any other type of graphic you may see on Test Day. We've chosen these as our examples because you're probably less familiar with scatter plots than with the other types of graphs commonly seen on the Integrated Reasoning section.

All graphics are accompanied by two incomplete sentences. Test takers must use a drop-down menu to select a word or phrase that completes the sentence according to the information presented in the graphic. Some of the sample graphs in this book are accompanied by more than two sentences in order to give you a better sense of the variety of questions you may be asked. The drop-down menus in this chapter are represented in multiple-choice format for ease of reading.

Let's take a look at some Graphics Interpretation questions.

Eruptions of the Old Faithful Geyser, Yellowstone National Park

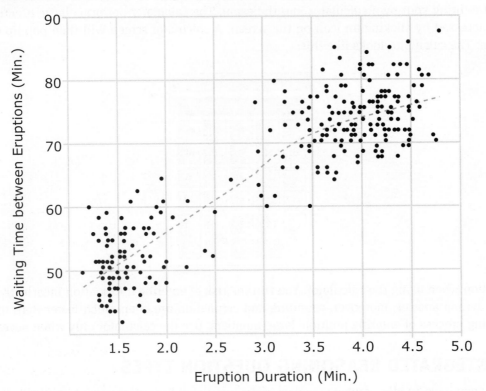

The graph above is a scatter plot with each point representing the duration of an eruption of Old Faithful, a geyser in Yellowstone National Park, and the time in minutes until the following eruption occurred. The dotted line represents a regression line. For each blank, select the answer choice that correctly completes the statement according to the information in the graph.

1a. The relationship between the duration of eruptions and the waiting time between eruptions is _____.

  ○ linear and positive
  ○ nonlinear and positive
  ○ linear and negative
  ○ nonlinear and negative

1b. The graph suggests that Old Faithful has _____ of eruption.

  ○ one type
  ○ two distinct types
  ○ more than two distinct types

1c. For an eruption of less than two minutes, the maximum recorded wait time is
_____ the minimum recorded wait time of an eruption of more than four
minutes.

- ○ greater than
- ○ equal to
- ○ less than

Get the Gist of the Graph

Your first step with a question of this type should be to read the text that accompanies the graph. You may see only a single sentence, or you may see (as in this case) a full paragraph. This text is important. Although most Graphics Interpretation questions can be answered without reference to the text, reading will give you an overview of the information the graph contains and how it is presented. On Test Day, taking a moment to paraphrase the written information will improve your understanding of the image, speeding up your analysis and reducing your chances of committing a careless error.

Here, the paragraph tells you that the graph shows the behavior of a single geyser, Old Faithful. The graph presents two types of information: how long the eruptions of Old Faithful last and how long it then takes before the next eruption happens. Each point on the graph represents an eruption.

Next, look at the graph itself. Get a bird's-eye view of the graph by reading the title and the labels of the axes and notice how the information from the paragraph is represented in the graph. Here, you'll notice that the duration, or length, of the eruption is measured against the waiting time that follows it before the next eruption. Now look at the units of measurement that correspond to each axis and determine whether the scales are similar. In this case, both axes are measured in minutes, but the scales are very different: the x-axis is measured in 0.5-minute increments, while the y-axis is measured in 10-minute increments. Furthermore, the x-axis starts at 1.0 and ends at 5.0, while the y-axis starts at 40 and goes to 90. Then notice if there are any specific features mentioned in the accompanying paragraph that you see represented on the graph, such as a regression line.

The final step before answering the questions is to look at the data to see if they fall into a general pattern. On this scatter plot, most of the data points separate into two distinct groups. With a pattern this clear, you can anticipate that this observation will be key to answering one or more of the accompanying questions. Making these observations before analyzing the questions will help you answer each question more effectively.

Answer the Questions

Question 1a: First, read and paraphrase the question. It asks about the relationship between the duration of eruptions and the waiting time between eruptions, which means that you are looking for a pattern in how the data points are arrayed on the graph. Before attempting to predict an answer, scan the answer choices. Here, you see the words *linear*, *nonlinear*, *positive*, and *negative*, which indicate that the pattern may take the shape and slope of a line. The regression line will help you here. There is more than one type of regression line, and in this case, the exact type of regression line has not been specified. But you should know that a regression line, however it is calculated, represents the overall trend of the points as a group. The regression line slopes upward—meaning the waiting time gets longer as the explosion duration gets longer. This is a positive relationship—both variables tend to increase and decrease together—so you can narrow the answer down to choices **(A)** and **(B)**. Next you need to determine whether the relationship is linear or nonlinear by looking at the shape of the regression line. You'll notice that the regression "line" isn't really a line, because its slope changes as the amounts of time get longer. Since the relationship isn't linear through the entire data set, the answer is **(B)**.

Question 1b: This question might seem a little tricky at first, since the way it's worded might make you think you need to know something qualitative about the types of eruptions the geyser experiences—perhaps something about their magnitude or geological characteristics. But the GMAT will never require you to have outside knowledge beyond high school math and general knowledge of grammar and logic. All the information you need to answer this question is contained in the graph. Begin by paraphrasing the question for yourself: Does Old Faithful have one, two, or more than two distinct types of eruption? As you noticed before, the data points separate themselves into two main clusters. There are a few stray data points scattered outside these clusters, but their number is not significant. Therefore, you can infer from the graph that Old Faithful has two types of eruptions, **(B)**.

Question 1c: For this question, you need to examine the data in the graph more closely. This statement contains a comparison between two data points: the maximum wait time for an eruption that lasts less than two minutes and the minimum wait time for an eruption that lasts more than four minutes. Note that you're asked to compare the wait times of these two points—that's their height along the y-axis. So this question asks you to find these two points and compare their heights. The first point is the highest point to the left of the two-minute line on the x-axis, which looks to be just below 65 on the y-axis. Now find the second point, the lowest point to the right of the four-minute line on the x-axis. The lowest point to the right of that line appears to be just below the 70-minute mark on the y-axis. The first point is therefore lower than the second, so you would choose "less than," **(C)**.

We've discussed how, before attacking any Graphics Interpretation question, you need to understand what the graph contains and how it is constructed. You can then target your research to answer each question correctly and efficiently. Try using these techniques on the next set of questions.

Public Elementary and High Schools, by State: 2008–2009

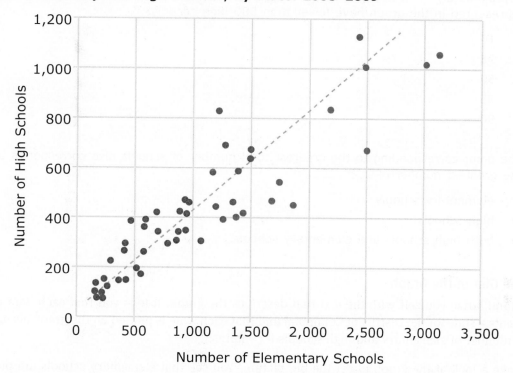

The graph above is a scatter plot with 49 points. The 49 points represent the number of elementary and high schools in 48 U.S. states and the District of Columbia (the numbers of schools in California and Texas are too large to appear on a graph of this scale). The dotted line represents a regression line. For each blank, select the answer choice that correctly completes the statement according to the information in the graph.

2a. The slope of the regression line is _____.

    O   greater than 1

    O   approximately 1

    O   less than 1

2b. Approximately _____ percent of the 49 states (including the District of Columbia) represented in the graph have fewer than 500 elementary schools.

    O   10

    O   25

    O   50

    O   75

    O   90

2c. Approximately _____ percent of the 49 states (including the District of Columbia) represented in the graph have fewer than 500 high schools.

- ○ 10
- ○ 25
- ○ 50
- ○ 75
- ○ 90

2d. The point corresponding to the greatest total number of schools also corresponds to the greatest number of _____.

- ○ elementary schools
- ○ high schools
- ○ both high schools and elementary schools

Get the Gist of the Graph

First, familiarize yourself with the text that describes the graph. It tells you that each data point represents a state (or the District of Columbia) and that each state is plotted on the graph according to the number of elementary and high schools it contains.

Now take a look at the graph to get the big picture. You see that elementary schools are plotted along the *x*-axis and high schools along the *y*-axis. In this case, both axes begin at zero, but again the scales of the two axes are different. The axis for elementary schools increases in increments of 500, while the axis for high schools moves up more slowly, in increments of 200. Looking at the points with these increments in mind, you can see that the states generally have more elementary schools than high schools. Again, you see a pattern in the graph; the data points and the regression line trend upward. That pattern makes sense—states that have more kids or higher populations are generally going to need more schools of both types.

Answer the Questions

Question 2a: First read the question; then glance at the answer choices. Again, as a Kaplan-trained test taker, you'll see how important it is to look at the answer choices before predicting an answer; this important step will save you time on Test Day. You'll notice that your only choices are a slope greater than, equal to, or less than 1. Think about what it means for a line to have a slope of 1. It rises at the same rate that it moves to the right. A line with a slope of 1 usually makes a 45-degree angle with the *x*- and *y*-axes. The line on this graph looks to be about 45 degrees, so does it have a slope of 1? If you said no, you just avoided an important trap in this question. A line with a slope of 1 makes a 45-degree angle with the *x*- and *y*-axes only when the scales of both axes are the same. But here, the scales are not the same; the numbers on the *y*-axis move upward much more slowly than the numbers on the *x*-axis. Remember the formula for the slope of a line:

$$\text{Slope} = \frac{\text{Change in } y}{\text{Change in } x}, \text{ or to put it another way, Slope} = \frac{\text{Rise}}{\text{Run}}$$

On this graph, the change in *y* is a lot less than the corresponding change in *x*. So the slope will be less than 1. You can test this out quickly using some approximate points from the graph. The regression line is close to the points (500, 200) and (1,000, 400). As the line moves up by 200, it moves to the right by 500. Plugging these points into the slope formula above, you get $\frac{400-200}{1000-500}$, which reduces to $\frac{2}{5}$, a positive fraction less than 1. **(C)** is correct.

Question 2b: This question asks about elementary schools only, so focus on the x-axis and count the number of points that fall to the left of the 500 mark on that axis. This number appears to be about 13 points. (The exact number does not matter, as the question is asking for an approximate percentage.) Since you want to know what percentage these states represent out of all the states on the graph, you can set up a fraction: 13 over the total number of data points, which the paragraph accompanying the graph tells you is 49. Using estimation, $\frac{13}{49} \approx \frac{13}{50}$, which when converted to a percentage is equal to 26 percent. The closest answer is **(B)**.

Question 2c: This question looks similar to the previous question, except it is asking about high schools, which are measured on the y-axis. This time, you need to estimate the percentage of schools that are below 500 on the y-axis. Rather than counting up all the points below 500, which would be a time-consuming task, count the points *above* 500, find the percentage that those points represent, and subtract that percentage from 100. In this case, you have about 13 points above 500, representing approximately 25% of the total (you might recall this same calculation from the previous question). Subtracting this percentage from 100% leaves you with 75%, or **(D)**.

Question 2d: Read the question and notice that you are looking for a particular point: the state with the greatest total number of schools. There are two points in the upper right portion of the graph that look like they could be the answer: the point highest on the y-axis and the point farthest to the right on the x-axis. Also, recall that the axes are scaled differently and the increments on the x-axis increase much more quickly than those on the y-axis. The point farthest to the right, then, will have the greatest number of schools. The state represented by this point has the greatest total number of elementary schools, but it does not have the greatest number of high schools. The answer is **(A)**.

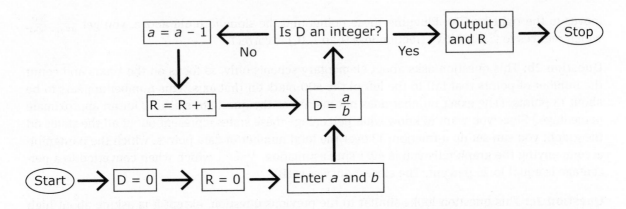

The flowchart represents a computer algorithm that takes two positive integers as the input and is intended to return two integers as the output. Each process is symbolized by an equation, such as $a = a - 1$. In this particular process, 1 is subtracted from the current value of the variable a, and the difference then becomes the value of a. For example, if the value of a is 5 before the process $a = a - 1$ is completed, then the value of a will be 4 after the process is completed. Algorithms that are incorrectly formed may sometimes get stuck in an infinite loop. An infinite loop is a sequence of instructions that never terminates. Complete the following statements by making selections from the drop-down menus in accordance with the algorithm represented by the flowchart.

3a. If 58 and 11 are entered as the values for a and b, respectively, then one of the outputs of the function will be _____.

○   D = 0
○   D = 4
○   D = 55
○   R = 3
○   R = 4

3b. The algorithm will get stuck in an infinite loop

○   if $a > b$
○   if $a = b$
○   if $a < b$
○   never

Get the Gist of the Flowchart

Paraphrase what the algorithm does. First, D is set to $\frac{a}{b}$. Then, if D is an integer, the algorithm outputs D and R and stops. If D is not an integer, then a is decreased by 1 and R is increased by 1, and the process repeats. Thus, the loop will keep repeating until $\frac{a}{b}$ is an integer, at which point it will output the value of D (which is $\frac{a}{b}$) and R (which is the number of times the algorithm divided a by b and didn't get an integer).

If you try a few examples, you might notice that this algorithm isn't just a random sequence of steps: the outputs are the integer part (D) and the remainder (R) when a is divided by b. R also acts as a "counter" of the number of times the algorithm loops before stopping. For example, given

$a = 13$ and $b = 5$, the outputs are D $= 2$ and R $= 3$, because $\frac{13}{5}$ equals 2 with a remainder of 3, and the algorithm will loop 3 times before it stops.

Answer the Questions

Question 3a: The first time through the loop, D will be set to $\frac{58}{11}$, a will be set to $58 - 1 = 57$, and R will be set to $0 + 1 = 1$. The second time through the loop, D will be set to $\frac{57}{11}$, a will be set to $57 - 1 = 56$, and R will be set to $1 + 1 = 2$. The third time through the loop, D will be set to $\frac{56}{11}$, a will be set to $56 - 1 = 55$, and R will be set to $2 + 1 = 3$. On the fourth time through the loop, D will be set to $\frac{55}{11} = 5$, which is an integer, so the algorithm will stop and the values of a and R will not be changed. Thus, the outputs are D $= 5$ and R $= 3$. D $= 5$ is not present among the selections, but R $= 3$ is. The correct answer is **(D)**.

Question 3b: If $a > b$, then you've already seen that the algorithm will stop. If $a = b$, then the algorithm will also stop, because a number divided by itself always equals 1 with a remainder of 0. If $a < b$, it may seem that the algorithm will get stuck because D will keep getting set to a fraction. For example, if $a = 9$ and $b = 10$, D will get set to $\frac{9}{10}$, then $\frac{8}{10}$, then $\frac{7}{10}$, and so on. However, a will eventually be reduced to 0, at which point $\frac{a}{b}$ will equal 0 (which is an integer) and the algorithm will stop. Thus, no matter the values of a and b, the algorithm's termination condition is always triggered. This means that it will never not stop, which is **(D)**.

MULTI-SOURCE REASONING

As its name suggests, Multi-Source Reasoning tests your ability to take information from multiple sources and synthesize it to answer questions. The information will be presented on two to three tabbed pages. You will have to click through the tabs to find the information you need. The data can be in the form of text, charts, or tables and may be presented in a combination of all three.

The information on the tabs may seem overwhelming, so you'll need to approach it similarly to how you approach Reading Comprehension. Get the gist of what the tabs contain and take brief notes highlighting the main points of each tab. Don't try to absorb all of the information at first, but make sure you scan all of the information on each tab so that you'll know where to find it when you answer the questions.

The tabbed pages are on the left side of the screen, and the questions are on the right. There may be more than one page of questions associated with a prompt, in which case you must click on the Next button to advance to the next page of questions. You can get hands-on experience with tabbed pages in your online resources. Take a few minutes to become familiar with the navigation of this section. Doing so will save you valuable time when answering the questions.

Some of the questions about the tabbed information will be in the standard multiple-choice format that you're familiar with from the Verbal and Quantitative sections. Others, called multiple dichotomous choice questions, will require you to evaluate multiple statements individually; you may be required to figure out whether statements are true or whether certain expenditures are within a given budget. Each of these yes/no or true/false questions will require you to evaluate three separate statements.

| American Pets | Table #1 | Table #2 |

78.4 million dogs and 86.4 million cats are owned as pets in the U.S. Though some pets come from breeders, many others are adopted from shelters and pounds. Even though 78 percent of pet dogs and 88 percent of pet cats are spayed or neutered, there has never been a shortage of animals available for adoption. The result of these staggering numbers of animals is a booming industry of pet supplies, services, and medical care.

Tables 1 and 2, respectively, indicate the average one-time adoption costs and average annual expenses associated with pet ownership. However, dogs vary significantly in size; small dogs such as chihuahuas cost on average 25 percent less than the values shown in the adoption and ownership cost tables, while larger canines such as mastiffs often cost 50 percent more.

| American Pets | Table #1 | Table #2 |

Average Per-Animal Adoption Expenses in America

	Dog	**Cat**
Spay/neuter	$100	$75
Collar/leash	$30	$10
Litter box	—	$20
Carrier	$40	$30
Sleeper crate	$80	—

| American Pets | Table #1 | Table #2 |

Average Per-Animal Annual Ownership Expenses in America

	Dog	**Cat**
Food	$250	$215
Veterinary	$240	$210
Litter	—	$150
Toys/treats	$60	$40
License	$25	—
House cleaning	$50	$50

4. Consider each of the following statements. Does the information in the passage and tables support the inference as stated? Choose *Yes* if the statement can be accurately inferred; otherwise choose *No*.

Yes	No	
○	○	Americans spend over $10 billion annually on toys and treats for their cats and dogs.
○	○	The average cost of adopting an average small dog and keeping it for a year is less than the cost of doing so for an average cat.
○	○	The number of categories of expenses unique to cats is the same as the number of categories unique to dogs.

5. Based on the information in the passage and tables, the total cost of spaying or neutering all unspayed and non-neutered pet cats and dogs in America would be closest to

- ○ $2.5 billion
- ○ $4.0 billion
- ○ $12 billion
- ○ $14.5 billion
- ○ $27.5 billion

Get the Gist of the Tabbed Pages

We approached Graphics Interpretation by first getting a general sense of how the graph works. Similarly, you need to know what is on each tabbed page before you begin answering Multi-Source Reasoning questions. Take brief notes on the content of each tab as you examine it. In the first tab, the text gives you data about the number of American pets and the frequency of spaying and neutering. It then goes on to describe the tables in the next two tabs. More specifically, the first table will show the one-time costs of adopting an animal in the United States, and the second table will focus on yearly expenses. Finally, it gives us an important warning: the data in the tabs are averages, and some dogs will require very different expenses according to their size.

Next, move to the second tab. Here, you are given a table with rows indicating several adoption expenses, separated into a column for dogs and a column for cats. Notice that not all expenses apply to both types of animal. The total cost of adoption isn't calculated for you, but you could find it with simple addition if necessary.

Switch to the third tab to view another table. This one also shows expenses for dogs and cats. Rather than listing one-time expenses, this lists the repeating yearly costs of those pets. Other than that, it's similar in structure to Table 1.

Answer the Questions

Question 4a: You can expect two things on a yes/no question like this. First, the answer will require you to look at two or three tabs. Second, the question will reward estimation.

Table 2 in the third tab gives the annual cost of toys and treats, but that cost is per animal. Calculating the total expenditure for all pets requires knowing the total number of pets. To look for that data you should check your notes, which will send you to the first tab. According to the combined data from Tabs 1 and 3, there are approximately 80 million (rounded from 78.4 million) dogs in America, and their treats and toys cost an average of $60 per dog, meaning the total toy and treat expense for dogs would be about $4.8 billion. The same tabs tell you that there are approximately 90 million (rounded from 86.4 million) cats and their owners spend an average of $40 for toys and treats per cat, meaning owners spend about $3.6 billion annually on toys and treats for cats. The combined total for money spent on cat and dog treats and toys is therefore only a little over $8 billion. Even though this is a high estimate (since both of the values above were estimated by rounding up), it's still less than $10 billion, so the answer is "No."

Question 4b: This problem requires you to total the adoption and annual ownership costs. You will need information from the tables in the second and third tabs. You'll also need to do some addition, if you haven't already, to total up the costs in each column.

If you add all of the expenses for cats, the total comes out to $800 for adopting and owning a cat for a year. For a dog the same costs $875, although if you were rounding to speed up the addition, you might have ended up with $850 or $900. Regardless, at first glance it seems clear-cut that the dog will cost more than the cat.

But something should have caught your eye: this question specifies a "small" dog. When you paraphrased the tabs, you noticed that size is mentioned briefly in Tab 1. Researching that tab will reveal that small dogs average 25% less money to adopt and keep. Because 25% (or one-fourth) of $875 is well over $200 ($875 × 0.25 = $218.75, but it's probably not worth calculating exactly), the cost reduction of having a small dog easily offsets the initial $75 difference you calculated between the cost of a dog and that of a cat. A small dog is therefore cheaper than a cat, so the answer is "Yes."

Question 4c: This question requires only simple counting, but you need to know what you're looking for. "Categories of expenses unique to cats" means expenses that are paid only for cats, not for dogs. Since this doesn't specify which expenses, look in both tabs that list expenses, Tables 1 and 2.

Litter box and litter are the two categories unique to cats. Sleeper crate and license are the two categories unique to dogs. Both animals have two unique categories, the same number, so the answer to this question is "Yes."

Question 5: This question asks you for the cost of spaying or neutering all unspayed and non-neutered dogs and cats in America. A glance at the answer choices can provide an important hint, as many of the answer choices are quite far apart. With numbers this big and this spread out in the answer choices, it's usually best to estimate.

Spaying and neutering statistics, as well as numbers of pets, are in the first tab. Researching this background information reveals that 22% of 78.4 million dogs and 12% of 86.4 million cats are unspayed or non-neutered. To estimate, instead say 20% of 80 million = 16 million dogs and 10% of 90 million = 9 million cats are unspayed or non-neutered.

Spaying and neutering are one-time expenditures, so the second tab contains the price. At $100 each, it will cost about $1.6 billion to spay or neuter 16 million dogs. At $75 per cat, it will cost $675 million, or about $0.68 billion, to spay or neuter 9 million cats.

The combined cost of spaying or neutering all unspayed and non-neutered dogs and cats is therefore about $2.3 billion. Although the estimate above rounds both percentages significantly down, it rounds the number of animals of both types up to compensate, so the resulting estimate is likely close to the real solution; regardless, the next closest answer choice ($4 billion) can't be correct unless the above estimation is off by more than 50%. Verify that you calculated the number of decimal places correctly and didn't confuse millions with billions. Once you've double-checked the accuracy of your estimations and calculations, you can see that $2.5 billion is closest and confidently choose **(A)** as the correct answer.

You've learned from working through this set of Multi-Source Reasoning questions that it's crucial to get the gist of each tabbed page and take brief notes highlighting the main points before attempting to answer any questions. Now apply these techniques to the next set of Multi-Source Reasoning questions.

Email #1	Email #2	Email #3

*Email from **project manager** to financial officer*

August 3, 9:43 a.m.

Did all three bids arrive on time last night? We need to minimize delays on construction, so if the contractors have submitted their estimates and our research team has compiled reports on the contractors' histories, we should make a decision on which firm to hire by the end of the day.

Email #1	Email #2	Email #3

*Email from **financial officer** in response to the project manager's August 3, 9:43 a.m. email*

August 3, 10:12 a.m.

Appaloosa Construction sent us a bid of $1.35 million. Its bid is the highest of the three, but its track record is spotless; none of the past 10 major projects it has worked on has gone over budget by more than 4 percent. Breton Construction did manage to underbid them—its representative claims that it can do the project for $1.25 million. However, in the past two years, Breton oversaw two different projects that went over budget by a full 25 percent. If our project were to exceed Breton's estimate by a comparable percentage, we would run out of funds before completion. Finally, Campolina Construction presented a $1.1 million plan, and its track record is as good as Appaloosa's. Unfortunately, although Appaloosa and Breton can both start tomorrow, Campolina would be unable to begin work until August 25, so we cannot accept Campolina's low bid.

Email #1	Email #2	Email #3

*Email from **project manager** in response to the financial officer's August 3, 10:12 a.m. email*

August 3, 10:38 a.m.

Even though Breton's work could potentially cost less than either of the other two, that savings does not justify the risk of being unable to complete the project. But as far as Campolina is concerned, you're not considering the actual cost of a delay. It's true that we are losing money at a constant rate each day we don't start building. But even after factoring in the losses of waiting until August 25, the estimated cost of working with Campolina still ends up $50,000 below Appaloosa's bid.

6. Consider each of the following statements. Does the information in the three emails support the inferences as stated? Choose *Yes* if the statement can be accurately inferred; otherwise, choose *No*.

Yes	No	
○	○	In making their decision, the project manager and the financial officer considered how much time the contractors would spend on construction.
○	○	The project manager and the financial officer disagree about the best choice of contractors for completing the project.
○	○	The project manager is willing to wait a few days before deciding on Campolina's bid.

7. The amount of money lost each day that construction is delayed is closest to

    ○ $2,500
    ○ $10,000
    ○ $20,000
    ○ $55,000
    ○ $65,000

Get the Gist of the Tabbed Pages

First, look through the tabbed pages and notice the basics: you have three emails, sent minutes apart, between a project manager and a financial officer. Use your Reading Comprehension Passage Mapping skills to create a brief synopsis of each email in your scratchwork:

Email 1—project manager to financial officer:

- Asking about the bids
- Start construction as soon as possible
- Make a decision by the end of the day

Email 2—financial officer to project manager:

- Appaloosa—$1.35 million—great track record
- Breton—$1.25 million—usually over budget—would run out of funds before completion
- Campolina—$1.1 million—can't begin work until August 25—can't accept

Think strategically here: although the financial officer never draws an explicit conclusion about which company should be hired, his opinion is clear. Breton could cause the company to run out of money for the project, and Campolina's delayed start date is unacceptable, so the financial officer must be in favor of Appaloosa.

Email 3—project manager to financial officer:

- Breton—not worth the risk
- Reminder about the cost of delay
- Campolina is still cheaper, even with the delay

It is not necessary to jot down all of the figures and calculations from the email. Just as with Reading Comprehension, if you need the details, they will be there for you to refer to later.

Answer the Questions

Question 6: Notice that you have another set of yes/no questions. As always, you'll want to read the introductory sentences very carefully. Your task is to consider whether the inferences in the questions are supported by the information in the three emails. Critical Reasoning skills will help you here; you must use *only* the evidence in the three emails to determine your answers.

Question 6a: Read carefully here. Time is discussed, but it is discussed in reference to when the construction can begin, not how long it will take. There isn't any mention of the length of construction in your notes, and if you glance through the three emails, there isn't any information there either. The answer is "No."

Question 6b: This question asks whether the project manager and financial officer disagree about who would be the best contractor. The answer to this question, as seen in your notes on the emails, is "Yes." The project manager thinks Campolina is the best choice, and the financial officer is in favor of Appaloosa.

Question 6c: The wording of this statement is tricky, so answer it by doing some careful research in the emails. Here, the question asks whether the project manager is willing to wait a few days to decide. Glance at your notes to find relevant keywords: "decide" is mentioned in the first email, and "delay," or waiting, is mentioned in the third. Going to the first email, you see that the project manager wants to reach a decision by the end of the day. This seems to contradict the inference given in the question, but don't stop just yet. Check the third email to see whether the project manager changed her mind. In the third email, the project manager discusses waiting, stating that it might be acceptable to wait to begin construction with Campolina—but there is nothing in this email about waiting to make a decision. Thus, you cannot infer that the project manager is willing to wait a few days, and the answer here is "No."

Question 7: By now, you can expect that you'll need to find information in multiple emails to answer this question. Looking at your notes, you see that the delay costs are discussed in the third email. The email states that a constant amount is lost every day that construction is delayed. From the second email, you find that the other two companies can start the next day, August 4, but Campolina can't start until August 25, a delay of 21 days. Next, use the information given to determine how much money is lost in those 21 days.

The third email says that even with the delay, Campolina would cost $50,000 less than Appaloosa's $1.35 million bid, or $1.3 million. That means the cost caused by the delay would be $1.3 million − $1.1 million, or $200,000. To determine the cost per day, calculate $\frac{\$200,000}{21} \approx \$9,524$. However, since the question asks for the number that's "closest to" the amount lost per day, you can save time by estimating. Round 21 to 20 and calculate much more easily that $200,000 divided by 20 is $10,000, or **(B)**.

Email #1	Email #2	Email #3

*Email from **CEO** to store manager*

April 10, 2:53 a.m.

I just got a call from the police. Our store on Thompson street was robbed again. This is the third time in exactly seven months. After the first robbery, you said you would heighten security, but the measures you took had no effect; 60 days later the same store was robbed. Then you said you'd install an alarm system, but I guess you never got around to that. After the second robbery, the insurance company threatened to cancel our account if the store was robbed again and we hadn't done anything to increase the security of the premises. What am I supposed to tell them?

Email #1	Email #2	Email #3

*Email from **store manager** in response to the CEO's April 10, 2:53 a.m. text*

April 10, 3:38 a.m.

I had an alarm system installed within a week after the second robbery. It took the police exactly four minutes to get to the store after the alarm was triggered; the robber was in and out in three. The alarm company called me after calling the police, and I still beat the police to the scene. I've told the alarm company to call me first next time—I missed the robber by no more than 30 seconds.

You can tell the insurance company that the measures I undertook after the first robbery did have a major impact. We started moving inventory from the shelves to the back room before closing the store each day. This cut our losses in the second robbery by nearly 70 percent as compared to the first robbery. I've attached the exact numbers for your perusal. After the second robbery, we began leaving even less inventory on the shelves. It's too soon to tell exactly how much money we lost in this morning's robbery, but my survey indicates that the losses are about another 40 percent smaller than those of the second robbery.

Email #1	Email #2	Email #3

*Attachment to the **store manager's** April 10, 3:38 a.m. email*

Value of Stolen Inventory

Robbery	Cameras	Tripods	Lenses	Accessories
First	$45,652	$9,834	$2,119	$589
Second	$11,000	$4,832	$1,003	$672

8. If the manager's estimates are correct and if the tripods stolen in the third robbery account for 15 percent of the value of the stolen inventory, then the value of the stolen tripods is closest to

   ○ $800
   ○ $1,100
   ○ $1,600
   ○ $2,100
   ○ $4,800

9. For each of the following statements, select *True* if the statement can be verified to be true assuming that the information in the emails (but not necessarily the attachment) is accurate. Otherwise, select *False*.

True	False	
○	○	An alarm system was installed at the store in November.
○	○	Upon being reached by phone, the store manager can make it to the store in under five minutes.
○	○	The attachment contradicts the store manager.

10. For each of the following statements, select *Yes* if the statement can be reasonably inferred from the emails and the attachment. Otherwise, select *No*.

Yes	No	
○	○	The robbery could have been prevented if the store manager had installed shatterproof windows.
○	○	The alarm company's phone call to the police lasted less than 45 seconds.
○	○	The value of the lenses stolen in the third robbery is less than that of the second robbery.

Get the Gist of the Tabbed Pages

Email 1—CEO to store manager

- 3 robberies
- Assumes manager's security measures had no effect/weren't done.
- Problem: What to tell the insurance company?

Email 2—Store manager to CEO

- After 1st robbery, moved inventory, cutting losses in 2nd robbery.
- After 2nd robbery, had alarm installed—but robber was fast.
- After 2nd robbery, moved more inventory, cutting losses in 3rd robbery.

Attachment to email 2—Value of stolen goods in 1st vs. 2nd robbery

- As manager claims, much less overall was stolen in 2nd robbery.

Answer the Questions

Question 8: The store manager's email states that there was an estimated 40% reduction in losses from the second robbery to the third. The total losses of the second robbery were about $18,000, so the losses of the third robbery were about $18,000 × 60%, or about $11,000. Then 15% of that is about $1,650, which is closest to **(C)**.

Question 9a: The CEO's text message states that the first robbery was exactly seven months ago and that the second robbery happened 60 days later. The current day is April 10, so the first robbery happened around September 10 and the second on November 10. The store manager's email states that the alarm was installed within a week of the second robbery, so there was indeed an alarm installed in November. The answer is "True."

Question 9b: According to the second email, the store manager missed the robber by 30 seconds. Since the robber was in and out in 3 minutes, the maximum time it could have taken for the store manager to reach the store was 3 minutes and 30 seconds. The answer is "True."

Question 9c: The total losses of the first robbery were $58,194. The total losses of the second robbery were $17,507. This is a percent change of $\frac{58,194 - 17,507}{58,194}$, or 69.9%, which confirms the store manager's claim that the reduction in losses was "nearly 70 percent." The answer is "False."

Question 10a: There's no information in the tabs about how the robber broke into the store. Thus, there's no way to tell whether shatterproof windows would have made any difference. The answer is "No."

Question 10b: The store manager's email states that he or she missed the robber by 30 seconds. This means that the alarm company's phone call to the police (whom they called first) lasted at least 30 seconds, but there's no way to tell whether that call was longer or shorter than 45 seconds. The answer is "No."

Question 10c: According to the store manager, the total losses of the third robbery are 40% less than those of the second robbery. However, the store manager doesn't say that the losses are proportional in all categories. It's possible that decreases in losses for other goods compensated for an increase in losses for lenses. The answer is "No."

TABLE ANALYSIS

Table Analysis questions measure your ability to interpret and analyze information presented in a sortable table similar to a spreadsheet. You will see a table, a paragraph of text that describes it, and one set of the same three-part multiple dichotomous choice questions you saw for Multi-Source Reasoning (i.e., yes/no, true/false, etc.).

Directly above the table, you will see a Sort button that, when clicked, opens a drop-down menu of options that correspond to the column headers in the table. When you select a category from the drop-down menu, the entire chart will be sorted based on the category you select. If the information in that column is numerical, it will be sorted from lowest to highest. If the information in that column is text, it will be sorted in alphabetical order. While working through the questions in this book, decide how you would sort the information before answering each question. To gain experience sorting tables in the test interface, use the questions in your online resources.

Read the text that accompanies the table first to get an overview of the table's content. Then look at the table itself, paying special attention to the column headings. Now let's look at some Table Analysis questions.

Total Fall Enrollment in Private Degree-Granting Institutions: 2008

Sort By Select... ▼

| | Undergraduate | | | | | Postbaccalaureate | | |
| | 4-year | | 2-year | | | | | |
	Total	Not-for-profit	For-profit	Not-for-profit	For-profit	Total	Not-for-profit	For-profit
Alabama	58,558	23,229	34,000	0	1,329	7,343	4,128	3,215
Arizona	291,869	3,539	275,530	0	12,800	81,066	4,507	76,559
California	264,775	136,304	76,356	2,375	49,740	147,979	129,522	18,457
Colorado	69,460	18,375	40,733	165	10,187	20,507	13,586	6,921
District of Columbia	71,465	37,967	33,498	0	0	49,061	36,575	12,486
Florida	206,477	106,089	79,732	152	20,504	56,629	48,067	8,562
Georgia	76,356	47,701	23,670	1,057	3,928	23,757	17,940	5,817
Illinois	200,263	134,075	56,676	1,126	8,386	98,568	86,235	12,333
Indiana	88,896	68,677	13,020	495	6,704	16,110	15,652	458
Iowa	113,385	45,397	67,601	151	236	16,487	10,919	5,568
Massachusetts	173,897	166,873	2,800	1,737	2,487	97,339	97,203	136
Michigan	101,252	93,562	4,649	0	3,041	23,507	22,870	637
Minnesota	78,855	50,793	25,723	106	2,233	75,567	21,232	54,335
Missouri	117,735	95,299	12,510	2,275	7,651	49,937	49,298	639
New York	390,435	341,205	24,241	6,575	18,414	168,531	166,449	2,082
North Carolina	75,228	68,524	4,635	572	1,497	18,773	18,039	734
Ohio	146,395	107,277	7,044	1,272	30,802	31,669	30,621	1,048
Pennsylvania	251,369	195,359	17,783	7,492	30,735	83,943	83,372	571
Tennessee	75,283	54,023	8,373	278	12,609	18,187	17,097	1,090
Texas	127,359	92,495	12,935	867	21,062	36,657	33,996	2,661
Virginia	90,439	59,959	24,416	0	6,064	27,236	24,789	2,447

The table above gives the 2008 enrollment in private degree-granting institutions for the 20 states with the highest total enrollment, as well as for the District of Columbia. These statistics do not include state-funded and federally funded public institutions. The data include both for-profit and not-for-profit institutions; enrollment for both of these categories is provided in addition to the total enrollment.

11. Consider the following statements about enrollment in the 21 states (including the District of Columbia) shown in the table. For each statement, indicate whether the statement is *True* or *False*, based on the information provided in the table.

True	False	
○	○	The state with the largest number of students enrolled in for-profit four-year undergraduate programs has the smallest number of students enrolled in not-for-profit four-year undergraduate programs.
○	○	The state with the median number of students enrolled in not-for-profit four-year undergraduate programs also has the median number of students enrolled in not-for-profit two-year undergraduate programs.
○	○	More than half of the students enrolled in degree-granting programs in Minnesota attend for-profit schools.

Get the Gist of the Table

As with Graphics Interpretation questions, your first step should be to read the text accompanying the table. Here, the text explains that the table shows the private school enrollment numbers for various states, as well as for the District of Columbia, in 2008. It also tells you that the table distinguishes between for-profit and not-for-profit institutions.

Next, look at the table itself and read the column headings. The private institutions are split into two main categories, undergraduate and postbaccalaureate, which are further broken down into for-profit and not-for-profit schools. The undergraduate schools are also divided into two- and four-year programs. Total enrollment numbers for undergraduate and postbaccalaureate programs are also provided. This is a lot of information, and you will need to pay attention to how it is organized in order to answer the questions.

Answer the Questions

Question 11a: Many Table Analysis questions ask you to compare pieces of information. Take each question one piece at a time. For this question, you first need to find the state with the largest enrollment in for-profit four-year undergraduate schools. Look at your table and find the column that contains that information. Here, it's easy to see that Arizona has the highest enrollment, with 275,530 students. If you weren't able to see that at a glance, you could sort the table by the for-profit four-year undergraduate column. Now that you have the first piece of information, it's time to find the second. You now know that you're looking for information about Arizona. Sort the table by the not-for-profit four-year undergraduate column, and you'll see that Arizona is by far the lowest, at 3,539 students. Arizona, the state with the largest for-profit four-year undergraduate enrollment, does in fact have the smallest not-for-profit four-year undergraduate enrollment, so the answer is "True."

Question 11b: Here, you are asked again to compare two pieces of information. By now, you should be zeroing in on the keywords in the statement that will tell you how to sort the table. In this case, you are looking for the "not-for-profit four-year undergraduate" column and the "not-for-profit two-year undergraduate" column. Also notice the keyword "median," which appears twice. You need to sort two columns and compare the median numbers. The median number of each set will appear exactly in the middle of the set when all the terms are placed in ascending or descending order. You won't be able to eyeball the median number, so get ready to use the Sort function. First, sort by not-for-profit four-year undergraduate institutions:

Sort By [Undergraduate 4-year Not-for-profit | ▼]

| | | Undergraduate | | | | Postbaccalaureate | | |
| | | 4-year | | 2-year | | | | |
	Total	Not-for-profit	For-profit	Not-for-profit	For-profit	Total	Not-for-profit	For-profit
Arizona	291,869	3,539	275,530	0	12,800	81,066	4,507	76,559
Colorado	69,460	18,375	40,733	165	10,187	20,507	13,586	6,921
Alabama	58,558	23,229	34,000	0	1,329	7,343	4,128	3,215
District of Columbia	71,465	37,967	33,498	0	0	49,061	36,575	12,486
Iowa	113,385	45,397	67,601	151	236	16,487	10,919	5,568
Georgia	76,356	47,701	23,670	1,057	3,928	23,757	17,940	5,817
Minnesota	78,855	50,793	25,723	106	2,233	75,567	21,232	54,335
Tennessee	75,283	54,023	8,373	278	12,609	18,187	17,097	1,090
Virginia	90,439	59,959	24,416	0	6,064	27,236	24,789	2,447
North Carolina	75,228	68,524	4,635	572	1,497	18,773	18,039	734
Indiana	88,896	68,677	13,020	495	6,704	16,110	15,652	458
Texas	127,359	92,495	12,935	867	21,062	36,657	33,996	2,661
Michigan	101,252	93,562	4,649	0	3,041	23,507	22,870	637
Missouri	117,735	95,299	12,510	2,275	7,651	49,937	49,298	639
Florida	206,477	106,089	79,732	152	20,504	56,629	48,067	8,562
Ohio	146,395	107,277	7,044	1,272	30,802	31,669	30,621	1,048
Illinois	200,263	134,075	56,676	1,126	8,386	98,568	86,235	12,333
California	264,775	136,304	76,356	2,375	49,740	147,979	129,522	18,457
Massachusetts	173,897	166,873	2,800	1,737	2,487	97,339	97,203	136
Pennsylvania	251,369	195,359	17,783	7,492	30,735	83,943	83,372	571
New York	390,435	341,205	24,241	6,575	18,414	168,531	166,449	2,082

There are 21 states in this table, so you will be looking for the 11th state. To calculate which line you're looking for in a table with an odd number of lines, you can always use the following formula: Median $= \frac{\text{Total} - 1}{2} + 1$.

In this example, $\frac{21-1}{2} + 1 = 10 + 1 = 11$. According to the sorted chart, the 11th state is Indiana. Once you know to focus on Indiana, sort the table by not-for-profit two-year undergraduate institutions:

Sort By [Undergraduate 2-year Not-for-profit ▼]

		Undergraduate				Postbaccalaureate		
		4-year		2-year				
	Total	Not-for-profit	For-profit	Not-for-profit	For-profit	Total	Not-for-profit	For-profit
Arizona	291,869	3,539	275,530	0	12,800	81,066	4,507	76,559
Michigan	101,252	93,562	4,649	0	3,041	23,507	22,870	637
Virginia	90,439	59,959	24,416	0	6,064	27,236	24,789	2,447
District of Columbia	71,465	37,967	33,498	0	0	49,061	36,575	12,486
Alabama	58,558	23,229	34,000	0	1,329	7,343	4,128	3,215
Minnesota	78,855	50,793	25,723	106	2,233	75,567	21,232	54,335
Iowa	113,385	45,397	67,601	151	236	16,487	10,919	5,568
Florida	206,477	106,089	79,732	152	20,504	56,629	48,067	8,562
Colorado	69,460	18,375	40,733	165	10,187	20,507	13,586	6,921
Tennessee	75,283	54,023	8,373	278	12,609	18,187	17,097	1,090
Indiana	88,896	68,677	13,020	495	6,704	16,110	15,652	458
North Carolina	75,228	68,524	4,635	572	1,497	18,773	18,039	734
Texas	127,359	92,495	12,935	867	21,062	36,657	33,996	2,661
Georgia	76,356	47,701	23,670	1,057	3,928	23,757	17,940	5,817
Illinois	200,263	134,075	56,676	1,126	8,386	98,568	86,235	12,333
Ohio	146,395	107,277	7,044	1,272	30,802	31,669	30,621	1,048
Massachusetts	173,897	166,873	2,800	1,737	2,487	97,339	97,203	136
Missouri	117,735	95,299	12,510	2,275	7,651	49,937	49,298	639
California	264,775	136,304	76,356	2,375	49,740	147,979	129,522	18,457
New York	390,435	341,205	24,241	6,575	18,414	168,531	166,449	2,082
Pennsylvania	251,369	195,359	17,783	7,492	30,735	83,943	83,372	571

Again, Indiana is the median (the 11th state), so the answer to this question is "True."

Question 11c: For this question, you'll be looking for information about Minnesota. Specifically, you'll need to find the number of students in that state who attend for-profit schools and then determine whether that number is more than half of Minnesota's total enrollment.

Approach strategically here—rather than add all the numbers, do some comparisons. In the four-year undergraduate programs, there are approximately 25,000 more students in not-for-profit schools. Look next at the two-year undergraduate enrollments. These numbers are probably too low to significantly affect the total, so turn your attention to the postbaccalaureate column: here there are approximately 33,000 more students enrolled in for-profit schools. Because 33,000 is significantly higher than 25,000, you know that there are more students enrolled in the for-profit schools, making the answer to this question "True."

Of course, if you have time to check your work, you can use the on-screen calculator:

For-profit: $25,723 + 2,233 + 54,335 = 82,291$

Not-for-profit: $50,793 + 106 + 21,232 = 72,131$

More than half the enrollments in Minnesota are in for-profit institutions, confirming our answer of "True."

Remember, for success in Table Analysis, you need to understand what information the table contains and how it is organized before attacking the questions. Pay close attention to the column headings and use the Sort function whenever possible, especially when finding the median. Apply this strategic approach to the next set of Table Analysis questions.

Household Size: Occupied Housing Units by State, 2010 Census

Sort By Select... ▾

	1-person households	2-person households	3-person households	4-person households	5-person households	6-person households	7-or-more-person households	Total households
Connecticut	373,648	443,095	226,658	197,116	84,916	29,348	16,306	1,371,087
Maine	159,533	213,695	84,340	64,010	23,840	7,854	3,947	557,219
Massachusetts	732,263	813,166	417,216	353,676	150,842	51,409	28,503	2,547,075
New Hampshire	133,057	188,923	85,046	70,835	27,365	9,286	4,461	518,973
Vermont	72,233	96,889	39,695	31,210	11,107	3,480	1,828	256,442

The above data are drawn from 2010 census data for New England (excluding Rhode Island, whose data is not available). The table provides the total number of households in each state and the distribution of households of various sizes within each state.

12. Consider the following statements about these states. For each statement, evaluate whether that statement is *True* or *False*, according to the information in the table.

True   False

○   ○   The median household size of all households in the five states combined is two people.

○   ○   Of the seven categories of household size, Maine has the median number of households in exactly three.

○   ○   In each of the seven categories of household size, Massachusetts has more households than the next highest two states combined.

Get the Gist of the Table

This table has fewer rows, but don't assume that means you're in for an easy time—the questions are likely to compensate for the graph's simplicity. They may require abstract reasoning, challenging math, or both. Begin as always by reading the paragraph of text that accompanies the table. It tells you that the table provides data about the number of households and the size of those households in several New England states.

Now look at the table itself. Note the column headings, which are broken down into households of seven different sizes, plus the total number of households, for each of the five states. Take note of the outliers in the data sets; a quick glance at the "Total" column shows you that Massachusetts has an overwhelmingly large number of households compared to the other states.

Answer the Questions

Question 12a: Now you're being asked to determine the median household size for all states combined. To do this, first sum up the total number of households for all five states (the far right column). Rounding to the nearest thousand, you get $1,000 \times (1,371 + 557 + 2,547 + 519 + 256) = 5,250,000$. That means that if you were to place all these households in order according to their size, the median household would be roughly the $\frac{5,250,000}{2} = 2,625,000$th household. The household size of the 2,625,000th household is therefore the median household size.

To determine the size of that particular household, you need to total the number of households of each size until you hit the 2.6-million mark. Starting at either end of the table will eventually get you to the middle, but because there are bigger numbers of smaller households, you'll reach the threshold faster if you start on the left with the one-person households. Rounding to the thousands place gets you $1,000 \times (374 + 160 + 732 + 133 + 72) = 1,471,000$, so you're a little over halfway to the 2,625,000th house.

Careful observation saves even more work on the next step of finding this solution. Every state has more two-person households than one-person households. If you actually tallied up the exact number of one- and two-person households, you'd end up with a number well above 2,900,000 (twice the previous total). Therefore, the 2,625,000th household must be a two-person household, so this statement can be marked "True."

Question 12b: This is another question about medians. You need to find the median number for each of the seven categories and determine whether Maine has the median for exactly three of them. It's time to use the Sort function again.

One-person households:

Sort By [1-person households ▼]

	1-person households	2-person households	3-person households	4-person households	5-person households	6-person households	7-or-more-person households	Total households
Vermont	72,233	96,889	39,695	31,210	11,107	3,480	1,828	256,442
New Hampshire	133,057	188,923	85,046	70,835	27,365	9,286	4,461	518,973
Maine	159,533	213,695	84,340	64,010	23,840	7,854	3,947	557,219
Connecticut	373,648	443,095	226,658	197,116	84,916	29,348	16,306	1,371,087
Massachusetts	732,263	813,166	417,216	353,676	150,842	51,409	28,503	2,547,075

Maine is the median for one-person households. That's one instance so far.

Two-person households:

Sort By [2-person households ▼]

	1-person households	2-person households	3-person households	4-person households	5-person households	6-person households	7-or-more-person households	Total households
Vermont	72,233	96,889	39,695	31,210	11,107	3,480	1,828	256,442
New Hampshire	133,057	188,923	85,046	70,835	27,365	9,286	4,461	518,973
Maine	159,533	213,695	84,340	64,010	23,840	7,854	3,947	557,219
Connecticut	373,648	443,095	226,658	197,116	84,916	29,348	16,306	1,371,087
Massachusetts	732,263	813,166	417,216	353,676	150,842	51,409	28,503	2,547,075

Maine is again the median; that makes two instances.

Three-person households:

Sort By [3-person households ▼]

	1-person households	2-person households	3-person households	4-person households	5-person households	6-person households	7-or-more-person households	Total households
Vermont	72,233	96,889	39,695	31,210	11,107	3,480	1,828	256,442
Maine	159,533	213,695	84,340	64,010	23,840	7,854	3,947	557,219
New Hampshire	133,057	188,923	85,046	70,835	27,365	9,286	4,461	518,973
Connecticut	373,648	443,095	226,658	197,116	84,916	29,348	16,306	1,371,087
Massachusetts	732,263	813,166	417,216	353,676	150,842	51,409	28,503	2,547,075

New Hampshire is the median; keep going.

Four-person households:

Sort By | 4-person households | ▾

	1-person households	2-person households	3-person households	4-person households	5-person households	6-person households	7-or-more-person households	Total households
Vermont	72,233	96,889	39,695	31,210	11,107	3,480	1,828	256,442
Maine	159,533	213,695	84,340	64,010	23,840	7,854	3,947	557,219
New Hampshire	133,057	188,923	85,046	70,835	27,365	9,286	4,461	518,973
Connecticut	373,648	443,095	226,658	197,116	84,916	29,348	16,306	1,371,087
Massachusetts	732,263	813,166	417,216	353,676	150,842	51,409	28,503	2,547,075

New Hampshire again; not what you're looking for.

Five-person households:

Sort By | 5-person households | ▾

	1-person households	2-person households	3-person households	4-person households	5-person households	6-person households	7-or-more-person households	Total households
Vermont	72,233	96,889	39,695	31,210	11,107	3,480	1,828	256,442
Maine	159,533	213,695	84,340	64,010	23,840	7,854	3,947	557,219
New Hampshire	133,057	188,923	85,046	70,835	27,365	9,286	4,461	518,973
Connecticut	373,648	443,095	226,658	197,116	84,916	29,348	16,306	1,371,087
Massachusetts	732,263	813,166	417,216	353,676	150,842	51,409	28,503	2,547,075

Still New Hampshire.

Six-person households:

Sort By | 6-person households | ▾

	1-person households	2-person households	3-person households	4-person households	5-person households	6-person households	7-or-more-person households	Total households
Vermont	72,233	96,889	39,695	31,210	11,107	3,480	1,828	256,442
Maine	159,533	213,695	84,340	64,010	23,840	7,854	3,947	557,219
New Hampshire	133,057	188,923	85,046	70,835	27,365	9,286	4,461	518,973
Connecticut	373,648	443,095	226,658	197,116	84,916	29,348	16,306	1,371,087
Massachusetts	732,263	813,166	417,216	353,676	150,842	51,409	28,503	2,547,075

New Hampshire is the median frequently in this table. There's only one more chance to find a third instance of Maine being the median.

Get the Gist of the Table

For each of 10 branch managers, three measures of job performance are given, as well as three features of their stores.

Answer the Questions

Question 13a: Sort the data by employee satisfaction rating to quickly find the median; it's about 49%. Six managers saw positive sales growth. Of these, four have an employee rating above 49%—Emerald, Xin, Szymes, and McDonough—and two have an employee rating below 49%—Jenkins and Stover. Four out of six is a majority. The correct answer is "True."

Question 13b: The second statement asserts that as the size of a branch's sales force increases, so too does its change in year-over-year sales. This is untrue: the three smallest branches saw positive growth, while the two biggest branches saw negative growth. There is in fact no correlation between sales force and change in sales, and the second statement is "False."

Question 13c: For the third statement, locate the branch that had the highest sales in the previous year. While Stover's branch had the highest sales this year, that's up 15.5% over the previous year, so Stover's sales in the previous year were under $100,000. The branch with the highest sales the previous year was Stripley's. $101,700 in sales this year with a 9.4% decrease over the previous year puts the previous year's sales at around $112,000. Stripley's branch does have underground parking, so this statement is "True."

Two-Part Analysis

Simply put, Two-Part Analysis questions have solutions in two parts. Two-Part Analysis questions consist of a few lines of text and instructions to select choices in a table based on the given information. These questions may test quantitative or verbal skills.

Solving an algebraic Two-Part Analysis usually necessitates setting up an algebraic equation with two variables. You'll want to begin by first reading the text and identifying the two unknowns, which may be provided or may need to be assigned variables. Then, you'll create one or more equations that relate the two values or variables. Once you've set up your equations, you can simplify them and look for a match (if the answer choices are algebraic equations or expressions) or start plugging in answer choices from the table until you find two corresponding values that work together.

Verbal Two-Part Analysis questions draw on many of the same logical reasoning skills, such as drawing supported inferences and finding assumptions, that you use on the Verbal section of the GMAT. For example, after reading about a type of dwelling used by a certain species of animal, you might identify from among the choices a characteristic that must be true of all dwellings of that type and a characteristic that can never be true. Alternatively, you might be asked to strengthen and weaken an author's argument.

All this will make much more sense with concrete examples, so let's take a look at some questions to see how Two-Part Analysis questions work.

14. At University X, there are 146 students who are taking economics and 97 students who are taking history.

In the table below, pick two numbers that are consistent with the information that is given. In the first column, select the row that shows the number of students at University X who are taking at least one of economics and history, and in the second column, select the row that shows the number of students at University X who are taking both economics and history.

Taking at Least One of Economics and History	Taking Both Economics and History	Possible Answers
○	○	78
○	○	83
○	○	104
○	○	154
○	○	160
○	○	164

Get the Gist of the Information

The text in Two-Part Analysis questions is likely to be brief, so read it thoroughly before doing anything else. Here, you are given information about students at University X: the number of students who are taking economics, 146, and the number of students who are taking history, 97. The question asks you to find two numbers: first, the number of students taking at least one of these two subjects and, second, the number of students taking both.

Answer the Questions

Start by solving for the number of students taking at least one subject. The most efficient way to determine this number is to think critically. If you add together the numbers of students taking each subject, you get: $146 + 97 = 243$. However, you know from the question stem and the column header that some students are taking both; if you rely on simple addition, you end up counting those students twice. Instead, set up an equation that relates the number of students in *at least* one subject, a, to the number of students in *both*, b.

Initial formula:	# in at least one = # in Group 1 + # in Group 2 − # in both
Fill in what you know:	$a = 146 + 97 − b$
Simplify:	$a = 243 − b$

Before you start plugging in the answer choices to find two values that satisfy this equation, think critically: Which number will be bigger? In this case, it has to be a. With that in mind, move to the answer choices.

Because your equation is $a = 243 − b$, start by plugging b into the equation to determine if there is a corresponding value for a in the chart. b must be the smaller of the two numbers, so start testing at the top of the column with $b = 78$. Your equation is now $a = 243 − 78 = 165$. Do you see 165 in the possible answer choices? Nope. The closest they get is 164, so this is not the correct answer. Once you know that 78 is not a possible answer for b, move on to 83. Plugging it into the formula, you have $a = 243 - 83 = 160$. Do you see 160 among the possible answer choices? Yes. This question format always has a single solution, so you don't need to test any further answer choices. You have your answer: $a = 160$ and $b = 83$.

Before submitting your answers, make sure that you enter each of your choices in the correct column. It would be unfortunate to do all of the work correctly, get the correct answers, and then not receive credit simply because you selected the numbers in the opposite columns. Look back at your scratch-work and remember that a represents the number of students in at least one subject and b represents the number of students in both subjects. You can now be sure that 160 belongs in the first column and 83 belongs in the second column.

Take what you've learned about solving for unknowns by using the given information to set up an equation and apply it to the next Two-Part Analysis question.

15. When Car P travels at a constant speed of x miles per hour for 84 minutes, and Car Q travels at an average speed of y miles per hour for 168 minutes, Car P travels 21 miles more than Car Q.

    In the table below, select a value for x and a value for y that together are consistent with the given information. In the first column, select the row that corresponds to the value of x, and in the second column, select the row that corresponds to the value of y.

Value of x	Value of y	Possible Answers
○	○	8
○	○	14
○	○	17
○	○	29
○	○	42
○	○	49

Get the Gist of the Information

When reading the information, remember that your goal is to use it to create an equation that relates the two unknowns, x and y. The text gives information about two cars and states one definitive relationship between them: Car P travels 21 more miles than Car Q. That is enough to indicate that your equation will focus on distance traveled. Go back to the beginning of the question stem to determine what you can about the distance the two cars travel.

Answer the Questions

Since the time traveled is given in terms of minutes, and speed in terms of miles per hour, you need to convert to get all of the times expressed in the same units.

$$\text{Car P time traveled} = 84 \; \text{minutes} \times \frac{1 \text{ hour}}{60 \text{ minutes}} = 1.4 \text{ hours}$$

$$\text{Car Q time traveled} = 168 \; \text{minutes} \times \frac{1 \text{ hour}}{60 \text{ minutes}} = 2.8 \text{ hours}$$

Since *distance = speed × time*, the distance each car traveled, in terms of x and y, is as follows:

$$\text{Car P distance traveled} = \frac{x \text{ miles}}{\text{hour}} \times 1.4 \text{ hours} = 1.4x \text{ miles}$$

$$\text{Car Q distance traveled} = \frac{y \text{ miles}}{\text{hour}} \times 2.8 \text{ hours} = 2.8y \text{ miles}$$

Once you have determined the distance traveled by each car, use the information that Car P travels 21 miles farther to set up the following equation: $1.4x = 2.8y + 21$. Before moving to the answer choices, be sure to get one variable entirely by itself. In this case, you can divide both sides by 1.4 to get $x = 2y + 15$. You can now plug possible values for y into this equation to see what value for x would result.

To simplify the process of plugging in answer choices, first determine which value is going to be bigger. Since all of the answer choices are positive (as they would have to be, since they represent the speed a car travels), you know that x must be greater than y. This makes sense when you think about the logic of the problem, which specifies that Car P travels a greater distance than Car Q in a shorter amount of time.

Use the possible answer choices to start testing for y. As before, since you are starting with the smaller value, y, you will start plugging in numbers from the top of the list and work down. Start with $y = 8$. Substituting into the equation, you get $x = 2(8) + 15 = 31$. Since 31 is not an option in the table, you know that 8 is not the value of y. Next, try $y = 14$. In this case, the calculation would be $x = 2(14) + 15 = 43$. Again, 43 is not one of the available choices, so keep going. If $y = 17$, then $x = 2(17) + 15 = 49$. Since 49 is among the answer choices, it must be the value for x. Again, be very careful when filling in the answer choices. Your answers are $x = 49$ and $y = 17$.

Now that you are familiar with the basic format and structure of Two-Part Analysis questions, try your hand at the following question, which focuses on your reasoning skills rather than on math.

16. A publisher has traditionally printed 10 abridged editions of Victorian or Edwardian writing each spring. In order to cut production costs, the publisher has decided to print only five of these books this spring and to offer the remaining five as e-books. The publisher wishes to print at least four abridged Victorian books. Moreover, the publisher has decided to include no single author more than twice in total and to offer at least three e-books that are detective fiction. Finally, in keeping with the strong British influence on Victorian and Edwardian literature in English-speaking countries everywhere, the publisher wants at least four e-books to be by British authors.

Four printed books and four e-books have already been chosen for publication:

Printed:

Dickens, *David Copperfield* (British Victorian autobiographical novel)

Thoreau, *Walden* (American Victorian nature writing)

Doyle, *The Hound of the Baskervilles* (British Edwardian detective fiction)

Collins, *The Woman in White* (British Victorian epistolary novel)

E-Books:

Doyle, *The Valley of Fear* (British Edwardian detective fiction)

Stoker, *Dracula* (British Victorian gothic novel)

Allen, *The Great Taboo* (Canadian Victorian adventure novel)

Freeman, *The Red Thumb Mark* (British Edwardian detective fiction)

Select a title that could be published as either a printed book or an e-book. Then select a title that could not be published as a printed book or as an e-book. Make only two selections, one in each column.

Either Printed or E-Book	Neither Printed nor E-Book	Possible Titles
○	○	Cooper, *Rural Hours* (American Victorian nature writing)
○	○	Doyle, *A Study in Scarlet* (British Victorian detective fiction)
○	○	Collins, *The Moonstone* (British Victorian detective fiction)
○	○	Freeman, *The Eye of Osiris* (British Edwardian detective fiction)
○	○	Orczy, *The Old Man in the Corner* (British Edwardian detective fiction)
○	○	Wells, *The Invisible Man* (British Victorian science fiction)

Get the Gist of the Information

You are given two lists of four book titles each; the fifth in each list is missing. The question asks you to find a book that would work on either list and to find a book that would work for neither list, given the publisher's selection criteria for printed books and e-books. In other words, the question wants one answer that "could be true" for either list and one that "must be false" for both lists.

Answer the Questions

You don't need to set up an equation to solve this problem, but you do need to use the GMAT Core Competency of Attention to the Right Detail as you consider the rules governing each set of books. Start by thinking about how to complete the list of printed books, which has only a single rule: there must be at least four Victorian titles. The list of printed books currently has only three Victorian titles, so you need a fourth. On Test Day, you would write, "Printed: need Victorian," on your scratchwork.

The list of e-books is governed by two rules: there must be at least three works of detective fiction and at least four books by British authors. The list already includes two detective titles and three titles by British authors. It follows that you need a work of detective fiction by a British author to complete the list of e-books. Your scratchwork might read, "E-books: need British detective fiction."

A book permissible for either list must have all the qualities that the rules for both lists require. The title that "could be true" for either list, therefore, must be a work of British Victorian detective fiction. There are two such books available among the answer choices—those by Doyle and Collins. If you have paid Attention to the Right Details, however, you know that another rule from the question states that no author may be included more than twice on both lists combined. Doyle shows up on both lists already, so it follows that the Collins book, *The Moonstone*, is the only one that would satisfy the requirements of either list.

Moreover, since Doyle has already appeared twice, he cannot appear again. So among the answer choices, the Doyle book is the "must be false" answer, the one that may not appear on either list.

Pay close attention to the column headings when filling in the answer choices. The correct answer for the first column (either printed or e-book) is *The Moonstone* by Collins, and the correct answer for the second column (neither printed nor e-book) is Doyle's *A Study in Scarlet*.

17. State A currently allows casino gambling while State B does not. The legislature of State B is considering a proposal under which a limited number of casino licenses would be granted within the state in order to compete with State A for gambling revenue. Given the fact that a great many citizens of State B currently visit casinos in State A, the legislature of State B would be foolish not to enact this proposal.

    In the table below, select one statement that would *strengthen* the proposal and another that would *weaken* it. Make exactly two selections, one in each column.

Would strengthen proposal	Would weaken proposal	Possible Statements
○	○	Some other states that have granted casino licenses have subsequently experienced an overall increase in revenue.
○	○	The residents of State B who currently visit casinos in State A travel to State A primarily to visit a nature preserve that serves as a major tourist attraction.
○	○	Currently, more State A residents than State B residents undertake international travel.
○	○	Before State A offered casinos, those residents of State B who wanted to visit casinos had to travel nearly twice as far in order to do so.
○	○	Most residents of State B who traveled to State A within the past year made the trip primarily to visit casinos.
○	○	Over the past five years, the gambling revenue that State A has taken in has more than offset the associated infrastructure costs associated with gambling tourism.

Get the Gist of the Information

In order to strengthen or weaken an argument, start by finding the conclusion, evidence, and assumption—exactly as you would do when attacking Strengthen or Weaken questions in Critical Reasoning. The author's conclusion is that State B should adopt the proposal to grant casino licenses. The evidence is that residents of State B currently visit casinos in State A. The author assumes that those same State B residents would visit casinos in State B if they had the opportunity to do so rather than visit the casinos in State A.

Answer the Questions

To strengthen the argument, look for a statement that supports the assumption that State B residents would stay home if there were casinos in State B rather than travel to State A. The fifth statement does so very well: "Most residents of State B who traveled to State A within the past year made the trip primarily to visit casinos." If State B residents are traveling to State A specifically to visit casinos, they might well save themselves the trip if there were casinos in State B.

To weaken the argument, look for a statement that undercuts the assumption—that is, find a statement that makes it less likely that residents of State B would visit casinos within their own state if given the opportunity to do so. That's the second statement: "The residents of State B who currently visit casinos in State A travel to State A primarily to visit a nature preserve that serves as a major tourist attraction." If State B residents are traveling to State A in order to visit a nature preserve, then they are not traveling specifically in order to visit casinos, and perhaps their casino visits are not all that important to them. They will likely continue to travel to State A (and perhaps continue to visit the casinos there as part of their visit), but there is no reason to believe that they might make separate trips to visit casinos within State B.

The correct answers are "Most residents of State B who traveled to State A within the past year made the trip primarily to visit casinos" to strengthen the proposal and "The residents of State B who currently visit casinos in State A travel to State A primarily to visit a nature preserve that serves as a major tourist attraction" to weaken the proposal.

Note that the first choice is incorrect because even if some states did see increased revenue from casino gambling, there may be more states that did not, or that even saw revenue decreases. The third and fourth choices are wrong because international travel and what happened before State A offered casinos both have no bearing on the argument. Finally, the last choice is wrong because the argument is about revenue only; infrastructure costs have no impact.

CONCLUSION

As you've seen from the examples in this chapter, Integrated Reasoning questions measure many of the same skills that you use for the Quantitative and Verbal sections of the test, such as paraphrasing information, finding keywords, determining whether an inference is supported, and using estimation instead of calculation. Regular review of the questions in this chapter, as well as those found in the quizzes and practice tests in your online resources, will help you get the best score you possibly can on Integrated Reasoning.

PART SIX

Test Day and Business School

CHAPTER 22

Take Control of Test Day

- Mental Conditioning
- Stress Management
- The Week Before Test Day
- On Test Day
- Cancellation and Multiple Scores Policy

In the earlier parts of this book, we looked at the content covered on the various sections of the GMAT. We also discussed the test expertise you'll need to move through those sections. Now we turn to the often overlooked topic of test mentality, that is, how to get into peak mental condition for the GMAT.

MENTAL CONDITIONING

Your frame of mind has a lot to do with the level of success you achieve. Here's what's involved in developing your best mindset for the GMAT.

TEST AWARENESS

To do your best on the GMAT, you must always keep in mind that the test is unlike other tests that you've taken in terms of both the content and the scoring system. If you took a test in high school or college and got a quarter of the questions wrong, you'd probably receive a pretty lousy grade. But due to the adaptive nature of the GMAT, missing only a quarter of the questions would give you a very high score. The test is designed to push test takers to their limits, so people rarely get every question right. In fact, you can get a handful of questions wrong and still score in the 99th percentile.

In other words, don't let what you consider to be a subpar performance on a handful of questions ruin your performance on the rest. A couple of missed questions won't, by themselves, spoil your score. But if you allow the frustration of those questions to unnerve you, you could end up compromising your performance on other questions or on the section as a whole. Missing a few points won't ruin your score, but losing your head will.

The test is designed to find your limits, so it should feel challenging. If you feel you've done poorly on a section, don't worry—you may have done just fine. Keep in mind that the questions that you are likely to struggle on most will be the hardest ones—the ones that hurt your score *least* if you miss them. To reach your highest potential score, you must remain calm and focused. Simply do your best on each question, and once a question or section is over, forget about it and move on.

Moreover, don't try to guess which questions are unscored (experimental questions). This kind of speculation has gotten countless test takers into trouble. They have a hunch that a certain question is one that doesn't count and then don't take it seriously. You cannot know which questions are experimental, so treat each one as if it counts. That way, you're covered no matter what. Likewise, don't worry if a question you get seems "too easy." This doesn't necessarily mean that you're doing poorly; it might be experimental. Or it might happen to align well with your individual strengths. Or perhaps you are just well prepared, have great strategies, and are beating the test! Do your best, get it right, and move on with confidence.

STAMINA

The GMAT is a grueling experience, and some test takers simply run out of gas when they reach the final questions. To avoid this, you must prepare by taking full-length practice tests (not skipping over any sections) every week or so leading up to the test so that on Test Day, that 4-hour test will seem like a breeze—or at least not a hurricane.

Your online resources include full-length CATs for just this purpose. If you finish the tests included with this book, a further option is to download the test maker's GMAT® Official Starter Kit software, which contains full-length exams and is available free from **mba.com**. One drawback to the software is that it does not include explanations, so you will want to rely on your Kaplan materials, which include thorough explanations, for the bulk of your study. However, the GMAT® Official Starter Kit CATs should give you a good indication of your score range.

CONFIDENCE

Confidence in your ability leads to quick, sure answers and a sense of poise that translates into more points. Confidence builds on itself, but unfortunately, so does self-doubt. If you lack confidence, you end up reading sentences and answer choices two, three, or four times until you confuse yourself and get off track. This uncertainty ruins your timing, only perpetuating a downward spiral.

If you cultivate a positive GMAT mindset, however, you'll gear your practice toward taking control of the test. And when you have achieved that goal—armed with the techniques and strategies explained in this book—you'll be ready to face the GMAT with supreme confidence.

POSITIVE ATTITUDE

Those who approach the GMAT as an obstacle and who rail against the necessity of taking it usually don't fare as well as those who see the GMAT as an opportunity. Those who look forward to doing battle with the GMAT—or, at least, who enjoy the opportunity to distinguish themselves from the rest of the applicant pack—tend to score better than do those who resent or dread it.

Take our word for it: developing a positive attitude is a proven test-taking technique. Here are a few steps you can take to make sure you develop the right GMAT attitude:

- Look at the GMAT as a challenge but try not to obsess over it; you certainly don't want to psych yourself out of the game.

- Remember that, yes, the GMAT is obviously important, but contrary to popular belief, this one test will not single-handedly determine the outcome of your life—or even of your business school admissions.
- Try to have fun with the test. Learning how to match your wits against those of the test makers can be a very satisfying experience, and the critical thinking skills you'll acquire will benefit you in business school, as well as in your future career.
- Remember that you're more prepared than most people. You've trained with Kaplan. You have the tools you need, plus the ability to use those tools.

STRESS MANAGEMENT

The countdown has begun. Your date with the test is looming on the horizon. Anxiety is on the rise. You have butterflies in your stomach, and your thinking is getting cloudy. Maybe you think you won't be ready. Maybe you already know your stuff, but you're going into panic mode anyway. Don't worry! It's possible to tame that anxiety and stress—before *and* during the test.

Remember, some stress is normal and good. Anxiety is a motivation to study. The adrenaline that gets pumped into your bloodstream when you're stressed helps you stay alert and think more clearly. But if you feel that the tension is so great that it's preventing you from using your study time effectively, here are some things you can do to get it under control.

TAKE CONTROL

Lack of control is a prime cause of stress. Research shows that if you don't have a sense of control over what's happening in your life, you can easily end up feeling helpless and hopeless. Try to identify the sources of the stress you feel. Which ones can you do something about? Can you find ways to reduce the stress you're feeling from any of these sources?

MAKE A STUDY SCHEDULE

Often the mere realization that you're procrastinating on your GMAT study can cause stress. To help you gain control over your preparation process, make study appointments with yourself on your calendar—and then keep these appointments with yourself! Without setting aside time to study for the GMAT, it's easy to keep putting it off due to looming work deadlines, business school applications, or other commitments on your calendar. The hardest part of studying is getting started, so get started soon and start small. Even committing to working on five problems a day will produce a pleasant feeling of accomplishment and momentum, leading you to be able to make longer and longer commitments to your Test Day success.

FOCUS ON YOUR STRENGTHS

Make a list of areas of strength you have that will help you do well on the test. We all have strengths, and recognizing your own is like having reserves of solid gold in the bank. You'll be able to draw on your reserves as you need them, helping you solve difficult questions, maintain confidence, and keep test stress and anxiety at a distance. And every time you recognize a new area of strength, solve a challenging problem, or score well on a practice test, congratulate yourself—you'll only increase your reserves.

IMAGINE YOURSELF SUCCEEDING

Close your eyes and imagine yourself in a relaxing situation. Breathe easily and naturally. Now think of a real-life situation in which you did well on an assignment. Focus on this success. Now turn your thoughts to the GMAT and keep your thoughts and feelings in line with that successful experience. Don't make comparisons between them; just imagine yourself taking the upcoming test with the same feelings of confidence and relaxed control.

SET REALISTIC GOALS

Facing your problem areas gives you some distinct advantages. What do you want to accomplish in the study time remaining? Make a list of realistic goals. You can't help feeling more confident when you know you're actively improving your chances of earning a higher GMAT score.

EXERCISE REGULARLY

Whether it's jogging, biking, push-ups, or a pickup basketball game, physical exercise will stimulate your mind and body and improve your ability to think and concentrate. A surprising number of test takers fall out of the habit of regular exercise, ironically because they're spending so much time prepping for the exam. A little physical exertion will help you to keep your mind and body in sync and to sleep better at night.

EAT WELL

Good nutrition will help you focus and think clearly. Eat plenty of fruits and vegetables; low-fat protein such as fish, skinless poultry, beans, and legumes; and whole grains such as brown rice, whole-wheat bread, and pastas. Don't eat a lot of sugary and high-fat snacks or salty foods. Note that on Test Day, you can't bring food or drink into the testing room. But you can keep a healthy snack in your locker to recharge you between sections.

SLEEP WELL

Every GMAT problem requires careful critical thinking. Unfortunately, that's the first mental skill to go away when you are sleep deprived. Get a full night's sleep as often as you can during your preparation, especially as Test Day approaches.

KEEP BREATHING

Conscious attention to breathing is an excellent way to manage stress while you're taking the test. Most of the people who get into trouble during the GMAT take shallow breaths; they breathe using only their upper chests and shoulder muscles and may even hold their breath for long periods of time. Conversely, test takers who breathe deeply in a slow, relaxed manner are likely to be in better control during the session.

STRETCH

If you find yourself getting spaced out or burned out as you're studying or taking the test, stop for a brief moment and stretch. Even though you'll be pausing for a moment, it's a moment well spent. Stretching will help to refresh you and refocus your thoughts.

STRESS MANAGEMENT QUIZ

Don't be alarmed: this is not a GMAT quiz. It is important to your score, though. Imagine that there are two people with equal GMAT knowledge, skill, and practice. Why might one still outperform the other? The biggest difference will likely be that one manages stress and anxiety better than the other.

This quiz is a chance to reinforce and expand upon the ideas and advice you've read so far in this chapter. Have fun with it and think about how to apply the correct answers to your own life and study schedule.

1. What is Test Day stress?

    O   A feeling of anxiety felt only by those aiming for a top score

    O   Any factor, physical or psychological, that impedes my performance on the GMAT

    O   A consequence of poor preparation

    O   A constant fear of not getting into my first-choice school

    O   Something that only poor test takers experience

2. It is most helpful to my Test Day success when my friends and family

    O   push me to study more

    O   tell me how much more I have to learn

    O   compete with me over test scores

    O   have positive attitudes about my ability to achieve my best score and help me get my mind off the test whenever I am not studying

    O   care little about my performance and prevent me from getting sufficient time to prep

3. In the weeks leading up to the exam, how can I reduce stress?

    O   List my weaknesses and create a study schedule to overcome them, one topic at a time

    O   Get some exercise

    O   Limit self-deprecating humor and keep a positive attitude

    O   Get sufficient sleep

    O   All of the above

4. In the final days before my exam, I should worry about all of the topics that I still have trouble with or haven't hit, rather than congratulate myself on how far I've come.

    O   True
    O   False

5. The night before the exam, what can I do to reduce stress?

    O   Try to learn topics that I have not mastered yet
    O   Go to my local bar with my friends, drink a few pitchers of beer, and try to get my mind off the exam
    O   Briefly review the topics that I mastered but haven't looked at in a while and get a good night's sleep
    O   Stay up all night, memorizing the grammar and math concepts
    O   Panic

6. On Test Day, what can I do to reduce stress?

    O   Make sure I know where the testing center is and allow plenty of time to get there early
    O   Eat a nutritious breakfast
    O   Dress in layers to be ready for any temperature in the testing room
    O   Expect a lot of paperwork before the test begins
    O   All of the above

7. During the exam, if I don't know how to answer a question and I begin to panic, I should

   O   keep rereading the question until I determine the correct approach, no matter how long it takes

   O   bite my fingernails and moan

   O   keep breathing, take a moment to get my bearings, and determine whether I should take a strategic guess or give the question another minute or two

   O   remind myself that if I miss the question, I will not get into business school, I will fail in life, and I will be forced to live with my parents forever

   O   choose an answer choice that I haven't chosen much so far in that section

8. During the GMAT, I should avoid worrying about questions that I have already answered.

   O   True

   O   False

9. What should I do next to make sure that I am prepared to overcome the natural stress that comes with taking an important test?

   O   Understand that anxiety is a sign of weakness and suppress it ruthlessly

   O   Take control of my preparation by following a study schedule and cultivating a positive attitude

   O   Forget about Test Day stress until Test Day and then figure out how to deal with it

   O   Decide not to take the GMAT

   O   Nothing. This exercise has taught me all I need to know about Test Day stress management.

ANSWER KEY

1. B
2. D
3. E
4. False
5. C
6. E
7. C
8. True
9. B

THE WEEK BEFORE TEST DAY

Is it starting to feel like your whole life is a buildup to the GMAT? You've known about it for years, worried about it for months, and have now spent at least a few weeks in solid preparation for it. As Test Day approaches, you may find your anxiety is on the rise. You shouldn't worry. After the preparation you've received from this book, you're in good shape for the test. To calm any jitters you may have, though, let's go over a few strategies for the days leading up to the test.

In the week or so leading up to Test Day, you should do the following:

- Visit the testing center. Sometimes seeing the actual room where your test will be administered and taking notice of little things—such as the kind of desk you'll be working on, whether the room is likely to be hot or cold, etc.—may help to calm your nerves. And if you've never been to the testing center, visiting beforehand is a good way to ensure that you don't get lost on Test Day. If you can go on the same day of the week and at the same time of day as your actual test, so much the better; you'll be able to scope out traffic patterns and parking. Remember, you must be on time—the computers at the testing centers are booked all day long. Consider using **Kaplan's Official Test Day Experience** to take a Kaplan practice test at a Pearson test center.
- Practice working on test material, preferably a full-length test, at the same time of day that your test is scheduled for as if it were the real Test Day.
- Practice using the test interface and get tips about what to expect at the test center by taking the tutorial at **mba.com/tutorial**.
- Time yourself while practicing so you don't feel as though you are rushing on Test Day.
- Evaluate thoroughly where you stand. Use the time remaining before the test to shore up your weak points, rereading the appropriate sections of this book. But make sure not to neglect your strong areas; after all, those are where you'll rack up most of your points.

THE DAY BEFORE TEST DAY

This advice might seem counterintuitive, but try to avoid intensive studying the day before the test. There's little you can do to improve your score at this late date, and you may just wind up exhausting yourself and burning out. Our advice is to review a few key concepts, get together everything you'll need for Test Day (acceptable photo identification, the names of schools to which you'd like to send your GMAT scores, directions to the testing center, a healthy snack for the break), and then take the night off entirely. Go to see a movie, rent a video, or watch some TV. Try not to think too much about the test; just relax and store up some energy for the big day.

ON TEST DAY

Test Day should contain no surprises. Test takers who feel in control of the events leading up to the test take that confidence with them into the testing center.

Leave early for the testing center, giving yourself plenty of time. Read something to warm up your brain; you don't want the GMAT to be the first written material your brain tries to assimilate that day. Dress in layers for maximum comfort. That way, you'll be able to adjust to the testing room's temperature. In traveling to the testing center, leave yourself enough time for traffic or mass transit delays.

Be ready for a long day. Total testing time, remember, is about 3.0 hours. When you add the administrative paperwork before and after, and the two 8-minute breaks, you're looking at an experience of 3.5 hours or more.

You will feel most prepared and confident if you have an understanding of how the logistics of Test Day will play out. Taking the full-length practice CATs in your online resources and those from **mba.com** will help you get the feel for the GMAT itself, but certain events are unique to the experience in the testing center. Here's what to expect:

At the testing center, you will...

- Check in.
- Place your belongings in a locker.
- Receive a noteboard and pen for your scratchwork.
- Go to the assigned computer. (Note that you will be videotaped as you take the test. Don't be disturbed by any video cameras facing you; this is just a tool that enables the test administrators to maintain a fair testing environment.)
- Select your score recipients. The computer will ask you where to send your results. You may send your scores to up to five schools free of charge. You should take advantage of this free service, as waiting until later has no advantage. If you specify your score recipients after the test or choose more than five schools, you will have to pay $35 per school (as this book goes to press) to send results.
- Complete the four sections of the test, taking advantage of the two 8-minute breaks offered to visit the restroom, eat your snack, and reboot your brain.
- Complete a brief optional survey.
- See your unofficial Quantitative, Verbal, and Integrated Reasoning scores.
- Choose whether to cancel or keep your scores.
- Check out.
- Remove your belongings from the locker and leave the testing facility.

Here are some strategic reminders to help guide your work on Test Day:

- Read each question stem carefully and reread it before making your final selection.
- Don't get bogged down in the middle of any section. You may find later questions more to your liking. So don't panic. Eliminate answer choices, guess, and move on.
- Don't fall behind early. Even if you get most of the first 10 questions right, you'll wind up rushing yourself into enough errors that you cancel out your early success. Keep a steady pace throughout the test and finish each section strong, avoiding the penalty for not completing all the questions.
- Don't bother trying to figure out which questions are unscored. It can't help you, and you might very well be wrong. Instead, just resolve to do your best on every question.
- Confidence is key. Accentuate the positives and don't dwell on the negatives. Your attitude and outlook are crucial to your performance on Test Day.

- During the exam, try not to speculate about how you're scoring. Imagine a baseball player who's focusing on the crowd's cheers and the sportswriters and his contract as he steps up to the plate: there's no surer way to strike out. Instead, focus on the question-by-question task of picking an answer choice. The correct answer is there. You don't have to come up with it; it's sitting right there in front of you!

What should you do if you...

- **Start to lose confidence?** If questions seem to be getting hard, don't lose confidence; since the GMAT is adaptive, it is practically guaranteed to feel like a struggle—for everyone! Trust in your preparation and in the skills and strategies you have practiced.

- **Start to lose concentration?** If you lose your concentration, pause, take a deep breath, exhale, and go back to the test. This will help you refocus and settle back in.

- **Take too long at the break?** If you take too long at the break, the test will continue without you. When the 8-minute countdown timer hits zero, the next section of the test—and its clock—will start.

- **Find the test environment too distracting?** If the test environment is too distracting, tell the proctor. If the proctor can't—or won't—do anything about it, mention the problem in the exit survey.

After Test Day, you should...

- Congratulate yourself for all the hard work you've put in. Make sure you celebrate afterward—and start thinking about all of the great times you'll be having at the business school of your choice!

- Plan your approach to business school applications, including references and essays.

- Go to **KaplanGMAT.com/businessadmissions/** to investigate options for admissions consulting programs through Kaplan's partner for business school admissions, mbaMission. Also, see the chapter of this book dealing with business school admissions for advice from mbaMission's founder and president, Jeremy Shinewald.

- Expect to wait approximately 20 days for your Official Score Report (which includes your Analytical Writing score) to be posted online.

CANCELLATION AND MULTIPLE SCORES POLICY

In late June 2014, the GMAT test maker announced that test takers will now be able to preview their unofficial scores on Test Day before deciding whether to report or cancel them. Before this change took place, GMAT test takers had been given the option of reporting or canceling their scores immediately after taking the test but only *before* seeing their unofficial scores. Under the updated process, test takers may now see their unofficial scores—Integrated Reasoning, Quantitative, Verbal, and Total—and are given two minutes to decide whether or not to accept them. If a choice is not made, the scores will be canceled by default. The test maker instituted another change in July of 2015: if a test taker cancels a score, no one else will know. Canceled scores are no longer included in score reports. In addition, in accord with new rules that went into effect in March of 2016, test takers who decide to cancel their scores at the test center will be able to reinstate them for a $50 fee. Any scores dating from January 1, 2014, or later are eligible for reinstatement. Moreover, scores not canceled at the testing center can be canceled for up to 72 hours after the test date for a $25 fee.

We at Kaplan feel that these changes in policy are good ones because they give test takers more control over their testing experience and how they present themselves to schools. You can show up on Test Day with more confidence knowing that if you perform below your goals, you don't necessarily need to submit your scores to schools.

To get the most out of the new features, the test maker recommends that you know what score you are willing to accept so that when asked whether you wish to send scores or cancel them, you have already considered your answer. We at Kaplan would echo that advice and add the following: because you only get 2 minutes to decide whether to cancel, and this comes after 4 full hours of testing that may leave you feeling exhausted and not in the best frame of mind for making high-stakes decisions, it is imperative that you enter the test knowing your lowest acceptable score. Know that if you need to, you can always take the test again and show improvement; any school you submit your scores to will be pleased to see an improvement.

However, you should not take this new policy to mean that you should devote less time to studying for the exam. Remember that you can take the GMAT only once every 16 days, only five times within a calendar year, and only eight times in total. In addition, it costs $250 to take the GMAT, so canceling your scores comes at a substantial price. As always, the best option of all is to prepare sufficiently with comprehensive materials and realistic practice so that you can test just once and achieve the score you need.

TAKEAWAYS

If you cancel your scores . . .

- They may be reinstated for a $50 fee.
- You will not receive a refund for the test.
- No one else will know. Canceled scores are no longer included in score reports.

If you do not cancel your scores . . .

- An official score report, including your AWA score, will be available online and sent to your designated schools within 20 days after you take the test.
- Your score and any other scores from within the past five years will appear on score reports sent to business schools. Most business schools consider only your highest GMAT score, but a few may average your scores. Check with individual schools for their policies on multiple scores.

CHAPTER 23

Business School Admissions Myths Destroyed (Before They Destroy You!)

By Jeremy Shinewald

Founder/President of mbaMission, Kaplan's Recommended Admissions Consulting Partner

ABOUT MBAMISSION

Your business school application is your ticket to a new and exciting phase of your life and career, so of course you want it to be the best it can be, and you might benefit from the advice of someone who is uniquely knowledgeable. But who? Someone with professional writing experience, perhaps? Someone with profound knowledge of the MBA application process? Maybe someone with an MBA who has been through the process? With mbaMission, you will work with a consultant who not only has all of these attributes and more, but who will also ensure that your business school application helps set you apart from the crowd. Our senior consultants are all published authors with elite MBA experience who will get to know you intimately and work one-on-one with you to discover, select, and articulate the unique stories that will force admissions committees to take notice. Your consultant will work with you on all aspects of your application, reducing your stress level and maximizing your chances of being admitted to the business school of your dreams.

Applicant blogs. Student tweets. Message board chatter. Competitive peers (some with agendas that run contrary to yours!). So many people try to influence you as you apply to business school, and these people frequently offer conflicting opinions and sources of information. In addition to managing your busy professional, community, and personal lives, you are suddenly attempting to process a seemingly infinite influx of application information. Welcome to the world of the MBA applicant! You'll need to find your way through an intensely competitive process whose rules are not clear and where questions sometimes seem unwelcome.

Given that the admissions process is not completely transparent—after all, decisions are still made behind closed doors—some armchair experts try to make sense of the process by simplifying it.

So, for example, a successful candidate may extrapolate from her own results and assume, "I had an alumni recommendation and I got in. So I'll tell my friend that she needs to have an alumni rec!" Similarly, an unsuccessful applicant might examine his results and conclude, "I submitted my application in Round 2, but my friend who got in submitted in Round 1. I am going to tell my colleagues that they'd better apply early if they want to be accepted!"

Can we really tell that much from the experiences of a single individual? After all, MBA candidates are not evaluated like data, their info run through a scanner that spits out a simple pass or fail determination. Rather, business school applicants are sophisticated human beings with interesting lives that cannot be measured quantitatively but can be understood subjectively. As candidates make snap judgments about the reasons behind their successful or unsuccessful applications and broadcast these simplifications to the world, and as these opinions are then retweeted and blogged about, opinions begin to propagate, and admissions myths start to develop. And once a myth develops, trying to change it—or to dissuade anxious business school applicants from believing it—is a real challenge. Yet these myths regularly cause candidates like you to inadvertently misdirect their energies and waste their time. So, here we present you with 10 myths and their opposing realities to help ensure that you stay on the right path and apply your energies appropriately.

MYTH #1: THE ADMISSIONS COMMITTEE WANTS A SPECIFIC TYPE

Many MBA candidates believe that admissions committees have narrowed down their criteria for selecting applicants over the years and that each school has one distinct "type" that it seeks. So, in this world of stereotypes, Harvard Business School (HBS) is looking only for leaders, Kellogg is looking only for marketing students, Chicago Booth is looking only for finance students, and MIT Sloan is looking only for "eggheads." Of course, these stereotypes—like most stereotypes—are not accurate. Chicago Booth wants far more than one-dimensional finance students in its classes, and it provides its MBA students with training in far more than just finance (offering, to the surprise of some, an excellent marketing program). HBS is not a school just for "generals"; among the 950 students in each of its classes, HBS has a wide variety of personalities, including some excellent "foot soldiers." Therefore, we strongly suggest that you ignore these stereotypes, because pandering to them can sink your applications.

For example, imagine that you have worked in operations at a manufacturing company. You have profound experience managing and motivating dozens of different types of people, at different levels, in both good and bad economic times. Even though your exposure to finance has been minimal, you erroneously determine that in order to get into New York University's Stern School of Business, you have to convince the school that you are a "finance guy." So in your application essays, you tell your best—but nonetheless weak—finance stories. What happens is that you are now competing in the Stern applicant pool with elite finance candidates whose stories are far more impressive. What if you had instead told your unique operations/management stories and stood out from the other applicants, rather than trying to compete in the school's most over-represented pool?

We believe that defying stereotypes and truly being yourself is the best course of action. But if you are still not convinced, consider this nugget of advice offered on Stanford's admissions website:

> Because we want to discover who you are, resist the urge to "package" yourself in order to come across in a way you think Stanford wants. Such attempts simply blur our understanding of who you are and what you can accomplish. We want to hear your genuine

voice throughout the essays that you write, and this is the time to think carefully about your values, your passions, your hopes and dreams.

Kind of makes sense, doesn't it?

MYTH #2: MY HIGH GMAT SCORE WILL GET ME IN

So you have taken the GMAT and exceeded even your highest expectations, scoring at the very top of the scale. Congratulations! But please, do not assume that earning a high score means you can pay less attention to the other components of your application. Every year, applicants who have scored 750 or even higher are rejected from their target business schools—even when their GMAT score falls within the top 10 percent of the schools' range. And many of these candidates were rejected because of a fatal, but ultimately avoidable, mistake: they got overconfident and assumed their GMAT score alone would get them in.

"I joke sometimes that I relish nothing more than rejecting people that have a 780 on the GMAT," Jonathan Fuller, senior associate director of admissions at the University of Michigan's Ross School of Business, said in an online chat, "because they come with the 780 GMAT and think they're golden, and they don't have to worry about anything else on the application. Well, you do. There are all these other pieces of information that we ask for, and you have to make sure that you are strong across the board." Similarly, candidates need not worry that a lower score will sink their candidacy entirely. We would never lie to you and tell you that being accepted with a lower GMAT score will be easy, but every year we see a few particularly accomplished individuals with scores in the 500s get into top-ten programs. It can be done!

Business schools want to learn a lot more about you than your GMAT score alone can convey. MBA programs are interested in hearing about your ambitions, accomplishments, leadership skills, teamwork experience, perseverance, motivation, integrity, compassion ... and the list goes on. Fundamentally, admissions committees need to be able to determine whether you will be a vital and contributing member of their school's community, and your GMAT score, while important, is only one piece of that puzzle.

Whether you have a 780 or a 580, heed our advice and commit yourself wholeheartedly to all the elements of your application. No single data point will result in a decision to admit or reject!

MYTH #3: MY SUPERVISOR GRADUATED FROM HBS—HE KNOWS

We know of a now 70-year-old man who graduated from a virtually unknown Canadian undergraduate school in 1963 and who, with no work experience at all, applied to HBS, the Wharton School of the University of Pennsylvania, and the Stanford Graduate School of Business (GSB), gaining acceptances at all three (though the GSB deferred his entry for one year so he could earn a little more experience first). He ultimately studied at HBS and now runs a small grain-trading business. You could not meet a nicer man, and although he is certainly wise in many respects, one thing he knows nothing about is MBA admissions. "I attended so long ago, things must have changed since then," he says. "I did not have any work experience at all. I had studied four years of commerce, and that was it!"

Why are we telling you this? Many candidates each year tell us that their bosses, who applied to business school during far different times, have given them "sage" advice about applying and that they feel they should follow it—after all, what worked for their boss in 1964, 1974, 1984, 1994, or even 2004 must still be applicable today, right? Wrong.

For a long time, the MBA was actually not all that desirable a degree, so admissions were not very competitive. To give you an idea of the relative popularity, Duke University (Fuqua) did not even start its MBA program until 1970, but its law school was founded in 1868. Yale University was founded in 1701, but it did not have an MBA program until 1976. So, the MBA is a relatively new degree that has only recently (in the late 1990s) reached its current level of popularity and prestige.

What does all of this mean with regard to your boss's advice? Although your supervisor may have gotten into one of your target schools, he or she likely did so years ago and therefore may not have had to contend with the steep competition you now face. Your boss may also not know anything about what the admissions process is like today and could—however inadvertently—be leading you astray. If your supervisor starts any bit of well-intended advice with the phrase "when I applied," you should view this guidance with tremendous caution.

MYTH #4: IF I DID NOT GO TO AN IVY, I'M NOT GETTING IN

Have you ever heard of Ateneo de Manila University in the Philippines? What about Universidad Metropolitana in Venezuela? Do you know anyone at New College of Florida or Carleton College? Why do we ask? HBS posted profiles of 33 students in its Class of 2012, and you might be surprised to learn that not all of them got their undergraduate degrees at Harvard. In fact, only a few among this group did. You may say, "Yes, but the school selectively released information on these students." True, but the school also offers a full list of the 500 undergraduate institutions represented in its previous three classes of 900 to 950 students each and notes that 243 different institutions are represented in the Class of 2013 alone. Meanwhile, the Stanford admissions office states that 156 schools were represented among the 397 students in its Class of 2013. And the list goes on ...

Although Harvard graduates are certainly well represented in each HBS class, most business schools attract a high number of applicants from among their undergrad alumni. Still, being an alumnus or alumna of an MBA program's undergraduate institution is neither a prerequisite nor a hindrance. The admissions committees are more interested in your performance—academic, professional, volunteer, personal—than your pedigree. The committees are also interested in diversity. We don't feel we are going out on a limb by stating that Wharton does not want—and indeed cannot have—a class made up of 850 UPenn undergrads; the school wants the best potential business leaders and thus must select from a much deeper pool.

So, if you graduated from a school that has no international profile or even a limited national profile, you should not worry. Your performance at your academic institution is far more important than your institution's name. Furthermore, you represent much more than your undergraduate institution. You should not be an apologist for your school but an advocate of your skills.

MYTH #5: IF I HAVE A GAP IN MY HISTORY, I'M NOT GETTING IN

The perfect MBA applicant simply does not exist. However, the perception of the perfect applicant certainly does: an individual who is on a very narrow course, scaling greater and greater academic, personal, community, and professional peaks (all of which are related to each other) unabated until he or she finally applies to business school. As a result, those who have taken some time off at any point in their professional lives tend to perceive themselves as being at a disadvantage in the business school application process. They worry that admissions committees will see these gaps and dismiss them outright. After all, don't the schools have many more determined individuals in the applicant pool whom they can choose to admit instead?

It's true that time off can potentially be detrimental to your application. If you spent a year on your couch watching reality TV, you are likely going to have difficulty presenting this in a positive way to the admissions committee. However, if you have a strong professional history overall and once spent a month between jobs sitting on your couch watching reality TV, your record should still speak favorably for itself. But even if you have taken an extended leave, as long as you were productive during that time and grew personally, you should be just fine. In fact, if you had some kind of an adventure during your break, this may even add to your story and help you differentiate yourself.

For example, if you spent six months or a year travelling before you started your professional career, you are certainly still eligible for a spot in a top MBA program. Similarly, if you took a personal leave to care for a family member in need, to do charity work, or even to pursue a personal passion (an art form, for example), an admissions officer should still see your merits as long as you can show purpose and reveal a broad record of competency.

Admissions officers are actual human beings. They understand that applicants are not robots and that they have interests, passions, and personal lives outside the workplace. If you have generally made good use of your time, they will not condemn you. In fact, they just might envy you.

MYTH #6: IF I HAVE NO MANAGERIAL EXPERIENCE, I'M NOT GETTING IN

It might seem ironic that having formal management experience is not a prerequisite for getting into a top MBA program. But keep in mind that an MBA education is meant for those who aspire to become managers—not only those who already *are* managers. So if you are fretting that you have not had any subordinates to date and feel that having supervised a staff is a requirement for getting into a top business school, you are actually adhering to a myth and can stop worrying. Instead, focus on the ways in which you have excelled in your positions thus far and made the most of the leadership opportunities that have presented themselves.

For example, consider the many investment banking analysts who apply to MBA programs each year. While analysts are at the bottom of most banks' organizational charts and therefore do not have staffs to manage, they still have demanding jobs and have to perform at a high level each day to succeed. Most analysts can therefore talk about thriving in an ultracompetitive environment and can reveal their professional excellence via their resumes, essays, and recommendations. And even if most analysts do not have a staff of their own, second-year analysts still have ample opportunity to train and mentor first-year analysts, and third-year analysts can mentor and train first- and second-year analysts. So even without direct subordinates, investment banking analysts can demonstrate strong leadership and de facto management skills.

Of course, there are ways other than through conventional professional management to show evidence of your leadership traits. If you have not yet had the opportunity in your professional life to demonstrate that you have the interpersonal skills necessary to lead others, you can look to your community activities and even personal leadership experiences to positively illustrate your potential in this capacity. The bottom line is that business schools are not looking exclusively for managers but for individuals who display true promise for their future careers. After all, an MBA program is designed to teach you management!

MYTH #7: I MUST SUBMIT IN ROUND 1

Many MBA admissions officers will tell candidates that if they can complete their applications in time to submit them in Round 1, then they should do so. Most programs will also tell applicants that they should try to avoid Round 3, because most of the places in the class will have been filled by then. So, what does that say about Round 2?

We have noticed a strange trend lately: candidates have taken to calling mbaMission the day after a school's Round 1 application deadline and asking whether submitting an application in Round 2 is worth the effort or whether the opportunity has passed at that point. Unfortunately, when one is being compared against a group of unknown competitors, being concerned about every perceived difference or deficiency is only natural. Some candidates grow concerned if they are a year older than the average at their target school, while others fret if they are a year younger. Many applicants worry if their GMAT score is 10 points below a school's average. And of course, some worry if they submit their application in Round 2. However, the overall strength of your candidacy, which is a measure of many factors, is far more important than where you fit in relation to any single statistic—which includes whether you apply in Round 1 or 2.

So we too would encourage candidates to apply early, if they are ready and able to do so, but we do not believe they should give up on their MBA dreams for a year if applying in Round 1 is just not practical. You may be surprised to discover that while admissions committees encourage early applications, they also concede that the difference in selectivity between the first and the second rounds is very small. To back up this statement, we offer a small selection of quotes from mbaMission's exclusive interviews with admissions officers:

> People ask, generally, is it better to apply in the first round or the second round or third round? We definitely advise people to avoid the third round if possible, because space can become an issue by the time the third round rolls around. But we do view the first two rounds as roughly equivalent.
>
> —Bruce DelMonico, admissions director, Yale School of Management

> [We] get about a third of our applications in Round 1, about 55 percent in Round 2, and the remainder in Round 3 ... We encourage people to submit their application when they feel that they offer their best possible applications ... So if you can get everything lined up and completed and you feel really good about it ... then I would encourage you to apply in Round 1. But if it takes you a bit longer, and you want to take the time to look at your application again and maybe have somebody else look at it, then Round 2 is fine, too.
>
> —Soojin Kwon Koh, admissions director, Michigan—Ross

> We look at statistics over the years—how many applications we got, how many we admitted, and how many we yielded—and we try to even it out so we're not being too generous in one round at the expense of another round.
>
> —Dawna Clarke, admissions director, Dartmouth—Tuck

MYTH #8: WRITING MY OWN RECOMMENDATION PUTS ME IN THE DRIVER'S SEAT

You get the courage to ask your boss for a recommendation and he not only agrees to do so, he goes even further and says, "Write it yourself and I will sign it." Writing your own recommendation letter can seem like a blessing. Suddenly, you have the power to oversee an aspect of the application process that was previously beyond your control. So, your downside risk in these letters is mitigated, and your upside is infinite, right? Well, things do not quite work that way.

Admissions committees are not seeking blustery rave reviews. Instead, they are seeking recommendations that are detailed and personal, intimate and sincere. Can you really write about yourself with dispassionate sincerity? And even if you are a master of "dispassionate sincerity," are you able to capture the subtleties that make you stand out? For example, let's say that among the many important things you do, you also do something thoughtful that you do not even perceive to be significant—you always take new team members out to lunch. Although you may regard "closing the big deal" as significant, others may appreciate and admire this small but influential act, which helps forge team unity. Unfortunately, you may lack the objectivity necessary to ensure that this distinctive and impressive detail is included in your letter.

This is only one simple example, of course, but our point is that you probably will not know what is missing from your letter if you write it yourself. So when you approach your supervisor for a recommendation, go in ready to push back a bit if he or she asks you to write the letter yourself. Some may be busy or lazy, and others may think that they are doing you a favor by giving you control. Be prepared to impress upon your recommender that you can't help yourself but that he or she can. After all, that is why you are approaching your boss in the first place!

MYTH #9: HBS IS FOR EVERYONE

As strong a program as it offers, Harvard Business School simply is not the right fit for every single MBA candidate. We are not writing this to bash HBS—in fact, you can even replace "HBS" in our myth with the name of any other business school, because *no* program is truly appropriate for *every* candidate—but we are hoping that you will use this statement as a trigger to critically appraise your target MBA programs and determine which schools are truly best for you. Ask yourself the following questions to start:

- Would I prefer to be in a larger program, or would I be overwhelmed by a larger program's size?
- Would I prefer to be in a smaller program, or would it feel claustrophobic?
- Would I prefer to have a flexible curriculum with a consistent stream of new classmates and where I could make my own academic choices early on?
- Would I prefer to have a comprehensive core curriculum set out for me so that I am, for a period of time, learning the same material as my classmates according to a predetermined course structure?
- Am I best suited for programs that use the case method, the lecture method, or strong experiential components? (And do I really understand what each entails, such as the teamwork and public speaking that are necessary for the case method?)
- Do my target schools match my academic objectives?

- Do my target firms recruit at my target schools?
- Are alumni well placed in my target industry/post-MBA location? (Are alumni even important to my career?)
- Do my target schools have facilities and an environment that appeals to me?

Again, these questions are just a start—we could certainly pose many more. Our point is that you will get far more than a brand from your MBA studies. You will get an education and an alumni network, and you will spend two years of your life and thousands of dollars on your experience. So skip the rankings, determine what is important to you in your selection process, and then do your homework so you can pick the program that truly fits you and your needs.

MYTH #10: IF MY APPLICATION HAS A TYPO, I'M NOT GETTING IN

You have worked painstakingly on your application. You have checked and rechecked your work. You finally press "submit" and then discover—to your horror!—that you are missing a comma and in one place inadvertently used *too* instead of *to*. The admissions committee is just going to throw your application out, right? Wrong.

There is a fine line between an isolated typo and pervasive sloppiness. If you have typos and grammatical errors throughout your application, you will send a negative message about your sense of professionalism and your ability to represent yourself—and in turn your target school—in a positive way. However, if you have just a minor mistake or two in your text, then you have an unfortunate situation, but not a devastating one. And let us note that there is no magic number of acceptable errors; three small mistakes will not necessarily disqualify you, either. Admissions committees understand that you are only human; if you are a strong candidate, the entirety of your professional, community, personal, and academic endeavors will outweigh these blips.

In short, don't dwell on the mistakes. Don't send new essays. Just accept your fallibility and move on.

So there you have it—ten pervasive admissions myths destroyed. Now the key is to avoid the noise that is out there and not fall prey to other such myths. At **mbaMission.com**, we have an extensive blog with admissions tips, essay writing advice, admissions officer interviews, and much more. In addition, every Kaplan GMAT Prep course and tutoring student is welcome to a free copy of our book *The Complete Start-to-Finish MBA Admissions Guide*. If you have further questions, we are always delighted to answer them via our free 30-minute consultation: learn more at **www.mbamission.com/consult.php**.

Appendices

Appendices

How Much Can a GMAT Score Change?

The following appendix is adapted from The GMAT Unlocked, *a white paper from Kaplan's Research Series. For more information, or if you're interested in any of our classroom or tutoring programs, please visit our website at* **KaplanGMAT.com**.

Whether you are just starting your studies or whether you have already taken the GMAT and are looking to retest, there's likely one question on your mind more than any other: how much can I improve my score?

This is an important practical question. If you have a baseline score that's far from your target, you need to know whether you can reach your target and how much work it will take. Or, you may have received a low score on the GMAT, and you're wondering how much it might go up if you retook the test in a month with a better mindset and some further study under your belt.

While the exact answer to the question of score improvement is as unique as your particular talents and circumstances, there is some information that's worth knowing. There are actually two questions regarding how much a person's GMAT score can change within a given period of time:

1. How much do scores vary?
2. How much can scores be improved?

Let's discuss some important facts related to these two questions and examine what these facts mean for your preparation.

HOW MUCH SCORES VARY

Scores can vary widely, but they tend not to. The test makers present two statistics on the subject that tell slightly different stories.

First is the reliability of the test. The GMAC says that you are 92 percent likely[1] to get the same score on the GMAT if you take the test and then retake it, unless your skills have improved or deteriorated in the interim. So there is little reason to retake the GMAT in the hope of improving your score by chance. If you retake the test, plan to do substantial preparation to improve your score.

The standard error of measurement also gives you some perspective on score improvement. Your score on the GMAT is an estimate of the "true" score of your ability, and the test makers say that "the standard error of measurement is 30–40 points" for the 200–800 score.[2] This means that your score on Test Day may well be 30 to 40 points below your "true" score, or it may be 30 to 40 points above your "true" score. Thus, a score improvement of 40 points or more constitutes a major accomplishment. In other words, 40 points may or may not sound like a lot on the GMAT scoring scale to you—but it is a lot.

The Magic Number Is 40 When Comparing Scores to True Performance

HAVING A "BAD DAY"

As GMAT teachers, we see applicants have a "bad day," recognize it as such, and walk away with unrealistically high hopes about how much their score will go up after a simple retake on a "good day." The figures above—the 92 percent reliability and the 30- to 40-point standard error—indicate that your score on a good day is likely to be the same as your score on a bad day. Furthermore, if your score on a good day is any higher, it's very, very unlikely to be more than 40 points higher, unless you have raised your skill level through preparation. There is hope for score improvement (we at Kaplan have seen hardworking students make tremendous score gains), but it lies along a path paved with practice.

One exception to this rule is the off day caused by sickness or a traumatic life event. If you have reason to believe that specific circumstances have caused you to underperform significantly, you should probably cancel your score on Test Day. This scenario is why it is so important to go into Test Day knowing both your goal score and the minimum score you will accept without canceling (see the section on "Cancellation and Multiple Scores Policy" in Chapter 21 for more detail). Even if you

---

[1] "Validity, Reliability, and Fairness." gmac.com/gmat-other-assessments/about-the-gmat-exam/validity-reliability-fairness.aspx

[2] *GMAT Handbook.* (2017, August 3). mba.com/gmathandbook

don't cancel, you might wish to schedule another testing appointment in the near future to have a good shot at the exam. Other disruptions that may affect your performance, such as a fire alarm going off or computer malfunctions during your test, can also be good reason to cancel your scores or retake the exam. If the disruption is caused by an irregularity in testing conditions, you should report it to the test administrators immediately and follow up through the appropriate channels to make sure that the situation is remedied fairly.

THE "GAMBLE RETAKE"

Maybe you had a fine day at the test, but you got a 690 and you're aiming for one of the top 10 or so programs, where the average score is close to 720. You hear the standard error is about 30 points, which is almost exactly the size of the increase you'd like. So you wonder whether you should gamble on a retake—simply take the test again and hope to do better. Knowing that you can simply cancel your score if you do the same or worse on the test provides a good measure of insurance against those risks. However, when you are contemplating such an investment of money ($250 for test registration), time, and stress, it's first worth considering logically what your actual chances are of improving your score without additional dedicated study in the interim.

Here's a breakdown of the gamble retake. Let's consider three cases:

1. Say your true score (at your current skill level) is 690. In this case, you are quite likely to get a 690, or close to it, on a gamble retake. Moreover, you're as likely to get a 660 on your gamble retake as a 720.

2. Say your true score at your current skill level is a 720. This is the possibility you want to believe is the case. In this case, your 690 score was somewhat lower than your true score—not necessarily because you had a bad day but perhaps due to statistical variation in scores. In this case, on your gamble retake, you're most likely to score at or near 720.

3. Say your true score at your current skill level is a 660. This case is the mirror image of case #2. In this case, your 690 was indeed a fluke, but in your favor. You're likely to score at or near a 660 on your gamble retake, and you're just as likely to score under 660 as above 660.

There are other possibilities, of course—your true score at your current skill level could be 680 or 700 or something near this range. It could even be as far away as 600 or 780—but such cases are very unlikely (and if you'd like to gamble on those odds, you may want to dedicate your B-school tuition to playing the lottery instead). But given the statistical reliability of the GMAT, the most likely case of all is #1. Cases #2 and #3 are less likely—and each of those is as likely as the other.

So even if you are only 30, 20, or 10 points shy of your goal, the gamble retake is not a particularly good gamble. The risk posed by case #3 is entirely mitigated by the fact that if you underperform on your retake, you may simply cancel your score. Nevertheless, a straight-up gamble retake will produce the same score more often than any other result—the most likely outcome is a simple waste of time and money. In general, a retake is the right move only if you have a month or two beforehand to devote to serious study.

IMPROVING YOUR SCORE

Devoting your time and focus to regular study, on the other hand, is no gamble; it's a proven way to gain familiarity with, and ultimately mastery over, the test. Rather than guessing at your true skill level as we discussed above, you can accurately assess your performance by looking at the range of scores after you've taken several Kaplan practice CATs. While the exact score will likely vary from test to test, the scores taken together should reveal a consistent pattern of performance. As you continue to practice, look for upward trends. Keeping the standard error of measurement in mind, don't focus too minutely on the individual scores but rather on the larger picture they reveal. Use this book and your online resources to move that range upward over time. Keep working to improve your performance until you're comfortable with the score range you are seeing consistently on your CATs. With practice, you can feel confident that you will receive a score on Test Day that reflects your highest attainable level of ability.

A Closer Look at GMAT Scoring

The following appendix is adapted from The GMAT Unlocked, *a white paper from Kaplan's Research Series. For more information, or if you're interested in any of our classroom or tutoring programs, please visit our website at* **KaplanGMAT.com**.

As you have seen throughout this book, every question has a difficulty level. This fact is an important part of the adaptive algorithm through which getting questions correct is "rewarded" with harder questions.

There's a little more to this story. After all, in Chapter 2 of this book, you learned that on the computer-adaptive GMAT, the first question you see is an "average difficulty" question; that means approximately half the people get the question right and half the people get it wrong. In a sense, for all the people who got the question right, it's an easy question, and in that same sense, it's a hard question for all the people who got it wrong. The difficulty of the question can be described by this entire pattern of responses, rather than just the percentage who answered it correctly.

EVERY QUESTION HAS A CURVE[1]

Let's take a closer look at such a pattern for a 550-level question. Imagine that a complete and representative population of GMAT test takers got to tango with this question and we tracked the results. The pattern of who got the question right and wrong would look something like this:

A Question Curve That Levels Around 550

---

[1]This section is based primarily on spoken remarks delivered at the 2009 and 2011 GMAC Test Prep Summits.

Notice what the axes represent in this graph. This graph shows the percentage of people who got the question correct, ordering those percentages by the test takers' ability—rather, their ability plus practice, since we know a great deal of practice goes into the test. When you count how many people get the question right at all their different skill levels, you end up with a pretty smooth curve. This curve makes a lot of sense when you examine the parts. Over on the right, where the test takers are very good, they are almost certain to get the question correct. Those individuals are destined for top-10 B-schools or to work as Kaplan faculty or both. On the left, where the test takers are at the bottom of the pool, the odds of getting the question correct are almost zero.

Finally, in the middle, the curve flattens out. The 540-, 550-, and 560-level test takers have about a 50 percent chance of getting the question right, and that's why the curve flattens out at a height corresponding to the 50 percent probability level. That part reflects what we've already said when discussing how the CAT works: a test taker who should ultimately score at the 550 level will get a question like this correct half of the time, on average. Also, the fact that the curve is nicely symmetrical indicates that when you take the entire test-taking population together, about half will get it right and half will get it wrong.

Now take a look at this one. It's a different question, so it has a different curve.

A Question Curve That Levels Around 650

It's a similar shape but stretched and shifted to the right. It's a harder question. Everyone below the 650 skill level is below the 50 percent level and therefore has a greater chance of getting this question wrong than getting it right. Also, if you look where the curve levels out for this one, you see that it's still at a height of 50 percent but that portion is now hovering at about the 650 skill level. Whereas for the first question, 550-level test takers had even odds of answering correctly, with this question, it's the 650-level test takers who have the even odds.

This conversation is getting fairly technical (we at Kaplan tend to be more interested in the behind-the-scenes details of the GMAT than our valued readers may be), but let's look at one more example, a trickier one.

The Curve for a 750-Level Question

This curve may appear deformed at first when compared to the previous question curves. Like the other curves, it moves generally upward from left to right, but unlike the other ones, the left side seems stretched out. Like the other curves, it has a flat part, but in this case the flat part stays close to 0 percent along the *y*-axis for a long time before curving upward. And that curve is *way* to the right.

According to the science of building test questions, you never really know what kind of curve a question is going to have when your mathematicians and wordsmiths devise it; you just have to write it and then collect the data to see what its curve is. That's true for the test makers (this is the reason they include experimental questions on the GMAT), and it's also true for us at Kaplan as we write and norm our practice tests to be the most accurate study tools for Test Day.

If you were the test maker and you had a question on your hands with this curve, you'd find this question to be not as useful in some respects and especially useful in others. First, consider the test takers at skill levels of 700 and below. They all are basically doomed. 700 level? 200 level? They all tend to get it wrong, so this question does not distinguish among them very efficiently. The first question we looked at does a much better job of telling those categories apart, because basically all 200-level test takers who see that question get it wrong and basically all 700-levelers get it right.

Nevertheless, this question is very good at one thing: it can distinguish among 700-, 750-, and 800-level scorers. If you look at the 700-level portion of the axis, you can see that the curve is riding low, and test takers on that part of the curve are, most likely, going to answer this question incorrectly. If your ability level is that of a 750-scorer, you have a good chance on this one. But if you're an 800-scorer, you're likely getting this question right. Telling the difference among these groups is what this question is perfect for: once you've progressed within a section and demonstrated that you're in the 700–800 range, the test will dish up questions with curves like this one to determine whether you belong at the top or the bottom of that range.

The whole point of the GMAT is that it's meant to discern the applicants who will be able to handle the coursework at a given business school program and the ones who won't. It's all about distinguishing among a competitive set of candidates in a fair and objective way. Toward that goal, each question has a job to do, which is to help in the task of distinguishing among test takers' ability levels, and each question does that job a little bit differently, based on the unique shape of its curve.

FAIR AND UNFAIR QUESTIONS

Apart from understanding better how the CAT algorithm chooses questions, you'll also note the following practical takeaways from the discussion of question curves:

- **"Bad" questions.** How do the test makers determine whether a question is clearly written? It all comes back to the curve. They collect information on each individual question and look at the curve for that question, and—as you've just seen—these curves give much more nuanced information than mere numbers or percentages can give. Questions that have nonsensical curves are thrown out.[2]

- **Fair and unfair questions.** This point is similar to the preceding takeaway—and it has to do with the issue of whether questions might be culturally biased or gender biased. An extremely important consideration in constructing the GMAT (so the test makers tell us) is to make a test that is fair to people from diverse geographies and backgrounds. To give an example: a Vice President of Research and Development at GMAC once narrated a story to members of our team about a Critical Reasoning question previously on the test that concerned skim milk. As it so happens, while the term *skim milk* is readily understood in the United States, it does not carry equal meaning in India. Moreover, the kind of milk at stake in the question had nothing to do with the argument, the argument's conclusion, its critical assumptions, or anything substantially related to the question's correct answer. But seeing a foreign expression in the first few words of the question was distracting to some Indian test takers. That distraction was one that test takers from the United States didn't have to endure, and therefore—however slight the inequity—the question was ultimately deemed unfair.

The test makers avoid many such inequities through diligence and common sense, but they can also spot and eradicate unfair questions using the curves we discussed above. Just as they can collect the curve for a particular question, so can they collect the curve for that question for a particular group and conduct analysis called Differential Item Functioning (DIF). And if, for example, they see that Indians are getting the skim-milk question wrong more than they should be, across all of the different skill levels of the Indian test takers, then the test makers have the opportunity to reexamine that question and uncover the point of cultural bias if human review hadn't already picked it up.

---

[2]For example, imagine a curve that looks like a parabola with negative concavity. This curve has a high point and then slopes downward on both sides from that point, symmetrical on the left and right, like a ∩ shape. It's an odd shape for a curve, but it can happen. The people whose skill level is at the parabola's high point (say, 670) are the ones who get the question correct most often. Then, we head to the left, and the percentage who get it right drops. That part makes sense: people at lower skill levels don't do as well on the question. The confusing part is when we head to the right of the topmost point. Those people are higher in skill level, but they get the question right *less* often? There's something wrong with the curve, because the most skilled test takers are getting the question wrong and being penalized. In fact, questions with curves such as this are often phrased confusingly or inaccurately. If a question is a good 670-level question but has a small error or grounds for misinterpretation that perceptive 700+ test takers are conditioned to notice, it may reward the 670-level test takers and falsely penalize the 700+ test takers. Such a question can be deemed "unfair" on scientific grounds—based on its curve—and it never graduates from being an experimental question into the ranks of questions that count toward GMAT scores.

NOT ALL QUESTIONS ARE WORTH THE SAME

Have you harbored a conviction all along that some GMAT questions are worth more than others? If so, you have been right, although perhaps not in exactly the way you thought. We saw in the previous examination that each question has a different curve. Each is unique in its ability to slice and dice test taker ability. And so it makes sense that each question has a different opportunity to impact your score. We saw a question above whose curve allowed it to distinguish 700-level scorers from 750- and 800-level scorers. If you are a 750-level scorer, or aspire to be, that may be one of the most important questions you see on Test Day. *It will actually create a larger swing in your running score than the previous or following question will.* Meanwhile, if you are a 680 scorer working to break 700 at this point, that particular question is of little relevance to you: if you see it (and you will likely not), you can get it wrong, and doing so would not do much to hurt your goal of scoring 700+.

Let's return to the first 10 questions of a Quant or Verbal section, which we discussed briefly in Chapter 2. As you've already seen, your performance on this first series of questions helps the CAT determine your rough placement on the difficulty scale. And you've also seen how questions appearing later in a section can be quite important as well, as they are the ones that are specifically targeted to evaluate your ability level compared to those test takers who will ultimately score slightly higher or lower than you.

The item curves help explain both points. Many of the questions near the beginning of the exam will have curves designed to separate 600 from 400, then 650 from 600, 670 from 630, and so on. As you progress through the test, the CAT tailors its questions to your ability level to learn more about you as a test taker. But all of these questions have a slightly different impact on your score. There are reasons to suspect that you might see questions later in a section that could make a big difference to your score. And there is every possibility that questions that could cause larger swings are inserted by the test makers later on intentionally, as the algorithm seeks to verify its estimate of your ability in different ways. As one study of an operational CAT pool found: "Findings refuted the myth that the beginning items are the most important."[3] The curves are key, not a question's placement per se.

On Test Day, you have only one choice: give every question your best effort. Give easy-looking questions a quick look for unseen pitfalls. Be open to guessing on harder-looking questions so that you can maximize the time you have available to answer all the questions you are capable of answering correctly. Take a balanced approach to time management. Don't be too quick to assume any question is one you'll definitely get right or definitely get wrong. And know that it's hard to fool a CAT. Its question selection and scoring algorithms are sophisticated, so your best defense is a good offense: practicing to improve your performance on questions across the range of difficulty levels.

---

[3]Talento-Miller, E., Han, K. T., & Guo, F. (2011). Guess again: The effect of correct guesses on scores in an operational CAT program. mba.com/~/media/Files/gmac/Research/research-report-series/guessagaintheeffectofcorrect.pdf